A SELECT LIBRARY

OF

NICENE AND POST-NICENE FATHERS

OF

THE CHRISTIAN CHURCH

Second Series

TRANSLATED INTO ENGLISH WITH PROLEGOMENA AND EXPLANATORY NOTES

UNDER THE EDITORIAL SUPERVISION OF

PHILIP SCHAFF, D.D., LL.D. AND **HENRY WACE, D.D.**

Professor of Church History in the
Union Theological Seminary, New York

Principal of King's College.
London.

IN CONNECTION WITH A NUMBER OF PATRISTIC SCHOLARS OF EUROPE
AND AMERICA

VOLUME XIV

THE SEVEN ECUMENICAL COUNCILS

T&T CLARK
EDINBURGH

WM. B. EERDMANS PUBLISHING COMPANY
GRAND RAPIDS, MICHIGAN

British Library Cataloguing in Publication Data

Nicene & Post-Nicene Fathers. — 2nd series
1. Fathers of the church
I. Schaff, Philip   II. Mace, Henry
230′.11   BR60.A62

Reprinted, June 1991

T&T Clark ISBN 0 567 09433 2

Eerdmans ISBN 0-8028-8129-7

PHOTOLITHOPRINTED BY EERDMANS PRINTING COMPANY
GRAND RAPIDS, MICHIGAN, UNITED STATES OF AMERICA

THE SEVEN ECUMENICAL COUNCILS

OF THE UNDIVIDED CHURCH

THEIR CANONS AND DOGMATIC DECREES,

TOGETHER WITH THE CANONS OF ALL THE LOCAL SYNODS WHICH
HAVE RECEIVED ECUMENICAL ACCEPTANCE.

*EDITED WITH NOTES GATHERED FROM THE WRITINGS OF THE
GREATEST SCHOLARS*

BY

HENRY R. PERCIVAL, M.A., D.D.

CONTENTS

PREFACE

THE work intrusted to me of preparing this volume evidently can be divided into two separate parts. The first, the collecting of the material needed and the setting of it before the reader in the English tongue; the other, the preparation of suitable introductions and notes to the matter thus provided. Now in each of these departments two courses were open to the editor: the one, to be original; the other, to be a copyist. I need hardly say that of these the former offered many temptations. But I could not fail to recognize the fact that such a course would greatly take from the real value of the work, and therefore without any hesitation I have adopted the other alternative, and have endeavoured, so far as was at all possible, to keep myself out of the question altogether; and as a general rule even the translation of the text (as distinguished from the notes) is not mine but that of some scholar of well-established reputation.

In the carrying out of this method of procedure I have availed myself of all the translations which I could find, and where, after comparing them with the original, I have thought them substantially accurate, I have adopted them and reproduced them. Where I have thought that the translation was misleading, I have amended it from some other translation, and, I think, in no case have I ventured a change of translation which rests upon my own judgment alone. A very considerable portion, however, of the matter found in this volume is now translated into English for the first time. For some of this I am indebted to my friends, who have most kindly given me every assistance in their power, but even here no translation has been made from the Greek without careful reference being had to the traditional understanding, as handed down in the Latin versions, and wherever the Latin and Greek texts differ on material points the difference has been noted. I have not thought it necessary nor desirable to specify the source of each particular translation, but I have provided for the use of the reader a list of all the translations which I have used. I should also add that I have not considered any one text sufficiently well established as to command any deference being paid to it, and that I have usually followed (for my own convenience rather than for any other reason) the text contained in Labbe and Cossart's *Concilia*. No doubt Hardouin and Mansi are in some respects superior, but old prejudices are very strong, and the reader will remember that these differing *Concilia* gave rise to a hard-fought battle in the history of the Gallican Church. I should add, however, that where more recent students of the subject have detected errors of importance in Labbe's text, I have corrected them, usually noting the variety of reading. With regard then to the text I entirely disclaim any responsibility, and the more so as on such a matter my opinion would be entirely valueless. And with regard to the translation my responsibility goes no further than the certifying the reader that, to all intents and purposes, the meaning of the original is presented to him in the English language and without interpretation being introduced under the specious guise of translation. Some portions are mere literal translations,

and some are done into more idiomatic English, but all—so far as I am able to judge—
are fair renderings of the original, *its ambiguities being duly preserved*. I have used as
the foundation of the translation of the canons of the first four synods and of the five
Provincial Synods that most convenient book, *Index Canonum*, by the Rev. John Fulton, D.D., D.C.L., in which united to a good translation is a Greek text, very well edited
and clearly printed.

In preparing the other division of the book, that is to say, the Introduction and
Notes, I have been guided by the same considerations. Here will be found no new and
brilliant guesses of my own, but a collection of the most reliable conclusions of the most
weighty critics and commentators. Where the notes are of any length I have traced the
source and given the exact reference, but for the brief notes, where I have not thought
this necessary, the reader may feel the greatest confidence that he is not reading any
surmises of mine, but that in every particular what he reads rests upon the authority of
the greatest names who have written on the subject. In the bibliographical table
already referred to I have placed the authorities most frequently cited.

I think it necessary to make a few remarks upon the rule which I have laid down
for myself with regard to my attitude on controverted questions bearing upon doctrine
or ecclesiastical discipline. It seems to me that in such a work as the present any
expression of the editor's views would be eminently out of place. I have therefore confined myself to a bare statement of what I conceive to be the facts of the case, and have
left the reader to draw from them what conclusions he pleases. I hope that this volume may be equally acceptable to the Catholic and to the Protestant, to the Eastern and
to the Western, and while I naturally think that the facts presented are clearly in
accordance with my own views, I hope that those who draw from the same premises
different conclusions will find these premises stated to their satisfaction in the following
pages. And should such be the case this volume may well be a step toward "the union
of all" and toward " the peace of all the holy churches of 'God," for which the unchanging East has so constantly prayed in her liturgy.

I wish to explain to the reader one other principle on which I have proceeded in
preparing this volume. It professes to be a translation of the decrees and canons of
certain ecclesiastical synods. It is not a history of those synods, nor is it a theological
treatise upon the truth or otherwise of the doctrines set forth by those synods in their
legislation. I have therefore carefully restricted my own historical introductions to a
bare statement of such facts as seemed needed to render the meaning of the matter subsequently presented intelligible to the reader. And with regard to doctrine I have
pursued the same course, merely explaining what the doctrine taught or condemned
was, without entering into any consideration of its truth or falsity. For the history of
the Church and its Councils the reader must consult the great historians ; for a defence
of the Church's faith he must read the works of her theologians.

I need hardly say that the overwhelming majority of the references found in this
volume I have had no opportunity of verifying, no copy of many of the books being (so
far as I know) to be found in America. I have, however, taken great pains to insure
accuracy in reproducing the references as given in the books from which I have cited
them ; this, however, does not give me any feeling of confidence that they may be relied
on, especially as in some cases where I have been able to look them up, I have found
errors of the most serious kind.

It now only remains that I thank all those who have assisted me in this work, and especially I must mention his Excellency the High Procurator of the Holy Governing Synod of Russia, who directed the bibliographical table of Russian editions of the Canons, etc., which is found in this volume, to be prepared for me by Professor Glubokoffski of the Ecclesiastical Academy at St. Petersburgh. My special thanks are due to the learned professor just named for the very admirable manner in which he has performed the work, and to Mr. W. J. Birkbeck, who has added one more to his numerous labours for making the West better acquainted with the East by translating the Russian MS. into English. I cannot but pause here to remark how deep my regret is that my ignorance of the Russian and Slavic tongues has prevented me from laying before my readers the treasures of learning and the stores of tradition and local illustration which these volumes must contain. I am, however, extremely well pleased in being able to put those, who are more fortunate than myself in this respect, in the way of investigating the matter for themselves, by supplying them with the titles of the books on the subject. I desire also to offer my thanks to Professor Bolotoff for the valuable information he sent me as well as for a copy of his learned (and often most just) strictures upon Professor Lauchert's book, " Die Kanones der wichtigsten altkirchlichen Concilien nebst den Apostolischen Kanones." (Freiburg in B. und Leipzig, 1896.)

The Rev. Wm. McGarvey has helped me most kindly by translating parts of the Second Council of Nice, and one or more of the African Canons; and by looking over the translation of the entire African Code.

The Rev. F. A. Sanborn translated two of St. Cyril's letters, and the Rev. Leighton Hoskins the Sardican Canons. To these and many other of my friends, who in one way or another helped me, I wish to return my deep thanks; also to the Nashotah Theological Seminary and to the Lutheran Theological Seminary at Mt. Airy, Philadelphia, for having placed their libraries entirely at my disposal; nor can I end this list without mention of my sister, who has assisted me most materially through the entire progress of the work, and without whom I never could have undertaken it.

When I think of the great number of authors cited, of the rapidity with which most of the translation has had to be done, of the difficulty of getting access to the necessary books, and of the vast range of subjects touched upon (including almost every branch of ecclesiastical and theological learning), I feel I must throw myself and my work upon the reader's indulgence and beg him to take all this in consideration in making his estimate of the value of the work done. As for me, now that it is all finished, I feel like crying out with the reader, in deep shame at the recollection of the many blunders he has made in reading the lesson,——" Tu autem, Domine, miserere nobis!"

In conclusion I would add that nothing I have written must be interpreted as meaning that the editor personally has any doubt of the truth of the doctrines set forth by the Ecumenical Councils of the Christian Church, and I wish to declare in the most distinct manner that I accept all the doctrinal decrees of the Seven Ecumenical Synods as infallible and irreformable.

HENRY R. PERCIVAL.

Pentecost, 1899.

GENERAL INTRODUCTION

I. METHOD OF TREATMENT

It is absolutely necessary that a few words should be said on the general arrangement of the work. The reader will find given him in the English tongue, so far as they have come down to us, all the doctrinal definitions of the Seven Ecumenical Councils (councils which have always, and still do, receive the unqualified acceptance of both East and West), and all the canons, disciplinary and doctrinal, which were enacted by them. To these has been added a translation in full of all the canons of the local synods which received the approval and sanction of the aforesaid Ecumenical Councils. Besides this, as throwing light upon the subject, large extracts from the *Acta* have been given, in fact all that seemed to illustrate the decrees ; and, that nothing might be lacking, in an appendix has been placed a collection of all the non-synodal canons which have received the sanction of the Ecumenical Synods, the " Canons of the Apostles " (so called) being given in full, and the others in a shortened form, for the most part in the words of the admirable and learned John Johnson.

This then is the text of the volume; but it is manifest that it stood in need of much comment to make its meaning clear to the reader, even if well informed on ordinary matters. To provide for this, to each synodal canon there has been added the Ancient Epitome.

Of this Epitome Bishop Beveridge treats with great learning in section xxvi. of his " Prolegomena " to his *Synodicon*, and shows that while some attributed this epitome to the Greek mediæval scholiast Aristenus, it cannot be his, as he has taken it for the text of his commentaries, and has in more than one instance pointed out that whoever he was who made it had, in his judgment, missed the sense.[1]

The Epitome must indeed be much older, for Nicholas Hydruntinus, who lived in the times of Alexis Angelus, when intending to quote one of the canons of Ephesus, actually quotes words which are not in that canon, but which are in the Epitome. " Wherefore," says Beveridge, " it is manifest that the Epitome is here cited, and that under the name of the whole canon." This being established we may justly look upon the Ancient Epitome as supplying us with a very ancient gloss upon the canons.

To this Epitome have been added Notes, taken from most of the great commentators, and Excursuses, largely made up from the writings of the greatest theologians, canonists, archæologists, etc., with regard to whom and their writings, all the information that seems necessary the reader will find in the Bibliographical Introduction.

II. CONCERNING ECUMENICAL COUNCILS IN GENERAL

An Ecumenical Synod may be defined as a synod the decrees of which have found acceptance by the Church in the whole world.[2] It is not necessary to make a council ecumenical that the number of bishops present should be large, there were but 325 at Nice, and 150 at I. Constantinople ; it is not necessary that it should be assembled with the intention of its being ecumenical, such was not the case with I. Constantinople ; it is

---

[1] Vide Apostolic Canon LXXV., and Ancyr. Canon XIX.

[2] This was until the division of the East and West the definition accepted by all the whole Christian world. But since the Church has been divided, while the East has kept to the old definition and has not pretended to have held any Ecumenical Councils, the Roman Church has made a new definition of the old term and has then proceeded to hold a very considerable number of synods which she recognizes as Ecumenical. I say " a very considerable number," for even among Roman Catholic theologians there is much dispute as to the number of these " Ecumenical Synods," the decrees of which, like those of Trent and the Vatican, have never been received by about half of the Christian world, including four of the five patriarchates, and of the fifth patriarchate all the Anglican communion. According to modern Roman writers the definition of these non-ecumenically received Ecumenical Synods is " Ecumenical councils are those to which the bishops and others entitled to vote are convoked from the whole world under the Presidency of the Pope or his legates, and the decrees of which, having received Papal confirmation, bind all Christians." Addis and Arnold, *A Catholic Dictionary. s. v.* Councils. The reader will notice that by this definition one at least (I. Constantinople), probably three, of the seven undisputed Ecumenical Synods cease to be such.

not necessary that all parts of the world should have been represented or even that the bishops of such parts should have been invited. All that is necessary is that its decrees find ecumenical acceptance afterwards, and its ecumenical character be universally recognized.

The reader will notice that in the foregoing I have not proceeded from the theological foundation of what an Ecumenical Synod should be (with this question the present volume has nothing to do), but from a consideration of the historical question as to what the Seven Councils have in common, which distinguishes them from the other councils of the Christian Church.

And here it is well to note that there have been many "General Councils" which have not been "Ecumenical." It is true that in ordinary parlance we often use the expressions as interchangeable, but such really is not the case. There are but seven universally recognized and undisputed "Ecumenical Councils"; on the other hand, the number of "General Councils" is very considerable, and as a matter of fact of these last several very large ones fell into heresy. It is only necessary to mention as examples the Latrocinium and the spurious "Seventh Council," held by the iconoclastic heretics. It is therefore the mere statement of an historical fact to say that General Councils have erred.

The Ecumenical Councils claimed for themselves an immunity from error in their doctrinal and moral teaching, resting such claim upon the promise of the presence and guidance of the Holy Ghost. The Council looked upon itself, not as revealing any new truth, but as setting forth the faith once for all delivered to the Saints, its decisions therefore were in themselves ecumenical, as being an expression of the mind of the whole body of the faithful both clerical and lay, the *sensus communis* of the Church. And by the then teaching of the Church that ecumenical consensus was considered free from the suspicion of error, guarded, (as was believed,) by the Lord's promise that the gates of hell should not prevail against his Church. This then is what Catholics mean when they affirm the infallibility of Ecumenical Councils. Whether this opinion is true or false is a question outside the scope of the present discussion. It was necessary, however, to state that these Councils looked upon themselves as divinely protected in their decisions from error in faith and morals, lest the reader should otherwise be at a loss to understand the anathematisms which follow the decrees, and which indeed would be singularly out of place, if the decrees which they thus emphatically affirm were supposed to rest only upon human wisdom and speculation, instead of upon divine authority.

Theologians consider that the decisions of Ecumenical Councils, like all juridical decrees, must be construed strictly, and that only the point at issue must be looked upon as decided. The *obiter dicta* of so august a body are no doubt of the greatest weight, but yet they have no claim to be possessed of that supreme authority which belongs to the definition of the particular point under consideration.[1]

The Seven Ecumenical Councils were all called together at the commandment and will of Princes; without any knowledge of the matter on the part of the Pope in one case at least (1st Constantinople)[2]; without any consultation with him in the case of I. Nice, so far as we know[3]; and contrary to his expressed desire in at least the case of Chalcedon, when he only gave a reluctant consent after the Emperor Marcian had already convoked the synod. From this it is historically evident that Ecumenical Councils can be summoned without either the knowledge or consent of the See of Rome.

In the history of the Christian Church, especially at a later period in connection with the Great Schism, much discussion has taken place among the learned as to the relative powers of a General Council and of the Pope. It will be remembered by everyone that the superior authority of the council was not only taught, but on one occasion

---

[1] Vide Vasquez, P. III., Disp. 181, c. 9; Bellarmin., *De Concil.*, Lib. II., cap. xvij.; Veron, *Rule* of the Cath. Faith, Chap. I., §§ 4, 5, and 6.

[2] See Hefele's answer to Baronius's special pleading. *Hist. Councils*, Vol. I., pp. 9, 10.

[3] It should be stated that at the Sixth Synod it was said that I. Nice was "summoned by the Emperor and Pope Sylvester," on what authority I know not.

acted on, by a council, but this is outside of the period covered by the Seven Ecumenical Synods, and I shall therefore only discuss the relations of these seven synods to the Roman See. And in the first place it is evident that no council has ever been received as ecumenical which has not been received and confirmed by the Roman Pontiff. But, after all, this is only saying that no council has been accepted as ecumenical which has not been ecumenically received, for it must be remembered that there was but one Patriarchate for the whole West, that of Rome; and this is true to all intents and purposes, whether or no certain sections had extrapatriarchal privileges, and were "autocephalous."

But it would be giving an entirely unfair impression of the matter to the reader were he left to suppose that this necessity for Rome's confirmation sprang necessarily from any idea of Rome's infallibility. So far as appears from any extant document, such an idea was as unknown in the whole world then as it is in four of the five patriarchates to-day. And it should be borne in mind that the confirmation by the Emperor was sought for and spoken of in quite as strong, if not stronger, terms. Before passing to a particular examination of what relation each of the Councils bore to the Roman See, it may be well to note that while as an historical fact each of the Seven Ecumenical Councils did eventually find acceptance at Rome, this fact does not prove that such acceptance is necessary in the nature of things. If we can imagine a time when Rome is not in communion with the greater part of the West, then it is quite possible to imagine that an Ecumenical Council could be held whose decrees would (for the time being) be rejected by the unworthy occupant of the Apostolic See. I am not asserting that such a state of affairs is possible from a theological standpoint, but merely stating an historical contingency which is perfectly within the range of imagination, even if cut off from any practical possibility by the faith of some.

We now come to a consideration of how, by its acts, each of the Seven Synods intimated its relation to the Roman See:

1. The First Council of Nice passed a canon in which some at least of the Roman rights are evidently looked upon as being exactly on the same plane as those of other metropolitans, declaring that they rest upon "custom."

It was the Emperor who originated this council and called it together, if we may believe his own words and those of the council; and while indeed it is possible that when the Emperor did not preside in person, Hosius of Cordova may have done so (even uniting the two Roman Presbyters who were the legates of the Roman See with him), yet there is no evidence that anything of the kind ever took place, and a pope, Felix III. (A.D. 483–492), in his Fifth Epistle (ad Imp. Zen.) declares that Eustathius, bishop of Antioch, presided at this council.[1]

The matter, however, is of little moment as no one would deny the right of the See of Rome to preside in a council of the whole Church.

2. The Second Ecumenical Council was called together by the Emperor without the knowledge of the Roman Pontiff. Nor was he invited to be present. Its first president was not in communion at the time of its session with the Roman Church. And, without any recourse to the first of all the patriarchs, it passed a canon changing the order of the patriarchates, and setting the new see of Constantinople in a higher place than the other ancient patriarchates, in fact immediately after Rome. Of course Protestants will consider this a matter of very minor importance, looking upon all patriarchal divisions and rank and priority (the Papacy included) as of a disciplinary character and as being *jure ecclesiastico*, and in no way affecting doctrine, but any fair reading of the third canon of this synod would seem plainly to assert that as the first rank of Rome rested upon the fact of its being the capital city, so the new capital city should have the second rank. If this interpretation is correct it affects very materially the Roman claim of *jure divino* primacy.

3. Before the third of the Ecumenical Synods was called to meet, Pope Celestine had already convicted Nestorius of heresy and deposed and excommunicated him. When

---

[1] Cf. Theod. *H. E.*, Lib. I., e. 6.

subsequently the synod was assembled, and before the papal legates had arrived, the Council met, treated Nestorius as in good standing, entirely ignoring the sentence already given by Rome, and having examined the case (after summoning him three times to appear that he might be heard in his own defence), proceeded to sentence Nestorius, and immediately published the sentence. On the 10th of July (more than a fortnight later), the papal legates having arrived, a second session was held, at which they were told what had been done, all of which they were good enough to approve of.[1]

4. The Council of Chalcedon refused to consider the Eutychian matter as settled by Rome's decision or to accept Leo's Tome without examination as to whether it was orthodox. Moreover it passed a canon at a session which the Papal legates refused to attend, ratifying the order of the Patriarchates fixed at I. Constantinople, and declaring that "the Fathers had very properly given privileges to Old Rome as the imperial city, and that now they gave the same ($\tau\grave{\alpha}$ $\acute{\iota}\sigma\alpha$ $\pi\rho\epsilon\sigma\beta\epsilon\hat{\iota}\alpha$) privileges" to Constantinople as the seat of the imperial government at that time.

5. The fifth of the Ecumenical Synods refused to receive any written doctrinal communication from the then pope (Vigilius), took his name from the diptychs, and refused him communion.

6. The Third Council of Constantinople, the sixth of the Ecumenical Synods, excommunicated Pope Honorius, who had been dead for years, for holding and teaching the Monothelite heresy.

7. It is certain that the Pope had nothing to do with the calling of the Seventh Synod,[2] and quite possible that it was presided over by Tarasius and not by the Papal legates.

Such is, in brief, the evidence which the Ecumenical Councils give on the subject of what, for lack of a better designation, may be called the Papal claims. Under these circumstances it may not be deemed strange that some extreme ultramontanists have arrived at the conclusion that much of the acts and decisions as we have them is spurious, or at least corrupted in an anti-papal direction. Vincenzi, who is the most learned of these writers, argues somewhat thus 'if the members of the Ecumenical Synods believed as we do to-day with regard to the Papacy it is impossible that they should have acted and spoken as they did, but we know they must have believed as we do, *ergo* they did not so act or speak.' The logic is admirable, but the truth of the conclusion depends upon the truth of the minor premise. The forgeries would have been very extensive, and who were they done by? Forgeries, as the false decretals, to advance papal claims we are unfortunately familiar with, but it is hard to imagine who could have forged in Greek and Latin the acts of the Ecumenical Synods. It is not necessary to pursue the matter any further, perhaps its very mention was uncalled for, but I wish to be absolutely fair, that no one may say that any evidence has been suppressed.[3]

---

[1] Protestant Controversialists, as well as others, have curious ways of stating historical events without any regard to the facts of the case. A notable instance of this is found in Dr. Salmon's *Infallibility of the Church* (p. 426 of the 2d Edition) where we are told that "the only one of the great controversies in which the Pope really did his part in teaching Christians what to believe was the Eutychian controversy. Leo the Great, instead of waiting, as Popes usually do, till the question was settled, published his sentiments at the beginning, and his letter to Flavian was adopted by the Council of Chalcedon. This is what would have always happened if God had really made the Pope the guide to the Church. But this case is quite exceptional, resulting from the accident that Leo was a good theologian, besides being a man of great vigour of character. No similar influence was exercised either by his predecessors or successors." This sentence is not pleasant reading, for it is an awe-inspiring display of one of two things, neither of which should be in the author of such a book. We need only remind the reader that Celestine had condemned Nestorius and his teaching before the Council of Ephesus; that Honorius had written letters defining the question with regard to the will or wills of the Incarnate Son before the III. Council of Constantinople (which excommunicated him as a heretic for these very letters); that Pope Vigilius condemned the "Three Chapters" before the II. Council of Constantinople; and that Gregory II. condemned the iconoclastic heresy before the Seventh Synod, if the letters attributed to him be genuine (which is not quite certain, as will be shewn in its proper place). Thus the only two great questions not decided, one way or another, by the See of Rome before the meeting of a General Council were Arianism and Macedonianism, and some have held (though mistakenly as is generally thought) that Arius was condemned by a synod held at Rome before that of Nice.

[2] See Michaud's brilliant answer to Hefele, *Discussion sur les Sept Conciles Œcuméniques*, p. 327.

[3] The reader may easily satisfy himself on this matter by reading the somewhat extensive works of Aloysius Vincenzi, published in Rome in 1875 and thereabouts.

III. THE NUMBER OF THE ECUMENICAL. SYNODS

IT may not be unjustly expected that some reasons should be assigned for limiting the number of the Ecumenical Synods to seven.   There is no need here to enter into any proof that Nice, I. Constantinople, Ephesus and Chalcedon are Ecumenical, since so long ago as the time of St. Gregory the Great, that Saint and Doctor said of them: " I venerate the first four Ecumenical Councils equally with the Four Gospels (sicut quatuor Evangelia)," [1] and no one has been found to question that in so saying he gave expression to the mind of the Church of his day.   Of the fifth and sixth synods there never was any real doubt, although there was trouble at first about the reception of the fifth in some places.   The ecumenical character of the seventh is not disputed by East or West and has not been for near a thousand years, and full proof of its ecumenicity will be found in connection with that council.   There is therefore no possible doubt that these seven must be included, but it may be asked why certain others are not here also.

The following is a list of those that might seem to have a claim: Sardica (343 circa), Quinisext (692), Constantinople (869), Lyons (1274), and Florence (1439).

The reasons for rejecting the claims of Sardica will be found in connection with the canons set forth by that council.   The same is the case with regard to the claims of the Synod in Trullo.   It is true that IV. Constantinople, holden in A.D. 869, was for a short while held as Ecumenical by both East and West, and continues to be held as such by the Latin Church down to this day, but it was soon rejected by the East and another synod of Constantinople (879), which undid much of its work, has for the Greeks taken its place.   However the Easterns do not claim for this synod an ecumenical character, but confine the number to seven.

The Councils of Lyons and Florence both fail of ecumenicity for the same reason. At both the East was represented, and at each an agreement was arrived at, but neither agreement was subsequently accepted in the East, and the decrees therefore have failed, as yet, of receiving ecumenical acceptance.

We are left therefore with Seven Ecumenical Councils, neither more nor less, and these are fully treated of in the pages that follow.

---

[1] Epistle XXIV. of Lib. I.

BIBLIOGRAPHICAL INTRODUCTION

To the student of the ancient synods of the Church of Christ, the name of William Beveridge must ever stand most illustrious; and his work on the canons of the undivided Church as received by the Greeks, published at Oxford in 1672, will remain a lasting glory to the Anglican Church, as the "Concilia" of Labbe and Cossart, which appeared in Paris about the same time, must ever redound to the glory of her sister, the Gallican Church.

Of the permanent value of Beveridge's work there can be no greater evidence than that to-day it is quoted all the world over, and not only are Anglicans proud of the bishop of St. Asaph, but Catholics and Protestants, Westerns and Easterns alike quote him as an authority. In illustration of this it will be sufficient to mention two examples, the most extensive and learned work on the councils of our own day, that by the Roman Catholic bishop Hefele, and the "Compendium of Canon Law," by the Metropolitan of the Orthodox Greek Hungarian Church,[1] in both of which the reader will find constant reference to Beveridge's "Synodicon."

This great work appeared in two volumes full folio, with the Greek text, beautifully printed, but of course with the ligatures so perplexing to the ordinary Greek reader of to-day. It should however be noted that the most learned and interesting *Prolegomena in Συνοδικὸν sive Pandectæ Canonum*, as well as the *Praefationem ad annotationes in Canones Apostolicos*, is reprinted as an Appendix to Vol. XII. of "The Theological Works of William Beveridge, sometime lord bishop of St. Asaph," in the "Library of Anglo-Catholic Theology," (published at Oxford, 1848), which also contains a reprint of the "Codex Canonum Ecclesiæ Primitivæ vindicatus ac illustratus," of which last work I shall have something to say in connection with the Apostolical Canons in the Appendix to this volume.

Nothing could exceed the value of the Prolegomena and it is greatly to be wished that this most unique preface were more read by students. It contains a fund of out-of-the-way information which can be found nowhere else collected together, and while indeed later research has thrown some further light upon the subject, yet the main conclusions of Bishop Beveridge are still accepted by the learned with but few exceptions. I have endeavoured, as far as possible to incorporate into this volume the most important part of the learned bishop's notes and observations, but the real student must consult the work itself. The reader will be interested to know that the greatest English scholars of his day assisted Bishop Beveridge in his work, among whom was John Pearson, the defender of the Ignatian Epistles.

I think I cannot do better than set out in full the contents of the Synodicon so that the student may know just what he will find in its pages:

"Συνοδικὸν sive Padectæ Canonum SS. Apostolorum, et Conciliorum ab Ecclesia Græca receptorum; necnon Canonicorum SS. Patrum Epistolarum: Unà cum Scholiis Antiquorum singulis eorum annexis, et scriptis aliis huc spectantibus; quorum plurima e Biblothecæ Bodleianæ aliarumque MSS. codicibus nunc primum edita: reliqua cum iisdem MSS. summâ fide et diligentiâ collata. Totum Opus in duos Tomos divisum, Guilielmus Beverigius, Ecclesiæ Anglicanæ Presbyter, Recensuit, Prolegomenis munivit, et Annotationibus auxit. Oxonii, E Theatro Sheldoniano. M.DC.LXXII."

Such is the title in full. I proceed to note the contents, premising that for all the Greek a Latin translation is given in a parallel column:

Volume I.

The Canons of the Holy Apostles, with the Ancient Epitome, and the scholia of Balsamon, Zonaras and Aristenus.

The Canons of the Council of Nice with notes *ut supra* and so throughout.

---

[1] As one of the few books of the Eastern Church ever translated into a Western tongue, the reader may be glad to have its full title. *Compendium des Kanonischen Rechtes der einen heiligen, allgemeinen und apostoliochen Kirche verfaszt von Andreas Freiherrn von Schaguna. Hermannstadt, Buchdruckerei des Josef Droklieff, 1868.*

The Canons of the Council of Constantinople.

The Canons of the Council of Ephesus.

The Canons of the Council of Chalcedon.

The Canons of the Sixth Council in Trullo.

The Canons of the Seventh Œcumenical Council.

The Canons of the Council of Constantinople called the First-and-Second [in the time of Photius].

The Canons of the Council held in the Temple of Wisdom [which confirmed the Seventh Œcumenical Synod]. All these with notes as before.

The Canons of the Council of Carthage [over which St. Cyprian, the Martyr, presided] with the notes of Balsamon and Zonaras.

The Canons of the Council of Ancyra.

The Canons of the Council of Neocæsarea.

The Canons of the Council of Gangra.

The Canons of the Council of Antioch.

The Canons of the Council of Laodicea.

The Canons of the Council of Sardica. All these with full notes as before.

The Canons of the 217 blessed Fathers who met at Carthage, with the epitome, and scholia by Balsamon and Aristenus, and on the actual canons by Zonaras also. To these some epistles are added, likewise annotated.

Then, ending Volume I. is a version of Josephus Ægyptius's Arabic Introduction and Paraphrase on the Canons of the first four General Councils, bearing the following title :

Josephi Ægyptii Proœmia et Paraphrasis Arabica in Quatuor Preorum Generalium Conciliorum Canones, interprete Guilielmo Beverigio, the Arabic being given in the left hand column.

Volume II.
Part I.

The Canons of Dionysius of Alexandria, with the scholia of Balsamon and Zonaras.

The Canons of Peter of Alexandria.

The Canons of Gregory Thaumaturgus.

The Canons of St. Athanasius. All these with scholia as above.

The Canons of St. Basil, with the Ancient Epitome and scholia of Balsamon, Zonaras, and Aristenus.

The Canons of St. Gregory Nyssen with scholia of Balsamon.

The Canonical Answer of Timothy, Bishop of Alexandria.

The Canons of Theophilus of Alexandria.

The Canonical Epistles of Cyril of Alexandria.

Extracts from the metrical poems of St. Gregory Theologus, concerning what books of the Old and New Testaments should be read.

Extracts from the iambics of St. Amphilochius the bishop to Seleucus on the same subject.

The Encyclical Letter of Gennadius, Patriarch of Constantinople.

The Epistle of Tarasius, Patriarch of Constantinople, to Adrian, Pope of Rome, concerning simony. All of these with Balsamon's scholia.

Part II.

The Synopsis by Alexius Aristenus of the letters called Canonical.

The questions of Certain Monks and the Answers sent by the Synod of Constantinople. With notes by Balsamon.[1]

The Alphabetical Syntagma of all that is contained in the Sacred and Divine Canons, by Mathew Blastares, the Monk.[2]

Concerning the Holy and Œcumenical Synod which restored Photius, the most holy Patriarch to the See of Constantinople, and dissolved the scandal of the two Churches

---

[1] According to the Eleuchus, in the beginning of this volume, both of these writings are found in the First Part and not in the Second Part of the volume.

[2] Schoell says that the text is not accurately given.

of Old and New Rome; [Styled by some the "Eighth Œcumenical Synod."] to which is added the Letter of the Blessed John Pope of Rome to the most holy Photius, Archbishop of Constantinople.

An Index Rerum et Verborum of both volumes.

Beveridge's own Notes on the Canons of the Councils.

An Index Rerum et Verborum of the Notes.

Such are the contents of Bishop Beveridge's great work, and it is impossible to exaggerate its value. But it will be noticed that it only covers the disciplinary action of the Councils, and does not give the dogmatic decrees, these being excluded from the author's plan.

Before leaving the collections of the canons we must mention the great work of Justellus (the Preface and notes of which are found reprinted in Migne's *Pat. Lat.*, Tom. LXVII.); *Canonum Ecclesiæ Universæ Gr. et Lat. cum Præfatione Notisque Christoph. Justelli.*

The author was counsellor and secretary to the King of France, was born in Paris 1580, and died in 1649. After his death there appeared at Paris in 1661 a work in 2 volumes folio, with the following title: *Bibliotheca juris canonici vetus . . . ex antiquis codicibus MSS. Bibliothecæ Christopheri Justelli. . . . Opera et studio Gul. Voelli et Henrici Justelli.*

The Church in Paris had the honour of having among its Cathedral clergy the first scholar who published a collection of the Acts of the councils. James Merlin was Canon and Grand Penitentiary of the Metropolitan Church, and the first edition of his work he put out in 1523 in one volume folio. This work passed through several editions within a few years, but soon gave place to fuller collections.[1]

In 1538, the Belgian Franciscan Peter Crabbe (Pierre Grable) issued at Cologne an enlarged collection in two volumes, and the second edition in 1551 was enlarged to three folio volumes. Besides these, there was Lawrence Surius's still more complete collection, published in 1557 (4 vols. folio), and the Venice collection compiled by Domenick Bollanus, O. P., and printed by Dominic Nicolini, 1585 (5 vols. folio).

But the renowned collection of Professor Severin Binius surpassed all its predecessors, and its historical and critical notes are quoted with respect even to-day. The first edition, in four volumes folio, was issued at Cologne in 1606, and later editions, better than the first, in 1618 and 1636. This last edition was published at Paris in nine volumes, and made use of the Roman collection.

To the learned Jesuit Sirmond belongs the chief glory of having compiled this Roman collection, and the "Introduction" is from his pen. The work was undertaken by the authority of Pope Paul V., and much of the Greek text, copied from MSS. in the Vatican Library, was now for the first time given to the reading public. This collection contains only the Ecumenical Councils according to the Roman method of reckoning, and its compilation took from 1608 to 1612.

No collection appeared from this date until the "Collectio Regia," a magnificent series of thirty-seven volumes folio, at the royal press at Paris in 1644. But while it was superb in get up, it left much to be desired when looked at critically, for many faults of the Roman edition already pointed out by Sirmond were not corrected.

And now we have reached the time when the first really great *Concilia* appeared, which while only filling seventeen volumes in folio was yet far more complete —Hefele says twenty-five per cent. more complete—than the great *Collectio Regia* just described. This edition was the work of Philip Labbe (Labbeus in Latin), S. J., and was completed after his death in 1667, by Father Gabriel Cossart of the same Society—"Almost all the French savants quote from this edition of Labbe's with Baluze's supplement,"[2] and I have followed their lead, availing myself of the corrections

---

[1] I am indebted to Hefele, *History of the Councils*, Vol. I.. p. 67 *et seqq.*, for this account of Merlin's *Collection*, as also for most of the statements that follow. Hefele says (footnote to page 67): "The longest details on Merlin's edition are found in a work of Salmon. Doctor and Librarian of the Sorbonne, *Traité de l'Etude des Conciles et de leurs Collections*, etc. Paris, 1726."

[2] Hefele, *Hist. Councils*, vol. I, p. 69.

made by later editors. The title of the edition used in this work is: "Sacrasancta Concilia ad Regiam Editionem exacta. Studio Philip. Labbei et Gabr. Cossartii, Soc. Jesu Presbyterorum. Lutetiæ Parisiorum. MDCLXXI. Cum Privilegio Regis Christianissimi."

Anything more perfect than these precious volumes it would be hard to conceive of, and while of course they contain the errors of chronology *et cetera* of their age, yet their general accuracy and marvellous completeness leave them even to-day as the greatest of the great, although the later edition of Hardouin is more often used by English and American scholars, and is the one quoted by Pope Benedict XIV. in his famous work *De Synodo Diœcesana*. Hardouin's edition did certainly correct many of the faults of Labbe and Cossart, yet had itself many faults and defects which are pointed out by Salmon [1] in a long list, although he fully acknowledges the value of Hardouin's improvements and additions. Perhaps, not unnaturally, as a Professor at the Sorbonne, he preferred Labbe and Cossart. It may not be amiss to add that Hardouin was very anti-Gallican and ultramontane.

The Dominican Archbishop of Lucca, Mansi, in 1759, put out his "Concilia" in thirty-one volumes folio at Florence, styled on the title-page "the most ample" edition ever printed, and claiming to contain all the old and much new matter. It was never finished, only reaching to the XVth century, has no indices, and (says Hefele) "is very inferior to Hardouin in accuracy. The order of the subjects in the later volumes is sometimes not sufficiently methodical, and is at variance with the chronology." [2]

I shall now present the reader with some bibliographical notes which I extract *verbatim* from Hefele (Hefele, *History of the Councils*, Vol. I., p. 74).

Among the numerous works on the history of the councils, the most useful to consult are:

1. John Cabassutius, *Notitia ecclesiastica historiarum conciliorum et canonum*. Lyons 1680, folio. Very often reprinted.

2. Hermant, *Histoire des Conciles*, Rouen 1730, four volumes, 8vo.

3. Labbe, *Synopsis historica Conciliorum*, in vol. i. of his Collection of Councils.

4. Edm. Richer, *Historia conciliorum generalium* (Paris, 1680), three volumes, 4to. Reprinted in 8vo. at Cologne.

5. Charles Ludovic Richard, *Analysis conciliorum generalium et particularium*. Translated from French into Latin by Dalmasus. Four volumes, 8vo, Augsburg, 1778.

6. Christ. Wilh. Franz Walch, *Entwurf einer vollständigen Historie der Kirchenversammlungen*, Leipzig, 1759.

7. Fabricius, *Bibliotheca Græca*, edit. Harless. t. xii., p. 422 sqq., in which is contained an alphabetical table of all the councils, and an estimate of the value of the principal collections.

8. Alletz, *Concilien-Lexikon*, translated from French into German by Father Maurus Disch, a Benedictine and professor at Augsburg, 1843.

9. *Dictionnaire universel et complet des Conciles, tant généraux que particuliers*, etc., rédigé par M. l'abbé P———, prêtre du Diocese de Paris, published by the Abbé Migne (Paris, 1846), two volumes, 4to.

In the great works on ecclesiastical history—for example, in the *Nouvelle Bibliothèque des Auteurs Ecclésiastiques*, by El. Dupin, and the *Historia Literaria* of Cave, and particularly in the excellent *Histoire des Auteurs Sacrés*, by Remi Ceillier—we find matter relating to the history of the councils. Salmon, l. c., p. 387, and Walch in his *Historie der Kirchenversammlungen*, pp. 48–67, have pointed out a large number of works on the history of the councils. There are also very valuable dissertations on the same subject in—

1. Christian Lupus, *Synodorum generalium ac provincialium decreta et canones, scholiis, notis ac historica actorum dissertatione illustrata*, Louv., 1665; Brussels, 1673; five volumes, 4to.

---

[1] Salmon, *l. c.*, pp. 315–331, 786–831.   [2] Hefele, *Hist. Councils*, vol. i, p. 72.

2. Lud. Thomassin, *Dissertationum in Concilia generalia et particularia*, t. i., Paris, 1667 ; reprinted in Rocaberti, *Bibl. pontificia*, tr. XV.

3. Van Espen, *Tractatus Historicus exhibens scholia in omnes canones conciliorum*, etc., in his complete works.

4. Barth. Caranza has written a very complete and useful abstract of the acts of the councils in his *Summa Conciliorum*, which has often been re-edited.

5. George Daniel Fuchs, deacon of Stuttgart, has, in his *Bibliothek der Kirchenversammlungen*, four volumes, Leipsic, 1780–1784, given German translations and abstracts of the acts of the councils in the fourth and fifth centuries.

6. Francis Salmon, Doctor and Librarian of the Sorbonne, has published an Introduction to the Study of the Councils, in his *Traité de l'Étude des Conciles et de leurs collections*, Paris, 1724, in 4to, which has often been reprinted.

To these I would add the following :

1. Fleury, *Histoire Ecclesiastique*. This work in many volumes, part of which has been translated into English, is most useful and accurate, and contains a resumé of the separate canons and definitions as well as the history of the proceedings.

2. Denziger, *Enchiridion Symbolorum et Definitionum quæ de rebus fidei et morum a Conciliis Œcumenicis et Summis Pontificibus emanarunt*. A most useful handbook in the original.

3. Hefele, *Conciliengeschicte*. This, the most recent work upon the subject, is also in some respects the most satisfactory, and it is a matter of real regret that only the first part of the work, down to the end of the Seventh Œcumenical Council, has been translated into English. The last volume of the author's revised edition appeared in 1890. The first volume of the first edition was published in 1855, and the seventh and last in 1874. The entire book was translated into French some years ago (with full indices) by M. l'abbé Goschlerand and M. l'abbé Delarc (Paris, Adrien le Clere et Cie). It should in fairness, however, be remarked that Bishop Hefele was one of the minority who opposed the opportuneness of the definition of Papal infallibility at the Vatican Council, and while indeed afterwards he submitted to the final decree, yet he has been a somewhat suspected person since to those who held extreme views on this doctrine.

So far as I am aware no serious work has been done upon the councils by any writer using the English tongue in recent times, with the exception of the useful *Notes on the Canons of the First Four General Councils*, by Canon Wm. Bright.

The following is a list of the English translations which I have consulted or followed :

John Johnson, *The Clergyman's Vade-mecum* (London, 2d Ed., 1714).

Wm. A. Hammond, *The Definitions of Faith and Canons of Discipline of the Six Œcumenical Councils*, etc.

William Lambert, *The Canons of the First Four General Councils of the Church and those of the Early Greek Synods* (London, s. d. Preface dated 1868).

John Fulton, *Index Canonum*. [This work ends with the Council of Chalcedon.] (New York, 1872. 3d Ed., 1892.)

John Mendham, *The Seventh General Council, the Second of Nice* (London, s. d.).

H. R. Percival, *The Decrees of the Seven Ecumenical Synods*. Appendix I. to *A Digest of Theology* (London, Masters, 1893).

It only remains that I mention two other works.

Dr. Pusey's book, *The Councils of the Church from the Council of Jerusalem A.D. 51 to the Council of Constantinople*, 381 (1857) should not be omitted, and certainly the reader's attention should be called to that most accurate and valuable volume by Herm. Theod. Bruns, *Canones Apostolorum et Conciliorum Veterum Selecti* (Berolini, 1839), which has been constantly referred to in preparing this work.

APPENDED NOTE ON THE EASTERN EDITIONS OF SYNOD- ICAL LITERATURE.

From the presses of the East, especially those at Athens, a number of editions more or less complete of the Greek text of the Canons of the Ecumenical and of the Local Councils have been issued, and the notes of Balsamon, Zonaras, and Aristenus have been added in some cases. Professor Bolotoff writes however that so far as Greek litera- ture on the subject is concerned, with the exception of purely topographical researches in the environs of Constantinople, it is simply putting into Greek what was originally in German.

The Russian Church has done somewhat more and as will be seen from the follow- ing table, some attempts have been made at providing scholia, but when the scheme of this present work was shewn him, Professor Bolotoff said : "We have nothing analo- gous to this undertaking in Russia." The learned professor remarks that all the best Russian literature upon the subject is contained in magazine articles, especially those of Professor Zaozersky of the Moscow Theological Academy, and of Professor A. S. Pavloff, of the University of Moscow ; he mentions also the latter's article in the *Ortho- dox Review*, and adds that "An Essay on a Course of Church Legislation," by Joann Smolensk (St. Petersburg, 1851) should be referred to.

BIBLIOGRAFIČESKIJ UKAZATEL' PEČATNYH IZDANIJ APOSTOL'SKIH I SOBORNYH PRAVIL NA SLAVJANSKOM I RUSSKOM JAZYKAH.

V pravoslavnoj Russkoj Cerkvi izdanija sobornyh pravil i opredělěnij soveršalis' tol'ko po neposredstvennomu rasporjaženiju i soizvoleniju vysšej cerknovnoj vlasti i faktičeski izjaty iz kompetencii častnoj učenoj predpriimčivosti. Poetomu podrobnyja izdanija vypuskalis' v Rossii liš' po měre praktičeskoj potrebnosti.

(1) Pervoe po vremeni pečatnoe izdanie nazvannyh pravil bylo v slavjanskoj "Kormčej Knigě" (=greč. Πηδάλιον), kotoraja načata pečataniem pri Moskovskom patriarhě Iosifě v Moskvě 7go oktjabrja 1649 g. i okončena 1go ijulja 1650 g., no patr. Nikon podverg ego sobornomu peresmotru, pri čem něskol'ko listov bylo perepečatano i vneseno vnov'.[1] Po semu ekzempljary etoj "Kormčej" byli razoslany po cerkvam dlja cerkovnago upotre- blenija i postupili v obrasčěnie ne raněe 1653 g. Vtoroe izdanie "Kormčej" bylo v 1787 g. poslě peresmotra eja mitropolitom Novgorodskim i S. Peterburgskim Gavriilom,[2] a zatěm i drugija (napr., v 1804 g., 1816 g. i 1823 g.) bez osobyh pereměn. Pozdnějšija izdanija otličajutsja ot Nikonovskago v častnostjah, no eto ne kasaetsja cerkovnyh pravil, kotoryja poměščajutsja v pervoj časti "Kormčej" i soderžat 85 apostol'skih pravil, pos- tanovlenija 16-i soborov (*Nikejskago*, Ankirskago, Neokesarijskago, Gangrskago, Antiohij- skago, Laodikijskago, *II-go, III-go, IV-go vselenskih*, Sardikskago, Karfagenskago, Kon- stantinopol'skago, pri Nekopargě, *Trull'skago 692 g., VII-go vselenskago*, Dvukratnago i v cerkvi sv. Sofii) i pravila 13-ti sv. otcov.

(2) V pečatnoj "Kormčej" kanony izloženy ne v polnom tekstě, a v sokrašcennom, inogda dajuščem liš' ves'ma nedostatočnoe predstavlenie o soderžanii podlinnika. Poetomu izdavna dělalis' popytki cělostnyh perevodov,[3] no poslědnie ne pojavljalis' v pečati. Tol'ko uže v 1839 g. sv. Sinodom vypuščeno bylo v S. Peterburgě takoe izdanie: "Kniga pravil

---

[1] Poetomu někotorye bibliografy spravedlivo sčitajut zděs' dva izdanija, iz koih 1653 g. — in folio — sostoit iz 37 +1 + 60 +1 +16 + 679 listov i bylo perepečatano staroobrjadcami (raskol'nikami) v 1785 g. v Varšavě.

[2] Eto izdanie in folio v Moskvě v dvuh častjah i knigah — v 1-j 2 nenum. + 38 + 5 + 60 + 300 + 39 numerovannyh listov, — vo 2-j 1 + 2 + 235 +16 + 37 listov.

[3] Vo vtoroj polovině XVII v. perevodil kanony Epifanij Slavineckij, a v pervoj polovině XVIII v. pravila apostol'ski- ja i sobornyja byli perevedeny Vasiliem Kozlovskim i Grigoriem Poletikoju po grečeskomu tekstu "Synodicon" a Beveregii, s kakovago izdanija sdělan byl novyj perevod v 1782 g.

sv. apostol, sv. soborov vselenskih i poměstnyh i sv. otec", napečatannaja v bol'šoj list v "carstvujuščem gradě sv. Petra pervym tisneniem, v lěto ot sozdanija mira 7347, ot Roždestva že po ploti Boga Slova 1839, indikta 12"; v nem 4 nenumerovannye lista i 455 numerovannyh strannic. Na každoj strannicě dvě kolonny dlja podlinnika i novago slavjanskago perevoda po polnomu tekstu, no bez tolkovanij vizantijskih kanonistov; rědko na osnovanii Zonary ili Val'samona dajutsja priměčanija, ne vsegda točnyja istoričeski (napr. k 10 pravilu Ankirsk., 3 Sard., 4 Karfag. i o dvukratnom soborě 861 g.), a po městam i samyj tekst ne ispraven (napr., v 13-m prav. I-go vsel. sobora). Eta "Kniga" iměla potom slědujuščija izdanija: (2) v Moskvě v Sinodal'noj tipografii v 1862, in folio 8 ll.+672+74 numer. strn., s tekstom grečeskim i slavjanskim (3) ibid. v 1866 g. in quarto, 3 ll.+373 strn.+1 l.+59 strn., s odnim slavjanskim tekstom; (4) ibid. v 1874 g., in octavo, 4 ll.+455 strn.+2 ll.+104+4 strn., tože s odnim slavjanskim tekstom; (5) ibid. v 1886 g., in folio, 3 ll.+395+42 strn.+1 l., opjat' v odnom slavjanskom tekstě.

(3) "Kniga pravil" ničut' ne predstavljaet avtorizovannago *textus receptus*, i poslě eja izdanija sam Sv. Sinod ne rědko privodil v svoih ukazah pravila po slavjanskoj redakcii "Kormčej knigi," a potom rekomendoval Afinskoe izdanie "Sintagmy" dlja vsěh duhovno-učebnyh zavedenij. Eto otkryvalo město dlja novoj obrabotki, kotoraja s razrěšenija vysšej duhovnoj vlasti i byla predprinjata Moskovskim "Obščestvom ljubitelej duhovnago prosvěščenija". Objavlenie ob etom bylo sdělano v N-rě 3 "Moskovskih Eparhialnyh Cerkovnyh Vědomostej" za 1875 g., a v janvarskoj knižkě togože goda Moskovskago žurnala "Čtenija v Obščestvě ljubitelej duhovnago prosvěščenija" byla napečatana i samaja "programma" izdanija (strn. 79-90 v otdělě bibliografii. Po povodu eja professor kanoni-českago prava v Novororossijskom Universitetě (skončavšijsja 16go avgusta 1898 g. pro-fessorom Moskovskago Universiteta) Aleksej Stepanovič Pavlov sdělal "Zaměčanija na programmu izdanija, v russkom perevodě, cerkovnyh pravil s tolkovanijami" v "Zapiskah Imperatorskago Novorossijskago Universiteta", t. XVI (Odessa 1875 g.) strn. 1-17 priloženij (i v otděl'noj brošurě), a poslě perepečatal ih—s někotorymi dopolnenijami— v Moskovskom žurnalě "Pravoslavnoe Obozrenie" za aprěl' 1876 g. (strn. 730-746) pod zaglaviem "O novom perevodě tolkovanij na cerkovnyja pravila". Na eti vozraženija otvěcal professor cerkovnago prava v Moskovskoj Duhovnoj Akademii Aleksandr Feo-dorovič Lavrov v žurnalě "Čtenija v Obščestvě ljubitelej duhovnago prosvěščenija" (č. II, strn. 158-194 za 1877 g.) "Pečatnym pis'mom k Alekseju Stepanoviču Pavlovu". Tak postepenno opredělilsja plan izdanija, kotoroe pečatalos' snačala v priloženijah k žurnalu "Čtenija v Obščestvě i pr.", a potom javilos' i otděl'no in octavo v slědujuščih vypuskah: (a) I-j "Pravila svjatih Apostol s tolkovanijami" v dvuh izdanijah—Moskva 1876 g. iz "Čtenij 1875 g., strn. 1-163) 4+12+175 strn., i ibid. 1887 g., 5+12+163 strn.; II-j "Pravila svjatyh vselennyh soborov s tolkovanijami" (iz "Čtenij" 1875 g., strn. 165-328; 1876 g., strn. 329-680; 1877 g., strn. 681-900) v dvuh častjah: 1-ja "pravila soborov 1-4" Moskva 1877 g., 260 strn., 2-ja "pravila soborov 5-7" ibid., 736 strn.; b) "Pravila svjatyh poměstnyh soborov s tolkovanijami" tože v dvuh vypuskah (iz "Čtenij" 1877 g., strn. 900-1066; 1878 g., strn. 1067-1306; 1879 g., strn. 1307-1410: 1-j (pravila soborov Ankirskago, Neokesarijskago, Gangrskago, Antiohijskago, Laodikijskago i Sardikijskago) Moskva 1880, strn. 359; 2-j (pravila soborov Karfagenskago [s poslanijami k papě Vonifatiju i papě Kelestinu], Konstantinopol'skago, Dvukratnago i vo hramě premudrosti slova Božija) ibid. 1881, strn. 876; c) "Pravila svjatyh otec s tolkovanijami" ibid. 1884, strn. 626. Pri nih iměetsja otděl'nyj "Ukazatel' predmetov, soderžaščihsja v izdanii pravil apostol'skih, sobornyh i svjatyh otcev s tolkovanijami", Moskva 1888, 58 strn. in octavo. Grečeskij tekst pravil privoditsja po izdaniju Σύνταγμα τῶν Θείων καὶ ἱερῶν κανόνων ... ὑπὸ Γ. Α. Ῥάλλη καὶ Μ. Πότλη, Ἀθήνησιν 1852-1854, rjadom s nim po-měščajetsja doslovnyj slavjanskij perevod tolkovanij vizantijskih kommentatorov (Zonary, Aristina, Val'samona), tekst i tolkovanija slavjanskoj Kormčej; vse eto soprovoždaetsja vydanijami i vsjakago roda pojasnenijami (istoričeskimi, filologičeskimi i t. p.). Izdanie

eto specialistami spravědlivo sčitaetsja ves'ma cěnnym v naučnom otnošenii.   Glavnym redaktorom i dějatelem ego byl prof. A. F. Lavrov (v monašestvě Aleksij, skončavšijsja arhiepiskopom Litovskim i Vilenskim), no privlekalis' k učastiju mnogija drugija lica i meždu nimi prof. A. S. Pavlov.

(4) Russkij perevod pravil iměetsja tol'ko pri izdanijah Kazanskoj Duhovnoj Akademii: *a*) "Dějanija vselenskih soborov v perevodě na russkij jazyk", t. I VII (7), Kazan' 1859-1878 (někotorye tomy vo vtorom izdanii) i *b*) "Dějanija devjati poměstnyh soborov v perevodě na russkij jazyk", odin tom, Kazan' 1878.   Etot perevod sdělan po poručenii Sv. Sinoda, a pravila peredajutsja v nem po tekstu sobornyh dějanij.

Iz predstavlennago očerka pečatnyh izdanij sobornyh pravil vidno, čto oni — v predělah svoej faktičeskoj priměnimosti — počitajutsja istočnikom *dějstvujuščago* prava v Russkoj pravoslavnoj cerkvi, počemu dlja neja osobennuju važnost' imějut liš' avtoritetnyja vizantijskija, tolkovanija, o kotoryh suščestvujut izslědovanija *V. Demidova*, harakter i značenie tolkovanij na kanoničeskij kodeks grečeskoj cerkvi — Aristina, Zonary i Val'samona — v "Pravoslavnom Obozrěnii" t.   II-j za 1888 g., Kazanskago prof. *V. A. Narbskago*, Tolkovanija Val'samona na nomokanon Fotija, Kazan' 1889, i Jur'evskago (= Derptskago) prof. *M. E. Krasnožena*, Tolkovateli kanoničeskago kodeksa vostočnoj cerkvi: Aristin, Zonara i Val'samon, Moskva 1892.

Otděl'nyh naučnyh tolkovanij vsěh sobornyh pravil v russkoj literaturě nět, no oni izlagajutsja i razjasnjajutsja v kursah cerkovnago prava (arhimandrit. [†ep. Smolenskago] Ioanna, prof. N. S. Suvorova, I. S. Berdnikova, P. A. Laskareva, M. A. Ostroumova), v sočinenijah po istorii vselenskih soborov (ep. Ioanna, prof. Alekšěja Petroviča Lebedeva), v kanoničeskih i cerkovno-istoričeskih monografijah.   Kasatel'no kritičeskago izdanija podlinnago teksta pravil est' učenaja i poleznaja stat'ja (o knigě Fr. Lauchert, Die Kanones usw., Freiburg i. Br. und Leipzig 1896) professora cerkovnnoj istorii v S. Peterburgskoj Duhovnoj Akademii Vasilija Vasilieviča Bolotova v "Hristianskom Čtenii", vyp.   IV-j za 1896 g., strn. 178–195.

Professor S.-Peterburgskoj Duhovnoj Akademii
po kafedrě Sv. Pisanija Novago Zavěta
NIKOLAJ GLUBOKOVSKIJ.
S.-Peterburg, 1898, X, 11-voskresenie.

A BIBLIOGRAPHICAL INDEX OF THE PRINTED EDITIONS OF THE CANONS OF THE APOSTLES AND OF THE COUNCILS IN THE SLAVONIC AND RUSSIAN LANGUAGES.

(Prepared by NICOLAS GLUBOKOFFSKI, Professor of the Chair of the Holy Scriptures of the New Testament in the Ecclesiastical Academy of St. Petersburgh.)[1]

IN the orthodox Russian Church, editions of the Conciliar Canons and Decrees have only been issued under the immediate disposition and sanction of the supreme ecclesiastical authority, and, in fact, are amongst those things which it is not within the competence of private scholars to undertake.   Such editions therefore have been published in Russia only in accordance with practical requirements.

1. The earliest printed edition of the afore-mentioned canons appeared in the Slavonic " Kormchaja Kniga "[2] (= Gk. πηδάλιον), the printing of which was commenced at Moscow, on October 7th, 1649, under the Patriarch Joseph of Moscow, and was finished on July 1, 1650 ; but the Patriarch Nicon caused it to be submitted to a Council for revision, in consequence of which certain pages were reprinted and inserted afresh into it.[3]   Thereupon copies of this " Kormchaja" were distributed for use amongst the

---

[1] Translated into English by W. J. Birkbeck, Esq., F. S. A.   [2] *Steering-Book.* W. J. B.
[3] Accordingly some bibliographers correctly reckon this as two editions, of which that of 1653 *in folio consists* of 37 + 1 + 60 + 1 + 16 + 679 pages, and was reprinted by the " Old Ritualists " (*Rascolniki*), in 1785 at Warsaw.
[4] *Rascolniki*, lit. *Schismatics;* i.e., the Russian Dissenting sects which in the 17th century left the Church rather than accept the service-books as corrected by the Patriarch Nicon.—W. J B.

churches, and came into general circulation not earlier than the year 1653. The second edition of the " Kormchaja " appeared in 1787, after a revision under the Metropolitan Gabriel of Novgorod and St. Petersburgh,[1] and was followed by others (e.g., those of 1804, 1816, and 1823) without any alterations of importance. The latest editions differ from that of Nicon in certain particulars, but these particulars do not concern the ecclesiastical Canons, which are placed in the first part of the " Kormchaja " and include the 85 Apostolic Canons, the decrees of the sixteen councils (of *Nicaea*, Ancyra, Neocæsarea, Gangra, Antioch, Laodicea, *the 2d, 3d, and 4th Ecumenical*, Sardica, Carthage, Constantinople under Nectarius, in *Trullo, A.D. 692, the 7th Ecumenical*, the First-and-Second [council of Constantinople] and that in the church of St. Sophia) and the Canons of the 13 Holy Fathers.

2. In the printed " Kormchaja " the canons are set forth, not in their full text, but in a shortened form which sometimes gives but a very insufficient representation of the contents of the original. On this account attempts·at full translations were made many years back, but these never appeared in print. It was not until 1839 that such an edition as this was put forth ·by the Holy Synod at St. Petersburgh, under the title : " The Book of the Canons of the Holy Apostles, of the Holy Ecumenical and local Councils, and of the Holy Fathers," printed in large folio in " the Imperial city of St. Peter, the first impression in the 7347th year from the creation of the world, and the 1839th from the Birth in the flesh of God the Word, indict. 12." In this edition there are 4 unnumbered leaves and 455 numbered pages. On each page there are two columns, for the original text and the new translation of the whole text into the Slavonic respectively, but without the commentaries of the Byzantine Canonists; occasionally, but rarely, notes based upon Zonaras or Balsamon are given, which are not always historically accurate (for instance, that to the 10th Canon of Ancyra, the 3d of Sardica the 4th of Carthage, and the one which deals with the First-and-Second Council of A.D. 861) while in some places the text itself is not correct (for instance, in the 13th Canon of the 1st Ecumenical Council). This " Book of the Canons " subsequently went through the following editions : the 2d, printed in Moscow at the Synodal Press in 1862, *in folio* 8 leaves + 672 + 74 numbered pages, with Greek and Slavonic texts; the 3d ibid in 1866, *in quarto*, 3 leaves + 373 pages + 1 leaf + 59 pages, with the Slavonic text only ; the 4th, ibid in 1874, *in octavo*, 4 leaves + 455 pages + 2 leaves + 104 + 4 pages, also with the Slavonic text only ; the 5th, ibid. in 1886, *in folio*, 3 leaves + 395 + 42 pages + 1 leaf, again with Slavonic text only.

3. The " Book of Canons " by no means represents an authorized *textus receptus*, and after its publication, the Holy Synod itself not unfrequently introduced the Canons as given in the Slavonic edition of the " Kormchaja Kniga "·into its edicts, and moreover recommended the Athenian Edition of the " Syntagma " for all the ecclesiastico-educational establishments. ·This opened the way for a new work, which, with the permission of the supreme ecclesiastical authority, was undertaken by the Moscow "Society of Amateurs of Spiritual Enlightenment." The announcement of this was made in No. 3 of the " Moscow Diocesan Church Gazette " of the year 1875, whilst in the same year in the January number of the Moscow Journal, " Lectures delivered in the Society of Amateurs of Spiritual Enlightenment," the " programme " of the edition itself was printed (pages 79–90 in the section devoted to bibliography). In criticism of it the Professor of Canonical Law in the University of Novorossiisk, Alexis Stepanovich Pavloff (who died on August 16, 1898, as Professor of the University of Moscow) wrote " Notes on the programme of an edition, in a Russian translation of the Canons of the Church with Commentaries " in the sixteenth volume of " Memoirs of the Imperial University of Novorossiisk " (Odessa, 1875), pages 1–17 of the Appendix (and in a separate pamphlet), which was afterwards reprinted with certain additions in the Moscow Journal, " Orthodox Review," of April, 1876 (pages 730–746), under the title : " A new translation of the Commentaries upon the canons of the church." To these criticisms the Professor of

---

[1] This edition was published at Moscow *in folio* in two parts and volumes, in the 1st there are 2 unnumbered + 38 + 5 — 60 + 300 + 39 numbered pages ; in the 2d 1 + 2 + 235 + 16 + 37 pages.

Ecclesiastical Law in the Moscow Ecclesiastical Academy, Alexander Theodorovich Lavroff, wrote a reply in "Lectures delivered in the Society of Amateurs of Spiritual Enlightenment" (for the year 1877, part 2, pages 158–194), entitled "A printed letter to Alexis Stepanovich Pavloff." Thus the plan of the edition gradually took shape. It was first printed in the Appendices to the Journal "Lectures in the Society, etc.," and subsequently was published separately *in octavo*. in the following parts (A) I. "The Canons of the Holy Apostles with Commentaries" in two editions—Moscow, 1876, (from "Lectures," 1875, pages 1–163) 4 + 12 + 175 pages, and ibid., 1887, 5–12 + 163 pages; II. "Canons of the Holy Ecuménical Councils with Commentaries" (from "Lectures" 1875, pages 165–325; 1876, pages 329–680; 1877, pages 891–900), in two parts: 1st "The Canons of the Councils I.-IV.," Moscow, 1877, 260 pages; 2d. "The Canons of Councils V.-VII.," ibid., 736 pages; (B) "The Canons of the Holy Local Councils with Commentaries," also in two parts (from "Lectures" 1877, pages 900–1066; 1878, pages 1067–1306; 1879, pages 1307–1410): the 1st (The Canons of the Councils of Ancyra, Neocæsarea, Gangra, Antioch, Laodicea, and Sardica) Moscow, 1880, 359 pages; the 2d (The Canons of the Councils of Carthage [with the letters to Pope Boniface and to Pope Celestine], Constantinople, the First-and-Second, and that in the Temple of the Wisdom of the Word of God) ibid., 1881, 876 pages; (C) "The Canons of the Holy Fathers with Commentaries," ibid., 1884, 626 pages. Together with these is a separate "Index of subjects contained in the edition of the Canons of the Apostles, Councils and Holy Fathers with Commentaries," Moscow, 1888, 58 pages *in octavo*. The Greek text of the canons follows the edition Σύνταγμα τῶν θείων καὶ ἱερῶν κανόνων . . . ὑπὸ Γ. Α. Ράλλη καὶ Μ. Πότλη, Αθήνησιν 1852–1854, and alongside of it is placed a literal Slavonic translation, after which follows a Russian translation of the Commentaries of the Byzantine Canonists (Zonaras, Aristenus, Balsamon), and the text and commentaries of the Slavonic "Kormchaja;" all this is accompanied by introductions and explanations of all sorts (historical, philological, etc.). This edition is rightly considered by specialists to be of very great value from a scientific point of view. Professor A. Th. Lavroff (who became a monk under the name Alexis, and died Archbishop of Lithuania and Vilna) was its chief editor and had most to do with it, but many others took part in the work, and amongst these Professor A. S. Pavloff.

4. The only *Russian* translation of the canons which exists is contained in the publications of the Ecclesiastical Academy of Kazan: (a) "The Acts of the Ecumenical Councils translated into Russian," 7 volumes. Kazan, 1859–1878 (some of these volumes have run into a second edition) and (b) "Acts of the nine local councils translated into Russian," 1 volume, Kazan, 1878. This translation was made under the direction of the Holy Synod, and the Canons are reproduced in it according to the text of the Acts of the Councils.

From the outline here presented of the printed editions of the Canons of the Councils, it will be seen that, within the limits of their practical applicability, they are reverenced as the source of the *operative* law in the Russian orthodox church, and therefore for her it is only the authoritative Byzantine commentaries which have any particular importance. There are works upon these by *V. Demidoff*, "The character and significance of the commentaries upon the Canonical Codex of the Greek Church—of Aristenus, Zonaras, and Balsamon," in the "Orthodox Review," vol. ii. of 1888, and of Professor *V. A. Narbekoff*, of Kazan, "The commentaries of Balsamon upon tne Nomocanon of Photius," Kazan, 1889, and of Professor *M. E. Krasnozhen*, of Jurieff (Dorpat) "The Commentators of the Canonical Codex of the Eastern Church: Aristenus, Zonaras, and Balsamon." Moscow, 1892.

No separate scientific commentaries upon all the canons of the councils exist in Russian literature, but they are described, and explained in courses of Ecclesiastical law (of the Archimandrite John [who, when he died, was Bishop of Smolensk] of Professors N. S. Suvoroff, T. S. Berdnikoff. N. A. Lashkareff, M. A. Ostroümoff) in our works upon the history of the Ecumenical Councils (by Bishop John, and Professor Alexis Petrovich Lebedeff), and in monographs dealing with Canon Law and Church History.   As far as a critical edition of the original text of the canons is concerned, there is a learned and useful article (upon a book by Fr. Lauchert, Die Kanones usw., Freiberg i. Br. und Leipsig, 1896), by Vasili Vasilievich Bolotoff, Professor of Ecclesiastical History in the St. Petersburgh Ecclesiastical Academy in the " Christian Reading," vol. iv. for 1896, pp. 178–195.

EXCURSUS ON THE HISTORY OF THE ROMAN LAW AND ITS RELATION TO THE CANON LAW.

THE foregoing bibliographical outline would be entirely incomplete did I not give the reader at least a sketch of how those canons adopted by the various councils gradually won admission to the law-code of the Empire, and how that code itself came into being. For those wishing to study the matter in detail I would name as the most recent authorities upon the Roman Law, Mr. Muirhead, who has published with additions and notes his article on the subject in the " Encyclopædia Britannica," and Mr. Bury's new edition of Gibbon's *Rome* just being issued with most learned notes.

But neither of these writers has put the matter exactly as I desire for this purpose, and I have therefore been forced to seek elsewhere the information I now lay before the reader.

The study of Jurisprudence did not form a separate department among the ancient Greeks, but among the Romans it was quite otherwise, and a very elaborate system was developed, so elaborate as to demand the care of a special class of men, who devoted themselves to this business alone and handed down to their successors a constantly increasing mass of legal matter.

When Greece fell under the Roman yoke the laws of the victor were imposed upon the vanquished, but even then the Greeks did not take to legal studies. In fact not until the seat of the Empire was removed to Constantinople did the East become a centre of jurisprudence or the residence of the chief legal experts. In the whole period before the fourth century of our era we know of but one barrister who wrote in Greek, and he came from the West, Herennius Modestinus. He was a disciple of Ulpian and preceptor to the Emperor Maximian the Younger.

From the time of Hadrian to that of Alexander Severus the influence of the legal schools of Rome had been paramount. The Emperors consulted them and asked them to decide difficult points. But after the death of Alexander this custom fell into entire disuse, and the Emperors themselves decided the matters formerly entrusted to the lawyers. After this time the Imperial Constitutions became the chief sources of Roman law. It is only in the time of Constantine the Great that we find once again the lawyers rising into prominence and a flourishing school at Beyroot in Syria. It was at this time that the Imperial Constitutions or Edicts were first collected, for until then they existed only in detached documents. This collection was made by two lawyers, Gregory or Gregorian, and Hermogenes. Gregory's collection contains the laws set forth from the time of Hadrian to Constantine, and Hermogenes wrote a supplement. Although this was but a private enterprise, yet it was cited in the courts of law, just as Lord Lyndwood's *Provinciale* is with us to-day.

It is interesting to note that it was about this same time that the first attempt was made to collect the ecclesiastical canons, and so the Civil Law and the Canon Law (as we know them in after times) had their rise about the same period.

The law of the Empire was not, however, to be left to private and unofficial action, but by the care of Theodosius the Younger its first official collection was made. This prince directed eight men learned in the law to gather into one body of laws all the Imperial Constitutions published since the last included in the collections of Gregory and Hermogenes. This is the " Theodosian Code," and contains the laws set forth by Constantine and his successors. It was promulgated in 438 in the East, and received by the then Emperor of the West, Valentinian III. To this were subsequently added such laws as each set forth, under the title of " New Constitutions."

The Emperor Justinian determined still further to simplify the attaining of judicial decisions. It is true that the making of the legal collections referred to had added greatly to the ease of determining the law in any given case, but there was a source of great confusion in the endless number of legal decisions which by custom had acquired the force of law, and which were by no means always consistent between themselves; these were the famous *responsa jurisperitorum*. To clear up this difficulty was no small task, but the Emperor went about it in the most determined fashion and appointed a commission, consisting of Tribonian and ten other experts, to make a new collection of all the imperial constitutions from Hadrian to his own day. This is the famous Justinian Code, which was promulgated in 529, and abrogated all previous collections.[1]

This, however, was not sufficient to remove the difficulty, and Tribonian next, together with sixteen lawyers, spent three years in making extracts from the great mass of decisions of the ancient jurists, filling as they did nearly two thousand volumes. These they digested and did their best to clear away the contradictions. When the work was finished it appeared to the world as the "Pandects," because it was intended to contain all there was to be said upon the subject. It is also known as the "Digest." This work was set forth in 533 and from that time such of the former decisions as were not incorporated ceased to have any force.

It must however be remembered that, while this was the case, all the decisions contained in the Pandects did not obtain the force of law. The Pandects are not a code of laws, but a system of public jurisprudence composed by public authority. To the Pandects were added by the Emperor two ordinances, the first to forbid any copyist to write them in an abbreviated form; and the second forbidding commentators to treat them in anything but their literal sense.

While this work was in progress some points were so complicated and obscure that the Emperor had to be appealed to, and his writings in these particulars are the origin of the "Fifty Decisions."

At the same time was prepared the "Institutes," containing the elements of the whole Roman law.[2]

Later, new laws having been made, the Code had to be revised; the former edition was abrogated in 534, and a new one set forth with the title "Codex repetitæ prælectionis."

The last of Justinian's labours in the field of jurisprudence (if indeed they were not collected after his death) are his "Novels," a series of imperial constitutions issued between 535 and 559 (Νεαραὶ Διατάξεις). There are one hundred and sixty-eight of these Novels, but the ancient glosses only know ninety-seven, and the rest have been added since, as they have been found.

Such is the origin of the *Corpus Juris Civilis*, and its history needed to be set forth in this place on account of its close connection with the *Corpus Juris Canonici*. In the foregoing I have followed M. Schœll in his admirable *Histoire de la Littérature Grecque Profane*, to which I am also chiefly indebted for the following notes upon the jurists of the sixth and ensuing centuries.

A work which is often looked upon as the origin of the Canon Law was composed by a lawyer of Antioch, somewhere near the middle of the sixth century. This jurist was John of Antioch, surnamed Scholasticus. He was representative or apocrisiarius of the Church of Antioch at Constantinople, and afterward was made Patriarch of that see, over which he ruled from 564 until his death in 578. While still a simple priest at Antioch he made his *Collection of the Canons of the Councils*.

"He was not the first who conceived the idea of such a work. Some writers, resting upon a passage in Socrates, have been of opinion that this honour belonged to Sabinus, bishop of Heraclea, in Thrace, at the beginning of the fifth century; but Socrates is not speaking of a collection of canons at all, but of the synodal acts, of the letters written by or addressed to the synods. If, however, Sabinus did not make a collection of canons, it is certain nevertheless that before John of Antioch there existed one, for he himself cites it many times, although he does not name the authors."[3]

---

[1] It was written in Latin but, says Bury (Appendix to Vol. V. of Gibbon's *Rome*, p. 525), "was also immediately after its publication in Latin, issued (perhaps incompletely) in a Greek form (Cf. Zacharia Von Lingenthal, *Gr. Röm. Recht.*, p. 6). Most of the later Novels are Greek, and Novel vij. [15, ed. Zach.] expressly recognizes the necessity of using 'the common Greek tongue.'"
[2] The Pandects or Digest was translated into Greek by Dorotheus, and Theophilus prepared a Greek paraphrase of the Institutes.
[3] Schœll, *Hist. Litt. Grec.*, Tome vii., Lib. vi., chap. xcvij., p. 226.

"In gathering together thus the canons of the councils John of Antioch did not form a complete body of ecclesiastical law. By his Novel CXLI., Justinian had indeed given to the canons of the Church the force of law, but he himself published a great number of constitutions upon Church matters. Now it was necessary to harmonize these constitutions and canons, and to accomplish this feat was the object of a second work undertaken by John of Antioch, to which he gave the title of Nomocanon (Νομοκάνων),[1] a word which from that time has served to designate any collection of this sort."[2]

Bury says, "In the troubles of the VIIth century the study of law, like many other things, declined, and in the practical administration of justice the prescriptions of the Code and Digest were often ignored or modified by the alien precepts of Christianity. The religion of the Empire had exerted but very slight influence—no fundamental influence, we may say—on the Justinian law. Leo III., the founder of the Syrian (vulgarly called Isaurian) dynasty, when he restored the Empire after a generation of anarchy, saw the necessity of legislation to meet the changed circumstances of the time. The settlements of foreigners—Slavs and Mardaites—in the provinces of the Empire created an agrarian question, which he dealt with in his Agrarian Code. The increase of Slavonic and Saracenic piracy demanded increased securities for maritime trade, and this was dealt with in a Navigation Code. But it was not only for special relations that Leo made laws ; he legislated also, and in an entirely new way, for the general relations of life. He issued a law book (in A.D. 740 in the name of himself and his son Constantine), which changed and modified the Roman law, as it had been fixed by Justinian. The Ecloga,[3] as it is called, may be described as a Christian law book. It is a deliberate attempt to change the legal system of the Empire by an application of Christian principles. Examples, to illustrate its tendency, will be given below. The horror in which the iconoclasts were held on account of their heresy by the image-worshippers, cast discredit upon all their works. This feeling had something to do with the great reaction, which was inaugurated by Basil I., against their legal reforms. The Christian Code of Leo prevailed in the empire for less than a century and a half ; and then, under the auspices of Basil, the Roman law of Justinian was (partially) restored. In legal activity the Basilian epoch faintly reflected the epoch of Justinian itself. A handbook of extracts from the Institutes, Digest, Code, and Novels, was published in A.D. 879, entitled the Prochiron, to diffuse a knowledge of the forgotten system. But the great achievement of the Basilian epoch is the 'Basilica'—begun under Basil, completed under Leo VI.—a huge collection of all the laws of the Empire, not only those still valid, but those which had become obsolete. It seems that two commissions of experts were appointed to prepare the material for this work. One of these commissions compiled the Prochiron by the way, and planned out the Basilica in sixty Books. The other commission also prepared a handbook called the Epanagoge, which was never actually published (though a sketch of the work is extant), and planned out the Basilica in forty Books. The Basilica, as actually published, are arranged in sixty Books, compiled from the materials prepared by both commissions.

"The Basilian revival of Justinianean law was permanent ; and it is outside our purpose to follow the history further, except to note the importance of the foundation of a school of law at Constantinople in the 11th century by the Emperor Constantine IX. The law enacting the institution of this school, under the direction of a salaried Nomophylax, is extant. John Xiphilin (see above) was the first director. This foundation may have possibly had some influence on the institution of the school at Bologna half a century later."[4]

I take from Schœll the following description of the "Basilica" :

"The 'Basilica' are a body of Roman law in the Greek language, extracted from the Institutes, the Pandects, the Codes and the Novels of Justinian as well as from the Im-

---

[1] The two collections of John are published with a translation in the *Bibliotheca Juris Canonici Veteris* of Voellus and Justellus. Vol. II.   [2] *Ibid ut supra*, p. 227.

[3] The "*Ecloga*" were edited in 1852 by Zacharia, and again in 1889 by Monferratus.

[4] Appendix to Vol. V. of Gibbon's *Decline and Fall of the Roman Empire*, pp. 525 and 526.

perial Constitutions posterior to that prince; also extracts from the interpretations of such jurists as had won a fixed authority in the courts, and the canons of the councils. Here is found together the civil and the ecclesiastical law of the Greeks, these two laws having been in an intimate union by reason of the authority which the Emperors exercised over the Church; on the other hand, in the West there was formed step by step a canon law separate from the civil law, and having a different source."[1]

Such, then, were the "Basilica," but what is most singular is that this collection was not given the force of law, neither by Leo VI. nor by Constantine VI., although it was prepared at their order, under their authority, and was written in the language which was spoken by their subjects. The Justinian code of law, although in Latin, still continued to be the only authority in the entire East. An anonymous writer prepared an Epitome of the Basilica, digested into Alphabetical order, and beginning with "Of the Orthodox faith of Christians."

In 883 Photius published a "Syntagma canonum" and a "Nomocanon" with the title Προκανὼν, because it was placed before the canons. This last work at the command of Constantine VI. was revised and soon took the place of the Nomocanon of John of Antioch, over which work it had the advantage of being more recent and of being digested in better order. In citing the canons, only the titles are given; but the text of the civil laws appears in full. "As in the Eastern Church the influence of the imperial authority increased at the expense of that of the councils, and as these princes made ecclesiastical affairs a principal part of their government, it came to pass that the *Nomocanon* of Photius became of more frequent and more necessary use than his *Syntagma*, [which contained the actual text of the canons of the councils down to 880]. Many commentators busied themselves with it, while the collection of the councils was neglected. Thus it has happened that the *Nomocanon* has become the true foundation of the ecclesiastical law of the East."[2]

But while this is true, yet there were not lacking commentators upon the Canon law, and of the three chiefest of these some notice must be taken in this place. As I have already pointed out it is to Bishop Beveridge that we owe the publication not only of Photius's Collection of Canons which are found in his "Συνοδικὸν sive Pandectæ," but also of the scholia of all three of these great commentators, Zonaras, Aristenus, and Balsamon, and from his most learned Prolegomena to the same work I have chiefly drawn the following facts, referring the curious reader to the introduction[3] itself for further particulars.

John Zonaras was probably the same person who wrote the Byzantine History which bears his name. He flourished under Alexis Comnenus, and enjoyed the high office of Grand Drungarius Viglæ (Δρουγγαριος τῆς Βίγλης) and Chief of the Clerks. After some years of secular life he retired to a monastery and devoted himself to literary pursuits. While here, at the command of his superiors, and moved by the persuasion of his friends, he wrote that great book which has made his fame, which he entitled "An Exposition of the Sacred and Divine Canons, as well those of the holy and venerable Apostles, as also those of the sacred Œcumenical Synods, and those of the local or particular councils, and those of the rest of the Holy Fathers; by the labour of John Zonaras the monk, who was formerly Grand Drungarius Viglæ and Chief of the Clerks."[4]

One of the greatest peculiarities of this work, and one which distinguishes it very markedly from the later work of Balsamon upon the same subject, is that Zonaras confines himself strictly to the canon law and rarely makes any references to the civil law whatever; and in such canons as bear no relation to the civil law Balsamon often adopts Zonaras's notes without change or addition.

These commentaries were first brought to light by John Quintin, a professor of canon law at Paris, who published a Latin translation of the scholia upon the Apostolic

---

[1] Schœll, *ut supra*, p. 229. The best edition of the *Basilica* is by W. E. Heimbach in 6 vols. (1833–70).
[2] Schœll, *ut ante*, p. 238.
[3] Beveridge, Συνοδικὸν sive Pandectæ, Tom. I. of the original ed. Reprinted in *Lib. Anglo. Cath. Theol.*, appendix to Vol. XII. of Beveridge's Works. pp. xxi.–xxxix.
[4] Ἐξήγησις τῶν ἱερῶν καὶ θείων κανόνων τῶν τε ἁγίων καὶ σεπτῶν Ἀποστόλων, κ. τ. λ.

Canons. This was in 1558. In 1618 Antonius Salmatia edited his commentaries on the canons of the Councils done into Latin. To this Latin version the Paris press added the Greek text from the MS. codex in the Royal Library and printed it in 1618. In 1622 the same press issued his commentaries upon the Epistles of the Holy Fathers, together with those of St. Gregory Thaumaturgus, Macarius of Egypt, and Basil. But Beveridge collected them in his Oxford Edition for the first time into one work; preparing a somewhat critical text by collation with some manuscripts he found at home.

The second of these great Greek scholiasts is Alexis Aristenus. As Beveridge points out, he must have flourished before or at the same time as Balsamon, for this latter speaks of him in high terms of commendation in his scholion on the Sixth of the Apostolic Canons, describing him as τον ὑπέρτιμον. Aristenus was Nomophylax, Orphanotrophe and Protecdekas, or chief of the Syndics of the Communes, called Ecdics (῎Εκδικοι). He wrote the excellent series of notes upon the Epitomes of the Canons which are given the reader in Beveridge's Pradects. Schœll says that it is an error to attribute to him the " Extract of the Ancient Ecclesiastical Laws," "which is none of his." [1] Aristenus was Grand Economus of the Church of Constantinople and a man of great distinction; and his opinion was sought after and his decision followed even when in opposition to one of the Patriarchs, viz.: Nicephorus of Jerusalem.

Beveridge was the first to print Aristenus's *Scholia*, and he did so from four MSS., in England, for a description of which I refer the reader to the bishop's prolegomena.

Theodore Balsamon is the last of the three great Greek scholiasts. He flourished in the time of the Emperor Isaac Angelus and bore the title of Patriarch of Antioch, although at that time the city was in the hands of the Latins and had been so since 1100. He was looked upon as the greatest jurist of his times both in ecclesiastical and civil matters. Somewhere about the year 1150, he wrote by the order of Manuel Comnenus a series of " Scholia upon the Nomocanon of Photius," and another set styled " Scholia upon the Canons of the Apostles, of the Councils and of the Fathers of the Church; " he also prepared a " Collection of [imperial] Constitutions upon ecclesiastical matters," [3] in three books, which has been published (by Lœwenklaw) at Frankfort, 1595, under the title "Paratitles." There remains also a great number of his opinions on cases presented to him, notably his " answers to sixty-four canonical questions by Mark, Patriarch of Alexandria."

These most learned writings were unknown and forgotten, at least in the West, until they were set forth in a Latin translation during the time the Council of Trent was sitting, in 1561, and not till 1620 did the Greek text appear in the Paris edition of that date. But this text was imperfect and corrupt, and Beveridge produced a pure text from an Oxford MS., with which he compared several others. Moreover in his Pandects he amended the Latin text as well in numberless particulars. For further particulars of the bibliography of the matter see Beveridge.[4]

It may not be amiss to add that abundant proof of the high esteem in which Balsamon was held is found in contemporary authors, and no words can give an exaggerated idea of the weight of his opinion on all legal matters, religious and profane; his works were undertaken at the command of the Emperor and of the Patriarch, and were received with an unmixed admiration.[5]

In the thirteenth century a certain Chumnus who had been Nomophylax and was afterwards elevated to the Archiepiscopal chair of Thessalonica wrote a little book on the "Degrees of Relationship." [6]

In the fourteenth century we find Matthew Blastares writing "An Alphabetical Table "[7] of the contents of the canons of the councils, and of the laws of the Emperors.

And in the same century we find Constantine Harmenopulus, who was born in 1320. He was, when thirty years of age, a member of the first court of civil justice (*Judex*

---

[1] Schœll, Hist. Lib. Grec., Tom VII., p. 241. [2] Beveridge, *Pandectœ.* Prol. § XXX.
[3] Τῶν ἐκκλησιαστικῶν διάταξεων Συλλογή. [4] Beveridge, *Pandects*, Prol. § XIX.-XXII.
[5] Ibid., Prol. § XVI.-XIX. [6] Found in Leunclavius, *Jur. Grec. Rom.*, Vol. ii.
[7] Σύνταγμα κατὰ Στοιχεῶν, found in Beveridge's Synodicon, but (says Schœll) "in a manner very little correct."

Dromi). Subsequently he was appointed Counsellor of the Emperor, John Cantacuzene, and finally Sebastos and Curopalatos under John Paleologus. In the year 1345 he published a "Manual of Jurisprudence." [1] This work is of great value to the student of Roman law as he completes the work of the Emperor Basil by adding the imperial constitutions since that time. But our chief concern with him is as the author of an "Epitome of the Divine and Sacred Canons." [2]

Constantine Harmenopulus was the last Greek jurist, and then Constantinople fell, to the everlasting disgrace of a divided Christendom, into the hands of the Infidel, and the law of the false Prophet supplanted the Roman Law, the Code of Civilization and Christianity.

I pass now to the history of the growth of the canon law in the West. No one reading even cursorily the canons contained in the present volume can fail to notice that, with the exception of those of the African code, they are primarily intended for the government of the East and of persons more immediately under the shadow of the imperial city. In fact in the canons of the Council in Trullo and in those of the Seventh Synod there are places which not even covertly are attacks, or at least reflections, upon the Western customs of the time. And it does not seem to be an unjust view of the matter to detect in the Council of Chalcedon and its canon on the position of the See of Rome, a beginning of that unhappy spirit which found its full expression in that most lamentable breaking off of communion between East and West.

While, then, as I have pointed out, in the East the Canon Law was developed and digested side by side and in consonance with the civil law, in the West the state of things was wholly different, and while in secular matters the secular power was supposed to be supreme, there grew up a great body of Ecclesiastical Law, often at variance with the secular decrees upon the subject. To trace this, step by step, is no part of my duty in this excursus, and I shall only give so brief an outline that the reader may be able to understand the references in the notes which accompany the Canons in the text.

Somewhere about the year 500 Dionysius Exiguus, who was Abbot of a Monastery in Rome, translated a collection of Greek Canons into Latin for Bishop Stephen of Salona. At the head of these he placed fifty of what we now know as the "Canons of the Apostles," but it must not be supposed that he was convinced of their Apostolic origin, for in the Preface to his translation he expressly styles them "Canons which are said to be by the Apostles," and adds "quibus plurimi consensum non prœbuere facilem." [3] To these he added the canons of Chalcedon with those that council had accepted, viz., those of Sardica, and a large number passed by African Synods, and lastly the Papal Decretals from Siricius to Anastasius II.

The next collection is that of St. Isidore of Seville, or which is supposed to have been made by him, early in the seventh century.

About the middle of the ninth century there appeared a collection bearing the name of Isidore Mercator, and containing the "false decretals" which have been so fruitful a theme of controversial writing. This collection was made somewhere about the year 850, and possibly at Mayence. Many writers in treating of these decretals, which are undoubtedly spurious, seem to forget that they must have expressed the prevailing opinions of the day in which they were forged, of what those early Popes would have been likely to have said, and that therefore even forgeries as they certainly are, they have a great historical value which no sound scholar can properly neglect.

After the collection of St. Isidore we have no great collection till that of Gratian in 1151. Gratian was a Benedictine monk, and he styled his work "A Reconciling of contradictory canons" (*Concordantia discordantium Canonum*), which well sets forth what his chief object in view was, but his work had a great future before it, and all the world

---

[1] Πρόχειρον τῶν νόμων. Of this there have been many editions since the first, which was that of Paris, 1540, edited by Snallenberg, without any Latin translation and without notes. The first Latin version was published at Cologne in 1547, a second at Lyons in 1556, and a third at Lausanne in 1580. At last in 1587, at Geneva, there appeared an edition in Greek and Latin.

[2] Ἐπιτομὴ τῶν θείων καὶ ἱερῶν κανόνων. This work is found with a Latin version in the Collection of Lœwenklaw.

[3] Hefele points out that Dr von Drey's contention that "plurimi" refers to the Greeks cannot be sustained if it is pushed so far as to exclude from the West an acquaintance with these canons in their Greek form, for, as he well points out, Greek was a perfectly well understood language at this time in the West, especially in Italy, where it was largely spoken. (*A Hist. Christ. Councils*, Vol. I. Appendix, p. 449.)

knows it as " Gratian's Decretum," and with it begins the "collections" of Canon law, if we consider it as a system in present force.

" This great work is divided into three parts. The first part, in 101 ' Distinctions,' treats of ecclesiastical law, its origin, principles, and authority, and then of the different ranks and duties of the clergy. The second part, in thirty-six ' Causes,' treats of ecclesiastical courts and their forms of procedure. The third part, usually called ' De Consecratione,' treats of things and rites employed in the service of religion. From its first appearance the *Decretum* obtained a wide popularity, but it was soon discovered that it contained numerous errors, which were corrected under the directions of successive Popes down to Gregory XIII. Nor, although every subsequent generation has resorted to its pages, is the *Decretum* an authority to this day—that is, whatever canons or maxims of law are found in it possess only that degree of legality which they would possess if they existed separately ; their being in the *Decretum* gives them no binding force. In the century after Gratian, several supplementary collections of Decretals appeared. These, with many of his own, were collected by the orders of Gregory IX., who employed in the work the extraordinary learning and acumen of St. Raymond of Pennafort, into five books, known as the *Decretals* of Gregory IX. These are in the fullest sense authoritative, having been deliberately ratified and published by that Pope (1234). The *Sext*, or sixth book of the Decretals, was added by Boniface VIII. (1298). The *Clementines* are named after Clement V., who compiled them out of the canons of the Council of Vienne (1316) and some of his own constitutions. The *Extravagantes* of John XXII., who succeeded Clement V., and the *Extravagantes Communes*, containing the decretals of twenty-five Popes, ending with Sixtus IV. (1484), complete the list. Of these five collections—namely the Decretals, the Sext, the Clementines, the Extravagants of John XXII. and the Extravagants Common—the ' Corpus Juris Ecclesiastici' of the West is made up." [1]

Into this body of canon law of course many of the canons we shall have to treat of in the following pages have been incorporated and so far as possible I shall give the reader a reference which will help his research in this particular.

---

[1] Addis and Arnold, *A Catholic Dictionary*, *sub voce* Canon Law.

THE FIRST ECUMENICAL COUNCIL

THE FIRST COUNCIL OF NICE

A.D. 325

Emperor.—Constantine.
Pope.—Silvester.

Elenchus.

HISTORICAL INTRODUCTION.

The history of the Council of Nice has been so often written by so many brilliant historians, from the time of its sitting down to to-day, that any historical notice of the causes leading to its assembling, or account of its proceedings, seems quite unnecessary. The editor, however, ventures to call the attention of the reader to the fact that in this, as in every other of the Seven Ecumenical Councils, the question the Fathers considered was not what they supposed Holy Scripture might mean, nor what they, from *à priori* arguments, thought would be consistent with the mind of God, but something entirely different, to wit, what they had received. They understood their position to be that of witnesses, not that of exegetes. They recognized but one duty resting upon them in this respect—to hand down to other faithful men that good thing the Church had received according to the command of God. The first requirement was not learning, but honesty. The question they were called upon to answer was not, What do I think probable, or even certain, from Holy Scripture? but, What have I been taught, what has been intrusted to me to hand down to others? When the time came, in the Fourth Council, to examine the Tome of Pope St. Leo, the question was not whether it could be proved to the satisfaction of the assembled fathers from Holy Scripture, but whether it was the traditional faith of the Church. It was not the doctrine of Leo in the fifth century, but the doctrine of Peter in the first, and of the Church since then, that they desired to believe and to teach, and so, when they had studied the Tome, they cried out:[1]

"This is the faith of the Fathers! This is the faith of the Apostles! . . . Peter hath thus spoken by Leo! The Apostles thus taught! Cyril thus taught!" etc.

No Acts of either of the first two Ecumenical Councils have been handed down.[2]

---

[1] This is clearly set forth by Pope Vigilius as follows : "No one can doubt that our fathers believed that they should receive with veneration the letter of blessed Leo if they declared it to agree with the doctrines of the Nicene and Constantinopolitan Councils, as also with those of blessed Cyril, set forth in the first of Ephesus. And if that letter of so great a Pontiff, shining with so bright a light of the orthodox Faith, needed to be approved by these comparisons, how can that letter to Maris the Persian, which specially rejects the First Council of Ephesus and declares to be heretical the expressed doctrines of the blessed Cyril, be believed to have been called orthodox by these same Fathers, condemning as it does those writings, by comparison with which, as we have said, the doctrine of so great a Pontiff deserved to be commended?"—Vigil., *Constitutum pro damnatione Trium Capitulorum.* Migne, *Pat. Lat.*, tom. lxix., col. 162.

[2] About twenty-five years ago Mr. Eugène Révillout discovered, in the Museum of Turin, two fragments in Coptic which he supposed to be portions of the Acts of this Council (of which the rest are still missing) incorporated into the Acts of a Council held at Alexandria in 362. But there is too little known about these fragments to attribute to them any fixed value. I therefore only refer the reader to the literature on the subject—*Journal Asiatique*, Fevrier–Mars, 1873 ; *Annales de Philosophie Chrétienne*, Juin, 1873 ; *Revue de Questions Historiques*, Avril, 1874 ; M. W. Guettée, *Histoire de l'Église*, t. III., p. 21 ; Eugène Révillout, *Le Concile de Nicée et le Concile d'Alexandrie . . . d'après les textes Coptes.*

THE NICENE CREED

(Found in the Acts of the Ecumenical Councils of Ephesus and Chalcedon, in the Epistle of Eusebius of Cæsarea to his own Church, in the Epistle of St. Athanasius Ad Jovianum Imp., in the Ecclesiastical Histories of Theodoret and Socrates, and elsewhere, The variations in the text are absolutely without importance.)

The Synod at Nice set forth this Creed.[1]

The Ecthesis of the Synod at Nice.[2]

We believe in one God, the Father Almighty, maker of all things visible and invisible; and in one Lord Jesus Christ, the Son of God, the only-begotten of his Father, of the substance of the Father, God of God, Light of Light, very God of very God, begotten (γεννηθέντα), not made, being of one substance (ὁμοούσιον, consubstantialem) with the Father. By whom all things were made, both which be in heaven and in earth. Who for us men and for our salvation came down [from heaven] and was incarnate and was made man. He suffered and the third day he rose again, and ascended into heaven. And he shall come again to judge both the quick and the dead. And [we believe] in the Holy Ghost. And whosoever shall say that there was a time when the Son of God was not (ἦν ποτε ὅτε οὐκ ἦν), or that before he was begotten he was not, or that he was made of things that were not, or that he is of a different substance or essence [from the Father] or that he is a creature, or subject to change or conversion [3]—all that so say, the Catholic and Apostolic Church anathematizes them.

NOTES

The Creed of Eusebius of Cæsarea, which he presented to the council, and which some suppose to have suggested the creed finally adopted.

(Found in his Epistle to his diocese; vide: St. Athanasius and Theodoret.)

We believe in one only God, Father Almighty, Creator of things visible and invisible; and in the Lord Jesus Christ, for he is the Word of God, God of God, Light of Light, life of life, his only Son, the first-born of all creatures, begotten of the Father before all time, by whom also everything was created, who became flesh for our redemption, who lived and suffered amongst men, rose again the third day, returned to the Father, and will come again one day in his glory to judge the quick and the dead. We believe also in the Holy Ghost. We believe that each of these three is and subsists; the Father truly as Father, the Son truly as Son, the Holy Ghost truly as Holy Ghost; as our Lord also said, when he sent his disciples to preach: Go and teach all nations, and baptize them in the name of the Father, and of the Son, and of the Holy Ghost.

EXCURSUS ON THE WORD HOMOUSIOS.[4]

The Fathers of the Council at Nice were at one time ready to accede to the request of some of the bishops and use only scriptural expressions in their definitions. But, after several attempts, they found that all these were capable of being explained away. Athanasius describes with much wit and penetration how he saw them nodding and winking to each other when the orthodox proposed expressions which they had thought of a way of escaping from the force of. After a series of attempts of this sort it was found that something clearer and more unequivocal must be adopted if real unity of faith was to be attained; and accordingly the word *homousios* was adopted. Just what the Council intended this

---

[1] This is the heading in the Acts of the IIId Council. Labbe, *Conc.*, tom. iii., 671.

[2] This is the heading in the Acts of the IVth Council. Labbe, *Conc.*, tom. iv., 339.

[3] This word, in the Greek τρεπτὸν, is translated in the Latin *convertibilem*, but see side note in Labbe.

[4] Our older English writers usually wrote this word "homousion," and thus spoke of the doctrine as "the doctrine of the homoousion." For the Arian word they wrote "homoiousion."

Later writers have used the nominative masculine, "homoousios" and "homoiousios." The great Latin writers did not thus transliterate the word, but, wrote "homousios," and for the heretical word "homœosios" or "homœsios." I have kept for the noun signifying the doctrine, our old English " Homoousion," but for the adjective, I have used the ordinary latinized form "homousios," in this copying Smith and Wace, *Dict. Christian Antiquities.*

expression to mean is set forth by St. Athanasius as follows : "That the Son is not only like to the Father, but that, as his image, he is the same as the Father ; that he is of the Father ; and that the resemblance of the Son to the Father, and his immutability, are different from ours : for in us they are something acquired, and arise from our fulfilling the divine commands. Moreover, they wished to indicate by this that his generation is different from that of human nature ; that the Son is not only like to the Father, but inseparable from the substance of the Father, that he and the Father are one and the same, as the Son himself said : 'The Logos is always in the Father, and, the Father always in the Logos,' as the sun and its splendour are inseparable." [1]

The word homousios had not had, although frequently used before the Council of Nice, a very happy history. It was probably rejected by the Council of Antioch,[2] and was suspected of being open to a Sabellian meaning. It was accepted by the heretic Paul of Samosata and this rendered it very offensive to many in the Asiatic Churches.

On the other hand the word is used four times by St. Irenæus, and Pamphilus the Martyr is quoted as asserting that Origen used the very word in the Nicene sense. Tertullian also uses the expression " of one substance " (unius substantiæ) in two places, and it would seem that more than half a century before the meeting of the Council of Nice, it was a common one among the Orthodox.

Vasquez treats this matter at some length in his *Disputations*,[3] and points out how well the distinction is drawn by Epiphanius between *Synousios* and *Homousios*, " for *synousios* signifies such an unity of substance as allows of no distinction : wherefore the Sabellians would admit this word : but on the contrary *homousios* signifies the same nature and substance but with a distinction between persons one from the other. Rightly, therefore, has the Church adopted this word as the one best calculated to confute the Arian heresy." [4]

It may perhaps be well to note that these words are formed like ὁμόβιος and ὁμοιόβιος, ὁμογνώμων and ὁμοιογνώμων, etc., etc.

The reader will find this whole doctrine treated at great length in all the bodies of divinity ; and in Alexander Natalis (*H.E.* t. iv., Diss. xiv.); he is also referred to Pearson, *On the Creed ;* Bull, *Defence of the Nicene Creed ;* Forbes, *An Explanation of the Nicene Creed ;* and especially to the little book, written in answer to the recent criticisms of Professor Harnack, by H. B. Swete, D.D., *The Apostles' Creed.*

EXCURSUS ON THE WORDS γεννηθέντα οὐ ποιηθέντα.

(J. B. Lightfoot. *The Apostolic Fathers*—Part II. Vol. ii. Sec. I. pp. 90, *et seqq.*)

The Son is here [Ignat. *Ad. Eph.* vii.] declared to be γεννητὸς as man and ἀγέννητος as God, for this is clearly shown to be the meaning from the parallel clauses. Such language is not in accordance with later theological definitions, which carefully distinguished between γενητός and γεννητός between ἀγένητος and ἀγέννητος ; so that γενητός, ἀγένητος respectively denied and affirmed the eternal existence, being equivalent to κτιστός, ἄκτιστος, while γεννητός, ἀγέννητος described certain ontological relations, whether in time or in eternity. In the later theological language, therefore, the Son was γεννητός even in his Godhead. See esp. Joann. Damasc. *de Fid. Orth.* i. 8 [where he draws the conclusion that only the Father is ἀγέννητος, and only the Son γεννητός].

There can be little doubt however, that Ignatius wrote γεννητός καὶ ἀγέννητος, though his editors frequently alter it into γενητὸς καὶ ἀγένητος. For (1) the Greek MS. still retains the double [Greek nun] ν, though the claims of orthodoxy would be a temptation to scribes to

---

[1] Athanas, *De Decret. Syn. Nic.*, c. xix. et seq.
[2] Vide Swainson, in Smith and Wace, *Dict. Christ. Biog.*, sub voce Homousios, p. 134.
[3] Vasquez, *Disput.* cix., cap. v. " Rightly doth the Church use the expression Homousios (that is Consubstantial) to express that the Father and the Son are of the same nature."
[4] Vasquez may also well be consulted on the expressions οὐσία, substantia, ὑπόστασις, etc.

substitute the single ν. And to this reading also the Latin *genitus et ingenitus* points. On the other hand it cannot be concluded that translators who give *factus et non factus* had the words with one ν, for this was after all what Ignatius meant by the double ν, and they would naturally render his words so as to make his orthodoxy apparent. (2) When Theodoret writes γεννητὸς ἐξ ἀγεννήτου, it is clear that he, or the person before him who first substituted this reading, must have read γεννητὸς καὶ ἀγέννητος, for there would be no temptation to alter the perfectly orthodox γενητὸς καὶ ἀγένητος, nor (if altered) would it have taken this form. (3) When the interpolator substitutes ὁ μόνος ἀληθινὸς Θεὸς ὁ ἀγέννητος . . . τοῦ δὲ μονογονοῦς πατὴρ καὶ γεννήτωρ, the natural inference is that he too, had the forms in double ν, which he retained, at the same time altering the whole run of the sentence so as not to do violence to his own doctrinal views ; see Bull *Def. Fid. Nic.* ii. 2 § 6. (4) The quotation in Athanasius is more difficult. The MSS. vary, and his editors write γενητὸς καὶ ἀγένητος. Zahn too, who has paid more attention to this point than any previous editor of Ignatius, in his former work (*Ign. v. Ant.* p. 564), supposed Athanasius to have read and written the words with a single ν, though in his subsequent edition of Ignatius (p. 338) he declares himself unable to determine between the single and double ν. I believe, however, that the argument of Athanasius decides in favour of the νν. Elsewhere he insists repeatedly on the distinction between κτίζειν and γεννᾶν, justifying the use of the latter term as applied to the divinity of the Son, and defending the statement in the Nicene Creed γεννητὸν ἐκ τῆς οὐσίας τοῦ πατρὸς τὸν υἱὸν ὁμοούσιον (*De Synod.* 54, 1, p. 612). Although he is not responsible for the language of the Macrostich (*De Synod.* 3, 1, p. 590), and would have regarded it as inadequate without the ὁμοούσιον, yet this use of terms entirely harmonizes with his own. In the passage before us, *ib.* §§ 46, 47 (p. 607), he is defending the use of *homousios* at Nicæa, notwithstanding that it had been previously rejected by the council which condemned Paul of Samosata, and he contends that both councils were orthodox, since they used *homousios* in a different sense. As a parallel instance he takes the word ἀγέννητος which like *homousios* is not a scriptural word, and like it also is used in two ways, signifying either (1) Τὸ ὂν μεν, μήτε δὲ γεννηθὲν μήτε ὅλως ἔχον τὸν αἴτιον, or (2) Τὸ ἄκτιστον. In the former sense the Son cannot be called ἀγέννητος, in the latter he may be so called. Both uses, he says, are found in the fathers. Of the latter he quotes the passage in Ignatius as an example ; of the former he says, that some writers subsequent to Ignatius declare ἕν τὸ ἀγέννητον ὁ πατήρ, καὶ εἷς ὁ ἐξ αὐτοῦ υἱὸς γνήσιος, γέννημα αληθίνον κ. τ. λ. [He may have been thinking of Clem. Alex. *Strom.* vi. 7, which I shall quote below.] He maintains that both are orthodox, as having in view two different senses of the word ἀγέννητον, and the same, he argues, is the case with the councils which seem to take opposite sides with regard to *homousios*. It is clear from this passage, as Zahn truly says, that Athanasius is dealing with one and the same word throughout ; and, if so, it follows that this word must be ἀγέννητον, since ἀγένητον would be intolerable in some places. I may add by way of caution that in two other passages, *de Decret. Syn. Nic.* 28 (1, p. 184), *Orat. c. Arian.* i. 30 (1, p. 343), St. Athanasius gives the various senses of ἀγένητον (for this is plain from the context), and that these passages ought not to be treated as parallels to the present passage which is concerned with the senses of ἀγέννητον. Much confusion is thus created, *e.g.* in Newman's notes on the several passages in the Oxford translation of Athanasius (pp. 51 sq., 224 sq.), where the three passages are treated as parallel, and no attempt is made to discriminate the readings in the several places, but "ingenerate" is given as the rendering of both alike. If then Athanasius who read γεννητὸς καὶ ἀγέννητος in Ignatius, there is absolutely no authority for the spelling with one ν. The earlier editors (Voss, Ussher, Cotelier, etc.), printed it as they found it in the MS.; but Smith substituted the forms with the single ν, and he has been followed more recently by Hefele, Dressel, and some other. In the Casanatensian copy of the MS., a marginal note is added, ἀναγνωστέον ἀγένητος τοῦτ' ἐστι μὴ ποιηθείς. Waterland (*Works*, III., p. 240 sq., Oxf. 1823) tries ineffectually to show that the form with the double ν was invented by the fathers at a later date to express their theological conception. He even "doubts whether there was any such word as ἀγέννητος so early as the time of Ignatius." In this he is certainly wrong.

The MSS. of early Christian writers exhibit much confusion between these words spelled with the double and the single ν. See *e.g.* Justin *Dial.* 2, with Otto's note ; Athenag. *Suppl.* 4 with Otto's note ; Theophil, *ad Autol.* ii. 3, 4 ; Iren. iv. 38, 1, 3 ; Orig. *c. Cels.* vi. 66 ; Method. *de Lib. Arbitr.*, p. 57 ; Jahn (see Jahn's note 11, p. 122) ; Maximus in Euseb. *Praep. Ev.* vii. 22 ; Hippol. *Haer.* v. 16 (from Sibylline Oracles) ; Clem. Alex. *Strom* v. 14 ; and very frequently in later writers. Yet notwithstanding the confusion into which later transcribers have thus thrown the subject, it is still possible to ascertain the main facts respecting the usage of the two forms. The distinction between the two terms, as indicated by their origin, is that ἀγένητος denies *the creation*, and ἀγέννητος *the generation or parentage*. Both are used at a very early date ; *e.g.* ἀγένητος by Parmenides in Clem. Alex. *Strom.* v. 14, and by Agothon in Arist. *Eth. Nic.* vii. 2 (comp. also *Orac. Sibyll.* prooem. 7, 17) ; and ἀγέννητος in Soph. *Trach.* 61 (where it is equivalent to δυσγενῶν). Here the distinction of meaning is strictly preserved, and so probably it always is in Classical writers ; for in Soph. *Trach.* 743 we should after Porson and Hermann read ἀγένητον with Suidas. In Christian writers also there is no reason to suppose that the distinction was ever lost, though in certain connexions the words might be used convertibly. Whenever, as here in Ignatius, we have the double ν where we should expect the single, we must ascribe the fact to the indistinctness or incorrectness of the writer's theological conceptions, not to any obliteration of the meaning of the terms themselves. To this early father for instance the eternal γέννησις of the Son was not a distinct theological idea, though substantially he held the same views as the Nicene fathers respecting the Person of Christ. The following passages from early Christian writers will serve at once to show how far the distinction was appreciated, and to what extent the Nicene conception prevailed in ante-Nicene Christianity ; Justin *Apol.* ii. 6, comp. *ib.* § 13 ; Athenag. *Suppl.* 10 (comp. *ib.* 4) ; Theoph. *ad. Aut.* ii. 3 ; Tatian *Orat.* 5 ; Rhodon in Euseb. *H. E.* v. 13 ; Clem. Alex. *Strom.* vi. 7 ; Orig. *c. Cels.* vi. 17, *ib.* vi. 52 ; Concil. Antioch (A.D. 269) in Routh *Rel. Sacr.* III., p. 290 ; Method. *de Creat.* 5. In no early Christian writing, however, is the distinction more obvious than in the *Clementine Homilies*, x. 10 (where the distinction is employed to support the writer's heretical theology) : see also viii. 16, and comp. xix. 3, 4, 9, 12. The following are instructive passages as regards the use of these words where the opinions of other heretical writers are given ; Saturninus, Iren. i. 24, 1 ; Hippol. *Haer.* vii. 28 ; Simon Magus, Hippol. *Haer.* vi. 17, 18 ; the Valentinians, Hippol. *Haer.* vi. 29, 30 ; the Ptolemæus in particular, Ptol. *Ep. ad. Flor.* 4 (in Stieren's Irenæus, p. 935) ; Basilides, Hippol. *Haer.* vii. 22 ; Carpocrates, Hippol. *Haer.* vii. 32.

From the above passages it will appear that Ante-Nicene writers were not indifferent to the distinction of meaning between the two words ; and when once the othodox Christology was formulated in the Nicene Creed in the words γεννηθέντα οὐ ποιηθέντα, it became henceforth impossible to overlook the difference. The Son was thus declared to be γεννητός but not γενητός. I am therefore unable to agree with Zahn (*Marcellus*, pp. 40, 104, 223, *Ign. von Ant.* p. 565), that at the time of the Arian controversy the disputants were not alive to the difference of meaning. See for example Epiphanius, *Haer.* lxiv. 8. But it had no especial interest for them. While the orthodox party clung to the *homousios* as enshrining the doctrine for which they fought, they had no liking for the terms ἀγέννητος and γεννητός as applied to the Father and the Son respectively, though unable to deny their propriety, because they were affected by the Arians and applied in their own way. To the orthodox mind the Arian formula οὐκ ἦν πρὶν γεννηθῆναι or some Semiarian formula hardly less dangerous, seemed always to be lurking under the expression Θεὸς γεννητός as applied to the Son.   Hence the language of Epiphanius *Haer.* lxxiii. 19 : "As you refuse to accept our *homousios* because though used by the fathers, it does not occur in the Scriptures, so will we decline on the same grounds to accept your ἀγέννητος."   Similarly Basil *c. Eunom.* i., iv., and especially *ib.* further on, in which last passage he argues at great length against the position of the heretics, εἰ ἀγέννητος, φασὶν, ὁ πατήρ, γεννητὸς δὲ ὁ υἱός, οὐ τῆς αὐτῆς οὐσίας.   See also the arguments against the Anomœans in [Athan.] *Dial. de Trin.* ii. passim.   This fully explains the reluctance of the orthodox party to handle terms which their adversaries used to endanger the *homousios*.   But, when the stress of the Arian controversy was removed, it became convenient to express the Catholic doctrine by saying that the Son in his divine nature was γέννητος but not γένητος.   And this distinction is staunchly maintained in later orthodox writers, *e.g.* John of Damascus, already quoted in the beginning of this Excursus.

THE CANONS OF THE 318 HOLY FATHERS ASSEMBLED IN THE CITY OF NICE, IN BITHYNIA.

CANON I.

If any one in sickness has been subjected by physicians to a surgical operation, or if he has been castrated by barbarians, let him remain among the clergy ; but, if any one in sound health has castrated himself, it behoves that such an one, if [already] enrolled among the clergy, should cease [from his ministry], and that from henceforth no such person should be promoted. But, as it is evident that this is said of those who wilfully do the thing and presume to castrate themselves, so if any have been made eunuchs by barbarians, or by their masters, and should otherwise be found worthy, such men the Canon admits to the clergy.

NOTES.

Ancient Epitome[1] of Canon I.

Eunuchs may be received into the number of the clergy, but those who castrate themselves shall not be received.

Balsamon.

The divine Apostolic Canons xxi., xxii., xxiii., and xxiv., have taught us sufficiently what ought to be done with those who castrate themselves, this canon provides as to what is to be done to these as well as to those who deliver themselves over to others to be emasculated by them, viz., that they are not to be admitted among the clergy nor advanced to the priesthood.

Daniel Butler.

(Smith & Cheetham, *Dict. Christ. Ant.*)

The feeling that one devoted to the sacred ministry should be unmutilated was strong in the Ancient Church. . . . This canon of Nice, and those in the Apostolic Canons and a later one in the Second Council of Arles (canon vii.) were aimed against that perverted notion of piety, originating in the misinterpretation of our Lord's saying (Matt. xix. 12) by which Origen, among others, was misled, and their observance was so carefully enforced in later times that not more than one or two instances of the practice which they condemn are noticed by the historian. The case was different if a man was born an eunuch or had suffered mutilation at the hands of persecutors ; an instance of the former, Dorotheus, presbyter of Antioch, is mentioned by Eusebius (*H. E.* vii., c. 32) ; of the latter, Tigris, presbyter of Constantinople, is referred to both by Socrates (*H. E.* vi. 15) and Sozomen (*H. E.* vi. 24) as the victim of a barbarian master.

Hefele.

We know, by the first apology of St. Justin (*Apol.* c. 29) that a century before Origen, a young man had desired to be mutilated by physicians, for the purpose of completely refuting the charge of vice which the heathen brought against the worship of Christians. St. Justin neither praises nor blames this young man : he only relates that he could not obtain the permission of the civil authorities for his project, that he renounced his intention, but nevertheless remained *virgo* all his life. It is very probable that the Council of Nice was induced by some fresh similar cases to renew the old injunctions ; it was perhaps the Arian bishop, Leontius, who was the principal cause of it.[1]

Lambert.

Constantine forbade by a law the practice condemned in this canon. "If anyone shall anywhere in the Roman Empire after this decree make eunuchs, he shall be punished with death. If the owner of the place where the deed was perpetrated was aware of it and hid the fact, his goods shall be confiscated." (Const. M. *Opera.* Migne Patrol. vol. viii., 396.)

Beveridge.

The Nicene fathers in this canon make no new enactment but only confirm by the authority of an Ecumenical synod the Apostolic Canons, and this is evident from the wording of this canon. For there can be no doubt that they had in mind some earlier canon when they said, "such men the canon admits to the clergy." Not, ὄυτος ὁ κανὼν, but ὁ κανὼν, as if they had said "the formerly set forth

---

[1] For the authority of this epitome *vide* Introduction.

[1] Leontius while still a presbyter lived with a *subintroducta* at Antioch, whose name was Eustolion, so we learn from St. Athanasius, Theodoret (*H. E.* ii. 24) and Socrates (*H. E.* ii. 26) ; as he could not part from her and wished to prevent her leaving him, he mutilated himself. His bishop deposed him for this act, but the Emperor Constantius (not Constantine, as by a mistake in the English Hefele, I. p. 377) practically forced him into the episcopal throne of Antioch.

and well-known canon" admits such to the clergy. But no other canon then existed in which this provision occurred except apostolical canon xxi. which therefore we are of opinion is here cited.

[In this conclusion Hefele also agrees.]

This law was frequently enacted by subsequent synods and is inserted in the *Corpus Juris Canonici, Decretum Gratiani.* Pars. I. Distinctio LV., C vij.

EXCURSUS ON THE USE OF THE WORD "CANON."

(Bright : *Notes on the Canons,* pp. 2 and 3.)

Κανών, as an ecclesiastical term, has a very interesting history. See Westcott's account of it, *On the New Testament Canon,* p. 498 ff. The original sense, "a straight rod" or "line," determines all its religious applications, which begin with St. Paul's use of it for a prescribed sphere of apostolic work (2 Cor. x. 13, 15), or a regulative principle of Christian life (Gal. vi. 16). It represents the element of definiteness in Christianity and in the order of the Christian Church. Clement of Rome uses it for the measure of Christian attainment (Ep. Cor. 7). Irenæus calls the baptismal creed "the canon of truth" (i. 9, 4): Polycrates (Euseb. v. 24) and probably Hippolytus (ib. v. 28) calls it "the canon of faith;" the Council of Antioch in A.D. 269, referring to the same standard of orthodox belief, speaks with significant absoluteness of "the canon" (ib. vii. 30). Eusebius himself mentions "the canon of truth" in iv. 23, and "the canon of the preaching" in iii. 32 ; and so Basil speaks of "the transmitted canon of true religion" (Epist. 204–6). Such language, like Tertullian's "regula fidei," amounted to saying, "We Christians know what we believe : it is not a vague 'idea' without substance or outline : it can be put into form, and by it we 'test the spirits whether they be of God.'" Thus it was natural for Socrates to call the Nicene Creed itself a "canon," ii. 27. Clement of Alexandria uses the phrase "canon of truth" for a standard of mystic interpretation, but proceeds to call the harmony between the two Testaments "a canon for the Church," Strom. vi. 15, 124, 125. Eusebius speaks of "the ecclesiastical canon" which recognized no other Gospels than the four (vi. 25). The use of the term and its cognates in reference to the Scriptures is explained by Westcott in a passive sense so that "canonized" books, as Athanasius calls them (Fest. Ep. 39), are books expressly recognized by the Church as portions of Holy Scripture. Again, as to matters of observance, Clement of Alexandria wrote a book against Judaizers, called "The Church's Canon" (Euseb. vi. 13) ; and Cornelius of Rome, in his letter to Fabius, speaks of the "canon" as to what we call confirmation (Euseb. vi. 43), and Dionysius of the "canon" as to reception of converts from heresy (*ib.* vii. 7). The Nicene Council in this canon refers to a standing "canon" of discipline (comp. Nic. 2, 5, 6, 9, 10, 15, 16, 18), but it does not apply the term to its own enactments, which are so described in the second canon of Constantinople (see below), and of which Socrates says "that it passed what are usually called 'canons'" (i. 13), as Julius of Rome calls a decree of this Council a "canon" (Athan. Apol. c. Ari. 25) ; so Athanasius applies the term generally to Church laws (Encycl. 2 ; cp. Apol. c. Ari. 69). The use of κανών for the clerical body (Nic. 16, 17, 19 ; Chalc. 2) is explained by Westcott with reference to the rule of clerical life, but Bingham traces it to the roll or official list on which the names of clerics were enrolled (i. 5, 10) ; and this appears to be the more natural derivation, see "the holy canon" in the first canon of the Council of Antioch, and compare Socrates (i. 17), "the Virgins enumerated ἐν τῷ τῶν ἐκκλησιῶν κανόνι," and (*ib.* v. 19) on the addition of a penitentiary "to the canon of the church ;" see also George of Laodicea in Sozomon, iv. 13. Hence any cleric might be called κανονικός, see Cyril of Jerusalem, *Procatech.* 4 ; so we read of "canonical singers." Laodicea, canon xv. The same notion of definiteness appears in the ritual use of the word for a series of nine "odes" in the Eastern Church service (Neale, *Introd. East. Ch.* ii. 832), for the central and unvarying element in the Liturgy, beginning after the Tersanctus (Hammond, Liturgies East and West, p. 377) ; or for any Church office (Ducange in v.) ; also in its application to a table for the calculation of Easter (Euseb. vi. 22 ; vii. 32) ; to a scheme for exhibiting the common and peculiar parts of the several Gospels (as the "Eusebian canons") and to a prescribed or ordinary payment to a church, a use which grew out of one found in Athanasius' Apol. c. Ari. 60.

In more recent times a tendency has appeared to restrict the term Canon to matters of discipline, but the Council of Trent continued the ancient use of the word, calling its doctrinal and disciplinary determinations alike "Canons."

CANON II.

Forasmuch as, either from necessity, or through the urgency of individuals, many things have been done contrary to the Ecclesiastical canon, so that men just converted from heathenism to the faith, and who have been instructed but a little while, are straightway brought to the spiritual laver, and as soon as they have been baptized, are advanced to the episcopate or the presbyterate, it has seemed right to us that for the time to come no such thing shall be done. For to the catechumen himself there is need of time and of a longer trial after baptism. For the apostolical saying is clear, "Not a novice ; lest, being lifted up with pride, he fall into condemnation and the snare of the devil." But if, as time goes on, any sensual sin should be found out about the person, and he should be convicted by two or three witnesses, let him cease from the clerical office. And whoso shall transgress these [enactments] will imperil his own clerical position, as a person who presumes to disobey the great Synod.

NOTES.

Ancient Epitome of Canon II.

Those who have come from the heathen shall not be immediately advanced to the presbyterate. For without a probation of some time a neophyte is of no advantage (κακός). But if after ordination it be found out that he had sinned previously, let him then be expelled from the clergy.

Hefele.

It may be seen by the very text of this canon, that it was already forbidden to baptize, and to raise to the episcopate or to the priesthood anyone who had only been a catechumen for a short time : this injunction is in fact contained in the eightieth (seventy-ninth) apostolical canon ; and according to that, it would be older than the Council of Nicæa. There have been, nevertheless, certain cases in which, for urgent reasons, an exception has been made to the rule of the Council of Nicæa—for instance, that of S. Ambrose. The canon of Nicæa does not seem to allow such an exception, but it might be justified by the apostolical canon, which says, at the close : "It is not right that any one who has not yet been proved should be a teacher of

others, unless by a peculiar divine grace." The expression of the canon of Nicæa, ψυχικὸν τι ἁμάρτημα, is not easy to explain : some render it by the Latin words *animale peccatam*, believing that the Council has here especially in view sins of the flesh ; but as Zonaras has said, all sins are ψυχικὰ ἁμαρτήματα. We must then understand the passage in question to refer to a capital and very serious offence, as the penalty of deposition annexed to it points out.

These words have also given offence, εἰ δὲ προϊόντος τοῦ χρόνον; that is to say, "It is necessary henceforward," etc., understanding that it is only those who have been too quickly ordained who are threatened with deposition in case they are guilty of crime ; but the canon is framed, and ought to be understood, in a general manner : it applies to all other clergymen, but it appears also to point out that greater severity should be shown toward those who have been too quickly ordained.

Others have explained the passage in this manner : "If it shall become known that any one who has been too quickly ordained was guilty before his baptism of any serious offence, he ought to be deposed." This is the interpretation given by Gratian, but it must be confessed that such a translation does violence to the text. This is, I believe, the general sense of the canon, and of this passage in particular : "Henceforward no one shall be baptized or ordained quickly. As to those already in orders (without any distinction between those who have been ordained in due course and those who have been ordained too quickly), the rule is that they shall be deposed if they commit a serious offence. Those who are guilty of disobedience to this great Synod, either by allowing themselves to be ordained or even by ordaining others prematurely, are threatened with deposition *ipso facto*, and for this fault alone." We consider, in short, that the last words of the canon may be understood as well of the ordained as of the ordainer.

CANON III.

THE great Synod has stringently forbidden any bishop, presbyter, deacon, or any one of the clergy whatever, to have a *subintroducta* dwelling with him, except only a mother, or sister, or aunt, or such persons only as are beyond all suspicion.

NOTES.

ANCIENT EPITOME OF CANON III.

No one shall have a woman in his house except his mother, and sister, and persons altogether beyond suspicion.

JUSTELLUS.

Who these mulieres subintroductæ were does not sufficiently appear . . . but they were neither wives nor concubines, but women of some third kind, which the clergy kept with them, not for the sake of offspring or lust, but from the desire, or certainly under the pretence, of piety.

JOHNSON.

For want of a proper English word to render it by, I translate " to retain any woman in their houses under pretence of her being a disciple to them."

VAN ESPEN

translates : And his sisters and aunts cannot remain unless they be free from all suspicion.

Fuchs in his *Bibliothek der kirchenver sammlungen* confesses that this canon shews that the practice of clerical celibacy had already spread widely. In connexion with this whole subject of the subintroductæ the text of St. Paul should be carefully considered. 1 Cor. ix. 5.

HEFELE.

It is very certain that the canon of Nice forbids such spiritual unions, but the context shows moreover that the Fathers had not these particular cases in view alone ; and the expression συνείσακτος should be understood of every woman who is *introduced* (συνείσακτος) into the house of a clergyman for the purpose of living there. If by the word συνείσακτος was only intended the wife in this spiritual marriage, the Council would not have said, any συνείσακτος, except his mother, etc. ; for neither his mother nor his sister could have formed this spiritual union with the cleric. The injunction, then, does not merely forbid the συνείσακτος in the specific sense, but orders that "no woman must live in the house of a cleric, unless she be his mother," etc.

This canon is found in the *Corpus Juris Canonici*, Gratian's *Decretum*, Pars I., Distinc. XXXII., C. xvj.

CANON IV.

IT is by all means proper that a bishop should be appointed by all the bishops in the province ; but should this be difficult, either on account of urgent necessity or because of distance, three at least should meet together, and the suffrages of the absent [bishops] also being given and communicated in writing, then the ordination should take place. But in every province the ratification of what is done should be left to the Metropolitan.

NOTES.

ANCIENT EPITOME OF CANON IV.

A bishop is to be chosen by all the bishops of the province, or at least by three, the rest giving by letter their assent; but this choice must be confirmed by the Metropolitan.

ZONARAS.

The present Canon might seem to be opposed to the first canon of the Holy Apostles, for the latter enjoins that a bishop be ordained by two or three bishops, but this by three, the absent also agreeing and testifying their assent by writing.   But they are not contradictory; for the Apostolical canon by ordination (χειροτονίαν) means consecration and imposition of hands, but the present canon by constitution (κατάστασιν) and ordination means the election, and enjoins that the election of a bishop do not take place unless three assemble, having the consent also of the absent by letter, or a declaration that they also will acquiesce in the election (or vote, ψήφῳ) made by the three who have assembled.   But after the election it gives the ratification or completion of the matter—the imposition of hands and consecration—to the metropolitan of the province, so that the election is to be ratified by him.   He does so when with two or three bishops, according to the apostolical canon, he consecrates with imposition of hands the one of the elected persons whom he himself selects.

BALSAMON

also understands καθίστασθαι to mean election by vote.

BRIGHT.

The Greek canonists are certainly in error when they interpret χειροτονία of election.   The canon is akin to the 1st Apostolic canon which, as the canonists admit, must refer to the consecration of a new bishop, and it was cited in that sense at the Council of Chalcedon—Session xiii. (Mansi., vii. 307).   We must follow Rufinus and the old Latin translators, who speak of "ordinari" "ordinatio" and "manus impositionem."

HEFELE.

The Council of Nice thought it necessary to define by precise rules the duties of the bishops who took part in these episcopal elections.   It decided (*a*) that a single bishop of the province was not sufficient for the appointment of another;   (*b*) three at least should meet, and (*c*) they were not to proceed to election without the written permission of the absent bishops; it was necessary (*d*) to obtain afterward the approval of the metropolitan.   The Council thus confirms the ordinary metropolitan division in its two most important points, namely, the nomination and ordination of bishops, and the superior position of the metropolitan.   The third point connected with this division — namely, the provincial synod—will be considered under the next canon.

Meletius was probably the occasion of this canon.   It may be remembered that he had nominated bishops without the concurrence of the other bishops of the province, and without the approval of the metropolitan of Alexandria, and had thus occasioned a schism.   This canon was intended to prevent the recurrence of such abuses.   The question has been raised as to whether the fourth canon speaks only of the choice of the bishop, or whether it also treats of the consecration of the newly elected.   We think, with Van Espen, that it treats equally of both,—as well of the part which the bishops of the province should take in an episcopal election, as of the consecration which completes it.

This canon has been interpreted in two ways.   The Greeks had learnt by bitter experience to distrust the interference of princes and earthly potentates in episcopal elections.   Accordingly, they tried to prove that this canon of Nice took away from the people the right of voting at the nomination of a bishop, and confined the nomination exclusively to the bishops of the province.

The Greek Commentators, Balsamon and others, therefore, only followed the example of the Seventh and [so-called] Eighth Œcumenical Councils in affirming that this fourth canon of Nice takes away from the people the right previously possessed of voting in the choice of bishops and makes the election depend entirely on the decision of the bishops of the province.

The Latin Church acted otherwise.   It is true that with it also the people have been removed from episcopal elections, but this did not happen till later, about the eleventh century; and it was not the people only who were removed, but the bishops of the province as well, and the election was conducted entirely by the clergy of the Cathedral Church.   The Latins then interpreted the canon of Nice as though it said nothing of the rights of the bishops of the province in the *election* of their future colleague (and it does not speak of it in a very explicit manner), and as though it determined these two points only ; (*a*) that for the *ordination* of a bishop three bishops at least are necessary ; (*b*) that the right of *confirmation* rests with the metropolitan.

The whole subject of episcopal elections is treated fully by Van Espen and by Thomassin, in *Ancienne et Nouvelle Discipline de l'Église*, P. II. l. 2.

This canon is found in the *Corpus Juris Canonici*, Gratian's *Decretum*, Pars I. Dist. LXIV. c. j.

CANON V.

CONCERNING those, whether of the clergy or of the laity, who have been excommunicated in the several provinces, let the provision of the canon be observed by the bishops which provides that persons cast out by some be not readmitted by others. Nevertheless, inquiry should be made whether they have been excommunicated through captiousness, or contentiousness, or any such like ungracious disposition in the bishop. And, that this matter may have due investigation, it is decreed that in every province synods shall be held twice a year, in order that when all the bishops of the province are assembled together, such questions may by them be thoroughly examined, that so those who have confessedly offended against their bishop, may be seen by all to be for just cause excommunicated, until it shall seem fit to a general meeting of the bishops to pronounce a milder sentence upon them. And let these synods be held, the one before Lent, (that the pure Gift may be offered to God after all bitterness has been put away), and let the second be held about autumn.

NOTES.

ANCIENT EPITOME OF CANON V.

Such as have been excommunicated by certain bishops shall not be restored by others, unless the excommunication was the result of pusillanimity, or strife, or some other similar cause. And that this may be duly attended to, there shall be in each year two synods in every province— the one before Lent, the other toward autumn.

There has always been found the greatest difficulty in securing the regular meetings of provincial and diocesan synods, and despite the very explicit canonical legislation upon the subject, and the severe penalties attached to those not answering the summons, in large parts of the Church for centuries these councils have been of the rarest occurrence. Zonaras complains that in his time "these synods were everywhere treated with great contempt," and that they had actually ceased to be held.

Possibly the opinion of St. Gregory Nazianzen had grown common, for it will be remembered that in refusing to go to the latter sessions of the Second Ecumenical he wrote, "I am resolved to avoid every meeting of bishops, for I have never seen any synod end well, nor assuage rather than aggravate disorders."[1]

HEFELE.

Gelasius has given in his history of the Council of Nice, the text of the canons passed by the Council; and it must be noticed that there is here a slight difference between his text and ours. Our reading is as follows: "The excommunication continues to be in force until it seem good to the assembly of bishops (τῷ κοινῷ) to soften it." Gelasius, on the other hand, writes: μέχρις ἂν τῷ κοινῷ ἢ τῷ ἐπισκόπῳ, κ. τ. λ., that is to say, "until it seem good to the assembly of bishops, *or to the bishop* (who has passed the sentence)," etc. . . . Dionysius the Less has also followed this variation, as his translation of the canon shows. It does not change the essential meaning of the passage; for it may be well understood that the bishop who has passed the sentence of excommunication has also the right to mitigate it. But the variation adopted by the *Prisca* alters, on the contrary, the whole sense of the canon: the *Prisca* has not τῷ κοινῷ, but only ἐπισκόπῳ: it is in this erroneous form that the canon has passed into the *Corpus jurisc an.*

This canon is found in the *Corpus Juris Canonici*, Gratian's *Decretum*, Pars II., Causa XI., Quæst. III., Canon lxxiij., and the latter part in Pars I., Distinc. XVIII., c. iij.

EXCURSUS ON THE WORD Προσφέρειν.

(Dr. Adolph Harnack : *Hist. of Dogma* [Eng. Tr.] Vol. I. p. 209.)

The idea of the whole transaction of the Supper as a sacrifice, is plainly found in the *Didache*, (c. 14), in Ignatius, and above all, in Justin (I. 65f.) But even Clement of Rome presupposes it, when (in cc. 40–44) he draws a parallel between bishops and deacons and the

---

[1] Greg. Naz. *Ep. ad Procop.*; Migne *Pat. Græc.*, No. cxxx.

Priests and Levites of the Old Testament, describing as the chief function of the former (44.4) προσφέρειν τὰ δῶρα. This is not the place to enquire whether the first celebration had, in the mind of its founder, the character of a sacrificial meal; but, certainly, the idea, as it was already developed at the time of Justin, had been created by the churches. Various reasons tended towards seeing in the Supper a sacrifice. In the first place, Malachi i. 11, demanded a solemn Christian sacrifice: see my notes on *Didache*, 14.3. In the second place, all prayers were regarded as a sacrifice, and therefore the solemn prayers at the Supper must be specially considered as such. In the third place, the words of institution τοῦτο ποιεῖτε, contained a command with regard to a definite religious action. Such an action, however, could only be represented as a sacrifice, and this the more, that the Gentile Christians might suppose that they had to understand ποιεῖν in the sense of θύειν. In the fourth place, payments in kind were necessary for the "agapæ" connected with the Supper, out of which were taken the bread and wine for the Holy celebration; in what other aspect could these offerings in the worship be regarded than as προσφοραί for the purpose of a sacrifice? Yet the spiritual idea so prevailed that only the prayers were regarded as the θυσία proper, even in the case of Justin (*Dial.* 117). The elements are only δῶρα, προσφοραί, which obtain their value from the prayers, in which thanks are given for the gifts of creation and redemption, as well as for the holy meal, and entreaty is made for the introduction of the community into the Kingdom of God (see *Didache*, 9. 10). Therefore, even the sacred meal itself is called εὐχαριστία (Justin, *Apol.* I. 66: ἡ τροφὴ αὕτη καλεῖται παρ' ἡμῖν εὐχαριστία. *Didache*, 9. 1: Ignat.), because it is τραφὴ εὐχαριστηθεῖσα. It is a mistake to suppose that Justin already understood the body of Christ to be the object of ποιεῖν,[1] and therefore thought of a sacrifice of this body (I. 66). The real sacrificial act in the Supper consists rather, according to Justin, only in the εὐχαριστίαν ποιεῖν, whereby the κοινὸς ἄρτος becomes the ἄρτος τῆς εὐχαριστίας.[2] The sacrifice of the Supper in its essence, apart from the offering of alms, which in the practice of the Church was closely united with it, is nothing but a sacrifice of prayer: the sacrificial act of the Christian here also is nothing else than an act of prayer (See *Apol.* I. 14, 65–67; *Dial.* 28, 29, 41, 70, 116–118).

Harnack (*lib. cit.* Vol. II. chapter III. p. 136) says that "Cyprian was the first to associate the specific offering, i.e. the Lord's Supper with the specific priesthood. Secondly, he was the first to designate the *passio Domini*, nay, the *sanguis Christi* and the *dominica hostia* as the object of the eucharistic offering." In a foot-note (on the same page) he explains that "*Sacrificare, Sacrificium celebrare* in all passages where they are unaccompanied by any qualifying words, mean to celebrate the Lord's Supper." But Harnack is confronted by the very evident objection that if this was an invention of St. Cyprian's, it is most extraordinary that it raised no protest, and he very frankly confesses (note 2, on same page) that "the transference of the sacrificial idea to the consecrated elements which in all probability Cyprian already found in existence, etc." Harnack further on (in the same note on p. 137) notes that he has pointed out in his notes on the *Didache* that in the "Apostolic Church Order" occurs the expression ἡ προσφορὰ τοῦ σώματος καὶ τοῦ αἵματος.

---

[1] Harnack seems to know only the printed (and almost certainly incorrect) reading of the modern texts of the I. Apology (Chapter LXVI) where τοῦτο ἐστι has taken the place of τούτεστι. The passage did read, τοῦτο ποιεῖτε, εἰς τὴν ἀνάμνησίν μου, τούτεστι τὸ σῶμά μου; in which it is evident that the words "my body" are in apposition with τοῦτο and the object of ποιεῖτε, which has its sacrificial sense "to offer," as in the Dialogue with Trypho, ὁ κύριος ἡμῶν παρέδωκε ποιεῖν (chapter xlj).

[2] Harnack evidently does not fully appreciate the Catholic doctrine of the Sacrifice in the Holy Eucharist. No Catholic theologian teaches that the essence of that sacrifice is to offer up the already present Body of Christ, but that the essence of the Sacrifice is the act of consecration; the "making the Eucharistic Sacrifice," as he accurately says, "whereby the common bread becomes the Bread of the Eucharist." Harnack says truly that "the sacrificial act of the Christian here also is nothing else than an act of prayer," but he does not seem to know that this is the Catholic doctrine to-day, nor to appreciate at its Catholic value the "Prayer of Consecration." The act of consecration is the essence of the Christian Sacrifice according to the teaching of all Catholics.

CANON VI.

LET the ancient customs in Egypt, Libya and Pentapolis prevail, that the Bishop of Alexandria have jurisdiction in all these, since the like is customary for the Bishop of Rome also. Likewise in Antioch and the other provinces, let the Churches retain their privileges. And this is to be universally understood, that if any one be made bishop without the consent of the Metropolitan, the great Synod has declared that such a man ought not to be a bishop. If, however, two or three bishops shall from natural love of contradiction, oppose the common suffrage of the rest, it being reasonable and in accordance with the ecclesiastical law, then let the choice of the majority prevail.

NOTES.

ANCIENT EPITOME OF CANON VI.

The Bishop of Alexandria shall have jurisdiction over Egypt, Libya, and Pentapolis. As also the Roman bishop over those subject to Rome. So, too, the Bishop of Antioch and the rest over those who are under them. If any be a bishop contrary to the judgment of the Metropolitan, let him be no bishop. Provided it be in accordance with the canons by the suffrage of the majority, if three object, their objection shall be of no force.

Many, probably most, commentators have considered this the most important and most interesting of all the Nicene canons, and a whole library of works has been written upon it, some of the works asserting and some denying what are commonly called the Papal claims. If any one wishes to see a list of the most famous of these works he will find it in Phillips's *Kirchenrecht* (Bd. ii. S. 35). I shall reserve what I have to say upon this subject to the notes on a canon which seems really to deal with it, confining myself here to an elucidation of the words found in the canon before us.

HAMMOND, W. A.

The object and intention of this canon seems clearly to have been, not to introduce any new powers or regulations into the Church, but to confirm and establish ancient customs already existing. This, indeed, is evident from the very first words of it: "Let the ancient customs be maintained." It appears to have been made with particular reference to the case of the Church of Alexandria, which had been troubled by the irregular proceedings of Miletius, and to confirm the ancient privileges of that see which he had invaded. The latter part of it, however, applies to all Metropolitans, and confirms all their ancient privileges.

FFOULKES.

(*Dict. Christ. Antiq. voce* Council of Nicæa).
The first half of the canon enacts merely that what had long been customary with respect to such persons in every province should become law, beginning with the province where this principle had been infringed; while the second half declares what was in future to be received as law on two points which custom had not as yet expressly ruled. . . . Nobody disputes the meaning of this last half; nor, in fact, would the meaning of the first half have been questioned, had it not included Rome. . . . Nobody can maintain that the bishops of Antioch and Alexandria were called patriarchs then, or that the jurisdiction they had then was co-extensive with what they had afterward, when they were so called. . . . It is on this clause ["since the like is customary for the Bishops of Rome also"] standing parenthetically between what is decreed for the particular cases of Egypt and Antioch, and in consequence of the interpretation given to it by Rufinus, more particularly, that so much strife has been raised. Rufinus may rank low as a translator, yet, being a native of Aquileia, he cannot have been ignorant of Roman ways, nor, on the other hand, had he greatly misrepresented them, would his version have waited till the seventeenth century to be impeached.

HEFELE.

The sense of the first words of the canon is as follows: "This ancient right is assigned to the Bishop of Alexandria which places under his jurisdiction the *whole* diocese of Egypt." It is without any reason, then, that the French Protestant Salmasius (Saumaise), the Anglican Beveridge, and the Gallican Launoy, try to show that the Council of Nice granted to the Bishop of Alexandria only the rights of ordinary metropolitans.

BISHOP STILLINGFLEET.

I do confess there was something peculiar in the case of the Bishop of Alexandria, for all the provinces of Egypt were under his immediate care, which was Patriarchal as to extent, but Metropolical in the administration.

JUSTELLUS.

This authority (ἐξουσία) is that of a Metropolitan which the Nicene Fathers decreed to be his due over the three provinces named in this canon, Egypt, Libya, and Pentapolis, which made up the whole diocese of Egypt, as well in matters civil as ecclesiastical.

On this important question Hefele refers to the dissertation of Dupin, in his work *De Antiqua Ecclesiæ Disciplina.* Hefele says: "It seems to me beyond a doubt that in this canon there is a question about that which was afterward called the patriarchate of the Bishop of Alexandria; that is to say that he had a certain recognized ecclesiastical authority, not only over several civil provinces, but also over several ecclesiastical provinces (which had their own metropolitans);" and further on (p. 392) he adds: "It is incontestable that the civil provinces of Egypt, Libya, Pentapolis and Thebaïs, which were all in subjection to the Bishop of Alexandria, were also ecclesiastical provinces with their own metropolitans; and consequently it is not the ordinary rights of metropolitans that the Sixth Canon of Nice confers on the Bishop of Alexandria, but the rights of a superior Metropolitan, that is, of a Patriarch."

There only remains to see what were the bounds of the jurisdiction of the Bishop of Antioch. The civil diocese of Oriens is shewn by the Second Canon of Constantinople to be conterminous with what was afterward called the Patriarchate of Antioch. The see of Antioch had, as we know, several metropolitans subject to it, among them Cæsarea, under whose jurisdiction was Palestine. Justellus, however, is of opinion that Pope Innocent I. was in error when he asserted that all the Metropolitans of Oriens were to be ordained by him by any peculiar authority, and goes so far as to stigmatize his words as "contrary to the mind of the Nicene Synod."[1]

EXCURSUS ON THE EXTENT OF THE JURISDICTION OF THE BISHOP OF ROME OVER THE SUBURBICAN CHURCHES.

Although, as Hefele well says, "It is evident that the Council has not in view here the primacy of the Bishop of Rome over the whole Church, but simply his power as a patriarch," yet it may not be unimportant to consider what his patriarchal limits may have been.

(Hefele, *Hist. Councils*, Vol. I., p. 397.)

The translation of this [VI.] canon by Rufinus has been especially an apple of discord. *Et ut apud Alexandriam et in urbe Roma vetusta consuetudo servetur, ut vel ille Egypti vel hic* suburbicariarum ecclesiarum *sollicitudinem gerat.* In the seventeenth century this sentence of Rufinus gave rise to a very lively discussion between the celebrated jurist, Jacob Gothfried (Gothofredus), and his friend, Salmasius, on one side, and the Jesuit, Sirmond, on the other. The great prefecture of Italy, which contained about a third of the whole Roman Empire, was divided into four vicariates, among which the vicariate of Rome was the first. At its head were two officers, the *præfectus urbi* and the *vicarius urbis.* The *præfectus urbi* exercised authority over the city of Rome, and further in a suburban circle as far as the hundredth milestone. The boundary of the *vicarius urbis* comprised ten provinces—Campania, Tuscia with Ombria, Picenum, Valeria, Samnium, Apulia with Calabria, Lucania and that of the Brutii, Sicily, Sardinia, and Corsica. Gothfried and Salmasius maintained, that by the *regiones suburbicariæ* the little territory of the *præfectus urbi* must be understood; while, according to Sirmond, these words designate the whole territory of the *vicarius urbis.* In our time Dr. Maasen has proved in his book,[2] already quoted several times, that Gothfried and Salmasius were right in maintaining that, by the *regiones suburbicariæ*, the little territory of the *præfectus urbi* must be alone understood.

Hefele thinks that Phillips "has proved" that the Bishop of Rome had patriarchal rights over places outside the limits of the ten provinces of the *vicarius urbis;* but does not agree

[1] *Contra mentem Synodi Nicæni.*
[2] Friedrich Maasen: *Der Primat des Bischofs von Rom. und die alten Patriarchalkirchen.* Bonn, 1853. § 100–110. Maasen goes on to express the opinion that the patriarchal power of Rome was much larger.

with Phillips in thinking Rufinus in error.   As a matter of fact the point is a difficult one, and has little to do with the gist of the meaning of the canon.   One thing is certain : the early Latin version of the canons, called the *Prisca*, was not satisfied with the Greek wording and made the Canon read thus : "It is of ancient custom that the bishop of the city of Rome should have a primacy (*principatum*), so that he should govern with care the suburbican places, AND ALL HIS OWN PROVINCE."[1]   Another interesting reading is that found in several MSS. which begins, "The Church of Rome hath always had a primacy (*primatum*)," and as a matter of fact the early date of this addition is evinced by the fact that the canon was actually quoted in this shape by Paschasinus at the Council of Chalcedon.

Hefele further on says, "The Greek commentators Zonaras and Balsamon (of the twelfth century) say very explicitly, in their explanation of the Canons of Nice, that this sixth canon confirms the rights of the Bishop of Rome as patriarch over the whole West," and refers to Beveridge's *Syodicon*, Tom. I., pp. 66 and 67.   After diligent search I can find nothing to warrant the great amplitude of this statement.   Balsamon's interpretation is very vague, being simply that the Bishop of Rome is over the Western Eparchies (τῶν ἐσπερίων ἐπάρχων) and Zonaras still more vaguely says that τῶν ἐσπερίων ἄρχειν ἔθος ἐκράτησε.   That the whole West was in a general way understood to be in the Roman Patriarchate I have no doubt, that the Greek scholiasts just quoted deemed it to be so I think most probably the case, but it does not seem to me that they have said so in the particular place cited.   It seems to me that all they meant to say was that the custom observed at Alexandria and Antioch was no purely Eastern and local thing, for a similar state of affairs was found in the West.

CANON VII.

SINCE custom and ancient tradition have prevailed that the Bishop of Ælia [*i.e.*, Jerusalem] should be honoured, let him, saving its due dignity to the Metropolis, have the next place of honour.

NOTES.

ANCIENT EPITOME OF CANON VII.

Let the Bishop of Ælia be honoured, the rights of the Metropolis being preserved intact.

There would seem to be a singular fitness in the Holy City Jerusalem holding a very exalted position among the sees of Christendom, and it may appear astonishing that in the earliest times it was only a suffragan see to the great Church of Cæsarea.   It must be remembered, however, that only about seventy years after our Lord's death the city of Jerusalem was entirely destroyed and ploughed as a field according to the prophet.   As a holy city Jerusalem was a thing of the past for long years, and it is only in the beginning of the second century that we find a strong Christian Church growing up in the rapidly increasing city, called no longer Jerusalem, but Ælia Capitolina.   Possibly by the end of the second century the idea of the holiness of the site began to lend dignity to the occupant of the see ; at all events Eusebius[2] tells us that "at a synod held on the subject of the Easter controversy in the time of Pope Victor, Theophilus of Cæsarea and Narcissus of Jerusalem were presidents."

It was this feeling of reverence which induced the passing of this seventh canon.   It is very hard to determine just what was the "precedence" granted to the Bishop of Ælia, nor is it clear which is the metropolis referred to in the last clause.   Most writers, including Hefele, Balsamon, Aristenus and Beveridge consider it to be Cæsarea ; while Zonaras thinks Jerusalem to be intended, a view recently adopted and defended by Fuchs ;[3] others again suppose it is Antioch that is referred to.

---

[1] *Vide* Labbe's *Observation.* Tom. II , col. 47.

[2] Eusebius : *Hist. Eccl.* Lib. v., c. 23.
[3] Fuchs : *Bib. der Kirchenversammlungen.* Bd. i., S. 399.

EXCURSUS ON THE RISE OF THE PATRIARCHATE OF JERUSALEM.

The narrative of the successive steps by which the See of Jerusalem rose from being nothing but Ælia, a Gentile city, into one of the five patriarchal sees is sad reading for a Christian. It is but the record of ambition and, worse still, of knavery. No Christian can for a moment grudge to the Holy City of the old dispensation the honour shewn it by the Church, but he may well wish that the honour had been otherwise obtained. A careful study of such records as we possess shews that until the fifth century the Metropolitan of Cæsarea as often took precedence of the Bishop of Jerusalem as *vice versa*, and Beveridge has taken great pains to shew that the learned De Marca is in error in supposing that the Council of Nice assigned to Jerusalem a dignity superior to Cæsarea, and only inferior to Rome, Alexandria, and Antioch. It is true that in the signatures the Bishop of Jerusalem does sign before his metropolitan, but to this Beveridge justly replies that the same is the case with the occupants of two other of his suffragan sees. Bishop Beveridge's opinion is that the Council assigned Jerusalem the second place in the province, such as London enjoys in the Province of Canterbury. This, however, would seem to be as much too little as De Marca's contention grants too much. It is certain that almost immediately after the Council had adjourned, the Bishop of Jerusalem, Maximus, convoked a synod of Palestine, without any reference to Cæsarea, which consecrated bishops and acquitted St. Athanasius. It is true that he was reprimanded for doing so,[1] but yet it clearly shews how he intended to understand the action of Nice. The matter was not decided for a century more, and then through the chicanery of Juvenal the bishop of Jerusalem.

(Canon Venables, *Dict. Christ. Biography*.)

Juvenalis succeeded Praylius as bishop of Jerusalem somewhere about 420 A.D. The exact year cannot be determined. The episcopate of Praylius, which commenced in 417 A.D., was but short, and we can hardly give it at most more than three years. The statement of Cyril of Scythopolis, in his Life of St. Euthymius (c. 96), that Juvenal died "in the forty-fourth year of his episcopate," 458 A.D., is certainly incorrect, as it would make his episcopate begin in 414 A.D., three years before that of his predecessor. Juvenal occupies a prominent position during the Nestorian and Eutychian troubles towards the middle of the fifth century. But the part played by him at the councils of Ephesus and Chalcedon, as well as at the disgraceful λῃστρικὴ σύνοδος of 449, was more conspicuous than creditable, and there are few of the actors in these turbulent and saddening scenes who leave a more unpleasing impression. The ruling object of Juvenal's episcopate, to which everything else was secondary, and which guided all his conduct, was the elevation of the see of Jerusalem from the subordinate position it held in accordance with the seventh of the canons of the council of Nicæa, as suffragan to the metropolitan see of Cæsarea, to a primary place in the episcopate. Not content with aspiring to metropolitan rank, Juvenal coveted patriarchal dignity, and, in defiance of all canonical authority, he claimed jurisdiction over the great see of Antioch, from which he sought to remove Arabia and the two Phœnicias to his own province. At the council of Ephesus, in 431, he asserted for "the apostolic see of Jerusalem the same rank and authority with the apostolic see of Rome" (Labbe, *Concil*. iii. 642). These falsehoods he did not scruple to support with forged documents ("insolenter ausus per commentitia scripta firmare," Leo. Mag. *Ep*. 119 [92]), and other disgraceful artifices. Scarcely had Juvenal been consecrated bishop of Jerusalem when he proceeded to assert his claims to the metropolitan rank by his acts. In the letter of remonstrance against the proceedings of the council of

---

[1] Socrates: *Hist. Eccl.*, ii. 24.

Ephesus, sent to Theodosius by the Oriental party, they complain that Juvenal, whose "ambitious designs and juggling tricks" they are only too well acquainted with, had ordained in provinces over which he had no jurisdiction (Labbe, *Concil.* iii. 728). This audacious attempt to set at nought the Nicene decrees, and to falsify both history and tradition was regarded with the utmost indignation by the leaders of the Christian church. Cyril of Alexandria shuddered at the impious design ("merito perhorrescens," Leo. *u. s.*), and wrote to Leo, then archdeacon of Rome, informing him of what Juvenal was undertaking, and begging that his unlawful attempts might have no sanction from the apostolic See ("ut nulla illicitis conatibus præberetur assensio," *u. s.*). Juvenal, however, was far too useful an ally in his campaign against Nestorius for Cyril lightly to discard. When the council met at Ephesus Juvenal was allowed, without the slightest remonstrance, to take precedence of his metropolitan of Cæsarea, and to occupy the position of vice-president of the council, coming next after Cyril himself (Labbe, *Concil.* iii. 445), and was regarded in all respects as the second prelate in the assembly. The arrogant assertion of his supremacy over the bishop of Antioch, and his claim to take rank next after Rome as an apostolical see, provoked no open remonstrance, and his pretensions were at least tacitly allowed. At the next council, the disgraceful *Latrocinium*, Juvenal occupied the third place, after Dioscorus and the papal legate, having been specially named by Theodosius, together with Thalassius of Cæsarea (who appears to have taken no umbrage at his suffragan being preferred before him), as next in authority to Dioscorus (Labbe, *Concil.* iv. 109), and he took a leading part in the violent proceedings of that assembly. When the council of Chalcedon met, one of the matters which came before it for settlement was the dispute as to priority between Juvenal and Maximus Bishop of Antioch. The contention was long and severe. It ended in a compromise agreed on in the Seventh Action, μετὰ πολλὴν φιλονεικίαν. Juvenal surrendered his claim to the two Phœnicias and to Arabia, on condition of his being allowed metropolitical jurisdiction over the three Palestines (Labbe, *Concil.* iv. 613). The claim to patriarchal authority over the Bishop of Antioch put forward at Ephesus was discreetly dropped. The difficulty presented by the Nicene canon does not appear to have presented itself to the council, nor was any one found to urge the undoubted claims of the see of Cæsarea. The terms arranged between Maximus and Juvenal were regarded as satisfactory, and received the consent of the assembled bishops (ibid. 618). Maximus, however, was not long in repenting of his too ready acquiescence in Juvenal's demands, and wrote a letter of complaint to pope Leo, who replied by the letter which has been already quoted, dated June 11, 453 A.D., in which he upheld the binding authority of the Nicene canons, and commenting in the strongest terms on the greediness and ambition of Juvenal, who allowed no opportunity of forwarding his ends to be lost, declared that as far as he was concerned he would do all he could to maintain the ancient dignity of the see of Antioch (Leo Magn. *Ep. ad Maximum*, 119 [92]). No further action, however, seems to have been taken either by Leo or by Maximus. Juvenal was left master of the situation, and the church of Jerusalem has from that epoch peaceably enjoyed the patriarchal dignity obtained for it by such base means.

CANON VIII.

CONCERNING those who call themselves Cathari, if they come over to the Catholic and Apostolic Church, the great and holy Synod decrees that they who are ordained shall continue as they are in the clergy. But it is before all things necessary that they should profess in writing that they will observe and follow the dogmas of the Catholic and Apostolic Church; in particular that they will communicate with persons who have been twice married, and with those who having lapsed in persecution have had a period [of penance] laid upon them, and a time [of restoration] fixed so that in all things they will follow the dogmas of the Catholic Church.   Wheresoever, then, whether in villages or in cities, all of the ordained are found to be of these only, let them remain in the clergy, and in the same rank in which they are found.   But if they come over where there is a bishop or presbyter of the Catholic Church, it is manifest that the Bishop of the Church must have the bishop's dignity; and he who was named bishop by those who are called Cathari shall have the rank of presbyter, unless it shall seem fit to the Bishop to admit him to partake in the honour of the title.   Or, if this should not be satisfactory, then shall the bishop provide for him a place as Chorepiscopus, or presbyter, in order that he may be evidently seen to be of the clergy, and that there may not be two bishops in the city.

NOTES.

Ancient Epitome of Canon VIII.

If those called Cathari come over, let them first make profession that they are willing to communicate with the twice married, and to grant pardon to the lapsed.   And on this condition he who happens to be in orders, shall continue in the same order, so that a bishop shall still be bishop.   Whoever was a bishop among the Cathari let him, however, become a Chorepiscopus, or let him enjoy the honour of a presbyter or of a bishop.   For in one church there shall not be two bishops.

The Cathari or Novatians were the followers of Novatian, a presbyter of Rome, who had been a Stoic philosopher and was delivered, according to his own story, from diabolical possession at his exorcising by the Church before his baptism, when becoming a Catechumen.   Being in peril of death by illness he received clinical baptism, and was ordained priest without any further sacred rites being administered to him.   During the persecution he constantly refused to assist his brethren, and afterwards raised his voice against what he considered their culpable laxity in admitting to penance the lapsed.   Many agreed with him in this, especially of the clergy, and eventually, in A.D. 251, he induced three bishops to consecrate him, thus becoming, as Fleury remarks,[1] "the first Anti-Pope."   His indignation was principally spent upon Pope Cornelius, and to overthrow the prevailing discipline of the Church he ordained bishops and sent them to different parts of the empire as the disseminators of his error.   It is well to remember that while beginning only as a schismatic, he soon fell into heresy, denying that the Church had the power to absolve the lapsed.   Although condemned by several councils his sect continued on, and like the Montanists they rebaptized Catholics who apostatized to them, and absolutely rejected all second marriages.   At the time of the Council of Nice

the Novatian bishop at Constantinople, Acesius, was greatly esteemed, and although a schismatic, was invited to attend the council.   After having in answer to the emperor's enquiry whether he was willing to sign the Creed, assured him that he was, he went on to explain that his separation was because the Church no longer observed the ancient discipline which forbade that those who had committed mortal sin should ever be readmitted to communion.   According to the Novatians he might be exhorted to repentance, but the Church had no power to assure him of forgiveness but must leave him to the judgment of God.   It was then that Constantine said, "Acesius, take a ladder, and climb up to heaven alone."[2]

Aristenus.

If any of them be bishops or chorepiscopi they shall remain in the same rank, unless perchance in the same city there be found a bishop of the Catholic Church, ordained before their coming.   For in this case he that was properly bishop from the first shall have the preference, and he alone shall retain the Episcopal throne.   For it is not right that in the same city there should be two bishops.   But he who by the Cathari was called bishop, shall be honoured as a presbyter, or (if it so please the bishop), he shall be sharer of the title bishop; but he shall exercise no episcopal jurisdiction.

Zonaras, Balsamon, Beveridge and Van Espen, are of opinion that χειροθετουμένους does not mean that they are to receive a new laying on of hands at their reception into the Church, but that it refers to their already condition of being ordained, the meaning being that as they have had Novatian ordination they must be reckoned among the clergy.   Dionysius Exiguus takes a different view, as does also the *Prisca* version, according to which the

---

[1] Fleury, *Hist. Eccles.* liv. VI., liij.

[2] Socrates, *Hist. Eccl.*, i. 10.   *Vide* also Tillemont, *Mémoires*, etc., tom. vi., art. 17, and Sozoman, *H. E.* i. 22.

clergy of the Novatians were to receive a laying on of hands, χειροθετουμένους, but that it was not to be a reordination. With this interpretation Hefele seems to agree, founding his opinion upon the fact that the article is wanting before χειροθετουμένους, and that αὐτοὺς is added. Gratian [1] supposes that this eighth canon orders a re-ordination.

EXCURSUS ON THE CHOREPISCOPI.

There has been much difference of opinion among the learned touching the status of the Chorepiscopus in the early Church. The main question in dispute is as to whether they were always, sometimes, or never, in episcopal orders. Most Anglican writers, including Beveridge, Hammond, Cave, and Routh, have affirmed the first proposition, that they were true bishops, but that, out of respect to the bishop of the City they were forbidden the exercise of certain of their episcopal functions, except upon extraordinary occasions. With this view Binterim [2] also agrees, and Augusti is of the same opinion.[3] But Thomassinus is of a different mind, thinking, so says Hefele,[4] that there were "two classes of chorepiscopi, of whom the one were real bishops, while the other had only the title without consecration."

The third opinion, that they were merely presbyters, is espoused by Morinus and Du Cange, and others who are named by Bingham.[5] This last opinion is now all but universally rejected, to the other two we shall now devote our attention.

For the first opinion no one can speak more learnedly nor more authoritatively than Arthur West Haddon, who writes as follows ;

(Haddon, *Dict. Christ. Antiq. s. v.* Chorepiscopus.)

The chorepiscopus was called into existence in the latter part of the third century, and first in Asia Minor, in order to meet the want of episcopal supervision in the country parts of the now enlarged dioceses without subdivision. [They are] first mentioned in the Councils of Ancyra and Neo-Cæsarea A. D. 314, and again in the Council of Nice (which is subscribed by fifteen, all from Asia Minor or Syria). [They became] sufficiently important to require restriction by the time of the Council of Antioch, A. D. 341 ; and continued to exist in the East until at least the ninth century, when they were supplanted by ἔξαρχοι. [Chorepiscopi are] first mentioned in the West in the Council of Riez, A. D. 439 (the Epistles of Pope Damasus I. and of Leo. M. respecting them being forgeries), and continued there (but not in Africa, principally in France) until about the tenth century, after which the name occurs (in a decree of Pope Damasus II. ap. Sigeb. *in an.* 1048) as equivalent to archdeacon, an office from which the Arabic Nicene canons expressly distinguish it. The functions of chorepiscopi, as well as their name, were of an episcopal, not of a presbyterial kind, although limited to minor offices. They overlooked the country district committed to them, "*loco episcopi*," ordaining readers, exorcists, subdeacons, but, as a rule, not deacons or presbyters (and of course not bishops), unless by express permission of their diocesan bishop. They confirmed in their own districts, and (in Gaul) are mentioned as consecrating churches (*vide* Du Cange). They granted εἰρενικαὶ, or letters dimissory, which country presbyters were forbidden to do. They had also the honorary privilege (τιμώμενοι) of assisting at the celebration of the Holy Eucharist in the mother city church, which country presbyters had not (*Conc. Ancyr.* can. xiii.; *Neo-Cæsar.* can. xiv. ; *Antioch*, can. x. ; St. Basil M. *Epist.* 181 ; Rab. Maur. *De Instit. Cler.* i. 5, etc. etc.). They were held therefore to have power of ordination, but to lack jurisdiction, save subordinately. And the actual ordination of a presbyter by Timotheus, a chorepiscopus, is recorded (Pallad., *Hist. Lausiac.* 106).

---

[1] Gratian, *Decretum, Corp. Juris Canon*, Pars. II. Causa I. Quæst. 7, Can. viij.
[2] Binterim, *Denkwürdigkeiten*, vol. i. part ii. pp. 386–414.
[3] Augusti, *Denkwürdigkeiten*, vol. xi. p. 159 *et seqq.*
[4] Hefele, *Hist. of the Councils*, vol. ii. p. 322.
[5] Bingham, *Antiquities*, ii. xiv. 2, 3.

In the West, i.e. chiefly in Gaul, the order appears to have prevailed more widely, to have usurped episcopal functions without due subordination to the diocesans, and to have been also taken advantage of by idle or worldly diocesans. In consequence it seems to have aroused a strong feeling of hostility, which showed itself, first in a series of papal bulls, condemning them ; headed, it is true, by two forged letters respectively of Damasus I. and Leo. M. (of which the latter is merely an interpolated version of *Conc. Hispal.* II. A.D. 619, can. 7, adding *chorepiscopi* to *presbyteri*, of which latter the council really treats), but continuing in a more genuine form, from Leo III. down to Pope Nicholas I. (to Rodolph, Archbishop of Bourges, A.D. 864) ; the last of whom, however, takes the more moderate line of affirming chorepiscopi to be really bishops, and consequently refusing to annul their ordinations of presbyters and deacons (as previous popes had done), but orders them to keep within canonical limits ; and secondly, in a series of conciliar decrees, *Conc. Ratispon.* A.D. 800, in *Capit.* lib. iv. c. 1, *Paris.* A.D. 829, lib. i. c. 27 ; *Meld.* A.D. 845, can. 44 ; *Metens.* A.D. 888, can. 8, and *Capitul.* v. 168, vi. 119, vii. 187, 310, 323, 324, annulling all episcopal acts of chorepiscopi, and ordering them to be repeated by "true" bishops ; and finally forbidding all further appointments of chorepiscopi at all.

That chorepiscopi as such—i.e. omitting the cases of reconciled or vacant bishops above mentioned, of whose episcopate of course no question is made—were at first truly bishops both in East and West, appears almost certain, both from their name and functions, and even from the arguments of their strong opponents just spoken of. If nothing more could be urged against them, than that the Council of Neo-Cæsarea compared them to the Seventy disciples, that the Council of Antioch authorises their consecration by a single bishop, and that they actually were so consecrated (the Antiochene decree *might* mean merely nomination by the word γίνεσθαι, but the actual history seems to rule the term to intend consecration, and the [one] exceptional case of a chorepiscopus recorded [*Actt. Episc. Cenoman. ap.* Du Cange] in late times to have been ordained by three bishops [in order that he *might* be a full bishop] merely proves the general rule to the contrary)—and that they were consecrated for "villages," contrary to canon,—then they certainly were bishops. And Pope Nicholas expressly says that they were so. Undoubtedly they ceased to be so in the East, and were practically merged in archdeacons in the West.

For the second opinion, its great champion, Thomassinus shall speak.

(Thomassin, *Ancienne et Nouvelle Discipline de l'Église*, Tom. I. Livre II. chap 1. § iii.)

The chorepiscopi were not duly consecrated bishops, unless some bishop had consecrated a bishop for a town and the bishop thus ordained contrary to the canons was tolerated on condition of his submitting himself to the diocesan as though he were only a chorepiscopus. This may be gathered from the fifty-seventh canon of Laodicea.

From this canon two conclusions may be drawn, 1st. That bishops ought not to be ordained for villages, and that as Chorepiscopi could only be placed in villages they could not be bishops. 2d. That sometimes by accident a chorepiscopus might be a bishop, but only through having been canonically lowered to that rank.

The Council of Nice furnishes another example of a bishop lowered to the rank of a chorepiscopus in Canon viii. This canon shows that they should not have been bishops, for two bishops could never be in a diocese, although this might accidentally be the case when a chorepiscopus happened to be a bishop.

This is the meaning which must be given to the tenth canon of Antioch, which directs that chorepiscopi, even if they have received episcopal orders, and have been consecrated bishops, shall keep within the limits prescribed by the canon ; that in cases of necessity, they ordain the lower clergy ; but that they be careful not to ordain priests or deacons, because this power is absolutely reserved to the Diocesan.   It must be added that as the council of Antioch commands that the Diocesan without any other bishop can ordain the chorepiscopus, the position can no longer be sustained that the chorepiscopi were bishops, such a method of consecrating a bishop being contrary to canon xix. of the same council, moreover the canon does not say the chorepiscopus is to be ordained, but uses the word γένεσθαι by the bishop of the city (canon x.).   The Council of Neocæsarea by referring them to the seventy disciples (in Canon XIV.) has shown the chorepiscopi to be only priests.

But the Council of Ancyra does furnish a difficulty, for the text seems to permit chorepiscopi to ordain priests.   But the Greek text must be corrected by the ancient Latin versions.   The letter attributed to pope Nicholas, A.D. 864, must be considered a forgery since he recognises the chorepiscopi as real bishops.

If Harmenopulus, Aristenus, Balsamon, and Zonaras seem to accord to the chorepiscopi the power to ordain priests and deacons with the permission of the Diocesan, it is because they are explaining the meaning and setting forth the practice of the ancient councils and not the practice of their own times.   But at all events it is past all doubt that before the seventh century there were, by different accidents, chorepiscopi who were really bishops and that these could, with the consent of the diocesan, ordain priests.   But at the time these authors wrote, there was not a single chorepiscopus in the entire East, as Balsamon frankly admits in commenting on Canon xiii. of Ancyra.

Whether in the foregoing the reader will think Thomassinus has proved his point, I do not know, but so far as the position of the chorepiscopi in synods is concerned there can be no doubt whatever, and I shall allow Hefele to speak on this point.

(Hefele, History of the Councils, Vol. I. pp. 17, 18.)

The *Chorepiscopi* (χωρεπίσκοποι), or bishops of country places, seem to have been considered in ancient times as quite on a par with the other bishops, as far as their position in synod was concerned.   We meet with them at the Councils of Neocæsarea in the year 314, of Nicæa in 325, of Ephesus in 431.   On the other hand, among the 600 bishops of the fourth Ecumenical Council at Chalcedon in 451, there is no chorepiscopus present, for by this time the office had been abolished ; but in the Middle Ages we again meet with chorepiscopi of a new kind at Western councils, particularly at those of the French Church, at Langres in 830, at Mayence in 847, at Pontion in 876, at Lyons in 886, at Douzy in 871.

CANON IX.

If any presbyters have been advanced without examination, or if upon examination they have made confession of crime, and men acting in violation of the canon have laid hands upon them, notwithstanding their confession, such the canon does not admit ; for the Catholic Church requires that [only] which is blameless.

NOTES.

ANCIENT EPITOME OF CANON IX.

Whoever are ordained without examination, shall be deposed if it be found out afterwards that they had been guilty.

HEFELE.

The crimes in question are those which were a bar to the priesthood—such as blasphemy, bigamy, heresy, idolatry, magic, etc.— as the Arabic paraphrase of Joseph explains. It is clear that these faults are punishable in the bishop no less than in the priest, and that consequently our canon refers to the bishops as well as to the πρεσβύτεροι in the more restricted sense. These words of the Greek text, "In the case in which any one might be induced, in opposition to the canon, to ordain such persons," allude to the ninth canon of the Synod of Neocæsarea. It was necessary to pass such ordinances; for even in the fifth century, as the twenty-second letter to Pope Innocent the First testifies, some held that as baptism effaces all former sins, so it takes away all the *impedimenta ordinationis* which are the result of those sins.

BALSAMON.

Some say that as baptism makes the baptized person a new man, so ordination takes away the sins committed before ordination, which opinion does not seem to agree with the canons.

This canon occurs twice in the *Corpus Juris Canonici. Decretum* Pars I. Dist. xxiv. c. vij., and Dist. lxxxj., c. iv.

CANON X.

IF any who have lapsed have been ordained through the ignorance, or even with the previous knowledge of the ordainers, this shall not prejudice the canon of the Church; for when they are discovered they shall be deposed.

NOTES.

ANCIENT EPITOME OF CANON X.

Whoso had lapsed are to be deposed whether those who ordained and promoted them did so conscious of their guilt or unknowing of it.

HEFELE.

The tenth canon differs from the ninth, inasmuch as it concerns only the *lapsi* and their elevation, not only to the priesthood, but to any other ecclesiastical preferment as well, and requires their deposition. The punishment of a bishop who should consciously perform such an ordination is not mentioned;

but it is incontestable that the *lapsi* could not be ordained, even after having performed penance; for, as the preceding canon states, the Church requires those who were faultless. It is to be observed that the word προχειρίζειν is evidently employed here in the sense of "ordain," and is used without any distinction from χειρίζειν, whilst in the synodal letter of the Council of Nicæa on the subject of the Meletians, there is a distinction between these two words, and προχειρίζειν is used to signify *eligere*.

This canon is found in *Corpus Juris Canonici. Decretum.* Pars I. Dist. lxxxi. c. v.

CANON XI.

CONCERNING those who have fallen without compulsion, without the spoiling of their property, without danger or the like, as happened during the tyranny of Licinius, the Synod declares that, though they have deserved no clemency, they shall be dealt with mercifully. As many as were communicants, if they heartily repent, shall pass three years among the hearers; for seven years they shall be prostrators; and for two years they shall communicate with the people in prayers, but without oblation.

NOTES.

ANCIENT EPITOME OF CANON XI.

As many as fell without necessity, even if therefore undeserving of indulgence, yet some indulgence shall be shown them and they shall be prostrators for twelve years.

On the expression "without oblation" (χωρὶς προσφορᾶς)see the notes to Ancyra, Canon V. where the matter is treated at some length.

LAMBERT.

The usual position of the hearers was just inside the church door. But Zonaras (and Balsamon agrees with him), in his comment on this canon, says, "they are ordered for three years to be hearers, or to stand without the church in the narthex."

I have read "as many as were communicants" (οἱ πιστοὶ) thus following Dr. Routh.

Vide his *Opuscula.* Caranza translates in his *Summary of the Councils* "if they were faithful" and seems to have read εἰ πιστοὶ, which is much simpler and makes better sense.

The prostrators stood within the body of the church behind the ambo [*i.e.* the reading desk] and went out with the catechumens.

EXCURSUS ON THE PUBLIC DISCIPLINE OR EXOMOLOGESIS OF THE EARLY CHURCH.

(Taken chiefly from Morinus, *De Disciplina in Administratione Sacramenti Pœnitentiæ;* Bingham, *Antiquities;* and Hammond, *The Definitions of Faith, etc.* Note to Canon XI. of Nice.)

"In the Primitive Church there was a godly discipline, that at the beginning of Lent, such persons as stood convicted of notorious sin were put to open penance, and punished in this world that their souls might be saved in the day of the Lord; and that others, admonished by their example, might be the more afraid to offend."

The foregoing words from the Commination Service of the Church of England may serve well to introduce this subject. In the history of the public administration of discipline in the Church, there are three periods sufficiently distinctly marked. The first of these ends at the rise of Novatianism in the middle of the second century; the second stretches down to about the eighth century; and the third period shews its gradual decline to its practical abandonment in the eleventh century. The period with which we are concerned is the second, when it was in full force.

In the first period it would seem that public penance was required only of those convicted of what then were called by pre-eminence "mortal sins" (*crimena mortalia* [1]), *viz:* idolatry, murder, and adultery. But in the second period the list of mortal sins was greatly enlarged, and Morinus says that "Many Fathers who wrote after Augustine's time, extended the necessity of public penance to all crimes which the civil law punished with death, exile, or other grave corporal penalty." [2] In the penitential canons ascribed to St. Basil and those which pass by the name of St. Gregory Nyssen, this increase of offences requiring public penance will be found intimated.

From the fourth century the penitents of the Church were divided into four classes. Three of these are mentioned in the eleventh canon, the fourth, which is not here referred to, was composed of those styled συγκλαίοντες, flentes or weepers. These were not allowed to enter into the body of the church at all, but stood or lay outside the gates, sometimes covered with sackcloth and ashes. This is the class which is sometimes styled χειμοζόμενοι, hybernantes, on account of their being obliged to endure the inclemency of the weather.

It may help to the better understanding of this and other canons which notice the different orders of penitents, to give a brief account of the usual form and arrangement of the ancient churches as well as of the different orders of the penitents.

Before the church there was commonly either an open area surrounded with porticoes, called μεσάυλιον or atrium, with a font of water in the centre, styled a cantharus or phiala, or sometimes only an open portico, or προπύλαιον. The first variety may still be seen at S. Ambrogio's in Milan, and the latter in Rome at S. Lorenzo's, and in Ravenna at the two S. Apollinares. This was the place at which the first and lowest order of penitents, the weepers, already referred to, stood exposed to the weather. Of these, St. Gregory Thaumaturgus says: "Weeping takes place outside the door of the church, where the sinner must stand and beg the prayers of the faithful as they go in."

The church itself usually consisted of three divisions within, besides these exterior courts

---

[1] Cyprian. *De Bono Patient.*, cap. xiv.　　　　　　[2] Morinus, *De Pœnitent.*, lib. v., cap. 5.

and porch. The first part after passing through "the great gates," or doors of the building, was called the Narthex in Greek, and Færula in Latin, and was a narrow vestibule extending the whole width of the church. In this part, to which Jews and Gentiles, and in most places even heretics and schismatics were admitted, stood the Catechumens, and the Energumens or those afflicted with evil spirits, and the second class of penitents (the first mentioned in the Canon), who were called the ἀκοώμενοι, audientes, or hearers. These were allowed to hear the Scriptures read, and the Sermon preached, but were obliged to depart before the celebration of the Divine Mysteries, with the Catechumens, and the others who went by the general name of hearers only.

The second division, or main body of the church, was called the Naos or Nave. This was separated from the Narthex by rails of wood, with gates in the centre, which were called "the beautiful or royal gates." In the middle of the Nave, but rather toward the lower or entrance part of it, stood the Ambo, or reading-desk, the place for the readers and singers, to which they went up by steps, whence the name, Ambo. Before coming to the Ambo, in the lowest part of the Nave, and just after passing the royal gates, was the place for the third order of penitents, called in Greek γονυκλίνοντες, or ὑποπίπτοντες, and in Latin Genuflectentes or Prostrati, i.e., kneelers or prostrators, because they were allowed to remain and join in certain prayers particularly made for them. Before going out they prostrated themselves to receive the imposition of the bishop's hands with prayer. This class of penitents left with the Catechumens.

In the other parts of the Nave stood the believers or faithful, i.e., those persons who were in full communion with the Church, the men and women generally on opposite sides, though in some places the men were below, and the women in galleries above. Amongst these were the fourth class of penitents, who were called συνεστῶτες, consistentes, i.e., co-standers, because they were allowed to stand with the faithful, and to remain and hear the prayers of the Church, after the Catechumens and the other penitents were dismissed, and to be present while the faithful offered and communicated, though they might not themselves make their offerings, nor partake of the Holy Communion. This class of penitents are frequently mentioned in the canons, as "communicating in prayers," or "without the oblation ;" and it was the last grade to be passed through previous to the being admitted again to full communion. The practice of "hearing mass" or "non-communicating attendance" clearly had its origin in this stage of discipline. At the upper end of the body of the church, and divided from it by rails which were called Cancelli, was that part which we now call the Chancel. This was anciently called by several names, as Bema or tribunal, from its being raised above the body of the church, and Sacrarium or Sanctuary. It was also called Apsis and Concha Bematis, from its semicircular end. In this part stood the Altar, or Holy Table (which names were indifferently used in the primitive Church), behind which, and against the wall of the chancel, was the Bishop's throne, with the seats of the Presbyters on each side of it, called synthronus. On one side of the chancel was the repository for the sacred utensils and vestments, called the Diaconicum, and answering to our Vestry ; and on the other the Prothesis, a side-table, or place, where the bread and wine were deposited before they were offered on the Altar. The gates in the chancel rail were called the holy gates, and none but the higher orders of the clergy, i.e., Bishops, Priests, and Deacons, were allowed to enter within them. The Emperor indeed was permitted to do so for the purpose of making his offering at the Altar, but then he was obliged to retire immediately, and to receive the communion without.

(Thomassin. *Ancienne et Nouvelle Discipline de l'Église.* Tom. I. Livre II. chap. xvj. somewhat abridged.)

In the West there existed always many cases of public penance, but in the East it is more difficult to find any traces of it, after it was abolished by the Patriarch Nectarius in the person of the Grand Penitentiary.

However, the Emperor Alexis Comnenus, who took the empire in the year 1080, did a penance like that of older days, and one which may well pass for miraculous. He called together a large number of bishops with the patriarch, and some holy religious; he presented himself before them in the garb of a criminal; he confessed to them his crime of usurpation with all its circumstances. They condemned the Emperor and all his accomplices to fasting, to lying prostrate upon the earth, to wearing haircloth, and to all the other ordinary austerities of penance. Their wives desired to share their griefs and their sufferings, although they had had no share in their crime. The whole palace became a theatre of sorrow and public penance. The emperor wore the hairshirt under the purple, and lay upon the earth for forty days, having only a stone for a pillow.

To all practical purposes Public Penance was a general institution but for a short while in the Church. But the reader must be careful to distinguish between this Public Penance and the private confession which in the Catholic Church both East and West is universally practised. What Nectarius did was to abolish the office of Penitentiary, whose duty it had been to assign *public* penance for *secret* sin ;[1] a thing wholly different from what Catholics understand by the "Sacrament of Penance." It would be out of place to do more in this place than to call the reader's attention to the bare fact, and to supply him, from a Roman Catholic point of view, with an explanation of why Public Penance died out. "It came to an end because it was of human institution. But sacramental confession, being of divine origin, lasted when the penitential discipline had been changed, and continues to this day among the Greeks and Oriental sects."[2] That the reader may judge of the absolute candour of the writer just quoted, I give a few sentences from the same article: "An opinion, however, did prevail to some extent in the middle ages, even among Catholics, that confession to God alone sufficed. The Council of Châlons in 813 (canon xxxiij.), says: 'Some assert that we should confess our sins to God alone, but some think that they should be confessed to the priest, each of which practices is followed not without great fruit in Holy Church. . . . Confession made to God purges sins, but that made to the priest teaches how they are to be purged.' This former opinion is also mentioned without reprobation by Peter Lombard (*In Sentent.* Lib. iv. dist. xvij.)."

CANON XII.

As many as were called by grace, and displayed the first zeal, having cast aside their military girdles, but afterwards returned, like dogs, to their own vomit, (so that some spent money and by means of gifts regained their military stations); let these, after they have passed the space of three years as hearers, be for ten years prostrators. But in all these cases it is necessary to examine well into their purpose and what their repentance appears to be like. For as many as give evidence of their conversions by deeds, and not pretence, with fear, and tears, and perseverance, and good works, when they have fulfilled their appointed time as hearers, may properly communicate in prayers; and after that the bishop may determine yet more favourably concerning them. But those who take [the matter] with indifference, and who think the form of [not] entering the Church is sufficient for their conversion, must fulfil the whole time.

---

[1] Vide, Thomassin. *Lib. cit.* Livre II. Chapitre vii. § xiii. where the whole matter of Nectarius's action is discussed.

[2] Addis and Arnold. *A Catholic Dictionary; sub voce* Penance, Sacrament of.

NOTES.

ANCIENT EPITOME OF CANON XII.

Those who endured violence and were seen to have resisted, but who afterwards yielded to wickedness, and returned to the army, shall be excommunicated for ten years. But in every case the way in which they do their penance must be scrutinized. And if anyone who is doing penance shews himself zealous in its performance, the bishop shall treat him more leniently than had he been cold and indifferent.

LAMBERT.

The abuse of this power, namely, of granting under certain circumstances a relaxation in the penitential exercises enjoined by the canons—led, in later times, to the practice of commuting such exercises for money payments, etc.

HEFELE.

In his last contests with Constantine, Licinius had made himself the representative of heathenism ; so that the final issue of the war would not be the mere triumph of one of the two competitors, but the triumph or fall of Christianity or heathenism. Accordingly, a Christian who had in this war supported the cause of Licinius and of heathenism might be considered as a *lapsus*, even if he did not formally fall away. With much more reason might those Christians be treated as *lapsi* who, having conscientiously given up military service (this is meant by the soldier's belt), afterwards retracted their resolution, and went so far as to give money and presents for the sake of readmission, on account of the numerous advantages which military service then afforded. It must not be forgotten that Licinius, as Zonaras and Eusebius relate, required from his soldiers a formal apostasy ; compelled them, for example, to take part in the heathen sacrifices which were held in the camps, and dismissed from his service those who would not apostatize.

BRIGHT.

This canon (which in the Prisca and the Isidorian version stands as part of canon 11) deals, like it, with cases which had arisen under the Eastern reign of Licinius, who having resolved to "purge his army of all ardent Christians" (Mason, *Persec. of Diocl.* p. 308), ordered his Christian officers to sacrifice to the gods on pain of being cashiered (compare Euseb. *H. E.* x. 8 ; *Vit. Con.* i. 54). It is to be observed here that military life as such was not deemed unchristian. The case of Cornelius was borne in mind. "We serve in your armies," says Tertullian, *Apol.* 42 (although later, as a Montanist, he took a rigorist and fanatical view, *De Cor.* 11), and compare the fact which underlies the tale of the "Thundering Legion,"—the presence of Christians in the army of Marcus Aurelius. It was the heathenish adjuncts to their calling which often brought Christian soldiers to a stand (see Routh. *Scr. Opusc.* i. 410), as when Marinus' succession to a centurionship was challenged on the ground that he could not sacrifice to the gods (Euseb. *H. E.* vii. 15). Sometimes, indeed, individual Christians thought like Maximilian in the Martyrology, who absolutely refused to enlist, and on being told by the proconsul that there were Christian soldiers in the imperial service, answered, "Ipsi sciunt quod ipsis expediat" (Ruinart, *Act. Sanc.* p. 341). But, says Bingham (*Antiq.* xi. 5, 10), "the ancient canons did not condemn the military life as a vocation simply unlawful. . . . I believe there is no instance of any man being refused baptism merely because he was a soldier, unless some unlawful circumstance, such as idolatry, or the like, made the vocation sinful." After the victory of Constantine in the West, the Council of Arles excommunicated those who in time of peace "threw away their arms" (can. 2). In the case before us, some Christian officers had at first stood firm under the trial imposed on them by Licinius. They had been "called by grace" to an act of self-sacrifice (the phrase is one which St. Augustine might have used) ; and had shown "their eagerness at the outset" ("primum suum ardorem," Dionysius ; Philo and Evarestus more laxly, "primordia bona ;" compare τὴν ἀγάπην σου τὴν πρώτην, Rev. ii. 4). Observe here how beautifully the ideas of grace and free will are harmonized. These men had responded to a Divine impulse : it might seem that they had committed themselves to a noble course : they had cast aside the "belts" which were their badge of office (compare the cases of Valentinian and Valens, Soc. iii. 13, and of Benevolus throwing down his belt at the feet of Justina, Soz. vii. 13). They had done, in fact, just what Auxentius, one of Licinius' notaries, had done when, according to the graphic anecdote of Philostorgius (*Fragm.* 5), his master bade him place a bunch of grapes before a statue of Bacchus in the palace-court ; but their zeal, unlike his, proved to be too impulsive—they reconsidered their position, and illustrated the maxim that in morals second thoughts are *not* best (Butler, *Serm.* 7), by making unworthy attempts—in some cases by bribery—to recover what they had worthily resigned. (Observe the Grecised Latinism βενεφικίοις and compare the Latinisms of St. Mark, and others in Euseb. iii. 20, vi. 40, x. 5.) This the Council describes in proverbial language, probably borrowed from 2 Pet. ii. 22, but, it is needless to say, without intending to censure enlistment as such. They now desired to be received to penance : accordingly they were ordered to spend three years as Hearers, during which time "their purpose, and the nature (εἶδος) of their repentance" were to be carefully "examined." Again we see the earnest resolution of the Council to make discipline a moral reality, and to prevent it from being turned into a formal routine ; to secure, as Rufinus' abridgment expresses it, a repentance "fructuosam et attentam." If the penitents were found to have "manifested their conversion by deeds, and not in outward show (σχήματι), by awe, and tears, and patience, and good works" (such, for instance, Zonaras comments, as almsgiving according to ability), "it would be then reasonable to admit them to a participation in the prayers," to the position of Consistentes, "with permission also to the bishop to come to a yet more indulgent resolution concerning them," by admitting them to full communion. This discretionary power of the bishop to dispense with part of a penance-time is recognized in the fifth canon of Ancyra and the sixteenth of Chalcedon, and mentioned by Basil,

Epist. 217, c. 74. It was the basis of "indulgences" in their original form (Bingham, xviii. 4, 9). But it was too possible that some at least of these "lapsi" might take the whole affair lightly, "with indifference" ἀδιαφόρως—not seriously enough, as Hervetas renders—just as if, in common parlance, it did not signify : the fourth Ancyrene canon speaks of *lapsi* who partook of the idol-feast ἀδιαφόρως as if it involved them in no sin (see below on Eph. 5, Chalc. 4). It was possible that they might "deem" the outward form of "entering the church" to stand in the narthex among the Hearers (here, as in c. 8, 19, σχῆμα denotes an external visible fact) sufficient to entitle them to the character of converted penitents, while their conduct out of church was utterly lacking in seriousness and self-humiliation. In that case there could be no question of shortening their penance-time, for they were not in a state to benefit by indulgence : it would be, as the Roman Presbyters wrote to Cyprian, and as he himself wrote to his own church, a "mere covering over of the wound" (*Epist.* 30, 3), an "injury" rather than "a kindness" (*De Lapsis*, 16) ; they must therefore "by all means" go through ten years as Kneelers, before they can become Consistentes.

There is great difficulty about the last phrase and Gelasius of Cyzicus, the *Prisca*, Dionysius Exiguus, the pseudo-Isidore, Zonaras and most others have considered the "not" an interpolation. I do not see how dropping the "not" makes the meaning materially clearer.

CANON XIII.

CONCERNING the departing, the ancient canonical law is still to be maintained, to wit, that, if any man be at the point of death, he must not be deprived of the last and most indispensable Viaticum. But, if any one should be restored to health again who has received the communion when his life was despaired of, let him remain among those who communicate in prayers only. But in general, and in the case of any dying person whatsoever asking to receive the Eucharist, let the Bishop, after examination made, give it him.

NOTES.

ANCIENT EPITOME OF CANON XIII.

The dying are to be communicated. But if any such get well, he must be placed in the number of those who share in the prayers, and with these only.

VAN ESPEN.

It cannot be denied that antiquity used the name "Viaticum" not only to denote the Eucharist which was given to the dying, but also to denote the reconciliation, and imposition of penance, and in general, everything that could be conducive to the happy death of the person concerned, and this has been shown by Aubespine (*lib.* 1, *Obs. cap.* ii.). But while this is so, the more usual sense of the word is the Eucharist. For this cannot be denied that the faithful of the first ages of the Church looked upon the Eucharist as the complement of Christian perfection, and as the last seal of hope and salvation. It was for this reason that at the beginning of life, after baptism and confirmation, the Eucharist was given even to infants, and at the close of life the Eucharist followed reconciliation and extreme unction, so that properly and literally it could be styled "the last Viaticum." Moreover for penitents it was considered especially necessary that through it they might return to the *peace* of the Church; for perfect peace is given by that very communion of the Eucharist. [A number of instances are then cited, and various ancient versions of the canon.]

Balsamon and Zonaras also understand the canon as I have done, as is *evident* from their commentaries, and so did Josephus Ægyptius, who in his Arabic *Paraphrase* gives the canon this title: "Concerning him who is excommunicated and has committed some deadly sin, and desires the Eucharist to be granted to him."

This canon is found in the *Corpus Juris Canonici*, Gratian, *Decretum* Pars. II. causa xxvi, Quæs. VI., c. ix.

EXCURSUS ON THE COMMUNION OF THE SICK.

There is nothing upon which the ancient church more strenuously insisted than the oral reception of the Holy Communion. What in later times was known as "Spiritual Communion" was outside of the view of those early days; and to them the issues of eternity were considered often to rest upon the sick man's receiving with his mouth "his food for the journey," the *Viaticum*, before he died. No greater proof of how important this matter was deemed could be found than the present canon, which provides that even the stern and invariable canons of the public penance are to give way before the awful necessity of fortifying the soul in the last hour of its earthly sojourn.

Possibly at first the holy Sacrament may have been consecrated in the presence of the sick person, but of this in early times the instances are rare and by no means clear. In fact it was considered a marked favour that such a thing should be allowed, and the saying of mass in private houses was prohibited (as it is in the Eastern and Latin churches still to-day) with the greatest rigour.

The necessity of having the consecrated bread and wine for the sick led to their reservation, a practice which has existed in the Church from the very beginning, so far as any records of which we are in possession shew.

St. Justin Martyr, writing less than a half century after St. John's death, mentions that "the deacons communicate each of those present, and carry away to the absent the blest bread, and wine and water." [1] It was evidently a long established custom in his day.

Tertullian tells us of a woman whose husband was a heathen and who was allowed to keep the Holy Sacrament in her house that she might receive every morning before other food. St. Cyprian also gives a most interesting example of reservation. In his treatise "On the Lapsed" written in A.D. 251, (chapter xxvi), he says: "Another woman, when she tried with unworthy hands to open her box, in which was the Holy of the Lord, was deterred from daring to touch it by fire rising from it."

It is impossible with any accuracy to fix the date, but certainly before the year four hundred, a perpetual reservation for the sick was made in the churches. A most interesting incidental proof of this is found in the thrilling description given by St. Chrysostom of the great riot in Constantinople in the year 403, when the soldiers "burst into the place where the Holy Things were stored, and saw all things therein," and "the most holy blood of Christ was spilled upon their clothes." [2] From this incident it is evident that in that church the Holy Sacrament was reserved in both kinds, and separately.

Whether this at the time was usual it is hard to say, but there can be no doubt that even in the earliest times the Sacrament was given, on rare occasions at least, in one kind,

---

[1] Just M. *Apol.* I. cap. lxv.   [2] Chrys. *Ep. ad Innoc.* Sec. 3.

sometimes under the form of bread alone, and when the sick persons could not swallow under the form of wine alone.   The practice called "intinction," that is the dipping of the bread into the wine and administering the two species together, was of very early introduction and still is universal in the East, not only when Communion is given with the reserved Sacrament, but also when the people are communicated in the Liturgy from the newly consecrated species.   The first mention of intinction in the West, is at Carthage in the fifth century.[1]   We know it was practised in the seventh century and by the twelfth it had become general, to give place to the withdrawal of the chalice altogether in the West.[2]   "Regino (*De Eccles. Discip.* Lib. I. c. lxx.) in 906, Burchard (*Decr.* Lib. V. cap. ix. fol. 95. colon. 1560.) in 996, and Ivo (*Decr.* Pars. II. cap. xix. p. 56, Paris 1647) in 1092 all cite a Canon, which they ascribe to a council of Tours ordering 'every presbyter to have a pyx or vessel meet for so great a sacrament, in which the Body of the Lord may be carefully laid up for the Viaticum to those departing from this world, which sacred oblation ought to be steeped in the Blood of Christ that the presbyter may be able to say truthfully to the sick man, The Body and Blood of the Lord avail thee, etc.' "[3]

The reservation of the Holy Sacrament was usually made in the church itself, and the learned W. E. Scudamore is of opinion that this was the case in Africa as early as the fourth century.[4]

It will not be uninteresting to quote in this connection the "Apostolic Constitutions," for while indeed there is much doubt of the date of the Eighth Book, yet it is certainly of great antiquity.   Here we read, "and after the communion of both men and women, the deacons take what remains and place it in the tabernacle."[5]

Perhaps it may not be amiss before closing the remark that so far as we are aware the reservation of the Holy Sacrament in the early church was only for the purposes of communion, and that the churches of the East reserve it to the present day only for this purpose.

Those who wish to read the matter treated of more at length, can do so in Muratorius's learned "Dissertations" which are prefixed to his edition of the Roman Sacramentaries (chapter XXIV) and in Scudamore's *Notitia Eucharistica*, a work which can be absolutely relied upon for the accuracy of its facts, however little one may feel constrained to accept the logical justness of its conclusions.

CANON XIV.

CONCERNING catechumens who have lapsed, the holy and great Synod has decreed that, after they have passed three years only as hearers, they shall pray with the catechumens.

NOTES.

ANCIENT EPITOME OF CANON XIV.

If any of the catechumens shall have fallen for three years he shall be a hearer only, and then let him pray with the catechumens.

JUSTELLUS.

The people formerly were divided into three classes in the church, for there were catechumens, faithful, and penitents; but it is clear from the present canon there were two kinds of catechumens: one consisting of those who heard the Word of God, and wished to become Christians, but had not yet desired baptism; these were called "hearers." Others who were of long standing, and were properly trained in the faith, and desired baptism—these were called "competentes."

[1] I give the reference as in Scudamore's *Not. Euch.* from which I have taken it. *De Prom. et Præd. Dei*; Dimid. Temp. c. 6; inter Opp. Prosperi. p. 161. ed. 1609.
[2] Cf. Scudamore. *Not. Euch.* p. 705.
[3] Scudamore. *Notit. Euch.* p. 707.
[4] W. E. Scudamore. *Notitia Eucharistica* [2d. Ed.] p. 1025.
[5] *Apost. Const.* Lib. viii. cap. xiij. The word used is παστοφόρια, this may possibly mean a side chapel, and does occur in the Book of Maccabees in this sense; but its classical use is to signify the shrine of a god, and while so distinguished a writer as Pierre Le Brun adopts the later meaning, the no less famous Durant, together with most commentators, translate as I have done above. In either case for the present purpose, the quotation is conclusive of the practice of the primitive church in regard to this matter. Liddell and Scott give "παστοφόρος, one carrying the image of a god in a shrine."

There is difference of opinion among the learned as to whether there was not a third or even a fourth class of catechumens. Bingham and Card. Bona, while not agreeing in particular points, agree in affirming that there were more than two classes. Bingham's first class are those not allowed to enter the church, the ἐξωθούμενοι, but the affirmation of the existence of such a class rests only on a very forced explanation of canon five of Neocæsarea. The second class, the hearers, audientes, rests on better evidence. These were not allowed to stay while the Holy Mysteries were celebrated, and their expulsion gave rise to the distinction between the " Mass of the Catechumens " (*Missa Catechumenorum*) and the " Mass of the Faithful " (*Missa Fidelium*). Nor were they suffered to hear the Creed or the Our Father. Writers who multiply the classes insert here some who knelt and prayed, called *Prostrati* or *Genuflectentes* (the same name as was given to one of the grades of penitence).

(Edw. H. Plumptre in *Dict. Christ. Antiq. s. v.* Catechumens.)

After these stages had been traversed each with its appropriate instruction, the catechumens gave in their names as applicants for baptism, and were known accordingly as *Competentes* (συναιτοῦντες). This was done commonly at the beginning of the Quadragesimal fast, and the instruction, carried on through the whole of that period, was fuller and more public in its nature (Cyril Hieros. *Catech.* i. 5 ; Hieron. *Ep.* 61, *ad Pammach.* c. 4). To catechumens in this stage the great articles of the Creed, the nature of the Sacraments, the

penitential discipline of the Church, were explained, as in the Catechetical Lectures of Cyril of Jerusalem, with dogmatic precision. Special examinations and inquiries into character were made at intervals during the forty days. It was a time for fasting and watching and prayer (*Constt. Apost.* viii. 5 ; 4 C. *Carth.* c. 85 ; Tertull. *De Bapt.* c. 20 ; Cyril. l. c.) and, in the case of those who were married, of the strictest continence (August. *De fide et oper.* v. 8). Those who passed through the ordeal were known as the *perfectiores* (τελειώτεροι) the *electi*, or in the nomenclature of the Eastern Church as βαπτιζόμενοι or φωτιζόμενοι, the present participle being used of course with a future or gerundial sense. Their names were inscribed as such in the *album* or register of the church. They were taught, but not till a few days before their baptism, the Creed and the Lord's Prayer which they were to use after it. The periods for this registration varied, naturally enough, in different churches. At Jerusalem it was done on the second (Cyril. *Catech.* iii.), in Africa on the fourth Sunday in Lent (August. *Serm.* 213), and this was the time at which the candidate, if so disposed, might lay aside his old heathen or Jewish name and take one more specifically Christian (Socrat. *H. E.* vii. 21). . . . It is only necessary to notice here that the *Sacramentum Catechumenorum* of which Augustine speaks (*De Peccat. Merit.* ii. 26) as given apparently at or about the time of their first admission by imposition of hands, was probably the εὐλογίαι or *panis benedictus*, and not, as Bingham and Angusti maintain, the *salt* which was given with milk and honey after baptism.

CANON XV.

ON account of the great disturbance and discords that occur, it is decreed that the custom prevailing in certain places contrary to the Canon, must wholly be done away ; so that neither bishop, presbyter, nor deacon shall pass from city to city. And if any one, after this decree of the holy and great Synod, shall attempt any such thing, or continue in any such course, his proceedings shall be utterly void, and he shall be restored to the Church for which he was ordained bishop or presbyter.

NOTES.

ANCIENT EPITOME OF CANON XV.

Neither bishop, presbyter, nor deacon shall pass from city to city. But they shall be sent back, should they attempt to do so, to the Churches in which they were ordained.

HEFELE.

The translation of a bishop, priest, or deacon from one church to another, had already

been forbidden in the primitive Church. Nevertheless, several translations had taken place, and even at the Council of Nice several eminent men were present who had left their first bishoprics to take others : thus Eusebius, Bishop of Nicomedia, had been before Bishop of Berytus ; Eustathius, Bishop of Antioch, had been before Bishop of Berrhœa in Syria. The Council of Nice thought it necessary to forbid in future these translations, and to declare them invalid. The chief reason of this prohibition was found in the irregularities and disputes occasioned by such change of sees; but even if such practical difficulties had not arisen, the whole doctrinal idea, so to speak, of the relationship between a cleric and the church to which he had been ordained, namely, the contracting of a mystical marriage between them, would be opposed to any translation or change. In 341 the Synod of Antioch renewed, in its twenty-first canon, the prohibition passed by the Council of Nice; but the interest of the Church often rendered it necessary to make exceptions, as happened in the case of St. Chrysostom. These exceptional cases increased almost immediately after the holding of the Council of Nice, so that in 382, St. Gregory of Nazianzum considered this law among those which had long been abrogated by custom. It was more strictly observed in the Latin Church; and even Gregory's contemporary, Pope Damasus, declared himself decidedly in favour of the rule of Nice.

This canon is found in the *Corpus Juris Canonici. Decretum*, Pars II. Causa VII, Q. 1, c. xix.

EXCURSUS ON THE TRANSLATION OF BISHOPS.

There are few points upon which the discipline of the Church has so completely changed as that which regulated, or rather which forbade, the translation of a bishop from the see for which he was consecrated to some other diocese. The grounds on which such prohibition rested were usually that such changes were the outcome of ambition, and that if tolerated the result would be that smaller and less important sees would be despised, and that there would be a constant temptation to the bishops of such sees to make themselves popular with the important persons in other dioceses with the hope of promotion. Besides this objection to translation, St. Athanasius mentions a spiritual one, that the diocese was the bishop's bride, and that to desert it and take another was an act of unjustifiable divorce, and subsequent adultery.[1] Canon XIV. of the Apostolic Canons does not forbid the practice absolutely, but allows it for just cause, and although the Council of Nice is more stringent so far as its words are concerned, apparently forbidding translation under any circumstances, yet, as a matter of fact, that very council did allow and approve a translation.[2] The general feeling, however, of the early Church was certainly very strong against all such changes of Episcopal cure, and there can be no doubt that the chief reason why St. Gregory Nazianzen resigned the Presidency of the First Council of Constantinople, was because he had been translated from his obscure see Sasima (not Nazianzum as Socrates and Jerome say) to the Imperial City.[3]

From the canons of some provincial councils, and especially from those of the Third and of the Fourth Council of Carthage, it is evident that despite the conciliar and papal prohibitions, translations did take place, being made by the authority of the provincial Synods, and without the consent of the pope,[4] but it is also evident that this authority was too weak, and that the aid of the secular power had often to be invoked.

This course, of having the matter decided by the synod, was exactly in accordance with the Apostolic Canon (no. xiv.). In this manner, for example, Alexander was translated from Cappadocia to Jerusalem, a translation made, so it is narrated, in obedience to heavenly revelation.

It will be noticed that the Nicene Canon does not forbid Provincial Councils to translate

---

[1] Athanas. *Apol.* ij.
[2] Sozom. *H. E.* I. 2.
[3] By no one has this whole matter of the translation of bishops been more carefully and thoroughly treated than by Thomassinus, and in what follows I shall use his discussion as a thesaurus of facts. The title of his book is *Ancienne et Nouvelle Discipline de l'Église* (There is also an edition in Latin). In the Third Part. and the Second Book,
Chapter LX. treats of "Translations of bishops in the Latin Church during the first five centuries"

Chapter LXI. "Translations in the Eastern Church, during the first five centuries."
Chapter LXII. "Translation of bishops and bishoprics between the years five hundred and eight hundred."
Chapter LXIII. "Translation under the empire of Charlemagne and his descendants."
Chapter LXIV. "Translation of bishops after the year one thousand."
Of all this I can in the text give but a brief *resumé.*
[4] Thomassin. *l. c.* lx. viij.

bishops, but forbids bishops to translate themselves, and the author of the tract *De Transla-*
tionibus in the *Jus Orient.* (i. 293, *Cit.* Haddon. Art. "Bishop," Smith and Cheetham, *Dict.*
Chr. Antiq.) sums up the matter tersely in the statement that ἡ μετάβασις κεκώλυται, οὐ μὴν ἡ
μετάθεσις: i.e., the thing prohibited is "transmigration" (which arises from the bishop himself,
from selfish motives) not "translation" (wherein the will of God and the good of the Church
is the ruling cause); the "going," not the "being taken" to another see. And this was the
practice both of East and West, for many centuries. Roman Catholic writers have tried to
prove that translations, at least to the chief sees, required the papal consent, but Thomassinus, considering the case of St. Meletius having translated St. Gregory of Nazianzum to
Constantinople, admits that in so doing he "would only have followed the example of many
great bishops of the first ages, when usage had not yet reserved translations to the first see
of the Church." [1]

But the same learned author frankly confesses that in France, Spain, and England, translations were made until the ninth century without consulting the pope at all, by bishops and
kings. When, however, from grounds of simple ambition, Anthimus was translated from
Trebizonde to Constantinople, the religious of the city wrote to the pope, as also did the
patriarchs of Antioch and Jerusalem, and as a result the Emperor Justinian allowed Anthimus to be deposed.[2]

Balsamon distinguishes three kinds of translations. The first, when a bishop of marked
learning and of equal piety is forced by a council to pass from a small diocese to one far
greater where he will be able to do the Church the most important services, as was the case
when St. Gregory of Nazianzum was transferred from Sasima to Constantinople, μετάθεσις;
the second when a bishop. whose see has been laid low by the barbarians, is transferred to
another see which is vacant, μετάβασις; and the third when a bishop, either having or lacking
a see, seizes on a bishopric which is vacant, on his own proper authority ἀνάβασις. And it is
this last which the Council of Sardica punishes so severely. In all these remarks of Balsamon there is no mention of the imperial power.

Demetrius Chomatenus, however, who was Archbishop of Thessalonica, and wrote a
series of answers to Cabasilas, Archbishop of Durazzo, says that by the command of the
Emperor a bishop, elected and confirmed, and even ready to be ordained for a diocese, may
be forced to take the charge of another one which is more important, and where his services
will be incomparably more useful to the public. Thus we read in the Book of Eastern Law
that "If a Metropolitan with his synod, moved by a praiseworthy cause and probable pretext, shall give his approbation to the translation of a bishop, this can, without doubt, be
done, for the good of souls and for the better administration of the church's affairs, etc."[3]
This was adopted at a synod held by the patriarch Manuel at Constantinople, in the presence of the imperial commissioners.

The same thing appears also in the synodal response of the patriarch Michael, which
only demands for translation the authority of the Metropolitan and "the greatest authority
of the Church."[4] But, soon after this, translation became the rule, and not the exception
both in East and West.

It was in vain that Simeon, Archbishop of Thessalonica, in the East raised his voice against
the constant translations made by the secular power, and the Emperors of Constantinople
were often absolute masters of the choice and translations of bishops; and Thomassinus
sums up the matter, "At the least we are forced to the conclusion that no translations could

---

[1] *Thomassin. l. cit.*, Chap. LI., § xiij.
[2] This is Thomassinus's version of the matter, in fact the charge of heresy was also made against Anthimus, but his unca-nonical translation was a real count in the accusation.

[3] *Juris. Orient.* tom. I. p. 240, 241.
[4] *Ibid.* p. 5. I am not at all clear as to what this last phrase means.

be made without the consent of the Emperor, especially when it was the See of Constantinople that was to be filled."

The same learned writer continues: "It was usually the bishop or archbishop of another church that was chosen to ascend the patriarchal throne of the imperial city. The Kings of England often used this same power to appoint to the Primatial See of Canterbury a bishop already approved in the government of another diocese." [1]

In the West, Cardinal Bellarmine disapproved the prevailing custom of translations and protested against it to his master, Pope Clement VIII., reminding him that they were contrary to the canons and contrary to the usage of the Ancient Church, except in cases of necessity and of great gain to the Church. The pope entirely agreed with these wise observations, and promised that he would himself make, and would urge princes to make, translations only "with difficulty." But translations are made universally, all the world over, to-day, and no attention whatever is paid to the ancient canons and discipline of the Church.[2]

CANON XVI.

NEITHER presbyters, nor deacons, nor any others enrolled among the clergy, who, not having the fear of God before their eyes, nor regarding the ecclesiastical Canon, shall recklessly remove from their own church, ought by any means to be received by another church ; but every constraint should be applied to restore them to their own parishes ; and, if they will not go, they must be excommunicated. And if anyone shall dare surreptitiously to carry off and in his own Church ordain a man belonging to another, without the consent of his own proper bishop, from whom although he was enrolled in the clergy list he has seceded, let the ordination be void.

NOTES.

ANCIENT EPITOME OF CANON XVI.

Such presbyters or deacons as desert their own Church are not to be admitted into another, but are to be sent back to their own diocese. But if any bishop should ordain one who belongs to another Church without the consent of his own bishop, the ordination shall be cancelled.

"Parish" in this canon, as so often elsewhere, means "diocese."

BALSAMON.

It seemed right that the clergy should have no power to move from city to city and to change their canonical residence without letters dimissory from the bishop who ordained them. But such clerics as are called by the bishops who ordained them and cannot be persuaded to return, are to be separated from communion, that is to say, not to be allowed to concelebrate (συνιερουργεῖν) with them, for this is the meaning of "excommunicated" in this place, and not that they should not enter the church nor receive the sacraments. This decree agrees with canon xv. of the Apostolical canons, which provides that such shall not celebrate the liturgy. Canon xvj. of the same Apostolical canons further provides that if a bishop receive a cleric coming to him from another diocese without his bishop's letters dimissory, and shall ordain him, such a bishop shall be separated. From all this it is evident that the Chartophylax of the Great Church for the time does rightly in refusing to allow priests ordained in other dioceses to offer the sacrifice unless they bring with them letters commendatory and dimissory from those who ordained them.

Zonaras had also in his Scholion given the same explanation of the canon.

This canon is found in the *Corpus Juris Canonici*, divided into two. *Decretum.* Pars II, Causa VII. Quæst. I. c. xxiij. ; and Pars I. Dist. LXXI., c. iij.

[1] *Thomassin. lib cit.*, chap. LXIV. § x.
[2] I believe this is true of all churches, Catholic and Protestant, having an episcopal form of government (including the Protestant Church of Sweden, and the Methodist Episcopal Church), with the exception of the Protestant Episcopal Church in the United States, in which the ancient prohibition of the translation of diocesan bishops is observed in all its Nicene strictness.

CANON XVII.

FORASMUCH as many enrolled among the Clergy, following covetousness and lust of gain, have forgotten the divine Scripture, which says, "He hath not given his money upon usury," and in lending money ask the hundredth of the sum [as monthly interest], the holy and great Synod thinks it just that if after this decree any one be found to receive usury, whether he accomplish it by secret transaction or otherwise, as by demanding the whole and one half, or by using any other contrivance whatever for filthy lucre's sake, he shall be deposed from the clergy and his name stricken from the list.

NOTES.

ANCIENT EPITOME OF CANON XVII.

If anyone shall receive usury or 150 per cent. he shall be cast forth and deposed, according to this decree of the Church.

VAN ESPEN.

Although the canon expresses only these two species of usury, if we bear in mind the grounds on which the prohibition was made, it will be manifest that every kind of usury is forbidden to clerics and under any circumstances, and therefore the translation of this canon sent by the Orientals to the Sixth Council of Carthage is in no respect alien to the true intent of the canon ; for in this version no mention is made of any particular kind of usury, but generally the penalty is assigned to any clerics who "shall be found after this decree taking usury" or thinking out any other scheme for the sake of filthy lucre.

This Canon is found in the *Corpus Juris Canonici*, in the first part of the *Decretum*, in Dionysius's version. *Dist.* xlvii, c. ii, and again in Isidore's version in Pars II, Causa xiv. Quæs. iv., c. viii.

EXCURSUS ON USURY.

The famous canonist Van Espen defines usury thus : "Usura definitur lucrum ex mutuo exactum aut speratum ;"[1] and then goes on to defend the proposition that, "Usury is forbidden by natural, by divine, and by human law. The first is proved thus. Natural law, as far as its first principles are concerned, is contained in the decalogue ; but usury is prohibited in the decalogue, inasmuch as theft is prohibited ; and this is the opinion of the Master of the Sentences, of St. Bonaventura, of St. Thomas and of a host of others : for by the name of theft in the Law all unlawful taking of another's goods is prohibited ; but usury is an unlawful, etc." For a proof of usury's being contrary to divine law he cites Ex. xxii. 25, and Deut. xxiii. 29 ; and from the New Testament Luke vi. 34. "The third assertion is proved thus. Usury is forbidden by human law : The First Council of Nice in Canon VII. deposed from the clergy and from all ecclesiastical rank, clerics who took usury ; and the same thing is the case with an infinite number of councils, in fact with nearly all e. g. Elvira, ij, Arles j, Carthage iij, Tours iij, etc. Nay, even the pagans themselves formerly forbid it by their laws." He then quotes Tacitus (*Annal.* lib. v.), and adds, "with what severe laws the French Kings coerced usurers is evident from the edicts of St. Louis, Philip IV., Charles IX., Henry III., etc."

There can be no doubt that Van Espen in the foregoing has accurately represented and without any exaggeration the universal opinion of all teachers of morals, theologians, doctors, Popes, and Councils of the Christian Church for the first fifteen hundred years. All interest exacted upon loans of money was looked upon as usury, and its reception was esteemed a form of theft and dishonesty. Those who wish to read the history of the matter in all its details are referred to Bossuet's work on the subject, *Traité de l'Usure*,[2] where they will find

---

[1] Van Espen. *Dissertatio de Usura*, Art. 1.   [2] Bossuet. *Œuvres Comp.* xxxj.

the old, traditional view of the Christian religion defended by one thoroughly acquainted with all that could be said on the other side.

The glory of inventing the new moral code on the subject, by which that which before was looked upon as mortal sin has been transfigured into innocence, if not virtue, belongs to John Calvin! He made the modern distinction between "interest" and "usury," and was the first to write in defence of this then new-fangled refinement of casuistry.[1] Luther violently opposed him, and Melancthon also kept to the old doctrine, though less violently (as was to be expected); to-day the whole Christian West, Protestant and Catholic alike, stake their salvation upon the truth of Calvin's distinction! Among Roman Catholics the new doctrine began to be defended about the beginning of the eighteenth century, the work of Scipio Maffei, *Dell' impiego dell danaro*, written on the laxer side, having attracted a widespread attention. The Ballerini affirm that the learned pope Benedict XIV. allowed books defending the new morals to be dedicated to him, and in 1830 the Congregation of the Holy Office with the approval of the reigning Pontiff, Pius VIII., decided that those who considered the taking of interest allowed by the state law justifiable, were "not to be disturbed." It is entirely disingenuous to attempt to reconcile the modern with the ancient doctrine; the Fathers expressly deny that the State has any power to make the receiving of interest just or to fix its rate, there is but one ground for those to take who accept the new teaching, viz. that all the ancients, while true on the moral principle that one must not defraud his neighbour nor take unjust advantage of his necessity, were in error concerning the facts, in that they supposed that money was barren, an opinion which the Schoolmen also held, following Aristotle. This we have found in modern times, and amid modern circumstances, to be an entire error, as Gury, the famous modern casuist, well says, "fructum producit et multiplicatur per se."[2]

That the student may have it in his power to read the Patristic view of the matter, I give a list of the passages most commonly cited, together with a review of the conciliar action, for all which I am indebted to a masterly article by Wharton B. Marriott in Smith and Cheetham's *Dictionary of Christian Antiquities* (s. v. Usury).

Although the conditions of the mercantile community in the East and the West differed materially in some respects, the fathers of the two churches are equally explicit and systematic in their condemnation of the practice of usury. Among those belonging to the Greek church we find Athanasius (*Expos. in Ps.* xiv); Basil the Great (*Hom. in Ps.* xiv). Gregory of Nazianzum (*Orat.* xiv. *in Patrem tacentem*). Gregory of Nyssa (*Orat. cont. Usurarios*); Cyril of Jerusalem (*Catech.* iv. c. 37), Epiphanius (*adv. Haeres. Epilog.* c. 24), Chrysostom (*Hom.* xli. *in Genes*), and Theodoret (*Interpr. in Ps.* xiv. 5, and liv. 11). Among those belonging to the Latin church, Hilary of Poitiers (*in Ps.* xiv); Ambrose (*de Tobia liber unus*). Jerome (*in Ezech.* vi. 18); Augustine *de Baptismo contr. Donatistas*, iv. 19); Leo the Great (*Epist.* iii. 4), and Cassiodorus (*in Ps.* xiv. 10).

The canons of later councils differ materially in relation to this subject, and indicate a distinct tendency to mitigate the rigour of the Nicæan interdict. That of the council of Carthage of the year 348 enforces the original prohibition, but without the penalty, and grounds the veto on both Old and New Testament authority, "nemo contra prophetas, nemo contra evangelia facit sine periculo" (Mansi, iii. 158). The language, however, when compared with that of the council of Carthage of the year 419, serves to suggest that, in the interval, the lower clergy had occasionally been found having recourse to the forbidden practice, for the general terms of the earlier canon, "ut non liceat clericis fenerari," are enforced with

---

[1] Funk (*Zins und Wucher*, p. 104) says that Eck and Hoogsträten had already verbally defended this distinction at Bologna.

[2] Gury, *Comp. Theol. Moral* (Ed. Ballerini) vol. ii. p. 611.

greater particularity in the latter, "Nec omnino *cuiquam clericorum* liceat de qualibet re foenus accipere" (Mansi, iv. 423). This supposition is supported by the language of the council of Orleans (A.D. 538), which appears to imply that deacons were not prohibited from lending money at interest, "Et clericus a diaconatu, et supra, pecuniam non commodet ad usuras" (*ib.* ix. 18). Similarly, at the second council of Trullanum (A.D. 692) a like liberty would appear to have been recognised among the lower clergy (Hardouin, iii. 1663). While, again, the Nicæan canon requires the immediate deposition of the ecclesiastic found guilty of the practice, the Apostolical canon enjoins that such deposition is to take place only after he has been admonished and has disregarded the admonition.

Generally speaking, the evidence points to the conclusion that the Church imposed no penalty on the layman. St. Basil (*Epist.* clxxxviii. can. 12), says that a usurer may even be admitted to orders, provided he gives his acquired wealth to the poor and abstains for the future from the pursuit of gain (Migne, *Patrol. Græc.* xxxii. 275). Gregory of Nyssa says that usury, unlike theft, the desecration of tombs, and sacrilege (ἱεροσυλία), is allowed to pass unpunished, although among the things forbidden by Scripture, nor is a candidate at ordination ever asked whether or no he has been guilty of the practice (Migne, ib. xlv. 233). A letter of Sidonius Apollinaris (*Epist.* vi. 24) relating an experience of his friend Maximus, appears to imply that no blame attached to lending money at the legal rate of interest, and that even a bishop might be a creditor on those terms. We find also Desideratus, bishop of Verdun, when applying for a loan to king Theodebert, for the relief of his impoverished diocese, promising repayment, "cum usuris legitimis," an expression which would seem to imply that in the Gallican church usury was recognised as lawful under certain conditions (Greg. Tur. *Hist. Franc.* iii. 34). So again a letter (*Epist.* ix. 38) of Gregory the Great seems to shew that he did not regard the payment of interest for money advanced by one layman to another as unlawful. But on the other hand, we find in what is known as archbishop Theodore's "Penitential" (*circ.* A.D. 690) what appears to be a general law on the subject, enjoining "Sie quis usuras undecunque exegerit . . . tres annos in pane et aqua" (c. xxv. 3); a penance again enjoined in the Penitential of Egbert of York (c. ii. 30). In like manner, the legates, George and Theophylact, in reporting their proceedings in England to pope Adrian I. (A.D. 787), state that they have prohibited "usurers," and cite the authority of the Psalmist and St. Augustine (Haddan and Stubbs, *Conc.* iii. 457). The councils of Mayence, Rheims, and Châlons, in the year 813, and that of Aix in the year 816, seem to have laid down the same prohibition as binding both on the clergy and the laity (Hardouin, *Conc.* iv. 1011, 1020, 1033, 1100).

Muratori, in his dissertation on the subject (*Antichità*, vol. i.), observes that "we do not know exactly how commerce was transacted in the five preceding centuries," and consequently are ignorant as to the terms on which loans of money were effected.

CANON XVIII.

It has come to the knowledge of the holy and great Synod that, in some districts and cities, the deacons administer the Eucharist to the presbyters, whereas neither canon nor custom permits that they who have no right to offer should give the Body of Christ to them that do offer. And this also has been made known, that certain deacons now touch the Eucharist even before the bishops. Let all such practices be utterly done away, and let the deacons remain within their own bounds, knowing that they are the ministers of the bishop and the inferiors of the presbyters. Let them receive the Eucharist according to their order, after the presbyters, and let either the bishop or the presbyter administer to them. Furthermore, let not the deacons sit among the presbyters, for that is contrary to canon and order. And if, after this decree, any one shall refuse to obey, let him be deposed from the diaconate.

NOTES.

ANCIENT EPITOME OF CANON XVIII.

Deacons must abide within their own bounds. They shall not administer the Eucharist to presbyters, nor touch it before them, nor sit among the presbyters. For all this is contrary to canon, and to decent order.

VAN ESPEN.

Four excesses of deacons this canon condemns, at least indirectly. The first was that they gave the holy Communion to presbyters. To understand more easily the meaning of the canon it must be remembered that the reference here is not to the presbyters who were sacrificing at the altar but to those who were offering together with the bishop who was sacrificing; by a rite not unlike that which to-day takes place, when the newly ordained presbyters or bishops celebrate mass with the ordaining bishop; and this rite in old times was of daily occurrence, for a full account of which see Morinus *De SS. Ordinat.* P. III. Exercit. viij. . . . The present canon does not take away from deacons the authority to distribute the Eucharist to laymen, or to the minor clergy, but only reproves their insolence and audacity in presuming to administer to presbyters who were concelebrating with the bishop or another presbyter. . . .

The second abuse was that certain deacons touched the sacred gifts before the bishop. The vulgar version of Isidore reads for "touched" "received," a meaning which Balsamon and Zonaras also adopt, and unless the Greek word, which signifies "to touch," is contrary to this translation, it seems by no means to be alien to the context of the canon.

"Let them receive the Eucharist according to their order, after the presbyters, and let the bishop or the presbyter administer to them." In these words it is implied that some deacons had presumed to receive Holy Communion before the presbyters, and this is the third excess of the deacon which is condemned by the Synod.

And lastly, the fourth excess was that they took a place among the presbyters at the very time of the sacrifice, or "at the holy altar," as Balsamon observes.

From this canon we see that the Nicene fathers entertained no doubt that the faithful in the holy Communion truly received "the body of Christ." Secondly, that that was "offered" in the church, which is the word by which sacrifice is designated in the New Testament, and therefore it was at that time a fixed tradition that there was a sacrifice in which the body of Christ was offered. Thirdly that not to all, nor even to deacons, but only to bishops and presbyters was given the power of offering. And lastly, that there was recognized a fixed hierarchy in the Church, made up of bishops and presbyters and deacons in subordination to these.

Of course even at that early date there was nothing new in this doctrine of the Eucharist. St. Ignatius more than a century and a half before, wrote as follows: "But mark ye those who hold strange doctrine touching the grace of Jesus Christ which came to us, how that they are contrary to the mind of God. They have no care for love, none for the widow, none for the orphan, none for the afflicted, none for the prisoner, none for the hungry or thirsty. They abstain from eucharist (thanksgiving) and prayer, because they allow not that the Eucharist is the flesh of our Saviour Jesus Christ, which flesh suffered for our sins, and which the Father of his goodness raised up." [1]

In one point the learned scholiast just quoted has most seriously understated his case. He says that the wording of the canon shews "that the Nicene fathers entertained no doubt that the faithful in the holy Communion truly received 'the body of Christ.'" Now this statement is of course true because it is included in what the canon says, but the doctrinal statement which is necessarily contained in the canon is that "the body of Christ is given" by the minister to the faithful. This doctrine is believed by all Catholics and by Lutherans, but is denied by all other Protestants; those Calvinists who kept most nearly to the ordinary Catholic phraseology only admitting that "the *sacrament* of the Body of Christ" was given in the supper by the minister, while "the body of Christ," they taught, was present only in the soul of the worthy communicant (and in no way connected with the form of bread, which was but the divinely appointed sign and assurance of the heavenly gift), and therefore could not be "given" by the priest. [2]

This canon is found in the *Corpus Juris Canonici, Decretum.* Pars I. Dist. XCIII., c. xiv.

[1] Ignat. *Ad Smyr.* § vi. Lightfoot's translation. *Apost. Fath.* Vol. II. Sec. I. p. 569.
[2] Cf. Art. xxviij. of the "Articles of Religion" of the Church of England, which declares that "The Body of Christ is given, taken, and eaten in the Supper," etc.

CANON XIX.

CONCERNING the Paulianists who have flown for refuge to the Catholic Church, it has been decreed that they must by all means be rebaptized; and if any of them who in past time have been numbered among their clergy should be found blameless and without reproach, let them be rebaptized and ordained by the Bishop of the Catholic Church; but if the examination should discover them to be unfit, they ought to be deposed. Likewise in the case of their deaconesses, and generally in the case of those who have been enrolled among their clergy, let the same form be observed. And we mean by deaconesses such as have assumed the habit, but who, since they have no imposition of hands, are to be numbered only among the laity.

NOTES.

ANCIENT EPITOME OF CANON XIX.

Paulianists must be rebaptised, and if such as are clergymen seem to be blameless let them be ordained. If they do not seem to be blameless, let them be deposed. Deaconesses who have been led astray, since they are not sharers of ordination, are to be reckoned among the laity.

FFOULKES.

(*Dict. Chr. Ant. s.v.* Nicæa, Councils of.)

That this is the true meaning of the phrase ὅρος ἐκτέθειται, viz. "a decree has now been made," is clear from the application of the words ὅρος in Canon xvii., and ὥρισεν, in Canon vi. It has been a pure mistake, therefore, which Bp. Hefele blindly follows, to understand it of some canon previously passed, whether at Arles or elsewhere.

JUSTELLUS.

Here χειροθεσία is taken for ordination or consecration, not for benediction, . . . for neither were deaconesses, sub-deacons, readers, and other ministers ordained, but a blessing was merely pronounced over them by prayer and imposition of hands.

ARISTENUS.

Their (the Paulicians') deaconesses also, since they have no imposition of hands, if they come over to the Catholic Church and are baptized, are ranked among the laity.

With this Zonaras and Balsamon also agree.

HEFELE.

By Paulianists must be understood the followers of Paul of Samosata the anti-Trinitarian who, about the year 260, had been made bishop of Antioch, but had been deposed by a great Synod in 269. As Paul of Samosata

was heretical in his teaching on the Holy Trinity the Synod of Nice applied to him the decree passed by the council of Arles in its eighth canon. "If anyone shall come from heresy to the Church, they shall ask him to say the creed; and if they shall perceive that he was baptized into the Father, and the Son, and the Holy Ghost,[1] he shall have a hand laid on him only that he may receive the Holy Ghost. But if in answer to their questioning he shall not answer this Trinity, let him be baptized."

The Samosatans, according to St. Athanasius, named the Father, Son and Holy Spirit in administering baptism (*Orat.* ii, *Contra Arian.* No. xliii), but as they gave a false meaning to the baptismal formula and did not use the words Son and Holy Spirit in the usual sense, the Council of Nice, like St. Athanasius himself, considered their baptism as invalid.

There is great difficulty about the text of the clause beginning "Likewise in the case, etc.," and Gelasius, the *Prisca*, Theilo and Thearistus, (who in 419 translated the canons of Nice for the African bishops), the Pseudo-Isidore, and Gratian have all followed a reading διακόνων, instead of διακονισσῶν. This change makes all clear, but many canonists keep the ordinary text, including Van Espen, with whose interpretation Hefele does not agree.

The clause I have rendered "And we mean by deaconesses" is most difficult of translation. I give the original, Ἐμνήσθημεν δὲ διακονισσῶν τῶν ἐν τῷ σχήματι ἐξετασθεισῶν, ἐπεὶ κ. τ. λ. Hefele's translation seems to me impossible, by σχήματι he understands the list of the clergy just mentioned.

---

[1] In Patre et Filio et Spiritu Sancto esse baptizatum.

EXCURSUS ON THE DEACONESS OF THE EARLY CHURCH.

It has been supposed by many that the deaconess of the Early Church had an Apostolic institution and that its existence may be referred to by St. Paul in his Epistle to the Romans (xvi. 1) where he speaks of Phœbe as being a διάκονος of the Church of Cenchrea. It moreover has been suggested that the "widows" of 1 Tim. v. 9 may have been deaconesses, and this seems not unlikely from the fact that the age for the admission of women to this ministry was fixed by Tertullian at sixty years (*De Vel. Virg.* Cap. ix.), and only changed to forty, two centuries later by the Council of Chalcedon, and from the further fact that these "widows" spoken of by St. Paul seem to have had a vow of chastity, for it is expressly said that if they marry they have "damnation, because they have cast off their first faith" (1 Tim. v. 12).

These women were called διακόνισσαι, πρεσβυτίδες (which must be distinguished from the πρεσβυτέραι, a poor class referred to in the *Apostolic Constitutions* (ii. 28) who are to be only invited frequently to the love-feasts, while the πρεσβυτίδες had a definite allotment of the offerings assigned to their support), χῆραι, *diaconissæ*, *presbyteræ*, and *viduæ*.

The one great characteristic of the deaconess was that she was vowed to perpetual chastity.[1] The *Apostolical Constitutions* (vi. 17) say that she must be a chaste virgin (παρθένος ἁγνή) or else a widow. The writer of the article "Deaconess" in the *Dictionary of Christian Antiquities* says: "It is evident that the ordination of deaconesses included a vow of celibacy." We have already seen the language used by St. Paul and of this the wording of the canon of Chalcedon is but an echo (Canon xv). "A woman shall not receive the laying on of hands as a deaconess under forty years of age, and then only after searching examination. And if, after she has had hands laid on her, and has continued for a time to minister, she shall despise the Grace of God and give herself in marriage, she shall be anathematized and the man who is united to her." The civil law went still further, and by Justinian's Sixth Novel (6) those who attempted to marry are subjected to forfeiture of property and capital punishment. In the collect in the ancient office there is a special petition that the newly admitted deaconess may have the gift of continence.

The principal work of the deaconess was to assist the female candidates for holy baptism. At that time the sacrament of baptism was always administered by immersion (except to those in extreme illness) and hence there was much that such an order of women could be useful in. Moreover they sometimes gave to the female catechumens preliminary instruction, but their work was wholly limited to women, and for a deaconess of the Early Church to teach a man or to nurse him in sickness would have been an impossibility. The duties of the deaconess are set forth in many ancient writings, I cite here what is commonly known as the XII Canon of the Fourth Council of Carthage, which met in the year 398:

"Widows and dedicated women (*sanctimoniales*) who are chosen to assist at the baptism of women, should be so well instructed in their office as to be able to teach aptly and properly unskilled and rustic women how to answer at the time of their baptism to the questions put to them, and also how to live godly after they have been baptized." This whole matter is treated clearly by St. Epiphanius who, while indeed speaking of deaconesses as an order (τάγμα), asserts that "they were only women-elders, not priestesses in any sense, that their

---

[1] In 1836, the Lutheran Pastor Fliedner, of a little town on the Rhine, opened a parish hospital the nurses of which he called "Deaconesses." This "Deaconess House" at Kaiserswerth. was the mother-house from which all the deaconess establishments of the present day have taken their origin. The Methodists have adopted the system successfully. Some efforts have been made to domesticate it, in a somewhat modified form, also in the Anglican Churches but thus far with but little success. Of course these "Deaconesses" resemble the Deaconesses of the Early Church only in name. The reader who may be interested in seeing an effort to connect the modern deaconess with the deaconess of antiquity is referred to *The Ministry of Deaconesses* by Deaconess Cecilia Robinson. This book, it should be said, contains much valuable and accurate information upon the subject, but accepts as proven facts the suppositions of the late Bishop Lightfoot upon the subject; who somewhat rashly asserted that "the female diaconate is as definite an institution as the male diaconate. Phœbe is as much a deacon as Stephen or Philip is a deacon!"

mission was not to interfere in any way with Sacerdotal functions, but simply to perform certain offices in the care of women" (*Hær.* lxxix, cap. iij).   From all this it is evident that they are entirely in error who suppose that "the laying on of hands" which the deaconesses received corresponded to that by which persons were ordained to the diaconate, presbyterate, and episcopate at that period of the church's history.   It was merely a solemn dedication and blessing and was not looked upon as "an outward sign of an inward grace given."   For further proof of this I must refer to Morinus, who has treated the matter most admirably. (*De Ordinationibus*, Exercitatio X.)

The deaconesses existed but a short while.   The council of Laodicea as early as A.D. 343–381, forbade the appointment of any who were called πρεσβύτιδες (*Vide* Canon xi) ; and the first council of Orange, A.D. 441, in its twenty-sixth canon forbids the appointment of deaconesses altogether, and the Second council of the same city in canons xvij and xviij, decrees that deaconesses who married were to be excommunicated unless they renounced the men they were living with, and that, on account of the weakness of the sex, none for the future were to be ordained.

Thomassinus, to whom I refer the reader for a very full treatment of the whole subject, is of opinion that the order was extinct in the West by the tenth or twelfth century, but that it lingered on a little later at Constantinople but only in conventual institutions. (Thomassin, *Ancienne et Nouvelle Discipline de l'Église*, I Partie, Livre III.)

CANON XX.

FORASMUCH as there are certain persons who kneel on the Lord's Day and in the days of Pentecost, therefore, to the intent that all things may be uniformly observed everywhere (in every parish), it seems good to the holy Synod that prayer be made to God standing.

NOTES.

ANCIENT EPITOME OF CANON XX.

On Lord's days and at Pentecost all must pray standing and not kneeling.

HAMMOND.

Although kneeling was the common posture for prayer in the primitive Church, yet the custom had prevailed, even from the earliest times, of standing at prayer on the Lord's day, and during the fifty days between Easter and Pentecost.   Tertullian, in a passage in his treatise *De Corona Militis*, which is often quoted, mentions it amongst other observances which, though not expressly commanded in Scripture, yet were universally practised upon the authority of tradition.   "We consider it unlawful," he says, "to fast, or to pray kneeling, upon the Lord's day ; we enjoy the same liberty from Easter-day to that of Pentecost." *De Cor. Mil.* s. 3, 4.   Many other of the Fathers notice the same practice, the reason of which, as given by Augustine and others, was to commemorate the resurrection of our Lord, and to signify the rest and joy of our own resurrection, which that of our Lord assured.   This canon, as Beveridge observes, is a proof of the importance formerly attached to an uniformity of sacred rites throughout the Church, which made the Nicene Fathers thus sanction and enforce by their authority a practice which in itself is indifferent, and not commanded directly or indirectly in Scripture, and assign this as their reason for doing so : "In order that all things may be observed in like manner in every parish " or diocese.

HEFELE.

All the churches did not, however, adopt this practice ; for we see in the Acts of the Apostles (xx. 36 and xxi. 5) that St. Paul prayed kneeling during the time between Pentecost and Easter.

This canon is found in the *Corpus Juris Canonici.*   *Decretum*, Pars III, *De Conc.* Dist. III. c. x.

EXCURSUS ON THE NUMBER OF THE NICENE CANONS.

There has come down to us a Latin letter purporting to have been written by St. Athanasius to Pope Marcus. This letter is found in the Benedictine edition of St. Athanasius's works (ed. Patav. ii. 599) but rejected as spurious by Montfaucon the learned editor. In this letter is contained the marvellous assertion that the Council of Nice at first adopted forty canons, which were in Greek, that it subsequently added twenty Latin canons, and that afterwards the council reassembled and set forth seventy altogether. A tradition that something of the kind had taken place was prevalent in parts of the East, and some collections did contain seventy canons.

In the Vatican Library is a MS. which was bought for it by the famous Asseman, from the Coptic Patriarch, John, and which contains not only seventy, but eighty canons attributed to the council of Nice. The MS. is in Arabic, and was discovered by J. B. Romanus, S. J., who first made its contents known, and translated into Latin a copy he had made of it. Another Jesuit, Pisanus, was writing a history of the Nicene Council at the time and he received the eighty newly found canons into his book; but, out of respect to the pseudo-Athanasian letter, he at first cut down the number to seventy; but in later editions he followed the MS. All this was in the latter half of the sixteenth century; and in 1578 Turrianus, who had had Father Romanus's translation revised before it was first published, now issued an entirely new translation with a *Proëmium* [1] containing a vast amount of information upon the whole subject, and setting up an attempted proof that the number of the Nicene Canons exceeded twenty. His argument for the time being carried the day.

Hefele says, " it is certain that the Orientals [2] believed the Council of Nice to have promulgated more than twenty canons : the learned Anglican, Beveridge,[3] has proved this, reproducing an ancient Arabic paraphrase of the canons of the first four Ecumenical Councils. According to this Arabic paraphrase, found in a MS. in the Bodleian Library, the Council of Nice must have put forth three books of canons. . . . The Arabic paraphrase of which we are speaking gives a paraphrase of all these canons, but Beveridge took only the part referring to the second book—that is to say, the paraphrase of the twenty genuine canons ; for, according to his view, which was perfectly correct, it was only these twenty canons which were really the work of the Council of Nice, and all the others were falsely attributed to it." [4]

Hefele goes on to prove that the canons he rejects must be of much later origin, some being laws of the times of Theodosius and Justinian according to the opinion of Renaudot.[5]

Before leaving this point I should notice the profound research on these Arabic canons of the Maronite, Abraham Echellensis. He gives eighty-four canons in his Latin translation of 1645, and was of opinion that they had been collected from different Oriental sources, and sects ; but that originally they had all been translated from the Greek, and were collected by James, the celebrated bishop of Nisibis, who was present at Nice. But this last supposition is utterly untenable.

Among the learned there have not been wanting some who have held that the Council of Nice passed more canons than the twenty we possess, and have arrived at the conclusion independently of the Arabic discovery, such are Baronius and Card. d'Aguirre, but their arguments have been sufficiently answered, and they cannot present anything able to weaken the conclusion that flows from the consideration of the following facts.

---

[1] *Vide* Labbe. *Conc.* ii. 287.
[2] Who exactly these "Orientals" were Hefele does not specify, but Ffoulkes well points out (*Dict. Christ. Antiq. sub voce* Councils of Nicæa) that it is an entire mistake to suppose that the Greek Church " ever quoted other canons [than the xx] as Nicene 'by mistake,' which were not Nicene, as popes Zosimus, Innocent and Leo did." [3] Beveridge *Synod. sive Pand.* i. 686.
[4] Hefele : *Hist. Councils*, I. 362.
[5] Renaudot : *Hist. Patriarcharum Alexandrianorum Jacobitarum.* Paris, 1713, p. 75.

(Hefele : *History of the Councils*, Vol. I. pp. 355 *et seqq.* [2d ed.])

Let us see first what is the testimony of those Greek and Latin authors who lived about the time of the Council, concerning the number.

a. The first to be consulted among the Greek authors is the learned Theodoret, who lived about a century after the Council of Nicæa. He says, in his *History of the Church :* "After the condemnation of the Arians, the bishops assembled once more, and decreed twenty canons on ecclesiastical discipline."

b. Twenty years later, Gelasius, Bishop of Cyzicus, after much research into the most ancient documents, wrote a history of the Nicene Council. Gelasius also says expressly that the Council decreed twenty canons ; and, what is more important, he gives the original text of these canons exactly in the same order, and according to the tenor which we find elsewhere.

c. Rufinus is more ancient than these two historians. He was born near the period when the Council of Nicæa was held, and about half a century after he wrote his celebrated history of the Church, in which he inserted a Latin translation of the Nicene canons. Rufinus also knew only of these twenty canons ; but as he has divided the sixth and the eighth into two parts, he has given twenty-two canons, which are exactly the same as the twenty furnished by the other historians.

d. The famous discussion between the African bishops and the Bishop of Rome, on the subject of appeals to Rome, gives us a very important testimony on the true number of the Nicene canons. The presbyter Apiarius of Sicca in Africa, having been deposed for many crimes, appealed to Rome. Pope Zosimus (417–418) took the appeal into consideration, sent legates to Africa ; and to prove that he had the right to act thus, he quoted a canon of the Council of Nicæa, containing these words : "When a bishop thinks he has been unjustly deposed by his colleagues he may appeal to Rome, and the Roman bishop shall have the business decided by *judices in partibus*." The canon quoted by the Pope does not belong to the Council of Nicæa, as he affirmed ; it was the fifth canon of the Council of Sardica (the seventh in the Latin version). What explains the error of Zosimus is that in the ancient copies the canons of Nicæa and Sardica are written consecutively, with the same figures, and under the common title of canons of the Council of Nicæa ; and Zosimus might *optima fide* fall into an error—which he shared with Greek authors, his contemporaries, who also mixed the canons of Nicæa with those of Sardica. The African bishops, not finding the canon quoted by the Pope either in their Greek or in their Latin copies, in vain consulted also the copy which Bishop Cecilian, who had himself been present at the Council of Nicæa, had brought to Carthage. The legates of the Pope then declared that they did not rely upon these copies, and they agreed to send to Alexandria and to Constantinople to ask the patriarchs of these two cities for authentic copies of the canons of the Council of Nicæa. The African bishops desired in their turn that Pope Boniface should take the same step (Pope Zosimus had died meanwhile in 418)—that he should ask for copies from the Archbishops of Constantinople, Alexandria, and Antioch. Cyril of Alexandria and Atticus of Constantinople, indeed, sent exact and faithful copies of the Creed and canons of Nicæa ; and two learned men of Constantinople, Theilo and Thearistus, even translated these canons into Latin. Their translation has been preserved to us in the acts of the sixth Council of Carthage, and it contains only the twenty ordinary canons. It might be thought at first sight that it contained twenty-one canons ; but on closer consideration we see, as Hardouin has proved, that this twenty-first article is nothing but an historical notice appended to the Nicene canons by the Fathers of Carthage. It is conceived in these terms : "After the bishops had decreed these rules at Nicæa, and after the holy Council had decided what was the ancient rule for the celebration of Easter, peace and unity of faith were re-established between the East and the West. This is what we (the African bishops) have thought it right to add according to the history of the Church."

The bishops of Africa despatched to Pope Boniface the copies which had been sent to them from Alexandria and Constantinople, in the month of November 419 ; and subsequently in their letters to Celestine I. (423–432), successor to Boniface, they appealed to the text of these documents.

e. All the ancient collections of canons, either in Latin or Greek, composed in the fourth, or quite certainly at least in the fifth century, agree in giving only these twenty canons to Nicæa. The most ancient of these collections were made in the Greek Church, and in the course of time a very great number of copies of them were written. Many of these copies have descended to us; many libraries possess copies ; thus Montfaucon enumerates several in his *Bibliotheca Coisliniana.* Fabricius makes a similar catalogue of the copies in his *Bibliotheca Græca* to those found in the libraries of Turin, Florence, Venice, Oxford, Moscow, etc.; and he adds that these copies also contain the so-called apostolic canons, and those of the most ancient councils. The French bishop John Tilius presented to Paris, in 1540, a MS. of one of these Greek collections as it existed in the ninth century. It contains exactly our twenty canons of Nicæa, besides the so-called apostolic canons, those of Ancyra, etc. Elias Ehmger published a new edition at Wittemberg in 1614, using a second MS. which was found at Augsburg ; but the Roman collection of the Councils had before given in 1608, the Greek text of the twenty canons of Nicæa. This text of the Roman editors, with the exception of some insignificant variations, was exactly the same as that of the edition of Tilius. Neither the learned Jesuit Sirmond nor his coadjutors have mentioned what manuscripts were consulted in preparing this edition ; probably they were manuscripts drawn from several libraries, and particularly from that of the Vatican. The text of this Roman edition passed into all the following collections, even into those of Hardouin and Mansi ; while Justell in his *Bibliotheca juris Canonici* and Beveridge in his *Synodicon* (both of the eighteenth century), give a somewhat different text, also collated from MSS., and very similar to the text given by Tilius. Bruns, in his recent *Bibliotheca Ecclesiastica*, compares the two texts. Now all these Greek MSS. consulted at such different times, and by all these editors, acknowledge only twenty canons of Nicæa, and always the same twenty which we possess.

The Latin collections of the canons of the Councils also give the same result—for example, the most ancient and the most remarkable of all, the *Prisca*, and that of Dionysius the Less, which was collected about the year 500. The testimony of this latter collection is the more important for the number twenty, as Dionysius refers to the *Græca auctoritas.*

f. Among the later Eastern witnesses we may further mention Photius, Zonaras and Balsamon. Photius, in his *Collection of the Canons*, and in his *Nomocanon*, as well as the two other writers in their commentaries upon the canons of the ancient Councils, quote only and know only twenty canons of Nicæa, and always those which we possess.

g. The Latin canonists of the Middle Ages also acknowledge only these twenty canons of Nicæa. We have proof of this in the celebrated Spanish collection, which is generally but erroneously attributed to St. Isidore (it was composed at the commencement of the seventh century), and in that of Adrian (so called because it was offered to Charles the Great by Pope Adrian I). The celebrated Hincmar,.Archbishop of Rheims, the first canonist of the ninth century, in his turn attributes only twenty canons to the Council of Nicæa, and even the pseudo-Isidore assigns it no more.

I add for the convenience of the reader the captions of the Eighty Canons as given by Turrianus, translating them from the reprint in Labbe and Cossart, *Concilia*, Tom. II. col. 291. The Eighty-four Canons as given by Echellensis together with numerous Constitutions and Decrees attributed to the Nicene Council are likewise to be found in Labbe (*ut supra*, col. 318).

THE CAPTIONS OF THE ARABIC CANONS ATTRIBUTED TO THE COUNCIL OF NICE.

Canon I.[1]

Insane persons and energumens should not be ordained.

Canon II.

Bond servants are not to be ordained.

Canon III.

Neophytes in the faith are not to be ordained to Holy Orders before they have a knowledge of Holy Scripture. And such, if convicted after their ordination of grave sin, are to be deposed with those who ordained them.

Canon IV.

The cohabitation of women with bishops, presbyters, and deacons prohibited on account of their celibacy.

We decree that bishops shall not live with women; nor shall a presbyter who is a widower; neither shall they escort them; nor be familiar with them, nor gaze upon them persistently. And the same decree is made with regard to every celibate priest, and the same concerning such deacons as have no wives. And this is to be the case whether the woman be beautiful or ugly, whether a young girl or beyond the age of puberty, whether great in birth, or an orphan taken out of charity under pretext of bringing her up. For the devil with such arms slays religious, bishops, presbyters, and deacons, and incites them to the fires of desire. But if she be an old woman, and of advanced age, or a sister, or mother, or aunt, or grandmother, it is permitted to live with these because such persons are free from all suspicion of scandal.[2]

Canon V.

Of the election of a bishop and of the confirmation of the election.

Canon VI.

That those excommunicated by one bishop are not to be received by another; and that those whose excommunication has been shown to have been unjust should be absolved by the archbishop or patriarch.

Canon VII.

That provincial Councils should be held twice a year, for the consideration of all things affecting the churches of the bishops of the province.

Canon VIII.

Of the patriarchs of Alexandria and Antioch, and of their jurisdiction.

Canon IX.

Of one who solicits the episcopate when the people do not wish him; or if they do desire him, but without the consent of the archbishop.

Canon X.

How the bishop of Jerusalem is to be honoured, the honour, however, of the metropolitan church of Cæsarea being preserved intact, to which he is subject.

Canon XI.

Of those who force themselves into the order of presbyters without election or examination.

Canon XII.

Of the bishop who ordains one whom he understands has denied the faith; also of one ordained who after that he had denied it, crept into orders.

Canon XIII.

Of one who of his own will goes to another church, having been chosen by it, and does not wish afterwards to stay there.

Of taking pains that he be transferred from his own church to another.

Canon XIV.

No one shall become a monk without the bishop's license, and why a license is required.

Canon XV.

That clerics or religious who lend on usury should be cast from their grade.

Canon XVI.

Of the honour to be paid to the bishop and to a presbyter by the deacons.

Canon XVII.

Of the system and of the manner of receiving those who are converted from the heresy of Paul of Samosata.

---

[1] Turrianus calls them "Chapters."
[2] I have translated this canon in full because the caption did not seem to give fairly its meaning. In Labbe will be found a long and most curious note.

CANON XVIII.

Of the system and manner of receiving those who are converted from the heresy of the Novatians.

CANON XIX.

Of the system and manner of receiving those who return after a lapse from the faith, and of receiving the relapsed, and of those brought into peril of death by sickness before their penance is finished, and concerning such as are convalescent.

CANON XX.

Of avoiding the conversation of evil workers and wizards, also of the penance of them that have not avoided such.

CANON XXI.

Of incestuous marriages contrary to the law of spiritual relationship, and of the penance of such as are in such marriages.
[The time of penance fixed is twenty years, only godfather and godmother are mentioned, and nothing is said of separation.]

CANON XXII.

Of sponsors in baptism.
Men shall not hold females at the font, neither women males; but women females, and men males.

CANON XXIII.

Of the prohibited marriages of spiritual brothers and sisters from receiving them in baptism.

CANON XXIV.

Of him who has married two wives at the same time, or who through lust has added another woman to his wife; and of his punishment.
Part of the canon. If he be a priest he is forbidden to sacrifice and is cut off from the communion of the faithful until he turn out of the house the second woman, and he ought to retain the first.

CANON XXV.

That no one should be forbidden Holy Communion unless such as are doing penance.

CANON XXVI.

Clerics are forbidden from suretyship or witness-giving in criminal causes.

CANON XXVII.

Of avoiding the excommunicate, and of not receiving the oblation from them; and of the excommunication of him who does not avoid the excommunicated.

CANON XXVIII.

How anger, indignation, and hatred should be avoided by the priest, especially because he has the power of excommunicating others.

CANON XXIX.

Of not kneeling in prayer.

CANON XXX.

Of giving [only] names of Christians in baptism, and of heretics who retain the faith in the Trinity and the perfect form of baptism; and of others not retaining it, worthy of a worse name, and of how such are to be received when they come to the faith.

CANON XXXI.

Of the system and manner of receiving converts to the Orthodox faith from the heresy of Arius and of other like.

CANON XXXII.

Of the system of receiving those who have kept the dogmas of the faith and the Church's laws, and yet have separated from us and afterwards come back.

CANON XXXIII.

Of the place of residence of the Patriarch, and of the honour which should be given to the bishop of Jerusalem and to the bishop of Seleucia.

CANON XXXIV.

Of the honour to be given to the Archbishop of Seleucia in the Synod of Greece.

CANON XXXV.

Of not holding a provincial synod in the province of Persia without the authority of the patriarch of Antioch, and how the bishops of Persia are subject to the metropolitans of Antioch.

CANON XXXVI.

Of the creation of a patriarch for Ethiopia, and of his power, and of the honour to be paid him in the Synod of Greece.

CANON XXXVII.

Of the election of the Archbishop of Cyprus, who is subject to the patriarch of Antioch.

CANON XXXVIII.

That the ordination of ministers of the Church by bishops in the dioceses of strangers is forbidden.

Canon XXXIX.

Of the care and power which a Patriarch has over the bishops and archbishops of his patriarchate ; and of the primacy of the Bishop of Rome over all.

Let the patriarch consider what things are done by the archbishops and bishops in their provinces ; and if he shall find anything done by them otherwise than it should be, let him change it, and order it, as seemeth him fit ; for he is the father of all, and they are his sons. And although the archbishop be among the bishops as an elder brother, who hath the care of his brethren, and to whom they owe obedience because he is over them ; yet the patriarch is to all those who are under his power, just as he who holds the seat of Rome, is the head and prince of all patriarchs ; inasmuch as he is first, as was Peter, to whom power is given over all Christian princes, and over all their peoples, as he who is the Vicar of Christ our Lord over all peoples and over the whole Christian Church, and whoever shall contradict this, is excommunicated by the Synod.[1]

[I add Canon XXXVII. of Echellensis's *Nova Versio LXXXIV. Arabic. Canonum Conc. Nicœni,* that the reader may compare it with the foregoing.]

Let there be only four patriarchs in the whole world as there are four writers of the Gospel, and four rivers, etc. And let there be a prince and chief over them, the lord of the see of the Divine Peter at Rome, according as the Apostles commanded. And after him the lord of the great Alexandria, which is the see of Mark. And the third is the lord of Ephesus, which is the see of John the Divine who speaks divine things. And the fourth and last is my lord of Antioch, which is another see of Peter. And let all the bishops be divided under the hands of these four patriarchs ; and the bishops of the little towns which are under the dominion of the great cities let them be under the authority of these metropolitans. But let every metropolitan of these great cities appoint the bishops of his province, but let none of the bishops appoint him, for he is greater than they. Therefore let every man know his own rank, and let him not usurp the rank of another. And whosoever shall contradict this law which we have established the Fathers of the Synod subject him to anathema.[2]

---

[1] I have translated the whole canon literally ; the reader will judge of its antiquity.
[2] Canon XXXIX. of this series has nothing to do with the Patriarchs or with the see of Rome and its prerogatives.

Canon XL.

Of the provincial synod which should be held twice every year, and of its utility ; together with the excommunication of such as oppose the decree.

Canon XLI.

Of the synod of Archbishops, which meets once a year with the Patriarch, and of its utility ; also of the collection to be made for the support of the patriarch throughout the provinces and places subject to the patriarch.

Canon XLII.

Of a cleric or monk who when fallen into sin, and summoned once, twice, and thrice, does not present himself for trial.

Canon XLIII.

What the patriarch should do in the case of a defendant set at liberty unpunished by the decision of the bishop, presbyter, or even of a deacon, as the case may be.

Canon XLIV.

How an archbishop ought to give trial to one of his suffragan bishops.

Canon XLV.

Of the receiving of complaints and condemnation of an archbishop against his patriarch.

Canon XLVI.

How a patriarch should admit a complaint or judgment of an Archbishop against an Archbishop.

Canon XLVII.

Of those excommunicated by a certain one, when they can be and when they cannot be absolved by another.

Canon XLVIII.

No bishop shall choose his own successor.

Canon XLIX.

No simoniacal ordinations shall be made.

Canon L.

There shall be but one bishop of one city, and one parochus of one town ; also the incumbent, whether bishop or parish priest, shall not be removed in favour of a successor desired by some of the people unless he has been convicted of manifest crime.

Canon LI.

Bishops shall not allow the separation of a wife from her husband on account of discord —[in American, "incompatibility of temper"].

Canon LII.

Usury and the base seeking of worldly gain is forbidden to the clergy, also conversation and fellowship with Jews.

Canon LIII.

Marriages with infidels to be avoided.

Canon LIV.

Of the election of a chorepiscopus, and of his duties in towns, and villages, and monasteries.

Canon LV.

How a chorepiscopus should visit the churches and monasteries which are under his jurisdiction.

Canon LVI.

Of how the presbyters of the towns and villages should go twice a year with their chorepiscopus to salute the bishop, and how religious should do so once a year from their monasteries, and how the new abbot of a monastery should go thrice.

Canon LVII.

Of the rank in sitting during the celebration of service in church by the bishop, the archdeacon and the chorepiscopus; and of the office of archdeacon, and of the honour due the archpresbyter.

Canon LVIII.

Of the honour due the archdeacon and the chorepiscopus when they sit in church during the absence of the bishop, and when they go about with the bishop.

Canon LIX.

How all the grades of the clergy and their duties should be publicly described and set forth.

Canon LX.

Of how men are to be chosen from the diocese for holy orders, and of how they should be examined.

Canon LXI.

Of the honour due to the deacons, and how the clerics must not put themselves in their way.

Canon LXII.

The number of presbyters and deacons is to be adapted to the work of the church and to its means.

Canon LXIII.

Of the Ecclesiastical Economist and of the others who with him care for the church's possessions.

Canon LXIV.

Of the offices said in the church, the night and day offices, and of the collect for all those who rule that church.

Canon LXV.

Of the order to be observed at the funeral of a bishop, of a chorepiscopus and of an archdeacon, and of the office of exequies.

Canon LXVI.

Of taking a second wife, after the former one has been disowned for any cause, or even not put away, and of him who falsely accuses his wife of adultery.

If any priest or deacon shall put away his wife on account of her fornication, or for other cause, as aforesaid, or cast her out of doors for external good, or that he may change her for another more beautiful, or better, or richer, or does so out of his lust which is displeasing to God; and after she has been put away for any of these causes he shall contract matrimony with another, or without having put her away shall take another, whether free or bond; and shall have both equally, they living separately and he sleeping every night with one or other of them, or else keeping both in the same house and bed, let him be deposed. If he were a layman let him be deprived of communion. But if anyone falsely defames his wife charging her with adultery, so that he turns her out of doors, the matter must be diligently examined; and if the accusation was false, he shall be deposed if a cleric, but if a layman shall be prohibited from entering the church and from the communion of the faithful; and shall be compelled to live with her whom he has defamed, even though she be deformed, and poor, and insane; and whoever shall not obey is excommunicated by the Synod.

[*Note.*—The reader will notice that by this canon a husband is deposed or excommunicated, as the case may be, if he marry another woman, after putting away his wife on account of her adultery. It is curious that in the parallel canon in the collection of Echellensis, which is numbered LXXI., the reading is quite different, although it is very awkward and inconsequent as given. Moreover, it should be remembered that in some codices and editions this canon is lacking altogether, one on the right of the Pope to receive appeals taking its place. As this canon is of considerable length, I only quote the interesting parts.]

Whatever presbyter or deacon shall put away his wife without the offence of fornication, or for any other cause of which we have spoken above, and shall cast her out of doors . . . such a person shall be cast out of the clergy, if he were a clergyman; if a layman he shall be forbidden the communion of the faithful. . . . But if that woman [untruly charged by her husband with adultery], that is to say his wife, spurns his society on account of the injury he has done her and the charge he has brought against her, of which she is innocent, let her freely be put away and let a bill of repudiation be written for her, noting the false accusation which had been brought against her. And then if she should wish to marry some other faithful man, it is right for her to do so, nor does the Church forbid it; and the same permission extends as well to men as to women, since there is equal reason for it for each. But if he shall return to better fruit which is of the same kind, and shall conciliate to himself the love and benevolence of his consort, and shall be willing to return to his pristine friendship, his fault shall be condoned to him after he has done suitable and sufficient penance. And whoever shall speak against this decree the fathers of the synod excommunicate him.

Canon LXVII.

Of having two wives at the same time, and of a woman who is one of the faithful marrying an infidel; and of the form of receiving her to penance.

[Her reception back is conditioned upon her leaving the infidel man.]

Canon LXVIII.

Of giving in marriage to an infidel a daughter or sister without her knowledge and contrary to her wish.

Canon LXIX.

Of one of the faithful who departs from the faith through lust and love of an infidel; and of the form of receiving him back, or admitting him to penance.

Canon LXX.

Of the hospital to be established in every city, and of the choice of a superintendent and concerning his duties.

[It is interesting to note that one of the duties of the superintendent is—"That if the goods of the hospital are not sufficient for its expenses, he ought to collect all the time and from all Christians provision according to the ability of each."]

Canon LXXI.

Of the placing a bishop or archbishop in his chair after ordination, which is enthronization.

Canon LXXII.

No one is allowed to transfer himself to another church [i.e., diocese] than that in which he was ordained; and what is to be done in the case of one cast out forcibly without any blame attaching to him.

Canon LXXIII.

The laity shall not choose for themselves priests in the towns and villages without the authority of the chorepiscopus; nor an abbot for a monastery; and that no one should give commands as to who should be elected his successor after his death, and when this is lawful for a superior.

Canon LXXIV.

How sisters, widows, and deaconesses should be made to keep their residence in their monasteries; and of the system of instructing them; and of the election of deaconesses, and of their duties and utility.

Canon LXXV.

How one seeking election should not be chosen, even if of conspicuous virtue; and how the election of a layman to the aforesaid grades is not prohibited, and that those chosen should not afterward be deprived before their deaths, except on account of crime.

Canon LXXVI.

Of the distinctive garb and distinctive names and conversation of monks and nuns.

Canon LXXVII.

That a bishop convicted of adultery or of other similar crime should be deposed without hope of restoration to the same grade; but shall not be excommunicated.

Canon LXXVIII.

Of presbyters and deacons who have fallen only once into adultery, if they have never been married; and of the same when fallen as widowers, and those who have fallen, all the while having their own wives. Also of those who return to the same sin as well widowers as those having living wives; and which of these ought not to be received to penance, and which once only, and which twice.

Canon LXXIX.

Each one of the faithful while his sin is yet not public should be mended by private exhortation and admonition; if he will not profit by this, he must be excommunicated.

Canon LXXX.

Of the election of a procurator of the poor, and of his duties.

PROPOSED ACTION ON CLERICAL CELIBACY.

[*The Acts are not extant.*]

NOTES.

Often the mind of a deliberative assembly is as clearly shown by the propositions it rejects as by those it adopts, and it would seem that this doctrine is of application in the case of the asserted attempt at this Council to pass a decree forbidding the priesthood to live in the use of marriage. This attempt is said to have failed. The particulars are as follows:

HEFELE.

(*Hist. Councils,* Vol. I., pp. 435 *et seqq.*)

Socrates, Sozomen, and Gelasius affirm that the Synod of Nicæa, as well as that of Elvira (can. 33), desired to pass a law respecting celibacy. This law was to forbid all bishops, priests and deacons (Sozomen adds subdeacons), who were married at the time of their ordination, to continue to live with their wives. But, say these historians, the law was opposed openly and decidedly by Paphnutius, bishop of a city of the Upper Thebaïs in Egypt, a man of a high reputation, who had lost an eye during the persecution under Maximian. He was also celebrated for his miracles, and was held in so great respect by the Emperor, that the latter often kissed the empty socket of the lost eye. Paphnutius declared with a loud voice, "that too heavy a yoke ought not to be laid upon the clergy; that marriage and married intercourse are of themselves honourable and undefiled; that the Church ought not to be injured by an extreme severity, for all could not live in absolute continency : in this way (by not prohibiting married intercourse) the virtue of the wife would be much more certainly preserved (viz the wife of a clergyman, because she might find injury elsewhere, if her husband withdrew from her married intercourse). The intercourse of a man with his lawful wife may also be a chaste intercourse. It would therefore be sufficient, according to the ancient tradition of the Church, if those who had taken holy orders without being married were prohibited from marrying afterwards; but those clergymen who had been married only once as laymen, were not to be separated from their wives (Gelasius adds, or being only a reader or cantor)." This discourse of Paphnutius made so much the more impression, because he had never lived in matrimony himself, and had had no conjugal intercourse. Paphnutius, indeed, had been brought up in a monastery, and his great purity of manners had rendered him especially celebrated. Therefore the Council took the serious words of the Egyptian bishop into consideration, stopped all discussion upon the law, and left to each cleric the responsibility of deciding the point as he would.

If this account be true, we must conclude that a law was proposed to the Council of Nicæa the same as one which had been carried twenty years previously at Elvira, in Spain ; this coincidence would lead us to believe that it was the Spaniard Hosius who proposed the law respecting celibacy at Nicæa. The discourse ascribed to Paphnutius, and the consequent decision of the Synod, agree very well with the text of the *Apostolic Constitutions*, and with the whole practice of the Greek Church in respect to celibacy. The Greek Church as well as the Latin accepted the principle, that whoever had taken holy orders before marriage, ought not to be married afterwards. In the Latin Church, bishops, priests, deacons, and even sub-deacons, were considered to be subject to this law, because the latter were at a very early period reckoned among the higher servants of the Church, which was not the case in the Greek Church. The Greek Church went so far as to allow deacons to marry after their ordination, if previously to it they had expressly obtained from their bishop permission to do so. The Council of Ancyra affirms this (c. 10). We see that the Greek Church wishes to leave the bishop free to decide the matter ; but in reference to priests, it also prohibited them from marrying after their ordination. Therefore, whilst the Latin Church exacted of those presenting themselves for ordination, even as subdeacons, that they should not continue to live with their wives if they were married, the Greek Church gave no such prohibition ; but if the wife of an ordained clergyman died, the Greek Church allowed no second marriage. The *Apostolic Constitutions* decided this point in the same way. To leave their wives from a pretext of piety was also forbidden to Greek priests ; and the Synod of Gangra (c. 4) took up the defence of married priests against the Eustathians. Eustathius, however, was not alone among the Greeks in opposing the marriage of all clerics, and in desiring to introduce into the Greek Church the Latin discipline on this point. St. Epiphanius also inclined towards this side. The Greek Church did not, however, adopt this rigour in reference to priests, deacons, and subdeacons, but by degrees it came to be required of bishops and of the higher order of clergy in general, that they should live in celibacy. Yet this was not until after the compilation of the *Apostolic Canons* (c. 5) and of the Constitutions; for in those documents mention is made of bishops living in wedlock, and Church history shows that there were married bishops, for instance Synesius, in the fifth century. But it is fair to remark, even as to Synesius, that he made it an express condition of his acceptation, on his election to the episcopate, that he might continue to live the married life. Thomassin believes that Synesius did not seriously require this condition, and only spoke thus for the sake of escaping the episcopal office; which would seem to imply that in his time Greek bishops had already begun to live in celibacy. At the Trullan Synod (c. 13.) the Greek Church finally settled the question of the marriage of priests. Baronius, Valesius, and other historians, have considered the account of the part taken by Paphnutius to be apocryphal. Baronius says, that as the Council of Nicæa in its third canon gave a law upon celibacy it is quite impossible to admit that it would alter such a law on account of Paphnutius. But Baronius is mistaken in seeing a law upon celibacy in that third canon; he thought it to be so, because, when mentioning the women who might live in the clergyman's house—his mother, sister, etc.—the canon does not say a word about the wife. It had no occasion to mention her, it was referring to the συνεισάκτοι whilst these συνεισάκτοι and married women have nothing in common. Natalis Alexander gives this anecdote about Paphnutius in full: he desired to refute Ballarmin, who considered it to be untrue and an invention of Socrates to please the Novatians. Natalis Alexander often maintains erroneous opinions, and on the present question he deserves no confidence. If, as St. Epiphanius relates, the Novatians maintained that the clergy might be married exactly like the laity, it cannot be said that Socrates shared that opinion, since he says, or rather makes Paphnutius say, that, according to *ancient* tradition, those not married at the time of ordination should not be so subsequently.

Moreover, if it may be said that Socrates had a partial sympathy with the Novatians, he certainly cannot be considered as belonging to them, still less can he be accused of falsifying history in their favour. He may sometimes have propounded erroneous opinions, but there is a great difference between that and the invention of a whole story. Valesius especially makes use of the argument *ex silentio* against Socrates. (a) Rufinus, he says, gives many particulars about Paphnutius in his *History of the Church;* he mentions his martyrdom, his miracles, and the Emperor's reverence for him, but not a single word of the business about celibacy. (b) The name of Paphnutius is wanting in the list of Egyptian bishops present at the Synod. These two arguments of Valesius are weak; the second has the authority of Rufinus himself against it, who expressly says that Bishop Paphnutius was present at the Council of Nicæa. If Valesius means by *lists* only the signatures at the end of the acts of the Council, this proves nothing; for these lists are very imperfect, and it is well known that many bishops whose names are not among these signatures were present at Nicæa. This argument *ex silentio* is evidently insufficient to prove that the anecdote about Paphnutius must be rejected as false, seeing that it is in perfect harmony with the practice of the ancient Church, and especially of the Greek Church, on the subject of clerical marriages. On the other hand, Thomassin pretends that there was no such practice, and endeavours to prove by quotations from St. Epiphanius, St. Jerome, Eusebius, and St. John Chrysostom, that even in the East priests who were married at the time of their ordination were prohibited from continuing to live with their wives. The texts quoted by Thomassin prove only that the Greeks gave especial honour to priests living in perfect continency, but they do not prove that this continence was a duty incumbent upon all priests; and so much the less, as the fifth and twenty-fifth Apostolic canons, the fourth canon of Gangra, and the thirteenth of the Trullan Synod, demonstrate clearly enough what was the universal custom of the Greek Church on this point. Lupus and Phillips explained the words of Paphnutius in another sense. According to them, the Egyptian bishop was not speaking in a general way; he simply desired that the contemplated law should not include the subdeacons. But this explanation does not agree with the extracts quoted from Socrates, Sozomen, and Gelasius, who believe Paphnutius intended deacons and priests as well.

THE SYNODAL LETTER.

(Found in Gelasius, Historia Concilii Nicæni, *lib. II., cap. xxxiii. ; Socr.*, H. E., *lib. I., cap. 6 ; Theodor.*, H. E., *lib. I., cap. 9.)*

To the Church of Alexandria, by the grace of GOD, holy and great; and to our well-beloved brethren, the orthodox clergy and laity throughout Egypt, and Pentapolis, and Lybia, and every nation under heaven, the holy and great synod, the bishops assembled at Nicea, wish health in the LORD.

FORASMUCH as the great and holy Synod, which was assembled at Nicea through the grace of Christ and our most religious Sovereign Constantine, who brought us together from our several provinces and cities, has considered matters which concern the faith of the Church, it seemed to us to be necessary that certain things should be communicated from us to you in writing, so that you might have the means of knowing what has been mooted and investigated, and also what has been decreed and confirmed.

First of all, then, in the presence of our most religious Sovereign Constantine, investigation was made of matters concerning the impiety and transgression of Arius and his adherents; and it was unanimously decreed that he and his impious opinion should be anathematized, together with the blasphemous words and speculations in which he indulged, blaspheming the Son of God, and saying that he is from things that are not, and that before he was begotten he was not, and that there was a time when he was not, and that the Son of God is by his free will capable of vice and virtue; saying also that he is a creature. All these things the holy Synod has anathematized, not even enduring to hear his impious doctrine and madness and blasphemous words. And of the charges against him and of the results they had, ye have either already heard or will hear the particulars, lest we should seem to be oppressing a man who has in fact received a fitting recompense for his own sin. So far indeed has his impiety prevailed, that he has even destroyed Theonas of Marmorica and Secundas of Ptolemais; for they also have received the same sentence as the rest.

But when the grace of God had delivered Egypt from that heresy and blasphemy, and from the persons who have dared to make disturbance and division among a people heretofore at peace, there remained the matter of the insolence of Meletius and those who have been ordained by him; and concerning this part of our work we now, beloved brethren, proceed to inform you of the decrees of the Synod. The Synod, then, being disposed to deal gently with Meletius (for in strict justice he deserved no leniency), decreed that he should remain in his own city, but have no authority either to ordain, or to administer affairs, or to make appointments; and that he should not appear in the country or in any other city for this purpose, but should enjoy the bare title of his rank; but that those who have been placed by him, after they have been confirmed by a more sacred laying on of hands, shall on these conditions be admitted to communion: that they shall both have their rank and the right to officiate, but that they shall be altogether the inferiors of all those who are enrolled in any church or parish, and have been appointed by our most honourable colleague Alexander. So that these men are to have no authority to make appointments of persons who may be pleasing to them, nor to suggest names, nor to do anything whatever, without the consent of the bishops of the Catholic and Apostolic Church, who are serving under our most holy colleague Alexander; while those who, by the grace of God and through your prayers, have been found in no schism, but on the contrary are without spot in the Catholic and Apostolic Church, are to have authority to make appointments and nominations of worthy persons among the clergy, and in short to do all things according to the law and ordinance of the Church. But, if it happen that any of the clergy who are now in the Church should die, then those who have been lately received are to succeed to the office of the deceased; always provided that they shall appear to be worthy, and that the people elect them, and that the bishop of Alexandria shall concur in the election and ratify it. This concession has been made to all the rest; but, on account of his disorderly conduct from the first, and the rashness and precipitation of his character, the same decree was not made concerning Meletius himself, but that, inasmuch as he is a man capable of committing again the same disorders, no authority nor privilege should be conceded to him.

These are the particulars, which are of special interest to Egypt and to the most holy Church of Alexandria; but if in the presence of our most honoured lord, our colleague and brother Alexander, anything else has been enacted by canon or other decree, he will himself convey it to you in greater detail, he having been both a guide and fellow-worker in what has been done.

We further proclaim to you the good news of the agreement concerning the holy Easter, that this particular also has through your prayers been rightly settled; so that all our brethren in the East who formerly followed the custom of the Jews are henceforth to celebrate the said most sacred feast of Easter at the same time with the Romans and yourselves and all those who have observed Easter from the beginning.

Wherefore, rejoicing in these wholesome results, and in our common peace and harmony, and in the cutting off of every heresy, receive ye with the greater honour and with increased love, our colleague your Bishop Alexander, who has gladdened us by his presence, and who at so great an age has undergone so great fatigue that peace might be established among you and all of us. Pray ye also for us all, that the things which have been deemed advisable may stand fast; for they have been done, as we believe, to the well-pleasing of Almighty God and of his only Begotten Son, our Lord Jesus Christ, and of the Holy Ghost, to whom be glory for ever. Amen.

ON THE KEEPING OF EASTER.

From the Letter of the Emperor to all those not present at the Council.

(*Found in Eusebius*, Vita Const., *Lib. iii.*, 18–20.)

When the question relative to the sacred festival of Easter arose, it was universally thought that it would be convenient that all should keep the feast on *one* day; for what could be more beautiful and more desirable, than to see this festival, through which we receive the hope of immortality, celebrated by all with one accord, and in the same manner? It was declared to be particularly unworthy for this, the holiest of all festivals, to follow the custom [the calculation] of the Jews, who had soiled their hands with the most fearful of crimes, and whose minds were blinded. In rejecting their custom,[1] we may transmit to our descendants the legitimate mode of celebrating Easter, which we have observed from the time of the Saviour's Passion to the present day [according to the day of the week]. We ought not, therefore, to have anything in common with the Jews, for the Saviour has shown us another way; our worship follows a more legitimate and more convenient course (the order of the days of the week); and consequently, in unanimously adopting this mode, we desire, dearest brethren, to separate ourselves from the detestable company of the Jews, for it is truly shameful for us to hear

them boast that without their direction we could not keep this feast. How can they be in the right, they who, after the death of the Saviour, have no longer been led by reason but by wild violence, as their delusion may urge them? They do not possess the truth in this Easter question; for, in their blindness and repugnance to all improvements, they frequently celebrate two passovers in the same year. We could not imitate those who are openly in error. How, then, could we follow these Jews, who are most certainly blinded by error? for to celebrate the passover twice in one year is totally inadmissible. But even if this were not so, it would still be your duty not to tarnish your soul by communications with such wicked people [the Jews]. Besides, consider well, that in such an important matter, and on a subject of such great solemnity, there ought not to be any division. Our Saviour has left us only *one* festal day of our redemption, that is to say, of his holy passion, and he desired [to establish] only *one* Catholic Church. Think, then, how unseemly it is, that on the same day some should be fasting whilst others are seated at a banquet; and that after Easter, some should be rejoicing at feasts, whilst others are still observing a strict fast. For this reason, a Divine Providence wills that this custom should be rectified and regulated in a uniform way; and everyone, I hope, will agree upon this point. As, on the one hand, it is our duty not to have anything in common with the murderers of our Lord; and as, on the other, the custom now followed by the Churches of the West, of the South, and of

---

[1] We must read ἔθους, not ἔθνους, as the Mayence impression of the edition of Valerius has it.

the North, and by some of those of the East, is the most acceptable, it has appeared good to all ; and I have been guarantee for your consent, that you would accept it with joy, as it is followed at Rome, in Africa, in all Italy, Egypt, Spain, Gaul, Britain, Libya, in all Achaia, and in the dioceses of Asia, of Pontus, and Cilicia. You should consider not only that the number of churches in these provinces make a majority, but also that it is right to demand what our reason approves, and that we should have nothing in common with the Jews. To sum up in few words : By the unanimous judgment of all, it has been decided that the most holy festival of Easter should be everywhere celebrated on one and the same day, and it is not seemly that in so holy a thing there should be any division. As this is the state of the case, accept joyfully the divine favour, and this truly divine command ; for all which takes place in assemblies of the bishops ought to be regarded as proceeding from the will of God. Make known to your brethren what has been decreed, keep this most holy day according to the prescribed mode ; we can thus celebrate this holy Easter day at the same time, if it is granted me, as I desire, to unite myself with you ; we can rejoice together, seeing that the divine power has made use of our instrumentality for destroying the evil designs of the devil, and thus causing faith, peace, and unity to flourish amongst us. May God graciously protect you, my beloved brethren.

EXCURSUS ON THE SUBSEQUENT HISTORY OF THE EASTER QUESTION.

(Hefele : *Hist. of the Councils,* Vol. I., pp. 328 *et seqq.*)

The differences in the way of fixing the period of Easter did not indeed disappear after the Council of Nicea. Alexandria and Rome could not agree, either because one of the two Churches neglected to make the calculation for Easter, or because the other considered it inaccurate. It is a fact, proved by the ancient Easter table of the Roman Church, that the cycle of eighty-four years continued to be used at Rome as before. Now this cycle differed in many ways from the Alexandrian, and did not always agree with it about the period for Easter—in fact (a), the Romans used quite another method from the Alexandrians ; they calculated from the epact, and began from the *feria prima* of January. (b.) The Romans were mistaken in placing the full moon a little too soon ; whilst the Alexandrians placed it a little too late. (c.) At Rome the equinox was supposed to fall on March 18th ; whilst the Alexandrians placed it on March 21st. (d.) Finally, the Romans differed in this from the Greeks also ; they did not celebrate Easter the next day when the full moon fell on the Saturday.

Even the year following the Council of Nicea—that is, in 326—as well as in the years 330, 333, 340, 341, 343, the Latins celebrated Easter on a different day from the Alexandrians. In order to put an end to this misunderstanding, the Synod of Sardica in 343, as we learn from the newly discovered festival letters of S. Athanasius, took up again the question of Easter, and brought the two parties (Alexandrians and Romans) to regulate, by means of mutual concessions, a common day for Easter for the next fifty years. This compromise, after a few years, was not observed. The troubles excited by the Arian heresy, and the division which it caused between the East and the West, prevented the decree of Sardica from being put into execution ; therefore the Emperor Theodosius the Great, after the re-establishment of peace in the Church, found himself obliged to take fresh steps for obtaining a complete uniformity in the manner of celebrating Easter. In 387, the Romans having kept Easter on March 21st, the Alexandrians did not do so for five weeks later—that is to say, till April 25th—because with the Alexandrians the equinox was not till March 21st. The Emperor Theodosius the Great then asked Theophilus, Bishop of Alexandria for an explanation of the difference. The bishop responded to the Emperor's desire, and drew up a chronological table of the Easter festivals, based upon the principles acknowledged by the Church of Alexandria. Unfortunately, we now possess only the prologue of his work.

Upon an invitation from Rome, S. Ambrose also mentioned the period of this same Easter in 387, in his letter to the bishops of Æmilia, and he sides with the Alexandrian computation.　Cyril of Alexandria abridged the paschal table of his uncle Theophilus, and fixed the time for the ninety-five following Easters—that is, from 436 to 531 after Christ. Besides this Cyril showed, in a letter to the Pope, what was defective in the Latin calculation ; and this demonstration was taken up again, some time after, by order of the Emperor, by Paschasinus, Bishop of Lilybæum and Proterius of Alexandria, in a letter written by them to Pope Leo I.　In consequence of these communications, Pope Leo often gave the preference to the Alexandrian computation, instead of that of the Church of Rome.　At the same time also was generally established, the opinion so little entertained by the ancient authorities of the Church—one might even say, so strongly in contradiction to their teaching—that Christ partook of the passover on the 14th Nisan, that he died on the 15th (not on the 14th, as the ancients considered), that he lay in the grave on the 16th, and rose again on the 17th.　In the letter we have just mentioned, Proterius of Alexandria openly admitted all these different points.

Some years afterwards, in 457, Victor of Aquitane, by order of the Roman Archdeacon Hilary, endeavoured to make the Roman and the Alexandrian calculations agree together. It has been conjectured that subsequently Hilary, when Pope, brought Victor's calculation into use, in 456—that is, at the time when the cycle of eighty-four years came to an end. In the latter cycle the new moons were marked more accurately, and the chief differences existing between the Latin and Greek calculations disappeared ; so that the Easter of the Latins generally coincided with that of Alexandria, or was only a very little removed from it.　In cases when the $\iota\delta'$ fell on a Saturday, Victor did not wish to decide whether Easter should be celebrated the next day, as the Alexandrians did, or should be postponed for a week.　He indicates both dates in his table, and leaves the Pope to decide what was to be done in each separate case.　Even after Victor's calculations, there still remained great differences in the manner of fixing the celebration of Easter ; and it was Dionysius the Less who first completely overcame them, by giving to the Latins a paschal table having as its basis the cycle of nineteen years.　This cycle perfectly corresponded to that of Alexandria, and thus established that harmony which had been so long sought in vain.　He showed the advantages of his calculation so strongly, that it was admitted by Rome and by the whole of Italy ; whilst almost the whole of Gaul remained faithful to Victor's canon, and Great Britain still held the cycle of eighty-four years, a little improved by Sulpicius Severus.　When the Heptarchy was evangelized by the Roman missionaries, the new converts accepted the calculation of Dionysius, whilst the ancient Churches of Wales held fast their old tradition. From this arose the well-known British dissensions about the celebration of Easter, which were transplanted by Columban into Gaul.　In 729, the majority of the ancient British Churches accepted the cycle of nineteen years.　It had before been introduced into Spain, immediately after the conversion of Reccared.　Finally, under Charles the Great, the cycle of nineteen years triumphed over all opposition ; and thus the whole of Christendom was united, for the Quartodecimans had gradually disappeared.[1]

---

[1] It is curious that after all the attempts that have been made to get this matter settled, the Church is still separated into East and West—the latter having accepted the Gregorian Calendar from which the Eastern Church, still using the Julian Calendar, differs in being twelve days behind. And even in the West we have succeeded in breaking the spirit of the Nicene decree, for in 1825 the Christian Easter coincided with the Jewish Passover !

THE CANONS OF THE COUNCILS OF ANCYRA, GANGRA, NEOCÆSAREA, ANTIOCH AND LAODICEA, WHICH CANONS WERE ACCEPTED AND RECEIVED BY THE ECUMENICAL SYNODS.

INTRODUCTORY NOTE TO THE CANONS OF THE PROVINCIAL SYNODS
WHICH IN THIS VOLUME ARE INTERJECTED BETWEEN THE FIRST
AND THE SECOND ECUMENICAL COUNCILS.

The First Canon of the Fourth Ecumenical Council, Chalcedon, reads as follows : " We
have judged it right that the canons of the Holy Fathers made in every synod even until
now, should remain in force." And the Council in Trullo, in its second canon, has enumerated these synods in the following words. "We set our seal to all the rest of the canons
which have been established by our holy and blessed fathers, that is to say by the 318 God-
inspired fathers who met at Nice, and by those who met at Ancyra, and by those who met
at Neocæsarea, as well as by those who met at Gangra : in addition to these the canons
adopted by those who met at Antioch in Syria, and by those who met at Laodicea in Phrygia ; moreover by the 150 fathers who assembled in this divinely kept and imperial city,
and by the 200 who were gathered in the metropolis of Ephesus, and by the 630 holy and
blessed fathers who met at Chalcedon," etc., etc.

There can be no doubt that this collection of canons was made at a very early date, and
from the fact that the canons of the First Council of Constantinople do not appear, as they
naturally would, immediately after those of Nice, we may not improbably conclude that the
collection was formed before that council assembled. For it will be noticed that Nice,
although not the earliest in date, takes the precedence as being of ecumenical rank. And
this is expressly stated in the caption to the canons of Ancyra according to the reading in the
Paris Edition of Balsamon. "The canons of the holy Fathers who assembled at Ancyra ;
which are indeed older than those made at Nice, but placed after them, on account of the
authority (αὐθεντίαν) of the Ecumenical Synod."

On the arrangement of this code much has been written and Archbishop Ussher has
made some interesting suggestions, but all appear to be attended with more or less difficulties. The reader will find in Bp: Beveridge, in the Prolegomena to his *Synodicon* a very
full treatment of the point,[1] the gist of the matter is admirably given in the following brief
note which I take from Hammond. In speaking of this early codex of the Church he says:

(Hammond, *Definitions of Faith and Canons of Discipline*, pp. 134 and 135.)

That this collection was made and received by the Church previous to the Council of
Chalcedon is evident from the manner in which several of the Canons are quoted in that
Council. Thus in the 4th Action, in the matter of Carosus and Dorotheus, who had acknowledged Dioscorus as Bishop, though he had been deposed from his bishopric, "the
holy Synod said, let the holy Canons of the Fathers be read, and inserted in the records ;
and Actius the Archdeacon taking the book read the 83d Canon, If any Bishops, etc. And
again the 84th Canon, concerning those who separate themselves, If any Presbyter," etc.
These Canons are the 4th and 5th of Antioch. Again, in the 11th Action, in the matter of
Bassianus and Stephanus who disputed about the Bishopric of Ephesus, both requested the
Canons to be read, "And the Judges said, Let the Canons be read. And Leontius Bishop
of Magnesia read the 95th Canon, If any Bishop, etc., and again out of the same book the
96th Canon, If any Bishop," etc. These Canons are the 16th and 17th of Antioch. Now if
we add together the different Canons in the Code of the Universal Church in the order in
which they follow in the enumeration of them by the Council of Trullo and in other documents, we find that the 4th and 5th of Antioch, are the 83d and 84th of the whole Code, and

---

[1] Beveridge, *Synodicon.*, tom. I., p. vi. *et seqq.* (Bev. *Works*, tom. II., Append. p. xiii. *et seqq.* [Anglo.-Cath. Lib.]).

the 16th and 17th of Antioch, the 95th and 96th. Nice 20, Ancyra 25, Neocæsarea 14, Gangra 20 ; all which make 79. Next come those of Antioch, the 4th and 5th of which therefore will be respectively the 83d and 84th, and the 16th and 17th the 95th and 96th.

The fact of the existence of such a code does not prove by any means that it was the only collection extant at the time nor that it was universally known. In fact we have good reason, as we shall see in connexion with the Council of Sardica, to believe that in many codices, probably especially in the West, the canons of that council followed immediately after those of Nice, and that without any break or note whatever. But we know that the number of canons attributed to Nice must have been twenty or else the numbering of the codex read from at Chalcedon would be quite inexplicable. It would naturally suggest itself to the mind that possibly the divergence in the canonical codes was the result of the local feelings of East and West with regard to the decrees of Sardica. But this supposition, plausible as it appears, must be rejected, since at the Quinisext Council, where it is not disputed there was a strong anti-Western bias, the canons of Sardica are expressly enumerated among those which the fathers receive as of Ecumenical authority. It will be noticed that the code set forth by the Council in Trullo differs from the code used at Chalcedon by having the so-called " Canons of the Apostles " prefixed to it, and by having a large number of other canons, including those of Sardica, appended, of which more will be said when treating of that Council.

The order which I have followed may justly be considered as that of the earliest accepted *codex canonum*, at least of the East.

THE COUNCIL OF ANCYRA

A.D. 314.

Emperors.—CONSTANTINE and LICINIUS.

Elenchus.

Historical Note.

The Canons with the Ancient Epitome and Notes.
Excursus to Canon XIX on Digamy.

HISTORICAL NOTE.

Soon after the death of the Emperor Maximin,[1] a council was held at Ancyra, the capital of Galatia. Only about a dozen bishops were present, and the lists of subscriptions which are found appended to the canons are not to be depended on, being evidently in their present form of later authorship ; as has been shewn by the Ballerini. If we may at all trust the lists, it would seem that nearly every part of Syria and Asia Minor was represented, and that therefore the council while small in numbers was of considerable weight. It is not certain whether Vitalis, (bishop of Antioch,) presided or Marcellus, who was at the time bishop of Ancyra. The honour is by the *Libellus Synodicus* assigned to the latter.

The disciplinary decrees of this council possess a singular interest as being the first enacted after the ceasing of the persecution of the Christians and as providing for the proper treatment of the lapsed. Recently two papyri have been recovered, containing the official certificates granted by the Roman government to those who had lapsed and offered sacrifice. These apostates were obliged to acknowledge in public their adhesion to the national religion of the empire, and then were provided with a document certifying to this fact to keep them from further trouble. Dr. Harnack (*Preussische Jahrbücher*) writing of the yielding of the lapsed says :

"The Church condemned this as lying and denial of the faith, and after the termination of the persecution, these unhappy people were partly excommunicated, partly obliged to submit to severe discipline. Who would ever suppose that the records of their shame would come down to our time?—and yet it has actually happened. Two of these papers have been preserved, contrary to all likelihood, by the sands of Egypt which so carefully keep what has been entrusted to them. The first was found by Krebs in a heap of papyrus, that had come to Berlin; the other was found by Wessely in the papyrus collection of Archduke Rainer. 'I, Diogenes, have constantly sacrificed and made offerings, and have eaten in your presence the sacrificial meat, and I petition you to give me a certificate.' Who to-day, without deep emotion, can read this paper and measure the trouble and terror of heart under which the Christians of that day collapsed?"

---

[1] Not " Maximilian," as in the English translation of Hefele's *History of the Councils*, Vol. I., p. 199 (revised edition). Max- imian died in 310, Galerius in 311, Maxentius in 312, and Diocletian in 313.

THE CANONS OF THE COUNCIL OF ANCYRA.

(Found in Labbe and Cossart's Concilia, *and all Collections, in the Greek text together with several Latin versions of different dates. Also in Justellus and Beveridge. There will also be found annotations by Routh, and a reprint of the notes of Christopher Justellus and of Bp. Beveridge in Vol. IV. of the* Reliquiæ Sacræ, *ed. altera, 1846.)*

CANON I.

WITH regard to those presbyters who have offered sacrifices and afterwards returned to the conflict, not with hypocrisy, but in sincerity, it has seemed good that they may retain the honour of their chair; provided they had not used management, arrangement, or persuasion, so as to appear to be subjected to the torture, when it was applied only in seeming and pretence. Nevertheless it is not lawful for them to make the oblation, nor to preach, nor in short to perform any act of sacerdotal function.

NOTES.

ANCIENT EPITOME TO CANONS I. AND II.

Presbyters and deacons who offered sacrifice and afterwards renewed the contest for the truth shall have only their seat and honour, but shall not perform any of the holy functions.

ZONARAS.

Of those that yielded to the tyrants in the persecution, and offered sacrifice, some, after having been subjected to torture, being unable to withstand to the end its force and intensity, were conquered, and denied the faith; some, through effeminacy, before they experienced any suffering, gave way, and lest they should seem to sacrifice voluntarily they persuaded the executioners, either by bribes or entreaties, to manifest perhaps a greater degree of severity against them, and seemingly to apply the torture to them, in order that sacrificing under these circumstances they might seem to have denied Christ, conquered by force, and not through effeminacy.

HEFELE.

It was quite justifiable, and in accordance with the ancient and severe discipline of the Church, when this Synod no longer allowed priests, even when sincerely penitent, to discharge priestly functions. It was for this same reason that the two Spanish bishops, Martial and Basilides, were deposed, and that the judgment given against them was confirmed in 254 by an African synod held under St. Cyprian.

The reader will notice how clearly the functions of a presbyter are set forth in this canon as they were understood at that time, they were "to offer" (προσφέρειν), "to preach" (ὁμιλεῖν), and "to perform any act of sacerdotal function" (λειτουργεῖν τι τῶν ἱερατικῶν λειτουργιῶν).

This canon is in the *Corpus Juris Canonici. Decretum.* Pars I., Dist. l., c. xxxii.

CANON II.

IT is likewise decreed that deacons who have sacrificed and afterwards resumed the conflict, shall enjoy their other honours, but shall abstain from every sacred ministry, neither bringing forth the bread and the cup, nor making proclamations. Nevertheless, if any of the bishops shall observe in them distress of mind and meek humiliation, it shall be lawful to the bishops to grant more indulgence, or to take away [what has been granted].

For Ancient Epitome see above under Canon I.

In this canon the work and office of a deacon as then understood is set forth, viz.: "to

bring forth" (whatever that may mean) "bread or wine" (ἄρτον ἢ ποτήριον ἀναφέρειν) and "to act the herald" (κηρύσσειν). There is considerable difference of opinion as to the meaning of the first of these expressions. It was always the duty of the deacon to serve the priest, especially when he ministered the Holy Communion, but this phrase may refer to one of two such ministrations, either to bringing the bread and wine to the priest at the offertory, and this is the view of Van Espen, or to the distribution of the Holy Sacrament to the people. It has been urged that the deacon had ceased to administer the species of bread before the time of this council, but Hefele shews that the custom had not entirely died out.

If I may be allowed to offer a suggestion, the use of the disjunctive ἤ seems rather to point to the administration of the sacrament than to the bringing of the oblations at the offertory.

The other diaconal function "to act the herald" refers to the reading of the Holy Gospel, and to the numerous proclamations made by the deacons at mass both according to the Greek and Latin Rite.

This canon is in the *Corpus Juris Canonici* united with the foregoing. *Decretum.*, Pars I., Dist. 1., c. xxxii.

CANON III.

THOSE who have fled and been apprehended, or have been betrayed by their servants; or those who have been otherwise despoiled of their goods, or have endured tortures, or have been imprisoned and abused, declaring themselves to be Christians; or who have been forced to receive something which their persecutors violently thrust into their hands, or meat [offered to idols], continually professing that they were Christians; and who, by their whole apparel, and demeanour, and humility of life, always give evidence of grief at what has happened; these persons, inasmuch as they are free from sin, are not to be repelled from the communion; and if, through an extreme strictness or ignorance of some things, they have been repelled, let them forthwith be re-admitted. This shall hold good alike of clergy and laity. It has also been considered whether laymen who have fallen under the same compulsion may be admitted to orders, and we have decreed that, since they have in no respect been guilty, they may be ordained; provided their past course of life be found to have been upright.

NOTES.

ANCIENT EPITOME OF CANON III.

Those who have been subjected to torments and have suffered violence, and have eaten food offered to idols after being tyrannized over, shall not be deprived of communion. And laymen who have endured the same sufferings, since they have in no way transgressed, if they wish to be ordained, they may be, if otherwise they be blameless.

In the translation the word "abused" is given as the equivalent of περισχισθέντας, which Zonaras translated, "if their clothes have been torn from their bodies," and this is quite accurate if the reading is correct, but Routh has found in the Bodleian several MSS. which had περισχεθέντας. Hefele adopts this reading and translates "declaring themselves to be Christians but who have subsequently been vanquished, whether their oppressors have by force put incense into their hands or have compelled them, etc." Hammond translates "and have been harassed by their persecutors forcibly putting something into their hands or who have been compelled, etc." The phrase is obscure at best with either reading.

This canon is in the *Corpus Juris Canonici* united to the two previous canons, *Decretum*, Pars I., Dist. 1., c. xxxii.

CANON IV.

CONCERNING those who have been forced to sacrifice, and who, in addition, have partaken of feasts in honour of the idols; as many as were haled away, but afterwards went up with a cheerful countenance, and wore their costliest apparel, and partook with indifference of the feast provided; it is decreed that all such be hearers for one year, and prostrators for three years, and that they communicate in prayers only for two years, and then return to full communion.

NOTES.

ANCIENT EPITOME OF CANON IV.

Such as have been led away and have with joy gone up and eaten are to be in subjection for six years.

In the Greek the word for "full communion" is τὸ τέλειον ("the perfection"), an expression frequently used by early writers to denote the Holy Communion. *Vide* Suicer, *Thesaurus ad h. v.*

BINGHAM.

[The Holy Communion was so called as being] that sacred mystery which unites us to Christ, and gives us the most consummate perfection that we are capable of in this world.

CANON V.

As many, however, as went up in mourning attire and sat down and ate, weeping throughout the whole entertainment, if they have fulfilled the three years as prostrators, let them be received without oblation ; and if they did not eat, let them be prostrators two years, and in the third year let them communicate without oblation, so that in the fourth year they may be received into full communion. But the bishops have the right, after considering the character of their conversion, either to deal with them more leniently, or to extend the time. But, first of all, let their life before and since be thoroughly examined, and let the indulgence be determined accordingly.

NOTES.

ANCIENT EPITOME OF CANON V.

Those who have gone up in mourning weeds, and have eaten with tears, shall be prostrators for three years ; but if they have not eaten, then for two years. And according to their former and after life, whether good or evil, they shall find the bishop gentle or severe.

Herbst and Routh have been followed by many in supposing that "oblation" (προσφορά) in this canon refers to the sacrament of the altar. But this seems to be a mistake, as the word while often used to denote the whole act of the celebration of the Holy Eucharist, is not used to mean the receiving alone of that sacrament.

Suicer (*Thesaurus* s. v. προσφορά) translates "They may take part in divine worship, but not actively," that is, "they may not mingle their offerings with those of the faithful."

HEFELE.

But as those who cannot present their offerings during the sacrifice are excluded from the communion, the complete meaning of the canon is : "They may be present at divine service, but may neither offer nor communicate with the faithful."

CANON VI.

CONCERNING those who have yielded merely upon threat of penalties and of the confiscation of their goods, or of banishment, and have sacrificed, and who till this present time have not repented nor been converted, but who now, at the time of this synod, have approached with a purpose of conversion, it is decreed that they be received as hearers till the Great Day, and that after the Great Day they be prostrators for three years, and for two years more communicate without oblation, and then come to full communion, so as to complete the period of six full years. And if any have been admitted to penance before this synod, let the beginning of the six years be reckoned to them from that time. Nevertheless, if there should be any danger or prospect of death whether from disease or any other cause, let them be received, but under limitation.

NOTES.

ANCIENT EPITOME OF CANON VI.

A man who yielded to threats alone, and has sacrificed, and then repented let him for five years be a prostrator.

ZONARAS.

But should any of those debarred from communion as penitents be seized with illness or in any other way be brought nigh to

death, they may be received to communion ;
but in accordance with this law or distinction, that if they escape death and recover
their health, they shall be altogether deprived
again of communion until they have finished
their six years penance.

HAMMOND.

"The Great Day," that is, Easter Day. The
great reverence which the Primitive Church
from the earliest ages felt for the holy festival of Easter is manifested by the application
of the epithet Great, to everything connected
with it. The preceding Friday, i.e., Good
Friday, was called the Great Preparation, the
Saturday, the Great Sabbath, and the whole
week, the Great Week.

CANON VII.

CONCERNING those who have partaken at a heathen feast in a place appointed for
heathens, but who have brought and eaten their own meats, it is decreed that they be
received after they have been prostrators two years ; but whether with oblation, every
bishop must determine after he has made examination into the rest of their life.

NOTES.

ANCIENT EPITOME OF CANON VII.

*If anyone having his own food, shall eat it
with heathen at their feasts, let him be a prostrator for two years.*

HEFELE.

Several Christians tried with worldly prudence, to take a middle course. On the one
hand, hoping to escape persecution, they were
present at the feasts of the heathen sacrifices,
which were held in the buildings adjoining
the temples ; and on the other, in order to
appease their consciences, they took their own
food, and touched nothing that had been offered to the gods. These Christians forgot
that St. Paul had ordered that meats sacrificed
to the gods should be avoided, not because
they were tainted in themselves, as the idols
were nothing, but from another, and in fact a
twofold reason : 1st, Because, in partaking
of them, some had still the idols in their
hearts, that is to say, were still attached to
the worship of idols, and thereby sinned ; and
2dly, Because others scandalized their brethren, and sinned in that way. To these two
reasons a third may be added, namely, the
hypocrisy and the duplicity of those Christians who wished to appear heathens, and
nevertheless to remain Christians. The Synod
punished them with two years of penance in
the third degree, and gave to each bishop the
right, at the expiration of this time, either to
admit them to communion, or to make them
remain some time longer in the fourth degree.

CANON VIII.

LET those who have twice or thrice sacrificed under compulsion, be prostrators four
years, and communicate without oblation two years, and the seventh year they shall be
received to full communion.

NOTES.

ANCIENT EPITOME OF CANON VIII.

*Whoever has sacrificed a second or third
time, but has been led thereto by force, shall be a
prostrator for seven years.*

VAN ESPEN.

This canon shews how in the Church it
was a received principle that greater pen-
ances ought to be imposed for the frequent
commission of the same crime, and consequently it was then believed that the number
of times the sin had been committed should
be expressed in confession, that the penance
might correspond to the sin, greater or less
as the case may be, and the time of probation
be accordingly protracted or remitted.

CANON IX.

As many as have not merely apostatized, but have risen against their brethren and
forced them [to apostatize], and have been guilty of their being forced, let these for
three years take the place of hearers, and for another term of six years that of prostra-

tors, and for another year let them communicate without oblation, in order that, when they have fulfilled the space of ten years, they may partake of the communion; but during this time the rest of their life must also be enquired into.

NOTES.

ANCIENT EPITOME OF CANON IX.

Whoever has not only sacrificed voluntarily but also has forced another to sacrifice, shall be a prostrator for ten years.

[It will be noticed that this epitome does not agree with the canon, although Aristenus does not note the discrepancy.]

VAN ESPEN.

From this canon we are taught that the circumstances of the sin that has been committed are to be taken into account in assigning the penance.

ARISTENUS.

When the ten years are past, he is worthy of perfection, and fit to receive the divine sacraments. Unless perchance an examination of the rest of his life demands his exclusion from the divine communion.

CANON X.

THEY who have been made deacons, declaring when they were ordained that they must marry, because they were not able to abide so, and who afterwards have married, shall continue in their ministry, because it was conceded to them by the bishop. But if any were silent on this matter, undertaking at their ordination to abide as they were, and afterwards proceeded to marriage, these shall cease from the diaconate.

NOTES.

ANCIENT EPITOME OF CANON X.

Whoso is to be ordained deacon, if he has before announced to the bishop that he cannot persevere unmarried, let him marry and let him be a deacon; but if he shall have kept silence, should he take a wife afterwards let him be cast out.

VAN ESPEN.

The case proposed to the synod and decided in this canon was as follows: When the bishop was willing to ordain two to the diaconate, one of them declared that he did not intend to bind himself to preserving perpetual continence, but intended to get married, because he had not the power to remain continent. The other said nothing. The bishop laid his hands on each and conferred the diaconate.

After the ordination it fell out that both got married, the question propounded is, What must be done in each case? The synod ruled that he who had made protestation at his ordination should remain in his ministry, " because of the license of the bishop," that is that he might contract matrimony after the reception of the diaconate. With regard to him who kept silence the synod declares that he should cease from his ministry.

The resolution of the synod to the first question shews that there was a general law which bound the deacons to continence; but this synod judged it meet that the bishops for just cause might dispense with this law, and this license or dispensation was deemed to have been given by the bishop if he ordained him after his protestation at the time of his ordination that he intended to be married, because he could not remain as he was; giving by the act of ordination his tacit approbation. Moreover from this decision it is also evident that not only was the ordained deacon allowed to enter but also to use matrimony after his ordination. . . . Moreover the deacon who after this protestation entered and used matrimony, not only remained a deacon, but continued in the exercise of his ministry.

On the whole subject of Clerical Celibacy in the Early Church see the Excursus devoted to that matter.

This canon is found in the *Corpus Juris Canonici*. *Decretum* Pars I., Dist. xxviii, c. viii.

CANON XI.

It is decreed that virgins who have been betrothed, and who have afterwards been carried off by others, shall be restored to those to whom they had formerly been betrothed, even though they may have suffered violence from the ravisher.

NOTES.

ANCIENT EPITOME OF CANON XI.

If a young girl who is engaged be stolen away by force by another man, let her be restored to the former.

HEFELE.

This canon treats only of betrothed women (of the *sponsalia de futuro*) not of those who are married (of the *sponsalia de præsenti*). In the case of the latter there could be no doubt as to the duty of restitution. The man who was betrothed was, moreover, at liberty to receive his affianced bride who had been carried off or not.

JOHNSON.

Here Balsamon puts in a very proper *cave*, viz.: If he to whom she was espoused demand her to be his wife.

Compare St. Basil's twenty-second canon in his letter to Amphilochius, where it is so ruled.

CANON XII.

It is decreed that they who have offered sacrifice before their baptism, and were afterwards baptized, may be promoted to orders, inasmuch as they have been cleansed.

NOTES.

ANCIENT EPITOME OF CANON XII.

Whoso has sacrificed before his baptism, after it shall be guiltless.

HEFELE.

This canon does not speak generally of all those who sacrificed before baptism ; for if a heathen sacrificed before having embraced Christianity, he certainly could not be reproached for it after his admission. It was quite a different case with a catechumen, who had already declared for Christianity, but who, during the persecution had lost courage, and sacrificed. In this case it might be asked whether he could still be admitted to the priesthood. The Council decided that a baptized catechumen could afterwards be promoted to holy orders.

CANON XIII.

It is not lawful for Chorepiscopi to ordain presbyters or deacons, and most assuredly not presbyters of a city, without the commission of the bishop given in writing, in another parish.

NOTES.

ANCIENT EPITOME OF CANON XIII.

A chorepiscopus is not to ordain without the consent of the bishop.

HEFELE.

If the first part of the thirteenth canon is easy to understand, the second, on the contrary, presents a great difficulty ; for a priest of a town could not in any case have the power of consecrating priests and deacons, least of all in a strange diocese. Many of the most learned men have, for this reason, supposed that the Greek text of the second half of the canon, as we have read it, is incorrect or defective. It wants, say they, ποιεῖν τι, or *aliquid agere, i.e., to complete a religious function.* To confirm this supposition, they have appealed to several ancient versions, especially to that of Isidore : *sed nec presbyteris civitatis sine episcopi præcepto amplius aliquid imperare, vel sine auctoritate literarum ejus in unaquaque* (some read ἐν ἑκάστῃ instead of ἐν ἑτέρᾳ) *parochia aliquid agere.* The ancient Roman MS. of the canons, *Codex Canonum*, has the same reading, only that it has *provincia* instead of *parochia*. Fulgentius Ferrandus, deacon of Carthage, who long ago made a collection of canons, translates in the same way in his *Breviatio Canonum: Ut presbyteri civitatis sine jussu episcopi nihil jubeant, nec in unaquaque parochia aliquid agant.* Van Espen has explained this canon in the same way.

Routh has given another interpretation. He maintained that there was not a word missing in this canon, but that at the commencement one ought to read, according to several MSS. χωρεπισκόποις in the dative, and further down ἀλλὰ μὴν μηδὲ instead of ἀλλα μηδὲ then πρεσβυτέρους (in the accusative) πόλεως and finally ἑκάστῃ instead of ἑτέρᾳ, and that we

must therefore translate, "*Chorepiscopi* are not permitted to consecrate priests and deacons (for the country) still less (ἀλλὰ μὴν μηδὲ) can they consecrate priests for the town without the consent of the bishop of the place." The Greek text, thus modified according to some MSS., especially those in the Bodleian Library, certainly gives a good meaning. Still ἀλλὰ μὴν μηδὲ does not mean, *but still less:* it means, *but certainly not,* which makes a considerable difference.

Besides this, it can very seldom have happened that the *chorepiscopi* ordained presbyters or deacons for a town; and if so, they were already forbidden, at least implicitly, in the first part of the canon.

CANON XIV.

It is decreed that among the clergy, presbyters and deacons who abstain from flesh shall taste of it, and afterwards, if they shall so please, may abstain. But if they disdain it, and will not even eat herbs served with flesh, but disobey the canon, let them be removed from their order.

NOTES.

ANCIENT EPITOME OF CANON XIV.

A priest who is an abstainer from flesh, let him merely taste it and so let him abstain. But if he will not taste even the vegetables cooked with the meat let him be deposed (πεπάνσθω).

There is a serious dispute about the reading of the Greek text. I have followed Routh, who, relying on three MSS. the *Collectio* of John of Antioch and the Latin versions, reads εἰ δὲ βδελύσσοιντο instead of the εἰ δὲ βούλοιντο

of the ordinary text, which as Bp. Beveridge had pointed out before has no meaning unless a μὴ be introduced.

Zonaras points out that the canon chiefly refers to the Love feasts.

I cannot agree with Hefele in his translation of the last clause. He makes the reference to "this present canon," I think it is clearly to the 53 (52) of the so-called Canons of the Apostles, τῷ κανόνι "the well-known canon."

CANON XV.

Concerning things belonging to the church, which presbyters may have sold when there was no bishop, it is decreed that the Church property shall be reclaimed; and it shall be in the discretion of the bishop whether it is better to receive the purchase price, or not; for oftentimes the revenue of the things sold might yield them the greater value.

NOTES.

ANCIENT EPITOME OF CANON XV.

Sales of Church goods made by presbyters are null, and the matter shall rest with the bishop.

HEFELE.

If the purchaser of ecclesiastical properties has realized more by the temporary revenue of such properties than the price of the purchase, the Synod thinks there is no occasion to restore him this price, as he has already

received a sufficient indemnity from the revenue, and as, according to the rules then in force, *interest* drawn from the purchase money was not permitted. Besides, the purchaser had done wrong in buying ecclesiastical property during the vacancy of a see (*sede vacante*). Beveridge and Routh have shown that in the text ἀνακαλεῖσθαι and πρόσοδον must be read.[1]

---

[1] ἀνακαλεῖσθαν for ἀναβαλεῖσθαι and πρόσοδον for εἴσοδον.

CANON XVI.

LET those who have ꙗeen or who are guilty of bestial lusts, if they have sinned while under twenty years of age, be prostrators fifteen years, and afterwards communicate in prayers; then, having passed five years in this communion, let them have a share in the oblation. But let their life as prostrators be examined, and so let them receive indulgence; and if any have been insatiable in their crimes, then let their time of prostration be prolonged. And if any who have passed this age and had wives, have fallen into this sin, let them be prostrators twenty-five years, and then communicate in prayers; and, after they have been five years in the communion of prayers, let them share the oblation. And if any married men of more than fifty years of age have so sinned, let them be admitted to communion only at the point of death.

NOTES.

ANCIENT EPITOME OF CANON XVI.

Whoever shall have commerce with animals devoid of reason being younger than twenty, shall be a prostrator for fifteen years If he is over that age and has a wife when he falls into this wickedness he shall be a prostrator for twenty-five years. But the married man who shall do so when over fifty years of age, shall be a prostrator to his life's end.

It is interesting to compare with this, as Van Espen does, the canon of the Church of England set forth in the tenth century under King Edgar, where, Part II., canon xvi., we read—

" If any one twenty years of age shall defile himself with a beast, or shall commit sodomy let him fast fifteen years; and if he have a wife and be forty years of age, and shall do such a deed let him abstain now and fast all the rest of his life, neither shall he presume until he is dying to receive the Lord's body. Youths and fools who shall do any such thing shall be soundly trounced."

CANON XVII.

DEFILERS of themselves with beasts, being also leprous, who have infected others [with the leprosy of this crime], the holy Synod commands to pray among the hiemantes.

NOTES.

ANCIENT EPITOME OF CANON XVII.

A leper who goes in to a beast or even to leprous women, shall pray with the hybernantes.

Λεπρώσαντας is from λεπρόω not from λεπράω and therefore cannot mean "have been lepers," but "have made others rough and scabby." It is only in the passive and in Alexandrian Greek that it has the meaning to become leprous. *Vide* Liddell and Scott.

There seems but little doubt that the word is to be understood spiritually as suggested above.

The last word of the canon is also a source of confusion. Both Beveridge and Routh understand by the χειμαζόμενοι those possessed with devils. Suicer however (*Thesaurus*) thinks that the penitents of the lowest degree are intended, who had no right to enter the church, but were exposed in the open porch to the inclemencies (χειμών) of the weather. But, after all it matters little, as the possessed also were forced to remain in the same place, and shared the same name.

Besides the grammatical reason for the meaning of λεπρώσαντας given above there is another argument of Hefele's, as follows:

HEFELE.

It is clear that λεπρώσαντας cannot possibly mean "those who have been lepers"; for there is no reason to be seen why those who were cured of that malady should have to remain outside the church among the flentes. Secondly, it is clear that the words λεπρούς ὄντας, etc. are added to give force to the expression ἀλογευσάμενοι. The preceding canon had decreed different penalties for different kinds of ἀλογευσάμενοι. But that pronounced by canon xvii. being much severer than the preceding ones, the ἀλογευσάμενοι of this canon must be greater sinners than those of the former one. This greater guilt cannot consist in the fact of a literal leprosy; for this malady was not a consequence of bestiality. But their sin was evidently greater when they tempted others to commit it. It is therefore λέπρα in the figurative sense that we are to understand, and our canon thus means; "Those who were spiritually leprous through this sin, and tempting others to commit it made them leprous."

CANON XVIII.

IF any who have been constituted bishops, but have not been received by the parish to which they were designated, shall invade other parishes and wrong the constituted [bishops] there, stirring up seditions against them, let such persons be suspended from office and communion. But if they are willing to accept a seat among the presbyterate, where they formerly were presbyters, let them not be deprived of that honour. But if they shall act seditiously against the bishops established there, the honour of the presbyterate also shall be taken from them and themselves expelled.

NOTES.

ANCIENT EPITOME OF CANON XVIII.

If a bishop who has been duly constituted, is not received by the Church to which he was elected, but gives trouble to other bishops, let him be excommunicated.

If he wishes to be numbered among the presbyters, let him be so numbered. But if he shall be at outs with the bishops duly constituted there, let him be deprived of the honour of being even a presbyter.

The word I have translated "suspended from office and communion" is ἀφορίζεσθαι. Suicer in his *Thesaurus* shews that this word does not mean only, as some have supposed, a deprivation of office and dignity (e.g., Van Espen), but also an exclusion from the communion of the Church.

CANON XIX.

IF any persons who profess virginity shall disregard their profession, let them fulfil the term of digamists. And, moreover, we prohibit women who are virgins from living with men as sisters.

NOTES.

ANCIENT EPITOME OF CANON XIX.

Whoever has professed virginity and afterwards annuls it, let him be cut off for four years. And virgins shall not go[1] to any as to brothers.

HAMMOND.

According to some of the ancient canons digamists were to be suspended from communion for one or two years, though Beveridge and others doubt whether the rule was not meant to apply to such marriages only as were contracted before a former one was dissolved. Bingham thinks that it was intended to discountenance marrying after an unlawful divorce. (*Ant.*, Bk. xv, c. iv., § 18.)[2]

HEFELE.

The first part of this canon regards all young persons—men as well as women—who have taken a vow of virginity, and who, having thus, so to speak, betrothed themselves to God are guilty of a *quasi* digamy in violating that promise. They must therefore incur the punishment of digamy (*successiva*) which, according to St. Basil the Great, consisted of one year's seclusion.

This canon is found in Gratian's *Decretum* (P. II., Causa xxvii., Q. i., c. xxiv.) as follows: "As many as have professed virginity and have broken their vow and contemned their profession shall be treated as digamists, that is as those who have contracted a second marriage."

---

[1] Aristenus understands this to mean to "live with," using the verb συναναστρέφεσθαι.
[2] This view of Bingham's would seem to be untenable, since the penance would have been for adultery not for digamy had the former marriage still been in force.

EXCURSUS ON SECOND MARRIAGES, CALLED DIGAMY.

To distinguish contemporaneous from successive bigamy I shall use throughout this volume the word " digamy " to denote the latter, and shall thus avoid much confusion which otherwise is unavoidable.

The whole subject of second, and even of third and fourth marriages has a great interest for the student of early ecclesiastical legislation, and I shall therefore treat the matter here (as I shall hope) sufficiently and refer the reader for its fuller treatment to books more especially upon the subject.

The general position of the Church seems to have been to discourage all second marriages, and to point to a single matrimonial connexion as the more excellent way. But at the same time the principle that the marriage obligation is severed by death was universally recognised, and however much such fresh marriages may have been disapproved of, such disapproval did not rest upon any supposed adulterous character in the new connexion. I cite a portion of an admirable article upon the subject by an English barrister of Lincoln's Inn.

(J. M. Ludlow, in Smith and Cheetham, *Dictionary of Christian Antiquities, sub voce* Digamy.)

Although among the earlier Romans [1] there was one form of marriage which was indissoluble, viz., that by *confarreatio*, still generally a second marriage either after death or divorce was by no means viewed with disfavour. . . . Meanwhile an intensifying spirit of asceticism was leading many in the Church to a condemnation of second marriage in all cases. Minucius Felix (*Octavius*, c. 31, § 5) only professes on behalf of the Christians a preference for monogamy. Clement of Alexandria (A.D. 150–220) seems to confine the term marriage to the first lawful union (*Stromata*, Bk. ii.). . . . It would seem, however, that when these views were carried to the extent of absolute prohibition of second marriages generally by several heretical sects, the Montanists (see Augustine, *De Hæresibus*, c. xxvi.), the Cathari (*ib.*, c. xxxviii.), and a portion at least of the Novatianists (see Cotel., *Patr. Apol.*, vol. i., p. 91, n. 16) the Church saw the necessity of not fixing such a yoke on the necks of the laity. The forbiddance of second marriage, or its assimilation to fornication, was treated as one of the marks of heresy (Augustin. *u. s.*; and see also his *De Bono Vid.*, c. vi.). The sentiment of Augustine (in the last referred to passage) may be taken to express the Church's judgment at the close of the fourth century : " Second marriages are not to be condemned, but had in less honour," and see also Epiphanius, in his *Exposition of the Catholic Faith*.

To these remarks of Mr. Ludlow's, I may add that St. Ambrose had written (*De Viduis*, c. xi.), " We do not prohibit second marriages, but we do not approve marriages frequently reiterated." St. Jerome had spoken still more strongly (Ep. lxvii., *Apol. pro libris adv. Jovin.*), " I do not condemn digamists, or even trigamists or, if such a thing can be said, octagamists." It does not seem that the penance which was imposed in the East upon those entering into second nuptials was imposed in the West. The *Corpus Juris Canonici* contains two decretals, one of Alexander III. and another of Urban III., forbidding priests to give the nuptial benediction in cases of reiterated marriage. In the East at second marriages the

---

[1] The reader may recall the words of Dido : Ille meos, primusqui me sibi junxit, amores
Abstulit ; ille habeat secum servetque sepulcro.

benediction of the crown is omitted and "propitiatory prayers" are to be said. Mr. Ludlow points out that in the "Sanctions and Decrees," falsely attributed to the Council of Nice and found in Mansi (vol. ii., col. 1029) it is expressly stated that widowers and widows may marry, but that "the blessing of the crowns is not to be imparted to them, for this is only once given, at first marriages, and is not to be repeated. . . . But if one of them be not a widower or widow, let such one alone receive the benediction with the paranymphs, those whom he will."

CANON XX.

IF the wife of anyone has committed adultery or if any man commit adultery it seems fit that he shall be restored to full communion after seven years passed in the prescribed degrees [of penance].

NOTES.

ANCIENT EPITOME OF CANON XX.

An adulteress and an adulterer are to be cut off for seven years.

HEFELE.

The simplest explanation of this canon is "that the man or woman who has violated the marriage bond shall undergo a seven years' penance"; but many reject this explanation, because the text says αὐτὸν τύχειν and consequently can refer only to the husband. Fleury and Routh think the canon speaks, as does the seventieth of Elvira, of a woman who has broken the marriage tie with the knowledge and consent of her husband. The husband would therefore in this case be punished for this permission, just as if he had himself committed adultery. Van Espen has given another explanation: "That he who marries a woman already divorced for adultery is as criminal as if he had himself committed adultery." But this explanation appears to us more forced than that already given; and we think that the Greek commentators Balsamon and Zonaras were right in giving the explanation we have offered first as the most natural. They think that the Synod punished every adulterer, whether man or woman, by a seven years' penance. There is no reason for making a mistake because only the word αὐτὸν occurs in the passage in which the penalty is fixed; for αὐτὸν here means the guilty party, and applies equally to the woman and the man: besides, in the preceding canon the masculine ὅσοι ἐπαγγελλόμενοι includes young men and young women also. It is probable that the Trullan Synod of 692, in forming its eighty-seventh canon, had in view the twentieth of Ancyra. The sixty-ninth canon of Elvira condemned to a lighter punishment—only five years of penance—him who had been only once guilty of adultery.

CANON XXI.

CONCERNING women who commit fornication, and destroy that which they have conceived, or who are employed in making drugs for abortion, a former decree excluded them until the hour of death, and to this some have assented. Nevertheless, being desirous to use somewhat greater lenity, we have ordained that they fulfil ten years [of penance], according to the prescribed degrees.

NOTES.

ANCIENT EPITOME OF CANON XXI.

Harlots taking injurious medicines are to be subjected to penance for ten years.

The phrase "and to this some have assented" is the translation of Hervetus, Van Espen, and Hefele. Dr. Routh suggests to understand ἅι and translate, "the same punishment will be inflicted on those who assist in causing miscarriages," but this seems rather an unnatural and strained rendering of the Greek.

CANON XXII.

CONCERNING wilful murderers let them remain prostrators; but at the end of life let them be indulged with full communion.

NOTES.

ANCIENT EPITOME OF CANON XXII.

A voluntary homicide may at the last attain perfection.[1]

VAN ESPEN.

It is noteworthy how singularly appositely Constantine] Harmenopulus the Scholiast in the *Epitom. Canonum.*, Sect. v., tit. 3, tells the following story: "In the time of the Patriarch Luke, a certain bishop gave absolution in writing to a soldier who had committed voluntary homicide, after a very short time of penace; and afterwards when he was accused before the synod of having done so, he defended himself by citing the canon which gives bishops the power of remitting or increasing the length of their penance to penitents. But he was told in answer that this was granted indeed to pontiffs but not that they should use it without examination, and with too great lenity. Wherefore the synod subjected the soldier to the canonical penance and the bishop it mulcted for a certain time, bidding him cease from the exercise of his ministry."

CANON XXIII.

CONCERNING involuntary homicides, a former decree directs that they be received to full communion after seven years [of penance], according to the prescribed degrees; but this second one, that they fulfil a term of five years.

NOTES.

ANCIENT EPITOME OF CANON XXIII.

An involuntary homicide shall be subjected to penance for five years.

VAN ESPEN.

Of voluntary and involuntary homicides St. Basil treats at length in his *Canonical Epistle ad Amphilochium,* can. viii., lvi. and lvii., and fixes the time of penance at twenty years for voluntary and ten years for involuntary homicides. It is evident that the penance given for this crime varied in different churches, although it is clear from the great length of the penance, how enormous the crime was considered, no light or short penance being sufficient.

CANON XXIV.

THEY who practice divination, and follow the customs of the heathen, or who take men to their houses for the invention of sorceries, or for lustrations, fall under the canon of five years' [penance], according to the prescribed degrees; that is, three years as prostrators, and two of prayer without oblation.

NOTES.

ANCIENT EPITOME OF CANON XXIV.

Whoso uses vaticination and whoso introduces anyone into his house for the sake of making a poison or a lustration let him be subject to penance for five years.

I read ἐθνῶν for χρόνων and accordingly translate "of the heathen."

VAN ESPEN.

It is greatly to be desired that bishops and pastors to-day would take example from the fathers of Ancyra and devote their attention strenuously to eliminate superstition from the people, and would expound with animation to the people the enormity of this crime.

---

[1] That is, receive the Sacraments.

CANON XXV.

ONE who had betrothed a maiden, corrupted her sister, so that she conceived. After that he married his betrothed, but she who had been corrupted hanged herself. The parties to this affair were ordered to be received among the co-standers after ten years [of penance] according to the prescribed degrees.

NOTES.

ANCIENT EPITOME TO CANON XXV.

A certain body after being engaged to marry a young girl, violates her sister and then takes her to wife. The first is suffocated. All who were cognizant of the affair are to be subject to penance for ten years.

I have followed the usual translation "hanged herself," which is the ordinary dictionary-meaning of ἀπάγχω, but Hefele says that it signifies any and every variety of suicides.

BALSAMON.

In this case we have many nefarious crimes committed, fornication, unlawful marriage [i.e. with the sister of one's mistress] and murder. In that case [mentioned by St. Basil in Canon lxxviij. where only seven years penance is enjoined] there is only a nefarious marriage [i.e. with a wife's sister].

THE COUNCIL OF NEOCÆSAREA

A.D. 315   (circa).

(Hefele thinks somewhat later, but before 325.)

Elenchus.

Historical Note.
The Canons with the Ancient Epitome and Notes.

HISTORICAL NOTE.

(Zonaras and Balsamon prefix to the canons this note.)

The Synod gathered together at Neocæsarea, which is a city of Pontus, is next in order after that of Ancyra, and earlier in date than the rest, even than the First Ecumenical Synod at Nice. In this synod the Holy Fathers gathered together, among whom was the holy Martyr Basil, bishop of Amasea, adopted canons for the establishing of ecclesiastical order as follow—

THE CANONS OF THE HOLY AND BLESSED FATHERS WHO ASSEMBLED AT NEOCÆSAREA, WHICH ARE INDEED LATER IN DATE THAN THOSE MADE AT ANCYRA, BUT MORE ANCIENT THAN THE NICENE: HOWEVER, THE SYNOD OF NICE HAS BEEN PLACED BEFORE THEM ON ACCOUNT OF ITS PECULIAR DIGNITY.[1]

(Annotations by Routh, and reprint of the Notes of Christopher Justellus and of Bp. Beveridge will be found in Vol. iv. of the *Reliquiæ Sacræ.*)

CANON I.

IF a presbyter marry, let him be removed from his order; but if he commit fornication or adultery, let him be altogether cast out [i.e. of communion] and put to penance.

NOTES.

ANCIENT EPITOME OF CANON I.

If a presbyter marries he shall be deposed from his order. If he commits adultery or whoredom he shall be expelled, and shall be put to penance.

ARISTENUS.

A presbyter who marries is removed from the exercise of the priesthood but retains his honour and seat. But he that commits fornication or adultery is cast forth altogether and put to penance.

VAN ESPEN.

These fathers [i.e. of Neocæsarea] shew how much graver seemed to them the sin of the presbyter who after ordination committed fornication or adultery, than his who took a wife. For the former they declare shall simply be deposed from his order or deprived of the dignity of the Priesthood, but the latter is to "be altogether cast out, and put to penance." . . . Therefore such a presbyter not only did they remove from the priestly functions, or the dignity of the priesthood, but perfectly or altogether cast him out of the Church.

This canon Gratian has inserted in the *Corpus Juris Canonici. Decretum.* Pars I., Dist. xxviii., c. ix. Gratian has followed Isidore in adding after the word "penance" the words "among the laity" (*inter laicos*) which do not occur in the Greek, (as is noted by the Roman Correctors) nor in the version of Dionysius Exiguus; these same correctors fall however themselves into a still graver error in supposing that criminous clerks in the early days of the Church were sent out to wander over the country, as Van Espen well points out.

On the whole subject of the marriage of the clergy in the Early Church see the Excursus devoted to that subject.

CANON II.

IF a woman shall have married two brothers, let her be cast out [i.e. of communion] until her death. Nevertheless, at the hour of death she may, as an act of mercy, be received to penance, provided she declare that she will break the marriage, should she recover. But if the woman in such a marriage, or the man, die, penance for the survivor shall be very difficult.

NOTES.

ANCIENT EPITOME OF CANON II.

A woman married to two brothers shall be expelled all her life. But if when near her death she promises that she will loose the marriage should she recover, she shall be admitted to penance.

But if one of those coupled together die, only with great difficulty shall penitence be allowed to the one still living.

It will be carefully observed that this canon has no provision for the case of a man marrying two sisters. It is the prohibited degree

---

[1] This is the title in the Paris edition of Zonaras.

of brother's wife, not that of wife's sister which is in consideration. Of course those who hold that the affinity is the same in each case will argue from this canon by parity of reasoning, and those who do not accept that position will refuse to do so.

In the Greek text of Balsamon (*Vide* Beveridge, *Synod.*) after the first clause is added, "if she will not be persuaded to loose the marriage."

Van Espen.

The meaning of this canon seems to be that which Balsamon sets forth, tó wit, that if a woman at the point of death or *in extremis* promises that if she gets better she will dissolve the marriage, or make a divorce, or abstain from the sacrilegious use of matrimony, then "she may be received to penance as an act of mercy"; and surely she is immediately absolved from the excommunication inflicted upon her when she was cast out and extruded from the Church. For it is certain that according to the discipline of the Fathers he was thought to be loosed from excommunication whoever was admitted to penance, and it is of this that the canon speaks;[1] but he did not obtain perfect reconciliation until his penance was done.

To this performance of penance this woman was to be admitted if she got well and dissolved the marriage according to her promise made when she was in peril of death, as the Greek commentators note; and this too is the sense given by Isidore.

CANON III.

CONCERNING those who fall into many marriages, the appointed time of penance is well known; but their manner of living and faith shortens the time.

NOTES.

ANCIENT EPITOME OF CANON III.

The time of polygamists is well known. A zeal for penance may shorten it.

HEFELE.

As the Greek commentators have remarked, this canon speaks of those who have been married more than twice. It is not known what were the ancient ordinances of penitence which the synod here refers to. In later times digamists were condemned to one year's penance, and trigamists from two to five years. St. Basil places the trigamists for three years among the "hearers," and then for some time among the *consistentes*.

VAN ESPEN.

"The appointed time of penance is well known." These words Zonaras notes must refer to a custom, for, says he, "before this synod no canon is found which prescribes the duration of the penance of bigamists [i.e. digamists]." It is for this reason that St. Basil says (*in Epist. ad Amphilogium*, Can. 4) in speaking of the penance of trigamists "we have received this by custom and not by canon, but from the following of precedent," hence the Fathers received many things by tradition, and observed these as having the force of law.

From the last clause of this canon we see the mind of the Fathers of this synod, which agrees with that of Ancyra and Nice, that with regard to the granting of indulgences, ro in shortening the time of penance, attention must be paid to the penitence, and conversetion, or "conversation and faith" of each one separately.

With this agrees Zonaras, whose remarks are worthy of consideration. On this whole subject of the commutation of the primitive penance and of the rise of the modern indulgences of the Roman Church Van Espen has written at length in his excursus *De Indulgentiis* (*Jure Eccles.*, P. I. i., Tit. vij.) in which he assigns the change to the end of the XIth century, and remarks that its introduction caused the "no small collapse of penitential discipline."[2]

This canon is found in the *Corpus Juris Canonici*, Gratian, *Decretum*, Pars II., Causa xxxi., Quæst. i., c. viij. where for "conversio," (ἀναστροφή) is read "conversatio," and the Greek word is used in this sense in Polybius, and frequently so in the New Testament.

---

[1] Van Espen gives "*fructum pœnitentiæ consequatur*" as the translation of ἕξει τὴν μετάνοιαν.

[2] The reader is referred also to Amort, *De Origine, progressu, valore ac fructu Indulgentiarum*, and to the article "Ablass" in the *Kirchen Lexicon* of Wetzer and Welte. Also for the English reader to T. L. Green, D.D., *Indulgences, Absolutions, and Tax tables, etc.* Some of the difficulties which Roman theologians experience in explaining what are called "Plenary Indulgences" are set forth by Dr. Littledale in his *Plain Reasons against joining the Church of Rome*, in which the matter is discussed in the usual witty, and unscrupulous fashion of that brilliant writer. But while this remark is just. it should also be remarked that ater the exaggeration is removed there yet remains a difficulty offthe most serious character.

CANON IV.

IF any man lusting after a woman purposes to lie with her, and his design does not come to effect, it is evident that he has been saved by grace.

NOTES.

ANCIENT EPITOME OF CANON IV.

Whoso lusteth but doth not accomplish his pleasure is preserved of God.

HEFELE.

Instead of ἐπιθυμῆσαι we must read, with Beveridge and Routh, who rely upon several MSS., ἐπιθυμήσας. They also replace μετ' αὐτῆς by αὐτῇ.

The meaning of the canon appears to me to be very obscure. Hefele refers to Van Espen and adopts his view, and Van Espen in turn has adopted Fleury's view and given him credit for it, referring to his *Histoire Ecclesiastique*, Lib. X., xvij. Zonaras' and Balsamon's notes are almost identical, I translate that of the latter in full.

BALSAMON.

In sins, the Fathers say, there are four stages, the first-motion, the struggle, the consent, and the act : the first two of these are not subject to punishment, but in the two others the case is different. For neither is the first impression nor the struggle against it to be condemned, provided that when the reason receives the impression it struggles with it and rejects the thought. But the consent thereto is subject to condemnation and accusation, and the action to punishment. If therefore anyone is assailed by the lust for a woman, and is overcome so that he would perform the act with her, he has given consent, indeed, but to the work he has not come, that is, he has not performed the act, and it is manifest that the grace of God has preserved him ; but he shall not go off with impunity. For the consent alone is worthy of punishment. And this is plain from canon lxx. of St. Basil, which says ; "A deacon polluted in lips (ἐν χείλεσι)" or who has approached to the kiss of a woman "and confesses that he has so sinned, is to be interdicted his ministry," that is to say is to be prohibited its exercise for a time. "But he shall not be deemed unworthy to communicate *in sacris* with the deacons. The same is also the case with a presbyter. But if anyone shall go any further in sin than this, no matter what his grade, he shall be deposed." Some, however, interpret the pollution of the lips in another way ; of this I shall speak in commenting on Canon lxx. of St. Basil.[1]

CANON V.

IF a catechumen coming into the Church have taken his place in the order of catechumens, and fall into sin, let him, if a kneeler, become a hearer and sin no more. But should he again sin while a hearer, let him be cast out.

NOTES.

ANCIENT EPITOME OF CANON V.

If a catechumen falls into a fault and if while a kneeler he sins no more, let him be among the hearers ; but should he sin while among the hearers, let him be cast out altogether.

ZONARAS.

There are two sorts of catechumens. For some have only just come in and these, as still imperfect, go out immediately after the reading of the scriptures and of the Gospels. But there are others who have been for some time in preparation and have attained some perfection ; these wait after the Gospel for the prayers for the catechumens, and when they hear the words "Catechumens, bow down your heads to the Lord," they kneel down. These, as being more perfect, having tasted the good words of God, if they fall, are removed from their position ; and are placed with the "hearers" ; but if any happen to sin while "hearers" they are cast out of the Church altogether.

---

[1] Balsamon's note is most curious reading, but beside being irrelevant to the present canon of Neocæsarea, would hardly bear translation into the vernacular.

CANON VI.

CONCERNING a woman with child, it is determined that she ought to be baptized whensoever she will; for in this the woman communicates nothing to the child, since the bringing forward to profession is evidently the individual [privilege] of every single person.

NOTES.

ANCIENT EPITOME OF CANON VI.

If a woman with child so desires, let her be baptized. For the choice of each one is judged of.

VAN ESPEN.

That the reason of the canon may be understood it must be noted that in the first ages of the Church catechumens were examined concerning their faith before they were baptized, and were made publicly to confess their faith and to renounce openly the pomps of the world, as Albaspinæus

(Aubespine) observes on this canon, "A short while before they were immersed they declared with a loud voice that they desired baptism and wished to be baptized. And since these confessions could not be made by those still shut up in their parent's womb, to them the thing (*res*) and grace of baptism could not come nor penetrate." And altogether in accord with this is the translation of Isidore—"because the free will of each one is declared in that confession," that is, in that confession he declares that he willingly desires to be baptized.

CANON VII.

A PRESBYTER shall not be a guest at the nuptials of persons contracting a second marriage; for, since the digamist is worthy of penance, what kind of a presbyter shall he be, who, by being present at the feast, sanctioned the marriage?

NOTES.

ANCIENT EPITOME OF CANON VII.

A presbyter ought not to be present at the marriage of digamists. For when that one[1] implores favour, who will deem him worthy of favour.

HEFELE.

The meaning of the canon is as follows: "If the digamist, after contracting his second marriage, comes to the priest to be told the punishment he has to undergo, how stands the priest himself who for the sake of the feast has become his accomplice in the offence?"

VAN ESPEN.

The present canon again shews that although the Church never disapproved of, nor reputed second or still later marriages illicit, nevertheless the Fathers enjoined a penance

upon digamists and those repeating marriage, because by this iteration they shewed their incontinence. As he that contracted a second marriage did not sin properly speaking, and committed no fault worthy of punishment, therefore whatever was amiss was believed to be paid off by a lighter penance, and Zonaras supposes that the canons inflicted a mulct upon digamists, for saith he, "Digamists are not allowed for one year to receive the Holy Gifts."

Zonaras seems to indicate that the discipline of the canon was not in force in his time, for he says, "Although this is found in our writings, yet we ourselves have seen the Patriarch and many Metropolitans present at the feast for the second nuptials of the Emperor."

CANON VIII.

IF the wife of a layman has committed adultery and been clearly convicted, such [a husband] cannot enter the ministry; and if she commit adultery after his ordination, he must put her away; but if he retain her, he can have no part in the ministry committed to him.

---

[1] Bp. Beveridge for "that one" translates "the digamist." The meaning is very obscure at best.

NOTES.

ANCIENT EPITOME OF CANON VIII.

A layman whose wife is an adulteress cannot be a clergyman, and a cleric who keeps an adulteress shall be expelled.

VAN ESPEN.

Although the Eastern Church allows the clergy to have wives, even priests, and permits to them the use of marriage after ordi-nation, nevertheless it requires of them the highest conjugal continency, as is seen by the present canon. For here it is evident that the Fathers wished even the smallest possible kind of incontinence to be absent from men dedicated to holiness.

This canon is found in the *Corpus Juris Canonici*, Gratian's *Decretum*, Pars I., Dist. xxxiv., c. xi.

CANON IX.

A PRESBYTER who has been promoted after having committed carnal sin, and who shall confess that he had sinned before his ordination, shall not make the oblation, though he may remain in his other functions on account of his zeal in other respects ; for the majority have affirmed that ordination blots out other kinds of sins. But if he do not confess and cannot be openly convicted, the decision shall depend upon himself.

NOTES.

ANCIENT EPITOME OF CANON IX.

If a presbyter confess that he has sinned,[1] let him abstain from the oblation, and from it only. For certain sins orders remit. If he neither confess nor is convicted, let him have power over himself.

VAN ESPEN.

Therefore if he who before his ordination had committed a sin of the flesh with a woman, confess it after ordination, when he is already a priest, he cannot perform the priestly office, he can neither offer nor consecrate the oblations, even though after his ordination he has preserved uprightness of living and been careful to exercise virtue ; as the words "zeal in other respects" ("studious of good") Zonaras rightly interprets.

And since here the consideration is of a sin committed before ordination, and also concerning a presbyter who after his ordination was of spotless life, and careful to exercise virtue, the Fathers rightly wished that he should not, against his will, be deposed from the priestly office.

It is certainly curious that this canon speaks of ordination as in the opinion of most persons taking away all sins except consummated carnal offences. And it will be noted that the ἀφιέναι must mean more than that they are forgiven by ordination, for they had been forgiven long ago by God upon true contrition, but that they were made to be non-existent, as if they had never been, so that they were no hinderance to the exercise of the spiritual office. I offer no explanation of the difficulty and only venture to doubt the satisfactory character of any of the explanations given by the commentators. Moreover it is hard to grasp the logical connexion of the clauses, and what this "blotting out" of τὰ λοιπὰ has to do with the matter I entirely fail to see. The καὶ after πολλοὶ may possibly suggest that something has dropped out.

This canon and the following are together in the *Corpus Juris Canonici*, Gratian's *Decretum*, Pars II., Causa xv., Quæst. viii., c. i.

CANON X.

LIKEWISE, if a deacon have fallen into the same sin, let him have the rank of a minister.

NOTES.

ANCIENT EPITOME OF CANON X.

A deacon found in the same crime shall remain a minister (ὑπηρέτης).

HEFELE.

By ministers (ὑπήρεται) are meant inferior officers of the Church—the so-called minor orders, often including the subdeacons.

---

[1] Aristenus understands this of fornication.

This canon is in the *Corpus Juris Canonici*, Gratian's *Decretum*, Pars II., Causa xv., Quæst. viii., united with canon ix., and in the following curious form: "Similiter et diaconus, si in eodem culpæ genere fuerit involutus, sese a ministerio cohibebit."

CANON XI.

LET not a presbyter be ordained before he is thirty years of age, even though he be in all respects a worthy man, but let him be made to wait. For our Lord Jesus Christ was baptized and began to teach in his thirtieth year.

NOTES.

ANCIENT EPITOME OF CANON XI.

Unless he be xxx. years of age none shall be presbyter, even should he be worthy, following the example of the baptism of our Saviour.

This canon is found in the *Corpus Juris Canonici*, Gratian's *Decretum*, Pars I., Dist. lxxviii., c. iv.

GRATIAN.

(*Ut supra*, Nota.)

This is the law, and we do not read that Christ, or John the Baptist, or Ezechiel, or some other of the Prophets prophesied or preached before that age. But Jeremiah and Daniel we read received the spirit of prophecy before they had arrived even at youth, and David and Solomon are found to have been anointed in their youth, also John the Evangelist, while still a youth, was chosen by the Lord for an Apostle, and we find that with the rest he was sent forth to preach: Paul also, as we know, while still a young man was called by the Lord, and was sent out to preach. The Church in like manner, when necessity compels, is wont to ordain some under thirty years of age.

For this reason Pope Zacharias in his Letter to Boniface the Bishop, number vi., which begins "Benedictus Deus" says,

C. v. *In case of necessity presbyters may be ordained at xxv. years of age.*

If men thirty years old cannot be found, and necessity so demand, Levites and priests may be ordained from twenty-five years of age upwards.

VAN ESPEN.

The power of dispensing was committed to the bishop, and at length it was so frequently exercised that in the space of one century [i.e. by the end of the xiith century] the law became abrogated, which was brought about by necessity, so that it passed into law that a presbyter could be ordained at twenty-five. And from this it may appear how true it is that there is no surer way of destroying discipline and abrogating law than the allowing of dispensations and relaxations. Vide Thomassinus, *De Disc. Eccles.*, Pars. IV., Lib. I., cap. 46.

CANON XII.

IF any one be baptized when he is ill, forasmuch as his [profession of] faith was not voluntary, but of necessity [i.e. though fear of death] he cannot be promoted to the presbyterate, unless on account of his subsequent [display of] zeal and faith, and because of a lack of men.

NOTES.

ANCIENT EPITOME OF CANON XII.

One baptized on account of sickness is not to be made presbyter, unless in reward for a contest which he afterwards sustains and on account of scarcity of men.

The word used in the Greek for "baptized," is "illuminated" (φωτισθῇ), a very common expression among the ancients.

ARISTENUS.

He that is baptised by reason of illness, and, therefore come to his illumination not freely but of necessity, shall not be admitted to the priesthood unless both these conditions concur, that there are few suitable men to be found and that he has endured a hard conflict after his baptism.

With this interpretation agree also Zonaras and Balsamon, the latter expressly saying, "If one of these conditions is lacking, the canon must be observed." Not only has Isidore therefore missed the meaning by changing the copulative into the disjunctive conjunction (as Van Espen points out) but Bp. Beveridge has fallen into the same error, not indeed in the canon itself, but in translating the Ancient Epitome.

Zonaras explains that the reason for this prohibition was the well-known fact that in those ages baptism was put off so as the longer to be free from the restraints which baptism was considered to impose. From this interpretation only Aubespine dissents, and Hefele points out how entirely without reason.

This canon is found in the *Corpus Juris Canonici*, Gratian's *Decretum.*, Pars. I., Dist. lvii., c. i.

CANON XIII.

COUNTRY presbyters may not make the oblation in the church of the city when the bishop or presbyters of the city are present; nor may they give the Bread or the Cup with prayer. If, however, they be absent, and he [*i.e.*, a country presbyter] alone be called to prayer, he may give them.

NOTES.

ANCIENT EPITOME OF CANONS XIII. AND XIV.

A country presbyter shall not offer in the city temple, unless the bishop and the whole body of the presbyters are away. But if wanted he can do so while they are away. The chorepiscopi can offer as fellow ministers, as they hold the place of the Seventy.

Routh reads the last clause in the plural, in this agreeing with Dionysius Exiguus and Isidore. In many MSS. this canon is united with the following and the whole number given as 14.

This canon is found in the *Corpus Juris Canonici*, Pars I., Dist. xcv., c. xii. And the

Roman correctors have added the following notes.

ROMAN CORRECTORS.

(Gratian *ut supra*.)

"Nor to give the sacrificed bread and to hand the chalice;" otherwise it is read "sanctified" [*sanctificatum* for *sacrificatum*]. The Greek of the council is ἄρτον διδόναι ἐν εὐχῇ; but Balsamon has ἄρτον εὐχῆς, that is, "the bread of the mystic prayer."

Instead of "let them only who are called for giving the prayer, etc.," read καὶ εἰς εὐχὴν κληθῇ μόνος δίδωσιν, that is: "and only he that shall have been called to the mystic prayer, shall distribute."

CANON XIV.

THE chorepiscopi, however, are indeed after the pattern of the Seventy; and as fellow-servants, on account of their devotion to the poor, they have the honour of making the oblation.

NOTES.

ANCIENT EPITOME OF CANON XIV.

[Vide ante, as in many MSS. the two canons are united in the Ancient Epitome.]

VAN ESPEN.

The reference to the Seventy seems to intimate that the Synod did not hold the chorepiscopi to be true bishops, as such were always reputed and called successors, not of the Seventy disciples but successors of the Twelve Apostles. It is also clear that their chief ministry was thought to be the care of the poor.

Zonaras and Balsamon would seem to agree in this with Van Espen. See on the whole subject the Excursus on the Chorepiscopi.

CANON XV.

THE deacons ought to be seven in number, according to the canon, even if the city be great. Of this you will be persuaded from the Book of the Acts.

NOTES.

ANCIENT EPITOME OF CANON XV.

Seven Deacons according to the Acts of the Apostles should be appointed for each great city.

This canon was observed in Rome and it was not until the xith century that the number of the Seven Cardinal Deacons was changed to fourteen. That Gratian received it into the *Decretum* (Pars. I., Dist. XCIII., c. xij.) is good evidence that he considered it part of the Roman discipline. Eusebius [1] gives a letter of Pope Cornelius, written about the middle of the third century, which says that at that time there were at Rome forty-four priests, seven deacons, and seven subdeacons; and that the number of those in inferior orders was very great. Thomassinus says that, "no doubt in this the Roman Church intended to imitate the Apostles who only ordained seven deacons. But the other Churches did not keep themselves so scrupulously to that number." [2]

In the acts of the Council of Chalcedon it is noted that the Church of Edessa had fifteen priests and thirty-eight deacons.[3] And Justinian, we know, appointed one hundred deacons for the Church of Constantinople. Van Espen well points out that while this canon refers to a previous law on the subject, neither the Council itself, nor the Greek commentators Balsamon or Zonaras give the least hint as to what that Canon was.

The Fathers of Neocæsarea base their limiting of the number of deacons to seven in one city upon the authority of Holy Scripture, but the sixteenth canon of the Quinisext Council expressly says that in doing so they showed they referred to ministers of alms, not to ministers at the divine mysteries, and that St. Stephen and the rest were not deacons at all in this latter sense. The reader is referred to this canon, where to defend the practice of Constantinople the meaning of the canon we are considering is entirely misrepresented.

[1] Eusebius, *H. E.*, Lib. VI., cap. xliij.
[2] Thomassin, *Ancienne et Nouvelle Discipline de l'Église*, Lib. II., Chap. xxix.

[3] Acta Conc. Chal., Actio x.

THE COUNCIL OF GANGRA.

A.D. 325–381.

Emperor.—CONSTANTINE.

Elenchus.

Historical Introduction.   *Synodal Letter.*

Canons with the Ancient Epitome and Notes.

HISTORICAL INTRODUCTION.

With regard to the Synod of Gangra we know little beside what we learn from its own synodal letter. Three great questions naturally arise with regard to it.

1. What was its date?
2. Who was the Eustathius it condemned?
3. Who was its presiding officer?

I shall briefly give the reader the salient points with regard to each of these matters.

1. With regard to the date, there can be no doubt that it was after Nice and before the First Council of Constantinople, that is between 325 and 381. Socrates[1] seems to place it about 365; but Sozomen[2] some twenty years earlier. On the other hand, Remi Ceillier[3] inconsistently with his other statements, seems to argue from St. Basil's letters that the true date is later than 376. Still another theory has been urged by the Ballerini, resting on the supposition that the Eusebius who presided was Eusebius of Cæsarea, and they therefore fix the date between 362 and 370. With this Mr. Ffoulkes agrees, and fixes the date,[4] with Pagi, at 358, and is bold enough to add, "and this was unquestionably the year of the Council." But in the old collections of canons almost without exception, the canons of Gangra precede those of Antioch, and Blondel and Tillemont[5] have sustained this, which perhaps I may call the traditional date.

2. There does not seem to be any reasonable ground to doubt that the person condemned, Eustathius by name, was the famous bishop of Sebaste. This may be gathered from both Sozomen[6] and Socrates,[7] and is confirmed incidentally by one of St. Basil's epistles.[8] Moreover, Eustathius's See of Sebaste is in Armenia, and it is to the bishops of Armenia that the Synod addresses its letter. It would seem in view of all this that Bp. Hefele's words are not too severe when he writes, "Under such circumstances the statement of Baronius, Du Pin, and others (supported by no single ancient testimony) that another Eustathius, or possibly the monk Eutactus, is here meant, deserves no serious consideration, though Tillemont did not express himself as opposed to it."[9]

The story that after his condemnation by the Synod of Gangra Eustathius gave up wearing his peculiar garb and other eccentricities, Sozomen only gives as a report.[10]

3. As to who was the president, it seems tolerably certain that his name was Eusebius—if Sozomen[11] indeed means it was "Eusebius of Constantinople," it is a blunder, yet he had the name right. In the heading of the Synodal letter Eusebius is first named, and as Gangra and Armenia were within the jurisdiction of Cæsarea, it certainly would seem natural to suppose that the Eusebius named was the Metropolitan of that province, but it must be remembered that Eusebius of Cappadocia was not made bishop until 362, four years after Mr. Ffoulkes makes him preside at Gangra. The names of thirteen bishops are given in the Greek text.

The Latin translations add other names, such as that of Hosius of Cordova, and some Latin writers have asserted that he presided as legate à latere from the pope, e.g., Baronius[12] and Binius.[13] Hefele denies this and says: "At the time of the Synod of Gangra Hosius was

[1] Socrat. *H. E.*, Lib. II., cap. xliij.
[2] Sozomen. *H. E.*, Lib. IV., cap. xxiv.
[3] Remi Ceillier. *Hist. Générale des Auteurs Sacrés*, Tom. IV., p. 735.
[4] E. S. Ffoulkes, in Smith and Cheetham, *Dict. Christ. Antiq.*, s. v. Gangra.
[5] I am indebted to Hefele for this reference, and he gives *Mémoires*, note xxvij., sur St. Basile.
[6] Sozom. *H. E.*, III., xiv.
[7] Socrat. *H. E.*, II., xliij.
[8] S. Basil. M., *Ep.* ccxxiij.
[9] Hefele. *Hist. Councils*, Vol. II., p. 337.

[10] Soz. *H. E.*, Lib. III., cap. xiv. It is curious that Canon Venables in his article "Eustathius" in Smith and Wace, *Dict. of Christ. Biog.*, gives the story on Sozomen's authority as quoted by Hefele, but without giving Hefele's warning that it was a mere rumour. It would seem that Canon Venables could not have consulted the Greek, where the word used is λόγος; Hefele gives no reference. I have supplied this in the beginning of this note.
[11] Sozomen. *H. E.*, Lib. IV., cap. xxiv.
[12] Baronius. *Annal.*, Tom. iii., *ad ann.* 361, n. 44.
[13] Binius. *Annotat. in Synod. Gang.*

without doubt dead." [1]   But such has not been the opinion of the learned, and Cave [2] is of opinion that Hosius's episcopate covered seventy years ending with 361, and (resting on the same opinion) Pagi thinks Hosius may have attended the Synod in 358 on his way back to Spain, an opinion with which, as I have said, Mr. Ffoulkes agrees.   It seems also clear that by the beginning of the sixth century the Synod of Gangra was looked upon at Rome as having been held under papal authority ; Pope Symmachus expressly saying so to the Roman Synod of 504.   (*Vide* Notes on Canons vij. and viij.)

It remains only further to remark that the *Libellus Synodicus* mentions a certain Dius as president of the Synod.   The Ballarini [3] suggest that it should be Βίος, an abbreviation of Eusebius.   Mr. Ffoulkes suggests that Dius is " probably Dianius, the predecessor of Eusebius."   Lightfoot [4] fixes the episcopate of Eusebius Pamphili as between 313 and 337; and states that that of Eusebius of Cæsarea in Cappadocia did not begin until 362, so that the enormous chronological difficulties will be evident to the reader.

As all the proposed new dates involve more or less contradiction, I have given the canons their usual position between Neocæsarea and Antioch, and have left the date undetermined.

---

[1] Hefele.   *Hist. Councils*, Vol. II., p. 327.
[2] Cave.   *Hist. Lit.*, Lib. I.. cap. v
[3] S. Leon., M., *Opp.*, ed. Ballerini, Tom. III., p. xxiv.

[4] Smith and Wace.   *Dict. Christ. Biog., s. v.* Eusebius of Cæsarea.

SYNODICAL LETTER OF THE COUNCIL OF GANGRA.

EUSEBIUS, Ælian, Eugenius, Olympius, Bithynicus, Gregory, Philetus, Pappus, Eulalius, Hypatius, Proæresius, Basil and Bassus,[1] assembled in the holy Synod at Gangra, to our most honoured lords and fellow-ministers in Armenia wish health in the Lord.

FORASMUCH as the most Holy Synod of Bishops, assembled on account of certain necessary matters of ecclesiastical business in the Church at Gangra, on inquiring also into the matters which concern Eustathius, found that many things had been unlawfully done by these very men who are partisans of Eustathius, it was compelled to make definitions, which it has hastened to make known to all, for the removal of whatever has by him been done amiss. For, from their utter abhorrence of marriage, and from their adoption of the proposition that no one living in a state of marriage has any hope towards God, many misguided married women have forsaken their husbands, and husbands their wives: then, afterwards, not being able to contain, they have fallen into adultery; and so, through such a principle as this, have come to shame. They were found, moreover, fomenting separations from the houses of God and of the Church; treating the Church and its members with disdain, and establishing separate meetings and assemblies, and different doctrines and other things in opposition to the Churches and those things which are done in the Church; wearing strange apparel, to the destruction of the common custom of dress; making distributions, among themselves and their adherents as saints, of the first-fruits of the Church, which have, from the first, been given to the Church; slaves also leaving their masters, and, on account of their own strange apparel, acting insolently towards their masters; women, too, disregarding decent custom, and, instead of womanly apparel, wearing men's clothes, thinking to be justified because of these; while many of them, under a pretext of piety, cut off the growth of hair, which is natural to woman; [and these persons were found] fasting on the Lord's Day, despising the sacredness of that free day, but disdaining and eating on the fasts appointed in the Church; and certain of them abhor the eating of flesh; neither do they tolerate prayers in the houses of married persons, but, on the contrary, despise such prayers when they are made, and often refuse to partake when Oblations are offered in the houses of married persons; contemning married presbyters, and refusing to touch their ministrations; condemning the services in honour of the Martyrs [2] and those who gather or minister therein, and the rich also who do not alienate all their wealth, as having nothing to hope from God; and many other things that no one could recount. For every one of them, when he forsook the canon of the Church, adopted laws that tended as it were to isolation; for neither was there any common judgment among all of them; but whatever any one conceived, that he propounded, to the scandal of the Church, and to his own destruction.

Wherefore, the Holy Synod present in Gangra was compelled, on these accounts, to condemn them, and to set forth definitions declaring them to be cast out of the Church; but that, if they should repent and anathematize every one of these false doctrines, then they should be capable of restoration. And therefore the Holy Synod has particularly set forth everything which they ought to anathematize before they are received. And if any one will not submit to the said decrees, he shall be anathematized as a heretic, and excommunicated, and cast out of the Church; and it will behove the bishops to observe a like rule in respect of all who may be found with them.

---

[1] This list of names varies in the different MSS. and versions.
[2] This phrase in the Greek has dropped out in Labbe, and Mansi; it is found in Zonaras, etc.

THE CANONS OF THE HOLY FATHERS ASSEMBLED AT GANGRA, WHICH WERE SET FORTH AFTER THE COUNCIL OF NICE.[1]

CANON I.

IF any one shall condemn marriage, or abominate and condemn a woman who is a believer and devout, and sleeps with her own husband, as though she could not enter the Kingdom [of heaven] let him be anathema.

NOTES.

ANCIENT EPITOME OF CANON I.

Anathema to him who disregards legitimate marriage.

When one considers how deeply the early church was impressed with those passages of Holy Scripture which she understood to set forth the superiority of the virgin over the married estate, it ceases to be any source of astonishment that some should have run into the error of condemning marriage as sinful. The saying of our Blessed Lord with reference to those who had become "eunuchs for the kingdom of heaven's sake," [2] and those words of St. Paul "He that giveth his virgin in marriage doeth well, but he that giveth her not in marriage doeth better," [3] together with the striking passage in the Revelation of those that were "not defiled with women, for they are virgins," [4] were considered as settling the matter for the new dispensation. The earliest writers are filled with the praises of virginity. Its superiority underlies the allegories of the Hermes Pastor ; [5] St. Justin Martyr speaks of "many men and women of sixty and seventy years of age who from their childhood have been the disciples of Christ, and have kept themselves uncorrupted," [6] and from that time on there is an ever-swelling tide of praise ; the reader must be referred to SS. Cyprian, Athanasius, Cyril of Jerusalem, Jerome, Augustine, etc., etc. In fact the Council of Trent (it cannot be denied) only gave expression to the view of all Christian antiquity both East and West, when it condemned those who denied that "it is more blessed to remain virgin or celibate than to be joined in marriage." [7]

This canon is found in the *Corpus Juris Canonici*, Gratian's *Decretum*, Pars I., Distinc. xxx., c. xii. (Isidore's version), and again Dist. xxxi., c. viii. (Dionysius's version). Gratian, however, supposes that the canon is directed against the Manichæans and refers to the marriage of priests, but in both matters he is mistaken, as the Roman Correctors and Van Espen point out.

CANON II.

IF any one shall condemn him who eats flesh, which is without blood and has not been offered to idols nor strangled, and is faithful and devout, as though the man were without hope [of salvation] because of his eating, let him be anathema.

NOTES.

ANCIENT EPITOME OF CANON II.

Anathema also to him who condemns the eating of flesh, except that of a suffocated animal or that offered to idols.

HEFELE.

This canon also, like the preceding one, is not directed against the Gnostics and Manicheans, but against an unenlightened hyperasceticism, which certainly approaches the Gnostic-Manichean error as to matter being Satanic. We further see that, at the time of the Synod of Gangra, the rule of the Apostolic Synod with regard to blood and things strangled was still in force. With the Greeks,

---

[1] This is the title in the Paris Edition of Zonaras. The Bodleian text simply reads "The Canons of the Synod at Gangra."
[2] Matt. xix. 12.
[3] I Cor. vii. 38.
[4] Rev. xiv. 4
[5] Hermes Pastor. *Sim.* x., xj.

[6] Justin. M. *Apol.*, i. 15.
[7] *Conc. Trid.*, sessio xxiv. *De Matr.*, can. x. It is curious to note that while Eustathius and his followers held all marriage to be sinful, Luther (at least at one time) taught that it was a sin for anyone to remain unmarried who could "increase and multiply!" The Synod of Gangra in this canon sets forth the unchanging position of the Catholic Church upon this point.

indeed, it continued always in force as their Euchologies still show. Balsamon also, the well-known commentator on the canons of the Middle Ages, in his commentary on the sixty-third Apostolic Canon, expressly blames the Latins because they had ceased to observe this command. What the Latin Church, however, thought on this subject about the year 400, is shown by St. Augustine in his work *Contra Faustum*, where he states that the Apostles had given this command in order to unite the heathens and Jews in the one ark of Noah ; but that then, when the barrier between Jewish and heathen converts had fallen, this command concerning things strangled and blood had lost its meaning, and was only observed by few. But still, as late as the eighth century, Pope Gregory the Third (731) forbade the eating of blood or things strangled under threat of a penance of forty days.

No one will pretend that the disciplinary enactments of any council, even though it be one of the undisputed Ecumenical Synods, can be of greater and more unchanging force than the decree of that first council, held by the Holy Apostles at Jerusalem, and the fact that its decree has been obsolete for centuries in the West is proof that even Ecumenical canons may be of only temporary utility and may be repealed by disuser, like other laws.

This canon is found in the *Corpus Juris Canonici*, Gratian's *Decretum*, Pars I., Dist. XXX., c. xiii.

CANON III.

IF any one shall teach a slave, under pretext of piety, to despise his master and to run away from his service, and not to serve his own master with good-will and all honour, let him be anathema.

NOTES.

ANCIENT EPITOME OF CANON III.

Anathema to him who persuades a slave to leave his master under pretence of religion.

VAN ESPEN.

This canon is framed in accordance with the doctrine of the Apostle, in I. Timothy, chapter six, verse 1. "Let as many servants as are under the yoke count their own masters worthy of all honour, that the name of God and his doctrine be not blasphemed." And again the same Apostle teaches his disciple Titus that he should "exhort servants to be obedient unto their own masters, and to please them well in all things; not answer-ing again ; not purloining, but shewing all good fidelity ; that they may adorn the doctrine of God our Saviour in all things." (Titus ii. 9 and 10.)

These texts are likewise cited by Balsamon and Zonaras.

This Canon is found in the *Corpus Juris Canonici*, Gratian's *Decretum*, Pars. II., Causa XVII., Q. IV., c. xxxvij. in the version of Isidore, and again in c. xxxviij. from the collections of Martin Bracarensis (so says Van Espen) and assigned to a council of Pope Martin, Canon xlvii.

CANON IV.

IF any one shall maintain, concerning a married presbyter, that is not lawful to partake of the oblation when he offers it, let him be anathema.

NOTES.

ANCIENT EPITOME OF CANON IV.

Anathema to him who hesitates to receive communion from presbyters joined in matrimony.

HEFELE.

As is well known, the ancient Church, as now the Greek Church, allowed those clergy who married before their ordination to con-tinue to live in matrimony. Compare what was said above in the history of the Council of Nicæa, in connection with Paphnutius, concerning the celibacy and marriage of priests in the ancient Church. Accordingly this canon speaks of those clergy who have wives and live in wedlock ; and Baronius, Binius, and Mitter-Müller gave themselves useless trouble in trying to interpret it as only protecting those clergy who, though married, have since their ordination ceased to cohabit with their wives.

The so-called *Codex Ecclesiæ Romanæ* published by Quesnel, which, however, as was shown by the Ballerini,[1] is of Gallican and not Roman origin, has not this canon, and consequently it only mentions nineteen canons of Gangra.

CANON V.

IF any one shall teach that the house of God and the assemblies held therein are to be despised, let him be anathema.

NOTES.

ANCIENT EPITOME OF CANON V.

Whoso styles the house of God contemptible, let him be anathema.

This canon is found in the *Corpus Juris Canonici*, Gratian's *Decretum*, Pars I., Dist. xxx., c. x. The commentators find nothing to say upon the canon, and in fact the despising of the worship of God's true church is and always has been so common a sin, that it hardly calls for comment ; no one will forget that the Prophet Malachi complains how in his days there were those who deemed "the table of the Lord contemptible" and said of his worship "what a weariness is it." (Mal. i., 7 and 13.)

CANON VI.

IF any one shall hold private assemblies outside of the Church, and, despising the canons, shall presume to perform ecclesiastical acts, the presbyter with the consent of the bishop refusing his permission, let him be anathema.

NOTES.

ANCIENT EPITOME OF CANON VI.

Whoso privately gathers a religious meeting let him be anathema.

HEFELE.

Both these canons, [V. and VI.] forbid the existence of conventicles, and conventicle services. It already appears from the second article of the Synodal Letter of Gangra, that the Eustathians, through spiritual pride, separated themselves from the rest of the congregation, as being the pure and holy, avoided the public worship, and held private services of their own. The ninth, tenth, and eleventh articles of the Synodal Letter give us to understand that the Eustathians especially avoided the public services, when married clergy officiated. We might possibly conclude, from the words of the sixth canon : μὴ συνόντος τοῦ πρεσβυτέρου κατὰ γνώμην τοῦ ἐπισκόπου, that no priest performed any part in their private services ; but it is more probable that the Eustathians, who did not reject the priesthood as such, but only abhorred the married clergy, had their own unmarried clergy, and that these officiated at their separate services. And the above-mentioned words of the canon do not the least contradict this supposition, for the very addition of the words κατὰ γνώμην τοῦ ἐπισκόπου indicate that the sectarian priests who performed the services of the Eustathians had received no permission to do so from the bishop of the place. Thus did the Greek commentators, Balsamon, etc., and likewise Van Espen, interpret this canon.

The meaning of this canon is very obscure. The Latin reads *non conveniente presbytero, de episcopi sententia ;* and Lambert translates "without the presence of a priest, with consent of the bishop." Hammond differs from this and renders thus, "without the concurrence of the presbyter and the consent of the bishop." I have translated literally and left the obscurity of the original.

[1] Vide their edition of *Opp. S. Leonis M.*, Tom. III., pp. 124, 685, 755.

CANON VII.

IF any one shall presume to take the fruits offered to the Church, or to give them out of the Church, without the consent of the bishop, or of the person charged with such things, and shall refuse to act according to his judgment, let him be anathema.

ANCIENT EPITOME OF CANON VII.

Whoso performs church acts contrary to the will of a bishop or of a presbyter, let him be anathema.

CANON VIII.

IF anyone, except the bishop or the person appointed for the stewardship of benefactions, shall either give or receive the revenue, let both the giver and the receiver be anathema.

NOTES.

ANCIENT EPITOME OF CANON VIII.

Whoso gives or receives offered fruits, except the bishop and the economist appointed to disburse charities, both he that gives, and he that receives shall be anathema.

POPE SYMMACHUS.

(*In his Address to the Synod of Rome* A.D. 504. *Labbe and Cossart,* Concilia, *tom. iv., col.* 1373.)

In the canons framed by Apostolic authority [i.e., by the authority of the Apostolic See of Rome, cf. Ffoulkes, Smith and Cheetham, *Dict. Christ. Antiq.,* art. Gangra] we find it written as follows concerning the offerings of fruits which are due to the clergy of the church, and concerning those things which are offered for the use of the poor ; "If anyone shall presume, etc." [Canon VII.] And again at the same council, "If anyone except the bishop, etc." [Canon VIII.] And truly

it is a crime and a great sacrilege for those whose duty it is chiefly to guard it, that is for Christians and God-fearing men and above all for princes and rulers of this world, to transfer and convert to other uses the wealth which has been bestowed or left by will to the venerable Church for the remedy of their sins, or for the health and repose of their souls.

Moreover, whosoever shall have no care for these, and contrary to these canons, shall seek for, accept, or hold, or shall unjustly defend and retain the treasures given to the Church unless he quickly repent himself shall be stricken with that anathema with which an angry God smites souls ; and to him that accepts, or gives, or possesses let there be anathema, and the constant accompaniment of the appointed penalty. For he can have no defence to offer before the tribunal of Christ, who nefariously without any regard to religion has scattered the substance left by pious souls for the poor.

CANON IX.

IF any one shall remain virgin, or observe continence, abstaining from marriage because he abhors it, and not on account of the beauty and holiness of virginity itself, let him be anathema.

NOTES.

ANCIENT EPITOME OF CANON IX.

Whoso preserves virginity not on account of its beauty but because he abhors marriage, let him be anathema.

The lesson taught by this canon and that which follows is that the practice of even the

highest Christian virtues, such as the preservation of virginity, if it does not spring from a worthy motive is only deserving of execration.

ZONARAS.

Virginity is most beautiful of all, and continence is likewise beautiful, but only if we follow them for their own sake and because of the sanctification which comes from them. But should anyone embrace virginity, because he detests marriage as impure, and keep himself chaste, and abstains from commerce with women and marriage, because he thinks that they

are in themselves wicked, he is subjected by this canon to the penalty of anathema.

This canon is found in the *Corpus Juris Canonici*, Gratian's *Decretum*, Pars I., Dist. xxx., c. v., and again Dist. xxxi., c. ix.

CANON X.

IF any one of those who are living a virgin life for the Lord's sake shall treat arrogantly the married, let him be anathema.

NOTES.

ANCIENT EPITOME OF CANON X.

Whoso treats arrogantly those joined in matrimony, let him be anathema.

On this point the fathers had spoken long before, I cite two as examples.

ST. CLEMENT.

(Epist. I., 38, Lightfoot's translation.)

So in our case let the whole body be saved in Christ Jesus, and let each man be subject unto his neighbour, according as also he was appointed with his special grace. Let not the strong neglect the weak; and let the weak respect the strong. Let the rich minister aid to the poor and let the poor give thanks to God, because he hath given him one through whom his wants may be supplied. Let the wise display his wisdom, not in words, but in good works. He that is lowly in mind, let him not bear testimony to himself, but leave testimony to be borne to him by his neighbour. He that is pure in the flesh, let him be so,[1] and not boast, knowing that it is Another who bestoweth his continence upon him. Let us consider, brethren, of what matter we were made; who and what manner of beings we were, when we came into the world; from what a sepulchre and what darkness he that moulded and created

us brought us into his world, having prepared his benefits aforehand ere ever we were born. Seeing therefore that we have all these things from him, we ought in all things to give thanks to him, to whom be the glory for ever and ever. Amen.

ST. IGNATIUS.

(Epist. ad Polyc. 5, Lightfoot's translation.)

Flee evil arts, or rather hold thou discourse about these, Tell my sisters to love the Lord and to be content with their husbands in flesh and in spirit. In like manner also charge my brothers in the name of Jesus Christ to love their wives, *as the Lord loved the Church.* If anyone is able to abide in chastity to the honour of the flesh of the Lord, let him so abide without boasting. If he boast, he is lost; and if it be known beyond the bishop, he is polluted. It becometh men and women, too, when they marry to unite themselves with the consent of the bishop, that the marriage may be after the Lord and not after concupiscence. Let all things be done to the honour of God.

This canon is found in the *Corpus Juris Canonici*, Gratian's *Decretum*, Pars I., Dist. xxx., c. iv.

CANON XI.

IF anyone shall despise those who out of faith make love-feasts and invite the brethren in honour of the Lord, and is not willing to accept these invitations because he despises what is done, let him be anathema.

NOTES.

ANCIENT EPITOME OF CANON XI.

Whoso spurns those who invite to the agape, and who when invited will not communicate with these, let him be anathema.

There are few subjects upon which there has been more difference of opinion than upon the history and significance of the *Agapæ* or Love-feasts of the Early Church.

[1] Lightfoot adopts Laurents' emendation and reads ἥτω. Σιγάτω has also been suggested, and Hort's thinks στήτω to be the genuine reading. It all comes to the same thing, however, the meaning being perfectly clear.

To cite here any writers would only mislead the reader, I shall therefore merely state the main outline of the discussion and leave every man to study the matter for himself.

All agree that these feasts are referred to by St. Jude in his Epistle, and, although Dean Plumptre has denied it (Smith and Cheetham, *Dict., Christ. Antiq.*, s.v. Agapæ), most writers add St. Paul in the First Epistle to the Corinthians xi. Estius (*in loc.*) argues with great cogency that the expression "Lord's Supper" in Holy Scripture never means the Holy Eucharist, but the love-feast, and in this view he has been followed by many moderns, but the prevalent opinion has been the opposite.

There is also much discussion as to the order in which the Agapæ and the celebrations of the Holy Sacrament were related, some holding that the love-feast preceded others that it followed the Divine Mysteries. There seems no doubt that in early times the two became separated, the Holy Sacrament being celebrated in the morning and the Agapæ in the evening.

All agree that these feasts were at first copies of the religious feasts common to the Jews and to the heathen world, and that soon abuses of one sort or another came in, so that they fell into ill repute and were finally prohibited at the Council in Trullo. This canon of Gangra is found in the *Corpus Juris Canonici*, Gratian's *Decretum*, Pars I., Dist. xlii., c. i.

Van Espen is of opinion that the agapæ of our canon have no real connexion with the religious feasts of earlier days, but were merely meals provided by the rich for the poor, and with this view Hefele agrees. But the matter is by no means plain. In fact at every point we are met with difficulties and uncertainties.

There would seem to be little doubt that the "pain beni" of the French Church, and the "Antidoron" of the Eastern Church are remains of the ancient Agapæ.

The meaning, however, of this canon is plain enough, to wit, people must not despise, out of a false asceticism, feasts made for the poor by those of the faithful who are rich and liberal.[1]

CANON XII.

IF any one, under pretence of asceticism, should wear a *periboloeum* and, as if this gave him righteousness, shall despise those who with piety wear the *berus* and use other common and customary dress, let him be anathema.

NOTES.

ANCIENT EPITOME OF CANON XII.

Whoso despises those who wear beruses, let him be anathema.

HEFELE.

The βῆροι (*lacernæ*) were the common upper garments worn by men over the tunic; but the περιβόλαια were rough mantles worn by philosophers to show their contempt for all luxury. Socrates (H. E., ii. 43) and the Synodal Letter of Gangra in its third article say that Eustathius of Sebaste wore the philosopher's mantle. But this canon in no way absolutely rejects a special dress for monks, for it is not the distinctive dress but the proud and superstitious over-estimation of its worth which the Synod here blames.

This canon is found in the *Corpus Juris Canonici*, Gratian's *Decretum*, Pars I., Dist. xxx., c. xv.

CANON XIII.

IF any woman, under pretence of asceticism, shall change her apparel and, instead of a woman's accustomed clothing, shall put on that of a man, let her be anathema.

NOTES.

ANCIENT EPITOME OF CANON XIII.

Whatever women wear men's clothes, anathema to them.

HEFELE.

The synodal letter in its sixth article also speaks of this. Exchange of dress, or the adoption by one sex of the dress of the other, was forbidden in the Pentateuch (Deut. xxii., 5), and was therefore most strictly interdicted by the whole ancient Church. Such

---

[1] Most interesting literature on the whole subject will be found in connexion with the frescoes and cups, etc., found in the catacombs.

change of attire was formerly adopted mainly for theatrical purposes, or from effeminacy, wantonness, the furtherance of unchastity, or the like. The Eustathians, from quite opposite and hyper-ascetical reasons, had recommended women to assume male, that is probably monk's attire, in order to show that for them, as the holy ones, there was no longer any distinction of sex; but the Church, also from ascetical reasons, forbade this change of attire, especially when joined to superstition and puritanical pride.

This canon is found in the *Corpus Juris Canonici*, Gratian's *Decretum*, Pars I., Dist. xxx., c. vi.

CANON XIV.

IF any woman shall forsake her husband, and resolve to depart from him because she abhors marriage, let her be anathema.

NOTES.

ANCIENT EPITOME OF CANON XIV.

Women who keep away from their husbands because they abominate marriage, anathema to them.

HEFELE.

This canon cannot in any way be employed in opposition to the practice of the Catholic Church. For though the Church allows one of a married couple, with the consent of the other, to give up matrimonial intercourse, and to enter the clerical order or the cloister, still this is not, as is the case with the Eustathians, the result of a false dogmatic theory, but takes place with a full recognition of the sanctity of marriage.

VAN ESPEN.

It would seem that the Eustathians chiefly disapproved of the use of marriage, and under pretext of preserving continence induced married women to abstain from its use as from something unlawful, and to leave their husbands, separating from them so far as the bed was concerned; and so the Greek interpreters understand this canon; for the Eustathians were never accused of persuading anyone to dissolve a marriage *a vinculo.*

This canon is found in the *Corpus Juris Canonici*, Gratian's *Decretum*, Pars I., Dist., xxx., c. iii., but in Isidore's version, which misses the sense by implying that a divorce *a vinculo* is intended. The Roman Correctors do not note this error.

CANON XV.

IF anyone shall forsake his own children and shall not nurture them, nor so far as in him lies, rear them in becoming piety, but shall neglect them, under pretence of asceticism, let him be anathema.

NOTES.

ANCIENT EPITOME OF CANON XV.

Whosoever they be that desert their children and do not instruct them in the fear of God let them be anathema.

VAN ESPEN.

The fathers of this Synod here teach that it is the office and duty of parents to provide for the bodily care of their children, and also, as far as in them lies, to mould them to the practice of piety. And this care for their children is to be preferred by parents to any private exercises of religion. In this connexion should be read the letter of St. Francis de Sales. (*Ep.* xxxii., Lib. 4.)

It may perhaps be noted that this canon has not infrequently been violated by those who are accepted as Saints in the Church.

This canon is found, in Isidore's version, in the *Corpus Juris Canonici*, Gratian's *Decretum*, Pars I., Dist. xxx., c. xiv.

CANON XVI.

IF, under any pretence of piety, any children shall forsake their parents, particularly [if the parents are] believers, and shall withhold becoming reverence from their parents, on the plea that they honour piety more than them, let them be anathema.

NOTES.

ANCIENT EPITOME OF CANON XVI.

If children leave their parents who are of the faithful let them be anathema.

Zonaras notes that the use of the word "particularly" shews that the obligation is universal. The commentators all refer here to St. Matthew xv., where our Lord speaks of the subterfuge by which the Jews under pretext of piety defrauded their parents and made the law of God of none effect.

VAN ESPEN.

Of the last clause this is the meaning; that according to the Eustathians "piety towards God" or "divine worship," or rather its pretence, should be preferred to the honour and reverence due to parents.

This canon, in Isidore's version, is found in the *Corpus Juris Canonici*, Gratian's *Decretum*, Pars I., Dist. xxx., c. i. The Roman correctors advertize the reader that the version of Dionysius Exiguus "is much nearer to the original Greek, although not altogether so."

CANON XVII.

IF any woman from pretended asceticism shall cut off her hair, which God gave her as the reminder of her subjection, thus annulling as it were the ordinance of subjection, let her be anathema.

NOTES.

ANCIENT EPITOME OF CANON XVII.

Whatever women shave their hair off, pretending to do so out of reverence for God, let them be anathema.

HEFELE.

The apostle Paul, in the first Epistle to the Corinthians, xi. 10, represents the long hair of women, which is given them as a natural veil, as a token of their subjection to man. We learn from the Synod of Gangra, that as many Eustathian women renounced this subjection, and left their husbands, so, as this canon says, they also did away with their long hair, which was the outward token of this subjection. An old proverb says: *duo si faciunt*

idem, non est idem. In the Catholic Church also, when women and girls enter the cloister, they have their hair cut off, but from quite other reasons than those of the Eustathian women. The former give up their hair, because it has gradually become the custom to consider the long hair of women as a special beauty, as their greatest ornament; but the Eustathians, like the ancient Church in general, regarded long hair as the token of subjection to the husband, and, because they renounced marriage and forsook their husbands, they cut it off.

This canon is found in the *Corpus Juris Canonici*, Gratian's *Decretum*, Pars I., Dist. xxx., c. ij.

CANON XVIII.

IF any one, under pretence of asceticism, shall fast on Sunday, let him be anathema.

NOTES.

ANCIENT EPITOME OF CANON XVIII.

Whoso fasts on the Lord's day or on the Sabbath let him be anathema.

ZONARAS.

Eustathius appointed the Lord's day as a fast, whereas, because Christ rose from the grave and delivered human nature from sin on that day, we should spend it in offering joyous thanks to God. But fasting carries with it the idea of grief and sorrow. For this reason those who fast on Sunday are subjected to the punishment of anathema.

BALSAMON.

By many canons we are warned against fasting or grieving on the festal and joyous Lord's day, in remembrance of the resurrection of the Lord; but that we should cele- brate it and offer thanks to God, that we be raised from the fall of sin. But this canon smites the Eustathians with anathema because they taught that the Lord's days should be fasted. Canon LXIV. of the Apostolic Canons cuts off such of the laity as shall so fast, and deposes such of the clergy. See also Canon LV. of the Council in Trullo.

This canon is found in the Corpus Juris Canonici, Gratian's *Decretum*, Pars I., Dist. xxx., c. vij.

CANON XIX.

IF any of the ascetics, without bodily necessity, shall behave with insolence and disregard the fasts commonly prescribed and observed by the Church, because of his perfect understanding in the matter, let him be anathema.

NOTES.

ANCIENT EPITOME OF CANON XIX.

Whoso neglects the fasts of the Church, let him be anathema.

I have followed Hefele's translation of the last clause, with which Van Espen seems to agree, as well as Zonaras. But Hardouin and Mansi take an entirely different view and translate "if the Eustathian deliberately rejects the Church fasts." Zonoras and Balsamon both refer to the LXIXth of the Apostolical Canons as being the law the Eustathians violated. Balsamon suggests that the Eustathians shared the error of the Bogomiles on the subject of fasting, but I see no reason to think that this was the case, Eustathius's action seems rather to be attributable to pride, and a desire to be different and original, "I thank thee that I am not as other men are," (as Van Espen points out). All that Socrates says (*H. E.,* II., xliii.,) is that "he commanded that the prescribed fasts should be neglected, and that the Lord's days should be fasted."

This canon is found in the *Corpus Juris Canonici,* Gratian's *Decretum,* Pars I., Dist. xxx., c. viii., in an imperfect translation but not that of either Isidore or Dionysius.

CANON XX.

IF any one shall, from a presumptuous disposition, **condemn** and abhor the assemblies [in honour] of the martyrs, or the services performed there, and the commemoration of them, let him be anathema.

NOTES.

ANCIENT EPITOME OF CANON XX.

Whoever thinks lightly of the meetings in honour of the holy martyrs, let him be anathema.

HEFELE.

Van Espen is of opinion that the Eustathians had generally rejected the common service as only fit for the less perfect, and that the martyr chapels are only mentioned here, because in old times service was usually held there. According to this view, no especial weight need be attached to the expression. But this canon plainly speaks of a disrespect shown by the Eustathians to the martyrs. Compare the twelfth article of the Synodal Letter. Fuchs thought that, as the Eustathians resembled the Aerians, who rejected the service for the dead, the same views might probably be ascribed to the Eustathians. But, in the first place, the Aerians are to be regarded rather as opposed than related in opinion to the Eustathians, being lax in contrast to these ultra-rigorists.

Besides which, Epiphanius only says that they rejected prayer for the salvation of the souls of the departed, but not that they did not honour the martyrs ; and there is surely a great difference between a feast in honour of a saint, and a requiem for the good of a departed soul. Why, however, the Eustathians rejected the veneration of martyrs is nowhere stated ; perhaps because they considered themselves as saints, κατ᾽ ἐξοχήν, exalted above the martyrs, who were for the most part only ordinary Christians, and many of whom had lived in marriage, while according to Eustathian views no married person could be saved, or consequently could be an object of veneration.

Lastly, it must be observed that the first meaning of σύναξις, is an assembly for divine service, or the service itself ; but here it seems to be taken to mean συναγωγή the place of worship, so that the συνάξεις τῶν μαρτύρων seems to be identical with martyria, and different from the λειτουργίαι held in them, of which the latter words of the canon speak.

EPILOGUE.

THESE things we write, not to cut off those who wish to lead in the Church of God an ascetic life, according to the Scriptures ; but those who carry the pretence of asceticism to superciliousness ; both exalting themselves above those who live more simply, and introducing novelties contrary to the Scriptures and the ecclesiastical Canons. We do, assuredly, admire virginity accompanied by humility ; and we have regard for continence, accompanied by godliness and gravity ; and we praise the leaving of worldly occupations, [when it is made] with lowliness of mind ; [but at the same time] we honour the holy companionship of marriage, and we do not contemn wealth enjoyed with uprightness and beneficence ; and we commend plainness and frugality in apparel, [which is worn] only from attention, [and that] not over-fastidious, to the body ; but dissolute and effeminate excess in dress we eschew ; and we reverence the houses of God and embrace the assemblies held therein as holy and helpful, not confining religion within the houses, but reverencing every place built in the name of God ; and we approve of gathering together in the Church itself for the common profit ; and we bless the exceeding charities done by the brethren to the poor, according to the traditions of the Church ; and, to sum up in a word, we wish that all things which have been delivered by the Holy Scriptures and the Apostolical traditions, may be observed in the Church.

NOTES.

This is lacking in the ancient epitome ; and while it occurs after Canon XX. in the versions of Dionysius Exiguus and of Isidore Mercator, it is not numbered as a canon. Moreover in John of Antioch's *Collection* and in Photius's *Nomocanon*, the number of canons is said to be 20. Only the Greek Scholiasts number it as Canon XXI., but its genuineness is unquestioned.

It is curiously enough found in the *Corpus Juris Canonici*, divided into two canons ! Gratian's *Decretum*, Pars I., Dist. XXX., c. xvj., and Dist. xli., c. v.

VAN ESPEN.

The Fathers of Gangra recognize not only the Holy Scriptures, but also the Apostolical traditions for the rule of morals.

From this [canon] it is by no means doubtful that the fathers of this Synod considered that the Eustathians had violated some already existing ecclesiastical canons. Beveridge is of opinion that these are those commonly called the Canons of the Apostles (*Synod.* I. 5). Nor is this unlikely to be true, for there can be no doubt that the doctrines of the Eustathians condemned by this synod are directly opposed to those very "Canons of the Apostles"; and no small argument is drawn for the authority and antiquity of the Canons of the Apostles from the large number of Eustathian teachings found to be therein condemned, as Beveridge has pointed out and as can easily be seen by comparing the two.

THE SYNOD OF ANTIOCH IN ENCÆNIIS.

A.D. 341.

Elenchus.

Historical Introduction.   *The Synodal Letter.*

The Canons, with the Ancient Epitome and Notes.

HISTORICAL INTRODUCTION.

Of the Synod of Antioch which adopted the canons subsequently received into the code of the universal church we know the exact date. This is fixed by the fact that the synod was held at the time of the dedication of the great church in Antioch, known as the "Golden," which had been begun by his father, Constantine the Great, and was finished in the days of Constantius. The synod has for this reason always been known as the Synod of Antioch *in Encœniis*, i.e., at the dedication (*in Dedicatione*), and was holden in the summer of the year 341. Ninety-seven bishops assembled together and a large number of them were hostile to St. Athanasius, being professed Eusebians, all of them were Orientals and most of them belonged to the patriarchate of Antioch. Not a single Western or Latin bishop was present and the pope, Julius, was in no way represented. This fact gave Socrates the historian the opportunity of making the statement (around which such polemics have raged), that "an ecclesiastical canon commands that the churches should not make decrees against the opinion of the bishop of Rome." [1]

But while this much is all clear, there is no council that presents a greater amount of difficulty to the historian as well as to the theologian. No one can deny that St. Hilary of Poictiers, who was a contemporary, styled it a Synod of Saints (Synodus Sanctorum) [2]; that two of its canons were read at Chalcedon as the "canons of the Holy Fathers"; and that Popes John II., Zacharias, and Leo. IV. all approved these canons, and attributed them to "Holy Fathers." And yet this synod set forth creeds to rival that of Nice, and, it is said, that some of the canons were adopted to condemn Athanasius.

Various attempts have been made to escape from these difficulties.

It has been suggested that there really were two Synods at Antioch, the one orthodox, which adopted the canons, the other heretical.

Father Emanuel Schelstraten, S. J. [3] improved on this theory. He supposed that the Eusebians stopped behind in Antioch after the orthodox bishops left and then passed the decrees against Athanasius, giving out that the synod was still in session. This has been adopted by Pagi, Remi Ceillier, Walch, and to a certain extent by Schröckh and others. But Tillemont demurs to this view, urging that according to Socrates [4] the deposition of Athanasius came first and the adoption of the canons afterwards. But Tillemont would seem to have misunderstood Socrates on this point and this objection falls to the ground. But another objection remains, viz., that both Socrates and Sozomen say that the creeds were drawn up *after* the deposition of Athanasius, "and yet" (as Hefele remarks, Vol. II., p. 63), "St. Hilary says that these creeds proceeded from a 'Synod of Saints.'"

Schelstraten's hypothesis not being satisfactory, the learned Ballerini, in their appendix to the *Opera S. Leonis M.*, have set forth another theory with which Mansi agrees in his "Notes on Alexander Natalis's *Church History*." These maintain that the canons did not come from the Council *in Encœniis* at all, but from another synod held before, in 332; but Hefele rejects this hypothesis altogether, on the following grounds. First and chiefest because it has no external evidence to support it; and secondly because the internal evidence is most unsatisfactory. But even if the 25 canons were adopted by a synod at Antioch in 332, the real difficulty would not be obviated, for Socrates says [5] of that synod that there too the

---

[1] Socrates. *H. E.*, Lib. II., cap viij. Hefele thinks the statement may rest upon nothing more than the letter of Julius I. that the matter should first have been referred to Rome (Hefele. *Hist. Councils*, Vol. II., p. 59, n. 2.) But the word used by Socrates is καυών!

[2] Hilar. Pict. *De Synodis, seu de Fide Orient.*, C. xxxii. Ed. Ben., 1170.

[3] Schelstraten, S. J. *Sacrum Antiochenum Concil. auctoritati suœ restitutum.* (Ant. 1680.)

[4] Socrates. *H. E.*, Lib. II., Cap. viij.

[5] Socrates. *H. E.*, Lib. I., Cap. xxiv.

"opposers of the Nicene faith" were able to elect their candidate to fill the place of the banished bishop Eustathius!

Hefele seems to give the true solution of the whole difficulty when he says: "Certainly Athanasius identified the Eusebians with the Arians and we regard them as at least Semi-arians; but at that time, after they had made the orthodox confession of faith, and repeatedly declared their disapproval of the heresies condemned at Nice, they were considered, by the greater number, as lawful bishops, and thoroughly orthodox and saintly men might without hesitation unite with them at a synod." [1]

Pope Julius styles the very Eusebian synod that deposed Athanasius "dear brethren" while blaming their action, and invited them to a common synod to enquire into the charges made against the Saint. In view of all this we may well believe that both orthodox and Eusebians met together at the consecration of the Emperor's new church, and that the whole church afterwards awarded the canons then adopted a rank in accordance with their intrinsic worth, and without any regard to the motives or shades of theological opinion that swayed those who drafted and voted for them.

---

[1] Hefele. *History of the Councils.* Vol., II., p. 66. I have in this introduction done little more than condense Hefele.

THE SYNODAL LETTER.

(*Found in Labbe and Cossart,* Concilia, Tom. II., col. 559. *It really is no part of the canons, but I have placed it here, because, as Labbe notes, " it is usually prefixed to the canons in the Greek."*)

The holy and most peaceful Synod which has been gathered together in Antioch from the provinces of Cœle-Syria, Phœnicia, Palestine, Arabia, Mesopotamia, Cilicia, and Isauria ; [1] to our like-minded and holy fellow Ministers in every Province, health in the Lord.

The grace and truth of our Lord and Saviour Jesus Christ hath regarded the holy Church of the Antiochians, and, by joining it together with unity of mind and concord and the Spirit of Peace, hath likewise bettered many other things; and in them all this betterment is wrought by the assistance of the holy and peace-giving Spirit. Wherefore, that which after much examination and investigation, was unanimously agreed upon by us bishops, who coming out of various Provinces have met together in Antioch, we have now brought to your knowledge ; trusting in the grace of Christ and in the Holy Spirit of Peace, that ye also will agree with us and stand by us as far as in you lies, striving with us in prayers, and being even more united with us, following the Holy Spirit, uniting in our definitions, and decreeing the same things as we ; ye, in the concord which proceedeth of the Holy Spirit, sealing and confirming what has been determined.

Now the Canons of the Church which have been settled are hereto appended.

---

[1] Hefele thinks this list of provinces is probably an interpolation. In the Latin version this letter is followed by the names of the bishops.

THE CANONS OF THE BLESSED AND HOLY FATHERS ASSEMBLED AT ANTIOCH IN SYRIA.[1]

CANON I.

WHOSOEVER shall presume to set aside the decree of the holy and great Synod which was assembled at Nice in the presence of the pious Emperor Constantine, beloved of God, concerning the holy and salutary feast of Easter; if they shall obstinately persist in opposing what was [then] rightly ordained, let them be excommunicated and cast out of the Church; this is said concerning the laity. But if any one of those who preside in the Church, whether he be bishop, presbyter, or deacon, shall presume, after this decree, to exercise his own private judgment to the subversion of the people and to the disturbance of the churches, by observing Easter [at the same time] with the Jews, the holy Synod decrees that he shall thenceforth be an alien from the Church, as one who not only heaps sins upon himself, but who is also the cause of destruction and subversion to many; and it deposes not only such persons themselves from their ministry, but those also who after their deposition shall presume to communicate with them. And the deposed shall be deprived even of that external honour, of which the holy Canon and God's priesthood partake.

NOTES.

ANCIENT EPITOME OF CANON I.

Whoso endeavours to change the lawful tradition of Easter, if he be a layman let him be excommunicated, but if a cleric let him be cast out of the Church.

The connexion between these canons of Antioch and the Apostolical Canons is so evident and so intimate that I shall note it, in each case, for the convenience of the student.

Zonaras and Balsamon both point out that from this first canon it is evident that the Council of Nice did take action upon the Paschal question, and in a form well known to the Church.

VAN ESPEN.

From this canon it appears that the fathers did not deem laymen deserving of excommunication who merely broke the decrees, but only those who "obstinately persist in opposing the decrees sanctioned and received by the Church; for by their refusal to obey they are attempting to overturn." And this being the case, why should such not be repelled or cast forth from the Church as rebels?

Finally this Canon proves that not only bishops and presbyters, but also deacons were reckoned among them who, "preside in the Church." An argument in favour of the opinion that the deacons of that time were entrusted with hierarchical functions.

It is curious that as a matter of fact the entire clergy and people of the West fell under the anathema of this canon in 1825, when they observed Easter on the same day as the Jews. This was owing to the adoption of the Gregorian calendar, and this misfortune while that calendar is followed it is almost impossible to prevent.[2]

Compare Apostolic Canons; Canon VII.

CANON II.

ALL who enter the church of God and hear the Holy Scriptures, but do not communicate with the people in prayers, or who turn away, by reason of some disorder, from the holy partaking of the Eucharist, are to be cast out of the Church, until, after they shall have made confession, and having brought forth the fruits of penance, and made

---

[1] This is the title in the codices of Zoraras; the Parisian edition of Balsamon simply reads "The Synod at Antioch." The Bodleian MS. reads "Canons of the Synod at Antioch in Syria."

[2] There seems but little doubt that the Gregorian Calendar will be introduced before many years into Russia.

earnest entreaty, they shall have obtained forgiveness; and it is unlawful to communicate with excommunicated persons, or to assemble in private houses and pray with those who do not pray in the Church; or to receive in one Church those who do not assemble with another Church. And, if any one of the bishops, presbyters, or deacons, or any one in the Canon shall be found communicating with excommunicated persons, let him also be excommunicated, as one who brings confusion on the order of the Church.

NOTES.

Ancient Epitome of Canon II.

Whoso comes to church, and attentively hears the holy Scriptures, and then despises, goes forth from, and turns his back upon the Communion, let him be cast out, until after having brought forth fruits of penance, he shall be indulged. And whoso communicates with one excommunicated, shall be excommunicated, and whoso prays with him who prays not with the Church is guilty, and even whoso receives him who does not attend the services of the Church is not without guilt.

Balsamon.

In the Eighth and Ninth canons of the Apostles it is set forth how those are to be punished who will not wait for the prayers, and the holy Communion: So, too, in the Tenth canon provision is made with respect to those who communicate with the excommunicated. In pursuance of this the present canon provides that they are to be cut off who come to church and do not wait for the prayer, and through disorder [? ἀταξίαν] [1] will not receive the holy Communion; for such are to be cast out until with confession they shew forth worthy penance.

Zonaras.

In this canon the Fathers refer to such as go to church but will not tarry to the prayer nor receive holy Communion, held back by some perversity or license, that is to say without any just cause, but petulantly, and by reason of some disorder [ἀταξίαν]; these are

forbidden to be expelled from the Church, that is to say cut off from the congregation of the faithful. But the Fathers call it a turning away from, not a hatred of the divine Communion, which holds them back from communion; a certain kind of flight from it, brought about perchance by reverence and lowliness of mind. Those who object to communicate by reason of hatred or disgust, such must be punished not with mere separation, but by an altogether absolute excommunication, and be cursed with anathema.

It need hardly be remarked that this canon has no reference to such of the faithful as tarry to the end of the service and yet do not partake of the holy sacrament, being held back by some good reason, recognized by the Church as such. It will be remembered that the highest grade of Penitents did this habitually, and that it was looked upon as a great privilege to be allowed to be present when the Divine Mysteries were performed, even though those assisting as spectators might not be partakers of them. What this canon condemns is leaving the Church before the service of the Holy Eucharist is done; this much is clear, the difficulty is to understand just why these particular people, against whom the canon is directed, did so.

This canon should be compared with the Apostolic canons viij., ix., x., xj., xij. and xiij.

CANON III.

If any presbyter or deacon, or any one whatever belonging to the priesthood, shall forsake his own parish, and shall depart, and, having wholly changed his residence, shall set himself to remain for a long time in another parish, let him no longer officiate; especially if his own bishop shall summon and urge him to return to his own parish and he shall disobey. And if he persist in his disorder, let him be wholly deposed from his ministry, so that no further room be left for his restoration. And if another bishop shall receive a man deposed for this cause, let him be punished by the Common Synod as one who nullifies the ecclesiastical laws.

---

[1] I confess I do not know what the phrase κατά τινα ἀταξίαν means, nor do the Greek Commentators give much help. I have translated "by reason of some disorder" in the canon itself, and in the notes, but Beveridge renders it *propter aliquam insolentiam*, which to me appears very unsatisfactory. The *pro quædam intemperantia* of the ordinary Latin seems no better. The same word is used in the next canon.

NOTES.

ANCIENT EPITOME OF CANON III.

If any cleric leaves his own parish and goes off to another, travelling here and there, and stays for a long time in that other, let him not offer the sacrifice (λειτουργείτω), especially if he do not return when called by his own bishop. But if he perseveres in his insolence let him be deposed, neither afterwards let him have any power to return. And if any bishop shall receive him thus deposed, he shall be punished by the Common Synod for breach of the ecclesiastical laws.

Compare with Canons of the Apostles xv. and xvi.

This canon is found in the *Corpus Juris Canonici*, Gratian's *Decretum*, Pars II., Causa VII., Quæst. I., Can. xxiv.[1]

CANON IV.

IF any bishop who has been deposed by a synod, or any presbyter or deacon who has been deposed by his bishop shall presume to execute any part of the ministry, whether it be a bishop according to his former custom, or a presbyter, or a deacon, he shall no longer have any prospect of restoration in another Synod; nor any opportunity of making his defence; but they who communicate with him shall all be cast out of the Church, and particularly if they have presumed to communicate with the persons aforementioned, knowing the sentence pronounced against them.

NOTES.

ANCIENT EPITOME OF CANON IV.

If a bishop deposed by a synod shall dare to celebrate the liturgy, let him have no chance of return.

This canon derives its chief interest from the fact that it is usually considered to have been adopted at the instigation of the party opposed to St. Athanasius and that afterwards it was used against St. Chrysostom. But while such may have been the secret reason why some voted for it and others prized it, it must be remembered that its provision is identical with that of the Apostolic Canons, and that it was read at the Council of Chalcedon as Canon eighty-three. Remi Ceillier (*Histoire Général des Autheurs*, p. 659) tries to prove that this is not the canon which St.

Chrysostom and his friends rejected, but Hefele thinks his position "altogether untenable" (*Hist. of the Councils*, Vol. II., p. 62, n. 1), and refers to Tillemont (*Mémoires*, p. 329, *Sur les Arians*, and Fuchs' *Bib. der Kirchenversammlungen*, P. II., p. 59.[2])

Compare Apostolic Canon xxviij.

This canon is found twice in the *Juris Corpus Canonici*, Gratian's *Decretum*, Pars II., Causa XI., Quæst. III., Can. vj., and Can. vij. in the version of Martin Bracarensis. This version is very interesting as expanding the phrase "to execute any part of the ministry" into "to make the oblation, or to perform the morning or evening sacrifice as though he were in office just as before, etc."

CANON V.

IF any presbyter or deacon, despising his own bishop, has separated himself from the Church, and gathered a private assembly, and set up an altar; and if, when summoned by his bishop, he shall refuse to be persuaded and will not obey, even though he summon him a first and a second time, let such an one be wholly deposed and have no further remedy, neither be capable of regaining his rank. And if he persist in troubling and disturbing the Church, let him be corrected, as a seditious person, by the civil power.

---

[1] Hefele seems to have overlooked this. The note referring to the Apostolic Canons is all wrong (p. 68, n. 1.)

[2] Hefele on the preceding page (p. 61, n. 1) says "Of course the sentence or canon to which the adversaries of Chrysostom referred must be distinguished from the fourth and twelfth true Antiochian canons. It seems somewhat difficult to reconcile this with what I have cited above, and with the following (p. 65): "In the affair of St. Chrysostom the canon employed against him was represented as proceeding from the Arians, and all attempts to deny its identity with our fourth and twelfth Antiochian canons are fruitless."

NOTES.

ANCIENT EPITOME OF CANON V.

Any presbyter or deacon who spurns his bishop, and withdraws from him, and sets up another altar, if after being thrice called by the bishop, he shall persist in his arrogancy, let him be deposed and be deprived of all hope of restoration.

It will be noted that the Ancient Epitome mentions three warnings, and the canon only two. The epitome in this evidently follows the Apostolical Canon, number thirty-one. It is somewhat curious that Aristenus in commenting on this canon does not note the discrepancy.

VAN ESPEN.

This canon, together with the preceding was read from the Code of Canons at the Council of Chalcedon, at the Fourth Session in connexion with the case of Carosus and Dorothœus, and of other monks who adhered to them. And a sentence in accordance with them was conceived in these words against those who would not obey the Council in the condemnation of Eutyches, "Let them know that they together with the monks who are with them, are deprived of grade, and of all dignity, and of communion, as well as he, so that they cease to preside over their monasteries: and if they attempt to escape, this holy and universal great council decrees the same punishment shall attach to them, that is to say the external authority, according to the divine and holy laws of the Fathers, shall carry out the sentence passed against the contumacious."

This canon shews that monks and clerics who were rebellious were sometimes coerced by the Secular Power, when the ecclesiastical power was not sufficient to coerce them, and hence it was that the secular arm was called in.

Compare with this Apostolic Canon XXXI.

The last clause of this canon is found in the *Corpus Juris Canonici*, Gratian's *Decretum*, Pars II. Causa XI., Quæst VIII. Can. vij. (The Latin however for "by the civil power" is, as is pointed out by the Roman Correctors, *per forinsecam potestatem* or *per forasticam potestatem.*

CANON VI.

IF any one has been excommunicated by his own bishop, let him not be received by others until he has either been restored by his own bishop, or until, when a synod is held, he shall have appeared and made his defence, and, having convinced the synod, shall have received a different sentence. And let this decree apply to the laity, and to presbyters and deacons, and all who are enrolled in the clergy-list.

NOTES.

ANCIENT EPITOME OF CANON VI.

The sentence of the greater synod upon a clerk excommunicated by his bishop, whether of acquittal or condemnation, shall stand.

Compare Apostolic Canons numbers XII. and XXXII.

This canon is found in the *Corpus Juris Canonici*, Gratian's *Decretum*, Pars II., Causa XI., Quæst. III., Can. ij.

CANON VII.

No stranger shall be received without letters pacifical.

NOTES.

ANCIENT EPITOME OF CANON VII.

A traveller having no letter pacific with him is not to be received.

Compare the Apostolic Canon number XXXIII.

For a discussion of the Letters styled *pacifici*, see notes on next canon.

This canon is found in the *Corpus Juris Canonici*, Gratian's *Decretum*, Pars I., Dist. lxxi., c. ix. in Isidore's version. The Roman Correctors note that Dionysius must have had a different reading from the Greek we know.

CANON VIII.

LET not country presbyters give letters canonical, or let them send such letters only to the neighbouring bishops.   But the chorepiscopi of good report may give letters pacifical.

NOTES.

ANCIENT EPITOME OF CANON VIII.

A country presbyter is not to give canonical letters, or [at most] only to a neighbouring bishop.

These "letters canonical" were called in the West letters "*formatæ*," and no greater proof of the great influence they had in the early days of the Church in binding the faithful together can be found than the fact that Julian the Apostate made an attempt to introduce something similar among the pagans of his empire.

"Commendatory letters" (ἐπιστολαὶ συστατικαὶ) are spoken of by St. Paul in 2 Cor. iii. 1, and the reader will find some interesting remarks on this and cognate subjects in J. J. Blunt's, *The Christian Church during the first three Centuries* (Chapter II).

By means of these letters even the lay people found hospitality and care in every part of the world, and it was thrown up against the Donatists as a mark of their being schismatics that their canonical letters were good only among themselves.

Pseudo-Isidore informs us that it was stated at the Council of Chalcedon by Atticus, bishop of Constantinople, that it was agreed at the Council of Nice that all such letters should be marked Π. Υ. Α. Π. (i. e. Father, Son, Holy Spirit), and it is asserted (Herzog, *Real-Encyk., s. v.* Literæ Formatæ) that this form is found in German documents of the sixth century.

As will be seen among the Canons of Chalcedon, the old name, Letters Commendatory, is continued, but in this canon and in the 41st of Laodicea the expression "Canonical Letters" is used. In the West, at least, these letters received the episcopal seal of the diocese to avoid all possibility of imposture. Dean Plumptre (whom I am following very closely in this note) believes the earliest evidence of this use of the diocesan seal is in St. Augustine (*Epist.* lix. *al.* ccxvij.) He also refers to Ducange, *s. v.* Formatæ.

As these letters admitted their bearers to communion they were sometimes called "Communion letters" (κοινωνικαὶ), and are so described by St. Cyril of Alexandria ; and by the Council of Elvira (canon xxv.), and by St. Augustine (*Epist.* xliii. *al.* clxii).

The "Letters Pacifical" appear to have been of an eleemosynary character, so that the bearers of them obtained bodily help. Chalcedon in its eleventh canon ordains that these "Letters pacifical" shall be given to the poor, whether they be clerics or laics. The same expression is used in the preceding canon of the synod.

A later form of ecclesiastical letter is that with which we are so familiar, the "letter dimissory." This expression first occurs in Canon XVII. of the Council in Trullo. On this expression Suicer (*Thesaurus, s. v.* ἀπολυτικὴ) draws from the context the conclusion that "letters dimissory" were given only for permanent change of ecclesiastical residence, while "letters commendatory" were given to those whose absence from their diocese was only temporary.

CANON IX.

IT behoves the bishops in every province to acknowledge the bishop who presides in the metropolis, and who has to take thought for the whole province ; because all men of business come together from every quarter to the metropolis. Wherefore it is decreed that he have precedence in rank, and that the other bishops do nothing extraordinary without him, (according to the ancient canon which prevailed from [the times of] our Fathers) or such things only as pertain to their own particular parishes and the districts subject to them. For each bishop has authority over his own parish, both to manage it with the piety which is incumbent on every one, and to make provision for the whole district which is dependent on his city ; to ordain presbyters and deacons ; and to settle everything with judgment. But let him undertake nothing further without the bishop of the metropolis ; neither the latter without the consent of the others.

NOTES.

ANCIENT EPITOME OF CANON IX.

Bishops should be bound to the opinion of the metropolitan, and nothing should they do without his knowledge except only such things as have reference to the diocese of each, and let them ordain men free from blame.

VAN ESPEN.

From this canon we see that causes of more importance and greater moment are to be considered in the Provincial Synod which consisted of the metropolitan and the other bishops of the province.

By the "ancient canon" of which mention is here made, there can scarcely be a doubt is intended the xxxiv. of the Canons of the Apostles, since in it are read the same provisions (and almost in the same words) as here are set forth somewhat more at length; nor is there any other canon in which these provisions are found earlier in date than this synod, wherefore from this is deduced a strong argument for the integrity of the Canons of the Apostles.

The wording of this canon should be compared with the famous sentence so often quoted of St. Irenæus. "Ad hanc enim ecclesiam [i. e. of Rome] propter potentiorem principalitatem necesse est omnem convenire ecclesiam, hoc est, eos qui sunt undique fideles, in quâ semper ab his, qui sunt undique, conservata est eaque est ab Apostolis traditio."

Is it not likely that in the lost Greek original the words translated *convenire ad* were συντρέχειν ἐν? *Vide* on the meaning of *convenire ad*, F. W. Puller, *The Primitive Saints and the See of Rome*, pp. 32 *et seqq.*

Compare Apostolic Canon XXXIV.

CANON X.

THE Holy Synod decrees that persons in villages and districts, or those who are called chorepiscopi, even though they may have received ordination to the Episcopate, shall regard their own limits and manage the churches subject to them, and be content with the care and administration of these; but they may ordain readers, sub-deacons and exorcists, and shall be content with promoting these, but shall not presume to ordain either a presbyter or a deacon, without the consent of bishop of the city to which he and his district are subject. And if he shall dare to transgress [these] decrees, he shall be deposed from the rank which he enjoys. And a chorepiscopus is to be appointed by the bishop of the city to which he is subject.

NOTES.

ANCIENT EPITOME OF CANON X.

A chorepiscopus makes Exorcists, Lectors, Subdeacons and Singers, but not a presbyter or a deacon without the bishop of the city. Who dares to transgress this law let him be deposed. The bishop of the city makes the chorepiscopus.

For the Minor Orders in the Early Church see the Excursus on the subject appended to Canon XXIV. of Laodicea.

"Ordination to the episcopate." In translating thus I have followed both Dionysius and Isidore. the former of whom translates "although they had received the imposition of the hand of the bishop and had been consecrated bishops;" and the latter "although they had received from bishops the imposition of the hand, and had been consecrated bishops."

VAN ESPEN.

There can be no doubt that the Chorepiscopi, the authority of whom is limited by this canon, are supposed to be endowed with episcopal character. Among the learned there is a controversy as to whether Chorepiscopi were true bishops by virtue of the ordination to that office, and endowed with the episcopal character or were only bishops when accidentally so. But whatever may be the merits of this controversy, there can be no doubt from the context of this canon that the Fathers of Antioch took it for granted that the chorepiscopi were true bishops by virtue of their ordination, but it is also evident that they were subject to the bishop of the greater city. It must also be noted that these chorepiscopi were not instituted by the canons of the Councils of Ancyra, Neocæsarea, or even of Nice, for these speak of them and make their decrees as concerning something already existing.

And from the very limitations of this canon it is by no means obscure that the fathers of Antioch supposed these chorepiscopi to be real bishops, for otherwise even with the license of the bishop of the city they could not ordain presbyters or deacons.

CANON XI.

If any bishop, or presbyter, or any one whatever of the canon shall presume to betake himself to the Emperor without the consent and letters of the bishop of the province, and particularly of the bishop of the metropolis, such a one shall be publicly deposed and cast out, not only from communion, but also from the rank which he happens to have; inasmuch as he dares to trouble the ears of our Emperor beloved of God, contrary to the law of the Church. But, if necessary business shall require any one to go to the Emperor, let him do it with the advice and consent of the metropolitan and other bishops in the province, and let him undertake his journey with letters from them.

NOTES.

ANCIENT EPITOME OF CANON XI.

A bishop or presbyter who of his own motion and not at the bidding of the Metropolitan of the province goes to the Emperor shall be deprived both of communion and dignity.

This canon is one of those magnificent efforts which the early church made to check the already growing inclination to what we have in later times learned to call Erastianism. Not only did the State, as soon as it became Christian, interfere in spiritual matters at its own motion, but there were found bishops and others of the clergy who not being able to attain their ends otherwise, appealed to the civil power, usually to the Emperor himself, and thus the whole discipline of the Church was threatened, and the authority of spiritual synods set aside. How unsuccessful the Church often was in this struggle is only too evident from the remarks of the Greek commentator Balsamon on this very canon.

HEFELE.

Kellner (*Das Buss. und Strafversahren*, p. 61) remarks with reference to this, that deposition is here treated as a heavier punishment than exclusion from communion, and therefore the latter cannot mean actual excommunication but only suspension.

CANON XII.

If any presbyter or deacon deposed by his own bishop, or any bishop deposed by a synod, shall dare to trouble the ears of the Emperor, when it is his duty to submit his case to a greater synod of bishops, and to refer to more bishops the things which he thinks right, and to abide by the examination and decision made by them; if, despising these, he shall trouble the Emperor, he shall be entitled to no pardon, neither shall he have an opportunity of defence, nor any hope of future restoration.

NOTES.

ANCIENT EPITOME OF CANON XII.

One deposed, if he shall have troubled the Emperor, shall seek the greater synod, and submit to its decree. But if he again misbehave himself, he shall not have any chance of restoration.

It is usually supposed that this canon, as well as the fourth, and the fourteenth and fifteenth, was directed against St. Athanasius, and it was used against St. Chrysostom by his enemies. *Vide* Socrates, *Ecclesiastical History*, Book II., Chapter viij., and Sozomen's *Ecclesiastical History*, Book III., chapter v.; also *ibid.* Book VII., chapter xx.

This canon is found in the *Corpus Juris Canonici*, Gratian's *Decretum*, Pars II., Causa XXI., Quest. V., Can. ij., in Isidore's Version.

CANON XIII.

No bishop shall presume to pass from one province to another, and ordain persons to the dignity of the ministry in the Church, not even should he have others with him, unless he should go at the written invitation of the metropolitan and bishops into whose country he goes. But if he should, without invitation, proceed irregularly to the ordination of any, or to the regulation of ecclesiastical affairs which do not concern him, the things done by him are null, and he himself shall suffer the due punishment of his irregularity and his unreasonable undertaking, by being forthwith deposed by the holy Synod.

NOTES.

ANCIENT EPITOME OF CANON XIII.

If without invitation a bishop shall go into another province, and shall ordain, and administer affairs, what he does shall be void and he himself shall be deposed.

Compare with this Apostolic Canon xxxv.; also canon xxii. of this same synod.

This canon is found in the *Corpus Juris Canonici*, Gratian's *Decretum*, Pars II., Causa ix., Quæst. II., Can. vj. in the *Versio Prisca*. The Roman Correctors are not satisfied with it, however, nor with any version and give the Greek text, to which they add an accurate translation.

CANON XIV.

IF a bishop shall be tried on any accusations, and it should then happen that the bishops of the province disagree concerning him, some pronouncing the accused innocent, and others guilty; for the settlement of all disputes, the holy Synod decrees that the metropolitan call on some others belonging to the neighbouring province, who shall add their judgment and resolve the dispute, and thus, with those of the province, confirm what is determined.

NOTES.

ANCIENT EPITOME OF CANON XIV.

If the bishops of the province disagree among themselves as to an accused bishop, that the controversy may be certainly settled, let other neighbouring bishops be called in.

ZONARAS.

When any bishop shall have been condemned with unanimous consent by all the bishops of the province, the condemnation cannot be called into doubt, as this synod has set forth in its fourth canon. But if all the bishops are not of the same mind, but some contend that he should be condemned and others the contrary, then other bishops may be called in by the metropolitan from the neighbouring provinces, and when their votes are added to one or other of the parties among the bishops, then controversy should be brought to a close.

This also is the law of the Synod of Sardica, canons iii. and v.

ARISTENUS.

Every bishop accused of crimes should be judged by his own synod, but if the bishops of the province differ, some saying that he is innocent and some that he is guilty, the metropolitan can call other bishops from a neighbouring province that they may solve the controversy agitated by the bishops.

This canon is found in the *Corpus Juris Canonici*, Gratian's *Decretum*, Pars II., Causa vi., Quæst. iv., can. j. The Roman Correctors note that the Latin translation implies that the neighbouring metropolitan is to be invited and say, " But, in truth, it hardly seems fitting that one metropolitan should come at the call of another, and that there should be two metropolitans in one synod."

CANON XV.

IF any bishop, lying under any accusation, shall be judged by all the bishops in the province, and all shall unanimously deliver the same verdict concerning him, he shall not be again judged by others, but the unanimous sentence of the bishops of the province shall stand firm.

NOTES.

If all the bishops of a province agree with regard to a bishop already sentenced, a new trial shall not be granted him.

VAN ESPEN.

By the phrase "by others" must be understood bishops called from a neighbouring province, of which mention is made in the previous canon, where in the case of an agreement among the bishops, the synod did not wish to be called in, even if it were demanded by the condemned bishop. This canon, therefore, is a supplement as it were to the preceding. And for this reason in the *Breviarium* and in Cresconius's *Collection* of Canons they are placed under a common title, cap. 144,

"Concerning the difference of opinion which happens in the judgment of bishops, or when a bishop is cut off by all the bishops of his province."

From these canons it is manifest that at first the causes of bishops were agitated and decided in provincial synods, and this discipline continued for many centuries, and was little by little departed from in the VIIIth and IXth centuries.

This canon is found in the *Corpus Juris Canonici*, Gratian's *Decretum*, Pars II., Causa VI., Quæst. IV., Can. v. Gratian adds a note which Van Espen remarks smacks of his own date rather than of that of the Synod of Antioch.

CANON XVI.

IF any bishop without a see shall throw himself upon a vacant church and seize its throne, without a full synod, he shall be cast out, even if all the people over whom he has usurped jurisdiction should choose him. And that shall be [accounted] a full synod, in which the metropolitan is present.

NOTES.

Whoever without the full synod and without the Metropolitan Council, shall go over to a vacant church, even if he has no position, he shall be ejected.

BEVERIDGE.

This, together with the following canon, was recited by Bishop Leontius in the Council of Chalcedon, from the book of the canons, in which this is called the 95th and the following the 96th, according to the order observed in that book of the canons.

This canon is found in the *Corpus Juris Canonici*, Gratian's *Decretum*, Pars I., Dist. XCII., Can. viij. in Isidore's version, and the Roman Correctors note its departure from the original.

CANON XVII.

IF any one having received the ordination of a bishop, and having been appointed to preside over a people, shall not accept his ministry, and will not be persuaded to proceed to the Church entrusted to him, he shall be excommunicated until he, being constrained, accept it, or until a full synod of the bishops of the province shall have determined concerning him.

NOTES.

Whoso has received orders and abandoned them let him be excommunicated, until he shall have repented and been received.

ZONARAS.

If any one called to the rule of the people refuse to undertake that office and ministry, let him be removed from communion, that is separated, until he accept the position. But should he persist in his refusal, he can by no means be absolved from his separation, unless perchance the full synod shall take some action in his case. For it is possible that he may assign reasonable causes why he should be excused from accepting the prelature offered him, reasons which would meet with the approbation of the synod.

Balsamon explains the canon in the same sense and adds that by "ordination" here is intended ordination proper, not merely election, as some have held.

Compare with this Apostolic Canon XXXVI.

This canon is found in the *Corpus Juris Canonici*, Gratian's *Decretum*, Pars I., Dist. XCII., C. vij. The Roman Correctors note that Dionysius's version is nearer the Greek.

CANON XVIII.

IF any bishop ordained to a parish shall not proceed to the parish to which he has been ordained, not through any fault of his own, but either because of the rejection of the people, or for any other reason not arising from himself, let him enjoy his rank and ministry; only he shall not disturb the affairs of the Church which he joins; and he shall abide by whatever the full synod of the province shall determine, after judging the case.

NOTES.

ANCIENT EPITOME OF CANON XVIII.

Let a bishop ordained but not received by his city have his part of the honour, and offer the liturgy only, waiting for the synod of the province to give judgment.

BALSAMON.

In canon xvij. the fathers punished him who when ordained could not be persuaded to go to the church to which he was assigned. In the present canon they grant pardon to him who is willing to take the charge of the diocese, for which he was consecrated, but is prevented from doing so by the impudence of the people or else by the incursions of the infidel; and therefore they allow him to enjoy, in whatever province he may happen to be, the honour due his rank, viz., his

throne, his title, and the exercise of the episcopal office, with the knowledge and consent of the bishop of the diocese. He must not, however, meddle with the affairs of the church of which he is a guest, that is to say he must not teach, nor ordain, nor perform any episcopal act without the consent of the bishop of the diocese; but he must observe quiet, until he learns what he ought to do by the determination of the full Synod.

Aristenus explains that by keeping quiet is intended that he should not "use any military help or other power."

This canon is found twice in the *Corpus Juris Canonici*, Gratian's *Decretum*, Pars I., Dist. xcii., c. iv. and v.; in the versions of Martin Bracarensis and of Dionysius.

CANON XIX.

A BISHOP shall not be ordained without a synod and the presence of the metropolitan of the province. And when he is present, it is by all means better that all his brethren in the ministry of the Province should assemble together with him; and these the metropolitan ought to invite by letter. And it were better that all should meet; but if this be difficult, it is indispensable that a majority should either be present or take part by letter in the election, and that thus the appointment should be made in the presence, or with the consent, of the majority; but if it should be done contrary to these decrees, the ordination shall be of no force. And if the appointment shall be made according to the prescribed canon, and any should object through natural love of contradiction, the decision of the majority shall prevail.

NOTES.

ANCIENT EPITOME OF CANON XIX.

If there be no synod and metropolitan, let there be no bishop. If on account of some difficulty all

do not meet together, at least let the greater number, or let them give their assent by letter. But if after the affair is all settled a few are contentious, let the vote of the majority stand firm.

ZONARAS.

In the first place it must be noted that by "ordination" in this place is meant election, and the laying on of the bishop's hand.

BALSAMON.

The method of choosing a bishop is laid down in the canons of Nice, number iv., but the present canon adds the provision that an election which takes place in violation of the provisions of this decree is null and invalid: and that when those who are electing are divided in opinion as to whom to choose, the votes of the majority shall prevail.   But

when you hear this canon saying that there should be no election without the presence of the Metropolitan, you must not say that he ought to be present at an election (for this was prohibited, as is found written in other canons) but rather say that his presence here is a permission or persuasion, without which no election could take place.

Compare Apostolic Canon number j.

This canon is found in the *Corpus Juris Canonici*, Gratian's *Decretum*, Pars I., Dist. LXV., can. iij.   Gratian has chosen Isidore's version, and the Roman Correctors point out that Dionysius' is preferable.

CANON XX.

WITH a view to the good of the Church and the settlement of disputes, it is decreed to be well that synods of the bishops, (of which the metropolitan shall give notice to the provincials), should be held in every province twice a year, one after the third week of the feast of Easter, so that the synod may be ended in the fourth week of the Pentecost ; and the second on the ides of October which is the tenth [or fifteenth] day of the month Hyperberetæus ; so that presbyters and deacons, and all who think themselves unjustly dealt with, may resort to these synods and obtain the judgment of the synod.   But it shall be unlawful for any to hold synods by themselves without those who are entrusted with the Metropolitan Sees.

NOTES.

ANCIENT EPITOME OF CANON XX.

On account of ecclesiastical necessities the synod in every province shall meet twice a year, in the fourth week of Pentecost and on the tenth day of Hyperberetæus.

SCHELESTRATIUS (*cit.* Van Espen).

The time fixed by the Council of Nice before Lent for the meeting of the synod was not received in the East, and the bishops kept on in the old custom of celebrating the council in the fourth week after Easter, for the time before Lent often presented the greatest difficulties for those in the far separated cities to come to the provincial metropolis.

VAN ESPEN.

In this canon the decree of Nice in canon v. is renewed, but with this difference that the Nicene synod orders one synod to be held

before Lent, but this synod that it should be held the fourth week after Easter.

It will be remembered that the whole period of the great fifty days from Easter to Whitsunday was known as "Pentecost."

Compare with this Apostolic Canon number XXXVII.

This canon is found in the *Corpus Juris Canonici*, Gratian's *Decretum*, Pars I., Dist. XVIII., c. xv., attributed to a council held by Pope Martin.   The Roman Correctors point out that this "Pope Martin" was a bishop of Braga (*Bracarensis*) from whose collection of the decrees of the Greek synods Gratian often quotes ; the Correctors also note, "For bishops in old times were usually called Popes" (*Antiquitus enim episcopi Papæ dicebantur*).

CANON XXI.

A BISHOP may not be translated from one parish to another, either intruding himself of his own suggestion, or under compulsion by the people, or by constraint of the bishops ; but he shall remain in the Church to which he was allotted by God from the beginning, and shall not be translated from it, according to the decree formerly passed on the subject.

NOTES.

A bishop even if compelled by the people, and compelled by the bishops, must not be translated to another diocese.

See the treatment of the translation of bishops in the Excursus to canon xv. of Nice.

Compare this canon with Apostolical Canon number xiv.

This canon is found in the *Corpus Juris Canonici*, Gratian's *Decretum*, Pars II., Causa VII., Quæst. I., can. xxv., from Isidore's version.

CANON XXII.

LET not a bishop go to a strange city, which is not subject to himself, nor into a district which does not belong to him, either to ordain any one, or to appoint presbyters or deacons to places within the jurisdiction of another bishop, unless with the consent of the proper bishop of the place. And if any one shall presume to do any such thing, the ordination shall be void, and he himself shall be punished by the synod.

NOTES.

A bishop shall not go from city to city ordaining people, except by the will of the bishop of the city : otherwise the ordination shall be without force, and he himself exposed to censure.

If we do not draw a rash conclusion, we should say that the interference of bishops in dioceses not their own, must have been very frequent in early days. This one synod enacted two canons (number XIII. and this present canon) on the subject. The same prohibition is found in canons XIV. and XXXV. of the Apostolic canons, in canon XV. of Nice, canon ij. of I. Constantinople and in many others. On account of the similarity of this canon to canon xiii. some have supposed it to be spurious, the enactment of some other synod, and this was the opinion of Godefrides Hermantius (*Vita S. Athanasii*, Lib. IV., cap. xij.) as well as of Alexander Natalis (*Hist. Sæc.*, IV., Dissert. xxv.). Van Espen, however, is of opinion that the two canons do not cover exactly the same ground,

for he says Canon XIII. requires letters both from the Metropolitan and from the other bishops of the province, while this canon XXII. requires only the consent of the diocesan. He concludes that Canon XIII. refers to a diocese *sede vacante*, when the Metropolitan with the other bishops took care of the widowed church, but that Canon XXII. refers to a diocese with its own bishop, whose will is all that is needed for the performance of episcopal acts by another bishop. And this distinction Schelestratius makes still more evident by his discussion of the matter in his scholion on Canon XIII.

Compare with this canon of the Apostolic Canons number XXXV. also number XIV.

This canon is found in the *Corpus Juris Canonici*, Gratian's *Decretum*, Pars II., Causa IX., Quæst. II., can. vij., but in a form differing far from the Greek original, as the Roman Correctors point out ; and even Gratian's present text is not as he wrote it, but amended.

CANON XXIII.

IT shall not be lawful for a bishop, even at the close of life, to appoint another as successor to himself ; and if any such thing should be done, the appointment shall be void. But the ecclesiastical law must be observed, that a bishop must not be appointed otherwise than by a synod and with the judgment of the bishops, who have the authority to promote the man who is worthy, after the falling asleep of him who has ceased from his labours.

NOTES.

A dying bishop shall not appoint another bishop. But when he is dead a worthy successor shall be provided by a synod of those who have this power.

Nothing could be more important than the provision of this canon. It is evidently intended to prevent nepotism in every form, and to leave the appointment to the vacant see absolutely to the free choice of the Metropolitan and his synod. The history of the Church, and its present practice, is a curious commentary upon the ancient legislation, and the appointment of coadjutor bishops *cum jure successionis*, so common in later days, seems to be a somewhat ingenious way of escaping the force of the canon. Van Espen, however, reminds his readers of the most interesting case of St. Augustine of Hippo (which he himself narrates in his Epistle CCXIII.) of how he was chosen by his predecessor as bishop of Hippo, both he and the then bishop being ignorant of the fact that it was prohibited by the canons. And how when in his old age the people wished him to have one chosen bishop to help him till his death and to succeed him afterwards, he declined saying: "What was worthy of blame in my own case, shall not be a blot likewise upon my son." He did not hesitate to say who he thought most worthy to succeed him, but he added, "he shall be a presbyter, as he is, and when God so wills he shall be a bishop." Van Espen adds; "All this should be read carefully that thence may be learned how St. Augustine set an example to bishops and pastors of taking all the pains possible that after their deaths true pastors, and not thieves and wolves, should enter into their flocks, who in a short time would destroy all they had accomplished by so much labour in so long a time." (Cf. Eusebius. *H. E.*, Lib. VI., cap. xj. and cap. xxxij.)

Compare Apostolic Canon number LXXVI.

This canon is found in the *Corpus Juris Canonici*, Gratian's *Decretum*, Pars II., Causa VIII., Quæst. I., can. III., in Dionysius's version, and again Canon IV. in that of Martin Bracarensis.

CANON XXIV.

It is right that what belongs to the Church be preserved with all care to the Church, with a good conscience and faith in God, the inspector and judge of all. And these things ought to be administered under the judgment and authority of the bishop, who is entrusted with the whole people and with the souls of the congregation. But it should be manifest what is church property, with the knowledge of the presbyters and deacons about him; so that these may know assuredly what things belong to the Church, and that nothing be concealed from them, in order that, when the bishop may happen to depart this life, the property belonging to the Church being well known, may not be embezzled nor lost, and in order that the private property of the bishop may not be disturbed on a pretence that it is part of the ecclesiastical goods. For it is just and well-pleasing to God and man that the private property of the bishop be bequeathed to whomsoever he will, but that for the Church be kept whatever belongs to the Church; so that neither the Church may suffer loss, nor the bishop be injured under pretext of the Church's interest, nor those who belong to him fall into lawsuits, and himself, after his death, be brought under reproach.

NOTES.

Ancient Epitome of Canon XXIV.

All the clergy should be cognizant of ecclesiastical matters; so that when the bishop dies the Church may preserve her own goods; but what belongs to the bishop shall be disposed of according to his directions.

Van Espen.

This canon shews the early discipline according to which the presbyters and deacons of the episcopal city, who were said to be "about him" or to pertain to his chair, represented the senate of the church, who together with the bishop administered the church affairs, and, when the see was vacant, had the charge of it. All this Martin of Braga sets forth more clearly in his version, and I have treated of the matter at large in my work on *Ecclesiastical Law*, Pars I., Tit. viii., cap. i., where I have shewn that the Cathedral chapter succeeded to this senate of presbyters and deacons.

Compare with this canon Apostolical Canon XL.

This canon in a somewhat changed form is found in the *Corpus Juris Canonici*, Gratian's *Decretum*, Pars II., Causa XII., Quæst. I., can. xx., and attributed to "Pope Martin's Council"; also compare with this the ensuing canon, number XXI.

CANON XXV.

LET the bishop have power over the funds of the Church, so as to dispense them with all piety and in the fear of God to all who need.   And if there be occasion, let him take what he requires for his own necessary uses and those of his brethren sojourning with him, so that they may in no way lack, according to the divine Apostle, who says, " Having food and raiment, let us therewith be content."   And if he shall not be content with these, but shall apply the funds to his own private uses, and not manage the revenues of the Church, or the rent of the farms, with the consent of the presbyters and deacons, but shall give the authority to his own domestics and kinsmen, or brothers, or sons, so that the accounts of the Church are secretly injured, he himself shall submit to an investigation by the synod of the province.   But if, on the other hand, the bishop or his presbyters shall be defamed as appropriating to themselves what belongs to the Church, (whether from lands or any other ecclesiastical resources), so that the poor are oppressed, and accusation and infamy are brought upon the account and on those who so administer it, let them also be subject to correction, the holy synod determining what is right.

NOTES.

ANCIENT EPITOME OF CANON XXV.

The bishop shall have power over ecclesiastical goods.   But should he not be content with those things which are sufficient for him but shall alienate the goods and revenues of the church, without the advice of the clergy, penalties shall be exacted from him in the presence of the synod.   But if he has converted to his own uses what was given for the poor, of this also let him give an explanation to the synod.

Compare with this canon Apostolic Canon number XLI.

This Canon is found in the *Corpus Juris Canonici*, Gratian's *Decretum*, Pars II., Causa XII., Quæst I., can. XXIII. and with this should be compared canon XXII. immediately preceding.

At the end of this canon in Labbe's version of Dionysius we find these words added. "And thirty bishops signed who were gathered together at this Synod." Isidore Mercator has a still fuller text, viz. : "I, Eusebius, being present subscribe to all things constituted by this holy Synod.   Theodore, Nicetas, Macedonius, Anatolius, Tarcodimantus, Æthereus, Narcissus, Eustachius, Hesychius, Mauricius, Paulus, and the rest, thirty bishops agreed and signed." Van Espen after noting that this addition is not found in the Greek, nor in Martin Bracarensis, adds "there is little probability that this clause is of the same antiquity as the canons."

SYNOD OF LAODICEA.

A.D. 343–381.

Elenchus.

HISTORICAL INTRODUCTION.

The Laodicea at which the Synod met is Laodicea in Phrygia Pacatiana, also called Lao-dicea ad Lycum, and to be carefully distinguished from the Laodicea in Syria. This much is certain, but as to the exact date of the Synod there is much discussion. Peter de Marca fixed it at the year 365, but Pagi in his *Critica* on Baronius's *Annals* [1] seems to have over-thrown the arguments upon which de Marca rested, and agrees with Gothofred in placing it *circa* 363. At first sight it would seem that the Seventh Canon gave a clue which would set-tle the date, inasmuch as the Photinians are mentioned, and Bishop Photinus began to be prominent in the middle of the fourth century and was anathematized by the Eusebians in a synod at Antioch in 344, and by the orthodox at Milan in 345 ; and finally, after several other condemnations, he died in banishment in 366. But it is not quite certain whether the word "Photinians" is not an interpolation. Something with regard to the date may perhaps be drawn from the word Πακατιανῆς as descriptive of Phrygia, for it is probable that this division was not yet made at the time of the Sardican Council in 343. Hefele concludes that "Under such circumstances, it is best, with Remi Ceillier, Tillemont, and others, to place the meeting of the synod of Laodicea generally somewhere between the years 343 and 381, i.e., between the Sardican and the Second Ecumenical Council—and to give up the at-tempt to discover a more exact date." [2]

But since the traditional position of the canons of this Council is after those of Antioch and immediately before those of First Constantinople, I have followed this order. Such is their position in "very many old collections of the Councils which have had their origin since the sixth or even in the fifth century," says Hefele. It is true that Matthew Blastares places these canons after those of Sardica, but the Quinisext Synod in its Second Canon and Pope Leo IV., according to the *Corpus Juris Canonici*,[3] give them the position which they hold in this volume.

---

[1] Pagi : *Crit. in Annal. Baron.*, A.D. 314, n. xxv. Baronius's view that this synod was held before that of Nice because the book of Judith is not mentioned among the books of the O. T., and because its canons are sometimes identical with those of Nice, is universally rejected.

[2] Hefele : *Hist. of the Councils*, Vol. II., p. 298.
[3] Gratian : *Decretum*, Pars I., Dist. xx., c. 1. It is from Leo's letter to the British Bishops.

THE CANONS OF THE SYNOD HELD IN THE CITY OF LAODICEA, IN PHRYGIA PACATIANA, IN WHICH MANY BLESSED FATHERS FROM DIVERS PROVINCES OF ASIA WERE GATHERED TOGETHER.[1]

The holy synod which assembled at Laodicea in Phrygia Pacatiana, from divers regions of Asia; set forth the ecclesiastical definitions which are hereunder annexed.

NOTE.

This brief preface, by some ancient collector, is found in the printed editions of Zonaras and of Balsamon and also in the Amerbachian manuscript.

CANON I.

It is right, according to the ecclesiastical Canon, that the Communion should by indulgence be given to those who have freely and lawfully joined in second marriages, not having previously made a secret marriage; after a short space, which is to be spent by them in prayer and fasting.

NOTES.

Ancient Epitome of Canon I.

A digamist not secretly married, after devoting himself for a short time to praying shall be held blameless afterwards.

Van Espen.

Many synods imposed a penance upon digamists, although the Church never condemned second marriages.

On this whole subject of second marriages see notes on Canon VIII. of Nice, on Canons III. and VII. of Neocæsarea, and on Canon XIX. of Ancyra. In treating of this canon Hefele does little but follow Van Espen, who accepts Bishop Beveridge's conclusions in opposition to Justellus and refers to him, as follows, "See this observation of Justellus' refuted more at length by William Beveridge in his notes on this canon," and Bp. Beveridge adopted and defended the exposition of the Greek commentators, viz.: there is some fault and some punishment, they are to be held back from communion for "a short space," but after that, it is according to the law of the Church that they should be admitted to communion. The phrase "not having previously made a secret marriage" means that there must not have been intercourse with the woman before the second marriage was "lawfully" contracted, for if so the punishment would have been for fornication, and neither light nor for "a short space." The person referred to in the canon is a real digamist and not a bigamist, this is proved by the word "lawfully" which could not be used of the second marriage of a man who already had a living wife.

CANON II.

They who have sinned in divers particulars, if they have persevered in the prayer of confession and penance, and are wholly converted from their faults, shall be received again to communion, through the mercy and goodness of God, after a time of penance appointed to them, in proportion to the nature of their offence.

NOTES.

Ancient Epitome of Canon II.

Those who have fallen into various faults and have confessed them with compunction, and done the penance suitable to them, shall be favourably received.

---

[1] Such is the caption in the Parisian edition of Zonaras; so too reads the Amerbachian codex; adding, however, that the number of canons is 60, and substituting for "Pacatiana" "Capatiana," a not unusual form of the same word.

HEFELE.

Van Espen and others were of opinion that this canon treated only of those who had themselves been guilty of various criminal acts, and it has been asked whether any one guilty not only of one gross sin, but of several of various kinds, might also be again received into communion. It seems to me, however, that this canon with the words, "those who have sinned in divers particulars," simply means that "sinners of various kinds shall be treated exactly in proportion to the extent of their fall." That the question is not necessarily of different sins committed by the same person appears from the words, "in proportion to the nature of their offence," as the singular, not the plural, is here used.

But Van Espen, with Aubespine, is clearly right in not referring the words, "if they persevere in confession and repentance," to sacramental confession, to which the expression "persevere" would not be well suited. Here is evidently meant the oft-repeated contrite confession before God and the congregation in prayer of sins committed, which preceded sacramental confession and absolution.

This canon is found in the *Corpus Juris Canonici*, Gratian's *Decretum*, Pars II., Causa XXVI., Quest. vii., can. iv.

CANON III.

HE who has been recently baptized ought not to be promoted to the sacerdotal order.

NOTES.

ANCIENT EPITOME OF CANON III.

A neophite is not ordainable.

This rule is laid down in the Second Nicene canon. Balsamon also compares Apostolic Canon lxxx.

BALSAMON.

Notwithstanding this provision, that great light, Nectarius, just separated from the flock of the catechumens, when he had washed away the sins of his life in the divine font, now pure himself, he put on the most pure dignity of the episcopate, and at the same time became bishop of the Imperial City, and president of the Second Holy Ecumenical Synod.

CANON IV.

THEY who are of the sacerdotal order ought not to lend and receive usury, nor what is called hemioliæ.

NOTES.

ANCIENT EPITOME OF CANON IV.

A priest is not to receive usury nor hemioliæ.

The same rule is laid down in the seventeenth Canon of Nice. For a treatment of the whole subject of usury see excursus to that canon.

Dionysius Exiguus and Isidore have numbered this canon v., and our fifth they have as iv.

This canon is found in the *Corpus Juris Canonici*, Gratian's *Decretum*, Pars I., Dist. XLVI., can. ix.

CANON V.

ORDINATIONS are not to be held in the presence of hearers.

NOTES.

ANCIENT EPITOME OF CANON V.

Ordinations are not to be performed in the presence of hearers.

BALSAMON.

This canon calls elections "laying on of hands," and says that since in elections unworthy things are often said with regard to those who are elected, therefore they should not take place in the presence of any that might happen to come to hear.

Zonaras also agrees that election is here intended, but Aristenus dissents and makes the reference to ordinations properly so-called, as follows :

ARISTENUS.

The prayers of ordination are not to be said out loud so that they may be heard by the people.

CANON VI.

IT is not permitted to heretics to enter the house of God while they continue in heresy.

NOTES.

ANCIENT EPITOME OF CANON VI.

The holy place is forbidden to heretics.

ARISTENUS.

Heretics are not to be permitted to enter the house of God, and yet Basil the Great, before this canon was set forth, admitted Valens to the perfecting of the faithful [i.e., to the witnessing the celebration of the Divine Mysteries].

VAN ESPEN.

A heretic who pertinaciously rejects the doctrine of the Church is rightly not allowed to enter the house of God, in which his doctrine is set forth, so long as he continues in his heresy. For this reason when Timothy, Archbishop of Alexandria, was consulted concerning the admission of heretics to church, answered in the IXth Canon of his *Canonical Epistle*, that unless they were ready to promise to do penance and to abandon their heresy, they could in no way be admitted to the prayers of the faithful.

Contrast with this Canon lxxxiv., of the so-called IVth Council of Carthage, A.D. 398.

CANON VII.

PERSONS converted from heresies, that is, of the Novatians, Photinians, and Quarto-decimans, whether they were catechumens or communicants among them, shall not be received until they shall have anathematized every heresy, and particularly that in which they were held ; and afterwards those who among them were called communicants, having thoroughly learned the symbols of the faith, and having been anointed with the holy chrism, shall so communicate in the holy Mysteries.

NOTES.

ANCIENT EPITOME OF CANON VII.

Novatians and Photinians, and Quartodeci-mans, unless they anathemathize their own and other heresies, are not to be received. When they have been anointed, after their abjuration, let them communicate.

I have allowed the word "Photinians" to stand in the text although whether it is not an interpolation is by no means certain. They certainly were heretical on the doctrine of the Holy Trinity, and therefore differed from the other dissidents mentioned in the canon, all of whom were orthodox on this matter. It is also worthy of note that the word is not found in Ferrandus's Condensation (*Breviatio Cano-num*, n. 177) nor in Isidore's version. More-over there is a Latin codex in Lucca, and also one in Paris (as is noted by Mansi, v. 585 ; ij. 591) in which it is lacking. It was rejected by Baronius, Binius, and Remi Ceillier.

The word "Catechumens" is wanting in many Greek MSS. but found in Balsamon, moreover, Dionysius and Isidore had it in their texts.

This canon possesses a great interest and value to the student from a different point of view. Its provisions, both doctrinal and disciplinary, are in contrariety with the provisions of the council held at Carthage in the time of St. Cyprian, and yet both these canons, contradictory as they are, are accepted by the Council in Trullo and are given such ecumenical authority as canons on discipline ever can possess, by the Seventh Ecumenical. This is not the only matter in which the various conciliar actions adopted and ratified do not agree *inter se*, and from this consideration it would seem evident that it was not intended that to each particular of each canon of each local synod adopted, the express sanction of the Universal Church was given, but that they were received in block as legislation well calculated for the good of the Church. And that this must have been the understanding at the time is evinced by the fact that while the Trullan canons condemned a number of Western customs and usages, as I shall have occasion to point out in its proper place, no objection was made by the Roman legates to the canon of the Seventh Ecumenical which received them as authoritative.

CANON VIII.

PERSONS converted from the heresy of those who are called Phrygians, even should they be among those reputed by them as clergymen, and even should they be called the very chiefest, are with all care to be both instructed and baptized by the bishops and presbyters of the Church.

NOTES.

ANCIENT EPITOME OF CANON VIII.

When Phrygians return they are to be baptized anew, even if among them they were reckoned clergymen.

HEFELE.

This synod here declares the baptism of the Montanists invalid, while in the preceding canon it recognised as valid the baptism of the Novatians and Quartodecimans. From this, it would appear that the Montanists were suspected of heresy with regard to the doctrine of the Trinity. Some other authorities of the ancient Church, however, judged differently, and for a long time it was a question in the Church whether to consider the baptism of the Montanists valid or not. Dionysius the Great of Alexandria was in favour of its validity: but this Synod and the Second General Council rejected it as invalid, not to mention the Synod of Iconium (235), which declared all heretical baptism invalid. This uncertainty of the ancient Church is accounted for thus: (*a*) On one side the Montanists, and especially Tertullian, asserted that they held the same faith and sacraments, especially the same baptism (*eadem lavacri sacramenta*) as the Catholics. St. Epiphanius concurred in this, and testified that the Montanists taught the same regarding the Father, the Son, and the Holy Ghost, as did the Catholic Church. (*b*) Other Fathers, however, thought less favourably of them, and for this reason, that the Montanists often expressed themselves so ambiguously, that they might, nay, must be said completely to iden-tify the Holy Ghost with Montanus. Thus Tertullian in quoting expressions of Montanus, actually says: "the Paraclete speaks"; and therefore Firmilian, Cyril of Jerusalem, Basil the Great, and other Fathers, did in fact, reproach the Montanists with this identification, and consequently held their baptism to be invalid. (*c*) Basil the Great goes to the greatest length in this direction in maintaining that the Montanists had baptized in the name of the Father, of the Son, and of Montanus and Priscilla. But it is very probable, as Tillemont conjectured, that Basil only founded these strange stories of their manner of baptizing upon his assumption that they identified Montanus with the Holy Ghost; and, as Baronius maintains, it is equally probable that the Montanists did not alter the form of baptism. But, even admitting all this, their ambiguous expressions concerning Montanus and the Holy Ghost would alone have rendered it advisable to declare their baptism invalid. (*d*) Besides this, a considerable number of Montanists, namely, the school of Æschines, fell into Sabellianism, and thus their baptism was decidedly invalid. (*Vide* Article in Wetzer and Welte *Kirchenlexicon s. v.* Montanus; by myself [i. e. Hefele]).

In conclusion, it must be observed that Balsamon and Zonaras rightly understood the words in our text, "even though they be called the very chiefest," "though they be held in the highest esteem," to refer to the most distinguished clergy and teachers of the Montanists.

CANON IX.

THE members of the Church are not allowed to meet in the cemeteries, nor attend the so-called martyries of any of the heretics, for prayer or service; but such as so do, if they be communicants, shall be excommunicated for a time; but if they repent and confess that they have sinned they shall be received.

NOTES.

ANCIENT EPITOME OF CANON IX.

Whoso prayeth in the cemeteries and martyries of heretics is to be excommunicated.

ZONARAS.

By the word "service" (θεραπείας) in this canon is to be understood the healing of sickness. The canon wishes that the faithful should under no pretence betake themselves to the prayers of heretical pseudo-martyrs nor pay them honour in the hope of obtaining the healing of sickness or the cure of their various temptations. And if any do so, they are to be cut off, that is for a time forbidden communion (and this refers to the faithful who are only laymen), but when they have done penance and made confession of their fault, the canon orders that they are to be received back again.

BALSAMON.

As canon vi. forbids heretics to enter the house of God, so this canon forbids the faithful to go to the cemeteries of heretics, which are called by them "Martyries." . . . For in the days of the persecution, certain of the heretics, calling themselves Christians, suffered even to death, and hence those who shared their opinions called them "martyrs."

VAN ESPEN.

As Catholics had their martyrs, so too had the heretics, and especially the Montanists or Phrygians, who greatly boasted of them. Apollinaris writes of these as may be seen in Eusebius (*H. E.*, Lib. v., cap. xvj.)

The places or cemeteries in which rested the bodies of those they boasted of as martyrs, they styled "Martyries" (*martyria*) as similar places among Catholics were wont to be called by the same name, from the bones of the martyrs that rested there.

From the Greek text, as also from Isidore's version it is clear that this canon refers to all the faithful generally, and that "the members of the Church" (Lat. *Ecclesiastici*, the word Dionysius uses) must be taken in this wide signification.

CANON X.

THE members of the Church shall not indiscriminately marry their children to heretics.

NOTES.

ANCIENT EPITOME OF CANON X.

Thou shalt not marry a heretic.

FUCHS.

(*Bib. der Kirchenvers.*, pt. ii., p. 324.)

"Indiscriminately" means not that they might be given in marriage to some heretics and not to others; but that it should not be considered a matter of indifference whether they were married to heretics or orthodox.

Zonaras and Balsamon, led astray by the similar canon enacted at Chalcedon (number xiv.), suppose this restriction only to apply to the children of the clergy, but Van Espen has shewn that the rule is of general application. He adds, however, the following:

VAN ESPEN.

Since by the custom of the Greeks, ecclesiastics are allowed to have wives, there is no doubt that the marriage of their children with heretics would be indecent in a very special degree, although there are many things which go to shew that marriage with heretics was universally deemed a thing to be avoided by Catholics, and was rightly forbidden.

CANON XI.

PRESBYTIDES, as they are called, or female presidents, are not to be appointed in the Church.

NOTES.

ANCIENT EPITOME OF CANON XI.

Widows called presidents shall not be appointed in churches.

BALSAMON.

In old days certain venerable women (πρεσβύτιδες) sat in Catholic churches, and took care that the other women kept good and modest order. But from their habit of using improperly that which was proper, either through their arrogancy or through their base self-seeking, scandal arose. Therefore the Fathers prohibited the existence in the Church thereafter of any more such women as are called presbytides or presidents. And that no one may object that in the monasteries of women one woman must preside over the rest, it should be remembered that the renunciation which they make of themselves to God and the tonsure brings it to pass that they are thought of as one body though many ; and all things which are theirs, relate only to the salvation of the soul. But for a woman to teach in a Catholic Church, where a multitude of men is gathered together, and women of different opinions, is, in the highest degree, indecorous and pernicious.

HEFELE.

It is doubtful what was here intended, and this canon has received very different interpretations. In the first place, what is the meaning of the words πρεσβύτιδες and προκαθήμεναι ("presbytides" and female presidents) ? I think the first light is thrown on the subject by Epiphanius, who in his treatise against the Collyridians (*Hær.*, lxxix. 4) says that "women had never been allowed to offer sacrifice, as the Collyridians presumed to do, but were only allowed to minister. Therefore there were only deaconesses in the Church, and even if the oldest among them were called 'presbytides,' this term must be clearly distinguished from presbyteresses. The latter would mean priestesses (ἱερίσσας), but 'presbytides' only designated their age, as seniors." According to this, the canon appears to treat of the superior deaconesses who were the overseers (προκαθήμεναι) of the other deaconesses ; and the further words of the text may then probably mean that in future no more such superior deaconesses or eldresses were to be appointed, probably because they had often outstepped their authority.

Neander, Fuchs, and others, however, think it more probable that the terms in question are in this canon to be taken as simply meaning deaconesses, for even in the church they had been wont to preside over the female portion of the congregation (whence their name of "presidents") ; and, according to St. Paul's rule, only widows over sixty years of age were to be chosen for this office (hence called "presbytides"). We may add, that this direction of the apostle was not very strictly adhered to subsequently, but still it was repeatedly enjoined that only elder persons should be chosen as deaconesses. Thus, for instance, the Council of Chalcedon, in its fifteenth canon, required that deaconesses should be at least forty years of age, while the Emperor Theodosius even prescribed the age of sixty.

Supposing now that this canon simply treats of deaconesses, a fresh doubt arises as to how the last words—"they are not to be appointed in the Church" are to be understood. For it may mean that "from henceforth no more deaconesses shall be appointed ; " or, that "in future they shall no more be solemnly ordained in the church." The first interpretation would, however, contradict the fact that the Greek Church had deaconesses long after the Synod of Laodicea. For instance, in 692 the Synod *in Trullo* (Can. xiv.) ordered that "no one under forty years of age should be ordained deaconess." Consequently the second interpretation, "they shall not be solemnly ordained in the church," seems a better one, and Neander decidedly prefers it. It is certainly true that several later synods distinctly forbade the old practice of conferring a sort of ordination upon deaconesses, as, for instance, the first Synod of Orange (*Arausicanum I.* of 441, Can. xxvj.) in the words—*diaconæ omnimodis non ordinandæ ;* also the Synod at Epaon in 517 (Can. xxj.), and the second Synod at Orleans in 533 (Can. xviij.) ; but in the Greek Church at least, an ordination, a χειροτονεῖσθαι, took place as late as the Council *in Trullo* (Can. xiv.). But this Canon of Laodicea does not speak of solemn dedication, and certainly not of ordination, but only of καθίστασθαι. These reasons induce us to return to the first interpretation of this canon, and to understand it as forbidding from that time forward the appointment of any more chief deaconesses or "presbytides."

Zonaras and Balsamon give yet another explanation. In their opinion, these "presbytides" were not chief deaconesses, but aged women in general (*ex populo*), to whom was given the supervision of the females, in church. The Synod of Laodicea, however, did away with this arrangement, probably because they had misused their office for purposes of pride, or money-making, bribery, etc.

Compare with the foregoing the Excursus on Deaconesses, appended to Canon XIX. of Nice.

This canon is found in the *Corpus Juris* *Canonici*, Gratian's *Decretum*, Pars I., Dist. XXXII., c. xix., in Isidore's version ; but Van Espen remarks that the Roman Correctors have pointed out that it departs widely from the Greek original. The Roman Correctors further say "The note of Balsamon on this point should be seen ; " and with this interpretation Morinus also agrees in his work on Holy Orders (*De Ordinationibus*, Pars III., Exercit. x., cap. iij., n. 3).

CANON XII.

BISHOPS are to be appointed to the ecclesiastical government by the judgment of the metropolitans and neighbouring bishops, after having been long proved both in the foundation of their faith and in the conversation of an honest life.

NOTE.

ANCIENT EPITOME OF CANON XII.

Whoever is most approved in faith and life and most learned, he is fit to be chosen bishop.

The first part of this canon is in conformity with the provision in the IV. canon of Nice.

CANON XIII.

THE election of those who are to be appointed to the priesthood is not to be committed to the multitude.

NOTES.

ANCIENT EPITOME OF CANON XIII.

Whoso is chosen by seculars is ineligible.

BALSAMON.

From this canon it is evident that in ancient times not only bishops but also priests were voted for by the multitude of the people. This is here forbidden.

ARISTENUS.

Bishops are elected by metropolitans and other bishops. If anyone in this manner shall not have been promoted to the Episcopate, but shall have been chosen by the multitude, he is not to be admitted nor elected.

[It is clear from this that by "the Priesthood" Aristenus understands the episcopate, and I think rightly:]

VAN ESPEN.

The word in the Greek to which "multitude" corresponds (ὄχλος) properly signifies a tumult.[1]

What the fathers intend to forbid are tumultuous elections, that is, that no attention is to be paid to riotous demonstrations

on the part of the people, when with acclamations they are demanding the ordination of anyone, with an appearance of sedition. Such a state of affairs St. Augustine admirably describes in his *Epistola ad Albinam* (*Epist.* cxxvi., Tom. II., col. 548, Ed. Gaume).

And it is manifest that by this canon the people were not excluded from all share in the election of bishops and priests from what St. Gregory Nazianzen says, in *Epistola ad Cæsarienses*, with regard to the election of St. Basil. From this what could be more evident than that after this canon was put out the people in the East still had their part in the election of a bishop? This also is clear from Justinian's "Novels" (*Novellæ*, cxxiij., c.j., and cxxxvij., c. ij.)

This canon is found in the *Corpus Juris Canonici*, Gratian's *Decretum*, Pars I., Dist. lxiii., can. vj., but in proof of the proposition that laymen were hereby forbidden to have any share in elections. Van Espen notes that Isidore's version favours Gratian's misunderstanding, and says that "no doubt that this version did much to exclude the people from the election of bishops."

---

[1] More accurately "a tumultuous and riotous mob" *vide* Liddell and Scott.

CANON XIV.

THE holy things are not to be sent into other dioceses at the feast of Easter by way of eulogiæ.

NOTES.

ANCIENT EPITOME OF CANON XIV.

It is not right to send the holy gifts to another parish.

HEFELE.

It was a custom in the ancient Church, not indeed to consecrate, but to bless such of the several breads of the same form laid on the altar as were not needed for the communion, and to employ them, partly for the maintenance of the clergy, and partly for distributing to those of the faithful who did not communicate at the Mass. The breads thus blessed were called *eulogiæ*. Another very ancient custom was, that bishops as a sign of Church fellowship, should send the *consecrated* bread to one another. That the Roman Popes of the first and second centuries did so, Irenæus testifies in his letter to Pope Victor in Eusebius. In course of time, however, instead of the consecrated bread, only bread which had been blessed, or *eulogiæ*, were sent abroad. For instance, Paulinus and Augustine sent one another these *eulogiæ*. But at Easter the older custom still prevailed; and to invest the matter with more solemnity, instead of the *eulogiæ*, the consecrated bread, *i.e.*, the Eucharist, was sent out. The Synod of Laodicea forbids this, probably out of reverence to the holy Sacrament.

Binterim (*Denkwürdegkeiten*, vol. IV., P. iij., p. 535.) gives another explanation. He starts from the fact that, with the Greeks as well as the Latins, the wafer intended for communion is generally called *sancta* or ἅγια even before the consecration. This is not only perfectly true, but a well-known fact; only it must not be forgotten that these wafers or oblations were only called *sancta* by anticipation, and because of the *sanctificatio* to which they were destined. Binterim then states that by ἅγια in the canon is to be understood not the breads already consecrated, but those still unconsecrated. He further conjectures that these unconsecrated breads were often sent about instead of the *eulogiæ*, and that the Synod of Laodicea had forbidden this, not during the whole year, but only at Easter. He cannot, however, give any reason, and his statement is the more doubtful, as he cannot prove that these unconsecrated communion breads really used before to be sent about as *eulogiæ*.

In connection with this, however, he adds another hypothesis. It is known that the Greeks only consecrate a square piece of the little loaf intended for communion, which is first cut out with the so-called holy spear. The remainder of the small loaf is divided into little pieces, which remain on or near the altar during Mass, after which they are distributed to the non-communicants. These remains of the small loaf intended for consecration are called ἀντίδωρα and Binterim's second conjecture is, that these ἀντίδωρα might perhaps have been sent as *eulogiæ* and may be the ἅγια of this canon. But he is unable to prove that these ἀντίδωρα were sent about, and is, moreover, obliged to confess that they are nowhere called *eulogiæ*, while this canon certainly speaks of *eulogiæ*. To this must be added that, as with regard to the unconsecrated wafer, so we see no sufficient cause why the Synod should have forbidden these ἀντίδωρα being sent.

CANON XV.

No others shall sing in the Church, save only the canonical singers, who go up into the ambo and sing from a book.

NOTES.

ANCIENT EPITOME OF CANON XV.

No one should ascend the ambon unless he is tonsured.

HEFELE.

The only question [presented by this canon] is whether this synod forbade the laity to take any part in the Church music, as Binius and others have understood the words of the text, or whether it only intended to forbid those who were not cantors taking the lead. Van Espen and Neander in particular were in favour of the latter meaning, pointing to the fact that certainly in the Greek Church after the Synod of Laodicea the people were accustomed to join in the singing, as Chrysostom and Basil the Great sufficiently testify. Bingham propounded a peculiar opinion, namely, that this Synod did indeed forbid the laity to sing in the church, or even to join in the singing, but this only temporarily, for certain reasons. I have no doubt, however, that Van Espen and Neander take the truer view.

CANON XVI.

THE Gospels are to be read on the Sabbath [i.e. Saturday], with the other Scriptures.

NOTES.

ANCIENT EPITOME OF CANON XVI.

The Gospel, the Epistle [ἀπόστολος] and the other Scriptures are to be read on the Sabbath.

BALSAMON.

Before the arrangement of the Ecclesiastical Psalmody was settled, neither the Gospel nor the other Scriptures were accustomed to be read on the Sabbath. But out of regard to the canons which forbade fasting or kneeling on the Sabbath, there were no services, so that there might be as much feasting as possible. This the fathers prohibit, and decree that on the Sabbath the whole ecclesiastical office shall be said.

Neander (*Kirchengesch.*, 2d ed., vol. iij., p. 565 *et seq.*) suggests in addition to the interpretation just given another, viz.: that it was the custom in many parts of the ancient Church to keep every Saturday as a feast in commemoration of the Creation. Neander also suggests that possibly some Judaizers

read on the Sabbath only the Old Testament; he, however, himself remarks that in this case εὐαγγέλια and ἑτέρων γραφῶν would require the article.

VAN ESPEN.

Among the Greeks the Sabbath was kept exactly as the Lord's day except so far as the cessation of work was concerned, wherefore the Council wishes that, as on Sundays, after the other lessons there should follow the Gospel.

For it is evident that by the intention of the Church the whole Divine Office was designed for the edification and instruction of the people, and especially was this the case on feast days, when the people were apt to be present in large numbers.

Here we may note the origin of our present [Western] discipline, by which on Sundays and feast days the Gospel is wont to be read with the other Scriptures in the canonical hours, while such is not the case on ferial days, or in the order for ferias and "simples."[1]

CANON XVII.

THE Psalms are not to be joined together in the congregations, but a lesson shall intervene after every psalm.

NOTES.

ANCIENT EPITOME OF CANON XVII.

In time of service lessons shall be interspersed with the Psalms.

ARISTENUS.

It was well to separate the Psalms by lessons when the congregation was gathered in church, and not to keep them continuously singing unbroken psalmody, lest those who had assembled might become careless through weariness.

ZONARAS.

This was an ancient custom which has been laid aside since the new order of ecclesiastical matters has been instituted.[2]

VAN ESPEN.

Here it may be remarked we find the real reason why in our present rite, the lections, verses, etc., of the nocturns are placed between the Psalms, so as to repel weariness.

---

[1] "Simples" (*simplici*) are distinguished from "doubles" (*duplici*) in not having their antiphons said double but only once.
[2] I do not understand this note, as to-day in the Divine Office of the Greek Church the Psalms are still divided by Lessons.

Vide *The Horologion* (ὡρόλογιον τὸ μέγα) and an English translation by G. V. Shann, entitled *Euchology, A Manual of Prayers of the Holy Orthodox Church.*

CANON XVIII.

THE same service of prayers is to be said always both at nones and at vespers.

NOTES.

ANCIENT EPITOME OF CANON XVIII.

The same prayers shall be said at nones and vespers.

HEFELE.

Some feasts ended at the ninth hour, others only in the evening, and both alike with prayer. The Synod here wills that in both cases the same prayers should be used. Thus does Van Espen explain the words of the text, and I think rightly. But the Greek commentator understands the Synod to order that the same prayers should be used in all places, thus excluding all individual caprice. According to this, the rule of conformity would refer to places; while, according to Van Espen, the nones and vespers were to be the same. If, however, this interpretation were correct, the Synod would not have only spoken of the prayers at nones and vespers, but would have said in general, " all dioceses shall use the same form of prayer."

EXCURSUS ON THE CHOIR OFFICES OF THE EARLY CHURCH.

Nothing is more marked in the lives of the early followers of Christ than the abiding sense which they had of the Divine Presence. Prayer was not to them an occasional exercise but an unceasing practice. If then the Psalmist sang in the old dispensation "Seven times a day do I praise thee" (Ps. cxix. 164), we may be quite certain that the Christians would never fall behind the Jewish example. We know that among the Jews there were the "Hours of Prayer," and nothing would be, *à priori*, more likely than that with new and deeper significance these should pass over into the Christian Church. I need not pause here to remind the reader of the observance of "the hour of prayer" which is mentioned in the New Testament, and shall pass on to my more immediate subject.

Most liturgiologists have been agreed that the "Choir Offices" of the Christian Church, that is to say the recitation of the Psalms of David, with lessons from other parts of Holy Scripture and collects,[1] was an actual continuation of the Jewish worship, the melodies even of the Psalms being carried over and modified through the ages into the plain song of to-day. For this view of the Jewish origin of the Canonical Hours there is so much to be said that one hesitates to accept a rival theory, recently set forth with much skill and learning, by a French priest, who had the inestimable happiness of sitting at the feet of De Rossi. M. Pierre Battifol[2] is of opinion that the Canonical Hours in no way come from the Jewish Hours of Prayer but are the outgrowth of the Saturday Vigil service, which was wholly of Christian origin, and which he tells us was divided into three parts, j., the evening service, or *lucernarium,* which was the service of Vespers ; ij., the midnight service, the origin of the Nocturns or Mattins ; iij., the service at daybreak, the origin of Lauds. Soon vigils were kept for all the martyr commemorations ; and by the time of Tertullian, if not before, Wednesdays and Fridays had their vigils. With the growth of monasticism they became daily. This Mr. Battifol thinks was introduced into Antioch about A.D. 350, and soon spread all over the East. The "little hours," that is Terce, Sext, and None, he thinks were monastic in origin and that Prime and Compline were transferred from the dormitory to the church, just as the martyrology was transferred from the refectory.

Such is the new theory, which, even if rejected, at least is valuable in drawing attention to the great importance of the vigil-service in the Early Church, an importance still attaching to it in Russia on the night of Easter Even.

---

[1] Vide Tertullian.

[2] *Histoire du Bréviaire Romain.* Paris. 1893. An English translation has since (1898) appeared by the Rev. A. M. Y. Bayley, which is not in principle changed so far as this discussion is concerned.

Of the twilight service we have a most exquisite remains in the hymn to be sung at the lighting of the lamps. This is one of the few *Psalmi idiotici* which has survived the condemnation of such compositions by the early councils, in fact the only two others are the *Gloria
in Excelsis* and the *Te Deum*.   The hymn at the lighting of the lamps is as follows:

> " O gladsome light
>   Of the Father Immortal,
>   And of the celestial
>   Sacred and blessed
>   Jesus, our Saviour!
>
> " Now to the sunset
>   Again hast thou brought us;
>   And seeing the evening
>   Twilight, we bless thee,
>   Praise thee, adore thee!
>
> " Father omnipotent!
>   Son, the Life-giver!
>   Spirit, the Comforter!
>   Worthy at all times
>   Of worship and wonder! " [1]

Dr. Battifol's new theory was promptly attacked by P. Suibbert Bäumer, a learned German Benedictine who had already written several magazine articles on the subject before
Battifol's book had appeared.

The title of Bäumer's book is *Geschichte des Breviers, Versuch einer quellenmässigen Darstel-
lung der Entwicklung des altkirchen und des römeschen Officiums bis auf unsere Tage.* (Freiburg in
Briesgau, 1895.)   The following [2] may be taken as a fair *resumé* of the position taken in this
work and most ably defended, a position which (if I may be allowed to express an opinion) is
more likely to prevail as being most in accordance with the previous researches of the
learned.

"The early Christians separated from the Synagogues about A.D. 65; that is, about the
same time as the first Epistle to Timothy was written, and at this moment of separation from
the Synagogue the Apostles had already established, besides the liturgy, at least one, probably two, canonical hours of prayer, Mattins and Evensong, Besides what we should call
sermons, the service of these hours was made up of psalms, readings from Holy Scripture,
and extempore prayers.   A few pages on (p. 42) Bäumer allows that even if this service had
been daily in Jerusalem in the Apostles' times, yet it had become limited to Sundays in the
sub-Apostolic times, when persecution would not allow the Apostolic custom of daily morning and evening public prayer.   Yet the practice of private prayer at the third, sixth, and
ninth hours continued, based upon an Apostolic tradition ; and thus, when the tyranny of
persecution was overpast, the idea of public prayer at these hours was saved and the practice carried on."

The student should by no means omit to read Dom Prosper Guéranger's *Institutions Liturgiques*, which while written in a bitter and most partisan spirit, is yet a work of the most profound learning.   Above all anyone professing any familiarity with the literature on the
subject must have mastered Cardinal Bona's invaluable *De Divina Psalmodia*, a mine of wisdom and a wonder of research.

---

[1] Longfellow.   *The Golden Legend* II. Liddon's remarks upon this hymn are well worth the reader's attention, *Bampton Lectures,*
Lect. VII., where Keble's translation will be found.
[2] Taken from the *Church Quarterly Review,* 1898.

CANON XIX.

AFTER the sermons of the Bishops, the prayer for the catechumens is to be made first by itself; and after the catechumens have gone out, the prayer for those who are under penance; and, after these have passed under the hand [of the Bishop] and departed, there should then be offered the three prayers of the faithful, the first to be said entirely in silence, the second and third aloud, and then the [kiss of] peace is to be given. And, after the presbyters have given the [kiss of] peace to the Bishop, then the laity are to give it [to one another], and so the Holy Oblation is to be completed. And it is lawful to the priesthood alone to go to the Altar and [there] communicate.

NOTES.

ANCIENT EPITOME OF CANON XIX.

After the prayers of the catechumens shall be said those of the Penitents, and afterwards those of the faithful. And after the peace, or embrace, has been given, the offering shall be made. Only priests shall enter the sanctuary and make there their communion.

The Greek commentators throw but little if any light upon this canon. A question has been raised as to who said the prayers mentioned. Van Espen, following Isidore's translation "they also pray who are doing penance," thinks the prayer of the penitents, said by themselves, is intended, and not the prayer said by the Bishop. But Hefele, following Dionysius's version—"the prayers over the catechumens," "over those who are doing penance"—thinks that the liturgical prayers are intended, which after the sermon were wont to be said "over" the different classes. Dionysius does not say "over" the faithful, but describes them as "the prayers of the faithful," which Hefele thinks means that the faithful joined in reciting them.

EXCURSUS ON THE WORSHIP OF THE EARLY CHURCH.

(Percival, H. R.: *Johnson's Universal Cyclopædia*, Vol. V., s. v. Liturgics.)

St. Paul is by some learned writers supposed to have quoted in several places the already existing liturgy, especially in I. Cor. ij. 9.,[1] and there can be no doubt that the Lord's prayer was used and certain other formulas which are referred to by St. Luke in the Acts of the Apostles[2] as "the Apostles' prayers." How early these forms were committed to writing has been much disputed among the learned, and it would be rash to attempt to rule this question. Pierre Le Brun[3] presents most strongly the denial of their having been written during the first three centuries, and Probst[4] argues against this opinion. While it does not seem possible to prove that before the fourth century the liturgical books were written out in full, owing no doubt to the influence of the *disciplina arcani*, it seems to be true that much earlier than this there was a definite and fixed order in the celebration of divine worship and in the administration of the sacraments. The famous passage in St Justin Martyr[5] seems to point to the existence of such a form in his day, shewing how even then the service for the Holy Eucharist began with the Epistle and Gospel. St. Augustine and St. Chrysostom bear witness to the same thing.[6]

Within, comparatively speaking, a few years, a good deal of information with regard to the worship of the early Church has been given us by the discovery of the Διδαχή, and of the fragments the Germans describe as the K. O., and by the publication of M. Gamurrini's transcript of the *Peregrinatio Silviæ*.[7]

---

[1] J. M. Neale. *Essays on Liturgiology.*
[2] Acts ij. 42.
[3] Pierre Le Brun. *Explic.* Tom. II., *Diss.* j. p. II., *et seqq.*
[4] Probst. *Liturgie der drei ersten Christichen Jahrhunderten.*
[5] *Apolog.* Cap. LXVII.
[6] I venture to draw the reader's attention to the rest of this article as containing information not readily found elsewhere.

[7] The MS. from which this was printed was found in a library in Arezzo. Silvia was a lady of rank, living in the times of Theodosius, who made a pilgrimage to Jerusalem and the Holy Places from Meridian Gaul. To us the chief interest of her book lies in the account she gives of the services. The following is the title, *S. Silviæ Aquitanæ peregrinatio ad loca Sancta.* It will be found in the *Biblioteca dell' Accademia storica giuridica.* Tom.

From all these it is thought that liturgical information of the greatest value can be obtained. Moreover the first two are thought to throw much light upon the age and construction of the Apostolical Constitutions. Without in any way committing myself to the views I now proceed to quote, I lay them before the reader as the results of the most advanced criticism in the matter.

(Duchesne. *Origines du Culte Chrétien*, p. 54 *et seqq.*)

All known liturgies may be reduced to four principal types—the Syrian, the Alexandrian, the Roman, and the Gallican. In the fourth century there certainly existed these four types at the least, for the Syrian had already given rise to several sub-types which were clearly marked.

The most ancient documents of the Syrian Liturgy are :

1. The Catechetical Lectures of St. Cyril of Jerusalem, delivered about the year 347.
2. The Apostolic Constitutions (Bk. II., 57, and Bk. VIII., 5–15).
3. The homilies of St. John Chrysostom.

St. John Chrysostom often quotes lines of thought and even prayers taken from the liturgy. Bingham [1] was the first to have the idea of gathering together and putting in order these scattered references. This work has been recently taken in hand afresh by Mr. Hammond.[2] From this one can find much interesting corroborative evidence, but the orator does not give anywhere a systematic description of the liturgy, in the order of its rites and prayers.

The *Catechetical Lectures* of St. Cyril are really a commentary upon the ceremonies of the mass, made to the neophytes after their initiation. The preacher does not treat of the *missa catechumenorum* because his hearers had so long been familiar with it ; he presupposes the bread and wine to have been brought to and placed upon the altar, and begins at the moment when the bishop prepares himself to celebrate the Holy Mysteries by washing his hands.

In the Apostolic Constitutions a distinction must be drawn between Book II. and Book VIII. The first is very sketchy ; it only contains a description of the rites without the words used, the other gives at length all the formulas of the prayers, but only from the end of the Gospel.

We know now that the Apostolical Constitutions in the present state of the Greek text represent a melting down and fusing together of two analogous books—the *Didaskale* of the Apostles, of which only a Syriac version is extant ; and the Didake of the Apostles, recently discovered by the metropolitan, Philotheus Bryennius. The first of these two books has served as a basis for the first six books of the Apostolical Constitutions. The second, much spread out, has become the seventh book of the same collection. The eighth book is more homogeneous. It must have been added to the seven others by the author of the recension of the *Didaskale* and of the *Didake*. This author is the same as he who made the interpolations in the seven authentic letters of St. Ignatius, and added to them six others of his own manufacture. He lived at Antioch in Syria, or else in the ecclesiastical region of which that city was the centre. He wrote about the middle of the fourth century, at the very high tide of the Subordination theology, which finds expression more than once in his different compositions. He is the author of the description of the liturgy, which is found in Book II. ; in fact, that whole passage is lacking in the Syriac *Didaskale*. Was it also he who composed the liturgy of the VIIIth book? This is open to doubt, for there are certain differences between this liturgy and that of the IId book. [3]

I shall now describe the religious service such as these documents suppose, noting, where necessary, their divergences.

IV. Rome, 1887, and again in the *Studi e Documenti di storia e dir itto*, April–September, 1888, and the liturgical parts in an appendix to Duchesne. Of the other books the best edition is Adolf Harnack's.
[1] Bingham, *Antiquities*, XIII. 6.

[2] Hammond. *The Ancient Liturgy of Antioch* (Oxford, 1879).
[3] The reader will, of course, recognize the foregoing as a piece of "Higher Criticism," and need not be told that it rests upon no foundation more secure than probable guess-work.

The congregation is gathered together, the men on one side the women on the other, the clergy in the apsidal chancel. The readings immediately begin ; they are interrupted by chants. A reader ascends the ambo, which stood in the middle of the church, between the clergy and the people, and read two lessons ; then another goes up in his place to sing a psalm. This he executes as a solo, but the congregation join in the last modulations of the chant and continue them. This is what is called the " Response " (*psalmus responsorius*), which must be distinguished carefully from the " Antiphon," which was a psalm executed alternately by two choirs. At this early date the antiphon did not exist, only the response was known. There must have been a considerable number of readings, but we are not told how many. The series ended with a lection from the Gospel, which is made not by a reader but by a priest or deacon. The congregation stands during this lesson.

When the lessons and psalmodies are done, the priests take the word, each in his turn, and after them the bishop. The homily is always preceded by a salutation to the people, to which they answer, " And with thy spirit."

After the sermon the sending out of the different categories of persons who should not assist at the holy Mysteries takes place. First of all the catechumens. Upon the invitation of the deacon they make a prayer in silence while the congregation prays for them. The deacon gives the outline of this prayer by detailing the intentions and the things to be prayed for. The faithful answer, and especially the children, by the supplication *Kyrie eleison*. Then the catechumens rise up, and the deacon asks them to join with him in the prayer which he pronounces ; next he makes them bow before the bishop to receive his benediction, after which he sends them home.

The same form is used for the energumens, for the competentes, *i.e.*, for the catechumens who are preparing to receive baptism, and last of all for the penitents.

When there remain in the church only the faithful communicants, these fall to prayer ; and prostrate toward the East they listen while the deacon says the litany—" For the peace and good estate of the world ; for the holy Catholic and Apostolic Church ; for bishops, priests ; for the Church's benefactors ; for the neophytes ; for the sick ; for travellers ; for little children ; for those who are erring," etc. And to all these petitions is added *Kyrie eleison*. The litany ends with this special form " Save us, and raise us up, O God, for thy mercy's sake." Then the voice of the bishop rises in the silence—he pronounces a solemn prayer of a grave and majestic style.

Here ends the first part of the liturgy ; that part which the Church had taken from the old use of the synagogues. The second part, the Christian liturgy, properly so-called, begins by the salutation of the bishop, followed by the response of the people. Then, at a sign given by a deacon, the clergy receive the kiss of peace from the bishop, and the faithful give it to each other, men to men, women to women.

Then the deacons and the other lower ministers divide themselves between watching and serving at the altar. The one division go through the congregation, keeping all in their proper place, and the little children on the outskirts of the sacred enclosure, and watching the door that no profane person may enter the church. The others bring and set upon the altar the breads and the chalices prepared for the Sacred Banquet ; two of them wave fans backwards and forwards to protect the holy offerings from insects. The bishop washes his hands and vests himself in festal habit ; the priests range themselves around him, and all together they approach the altar. This is a solemn moment. After private prayer the bishop makes the sign of the cross upon his brow and begins,

" The grace of God Almighty, and the love of our Lord Jesus Christ, and the communion of the Holy Ghost be with you always !

" And with thy spirit.

" Lift up your hearts.

" We lift them up unto the Lord.

" Let us give thanks unto our Lord.

" It is meet and right so to do.

" It is very meet," etc.

And the eucharistic prayer goes on . . .   concluding at last with a return to the mysterious Sanctuary where God abides in the midst of spirits, where the Cherubims and the Seraphims eternally make heaven ring with the trisagion.

Here the whole multitude of the people lift up their voices and joining their song with that of the choir of Angels, sing, " Holy, Holy, Holy," etc.

When the hymn is done and silence returns, the bishop continues the interrupted eucharistic prayer.

" Thou truly art holy," etc., and goes on to commemorate the work of Redemption, the Incarnation of the Word, his mortal life, his passion ; now the officiant keeps close to the Gospel account of the last supper ; the mysterious words pronounced at first by Jesus on the night before his death are heard over the holy table. Then, taking his inspiration from the last words, " Do this in remembrance of me," the bishop develops the idea, recalling the Passion of the Son of God, his death, his resurrection, his ascension, the hope of his glorious return, and declaring that it is in order to observe this precept and make this memorial that the congregation offers to God this eucharistic bread and wine. Finally he prays the Lord to turn upon the Oblation a favourable regard, and to send down upon it the power of his Holy Spirit, to make it the Body and Blood of Christ, the spiritual food of his faithful, and the pledge of their immortality.

Thus ends the eucharistic prayer, properly so-called. The mystery is consummated. . . . The bishop then directs the prayers . . . and when this long prayer is finished by a doxology, all the congregation answer " Amen," and thus ratify his acts of thanks and intercession.

After this is said " Our Father," accompanied by a short litany. . . . The bishop then pronounces his benediction on the people.

The deacon awakes the attention of the faithful and the bishop cries aloud, " Holy things for holy persons." And the people answer, " There is one only holy, one only Lord Jesus Christ, to the glory of God the Father," etc.

No doubt at this moment took place the fraction of the bread, a ceremony which the documents of the fourth century do not mention in express terms.

The communion then follows. The bishop receives first, then the priests, the deacons, the sub-deacons, the readers, the singers, the ascetics, the deaconesses, the virgins, the widows, the little children, and last of all the people.

The bishop places the consecrated bread in the right hand, which is open, and supported by the left ; the deacon holds the chalice—they drink out of it directly. To each communicant the bishop says, " The Body of Christ " ; and the deacon says, " The Blood of Christ, the Cup of life," to which the answer is made, " Amen."

During the communion the singers execute Psalm XXXIII. [XXXIV. Heb. numbering] *Benedicam Dominum*, in which the words " O, taste and see how gracious the Lord is," have a special suitability.

When the communion is done, the deacon gives the sign for prayer, which the bishop offers in the name of all ; then all bow to receive his blessing. Finally the deacon dismisses the congregation, saying, " Go in peace." [1]

---

[1] An interesting and instructive book has recently been published on this subject by F. E. Warren, F.S.A., entitled *The Liturgy and Ritual of the Ante-Nicene Church*, in which all the theories from Vitringa to Bickell are carefully considered. The book is one of the S. P. C. K. series, "Side-lights of Church History."

CANON XX.

It is not right for a deacon to sit in the presence of a presbyter, unless he be bidden by the presbyter to sit down.   Likewise the deacons shall have worship of the subdeacons and all the [inferior] clergy.

NOTES.

ANCIENT EPITOME OF CANON XX.

A deacon shall not sit down unless bidden.

This is another canon to curb the ambition of Levites who wish to take upon themselves the honours of the priesthood also.   Spiritual Cores seem to have been common in early times among the deacons and this is but one of many canons on the subject.   Compare Canon XVIII of the Council of Nice.   Van Espen points out that in the *Apostolic Constitutions* (Lib. II., cap. lvij), occurs the following passage, "Let the seat for the bishop be set in the midst, and on each side of him let the presbyters sit, and let the deacons stand, having their loins girded."

VAN ESPEN.

Here it should be noted, by the way, that in this canon there is presented a hierarchy consisting of bishops, presbyters, and deacons and other inferior ministers, each with their mutual subordination one to the other.

This canon is found in the *Corpus Juris Canonici*, Gratian's *Decretum*, Pars I., Dist. xciii., c. xv., in Dionysius's version.

CANON XXI.

The subdeacons have no right to a place in the Diaconicum, nor to touch the Lord's vessels.

NOTES.

ANCIENT EPITOME OF CANON XXI.

A subdeacon shall not touch the vessels.

The "Lord's vessels" are the chalice and what we call the sacred vessels.

ARISTENUS.

The ecclesiastical ministers shall not take into their hands the Lord's vessels, but they shall be carried to the Table by the priests or deacons.

Both Balsamon and Zonaras agree that by ὑπέρεται is here meant subdeacons.

HEFELE.

It is doubtful whether by *diaconicum* is here meant the place where the deacons stood during service, or the *diaconicum* generally so called, which answers to our sacristy of the present day.   In this *diaconicum* the sacred vessels and vestments were kept; and as the last part of the canon especially mentions these, I have no doubt that the *diaconicum* must mean the sacristy.   For the rest, this canon is only the concrete expression of the rule, that the subdeacons shall not assume the functions of the deacons.

With regard to the last words of this canon, Morinus and Van Espen are of opinion that the subdeacons were not altogether forbidden to touch the sacred vessels, for this had never been the case, but that it was intended that at the solemn entrance to the altar, peculiar to the Greek service, the sacred vessels which were then carried should not be borne by the subdeacons.

This canon is found in the *Corpus Juris Canonici*, Gratian's *Decretum*, Pars I., Dist. xxiii., c. xxvj.

CANON XXII.

The subdeacon has no right to wear an orarium [*i.e.*, stole], nor to leave the doors.

NOTES.

ANCIENT EPITOME OF CANON XXII.

A subdeacon must not wear an orarium nor leave the doors.

The "orarium" is what we call now the stole.

In old times, so we are told by Zonaras

and Balsamon, it was the place of the sub-deacons to stand at the church doors and to bring in and take out the catechumens and the penitents at the proper points in the service. Zonaras remarks that no one need be surprised if this, like many other ancient customs, has been entirely changed and abandoned.

This canon is found in the *Corpus Juris Canonici*, Gratian's *Decretum*, Pars I., Dist. xxxii., canon xxvij., but reads *hostias* instead of *ostia*, thus making the canon forbid the subdeacons to leave the Hosts ; and to make this worse the ancient Glossator adds, "but the subdeacon should remain and consume them with the other ministers." The Roman Correctors indeed note the error but have not felt themselves at liberty to correct it on account of the authority of the gloss. Van Espen remarks "To-day if any Hosts remain which are not to be reserved, the celebrant consumes them himself, but perchance in the time the gloss was written, it was the custom that the subdeacons and other ministers of the altar were accustomed to do this, but whenever the ministers present gradually fell into the habit of not receiving the sacra-ment, this consumption of what remained devolved upon the celebrant."[1]

EXCURSUS ON THE VESTMENTS OF THE EARLY CHURCH.

It would be out of place to enter into any specific treatment of the different vestments worn by the clergy in the performance of their various duties. For a full discussion of this whole matter I must refer my readers to the great writers on liturgical and kindred matters, especially to Cardinal Bona, *De Rebus Liturgicis ;* Pugin, *Ecclesiastical Glossary ;* Rock, *Church of our Fathers ;* Hefele, *Beiträge zu Kircheschichte, Archäologie und Liturgik* (essay in Die Lit-urgischen Gervänder, vol. ij., p. 184 *sqq.*). And I would take this opportunity of warning the student against the entirely unwarranted conclusions of Durandus's *Rationale Divinorum Officiorum* and of Marriott's *Vestiarium Christianum.*

The manner in which the use of the stole is spoken of in this canon shews not only the great antiquity of that vestment but of other ecclesiastical vestments as well. Before, how-ever, giving the details of our knowledge with regard to this particular vestment I shall need no apology for quoting a passage, very germane to the whole subject, from the pen of that most delightful writer Curzon, to whose care and erudition all scholars and students of manuscripts are so deeply indebted.

(Robert Curzon, *Armenia*, p. 202.)

Here I will remark that the sacred vestures of the Christian Church are the same, with very insignificant modifications, among every denomination of Christians in the world ; that they have always been the same, and never were otherwise in any country, from the remotest times when we have any written accounts of them, or any mosaics, sculptures, or pictures to explain their forms. They are no more a Popish invention, or have anything more to do with the Roman Church, than any other usage which is common to all denominations of Christians. They are and always have been, of general and universal—that is, of Catholic—use ; they have never been used for many centuries for ornament or dress by the laity, having been considered as set apart to be used only by priests in the church during the celebration of the worship of Almighty God.

Thus far the very learned Curzon. As is natural the distinctive dress of the bishops is the first that we hear of, and that in connexion with St. John, who is said to have worn a golden mitre or fillet.[2]

---

[1] It is interesting to note that the ancient custom is in full use in the Anglican Church to-day, ordered expressly by the rubrics of the Prayer Book.
[2] Eusebius. *Hist. Eccl.*, v. 24.

(Duchesne, *Origines du Culte Chrétien*, p. 376 *et sqq.*)

It was not the bishops alone who were distinguished by insignia from the other ecclesi-astics. Priests and deacons had their distinctive insignia as well. There was, however, a difference between Rome and the rest of the world in this matter. At Rome it would seem that but little favour was extended at first to these marks of rank ; the letter of Pope Celes-tine to the bishops shews this already. But what makes it evident still more clearly, is that the *orarium* of the priest and of the deacon, looked upon as a visible and distinctive mark of these orders, was unknown at Rome, at least down to the tenth century, while it had been adopted everywhere else.

To be sure, the *orarium* is spoken of in the *ordines* of the ninth century ; but from these it is also evident that this vestment was worn by acolytes and subdeacons, as well as by the superior clergy, and that its place was under the top vestment, whether dalmatic or chasuble, and not over it. But that *orarium* is nothing more than the ancient sweat-cloth (*sudarium*), the handkerchief, or cravat which has ended up by taking a special form and even by becom-ing an accessory of a ceremonial vestment : but it is not an insignia. I know no Roman representation of this earlier than the twelfth century. The priests and deacons who figure in the mosaics never display this detail of costume.

But such is not the case elsewhere. Towards the end of the fourth century, the Council of Laodicea in Phrygia forbade inferior classes, subdeacons, readers, etc., to usurp the *orarium*. St. Isidore of Pelusium knew it as somewhat analogous to the episcopal *pallium*, except that it was of linen, while the pallium was of wool. The sermon on the Prodigal Son, sometimes attributed to St. John Chrysostom [Migne's Ed., vol. viij., 520], uses the same term, ὀθόνη ; it adds that this piece of dress was worn over the left shoulder, and that as it swung back and forth it called to mind the wings of the angels.

The deacons among the Greeks wear the stole in this fashion down to to-day, perfectly visible, over the top of the upper vestment, and fastened upon the left shoulder. Its ancient name (ὠράριον) still clings to it. As for the *orarium* of the priests it is worn, like the stole of Latin priests, round the neck, the two ends falling in front, almost to the feet. This is called the epitrachilion (ἐπιτραχήλιον).

These distinctions were also found in Spain and Gaul. The Council of Braga, in 561, ordered that deacons should wear these *oraria*, not under the tunicle, which caused them to be confounded with the subdeacon, but over it, over the shoulder. The Council of Toledo, in 633, describes the *orarium* as the common mark of the three superior orders, bishops, priests, and deacons ; and specifies that the deacon should wear his over his left shoulder, and that it should be white, without any mixture of colours or any gold embroidery. An-other Council of Braga forbade priests to say mass without having a stole around their necks and crossed upon the breast, exactly as Latin priests wear it to-day. St. Germanus of Paris speaks of the insignia of a bishop and of a deacon ; to the first he assigns the name of *pallium*, and says that it is worn around the neck, and falls down upon the breast where it ends with a fringe. As for the insignia of a deacon he calls it a stole (*stola*) ; and says that deacons wear it over the alb. This fashion of wearing the stole of the deacon spread during the middle ages over nearly the whole of Italy and to the very gates of Rome. And even at Rome the ancient usage seems to have been maintained with a compromise. They ended up by adopting the stole for deacons and by placing it over the left shoulder, but they covered it up with the dalmatic or the chasuble.

The priest's stole was also accepted : and in the mosaics of Sta. Maria in Trastevere is seen a priest ornamented with this insignia. It is worthy of notice that the four popes who are represented in the same mosaic wear the pallium but no stole. The one seems to exclude the other.   And as a matter of fact the *ordines* of the ninth century in describing the costume of the pope omit always the stole.   One can readily understand that who bore one of these insignia should not wear the other.

However, they ended by combining them, and at Ravenna, where they always had a taste for decorations, bishop Ecclesius in the mosaics of San Vitale wears both the priest's stole and the Roman pallium.   This, however, seems to be unique, and his successors have the pallium only.   The two are found together again in the Sacramentary of Autun (*Vide* M. Lelisle's reproduction in the *Gazette Archéologique*, 1884, pl. 20), and on the paliotto of St. Ambrose of Milan ; such seems to have been the usage of the Franks.

In view of these facts one is led to the conclusion that all these insignia, called *pallium, omophorion, orarium*, stole, *epitrachilion*, have the same origin.   They are the marks of dignity, introduced into church usage during the fourth century, analogous to those which the Theodosian code orders for certain kinds of civil functionaries.   For one reason or another the Roman Church refused to receive these marks, or rather confined itself to the papal pallium, which then took a wholly technical signification.   But everywhere else, this mark of the then superior orders of the hierarchy was adopted, only varying slightly to mark the degree, the deacon wearing it over the left shoulder, the bishop and priest around the neck, the deacon over the tunicle which is his uppermost vestment, the priest under the chasuble; the bishop over his chasuble.   *However, for this distinction between a bishop and priest we have very little evidence.   The Canon of III Braga, already cited, which prescribes that priests shall wear the stole crossed over the breast, presupposes that it is worn under the chasuble, but the council understands that this method of wearing it pertains distinctively to priests, and that bishops have another method which they should observe ; for the word *sacerdotes*, used by the council, includes bishops as well as priests.   The rest of the Spanish ecclesiastical literature gives us no information upon the point.   In Gaul, St. Germanus of Paris (as we have seen) speaks of the episcopal *pallium* after having described the chasuble, which makes one believe that it was worn on top.   I have already said that Bishop Ecclesius of Ravenna is represented with the stole pendant before, under the chasuble and at the same time with the pallium on top of it ; and that this usage was adopted in France in the Carlovingian times.   Greek bishops also wear at the same time the *epitrachilion* and the *omophorion*.   This accumulation of insignia was forbidden in Spain in the seventh century (*Vide* IV Toledo, Canon XXXIX), and (as we have stated) the Pope abstained from it until about the twelfth century, contenting himself with the pallium without adding to it the stole.*

The pallium, with the exception of the crosses which adorn its ends, was always white ; so too was the deacon's stole and also that of the priest and bishop.   The pallium was always and everywhere made of wool ; in the East the deacon's stole was of linen ; I cannot say of what material the priest's and deacon's stole was in the West.

CANON XXIII.

THE readers and singers have no right to wear an orarium, and to read or sing thus [habited].

NOTES.

Cantors and lectors shall not wear the orarium.

* What follows down to the next asterisk is a foot-note to p. 379 of Duchesne's book.

VAN ESPEN.

Rightly Zonoras here remarks, "for the same reason (that they should not seem to wish to usurp a ministry not their own) it is not permitted to these to wear the stole, for readers are for the work of reading, and singers for singing," so each one should perform his own office.

This canon is found in the *Corpus Juris Canonici*, Gratian's *Decretum*, Pars I., Dist. xxiii., can. xxviij.

CANON XXIV.

No one of the priesthood, from presbyters to deacons, and so on in the ecclesiastical order to subdeacons, readers, singers, exorcists, door-keepers, or any of the class of the Ascetics, ought to enter a tavern.

NOTES.

ANCIENT EPITOME OF CANON XXIV.

No clergyman should enter a tavern.

Compare this with Apostolic Canon LIV.,

which contains exceptions not here specified.

This canon is contained in the *Corpus Juris Canonici*, Gratian's *Decretum*, Pars I., Dist. xliv., c. ij.

EXCURSUS ON THE MINOR ORDERS OF THE EARLY CHURCH.

(Lightfoot, *Apostolic Fathers*, Ignatius, Vol. I., p. 258.)

Some of these lower orders, the subdeacons, readers, door-keepers, and exorcists, are mentioned in the celebrated letter of Cornelius bishop of Rome (A.D. 251) preserved by Eusebius (*H.E.*, vi., 43), and the readers existed at least half a century earlier (Tertull., *de Praescr.*, 41). In the Eastern Church, however, if we except the *Apostolic Constitutions*, of which the date and country are uncertain, the first reference to such offices is found in a canon of the Council of Antioch, A.D. 341, where readers, subdeacons, and exorcists, are mentioned, this being apparently intended as an exhaustive enumeration of the ecclesiastical orders below the diaconate ; and for the first mention of door-keepers in the East, we must go to the still later Council of Laodicea, about A.D. 363, (see III., p. 240, for the references, where also fuller information is given). But while most of these lower orders certainly existed in the West, and probably in the East, as early as the middle of the third century the case is different with the "singers" (ψάλται) and the "labourers" (κοπιᾶται). Setting aside the *Apostolic Constitutions*, the first notice of the "singers" occurs in the canons of the above-mentioned Council of Laodicea. This, however, may be accidental. The history of the word *copiatai* affords a more precise and conclusive indication of date. The term first occurs in a rescript of Constantius (A.D. 357), "clerici qui copiatai appellantur," and a little later (A.D. 361), the same emperor speaks of them as "hi quos copiatas *recens usus* instituit nuncupari."

(Adolf Harnack, in his little book ridiculously intituled in the English version *Sources of the Apostolic Canons*, page 85.)

Exorcists and readers there had been in the Church from old times, subdeacons are not essentially strange, as they participate in a name (deacon) which dates from the earliest days of Christianity. But acolytes and door-keepers (πυλωροί) are quite strange, are really novelties. And these acolytes even at the time of Cornelius stand at the head of the *ordines minores :* for that the subdeacons follow on the deacons is self-evident. Whence do they come ? Now if they do not spring out of the Christian tradition, their origin must be explained from the Roman. It can in fact be shown there with desirable plainness.

With regard to subdeacons the reader may also like to see some of Harnack's speculations. In the volume just quoted he writes as follows (p. 85 note) :

According to Cornelius and Cyprian subdeacons were mentioned in the thirtieth canon of the Synod of Elvira (about 305), so that the sub diaconate must then have been acknowledged as a fixed general institution in the whole west (see Dale, *The Synod of Elvira*, Lond., 1882). The same is seen in the "gesta apud Zenophilum." As the appointment of the lower orders took place at Rome between about the years 222–249, the announcement in the *Liber Pontificalis* (see Duchesne's edition, fasc. 2, 1885, p. 148) is not to be despised, as according to it Bishop Fabian appointed seven subdeacons: "Hic regiones dividit diaconibus et fecit vii. subdiaconos." The Codex Liberianus indeed (see Duchesne, fasc. 1, pp. 4 and 5; Lipsius, *Chronologie d. röm Bischöfe*, p. 267), only contains the first half of the sentence, and what the *Liber Pontif.* has added of the account of the appointment of subdeacons (. . . qui vii notariis imminerent, ut gestas martyrum in integro fideliter colligerent) is, in spite of the explanation of Duchesne, not convincing. According to Probst and other Catholic scholars the subdiaconate existed in Rome a long time before Fabian (*Kirchl. Disciplin*, p. 109), but Hippolytus is against them. Besides, it should be observed that the officials first, even in Carthage, are called hypo-deacons, though the word subdiaconus was by degrees used in the West. This also points to a Roman origin of the office, for in the Roman church in the first part of the third century the Greek language was the prevailing one, but not at Carthage.

But to return to the Acolythes, and door-keepers, whom Harnack thinks to be copies of the old Roman temple officers. He refers to Marquardt's explanation of the sacrificial system of the Romans, and gives the following resumé (page 85 *et seqq.*) :

1. The temples have only partially their own priests, but they all have a superintendent (*œdituus-curator templi*). These *œditui*, who lived in the temple, fall again into two classes. At least "in the most important brotherhoods the chosen *œdituus* was not in a position to undertake in person the watching and cleaning of the *sacellum*. He charged therefore with this service a freedman or slave." "In this case the *sacellum* had two *œditui*, the temple-keeper, originally called *magister œdituus*, and the temple-servant, who appears to be called the *œdituus minister*." "To both it is common that they live in the temple, although in small chapels the presence of the servant is sufficient. The temple-servant *opens, shuts, and cleans the sacred place, and shows to strangers its curiosities, and allows, according to the rules of the temple, those persons to offer up prayers and sacrifices to whom this is permitted, while he sends away the others*."

2. "Besides the endowment, the colleges of priests were also supplied with a body of servants"—the under officials— ; "they were appointed to the priests, . . . by all of whom they were used partly as letter-carriers (tabellarii), partly as scribes, partly as assistants at the sacrifices." Marquardt reckons, (page 218 and fol.) the various categories of them among the sacerdotes publici, lictores, pullarii, victimarii, tibicines, viatores, sixthly the calatores, in the priests' colleges free men or freedmen, not slaves, *and in fact one* for the personal service of each member.

Here we have the forerunners of the Church door-keepers and acolytes. Thus says the fourth Council of Carthage, as far as refers to the former: "Ostiarius cum ordinatur, postquam ab archidiacono instructus fuerit, qualiter in domo dei debeat conversari, ad suggestionem archidiaconi, tradat ei episcopus claves ecclesiæ de altari, dicens. Sic age, quasi redditurus deo rationem pro his rebus, quæ hisce clavibus recluduntur." The ostiarius (πυλωρός) is thus the ædituus minister. He had to look after the opening and shutting of the doors, to watch over the coming in and going out of the faithful, to refuse entrance to suspicious persons, and, from the date of the more strict separation between the missa catechumenorum and the missa fidelium, to close the doors, after the dismissal of the catechumens, against those doing penance and unbelievers. He first became necessary when there were special church buildings (there were such even in the second century), and they like the temples, together with the ceremonial of divine service, had come to be considered as holy, that is, since about 225. The church acolytes are without difficulty to be recognised in the under officials of the priests, especially in the "calatores," the personal servants of the priests. According to Cyprian the acolytes and others are used by preference as tabellarii. According to Cornelius there were in Rome forty-two acolytes. As he gives the number of priests as forty-six, it may be concluded with something like certainty that the rule was that the number of the priests and of the acolytes should be equal, and that the little difference may have been caused by temporary vacancies. If this view is correct, the identity of the calator with the acolyte is strikingly proved. But the name "acolyte" plainly shows the acolyte was not, like the door-keeper, attached to a sacred thing, but to a sacred person.

(Lightfoot. *Apostolic Fathers*. Ignatius, *ad Antioch*, xj., note. Vol. II., Sec. II., p. 240.)

The acolytes were confined to the Western Church and so are not mentioned here. On the other hand the "deaconesses" seem to have been confined to the Eastern Church at this time. See also ∴post. Const., iii., 11.; viii., 12; comp. viii., 19-28, 31; *Apost. Can.*, 43; *Conc. Laodic.*, Can. 24; Conc. Antioch, Can. 10. Of these lower orders the "subdeacons" are first mentioned in the middle of the third century, in the passage of Cornelius already quoted and in the contemporary letters of Cyprian. The "readers" occur as early as Tertullian *de Præscr.* 41 "hodie diaconus, qui cras lector," where the language shows that this was already a firmly established order in the Church. Of the "singers" the notices in the *Apostolical Constitutions* are probably the most ancient. The "door-keepers," like the subdeacons, seem to be first mentioned in the letter of Cornelius. The κοπιῶντες first appear a full century later; see the next note. The "exorcists," as we have seen, are mentioned as a distinct order by Cornelius, while in *Apost. Const.*, viii., 26, it is ordered that they shall not be ordained, because it is a spiritual function which comes direct from God and manifests itself by its results. The name and the function, however, appear much earlier in the Christian Church; e.g., Justin Mart., *Apol.* ii., 6 (p. 45). The forms ἐπορκιστὴς and ἐξορκιστὴς are convertible; e.g., Justin Mart., *Dial.*, 85 (p. 311). The "confessors" hardly deserve to be reckoned a distinct order, though accidentally they are mentioned in proximity with the different grades of clergy in *Apost. Const.*, viii., 12, already quoted. Perhaps the accidental connexion in this work has led to their confusion with the offices of the Christian ministry in our false Ignatius. In *Apost. Const.*, viii., 23, they are treated in much the same way as the exorcists, being regarded as in some sense an order and yet not subject to ordination. Possibly, however, the word ὁμολογηταὶ has here a different sense, "chanters," as the corresponding Latin "confessores" seems sometimes to have, e.g., in the Sacramentary of Gregory "Oremus et pro omnibus episcopis, presbyteris, diaconibus, acolythis, exorcistis, lectoribus, ostiariis, confessoribus, virginibus, viduis, et pro omni populo sancto Dei;" see Ducange, *Gloss. Lat.*, s. v. (11. p. 530, Henschel).

In a law of the year 357 (*Cod. Theod.*, xiii., 1) mention is made of "clerici qui copiatæ appellantur," and another law of the year 361 (*Cod. Theod.*, xvi., 2, 15) runs "clerici vero vel his quos copiatas recens usus instituit nuncupari," etc. From these passages it is clear that the name κοπιῶντες was not in use much before the middle of the fourth century, though the office under its Latin name "fossores" or "fossarii" appears somewhat earlier. Even later Epiphanius (*Expos. Fid.*, 21) writes as if the word still needed some explanation. In accordance with these facts, Zahn (I. *v.*, A. p. 129), correctly argues with regard to our Ignatian writer, urging that on the one hand he would not have ascribed such language to Ignatius if the word had been quite recent, while on the other hand his using the participle (τοὺς κοπιῶντας) rather than the substantive indicates that it had not yet firmly established itself. For these "copiatæ" see especially de Rossi, *Roma Sotteranea*, III., p. 533 sq., Gothofred on *Cod. Theod.*, II., cc., and for the Latin "fossores" Martigny, *Dict. des Antiq. Chrit.* s.v. See also the inscriptions, *C. I. G.*, 9227, *Bull. de Corr. Hellen.*, vii., p. 238, *Journ. of Hellen. Stud.*, vi., p. 362.

CANON XXV.

A SUBDEACON must not give the Bread, nor bless the Cup.

NOTES.

ANCIENT EPITOME OF CANON XXV.

A subdeacon may not give the bread and the cup.

ARISTENUS.

Subdeacons are not allowed to perform the work of presbyters and deacons. Wherefore they neither deliver the bread nor the cup to the people.

HEFELE.

According to the Apostolic Constitutions, the communion was administered in the following manner : the bishop gave to each the holy bread with the words : "the Body of the Lord," and the recipient said, "Amen." The deacon then gave the chalice with the words : "the Blood of Christ, the chalice of life," and the recipient again answered, "Amen." This giving of the chalice with the words : "the Blood of Christ," etc., is called in the canon of Laodicea a "blessing" (εὐλογεῖν). The Greek commentator Aristenus in accordance with this, and quite rightly, gives the meaning of this canon.

This canon is found in the *Corpus Juris Canonici*, Gratian's *Decretum*, Pars I., Dist. XCIII., c. xix. ; but reads "Deacons" instead of "Subdeacons." The Roman Correctors point out the error.

CANON XXVI.

THEY who have not been promoted [to that office] by the bishop, ought not to adjure, either in churches or in private houses.

NOTES.

ANCIENT EPITOME OF CANON XXVI.

No one shall adjure without the bishop's promotion to that office.

BALSAMON.

Some were in the habit of "adjuring," that is catechising the unbelievers, who had never received the imposition of the bishop's hands for that purpose ; and when they were accused of doing so, contended that as they did not do it in church but only at home, they could not be considered as deserving of any punishment. For this reason the Fathers rule that even to "adjure" (ἐφορκίζειν) is an ecclesiastical ministry, and must not be executed by anyone who shall not have been promoted thereto by a bishop. But the "Exorcist" must be excepted who has been promoted by a Chorepiscopus, for he can indeed properly catechize although not promoted by a bishop ; for from Canon X. of Antioch we learn that even a Chorepiscopus can make an Exorcist.

Zonaras notes that from this canon it appears that "Chorepiscopi are considered to be in the number of bishops."

VAN ESPEN.

"Promoted" (προαχθέντας) by the bishops, by which is signified a mere designation or appointment, in conformity with the Greek discipline which never counted exorcism among the orders, but among the simple ministries which were committed to certain persons by the bishops, as Morinus proves at length in his work on Orders (*De Ordinationibus*, Pars III., Ex. XIV., cap. ij.).

Double is the power of devils over men, the one part internal the other external. The former is when they hold the soul captive by vice and sin. The latter when they disturb the exterior and interior senses and lead anyone on to fury. Those who are subject to the interior evils are the Catechumens and Penitents, and those who are subject to the exterior are the Energumens. Whoever are occupied with the freeing from the power of the devil of either of these kinds, by prayers, exhortations, and exorcisms, are said "to exorcize" them ; which seems to be what Balsamon means when he says—"'exorcize' that is 'to catechize the unbelievers.'" Vide

this matter more at length in Ducange's *Glossary* (*Gloss.*, s. v. Exorcizare).

This canon is found in the *Corpus Juris Canonici*, Gratian's *Decretum*, Pars I., Dist. LXIX. c. ij., Isidore's version.

CANON XXVII.

NEITHER they of the priesthood, nor clergymen, nor laymen, who are invited to a love feast, may take away their portions, for this is to cast reproach on the ecclesiastical order.

NOTES.

ANCIENT EPITOME OF CANON XXVII.

A clergyman invited to a love feast shall carry nothing away with him ; for this would bring his order into shame.

HEFELE.

Van Espen translates : "no one holding any office in the Church, be he cleric or layman," and appeals to the fact that already in early times among the Greeks many held offices in the Church without being ordained, as do now our sacristans and acolytes. I do not think, however, with Van Espen, that by "they of the priesthood" is meant in general any one holding office in the Church, but only

the higher ranks of the clergy, priests and deacons, as in the preceding twenty-fourth canon the presbyters and deacons alone are expressly numbered among the ἱερατικοῖς and distinguished from the other (minor) clerics. And afterwards, in canon XXX., there is a similar mention of three different grades, ἱερατικοί, κληρικοί, and ἀσκηταί.

The taking away of the remains of the *agape* is here forbidden, because, on the one hand, it showed covetousness, and, on the other, was perhaps considered a profanation.

This canon is found in the *Corpus Juris Canonici*, Gratian's *Decretum*, Pars I., Dist. XLII., c. iij.

CANON XXVIII.

IT is not permitted to hold love feasts, as they are called, in the Lord's Houses, or Churches, nor to eat and to spread couches in the house of God.

NOTES.

ANCIENT EPITOME OF CANON XXVIII.

Beds shall not be set up in churches, nor shall love feasts be held there.

HEFELE.

Eusebius (*H. E.*, Lib. IX., Cap. X.) employs the expression κυριακά in the same sense as does this canon as identical with churches. The prohibition itself, however, here given, as well as the preceding canon, proves that as

early as the time of the Synod of Laodicea, many irregularities had crept into the *agape*. For the rest, this Synod was not in a position permanently to banish the usage from the Church ; for which reason the Trullan Synod in its seventy-fourth canon repeated this rule word for word.

This canon is found in the *Corpus Juris Canonici*, Gratian's *Decretum*, Pars I., Dist. XLII., c. iv.

CANON XXIX.

CHRISTIANS must not judaize by resting on the Sabbath, but must work on that day, rather honouring the Lord's Day ; and, if they can, resting then as Christians. But if any shall be found to be judaizers, let them be anathema from Christ.

NOTES.

ANCIENT EPITOME OF CANON XXIX.

A Christian shall not stop work on the Sabbath, but on the Lord's Day.

BALSAMON.

Here the Fathers order that no one of the faithful shall stop work on the Sabbath as do the Jews, but that they should honour the Lord's Day, on account of the Lord's resurrection, and that on that day they should abstain from manual labour and go to church. But thus abstaining from work on Sunday they do not lay down as a necessity, but they add, "if they can." For if through need or any other necessity any one worked on the Lord's day this was not reckoned against him.

CANON XXX.

NONE of the priesthood, nor clerics [of lower rank] nor ascetics, nor any Christian or layman, shall wash in a bath with women; for this is the greatest reproach among the heathen.

NOTES.

ANCIENT EPITOME OF CANON XXX.

It is an abomination to bathe with women.

This canon was renewed by the Synod in Trullo, canon lxxvij.

Zonaras explains that the bathers were en-tirely nude and hence arose the objection which was also felt by the heathen.

This canon is found in the *Corpus Juris Canonici*, Gratian's *Decretum*, Pars I., Dist. LXXXI., c. xxviij.

CANON XXXI.

IT is not lawful to make marriages with all [sorts of] heretics, nor to give our sons and daughters to them; but rather to take of them, if they promise to become Christians.

NOTES.

ANCIENT EPITOME OF CANON XXXI.

It is not right to give children in marriage to heretics, but they should be received if they promise to become Christians.

VAN ESPEN.

By this canon the faithful are forbidden to contract marriage with heretics or to join their children in such; for, as both Balsamon and Zonaras remark, "they imbue them with their errors, and lead them to embrace their own perverse opinions."

CANON XXXII.

IT is unlawful to receive the eulogiæ of heretics, for they are rather ἀλογίαι [*i.e.*, follies], than eulogiæ [*i.e.*, blessings].

NOTES.

ANCIENT EPITOME OF CANON XXXII.

The blessings of heretics are cursings.

To keep the Latin play upon the words the translator has used *bene-dictiones* and *male-dictiones*, but at the expense of the accuracy of translation.

This canon is found in the *Corpus Juris Canonici*, Gratian's *Decretum*, Pars II., Causa II., Quæst. I., Can. lxvj.

CANON XXXIII.

No one shall join in prayers with heretics or schismatics.

NOTES.

ANCIENT EPITOME OF CANON XXXIII.

Thou shalt not pray with heretics or schismatics.

VAN ESPEN.

The underlying principle of this canon is the same as the last, for as the receiving of the Eulogiæ which were sent by heretics as a sign of communion, signified a communion with them in religious matters, so the sharing with them common prayer is a declaration of the same communion, and therefore to be avoided. This is also set forth in Apostolical Canon number xlv.

CANON XXXIV.

No Christian shall forsake the martyrs of Christ, and turn to false martyrs, that is, to those of the heretics, or those who formerly were heretics ; for they are aliens from God. Let those, therefore, who go after them, be anathema.

NOTES.

ANCIENT EPITOME OF CANON XXXIV.

Whoso honours an heretical pseudo-martyr let him be anathema.

HEFELE.

This canon forbids the honouring of martyrs not belonging to the orthodox church. The number of Montanist martyrs of Phrygia was probably the occasion of this canon.

The phrase which I have translated "to those who formerly were heretics" has caused great difficulty to all translators and scarcely two agree. Hammond reads "those who have been reputed to have been heretics ; " and with him Fulton agrees, but wrongly (as I think) by omitting the "to." Lambert translates "to those who before were heretics" and correctly. With him agrees Van Espen, thus, *vel eos qui prius heretici fuere.*

CANON XXXV.

CHRISTIANS must not forsake the Church of God, and go away and invoke angels and gather assemblies, which things are forbidden. If, therefore, any one shall be found engaged in this covert idolatry, let him be anathema ; for he has forsaken our Lord Jesus Christ, the Son of God, and has gone over to idolatry.

NOTES.

ANCIENT EPITOME OF CANON XXXV.

Whoso calls assemblies in opposition to those of the Church and names angels, is near to idolatry and let him be anathema.

VAN ESPEN.

Whatever the worship of angels condemned by this canon may have been, one thing is manifest, that it was a species of idolatry, and detracted from the worship due to Christ.

Theodoret makes mention of this superstitious cult in his exposition of the text of St. Paul, Col. ii., 18, and when writing of its condemnation by this synod he says, "they were leading to worship angels such as were defending the Law ; for, said they, the Law was given through angels. And this vice lasted for a long time in Phrygia and Pisidia. Therefore it was that the synod which met at Laodicea in Phrygia, prohibited by a canon, that prayer should be offered to angels, and even to-day an oratory of St. Michael can be seen among them, and their neighbours."

In the Capitular of Charlemagne, A.D 789

(cap. xvi.), it is said, "In that same council (Laodicea) it was ordered that angels should not be given unknown names, and that such should not be affixed to them, but that only they should be named by the names which we have by authority. These are Michael, Gabriel, Raphael." And then is subjoined the present canon. The canon forbids "to name" (ὀνομάζειν) angels, and this was understood as meaning to give them names instead of to call upon them by name.

Perchance the authors of the Capitular had in mind the Roman Council under Pope Zachary, A.D. 745, against Aldebert, who was found to invoke by name eight angels in his prayers.

It should be noted that some Latin versions of great authority and antiquity read *angulos* for *angelos.* This would refer to doing these idolatrous rites in corners, hiddenly, secretly, *occulte* as in the Latin. But this reading, though so respectable in the Latin, has no Greek authority for it.

This canon has often been used in controversy as condemning the cultus which the Catholic Church has always given to the angels, but those who would make such a use of this canon should explain how these interpretations can be consistent with the cultus of the Martyrs so evidently approved by the same council ; and how this canon came to be accepted by the Fathers of the Second Council of Nice, if it condemned the then universal practice of the Church, East and West. *Cf.* Forbes, *Considerationes Modestœ.*

CANON XXXVI.

THEY who are of the priesthood, or of the clergy, shall not be magicians, enchanters, mathematicians, or astrologers ; nor shall they make what are called amulets, which are chains for their own souls. And those who wear such, we command to be cast out of the Church.

NOTES.

ANCIENT EPITOME OF CANON XXXVI.

Whoso will be priest must not be a magician, nor one who uses incantations, or mathematical or astrological charms, nor a putter on of amulets.

Some interesting and valuable information on charms will be found in Ducange (*Glossarium, s. v.* Phylacterea).

BALSAMON.

"Magicians" are those who for any purpose call Satan to their aid. "Enchantors" are those who sing charms or incantations, and through them draw demons to obey them. "Mathematicians" are they who hold the opinion that the celestial bodies rule the universe, and that all earthly things are ruled by their influence. "Astrologers" are they who divine by the stars through the agency of demons, and place their faith in them.

VAN ESPEN.

Zonaras also notes that the science of mathematics or astronomy is not at all hereby forbidden to the clergy, but the excess and abuse of that science, which even more easily may happen in the case of clergymen and consecrated persons than in that of laymen.

CANON XXXVII.

IT is not lawful to receive portions sent from the feasts of Jews or heretics, nor to feast together with them.

CANON XXXVIII.

IT is not lawful to receive unleavened bread from the Jews, nor to be partakers of their impiety.

CANON XXXIX.

IT is not lawful to feast together with the heathen, and to be partakers of their godlessness.

NOTES.

ANCIENT EPITOME OF CANONS XXXVII., XXXVIII. AND XXXIX.

Thou shalt not keep feasts with Hebrews or heretics, nor receive festival offerings from them.

BALSAMON.

Read canon lxx. and canon lxxj. of the Holy Apostles, and Canon lx[1] of the Synod of Carthage.

ARISTENUS.

Light hath no communion with darkness. Therefore no Christian should celebrate a feast with heretics or Jews, neither should he receive anything connected with these feasts such as azymes and the like.

---

[1] So both Zonaras and Balsamon give the number, but in this they follow the Latin numbers of the African Code, the Greek number is lxiij.

CANON XL.

BISHOPS called to a synod must not be guilty of contempt, but must attend, and either teach, or be taught, for the reformation of the Church and of others. And if such an one shall be guilty of contempt, he will condemn himself, unless he be detained by ill health.

NOTES.

ANCIENT EPITOME OF CANON XL.

Whoso summoned to a synod shall spurn the invitation, unless hindered by the force of circumstances, shall not be free from blame.

HEFELE.

By ἀνωμαλία, illness is commonly understood, and Dionysius Exiguus and Isidore translated it, the former *œgritudinem*, and the latter *infirmitatem*. But Balsamon justly remarks that the term has a wider meaning, and, besides cases of illness includes other unavoidable hinderances or obstacles.

This Canon is found in the *Corpus Juris Canonici*, Gratian's *Decretum*, Pars I., Dist. XVIII., c. v.

CANON XLI.

NONE of the priesthood nor of the clergy may go on a journey, without the bidding of the Bishop.

CANON XLII.

NONE of the priesthood nor of the clergy may travel without letters canonical.

NOTES.

ANCIENT EPITOME OF CANONS XLI. AND XLII.

No clergyman shall undertake a journey without canonical letters or unless he is ordered to do so.

VAN ESPEN

(On Canon xli.)

It is well known that according to the true discipline of the Church no one should be ordained unless he be attached to some church, which as an ecclesiastical soldier he shall fight for and preserve. As, then, a secular soldier cannot without his prefect's bidding leave his post and go to another, so the canons decree that no one in the ranks of the ecclesiastical military can travel about except at the bidding of the bishop who is in command of the army. A slight trace of this discipline is observed even to-day in the fact that priests of other dioceses are not allowed to celebrate unless they are provided with Canonical letters or testimonials from their own bishops.

(On Canon xlii.)

The whole subject of Commendatory and other letters is treated of in the note to Canon VIII. of the Council of Antioch.

Canon xlj. is found in the *Corpus Juris Canonici*, Gratian's *Decretum*, Pars III., Dist. V., *De Consecrat*, can. xxxvj.

Canon xlij. is appended to the preceding, but, curiously enough, limited to laymen, reading as follows : "a layman also without canonical letters," that is "formed letters," should not travel anywhere. The Roman Correctors remark that in the Greek order this last is canon xli., and the former part of Gratian's canon, canon xlij. of the Greek, but such is not the order of the Greek in Zonaras nor in Balsamon. The correctors add that in neither canon is there any mention made of laymen, nor in Dionysius's version ; the Prisca, however, read for canon xlj., "It is not right for a minister of the altar, even for a layman, to travel, etc."

CANON XLIII.

THE subdeacons may not leave the doors to engage in the prayer, even for a short time.

NOTES.

ANCIENT EPITOME OF CANON XLIII.

A subdeacon should not leave the gates, even for a short time, to pray.

On this canon the commentators find nothing to say in addition to their remarks on Canons xxj., and xxij., except that the "prayer" is not their own private prayer, but the prayer of the Liturgy. It has struck me that possibly when there was no deacon to sing the litany outside the Holy Gates while the priest was going on with the holy action within, subdeacons may have left their places at the doors, assumed the deacon's stole and done his part of the office, and that it was to prevent this abuse that this canon was enacted, the "prayer" being the litany. But as this is purely my own suggestion it is probably valueless.

CANON XLIV.

WOMEN may not go to the altar.

NOTES.

ANCIENT EPITOME OF CANON XLIV.

The altar must not be approached by women.

VAN ESPEN.

The discipline of this canon was often renewed even in the Latin Church, and therefore Balsamon unjustly attacks the Latins when he says; "Among the Latins women go without any shame up to the altar whenever they wish." For the Latins have forbidden and do forbid this approach of women to the altar no less than the Greeks; and look upon the contrary custom as an abuse sprung of the insolence of the women and of the negligence of bishops and pastors.

ZONARAS.

If it is prohibited to laymen to enter the Sanctuary by the lxixth canon of the Sixth synod [i.e. Quinisext], much more are women forbidden to do so who are unwillingly indeed, but yet truly, polluted by the monthly flux of blood.

CANON XLV.

[CANDIDATES] for baptism are not to be received after the second week in Lent.

NOTES.

ANCIENT EPITOME OF CANON XLV.

After two weeks of Lent no one must be admitted for illumination, for all such should fast from its beginning.

VAN ESPEN.

To the understanding of this canon it must be remembered that such of the Gentiles as desired to become Catholics and to be baptized, at first were privately instructed by the catechists. After this, having acquired some knowledge of the Christian religion, they were admitted to the public instructions given by the bishop in church; and were therefore called *Audientes* and for the first time properly-speaking *Catechumens*. But when these catechumens had been kept in this rank a sufficient time and had been there tried, they were allowed to go up to the higher grade called *Genuflectentes*.

And when their exercises had been completed in this order they were brought by the catechists who had had the charge of them, to the bishop, that on the Holy Sabbath [Easter Even] they might receive baptism, and the catechumens gave their names at the same time, so that they might be set down for baptism at the coming Holy Sabbath.

Moreover we learn from St. Augustine (Serm. xiii., Ad Neophitos,) that the time for the giving in of the names was the beginning of Lent.

This council therefore in this canon decrees that such as do not hand in their names at the beginning of Lent, but after two weeks are past, shall not be admitted to baptism on the next Holy Sabbath.

CANON XLVI.

THEY who are to be baptized must learn the faith [Creed] by heart, and recite it to the bishop, or to the presbyters, on the fifth day of the week.

NOTES.

ANCIENT EPITOME OF CANON XLVI.

Vide *infra.*

HEFELE.

It is doubtful whether by the Thursday of the text was meant only the Thursday of Holy Week, or every Thursday of the time during which the catechumens received instruction. The Greek commentators are in favour of the latter, but Dionysius Exiguus and Isidore, and after them Bingham, are, and probably rightly, in favour of the former meaning. This canon was repeated by the Trullan Synod in its seventy-eighth canon.

CANON XLVII.

THEY who are baptized in sickness and afterwards recover, must learn the Creed by heart and know that the Divine gifts have been vouchsafed them.

NOTES.

ANCIENT EPITOME OF CANONS XLVI. AND XLVII.

Whoso is baptised by a bishop or presbyter let him recite the faith on the fifth feria of the week. Also anyone baptized clinically a short while afterwards.

BALSAMON.

Some unbelievers were baptized before they had been catechized, by reason of the urgency of the illness. Now some thought that as their baptism did not follow their being cate-chumens, they ought to be catechized and baptized over again. And in support of this opinion they urged Canon XII. of Neocæsarea, which does not permit one clinically baptized to become a priest rashly. For this reason it is that the Fathers decree that such an one shall not be baptized a second time, but as soon as he gets well he shall learn the faith and the mystery of baptism, and to appreciate the divine gifts he has received, viz., the confession of the one true God and the remission of sins which comes to us in holy baptism.

CANON XLVIII.

THEY who are baptized must after Baptism be anointed with the heavenly chrism, and be partakers of the Kingdom of Christ.

NOTES.

ANCIENT EPITOME OF CANON XLVIII.

Those illuminated should after their baptism be anointed.

VAN ESPEN.

That this canon refers to the anointing with chrism on the forehead of the baptized, that is to say of the sacrament of confirmation, is the unanimous opinion of the Greek commentators, and Balsamon notes that this anointing is not simply styled "chrism" but "the heavenly chrism," viz.: "that which is sanctified by holy prayers and through the invocation of the Holy Spirit ; and those who are anointed therewith, it sanctifies and makes partakers of the kingdom of heaven."

AUBESPINE.

(*Lib.* i., *Observat. cap.* xv.)

Formerly no one was esteemed worthy of the name Christian or reckoned among the perfect who had not been confirmed and endowed with the gift of the Holy Ghost.

The prayers for the consecration of the Holy Chrism according to the rites of the East and of the West should be carefully read by the student. Those of the East are found in the Euchologion, and those of the West in the *Pontificale Romanum*, De Officio in feria v. Cœna Domini.

CANON XLIX.

DURING Lent the Bread must not be offered except on the Sabbath Day and on the Lord's Day only.

NOTES.

In Lent the offering should be made only on the Sabbath and on the Lord's day.

HEFELE.

This canon, which was repeated by the Trullan Synod in its fifty-second canon, orders that on ordinary week days during Lent, only a *Missa Præsanctificatorum* should take place, as is still the custom with the Greeks on all days of penitence and mourning, when it appears to them unsuitable to have the full liturgy, and as Leo Allatius says, for this reason, that the consecration is a joyful act. A comparison of the above sixteenth canon, however, shows that Saturday was a special exception.

To the Saturdays and Sundays mentioned by Hefele must be added the feast of the Annunciation, which is always solemnized with a full celebration of the Liturgy, even when it falls upon Good Friday.

CANON L.

THE fast must not be broken on the fifth day of the last week in Lent [*i.e.*, on Maunday Thursday], and the whole of Lent be dishonoured ; but it is necessary to fast during all the Lenten season by eating only dry meats.

NOTES.

It is not right on the fifth feria of the last week of Lent to break the fast, and thus spoil the whole of Lent ; but the whole of Lent should be kept with fasting on dry food.

That long before the date of the Quinisext Synod the fasting reception of the Holy Eucharist was the universal law of the Church no one can doubt who has devoted the slightest study to the point. To produce the evidence here would be out of place, but the reader may be referred to the excellent presentation of it in Cardinal Bona's *De Rebus Liturgicis.*

I shall here cite but one passage, from St. Augustine:

"It is clear that when the disciples first received the body and blood of the Lord they had not been fasting. Must we then censure the Universal Church because *the sacrament is everywhere partaken of by persons fasting?* Nay, verily ; for from that time it pleased the Holy Spirit to appoint, for the honour of so great a sacrament, that the body of the Lord should take the precedence of all other food entering the mouth of a Christian ; and it is for this reason that *the custom referred to is universally observed.* For the fact that the Lord instituted the sacrament after other food had been partaken of does not prove that brethren should come together to partake of that sacrament after having dined or supped, or imitate those whom the Apostle reproved and corrected for not distinguishing between the Lord's Supper and an ordinary meal. The Saviour, indeed, in order to commend the depths of that mystery more affectingly to his disciples, was pleased to impress it on their hearts and memories by making its institution his last act before going from them to his passion. And, therefore, he did not prescribe the order in which it was to be observed, reserving this to be done by the Apostles, through whom he intended to arrange all things pertaining to the churches. Had he appointed that the sacrament should be always partaken of after other food, I believe that no one would have departed from that practice. But when the Apostle, speaking of this sacrament, says, 'Wherefore, my brethren, when ye come together to eat, tarry one for another, and if any man hunger let him eat at home, that ye come not together unto condemnation,' he immediately adds, 'And the rest will I set in order when I come.' Whence we are given to understand that, since it was too much for him to prescribe completely in an epistle the method observed by the Universal Church throughout the world it was one of the things set in order by him in person ; for we find its observance uniform amid all the variety of other customs."[1]

[1] Aug. *Epist. ad Januar.*

In fact the utter absurdity of the attempt to maintain the opposite cannot better be seen than in reading Kingdon's *Fasting Communion*, an example of special pleading and disingenuousness rarely equalled even in controversial theological literature. A brief but crushing refutation of the position taken by that writer will be found in an appendix to a pamphlet by H. P. Liddon, *Evening Communions contrary to the Teaching and Practice of the Church in all Ages.*

But while this is true, it is also true that in some few places the custom had lingered on of making Maundy Thursday night an exception to this rule, and of having then a feast, in memory of our Lord's Last Supper, and after this having a celebration of the Divine Mysteries. This is the custom which is prohibited by this canon, but it is manifest both from the wording of the canon itself and from the remarks of the Greek commentators that the custom was condemned not because it necessitated an unfasting reception of the Holy Eucharist, but because it connoted a feast which was a breaking of the Lenten fast and a dishonour to the whole of the holy season.

It is somewhat curious and a trifle amusing to read Zonaras gravely arguing the point as to whether the drinking of water is forbidden by this canon because it speaks of "dry meats," which he decides in the negative !

BALSAMON.

Those, therefore, who without being ill, fast on oil and shell-fish, do contrary to this law ; and much more they who eat on the fourth and sixth ferias fish.

CANON LI.

THE nativities of Martyrs are not to be celebrated in Lent, but commemorations of the holy Martyrs are to be made on the Sabbaths and Lord's days.

NOTES.

ANCIENT EPITOME OF CANON LI.

Commemorations of Martyrs shall only be held on Lord's days and Sabbaths.

By this canon all Saints-days are forbidden to be observed in Lent on the days on which they fall, but must be transferred to a Sabbath or else to the Sunday, when they can be kept with the festival service of the full liturgy and not with the penitential incompleteness of the Mass of the Presanctified. Compare canon xlix. of this Synod, and canon lij. of the Quinisext Council.

BALSAMON.

The whole of Lent is a time of grief for our sins, and the memories of the Saints are not kept except on the Sabbaths.

Van Espen remarks how in old calendars there are but few Saints-days in those months in which Lent ordinarily falls, and that the multitude of days now kept by the Roman *ordo* are mostly of modern introduction.

CANON LII.

MARRIAGES and birthday feasts are not to be celebrated in Lent.

NOTES.

ANCIENT EPITOME OF CANON LII.

Marriage shall not be celebrated in Lent, nor birthdays.

HEFELE.

By "birthday feasts" in this canon the *natalitia martyrum* is not to be understood as in the preceding canon, but the birthday feasts of princes. This, as well as the preceding rule, was renewed in the sixth century by Bishop Martin of Bracara, now Braga, in Portugal.

CANON LIII.

CHRISTIANS, when they attend weddings, must not join in wanton dances, but modestly dine or breakfast, as is becoming to Christians.

NOTES.

It is unsuitable to dance or leap at weddings.

VAN ESPEN.

This canon does not call for explanation but for reflexion, and greatly it is to be desired that it should be observed by Christians, and that through like improprieties, wedding-days, which should be days of holy joy and blessing, be not turned, even to the bride and groom themselves, into days of cursing. Moreover the Synod of Trent admonishes bishops (*Sess.* xxiv., *De Reform. Mat.,* cap. x.) to take care that at weddings there be only that which is modest and proper.

CANON LIV.

MEMBERS of the priesthood and of the clergy must not witness the plays at weddings or banquets; but, before the players enter, they must rise and depart.

NOTES.

ANCIENT EPITOME OF CANON LIV.

Priests and clerics should leave before the play.

ARISTENUS.

Christians are admonished to feast modestly when they go to weddings and not to dance nor βαλλίζειν, that is to clap their hands and make a noise with them. For this is unworthy of the Christian standing. But consecrated persons must not see the play at weddings, but before the *thymelici* begin, they must go out.

Compare with this Canons XXIV. and LI., of the Synod in Trullo.

This canon is found in the *Corpus Juris Canonici,* Gratian's *Decretum,* Pars III., *De Consecrat.* Dist. v., can. xxxvij.

CANON LV.

NEITHER members of the priesthood nor of the clergy, nor yet laymen, may club together for drinking entertainments.

NOTES.

ANCIENT EPITOME OF CANON LV.

Neither a layman nor a cleric shall celebrate a club feast.

These meals, the expenses of which were defrayed by a number clubbing together and sharing the cost, were called "symbola" by Isidore, and by Melinus and Crabbe "comissalia," although the more ordinary form is "commensalia" or "comessalia." *Cf.* Ducange *Gloss., s. v.* Commensalia *and* Confertum.

This Canon is found in the *Corpus Juris Canonici,* Gratian's *Decretum,* Pars I., Dist. XLIV., c. x. (Isidore's version), and c. xij., (Martin of Braga's version).

CANON LVI.

PRESBYTERS may not enter and take their seats in the bema before the entrance of the Bishop: but they must enter with the Bishop, unless he be at home sick, or absent.

NOTES.

ANCIENT EPITOME OF CANON LVI.

A presbyter shall not enter the bema before the bishop, nor sit down.

It is difficult to translate this canon without giving a false idea of its meaning. It does not determine the order of dignity in an ecclesiastical procession, but something entirely different, viz., it provides that when the bishop enters the sanctuary he should not be alone and walk into a place already occupied, but that he should have with him, as a guard of honour, the clergy. Whether these should walk before or after him would be a mere matter of local custom, the rule *juniores priores* did not universally prevail.

This canon is found in the *Corpus Juris Canonici*, Gratian's *Decretum*, Pars I., Dist. XCV., can. viij.

CANON LVII.

BISHOPS must not be appointed in villages or country districts, but visitors; and those who have been already appointed must do nothing without the consent of the bishop of the city. Presbyters, in like manner, must do nothing without the consent of the bishop.

NOTES.

ANCIENT EPITOME OF CANON LVII.

A bishop shall not be established in a village or in the country, but a periodeutes. But should one be appointed he shall not perform any function without the bishop of the city.

On the whole subject of Chorepiscopi see the Excursus to Canon VIII. of Nice, in this volume.

HEFELE.

Compare the eighth and tenth canons of the Synod of Antioch of 341, the thirteenth of the Synod of Ancyra, and the second clause of the sixth canon of the Synod of Sardica. The above canon orders that from henceforth, in the place of the rural bishops, priests of higher rank shall act as visitors of the country dioceses and country clergy. Dionysius Exiguus, Isidore, the Greek commentators, Van Espen, Remi Ceillier, Neander, and others thus interpret this canon; but Herbst, in the *Tübingen Review*, translates the word (περιοδευταί) not visitors but physicians—physicians of the soul,—and for this he appeals to passages from the Fathers of the Church collected by Suicer in his *Thesaurus*.

This canon is found in the *Corpus Juris Canonici*, Gratian's *Decretum*, Pars I., Dist. LXXX., c. v.

CANON LVIII.

THE Oblation must not be made by bishops or presbyters in any private houses.

NOTES.

ANCIENT EPITOME OF CANON LVIII.

Neither a bishop nor a presbyter shall make the offering in private houses.

VAN ESPEN.

By "the oblation" here is intended the oblation of the unbloody sacrifice according to the mind of the Greek interpreters. Zonaras says: "The faithful can pray to God and be intent upon their prayers everywhere, whether in the house, in the field, or in any place they possess: but to offer or perform the oblation must by no means be done except in a church and at an altar."

CANON LIX.

No psalms composed by private individuals nor any uncanonical books may be read in the church, but only the Canonical Books of the Old and New Testaments.

NOTES.

ANCIENT EPITOME OF CANON LIX.

Psalms of private origin, or books uncanonical are not to be sung in temples; but the canonical writings of the old and new testaments.

HEFELE.

Several heretics, for instance Bardesanes, Paul of Samosata, and Apollinaris — had composed psalms, *i.e.*, Church hymns. The Synod of Laodicea forbade the use of any composed by private individuals, namely all unauthorized Church hymns. Lüft remarks that by this it was not intended to forbid the use of all but the Bible psalms and hymns, for it is known that even after this Synod many hymns composed by individual Christians, for instance, Prudentius, Clement, and Ambrose, came into use in the Church. Only those not sanctioned were to be banished.

This idea was greatly exaggerated by some Gallicans in the seventeenth century who wished that all the Antiphons, etc., should be in the words of Holy Scripture. A learned but somewhat distorted account of this whole matter will be found in the *Institutions Liturgiques* by Dom Prosper Guéranger, tome ij., and a shorter but more temperate account in Dr. Batiffol's *Histoire du Bréviaire Romain*, Chap. vj.

CANON LX.

[*N. B.—This Canon is of most questionable genuineness.*]

THESE are all the books of the Old Testament appointed to be read: 1, Genesis of the world; 2, The Exodus from Egypt; 3, Leviticus; 4, Numbers; 5, Deuteronomy; 6, Joshua, the son of Nun; 7, Judges, Ruth; 8, Esther; 9, Of the Kings, First and Second; 10, Of the Kings, Third and Fourth; 11, Chronicles, First and Second; 12, Esdras, First and Second; 13, The Book of Psalms; 14, The Proverbs of Solomon; 15, Ecclesiastes; 16, The Song of Songs; 17, Job; 18, The Twelve Prophets; 19, Isaiah; 20, Jeremiah, and Baruch, the Lamentations, and the Epistle; 21, Ezekiel; 22, Daniel.

And these are the books of the New Testament: Four Gospels, according to Matthew, Mark, Luke and John; The Acts of the Apostles; Seven Catholic Epistles, to wit, one of James, two of Peter, three of John, one of Jude; Fourteen Epistles of Paul, one to the Romans, two to the Corinthians, one to the Galatians, one to the Ephesians, one to the Philippians, one to the Colossians, two to the Thessalonians, one to the Hebrews, two to Timothy, one to Titus, and one to Philemon.

NOTES.

ANCIENT EPITOME OF CANON LX.

But of the new, the four Gospels—of Matthew, of Mark, of Luke, of John; Acts; Seven Catholic epistles, viz. of James one, of Peter two, of John three, of Jude one; of Paul fourteen, viz.: to the Romans one, to the Corinthians two, to the Galatians one, to the Ephesians one, to the Philippians one, to the Colossians one, to the Thessalonians two, to the Hebrews one, to Timothy two, to Titus one, and to Philemon one.

It will be noticed that while this canon has often been used for controversial purposes it really has little or no value in this connexion, for the absence of the Revelation of St. John from the New Testament to all orthodox Christians is, to say the least, as fatal to its reception as an ecumenical definition of the canon of Holy Scripture, as the absence of the book of Wisdom, etc., from the Old Testament is to its reception by those who accept the books of what we may call for convenience the Greek canon, as distinguished from the Hebrew, as canonical.

We may therefore leave this question wholly out of account, and merely consider the matter from the evidence we possess.

In 1777 Spittler published a special treatise [1] to shew that the list of scriptural books was no part of the original canon adopted by Laodicea. Hefele gives the following resumé of his argument: [2]

(a) That Dionysius Exiguus has not this canon in his translation of the Laodicean decrees. It might, indeed, be said with Dallæus and Van Espen, that Dionysius omitted this list of the books of Scripture because in Rome, where he composed his work, another by Innocent I. was in general use.

(b) But, apart from the fact that Dionysius is always a most faithful translator, this sixtieth canon is also omitted by John of Antioch, one of the most esteemed and oldest Greek collectors of canons, who could have had no such reasons as Dionysius for his omission.

(c) Lastly, Bishop Martin of Braga in the sixth century, though he has the fifty-ninth, has also not included in his collection the sixtieth canon so nearly related to it, nor does the Isidorian translation appear at first to have

---

[1] See new edition of his collected works, vol. viij., pp. 66 *et seqq.*　　[2] Hefele. *Hist. of the Concils*, Vol. II., pp. 323, 324.

had this canon.[1]   Herbst, in the *Tübingen Review*, also accedes to these arguments of Spittler's, as did Fuchs and others before him. Mr. Ffoulkes in his article on the Council of Laodicea in Smith and Cheetham's *Dictionary of Christian Antiquities* at length attempts to refute all objections, and affirms the genuineness of the list, but his conclusions can hardly be accepted when the careful consideration and discussion of the matter by Bishop Westcott is kept in mind.   (*History of the Canon of the New Testament*, IIId. Period, chapter ii. [p. 428 of the 4th Edition.])

---

[1] Leonis, *Opp.*, Ed. Ballerini, tom. iii., p. 441, n. xlviij.

THE SECOND ECUMENICAL COUNCIL.

THE FIRST COUNCIL OF CONSTANTINOPLE.

A.D. 381.

Emperor.—THEODOSIUS.[1]
Pope.—DAMASUS.

Elenchus.

---

[1] Theodosius was Emperor of the East. Gratian was Emperor of the West, but had no share in calling this council.

HISTORICAL INTRODUCTION.

In the whole history of the Church there is no council which bristles with such astonishing facts as the First Council of Constantinople. It is one of the "undisputed General Councils," one of the four which St. Gregory said he revered as he did the four holy Gospels, and he would be rash indeed who denied its right to the position it has so long occupied; and yet

1. It was not intended to be an Ecumenical Synod at all.

2. It was a local gathering of only one hundred and fifty bishops.

3. It was not summoned by the Pope, nor was he invited to it.

4. No diocese of the West was present either by representation or in the person of its bishop; neither the see of Rome, nor any other see.

5. It was a council of Saints, Cardinal Orsi, the Roman Historian, says: "Besides St. Gregory of Nyssa, and St. Peter of Sebaste, there were also at Constantinople on account of the Synod many other Bishops, remarkable either for the holiness of their life, or for their zeal for the faith, or for their learning, or for the eminence of their Sees, as St. Amphilochius of Iconium, Helladius of Cesarea in Cappadocia, Optimus of Antioch in Pisidia, Diodorus of Tarsus, St. Pelagius of Laodicea, St. Eulogius of Edessa, Acacius of Berea, Isidorus of Cyrus, St. Cyril of Jerusalem, Gelasius of Cesarea in Palestine, Vitus of Carres, Dionysius of Diospolis, Abram of Batnes, and Antiochus of Samosata, all three Confessors, Bosphorus of Colonia, and Otreius of Melitina, and various others whose names appear with honour in history. So that perhaps there has not been a council, in which has been found a greater number of Confessors and of Saints." [1]

6. It was presided over at first by St. Meletius, the bishop of Antioch who was the bishop not in communion with Rome, [2] who died during its session and was styled a Saint in the panegyric delivered over him and who has since been canonized as a Saint of the Roman Church by the Pope.

7. Its second president was St. Gregory Nazianzen, who was at that time liable to censure for a breach of the canons which forbade his translation to Constantinople.

8. Its action in continuing the Meletian Schism was condemned at Rome, and its Canons rejected for a thousand years.

9. Its canons were not placed in their natural position after those of Nice in the codex which was used at the Council of Chalcedon, although this was an Eastern codex.

10. Its Creed was not read nor mentioned, so far as the acts record, at the Council of Ephesus, fifty years afterwards.

11. Its title to being (as it undoubtedly is) the Second of the Ecumenical Synods rests upon its Creed having found a reception in the whole world. And now—*mirabile dictu*—an English scholar comes forward, ready to defend the proposition that the First Council of Constantinople never set forth any creed at all! [3]

[1] Orsi, *Ist. Eccl*, xviii., 63.

[2] E. B. Pusey. *The Councils of the Church, A.D.* 51–381, p. 306. Tillemont, *Mémoires*, xvj., 662, who says, "If none of those who die out of communion with Rome can merit the title of Saints and Confessors, Baronius should have the names of St. Meletius, St. Elias of Jerusalem and St. Daniel the Stylite stricken from the Martyrology." *Cf.* F. W. Puller, *The Primitive Saints and the See of Rome*, pp. 174 and 238.

Many attempts have been made to explain this fact away, but without success. Not only was the president of the Council a *persona non grata* to the Pope, but the members of the Council were well aware of the fact, and much pleased that such was the case, and Hefele acknowledges that the reason the council determined to continue the Meletian Schism was because allowing Paulinus to succeed to Meletius would be "too great a concession to the Latins" (vol. III., p. 346).

[3] F. J. A. Hort, *Two Dissertations*. I. *On μονογένης Θεός in Scripture and tradition*, II. *On the Constantinopolitan Creed and other Eastern Creeds of the 4th Century*. It should be added that Dr. Hort acknowledges that, "we may well believe that they [i.e. the 150 fathers of Constantinople] had expressed approval" of the creed ordinarily attributed to them (p. 115). The whole dissertation is a fine example of what Dr. Salmon so well called Dr. Hort's "*perfervidum ingenium* as an advocate," and of

his "exaggeration of judgment." (Salmon. *Criticism of the Text of the New Testament*, p. 12, also see p. 34.) Swainson. in his *The Nicene and Apostles' Creeds*, has all the material points found in Hort's *Dissertation*. Harnack goes much further. He is of opinion that the Creed of Constantinople (as we call it), the Creed which has been the symbol of orthodoxy for fifteen hundred years, is really a Semi-Arian, anti-Nicene, and *quasi* Macedonian confession! The first contention he supports, not without a shew of plausibility, by the fact that it omits the words (which were really most crucial) "that is to say of the substance of the Father." In support of the second opinion he writes as follows: "The words [with regard to the Holy Ghost] are in entire harmony with the form which the doctrine of the Holy Spirit had in the sixties. A Pneumatochian could have subscribed this formula at a pinch; and just because of this it is certain that the Council of 381 did not accept this creed." Some scholars arrive at "certainty" more easily than others. even Harnack himself only attains this "certainty" in the foot-note! The reader will remark that what Harnack is "certain" of in the foot-note is that the Council "did not accept" this creed, not that it "did not frame" it. which is entirely a different question. (Adolf Harnack, *History of Dogma*, [Eng. Trans.], Vol. iv., p. 99.)

THE HOLY CREED WHICH THE 150 HOLY FATHERS SET FORTH, WHICH IS CONSONANT WITH THE HOLY AND GREAT SYNOD OF NICE.[1]

(Found in all the Collections in the Acts of the Council of Chalcedon.)

INTRODUCTORY NOTE.

The reader should know that Tillemont (*Mémoires*, t. ix., art. 78 in the treatise on St. Greg. Naz.) broached the theory that the Creed adopted at Constantinople was not a new expansion of the Nicene but rather the adoption of a Creed already in use. Hefele is of the same opinion (*Hist. of the Councils*, II., p. 349), and the learned Professor of Divinity in the University of Jena, Dr. Lipsius, says, of St. Epiphanius: "Though not himself present at the Ecumenical Council of Constantinople, A.D: 381, which ensured the triumph of the Nicene doctrine in the Oriental Churches, his shorter confession of faith, which is found at the end of his *Ancoratus*, and seems to have been the baptismal creed of the Church of Salamis, agrees almost word for word with the Constantinopolitan formula." (Smith and Wace, *Dict. Chr. Biog.*, *s. v.* Epiphanius). "The Ancoratus," St. Epiphanius distinctly tells us, was written as early as A.D. 374, and toward the end of chapter cxix., he writes as follows. "The children of the Church have received from the holy fathers, that is from the holy Apostles, the faith to keep, and to hand down, and to teach their children. To these children you belong, and I beg you to receive it and pass it on. And whilst you teach your children these things and such as these from the holy Scriptures, cease not to confirm and strengthen them, and indeed all who hear you: tell them that this is the holy faith of the Holy Catholic Church, as the one holy Virgin of God received it from the holy Apostles of the Lord to keep: and thus every person who is in preparation for the holy laver of baptism must learn it: they must learn it themselves, and teach it expressly, as the one Mother of all, of you and of us, proclaims it, saying." Then follows the Creed as on page 164.

We believe in one God, the Father Almighty, maker of heaven and earth and of all things visible and invisible. And in one Lord Jesus Christ, the only begotten Son of God, begotten of his Father before all worlds, Light of Light, very God of very God, begotten not made, being of one substance with the Father, by whom all things were made. Who for us men and for our salvation came down from heaven and was incarnate by the Holy Ghost and the Virgin Mary, and was made man, and was crucified also for us under Pontius Pilate. He suffered and was buried, and the third day he rose again according to the Scriptures, and ascended into heaven, and sitteth at the Right Hand of the Father. And he shall come again with glory to judge both the quick and the dead. Whose kingdom shall have no end. (*I*)

And [we believe] in the Holy Ghost, the Lord and Giver-of-Life, who proceedeth from the Father, who with the Father and the Son together is worshipped and glorified, who spake by the prophets. And [we believe] in one, holy, (*II*) Catholic and Apostolic Church. We acknowledge one Baptism for the remission of sins, [and] we look for the resurrection of the dead and the life of the world to come. Amen.

NOTE I.

This clause had already, so far as the meaning is concerned, been added to the Nicene Creed, years before, in correction of the heresy of Marcellus of Ancyra, of whose heresy a statement will be found in the notes on Canon I. of this Council. One of the creeds of the Council of Antioch in Encæniis (A.D. 341) reads: "and he sitteth at the right hand of

---

[1] This is the title in the Acts of the IVth Council. Labbe, *Conc.*, iv., 342.

the Father, and he shall come again to judge both the quick and the dead, and he remaineth God and King to all eternity."[1]

NOTE II.

The word "Holy" is omitted in some texts of this Creed, notably in the Latin version in the collection of Isidore Mercator. *Vide* Labbe, *Conc.*, II., 960. Cf. Creed in English Prayer-Book.

NOTES.

THE CREED FOUND IN EPIPHANIUS'S *Ancoratus* (*Cap.* cxx.)[2]

We believe in one God the Father Almighty, maker of heaven and earth, and of all things visible and invisible: and in one Lord Jesus Christ, the only begotten Son of God, begotten of the Father before all worlds, that is of the substance of the Father, Light of Light, very God of very God, begotten not made, consubstantial with the Father: by whom all things were made, both in heaven and earth: who for us men and for our salvation came down from heaven, and was incarnate of the Holy Ghost and the Virgin Mary, and was made man, was crucified also for us under Pontius Pilate, and suffered, and was buried, and on the third day he rose again according to the Scriptures, and ascended into heaven, and sitteth on the right hand of the Father, and from thence he shall come again with glory to judge both the quick and the dead, whose kingdom shall have no end. And in the Holy Ghost, the Lord and Giver of life, who proceedeth from the Father; who, with the Father and the Son together is worshipped and glorified, who spake by the prophets: in one holy Catholic and Apostolic Church. We acknowledge one baptism for the remission of sins; we look for the resurrection of the dead, and the life of the world to come. And those who say that there was a time when the Son of God was not, and before he was begotten he was not, or that he was of things which are not, or that he is of a different hypostasis or substance, or pretend that he is effluent or changeable, these the Catholic and Apostolic Church anathematizes.

Epiphanius thus continues:

"And this faith was delivered from the Holy Apostles and in the Church, the Holy City, from all the Holy Bishops together more than three hundred and ten in number."

"In our generation, that is in the times of Valentinus and Valens, and the ninetieth year from the succession of Diocletian the tyrant,[3] you and we and all the orthodox bishops of the whole Catholic Church together, make this address to those who come to baptism, in order that they may proclaim and say as follows:"

Epiphanius then gives this creed:

We believe in one God, the Father Almighty, maker of all things, invisible and visible. And in one Lord Jesus Christ the Son of God, begotten of God the Father, only begotten, that is of the substance of the Father, God of God, Light of Light, very God of very God, begotten not made, being of one substance with the Father, by whom all things were made, both which be in heaven and in earth, whether they be visible or invisible. Who for us men and for our salvation came down, and was incarnate, that is to say was conceived perfectly through the Holy Ghost of the holy ever-virgin Mary, and was made man, that is to say a perfect man, receiving a soul, and body, and intellect, and all that make up a man, but without sin, not from human seed, nor [that he dwelt] in a man, but taking flesh to himself into one holy entity; not as he inspired the prophets and spake and worked [in them], but was perfectly made man, for the Word was made flesh; neither did he experience any change, nor did he convert his divine nature into the nature of man, but united it to his one holy perfection and Divinity.

For there is one Lord Jesus Christ, not two, the same is God, the same is Lord, the same is King. He suffered in the flesh, and rose again, and ascended into heaven in the same body, and with glory he sat down at the right hand of the Father, and in the same body he will come in glory to judge both the quick and the dead, and of his kingdom there shall be no end.

And we believe in the Holy Ghost, who spake in the Law, and preached in the Prophets, and descended at Jordan, and spake in the Apostles, and indwells the Saints. And thus we believe in him, that he is the Holy Spirit, the Spirit of God, the perfect Spirit, the Spirit the Comforter, uncreate, who proceedeth from the Father, receiving of the Son (ἐκ τοῦ Πατρὸς ἐκπορευόμενον, καὶ ἐκ τοῦ Υἱοῦ λαμβανόμενον), and believed on. (καὶ πιστευόμενον,

---

[1] Soc., *H. E.*, II., 10; Soz., *H. E.*, III. 5; Athanas., *De Synod.*, C. xxij.

[2] I have used Petavius's edition, Cologne, 1682; there are some differences in the various editions about the numbering of the chapters, and this seems to be the origin of the curious mistake Hefele makes in confounding the longer with the shorter creed.

[3] This would be the year 374, that is to say seven years before this Second Ecumenical Council which was held at Constantinople in 381.

which the Latin version gives *in quem credimus;* and proceeds to insert, *Præterea credimus in unam,* etc. It certainly looks as if it had read πιστεύομεν, and had belonged to the following phrase.)

[We believe] in one Catholic and Apostolic Church. And in one baptism of penitence, and in the resurrection of the dead, and the just judgment of souls and bodies, and in the Kingdom of heaven and in life everlasting.

And those who say that there was a time when the Son was not, or when the Holy Ghost was not, or that either was made of that which previously had no being, or that he is of a different nature or substance, and affirm that the Son of God and the Holy Spirit are subject to change and mutation ; all such the Catholic and Apostolic Church, the mother both of you and of us, anathematizes. And further we anathematize such as do not confess the resurrection of the dead, as well as all heresies which are not in accord with the true faith.

Finally, you and your children thus believing and keeping the commandments of this same faith, we trust that you will always pray for us, that we may have a share and lot in that same faith and in the keeping of these same commandments. For us make your intercessions you and all who believe thus, and keep the commandments of the Lord in our Lord Jesus Christ, through whom and with whom, glory be to the Father with the Holy Spirit for ever and ever. Amen.

HISTORICAL EXCURSUS ON THE INTRODUCTION INTO THE CREED OF THE WORDS "AND THE SON."

The introduction into the Nicene Creed of the words "and the Son" (*Filioque*) has given rise to, or has been the pretext for, such bitter reviling between East and West (during which many statements unsupported by fact have become more or less commonly believed) that I think it well in this place to set forth as dispassionately as possible the real facts of the case. I shall briefly then give the proof of the following propositions :

1. That no pretence is made by the West that the words in dispute formed part of the original creed as adopted at Constantinople, or that they now form part of that Creed.

2. That so far from the insertion being made by the Pope, it was made in direct opposition to his wishes and command.

3. That it never was intended by the words to assert that there were two Ἀρχαὶ in the Trinity, nor in any respect on this point to differ from the teaching of the East.

4. That it is quite possible that the words were not an intentional insertion at all.

5. And finally that the doctrine of the East as set forth by St. John Damascene is now and always has been the doctrine of the West on the procession of the Holy Spirit, however much through ecclesiastico-political contingencies this fact may have become obscured.

With the truth or falsity of the doctrine set forth by the Western addition to the creed this work has no concern, nor even am I called upon to treat the historical question as to when and where the expression "and the Son" was first used. For a temperate and eminently scholarly treatment of this point from a Western point of view, I would refer the reader to Professor Swete's *On the History of the Doctrine of the Procession of the Holy Spirit.* In J. M. Neale's *History of the Holy Eastern Church* will be found a statement from the opposite point of view. The great treatises of past years I need not mention here, but may be allowed to enter a warning to the reader, that they were often written in the period of hot controversy, and make more for strife than for peace, magnifying rather than lessening differences both of thought and expression.

Perhaps, too, I may be allowed here to remind the readers that it has been said that while " ex Patre Filioque procedens " in Latin does not necessitate a double source of the Holy Spirit, the expression ἐκπορευόμενον ἐκ τοῦ πατρὸς καὶ ἐκ τοῦ Υἱοῦ does. On such a point I am not fit to give an opinion, but St. John Damascene does not use this expression.

1. That no pretence is made by the West that the words in dispute ever formed part of

the creed as adopted at Constantinople is evidently proved by the patent fact that it is printed without those words in all our *Concilias* and in all our histories. It is true that at the Council of Florence it was asserted that the words were found in a copy of the Acts of the Seventh Ecumenical which they had, but no stress was even at that eminently Western council laid upon the point, which even if it had been the case would have shewn nothing with regard to the true reading of the Creed as adopted by the Second Synod.[1] On this point there never was nor can be any doubt.

2. The addition was not made at the will and at the bidding of the Pope. It has frequently been said that it was a proof of the insufferable arrogancy of the See of Rome that it dared to tamper with the creed set forth by the authority of an Ecumenical Synod and which had been received by the world. Now so far from the history of this addition to the creed being a ground of pride and complacency to the advocates of the Papal claims, it is a most marked instance of the weakness of the papal power even in the West.

"Baronius," says Dr. Pusey, " endeavours in vain to find any Pope, to whom the ' formal addition' may be ascribed, and rests at last on a statement of a writer towards the end of the 12th century, writing against the Greeks. ' If the Council of Constantinople added to the Nicene Creed, " in the Holy Ghost, the Lord, and Giver of life," and the Council of Chalcedon to that of Constantinople, " perfect in Divinity and perfect in Humanity, consubstantial with the Father as touching his Godhead, consubstantial with us as touching his manhood," and some other things as aforesaid, the Bishop of the elder Rome ought not to be calumniated, because for explanation, he added one word [that the Holy Spirit proceeds from the Son] having the consent of very many bishops and most learned Cardinals.' ' For the truth of which,' says Le Quien, ' be the author responsible !' It seems to me inconceivable, that all account of any such proceeding, if it ever took place, should have been lost." [2]

We may then dismiss this point and briefly review the history of the matter.

There seems little doubt that the words were first inserted in Spain. As early as the year 400 it had been found necessary at a Council of Toledo to affirm the double procession against the Priscillianists,[3] and in 589 by the authority of the Third Council of Toledo the newly converted Goths were required to sign the creed with the addition.[4] From this time it became for Spain the accepted form, and was so recited at the Eighth Council of Toledo in 653, and again in 681 at the Twelfth Council of Toledo.[5]

But this was at first only true of Spain, and at Rome nothing of the kind was known. In the Gelasian Sacramentary the Creed is found in its original form.[6] The same is the case with the old Gallican Sacramentary of the viith or viiith century.[7]

However, there can be no doubt that its introduction spread very rapidly through the West and that before long it was received practically everywhere except at Rome.

In 809 a council was held at Aix-la-Chapelle by Charlemagne, and from it three divines were sent to confer with the Pope, Leo III, upon the subject. The Pope opposed the insertion of the Filioque on the express ground that the General Councils had forbidden any addition to be made to their formulary.[8] Later on, the Frankish Emperor asked his bishops what was "the meaning of the Creed according to the Latins," [9] and Fleury gives the result of the investigations to have been, "In France they continued to chant the creed with the word *Filioque,* and at Rome they continued not to chant it." [10]

---

[1] In fact the contention of the Latins was that the words were inserted by II. Nice! To this the Easterns answered most pertinently " Why did you not tell us this long ago ?" They were not so fortunate when they insisted that St. Thomas would have quoted it. for some scholars have thought St. Thomas but ill acquainted with the proceedings at the Seventh Synod. Vide Hefele, *Concil.* XLVIII., § 810.

[2] E. B. Pusey. *On the clause* " and The Son." p. 68.

[3] Hefele. *Hist. of the Councils,* Vol. III., p. 175.
[4] Hefele. *Hist. Counc.,* Vol. IV., p. 416.
[5] Hefele. *Hist. Counc.,* Vol. IV., p. 470 ; Vol. V., p. 208.
[6] Muratorius. *Ord. Rom.,* Tom. I., col. 541.
[7] Mabillon. *Mus. Ital.,* Tom. I., p. 313 and p. 376.
[8] Labbe and Cossart. *Concilia.,* Tom. vij., col. 1194.
[9] Capit. Reg. Franc., Tom. I., p. 483.
[10] Fleury. *Hist. Eccl.,* Liv. xiv., chap. 48.

So firmly resolved was the Pope that the clause should not be introduced into the creed that he presented two silver shields to the *Confessio* in St. Peter's at Rome, on one of which was engraved the creed in Latin and on the other in Greek, without the addition.   This act the Greeks never forgot during the controversy.   Photius refers to it in writing to the Patriarch of Acquileia.   About two centuries later St. Peter Damian [1] mentions them as still in place; and about two centuries later on, Veccur, Patriarch of Constantinople, declares they hung there still. [2]

It was not till 1014 that for the first time the interpolated creed was used at mass with the sanction of the Pope.   In that year Benedict VIII. acceded to the urgent request of Henry II. of Germany and so the papal authority was forced to yield, and the silver shields have disappeared from St. Peter's.

3. Nothing could be clearer than that the theologians of the West never had any idea of teaching a double source of the Godhead.   The doctrine of the Divine Monarchy was always intended to be preserved, and while in the heat of the controversy sometimes expressions highly dangerous, or at least clearly inaccurate, may have been used, yet the intention must be judged from the prevailing teaching of the approved theologians.   And what this was is evident from the definition of the Council of Florence, which, while indeed it was not received by the Eastern Church, and therefore cannot be accepted as an authoritative exposition of its views, yet certainly must be regarded as a true and full expression of the teaching of the West.   "The Greeks asserted that when they say the Holy Ghost proceeds from the Father, they do not use it because they wish to exclude the Son; but because it seemed to them, as they say, that the Latins assert the Holy Spirit to proceed from the Father and the Son, as from two principles and by two spirations, and therefore they abstain from saying that the Holy Spirit proceeds from the Father and the Son.   But the Latins affirm that they have no intention when they say the Holy Ghost proceeds from the Father and the Son to deprive the Father of his prerogative of being the fountain and principle of the entire Godhead, viz. of the Son and of the Holy Ghost; nor do they deny that the very procession of the Holy Ghost from the Son, the Son derives from the Father; nor do they teach two principles or two spirations; but they assert that there is one only principle, one only spiration, as they have always asserted up to this time."

4. It is quite possible that when these words were first used there was no knowledge on the part of those using them that there had been made any addition to the Creed.   As I have already pointed out, the year 589 is the earliest date at which we find the words actually introduced into the Creed.   Now there can be no doubt whatever that the Council of Toledo of that year had no suspicion that the creed as they had it was not the creed exactly as adopted at Constantinople.   This is capable of the most ample proof.

In the first place they declared, "Whosoever believes that there is any other Catholic faith and communion, besides that of the Universal Church, that Church which holds and honours the decrees of the Councils of Nice, Constantinople, I. Ephesus, and Chalcedon, let him be anathema."   After some further anathemas in the same sense they repeat "the creed published at the council of Nice," and next, "The holy faith which the 150 fathers of the Council of Constantinople explained, consonant with the great Council of Nice."   And then lastly, "The holy faith which the translators of the council of Chalcedon explained." The creed of Constantinople as recited contained the words "and from the Son."   Now the fathers at Toledo were not ignorant of the decree of Ephesus forbidding the making of "another faith" (ἑτέραν πίστιν) for they themselves cite it, as follows from the acts of Chalcedon; "The holy and universal Synod forbids to bring forward any other faith; or to write or

---

[1] Pet. Damian.   *Opusc.*, xxxviij.   [2] Leo Allat.   *Græc. Orthod.*, Tom. I., p. 173.

believe or to teach other, or be otherwise minded. But whoso shall dare either to expound or produce or deliver any other faith to those who wish to be converted etc." Upon this Dr. Pusey well remarks,[1] "It is, of course, impossible to suppose that they can have believed any addition to the creed to have been forbidden by the clause, and, accepting it with its anathema, themselves to have added to the creed of Constantinople."

But while this is the case it might be that they understood ἑτέραν of the Ephesine decree to forbid the making of contradictory and new creeds and not explanatory additions to the existing one. Of this interpretation of the decree, which would seem without any doubt to be the only tenable one, I shall treat in its proper place.

We have however further proof that the Council of Toledo thought they were using the unaltered creed of Constantinople. In these acts we find they adopted the following; "for reverence of the most holy faith and for the strengthening of the weak minds of men, the holy Synod enacts, with the advice of our most pious and most glorious Lord, King Recarede, that through all the churches of Spain and Gallæcia, the symbol of faith of the council of Constantinople, i.e. of the 150 bishops, should be recited according to the form of the Eastern Church, etc."

This seems to make the matter clear and the next question which arises is, How the words could have got into the Spanish creed? I venture to suggest a possible explanation. Epiphanius tells us that in the year 374 "all the orthodox bishops of the whole Catholic Church together make this address to those who come to baptism, in order that they may proclaim and say as follows."[2] If this is to be understood literally of course Spain was included. Now the creed thus taught the catechumens reads as follows at the point about which our interest centres:

Καὶ εἰς τὸ ἅγιον πνεῦμα πιστεύομεν, . . . ἐκ τοῦ πατρὸς ἐκπορευόμενον καὶ ἐκ τοῦ Υἱοῦ λαμβανό-μενον καὶ πιστευόμενον, εἰς μίαν καθολικὴν κ. τ. λ. Now it looks to me as if the text had got corrupted and that there should be a full stop after λαμβανόμενον, and that πιστευόμενον should be πιστεύομεν. These emendations are not necessary however for my suggestion although they would make it more perfect, for in that case by the single omission of the word λαμβανόμενον the Western form is obtained. It will be noticed that this was some years before the Constantinopolitan Council and therefore nothing would be more natural than that a scribe accustomed to writing the old baptismal creed and now given the Constantinopolitan creed, so similar to it, to copy, should have gone on and added the καὶ ἐκ τοῦ Υἱοῦ, according to habit.

However this is a mere suggestion, I think I have shewn that there is strong reason to believe that whatever the explanation may be, the Spanish Church was unaware that it had added to or changed the Constantinopolitan creed.

5. There remains now only the last point, which is the most important of all, but which does not belong to the subject matter of this volume and which therefore I shall treat with the greatest brevity. The writings of St. John Damascene are certainly deemed entirely orthodox by the Easterns and always have been. On the other hand their entire orthodoxy has never been disputed in the West, but a citation from Damascene is considered by St. Thomas as conclusive. Under these circumstances it seems hard to resist the conclusion that the faith of the East and the West, so far as its official setting forth is concerned, is the same and always has been. And perhaps no better proof of the Western acceptance of the Eastern doctrine concerning the eternal procession of the Holy Spirit can be found than the fact that St. John Damascene has been in recent years raised by the pope for his followers to the rank of a Doctor of the Catholic Church.

---

[1] E. B. Pusey. *On the clause,* " and the Son," p. 48.　　　　[2] Epiphanius, *Ancoratus,* cxx.

Perhaps I may be allowed to close with two moderate statements of the Western position, the one by the learned and pious Dr. Pusey and the other by the none less famous Bishop Pearson.

Dr. Pusey says :

" Since, however, the clause, which found its way into the Creed, was, in the first instance, admitted, as being supposed to be part of the Constantinopolitan Creed, and, since after it had been rooted for 200 years, it was not uprooted, for fear of uprooting also or perplexing the faith of the people, there was no *fault* either in its first reception or in its subsequent retention.

"The Greeks would condemn forefathers of their own, if they were to pronounce the clause to be heretical. For it would be against the principles of the Church to be in communion with an heretical body. But from the deposition of Photius, A.D. 886 to at least A.D. 1009, East and West retained their own expression of faith without schism.[1]

" A.D. 1077, Theophylact did not object to the West, retaining for itself the confession of faith contained in the words, but only excepted against the insertion of the words in the Creed." [2]

And Bp. Pearson, explaining Article VIII. of the Creed says : " Now although the addition of words to the formal Creed without the consent, and against the protestations of the Oriental Church be not justifiable ; yet that which was added is nevertheless a certain truth, and may be so used in that Creed by them who believe the same to be a truth ; so long as they pretend it not to be a definition of that Council, but an addition or explication inserted, and condemn not those who, out of a greater respect to such synodical determinations, will admit of no such insertions, nor speak any other language than the Scriptures and their Fathers spake."

HISTORICAL NOTE ON THE LOST "TOME" OF THE SECOND COUNCIL.

We know from the Synodical letter sent by the bishops who assembled at Constantinople in A.D. 382 (the next year after the Second Ecumenical Council) sent to Pope Damasus and other Western bishops, that the Second Council set forth a "Tome," containing a statement of the doctrinal points at issue. This letter will be found in full at the end of the treatment of this council. The Council of Chalcedon in its address to the Emperor says : "The bishops who at Constantinople detected the taint of Apollinarianism, communicated to the Westerns their decision in the matter." From this we may reasonably conclude, with Tillemont,[3] that the lost Tome treated also of the Apollinarian heresy. It is moreover by no means unlikely that the Creed as it has come down to us, was the summary at the end of the Tome, and was followed by the anathemas which now form our Canon I. It also is likely that the very accurate doctrinal statements contained in the Letter of the Synod of 382 may be taken almost, if not quite, *verbatim* from this Tome. It seems perfectly evident that at least one copy of the Tome was sent to the West but how it got lost is a matter on which at present we are entirely in the dark.

---

[1] Peter of Antioch about A.D. 1054, says that he had heard the name of the Roman Pontiff recited from the Diptychs at the mass at Constantinople forty-five years before. Le Quien, p. xii.

[2] E. B. Pusey. *On the clause* "and the Son," p. 72.
[3] Tillemont. *Mémoires*, Tom. ix., art. 78, in the treatise on St. Greg. Nonz.

LETTER OF THE SAME HOLY SYNOD TO THE MOST PIOUS EMPEROR THEODOSIUS THE GREAT, TO WHICH ARE APPENDED THE CANONS ENACTED BY THEM.

(Found in Labbe, Concilia, *Tom. II., 945.)*

To the most religious Emperor Theodosius, the Holy Synod of Bishops assembled in Constantinople out of different Provinces.

We begin our letter to your Piety with thanks to God, who has established the empire of your Piety for the common peace of the Churches and for the support of the true Faith. And, after rendering due thanks unto God, as in duty bound we lay before your Piety the things which have been done in the Holy Synod. When, then, we had assembled in Constantinople, according to the letter of your Piety, we first of all renewed our unity of heart each with the other, and then we pronounced some concise definitions, ratifying the Faith of the Nicene Fathers, and anathematizing the heresies which have sprung up, contrary thereto. Besides these things, we also framed certain Canons for the better ordering of the Churches, all which we have subjoined to this our letter. Wherefore we beseech your Piety that the decree of the Synod may be ratified, to the end that, as you have honoured the Church by your letter of citation, so you should set your seal to the conclusion of what has been decreed. May the Lord establish your empire in peace and righteousness, and prolong it from generation to generation; and may he add unto your earthly power the fruition of the heavenly kingdom also. May God by the prayers (εὐχαῖς τῶν ἁγίων) of the Saints,[1] shew favour to the world, that you may be strong and eminent in all good things as an Emperor most truly pious and beloved of God.

---

[1] On the whole subject of the prayers of the Saints see H. R. Percival, *The Invocation of Saints.* (Longmans. London, 1896.) I have the less hesitation in referring to my own work as it is, so far as I can discover, the only book in the English language devoted to an historical and theological consideration of the subject. Of course the subject is treated of cursorily in numerous theological treatises and dictionaries.

INTRODUCTION ON THE NUMBER OF THE CANONS.

(HEFELE, *History of the Councils*, Vol. II., p. 351.)

The number of canons drawn up by this synod is doubtful. The old Greek codices and the Greek commentators of the Middle Ages, Zonaras and Balsamon, enumerate seven ; but the old Latin translations—viz. the *Prisca*, those by Dionysius Exiguus and Isidore, as well as the Codex of Luna—only recognize the first four canons of the Greek text, and the fact that they agree in this point is the more important as they are wholly independent of each other, and divide and arrange those canons of Constantinople which they do acknowledge quite differently.

Because, however, in the *Prisca* the canons of Constantinople are only placed after those of the fourth General Council, the Ballerini brothers conclude that they were not contained at all in the oldest Greek collections of canons, and were inserted after the Council of Chalcedon. But it was at this very Council of Chalcedon that the first three canons of Constantinople were read out word for word. As however, they were not separately numbered, but were there read under the general title of Synodicon Synodi Secundæ, Fuchs concluded that they were not originally in the form in which we now possess them, but, without being divided into numbers, formed a larger and unbroken decree, the contents of which were divided by later copyists and translators into several different canons. And hence the very different divisions of these canons in the *Prisca*, Dionysius, and Isidore may be explained. The fact, however, that the old Latin translations all agree in only giving the first four canons of the Greek text, seems to show that the oldest Greek manuscripts, from which those translations were made, did not contain the fifth, sixth, and seventh, and that these last did not properly belong to this Synod, but were later additions. To this must be added that the old Greek Church-historians, in speaking of the affairs of the second General Council, only mention those points which are contained in the first four canons, and say nothing of what, according to the fifth, sixth, and seventh canons, had also been decided at Constantinople. At the very least, the seventh canon cannot have emanated from this Council, since in the sixth century John Scholasticus did not receive it into his collection, although he adopted the fifth and sixth. It is also missing in many other collections ; and in treating specially of this canon further on, we shall endeavour to show the time and manner of its origin. But the fifth and sixth canons probably belong to the Synod of Constantinople of the following year, as Beveridge, the Ballerini, and others conjectured. The Greek scholiasts, Zonaras and Balsamon, and later on Tillemont, Beveridge, Van Espen and Herbst, have given more or less detailed commentaries on all these canons.

CANONS OF THE ONE HUNDRED AND FIFTY FATHERS WHO ASSEMBLED AT CONSTANTINOPLE DURING THE CONSULATE OF THOSE ILLUSTRIOUS MEN, FLAVIUS EUCHERIUS AND FLAVIUS EVAGRIUS ON THE VII OF THE IDES OF JULY.[1]

THE Bishops out of different provinces assembled by the grace of God in Constantinople, on the summons of the most religious Emperor Theodosius, have decreed as follows :

CANON I.

THE Faith of the Three Hundred and Eighteen Fathers assembled at Nice in Bithynia shall not be set aside, but shall remain firm. And every heresy shall be anathematized, particularly that of the Eunomians or [*Anomœans, the Arians or*] Eudoxians, and that of the Semi-Arians or Pneumatomachi, and that of the Sabellians, and that of the Marcellians, and that of the Photinians, and that of the Apollinarians.

NOTES.

ANCIENT EPITOME OF CANON I.

Let the Nicene faith stand firm. Anathema *to heresy.*

There is a difference of reading in the list of the heretics. The reading I have followed in the text is that given in Beveridge's *Synodicon*. The Greek text, however, in Labbe, and with it agree the version of Hervetus and the text of Hefele, reads : "the Eunomians or Anomæans, the Arians or Eudoxians, the Semi-Arians or Pneumatomachi, the Sabellians, Marcellians, Photinians and Apollinarians." From this Dionysius only varies by substituting "Macedonians" for "Semi-Arians." It would seem that this was the correct reading. I, however, have followed the other as being the more usual.

HEFELE.

By the Eudoxians, whom this canon identifies with the Arians [according to his text, *vide supra*,] is meant that faction who, in contradistinction to the strict Arians or Anomæans on one side, and the Semi-Arians on the other side, followed the leadership of the Court Bishop Eudoxius (Bishop of Constantinople under the Emperor Valens), and without being entirely Anomæan, yet very decidedly inclined to the left of the Arian party—probably claiming to represent the old and original Arianism. But this canon makes the Semi-Arians identical with the Pneumatomachians, and so far rightly, that the latter sprang from the Semi-Arian party, and applied the Arian principle to their doctrine of the Holy Ghost. Lastly, by the Marcellians are meant those pupils of Marcellus of Ancyra who remained in the errors formerly propounded by him, while afterwards others, and indeed he himself, once more acknowledged the truth.

EXCURSUS ON THE HERESIES CONDEMNED IN CANON I.

In treating of these heresies I shall invert the order of the canon, and shall speak of the Macedonian and Apollinarian heresies first, as being most nearly connected with the object for which the Constantinopolitan Synod was assembled.

THE SEMI-ARIANS, MACEDONIANS OR PNEUMATOMACHI.

Peace indeed seemed to have been secured by the Nicene decision but there was an element of discord still extant, and so shortly afterwards as in 359 the double-synod of Rimini

---

[1] Such is the caption in the old Greek codices. The vijth of the Ides is July 9th. "From this (says Hefele) we may conclude that this synod which according to Socrates May 381, lasted until July of that year." *E.*, v. 8) begun

(Ariminum) and Selencia rejected the expressions *homousion* and *homœusion* equally, and Jerome gave birth to his famous phrase, "the world awoke to find itself Arian." The cause of this was the weight attaching to the Semi-Arian party, which counted among its numbers men of note and holiness, such as St. Cyril of Jerusalem. Of the developments of this party it seems right that some mention should be made in this place, since it brought forth the Macedonian heresy.

(Wm. Bright, D.D., *St. Leo on the Incarnation*, pp. 213 *et seqq.*)

The Semi-Arian party in the fourth century attempted to steer a middle course between calling the Son Consubstantial and calling him a creature. Their position, indeed, was untenable, but several persisted in clinging to it; and it was adopted by Macedonius, who occupied the see of Constantinople. It was through their adoption of a more reverential language about the Son than had been used by the old Arians, that what is called the Macedonian heresy showed itself. Arianism had spoken both of the Son and the Holy Spirit as creatures. The Macedonians, rising up out of Semi-Arianism, gradually reached the Church's belief as to the uncreated majesty of the Son, even if they retained their objection to the homoousion as a formula. But having, in their previously Semi-Arian position, refused to extend their own "homoiousion" to the Holy Spirit, they afterwards persisted in regarding him as "external to the one indivisible Godhead," Newman's *Arians*, p. 226; or as Tillemont says (*Mém.* vi., 527), "the denial of the divinity of the Holy Spirit was at last their capital or only error." St. Athanasius, while an exile under Constantius for the second time, "heard with pain," as he says (*Ep.* i. *ad Serap.*, 1) that "some who had left the Arians from disgust at their blasphemy against the Son of God, yet called the Spirit a creature, and one of the ministering spirits, differing only in degree from the Angels:" and soon afterwards, in 362, the Council of Alexandria condemned the notion that the Spirit was a creature, as being "no true avoidance of the detestable Arian heresy." See "Later Treatises of St. Athanasius," p. 5. Athanasius insisted that the Nicene Fathers, although silent on the nature of the Holy Spirit, had by implication ranked him with the Father and the Son as an object of belief (*ad Afros*, 11). After the death of St. Athanasius, the new heresy was rejected on behalf of the West by Pope Damasus, who declared the Spirit to be truly and properly from the Father (as the Son from the Divine substance) and very God, "omnia posse et omnia nosse, et ubique esse," coequal and adorable (Mansi, iii., 483). The Illyrian bishops also, in 374, wrote to the bishops of Asia Minor, affirming the consubstantiality of the Three Divine Persons (Theodoret, *H. E.*, iv., 9). St. Basil wrote his *De Spiritu Sancto* in the same sense (see Swete, *Early History of the Doctrine of the Holy Spirit*, pp. 58, 67), and in order to vindicate this truth against the Pneumatomachi, as the Macedonians were called by the Catholics, the Constantinopolitan recension of the Nicene Creed added the words, "the Lord and the Life-giver, proceeding from the Father, with the Father and the Son worshipped and glorified" etc., which had already formed part of local Creeds in the East.

From the foregoing by Canon Bright, the reader will be able to understand the connexion between the Semi-Arians and Pneumatomachi, as well as to see how the undestroyed heretical germs of the Semi-Arian heresy necessitated by their development the condemnation of a second synod.

THE APOLLINARIANS.

(Philip Schaff, in Smith and Wace, *Dict. Christ. Biog., s. v.* Apollinaris.)

Apollinaris was the first to apply the results of the Nicene controversy to Christology proper, and to call the attention of the Church to the psychical and pneumatic element in the humanity of Christ; but in his zeal for the true deity of Christ, and fear of a double personality, he fell into the error of a partial denial of his true humanity. Adopting the psychological trichotomy of Plato (σῶμα, ψυχὴ, πνεῦμα), for which he quoted I. Thess. v. 23 and Gal. v. 17, he attributed to Christ a human body (σῶμα) and a human soul (the ψυχὴ ἄλογος, the *anima animans* which man has in common with the animal), but not a rational spirit (νοῦς, πνεῦμα, ψυχὴ λογικὴ, *anima rationalis*,) and put in the place of the latter the divine Logos. In opposition to the idea of a mere connection of the Logos with the man Jesus, he wished to secure an organic unity of the two, and so a true incarnation; but he sought this at the expense of the most important constituent of man. He reached only a Θεὸς σαρκοφόρος as Nestorianism only an ἄνθρωπος θεοφόρος instead of the proper θεάνδρωτος. He appealed to the fact that the Scripture says, "the Word was made *flesh*"—not *spirit;* "God was manifest in the *flesh*" etc. To which Gregory Nazianzen justly replied that in these passages the term σάρξ was used by synecdoche for the whole human nature. In this way Apollinaris established so close a connection of the Logos with human flesh, that all the divine attributes were transferred to the human nature, and all the human attributes to the divine, and the two merged in *one* nature in Christ. Hence he could speak of a crucifixion of the Logos, and a worship of his flesh. He made Christ a middle being between God and man, in whom, as it were, one part divine and two parts human were fused in the unity of a new nature. He even ventured to adduce created analogies, such as the mule, midway between the horse and the ass; the grey colour, a mixture of white and black; and spring, in distinction from winter and summer. Christ, said he, is neither whole man, nor God, but a mixture (μίξις) of God and man. On the other hand, he regarded the orthodox view of a union of full humanity with a full divinity in one person—of two wholes in one whole—as an absurdity. He called the result of this construction ἀνθρωπόθεος, a sort of monstrosity, which he put in the same category with the mythological figure of the Minotaur. But the Apollinarian idea of the union of the Logos with a truncated human nature might be itself more justly compared with this monster. Starting from the Nicene *homoousion* as to the Logos, but denying the completeness of Christ's humanity, he met Arianism half-way, which likewise put the divine Logos in the place of the human spirit in Christ. But he strongly asserted his unchangeableness, while Arians taught his changeableness (τρεπτότης).

The faith of the Church revolted against such a mutilated and stunted humanity of Christ which necessarily involved also a merely partial redemption. The incarnation is an assumption of the entire human nature, sin only excluded. The ἐνσάρκωσις is ἐνανθρώπησις. To be a full and complete Redeemer, Christ must be a perfect man (τέλειος ἄνθρωπος). The spirit or rational soul is the most important element in man, his crowning glory, the seat of intelligence and freedom, and needs redemption as well as the soul and the body; for sin has entered and corrupted all the faculties.

In the sentence immediately preceding the above Dr. Schaff remarks "but the peculiar Christology of Apollinaris has reappeared from time to time in a modified shape, as isolated theological opinion." No doubt Dr. Schaff had in mind the fathers of the so-called "Kenoticism" of to-day, Gess and Ebrard, who teach, unless they have been misunderstood, that the incarnate Son had no human intellect or rational soul (νοῦς) but that the divine personality took its place, by being changed into it. By this last modification, they claim to escape from the taint of the Apollinarian heresy.[1]

---

[1] The theological views of Gess and Ebrard I know only from the statements of them in writers on the subject of the Incarnation, especially from those made by the Rev. A. B. Bruce, D D., Professor at Free Church College, Glasgow, in his work "The Humiliation of Christ." (Lecture IV.) The following passage cited by Dr. Bruce) seems to prove his contention so far as Gess is concerned. "Dass eine wahrhaft menschliche Seele in Jesu war. versteht sich für und von se!bt: er war ja sonst kein wirklicher Mensch. Aber die Frage ist, ob der in's Werden eingegangene Logos selbst diese menschliche Seele, oder ob neben dem in's Werden eingegangenen Logos noch eine becondere menschliche Seele in Jesu war?" (Gess. *Die Lehre v. d. Person Christi*, ii.. p. 321.) Bruce understands Gess to teach that "The only difference between the Logos and a human soul was, that he became human by voluntary kenosis, while an ordinary human soul derives its existence from a creative act." (And refers to Gess, *ut supra*, p. 325 *et seqq*.) For Ebrard's view, see his *Christlche Dogmatik*, ii., p. 40. Ritschl dubbed the whole kenotic theory as "Verschämter Socinianismus."

The Eunomians or Anomœans.

(Bright, *Notes on the Canons*, Canon I. of I. Const.)

"The Eunomians or Anomœans." These were the ultra-Arians, who carried to its legitimate issue the original Arian denial of the eternity and uncreatedness of the Son, while they further rejected what Arius had affirmed as to the essential mysteriousness of the Divine nature (Soc., *H. E.*, iv., 7; comp. Athan., *De Synod.*, 15). Their founder was Aetius, the most versatile of theological adventurers (*cf.* Athan., *De Synod.*, 31; Soc., *H. E.*, ii., 45; and see a summary of his career in Newman's *Arians*, p. 347); but their leader at the time of the Council was the daring and indefatigable Eunomius (for whose personal characteristics, see his admirer Philostorgius, x., 6) He, too, had gone through many vicissitudes from his first employment as the secretary of Aetius, and his ordination as deacon by Eudoxius; as bishop of Cyzicus, he had been lured into a disclosure of his true sentiments, and then denounced as a heretic (Theod., *H. E.*, ii., 29); with Aetius he had openly separated from Eudoxius as a disingenuous time-server, and had gone into retirement at Chalcedon (Philostorg., ix., 4). The distinctive formula of his adherents was the "Anomoion." The Son, they said, was not "like to the Father in essence"; even to call him simply "like" was to obscure the fact that he was simply a creature, and, as such, "unlike" to his Creator. In other words, they thought the Semi-Arian "homoiousion" little better than the Catholic "homoousion": the "homoion" of the more "respectable" Arians represented in their eyes an ignoble reticence; the plain truth, however it might shock devout prejudice, must be put into words which would bar all misunderstanding: the Son might be called "God," but in a sense merely titular, so as to leave an impassable gulf between him and the uncreated Godhead (see Eunomius's *Exposition* in Valesius's note on Soc., *H. E.*, v., 10). Compare Basil (*Epist.*, 233, and his work against Eunomius), and Epiphanius (*Hær.*, 76).

The Arians or Eudoxians.

(Bright.   *Ut supra.*)

"The Arians or Eudoxians." By these are meant the ordinary Arians of the period, or, as they may be called, the Acacian party, directed for several years by the essentially worldly and unconscientious Eudoxius. His real sympathies were with the Anomœans (see Tillemont, *Mémoires*, vi., 423, and compare his profane speech recorded by Socrates, *H. E.*, ii., 43): but, as a bishop of Constantinople, he felt it necessary to discourage them, and to abide by the vague formula invented by Acacius of Cæsarea, which described the Son as "like to the Father," without saying whether this likeness was supposed to be more than moral (*cf.* Newman, *Arians*, p. 317), so that the practical effect of this "homoion" was to prepare the way for that very Anomœanism which its maintainers were ready for political purposes to disown.

The Sabellians.

(Bright.   *Ut supra.*)

"The Sabellians," whose theory is traceable to Noetus and Praxeas in the latter part of the second century: they regarded the Son and the Holy Spirit as aspects and modes of, or as emanations from, the One Person of the Father (see Newman's *Arians*, pp. 120 *et seqq.*). Such a view tended directly to dissolve Christian belief in the Trinity and in the Incarnation (*Vide* Wilberforce, *Incarnation*, pp. 112, 197). Hence the gentle Dionysius of Alexandria characterised it in severe terms as involving "blasphemy, unbelief, and irreverence, towards the Father, the Son, and the Holy Spirit" (Euseb., *H. E.*, vii.. 6). Hence the deep repugnance which it excited, and the facility with which the imputation of "Sabellianizing" could be utilised by the Arians against maintainers of the Consubstantiality (Hilary, *De Trinit.*, iv., 4; *De Synod.*, 68; *Fragm.*, 11; Basil, *Epist.*, 189, 2). No organized Sabellian sect was in existence at the date of this anathema : but Sabellian ideas were "in the air," and St. Basil could speak of a revival of this old misbelief (*Epist.*, 126). We find it again asserted by Chilperic I., King of Neustria, in the latter part of the sixth century (Greg. Turon., *Hist. Fr.*, v., 45).

The Marcellians.

(Bright. *Ut supra.*)

"The Marcellians," called after Marcellus bishop of Ancyra, who was persistently denounced not only by the Arianizers, but by St. Basil, and for a time, at least, suspected by St. Athanasius (*Vide* Epiphan., *Hær.*, 72, 4) as one who held notions akin to Sabellianism, and fatal to a true belief in the Divine Sonship and the Incarnation. The theory ascribed to him was that the Logos was an impersonal Divine power, immanent from eternity in God, but issuing from him in the act of creation, and entering at last into relations with the human person of Jesus, who thus became God's Son. But this expansion of the original divine unity would be followed by a "contraction," when the Logos would retire from Jesus, and God would again be all in all. Some nine years before the council, Marcellus, then in extreme old age, had sent his deacon Eugenius to St. Athanasius, with a written confession of faith, quite orthodox as to the eternity of the Trinity, and the identity of the Logos with a pre-existing and personal Son, although not verbally explicit as to the permanence of Christ's "kingdom,"—the point insisted on in one of the Epiphanian-Constantinopolitan additions to the Creed (Montfaucon, *Collect. Nov.*, ii., 1). The question whether Marcellus was personally heterodox—i.e. whether the extracts from his treatise, made by his adversary Eusebius of Cæsarea, give a fair account of his real views—has been answered unfavourably by some writers, as Newman (*Athanasian Treatises*, ii., 200, ed. 2), and Döllinger (*Hippolytus and Callistus*, p. 217, E. T. p. 201), while others, like Neale, think that "charity and truth" suggest his "acquittal" (*Hist. Patr. Antioch.*, p. 106). Montfaucon thinks that his written statements might be favourably interpreted, but that his oral statements must have given ground for suspicion.

The Photinians.

(Bright. *Ut supra.*)

"The Photinians," or followers of Marcellus's disciple Photinus, bishop of Sirmium, the ready-witted and pertinacious disputant whom four successive synods condemned before he could be got rid of, by State power, in A.D. 351. (See St. Athanasius's *Historical Writings*, Introd. p. lxxxix.) In his representation of the "Marcellian" theology, he laid special stress on its Christological position—that Jesus, on whom the Logos rested with exceptional fulness, was a mere man. See Athanasius, *De Synodis*, 26, 27, for two creeds in which Photinianism is censured; also Soc. *H. E.* ii., 18, 29, 30 ; vii., 32. There is an obvious affinity between it and the "Samosatene" or Paulionist theory.

CANON II.

The bishops are not to go beyond their dioceses to churches lying outside of their bounds, nor bring confusion on the churches; but let the Bishop of Alexandria, according to the canons, alone administer the affairs of Egypt; and let the bishops of the East manage the East alone, the privileges of the Church in Antioch, which are mentioned in the canons of Nice, being preserved ; and let the bishops of the Asian Diocese administer the Asian affairs only; and the Pontic bishops only Pontic matters; and the Thracian bishops only Thracian affairs. And let not bishops go beyond their dioceses for ordination or any other ecclesiastical ministrations, unless they be invited. And the aforesaid canon concerning dioceses being observed, it is evident that the synod of every province will administer the affairs of that particular province as was decreed at Nice. But the Churches of God in heathen nations must be governed according to the custom which has prevailed from the times of the Fathers.

NOTES.

Ancient Epitome of Canon II.

No traveller shall introduce confusion into the Churches either by ordaining or by enthroning. Nevertheless in Churches which are among the heathen the tradition of the Fathers shall be preserved.

In the above Ancient Epitome it will be noticed that not only is ordination mentioned but also the "inthronization" of bishops. Few ceremonies are of greater antiquity in the Christian Church than the solemn placing of the newly chosen bishop in the episcopal chair of his diocese. It is mentioned in the Apostolical Constitutions, and in the Greek Pontificals. Also in the Arabic version of the Nicene Canons. (No. lxxi.). A sermon was usually delivered by the newly consecrated bishop, called the "sermo enthronisticus." He also sent to neighbouring bishops συλλαβαὶ ἐνθρονιστικαὶ, and the fees the new bishops paid were called τὰ ἐνθρονιστικὰ.

Valesius.

(Note on Socrates, *H. E.* v., 8).

This rule seems to have been made chiefly on account of Meletius, Bishop of Antioch, Gregory Nazianzen, and Peter of Alexandria. For Meletius leaving the Eastern diocese had come to Constantinople to ordain Gregory bishop there. And Gregory having abandoned the bishoprick of Sasima, which was in the Pontic diocese, had removed to Constantinople. While Peter of Alexandria had sent to Constantinople seven Egyptian bishops to ordain Maximus the Cynic. For the purpose therefore of repressing these [disorders], the fathers of the Synod of Constantinople made this canon.

Balsamon.

Take notice from the present canon that formerly all the Metropolitans of provinces were themselves the heads of their own provinces, and were ordained by their own synods. But all this was changed by Canon xxviij of the Synod of Chalcedon, which directs that the Metropolitans of the dioceses of Pontus, Asia, and Thrace, and certain others which are mentioned in this Canon should be ordained by the Patriarch of Constantinople and should be subject to him. But if you find other churches which are autocephalous as the Church of Bulgaria, of Cyprus, of Iberia, you need not be astonished. For the Emperor Justinian gave this honour to the Archbishop of Bulgaria. . . . The third Synod gave this honour to the Archbishop of Cyprus, and by the law of the same synod (Canon viii.), and by the Sixth Synod in its xxxixth Canon, the judgment of the Synod of Antioch is annulled and this honour granted to the bishop of Iberia.

Tillemont.

(*Mém.* ix., 489).

The Council seems likewise to reject, whether designedly or inadvertently, what had been ordained by the Council of Sardica in favour of Rome. But as assuredly it did not affect to prevent either Ecumenical Councils, or even general Councils of the East, from judging of matters brought before them, so I do not know if one may conclude absolutely that they intended to forbid appeals to Rome. It regulates proceedings between Dioceses, but not what might concern superior tribunals.

Fleury.

(*Hist. Eccl. in loc.*).

This Canon, which gives to the councils of particular places full authority in Ecclesiastical matters, seems to take away the power of appealing to the Pope granted by the Council of Sardica, and to restore the ancient right.

Hefele.

An exception to the rule against interference in other patriarchates was made with regard to those Churches newly founded amongst barbarous nations (not belonging to the Roman Empire), as these were of course obliged to receive their first bishops from strange patriarchates, and remained afterwards too few in number to form patriarchates of their own and were therefore governed as belonging to other patriarchates, as, for instance, Abyssinia by the patriarchate of Alexandria.

CANON III.

THE Bishop of Constantinople, however, shall have the prerogative of honour after the Bishop of Rome; because Constantinople is New Rome.

NOTES.

ANCIENT EPITOME OF CANON III.

The bishop of Constantinople is to be honoured next after the bishop of Rome.

It should be remembered that the change effected by this canon did not affect Rome directly in any way, but did seriously affect Alexandria and Antioch, which till then had ranked next after the see of Rome. When the pope refused to acknowledge the authority of this canon, he was in reality defending the principle laid down in the canon of Nice, that in such matters the ancient customs should continue. Even the last clause, it would seem, could give no offence to the most sensitive on the papal claims, for it implies a wonderful power in the rank of Old Rome, if a see is to rank next to it because it happens to be "New Rome." Of course these remarks only refer to the wording of the canon which is carefully guarded; the intention doubtless was to exalt the see of Constantinople, the chief see of the East, to a position of as near equality as possible with the chief see of the West.

ZONARAS.

In this place the Council takes action concerning Constantinople, to which it decrees the prerogative of honour, the priority, and the glory after the Bishop of Rome as being New Rome and the Queen of cities. Some indeed wish to understand the preposition μετὰ here of time and not of inferiority of grade. And they strive to confirm this interpretation by a consideration of the XXVIII canon of Chalcedon, urging that if Constantinople is to enjoy equal honours, the preposition "after" cannot signify subjection. But on the other hand the hundred and thirtieth novel of Justinian,[1] Book V of the Imperial Constitutions, title three, understands the canon otherwise. For, it says, "we decree that the most holy Pope of Old Rome, according to the decrees of the holy synods, is the first of all priests, and that the most blessed bishop of Constantinople and of New Rome, should have the second place after the Apostolic Throne of the Elder Rome, and should be superior in honour to all others." From

this therefore it is abundantly evident that "after" denotes subjection (ὑποβιβασμὸν) and diminution. And otherwise it would be impossible to guard this equality of honour in each see. For in reciting their names, or assigning them seats when they are to sit together, or arranging the order of their signatures to documents, one must come before the other. Whoever therefore shall explain this particle μετὰ as only referring to time, and does not admit that it signifies an inferior grade of dignity, does violence to the passage and draws from it a meaning neither true nor good. Moreover in Canon xxxvj of the Council in Trullo, μετὰ manifestly denotes subjection, assigning to Constantinople the second place after the throne of Old Rome; and then adds, after this Alexandria, then Antioch, and last of all shall be placed Jerusalem.

HEFELE.

If we enquire the reason why this Council tried to change the order of rank of the great Sees, which had been established in the sixth Nicene canon, we must first take into consideration that, since the elevation of Constantinople to the Imperial residence, as New Rome, the bishops as well as the Emperors naturally wished to see the new imperial residence, New Rome, placed immediately after Old Rome in ecclesiastical rank also; the rather, as with the Greeks it was the rule for the ecclesiastical rank of a See to follow the civil rank of the city. The Synod of Antioch in 341, in its ninth canon, had plainly declared this, and subsequently the fourth General Council, in its seventeenth canon, spoke in the same sense. But how these principles were protested against on the side of Rome, we shall see further on in the history of the fourth General Council. For the present, it may suffice to add that the aversion to Alexandria which, by favouring Maximus, had exercised such a disturbing influence on Church affairs in Constantinople, may well have helped to effect the elevation of the See of Constantinople over that of Alexandria. Moreover, for many centuries Rome did not recognize this change of the old ecclesiastical order. In the sixteenth session of the fourth General

---

[1] The reader will notice that this is not even an approximately contemporaneous interpretation, but more than a century and a half later, after Leo I. had done so much to establish the power of his see.

Council, the Papal Legate, Lucentius, expressly declared this. In like manner the Popes Leo the Great and Gregory the Great pronounced against it ; and though even Gratian adopted this canon in his collection the Roman critics added the following note : *Canon hic ex iis est, quos Apostolica Romana Sedes a principio et longo post tempore non recepit.* It was only wh.n, after the conquest of Constantinople by the Latins, a Latin patriarchate was founded there in 1204, that Pope Innocent III, and the twelfth General Council, in 1215, allowed this patriarch the first rank after the Roman ; and the same recognition was expressly awarded to the Greek Patriarch at the Florentine Union in 1439.

T. W. ALLIES.[1]

Remarkable enough it is that when, in the Council of Chalcedon, appeal was made to this third Canon, the Pope St. Leo declared that it had never been notified to Rome. As in the mean time it had taken effect throughout the whole East, as in this very council Nectarius, as soon as he is elected, presides instead of Timothy of Alexandria, it puts in a strong point of view the real self-government of the Eastern Church at this time ; for the giving the Bishop of Constantinople precedence over Alexandria and Antioch was a proceeding which affected the whole Church, and so far altered its original order—one in which certainly the West might claim to have a voice. Tillemont goes on : " It would be very difficult to justify St. Leo, if he meant that the Roman Church had never known that the Bishop of Constantinople took the second place in the Church, and the first in the East, since his legates, whose conduct he entirely approves, had just themselves authorized it as a thing beyond dispute, and Eusebius of Dory-

læum maintained that St. Leo himself had approved it." The simple fact is, that, exceedingly unwilling as the Bishops of Rome were to sanction it, from this time, 381, to say the least, the Bishop of Constantinople appears uniformly as first bishop of the East.

Cardinal Baronius in his *Annals* (A.D. 381, n. 35, 36) has disputed the genuineness of this Canon ! As already mentioned it is found in the *Corpus Juris Canonici, Decretum,* Pars I., Dist. XXII., c. iij. The note added to this in Gratian reads as follows :

NOTE IN GRATIAN'S "DECRETUM."

This canon is of the number of those which the Apostolic See of Rome did not at first nor for long years afterwards receive. This is evident from Epistle LI. (or LIII.) of Pope Leo I. to Anatolius of Constantinople and from several other of his letters. The same thing also is shewn by two letters of Leo IX.'s, the one against the presumptuous acts of Michael and Leo (cap. 28) and the other addressed to the same Michael. But still more clearly is this seen from the letter of Blessed Gregory (xxxj., lib. VI.) to Eulogius of Alexandria and Anastasius of Antioch, and from the letter of Nicholas I. to the Emperor Michel which begins "Proposueramus." However, the bishops of Constantinople, sustained by the authority of the Emperors, usurped to themselves the second place among the patriarchs, and this at length was granted to them for the sake of peace and tranquillity, as Pope Innocent III. declares (in *cap. antiqua de privileg.*).[2]

This canon Dionysius Exiguus appends to Canon 2, and dropping 5, 6, and 7 he has but three canons of this Synod.

CANON IV.

CONCERNING Maximus the Cynic and the disorder which has happened in Constantinople on his account, it is decreed that Maximus never was and is not now a Bishop ; that those who have been ordained by him are in no order whatever of the clergy ; since all which has been done concerning him or by him, is declared to be invalid.

NOTES.

ANCIENT EPITOME OF CANON IV.

Let Maximus the Cynic be cast out from among the bishops, and anyone who was inscribed by him on the clergy list shall be held as profane.

EDMUND VENABLES.

(Smith and Wace, *Dict. Christ. Biog.*)

MAXIMUS the Cynic ; the intrusive bishop of Constantinople, A.D. 380. Ecclesiastical history hardly presents a more extraordinary

---

[1] T. W. Allies. *The Ch. of Eng. cleared from the Charge of Schism.* (Written while an Anglican) p. 94 (2d Edition).

[2] For some reason this canon does not seem to be any more acceptable to modern champions of the Papacy than it was to the

career than that of this man, who, after a most disreputable youth, more than once brought to justice for his misdeeds, and bearing the scars of his punishments, by sheer impudence, clever flattery, and adroit management of opportunities, contrived to gain the confidence successively of no less men than Peter of Alexandria, Gregory Nazianzen, and Ambrose, and to install himself in one of the first sees of the church, from which he was with difficulty dislodged by a decree of an ecumenical council. His history also illustrates the jealousy felt by the churches of Alexandria and Rome towards their young and vigorous rival for patriarchal honours, the church of Constantinople; as well as their claim to interfere with her government, and to impose prelates upon her according to their pleasure. Alexandria, as the chief see of the Eastern world, from the first asserted a jurisdiction which she has never formally relinquished over the see of Constantinople, more particularly in a vacancy in the episcopate (Neale, *Patr. of Alexandria*, i., 206). The conduct of Peter, the successor of Athanasius, first in instituting Gregory Nazianzen bishop of Constantinople by his letters and sending a formal recognition of his appointment and then in substituting Maximus, as has been remarked by Milman (*History of Christianity*, iii., 115, note) and Ullman (Greg. Naz., p. 203 [Cox's translation]), furnish unmistakable indications of the desire to erect an Oriental papacy, by establishing the primacy of Alexandria over Constantinople and so over the East, which was still further illustrated a few years later by the high-handed behaviour of Theophilus towards Chrysostom.

Maximus was a native of Alexandria of low parentage. He boasted that his family had produced martyrs. He got instructed in the rudiments of the Christian faith and received baptism, but strangely enough sought to combine the Christian profession with Cynic philosophy.

When he presented himself at the Eastern capital he wore the white robe of a Cynic, and carried a philosopher's staff, his head being laden with a huge crop of crisp curling hair, dyed a golden yellow, and swinging over his shoulders in long ringlets. He represented himself as a confessor for the Nicene faith, and his banishment to the Oasis as a suffering for the truth (*Orat.* xxiii., p. 419). Before long he completely gained the ear and heart of Gregory, who admitted him to the closest companionship. Maximus proclaimed the most unbounded admiration for Gregory's discourses, which he praised in private, and, according to the custom of the age, applauded in public. His zeal against heretics was most fierce, and his denunciation of them uncompromising. The simple-hearted Gregory became the complete dupe of Maximus.

All this time Maximus was secretly maturing a plot for ousting his unsuspicious patron from his throne. He gained the ear and the confidence of Peter of Alexandria, and induced him to favour his ambitious views. Gregory, he asserted, had never been formally enthroned bishop of Constantinople; his translation thither was a violation of the canons of the church; rustic in manners, he had proved himself quite unfitted for the place. Constantinople was getting weary of him. It was time the patriarch of the Eastern world should exercise his prerogative and give New Rome a more suitable bishop. The old man was imposed on as Gregory had been, and lent himself to Maximus's projects. Maximus found a ready tool in a presbyter of Constantinople, envious of Gregory's talents and popularity (*de Vit.*, p. 13). Others were gained by bribes. Seven unscrupulous sailor fellows were despatched from Alexandria to mix with the people, and watch for a favourable opportunity for carrying out the plot. When all was ripe they were followed by a bevy of bishops, with secret instructions from the patriarch to consecrate Maximus.

The conspirators chose the night for the accomplishment of their enterprise. Gregory they knew was confined by illness. They forced their way into the cathedral, and commenced the rite of ordination. By the time they had set the Cynic on the archiepiscopal throne, and had just begun shearing away his long curls, they were surprised by the dawn. The news quickly spread, and everybody rushed to the church. The magistrates appeared on the scene with their officers; Maximus and his consecrators were driven from the sacred precincts, and in the house or shop of a flute-player the tonsure was completed. Maximus repaired to Thessalonica to lay his cause before Theodosius. He met with a cold reception from the emperor, who committed the matter to Ascholius, the much respected bishop of that city, charging him to refer it to pope Damasus. We have two letters of Damasus's on this subject. In the first, addressed to Ascholius and the Mace-

nople was the germ of the successful mendacity of the arch-rebel Photius." (Rivington. *The Prim. Ch.*, p. 263). The phraseology seems to suggest warm discontent at the canon.

donian bishops, he vehemently condemns the "ardor animi et fœda presumptio" which had led certain persons coming from Egypt, in violation of the rule of ecclesiastical discipline, to have proposed to consecrate a restless man, an alien from the Christian profession, not worthy to be called a Christian, who wore an idolatrous garb ("habitus idoli") and the long hair which St. Paul said was a shame to a man, and remarks on the fact that being expelled from the church they were compelled to complete the ordination "intra parietes alienos." In the second letter, addressed to Ascholius individually (*Ep*. vi.) he repeats his condemnation of the ordination of the long-haired Maximus ("comatum") and asks him to take special care that a Catholic bishop may be ordained (Migne, *Patrolog*., xiii., pp. 366–369 ; *Ep*. 5 ; 5, 6).

Maximus returned to Alexandria, and demanded that Peter should assist him in re-establishing himself at Constantinople. But Peter had discovered the man's true character, and received him as coldly as Theodosius had done. Determined to carry his point he presented himself to the patriarch at the head of a disorderly mob, with the threat that if he did not help him to gain the throne of Constantinople he would have that of Alexandria. Peter appealed to the prefect, by whom Maximus was driven out of Egypt. The death of Peter and the accession of Timotheus are placed Feb. 14, 380. The events described must therefore have occurred in 379. When the second ecumenical council met at Constantinople in 381, the question of Maximus's claim to the see of Constantinople came up for consideration. His pretensions were unanimously rejected.

BRIGHT.
(Notes on the Canons, in loc.)

Maximus, however, having been expelled from Egypt, made his way into Northern Italy, presented to Gratian at Milan a large work which he had written against the Arians (as to which Gregory sarcastically remarks—"Saul a prophet, Maximus an author ! " *Carm. adv. Max.*, 21), and deceived St. Ambrose and his suffragans by showing the record of his consecration, with letters which Peter had once written in his behalf. To these prelates of the "Italic diocese" the appeal of Maximus seemed like the appeal of Athanasius, and more recently of Peter himself, to the sympathy of the church of Rome ; and they requested Theodosius to let the case be heard before a really General Council (Mansi, iii., 631). Nothing further came of it ; perhaps, says Tillemont, those who thus wrote in favour of Maximus "reconnurent bientôt quel il était " (ix., 502) : so that when a Council did meet at Rome towards the end of 382, no steps were taken in his behalf.

CANON V.

(Probably adopted at a Council held in Constantinople the next year, 382. *Vide*. Introduction on the number of the Canons.)

In regard to the tome of the Western [Bishops], we receive those in Antioch also who confess the unity of the Godhead of the Father, and of the Son, and of the Holy Ghost.

NOTES.

ANCIENT EPITOME OF CANON V.

The Tome of the Westerns which recognizes the Father, the Son, and the Holy Spirit as consubstantial is highly acceptable.

Beveridge and Van Espen translate this canon differently, thus, " With regard to the tome of the Westerns, we agree with those in Antioch [i.e. the Synod of 378] who (accepted it and) acknowledged the unity of the Godhead of the Father etc." In opposition to this translation Hefele urges that ἀποδέχεσθαι in ecclesiastical language usually refers to receiving persons and recognizing them, not opinions or doctrines.

HEFELE.

This canon probably does not belong to the second General Council, but to the Synod held in the following year at Constantinople consisting of nearly the same bishops.

It is certain that by the "Tome of the Westerns " a dogmatic work of the Western bishops is to be understood, and the only question is which Tome of the Westerns is here meant. Several—for instance, the Greek commentators, Balsamon and Zonaras, and the spokesman of the Latins at the Synod of Florence in 1439 (Archbishop Andrew of Rhodes)—understood by it the decrees of the Synod of Sardica ; but it seems to me that this canon undoubtedly indicates that the Tome of the Westerns also mentioned the condition of the Antiochian Church, and the division into two parties of the orthodox of that place—the Meletian schism.   Now, as this was not mentioned, nay, could not have been, at the Synod of Sardica—for this schism at Antioch only broke out seventeen years later —some other document of the Latins must certainly be meant.   But we know that Pope Damasus, and the synod assembled by him in 369, addressed a Tome to the Orientals, of which fragments are still preserved, and that nine years later, in 379, a great synod at Antioch of one hundred and forty-six orthodox Oriental bishops, under Meletius, accepted and signed this Tome, and at the same time sought to put a stop to the Meletian schism.   Soon afterwards, in 380, Pope Damasus and his fourth Roman Synod again sent a treatise on the faith, of which we still possess a portion, containing anathemas, to the Orientals, especially to Bishop Paul of Antioch, head of the Eustathians of that city. Under these circumstances, we are justified in referring the expression "the tome of the Westerns" either to the Roman treatise of 369 or to that of 380, and I am disposed to give the preference to the former, for the following reasons :—

(1.) As has been already observed, this canon belongs to the Synod held at Constantinople in 382.

(2.) We still possess in Theodoret a Synodal Letter to the Latins from this later Synod.

(3.) The canon in question, as proceeding from the same source, is, of course to a certain extent, connected with this letter.

(4.) In this Synodal Letter, the Eastern bishops, in order to convince the Latins of their orthodoxy, appeal to two documents, the one a "tome" of an Antiochian Synod, and the other a "tome" of the Ecumenical Council held at Constantinople in 381.

(5.) By the Antiochian Synod here mentioned, I understand the great synod of 378, and, as a necessary consequence, believe the "tome" there produced to be none other than the Roman Tome of 369, which was then accepted at Antioch.

(6.) It is quite certain that the Synod of Antioch sent a copy of this Tome, with the declaration of its acceptance and the signatures of the members, back to Rome, as a supplement to its Synodal Letter ; and hence Lucas Holstenius was still able to find fragments of it in Rome.

(7.) The Synod of Constantinople of 382 might well call this Tome, sent back to Rome with the acceptance and signatures of the Easterns, a "Tome established at Antioch," although it was really drawn up at Rome.

(8.) If, however, the Synod of Constantinople in its Synodal Letter speaks of this Tome, we are justified in supposing that the one mentioned in its canon is the same.

(9.) That which still remains of the Roman Tome of 369, treats expressly of the oneness of the Godhead of the Father, the Son, and the Holy Ghost ; and such were the contents of the Tome according to this canon.

(10.) It is true that the fragments still preserved of this Tome contain no passage directly referring to the Antiochian schism ; but, in the first place, very little remains of it, and there is the more reason to suppose that the Meletian schism was spoken of in the portion which has been lost, as it was the same Antiochian Synod that accepted the Tome which urged the putting an end to that schism.   It is still more to the purpose that the Italian bishops, in their letter to the Easterns in 381, expressly say that they had already long before (*dudum*) written to the Orientals in order to put an end to the division between the orthodox at Antioch.   By this "*dudum*" I conclude that they refer to the Roman Tome of 369 ; and if the Westerns in their letter to the Easterns in 381 pointed to this Tome, it was natural that the Synod of Constantinople of 382 should also have referred to it, for it was that very letter of the Latins which occasioned and called the synod into being.

Lastly, for the full understanding of this canon, it is necessary to observe that the Latins, in their letter just mentioned of 381, say that "they had already in their earlier missive (*i.e.* as we suppose, in the Tome of 369) spoken to the effect that both parties at Antioch, one as much as the other, were orthodox."   Agreeing with this remark of the Westerns, repeated in their letter of 381, the Easterns in this canon say, "We also recognise all Antiochians as orthodox who acknowledge the oneness of the Godhead of the Father, the Son, and the Holy Ghost."

CANON VI.

(Probably adopted at a Council held in Constantinople the next year, 382. *Vide* Introduction on the number of Canons.)

FORASMUCH as many wishing to confuse and overturn ecclesiastical order, do contentiously and slanderously fabricate charges against the orthodox bishops who have the administration of the Churches, intending nothing else than to stain the reputation of the priests and raise up disturbances amongst the peaceful laity; therefore it seemed right to the Holy Synod of Bishops assembled together in Constantinople, not to admit accusers without examination; and neither to allow all persons whatsoever to bring accusations against the rulers of the Church, nor, on the other hand, to exclude all. If then, any one shall bring a private complaint against the Bishop, that is, one relating to his own affairs, as, for example, that he has been defrauded, or otherwise unjustly treated by him, in such accusations no examination shall be made, either of the person or of the religion of the accuser; for it is by all means necessary that the conscience of the Bishop should be free, and that he who says he has been wronged should meet with righteous judgment, of whatever religion he may be. But if the charge alleged against the Bishop be that of some ecclesiastical offence, then it is necessary to examine carefully the persons of the accusers, so that, in the first place, heretics may not be suffered to bring accusations touching ecclesiastical matters against orthodox bishops. And by heretics we mean both those who were aforetime cast out and those whom we ourselves have since anathematized, and also those professing to hold the true faith who have separated from our canonical bishops, and set up conventicles in opposition [to them]. Moreover, if there be any who have been condemned for faults and cast out of the Church, or excommunicated, whether of the clergy or the laity, neither shall it be lawful for these to bring an accusation against the bishop, until they have cleared away the charge against themselves. In like manner, persons who are under previous accusations are not to be permitted to bring charges against a bishop or any other clergyman, until they shall have proved their own innocence of the accusation brought against them. But if any, being neither heretics, nor excommunicate, nor condemned, nor under previous accusation for alleged faults, should declare that they have any ecclesiastical charge against the bishop, the Holy Synod bids them first lay their charges before all the Bishops of the Province, and before them prove the accusations, whatsoever they may be, which they have brought against the bishop. And if the comprovincials should be unable rightly to settle the charges brought against the bishop, then the parties must betake themselves to a greater synod of the bishops of that diocese called together for this purpose; and they shall not produce their allegations before they have promised in writing to undergo an equal penalty to be exacted from themselves, if, in the course of the examination, they shall be proved to have slandered the accused bishop. And if anyone, despising what has been decreed concerning these things, shall presume to annoy the ears of the Emperor, or the courts of temporal judges, or, to the dishonour of all the Bishops of his Province, shall trouble an Ecumenical Synod, such an one shall by no means be admitted as an accuser; forasmuch as he has cast contempt upon the Canons, and brought reproach upon the order of the Church.

NOTES.

ANCIENT EPITOME OF CANON VI.

Even one that is of ill repute, if he have suffered any injury, let him bring a charge against the bishop. If however it be a crime of ecclesiastical matters let him not speak. Nor shall another condemned before, speak. Let not one excommunicated, or cast forth, or charged with any crimes speak, until he is cleared of them. But those who should bring the charge are the orthodox, who are communicants, uncondemned, unaccused. Let the case be heard by the provincials. If however they are not able to decide the case, let them have recourse to a greater synod and let them not be heard, without a written declaration of liability to the same sufferings [i.e. *of their readiness to be tried by the* lex talionis.] *But should anyone contrary to the provisions appeal to the Emperor and trouble him, let such be cast forth.*

The phrase "who have the administration of the Churches," Hatch in his Bampton Lectures (Lect. I., p. 41) erroneously supposes to refer only to the administration of the Church's alms. But this, as Dr. Bright well points out ("Notes on the Canons," *in loc.*) cannot be the meaning of οἰκονομεῖν when used absolutely as in this canon. He says, "When a merely 'economic' function is intended, the context shews it, as in Chalcedon, Canon xxvj." He also points out that in Canon ij., and in Eusebius (H. E. iv., 4), and when St. Basil wishes his brother to οἰκονομεῖν a church suited to his temperament (*Epist.* xcviij., 2) the meaning of the word is evidently spiritual stewardship.

ZONARAS.

By "those who were cast out of the Church" are to be understood those who were altogether cut off from the Church; but by those who were "excommunicated" the holy fathers intend all those, whether clerics or laymen, who are deprived of communion for a set time.

VAN ESPEN.

It is evident from the context of this canon that "Diocese" here does not signify the district or territory assigned to any one bishop, as we to-day use the word; but for a district, which not only contained many episcopal districts, as to-day do ecclesiastical provinces, but which contained also many provinces, and this was the meaning of the word at the time of this Council's session.

ZONARAS.

We call Adrianople, for example, or Philoppopolis with the bishops of each a "Province," but the whole of Thrace or Macedonia we call a "Diocese." When these crimes were brought forward to be corrected, for the judging of which the provincial bishops were by no means sufficient, then the Canon orders the bishops of the diocese to assemble, and determine the charges preferred against the bishop.

VAN ESPEN.

Both the Canon and the Civil Law require the accusers to submit themselves to the law of retaliation (*lex talionis*). *Vide* Gratian, Pt. II., Causa II., Quæst. III., 2 and 3, where we read from the decree of Pope Hadrian; "Whoever shall not prove what he advances, shall himself suffer the penalty due the crime he charged." And under the name of Damasus, "The calumniator, if he fail in proving his accusation, shall receive his tale." The Civil Law is in L. x., Cod. *de Calumniatoribus*, and reads, "Whoso charges a crime, shall not have licence to lie with impunity, since justice requires that calumniators shall endure the punishment due the crime which they failed to prove."

The Council wishes that all accusations of bishops for ecclesiastical offences shall be kept out of the secular courts, and shall be heard by synods of bishops, in the manner and form here prescribed, which is in accordance with the Constitution which under the names of Valens, Gratian, and Valentinian, the Emperors, is referred to in law xxiij. of the Code of Theodosius, *De Episcopis et Clericis.*

Whatever may be said of the meeting of bishops at which this canon was enacted, this is clear, no mention was made of the Roman Pontiff, nor of the Council of Sardica, as Fleury notes in his *Histoire Ecclesiastique*, Lib. xviij., n. 8. From this it is evident either that at that time the Orientals did not admit, especially for bishops, appeals to the Roman Pontiff; nor did they accept the authority of the Synod of Sardica, in so far as it permitted that the sentence given in a provincial synod, should be reopened by the neighbouring bishops together with the bishops of the province, and if it seemed good, that the cause might be referred to Rome.

WARNING TO THE READER TOUCHING CANON VII.

(Beveridge, *Synodicon*, Tom. II., *in loc.*)

This canon, I confess, is contained in all the editions of the Commentaries of Balsamon and Zonaras. It is cited also by Photius in *Nomocanon*, Tit. xii., ch. xiv., besides it is extant in a contracted form in the Epitome of Alexius Aristenus. But it is wanting in all the Latin versions of the Canons, in the ancient translations of Dionys. Exig., Isidore Mercator, etc.; also in the Epitome of Sym. Logothet., and the Arabic paraphrase of Josephus Ægyp., and what is particularly to be observed, in the collection and nomocanon of John of Antioch; and this not through want of attention on his part, as is clear from this namely, that in the order of the Canons as given by him he attributes six Canons only to this second General Council, saying ". . . of the Fathers who assembled at Constantinople, by whom six Canons were set forth," so that it is clear the present was not reckoned among the canons of this council in those days. Nay, the whole composition of this canon clearly indicates that it is to be ascribed, neither to this present council, nor to any other (unless perhaps to that of Trullo, of which we shall speak afterwards). For nothing is appointed in it, nothing confirmed, but a certain ancient custom of receiving converted heretics, is here merely recited.

(Hefele, History of the Councils, Vol. II., p. 368.)

As we possess a letter from the Church at Constantinople in the middle of the fifth century to Bishop Martyrius of Antioch, in which the same subject is referred to in a precisely similar way, Beveridge is probably right in conjecturing that the canon was only an extract from this letter to Martyrius; therefore in no way a decree of the second General Council, nor even of the Synod of 382, but at least eighty years later than the latter. This canon, with an addition, was afterwards adopted by the Quinisext Synod as its ninety-fifth, without, however, giving its origin.

CANON VII.

THOSE who from heresy turn to orthodoxy, and to the portion of those who are being saved, we receive according to the following method and custom: Arians, and Macedonians, and Sabbatians, and Novatians, who call themselves Cathari or Aristeri, and Quarto-decimans or Tetradites, and Apollinarians, we receive, upon their giving a written renunciation [of their errors] and anathematize every heresy which is not in accordance with the Holy, Catholic, and Apostolic Church of God. Thereupon, they are first sealed or anointed with the holy oil upon the forehead, eyes, nostrils, mouth, and ears; and when we seal them, we say, "The Seal of the gift of the Holy Ghost." But Eunomians, who are baptized with only one immersion, and Montanists, who are here called Phrygians, and Sabellians, who teach the identity of Father and Son, and do sundry other mischievous things, and [the partisans of] all other heresies—for there are many such here, particularly among those who come from the country of the Galatians:—all these, when they desire to turn to orthodoxy, we receive as heathen. On the first day we make them Christians; on the second, catechumens; on the third, we exorcise them by breathing thrice in their face and ears; and thus we instruct them and oblige them to spend some time in the Church, and to hear the Scriptures; and then we baptize them.

NOTES.

ANCIENT EPITOME OF CANON VII.[1]

Quarto-decimans or Tetradites, Arians, Macedonians, Sabbatians, and Apollinarians ought to be received with their books and anointed in all their organs of sense.

ANCIENT EPITOME OF CANON VIII.

Eunomians baptized with one immersion, Sabellians, and Phrygians are to be received as heathen.

ARISTEMUS (*in Can.* vij.).

Those giving up their books and execrating every heresy are received with only anointing with chrism of the eyes, the nostrils, the ears, the mouth, and the brow; and signing them with the words, "The Seal of the gift of the Holy Ghost."

For the "Cathari," see Notes on Canon viij. of I. Nice.

HAMMOND.

Sabbatians. Sabbatius was a presbyter who adopted the sentiments of Novatius, but as it is clear from the histories of Socrates and Sozomen, that he did not do so till at least eight years after the celebration of this council, it is of course equally clear that this canon could not have been framed by this council.

---

[1] This canon is broken into two by the Ancient Epitome.

Aristeri. This is probably a false reading for Aristi, i.e. the best. In the letter above mentioned the expression is Cathari and Catheroteri, i.e. the pure, and the more pure.

The Quarto-decimans, or Tetradites, were those persons who persisted in observing the Easter festival with the Jews, on the fourteenth day of the first month, whatever day of the week it happened to be.

Montanists. One of the older sects, so called from Montanus, who embraced Christianity in the second century. He professed to be inspired in a peculiar way by the Holy Ghost, and to prophesy. He was supported in his errors by two women, Priscilla and Maximilla, who also pretended to prophesy. His heresy infected many persons, amongst others Tertullian, but being condemned by the Church, his followers formed a sect remarkable for extreme austerity. But although they asserted that the Holy Ghost had inspired Montanus to introduce a system of greater perfection than the Church had before known, and condemned those who would not join them as carnal, they did not at first innovate in any of the articles of the Creed. This sect lasted a long time, and spread much in Phrygia and the neighbouring districts, whence they were called Phryges and Cataphryges, and latterly adopted the errors of Sabellius respecting the Trinity.

The other heresies mentioned in this canon have been treated of in the excursus to Canon j.

EXCURSUS ON THE AUTHORITY OF THE SECOND ECUMENICAL COUNCIL.

(Hefele, *History of the Councils*, Vol. II., pp. 370, *et seqq.*)

Lastly, to turn to the question of the authority of this Council, it appears, first of all, that immediately after its close, in the same year, 381, several of its acts were censured by a Council of Latins, namely, the prolongation of the Meletian schism (by the elevation of Flavian), and the choice of Nectarius as Bishop of Constantinople, while, as is known, the Westerns held (the Cynic) Maximus to be the rightful bishop of that city.

In consequence of this, the new Synod assembled in the following year, 382, at Constantinople, sent the Latins a copy of the decrees of faith composed the year before, expressly calling this Synod οἰκουμενική and at the same time seeking to justify it in those points which had been censured. Photius[1] maintains that soon afterwards Pope Damasus confirmed this synod; but, as the following will show, this confirmation could only have referred to the creed and not to the canons. As late as about the middle of the fifth century, Pope Leo I. spoke in a very depreciatory manner of these canons, especially of the third, which concerned the ecclesiastical rank of Constantinople, remarking that it was never sent to the See of Rome. Still later, Gregory the Great wrote in the same sense: *Romana autem Ecclesia eosdam canones vel gesta Synodi illius hactenus non habet, nec accepit; in hoc autem eam accepit, quod est per eam contra Macedonium definitum.*[2]

Thus, as late as the year 600, only the creed, but not the canons of the Synod of Constantinople were accepted at Rome; but on account of its creed, Gregory the Great reckons it as one of the four Ecumenical Councils, which he compares to the four Gospels. So also before him the popes Vigilius and Pelagius II., reckoned this Synod among the Ecumenical Councils.

The question is, from what date the Council of Constantinople was considered ecumenical by the Latins as well as by the Greeks. We will begin with the latter. Although as we have seen, the Synod of 382 had already designated this council as ecumenical, yet it could not for a long time obtain an equal rank with the Council of Nicæa, for which reason the General Council of Ephesus mentions that of Nicæa and its creed with the greatest respect, but is totally silent as to this Synod. Soon afterwards, the so-called Robber-Synod in 449, spoke of two (General) Councils, at Nicæa and Ephesus, and designated the latter as ἡ δευτέρα σύνοδος, as a plain token that it did not ascribe such a high rank to the assembly

---

[1] Photius, *De Synodis*, p. 1143, ed. Justelli.   [2] Greg., *Epist.*, Lib. I., 25.

at Constantinople. It might perhaps be objected that only the Monophysites, who notoriously ruled the Robber-Synod, used this language; but the most determined opponent of the Monophysites, their accuser, Bishop Eusebius of Doylæum, in like manner also brought forward only the two Synods of Nicæa and Ephesus, and declared that "he held to the faith of the three hundred and eighteen Fathers assembled at Nicæa, and to all that was done at the great and Holy Synod at Ephesus."

The Creed of Constantinople appears for the first time to have been highly honoured at the fourth General Council, which had it recited after that of Nicæa, and thus solemnly approved it. Since then this Synod has been universally honoured as ecumenical by the Greeks, and was mentioned by the Emperor Justinian with the Councils of Nicæa, Ephesus, and Chalcedon, as of equal rank.[1]

But in the West, and especially in Rome, however satisfied people were with the decree of faith enacted by this Synod, and its completion of the creed, yet its third canon, respecting the rank of Constantinople, for a long time proved a hindrance to its acknowledgment. This was especially shown at the Council of Chalcedon, and during the time immediately following. When at that Council the creed of Constantinople was praised, repeated, and confirmed the Papal Legates fully concurred; but when the Council also renewed and confirmed the third canon of Constantinople, the Legates left the assembly, lodged a protest against it on the following day, and declared that the rules of the hundred and fifty bishops at Constantinople were never inserted among the Synodal canons (which were recognised at Rome). The same was mentioned by Pope Leo himself, who, immediately after the close of the Council of Chalcedon wrote to Bishop Anatolius of Constantinople: "that document of certain bishops (i.e. the third canon of Constantinople) was never brought by your predecessors to the knowledge of the Apostolic See."[2] Leo also, in his 105th letter to the Empress Pulcheria, speaks just as depreciatingly of this Council of Constantinople; and Quesnel is entirely wrong in maintaining that the Papal Legates at the Synod of Chalcedon at first practically acknowledged the validity of the third canon of Constantinople. Bishop Eusebius of Doylæum was equally mistaken in maintaining at Chalcedon itself, that the third canon had been sanctioned by the Pope; and we shall have occasion further on, in the history of the Council of Chalcedon, to show the untenable character of both statements.

Pope Felix III. took the same view as Pope Leo, when, in his letter to the monks at Constantinople and Bithynia in 485, he only spoke of three General Councils at Nicæa, Ephesus, and Chalcedon; neither did his successor Gelasius (492–496) in his genuine decree, De libris recipiendis, mention this Synod. It may certainly be said, on the other hand, that in the sixth century its ecumenical character had come to be most distinctly acknowledged in the Latin Church also, and, as we have seen above, had been expressly affirmed by the Popes Vigilius, Pelagius II., and Gregory the Great. But this acknowledgment, even when it is not expressly stated, only referred to the decrees on faith of the Council of Constantinople, and not to its canons, as we have already observed in reference to the third and sixth of them.

---

[1] In his edict against the Three Chapters.   [2] Leo, Epist. cvi. n., ed. Ballerini, t. i., p. 1165.

COUNCIL OF CONSTANTINOPLE.

A.D. 382.

THE SYNODICAL LETTER.[1]

To the right honourable lords our right reverend brethren and colleagues, Damasus, Ambrosius, Britton, Valerianus, Ascholius, Anemius, Basilius and the rest of the holy bishops assembled in the great city of Rome, the holy synod of the orthodox bishops assembled at the great city of Constantinople sends greeting in the Lord.

To recount all the sufferings inflicted on us by the power of the Arians, and to attempt to give information to your reverences, as though you were not already well acquainted with them, might seem superfluous. For we do not suppose your piety to hold what is befalling us as of such secondary importance as that you stand in any need of information on matters which cannot but evoke your sympathy. Nor indeed were the storms which beset us such as to escape notice from their insignificance. Our persecutions are but of yesterday. The sound of them still rings in the ears alike of those who suffered them and of those whose love made the sufferers' pain their own. It was but a day or two ago, so to speak, that some released from chains in foreign lands returned to their own churches through manifold afflictions; of others who had died in exile the relics were brought home; others again, even after their return from exile, found the passion of the heretics still at the boiling heat, and, slain by them with stones as was the blessed Stephen, met with a sadder fate in their own than in a stranger's land. Others, worn away with various cruelties, still bear in their bodies the scars of their wounds and the marks of Christ. Who could tell the tale of fines, of disfranchisements, of individual confiscations, of intrigues, of outrages, of prisons? In truth all kinds of tribulation were wrought out beyond number in us, perhaps because we were paying the penalty of sins, perhaps because the merciful God was trying us by means of the multitude of our sufferings. For these all thanks to God, who by means of such afflictions trained his servants and, according to the multitude of his mercies, brought us again to refreshment. We indeed needed long leisure, time, and toil to restore the church once more, that so, like physicians healing the body after long sickness and expelling its disease by gradual treatment, we might bring her back to her ancient health of true religion. It is true that on the whole we seem to have been delivered from the violence of our persecutions and to be just now recovering the churches which have for a long time been the prey of the heretics. But wolves are troublesome to us who, though they have been driven from the fold, yet harry the flock up and down the glades, daring to hold rival assemblies, stirring seditions among the people, and shrinking from nothing which can do damage to the churches. So, as we have already said, we needs must labour all the longer. Since, however, you showed your brotherly love to us by inviting us (as though we were your own members) by the letters of our most religious emperor to the synod which you are gathering by divine permission at Rome, to the end that since we alone were then condemned to suffer persecution, you should not now, when our emperors are at one with us as to true religion, reign apart from us, but that we, to use the Apostle's phrase, should reign with you, our prayer was, if it were possible, all in company to leave our churches, and rather gratify our longing to see you than consult their needs. For who will give us wings as of a dove, and we will fly and be at rest? But this course seemed likely to leave the churches who were just recovering quite undefended, and the undertaking was to most of us impossible, for, in accordance with the letters sent a year ago from your holiness after the synod at Aquileia to the most pious emperor Theodosius, we had journeyed to Constantinople, equipped only for travelling

---

[1] Found in Theod., *H. E.* v. 9. The reader is warned against inaccurate translations of the dogmatic portions.

so far as Constantinople, and bringing the consent of the bishops remaining in the provinces of this synod alone. We had been in no expectation of any longer journey nor had heard a word about it, before our arrival at Constantinople. In addition to all this, and on account of the narrow limits of the appointed time which allowed of no preparation for a longer journey, nor of communicating with the bishops of our communion in the provinces and of obtaining their consent, the journey to Rome was for the majority impossible. We have therefore adopted the next best course open to us under the circumstances, both for the better administration of the church, and for manifesting our love towards you, by strongly urging our most venerated, and honoured colleagues and brother bishops Cyriacus, Eusebius and Priscianus, to consent to travel to you.

Through them we wish to make it plain that our disposition is all for peace with unity for its sole object, and that we are full of zeal for the right faith. For we, whether we suffered persecutions, or afflictions, or the threats of emperors, or the cruelties of princes, or any other trial at the hands of heretics, have undergone all for the sake of the evangelic faith, ratified by the three hundred and eighteen fathers at Nicæa in Bithynia. This is the faith which ought to be sufficient for you, for us, for all who wrest not the word of the true faith; for it is the ancient faith; it is the faith of our baptism; it is the faith that teaches us to believe in the name of the Father, of the Son, and of the Holy Ghost. According to this faith there is one Godhead, Power and Substance of the Father and of the Son and of the Holy Ghost; the dignity being equal, and the majesty being equal in three perfect hypostases, i.e. three perfect persons. Thus there is no room for the heresy of Sabellius by the confusion of the hypostases, i.e. the destruction of the personalities; thus the blasphemy of the Eunomians, of the Arians, and of the Pneumatomachi is nullified, which divides the substance, the nature, and the godhead, and superinduces on the uncreated consubstantial and co-eternal Trinity a nature posterior, created and of a different substance. We moreover preserve unperverted the doctrine of the incarnation of the Lord, holding the tradition that the dispensation of the flesh is neither soulless nor mindless nor imperfect; and knowing full well that God's Word was perfect before the ages, and became perfect man in the last days for our salvation.

Let this suffice for a summary of the doctrine which is fearlessly and frankly preached by us, and concerning which you will be able to be still further satisfied if you will deign to read the tome of the synod of Antioch, and also that tome issued last year by the Ecumenical Council held at Constantinople, in which we have set forth our confession of the faith at greater length, and have appended an anathema against the heresies which innovators have recently inscribed.

Now as to the particular administration of individual churches, an ancient custom, as you know, has obtained, confirmed by the enactment of the holy fathers of Nicæa, that in every province, the bishops of the province, and, with their consent, the neighbouring bishops with them, should perform ordinations as expediency may require. In conforming with these customs note that other churches have been administered by us and the priests of the most famous churches publicly appointed. Accordingly over the new made (if the expression be allowable) church at Constantinople, which, as though from a lion's mouth, we have lately snatched by God's mercy from the blasphemy of the heretics, we have ordained bishop the right reverend and most religious Nectarius, in the presence of the Ecumenical Council, with common consent, before the most religious emperor Theodosius, and with the assent of all the clergy and of the whole city. And over the most ancient and truly apostolic church in Syria, where first the noble name of Christians was given them, the bishops of the province and of the eastern diocese have met together and canonically ordained bishop the right reverend and most religious Flavianus, with the consent of all the church, who as though with one voice joined in expressing their respect for him. This rightful ordination also received the sanction of the General Council. Of the church at Jerusalem, mother of all the churches, we make known that the right reverend and most religious Cyril is bishop, who was some time ago canonically ordained by the bishops of the province, and has in several places fought a good fight against the Arians. We beseech your reverence to rejoice at what has thus been rightly and canonically settled by us, by the intervention of spiritual love and by the influence of the fear of the

Lord, compelling the feelings of men, and making the edification of churches of more importance than individual grace or favour. Thus since among us there is agreement in the faith and Christian charity has been established, we shall cease to use the phrase condemned by the apostles, I am of Paul and I of Apollos and I of Cephas, and all appearing as Christ's, who in us is not divided, by God's grace we will keep the body of the church unrent, and will boldly stand at the judgment seat of the Lord.

THE THIRD ECUMENICAL COUNCIL.

THE COUNCIL OF EPHESUS.

A.D. 431

Emperors.—Theodosius II. and Valentinian III.
Pope.—Celestine I.

Elenchus.

HISTORICAL INTRODUCTION.

(Bossuet, *Def. Cler. Gall.*, Lib. vij., Cap. ix. *et seqq.* Abridged. Translation by Allies.)

The innovation of Nestorius, Bishop of Constantinople, is known ; how he divided into two the person of Christ. Pope St. Celestine, watchful, according to his office, over the affairs of the Church, had charged the blessed Cyril, Bishop of Alexandria, to send him a certain report of the doctrine of Nestorius, already in bad repute. Cyril declares this in his letter to Nestorius ; and so he writes to Celestine a complete account, and sets forth the doctrines of Nestorius and his own ; he sends him two letters from himself to Nestorius, who likewise, by his own letters and explanations, endeavoured to draw Celestine to his side. Thus the holy Pontiff, having been most fully informed by letters from both sides, is thus inquired of by Cyril. " We have not confidently abstained from Communion with him (Nestorius) before informing you of this ; condescend, therefore, to unfold your judgment, that we may clearly know whether we ought to communicate with him who cherishes such erroneous doctrine." And he adds, that his judgment should be written to the other Bishops also, " that all with one mind may hold firm in one sentence." Here is the Apostolic See manifestly consulted by so great a man, presiding over the second, or at least the third, Patriarchal See, and its judgment awaited ; and nothing remained but that Celestine, being duly consulted, should perform his Apostolic office. But how he did this, the Acts have shewn. In those Acts he not only approves the letters and doctrine of Cyril, but disapproves, too, the perverse dogma of Nestorius, and that distinctly, because he was unwilling to call the blessed Virgin Mother of God : and he decrees that he should be deprived of the Episcopate and Communion unless, within ten days from the date of the announcing of the sentence, he openly rejects this faithless innovation, which endeavours to separate what Scripture joineth together—that is, the Person of Christ. Here is the doctrine of Nestorius expressly disapproved, and a sentence of the Roman Pontiff on a matter of Faith most clearly pronounced under threat of deposition and excommunication : then, that nothing be wanting, the holy Pope commits his authority to Cyril to carry into execution that sentence " associating," he saith to Cyril, " the authority of our See, and using our person, and place, with power." So to Cyril ; so to Nestorius himself ; so to the clergy of Constantinople ; so to John of Antioch, then the Bishop of the third or fourth Patriarchal See ; so to Juvenal, Bishop of the Holy City, whom the Council of Nice had ordered to be especially honoured : so he writes to the other Bishops also, that the sentence given may be duly and in order made known to all. Cyril proceeds to execute his office, and performs all that he had been commanded. He promulgates and executes the decrees of Celestine ; declares to Nestorius, that after the ten days prescribed and set forth by Celestine, he would have no portion, intercourse, or place with the priesthood. Nothing evidently is wanting to the Apostolical authority being most fully exercised.

But Nestorius, bishop of the royal city, possessed such influence, had deceived men's minds with such an appearance of piety, had gained so many bishops and enjoyed such favour with the younger Theodosius and the great men, that he could easily throw everything into commotion ; and thus there was need of an Ecumenical Council, the question being most important, and the person of the highest dignity ; because many bishops, amongst these almost all of the East—that is, of the Patriarchate of Antioch, and the Patriarch John himself—were ill disposed to Cyril, and seemed to favour Nestorius : because men's feelings were divided, and the whole empire of the East seemed to fluctuate between Cyril and Nestorius. Such was the need of an Ecumenical Council.

The Emperor, moved by these and other reasons, wrote to Cyril,—" It is our will that the holy doctrine be discussed and examined in a sacred Synod, and that be ratified which appeareth agreeable to the right faith, whether the wrong party be pardoned by the Fathers or no."

Here we see three things: First, after the judgment of St. Celestine, another is still required, that of the Council; secondly, that these two things would rest with the Fathers, to judge of doctrine and of persons; thirdly, that the judgment of the Council would be decisive and final.

He adds, "those who everywhere preside over the Priesthood, and through whom we ourselves are and shall be professing the truth, must be judges of this matter." See on whose faith we rest. See in whose judgment is the final and irreversible authority.

Both the Emperor affirmed, and the bishops confessed, that this was done according to the Ecclesiastical Canons. And so all, and Celestine himself, prepared themselves for the Council. Cyril does no more, though named by Celestine to execute the pontifical decree. Nestorius remained in his original rank; the sentence of the universal Council is awaited; and the Emperor had expressly decreed, "that before the assembling and common sentence of the most holy Council, no change should be made in any matter at all, on any private authority." Rightly, and in order; for this was demanded by the majesty of an universal Council. Wherefore, both Cyril obeyed and the bishops rested. And it was established, that although the sentence of the Roman Pontiff on matters of Faith, and on persons judged for violation of the Faith, had been passed and promulged, all was suspended, while the authority of the universal Council was awaited.

Having gone over what preceded the Council, we review the acts of the Council itself, and begin with the first course of proceeding. After, therefore, the bishops and Nestorius himself were come to Ephesus, the universal Council began, Cyril being president, and representing Celestine, as being appointed by the Pontiff himself to execute his sentence. In the first course of proceeding this was done. First, the above-mentioned letter of the Emperor was read, that an Ecumenical Council should be held, and all proceedings in the mean time be suspended; this letter, I say, was read, and placed on the Acts, and it was approved by the Fathers, that all the decrees of Celestine in the matter of Nestorius had been suspended until the holy Council should give its sentence. You will ask if it was the will of the Council merely that the Emperor should be allowed to prohibit, in the interim, effect being given to the sentence of the Apostolic See. Not so, according to the Acts; but rather, by the intervention of a General Council's authority (the convocation of which, according to the discipline of those times, was left to the Emperor), the Council itself understood that all proceedings were of course suspended, and depended on the sentence of the Council. Wherefore, though the decree of the Pontiff had been promulged and notified, and the ten days had long been past, Nestorius was held by the Council itself to be a bishop, and called by the name of most religious bishop, and by that name, too, thrice cited and summoned to take his seat with the other bishops in the holy Council; for this expression, "to take his seat," is distinctly written; and it is added, "in order to answer to what was charged against him." For it was their full purpose that he should recognise in whatever way, the Ecumenical Council, as he would then afterwards be, beyond doubt, answerable to it; but he refused to come, and chose to have his doors besieged with an armed force, that no one might approach him.

Thereupon, as the Emperor commanded, and the Canons required, the rule of Faith was set forth, and the Nicene Creed read, as the standard to which all should be referred, and then the letters of Cyril and Nestorius were examined in order. The letter of Cyril was first brought before the judgment of the Council. That letter, I mean, concerning the Faith, to Nestorius, so expressly approved by Pope Celestine, of which he had declared to Cyril, " We

see that you hold and maintain all that we hold and maintain"; which, by the decree against
Nestorius, published to all Churches, he had approved, and wishes to be considered as a
canonical monition against Nestorius : that letter, I repeat, was examined, at the proposition
of Cyril himself, in these words : "I am persuaded that I have in nothing departed from
the orthodox Faith, or the Nicene Creed ; wherefore I beseech your Holiness to set forth
openly whether I have written this correctly, blamelessly, and in accordance with that
holy Council."

And are there those who say that questions concerning the Faith, once judged by the
Roman Pontiff on his Apostolical authority, are examined in general Councils, in order to
understand their contents, but not to decide on their substance, as being still a matter of
question ?   Let them hear Cyril, the President of the Council ; let them attend to what he
proposes for the inquiry of the Council ; and though he were conscious of no error in himself yet, not to trust himself, he asked for the sentence of the Council in these words—
"whether I have written correctly and blamelessly, or not." This Cyril, the chief of the
Council, proposes for their consideration.   Who ever even heard it whispered that, after a
final and irreversible judgment of the Church on a matter of Faith, any such inquiry or
question was made ?   It was never done, for that would be to doubt about the Faith itself,
when declared and discussed.   But this was done after the judgment of Pope Celestine ;
neither Cyril, nor anyone else, thought of any other course : that, therefore, was not a final
and irreversible judgment.

In answer to this question the Fathers in order give their judgment—"that the Nicene
Creed, and the letter of Cyril, in all things agree and harmonise." Here is inquiry and examination, and then judgment.   The Acts speak for themselves—we say not here a word.

Next that letter of Nestorius was produced, which Celestine had pronounced blasphemous and impious.   It is read : then at the instance of Cyril it is examined, "whether this,
too, be agreeable to the Faith set forth by the holy Council of the Nicene Fathers, or not."
It is precisely the same form according to which Cyril's letter was examined.   The Fathers,
in order, give judgment that it disagreed from the Nicene Creed, and was, therefore, censur-
able.   The letter of Nestorius is disapproved in the same manner, by the same rule, by
which that of Cyril was approved.   Here, twice in the same proceeding of the Council of
Ephesus, a judgment of the Roman Pontiff concerning the Catholic Faith, uttered and published, is reconsidered.   What he had approved, and what he had disapproved, is equally
examined, and, only after examination, confirmed.

In the mean time, the bishops Arcadius and Projectus, and the presbyter Philip, had been
chosen by Celestine to be present at the Council of Ephesus, with a special commission
from the Apostolic See, and the whole Council of the West.   So they come from Rome to
Ephesus, and appear at the holy Council, and here the second procedure commences.

After reading the letter of Celestine, the Legates, in pursuance, say to the bishops :
"Let your Holiness consider the form of the letters of the holy and venerable Pope Celestine the Bishop, who hath exhorted your Holiness, not as instructing those who are ignorant, but as reminding those who are aware : in order that you may command to be completely and finally settled according to the Canon of our common Faith, and the utility of
the Catholic Church, what he has before determined, and has now the goodness to remind
you of." This is the advantage of a Council ; after whose sentence there is no new discussion, or new judgment, but merely execution.   And this the Legates request to be commanded by the Council, in which they recognise that supreme authority.

It behoved, also, that the Legates, sent to the Council on a special mission, should
understand whether the proceedings against Nestorius had been pursued according to the
requisition of the Canons, and due respect to the Apostolic See.   This we have already often

said. Wherefore, with reason, they require the Acts to be communicated, "that we, too," say they, "may confirm them." The proceedings themselves will declare what that confirmation means. After that, at the request of the Legates, the Acts against Nestorius were given them, they thus report about them at the third procedure: "We have found all things judged canonically, and according to the Church's discipline." Therefore judgments of the Apostolic See are canonically and, according to the Church's discipline, reconsidered, after deliberation, in a General Council, and judgment passed upon them. After the Legates had approved the Acts against Nestorius communicated to them, they request that all which had been read and done at Ephesus from the beginning, should be read afresh in public Session, "in order," they say, "that obeying the form of the most holy Pope Celestine, who hath committed this care to us, we may be enabled to confirm the judgment also of your Holiness." After these all had been read afresh, and the Legates agreed to them, Cyril proposes to the holy Council, "That the Legates, by their signature, as was customary, should make plain and manifest their canonical agreement with the Council." To this question of Cyril the Council thus answers, and decrees that the Legates, by their subscription, confirm the Acts; by which place this confirmation, spoken of by the Council, is clearly nothing else but to make their assent plain and manifest, as Cyril proposed.

Finally, Celestine himself, after the conclusion of the whole matter, sends a letter to the holy Council of Ephesus, which he thus begins: "At length we must rejoice at the conclusion of evils." The learned reader understands where he recognizes the *conclusion;* that is, after the condemnation of Nestorius by the infallible authority of an Ecumenical Council, viz., of the whole Catholic Church. He proceeds: "We see, that you, with us, have executed this matter so faithfully transacted." All decree, and all execute, that is, by giving a common judgment. Whence Celestine adds, "We have been informed of a just deposition, and a still juster exaltation:" the deposition of Nestorius, begun, indeed, by the Roman See, but brought to a conclusion by the sentence of the Council; to a full and complete settlement, as we have seen above: the exaltation of Maximianus, who was substituted in place of Nestorius immediately after the Ephesine decrees; this is the conclusion of the question. Even Celestine himself recognises this conclusion to lie not in his own examination and judgment, but in that of an Ecumenical Council. And this was done in that Council in which it is admitted that the authority of the Apostolic See was most clearly set forth, not only by words, but by deeds, of any since the birth of Christ. At least the Holy Council gives credence to Philip uttering these true and magnificent encomiums, concerning the dignity of the Apostolic See, and "Peter the head and pillar of the Faith, and foundation of the Catholic Church, and by Christ's authority administering the keys, who to this very time lives ever, and exercises judgment, in his successors." This, he says, after having seen all the Acts of the Council itself, which we have mentioned, so that we may indeed understand, that all these privileges of Peter and the Apostolic See entirely agree with the decrees of the Council, and the judgment entered into afresh, and deliberation upon matters of Faith held after the Apostolic See.

NOTE ON THE EMPEROR'S EDICT TO THE SYNOD.

Neither of the Emperors could personally attend the Council of Ephesus and accordingly Theodosius II., appointed the Count Candidian, Captain of the imperial bodyguard, the protector of the council, to sit in the room of the Emperors. In making this appointment he addressed an edict to the synod which will be found in the *Concilia* and of which Hefele gives the following synopsis.

(Hefele, *Hist. of the Councils*, Vol. III., p. 43.)

Candidian is to take no immediate part in the discussions on contested points of faith, for it is not becoming that one who does not belong to the number of the bishops should mix himself up in the examination and decision of theological controversies. On the contrary, Candidian was to remove from the city the monks and laymen who had come or should afterwards come to Ephesus out of curiosity, so that disorder and confusion should not be caused by those who were in no way needed for the examination of the sacred doctrines. He was, besides, to watch lest the discussions among the members of the Synod themselves should degenerate into violent disputes and hinder the more exact investigation of truth ; and, on the contrary, see that every statement should be heard with attention, and that every one put forward in view, or his objections, without let or hindrance, so that at last an unanimous decision might be arrived at in peace by the holy Synod. But above all, Candidian was to take care that no member of the Synod should attempt, before the close of the transactions, to go home, or to the court, or elsewhere. Moreover, he was not to allow that any other matter of controversy should be taken into consideration before the settlement of the principal point of doctrine before the Council.

EXTRACTS FROM THE ACTS.

SESSION I.

[Before the arrival of the Papal Legates.]

(Labbe and Cossart, *Concilia*, Tom. III., col. 459 *et seqq.*)

The Nicene Synod set forth this faith: We believe in one God, etc.

When this creed had been recited, Peter the Presbyter of Alexandria, and primicerius of the notaries said:

We have in our hands the letter of the most holy and most reverend archbishop Cyril, which he wrote to the most reverend Nestorius, filled with counsel and advice, on account of his aberration from the right faith. I will read this if your holiness [i.e., the holy Synod] so orders. . . . The letter began as follows:

Καταφλυαροῦσι μὲν, ὡς ἀκούω, κ τ. λ. Intelligo quosdam meæ, etc.

THE EPISTLE OF CYRIL TO NESTORIUS.

(Labbe and Cossart, *Concilia*, Tom. III., col. 315; Migne, *Patr. Græc.*, Tom. LXXVII. [Cyril., *Opera*, Tom. X.]; *Epist.* iv., col. 43.)

To the most religious and beloved of God, fellow minister Nestorius, Cyril sends greeting in the Lord.

I hear that some are rashly talking of the estimation in which I hold your holiness, and that this is frequently the case especially at the times that meetings are held of those in authority. And perchance they think in so doing to say something agreeable to you, but they speak senselessly, for they have suffered no injustice at my hands, but have been exposed by me only to their profit; this man as an oppressor of the blind and needy, and that as one who wounded his mother with a sword. Another because he stole, in collusion with his waiting maid, another's money, and had always laboured under the imputation of such like crimes as no one would wish even one of his bitterest enemies to be laden with.[1] I take little reckoning of the words of such people, for the disciple is not above his Master, nor would I stretch the measure of my narrow brain above the Fathers, for no matter what path of life one pursues it is hardly possible to escape the smirching of the wicked, whose mouths are full of cursing and bitterness, and who at the last must give an account to the Judge of all.

But I return to the point which especially I had in mind. And now I urge you, as a brother in the Lord, to propose the word of teaching and the doctrine of the faith with all accuracy to the people, and to consider that the giving of scandal to one even of the least of those who believe in Christ, exposes a body to the unbearable indignation of God. And of how great diligence and skill there is need when the multitude of those grieved is so great, so that we may administer the healing word of truth to them that seek it. But this we shall accomplish most excellently if we shall turn over the words of the holy Fathers, and are zealous to obey their commands, proving ourselves, whether we be in the faith according to that which is written, and conform our thoughts to their upright and irreprehensible teaching.

The holy and great Synod therefore says, that the only begotten Son, born according to nature of God the Father, very God of very God, Light of Light, by whom the Father made all things, came down, and was incarnate, and was made man, suffered, and rose again the third day, and ascended into heaven. These words and these decrees we ought to follow, considering what is meant by the Word of God being incarnate and made man. For we do not say that the nature of the Word was changed and became flesh, or that it was

---

[1] Rohrbacher, in his famous *Histoire Universelle de l'Élise Catholique*, Tome IV. (Septième Edition), Livre xxxix., p. 394, informs us that this letter gives the names of some of Cyril's calumniators! The text he used must have been different from the one now accessible to scholars.

converted into a whole man consisting of soul and body; but rather that the Word having personally united to himself flesh animated by a rational soul, did in an ineffable and inconceivable manner become man, and was called the Son of Man, not merely as willing or being pleased to be so called, neither on account of taking to himself a person, but because the two natures being brought together in a true union, there is of both one Christ and one Son; for the difference of the natures is not taken away by the union, but rather the divinity and the humanity make perfect for us the one Lord Jesus Christ by their ineffable and inexpressible union.   So then he who had an existence before all ages and was born of the Father, is said to have been born according to the flesh of a woman, not as though his divine nature received its beginning of existence in the holy Virgin, for it needed not any second generation after that of the Father (for it would be absurd and foolish to say that he who existed before all ages, coeternal with the Father, needed any second beginning of existence), but since, for us and for our salvation, he personally united to himself an human body, and came forth of a woman, he is in this way said to be born after the flesh; for he was not first born a common man of the holy Virgin, and then the Word came down and entered into him, but the union being made in the womb itself, he is said to endure a birth after the flesh, ascribing to himself the birth of his own flesh.   On this account we say that he suffered and rose again; not as if God the Word suffered in his own nature stripes, or the piercing of the nails, or any other wounds, for the Divine nature is incapable of suffering, inasmuch as it is incorporeal, but since that which had become his own body suffered in this way, he is also said to suffer for us; for he who is in himself incapable of suffering was in a suffering body.   In the same manner also we conceive respecting his dying; for the Word of God is by nature immortal and incorruptible, and life and life-giving; since, however, his own body did, as Paul says, by the grace of God taste death for every man, he himself is said to have suffered death for us, not as if he had any experience of death in his own nature (for it would be madness to say or think this), but because, as I have just said, his flesh tasted death.   In like manner his flesh being raised again, it is spoken of as his resurrection, not as if he had fallen into corruption (God forbid), but because his own body was raised again. We, therefore, confess one Christ and Lord, not as worshipping a man *with* the Word (lest this expression "with the Word" should suggest to the mind the idea of division), but worshipping him as one and the same, forasmuch as the body of the Word, with which he sits with the Father, is not separated from the Word himself, not as if two sons were sitting with him, but one by the union with the flesh.   If, however, we reject the personal union as impossible or unbecoming, we fall into the error of speaking of two sons, for it will be necessary to distinguish, and to say, that he who was properly man was honoured with the appellation of Son, and that he who is properly the Word of God, has by nature both the name and the reality of Sonship.   We must not, therefore, divide the one Lord Jesus Christ into two Sons.   Neither will it at all avail to a sound faith to hold, as some do, an union of persons; for the Scripture has not said that the Word united to himself the person of man, but that he was made flesh. This expression, however, "the Word was made flesh," can mean nothing else but that he partook of flesh and blood like to us; he made our body his own, and came forth man from a woman, not casting off his existence as God, or his generation of God the Father, but even in taking to himself flesh remaining what he was.   This the declaration of the correct faith proclaims everywhere.   This was the sentiment of the holy Fathers; therefore they ventured to call the holy Virgin, the Mother of God, not as if the nature of the Word or his divinity had its beginning from the holy Virgin, but because of her was born that holy body with a rational soul, to which the Word being personally united is said to be born according to the flesh.   These things, therefore, I now write unto you for the love of Christ, beseeching you as a brother, and testifying to you before Christ and the elect angels, that you would both think and teach these things with us, that the peace of the Churches may be preserved and the bond of concord and love continue unbroken amongst the Priests of God.

EXTRACTS FROM THE ACTS.

SESSION I. (CONTINUED).

(Labbe and Cossart, *Concilia*, Tom. III., col. 462.)

And after the letter was read, Cyril, the bishop of Alexandria, said : This holy and great Synod has heard what I wrote to the most religious Nestorius, defending the right faith. I think that I have in no respect departed from the true statement of the faith, that is from the creed set forth by the holy and great synod formerly assembled at Nice. Wherefore I desire your holiness [i.e. the Council] to say whether rightly and blamelessly and in accordance with that holy synod I have written these things or no.

[*A number of bishops then gave their opinion, all favourable to Cyril ; after these individual opinions the Acts continue* (col. 491):]

And all the rest of the bishops in the order of their rank deposed to the same things, and so believed, according as the Fathers had set forth, and as the Epistle of the most holy Archbishop Cyril to Nestorius the bishop declared.

Palladius, the bishop of Amasea, said, The next thing to be done is to read the letter of the most reverend Nestorius, of which the most religious presbyter Peter made mention ; so that we may understand whether or no it agrees with the exposition of the Nicene fathers. . . .

And after this letter was read, Cyril, the bishop of Alexandria, said, What seems good to this holy and great synod with regard to the letter just read ? Does it also seem to be consonant to the faith set forth by the holy Synod assembled in the city of Nice ?

[*The bishops, then as before, individually express their opinion, and at last the Acts continue* (col. 502) :]

All the bishops cried out together : Whoever does not anathematize Nestorius let him be anathema. Such an one the right faith anathematizes ; such an one the holy Synod anathematizes. Whoever communicates with Nestorius let him be anathema ! We anathematize all the apostles of Nestorius : we all anathematize Nestorius as a heretic : let all such as communicate with Nestorius be anathema, etc., etc.

Juvenal, the bishop of Jerusalem, said : Let the letter of the most holy and reverend Cælestine, archbishop of the Church of Rome, be read, which he wrote concerning the faith.

[*The letter of Cælestine was read and no opinion expressed.*]

Peter the presbyter of Alexandria, and primicerius of the notaries said : Altogether in agreement with the things just read are those which his holiness Cyril our most pious bishop wrote, which I now have at hand, and will read if your piety so shall order.

[*The letter was read which begins thus* :]

Τοῦ Σωτῆρος ἡμῶν λέγοντος ἐναργῶς, κ. τ. λ.

Cum Salvator noster, etc.

HISTORICAL INTRODUCTION TO ST. CYRIL'S ANATHEMATISMS.

There has been some difference of opinion among the learned as to whether St. Cyril's Synodal letter which has at its end the anathemas against Nestorius, which hereafter follow, was formally approved at the Council of Ephesus. The matter is one only of archeological and historical interest, for from a theological point of view the question is entirely uninteresting, since there is no possible doubt that the synod endorsed St. Cyril's teaching and for that express reason proceeded at their first session to excommunicate Nestorius. Further there is no one that disputes that the anathematisms were received at the next General Council. i.e., of Chalcedon, only twenty years later, and that Theodoret was condemned by the Fifth Ecumenical Council because he wrote against these very Anathemas. This being the case, to those who value the decrees of Ecumenical Councils because of their ecumenical character, it is quite immaterial whether these anathematisms were received and approved by the third Council or no, provided, which is indisputably the case, they have been approved by some one council of ecumenical authority, so as to become thereby part and parcel of the ecumenical faith of the Church.

But the historical question is one of some interest, and I shall very briefly consider it. We have indeed the "Acta" of this council, but I cannot but agree with the very learned Jesuit Petavius and the Gallican Tillemont in thinking them in a very unsatisfactory condition. I am fully aware of the temerity of making such a suggestion, but I cannot help feeling that in the remarks of the Roman representatives, especially in those of the presbyter-legate, there is some anachronism. Be this as it may, it is a fact that the Acts do not recite that this letter of Cyril's was read, nor do they state that the Anathemas were received. I would suggest, however, that for those who defend John of Antioch, and criticise the action of St. Cyril, it is the height of inconsistency to deny that the Council adopted the Anathemas. If it was the bitterly partisan assembly that they would have us believe, absolutely under the control of Cyril, there is nothing that, à priori, they would have been more sure to do than adopt the Anathemas which were universally looked upon as the very fulcrum on which the whole matter turned.

Bishop Hefele was at first of opinion that the letter was merely read, being led to this conclusion by the silence of the Acts with regard to any acceptance of it, and indeed at first wrote on that side, but he afterwards saw grounds to change his mind and expresses them with his usual clearness, in the following words :

(Hefele,   *Hist. of Councils.* Vol. III., p. 48, note 2.)

We were formerly of opinion that these anathematisms were read at Ephesus, but not expressly confirmed, as there is hardly anything on the subject in the Acts. But in the Fifth Ecumenical Council (collatio vj.) it is said : "The holy Council at Chalcedon approved this teaching of Cyril of blessed memory, and received his Synodical letters, to one of which are appended the xij. anathemas" (Mansi, t. ix., p. 341 ; Hardouin, t. iij., p. 167). If, however, the anathematisms of Cyril were expressly confirmed at Chalcedon, there was even more reason for doing so at Ephesus. And Ibas, in his well-known letter to Maris, says expressly that the Synod of Ephesus confirmed the anathematisms of Cyril, and the same was asserted even by the bishops of Antioch at Ephesus in a letter to the Emperor.

From all these considerations it would seem that Tillemont's [1] conclusion is well founded that the Synod certainly discussed the anathemas of Cyril in detail, but that here, as in many other places, there are parts of the Acts lacking. I shall add the opinion of Petavius.

(Petavius, *De Incarnatione,* Lib. VI., cap. xvij.)

The Acts do not tell us what judgment the Synod of Ephesus gave with respect to the third letter of Cyril, and with regard to the anathemas attached to it. But the Acts in other respects also have not come down to us in their integrity. That that third letter was received and approved by the Ephesine Council there can be no doubt, and this the Catholics shewed in their dispute with the Acephali in the Collation held at Constantinople under the Emperor Justinian in the year of Christ 811. For at that memorable meeting something was shewn forth concerning this letter and its anathemas, which has a connexion with the matter in hand, and therefore must not be omitted. At that meeting the Opposers, that is the Acephali, the enemies of the Council of Chalcedon, made this objection against that

---

[1] Tillemont, Mémoires. Tom. XIV., p. 405.

Council: "The [letter] of the Twelve Anathemas which is inserted in the holy Council of Ephesus, and which you cannot deny to be synodical, why did not Chalcedon receive it?" etc., etc.

From this it is evident that the prevailing opinion, then as now, was that the Twelve Anathemas were defined as part of the faith by the Council of Ephesus. Perhaps I may close this treatment of the subject in the words of Denziger, being the caption he gives the xij. Anathematisms in his *Enchiridion*, under "Decrees of the Third Ecumenical Council, that of Ephesus." "The Third Synod received these anathematisms; the Fourth Synod placed them in its Acts and styled the Epistles of Cyril 'Canonical'; the Fifth Synod defended them."

THE EPISTLE OF CYRIL TO NESTORIUS WITH THE XII. ANATHE-MATISMS.

(Labbe and Cossart, *Concilia*, Tom. III., col. 395; Migne, *Patr. Græc.*, Tom. LXXVII. [Cyril, *Opera*, Tom. X.], col. 105 *et seqq.*)

To the most reverend and God-loving fellow-minister Nestorius, Cyril and the synod assembled in Alexandria, of the Egyptian Province, Greeting in the Lord.

When our Saviour says, clearly: "He that loveth father or mother more than me is not worthy of me: and he that loveth son or daughter more than me is not worthy of me," what is to become of us, from whom your Holiness requires that we love you more than Christ the Saviour of us all? Who can help us in the day of judgment, or what kind of excuse shall we find for thus keeping silence so long, with regard to the blasphemies made by you against him? If you injured yourself alone, by teaching and holding such things, perhaps it would be less matter; but you have greatly scandalized the whole Church, and have cast among the people the leaven of a strange and new heresy. And not to those there [i.e. at Constantinople] only; but also to those everywhere [the books of your explanation were sent]. How can we any longer, under these circumstances, make a defence for our silence, or how shall we not be forced to remember that Christ said: "Think not that I am come to send peace on earth: I came not to send peace, but a sword. For I am come to set a man at variance against his father, and the daughter against her mother." For if faith be injured, let there be lost the honour due to parents, as stale and tottering, let even the law of tender love towards children and brothers be silenced, let death be better to the pious than living; "that they might obtain a better resurrection," as it is written.

Behold, therefore, how we, together with the holy synod which met in great Rome, presided over by the most holy and most reverend brother and fellow-minister, Celestine the Bishop, also testify by this third letter to you, and counsel you to abstain from these mischievous and distorted dogmas, which you hold and teach, and to receive the right faith, handed down to the churches from the beginning through the holy Apostles and Evangelists, who "were eye-witnesses, and ministers of the Word." And if your holiness have not a mind to this according to the limits defined in the writings of our brother of blessed memory and most reverend fellow-minister Celestine, Bishop of the Church of Rome, be well assured then that you have no lot with us, nor place or standing (λόγον) among the priests and bishops of God. For it is not possible for us to overlook the churches thus troubled, and the people scandalized, and the right faith set aside, and the sheep scattered by you, who ought to save them, if indeed we are ourselves adherents of the right faith, and followers of the devotion of the holy fathers. And we are in communion with all those laymen and clergymen cast out or deposed by your holiness on account of the faith; for it is not right that those, who resolved to believe rightly, should suffer by your choice; for they do well in opposing you. This very thing you have mentioned in your epistle written to our most holy and fellow-bishop Celestine of great Rome.

But it would not be sufficient for your reverence to confess with us only the sym-

bol of the faith set out some time ago by
the Holy Ghost at the great and holy
synod convened in Nice : for you have
not held and interpreted it rightly, but
rather perversely ; even though you confess
with your voice the form of words. But
in addition, in writing and by oath, you
must confess that you also anathematize
those polluted and unholy dogmas of yours,
and that you will hold and teach that which
we all, bishops, teachers, and leaders of the
people both East and West, hold. The
holy synod of Rome and we all agreed on
the epistle written to your Holiness from
the Alexandrian Church as being right and
blameless. We have added to these our
own letters and that which it is necessary
for you to hold and teach, and what you
should be careful to avoid. Now this is
the Faith of the Catholic and Apostolic
Church to which all Orthodox Bishops,
both East and West, agree:

"We believe in one God, the Father
Almighty, Maker of all things visible and
invisible, and in one Lord Jesus Christ, the
Only-begotten Son of God, begotten of his
Father, that is, of the substance of the
Father ; God of God, Light of Light, Very
God of very God, begotten, not made, being of one substance with the Father, by
whom all things were made, both those in
heaven and those in the earth. Who for us
men and for our salvation, came down, and
was incarnate, and was made man. He
suffered, and rose again the third day. He
ascended into the heavens, from thence he
shall come to judge both the quick and the
dead. And in the Holy Ghost. But those
that say, There was a time when he was
not, and, before he was begotten he was
not, and that he was made of that which
previously was not, or that he was of some
other substance or essence ; and that the
Son of God was capable of change or alteration ; those the Catholic and Apostolic
Church anathematizes."

Following in all points the confessions
of the Holy Fathers which they made (the
Holy Ghost speaking in them), and following the scope of their opinions, and going,
as it were, in the royal way, we confess that
the Only begotten Word of God, begotten
of the same substance of the Father, True
God from True God, Light from Light,
through Whom all things were made, the

things in heaven and the things in the
earth, coming down for our salvation, making himself of no reputation (καθεὶς ἑαυτὸν
εἰς κένωσιν), was incarnate and made man ;
that is, taking flesh of the holy Virgin, and
having made it his own from the womb, he
subjected himself to birth for us, and came
forth man from a woman, without casting
off that which he was ; but although he
assumed flesh and blood, he remained
what he was, God in essence and in truth.
Neither do we say that his flesh was
changed into the nature of divinity, nor
that the ineffable nature of the Word of
God was laid aside for the nature of flesh ;
for he is unchanged and absolutely unchangeable, being the same always, according to the Scriptures. For although visible
and a child in swaddling clothes, and even
in the bosom of his Virgin Mother, he filled
all creation as God, and was a fellow-ruler
with him who begat him, for the Godhead
is without quantity and dimension, and cannot have limits.

Confessing the Word to be made one
with the flesh according to substance, we
adore one Son and Lord Jesus Christ : we
do not divide the God from the man, nor
separate him into parts, as though the two
natures were mutually united in him only
through a sharing of dignity and authority
(for that is a novelty and nothing else),
neither do we give separately to the Word
of God the name Christ and the same
name separately to a different one born of
a woman ; but we know only one Christ,
the Word from God the Father with his
own Flesh. For as man he was anointed
with us, although it is he himself who
gives the Spirit to those who are worthy
and not in measure, according to the saying
of the blessed Evangelist John.

But we do not say that the Word of God
dwelt in him as in a common man born of
the holy Virgin, lest Christ be thought of
as a God-bearing man ; for although the
Word tabernacled among us, it is also said
that in Christ "dwelt all the fulness of the
Godhead bodily " ; but we understand that
he became flesh, not just as he is said
to dwell in the saints, but we define that
that tabernacling in him was according to
equality (κατὰ τον ἴσον ἐν αὐτῷ τρόπον).
But being made one κατὰ φύσιν,[1] and not
converted into flesh, he made his indwell-

---

[1] *Vide* notes on this expression.

ing in such a way, as we may say that the soul of man does in his own body.

One therefore is Christ both Son and Lord, not as if a man had attained only such a conjunction with God as consists in a unity [1] of dignity alone or of authority. For it is not equality of honour which unites natures; for then Peter and John, who were of equal honour with each other, being both Apostles and holy disciples [would have been one, and], yet the two are not one. Neither do we understand the manner of conjunction to be apposition, for this does not suffice for natural oneness (πρὸς ἕνωσον φυσικήν). Nor yet according to relative participation, as we are also joined to the Lord, as it is written "we are one Spirit in him." Rather we deprecate the term of "junction" (συναφείας) as not having sufficiently signified the oneness. But we do not call the Word of God the Father, the God nor the Lord of Christ, lest we openly cut in two the one Christ, the Son and Lord, and fall under the charge of blasphemy, making him the God and Lord of himself. For the Word of God, as we have said already, was made hypostatically one in flesh, yet he is God of all and he rules all; but he is not the slave of himself, nor his own Lord. For it is foolish, or rather impious, to think or teach thus. For he said that God was his Father, although he was God by nature, and of his substance. Yet we are not ignorant that while he remained God, he also became man and subject to God, according to the law suitable to the nature of the manhood. But how could he become the God or Lord of himself? Consequently as man, and with regard to the measure of his humiliation, it is said that he is equally with us subject to God; thus he became under the Law, although as God he spake the Law and was the Law-giver.

We are careful also how we say about Christ: "I worship the One clothed on account of the One clothing him, and on account of the Unseen, I worship the Seen." It is horrible to say in this connexion as follows: "The assumed as well as the assuming have the name of God." For the saying of this divides again Christ into two, and puts the man separately by himself and God also by himself. For this saying denies openly the Unity according to which one is not worshipped in the other, nor does God exist together with the other; but Jesus Christ is considered as One, the Only-begotten Son, to be honoured with one adoration together with his own flesh.

We confess that he is the Son, begotten of God the Father, and Only-begotten God; and although according to his own nature he was not subject to suffering, yet he suffered for us in the flesh according to the Scriptures, and although impassible, yet in his Crucified Body he made his own the sufferings of his own flesh; and by the grace of God he tasted death for all: he gave his own Body thereto, although he was by nature himself the life and the resurrection, in order that, having trodden down death by his unspeakable power, first in his own flesh, he might become the first born from the dead, and the first-fruits of them that slept. And that he might make a way for the nature of man to attain incorruption, by the grace of God (as we just now said), he tasted death for every man, and after three days rose again, having despoiled hell. So although it is said that the resurrection of the dead was through man, yet we understand that man to have been the Word of God, and the power of death was loosed through him, and he shall come in the fulness of time as the One Son and Lord, in the glory of the Father, in order to judge the world in righteousness, as it is written.

We will necessarily add this also. Proclaiming the death, according to the flesh, of the Only-begotten Son of God, that is Jesus Christ, confessing his resurrection from the dead, and his ascension into heaven, we offer the Unbloody Sacrifice in the churches, and so go on to the mystical thanksgivings, and are sanctified, having received his Holy Flesh and the Precious Blood of Christ the Saviour of us all. And not as common flesh do we receive it; God forbid; nor as of a man sanctified and associated with the Word according to the unity of worth, or as having a divine indwelling, but as truly the Life-giving and very flesh of the Word himself. For he is the Life according to his nature as God, and when he became united to his Flesh, he made it also to be Life-giving, as also he said to us: Verily, verily, I say unto

---

[1] This passage is very difficult, and I have followed the Latin in omitting one Θεόν.

you, Except ye eat the flesh of the Son of Man and drink his Blood. For we must not think that it is flesh of a man like us (for how can the flesh of man be life-giving by its own nature?) but as having become truly the very own of him who for us both became and was called Son of Man. Besides, what the Gospels say our Saviour said of himself, we do not divide between two hypostases or persons. For neither is he, the one and only Christ, to be thought of as double, although of two (ἐκ δύο) and they diverse, yet he has joined them in an indivisible union, just as everyone knows a man is not double although made up of soul and body, but is one of both. Wherefore when thinking rightly, we transfer the human and the divine to the same person (παρ' ἑνὸς εἰρῆσθαι).

For when as God he speaks about himself: "He who hath seen me hath seen the Father," and "I and my Father are one," we consider his ineffable divine nature according to which he is One with his Father through the identity of essence— "The image and impress and brightness of his glory." But when not scorning the measure of his humanity, he said to the Jews: "But now ye seek to kill me, a man that hath told you the truth." Again no less than before we recognize that he is the Word of God from his identity and likeness to the Father and from the circumstances of his humanity. For if it is necessary to believe that being by nature God, he became flesh, that is, a man endowed with a reasonable soul, what reason can certain ones have to be ashamed of this language about him, which is suitable to him as man? For if he should reject the words suitable to him as man, who compelled him to become man like us? And as he humbled himself to a voluntary abasement (κένωσιν) for us, for what cause can any one reject the words suitable to such abasement? Therefore all the words which are read in the Gospels are to be applied to One Person, to One hypostasis of the Word Incarnate. For the Lord Jesus Christ is One, according to the Scriptures, although he is called "the Apostle and High Priest of our profession," as offering to God and the Father the confession of faith which we make to him, and through him to God even the Father and also to the Holy Spirit; yet we say he is, according to nature, the Only-begotten of God. And not to any man different from him do we assign the name of priesthood, and the thing, for he became "the Mediator between God and men," and a Reconciler unto peace, having offered himself as a sweet smelling savour to God and the Father. Therefore also he said: "Sacrifice and offering thou wouldest not; but a body hast thou prepared me: In burnt offerings and sacrifices for sin thou hast had no pleasure. Then said I, Lo, I come (in the volume of the book it is written of me) to do thy will, O God." For on account of us he offered his body as a sweet smelling savour, and not for himself; for what offering or sacrifice was needed for himself, who as God existed above all sins? For "all have sinned and come short of the glory of God," so that we became prone to fall, and the nature of man has fallen into sin, yet not so he (and therefore we fall short of his glory). How then can there be further doubt that the true Lamb died for us and on our account? And to say that he offered himself for himself and us, could in no way escape the charge of impiety. For he never committed a fault at all, neither did he sin. What offering then did he need, not having sin for which sacrifices are rightly offered? But when he spoke about the Spirit, he said: "He shall glorify me." If we think rightly, we do not say that the One Christ and Son as needing glory from another received glory from the Holy Spirit; for neither greater than he nor above him is his Spirit, but because he used the Holy Spirit to show forth his own divinity in his mighty works, therefore he is said to have been glorified by him just as if any one of us should say concerning his inherent strength for example, or his knowledge of anything, "They glorified me." For although the Spirit is the same essence, yet we think of him by himself, as he is the Spirit and not the Son; but he is not different from him; for he is called the Spirit of truth and Christ is the Truth, and he is sent by him, just as, moreover, he is from God and the Father. When then the Spirit worked miracles through the hands of the holy apostles after the Ascension of Our Lord Jesus Christ into heaven, he glorified him. For it is believed that he who works through his own Spirit is God according to nature. Therefore he said: "He shall receive of mine, and shall shew it unto you." But we do not say this as if the Spirit is wise and powerful through some sharing with another; for he is all perfect and in need of no good thing. Since, therefore, he is the Spirit of the Power and Wisdom of the Father (that is, of the Son), he is evidently Wisdom and Power.

And since the holy Virgin brought forth corporally God made one with flesh according to nature, for this reason we also call her Mother of God, not as if the nature of the Word had the beginning of its existence from the flesh.

For "In the beginning was the Word, and the Word was God, and the Word was with God," and he is the Maker of the ages, coeternal with the Father, and Creator of all; but, as we have already said, since he united to himself hypostatically human nature from her womb, also he subjected himself to birth as man, not as needing necessarily in his own nature birth in time and in these last times of the world, but in order that he might bless the beginning of our existence, and that that which sent the earthly bodies of our whole race to death, might lose its power for the future by his being born of a woman in the flesh. And this: "In sorrow thou shalt bring forth children," being removed through him, he showed the truth of that spoken by the prophet, "Strong death swallowed them up, and again God hath wiped away every tear from off all faces." [1] For this cause also we say that he attended, having been called, and also blessed, the marriage in Cana of Galilee, with his holy Apostles in accordance with the economy. We have been taught to hold these things by the holy Apostles and Evangelists, and all the God-inspired Scriptures, and in the true confessions of the blessed Fathers.

To all these your reverence also should agree, and give heed, without any guile. And what it is necessary your reverence should anathematize we have subjoined to our epistle. [2]

---

[1] There is a most curious blunder in the editing of this Epistle in Migne, where this passage, which is but one text, viz.: Isaiah xxv. 8, is made into two, the first few words being assigned in the margin to Hosea, xiii. 14. As a matter of fact the whole sentence is turned into nonsense by making the words και πάλιν as a connective supplied by St. Cyril. What the text really says is that Death prevailed indeed, but God wiped away again the tears death had caused. The same error is found in the letter as it occurs in Labbe and Cossart, and it should be remarked that it is both in the Greek and Latin. I rather suspect that St. Cyril had a purer text of the LXX. than ours which read—" And he hath swallowed death up and hath wiped away, etc.," as the Vulgate and A. V. read This is the reading the context certainly seems to call for.

[2] For critical notes and proposed emendations of the text, see Routh's *Scriptorum Eccles. Opuscula.* Tom. II. (Ed. III.), p. 17.

THE XII. ANATHEMATISMS OF ST. CYRIL AGAINST NESTORIUS.

(*Found in St. Cyril's Opera. Migne, Pat. Græc, Tom. LXXVII., Col. 119; and the Concilia.*)

I.

IF anyone will not confess that the Emmanuel is very God, and that therefore the Holy Virgin is the Mother of God (Θεοτόκος), inasmuch as in the flesh she bore the Word of God made flesh [as it is written, "The Word was made flesh"]: let him be anathema.

NOTES.

THE ANATHEMATISMS OF THE HERETIC NESTORIUS AGAINST CYRIL.

(*Found best in Migne's edition of Marius Mercator.*)

I.

If anyone says that the Emmanuel is true God, and not rather *God with us*, that is, that he has united himself to a like nature with ours, which he assumed from the Virgin Mary, and dwelt in it; and if anyone calls Mary the mother of God the Word, and not rather mother of him who is Emmanuel; and if he maintains that God the Word has *changed* himself into the flesh, which he only assumed in order to make his Godhead visible, and to be found in form as a man, let him be anathema.

PETAVIUS.[1]

(*De Incarnatione, Lib. vj. cap. xvij.*)

In this anathematism certain words are found in the Greek copy of Dionysius which are lacking in the ordinary copies, viz. " according as it is written, 'And the Word was made flesh';" unless forsooth Dionysius supplied them of his own authority. For in the Lateran Synod in the time of Martin I. this anathematism was quoted without the appended words.

This anathematism breaks to pieces the chief strength of the Nestorian impiety. For it sets forth two facts. The one that the Emmanuel, that is he who was born of a woman and dwelt with us, is God: the other, that Mary who bare such an one is Mother of God. That Christ is God is clearly proved from the Nicene Creed, and he shews that the same that was in the beginning the Son of God, afterwards took flesh and was born of Mary, without any change or confusion of natures.

St. Cyril explains that by σαρκικῶς, *carnaliter*, he meant nothing else than κατα σάρκα, *secundum carnem*, "according to the flesh." And it was necessary to use this expression to overthrow the perfidy of Nestorius; so that we may understand that the most holy Virgin was the parent not of a simple and bare man, but of God the Word, not in that he was God, but in that he had taken flesh. For God the Father was the parent of the same Son θεϊκῶς[2] (divinely) as his mother was σαρκικῶς (after the flesh). And the word (σαρκικῶς) in no degree lessens the dignity of his begetting and bringing forth; for it shews that his flesh was not simulated or shadowed forth; but true and like to ours. Amphilochius distinctly uses the word, saying "Except he had been born carnally (σαρκικῶς), never wouldest thou have been born spiritually (πνευματικῶς)." Cf. St. Gregory Nazianzen (*Orat.* 51).

Theodoret misunderstood St. Cyril to teach in this first anathematism that the Word was changed into the flesh he assumed. But Cyril rightly treated this whole accusation as a foolish calumny.

EXCURSUS ON THE WORD Θεοτόκος.

There have been some who have tried to reduce all the great theological controversies on the Trinity and on the Incarnation to mere logomachies, and have jeered at those who could waste their time and energies over such trivialities. For example, it has been said that the

---

[1] Petavius gives a scholion on every anathematism and a résumé of the Orientals' objections and of Theodoret's criticisms, with answers.

[2] This is a late form of θείως, but used only in its secondary sense.

real difference between Arius and Athanasius was nothing more nor less than an iota, and that even Athanasius himself, in his more placid, and therefore presumably more rational moods, was willing to hold communion with those who differed from him and who still rejected the homousion. But however catching and brilliant such remarks may be, they lack all solid foundation in truth. It is perfectly manifest that a person so entirely lacking in discrimination as not to see the enormous difference between identity and likeness is not one whose opinion on such a point can be of much value. A brilliant historian is not necessarily an accurate historian, far less need he be a safe guide in matters of theological definition.[1]

A similar attempt to reduce to a logomachy the difference between the Catholic faith and Nestorianism has been made by some writers of undoubted learning among Protestants, notably by Fuchs and Schröckh. But as in the case of the *homousios* so, too, in the case of the *theotocos* the word expresses a great, necessary, and fundamental doctrine of the Catholic faith. It is not a matter of words, but of things, and the mind most unskilled in theology cannot fail to grasp the enormous difference there is between affirming, as does Nestorianism, that a God indwelt a man with a human personality of his own distinct from the personality of the indwelling god ; and that God assumed to himself human nature, that is a human body and a human soul, but without human personality.

(Wm. Bright, *St. Leo on the Incarnation*, pp. 160, 161.)

It is, then, clear that the question raised by the wide circulation of the discourses of Nestorius as archbishop of Constantinople was not verbal, but vital. Much of his language was irrelevant, and indicated some confusedness of thought : much would, of itself, admit of an orthodox construction ; in one of the latest of his sermons, which Garnier dates on Sunday, December 14, 430, he grants that " Theotocos " might be used as signifying that " the temple which was formed in Mary by the Holy Spirit was united to the Godhead ; " but it was impossible not to ask whether by " the temple " he meant the body of Jesus, or Jesus himself regarded as a human individual existing ἰδίᾳ, ἰδικῶς, ἀνὰ μέρος—as Cyril represents his theory—and whether by " union " he meant more than a close alliance, *ejusdem generis*, in the last analysis, with the relation between God and every saint, or, indeed, every Christian in true moral fellowship with him—an alliance which would amount, in Cyril's phrase, to no more than a " relative union," and would reduce the Saviour to a "Theophoros," the title claimed of old by one of his chief martyrs. And the real identity of Nestorius's view with that of Theodore [of Mopsuestia] was but too plainly exhibited by such statements as occur in some of the extracts preserved in Cyril's treatise *Against Nestorius*—to the effect that Christ was one with the Word by participation in dignity ; that " the man " was partaker of Divine power, and in *that* sense not mere man; that he was adored together with the Word ; and that " My Lord and my God " was a doxology to the Father ; and above all, by the words spoken at Ephesus, "I can never allow that a child of three months old was God."

It is no part of my duty to defend the truth of either the Catholic or Nestorian proposition—each has found many adherents in most ages since it was first started, and probably what is virtually Nestorianism is to-day far more widely held among persons deemed to be orthodox than is commonly supposed: Be this as it may, Nestorianism is clearly subversive of the whole Catholic Doctrine of the Incarnation, and therefore the importance of the word Θεοτόκος cannot be exaggerated.

---

[1] Cf. Bp. Lightfoot's criticism on Gibbon as an historian, *The Apostolic Fathers*, Vol. I., p. 46 n. Macaulay's *History of England* will of course instantly present itself to the reader as a sample of the brilliant variety of histories referred to in the text.

I shall treat the word Theotocos under two heads ; (1) Its history (2) its meaning, first how-ever quoting Bp. Pearson's words on its Conciliar authority.   (Pearson, *Exp. of the Creed*, Art. III., n. 37).   "It is plain that the Council of Ephesus which condemned Nestorius con-firmed this title Θεοτόκος ; I say confirmed it; for it is evident that it was before used in the Church, by the tumult which arose at the first denial of it by Anastasius [Nestorius's presby-ter] ; and so confirmed it as received before, because they approved the Epistles of St. Cyril, who proved it by the usage of those Fathers which preceded him."

(1) *History of Word* Θεοτόκος.

It has not been unfrequently assumed that the word Theotocos was coined to express the peculiar view of the Incarnation held by St. Cyril. Such, however, is an entire mistake. It was an old term of Catholic Theology, and the very word was used by bishop Alexander in a letter from the synod held at Alexandria in A.D. 320,[1] to condemn the Arian heresy (more than a hundred years before the meeting of the Council of Ephesus) ; "After this, we receive the doc-trine of the resurrection from the dead, of which Jesus Christ our Lord became the first-fruits ; who bore a body in truth, not in semblance, which he derived from Mary the Mother of God (ἐκ τῆς Θεοτόκου Μαρίας)."[2] The same word had been used by many church writers among whom may be mentioned St. Athanasius, who says, "As the flesh was born of Mary, the Mother of God, so we say that he, the Word, was himself born of Mary" (*Orat. c. Arian.*, iij., 14, 29, 33 ; also iv., 32). See also Eusebius (*Vit.Const.*, iij., 43) ; St. Cyril of Jerusalem (*Cat.*, x., 9); and especially Origen, who (says Bp. Pearson) "did not only use, but expound at large the meaning of that title Θεοτόκος in his first tome on the Epistle to the Romans, as Socrates and Liberatus testify."[3] (Cf. Origen *in Deut.* xxii., 23 ; vol. ij., p. 391. A ; in Luc. apud Galland, *Bib. Patr.*, vol. xiv., append., p. 87, D). A list is given by Dr. Routh, in his *Reliquiæ Sacræ.* Vol. ij., p. 215 (1st Ed.), 332 (2d Ed.).

In fact Theodore of Mopsuestia was the first to object to it, so far as we know, writing as follows : "Mary bare Jesus, not the Word, for the Word was and remained omnipresent, although from the beginning he dwelt in Jesus in a peculiar manner. Thus Mary is properly the Mother of Christ (Christotocos) but not the mother of God (Theotocos). Only figura-tively, *per anaphoram*, can she be called Theotocos also, because God was in Christ in a re-markable manner. Properly she bare a man, in whom the union with the Word was begun, but was still so little completed, that he was not yet called the Son of God." And in another place he says : "It is madness to say that God is born of the Virgin. . . . Not God, but the temple in which God dwelt, is born of Mary."[4] How far Theodore had departed from the teaching of the Apostolic days may be seen by the following quotations from St. Igna-tius. "There is one only physician, of flesh and spirit, generate and ingenerate, God in man, true Life in death, Son of Mary and of God, first passible and then impassible, Jesus Christ our Lord."[5] Further on in the same epistle he says : "For our God, Jesus the Christ, was borne in the womb by Mary etc."[6] With the first of these passages Bp. Light-foot very aptly compares the following from Melito. "Since he was incorporeal, he fashioned a body for himself of our likeness . . . he was carried by Mary and clothed by his Father, he trod the earth and he filled the heavens."[7]

Theodore was forced by the exigencies of his position to deny the doctrine of the *com-municatio idiomatum* which had already at that early date come to be well understood, at least so far as practice is concerned.

---

[1] The date is not certain, it may have been a year or so differ-ent.
[2] Theod., *Hist. Eccl.*, I., 4.
[3] Pearson, *An Expos. of the Creed*, Art. III., n. 36.

[4] I take this passage as cited by Hefele, *Hist. Counc.*, Vol. III., 9.
[5] Ignat., *Ad. Eph.*, vii.   [6] *Ibid.* xviij.
[7] Melito, *Fragm.* 14 (ed. Otto) ; cit. Lightfoot, *Apost. Fath.*, II.,. 1, p. 48, n.

(Hefele, *Hist. of the Councils*, Vol. iii., p. 8.)

This doctrine, as is well known is predicating the same properties of the two natures in Christ, not *in abstracto* (Godhead and manhood), but *in concreto* (God and man).   Christ himself had declared in St. John iii., 16: "God . . . gave his only begotten Son" (namely, to death), and similarly St. Peter declared (Acts iii., 15): "ye . . . killed the Prince of Life," when in fact the being given up and being killed is a property (ἰδίωμα = predicate) of *man*, not of *God* (the only begotten, the Prince of Life).   In the same way Clement of Rome, for example, spoke of " the sufferings of God " (παθήματα Θεοῦ) (1 *Ad Cor.* 2), Ignatius of Antioch (*Ad Ephes.*, c. 1, and *Ad Rom.*, 6) of an αἷμα and πάθος Θεοῦ, Tatian of a Θεὸς πεπονθὼς (*Ad Græcos*, c. 13) ; Barnabas teaches (c. 7) that " the Son of God could not suffer except on our behalf . . . and on our behalf he has brought the vessel of his Spirit as a sacrifice."   Similarly Irenæus (iii., 16, 6) says, " The Only-begotten impassible Word (*unigenitus impassibilis*) has become passible " (*passibilis*) ; and Athanasius, ἐσταυρωμένον εἶναι Θεὸν (*Ep. ad Epictet.*, n. 10, t. j., p. 726. ed. Patav.)

It is, however, to be remarked that the properties of the one nature were never transferred to the other *nature in itself*, but always to the *Person* who is at the same time both man and God.   Human attributes were not ascribed to the Godhead, but to God, and *vice versâ*.

For a full treatment of the figure of speech called the *communicatio idiomatum* the reader is referred to the great works on Theology where it will be found set forth at large, with its restrictions specified and with examples of its use.   A brief but interesting note on it will be found in St. John Damascene's famous treatise *De Fide Orthodoxa*, Book III., iij. (Migne's *Pat. Græc.*, col. 994).

(2) *Meaning of the Word* Θεοτόκος.

We pass now to the meaning of the word, having sufficiently traced the history of its use.   Bishop Pearson says : "This name was first in use in the Greek Church, who, delighting in the happy compositions of that language, called the blessed Virgin Theotocos. From whence the Latins in imitation styled her *Virginem Deiparam et Deigenitricem.*"[1]   In the passage to which the words just quoted are a portion of a foot-note, he says : "Wherefore from these three, a true conception, nutrition, and parturition, we must acknowledge that the blessed Virgin was truly and properly the Mother of our Saviour.   And so is she frequently styled the Mother of Jesus in the language of the Evangelists, and by Elizabeth particularly the 'Mother of her Lord,' as also by the general consent of the Church (because he which was so born of her was God,) the *Deipara ;* which being a compound title begun in the Greek Church, was resolved into its parts by the Latins and so the Virgin was plainly named the Mother of God."

Pearson is mistaken in supposing that the resolution of the compound Theotocos into μήτηρ τοῦ Θεοῦ was unknown to the early Greek writers.   Dionysius expressly calls Mary ἡ μήτηρ τοῦ Θεοῦ μου (*Contr. Paul. Samos.*, Quæst. viij.) ; and among the Latins *Mater Dei* and *Dei Genetrix* were (as Pearson himself confesses in note 37) used before the time of St. Leo I.   It is not an open question whether *Mater Dei, Dei Genetrix, Deipara*, μήτηρ τοῦ Θεοῦ are proper equivalents for Θεοτόκος.   This point has been settled by the unvarying use of the whole Church of God throughout all the ages from that day to this, but there is, or at least some persons have thought that there was, some question as to how Theotocos should be translated into English.

Throughout this volume I have translated it " Mother of God," and I propose giving my

---

[1] Pearson, *An Expos. of the Creed*, Art. III., n. 36.

reasons for considering this the only accurate translation of the word, both from a lexico-graphical and from a theological point of view.

(a) It is evident that the word is a composite formed of Θεός = God, and τίκτειν = to be the mother of a child. Now I have translated the verbal part "to be the mother of a child" because "to bear" in English does not necessarily carry the full meaning of the Greek word, which (as Bp. Pearson has well remarked in the passage cited above) includes "conception, nutrition, and parturition." It has been suggested that "God-bearer" is an exact translation. To this I object, that in the first place it is not English; and in the second that it would be an equally and, to my mind, more accurate translation of Θεοφόρος than of Θεοτόκος.

Another suggestion is that it be rendered "the bringer forth of God." Again I object that, from a rhetorical standpoint, the expression is very open to criticism; and from a lexicographical point of view it is entirely inadequate, for while indeed the parturition does necessarily involve in the course of nature the previous conception and nutrition, it certainly does not express it.

Now the word Mother does necessarily express all three of these when used in relation to her child. The reader will remember that the question I am discussing is not whether Mary can properly be called the Mother of God; this Nestorius denied and many in ancient and modern times have been found to agree with him. The question I am considering is what the Greek word Theotocos means in English. I do not think anyone would hesitate to translate Nestorius's *Christotocos* by "Mother of Christ" and surely the expressions are identical from a lexicographical point of view.

Liddell and Scott in their *Lexicon* insert the word Θεοτόκος as an adjective and translate "bearing God" and add : "especially ἡ Θεοτόκος, Mother of God, of the Virgin, Eccl."

(b) It only remains to consider whether there is from a theological point of view any objection to the translation, "Mother of· God." It is true that some persons have thought that such a rendering implied that the Godhead has its origin in Mary, but this was the very objection which Nestorius and his followers urged against the word Theotocos, and this being the case, it constitutes a strong argument in favour of the accuracy of the rendering. Of course the answer to the objection in each case is the same, it is not of the Godhead that Mary is the Mother, but of the Incarnate Son, who is God. "Mother" expresses exactly the relation to the incarnate Son which St. Cyril, the Council of Ephesus, and all succeeding, not to say also preceding, ages of Catholics, rightly or wrongly, ascribe to Mary. All that every child derives from its Mother that God the Son derived from Mary, and this without the co-operation of any man, but by the direct operation of the Holy Ghost, so that in a fuller, truer, and more perfect sense, Mary is the Mother of God the Son in his incarnation, than any other earthly mother is of her son.

I therefore consider it certain that no scholar who can and will divest himself of theological bias, can doubt that "Mother of God" is the most accurate translation of the term Theotocos.

II.

IF anyone shall not confess that the Word of God the Father is united hypostatically to flesh, and that with that flesh of his own, he is one only Christ both God and man at the same time : let him be anathema.

NOTES.

NESTORIUS.

II.

If any one asserts that, at the union of the Logos with the flesh, the divine Essence moved from one place to another; or says that the flesh is capable of receiving the divine nature, and that it has been partially united with the flesh; or ascribes to the flesh,

by reason of its reception of God, an extension to the infinite and boundless, and says
that God and man are one and the same in
nature; let him be anathema.

III.

IF anyone shall after the [hypostatic] union divide the hypostases in the one Christ, joining them by that connexion alone, which happens according to worthiness, or even authority and power, and not rather by a coming together (συνόδῳ), which is made by natural union (ἕνωσιν φυσικὴν): let him be anathema.

NOTES.

NESTORIUS.

III.

If any one says that Christ, who is also Emmanuel, is One, not [merely] in consequence of *connection*, but [also] in *nature*, and does not acknowledge the *connection* (συνάφεια) of the two natures, that of the Logos and of the assumed manhood, in one Son, as still continuing without *mingling*; let him be anathema.

HEFELE.

(*Hist. of the Counc.*, Vol. III., p. 7.)

Theodore [of Mopsuestia, and in this he was followed by Nestorius,] (and here is his fundamental error,) not merely maintained the existence of two *natures* in Christ, but of two *persons*, as, he says himself, no subsistence can be thought of as perfect without personality. As however, he did not ignore the fact that the consciousness of the Church rejected such a double personality in Christ, he endeavoured to get rid of the difficulty, and he repeatedly says expressly: "The two natures united together make only one Person, as man and wife are only one flesh. . . . If we consider the natures in their distinction, we should define the nature of the Logos as perfect and complete, and so also his Person, and again the nature and the person of the man as perfect and complete. If, on the other hand, we have regard to the union (συνάφεια), we say it is one Person." The very illustration of the union of man and wife shows that Theodore did not suppose a true union of the two natures in Christ, but that his notion was rather that of an external connection of the two. The expression συνάφεια, moreover, which he selected here instead of the term ἕνωσιν, which he elsewhere employs, being derived from συνάπτω [to join together], expresses only an external connection, a fixing together. and is therefore expressly rejected in later times by the doctors of the Church. And again, Theodore designates a merely external connection also in the phrase already quoted, to the effect that " the Logos dwells in the man assumed as in a temple." As a temple and the statue set up within it are one whole merely in outward appearance, so the Godhead and manhood in Christ appear only from without in their actuality as one Person, while they remain essentially two Persons.

IV.

IF anyone shall divide between two persons or subsistences those expressions (φωνάς) which are contained in the Evangelical and Apostolical writings, or which have been said concerning Christ by the Saints, or by himself, and shall apply some to him as to a man separate from the Word of God, and shall apply others to the only Word of God the Father, on the ground that they are fit to be applied to God: let him be anathema.

NOTES.

NESTORIUS.

IV.

If any one assigns the expressions of the Gospels and Apostolic letters, which refer to the two natures of Christ, to one only of those natures, and even ascribes suffering to the divine Word, both in the flesh and in the Godhead; let him be anathema.

ST. CYRIL.

(*Apol. contra Orientales.*)

For we neither teach the division of the hypostases after the union, nor do we say that the nature of the Deity needs increase and growth; but this rather we hold, that by way of an economical appropriation (κατ' οἰκείωσιν οἰκονομικὴν), he made his own the properties of the flesh, as having become flesh.

(*Quod unus est Christus.*)

For the wise Evangelist, introducing the Word as become flesh, shows him economically submitting himself to his own flesh and going through the laws of his own nature. But it belongs to humanity to increase in stature and in wisdom, and, I might add, in grace, intelligence keeping pace with the measure of the body, and differing according to age. For it was not impossible for the Word born of the Father to have raised the body united to himself to its full height from the very swaddling-clothes. I would say also, that in the babe a wonderful wisdom might easily have *appeared*. But that would have approached the thaumaturgical, and would have been incongruous to the laws of the economy. For the mystery was accomplished noiselessly. Therefore he economically allowed the measures of humanity to have power over himself.

A. B. BRUCE.

(*The Humiliation of Christ.* Appendix to Lect. II.)

The accommodation to the laws of the economy, according to this passage, consisted in this—in stature, real growth ; in wisdom, apparent growth. The wonderful wisdom was there from the first, but it was not allowed to appear (ἐκφῆναι), to avoid an aspect of monstrosity.

ST. CYRIL.

(*Adversus Nestorium.*)

Therefore there would have been shown to all an unwonted and strange thing, if, being yet an infant, he had made a demonstration of his wisdom worthy of God ; but expanding it gradually and in proportion to the age of the body, and (in this gradual manner) making it manifest to all, he might be said to increase (in wisdom) very appropriately.

(*Ad Reginas de recta fide,* Orat. II., cap. xvi.)

"But the boy increased and waxed strong in spirit, being filled with wisdom, and the grace of God was upon him." And again : " Jesus increased in stature and wisdom, and in favour with God and men." In affirming our Lord Jesus Christ to be one, and assigning to him both divine and human properties, we truly assert that it was congruous to the measures of the kenosis, on the one hand, that he should receive bodily increase and grow strong, the parts of the body gradually attaining their full development ; and, on the other hand, that he should *seem* to be filled with wisdom, in so far as the *manifestation* of the wisdom dwelling within him proceeded, as by addition, most congruously to the stature of the body ; and this, as I said, agreed with the economy of the Incarnation, and the measures of the state of humiliation.

(*Apol. contra Theod.,* ad Anath. iv.)

And if he is one and the same in virtue of the true unity of natures, and is not one and another (two persons) disjunctively and partitively, to him will belong both to know and to *seem* not to know. Therefore he knows on the divine side as the Wisdom of the Father. But since he subjected himself to the measure of humanity, he economically appropriates this also with the rest, although, as I said a little ago, being ignorant of nothing, but knowing all things with the Father.

V.

IF anyone shall dare to say that the Christ is a Theophorus [that is, God-bearing] man and not rather that he is very God, as an only Son through nature, because "the Word was made flesh," and "hath a share in flesh and blood as we do :" let him be anathema.

NOTES.

NESTORIUS.

v.

If any one ventures to say that, even after the assumption of human nature, there is only one Son of God, namely, he who is so in nature (*naturaliter filius* = Logos), while he (since the assumption of the flesh) is certainly Emmanuel ; let him be anathema.

PETAVIUS.

It is manifest that this anathematism is directed against the blasphemy of Nestorius, by which he said that Christ was in this sense Emmanuel, that a man was united and associated with God, just as God had been said to have been with the Prophets and other holy men, and to have had his abode in them ;

so that they were properly styled Θεοφόροι, because, as it were, they carried God about with them ; but there was no one made of the two. But he held that our Lord as man was bound and united with God only by a communion of dignity.

Nestorius [in his Counter Anathematism] displays the hidden meaning of his heresy, when he says, that the Son of God is not one after the assumption of the humanity ; for he who denied that he was one, no doubt thought that he was two.

Theodoret in his criticism of this Anathematism remarks that many of the Ancients, including St. Basil had used this very word, Θεοφόρος, for the Lord ; but the objection has no real foundation, for the orthodoxy or heterodoxy of such a word must be determined by the context in which it is used, and also by the known opinions of him that uses it.   Expressions which are in a loose sense orthodox and quite excusable before a heresy arises, may become afterwards the very distinctive marks and shibboleths of error.   Petavius has pointed out how far from orthodox many of the earliest Christian writers were, at least verbally, and Bp. Bull defended them by the same line of argument I have just used and which Petavius himself employs in this very connection.

VI.

IF anyone shall dare say that the Word of God the Father is the God of Christ or the Lord of Christ, and shall not rather confess him as at the same time both God and Man, since according to the Scriptures, "The Word was made flesh " : let him be anathema.

NOTES.

NESTORIUS.

VI.

If anyone, after the Incarnation calls another than Christ the Word, and ventures to say that the form of a servant is equally with the Word of God, without beginning and uncreated, and not rather that it is made by him as its natural Lord and Creator and God, and that he has promised to raise it again in the words : "Destroy this temple, and in three days I will build it up again " ; let him be anathema.

HEFELE.

This [statement of Nestorius's that any should call "another than Christ the Word "] has no reference to Cyril ; but is a hyper-Nestorianism, which Nestorius here rejects. This [that "the form of a servant is without beginning and uncreated "] was asserted by some Apollinarists ; and Nestorius accused St. Cyril of Apollinarianism.

PETAVIUS.

As Nestorius believed that in Christ there were two distinct entities (*re ipsa duos*) that is to say two persons joined together ; it was natural that he should hold that the Word was the God and Lord of the other, that is of the man.   Cyril contradicts this, and since he taught that there was, not two, but one of two natures, that is one person or suppositum, therefore he denied that the Word was the God or Lord of the man ; since no one should be called the Lord of himself.

Theodoret in his answer shuffles as usual, and points out that Christ is styled a servant by the Prophet Isaiah, because of the form of a servant which he had received.   But to this Cyril answers ; that although Christ, inasmuch as he was man, is called the servant of the Father, as of a person distinct from himself ; yet he denies that the same person can be his own lord or servant, lest a separation of the person be introduced.

VII.

IF anyone shall say that Jesus as man is only energized by the Word of God, and that the glory of the Only-begotten is attributed to him as something not properly his : let him be anathema.

NOTES.

NESTORIUS.

VII.

If any one says that the man who was formed of the Virgin is the *Only-begotten*, who was born from the bosom of the Father, before the morning star was (Ps. cix., 3)[1], and does not rather confess that he has obtained the desig-

---

[1] The editor of the English translation to this reference adds the following note : " This is the reference in the original ; but the editor is unable to say to what it refers." (l) (Hefele, *Hist. of the Councils*, Vol. III.. p. 36, n. 3.) " Ex utero ante Luciferum genui te," the third verse of the Psalm *Dixit Dominus*, cix., by the Hebrew numbering cx.

nation of *Only-begotten* on account of his connection with him who in nature is the Only-begotten of the Father; and besides. if any one calls another than the Emmanuel Christ; let him be anathema.

St. Cyril.

(*Declaratio Septima.*)

When the blessed Gabriel announced to the holy Virgin the generation of the only-begotten Son of God according to the flesh, he said, "Thou shalt bear a son; and thou shalt call his name Jesus, for he shall save his people from their sins." But he was named also Christ, because that according to his human nature he was anointed with us, according to the words of the Psalmist: "Thou hast loved righteousness and hated iniquity: therefore God, even thy God hath anointed thee with the oil of gladness above thy fellows." For

although he was the giver of the Holy Spirit, neither did he give it by measure to them that were worthy (for he was full of the Holy Ghost, and of his fulness have we all received, as it is written), nevertheless as he is man he was called anointed economically, the Holy Spirit resting upon him spiritually (νοητῶς) and not after the manner of men, in order that he might abide in us, although he had been driven forth from us in the beginning by Adam's fall. He therefore the only begotten Word of God made flesh was called Christ. And since he possessed as his own the power proper to God, he wrought his wonders. Whosoever therefore shall say that the glory of the Only-begotten was added to the power of Christ, as though the Only-begotten was different from Christ, they are thinking of two sons; the one truly working and the other impelled (by the strength of another, *Lat.*) as a man like to us; and all such fall under the penalty of this anathematism.

VIII.

If anyone shall dare to say that the assumed man (ἀναληφθέντα) ought to be worshipped together with God the Word, and glorified together with him, and recognised together with him as God, and yet as two different things, the one with the other (for this "Together with" is added [*i. e.*, by the Nestorians] to convey this meaning); and shall not rather with one adoration worship the Emmanuel and pay to him one glorification, as [it is written] "The Word was made flesh": let him be anathema.

NOTES.

Nestorius.

VIII.

If any one says that the form of a servant should, for its own sake, that is, in reference to its own nature, be reverenced, and that it is the ruler of all things, and not rather. that [merely] on account of its connection with the holy and in itself universally-ruling nature of the Only-begotten, it is to be reverenced; let him be anathema.

Hefele.

On this point [made by Nestorius, that "the form of a servant is the ruler of all things"] Marius Mercator has already remarked with justice, that no Catholic had ever asserted anything of the kind.

Petavius notes that the version of Dionysius Exiguus is defective.

Petavius.

Nestorius captiously and maliciously interpreted this as if the "form of a servant" according to its very nature (*ratio*) was to be adored, that is should receive divine worship. But this is nefarious and far removed from the mind of Cyril. Since to such an extent only the human nature of Christ is one suppositum with the divine, that he declares that each is the object of one and an undivided adoration; lest if a double and dissimilar cultus be attributed to each one, the divine person should be divided into two adorable Sons and Christs, as we have heard Cyril often complaining.

IX.

If any man shall say that the one Lord Jesus Christ was glorified by the Holy Ghost, so that he used through him a power not his own and from him received power against unclean spirits and power to work miracles before men and shall not rather confess that it was his own Spirit through which he worked these divine signs; let him be anathema.

NOTES.

NESTORIUS.

IX.

If anyone says that the form of a servant is of like nature with the Holy Ghost, and not rather that it owes its union with the Word which has existed since the conception, to his mediation, by which it works miraculous healings among men, and possesses the power of expelling demons ; let him be anathema.

PETAVIUS.

The scope of this anathematism is to shew that the Word of God, when he assumed flesh remaining what he was, and lacking nothing which the Father possessed except only paternity, had as his own the Holy Spirit which is from him and substantially abides in him. From this it follows that through him, as through a power and strength which was his own, and not one alien or adventitious, he wrought his wonders and cast forth devils, but he did not receive that Holy Spirit and his power as formerly the Prophets had done, or as afterwards his disciples did, as a kind of gift (*beneficii loco*).

The Orientals objected that St. Cyril here contradicts himself, for here he says that Christ did not work his wonders by the Holy Ghost and in another place he frankly confesses that he did so work them. But the whole point is what is intended by working through the Holy Ghost. For the Apostles worked miracles through the Holy Ghost but as by a power external to themselves, but not so Christ. When Christ worked wonders through the Holy Ghost, he was working through a power which was his own, viz.: the Third Person of the Holy Trinity; from whom he never was and never could be separated, ever abiding with him and the Eternal Father in the Divine Unity.

The Westerns have always pointed to this anathematism as shewing that St. Cyril recognized the eternal relation of the Holy Spirit as being from the Son.

EXCURSUS ON HOW OUR LORD WORKED MIRACLES.

In view of the fact that many are now presenting as if something newly discovered, and as the latest results of biblical study, the interpretations of the early heretics with regard to our Lord's powers and to his relation to the Holy Ghost, I have here set down in full Theodoret's Counter-statement to the faith accepted by the Ecumenical Councils of the Church.

THEODORET.

(*Counter Statement to Anath. IX. of Cyril.*)

Here he has plainly had the hardihood to anathematize not only those who at the present time hold pious opinions, but also those who were in former days heralds of truth ; aye even the writers of the divine Gospels, the band of the holy Apostles, and, in addition to these, Gabriel the archangel. For he indeed it was who first, even before the conception, announced the birth of the Christ according to the flesh ; saying in reply to Mary when she asked, "How shall this be, seeing I know not a man?" "The Holy Ghost shall come upon thee and the power of the Highest shall overshadow thee ; therefore also that holy thing that shall be born of thee shall be called the Son of God." And to Joseph he said, "Fear not to take unto thee Mary thy wife, for that which is conceived in her is of the Holy Ghost." And the Evangelist says, "When as his mother Mary was espoused to Joseph . . . she was found with child of the Holy Ghost." And the Lord himself when he had come into the synagogue of the Jews and had taken the prophet Isaiah, after reading the passage in which he says, "The Spirit of the Lord is upon me because he hath anointed me" and so on, added, "This day is this scripture fulfilled in your ears." And the blessed Peter in his sermon to the Jews said, "God anointed Jesus of Nazareth with the Holy Ghost." And Isaiah many ages before had predicted "There shall come forth a rod out of the stem of Jesse, and a branch shall grow out of his roots ; and the Spirit of the Lord shall rest upon him, the spirit of wisdom and understanding, the spirit of counsel and might, the spirit of knowledge and of the fear of the Lord"; and again, "Behold my servant whom I uphold, my beloved in whom my soul delighteth. I will put my Spirit upon him : he shall bring forth judgment to the Gentiles." This testimony the Evangelist too has inserted in his own writings. And the Lord himself in the Gospels says to the Jews, "If I with the Spirit of God cast out devils, no doubt the kingdom of God is come upon you." And John says, "He that sent me to baptize with water, the same said unto me, Upon whom thou shalt see the Spirit descending and remaining on him, the same is he which baptizeth with the Holy Ghost." So this exact examiner of the divine decrees has not only anathematized prophets, apostles, and even the archangel Gabriel, but has suffered his blasphemy to reach even the Saviour of the world himself. For we have shewn that the Lord himself after reading the passage "The Spirit of the Lord is upon me because he had anointed me," said to the Jews, "This day is this scripture fulfilled in your ears." And to those who said that he was casting out devils by Beelzebub he replied that he was casting them out by the Spirit of God. But we maintain that it was not God the Word, of one substance and co-eternal with the Father, that was formed by the Holy Ghost and anointed, but the human nature which was assumed by him at the end of days. We shall confess that the Spirit of the Son was his own if he spoke of it as of the same nature and proceeding from the Father, and shall accept the expression as consistent with true piety. But if he speaks of the Spirit as being of the Son, or as having its origin through the Son we shall reject this statement as blasphemous and impious. For we believe the Lord when he says, "The spirit which proceedeth from the Father"; and likewise the very divine Paul saying, "We have received not the spirit of the world, but the spirit which is of God."

In the foregoing will be found the very same arguments used and the same texts cited against the Catholic faith as are urged and cited by the Rev. A. J. Mason. *The Conditions of Our Lord's Life on Earth,* and by several other recent writers.

X.

WHOSOEVER shall say that it is not the divine Word himself, when he was made flesh and had become man as we are, but another than he, a man born of a woman, yet different from him (ἰδικῶς ἄνθρωπον), who is become our Great High Priest and Apostle ; or if any man shall say that he offered himself in sacrifice for himself and not rather for us, whereas, being without sin, he had no need of offering or sacrifice : let him be anathema.

NOTES.

NESTORIUS.	ST. CYRIL.
x.	*(Declaratio decima.)*
If any one maintains that the Word, who is from the beginning, has become the high priest and apostle of our confession, and has offered himself for us, and does not rather say that it is the work of Emmanuel to be an apostle ; and if any one in such a manner divides the sacrifice between him who united [the Word] and him who was united [the manhood] referring it to a common sonship, that is, not giving to God that which is God's, and to man that which is man's ; let him be anathema.	But I do not know how those who think otherwise contend that the very Word of God made man, was not the apostle and high-priest of our profession, but a man different from him ; who was born of the holy Virgin, was called our apostle and high-priest, and came to this gradually ; and that not only for us did he offer himself a sacrifice to God and the Father, but also for himself. A statement which is wholly contrary to the right and undefiled faith, for he did no sin, but was supe-

rior to fault and altogether free from sin, and needed no sacrifice for himself. Since those who think differently were again unreasonably thinking of two sons, this anathematism became necessary that their impiety might appear.

XI.

Whosoever shall not confess that the flesh of the Lord giveth life and that it pertains to the Word of God the Father as his very own, but shall pretend that it belongs to another person who is united to him [*i.e.*, the Word] only according to honour, and who has served as a dwelling for the divinity; and shall not rather confess, as we say, that that flesh giveth life because it is that of the Word who giveth life to all: let him be anathema.

NOTES.

Nestorius.

XI.

If any one maintains that the flesh which is united with God the Word is by the power of its own nature life-giving, whereas the Lord himself says, "It is the Spirit that quickeneth; the flesh profiteth nothing" (St. John vi. 64), let him be anathema. [He adds, "God is a Spirit" (St. John iv. 24). If, then, any one maintains that God the Logos has in a carnal manner, in his substance, become flesh, and persists in this with reference to the Lord Christ; who himself after his resurrection said to his disciples, "Handle me and see; for a spirit hath not flesh and bones, as ye behold me having" (St. Luke xxiv. 39); let him be anathema.]

Hefele.

The part enclosed in brackets is certainly a spurious addition and is wanting in many manuscripts. *Cf.* Marius Mercator [ed. Migne], p. 919.

St. Cyril.

(*Declaratio undecima.*)

We perform in the churches the holy, life-giving, and unbloody sacrifice; the body, as also the precious blood, which is exhibited we believe not to be that of a common man and of any one like unto us, but receiving it rather as his own body and as the blood of the Word which gives all things life. For common flesh cannot give life. And this our Saviour himself testified when he said: "The flesh profiteth nothing, it is the Spirit that giveth life." For since the flesh became the very own of the Word, therefore we understand that it is life-giving, as the Saviour himself said: "As the living Father hath sent me, and I live by the Father; so he that eateth me shall live by me." Since therefore Nestorius and those who think with him rashly dissolve the power of this mystery; therefore it was convenient that this anathematism should be put forth.

XII.

Whosoever shall not recognize that the Word of God suffered in the flesh, that he was crucified in the flesh, and that likewise in that same flesh he tasted death and that he is become the first-begotten of the dead, for, as he is God, he is the life and it is he that giveth life: let him be anathema.

NOTES.

Nestorius.

XII.

If any one, in confessing the sufferings of the flesh, ascribes these also to the Word of God as to the flesh in which he appeared, and thus does not distinguish the dignity of the natures; let him be anathema.

St. Cyril.

(*Adv. Orientales*, ad XII. Quoting Athanasius.)

For if the body is of another, to him also must the sufferings be ascribed. But if the flesh is the Word's (for "The Word was made flesh") it is necessary that the sufferings of the flesh be called his also whose is the flesh. But whose are the sufferings, such especially as condemnation, flagellation, thirst, the cross, death, and other such like infirmities of the body, his also is the merit and the grace. Therefore rightly and properly to none other are these sufferings attributed than to the Lord, as also the grace is from him; and we shall not be guilty of idolatry, but be the true worshippers of God, for we invoke him who is no creature nor any common man, but the natural and true Son of God, made man, and yet the same Lord and God and Saviour.

As I think, these quotations will suffice to the learned for the proof of the propositions advanced, the Divine Law plainly saying that "In the mouth of two or three witnesses every word shall be established." But if after this any one would still seem to be contentious, we would say to him : "Go thine own way. We however shall follow the divine Scriptures and the faith of the Holy Fathers."

The student should read at full length all Cyril's defence of his anathematisms, also his answers to the criticisms of Theodoret, and to those of the Orientals, all of which will be found in his works, and in Labbe and Cossart, *Concilia*, Tom. III., 811 *et seqq.*

EXTRACTS FROM THE ACTS.

SESSION I. (*Continued*).

(L. and C., *Conc.*, Tom. III., Col. 503.)

[*No action is recorded in the Acts as having been taken. A verbal report was made by certain who had seen Nestorius during the past three days, that they were hopeless of any repentance on his part. On the motion of Flavian, bishop of Philippi, a number of passages from the Fathers were read ; and after that some selections from the writings of Nestorius. A letter from Capreolus, Archbishop of Carthage, was next read, excusing his absence ; after the reading of the letter, which makes no direct reference to Nestorius whatever, but prays the Synod to see to it that no novelties be tolerated, the Acts proceed.* (Col. 534).]

Cyril, the bishop of the Church of Alexandria, said : As this letter of the most reverend and pious Capreolus, bishop of Carthage, which has been read, contains a most lucid expression of opinion, let it be inserted in the Acts. For it wishes that the ancient dogmas of the faith should be confirmed, and that novelties, absurdly conceived and impiously brought forth, should be reprobated and proscribed.

All the bishops at the same time cried out : These are the sentiments (φωναί) of all of us, these are the things we all say— the accomplishment of this is the desire of us all.

[*Immediately follows the sentence of deposition and the subscriptions. It seems almost certain that something has dropped out here, most probably the whole discussion of Cyril's XII. Anathematisms.*]

DECREE OF THE COUNCIL AGAINST NESTORIUS.

(*Found in all the* Concilia *in Greek with Latin Versions.*)

As, in addition to other things, the impious Nestorius has not obeyed our citation, and did not receive the holy bishops who were sent by us to him, we were compelled to examine his ungodly doctrines. We discovered that he had held and published impious doctrines in his letters and treatises, as well as in discourses which he delivered in this city, and which have been testified to. Compelled thereto by the canons and by the letter (ἀναγκαίως κατεπειχθέντες ἀπό τε τῶν κανόνων, καὶ ἐκ τῆς ἐπιστολῆς, κ. τ. λ.) of our most holy father and fellow-servant Cœlestine, the Roman bishop, we have come, with many tears, to this sorrowful sentence against him, namely, that our Lord Jesus Christ, whom he has blasphemed, decrees by the holy Synod that Nestorius be excluded from the episcopal dignity, and from all priestly communion.

NOTES.

The words for which I have given the original Greek, are not mentioned by Canon Bright in his Article on St. Cyril in Smith and Wace's *Dictionary of Christian Biography ;* nor by Ffoulkes in his article on the Council of Ephesus in Smith and Cheetham's *Dictionary of Christian Antiquities.* They do not appear in Canon Robertson s *History of the Church.*

And strangest of all, Dean Milman cites the sentence in English in the text and in Greek in a note but in each case omits all mention of the letter of the Pope, marking however in the Greek that there is an omission. (*Lat. Chr.*, Bk. II., Chap. III.)[1] I also note that the translation in the English edition of Hefele's *History of the Councils* (Vol. III., p. 51) is misleading and inaccurate, "Urged by the canons, and in accordance with the letter etc." The participle by itself might mean nothing more than "urged" (*vide* Liddell and Scott on this verb and also ἐπείγω) but the adverb which precedes it, ἀναγκαίως, certainly is sufficient to necessitate the *coacti* of the old Latin version which I have followed, translating "compelled thereto." It will also be noticed that while the prepositions used with regard to the "canons" and the "letter" are different, yet that their grammatical relation to the verb is identical is shewn by the τε—καὶ, which proves the translation cited above to be utterly incorrect.

Hefele for the "canons" refers to canon number lxxiv. of the Apostolic Canons; which orders an absent bishop to be summoned thrice before sentence be given against him.

EXTRACTS FROM THE ACTS.

SESSION II.

(Labbe and Cossart, *Concilia*, Tom. III., col. 609.)

The most pious and God-beloved bishops, Arcadius and Projectus, as also the most beloved-of-God Philip, a presbyter and legate of the Apostolic See, then entered and took their seats.[2]

Philip the presbyter and legate of the Apostolic See said: We bless the holy and adorable Trinity that our lowliness has been deemed worthy to attend your holy Synod. For a long time ago (πάλαι) our most holy and blessed pope Cœlestine, bishop of the Apostolic See, through his letters to that holy and most pious man Cyril, bishop of Alexandria, gave judgment concerning the present cause and affair (ὥρισεν) which letters have been shewn to your holy assembly. And now again for the corroboration of the Catholic (καθολικῆς) faith, he has sent through us letters to all your holinesses, which you will bid (κελούσατε) to be read with becoming reverence (πρεπόντως) and to be entered on the ecclesiastical minutes.

Arcadius, a bishop and legate of the Roman Church said: May it please your blessedness to give order that the letters of the holy and ever-to-be-mentioned-with-veneration Pope Cœlestine, bishop of the Apostolic See, which have been brought by us, be read, from which your reverence will be able to see what care he has for all the Churches.

Projectus, a bishop and legate of the Roman Church said, May it please, etc. [*The same as Arcadius had said* verbatim!]

And afterwards the most holy and beloved-of-God Cyril, bishop of the Church of Alexandria, spoke as is next in order contained; Siricius, notary of the holy Catholic (καθολικῆς) Church of Rome read it.

Cyril, the bishop of Alexandria said: Let the letter received from the most holy and altogether most blessed Cœlestine, bishop of the Apostolic See of Rome be read to the holy Synod with fitting honour.

Siricius, notary of the holy Catholic (καθολικῆς) Church of the city of Rome read it.

And after it was read in Latin, Juvenal, the bishop of Jerusalem said: Let the writings of the most holy and blessed bishop of great Rome which have just been read, be entered on the minutes.

And all the most reverend bishops prayed that the letter might be translated and read.

Philip, the presbyter of the Apostolic See and Legate said: The custom has been sufficiently complied with, that the writings of the Apostolic See should first be read in Latin.[3] But now since your holiness has

---

[1] Complaint of all this has very justly been made recently by the Rev. Luke Rivington, a Roman Catholic writer, in his work *The Primitive Church and the See of Peter*, p 336.

[2] It should be noted that in the Acts Cyril is described as having "the place of the most holy and sacred Archbishop of the Roman Church Cœlestine." Hefele says "that Cyril presided as Pope's vicar is asserted also by Mennas of Constantinople and other Greek bishops in their letter to Pope Vigilius, in Mansi, t. ix., p. 62; Hardouin, t. iii., p. 10." (Hef., *Hist. of the Councils*, Vol. III., p. 46, n. 4.)

[3] This seems to me to be the climax of improbable statements. There are many other things which will induce the curious reader to suspect that the Acts are not in good shape.

demanded that they be read in Greek also, it is necessary that your holiness's desire should be satisfied; We have taken care that this be done, and that the Latin be turned into Greek. Give order therefore that it be received and read in your holy hearing.

Arcadius and Projectus, bishops and legates said, As your blessedness ordered that the writings which we brought should be brought to the knowledge of all, for of our holy brethren bishops there are not a few who do not understand Latin, therefore the letter has been translated into Greek and if you so command let it be read.

Flavian, the bishop of Philippi said: Let the translation of the letter of the most holy and beloved of God, bishop of the Roman Church be received and read.

Peter, the presbyter of Alexandria and primicerius of the notaries read as follows:

THE LETTER OF POPE CŒLESTINE TO THE SYNOD OF EPHESUS.

(Labbe and Cossart, *Concilia*, Tom. III., col. 613.   Also Migne, *Pat. Lat.*, Tom. L., col. 505.[1])

Cœlestine the bishop to the holy Synod assembled at Ephesus, brethren beloved and most longed for, greeting in the Lord.

A Synod of priests gives witness to the presence of the Holy Spirit. For true is that which we read, since the Truth cannot lie, to wit, the promise of the Gospel; "Where two or three are gathered together in my name, there am I in the midst of them." And since this is so, if the Holy Spirit is not absent from so small a number how much more may we believe he is present when so great a multitude of holy ones are assembled together! Every council is holy on account of a peculiar veneration which is its due; for in every such council the reverence which should be paid to that most famous council of the Apostles of which we read is to be had regard to. Never was the Master, whom they had received to preach, lacking to this, but ever was present as Lord and Master; and never were those who taught deserted by their teacher. For he that had sent them was their teacher; he who had commanded what was to be taught, was their teacher; he who affirms that he himself is heard in his Apostles, was their teacher. This duty of preaching has been entrusted to all the Lord's priests in common, for by right of inheritance we are bound to undertake this solicitude, whoever of us preach the name of the Lord in divers lands in their stead: for he said to them, "Go, teach all nations." You, dear brethren, should observe that we have received a general command: for he wills that all of us should perform that office, which he thus entrusted in common to all the Apostles. We must needs follow our predecessors. Let us all, then, undertake their labours, since we are the successors in their honour. And we shew forth our diligence in preaching the same doctrines that they taught, beside which, according to the admonition of the Apostle, we are forbidden to add aught. For the office of keeping what is committed to our trust is no less dignified than that of handing it down.

They sowed the seed of the faith. This shall be our care that the coming of our great father of the family, to whom alone assuredly this fulness of the Apostles is assigned, may find fruit uncorrupt and many fold. For the vase of election tells us that it is not sufficient to plant and to water unless God gives the increase. We must strive therefore in common to keep the faith which has come down to us to-day, through the Apostolic Succession. For we are expected to walk according to the Apostle. For now not our appearance (*species*) but our faith is called in question. Spiritual weapons are those we must take, because the war is one of minds, and the weapons are words; so shall we be strong in the faith of our King. Now the Blessed Apostle Paul admonishes that all should remain in that place in which he bid Timothy remain. The same place therefore, the same cause, lays upon us the same duty. Let us now also do and study

---

[1] This letter we know was originally written in Latin, and that it was translated into Greek and then read afterwards in that language to the Council. There would seem to be no doubt that the Greek text we now find in the Acts is that first translation, but whether the Latin is the original or whether it is a translation back again from the Greek is not known, so far as I am aware. Certainly the Latin is of the most extraordinary character, and suggests that it was the work of one not skilled in that tongue. The text in several places is manifestly corrupt and the Greek and Latin do not always agree. If I may venture to express an opinion I should say that the Greek was more lucid. Although in nineteen places Labbe considers the true reading uncertain.

that which he then commanded him to do. And let no one think otherwise, and let no one pay heed to over strange fables, as he himself ordered. Let us be unanimous, thinking the same thing, for this is expedient: let us do nothing out of contention, nothing out of vain glory: let us be in all things of one mind, of one heart, when the faith which is one, is attacked. Let the whole body grieve and mourn in common with us. He who is to judge the world is called into judgment; he who is to criticise all, is himself made the object of criticism, he who redeemed us is made to suffer calumny. Dear Brethren, gird ye with the armour of God. Ye know what helmet must protect our head, what breast-plate our breast. For this is not the first time the ecclesiastical camps have received you as their rulers. Let no one doubt that by the favour of the Lord who maketh twain to be one, there will be peace, and that arms will be laid aside since the very cause defends itself.

Let us look once again at these words of our Doctor, which he uses with express reference to bishops, saying, "Take heed to yourselves and to the whole flock, over which the Holy Ghost has placed you as bishop, that ye rule the church of God, which he hath purchased with his blood."

We read that they who heard this at Ephesus, the same place at which your holiness is come together, were called thence. To them therefore to whom this preaching of the faith was known, to them also let your defence of the same faith also be known. Let us shew them the constancy of our mind with that reverence which is due to matters of great importance; which things peace has guarded for a long time with pious understanding.

Let there be announced by you what things have been preserved intact from the Apostles; for the words of tyrannical opposition are never admitted against the King of Kings, nor can the business of truth be oppressed by falsehood.

I exhort you, most blessed brethren, that love alone be regarded in which we ought to remain, according to the voice of John the Apostle whose reliques we venerate in this city. Let common prayer be offered to the Lord. For we can form some idea of what will be the power of the divine presence at the united intercession of such a multitude of priests, by considering how the very place was moved where, as we read, the Twelve made together their supplication. And what was the purport of that prayer of the Apostles? It was that they might receive grace to speak the word of God with confidence, and to act through its power, both of which they received by the favour of Christ our God. And now what else is to be asked for by your holy council, except that ye may speak the Word of the Lord with confidence? What else than that he would give you grace to preserve that which he has given you to preach? that being filled with the Holy Ghost, as it is written, ye may set forth that one truth which the Spirit himself has taught you, although with divers voices.

Animated, in brief, by all these considerations (for, as the Apostle says: "I speak to them that know the law, and I speak wisdom among them that are perfect"), stand fast by the Catholic faith, and defend the peace of the Churches, for so it is said, both to those past, present, and future, asking and preserving "those things which belong to the peace of Jerusalem."

Out of our solicitude, we have sent our holy brethren and fellow priests, who are at one with us and are most approved men, Arcadius, and Projectus, the bishops, and our presbyter, Philip, that they may be present at what is done and may carry out what things have been already decreed by us (*quæ a nobis antea statuta sunt, exequantur*).

To the performing of which we have no doubt that your holiness will assent when it is seen that what has been decreed is for the security of the whole church. Given the viij of the Ides of May, in the consulate of Bassus and Antiochus.

EXTRACTS FROM THE ACTS.

SESSION II. (Continued.)

(Labbe and Cossart, *Concilia*, Tom. III., col. 617.)

And all the most reverend bishops at the same time cried out. This is a just judgment. To Cœlestine, a new Paul! To Cyril a new Paul! To Cœlestine the guardian of the faith! To Cœlestine of one mind with the synod! To Cœlestine the whole Synod offers its thanks! One Cœlestine! One Cyril! One faith of the Synod! One faith of the world!

Projectus, the most reverend bishop and legate, said: Let your holiness consider the form (τύπον) of the writings of the holy and venerable pope Cœlestine, the bishop, who has exhorted your holiness (not as if teaching the ignorant, but as reminding them that know) that those things which he had long ago defined, and now thought it right to remind you of, ye might give command to be carried out to the uttermost, according to the canon of the common faith, and according to the use of the Catholic Church.

Firmus, the bishop of Cæsarea in Cappadocia said: The Apostolic and holy see of the most holy bishop Cœlestine, hath previously given a decision and type (τύπον) in this matter, through the writings which were sent to the most God beloved bishops, to wit to Cyril of Alexandria, and to Juvenal of Jerusalem, and to Rufus of Thessalonica, and to the holy churches, both of Constantinople and of Antioch. This we have also followed and (since the limit set for Nestorius's emendation was long gone by, and much time has passed since our arrival at the city of Ephesus in accordance with the decree of the most pious emperor, and thereupon having delayed no little time so that the day fixed by the emperor was past; and since Nestorius although cited had not appeared) we carried into effect the type (τύπον) having pronounced against him a canonical and apostolical judgment.

Arcadius the most reverend bishop and legate, said: Although our sailing was slow, and contrary winds hindered us especially, so that we did not know whether we should arrive at the destined place, as we had hoped, nevertheless by God's good providence . . .   Wherefore we desire to ask your blessedness, that you command that we be taught what has been already decreed by your holiness.

Philip, presbyter and legate of the Apostolic See said: We offer our thanks to the holy and venerable Synod, that when the writings of our holy and blessed pope had been read to you, the holy members by our [or your] holy voices,[1] ye joined yourselves to the holy head also by your holy acclamations. For your blessedness is not ignorant that the head of the whole faith, the head of the Apostles, is blessed Peter the Apostle. And since now our mediocrity, after having been tempest-tossed and much vexed, has arrived, we ask that ye give order that there be laid before us what things were done in this holy Synod before our arrival; in order that according to the opinion of our blessed pope and of this present holy assembly, we likewise may ratify their determination.

Theodotus, the bishop of Ancyra said: The God of the whole world has made manifest the justice of the judgment pronounced by the holy Synod by the writings of the most religious bishop Cœlestine, and by the coming of your holiness. For ye have made manifest the zeal of the most holy and reverend bishop Cœlestine, and his care for the pious faith. And since very reasonably your reverence is desirous of learning what has been done from the minutes of the acts concerning the deposition of Nestorius your reverence will be fully convinced of the justice of the sentence, and of the zeal of the holy Synod, and the symphony of the faith which the most pious and holy bishop Cœlestine has

---

[1] This seems to be certainly corrupt. I have literally followed the Greek.

proclaimed with a great voice, of course after your full conviction, the rest shall be added to the present action.

[*In the Acts follow two short letters from*

Cœlestine, one to the Emperor and the other to Cyril, but nothing is said about them, or how they got there, and thus abruptly ends the account of this session.]

EXTRACTS FROM· THE ACTS.

SESSION III.

(Labbe and Cossart, *Concilia*, Tom. III., col. 621.)

Juvenal the bishop of Jerusalem said to Arcadius and Projectus the most reverend bishops, and to Philip the most ·reverend presbyter: Yesterday while this holy and great synod was in session, when your holiness was present, you demanded after the reading of the letter of the most holy and blessed bishop of ·Great Rome, Cœlestine, that the minutes made in the Acts with regard to the deposition of Nestorius the heretic should be read. And thereupon the Synod ordered this to be done. Your holiness will be good enough to inform us whether you have read them and understand their power.

Philip the presbyter and legate of the Apostolic See said: From reading the Acts we have found what things have been done in your holy synod with ·regard to Nestorius. We have found from the minutes that all things have been decided in accordance with the canons and with ecclesiastical discipline. And now also we seek from your honour, although it may be useless, that what things have been read in your synod, the same should now again be read to us also; so that we may follow the formula (τύπῳ) of the most holy pope Cœlestine (who committed this· same care to us), and of your holiness also, and may be able to confirm (βεβαιῶσαι) the judgment.

[*Arcadius having seconded Philip's motion, Memnon directed the acts to be read which was done by the primicerius of the notaries.*]

Philip the presbyter and legate of the Apostolic See said: There is no doubt, and in fact it has been known in all ages, that the holy and most blessed Peter, prince (ἔξαρχος) and head of the Apostles, pillar of the faith, and foundation (θεμέλιος) of the Catholic Church, received the keys of the kingdom from our Lord Jesus Christ, the Saviour and Redeemer of the human

race, and that to him was given the power of loosing and binding sins: who down even to to-day and forever both lives and judges in his successors. The holy and most blessed pope Cœlestine, according to due order, is his successor and holds his place, and us he sent to supply his place in this holy synod, which the most humane and Christian Emperors have commanded to assemble, bearing in mind and continually watching over the Catholic faith. For they both have kept and are now keeping intact the apostolic doctrine handed down to them from their most pious and humane grandfathers and fathers of holy memory down to the present time, etc.

[*There is no further reference in the speech to the papal prerogatives.*]

Arcadius the most reverend bishop and legate of the Apostolic See said: Nestorius hath brought us great sorrow. . . . And since of his own accord he hath made himself an alien and an exile from us, we following the sanctions handed down from the beginning by the holy Apostles, and by the Catholic Church (for they taught what they had received from our Lord Jesus Christ), also following the types (τύποις) of Cœlestine, most holy pope of the Apostolic See, who has condescended to send us as his executors of this business, and also following the decrees of the holy Synod [we give this as our conclusion]: Let Nestorius know that he is deprived of all episcopal dignity, and is an alien from the whole Church and from the communion of all its priests.

Projectus, bishop and legate of the Roman Church said: Most clearly from the reading, etc. . . . Moreover I also, by my authority as legate of the holy Apostolic See, define, being with my brethren an executor (ἐκβιβαστής) of the aforesaid sentence, that the beforenamed Nestorius is an enemy of the truth, a corrupter of the faith, and as guilty of the things of which he was accused, has been removed from the grade of Episcopal honour, and moreover from the communion of all orthodox priests.

Cyril, the bishop of Alexandria said : The professions which have been made by Arcadius and Projectus, the most holy and pious bishops, as also by Philip, the most religious presbyter of the Roman Church, stand manifest to the holy Synod. For they have made their profession in the place of the Apostolic See, and of the whole of the holy synod of the God-beloved and most holy bishops of the West. Wherefore let those things which were defined by the most holy Cœlestine, the God-beloved bishop, be carried into effect, and the vote cast against Nestorius the heretic, by the holy Synod, which met in the metropolis of Ephesus be agreed to universally ; for this purpose let there be added to the already prepared acts the proceedings of yesterday and to-day, and let them be shewn to their holiness, so that by their subscription according to custom, their canonical agreement with all of us may be manifest.

Arcadius the most reverend bishop and legate of the Roman Church, said : According to the acts of this holy Synod, we necessarily confirm with our subscriptions their doctrines.

The Holy Synod said : Since Arcadius and Projectus the most reverend and most religious bishops and legates and Philip, the presbyter and legate of the Apostolic See, have said that they are of the same mind with us, it only remains, that they redeem their promises and confirm the acts with their signatures, and then let the minutes of the acts be shewn to them.

[*The three then signed.*]

THE CANONS OF THE TWO HUNDRED HOLY AND BLESSED FATHERS WHO MET AT EPHESUS.[1]

(*Critical Annotations on the text will be found in Dr. Routh's* Scriptorum Eccl. Opusc. *Tom. II.* [*Ed. III.*] *p. 85.*)

The holy and ecumenical Synod, gathered together in Ephesus by the decree of our most religious Emperors, to the bishops, presbyters, deacons, and all the people in every province and city:

When we had assembled, according to the religious decree [of the Emperors], in the Metropolis of Ephesus, certain persons, a little more than thirty in number, withdrew from amongst us, having for the leader of their schism John, Bishop of Antioch. Their names are as follows: first, the said John of Antioch in Syria, John of Damascus, Alexander of Apamea, Alexander of Hierapolis, Himerius of Nicomedia, Fritilas of Heraclea, Helladius of Tarsus, Maximin of Anazarbus, Theodore of Marcianopolis, Peter of Trajanopolis, Paul of Emissa, Polychronius of Heracleopolis, Euthyrius of Tyana, Meletius of Neocæsarea, Theodoret of Cyrus, Apringius of Chalcedon, Macarius of Laodicea Magna, Zosys of Esbus, Sallust of Corycus in Cilicia, Hesychius of Castabala in Cilicia, Valentine of Mutloblaca, Eustathius of Parnassus, Philip of Theodosia, and Daniel, and Dexianus, and Julian, and Cyril, and Olympius, and Diogenes, Polius, Theophanes of Philadelphia, Trajan of Augusta, Aurelius of Irenopolis, Mysæus of Aradus, Helladius of Ptolemais. These men, having no privilege of ecclesiastical communion on the ground of a priestly authority, by which they could injure or benefit any persons; since some of them had already been deposed; and since from their refusing to join in our decree against Nestorius, it was manifestly evident to all men that they were all promoting the opinions of Nestorius and Celestius; the Holy Synod, by one common decree, deposed them from all ecclesiastical communion, and deprived them of all their priestly power by which they might injure or profit any persons.

CANON I.

WHEREAS it is needful that they who were detained from the holy Synod and remained in their own district or city, for any reason, ecclesiastical or personal, should not be ignorant of the matters which were thereby decreed; we, therefore, notify your holiness and charity that if any Metropolitan of a Province, forsaking the holy and Ecumenical Synod, has joined the assembly of the apostates, or shall join the same hereafter; or, if he has adopted, or shall hereafter adopt, the doctrines of Celestius, he has no power in any way to do anything in opposition to the bishops of the province, since he is already cast forth from all ecclesiastical communion and made incapable of exercising his ministry; but he shall himself be subject in all things to those very bishops of the province and to the neighbouring orthodox metropolitans, and shall be degraded from his episcopal rank.

NOTES.

ANCIENT EPITOME OF CANON I.

If a metropolitan, having deserted his synod, adheres or shall adhere to Celestine, let him be cast out.

NICHOLAS HYDRUNTINUS.

Scholion concerning Celestine and Celestius. Whoso finds at the end of the fourth canon of the Holy Synod of Ephesus [and the

same is true of this first canon. *Ed.*] "Clerics who shall have consented to Celestine or Nestorius, should be deposed," let him not read "Celestine" with an "n," but "Celestius" without the "n." For Celestine was the holy and orthodox Pope of Rome, Celestius was the heretic.

It is perfectly certain that this was no accident on the part of Aristenus, for in his commentary on Canon V., he expressly says that "Celestine was Bishop of Rome" and goes on to affirm that, "The Holy Synod decreed that they who embraced the opinions of Nestorius and Celestine," etc. What perhaps is equally astonishing is that Nicholas Hydruntinus, while correcting the name, still is of opinion that Celestius was a pope of Rome and begins his scholion with the title, περὶ Κελεστίνου καὶ Κελεστίου, Παπῶν Ρώμης. Bev-

eridge well points out that this confusion is all the more remarkable as in the Kalendar of the Saints observed at that very time by the Greeks, on the eighth day of April was kept the memory of "Celestine, Pope of Rome, as a Saint and Champion against the Nestorian heretics." (Bev., *Annot*, in C. v.).

Simeon the Logothete adds to this epitome the words, καὶ τὸ ἑξῆς ἀδιοίκητος which are necessary to make the sense complete.

EXCURSUS ON THE CONCILIABULUM OF JOHN OF ANTIOCH.

The assembly referred to in this canon is one held by John of Antioch who had delayed his coming so as to hamper the meeting of the synod. John was a friend of Nestorius and made many fruitless attempts to induce him to accept the orthodox faith. It will be noticed that the conciliabulum was absolutely silent with respect to Nestorius and his doctrine and contented itself with attacking St. Cyril and the orthodox Memnon, the bishop of Ephesus. St. Cyril and his friends did indeed accuse the Antiochenes of being adherents of Nestorius, and in a negative way they certainly were so, and were in open opposition to the defenders of the orthodox faith ; but, as Tillemont [1] has well pointed out, they did not theologically agree with the heresy of Nestorius, gladly accepted the orthodox watchword "Mother of God," and subsequently agreed to his deposition.

The first session of the Council of Ephesus had already taken place on June 22, and it was only on June 26th or 27th, that John of Antioch arrived at last at Ephesus.

(Hefele, *History of the Councils*, Vol. III., p. 55 *et seqq.*)

The Synod immediately sent a deputation to meet him, consisting of several bishops and clerics, to show him proper respect, and at the same time to make him acquainted with the deposition of Nestorius, so that he might not be drawn into any intercourse with him.   The soldiers who surrounded Archbishop John prevented the deputation from speaking to him in the street ; consequently they accompanied him to his abode, but were compelled to wait here for several hours, exposed to the insults of the soldiers, and at last, when they had discharged their commission, were driven home, ill-treated and beaten. Count Irenæus, the friend of Nestorius, had suggested this treatment, and approved of it. The envoys immediately informed the Synod of what had happened, and showed the wounds which they had received, which called forth great indignation against John of Antioch. According to the representation of Memnon, excommunication was for this reason pronounced against him ; but we shall see further on that this did not take place until afterwards, and it is clear that Memnon, in his brief narrative, has passed over an intermediate portion—the threefold invitation of John.   In the meantime, Candidian had gone still further in his opposition to the members of the synod, causing them to be annoyed and insulted by his soldiers, and even cutting off their supply of food, while he provided Nestorius with a regular body-guard of armed peasants.   John of Antioch, immediately after his arrival, while still dusty from the journey, and at the time when he was allowing the envoys of the synod to wait, held at his own residence a Conciliabulum with his adherents, at which, first of all Count Candidian related how Cyril and his friends, in spite of all warnings, and in opposition to the imperial decrees, had held a session five days before, had contested his (the count's) right to be present, had dismissed the bishops sent by Nestorius, and had paid no attention to the letters of

---

[1] Tillemont, *Mémoires*, Tom. xiv.

others. Before he proceeded further, John of Antioch requested that the Emperor's edict of convocation should be read, whereupon Candidian went on with his account of what had taken place, and in answer to a fresh question of John's declared that Nestorius had been condemned unheard. John found this quite in keeping with the disposition of the synod since, instead of receiving him and his companions in a friendly manner, they had rushed upon them tumultuously (it was thus that he described what had happened). *But the holy Synod, which was now assembled*, would decide what was proper with respect to them. And this synod, of which John speaks in such grandiloquent terms, numbered only forty-three members, including himself, while on the other side there were more than two hundred.

John then proposed the question' [as to] what was to be decided respecting Cyril and his adherents ; and several who were not particularly pronounced Nestorian bishops came forward to relate how Cyril and Memnon of Ephesus had, from the beginning, maltreated the Nestorians, had allowed them no church, and even on the festival of Pentecost had permitted them to hold no service. Besides Memnon had sent his clerics into the residences of the bishops, and had ordered them with threats to take part in his council. And in this way he and Cyril had confused everything, so that their own heresies might not be examined. Heresies, such as the Arian, the Apollinarian, and the Eunomian, were certainly contained in the last letter of Cyril [to Nestorius, along with the anathematisms]. It was therefore John's duty to see to it that the heads of these heresies (Cyril and Memnon) should be suitably punished for such grave offences, and that the bishops who had been misguided by them should be subjected to ecclesiastical penalties.

To these impudent and false accusations John replied with hypocritical meekness " that he had certainly wished that he should not be compelled to exclude from the Church any one who had been received into the sacred priesthood, but diseased members must certainly be cut off in order to save the whole body ; and for this reason Cyril and Memnon deserved to be deposed, because they had given occasion to disorders, and had acted in opposition to the commands of the Emperors, and besides, were in the chapters mentioned [the anathematisms] guilty of heresy. All who had been misled by them were to be excommunicated until they confessed their error, anathematized the heretical propositions of Cyril, adhered strictly to the creed of Nice, without any foreign addition, and joined the synod of John."

The assembly approved of this proposal, and John then announced the sentence in the following manner :—

"The holy Synod, assembled in Ephesus, by the grace of God and the command of the pious Emperors, declares : We should indeed have wished to be able to hold a Synod in peace, but because you held a separate assembly from a heretical, insolent, and obstinate disposition, although we were already in the neighbourhood, and have filled both the city and the holy Synod with confusion, in order to prevent the examination of your Apollinarian, Arian, and Eunomian heresies, and have not waited for the arrival of the holy bishops of all regions, and have also disregarded the warnings and admonitions of Candidian, therefore shall you, Cyril of Alexandria, and you Memnon of this place, know that you are deposed and dismissed from all sacerdotal functions, as the originators of the whole disorder, etc. You others, who gave your consent, are excommunicated, until you acknowledge your fault and reform, accept anew the Nicene faith [as if they had surrendered it !] without foreign addition, anathematize the heretical propositions of Cyril, and in all things comply with the command of the Emperors, who require a peaceful and more accurate consideration of the dogma."

This decree was subscribed by all the forty-three members of the Conciliabulum :

The Conciliabulum then, in very one-sided letters informed the Emperor, the imperial ladies (the wife and sister of the Emperor Theodosius II.), the clergy, the senate, and the people of Constantinople, of all that had taken place, and a little later once more required the members of the genuine Synod, in writing, no longer to delay the time for repentance and conversion, and to separate themselves from Cyril and Memnon, etc., otherwise they would very soon be forced to lament their own folly.

On Saturday evening the Conciliabulum asked Count Candidian to take care that neither Cyril nor Memnon, nor any one of their (excommunicated) adherents should hold divine service on Sunday.   Candidian now wished that no member of either synodal party should officiate, but only the ordinary clergy of the city ; but Memnon declared that he would in no way submit to John and his synod, and Cyril and his adherents held divine service.   All the efforts of John to appoint by force another bishop of Ephesus in the place of Memnon were frustrated by the opposition of the orthodox inhabitants.

CANON II.

If any provincial bishops were not present at the holy Synod and have joined or attempted to join the apostacy ; or if, after subscribing the deposition of Nestorius, they went back into the assembly of apostates ; these men, according to the decree of the holy Synod, are to be deposed from the priesthood and degraded from their rank.

NOTES.

ANCIENT EPITOME OF CANON II.

If any bishop assents to or favours Nestorius, let him be discharged.

It was not unnatural that when it was seen that the Imperial authority was in favour of the Antiochene party that some of the clergy should have been weak enough to vacillate in their course, the more so as the Conciliabulum was not either avowedly, nor really, a Nestorian assembly, but one made up of those not sympathizing with Nestorius's heresy, yet friendly to the heretic himself, and disapproving of what they looked upon as the uncalled-for harshness and precipitancy of Cyril's course.

CANON III.

If any of the city or country clergy have been inhibited by Nestorius or his followers from the exercise of the priesthood, on account of their orthodoxy, we have declared it just that these should be restored to their proper rank.   And in general we forbid all the clergy who adhere to the Orthodox and Ecumenical Synod in any way to submit to the bishops who have already apostatized or shall hereafter apostatize.

NOTES.

ANCIENT EPITOME OF CANON III.

To whom Nestorius forbids the priesthood, he is most worthy ; but whom he approves is profane.

It would seem from this canon that any bishop who had become a member of the Conciliabulum of John, was considered as *eo ipso* having lost all jurisdiction.   Also it would seem that the clergy were to disregard the inhibition of Nestorian prelates or at least these inhibitions were by some one to be removed. This principle, if generally applied, would seem to be somewhat revolutionary.

LIGHTFOOT.

(*Apos. Fath.* Ign. *Ad Rom.* i., Vol. II., Sec. I., p. 191.)

The words χῶρος ("place"), χώρα ("country"), and χωρίον ("district"), may be distinguished as implying *locality, extension,* and *limitation,* respectively.   The last word commonly denotes either "an estate, a farm," or "a fastness, a stronghold," or (as a mathematical term) "an area."   Here, as not unfrequently in later writers, it is "a region, a district," but the same fundamental idea is presumed. The relation of χῶρος to χωρίον is the same as that of ἄργυρος, χρυσός to ἀργύριον, χρυσίον, the

former being the metals themselves, the latter | plate or trinkets or images, e.g. Macar. Magn.
the metals worked up into bullion or coins or | *Apocr.* iii. 42 (p. 147).

CANON IV.

IF any of the clergy should fall away, and publicly or privately presume to maintain the doctrines of Nestorius or Celestius, it is declared just by the holy Synod that these also should be deposed.

NOTES.

ANCIENT EPITOME OF CANON IV.

If any of the clergy shall consent to Celestine[1] *or Nestorius, let them be deposed.*

EXCURSUS ON PELAGIANISM.

The only point which is material to the main object of this volume is that Pelagius and his fellow heretic Celestius were condemned by the Ecumenical Council of Ephesus for their heresy.   On this point there can be no possible doubt.   And further than this the Seventh Council by ratifying the Canons of Trullo received the Canons of the African Code which include those of the Carthaginian conciliar condemnations of the Pelagian heresy to which the attention of the reader is particularly drawn.   The condemnation of these heretics at Ephesus is said to have been due chiefly to the energy of St. Augustine, assisted very materially by a layman living in Constantinople by the name of Marius Mercator.

Pelagius and his heresy have a sad interest to us as he is said to have been born in Britain. He was a monk and preached at Rome with great applause in the early years of the fifth century.   But in his extreme horror of Manichæism and Gnosticism he fell into the opposite extreme ; and from the hatred of the doctrine of the inherent evilness of humanity he fell into the error of denying the necessity of grace.

Pelagius's doctrines may be briefly stated thus.   Adam's sin injured only himself, so that there is no such thing as original sin.   Infants therefore are not born in sin and the children of wrath, but are born innocent, and only need baptism so as to be knit into Christ, not "for the remission of sins" as is declared in the creed.   Further he taught that man could live without committing any sin at all.   And for this there was no need of grace ; indeed grace was not possible, according to his teaching.   The only " grace," which he would admit the existence of, was what we may call external grace, e.g. the example of Christ, the teaching of his ministers, and the like.   Petavius[2] indeed thinks that he allowed the activity of internal grace to illumine the intellect, but this seems quite doubtful.

Pelagius's writings have come down to us in a more or less—generally the latter—pure form.   There are fourteen books on the Epistles of St. Paul, also a letter to Demetrius and his *Libellus fidei ad Innocentium*.   In the writings of St. Augustine are found fragments of Pelagius's writings on free will.

It would be absurd to attempt in the limits possible to this volume to give any, even the most sketchy, treatment of the doctrine involved in the Pelagian controversy : the reader must be referred to the great theologians for this and to aid him I append a bibliographical table on the subject.

St. Augustine.

St. Jerome.

Marius Mercator, *Commonitorium super nomine Cœlestii.*

Vossius, G. J., *Histor. de controv. quas Pel. ejusque reliquiæ moverunt.*

---

[1] It should read "Celestius"; see Scholion on Canon I.   [2] Petav. *De Pelag. et Semi-Pelag. Hær.*, Cap. iv.

Noris. *Historia Pelagiana.*

Garnier, J. *Dissertat. in Pelag.* in *Opera* Mar. Mercator.

Quesnel, *Dissert. de conc. Africanis in Pelag. causa celebratis* etc.

Fuchs, G. D., *Bibliothek der Kirchenversammlungen.*

Horn, *De sentent. Pat. de peccato orig.*

Habert, P. L., *Theologiæ Græcorum Patrum vindicatæ circa univers. materiam gratiæ.*

Petavius, *De Pelag. et Semi-Pelag.*[1]

The English works on the subject are so well known to the English reader as to need no mention.

As it is impossible to treat the theological question here, so too is it impossible to treat the historical question.   However I may remind the reader that Nestorius and his heresy were defended by Theodore of Mopsuestia, and that he and Celestius were declared by Pope Zosimus to be innocent in the year 417, a decision which was entirely disregarded by the rest of the world, a Carthaginian Synod subsequently anathematizing him.   Finally the Pope retracted his former decision, and in 418 anathematized him and his fellow, and gave notice of this in his "epistola tractoria" to the bishops.   Eighteen Italian bishops, who had followed the Pope in his former decision of a twelve month before, refused to change their minds at his bidding now, and were accordingly deposed, among them Julian of Eclanum.   After this Pelagius and Celestius found a fitting harbour of refuge with Nestorius of Constantinople, and so all three were condemned together by the council of Ephesus, he that denied the incarnation of the Word, and they twain that denied the necessity of that incarnation and of the grace purchased thereby.

CANON V.

IF any have been condemned for evil practices by the holy Synod, or by their own bishops; and if, with his usual lack of discrimination, Nestorius (or his followers) has attempted, or shall hereafter attempt, uncanonically to restore such persons to communion and to their former rank, we have declared that they shall not be profited thereby, but shall remain deposed nevertheless.

NOTES.

ANCIENT EPITOME OF CANON V.

If one condemned by his bishop is received by Nestorius it shall profit him nothing.

This canon is interesting as shewing that thus early in the history of the Church, it was not unusual for those disciplined for their faults in one communion to go to another and there be welcomed and restored, to the overthrow of discipline and to the lowering of the moral sense of the people to whom they minister.

CANON VI.

LIKEWISE, if any should in any way attempt to set aside the orders in each case made by the holy Synod at Ephesus, the holy Synod decrees that, if they be bishops or clergymen, they shall absolutely forfeit their office; and, if laymen, that they shall be excommunicated.

NOTES.

ANCIENT EPITOME OF CANON VI.

If any layman shall resist the Synod, let him be excommunicated.   But if it be a cleric let him be discharged.

How courageous the passing of this canon was can only be justly appreciated by those who are familiar with the weight of the imperial authority at that day in ecclesiastical matters and who will remember that at the very time this canon was passed it was extremely difficult to say whether the Emperor would support Cyril's or John's synod.

---

[1] I am chiefly indebted to Michaud for this list.

OBSERVATION OF THE ROMAN EDITORS (Ed: 1608).

In the Vatican books and in some others only these six canons are found ; but in certain texts there is added, under the name of Canon VII., the definition of the same holy Synod put forth after the Presbyter Charisius had stated his case, and for Canon VIII. another decree of the synod concerning the bishops of Cyprus.

OBSERVATION OF PHILIP LABBE, S.J.P.

In the Collections of John Zonaras and of Theodore Balsamon, also in the "Code of the Universal Church" which has John Tilius, Bishop of St. Brieuc and Christopher Justellus for its editors, are found eight canons of the Ephesine council, to wit the six which are appended to the foregoing epistle and two others : but it is altogether a subject of wonder that in the Codex of Canons, made for the Roman Church by Dionysius Exiguus, none of these canons are found at all. I suppose that the reason of this is that the Latins saw that they were not decrees affecting the Universal Church, but that the Canons set forth by the Ephesine fathers dealt merely with the peculiar and private matters of Nestorius and of his followers.

The Decree of the same holy Synod, pronounced after hearing the Exposition [of the Faith] by the Three hundred and eighteen holy and blessed Fathers in the city of Nice, and the impious formula composed by Theodore of Mopsuestia, and given to the same holy Synod at Ephesus by the Presbyter Charisius, of Philadelphia :

CANON VII.

WHEN these things had been read, the holy Synod decreed that it is unlawful for any man to bring forward, or to write, or to compose a different ($\dot{\epsilon}\tau\dot{\epsilon}\rho\alpha\nu$) Faith as a rival to that established by the holy Fathers assembled with the Holy Ghost in Nicæa.

But those who shall dare to compose a different faith, or to introduce or offer it to persons desiring to turn to the acknowledgment of the truth, whether from Heathenism or from Judaism, or from any heresy whatsoever, shall be deposed, if they be bishops or clergymen ; bishops from the episcopate and clergymen from the clergy ; and if they be laymen, they shall be anathematized.

And in like manner, if any, whether bishops, clergymen, or laymen, should be discovered to hold or teach the doctrines contained in the Exposition introduced by the Presbyter Charisius concerning the Incarnation of the Only-Begotten Son of God, or the abominable and profane doctrines of Nestorius, which are subjoined, they shall be subjected to the sentence of this holy and ecumenical Synod. So that, if it be a bishop, he shall be removed from his bishopric and degraded ; if it be a clergyman, he shall likewise be stricken from the clergy ; and if it be a layman, he shall be anathematized, as has been afore said.

NOTES.

ANCIENT EPITOME OF CANON VII.

Any bishop who sets forth a faith other than that of Nice shall be an alien from the Church : if a layman do so let him be cast out.

The heading is that found in the ordinary Greek texts. The canon itself is found *verbatim* in the Acts—Actio VI. (Labbe and Cossart, *Concilia*, Tom. III., col. 689.)

BEVERIDGE.

"When these things had been read." Balsamon here makes an egregious mistake, for it was not after the reading of the decree of this council and of the Nicene Creed, that this canon was set forth, as Balsamon affirms ; but after the reading of the *libellum* of Charisius, and of the Nestorian Creed, as is abundantly evident from what we read in the Acts of the

council.   From this it is clear that Balsamon
had never seen the Acts of this council, or at
least had never carefully studied them, else he
could not have written such a comment.

[With regard to Charisius, Balsamon] makes
another mistake.   For not only did this presbyter not follow the evil opinions of Nestorius,

but as a matter of fact exhibited to the synod
his *libellum* written against Nestorius; in
which so far from asserting that Nestorius
was orthodox, he distinctly calls him κακόδοξος.

Photius has included this canon in his No-
mocanons, Title I., cap. j.

EXCURSUS ON THE WORDS πίστιν ἑτέραν.

It has been held by some and was urged by the Greeks at the Council of Florence,[1] and
often before and since, as well as by Pope Leo III., in answer to the ambassadors of Charlemagne, that the prohibition of the Council of Ephesus to make, hold, or teach any other faith
than that of Nice forbade anyone, even a subsequent General Council, to add anything to the
creed.   This interpretation seems to be shewn to be incorrect from the following circumstances.

1. That the prohibition was passed by the Council immediately after it had heard Charisius read his creed, which it had approved, and on the strength of which it had received its
author, and after the reading of a Nestorian creed which it condemned.   From this it seems
clear that ἑτέραν must mean " different," " contradictory," and not " another" in the sense of
mere explanatory additions to the already existing creed.

(E. B. Pusey, On the Clause "and the Son," p. 81.)

St. Cyril ought to understand the canon, which he probably himself framed, as presiding
over the Council of Ephesus, as Archbishop of Alexandria and representative of Celestine,
Bishop of Rome.   His signature immediately succeeds the Canon.   We can hardly think
that we understand it better than he who probably framed it, nay who presided over the
Council which passed it.   He, however, explained that what was not *against* the Creed was
not *beside* it.   The Orientals had proposed to him, as terms of communion, that he should
"do away with all he had written in epistles, tomes, or books, and agree with that only faith
which had been defined by our holy Fathers 'at Nice."   But, St. Cyril wrote back: "We
all follow that exposition of faith which was defined by the holy fathers in the city of Nice,
sapping absolutely nothing of the things contained in it.   For they are all right and unex-
ceptionable; and anything curious, after it, is not safe.   But what I have rightly written
against the blasphemies of Nestorius no words will persuade me to say that they were not
done well:" and against the imputation that he "had received an exposition of faith or new
Creed, as dishonouring that old and venerable Creed," he says :

"Neither have we demanded of any an exposition of faith, nor have we received one newly
framed by others.   For Divine Scripture suffices us, and the prudence of the holy fathers,
and the symbol of faith, framed perfectly as to all right doctrine.   But since the most holy
Eastern Bishops differed from us as to that of Ephesus and were somehow suspected of
being entangled in the meshes of Nestorius, therefore they very wisely made a defence, to
free themselves from blame, and eager to satisfy the lovers of the blameless faith that they
were minded to have no share in his impiety; and the thing is far from all note of blame.
If Nestorius himself, when we all held out to him that he ought to condemn his own dogmas and choose the truth instead thereof, had made a written confession thereon, who would
say that he framed for us a new exposition of faith?   Why then do they calumniate the
assent of the most holy Bishops of Phœnicia, calling it a new setting forth of the Creed,
whereas they made it for a good and necessary end, to defend themselves and soothe those

---

[1] Hefele, *Conciliengesch.* XLVIII., § 810.

who thought that they followed the innovations of Nestorius? For the holy Ecumenical Synod gathered at Ephesus provided, of necessity, that no other exposition of faith besides that which existed, which the most blessed fathers, speaking in the Holy Ghost, defined, should be brought into the Churches of God. But they who at one time, I know not how, differed from it, and were suspected of not being right-minded, following the Apostolic and Evangelic doctrines, how should they free themselves from this ill-report? by silence? or rather by self-defence, and by manifesting the power of the faith which was in them? The divine disciple wrote, "be ready always to give an answer to every one who asketh you an account of the hope which is in you." But he who willeth to do this, innovates in nothing, nor doth he frame any new exposition of faith, but rather maketh plain to those who ask him, what faith he hath concerning Christ."[1]

2. The fathers of the Council of Chalcedon, by their practice, are authoritative exponents of the Canon of Ephesus. For they renewed the prohibition of the Council of Ephesus to "adduce any other faith," but, in "the faith" which is not to be set aside, they included not only the Creeds of Nice and Constantinople, but the definitions at Ephesus and Chalcedon itself. The statements of the faith were expanded, because fresh contradictions of the faith had emerged. After directing that both Creeds should be read, the Council says, "This wise and saving Symbol of Divine grace would have sufficed to the full knowledge and confirmation of the faith; for it teaches thoroughly the perfect truth of the Father, Son, and Holy Ghost, and presents to those who receive it faithfully the Incarnation of the Lord." Then, having in detail shewn how both heresies were confuted by it, and having set forth the true doctrine, they sum up.

"These things being framed by us with all accuracy and care on every side, the holy and ecumenical Synod defines, that it shall be lawful for no one to produce or compose, or put together, or hold, or teach others another faith, and those who venture, etc." (as in the Council of Ephesus).

The Council of Chalcedon enlarged greatly the terms although not the substance of the faith contained in the Nicene Creed; and that, in view of the heresies, which had since arisen; and yet renewed in terms the prohibition of the Canon of Ephesus and the penalties annexed to its infringement. It shewed, then, in practice, that it did not hold the enlargement of the things proposed as *de fide* to be prohibited, but only the producing of things contradictory to the faith once delivered to the saints. Its prohibition, moreover, to "hold" another faith shews the more that they meant only to prohibit any contradictory statement of faith. For if they had prohibited any additional statement not being a contradiction of its truth, then (as Cardinal Julian acutely argued in the Council of Florence), any one would fall under its anathema, who held (as all must) anything not expressed in set terms in the Nicene Creed; such as that God is eternal or incomprehensible.

It may not be amiss to remember that the argument that πίστιν ἑτέραν forbids any addition to the Creed or any further definition of the faith, was that urged by the heretics at the Latrocinium, and the orthodox were there condemned on the ground that they had added to the faith and laid themselves under the Anathema of Ephesus. How far this interpretation was from being that of the Council of Chalcedon is evinced by the fact that it immediately declared that St. Flavian and Bishop Eusebius had been unjustly deposed, and proceeded to depose those who had deposed them. After stating these facts Dr. Pusey remarks, "Protestants may reject consistently the authority of all councils; but on what grounds any who accept their authority can insist on their own private interpretation of a canon of one council against the authority of another General Council which rejected that interpretation, I see not."[2]

---

[1] Cyril. Alex., *Ep.* xxxv., *Ad Acac. Melit.*   [2] E. B. Pusey, *Lib. cit.*, p. 86.

4. The Fifth Ecumenical Council, the Second of Constantinople, received both the creeds of Nice and that of Constantinople, as well of the definitions of Ephesus and Chalcedon, and yet at the end of the fourth Session we find in the acts that the fathers cried out, with respect to the creed of Theodore of Mopsuestia: "This creed Satan composed. Anathema to him that composed this creed! The First Council of Ephesus anathematized this creed and its author. We know only one symbol of faith, that which the holy fathers of Nice set forth and handed down. This also the three holy Synods handed down. Into this we were baptized, and into this we baptize, etc., etc." [1]

From this it is clearer than day that these fathers looked upon the creed of Constantinople, with its additions, to be yet the same creed as that of Nice.

(Le Quien, Diss. Dam., n. 37.)

In the Sixth Council also, no one objecting, Peter of Nicomedia, Theodore, and other bishops, clerks, and monks, who had embraced the Monothelite heresy, openly recited a Creed longer and fuller than the Nicene.

In the Seventh Synod also, another was read written by Theodore of Jerusalem : and again, Basil of Ancyra, and the other Bishops, who had embraced the errors of the Iconoclasts, again offered another, although the Canon of Ephesus pronounced, that "it should not be lawful to offer to heretics, who wished to be converted to the Church, any other creed than the Nicene." In this same Synod, was read another profession of faith, which Tarasius had sent to the Patriarchs of the Eastern sees. It contains the Nicene, or Constantinopolitan Creed, variously enlarged and interpolated. But of the Holy Spirit it has specifically this : "And in the Holy Spirit, the Lord, the Giver of Life, which proceedeth from the Father through the Son." But since the Greeks at the Council of Florence said, that these were individual, not common, formulæ of faith, here are others, which are plainly common and solemn, which are contained in their own rituals. They do not baptize a Hebrew or a Jew, until he have pronounced a profession of Christian Faith, altogether different from the Creed of Constantinople, as may be seen in the Euchologion. In the consecration of a Bishop, the Bishop elect is first bidden to recite the Creed of Constantinople ; and then, as if this did not suffice, a second and a third are demanded of him ; of which the last contains that aforesaid symbol, intermingled with various declarations. Nay, Photius himself is pointed out to be the author of this interpolated symbol.[2] I pass by other formulæ, which the Greeks have framed for those who return to the Church from divers heresies or sects, although the terms of the Canon of Ephesus are, that "it is unlawful to propose any other faith to those who wish to be converted to the Church, from heathenism, or Judaism, or any heresy whatever."

The Judgment of the same Holy Synod, pronounced on the petition presented to it by the Bishops of Cyprus :

CANON VIII.

OUR brother bishop Rheginus, the beloved of God, and his fellow beloved of God bishops, Zeno and Evagrius, of the Province of Cyprus, have reported to us an innovation which has been introduced contrary to the ecclessiastical constitutions and the Canons of the Holy Apostles, and which touches the liberties of all. Wherefore, since injuries affecting all require the more attention, as they cause the greater damage, and particularly when they are transgressions of an ancient custom ; and since those excellent men, who have petitioned the Synod, have told us in writing and by word of mouth

---

[1] Labbe and Cossart, Tom. v.. col. 455.
[2] In the Codex Cæsareus, mentioned by Lambecius, Lib. vii., cod 77.

that the Bishop of Antioch has in this way held ordinations in Cyprus; therefore the Rulers of the holy churches in Cyprus shall enjoy, without dispute or injury, according to the Canons of the blessed Fathers and ancient custom, the right of performing for themselves the ordination of their excellent Bishops. The same rule shall be observed in the other dioceses and provinces everywhere, so that none of the God-beloved Bishops shall assume control of any province which has not heretofore, from the very beginning, been under his own hand or that of his predecessors. But if any one has violently taken and subjected [a Province], he shall give it up; lest the Canons of the Fathers be transgressed; or the vanities of worldly honour be brought in under pretext of sacred office; or we lose, without knowing it, little by little, the liberty which Our Lord Jesus Christ, the Deliverer of all men, hath given us by his own Blood.

Wherefore, this holy and ecumenical Synod has decreed that in every province the rights which heretofore, from the beginning, have belonged to it, shall be preserved to it, according to the old prevailing custom, unchanged and uninjured: every Metropolitan having permission to take, for his own security, a copy of these acts. And if any one shall bring forward a rule contrary to what is here determined, this holy and ecumenical Synod unanimously decrees that it shall be of no effect.

NOTES.

ANCIENT EPITOME OF CANON VIII.

Let the rights of each province be preserved pure and inviolate. No attempt to introduce any form contrary to these shall be of any avail.

The caption is the one given in the ordinary Greek texts. The canon is found word for word in the VII Session of the Council, with the heading, "A decree of the same holy Synod." (Labbe and Cossart, *Concilia*, Tom. III., col. 802.)

I have followed in reading "the Canons of the Holy Apostles" the reading in Balsamon and Zonaras, and that of Elias Ehingerus Augustanus (so says Beveridge) in his edition of the Greek canons, A.D. 1614. But the Bodleian MS. and John of Antioch in his collection of the Canons, and the Codex edited by Christopher Justellus read "of the Holy Fathers" instead of "of the Holy Apostles." Beveridge is of opinion that this is the truer reading, for while no doubt the Ephesine Fathers had in mind the Apostolic Canons, yet they seem to have more particularly referred in this place to the canons of Nice. And this seems to be intimated in the *libellum* of the Bishops of Cyprus, who gave rise to this very decree, in which the condemned practice is said to be "contrary to the Apostolic Canons and to the definitions of the most holy Council of Nice."

This canon Photius does not recognize, for in the Preface to his Nomocanon he distinctly writes that there were but seven canons adopted by the Ephesine Synod, and in the first chapter of the first title he cites the preceding canon as the seventh, that is the last. John of Antioch likewise says that there are but seven canons of Ephesus, but reckons this present canon as the seventh, from which Beveridge concludes that he rejects the Canon concerning Charisius (vij).

BEVERIDGE.

Concerning the present canon, of rather decree, the Bishop of Antioch, who had given occasion to the six former canons, gave also occasion for the enacting of this, by arrogating to himself the right of ordaining in the Island of Cyprus, in violation of former usage. After the bishops of that island, who are mentioned in the canon, had presented their statements (*libellum*) to the Synod, the present decree was set forth, in which warning was given that no innovation should be tolerated in Ecclesiastical administration, whether in Cyprus or elsewhere; but that in all Dioceses and Provinces their ancient rights and privileges should be preserved.

THE LETTER OF THE SAME HOLY SYNOD OF EPHESUS, TO THE SACRED SYNOD IN PAMPHYLIA CONCERNING EUSTATHIUS WHO HAD BEEN THEIR METROPOLITAN.

(Labbe and Cossart, *Concilia*, Tome III., col. 806.)

Forasmuch as the divinely inspired Scripture says, "Do all things with advice,"[1] it is especially their duty who have had the priestly ministry allotted to them to examine with all diligence whatever matters are to be transacted. For to those who will so spend their lives, it comes to pass both that they are established in [the enjoyment of] an honest hope concerning what belongs to them, and that they are borne along, as by a favouring breeze, in things that they desire: so that, in truth, the saying [of the Scripture] has much reason [to commend it]. But there are times when bitter and intolerable grief swoops down upon the mind, and has the effect of cruelly beclouding it, so as to carry it away from the pursuit of what is needful, and persuade it to consider that to be of service which is in its [very] nature mischievous. Something of this kind we have seen endured by that most excellent and most religious Bishop Eustathius. For it is in evidence that he has been ordained canonically; but having been much disturbed, as he declares, by certain parties, and having entered upon circumstances he had not foreseen, therefore, though fully able to repel the slanders of his persecutors, he nevertheless, through an extraordinary inexperience of affairs, declined to battle with the difficulties which beset him, and in some way that we know not set forth an act of resignation. Yet it behooved him, when he had been once entrusted with the priestly care, to cling to it with spiritual energy, and, as it were, to strip himself to strive against the troubles and gladly to endure the sweat for which he had bargained. But inasmuch as he proved himself to be deficient in practical capacity, having met with this misfortune rather from inexperience than from cowardice and sloth, your holiness has of necessity ordained our most excellent and most religious brother and fellow-bishop, Theodore, as the overseer of the Church; for it was not reasonable that it should remain in widowhood, and that the Saviour's sheep should pass their time without a shepherd. But when he came to us weeping, not contending with the aforenamed most religious Bishop Theodore for his See or Church, but in the meantime seeking only for his rank and title as a bishop, we all suffered with the old man in his grief, and considering his weeping as our own, we hastened to discover whether the aforenamed [Eustathius] had been subjected to a legal deposition, or whether, forsooth, he had been convicted on any of the absurd charges alleged by certain parties who had poured forth idle gossip against his reputation. And indeed we learned that nothing of such a kind had taken place, but rather that his resignation had been counted against the said Eustathius instead of a [regular] indictment. Wherefore, we did by no means blame your holiness for being compelled to ordain into his place the aforenamed most excellent Bishop Theodore. But forasmuch as it was not seemly to contend much against the unpractical character of the man, while it was rather necessary to have pity on the elder who, at so advanced an age, was now so far away from the city which had given him birth, and from the dwelling-places of his fathers, we have judicially pronounced and decreed without any opposition, that he shall have both the name, and the rank, and the communion of the episcopate. On this condition, however, only, that he shall not ordain, and that he shall not take and minister to a Church of his own individual authority; but that [he shall do so only] if taken as an assistant, or when appointed, if it should so chance, by a brother and fellow-bishop, in accordance with the ordinance and the love which is in Christ. If, however, ye shall determine anything more favourable towards him, either now or hereafter, this also will be pleasing to the Holy Synod.

---

[1] Ecclesiasticus, xxxii., 19— "Do nothing without advice" (*sine consilio nihil facias*) : The deutero-canonical book of Ecclesiasticus is here by an Ecumenical Council styled "divinely inspired Scripture."

THE LETTER OF THE SYNOD TO POPE CELESTINE.

(Labbe and Cossart, *Concilia*, Tom. III., col. 659; also in Migne, *Pat. Lat.* [reprinted from Galland., *Vett. Patr.*, Tom. ix.], Tom. L., Ep. xx., col. 511.)

THE RELATION WHICH THE HOLY COUNCIL OF EPHESUS SENT TO POPE CELESTINE; IN WHICH ARE EXPLAINED WHAT THINGS WERE DONE IN THAT HOLY AND GREAT COUNCIL.

The Holy Synod which by the grace of God was assembled at Ephesus the Metropolis to the most holy and our fellow-minister Cœlestine, health in the Lord.

The zeal of your holiness for piety, and your care for the right faith, so grateful and highly pleasing to God the Saviour of us all, are worthy of all admiration. For it is your custom in such great matters to make trial of all things, and the confirmation of the Churches you have made your own care. But since it is right that all things which have taken place should be brought to the knowledge of your holiness, we are writing of necessity [to inform you] that, by the will of Christ the Saviour of us all, and in accordance with the orders of the most pious and Christ-loving Emperors, we assembled together in the Metropolis of the Ephesians from many and far scattered regions, being in all over two hundred bishops. Then, in accordance with the decrees of the Christ-loving Emperors by whom we were assembled, we fixed the date of the meeting of the holy Synod as the Feast of the Holy Pentecost, all agreeing thereto, especially as it was contained in the letters of the Emperors that if anyone did not arrive at the appointed time, he was absent with no good conscience, and was inexcusable both before God and man. The most reverend John bishop of Antioch stopped behind; not in singleness of heart, nor because the length of the journey made the impediment, but hiding in his mind his plan and his thought (which was so displeasing to God,) [a plan and thought] which he made clear when not long afterwards he arrived at Ephesus. Therefore we put off the assembling [of the council] after the appointed day of the Holy Pentecost for sixteen whole days; in

the meanwhile many of the bishops and clerics were overtaken with illness, and much burdened by the expense, and some even died. A great injury was thus being done to the great Synod, as your holiness easily perceives. For he used perversely such long delay that many from much greater distances arrived before him.

Nevertheless after sixteen days had passed, certain of the bishops who were with him, to wit, two Metropolitans, the one Alexander of Apamea, and the other Alexander of Hierapolis, arrived before him. And when we complained of the tardy coming of the most reverend bishop John, not once, but often, we were told, "He gave us command to announce to your reverence, that if anything should happen to delay him, not to put off the Synod, but to do what was right." After having received this message,—and as it was manifest, as well from his delay as from the announcements just made to us, that he refused to attend the Council, whether out of friendship to Nestorius, or because he had been a cleric of a church under his sway, or out of regard to petitions made by some in his favour,—the Holy Council sat in the great church of Ephesus, which bears the name of Mary.

But when all with zeal had come together, Nestorius alone was found missing from the council, thereupon the holy Synod sent him admonition in accordance with the canons by bishops, a first, second, and third time. But he surrounding his house with soldiers, set himself up against the ecclesiastical laws, neither did he shew himself, nor give any satisfaction for his iniquitous blasphemies.

After this the letters were read which were written to him by the most holy and most reverend bishop of the Church of Alexandria, Cyril, which the Holy Synod approved as being orthodox and without fault (ὀρθῶς καὶ ἀλήπτως ἔχειν), and in no point out of agreement either with the divinely inspired Scriptures, or with the faith handed down and set forth in the great synod of holy Fathers, which assembled sometime ago at Nice in Bithynia, as your holiness also rightly having examined this has given witness.

On the other hand there was read the letter of Nestorius, which was written to the already mentioned most holy and reverend brother of ours and fellow-minister, Cyril, and the Holy Synod was of opinion that those things which were taught in it were wholly alien from the Apostolic and Evangelical faith, sick with many and strange blasphemies.

His most impious expositions were likewise read, and also the letter written to him by your holiness, in which he was properly condemned as one who had written blasphemy and had inserted irreligious views (φωνᾶς) in his private exegesis, and after this a just sentence of deposition was pronounced against him; especially is this sentence just, because he is so far removed from being penitent, or from a confession of the matters in which he blasphemed, while yet he had the Church of Constantinople, that even in the very metropolis of the Ephesians, he delivered a sermon to certain of the Metropolitical bishops, men who were not ignorant, but learned and God-fearing, in which he was bold enough to say, "I do not confess a two or three months old God," and he said other things more outrageous than this.

Therefore as an impious and most pestilent heresy, which perverts our most pure religion (θρησκείαν) and which overthrows from the foundation the whole economy of the mystery [i.e. the Incarnation], we cast it down, as we have said above. But it was not possible, as it seemed, that those who had the sincere love of Christ, and were zealous in the Lord should not experience many trials. For we had hoped that the most reverend John, bishop of Antioch would have praised the sedulous care and piety of the Synod, and that perchance he would have blamed the slowness of Nestorius's deposition. But all things turned out contrary to our hope. For he was found to be an enemy, and a most warlike one, to the holy Synod, and even to the orthodox faith of the churches, as these things indicate.

For as soon as he was come to Ephesus, before he had even shaken off the dust of the journey, or changed his travelling dress, he assembled those who had sided with Nestorius and who had uttered blasphemies against their head, and only not derided the glory of Christ, and gathering as a college to himself, I suppose, thirty men, having the name of bishops (some of whom were without sees, wandering about and having no dioceses, others again had for many years been deposed for serious causes from their metropolises, and with these were Pelagians and the followers of Celestius, and some of those who were turned out of Thessaly), he had the presumption to commit a piece of iniquity no man had ever done before. For all by himself he drew up a paper which he called a deposition, and reviled and reproached the most holy and reverend Cyril, bishop of Alexandria, and the most reverend Memnon, bishop of Ephesus, our brother, and fellow-minister, none of us knowing anything about it, and not even those who were thus reviling knew what was being done, nor for what reason they had presumed to do this. But ignoring the anger of God for such behaviour, and unheeding the ecclesiastical canons, and forgetting that they were hastening to destruction by such a course of action, under the name of an excommunication, they then reviled the whole Synod. And placing these acts of theirs on the public bulletin boards, they exposed them to be read by such as chose to do so, having posted them on the outside of the theatres, that they might make a spectacle of their impiety. But not even was this the limit of their audacity; but as if they had done something in accordance with the canons, they dared to bring what they had done to the ears of the most pious and Christ-loving Emperors.

Things being in this condition, the most holy and reverend Cyril, bishop of Alexandria and the most reverend Memnon bishop of the city of Ephesus, offered some books composed by themselves and accusing the most reverend Bishop John and those who with him had done this thing, and conjuring our holy Synod that John and those with him should be summoned according to the canons, so that they might apologize for their daring acts, and if they had any complaints to make they might speak and prove them, for in their written deposition, or rather sheet of abuse, they made this statement as a pretext, "They are Apollinarians, and Arians, and Eunomians, and therefore they have been deposed by us."

When, therefore, those who had endured their reviling were present, we again necessarily assembled in the great church, being more than two hundred bishops, and by a first, second, and third call on two days, we summoned John and his companions to the Synod, in order that they might examine those who had been reviled, and might make explanations, and tell the causes which led them to draw up the sentence of deposition; but he[1] did not dare to come.

But it was right that he, if he could truly prove the before-mentioned holy men to be heretics, both should come and prove the truth of that which, accepted as a true and indubitable crime, induced the temerarious sentence against them. But being condemned by his own conscience he did not come. Now what he had planned was this. For he thought that when that foundationless and most unjust reviling was done away, the just vote of the Synod which it cast against the heretic Nestorius would likewise be dissolved. Being justly vexed, therefore, we determined to inflict according to law the same penalty upon him and those who were with him, which he contrary to law had pronounced against those who had been convicted of no fault. But although most justly and in accordance with law he would have suffered this punishment yet in the hope that by our patience his temerity might be conquered, we have reserved this to the decision of your holiness. In the meanwhile, we have deprived them of communion and have taken from them all priestly power, so that they may not be able to do any harm by their opinions. For those who thus ferociously, and cruelly, and uncanonically are wont to rush to such frightful and most wicked things, how was it not necessary that they should be stripped of the powers which [as a matter of fact] they did not possess,[2] of being able to do harm.

With our brethren and fellow-ministers, both Cyril the bishop and Memnon, who had endured reproval at their hands, we are all in communion, and after the rashness [of their accusers] we both have and do per-form the liturgy in common, all together celebrating the Synaxis, having made of none effect their play in writing, and having thus shewn that it lacked all validity and effect. For it was mere reviling and nothing else. For what kind of a synod could thirty men hold, some of whom were marked with the stamp of heresy, and some without sees and ejected [from their dioceses]? Or what strength could it have in opposition to a synod gathered from all the whole world? For there were sitting with us the most reverend bishops Arcadius and Projectus, and with them the most holy presbyter Philip, all of whom were sent by your holiness, who gave to us your presence and filled the place of the Apostolic See (τῆς ἀποστολικῆς καθέδρας). Let then your holiness be angered at what took place. But if license were granted to such as wished to pour reproval upon the greater sees, and thus unlawfully and uncanonically to give sentence or rather to utter revilings against those over whom they have no power, against those who for religion have endured such great conflicts, by reason of which now also piety shines forth through the prayers of your holiness [if, I say, all this should be tolerated], the affairs of the Church would fall into the greatest confusion. But when those who dare to do such things shall have been chastised aright, all disturbance will cease, and the reverence due to the canons will be observed by all.

When there had been read in the holy Synod what had been done touching the deposition of the most irreligious Pelagians and Cœlestines, of Cœlestius, and Pelagius, and Julian, and Præsidius, and Florus, and Marcellian, and Orontius, and those inclined to like errors, we also deemed it right (ἐδικαιώσαμεν) that the determinations of your holiness concerning them should stand strong and firm. And we all were of the same mind, holding them deposed. And that you may know in full all things that have been done, we have sent you a copy of the Acts, and of the subscriptions of the Synod. We pray that you, dearly beloved and most longed for, may be strong and mindful of us in the Lord.[3]

---

[1] Plural in the Greek but singular in the Latin, which the critical editors consider the correct reading.

[2] It seems that ἔχοντας, and not ἐκόντας, is the true reading.

[3] The Latin adds, "Then all the bishops subscribed their names."

THE DEFINITION OF THE HOLY AND ECUMENICAL SYNOD OF EPHESUS AGAINST THE IMPIOUS MESSALIANS WHO ARE ALSO 'ALLED EUCHETÆ AND ENTHUSIASTS.

(Found in Latin only.   Labbe and Cossart, *Concilia,* Tom. III., col. 809.)*

When the most pious and religious bishops, Valerian and Amphilochius had come to us, they proposed that we should consider in common the case of the Messalians, that is the Euchetes or Enthusiasts, who were flourishing in Pamphylia, or by what other name this most contaminating heresy is called.   And when we were considering the question, the most pious and religious bishop Valerian, presented to us a synodical schedule which had been drawn up concerning them in the great city of Constantinople, under Sisinnius of blessed memory: What we read therein was approved by all, as well composed and as a due presentation of the case.   And it seemed good to us all, and to the most pious bishops Valerian and Amphilochius and to all the most pious bishops of the provinces of Pamphylia and Lycaonia, that all things contained in that Synodical chart should be confirmed and in no way rescinded; also that the action taken at Alexandria might also be made firm, so that all those who throughout the whole province are of the Messalian or Enthusiastic heresy, or suspected of being tainted with that heresy, whether clerics or laymen, may come together ; and if they shall anathematize in writing, according to the decrees pronounced in the aforesaid synod [their errors], if they are clergymen they may remain such; and if laymen they may be admitted to communion.   But if they refuse to anathematize, if they were presbyters or deacons or in any other ecclesiastical grade, let them be cast out of the clergy and from their grade, and also from communion ; if they be laymen let them be anathematized.

Furthermore those convicted of this heresy are no more to be permitted to have the rule of our monasteries, lest tares be sown and increase.   And we give command that the most pious bishops Valerian and Amphilochius, and the rest of the most reverend bishops of the whole province shall pay attention that this decree be carried into effect.   In addition to this it seemed good that the filthy book of this heresy, which is called the "Asceticon," should be anathematized, as composed by heretics, a copy of which the most religious and pious Valerian brought with him.   Likewise anything savouring of their impiety which may be found among the people, let it be anathema.

Moreover when they come together, let there be commended by them in writing such things as are useful and necessary for concord, and communion, and arrangement (*dispositionem vel dispensationem*).   But should any question arise in connexion with the present business, and if it should prove to be difficult and ambiguous, what is not approved by the most pious bishops Valerian and Amphilochius, and the other bishops throughout the province, they ought to discuss all things by reference to what is written.   And if the most pious bishops of the Lycians or of the Lycaonians shall have been passed over ; nevertheless let not a Metropolitan be left out of whatever province he may be.   And let these things be inserted in the Acts so that if any have need of them they would find how also to expound these things more diligently to others.

NOTE ON THE MESSALIANS OR MASSALIANS.

(Tillemont, *Mémoires,* Tom. VIII., Seconde Partie.   Condensed.)

St. Epiphanius distinguishes two sorts of persons who were called by the name of Messalians, the one and the more ancient were heathen, the other were Christian in name.

The Messalians who bore the Christian name had no beginning, nor end, nor chief, nor fixed faith.   Their first writers were Dadoes, Sabas, Adelphus, Hermes, Simeon and some others. Adelphus was neither monk nor clerk, but a layman. Sabas had taken the habit of an anchorite and was surnamed "the Eunuch," because he had mutilated himself. Adelphus was of Mesopotamia and was considered their leader, so that they are sometimes called "Adelphians." They are also called "Eustathians." "Euchites" is the Greek equivalent of "Messalians" in Hebrew. They were also called "Enthusiasts" or "Corentes" because of the agitation the devils caused them, which they attributed to the Holy Spirit.

St. Epiphanius thought that these heretics sprang up in the time of Constance, although Theodoret does not put them down until the days of Valentinian. They came from Mesopotamia, but spread as far as Antioch by the year 376.

They pretended to renounce the world, and to give up their possessions, and under the habit of monks they taught Manichæan impieties, and others still more detestable.

Their principal tenet was that everyone inherited from his ancestors a demon, who had possession of his soul from the moment of his birth, and always led it to evil. That baptism cut away the outside branches of sin, but could not free the soul of this demon, and that therefore its reception was useless. That only constant prayer could drive out this demon. That when it was expelled, the Holy Spirit descended and gave visible and sensible marks of his presence, and delivered the body from all the uprisings of passion, and the soul from the inclination to evil, so that afterwards there was no need of fasting, nor of controlling lust by the precepts of the Gospel.

Besides this chief dogma, gross errors, contrary to the first principles of religion, were attributed to them. That the divinity changed itself in different manners to unite itself to their souls. They held that the body of Christ was infinite like his divine nature; they did not hesitate to say that his body was at first full of devils which were driven out when the Word took it upon him.[1] They claimed that they possessed clear knowledge of the state of souls after death, read the hearts and desires of man, the secrets of the future and saw the Holy Trinity with their bodily eyes. They affirmed that man could not only attain perfection but equal the deity in virtue and knowledge.

They never fasted, slept men and women together, in warm weather in the open streets. But certain say that before attaining to this liberty of license three years of mortification were required.

The most well-known point of their discipline is that they forbade all manual labour as evil, and unworthy of the spiritual.

Harmenopulus in his *Basilicæ* (Tom. I., Lib. ix.) says that they held the Cross in horror, that they refused to honour the Holy Virgin, or St. John the Baptist, or any of the Saints unless they were Martyrs; that they mutilated themselves at will, that they dissolved marriages, that they foreswore and perjured themselves without scruple, that women were appointed as mistresses of the sect to instruct and govern men, even priests.

Although so opposed to the faith of the Church, yet for all this the Messalians did not separate themselves from her communion. They did not believe in the Communion as a mystery which sanctifies us, which must be approached with fear and faith, but only came to the holy Table to hide themselves and to pass for Catholics, for this was one of their artifices. When asked, they had no hesitation in denying all that they believed, and were willing to anathematize those who thought with them. And all this they did without fear, because they were taught they had attained perfection, that is impassibility.

Vide Theodoret, *H. E.*, Lib. iv., cap. xi.

Photius tells us that John of Antioch wrote against these heretics.

St. Maximus the Abbot speaks of this heresy as still existing in the VIIth Century, and as practising the most abominable infamies. Photius bears witness of its resuscitation

---

[1] They were therefore Nestorians.

in his days in Cappadocia with its wonted corruptions. Harmenopulus remarks that a certain Eleutherius of Paphlagonia had added to it new crimes, and that in part it became the source of the sect of the Bogomiles, so well known in the decadence of the Greek empire.

DECREE OF THE SYNOD IN THE MATTER OF EUPREPIUS AND CYRIL.

(Found in Latin only. Labbe and Cossart, *Concilia*, Tom. III., col. 810.)

The petition of the most pious bishops Euprepius and Cyril, which is set forth in the papers they offered, is honest. Therefore from the holy canons and the external laws, which have from ancient custom the force of law,[1] let no innovation be made in the cities of Europa, but according to the ancient custom they shall be governed by the bishops by whom they have been formerly governed. For since there never was a metropolitan who had power otherwise, so neither hereafter shall there be any departure from the ancient custom.

NOTE.

Hefele.

(Hist. of the Councils, Vol. III., p. 77.)

Two Thracian bishops, Euprepius of Biza (Bizya) and Cyril of Cœle, gave occasion for a decree, praying for protection against their Metropolitan, Fritilas of Heraclea, who had gone over to the party of John of Antioch, and at the same time for the confirmation of the previous practice of holding two bishoprics at the same time. The Synod granted both.

---

[1] The text, as the side note remarks, "seems to be mutilated and depraved" in this passage, but the meaning is clear enough as given by Hefele in the note.

THE FOURTH ECUMENICAL COUNCIL.

THE COUNCIL OF CHALCEDON.

A.D. 451.

Emperors.—Marcian and Pulcheria (in the East).
Valentinian III. (in the West).
Pope.—Leo I.

Elenchus.

GENERAL INTRODUCTION.

I should consider it a piece of impertinence were I to attempt to add anything to what has been already said with regard to the Council of Chalcedon. The literature upon the subject is so great and so bitterly polemical that I think I shall do well in laying before my readers the Acts, practically complete on all disputed points, and to leave them to draw their own conclusions. I shall not, however, be liable to the charge of unfairness if I quote at some length the deductions of the Eagle of Meaux, the famous Bossuet, from these acts; and since his somewhat isolated position as a Gallican gives him a singular fitness to serve in this and similar questions as a mediator between Catholics and Protestants, his remarks upon this Council will, I think, be read with great interest and respect.

(Bossuet. *Defensio Dec. Cleri Gallic.* Lib. VII., cap. xvij. [Translation by Allies].)

An important point treated in the Council of Chalcedon, that is, the establishing of the faith, and the approval of Leo's letter, is as follows: Already almost the whole West, and most of the Easterns, with Anatolius himself, Bishop of Constantinople, had gone so far as to confirm by subscription that letter, before the council took place; and in the council itself the Fathers had often cried out, "We believe, as Leo: Peter hath spoken by Leo: we have all subscribed the letter: what has been set forth is sufficient for the Faith: no other exposition may be made." Things went so far, that they would hardly permit a definition to be made by the council. But neither subscriptions privately made before the council, nor these vehement cries of the Fathers in the council, were thought sufficient to tranquillize minds in so unsettled a state of the Church, for fear that a matter so important might seem determined rather by outcries than by fair and legitimate discussion. And the clergy of Constantinople exclaimed, "It is a few who cry out, not the whole council which speaks." So it was determined, that the letter of Leo should be lawfully examined by the council, and a definition of faith be written by the synod itself. So the acts of foregoing councils being previously read, the magistrates proposed concerning Leo's letter, "As we see the divine Gospels laid before your Piety, let each one of the assembled bishops declare, whether the exposition of the 318 Fathers at Nice, and of the 150 who afterwards assembled in the imperial city, agrees with the letter of the most reverend Archbishop Leo."

After the question as to examining the letter of Leo was put in this form, it will be worth while to weigh the sentences and, as they are called, the votes of the Fathers, in order to understand from the beginning why they approved of the letter; why they afterwards defended it with so much zeal; why, finally, it was ratified after so exact an examination of the council. Anatolius first gives his sentence. "The letter of the most holy and religious Archbishop Leo agrees with the creed of our 318 Fathers at Nice, and of the 150 who afterwards assembled at Constantinople, and confirmed the same faith, and with the proceedings at Ephesus under the most blessed Cyril, who is among the saints, by the Ecumenical and holy Council, when it condemned Nestorius. I therefore agree to it, and willingly subscribe to it." These are the words of one plainly deliberating, not blindly subscribing out of obedience. The rest say to the same effect: "It agrees, and I subscribe." Many plainly and expressly, "It agrees, and I therefore subscribe." Some add, "It agrees, and I subscribe, as it is correct." Others, "I am sure that it agrees." Others, "As it is concordant, and has the same aim, we embrace it, and subscribe." Others, "This is the faith we have long held: this we hold: in this we were baptized: in this we baptize." Others, and a great part, "As I see, as I feel, as I have proved, as I find that it agrees, I subscribe." Others, "As I am persuaded, instructed, informed, that all agrees, I subscribe." Many set forth their difficulties, mostly arising from a foreign language ; others from the subject matter, saying, that they had heard the letter, "and in very many points were assured it was right ; some few words stood in their way, which seemed to point at a certain division in the person of Christ." They add, that they had been informed by Paschasinus and the Legates "that there is no division, but one Christ ; therefore," they say, "we agree and subscribe." Others after mentioning what Paschasinus and Lucentius had said, thus conclude : "By this we have been satisfied and, considering that it agrees in all things with the holy Fathers, we agree and subscribe." Where the Illyrian bishops, and others who before that examination had expressed their acclamations to the letter, again cry out, "We all say the same thing, and agree with this." So that, indeed, it is evident that, in the council itself, and before it their agreement is based on this that, after weighing the matter, they considered, they judged, they were persuaded, that all agreed with the Fathers, and perceived that the common faith of all and each had been set forth by Leo. This is that examination of Leo's letter, synodically made at Chalcedon, and placed among the acts.

(*Gallia Orthod.*, LIX.)

Nor did Anatolius and the other bishops receive it, until they had deliberated, and found that Leo's letter agreed with the preceding councils.

(*Gallia Orthod.*, LX.)

But here a singular discussion arises between the eminent Cardinals Bellarmine and Baronius. The latter, and with him a large number of our theologians, recognize the letter of Leo as the *Type and Rule* of faith, by which all Churches were bound : but Bellarmine, alarmed at the examination which he could not deny, answers thus : " Leo had sent his letter to the council, not as containing his final and definitive sentence, but as an instruction, assisted by which the bishops might form a better judgment." But, most eminent man, allow me to say that Leo, upon the appeal of Eutyches, and at the demand of Flavian, composed this letter for a summary of the faith, and sent it to every Church in all parts, when as yet no one thought about a council. Therefore it was not an instruction to the council which he provided, but an Apostolic sentence which he put forth. The fact is that out of this strait there was no other escape : Baronius will not allow that a letter, confirmed by so great an authority of the Apostolic See, should be attributed to any other power but that which is supreme and indefectible : Bellarmine will not take that to emanate from the supreme and indefectible authority, which was subjected to synodical inquiry, and deliberation. What, then, is the issue of this conflict, unless that it is equally evident that the letter was written with the whole authority of the Apostolic See, and yet subjected, as usual, to the examination of an Universal Council.

(*Ib.* LXI.)

And in this we follow no other authority than Leo himself, who speaks thus in his letter to Theodoret : "What God had before decreed by our ministry, he confirmed by the irreversible assent of the whole brotherhood, to shew that what was first put forth in form by the First See of all, and then received by the *judgment* of the whole Christian world, really proceeded from himself." Here is a decree, as Baronius says, but not as Bellarmine says, an instruction : here is a *judgment* of the whole world upon a decree of the Apostolic See. He proceeds : " For in order that the consent of other sees to that which the Lord of all appointed to preside over the rest might not appear flattery, nor any other adverse suspicion creep in, persons were at first found who doubted concerning our judgments." And not only heretics, but even the Fathers of the council themselves, as the acts bear witness.

Here the First See shews a fear of flattery, if doubt about its judgments were forbidden. Moreover, "The truth itself likewise is both more clearly conspicuous, and more strongly maintained, when after examination confirms what previous faith had taught." Here in plain words he speaks of an examination by the council, *de fide*, not by himself, as they wretchedly object, but of that faith which the decretal letter set forth. And at length that same letter is issued as the Rule, but confirmed by the assent of the universal holy Council, or as he had before said, after that it is confirmed by the irreversible assent of the whole Brother-hood. Out of this expression of that great Pontiff, the Gallican clergy drew theirs, that in questions of faith the judgment is, what Tertullian calls, "not to be altered;" what Leo calls, "not to be reconsidered," only when the assent of the Church is added.

(Defens. Dec. Cleri Gall. **VII.** xvij.)

This certainly no one can be blamed for holding with him and with the Fathers of Chalcedon. The forma is set forth by the Apostolic See, yet it is to be received with a judgment, and that free, and each bishop individually is inferior to the First, yet so that all together pass judgment even on his decree.

They conceived no other way of removing all doubt; for, after the conclusion of the synod, the Emperor thus proclaims: "Let then all profane contentions cease, for he is indeed impious and sacrilegious, who, after the sentence of so many priests, leaves anything for his own opinion to consider." He then prohibits all discussion concerning religion; for, says he, "he does an injury to the judgment of the most religious council, who endeavours to open afresh, and publicly discuss, what has been once judged, and rightly ordered." Here in the condemnation of Eutyches is the order of Ecclesiastical judgments in questions of faith. He is judged by his proper Bishop, Flavian: the cause is reheard, reconsidered by the Pope St. Leo; it is decided by a declaration of the Apostolic See: after that declaration follows the examination, inquiry, judgment of the Fathers or bishops, in a General Council: after the declaration has been approved by the judgment of the Fathers no place is any longer left for doubt or discussion.

EXTRACTS FROM THE ACTS.

SESSION I.

(Labbe and Cossart, *Concilia*, Tom. IV., col. 93.)

Paschasinus, the most reverend bishop and legate of the Apostolic See, stood up in the midst with his most reverend colleagues and said: We received directions at the hands of the most blessed and apostolic bishop of the Roman city, which is the head of all the churches, which directions say that Dioscorus is not to be allowed a seat in this assembly, but that if he should attempt to take his seat he is to be cast out. This instruction we must carry out; if now your holiness so commands let him be expelled or else we leave.[1]

The most glorious judges and the full senate said: What special charge do you prefer against the most reverend bishop Dioscorus?

Paschasinus, the most reverend bishop and legate of the Apostolic See, said: Since he has come, it is necessary that objection be made to him.

The most glorious judges and the whole senate said: In accordance with what has been said, let the charge under which he lies, be specifically made.

Lucentius, the most reverend bishop having the place of the Apostolic See, said: Let him give a reason for his judgment. For he undertook to give sentence against one over whom he had no jurisdiction. And he dared to hold a synod without the authority of the Apostolic See, a thing which had never taken place nor can take place.[2]

Paschasinus the most reverend bishop, holding the place of the Apostolic See, said: We cannot go counter to the decrees of the most blessed and apostolic bishop ["Pope" for "bishop" in the Latin], who governs the Apostolic See, nor against the ecclesiastical canons nor the patristic traditions.

The most glorious judges and the full senate, said: It is proper that you should set forth specifically in what he hath gone astray.

Lucentius, the venerable bishop and holding the place of the Apostolic See, said: We will not suffer so great a wrong to be done us and you, as that he who is come to be judged should sit down [as one to give judgment].

The glorious judges and the whole senate said: If you hold the office of judge, you ought not to defend yourself as if you were to be judged.

And when Dioscorus the most religious bishop of Alexandria at the bidding of the most glorious judges and of the sacred assembly (τῆς ἱερᾶς συγκλήτου [3]) had sat down in the midst, and the most reverend Roman bishops also had had sat down in their proper places, and kept silence, Eusebius, the most reverend bishop of the city of Dorylæum, stepping into the midst, said:

[*He then presented a petition, and the Acts of the Latrocinium were read. Also the Acts of the council of Constantinople under Flavian against Eutyches* (col. 175).]

And when they were read, the most glorious judges and immense assembly (ὑπερφυὴς σύγκλητος) said: What do the most reverend bishops of the present holy synod say? When he thus expounded the faith did Flavian, of holy memory, preserve the orthodox and catholic religion, or did he in any respect err concerning it?

Paschasinus the most reverend bishop, representing the Apostolic See, said; Flavian of blessed memory hath most holily and perfectly expounded the faith. His faith and exposition agrees with the epistle of the most blessed and apostolic man, the bishop of Rome.

Anatolius the most reverend archbishop of Constantinople said; The blessed Fla-

---

[1] This whole paragraph reads with material differences in the Latin. Moreover while the Greek text is clear and grammatical, the Latin is most incorrect and halting. Leo is described as "Pope of the city of Rome," instead of "bishop of Rome."

[2] This statement, so absolutely contrary to fact, has been a sore difficulty to the commentators. Arendt (*Leo the Great and his Times*, § 270) says that this meant only that "he had, without per-mission of the Pope, taken the presidency there, and conducted the proceedings, for Leo himself had acknowledged the synod by the fact that he allowed his legates to be present at it." Almost the same is the explanation of the Ballerini (Leo M. *Opera*, Tom. ii. 460, n. 15.)

[3] The Latin here has the usual form "amplissimus senatus," for which the Greek is περιφανέστατοι συγκλητικοί.

vian hath beautifully and orthodoxly set forth the faith of our fathers.

Lucentius, the most reverend bishop, and legate of the Apostolic See, said; Since the faith of Flavian of blessed memory agrees with the Apostolic See and the tradition of the fathers it is just that the sentence by which he was condemned by the heretics should be turned back upon them by this most holy synod.

Maximus the most reverend bishop of Antioch in Syria, said: Archbishop Flavian of blessed memory hath set forth the faith orthodoxly and in accordance with the most beloved-of-God and most holy Archbishop Leo. And this we all receive with zeal.

Thalassius, the most reverend bishop of Cæsarea in Cappadocia said; Flavian of blessed memory hath spoken in accordance with Cyril of blessed memory.

[*And so, one after another, the bishops expressed their opinions. The reading of the acts of the Council of Constantinople was then continued.*]

And at this point of the reading, Dioscorus, the most reverend Archbishop of Alexandria said, I receive "the of two;" "the two" I do not receive (τὸ ἐκ δύο δέχομαι· τὸ δύο, οὐ δέχομαι). I am forced to be impudent, but the matter is one which touches my soul.

[*After a few remarks the reading was continued and the rest of the acts of the Latro-*
cinium of Ephesus completed. The judges then postponed to the morrow the setting forth a decree on the faith but intimated that Dioscorus and his associates should suffer the punishment to which they unjustly sentenced Flavian. This met with the approval of all the bishops except those of Illyrica who said: " We all have erred, let us all be pardoned."* (col. 323.)]

The most glorious judges and the whole senate said; Let each one of the most reverend bishops of the present synod, hasten to set forth how he believes, writing without any fear, but placing the fear of God before his eyes; knowing that our most divine and pious lord believes according to the ecthesis of the three hundred and eighteen holy fathers at Nice, and according to the ecthesis of the one hundred and fifty after them, and according to the Canonical epistles and ectheses of the holy fathers Gregory, Basil, Athanasius, Hilary, Ambrose, and according to the two canonical epistles of Cyril, which were confirmed and published in the first Council of Ephesus, nor does he in any point depart from the faith of the same. For the most reverend archbishop of Old Rome, Leo, appears to have sent a letter to Flavian of blessed memory, with reference to Eutyches's unbelieving doubt which was springing up against the Catholic Church.

End of the first Actio.

EXTRACTS FROM THE ACTS.

SESSION II.

(L. and C., *Concilia*, Tom. IV., col. 338.)

When all were seated before the rails of the most holy altar, the most superb and glorious judges and the great (ὑπερφυὴς) senate said; At a former meeting the question was examined of the condemnation of the most reverend bishop Flavian of blessed memory and Eusebius, and it was patent to you all with what justice and accuracy the examination was conducted: and it was proved that they had been cruelly and improperly condemned. What course we should pursue in this matter became clear after your deliberations. Now however the question to be enquired into, studied, and decided, is how the true faith is to be established, which is the chief end for which this Council has been assembled. As we know that ye are to render to God a strict account not only for your own souls in particular, but as well for the souls of all of us who desire rightly to be taught all things that pertain to religion, and that all ambiguity be taken away, by the agreement and consent of all the holy fathers, and by their united exposition and doctrine; hasten therefore without any fear of pleasing or displeasing, to set forth (ἐκθέσθαι) the pure faith, so that they who do not seem to believe with all the rest, may be brought to unity through the acknowledging of the truth. For we wish you to know that the most divine and pious lord of the whole world and ourselves hold the orthodox faith set forth by the 318 and by the 150 holy fathers, and what also has been taught by the rest of the most holy and glorious fathers, and in accordance with this is our belief.

The most reverend bishops cried; Any other setting forth (ἔκθεσιν ἄλλην) no one makes, neither will we attempt it, neither will we dare to set forth [anything new] (ἐκθέσθαι). For the fathers taught, and in their writings are preserved, what things were set forth by them, and further than this we can say nothing.

Cecropius, the most reverend bishop of Sebastopol said : The matters concerning Eutyches have been examined, and the most holy archbishop of Rome has given a form (τύπον) which we follow and to his letter we all [i. e. those in his neighbourhood] have subscribed.

The most reverend bishops cried : These are the opinions of all of us. The expositions (ἐκτεθέντα) already made are quite sufficient : it is not lawful to make any other.

The most glorious judges and great senate said, If it pleases your reverence, let the most holy patriarch of each province, choosing one or two of his own province and going into the midst, and together considering the faith, make known to all what is agreed upon. So that if, as we desire, all be of one mind, all ambiguity may be removed : But if some entertain contrary opinions (which we do not believe to be the case) we may know what their opinions are.

The most reverend bishops cried out, we make no new exposition in writing. This is the law, [i. e. of the Third Synod] which teaches that what has been set forth is sufficient. The law wills that no other exposition should be made. Let the sayings of the Fathers remain fast.

Florentius, the most reverend bishop of Sardis, said, since it is not possible for those who follow the teaching of the holy Synod of Nice, which was confirmed rightly and piously at Ephesus, to draw up suddenly a declaration of faith in accordance with the faith of the holy fathers Cyril and Celestine, and of the letter of the most holy

Leo, we therefore pray your magnificence to give us time, so that we may be able to arrive at the truth of the matter with a fitting document, although so far as we are concerned, who have subscribed the letter of the most holy Leo, nothing further is needed.

Cecropius, the most reverend bishop of Sebastopol, said, The faith has been well defined by the 318 holy fathers and confirmed by the holy fathers Athanasius, Cyril, Celestine, Hilary, Basil, Gregory, and now once again by the most holy Leo : and we pray that those things which were decreed by the 318 holy fathers, and by the most holy Leo be read.

The most glorious judges and great Senate said : Let there be read the expositions (ἐκτεθέντα) of the 318 fathers gathered together at Nice.

Eunomius, the most reverend bishop of Nicomedia read from a book [the Exposition of faith of the 318 fathers.[1]]

The Exposition of faith of the Council held at Nice.

" In the consulate of Paul and Julian " etc.

" We believe in one God," etc.

" But those who say," etc.

The most reverend bishops cried out; This is the orthodox faith; this we all believe : into this we were baptized; into this we baptize : Blessed Cyril so taught : this is the true faith : this is the holy faith : this is the everlasting faith : into this we were baptized : into this we baptize : we all so believe : so believes Leo, the Pope (ὁ πάπας) : Cyril thus believed : Pope Leo so interpreted it.

The most glorious judges and great senate said, Let there be read what was set forth by the 150 holy fathers.

Aetius, the reverend deacon of Constantinople read from a book [the creed of the 150 fathers.[2]]

The holy faith which the 150 fathers set forth as consonant to the holy and great Synod of Nice.

" We believe in one God," etc.

All the most reverend bishops cried out: This is the faith of all of us : we all so believe.

The reverend archdeacon Aetius said, There remains the letter of Cyril of holy

---

[1] Added in the Latin acts.   [2] Ibid.

and blessed memory, sometime bishop of the great city Alexandria, which he wrote to Nestorius, which was approved by all the most holy bishops assembled in the first Council at Ephesus, called to condemn the same Nestorius, and which was confirmed by the subscription of all. There is also another letter of the same Cyril, of blessed memory, which he wrote to John, of blessed memory, sometime bishop of the great city of Antioch, which likewise was confirmed. If it be so ordered, I shall read these.

The most glorious judges and great senate said, Let the letters of Cyril of blessed memory be read.

Aetius, the Archdeacon of the imperial city Constantinople read.

To the most reverend and most religious fellow-priest Nestorius, Cyril sends greeting in the Lord.

[Καταφλυαροῦσι μὴν κ. τ. λ.   *Lat.* Obloquuntur quidem, etc.   *This letter is found among the acts of the Council of Ephesus.*]

Likewise the same Archdeacon Aetius read [the letter of the same holy Cyril of blessed memory to John of Antioch, on the peace].

[*This letter begins,* Εὐφραινέϑωσαν οἱ οὐρανοὶ κ. τ. λ.; *and in the Latin* Lætentur cæli.]

THE LETTER OF CYRIL TO JOHN OF ANTIOCH.

(*Found in Labbe and Cossart*, Concilia, *Tom. IV., col.* 343 *and col.* 164; *and in Migne,* Pat. Græc., *Tom. LXXVII.* [*Cyrilli* Opera, *Tom. X.*], *col.* 173. *This is the letter which is often styled "the Ephesine Creed."*)

Cyril to my lord, beloved brother, and fellow minister John, greeting in the Lord.

"Let the heavens rejoice, and let the earth be glad" for the middle wall of partition has been taken away, and grief has been silenced, and all kind of difference of opinion has been removed; Christ the Saviour of us all having awarded peace to his churches, through our being called to this by our most devout and beloved of God kings, who are the best imitators of the piety of their ancestors in keeping the right faith in their souls firm and immovable, for they chiefly give their mind to the affairs of the holy Churches, in order that they may have the noted glory forever and show forth their most renowned kingdom, to whom also Christ himself the Lord of powers distributes good things with plenteous hand, and gives to prevail over their enemies and grants them victory. For he does not lie in saying: "As I live saith the Lord, them that honour me, I will honour." For when my lord, my most-beloved-of-God, fellow-minister and brother Paul, had arrived in Alexandria, we were filled with gladness, and most naturally at the coming of such a man as a mediator, who was ready to work beyond measure that he might overcome the envy of the devil and heal our divisions, and who by removing the offences scattered between us, would crown your Church and ours with harmony and peace.

Of the reason of the disagreement it is superfluous to speak. I deem it more useful both to think and speak of things suitable to the time of peace. We were therefore delighted at meeting with that distinguished and most pious man, who expected perhaps to have no small struggle, persuading us that it is necessary to form an alliance for the peace of the Church, and to drive away the laughter of the heterodox, and for this end to blunt the goads of the stubbornness of the devil. He found us ready for this, so as absolutely to need no labour to be bestowed upon us. For we remembered the Saviour's saying; "My peace I give unto you, my peace I leave with you." We have been taught also to say in prayers : "O Lord our God give us peace, for thou hast given us all things." So that if anyone should be in the participation of the peace furnished from God, he is not lacking in any good. That as a matter of fact, the disagreement of the Churches happened altogether unnecessarily and inopportunely, we now have been fully satisfied by the document brought by my lord, the most pious bishop Paul, which contains an unimpeachable confession of faith, and this he asserted to have been prepared, by your holiness and by the God-beloved Bishops there. The document is as follows, and is set down verbatim in this our epistle.

Concerning the Virgin Mother of God, we thus think and speak; and of the manner of the Incarnation of the Only Begotten Son of God, necessarily, not by way of addition but for the sake of certainty, as we have received from the beginning from the divine Scriptures and from the tradition of the holy fathers, we will speak briefly, adding nothing whatever to the Faith set forth by the holy Fathers in Nice. For, as we said before, it suffices for all knowledge of piety and the refutation of all false doctrine of heretics. But we speak, not presuming on the impossible; but with the confession of our own weakness, excluding those who wish us to cling to those things which transcend human consideration.

We confess, therefore, our Lord Jesus Christ, the Only Begotten Son of God, perfect God, and perfect Man of a reasonable soul and flesh consisting; begotten before the ages of the Father according to his Divinity, and in the last days, for us and for our salvation, of Mary the Virgin according to his humanity, of the same substance with his Father according to his Divinity, and of the same substance with us according to his humanity; for there became a union of two natures. Wherefore we confess one Christ, one Son, one Lord.

According to this understanding of this

unmixed union, we confess the holy Virgin to be Mother of God; because God the Word was incarnate and became Man, and from this conception he united the temple taken from her with himself.

For we know the theologians make some things of the Evangelical and Apostolic teaching about the Lord common as pertaining to the one person, and other things they divide as to the two natures, and attribute the worthy ones to God on account of the Divinity of Christ, and the lowly ones on account of his humanity [to his humanity].

These being your holy voices, and finding ourselves thinking the same with them ("One Lord, One Faith, One Baptism,") we glorified God the Saviour of all, congratulating one another that our churches and yours have the Faith which agrees with the God-inspired Scriptures and the traditions of our holy Fathers.

Since I learned that certain of those accustomed to find fault were humming around like vicious wasps, and vomiting out wretched words against me, as that I say the holy Body of Christ was brought from heaven, and not of the holy Virgin, I thought it necessary to say a few words concerning this to them:

O fools, and only knowing how to misrepresent, how have ye been led to such a judgment, how have ye fallen into so foolish a sickness? For it is necessary, it is undoubtedly necessary, to understand that almost all the opposition to us concerning the faith, arose from our affirming that the holy Virgin is Mother of God. But if from heaven and not from her the holy Body of the Saviour of all was born, how then is she understood to be Mother of God? What then did she bring forth except it be true that she brought forth the Emmanuel according to the flesh? They are to be laughed at who babble such things about me.

For the blessed prophet Isaiah does not lie in saying "Behold the Virgin shall conceive and bear a Son, and shall call his name Emmanuel, which being interpreted is God with us." Truly also the holy Gabriel said to the Blessed Virgin: "Fear not, Mary, for thou hast found favour with God. And, behold, thou shalt conceive in thy womb, and bring forth a Son, and shalt call his name Jesus. He shall save his people from their sins."

For when we say our Lord Jesus Christ descended from heaven, and from above, we do not so say this as if from above and from heaven was his Holy Flesh taken, but rather by way of following the divine Paul, who distinctly declares: "The first man is of the earth, earthy; the Second Man is the Lord from heaven."

We remember too, the Saviour himself saying, "And no man hath ascended up to heaven, but he that came down from heaven, even the Son of Man." Although he was born according to his flesh, as just said, of the holy Virgin, yet God the Word came down from above and from heaven. He "made himself of no reputation, and took upon him the form of a servant," and was called the Son of Man, yet remaining what he was, that is to say God. For he is unchanging and unchangeable according to nature; considered already as one with his own Flesh, he is said to have come down from heaven.

He is also called the Man from heaven, being perfect in his Divinity and perfect in his Humanity, and considered as in one Person. For one is the Lord Jesus Christ, although the difference of his natures is not unknown, from which we say the ineffable union was made.

Will your holiness vouchsafe to silence those who say that a crasis, or mingling or mixture took place between the Word of God and flesh. For it is likely that certain also gossip about me as having thought or said such things.

But I am far from any such thought as that, and I also consider them wholly to rave who think a shadow of change could occur concerning the Nature of the Word of God. For he remains that which he always was, and has not been changed, nor can he ever be changed, nor is he capable of change. For we all confess in addition to this, that the Word of God is impassible, even though when he dispenses most wisely this mystery, he appears to ascribe to himself the sufferings endured in his own flesh. To the same purpose the all-wise Peter also said when he wrote of Christ as having "suffered in the flesh," and not in the nature of his ineffable godhead. In order that he should be believed to be the Saviour of all, by an economic appropriation to himself, as just said, he assumed the sufferings of his own Flesh.

Like to this is the prophecy through the voice of the prophet, as from him, "I gave my back to the smiters, and my cheeks to them that plucked off the hair: I hid not my face from shame and spitting." Let your holiness be convinced nor let anyone else be doubtful that we altogether follow the teachings of the holy fathers, especially of our blessed and celebrated Father Athanasius, deprecating the least departure from it.

I might have added many quotations from them also establishing my words, but that it would have added to the length of my letter and it might become wearisome. And we will allow the defined Faith, the symbol of the Faith set forth by our holy Fathers who assembled some time ago at Nice, to be shaken by no one. Nor would we permit ourselves or others, to alter a single word of those set forth, or to add one syllable, remembering the saying: "Remove not the ancient landmark which thy fathers have set," for it was not they who spoke but the Spirit himself of God and the Father, who proceedeth also from him, and is not alien from the Son, according to his essence. And this the words of the holy initiators into mysteries confirm to us. For in the Acts of the Apostles it is written: "And after they were come to Mysia, they assayed to go into Bithynia; but the Spirit of Jesus suffered them not." And the divine Paul wrote: "So then they that are in the flesh cannot please God. But ye are not in the flesh, but in the Spirit, if so be that the Spirit of God dwell in you. Now if any man have not the Spirit of Christ, he is none of his."

When some of those who are accustomed to turn from the right, twist my speech to their views, I pray your holiness not to wonder; but be well assured that the followers of every heresy gather the occasions of their error from the God-inspired Scriptures, corrupting in their evil minds the things rightly said through the Holy Spirit, and drawing down upon their own heads the unquenchable flame.

Since we have learned that certain, after having corrupted it, have set forth the orthodox epistle of our most distinguished Father Athanasius to the Blessed Epictetus, so as thereby to injure many; therefore it appeared to the brethren to be useful and necessary that we should send to your holiness a copy of it from some correct ancient transcripts which exist among us. Farewell.

EXTRACTS FROM THE ACTS.

SESSION II. (continued).

(L. and C., *Conc.*, Tom. IV., col. 343.)

And when these letters [i.e. Cyril's letter to Nestorius Καταφλυαροῦσι and his letter to John of Antioch Εὐφραινέσθωσαν] had been read, the most reverend bishops cried out: We all so believe: Pope Leo thus believes: anathema to him who divides and to him who confounds: this is the faith of Archbishop Leo: Leo thus believes: Leo and Anatolius so believe: we all thus believe. As Cyril so believe we, all of us: eternal be the memory of Cyril: as the epistles of Cyril teach such is our mind, such has been our faith: such is our faith: this is the mind of Archbishop Leo, so he believes, so he has written.

The most glorious judges and the great senate said: Let there be read also the epistle of the most worthy Leo, Archbishop of Old Rome, the Imperial City.

Beronician, the most devout clerk of the sacred consistory, read from a book handed him by Aetius, Archdeacon of the holy Church of Constantinople, the encyclical or synodical letter of the most holy Leo, the Archbishop, written to Flavian, Archbishop of Constantinople.

THE TOME OF ST. LEO.

(Labbe and Cossart, *Concilia*, Tom. IV., col. 343; also Migne, *Pat. Lat.*, Tom. LIV. [Leo. M. *Opera*, Tom. I.] col. 756.)[1]

Leo [the bishop] to his [most] dear brother Flavian.

Having read your Affection's letter, the late arrival of which is matter of surprise to us, and having gone through the record of the proceedings of the bishops, we have now, at last, gained a clear view of the scandal which has risen up among you, against the integrity of the faith; and what at first seemed obscure has now been elucidated and explained. By this means Eutyches, who seemed to be deserving of honour under the title of Presbyter, is now shown to be exceedingly thoughtless and sadly inexperienced, so that to him also we may apply the prophet's words, " He refused to understand in order to act well: he meditated unrighteousness on his bed." What, indeed, is more unrighteous than to entertain ungodly thoughts, and not to yield to persons wiser and more learned? But into this folly do they fall who, when hindered by some obscurity from apprehending the truth, have recourse, not to the words of the Prophets, not to the letters of the Apostles, nor to the authority of the Gospels, but to themselves; and become teachers of error, just because they have not been disciples of the truth. For what learning has *he* received from the sacred pages of the New and the Old Testament, who does not so much as understand the very beginning of the Creed? And that which, all the world over, is uttered by the voices of all applicants for regeneration, is still not grasped by the mind of this aged man. If, then, he knew not what he ought to think about the Incarnation of the Word of God, and was not willing, for the sake of obtaining the light of intelligence, to make laborious search through the whole extent of the Holy Scriptures, he should at least have received with heedful attention that general Confession common to all, whereby the whole body of the faithful profess that they "believe in God the Father Almighty, and in Jesus Christ his only Son our Lord, who was born of the Holy Ghost and the Virgin Mary." By which three clauses the engines of almost all heretics are shattered. For when God is believed to be both " Almighty " and "Father," it is proved that the Son is everlasting together with himself, differing in nothing from the Father, because he was born as " God from God," Almighty from Almighty, Coeternal from Eternal; not later in time, not inferior in power, not unlike him in glory, not divided from him in essence, but the same Onlybegotten and Everlasting Son of an Everlasting Parent was " born of the Holy Ghost and the Virgin Mary." This birth in time in no way detracted from, in no way added to, that divine and everlasting birth; but expended itself wholly in the work of restoring man, who had been deceived; so that it might both overcome death, and by its power " destroy the devil who had the power of death." For we could not have overcome the author of sin and of death, unless he who could neither be contaminated by sin, nor detained by death, had taken upon himself our nature, and made it his own. For, in fact, he was "conceived of the Holy Ghost " within the womb of a Virgin Mother, who bore him as she had conceived him, without loss of virginity.[2] But if he (Eutyches) was not able to obtain a true conception from this pure fountain of Christian faith because by his own blindness he had darkened for himself the brightness of a truth so clear, he should have submitted himself to the Evangelist's teaching; and after reading what Matthew says, "The book of the generation of Jesus Christ, the Son of David, the Son of Abraham," he should also have sought instruction from the Apostle's preaching; and after reading in the Epistle to the Romans, " Paul, a servant of Jesus Christ, called an Apostle, separated unto the gospel of God, which he had promised before by the prophets in the Holy Scriptures, concerning

[1] The translation here given is that of Rev. Wm. Bright, D.D., found in his *Select Sermons of S. Leo the Great on the Incarnation with his XXVIIIth Epistle called the " Tome."* London, 1886.

[2] It will be noticed here that the virgin-birth is as distinctly defined as the virgin-conception.

his Son, who was made unto him of the seed of David according to the flesh," he should have bestowed some devout study on the pages of the Prophets ; and finding that God's promise said to Abraham, "in thy seed shall all nations be blessed," in order to avoid all doubt as to the proper meaning of this "seed," he should have attended to the Apostle's words, "To Abraham and to his seed were the promises made. He saith not, 'and to seeds,' as in the case of many, but as in the case of one, 'and to thy seed,' which is Christ." He should also have apprehended with his inward ear the declaration of Isaiah, "Behold, a Virgin shall conceive and bear a Son, and they shall call his name Emmanuel, which is, being interpreted, God with us ; " and should have read with faith the words of the same prophet, "Unto us a Child has been born, unto us a Son has been given, whose power is on his shoulder ; and they shall call his name Angel of great counsel, Wonderful, Counsellor, Strong God, Prince of Peace, Father of the age to come." And he should not have spoken idly to the effect that the Word was in such a sense made flesh, that the Christ who was brought forth from the Virgin's womb had the form of a man, and had not a body really derived from his Mother's body. Possibly his reason for thinking that our Lord Jesus Christ was not of our nature was this—that the Angel who was sent to the blessed and ever Virgin Mary said, "The Holy Ghost shall come upon thee, and the power of the Highest shall overshadow thee, and therefore also that holy thing which shall be born of thee shall be called the Son of God ; " as if, because the Virgin's conception was caused by a divine act, therefore the flesh of him whom she conceived was not of the nature of her who conceived him. But we are not to understand that "generation," peerlessly wonderful, and wonderfully peerless, in such a sense as that the newness of the mode of production did away with the proper character of the kind. For it was the Holy Ghost who gave fecundity to the Virgin, but it was from a body that a real body was derived ; and "when Wisdom was building herself a house," the "Word was made flesh, and dwelt among us," that is, in that flesh which he assumed from a human being, and which he animated with the spirit of rational life. Accordingly, while the distinctness of both natures and substances was preserved, and both met in one Person, lowliness was assumed by majesty, weakness by power, mortality by eternity ; and, in order to pay the debt of our condition, the inviolable nature was united to the passible, so that as the appropriate remedy for our ills, one and the same "Mediator between God and man, the Man Christ Jesus," might from one element be capable of dying and also from the other be incapable. Therefore in the entire and perfect nature of very man was born very God, whole in what was his, whole in what was ours. By "ours" we mean what the Creator formed in us at the beginning and what he assumed in order to restore ; for of that which the deceiver brought in, and man, thus deceived, admitted, there was not a trace in the Saviour ; and the fact that he took on himself a share in our infirmities did not make him a partaker in our transgressions. He assumed "the form of a servant" without the defilement of sin, enriching what was human, not impairing what was divine : because that "emptying of himself," whereby the Invisible made himself visible, and the Creator and Lord of all things willed to be one among mortals, was a stooping down in compassion, not a failure of power. Accordingly, the same who, remaining in the form of God, made man, was made man in the form of a servant. For each of the natures retains its proper character without defect ; and as the form of God does not take away the form of a servant, so the form of a servant does not impair the form of God. For since the devil was glorying in the fact that man, deceived by his craft, was bereft of divine gifts and, being stripped of his endowment of immortality, had come under the grievous sentence of death, and that he himself, amid his miseries, had found a sort of consolation in having a transgressor as his companion, and that God, according to the requirements of the principle of justice, had changed his own resolution in regard to man, whom he had created in so high a position of honour ; there was need of a dispensation of secret counsel, in order that the unchangeable God, whose will could not be deprived of its own benignity, should fulfil by a more secret mystery his original plan of loving kindness toward us, and that man, who had been led into fault by the wicked subtlety of the devil, should not perish contrary to God's purpose. Accordingly, the Son of God, descending from his seat in heaven, and not departing from the glory of the Father, enters this lower world, born after a new order, by a new mode of birth. After a new order; because he who in his own sphere is invisible, became visible in ours; He who could not be enclosed in space, willed to be enclosed; continuing to be before times, he began to exist in time; the Lord of the universe allowed his infinite majesty to be overshadowed, and took upon him the form of a servant; the impassible God did not disdain to be passible Man, and the immortal One to be subjected to the laws of death. And born by a new mode of birth; because inviolate virginity, while ignorant of concupiscence, supplied the matter of his flesh. What was assumed from the Lord's mother was nature, not fault; nor does the wondrousness of the nativity of our Lord Jesus Christ, as born of a Virgin's womb, imply that his nature is unlike ours. For the selfsame who is very God, is also very man; and there is no illusion in this union, while the lowliness of man and the loftiness of Godhead meet together. For as "God" is not changed by the compassion [exhibited], so "Man" is not consumed by the dignity [bestowed]. For each "form" does the acts which belong to it, in communion with the other; the Word, that is, performing what belongs to the Word, and the flesh carrying out what belongs to the flesh; the one of these shines out in miracles, the other succumbs to injuries. And as the Word does not withdraw from equality with the Father in glory, so the flesh does not abandon the nature of our kind. For, as we must often be saying, he is one and the same, truly Son of God, and truly Son of Man. God, inasmuch as "in the beginning was the Word, and the Word was with God, and the Word was God." Man, inasmuch as "the Word was made flesh, and dwelt among us." God, inasmuch as "all things were made by him, and without him nothing was made." Man, inasmuch as he was "made of a woman, made under the law." The nativity of the flesh is a manifestation of human nature; the Virgin's child-bearing is an indication of Divine power. The infancy of the Babe is exhibited by the humiliation of swaddling clothes: the greatness of the Highest is declared by the voices of angels. He whom Herod impiously designs to slay is like humanity in its beginnings; but he whom the Magi rejoice to adore on their knees is Lord of all. Now when he came to the baptism of John his forerunner, lest the fact that the Godhead was covered with a veil of flesh should be concealed, the voice of the Father spake in thunder from heaven, "This is my beloved Son, in whom I am well pleased." Accordingly, he who, as man, is tempted by the devil's subtlety, is the same to whom, as God, angels pay duteous service. To hunger, to thirst, to be weary, and to sleep, is evidently human. But to satisfy five thousand men with five loaves, and give to the Samaritan woman that living water, to draw which can secure him that drinks of it from ever thirsting again; to walk on the surface of the sea with feet that sink not, and by rebuking the storm to bring down the "uplifted waves," is unquestionably Divine. As then—to pass by many points —it does not belong to the same nature to weep with feelings of pity over a dead friend and, after the mass of stone had been removed from the grave where he had lain four days, by a voice of command to raise him up to life again; or to hang on the wood, and to make all the elements tremble after daylight had been turned into night; or to be transfixed with nails, and to open the gates of paradise to the faith of the robber; so it does not belong to the same nature to say, "I and the Father are one," and to say, "the Father is greater than I." For although in the Lord Jesus Christ there is one Person of God and man, yet that whereby contumely attaches to both is one thing, and that whereby glory attaches to both is another; for from what belongs to us he has that manhood which is inferior to the Father; while from the Father he has equal Godhead with the Father. Accordingly, on account of this unity of Person which is to be understood as existing in both the natures, we read, on the one hand, that "the Son of Man came down from heaven," inasmuch as the Son of God took flesh from that Virgin of whom he was born; and on the other hand, the Son of God is said to have been crucified and buried, inasmuch as he underwent this, not in his actual Godhead; wherein the Only-begotten is coeternal and consubstantial with the Father, but in the weakness of human nature. Wherefore we all, in the very Creed, confess that "the only-begotten Son of God was crucified and buried," according to that saying of the Apostle, "for if they had known it, they would not have crucified the Lord of Majesty." But when our Lord and Saviour himself was by his questions instructing the faith of the disciples, he said, "Whom do men say that I the Son of Man am?" And when they had mentioned various opinions held by others, he said, "But whom say ye that I am?" that is, "I who am Son of Man, and whom you see in the form of a servant, and in reality of flesh, whom say ye that I am?" Whereupon the blessed Peter, as inspired by God, and about to benefit all nations by his confession, said, "Thou art the Christ, the Son of the living God." Not undeservedly, therefore, was he pronounced blessed by the Lord, and derived from the original Rock that solidity which belonged both to his virtue and to his name, who through revelation from the Father confessed the selfsame to be both the Son of God and the Christ; because one of these truths, accepted without the other, would not profit unto salvation, and it was equally dangerous to believe the Lord Jesus Christ to be merely God and not man, or merely man and not God. But after the resurrection of the Lord—which was in truth the resurrection of a real body, for no other person was raised again than he who had been crucified and had died—what else was accomplished during that interval of forty days than to make our faith entire and clear of all darkness? For while he conversed with his disciples, and dwelt with them, and ate with them, and allowed himself to be handled with careful and inquisitive touch by those who were under the influence of doubt, for this end he came in to the disciples when the doors were shut, and by his breath gave them the Holy Ghost, and opened the secrets of Holy Scripture after bestowing on them the light of intelligence, and again in his selfsame person showed to them the wound in the side, the prints of the nails, and all the fresh tokens of the Passion, saying, "Behold my hands and my feet, that it is I myself; handle me and see, for a spirit hath not flesh and bones, as ye see me

have:" that the properties of the Divine and the human nature might be acknowledged to remain in him without causing a division, and that we might in such sort know that the Word is not what the flesh is, as to confess that the one Son of God is both Word and flesh. On which mystery of the faith this Eutyches must be regarded as unhappily having no hold, who does not recognise our nature to exist in the Only-begotten Son of God, either by way of the lowliness of mortality, or of the glory of resurrection. Nor has he been overawed by the declaration of the blessed Apostle and Evangelist John, saying, "Every spirit that confesseth that Jesus Christ has come in the flesh is of God; and every spirit which dissolveth Jesus is not of God, and this is Antichrist." Now what is to dissolve Jesus, but to separate the human nature from him, and to make void by shameless inventions that mystery by which alone we have been saved? Moreover, being in the dark as to the nature of Christ's body, he must needs be involved in the like senseless blindness with regard to his Passion also. For if he does not think the Lord's crucifixion to be unreal, and does not doubt that he really accepted suffering, even unto death, for the sake of the world's salvation; as he believes in his death, let him acknowledge his flesh also, and not doubt that he whom he recognises as having been capable of suffering is also Man with a body like ours; since to deny his true flesh is also to deny his bodily sufferings. If then he accepts the Christian faith, and does not turn away his ear from the preaching of the Gospel, let him see what nature it was that was transfixed with nails and hung on the wood of the cross; and let him understand whence it was that, after the side of the Crucified had been pierced by the soldier's spear, blood and water flowed out, that the Church of God might be refreshed both with a Laver and with a Cup. Let him listen also to the blessed Apostle Peter when he declares, that "sanctification by the Spirit" takes place through the "sprinkling of the blood of Christ," and let him not give a mere cursory reading to the words of the same Apostle, "Knowing that ye were not redeemed with corruptible things, as silver and gold, from your vain way of life received by tradition from your fathers, but with the precious blood of Jesus

Christ as of a Lamb without blemish and without spot." Let him also not resist the testimony of Blessed John the Apostle, "And the blood of Jesus the Son of God cleanseth us from all sin." And again, "This is the victory which overcometh the world, even our faith;" and, "who is he that overcometh the world, but he that believeth that Jesus is the Son of God? This is he that came by water and blood, even Jesus Christ; not in water only, but in water and blood; and it is the Spirit that beareth witness, because the Spirit is truth. For there are three that bear witness—the Spirit, the water, and the blood; and the three are one." That is, the Spirit of sanctification, and the blood of redemption, and the water of baptism; which three things are one, and remain undivided, and not one of them is disjoined from connection with the others; because the Catholic Church lives and advances by this faith, that in Christ Jesus we should believe neither manhood to exist without true Godhead, nor Godhead without true manhood. But when Eutyches, on being questioned in your examination of him, answered, "I confess that our Lord was of two natures before the union, but after the union I confess one nature;" I am astonished that so absurd and perverse a profession as this of his was not rebuked by a censure on the part of any of his judges, and that an utterance extremely foolish and extremely blasphemous was passed over, just as if nothing had been heard which could give offence: seeing that it is as impious to say that the Only-begotten Son of God was of two natures before the Incarnation as it is shocking to affirm that, since the Word became flesh, there has been in him one nature only. But lest Eutyches should think that what he said was correct, or was tolerable, because it was not confuted by any assertion of yours, we exhort your earnest solicitude, dearly beloved brother, to see that, if by God's merciful inspiration the case is brought to a satisfactory issue, the inconsiderate and inexperienced man be cleansed also from this pestilent notion of his; seeing that, as the record of the proceedings has clearly shown, he had fairly begun to abandon his own opinion when on being driven into a corner by authoritative words of yours, he professed himself ready to say what he had not said before, and to give his adhesion to that faith from which he had previously stood aloof. But when he would not consent to anathematize the impious dogma you understood, brother, that he continued in his own misbelief, and deserved to receive sentence of condemnation. For which if he grieves sincerely and to good purpose, and understands, even though too late, how properly the Episcopal authority has been put in motion, or if, in order to make full satisfaction, he shall condemn *viva voce*, and under his own hand, all that he has held amiss, no compassion, to whatever extent, which can be shown him when he has been set right, will be worthy of blame, for our Lord, the true and good Shepherd, who laid down his life for his sheep, and who came to save men's souls and not to destroy them, wills us to imitate his own loving kindness; so that justice should indeed constrain those who sin, but mercy should not reject those who are converted. For then indeed is the true faith defended with the best results, when a false opinion is condemned even by those who have followed it. But in order that the whole matter may be piously and faithfully carried out, we have appointed our brethren, Julius, Bishop, and Reatus, Presbyter (of the title of St. Clement) and also my son Hilarus, Deacon, to represent us; and with them we have associated Dulcitius, our Notary, of whose fidelity we have had good proof: trusting that the Divine assistance will be with you, so that he who has gone astray may be saved by condemning his own unsound opinion. May God keep you in good health, dearly beloved brother. Given on the Ides of June, in the Consulate of the illustrious men, Asterius and Protogenes.

[*Next was read a long catena of quotations from the Fathers sustaining the teaching of the Tome.* (L. and C., *Conc.*, Tom. IV., cols. 357–368.)]

EXTRACTS FROM THE ACTS.

SESSION II. (continued).

(Labbe and Cossart, Concilia, Tom. IV., col. 368.)

After the reading of the foregoing epistle, the most reverend bishops cried out: This is the faith of the fathers, this is the faith of the Apostles. So we all believe, thus the orthodox believe. Anathema to him who does not thus believe. Peter has spoken thus through Leo. So taught the Apostles. Piously and truly did Leo teach, so taught Cyril. Everlasting be the memory of Cyril. Leo and Cyril taught the same thing, anathema to him who does not so believe. This is the true faith. Those of us who are orthodox thus believe. This is the faith of the fathers. Why were not these things read at Ephesus [i.e. at the heretical synod held there]? These are the things Dioscorus hid away.

[*Some explanations were asked by the Illyrian bishops and the answers were found satisfactory, but yet a delay of a few days was asked for, and some bishops petitioned for a general pardon of all who had been kept out. This proposition made great confusion, in the midst of which the session was dissolved by the judges.* (Col. 371.)]

SESSION III.

[*The imperial representatives do not seem to have been present, and after Aetius the Archdeacon of Constantinople had opened the Session,*]

Paschasinus the bishop of Lilybæum, in the province of Silicia, and holding the place of the most holy Leo, archbishop of the Apostolic see of old Rome, said in Latin what being interpreted is as follows: It is well known to this beloved of God synod, that divine[1] letters were sent to the blessed and apostolic pope Leo, inviting him to deign to be present at the holy synod. But since ancient custom did not sanction this, nor the general necessity of the time seemed to permit it, our littleness in the place of himself he τὰ τῆς ἁγίας συνόδου ἐπέτρεψε, and therefore it is necessary that whatever things are brought into discussion should be examined by our interference (διαλαλιᾶς). [The Latin reads where I have placed the Greek of the ordinary text, thus, "commanded our littleness to preside in his place over this holy council."] Therefore let the book presented by our most beloved-of-God brother, and fellow-bishop Eusebius be received, and read by the beloved of God archdeacon and primicerius of the notaries, Aetius.

And Aetius, the archdeacon and primicerius of the notaries, took the book and read as follows.

[*Next follows the petition of Eusebius* et post nonnulla *four petitions each addressed to* "The most holy and beloved-of-God ecumenical archbishop and patriarch of great Rome Leo, and to the holy and ecumenical Synod assembled at Chalcedon, etc., etc.;" *The first two by deacons of Alexandria, the third by a quondam presbyter of the diocese, and the fourth by a layman also of Alexandria. After this Dioscorus was again summoned and, as he did not come, sentence was given against him, which was communicated to him in a letter contained in the acts.* (L. and C., Conc., Tom IV., col. 418.) *The Bishops expressed their opinions for the most part one by one, but the Roman Legates spoke together, and in their speech occurs the following* (Col. 426 :)]

Wherefore the most holy and blessed Leo, archbishop of the great and elder Rome, through us, and through this present most holy synod together with[2] the thrice blessed and all-glorious Peter the Apostle, who is the rock and foundation of the Catholic Church, and the foundation of

---

[1] i. e. Imperial.

[2] The translation of the English Hefele (iv. 328) "in communion with" is most extraordinary.

the orthodox faith, hath stripped him of the episcopate, and hath alienated from him all hieratic worthiness. Therefore let this most holy and great synod sentence the before mentioned Dioscorus to the canonical penalties.

[*The bishops then, one by one, spoke in favour of the deposition of Dioscorus, but usually on the ground of his refusal to appear when thrice summoned.*]

And when all the most holy bishops had spoken on the subject, they signed this which follows.

THE CONDEMNATION SENT BY THE HOLY AND ECUMENICAL SYNOD TO DIOSCORUS.

(Labbe and Cossart, *Concilia*, Tom. IV., col. 459.)

The holy and great and ecumenical Synod, which by the grace of God according to the constitution of our most pious and beloved of God emperors assembled together at Chalcedom the city of Bithynia, in the martyry of the most holy and victorious Martyr Euphemia to Dioscorus.

We do you to wit that on the thirteenth day of the month of October you were deposed from the episcopate and made a stranger to all ecclesiastical order (θεσμοῦ) by the holy and ecumenical synod, on account of your disregard of the divine canons, and of your disobedience to this holy and ecumenical synod and on account of the other crimes of which you have been found guilty, for even when called to answer your accusers three times by this holy and great synod according to the divine canons you did not come.

EXTRACTS FROM THE ACTS.

SESSION IV.

(Labbe and Cossart, *Concilia*, Tom. IV., col. 469.)

The most magnificent and glorious judges and the great Senate said:

Let the reverend council now declare what seems good concerning the faith, since those things which have already been disposed of have been made manifest. Paschasinus and Lucentius, the most reverend bishops, and Boniface the most reverend presbyter, legates of the Apostolic See, through that most reverend man, bishop Paschasinus said: As the holy and blessed and Ecumenical Synod holds fast and follows the rule of faith (*fidei regulam* in the Latin Acts) which was set forth by the fathers at Nice, it also confirms the faith set forth by the Synod of 150 fathers gathered at Constantinople at the bidding of the great Theodosius of blessed memory. Moreover the exposition of their faith, of the illustrious Cyril of blessed memory set forth at the Council of Ephesus (in which Nestorius was condemned) is received. And in the third place the writings of that blessed man, Leo, Archbishop of all the churches, who condemned the heresy of Nestorius and Eutyches, shew what the true faith is. Likewise the holy Synod holds this faith, this it follows—nothing further can it add nor can it take aught away.

When this had been translated into Greek by Beronician, the devout secretary of the divine consistory, the most reverend bishops cried out: So we all believe, so we were baptized, so we baptize, so we have believed, so we now believe.

The most glorious judges and the great senate said: Since we see that the Holy Gospels have been placed alongside of your holiness, let each one of the bishops here assembled declare whether the epistle of most blessed archbishop Leo is in accordance with the exposition of the 318 fathers assembled at Nice and with the decrees of the 150 fathers afterwards assembled in the royal city.

[*To this question the bishops answered one by one, until 161 separate opinions had been given, when the rest of the bishops were asked* by *the imperial judges to give their votes in a body (col. 508).*]

All the most reverend bishops cried out: We all acquiesce, we all believe thus; we are all of the same mind. So are we minded, so we believe, etc., etc.

SESSION V.

(Labbe and Cossart, *Concilia*, Tom. IV., col. 555.)

Paschasinus and Lucentius the most reverend bishops and Boniface a presbyter, vicars of the Apostolic See of Rome, said: If they do not agree to the letter of that apostolic and blessed man, Pope Leo, give directions that we be given our letters of dismission, and let a synod be held there [i. e. in the West].

[*A long debate then followed as to whether the decree drawn up and presented should be accepted. This seems to have been the mind of most of the bishops. At last the commissioners proposed a committee of twenty-two to meet with them and report to the council, and the Emperor imposed this with the threat that otherwise they all should be sent home and a new council called in the West. Even this did not make them yield* (col. 560.)]

The most reverend bishops cried out: Many years to the Emperor! Either let the definition [i.e. the one presented at this session] stand or we go. Many years to the Emperor!

Cecropius, the most reverend bishop of Sebastopol, said: We ask that the definition be read again and that those who dissent from it, and will not sign, may go about their business; for we give our consent to these things which have been so beautifully drafted, and make no criticisms.

The most blessed bishops of Illyria said: Let those who contradict be made manifest. Those who contradict are Nestorians. Those who contradict, let them go to Rome.

The most magnificent and most glorious judges said: Dioscorus acknowledged that he accepted the expression "of two natures," but not that there were two natures. But the most holy archbishop Leo says that there are two natures in Christ unchangeably, inseparably, unconfusedly united in the one only-begotten Son our Saviour. Which would you follow, the most holy Leo or Dioscorus?

The most reverend bishops cried out: We believe as Leo. Those who contradict are Eutychians. Leo hath rightly expounded the faith.

The most magnificent and glorious judges said: Add then to the definition, according to the judgment of our most holy father Leo, that there are two natures in Christ united unchangeably, inseparably, unconfusedly.

[*The Committee then sat in the oratory of the most holy martyr Euphemis and afterwards reported a definition of faith which while teaching the same doctrine was not the Tome of Leo* (col. 562).]

THE DEFINITION OF FAITH OF THE COUNCIL OF CHALCEDON.

(Labbe and Cossart, *Concilia*, Tom. IV., col. 562.)

The holy, great, and ecumenical synod, assembled by the grace of God and the command of our most religious and Christian Emperors, Marcian and Valentinan, Augusti, at Chalcedon, the metropolis of the Bithynian Province, in the martyry of the holy and victorious martyr Euphemia, has decreed as follows:

Our Lord and Saviour Jesus Christ, when strengthening the knowledge of the Faith in his disciples, to the end that no one might disagree with his neighbour concerning the doctrines of religion, and that the proclamation of the truth might be set forth equally to all men, said, "My peace I leave with you, my peace I give unto you." But, since the evil one does not desist from sowing tares among the seeds of godliness, but ever invents some new device against the truth; therefore the Lord, providing, as he ever does, for the human race, has raised up this pious, faithful, and zealous Sovereign, and has called together unto him from all parts the chief rulers of the priesthood; so that, the grace of Christ our common Lord inspiring us, we may cast off every plague of falsehood from the sheep of Christ, and feed them with the tender leaves of truth. And this have we done with one unanimous consent, driving away erroneous doctrines and renewing the unerring faith of the Fathers, publishing to all men the Creed of the Three Hundred and Eighteen, and to their number adding, as their peers, the Fathers who have received the same summary of religion. Such are the One Hundred and Fifty holy Fathers who afterwards assembled in the great Constantinople and ratified the same faith. Moreover, observing the order and every form relating to the faith, which was observed by the holy synod formerly held in Ephesus, of which Celestine of Rome and Cyril of Alexandria, of holy memory, were the leaders, we do declare that the exposition of the right and blameless faith made by the Three Hundred and Eighteen holy and blessed Fathers, assembled at Nice in the reign of Constantine of pious memory, shall be pre-eminent: and that those things shall be of force also,

NOTES.

ANATOLIUS OF CONSTANTINOPLE.

(Ep. to St. Leo. Migne, *Pat. Lat.*, Tom. LIV. [Leo. M., *Opera*, Tom. I.] col. 978.)

Since after judgment had been delivered concerning him, there was need that all should agree in the right faith (for which purpose the most pious emperor had with the greatest pains assembled the holy Synod) with prayer and tears, your holiness being present with us in spirit and co-operating with us through those most God-beloved men whom you had sent to us, having as our protector the most holy and most comely Martyr Euphemia, we gave ourselves up entirely to this salutary work, all other matters being laid aside. And when the crisis demanded that all the most holy bishops gathered together should set forth an unanimous definition (σύμφωνον ὅρον) for the explanation and clearer understanding of our confession of our Lord Jesus Christ, our Lord God was found appearing to them that sought him not, and even to them that asked not for him. And although some from the beginning contentiously made opposition, he shewed forth nevertheless his truth and so disposed things that an unanimous and uncontradicted writing was published by us all, which confirmed the souls of the stable, and inviting to the way of truth all who had declined therefrom. And when we had subscribed with unanimous consent the chart, we all with one consent, that is our whole synod, entered the martyry of the most holy and triumphant martyr Euphemia, and when at the prayer of our most pious and beloved of Christ Emperor Marcian, and of our most pious and in all respects faithful Empress, our daughter and Augusta Pulcheria, with joy, and hilarity we placed upon the holy altar the decision which we had written for the confirmation of the faith of our fathers in accordance with that holy letter you sent us; and then handed it to their piety, that they might receive it as they had asked for it. And when they had received it they gave glory with us to Christ the Lord, who had driven away the darkness of wicked opinion, and had illustrated with the greatest unanimity the word of truth, etc.

which were decreed by the One Hundred and Fifty holy Fathers at Constantinople, for the uprooting of the heresies which had then sprung up, and for the confirmation of the same Catholic and Apostolic Faith of ours.

The Creed of the three hundred and eighteen Fathers at Nice.

We believe in one God, etc.

Item, the Creed of the one hundred and fifty holy Fathers who were assembled at Constantinople.

We believe in one God, etc.

This wise and salutary formula of divine grace sufficed for the perfect knowledge and confirmation of religion; for it teaches the perfect [doctrine] concerning Father, Son, and Holy Ghost, and sets forth the Incarnation of the Lord to them that faithfully receive it. But, forasmuch as persons undertaking to make void the preaching of the truth have through their individual heresies given rise to empty babblings; some of them daring to corrupt the mystery of the Lord's incarnation for us and refusing [to use] the name Mother of God (Θεοτοκος) in reference to the Virgin, while others, bringing in a confusion and mixture, and idly conceiving that the nature of the flesh and of the Godhead is all one, maintaining that the divine Nature of the Only Begotten is, by mixture, capable of suffering; therefore this present holy, great, and ecumenical synod, desiring to exclude every device against the Truth, and teaching that which is unchanged from the beginning, has at the very outset decreed that the faith of the Three Hundred and Eighteen Fathers shall be preserved inviolate. And on account of them that contend against the Holy Ghost, it confirms the doctrine afterwards delivered concerning the substance of the Spirit by the One Hundred and Fifty holy Fathers who assembled in the imperial City; which doctrine they declared unto all men, not as though they were introducing anything that had been lacking in their predecessors, but in order to explain through written documents their faith concerning the Holy Ghost against those who were seeking to destroy his sovereignty. And,

From this passage can easily be understood the very obscure passage in the letter of the Council to Leo, where it says that the definition was delivered by St. Euphemia as her own confession of faith. *Vide* note of the Ballerini on this epistle of Anatolius.

HEFELE.

(*Hist. of the Councils.* Vol. III., p. 348.)

The present Greek text has ἐκ δύο φύσεων while the old Latin translation has, *in duabus naturis.* After what had been repeatedly said in this session on the difference between "in two natures" and "of two natures," and in opposition to the latter formula, there can be no doubt whatever that the old Latin translator had the more accurate text before him, and that it was originally ἐν δύο φύσεσιν. This, however, is not mere supposition, but is expressly testified by antiquity: (1) by the famous Abbot Euthymius of Palestine, a contemporary of the Council of Chalcedon, of whose disciples several were present as bishops at our Council (cf. Baron. *ad. ann.* 451, n. 152 sq.). We still have a judgment of his which he gave respecting the decree of Chalcedon concerning the faith, and in which he repeats the leading doctrine in the words of the Synod itself. At our passage he remarks : ἐν δύο φύσεσι γνωρίζεσθαι ὁμολογεῖ τὸν ἕνα Χριστὸν κ. τ. λ. The fragment of his writings on the subject is found in the Vita S. Euthymii Abbatis, written by his pupil Cyril in the *Analecta Græca* of the monks of St. Maur, t. i., p. 57, printed in Mansi, t. vii., p. 774 sq. (2) The second ancient witness is Severus, from A.D. 513 Monophysite patriarch of Antioch, who represents it as a great reproach and an unpardonable offence in the fathers of Chalcedon that they had declared : ἐν δύο φύσεσιν ἀδιαιρέτοις γνωρίζεσθαι τον Χριστὸν (see the *Sententiæ Severi* in Mansi, t. vii., p. 839). (3) Somewhat more than a hundred years after the Council of Chalcedon, Evagrius copied its decree concerning the faith *in extenso* into his *Church History* (lib. ii., 4), and, in fact, with the words : ἐν δύο φύσεσιν ἀσυγχύτως κ. τ. λ. (ed. Mog., p. 294). (4) In the conference on religion held between the Severians and the orthodox at Constantinople, A.D. 553, the former reproached the Synod of Chalcedon with having put *in duabus naturis,* instead of *ex duabus naturis,* as Cyril and the old fathers had taught (Mansi, t. viii., p. 892 ; Hardouin, t. ii., p. 1162). (5) Leontius of Byzantium maintains quite on account of those who have taken in hand to corrupt the mystery of the dispensation [i.e. the Incarnation] and who shamelessly pretend that he who was born of the holy Virgin Mary was a mere man, it receives the synodical letters of the Blessed Cyril, Pastor of the Church of Alexandria, addressed to Nestorius and the Easterns, judging them suitable, for the refutation of the frenzied folly of Nestorius, and for the instruction of those who long with holy ardour for a knowledge of the saving symbol.   And, for the confirmation of the orthodox doctrines, it has rightly added to these the letter of the President of the great and old Rome, the most blessed and holy Archbishop Leo, which was addressed to Archbishop Flavian of blessed memory, for the removal of the false doctrines of Eutyches, judging them to be agreeable to the confession of the great Peter, and as it were a common pillar against misbelievers.   For it opposes those who would rend the mystery of the dispensation into a Duad of Sons; it repels from the sacred assembly those who dare to say that the Godhead of the Only Begotten is capable of suffering; it resists those who imagine a mixture or confusion of the two natures of Christ; it drives away those who fancy his form of a servant is of an heavenly or some substance other than that which was taken of us, and it anathematizes those who foolishly talk of two natures of our Lord before the union, conceiving that after the union there was only one.

Following the holy Fathers we teach with one voice that the Son [of God] and our Lord Jesus Christ is to be confessed as one and the same [Person], that he is perfect in Godhead and perfect in manhood, very God and very man, of a reasonable soul and [human] body consisting, consubstantial with the Father as touching his Godhead, and consubstantial with us as touching his manhood; made in all things like unto us, sin only excepted; begotten of his Father before the worlds according to his Godhead; but in these last days for us men and for our salvation born [into the world] of the Virgin Mary, the Mother of God according to his manhood.   This one and the same Jesus Christ, the only-begotten Son [of God] must be confessed to be in two natures,[1] unconfusedly, immutably, indivisibly,

distinctly, in the year 610, in his work *De Sectis*, that the Synod taught ἕνα Χριστὸν ἐν δύο φύσεσιν ἀσυγχύτως κ. π. λ.

It is clear that if any doubt had then existed as to the correct reading, Leontius could not have opposed the Monophysites with such certainty.   The passage adduced by him is *Actio* iv., c. 7., in Galland.   *Bibliotheca PP.*, t. xii., p. 633.   Gieseler (*Kirchengesch.* i., S. 465), and after him Hahn (*Biblioth. der Symbole*, S. 118, note 6), cites incorrectly the fourth instead of the fifth *Actio*.   Perhaps neither of them had consulted the passage itself.   (6) No less weight is to be attached to the fact that all the Latin translations, that of Rusticus and those before him, have *in duabus naturis*; and (7) that the Lateran Synod, A.D. 649, had the same reading in their Acts (Hardouin, t. iii., p. 835).   (8) Pope Agatho, also, in his letter to the Emperor Constans II., which was read in the sixth Ecumenical Synod, adduced the creed of Chalcedon with the words *in duabus naturis* (in the Acts of the sixth Ecumenical Council, *Actio* iv.; in Mansi, t. xi., p. 256; Hardouin, t. iii., p. 1091).   In consequence of this, most scholars of recent times, e. g., Tillemont, Walch (*Bibloth. symbol veter.*, p. 106), Hahn (l. c.), Gieseler (l. c.), Neander (Abthl. ii., 2 of Bd. iv., S. 988), have declared ἐν δύο φύσεσιν to be the original and correct reading. Neander adds: "The whole process of the transactions of the Council shows this (that ἐν δύο is the correct reading).   Evidently the earlier creed, which was more favourable to the Egyptian doctrine, contained the ἐκ δύο φύσεων and the favour shown to the other party came out chiefly in the change of the ἐκ into ἐν.   The expression ἐκ δύο φύσεων besides, does not fit the place, the verb γνωριζόμενον points rather to the original ἐν. The ἐν δύο φύσεσιν or ἐκ δύο φύσεων was the turning-point of the whole controversy between Monophysitism and Dyophysitism." Cf., on the other side, Baur, *Trinitätslehre*, Bd. i., S. 820, and Dorner (*Lehre v. der Person Christi*, Thl. ii., S. 129), where it is maintained that ἐκ is the correct and original reading, but that it was from the beginning purposely altered by the Westerns into *in*; moreover, that ἐκ fits better than ἐν with γνωριζόμενον, and therefore that it had been allowed as a concession to the Monophysites. The meaning, moreover, they say, of ἐκ and ἐν is essentially the same, and the one and the other alike excluded Monophysitism.

---

[1] *Vide* parallel note from Hefele.

inseparably [united], and that without the distinction of natures being taken away by such union, but rather the peculiar property of each nature being preserved and being united in one Person and subsistence, not separated or divided into two persons, but one and the same Son and only-begotten, God the Word, our Lord Jesus Christ, as the Prophets of old time have spoken concerning him, and as the Lord Jesus Christ hath taught us, and as the Creed of the Fathers hath delivered to us.

These things, therefore, having been expressed by us with the greatest accuracy and attention, the holy Ecumenical Synod defines that no one shall be suffered to bring forward a different faith (ἑτέραν πίστιν), nor to write, nor to put together, nor to excogitate, nor to teach it to others. But such as dare either to put together another faith, or to bring forward or to teach or to deliver a different Creed (ἕτερον σύμβολον) to such as wish to be converted to the knowledge of the truth from the Gentiles, or Jews or any heresy whatever, if they be Bishops or clerics let them be deposed, the Bishops from the Episcopate, and the clerics from the clergy; but if they be monks or laics: let them be anathematized.

After the reading of the definition, all the most religious Bishops cried out: This is the faith of the fathers: let the metropolitans forthwith subscribe it: let them forthwith, in the presence of the judges, subscribe it: let that which has been well defined have no delay: this is the faith of the Apostles: by this we all stand: thus we all believe.

EXTRACTS FROM THE ACTS.

SESSION VI.

(Labbe and Cossart, *Concilia*, Tom. IV., col. 611.)

[*The Emperor was present in person and addressed the Council and afterwards suggested legislation under three heads, the drafts for which were read.*]

After this reading, the capitulas were handed by our most sacred and pious prince to the most beloved of God Anatolius, archbishop of royal Constantinople, which is New Rome, and all the most God-beloved bishops cried out: Many years to our Emperor and Empress, the pious, the Christian. May Christ whom thou servest keep thee. These things are worthy of the faith. To the Priest, the Emperor. Thou hast straightened out the churches, victor of thine enemies, teacher of the faith. Many years to the pious Empress, the lover of Christ. Many years to her that is orthodox. May God save your kingdom. Ye have put down the heretics, ye have kept the faith. May hatred be far removed from your empire, and may your kingdom endure for ever!

Our most sacred and pious prince said to the holy synod: To the honour of the holy martyr Euphemia, and of your holiness, we decree that the city of Chalcedon, in which the synod of the holy faith has been held, shall have the honours of a metropolis, in name only giving it this honour, the proper dignity of the city of Nicomedia being preserved.

All cried out, etc., etc.

DECREE ON THE JURISDICTION OF JERUSALEM AND ANTIOCH.

SESSION VII.

(Labbe and Cossart, *Concilia*, Tom. IV., col. 618.)

The most magnificent and glorious judges said: . . . The arrangement arrived at through the agreement of the most holy Maximus, the bishop of the city of Antioch, and of the most holy Juvenal, the bishop of Jerusalem, as the attestation of each of them declares, shall remain firm for ever, through our decree and the sentence of the holy synod; to wit, that the most holy bishop Maximus, or rather the most holy church of Antioch, shall have under its own jurisdiction the two Phœnicias and Arabia; but the most holy Juvenal, bishop of Jerusalem, or rather the most holy Church which is under him, shall have under his own power the three Palestines, all imperial pragmatics and letters and penalties being done away according to the bidding of our most sacred and pious prince.

NOTE.

The Ballerini, in their notes to the Works of St. Leo (Migne, *Pat. Lat.*, LV., col. 733 *et seqq.*), cite fragments of the Acts of this council, which if they can be trusted, shew that this matter of the rights of Antioch and Jerusalem was treated of again at a subsequent session (on Oct. 31) and determined in the same fashion. These fragments have generally been received as genuine, and have been inserted by Mansi (Tom. vii., 722 C.) in his *Concilia*.

The notes of the Ballerini may also be read with profit, in the same volume of Migne's *Latin Patrology*, col. 737 *et seq.*

THE DECREE WITH REGARD TO THE BISHOP OF EPHESUS.

SESSION XII.

(Labbe and Cossart, *Concilia*, Tom. IV., col. 706.)

The most glorious judges said: Since the proposition of the God-beloved archbishop of royal Constantinople, Anatolius, and of the most reverend bishop Paschasinus, holding the place of Leo, the most God-beloved archbishop of old Rome, which orders that because both of them [i.e., Bassianus and Stephen] acted uncanonically, neither of them should rule, nor be called bishop of the most holy church of Ephesus, and since the whole holy synod taught that uncanonically they had performed these ordinations, and had agreed with the speeches of the most reverend bishops; the most reverend Bassianus and the most reverend Stephen will be removed from the holy church of Ephesus; but they shall enjoy the episcopal dignity, and from the revenues of the before-mentioned most holy church, for their nourishment and consolation, they shall receive each year two hundred gold pieces; and another bishop shall be ordained according to the canons for the most holy church.[1]

And the whole holy synod cried out: This is a just sentence. This is a pious scheme. These things are fair to look upon.

The most reverend bishop Bassianus said: Pray give order that what was stolen from me be restored.

The most glorious judges said: If anything belonging to the most reverend bishop Bassianus personally has been taken from him, either by the most reverend bishop Stephen, or by any other persons whatsoever, this shall be restored, after judicial proof, by them who took it away or caused it to be taken.

---

[1] The English translation of Hefele asserts twice (*Hist. of the Councils*, Vol. III., pp. 173 and 376), that Bassianus was "deposed." This is entirely a mistake, he was deprived of his diocese, but retained his episcopal rank.

DECREE WITH REGARD TO NICOMEDIA.

SESSION XIII.

(Labbe and Cossart, *Concilia*, Tom. IV., col. 715.)

The most glorious judges said [after the reading of the imperial letters was finished]: These divine letters say nothing whatever with regard to the episcopate, but both refer to honour belonging to metropolitan cities. But the sacred letters of Valentinian and Valens of divine memory, which then bestowed metropolitan rights upon the city of Nice, carefully provided that nothing should be taken away from other cities. And the canon of the holy fathers decreed that there should be one metropolis in each province. What therefore is the pleasure of the holy synod in this matter?

The holy synod cried out: Let the canons be kept. Let the canons be sufficient.

Atticus the most reverend bishop of old Nicopolis in Epirus said: The canon thus defines, that a metropolitan should have jurisdiction in each province, and he should constitute all the bishops who are in that province. And this is the meaning of the canon. Now the bishop of Nicomedia, since from the beginning this was a metropolis, ought to ordain all the bishops who are in that province.

The holy synod said: This is what we all wish, this we all pray for, let this everywhere be observed, this is pleasing to all of us.

John, Constantine, Patrick [Peter] and the rest of the most reverend bishops of the Pontic diocese [through John who was one of them] said: The canons recognize the one more ancient as the metropolitan. And it is manifest that the most religious bishop of Nicomedia has the right of the ordination, and since the laws (as your magnificence has seen) have honoured Nice with the name only of metropolis, and so made its bishop superior to the rest of the bishops of the province in honour only.

The holy synod said: They have taught in accordance with the canons, beautifully have they taught. We all say the same things.

[*Aetius, Archdeacon of Constantinople, then put in a plea to save the rights of the throne of the royal city.*]

The most glorious judges said: The most reverend the bishop of Nicomedia shall have the authority of metropolitan over the churches of the province of Bithynia, and Nice shall have the honour only of Metropolitical rank, submitting itself according to the example of the other bishops of the province of Nicomedia. For such is the pleasure of the Holy Synod.

THE XXX CANONS OF THE HOLY AND FOURTH SYNODS, OF CHALCEDON.

CANON I.

WE have judged it right that the canons of the Holy Fathers made in every synod even until now, should remain in force.

NOTES.

ANCIENT EPITOME OF CANON I.

The canons of every Synod of the holy Fathers shall be observed.

HEFELE.

Before the holding of the Council of Chalcedon, in the Greek Church, the canons of several synods, which were held previously, were gathered into one collection and provided with continuous numbers, and such a collection of canons, as we have seen, lay before the Synod of Chalcedon. As, however, most of the synods whose canons were received into the collection, *e.g.* those of Neocæsarea, Ancyra, Gangra, Antioch, were certainly not Ecumenical Councils, and were even to some extent of doubtful authority, such as the Antiochene Synod of 341, the confirmation of the Ecumenical Synod was now given to them, in order to raise them to the position of universally and unconditionally valid ecclesiastical rules. It is admirably remarked by the Emperor Justinian, in his 131st Novel, cap.j.; "We honour the doctrinal decrees of the first four Councils as we do Holy Scripture, but the canons given or *approved* by them as we do the laws."

It seems quite impossible to determine just what councils are included in this list, the Council in Trullo has entirely removed this ambiguity in its second canon.

This canon is found in the *Corpus Juris Canonici*, Gratian's *Decretum*, Pars II., Causa XXV., Quæst. 1, can. xiv.

CANON II.

If any Bishop should ordain for money, and put to sale a grace which cannot be sold, and for money ordain a bishop, or chorepiscopus, or presbyters, or deacons, or any other of those who are counted among the clergy; or if through lust of gain he should nominate for money a steward, or advocate, or prosmonarius, or any one whatever who is on the roll of the Church, let him who is convicted of this forfeit his own rank; and let him who is ordained be nothing profited by the purchased ordination or promotion; but let him be removed from the dignity or charge he has obtained for money. And if any one should be found negotiating such shameful and unlawful transactions, let him also, if he is a clergyman, be deposed from his rank, and if he is a layman or monk, let him be anathematized.

NOTES.

ANCIENT EPITOME OF CANON XIX.

Whoso buys or sells an ordination, down to a Prosmonarius, shall be in danger of losing his grade. Such shall also be the case with go-betweens, if they be clerics they shall be cut off from their rank, if laymen or monks, they shall be anathematized.

BRIGHT.

A great scandal in the "Asian diocese" had led to St. Chrysostom's intervention. Antoninus, bishop of Ephesus, was charged, with "making it a rule to sell ordinations of bishops at rates proportionate to the value of their sees" (Palladius, *Dial. de vita Chrysost*, p. 50). Chrysostom held a synod at Ephesus, at which six bishops were deposed for having obtained their sees in this manner. Isidore of Pelasium repeatedly remonstrated with his bishop Eusebius on the heinousness of "selling the gift" of ordinations (*Epist.* I., 26, 30, 37); and names Zosimus, a priest, and Maron, a deacon, as thus ordained (*ib.* 111, 119). A few years before the council, a court of three bishops sat at Berytus to hear charges brought against Ibas, bishop of Edessa, by clerics of his diocese. The third charge was thus curtly worded: "Moreover he receives for laying on hands" (Mansi, vii. 224). The xxvijth Trullan canon repeated this canon of Chalcedon against persons ordained for money, doubtless in view of such a state of things as Gregory the Great had heard of nearly a century earlier, "that in the Eastern Churches no one comes to holy order except by the payment of premiums" (*Epist.* xi. 46, to the bishop of Jerusalem; compare Evagrius's assertion that Justin II. openly sold bishoprics, V. 1). It is easy to understand how the scruples of ecclesiastics could be abated by the courtly fashion of calling bribes "eulogiæ" (Fleury, XXVI, 20), just as the six prelates above referred to had regarded their payments as an equivalent for that "making over of property to the Curia," which was required by a law of 399 (Cod. Theod., xii. 1, 163, see notes in Transl. of Fleury, i. 163, ij. 16).

The ἔκδικος, "defensor," was an official Advocate or counsel for the Church. The legal force of the term "defensor" is indicated by a law of Valentinian I. "Nec idem in eodem negotio defensor sit et quaesitor" (Cod. Theod., ii. 10, 2). In the East the office was held by ecclesiastics; thus, John, presbyter and "advocate" was employed, at the Council of Constantinople in 448, to summon Eutyches (Mansi, vii. 697). About 496, Paul the "Advocate" of Constantinople saved his archbishop from the sword of a murderer at the cost of his own life (Theodor., Lect. ii. 11). In the list of the functionaries of St. Sophia, given by Goar in his Euchologion (p. 270), the Protecdicos is discribed as adjudicating, with twelve assessors, in smaller causes, on which he afterwards reports to the bishop. In Africa, on the other hand, from A. D. 407 (see Cod. Theod., xvi. 2, 38), the office was held by barristers, in accordance with a request of the African bishops (Cod. Afric., 97 ; Mansi, iii., 802), who, six years earlier, had asked for "defensores," with special reference to the oppression of the poor by the rich (Cod. Afric., 75 ; Mansi, iii. 778, 970). The "defensores" mentioned by Gregory the Great had primarily to take care of the poor (*Epist.*, v. 29), and of the church property (*ib.*, i. 36), but also to be advocates of injured clerics (*ib.*, ix. 64) and act as assessors (*ib.*, x. 1), etc.

The next office is that of the Prosmonarius or, according to a various reading adopted by many (e.g. Justellus, Hervetus, Beveridge, Bingham), the Paramonarius. Opinions differ as to the functions intended. Isidore gives simply "paramonarius :" Dionysius (see Justellus, *Biblioth.*, i., 134) omits the word ; but in the "interpretatio Dionysii," as given in the Concilia, freedom has been taken to insert "vel mansionarium" in a parenthesis (vii. 373 ; see Beveridge, *in loc.*). Mansionarius is a literal rendering ; but what was the function of a mansionarius ? In Gregory the Great's time he was a sacristan who had the duty of lighting the church (*Dial.*, i. 5) ; and "ostiarium" in the Prisca implies the same idea. Tillemont, without deciding between the two Greek readings, thinks that the person intended had "some charge of what pertained

to the church itself, perhaps like our present bedells" (xv. 694). So Fleury renders, "concièrge" (xxviij. 29) ; and Newman, reading "paramonarion," takes a like view (note in Transl. of Fleury, vol. iii., p. 392). But Justellus (i. 91) derives "paramonarius" from μονή "mansio," a halting-place, so that the sense would be a manager of one of the church's farms, a "villicus," or, as Bingham expresses it, "a bailiff" (iii. 3, 1). Beveridge agrees with Justellus, except in giving to μονή the sense of "monastery" (compare the use of μονή in Athan., *Apol. c. Arion*, 67, where Valesius understands it as "a station" on a road, but others as "a monastery," see Historical Writings of St. Athanasius, Introd., p. xliv.). Bingham also prefers this interpretation. Suicer takes it as required by "paramonarios" which he treats as the true reading : "prosmonarios" he thinks would have the sense of "sacristan."

HEFELE.

According to Van Espen, however, who here supports himself upon Du Cange, by "prosmonarios" or "mansionarius," in the same way as by "oiconomos," a steward of church property was to be understood.

The canon is found in the *Corpus Juris Canonici*, Gratian's *Decretum*, Pars II., Causa I., Quæst. i., can. viij.

CANON III.

IT has come to [the knowledge of] the holy Synod that certain of those who are enrolled among the clergy have, through lust of gain, become hirers of other men's possessions, and make contracts pertaining to secular affairs, lightly esteeming the service of God, and slip into the houses of secular persons, whose property they undertake through covetousness to manage. Wherefore the great and holy Synod decrees that henceforth no bishop, clergyman, nor monk shall hire possessions, or engage in business, or occupy himself in worldly engagements, unless he shall be called by the law to the guardianship of minors, from which there is no escape ; or unless the bishop of the city shall commit to him the care of ecclesiastical business, or of unprovided orphans or widows and of persons who stand especially in need of the Church's help, through the fear of God. And if any one shall hereafter transgress these decrees, he shall be subjected to ecclesiastical penalties.

NOTES.

ANCIENT EPITOME OF CANON III.

Those who assume the care of secular houses should be corrected, unless perchance the law called them to the administration of those not yet come of age, from which there is no exemption. Unless further their Bishop permits them to take care of orphans and widows.

BRIGHT.

These two cases excepted, the undertaking of secular business was made ecclesiastically penal. Yet this is not to be construed as forbidding clerics to work at trades either (1) when the church-funds were insufficient to maintain them, or (2) in order to have more to bestow in alms, or (3) as an example of industry or humility. Thus, most of the clergy of Cæsarea in Cappadocia practised sedentary trades for a livelihood (Basil, *Epist.*, cxcviii., 1); and some African canons allow, or even direct, a cleric to live by a trade, provided that his clerical duties are not neglected (Mansi, iii., 955). At an earlier time Spyridion, the famous Cypriot bishop, still one of the most popular saints in the Levant (Stanley's *East. Church*, p. 126), retained, out of humility (ἀτυφιαν πολλήν, Soc., i. 12), his occupation as a shepherd; and in the latter part of the fourth century Zeno, bishop of Maiuma, wove linen, partly to supply his own wants, and partly to obtain means of helping the poor (Soz., vii. 28). Sidonius mentions a "reader" who maintained himself by commercial transactions (*Epist.*, vi. 8), and in the Anglo-Saxon Church, although presbyters were forbidden to become "negotiorum sæcularium dispositores" (Cl. of Clovesho in 747, c. 8), or to be "*mongers* and covetous merchants" (Elfric's canons, xxx.), yet the canons of King Edgar's reign ordered every priest "diligently to learn a handicraft" (No. 11; Wilkins, i. 225). In short, it was not the mere fact of secular employment, but secularity of motive and of tone that was condemned.

This canon was the second of these proposed by the Emperor, and is found in the *Corpus Juris Canonici*, Gratian's *Decretum*, Pars I., Dist. lxxxvi., C. xxvj.

CANON IV.

LET those who truly and sincerely lead the monastic life be counted worthy of becoming honour; but, forasmuch as certain persons using the pretext of monasticism bring confusion both upon the churches and into political affairs by going about promiscuously in the cities, and at the same time seeking to establish Monasteries for themselves; it is decreed that no one anywhere build or found a monastery or oratory contrary to the will of the bishop of the city; and that the monks in every city and district shall be subject to the bishop, and embrace a quiet course of life, and give themselves only to fasting and prayer, remaining permanently in the places in which they were set apart; and they shall meddle neither in ecclesiastical nor in secular affairs, nor leave their own monasteries to take part in such; unless, indeed, they should at any time through urgent necessity be appointed thereto by the bishop of the city. And no slave shall be received into any monastery to become a monk against the will of his master. And if any one shall transgress this our judgment, we have decreed that he shall be excommunicated, that the name of God be not blasphemed. But the bishop of the city must make the needful provision for the monasteries.

NOTES.

ANCIENT EPITOME OF CANON IV.

Domestic oratories and monasteries are not to be erected contrary to the judgment of the bishop. Every monk must be subject to his bishop, and must not leave his house except at his suggestion. A slave, however, can not enter the monastic life without the consent of his master.

HEFELE.

Like the previous canon, this one was brought forward by the Emperor Marcian in the sixth session, and then as number one, and the synod accepted the Emperor's proposed canon almost verbally. Occasion for this canon seems to have been given by monks of Eutychian tendencies, and especially by the Syrian Barsumas, as appears from the fourth session. He and his monks had, as Eutychians, withdrawn themselves from the jurisdiction of their bishops, whom they suspected of Nestorianism.

BRIGHT.

Here observe (1) the definite assertion of episcopal authority over monks, as it is repeated for greater clearness in the last words of the canon, which are not found in Marcian's draft, "It is the duty of the bishop of the city to make due provision for the monasteries," and compare canons 8, 24. Isidore says that the bishop must "keep an eye on the negligences of monks" (*Epist.*, i. 149). The Western Church followed in this track (see Council of Agde, canon xxvii., that "no new monastery is to be founded without the bishop's approval," and 1st of Orleans, canon xix., "Let abbots be under the bishop's power," and also Vth of Paris, canon xij., Mansi, viii., 329, 354, 542, etc.), until a reaction set in against the oppressiveness of bishops, was encouraged by Gregory the Great (*Epist.*, i. 12 ; ii. 41), the IVth Council of Toledo (canon li.), and the English Council of Hertford (canon iij., Bede, iv. 5, and Bright's *Chapters of Early Engl. Ch. Hist.*, p. 244), and culminated in the system of monastic exemptions, of which Monte Cassino, St. Martin's of Tours, Fulda, Westminster, Battle (see Freeman, *Norm. Conquest*, iv. 409), and St Alban's were eminent instances.

This canon, cut up and mutilated, is found

in the *Corpus Juris Canonici*, Gratian's *Decretum*, Pars II., Causa XVI., Quest. I., can. xij., and Causa XVIII., Quest. II., Canon X.

I have followed the reading of the *Prisca*, and of Dionysius, of Routh, and of Balsamon, " they were set apart," i.e. (as Balsamon explains) where they received the monastic tonsure. This reading substitutes ἀπετάξαντο for ἐπετάξαντο, which would mean " over which they had been put in authority," or possibly (as Johnson) "where they are appointed," or as Hammond, "in which they have been settled." Isidore reads " *ordinati sunt.*"

CANON V.

CONCERNING bishops or clergymen who go about from city to city, it is decreed that the canons enacted by the Holy Fathers shall still retain their force.

NOTES.

ANCIENT EPITOME OF CANON V.

Those who go from city to city shall be subject to the canon law on the subject.

Clerical adventurers and brief pastorates are not the peculiar characteristics of any one century.

BRIGHT.

It is supposed by Hefele that the bishops were thinking of the case of Bassian, who, in the eleventh session (Oct. 29), pleaded that he had been violently ejected from the see of Ephesus. Stephen, the actual bishop, answered that Bassian had not been "ordained"

for that see, but had invaded it and been justly expelled. Bassian rejoined that his original consecration for the see of Evasa had been forcible even to brutality ; that he had never even visited Evasa, that therefore his appointment to Ephesus was not a translation. Ultimately, the Council cut the knot by ordering that a new bishop should be elected, Bassian and Stephen retaining the episcopal title and receiving allowances from the revenues of the see (Mansi, vii. 273 *et seqq.*)

This canon is found in the *Corpus Juris Canonici*, Gratian's *Decretum*, Pars II., Causa VII., Quæst. I., can. xxij.[1]

CANON VI.

NEITHER presbyter, deacon, nor any of the ecclesiastical order shall be ordained at large, nor unless the person ordained is particularly appointed to a church in a city or village, or to a martyry, or to a monastery. And if any have been ordained without a charge, the holy Synod decrees, to the reproach of the ordainer, that such an ordination shall be inoperative, and that such shall nowhere be suffered to officiate.

NOTES.

ANCIENT EPITOME OF CANON VI.

In Martyries and Monasteries ordinations are strictly forbidden. Should any one be ordained therein, his ordination shall be reputed of no effect.

VAN ESPEN.

The wording of the canon seems to intimate

that the synod of Chalcedon held ordinations of this sort to be not only *illicit* but also invalid, *irritis* and *cassis*. Nor is this to be wondered at, if we take into account the pristine and ancient discipline of the church and the opinion of many of the Scholastics (Morinus, *De SS. Ordinat.*, Parte III., Exercit. V., cap ix.).

---

[1] Not given in Hefele, and incorrectly printed in Van Espen as Causa XII. instead of VII.

HEFELE.

It is clear that our canon forbids the so-called absolute ordinations, and requires that every cleric must at the time of his ordination be designated to a definite church. The only *titulus* which is here recognized is that which was later known as *titulus beneficii*. As various kinds of this title we find here (*a*) the appointment to a church in the city ; (*b*) to a village church ; (*c*) that to the chapel of a martyr ; (*d*) the appointment as chaplain of a monastery. For the right understanding of the last point, it must be remembered that the earliest monks were in no wise clerics, but that soon the custom was introduced in every larger convent, of having at least one monk ordained presbyter, that he might provide for divine service in the monastery.

Similar prohibitions of *ordinationes absolutæ* were also put forth in after times.

According to existing law, absolute ordinations, as is well known, are still *illicitæ*, but yet *validæ*, and even the Council of Chalcedon has not declared them to be properly *invalidæ*, but only as without effect (by permanent suspension). *Cf.* Kober, *Suspension*, S. 220, and Hergenröther, *Photius*, etc., Bd. ii., S. 324.

BRIGHT.

By the word μαρτυρίῳ ("martyry") is meant a church or chapel raised over a martyr's grave. So the Laodicene Council forbids Churchmen to visit the "martyries of heretics" (can. ix.). So Gregory of Nyssa speaks of "the martyry" of the Holy Martyrs (*Op.* ii., 212) ; Chrysostom of a "martyry," and Palladius of "martyries" near Antioch (*In Act. Apost. Hom.*, xxxviii., 5 ; *Dial.*, p. 17), and Palladius of "the martyry of St. John" at Constantinople (*Dial.*, p. 25). See Socrates, iv. 18, 23, on the "martyry" of St. Thomas at Edessa, and that of SS. Peter and Paul at Rome ; and vi. 6, on the "martyry" of St. Euphenia at Chalcedon in which the Council actually met. In the distinct sense of a visible testimony, the word was applied to the church of the Resurrection at Jerusalem (Eusebius, *Vit. Con.*, iii. 40, iv. 40 ; Mansi, vi. 564 ; Cyril, *Catech.*, xiv. 3), and to the Holy Sepulchre itself (*Vit. Con.*, iii. 28). Churches raised over martyrs' tombs were called in the West "*memoriæ martyrum*," see Cod. Afric., lxxxiii. (compare Augustine, *De Cura pro Mortuis*, VI.).

This canon is found in the *Corpus Juris Canonici*, Gratian's *Decretum*, Pars I., Dist. lxx., can. j.

CANON VII.

WE have decreed that those who have once been enrolled among the clergy, or have been made monks, shall accept neither a military charge nor any secular dignity ; and if they shall presume to do so and not repent in such wise as to turn again to that which they had first chosen for the love of God, they shall be anathematized.

NOTES.

ANCIENT EPITOME OF CANON VII.

If any cleric or monk arrogantly affects the military or any other dignity, let him be cursed.

HEFELE.

Something similar was ordered by the lxxxiii. (lxxxii.) Apostolic Canon, only that it threatens the cleric who takes military service merely with deposition from his clerical office, while our canon subjects him to excommunication. . . . The Greek commentators, Balsamon and Zonaras, think that our canon selects a more severe punishment, that of excommunication, because it has in view those clerics who have not merely taken military service, etc., but at the same time have laid aside their clerical dress and put on secular clothing.

BRIGHT.

By στρατείαν [which I have translated (or, as Canon Bright thinks, mistranslated) "military charge"], "militiam," is here meant, not military employment as such, but the public service in general. This use of the term is a relic and token of the military basis of the Roman monarchy. The court of the Imperator was called his camp, στρατόπεδον (Cod. Theod., tom. ii., p. 22), as in Constantine's letters to John Archaph and the Council of Tyre (Athan., *Apol. c. Ari.*, lxx. 86), and in the VIIth canon of Sardica, so Athanasius speaks of the "camp" of Constans (*Apol. ad Constant*, iv.), and of that of Constantius at Milan (*Hist. Ari.*, xxxvij.) ; so Hosius uses the same phrase in his letter to Constantius (*ib.* xliv.) ; so the Semi-Arian bishops, when addressing Jovian

(Soz., vi. 4); so Chrysostom in the reign of Theodosius I. (*Hom. ad Pop. Antioch*, vi. 2). Similarly, there were officers of the palace called Castrensians (Tertull., *De Cor.*, 12), as being "milites alius generis—de imperatoria familia" (Gothofred, Cod. Theod., tom. ii., p. 526). So στρατεύεσθαι is used for holding a place at court, as in Soc., iv. 9; Soz., vi. 9, on Marcian's case, and a very clear passage in Soc., v. 25, where the verb is applied to an imperial secretary. It occurs in combination with στρατεία in a petition of an Alexandrian deacon named Theodore, which was read in the third session of Chalcedon: he says, "Ἐστρατευσάμεν for about twenty-two years in

the Schola of the magistrians" (under the Magister officionum, or chief magistrate of the palace), "but I disregarded στρατείας τοσοῦτον χρόναν in order to enter the ministry" (Mansi, vi., 1008). See also Theodoret, *Relig. Hist.*, xij., on the emperor's letter-carriers. In the same sense Honorius, by a law of 408, forbids non-Catholics "intra palatium militare" (Cod. Theod., xvi., 5, 42); and the Vandal king Hunneric speaks of "domus nostræ militiæ" (Vict r Vitens, iv. 2).

This canon is found in the *Corpus Juris Canonici*, Gratian's *Decretum*, Pars II., Causa xx., Quæst. iii., Can. iij.

CANON VIII.

LET the clergy of the poor-houses, monasteries, and martyries remain under the authority of the bishops in every city according to the tradition of the holy Fathers; and let no one arrogantly cast off the rule of his own bishop; and if any shall contravene this canon in any way whatever, and will not be subject to their own bishop, if they be clergy, let them be subjected to canonical censure, and if they be monks or laymen, let them be excommunicated.

NOTES.

ANCIENT EPITOME OF CANON VIII.

Any clergyman in an almshouse or monastery must submit himself to the authority of the bishop of the city. But he who rebels against this let him pay the penalty.

VAN ESPEN.

From this canon we learn that the synod of Chalcedon willed that all who were in charge of such pious institutions should be subject to the bishop, and in making this decree the synod only followed the tradition of the Fathers and Canons. Although in its first part the canon only mentions "clergymen," yet in the second part monks are named, and, as Balsamon and Zonoras point out, both are included.

BRIGHT.

What a πτωχεῖόν was may be seen from what Gibbon calls the "noble and charitable foundation, almost a new city" (iii. 252), established by St. Basil at a little distance from Cæsarea, and called in consequence the Basiliad. Gregory Nazianzen describes it as a large set of buildings with rooms for the sick, especially for lepers, and also for houseless travellers; "a storehouse of piety, where disease was borne philosophically, and sympathy was tested" (*Orat.*, xliii., 63, compare Basil himself, *Epist.*, xciv., on its staff of

nurses and physicians and cl., 3). Sozomen calls it "a most celebrated resting-place for the poor," and names Prapidius as having been its warden while acting as "bishop over many villages" (vi. 34, see on Nic., viij.). Another πτωχοτροφεῖον is mentioned by Basil (*Epist.*, cxliij.) as governed by a chorepiscopus. St. Chrysostom, on coming to the see of Constantinople, ordered the excess of episcopal expenditure to be transferred to the hospital for the sick (νοσοκομεῖον), and "founded other such hospitals, setting over them two pious presbyters, with physicians and cooks. . . . so that foreigners arriving in the city, on being attacked by disease, might receive aid, both because it was a good work in itself, and for the glory of the Saviour" (Palladius, *Dial.*, p. 19). At Ephesus Bassian founded a πτωχεῖτον with seventy pallets for the sick (Mansi, vii., 277), and there were several such houses in Egypt (*ib.*, vi., 1013; in the next century there was a hospital for the sick at Daphne near Antioch (Evagr., iv., 35). "The tradition of the holy fathers" is here cited as barring any claim on the part of clerics officiating in these institutions, or in monasteries or martyries, to be exempt from the jurisdiction of the ordinary. They are to "abide under it," and not to indulge selfwill by "turning restive" against their bishop's authority" (ἀσχηνιάζω is literally to get the bit between the teeth, and is used by Aetius for "not choosing to obey," Mansi, vii., 72). Those who dare to violate this clearly defined rule (διατύπωσιν, comp. τύπος in Nic., xix.), and to refuse subjection to their own bishop, are, if clerics, to incur canonical censure, if monks or laics, to be excommunicated. The allu-

sion to laics points to laymen as founders or benefactors of such institutions.

This canon is found in the *Corpus Juris Canonici*, Gratian's *Decretum*, Pars II., Causa XVIII., Q. II., canon x., § 3.

CANON IX.

IF any Clergyman have a matter against another clergyman, he shall not forsake his bishop and run to secular courts; but let him first lay open the matter before his own Bishop, or let the matter be submitted to any person whom each of the parties may, with the Bishop's consent, select. And if any one shall contravene these decrees, let him be subjected to canonical penalties. And if a clergyman have a complaint against his own or any other bishop, let it be decided by the synod of the province. And if a bishop or clergyman should have a difference with the metropolitan of the province, let him have recourse to the Exarch of the Diocese, or to the throne of the Imperial City of Constantinople, and there let it be tried.

NOTES.

ANCIENT EPITOME OF CANON IX.

Litigious clerics shall be punished according to canon, if they despise the episcopal and resort to the secular tribunal. When a cleric has a contention with a bishop let him wait till the synod sits, and if a bishop have a contention with his metropolitan let him carry the case to Constantinople.

JOHNSON.

Let the reader observe that here is a greater privilege given by a General Council to the see of Constantinople than ever was given by any council, even that of Sardica, to the bishop of Rome, viz., that any bishop or clergyman might at the first instance bring his cause before the bishop of Constantinople if the defendant were a metropolitan.

HEFELE.

That our canon would refer not merely the ecclesiastical, but the civil differences of the clergy, in the first case, to the bishop, is beyond a doubt. And it comes out as clearly from the word πρότερον (= at first) that it does not absolutely exclude a reference to the secular judges, but regards it as allowable only when the first attempt at an adjustment of the controversy by the bishop has miscarried. This was quite clearly recognized by Justinian in his 123d Novel, c. 21: "If any one has a case against a cleric, or a monk, or a deaconess, or a nun, or an ascetic, he shall first make application to the bishop of his opponent, and he shall decide. If both parties are satisfied with his decision, it shall then be

carried into effect by the imperial judge of the locality. If, however, one of the contending parties lodges an appeal against the bishop's judgment within ten days, then the imperial judge of the locality shall decide the matter. There is no doubt that the expression "Exarch" employed in our canon, and also in canon 17, means, in the first place, those superior metropolitans who have several ecclesiastical provinces under them. Whether, however, the great patriarchs, properly so called, are to be included under it, may be doubted. The Emperor Justinian, in c. 22 of his Novel just quoted (*l. c.*) in our text has, without further explanation, substituted the expression *Patriarch* for *Exarch*, and in the same way the commentator Aristenus has declared both terms to be identical; adding that only the Patriarch of Constantinople has the privilege of having a metropolitan tried before him who does not belong to his patriarchate, but is subject to another patriarch. In the same way our canon was understood by Beveridge. Van Espen, on the contrary, thinks that the Synod had here in view only the exarchs in the narrower sense (of Ephesus, Cæsarea), but not the Patriarchs, properly so called, of Rome, Alexandria, Antioch, and Jerusalem, as it would be too great a violation of the ancient canons, particularly of the 6th of Nicæa, to have set aside the proper patriarch and have allowed an appeal to the Bishop of Constantinople (with this Zonaras also agrees in his explanation of canon 17). Least of all, however, would the Synod have made such a rule for the West, *i.e.*, have allowed that any one should set aside the Patriarch of

Rome and appeal to the Patriarch of Constantinople, since they themselves, in canon 28, assigned the first place in rank to Rome.

It appears to me that neither Beveridge, etc., nor Van Espen are fully in the right, while each is partially so. With Van Espen we must assume that our Synod, in drawing up this canon, had in view only the Greek Church, and not the Latin as well, particularly as neither the papal legates nor any Latin bishop whatever was present at the drawing up of these canons. On the other hand, Beveridge is also right in maintaining that the Synod made no distinction between the patriarchs proper and the exarchs (such a distinction must otherwise have been indicated in the text), and allowed that quarrels which should arise among the bishops of other patriarchates might be tried at Constantinople. Only that Beveridge ought to have excepted the West and Rome.

The strange part of our canon may be explained in the following manner. There were always many bishops at Constantinople from the most different places, who came there to lay their contentions and the like before the Emperor. The latter frequently referred the decision to the bishop of Constantinople, who then, in union with the then present bishops from the most different provinces, held a "Home Synod" and gave the sentence required at this. Thus gradually the practice was formed of controversies being decided by bishops of other patriarchates or exarchates at Constantinople, to the setting aside of the proper superior metropolitan, an example of which we have seen in that famous Synod of Constantinople, A.D. 448, at which the case of Eutyches was the first time brought forward.

This canon is found in the *Corpus Juris Canonici*, Gratian's *Decretum*, Pars II., Causa XI., Q. I., canon xlvj.

CANON X.

IT shall not be lawful for a clergyman to be at the same time enrolled in the churches of two cities, that is, in the church in which he was at first ordained, and in another to which, because it is greater, he has removed from lust of empty honour. And those who do so shall be returned to their own church in which they were originally ordained, and there only shall they minister. But if any one has heretofore been removed from one church to another, he shall not intermeddle with the affairs of his former church, nor with the martyries, almshouses, and hostels belonging to it. And if, after the decree of this great and ecumenical Synod, any shall dare to do any of these things now forbidden, the synod decrees that he shall be degraded from his rank.

NOTES.

ANCIENT EPITOME OF CANON X.

No cleric shall be recorded on the clergy-list of the churches of two cities. But if he shall have strayed forth, let him be returned to his former place. But if he has been transferred, let him have no share in the affairs of his former church.

Van Espen, following Christian Lupus, remarks that this canon is opposed to pluralities. For if a clergyman has by presentation and institution obtained two churches, he is enrolled in two churches at the same time, contrary to this canon; but surely that this be the case, the two churches must needs be in two cities, and that, in the days of Chalcedon, meant in two dioceses.

BRIGHT.

Here a new institution comes into view, of which there were many instances. Julian had directed Pagan hospices (ξενοδοχεῖα) to be established on the Christian model (*Epist.* xlix.). The Basiliad at Cæsarea was a ξενοδοχεῖον as well as a πτωχεῖον; it contained καταγώγια τοῖς ξένοις, as well as for wayfarers, and those who needed assistance on account of illness, and Basil distinguished various classes of persons engaged in charitable ministrations, including those who escorted the traveller on his way (τοὺς παραπέμποντας, *Epist.* xciv.). Jerome writes to Pammachius: "I hear that you have made a 'xenodochion' in the port of Rome," and adds that he himself had built a "diversorium" for pilgrims to Bethlehem (*Epist.* xvi., 11, 14). Chrysostom reminds his auditors at Constantinople that "there is a common dwelling set apart by the Church," and "called a xenōn" (*in Act. Hom.*, xlv. 4). His friend Olympias was munificent to "xenotrophia" (*Hist. Lausiac*, 144). There was a xenodochion near the church of the monastic settlement at

Nitria (*ib.*, 7). Ischyrion, in his memorial read in the 3d session of Chalcedon, complains of his patriarch Dioscorus for having misapplied funds bequeathed by a charitable lady τοῖς ξενεῶσι καὶ πτωχείοις in Egypt, and says that he himself had been confined by Dioscorus in a "xenōn" for lepers (Mansi, vi. 1013, 1017). Justinian mentions xenodochia in Cod., i. 3, 49, and their wardens in Novell., 134, 16. Gregory the Great orders that the accounts of xenodochia should be audited by the bishop (*Epist.* iv., 27). Charles the Great provides for the restoration of decayed "senodochia" (Capitul. of 803; Pertz, Leg., i. 110); and Alcuin exhorts his pupil, archbishop Eanbald, to think where in the diocese of York he could establish "xenodochia, id est, hospitalia" (*Epist. L.*).

This canon is found in the *Corpus Juris Canonici*, Gratian's *Decretum*, Pars II., Causa XXI., Q. I., canon ij., and again Causa XXI., Q. II., canon iij.

CANON XI.

WE have decreed that the poor and those needing assistance shall travel, after examination, with letters merely pacifical from the church, and not with letters commendatory, inasmuch as letters commendatory ought to be given only to persons who are open to suspicion.

NOTES.

ANCIENT EPITOME OF CANON XI.

Let the poor who stand in need of help make their journey with letters pacificatory and not commendatory : For letters commendatory should only be given to those who are open to suspicion.

ARISTENUS.

. . . The poor who need help should journey with letters pacificatory from the bishop, so that those who have the ability to help them may be moved with pity. These need no letters commendatory, such letters should be shown, however, by presbyters and deacons, and by the rest of the clergy.

See notes on canons vij., viij., and xj. of Antioch ; and on canon xlij. of Laodicea.

HEFELE.

The mediæval commentators, Balsamon, Zonaras, and Aristenus, understand this canon to mean that letters of commendation, συστατικαὶ, *commendatitiæ litteræ* were given to those laymen and clerics who were previously subject to ecclesiastical censure, and therefore were suspected by other bishops, and for this reason needed a special recommendation, in order to be received in another church into the number of the faithful. The letters of peace (εἰρηνικαί) on the contrary, were given to those who were in undisturbed communion with their bishop, and had not the least evil reputation abroad.

Our canon was understood quite differently by the old Latin writers, Dionysius Exiguus and Isidore, who translate the words ἐν ὑπολήψει by *personæ honoratiores* and *clariores*, and the learned Bishop Gabriel Aubespine of Orleans has endeavored to prove, in his notes to our canon, that the *litteræ pacificæ* were given to ordinary believers, and the *commendatitiæ* (συστατικαί) on the contrary, only to clerics and to distinguished laymen ; and in favour of this view is the xiii. canon of Chalcedon.

With regard to this much-vexed point, authorities are so divided that no absolute judgment can be arrived at. The interpretation I have followed is that of the Greeks and of Hervetus, which seems to be supported by Apostolic Canon XIII., and was that adopted by Johnson and Hammond. On the other hand are the *Prisca*, Dionysius, Isidore, Tillemont, Routh, and to these Bright seems to unite himself by saying that this "sense is the more natural."

CANON XII.

IT has come to our knowledge that certain persons, contrary to the laws of the Church, having had recourse to secular powers, have by means of imperial rescripts divided one Province into two, so that there are consequently two metropolitans in one province; therefore the holy Synod has decreed that for the future no such thing shall be attempted by a bishop, since he who shall undertake it shall be degraded from his rank. But the cities which have already been honoured by means of imperial letters with the name of metropolis, and the bishops in charge of them, shall take the bare title, all metropolitan rights being preserved to the true Metropolis.

NOTES.

ANCIENT EPITOME OF CANON XII.

One province shall not be cut into two. Whoever shall do this shall be cast out of the episcopate. Such cities as are cut off by imperial rescript shall enjoy only the honour of having a bishop settled in them: but all the rights pertaining to the true metropolis shall be preserved.

BRIGHT.

We learn from this canon, there were cases in which an ambitious prelate, "by making application to the government" ("secular powers") had obtained what are called "pragmatic letters," and employed them for the purpose of "dividing one province into two," and exalting himself as a metropolitan. The name of a "pragmatic sanction" is more familiar in regard to mediæval and modern history; it recalls the name of St. Louis, and, still more, that of the Emperor Charles VI. the father of Maria Theresa. Properly a "pragmatic" was a deliberate order promulgated by the Emperor after full hearing of advice, on some public affair. We find "pragmatici nostri statuta" in a law of A.D. 431. (Cod. Theod., xi. 1, 36); and pragmatici prioris," "sub hac pragmatica jussione," in ordinances in Append. to Cod. Theod., pp. 95, 162; and the empress Pulcheria, about a year before the Council, had informed Leo that her husband Marcian had recalled some exiled orthodox bishops "robore pragmatici sui" (Leon., *Epist.* lxxvij.). Justinian speaks of "pragmaticas nostras formas" and "pragmaticum typum" (Novel., 7, 9, etc.). The phrase was adopted from his legislation by Louis the Pious and his colleague-son Lothar (compare Novel. 7, 2 with Pertz, *Mon. Germ, Hist. Leg.*, i., 254), and hence it came to be used both by later German emperors (see, e.g., Bryce's *Holy Roman Empire*, p. 212), and by the French kings (Kitchin, *Hist. France*, i. 343, 544). Augustine explains it by "præceptum imperatoris" (*Brev. Collat. cum Donatist.* iii., 2), and Balsamon in his comment uses an equivalent phrase; and so in the record of the fourth session of Chalcedon we have θεῖα γράμματα ("divine" being practically equivalent to "imperial") explained by πραγματικοὺς τύπους (Mansi, vii., 89). We must ob-

serve that the imperial order, in the cases contemplated by the canon, had only conferred the title of "metropolis" on the city, and had not professed to divide the province for civil, much less for ecclesiastical, purposes. Valens, indeed, had divided the province of Cappadocia, when in 371 he made Tyana a metropolis : and therefore Anthimus, bishop of Tyana, when he claimed the position of a metropolitan, with authority over suffragans, was making a not unnatural inference in regard to ecclesiastical limits from political rearrangements of territory, as Gregory of Nazianzus says (*Orat.* xliii., 58), whereas Basil "held to the old custom," i.e., to the traditional unity of his provincial church, although after a while he submitted to what he could not hinder (see Tillemont, ix., 175, 182, 670). But in the case of Eustathius of Berytus, which was clearly in the Council's mind, the Phœnician province had not been divided; it was in reliance on a mere title bestowed upon his city, and also on an alleged synodical ordinance which issued in fact from the so-called "Home Synod" that he declared himself independent of his metropolitan, Photius of Tyre, and brought six bishoprics under his assumed jurisdiction. Thus while the province remained politically one, he had *de facto* divided it ecclesiastically into two. Photius petitioned Marcian, who referred the case to the Council of Chalcedon, and it was taken up in the fourth session. The imperial commissioners announced that it was to be settled not according to "pragmatic forms," but according to those which had been enacted by the Fathers (Mansi, vii., 89). This encouraged the Council to say, "A pragmatic can have no force against the canons." The commissioners asked whether it was lawful for bishops, on the ground of a pragmatic, to steal away the rights of other churches? The answer was explicit : "No, it is against the canon." The Council proceeded to cancel the resolution of the Home Synod in favour of the elevation of Berytus, ordered the 4th Nicene canon to be read, and upheld the metropolitical rights of Tyre. The commissioners also pronounced against Eustathius. Cecropius, bishop of Sebastopolis, requested them to put an end to the issue of pragmatics made to the detriment of the canons; the Council echoed this request; and the commissioners granted it by declaring that the canons should everywhere stand good (Mansi, vii., 89–97). We may connect with this incident a law of Marcian dated in 454, by which "all pragmatic sanctions, obtained by means of favour or ambition in opposition to the canon of the Church, are declared to be deprived of effect" (Cod. Justin, i., 2, 12).

To this decision the present canon looks back, when it forbids any bishop, on pain of deposition, to presume to do as Eustathius had done, since it decrees that "he who attempts to do so shall fall from his own rank (βαθμοῦ) in the Church. And cities which have already obtained the honorary title of a metropolis from the emperor are to enjoy the honour only, and their bishops to be but honorary metropolitans, so that all the rights of the real metropolis are to be reserved to it." So, at the end of the 6th session the emperor had announced that Chalcedon was to be a titular metropolis, saving all the rights of Nicomedia; and the Council had expressed its assent (Mansi, xii., 177; cf. Le Quien, i., 602). Another case was discussed in the 13th session of the Council. Anastasius of Nicæa had claimed to be independent of his metropolitan

Eunomius of Nicomedia, on the ground of an ordinance of Valens, recognising the city of Nicæa as by old custom a "metropolis." Eunomius, who complained of Anastasius's encroachments, appealed to a later ordinance, guaranteeing to the capital of Bithynia its rights as unaffected by the honour conferred on Nicæa : the Council expressed its mind in favour of Eunomius, and the dispute was settled by a decision "that the bishop of Nicomedia should have metropolitical authority over the Bithynian churches, while the bishop of Nicæa should have merely the honour of a metropolitan, being subjected, like the other comprovincials, to the bishop of Nicomedia (Mansi, vii., 313). Zonaras says that this canon was in his time no longer observed; and Balsamon says that when the primates of Heraclea and Ancyra cited it as upholding their claim to perform the consecration of two "honorary metropolitans," they were overruled by a decree of Alexius Comnenus, "in presence and with consent" of a synod (on Trullan, canon xxxviij.).

The first part of this canon is found in the *Corpus Juris Canonici*, Grat *Decretum,* Pars I., Dist. ci., canon j.

CANON XIII.

STRANGE and unknown clergymen without letters commendatory from their own Bishop, are absolutely prohibited from officiating in another city.

NOTES.

ANCIENT EPITOME OF CANON XIII.

No cleric shall be received to communion in another city without a letter commendatory.

"Unknown clergymen." I have here followed the reading of the Greek commentators. But the translators of the Prisca, and Dionysius, and Isidore must have all read ἀναγνώστας (i.e., Readers) instead of ἀγνώστους. Justellus, Hervetus, and Beveridge, as also Johnson and Hammond, follow the reading of the text. Hefele suggests that if "Readers" is the correct reading perhaps it means, "all clergymen even readers."

CANON XIV.

SINCE in certain provinces it is permitted to the readers and singers to marry, the holy Synod has decreed that it shall not be lawful for any of them to take a wife that is heterodox. But those who have already begotten children of such a marriage, if they have already had their children baptized among the heretics, must bring them into the communion of the Catholic Church; but if they have not had them baptized, they may not hereafter baptize them among heretics, nor give them in marriage to a heretic, or a Jew, or a heathen, unless the person marrying the orthodox child shall promise to come over to the orthodox faith. And if any one shall transgress this decree of the holy synod, let him be subjected to canonical censure.

NOTES.

A Cantor or Lector alien to the sound faith, if being then married, he shall have begotten children let him bring them to communion, if they had there been baptized. But if they had not yet been baptized they shall not be baptized afterwards by the heretics.

ARISTENUS.

The tenth and thirty-first canons of the Synod of Laodicea and the second of the Sixth Synod in Trullo, and this present canon forbid one of the orthodox to be joined in marriage with a woman who is a heretic, or *vice versa*. But if any of the Cantors or Lectors had taken a wife of another sect before these canons were set forth, and had had children by her, and had had them baptized while yet he remained among the heretics, these he should bring to the communion of the Catholic Church. But if they had not yet been baptized, he must not turn back and have them baptized among heretics. But departing thence let him lead them to the Catholic Church and enrich them with divine baptism.

HEFELE.

According to the Latin translation of Dionysius Exiguus, who speaks only of the *daughters* of the lectors, etc., the meaning may be understood, with Christian Lupus, as being that only their *daughters* must not be married to heretics or Jews or heathen, but that the sons of readers may take wives who are heretics, etc., because that men are less easily led to fall away from the faith than women. But the Greek text makes here no distinction between sons and daughters.

BRIGHT.

It is to Victor that we owe the most striking of all anecdotes about readers. During the former persecution under Genseric (or Gaiseric), the Arians attacked a Catholic congregation on Easter Sunday; and while a reader was standing alone in the pulpit, and chanting the "Alleluia melody" (*cf.* Hammond, *Liturgies*, p. 95), an arrow pierced his throat, the "codex" dropped from his hands, and he fell down dead (*De Persec. Vand.*, i., 13). Five years before the Council, a boy of eight named Epiphanius was made a reader in the church of Pavia, and in process of time became famous as its bishop. Justinian forbade readers to be appointed under eighteen (*Novel.*, 134, 13). The office is described in the Greek Euchologion as "the first step to the priesthood," and is conferred with delivery of the book containing the Epistles. Isidore of Seville, in the seventh century, tells us that the bishop ordained a reader by delivering to him "coram plebe," the "codex" of Scripture: and after giving precise directions as to pronunciation and accentuation, says that the readers were of old called "heralds" (*De Eccl. Offic.*, ii., 11). (b) The Singers are placed by the xliijrd. Apostolic canon between subdeacons and readers, but they rank below readers in Laodic., c. 23, in the Liturgy of St. Mark (Hammond, p. 173), and in the canons wrongly ascribed to a IVth Council of Carthage, which permit a presbyter to appoint a "psalmist" without the bishop's knowledge, and rank him even below the doorkeepers (Mansi, iii., 952). The chief passage respecting the ancient "singers" is Laodic., xv.

The first part of this canon is found in the *Corpus Juris Canonici*, Gratian's *Decretum*, Pars I., Dist. xxxii., c. xv.

CANON XV.

A WOMAN shall not receive the laying on of hands as a deaconess under forty years of age, and then only after searching examination. And if, after she has had hands laid on her and has continued for a time to minister, she shall despise the grace of God and give herself in marriage, she shall be anathematized and the man united to her.

NOTES.

No person shall be ordained deaconess except she be forty years of age. If she shall dishonour her ministry by contracting a marriage, let her be anathema.

This canon should be read carefully in connexion with what is said in the Excursus on deaconesses to canon xix. of Nice.

This canon is found in the *Corpus Juris Canonici*, Gratian's *Decretum*, Pars II., **Causa** XXVII, Quæst. I., Canon xxiij.

CANON XVI.

IT is not lawful for a virgin who has dedicated herself to the Lord God, nor for monks, to marry; and if they are found to have done this, let them be excommunicated. But we decree that in every place the bishop shall have the power of indulgence towards them.

NOTES.

ANCIENT EPITOME OF CANON XVI.

Monks or nuns shall not contract marriage, and if they do so let them be excommunicated.

VAN ESPEN.

Since this canon says nothing at all of separation in connexion with a marriage made contrary to a vow, but only orders separation from communion, it seems very likely that vows of this kind at the time of the synod were not considered diriment but only impedient impediments from which the bishop of the diocese could dispense at least as far as the canonical punishment was concerned.

HEFELE.

The last part of the canon gives the bishop authority in certain circumstances not to inflict the excommunication which is threatened in the first part, or again to remove it. Thus all the old Latin translators understood our text; but Dionysius Exiguus and the Prisca added *confitentibus*, meaning, " if such a virgin or monk *confess and repent* their fault, then the bishop may be kind to them." That the marriage of a monk is invalid, as was ruled by later ecclesiastical law, our canon does not say; on the contrary, it assumes its validity, as also the marriages contracted by priests until the beginning of the twelfth century were regarded as valid.

This canon is found in the *Corpus Juris Canonici*, Gratian's *Decretum*, Pars II., Causa xxvii., Quæst. I., canon xxii., from Isidore's version; it is also found in Dionysius's version as canon xij. of the same Quæstio, Causa, and Part, where it is said to be taken " ex Concilio Triburiensi."

CANON XVII.

OUTLYING or rural parishes shall in every province remain subject to the bishops who now have jurisdiction over them, particularly if the bishops have peaceably and continuously governed them for the space of thirty years. But if within thirty years there has been, or is, any dispute concerning them, it is lawful for those who hold themselves aggrieved to bring their cause before the synod of the province. And if any one be wronged by his metropolitan, let the matter be decided by the exarch of the diocese or by the throne of Constantinople, as aforesaid. And if any city has been, or shall hereafter be newly erected by imperial authority, let the order of the ecclesiastical parishes follow the political and municipal example.

NOTES.

ANCIENT EPITOME OF CANON XVII.

Village and rural parishes if they have been possessed for thirty years, they shall so continue. But if within that time, the matter shall be subject to adjudication. But if by the command of the Emperor a city be renewed, the order of ecclesiastical parishes shall follow the civil and public forms.

BRIGHT.

The adjective ἐγχωρίους is probably synonymous with ἀγροικικάς (" rusticas," Prisca), although Dionysius and Isidorian take in as " situated on estates," *cf*. Routh, *Scr. Opusc.*, ii., 109. It was conceivable that some such outlying districts might form, ecclesiastically, a border-land, it might not be easy to assign them definitively to this or that bishopric. In such a case, says the Council, if the bishop who is now in possession of these rural churches can show a prescription of thirty years in favour of his see, let them remain undisturbed in his obedience. (Here ἀβιάστως may be illustrated from βιασάμενος in Eph. viij. and for the use of οἰκονομεῖν see I. Const., ij.) But the border-land might be the " debateable" land: the two neighbour bishops might dispute as to the right to tend these " sheep in the wilderness;" as we read in Cod. Afric.,

117, "multæ controversiæ postea inter episcopos de diœcesibus ortæ sunt, et oriuntur" (see on I. Const., ij.) ; as archbishop Thomas of York, and Remigius of Dorchester, were at issue for years "with reference to Lindsey" (Raine, *Fasti Eborac.*, i. 150). Accordingly, the canon provides that if such a contest had arisen within the thirty years, or should thereafter arise, the prelate who considered himself wronged might appeal to the provincial synod. If he should be aggrieved at the decision of his metropolitan in synod, he might apply for redress to the *eparch* (or prefect, a substitute for exarch) of the "diocese," or to the see of Constantinople (in the manner provided by canon ix.). It is curious "that in Russia all the sees are divided into eparchies of the first, second, and third class" (Neale, *Essays on Liturgiology*, p. 302).

This canon is found in the *Corpus Juris Canonici*, Gratian's *Decretum*, Pars II., Causa XVI., Quæst. iii., can. j., in Isidore Mercator's version.[1]

CANON XVIII.

THE crime of conspiracy or banding together is utterly prohibited even by the secular law, and much more ought it to be forbidden in the Church of God. Therefore, if any, whether clergymen or monks, should be detected in conspiring or banding together, or hatching plots against their bishops or fellow-clergy, they shall by all means be deposed from their own rank.

NOTES.

ANCIENT EPITOME OF CANON XVIII.

Clerics and Monks, if they shall have dared to hold conventicles and to conspire against the bishop, shall be cast out of their rank.

BRIGHT.

In order to appreciate this canon, we must consider the case of Ibas bishop of Edessa. He had been attached to the Nestorians, but after the reunion between Cyril and John of Antioch had re-entered into communion with Cyril on the ground that Cyril had explained his anathemas (Mansi, vii., 240), or, as he wrote to Maris (in a letter famous as one of the "Three Chapters") that God had "softened the Egyptian's heart" (*ib.*, 248). Four of his priests (Samuel, Cyrus, Maras, and Eulegius), stimulated, says Fleury (xxvij. 19) by Uranius bishop of Himeria, accused Ibas of Nestorianism before his patriarch Domnus of Antioch, who held a synod, but, as Samuel and Cyrus failed to appear, pronounced them defaulters and set aside the case (Mansi, vii., 217). They went up to Constantinople, and persuaded Theodosius and archbishop Flavian to appoint a commission for inquiring into the matter. Two sessions, so to speak, were held by the three prelates thus appointed, one at Berytus the other at Tyre. At Berytus, according to the extant minutes (Mansi, vii., 212 ff.), five new accusers joined the original four, and charges were brought which affected the moral character of Ibas as well as his orthodoxy. The charge of having used a "blasphemous" speech implying that Christ was but a man deified, was rebutted by a statement signed by some sixty clerics of Edessa, who according to the accusers, had been present when Ibas uttered it. At Tyre the episcopal judges succeeded in making peace, and accusers and accused partook of the communion together (*ib.*, vii., 209). The sequence of these proceedings cannot be thoroughly ascertained, but Hefele (sect. 169) agrees with Tillemont (xv., 474 *et seqq.*) in dating the trial at Berytus slightly earlier than that at Tyre, and assigning both to the February of 448 or 449. Fleury inverts this order, and thinks that, "notwithstanding the reconciliation" at Tyre, the four accusers renewed their prosecution of Ibas (xxvij. 20) ; but he has to suppose two applications on their part to Theodosius and Flavian, which seems improbable. "The Council is believed," says Tillemont (xv., 698), "to have had this case in mind when drawing up the present canon:" and one can hardly help thinking that, on a spot within sight of Constantinople, they must have recalled the protracted sufferings which malignant plotters had inflicted on St. Chrysostom.

This canon is found in part in the *Corpus Juris Canonici*, Gratian's *Decretum*, Pars II., Causa XI., Quæst. I., canons xxj. and xxiij.

---

[1] Hefele does not give this reference, and Van Espen gives it incorrectly as causa xix. instead of xvi.

CANON XIX.

WHEREAS it has come to our ears that in the provinces the Canonical Synods of Bishops are not held, and that on this account many ecclesiastical matters which need reformation are neglected; therefore, according to the canons of the holy Fathers, the holy Synod decrees that the bishops of every province shall twice in the year assemble together where the bishop of the Metropolis shall approve, and shall then settle whatever matters may have arisen. And bishops, who do not attend, but remain in their own cities, though they are in good health and free from any unavoidable and necessary business, shall receive a brotherly admonition.

NOTES.

ANCIENT EPITOME OF CANON XIX.

Twice each year the Synod shall be held wherever the bishop of the Metropolis shall designate, and all matters of pressing interest shall be determined.

See notes on Canon V. of Nice, and on Canon XX. of Antioch, and compare canon VIII. of the council in Trullo.

BRIGHT.

Hilary of Arles and his suffragans, assembled at Riez, had already, in 439 qualified the provision for two by adding significantly "if the times are quiet" (Mansi, v., 1194). The words were written at the close of ten years' war, during which the Visigoths of Septimania "were endeavouring to take Arles and Narbonne" (Hodgkin, *Italy and her Invaders*, ii., 121).

This canon is found in the *Corpus Juris Canonici*, Gratian's *Decretum*, Pars I., Dist. XVIII., canon vj.

CANON XX.

IT shall not be lawful, as we have already decreed, for clergymen officiating in one church to be appointed to the church of another city, but they shall cleave to that in which they were first thought worthy to minister; those, however, being excepted, who have been driven by necessity from their own country, and have therefore removed to another church. And if, after this decree, any bishop shall receive a clergyman belonging to another bishop, it is decreed that both the received and the receiver shall be excommunicated until such time as the clergyman who has removed shall have returned to his own church.

NOTES.

ANCIENT EPITOME OF CANON XX.

A clergyman of one city shall not be given a cure in another. But if he has been driven from his native place and shall go into another he shall be without blame. If any bishop receives clergymen from without his diocese he shall be excommunicated as well as the cleric he receives.

It is quite doubtful as to what "excommunication" means in this canon, probably not anathematism (so think the commentators) but separation from the communion of the other bishops, and suspension from the performance of clerical functions.

BRIGHT.

This canon is the third of those which were originally proposed by Marcian in the end of the sixth session, as certain articles for which synodical sanction was desirable (see above Canons iij. and iv.). It was after they had been delivered by the Emperor's own hand to Anatolius of Constantinople that the Council broke out into plaudits, one of which is sufficiently startling, τῷ ἱερεῖ, τῷ βασιλεῖ (Mansi, vii., 177). The imperial draft is in this case very slightly altered. A reference is made to a previous determination (*i.e.*, canon x.) against clerical pluralities, and it is ordered that "clerics registered as belonging to one church shall not be ranked as belonging to the church of another city, but must be content with the one in which they were originally admitted to minister, excepting those who, having lost their own country, have been compelled to migrate to another church,"— an exception intelligible enough at such a period. Eleven years before, the Vandal Gaiseric had expelled the Catholic bishops and priests of Western Africa from their churches : Quodvultdeus, bishop of Carthage with many of his clergy, had been "placed on board some unseaworthy vessels," and yet, "by the Divine mercy, had been carried safe to Naples" (Vict. Vitens., *De Persec. Vandal.*, i., 5 : he mentions other bishops as driven into exile). Somewhat later, the surge of the Hunnish invasion had frightened the bishop of Sirmium into sending his church vessels to Attila's Gaulish secretary and had swept onward in 447 to within a short distance of the "New Rome" (Hodgkin, *Italy and her Invaders*, ii., 54–56). And the very year of the Council was the most momentous in the

whole history of the "Barbaric" movement. The bishops who assembled in October at Chalcedon must have heard by that time of the massacre of the Metz clergy on Easter Eve, of a bishop of Rheims slain at his own altar, of the deliverance of Orleans at the prayer of St. Anianus, of "the supreme battle" in the plain of Chalons, which turned back Attila and rescued Christian Gaul (Hodgkin, ii., 129–152 ; Kitchin, *Hist. France*, i. 61).

This canon is found in the *Corpus Juris Canonici*, Gratian's *Decretum*, Pars I., Dist. lxxi., c. iv.

CANON XXI.

CLERGYMEN and laymen bringing charges against bishops or clergymen are not to be received loosely and without examination, as accusers, but their own character shall first be investigated.

NOTES.

ANCIENT EPITOME OF CANON XXI.

A cleric or layman making charges rashly against his bishop shall not be received.

Compare with this canon the VIth Canon

of those credited to the First Synod at Constantinople, the second ecumenical.

This canon is found in the *Corpus Juris Canonici*, Gratian's *Decretum*, Pars II., Causa II., Quest. VII., canon xlix., in Isidore's first version.

CANON XXII.

IT is not lawful for clergymen, after the death of their bishop, to seize what belongs to him, as has been forbidden also by the ancient canons ; and those who do so shall be in danger of degradation from their own rank.

NOTES.

ANCIENT EPITOME OF CANON XXII.

Whoever seizes the goods of his deceased bishop shall be cast forth from his rank.

It is curious that the Greek text which Zonaras and Balsamon produce, and which Hervetus translated, had instead of τοῖς πάλαι κανόσι, τοις παραλαμβάνουσιν. Van Espen thinks that the Greek commentators have tried without success to attach any meaning to these

words, accepting the arguments of Bp. Beveridge (which see). The reading adopted in the text does not lack MS. authority, and is the one printed by Justellus in his "Codex of the Canons of the Universal Church."

This canon is found in the *Corpus Juris Canonici*, Gratian's *Decretum*, Pars II., Causa XII., Quest. II., canon xliii., in Isidore's version.

CANON XXIII.

IT has come to the hearing of the holy Synod that certain clergymen and monks, having no authority from their own bishop, and sometimes, indeed, while under sentence of excommunication by him, betake themselves to the imperial Constantinople, and remain there for a long time, raising disturbances and troubling the ecclesiastical state, and turning men's houses upside down. Therefore the holy Synod has determined that such persons be first notified by the Advocate of the most holy Church of Constantinople to depart from the imperial city; and if they shall shamelessly continue in the same practices, that they shall be expelled by the same Advocate even against their will, and return to their own places.

NOTES.

ANCIENT EPITOME OF CANON XXIII.

Clerics or monks who spend much time at Constantinople contrary to the will of their bishop, and stir up seditions, shall be cast out of the city.[1]

This canon is found in the *Corpus Juris Canonici*, Gratian's *Decretum*, Pars II., Causa XVI., Quæst. I., canon xvij., but with the last part epitomized, as the Roman correctors point out.

CANON XXIV.

MONASTERIES, which have once been consecrated with the consent of the bishop, shall remain monasteries for ever, and the property belonging to them shall be preserved, and they shall never again become secular dwellings. And they who shall permit this to be done shall be liable to ecclesiastical penalties.

NOTES.

ANCIENT EPITOME OF CANON XXIV.

A monastery erected with the consent of the bishop shall be immovable. And whatever pertains to it shall not be alienated. Whoever shall take upon him to do otherwise, shall not be held guiltless.

Joseph Ægyptius, in turning this into Arabic, reads: "And whoever shall turn any monastery into a dwelling house for himself . . . let him be cursed and anathema." The curious reader is referred on this whole subject to Sir Henry Spelman's *History and Fate of Sacrilege*, or to the more handy book on the subject by James Wayland Joyce, *The Doom of Sacrilege*.[2]

BRIGHT.

The secularization of monasteries was an evil which grew with their wealth and influence. At a Council held by the patriarch Photius in the Apostles' church at Constantinople, it is complained that some persons attach the name of "monastery" to property of their own, and while professing to dedicate it to God, write themselves down as lords of

what has been thus consecrated, and are not ashamed to claim after such consecration the same power over it which they had before. In the West, we find this abuse attracting the attention of Gregory the Great, who writes to a bishop that "rationalis ordo" would not allow a layman to pervert a monastic foundation at will to his own uses (*Epist.* viii., 31). In ancient Scotland, the occasional dispersion of religious communities, and, still more, the clan-principle which assigned chieftain-rights over monasteries to the descendants of the founder, left at Dunkeld, Brechin, Abernethy, and elsewhere, "nothing but the mere name of abbacy applied to the lands, and of abbot borne by the secular lord for the time" (Skene's *Celtic Scotland*, ii., 365 ; *cf.* Anderson's *Scotland in Early Christian Times*, p. 235). So, after the great Irish monastery of Bangor in Down was destroyed by the Northmen, "non defuit," says St. Bernard, "qui illud teneret cum possessionibus suis ; nam et constituebantur per electionem etiam, et abbates appellabantur, servantes nomine, etsi non re, quod olim exstiterat" (*De Vita S. Malachiæ*, vj.). So in 1188 Giraldus Cambrensis found a lay abbot in possession of the venerable church of Llanbadarn Vawr ; a "bad custom,"

[1] "The City," that is to say Constantinople.
[2] The reader may like to see the vow on this subject taken by King Charles I. of England, and which was made public by Archbishop Sheldon after the Restoration. The vow is as follows :

"I do here promise and solemnly vow, in the presence and service of Almighty God, that if it shall please the Divine Majesty of his infinite goodness to restore me to my just kingly rights, and to re-establish me in my throne, I will wholly give back to his Church all those impropriations which are now held by the Crown; and what lands soever I do now or should enjoy, which have been

taken away either from any episcopal see or any cathedral or collegiate church, from any abbey or other religious house, I likewise promise for hereafter to hold them from the Church under such reasonable fines and rents as shall be set down by some conscientious persons, whom I propose to choose with all uprightness of heart to direct me in this particular And I humbly beseech God to accept of this my vow. and to bless me in the design I have now in hand through Jesus Christ our Lord.
"CHARLES R.

" OXFORD, April 13, 1646."

he says, "had grown up, whereby powerful laymen, at first chosen by the clergy to be "œconomi" or "patroni et defensores," had usurped "totum jus," appropriated the lands, and left to the clergy nothing but the altars, with tithes and offerings (*Itin. Camb.*, ii., 4). This abuse must be distinguished from the corrupt device whereby, in Bede's later years, Northumbrian nobles contrived to gain for their estates the immunities of abbey-lands by professing to found monasteries, which they filled with disorderly monks, who lived there in contempt of all rule (Bede, *Ep. to Egbert*, vij.). In the year of his birth, the first English synod had forbidden *bishops* to despoil consecrated monasteries (Bede, iv., 5).

This canon is found in the *Corpus Juris Canonici*, Gratian's *Decretum*, Pars II., Causa XIX., Quæst. III., canon iv.

CANON XXV.

FORASMUCH as certain of the metropolitans, as we have heard, neglect the flocks committed to them, and delay the ordinations of bishops the holy Synod has decided that the ordinations of bishops shall take place within three months, unless an inevitable necessity should some time require the term of delay to be prolonged. And if he shall not do this, he shall be liable to ecclesiastical penalties, and the income of the widowed church shall be kept safe by the steward of the same Church.

NOTES.

ANCIENT EPITOME OF CANON XXV.

Let the ordination of bishops be within three months: necessity however may make the time longer. But if anyone shall ordain counter to this decree, he shall be liable to punishment. The revenue shall remain with the œconomus.

BRIGHT.

The "Steward of the Church" was to "take care of the revenues of the church widowed" by the death of its bishop, who was regarded as representing Him to whom the whole Church was espoused (see Eph. v. 23 ff.). So in the "order of the holy and great church" of St. Sophia, the "Great Steward is described as "taking the oversight of the widowed church" (Goar, *Eucholog.*, p. 269); so Hincmar says: "Si fuerit defunctus episeopus, ego

. . . visitatorem ipsi viduatæ designabo ecclesiæ;" and the phrase, "viduata per mortem N. nuper episcopi" became common in the West (F. G. Lee, *Validity of English Orders*, p. 373). The episcopal ring was a symbol of the same idea. So at St. Chrysostom's restoration Eudoxia claimed to have "given back the bridegroom" (*Serm. post redit.*, iv.). So Bishop Wilson told Queen Caroline that he "would not leave his wife in his old age because she was poor" (Keble's *Life of Wilson*, ii., 767); and Peter Mongus, having invaded the Alexandrian see while its legitimate occupant, Timothy Salophaciolus, was alive, was expelled as an "adulterer" (Liberatus, *Breviar.*, xviij.).

This canon is found in the *Corpus Juris Canonici*, Gratian's *Decretum*, Pars I., Dist. LXXV., C. ij.[1]

CANON XXVI.

FORASMUCH as we have heard that in certain churches the bishops managed the church-business without stewards, it has seemed good that every church having a bishop shall have also a steward from among its own clergy, who shall manage the church business under the sanction of his own bishop; that so the administration of the church may not be without a witness; and that thus the goods of the church may not be squandered, nor reproach be brought upon the priesthood; and if he [i.e., the Bishop] will not do this, he shall be subjected to the divine canons.

NOTES.

ANCIENT EPITOME OF CANON XXVI.

The Œconomus in all churches must be chosen from the clergy. And the bishop who neglects to do this is not without blame.

BRIGHT.

As the stream of offerings became fuller, the work of dispensing them became more complex, until the archdeacons could no

---

[1] I think this is the first time I have ever noticed Van Espen to have omitted giving the reference.

longer find time for it, and it was committed to a special officer called "œconomus" or steward (Bingham, iii., 12, 1; Transl. of Fleury, iii., 120). So the Council of Gangra, in the middle of the fourth century, forbids the church offerings to be disposed of without consent of the bishop or of the person appointed, εἰς οἰκονομίαν εὐποιίας (canon viij.); and St Basil mentions the œconomi of his own church (*Epist.*, xxiij. 1), and the "ταμίαι of the sacred goods" of his brother's at Nyssa (*ib.*, 225). And although Gregory Nazianzen took credit to himself for declining to appoint a "stranger" to make an estimate of the property which of right belonged to the church of Constantinople, and in fact, with a strange confusion between personal and official obligations, gave the go-by to the whole question (*Carm. de Vita sua*, 1479 ff.), his successor, Nectarius, being a man of business, took care to appoint a "church-steward"; and Chrysostom, on coming to the see, examined his accounts, and found much superfluous expenditure (Palladius, *Dial*, p. 19). Theophilus of Alexandria compelled two of the Tall Brothers to undertake the οἰκονομία of the Alexandrian church (Soc., vi., 7); and in one of his extant directions observes that the clergy of Lyco wish for another "œconomus," and that the bishop has consented, in order that the church-funds may be properly spent (Mansi, iii., 1257). At Hippo St. Augustine had a "præpositus domus" who acted as Church-steward (Possidius, *Vit. August.*, xxiv.). Isidore of Pelusium denounces Martinianus as a fraudulent "œconomus," and requests Cyril to appoint an upright one (*Epist.* ii., 127), and in another letter urges him to put a stop to the dishonest greed of those who acted as stewards of the same church (*ib.*, v. 79). The records of the Council of Ephesus mention the "œconomus" of Constantinople, the "œconomus" of Ephesus (Mansi, iv., 1228–1398), and, the "œconomus" of Philadelphia. According to an extant letter of Cyril, the "œconomi" of Perrha in Syria were mistrusted by the clergy, who wished to get rid of them "and appoint others by their own authority" (*ib.*, vii., 321). Ibas of Edessa had been complained of for his administration of church property; he was accused, e.g., of secreting a jewelled chalice, and bestowing the church revenues, and gold and silver crosses, on his brother and cousins; he ultimately undertook to appoint "œconomi" after the model of Antioch (Mansi, vii., 201). Proterius, afterwards patriarch of Alexandria and a martyr for Chalcedonian orthodoxy, was "œconomus" under Dioscorus (*ib.*, iv., 1017), as was John Talaia, a man accused of bribery, under his successor (Evag., iii., 12). There

may have been many cases in which there was no "œconomus," or in which the management was in the hands of private agents of the bishop, in whom the Church could put no confidence; and the Council, having alluded to the office of "œconomus" in canons ij. and xxv., now observes that some bishops had been managing their church property without "œconomi," and thereupon resolves "that every church which has a bishop shall also have an œconomus" from among its own clergy, to administer the property of the church under the direction of its own bishop; so that the administration of the church property may not be unattested, and thereby waste ensue, and the episcopate incur reproach." Any bishop who should neglect to appoint such an officer should be punishable under "the divine" (or sacred) "canons."

Nearly three years after the Council, Leo saw reason for requesting Marcian not to allow civil judges, "novo exemplo," to audit the accounts of "the œconomi of the church of Constantinople," which ought, "secundum traditum morem," to be examined by the bishop alone (*Epist.* cxxxvij. 2). In after days the "great steward" of St. Sophia was always a deacon; he was a conspicuous figure at the Patriarch's celebrations, standing on the right of the altar, vested in alb and stole, and holding the sacred fan (ῥιπίδιον); his duty was to enter all incomings and outgoings of the church's revenue in a charterlary, and exhibit it quarterly, or half yearly, to the patriarchs; and he governed the church during a vacancy of the see (Eucholog., pp. 268, 275). In the West, Isidore of Seville describes the duties of the "œconomus"; he has to see to the repair and building of churches, the care of church lands, the cultivation of vineyards, the payment of clerical stipends, of doles to the widows and the poor, and of food and clothing to church servants, and even the carrying on of church law suits,—all "cum jussu et arbitrio sui episcopi" (*Ep. to Leudefred, Op.* ii., 520); and before Isidore's death the IVth Council of Toledo refers to this canon, and orders the bishops to appoint "from their own clergy those whom the Greeks call œconomi, hoc est, qui vici episcoporum res ecclesiasticas tractant (canon xlviij., Mansi, x., 631). There was an officer named "œconomus" in the old Irish monasteries; see Reeves' edition of Adamnan, p. 47.

This Canon is found twice in the *Corpus Juris Canonici*, Gratian's *Decretum*, Pars II., Causa XVI., Q. VII., Canon xxi., and again in Pars I., Dist. LXXXIX., c. iv.[1]

---

[1] It is curious that both the French and English translations of Hefele give this reference incorrectly, and each makes the same e.ror, giving Dist. lxxix. instead of lxxxix.

CANON XXVII.

THE holy Synod has decreed that those who forcibly carry off women under pretence of marriage, and the aiders or abettors of such ravishers, shall be degraded if clergymen, and if laymen be anathematized.

NOTES.

ANCIENT EPITOME OF CANON XXVII.

If a clergyman elope with a woman, let him be expelled from the Church. If a layman, let him be anathema. The same shall be the lot of any that assist him.

This canon is found in the *Corpus Juris Canonici*, Gratian's *Decretum*, Pars II., Causa XXXVI., Q. II., canon j.

In many old collections this is the last canon of this Council, e.g., Dionysius Exiguus, Isidore, the *Prisca*, the Greek by John of Antioch, and the Arabic by Joseph Ægyptius. The reader familiar with the subject will have but little difficulty in explaining to his own satisfaction the omission of canon xxviij. in these instances.

CANON XXVIII.

FOLLOWING in all things the decisions of the holy Fathers, and acknowledging the canon, which has been just read, of the One Hundred and Fifty Bishops beloved-of-God (who assembled in the imperial city of Constantinople, which is New Rome, in the time of the Emperor Theodosius of happy memory), we also do enact and decree the same things concerning the privileges of the most holy Church of Constantinople, which is New Rome. For the Fathers rightly granted privileges to the throne of old Rome, because it was the royal city. And the One Hundred and Fifty most religious Bishops, actuated by the same consideration, gave equal privileges ($\check{\iota}\sigma\alpha\ \pi\rho\epsilon\sigma\beta\epsilon\hat{\iota}\alpha$) to the most holy throne of New Rome, justly judging that the city which is honoured with the Sovereignty and the Senate, and enjoys equal privileges with the old imperial Rome, should in ecclesiastical matters also be magnified as she is, and rank next after her; so that, in the Pontic, the Asian, and the Thracian dioceses, the metropolitans only and such bishops also of the Dioceses aforesaid as are among the barbarians, should be ordained by the aforesaid most holy throne of the most holy Church of Constantinople; every metropolitan of the aforesaid dioceses, together with the bishops of his province, ordaining his own provincial bishops, as has been declared by the divine canons; but that, as has been above said, the metropolitans of the aforesaid Dioceses should be ordained by the archbishop of Constantinople, after the proper elections have been held according to custom and have been reported to him.

NOTE.

ANCIENT EPITOME OF CANON XXVIII.

The bishop of New Rome shall enjoy the same honour as the bishop of Old Rome, on account of the removal of the Empire. For this reason the [metropolitans] of Pontus, of Asia, and of Thrace, as well as the Barbarian bishops shall be ordained by the bishop of Constantinople.

VAN ESPEN.

It is certain that this canon was expressly renewed by canon xxxvi. of the Council of Trullo and from that time has been numbered by the Greeks among the canons; and at last it was acknowledged by some Latin collectors also, and was placed by Gratian in

his *Decretum*, although clearly with a different sense. (Pars I., Dist. xxii., C. vj.)

BRIGHT.

Here is a great addition to the canon of 381, so ingeniously linked on to it as to seem at first sight a part of it. The words καὶ ὥστε are meant to suggest that what follows is in fact involved in what has preceded: whereas a new point of departure is here taken, and instead of a mere "honorary pre-eminence" the bishop of Constantinople acquires a vast jurisdiction, the independent authority of three exarchs being annulled in order to make him patriarch. Previously he had προεδρία now he gains προστασία. As we have seen, a series of aggrandizements in fact had prepared for this aggrandizement in law; and various metropolitans of Asia Minor expressed their contentment at seeing it effected. "It is, indeed, more than probable that the self-assertion of Rome excited the jealousy of her rival of the East," and thus "Eastern bishops secretly felt that the cause of Constantinople was theirs" (Gore's *Leo the Great*, p. 120); but the gratification of Constantinople ambition was not the less, in a canonical sense, a novelty, and the attempt to enfold it in the authority of the Council of 381 was rather astute than candid. The true plea, whatever might be its value, was that the Council had to deal with a *fait accompli*, which it was wise at once to legalize and to regulate; that the "boundaries of the respective exarchates . . . were ecclesiastical arrangements made with a view to the general good and peace of the Church, and liable to vary with the dispensations to which the Church was providentially subjected," so that "by confirming the ἐκ πολλοῦ κρατῆσαν ἔθος" in regard to the ordination of certain metropolitans (see *Ep. of Council to Leo*, Leon. *Epist.* xcviij., 4), "they were acting in the spirit, while violating the letter, of the ever-famous rule of Nicæa, τὰ ἀρχεῖα ἔθη κρατείτο (cp. Newman, Transl. of Fleury, iii., 407). It is observable that Aristenus[1] and Symeon Logothetes reckon this decree as a XXIXth canon (Justellus, ii., 694, 720).

After the renewal of this canon by the Council of Trullo, Gratian adds "The VIIIth Synod held under Pope Hadrian II., canon xxj." (*Decretum*, Pars I., Dist. xxij., C. vij.) "We define that no secular power shall hereafter dishonour anyone of these who rule our patriarchal sees, or attempt to move them from their proper throne, but shall judge them worthy of all reverence and honour;

chiefly the most holy Pope of Old Rome, and then the Patriarch of Constantinople, and then those of Alexandria, and Antioch, and Jerusalem."

Some Greek codices have the following heading to this canon.
"Decree of the same holy Synod published on account of the privileges of the throne of the most holy Church of Constantinople."

TILLEMONT.

This canon seems to recognise no particular authority in the Church of Rome, save what the Fathers had granted it, as the seat of the empire. And it attributes in plain words as much to Constantinople as to Rome, with the exception of the first place. Nevertheless I do not observe that the Popes took up a thing so injurious to their dignity, and of so dangerous a consequence to the whole Church. For what Lupus quotes of St. Leo's lxxviij. (civ) letter, refers rather to Alexandria and to Antioch, than to Rome. St. Leo is contented to destroy the foundation on which they built the elevation of Constantinople, maintaining that a thing so entirely ecclesiastical as the episcopate ought not to be regulated by the temporal dignity of cities, which, nevertheless, has been almost always followed in the establishment of the metropolis, according to the Council of Nicea.

St. Leo also complains that the Council of Chalcedon broke the decrees of the Council of Nice, the practice of antiquity, and the rights of Metropolitans. Certainly it was an odious innovation to see a Bishop made the chief, not of one department but of three; for which no example could be found save in the authority which the Popes took over Illyricum, where, however, they did not claim the power to ordain any Bishop.

EXCURSUS ON THE LATER HISTORY OF CANON XXVIII.

Among the bishops who gave their answers at the last session to the question whether their subscription to the canons was voluntary or forced was Eusebius, bishop of Doryloeum, an Asiatic bishop who said that he had read the Constantinopolitan canon to "the holy pope of Rome in presence of clerics of Constantinople, and that he had accepted it" (L. and C., *Conc.*, iv. 815). But quite possibly this evidence is of little value. But what is more to the point is that the Papal legates most probably had already at this very council recognized the right of Constantinople to rank immediately after Rome. For at the very first session when the Acts of the Latrocinium were read, it was found that to Flavian, the Archbishop of Constantinople, was given only the fifth place. Against this the bishop protested and asked, "Why

---

[1] Such is not the case in Aristenus as found in Beveridge, Tom. I., p. 147.

did not Flavian receive his position?" and the papal legate Paschasinus answered: "We will, please God, recognize the present bishop Anatolius of Constantinople as the first [i.e. after us], but Dioscorus made Flavian the fifth." It would seem to be in vain to attempt to escape the force of these words by comparing with them the statement made in the last session, in a moment of heat and indignation, by Lucentius the papal legate, that the canons of Constantinople were not found among those of the Roman Code. It may well be that this statement was true, and yet it does not in any way lessen the importance of the fact that at the first session (a very different thing from the sixteenth) Paschasinus had admitted that Constantinople enjoyed the second place. It would seem that Quesnel has proved his point, notwithstanding the attempts of the Ballerini to counteract and overthrow his arguments.

It would be the height of absurdity for any one to attempt to deny that the canon of Constantinople was entirely in force and practical execution, as far of those most interested were concerned, long before the meeting of the council of Chalcedon, and in 394, only thirteen years after the adoption of the canon, we find the bishop of Constantinople presiding at a synod at which both the bishop of Alexandria and the bishop of Antioch were present.

St. Leo made, in connexion with this matter, some statements which perhaps need not be commented upon, but should certainly not be forgotten. In his epistle to Anatolius (no. cvi.) in speaking of the third canon of Constantinople he says: "That document of certain bishops has never been brought by your predecessors to the knowledge of the Apostolic See." And in writing to the Empress (*Ep.* cv., *ad Pulch.*) he makes the following statement, strangely contrary to what she at least knew to be the fact, "To this concession a long course of years has given no effect!"

We need not stop to consider the question why Leo rejected the xxviijth canon of Chalcedon. It is certain that he rejected it and those who wish to see the motive of this rejection considered at length are referred to Quesnel and to the Ballerini; the former affirming that it was because of its encroachments upon the prerogatives of his own see, the latter urging that it was only out of his zeal for the keeping in full force of the Nicene decree.

Leo can never be charged with weakness. His rejection of the canon was absolute and unequivocal. In writing to the Emperor he says that Anatolius only got the See of Constantinople by his consent, that he should behave himself modestly, and that there is no way he can make of Constantinople "an Apostolic See," and adds that "only from love of peace and for the restoration of the unity of the faith" he has "abstained from annulling this ordination" (*Ep.* civ.).

To the Empress he wrote with still greater violence: "As for the resolution of the bishops which is contrary to the Nicene decree, in union with your faithful piety, I declare it to be invalid and annul it by the authority of the holy Apostle Peter" (*Ep.* cv.).

The papal annulling does not appear to have been of much force, for Leo himself confesses, in a letter written about a year later to the Empress Pulcheria (*Ep.* cxvi.), that the Illyrian bishops had since the council subscribed the xxviiith canon.

The pope had taken occasion in his letter in which he announced his acceptance of the doctrinal decrees of Chalcedon to go on further and express his rejection of the canons. This part of the letter was left unread throughout the Greek empire, and Leo complains of it to Julian of Cos (*Ep.* cxxvij.).

Leo never gave over his opposition, although the breach was made up between him and Anatolius by an apparently insincere letter on the part of the latter (*Ep.* cxxxii.). Leo's successors followed his example in rejecting the canons, both the IIId of Constantinople and the XXVIIIth of Chalcedon, but as M. l'abbé Duchesne so admirably says: "Mais leur voix fut peu écoutée; on leur accorda sans doute des satisfactions, mais de pure cérémonie."[1] But

---

[1] Duchesne, *Origines du Culte Chrétien*, p. 24.

Justinian acknowledged the Constantinopolitan and Chalcedonian rank of Constantinople
in his CXXXIst Novel. (cap. j.), and the Synod in Trullo in canon xxxvj. renewed exactly
canon xxviij. of Chalcedon.   Moreover the Seventh Ecumenical with the approval of the
Papal Legates gave a general sanction to all the canons accepted by the Trullan Synod.   And
finally in 1215 the Fourth Council of the Lateran in its Vth Canon acknowledged Constantinople's rank as immediately after Rome, but this was while Constantinople was in the hands
of the Latins !   Subsequently at Florence the second rank, in accordance with the canons of
I. Constantinople and of Chalcedon (which had been annulled by Leo) was given to the Greek
Patriarch of Constantinople, and so the opposition of Rome gave way after seven centuries
and a half, and the Nicene Canon which Leo declared to be "inspired by the Holy Ghost"
and "valid to the end of time" (*Ep.* cvi.), was set at nought by Leo's successor in the Apostolic See.

From the Acts of the same Holy Synod concerning Photius, Bishop of Tyre, and
Eustathius, Bishop of Berytus.
The most magnificent and glorious judges said :
What is determined by the Holy Synod [in the matter of the Bishops ordained by
the most religious Bishop Photius, but removed by the most religious Bishop Eusta-
thius and ordered to be Presbyters after (having held) the Episcopate] ?
The most religious Bishops Paschasinus and Lucentius, and the Priest Boniface,
representatives of the Church [1] of Rome, said :

CANON XXIX.

It is sacrilege to degrade a bishop to the rank of a presbyter; but, if they are for
just cause removed from episcopal functions, neither ought they to have the position of
a Presbyter; and if they have been displaced without any charge, they shall be restored
to their episcopal dignity.

And Anatolius, the most reverend Archbishop of Constantinople, said : If those who
are alleged to have been removed from the episcopal dignity to the order of presbyter,
have indeed been condemned for any sufficient causes, clearly they are not worthy of
the honour of a presbyter.   But if they have been forced down into the lower rank
without just cause, they are worthy, if they appear guiltless, to receive again both the
dignity and priesthood of the Episcopate.
And all the most reverend Bishops cried out:
The judgment of the Fathers is right.   We all say the same.   The Fathers have
righteously decided.   Let the sentence of the Archbishops prevail.
And the most magnificent and glorious judges said :
Let the pleasure of the Holy Synod be established for all time.

NOTES.

ANCIENT EPITOME OF CANON XXIX.

He is sacrilegious who degrades a bishop to
the rank of a presbyter.   For he that is guilty
of crime is unworthy of the priesthood.   But he
that was deposed without cause, let him be [still]
bishop.

What precedes and follows the so-called

canon is abbreviated from the IVth Session
of the Council (L. and C., *Conc.*, Tom. IV.,
col. 550).   I have followed a usual Greek
method of printing it.

HEFELE.

This so-called canon is nothing but a verbal copy of a passage from the minutes of the

---

[1] "Apostolic Chair of Rome" in the Greek of the acts.

fourth session in the matter of Photius of Tyre and Eustathius of Berytus. Moreover, it does not possess the peculiar form which we find in all the genuine canons of Chalcedon, and in almost all ecclesiastical canons in general ; on the contrary, there adheres to it a portion of the debate, of which it is a fragment, in which Anatolius is introduced as speaking. Besides it is wanting in all the old Greek, as well as in the Latin collections of canons, and in those of John of Antioch and of Photius, and has only been appended to the twenty-eight genuine canons of Chalcedon from the fact that a later transcriber thought fit to add to the genuine canons the general and important principle contained in the place in question of the fourth session. Accordingly, this so-called canon is certainly an ecclesiastical rule declared at Chalcedon, and in so far a κανών, but it was not added as a canon proper to the other twenty-eight by the Synod.

From the Fourth Session of the same Holy Synod, having reference to the matter of the Egyptian Bishops.

The most magnificent and glorious judges, and the whole Senate, said :

CANON XXX.

SINCE the most religious bishops of Egypt have postponed for the present their subscription to the letter of the most holy Archbishop Leo, not because they oppose the Catholic Faith, but because they declare that it is the custom in the Egyptian diocese to do no such thing without the consent and order of their Archbishop, and ask to be excused until the ordination of the new bishop of the metropolis of Alexandria, it has seemed to us reasonable and kind that this concession should be made to them, they remaining in their official habit in the imperial city until the Archbishop of the Metropolis of Alexandria shall have been ordained.

And the most religious Bishop Paschasinus, representative of the Apostolic throne [of Rome [1]], said :

If your authority suggests and commands that any indulgence be shewn to them, let them give securities that they will not depart from this city until the city of Alexandria receives a Bishop.

And the most magnificent and glorious judges, and the whole Senate, said :

Let the sentence of the most holy Paschasinus be confirmed.

And therefore let them [*i.e.*, the most religious Bishops of the Egyptians] remain in their official habit, either giving securities, if they can, or being bound by the obligation of an oath.

NOTES.

ANCIENT EPITOME OF CANON XXX.

It is the custom of the Egyptians that none subscribe [2] without the permission of their Archbishop. Wherefore they are not to be blamed who did not subscribe the Epistle of the holy Leo until an Archbishop had been appointed for them.

As in the case of the last so-called "canon" I have followed a usual Greek method, the wording departs but little from that of the acts (*Vide* L. and C., *Conc.*, Tom. IV., col. 517).

HEFELE.

This paragraph, like the previous one, is not a proper canon, but a verbal repetition of a proposal made in the fourth session by the imperial commissioners, improved by the legate Paschasinus, and approved by the Synod. Moreover, this so-called canon is not found in the ancient collections, and was probably added to the twenty-eight canons in the same manner and for the same reasons as the preceding.

BRIGHT.

The council could insist with all plainness on the duty of hearing before condemning (see on Canon XXIX.) ; yet on this occasion

---

[1] These words do not occur in the Acts.   [2] i.e., a conciliar decree.

bishop after bishop gave vent to harsh un-feeling absolutism, the only excuse for which consists in the fact that the outrages of the Latrocinium were fresh in their minds, and that three of the Egyptian supplicants, whom they were so eager to terrify or crush, had actually supported Dioscorus on the tragical August 8, 449. It was not in human nature to forget this ; but the result is a blot on the history of the Council of Chalcedon.

EXTRACTS FROM THE ACTS.

SESSION XVI.

(Labbe and Cossart, *Concilia*, Tom. IV., col. 794.)

Paschasinus and Lucentius, the most reverend bishops, holding the place of the Apostolic See, said : If your magnificence so orders, we have something to lay before you.

The most glorious judges, said : Say what you wish. The most holy Paschasi-nus the bishop, holding the place of Rome, said : The rulers of the world, taking care of the holy Catholic faith, by which their kingdom and glory is increased, have deigned to define this, in order that unity through a holy peace may be preserved through all the churches. But with still greater care their clemency has vouchsafed to provide for the future, so that no con-tention may spring up again between God's bishops, nor any schisms, nor any scandal. But yesterday after your excellencies and our humility had left, it is said that certain decrees were made, which we esteem to have been done contrary to the canons, and contrary to ecclesiastical discipline. We request that your magnificence order these things to be read, that all the breth-ren may know whether the things done are just or unjust.

The most glorious judges said : If any-thing was done after our leaving let it be read.

And before the reading, Aetius, the Arch-deacon of the Church of Constantinople said : It is certain that the matters touch-ing the faith received a suitable form. But it is customary at synods, after those things which are chiefest of all shall have been defined, that other things also which are necessary should be examined and put into shape. We have, I mean the most holy Church of Constantinople has, manifestly things to be attended to. We asked the lord bishops (κυρίοις τοις ἐπισκόποις) from Rome, to join with us in these matters, but they declined, saying they had received no instructions on the subject, We referred the matter to your magnificence and you bid the holy Synod to consider this very point. And when your magnificence had gone forth, as the affair was one of com-mon interest, the most holy bishops, stand-ing up, prayed that this thing might be done. And they were present here, and this was done in no hidden nor secret fash-ion, but in due course and in accordance with the canons.

The most glorious judges said : Let the acts be read.

[*The canon (number* **XXVIII.**), *was then read, and the signatures, in all* 192, *inclu-ding the bishops of Antioch, Jerusalem, and Heraclea, but not Thalassius of Cæsarea who afterwards assented. Only a week be-fore* 350 *had signed the Definition of faith. When the last name was read a debate arose as follows.*   (Col. 810.).]

Lucentius, the most reverend bishop and legate of the Apostolic See, said : In the first place let your excellency notice that it was brought to pass by circumventing the holy bishops so that they were forced to sign the as yet unwritten canons, of which they made mention. [*The Greek reads a little differently (I have followed the Latin as it is supposed by the critics to be more pure than the Greek we now have*) : Your excellency has perceived how many things were done in the presence of the bishops, in order that no one might be forced to sign the afore-mentioned canons ; defining by necessity.]

The most reverend bishops cried out : No one was forced.

Lucentius the most reverend bishop and legate of the Apostolic See, said: It is manifest that the decrees of the 318 have been put aside, and that mention only has been made of those of the 150, which are not found to have any place in the synodical canons, and which were made as they acknowledge eighty years ago. If therefore they enjoyed this privilege during these years, what do they seek for now? If they never used it, why seek it? [*The Greek reads:* "It is manifest that the present decrees have been added to the decrees of the 318 and to those of the 150 after them, decrees not received into the synodical canons, these things they pretend to be defined. If therefore in these times they used this benefit what now do they seek which according to the canons they had not used?]

Paschasinus, the most reverend bishop and representative, read: Canon Six of the 318 holy fathers, "The Roman Church hath always had the primacy. Let Egypt therefore so hold itself that the bishop of Alexandria have the authority over all, for this is also the custom as regards the bishop of Rome. So too at Antioch and in the other provinces let the churches of the larger cities have the primacy. [*In the Greek* "let the primacy be kept to the churches;" *a sentence which I do not understand, unless it means that for the advantage of the churches the primatial rights of Antioch must be upheld. But such a sentiment one would expect to find rather in the Latin than in the Greek.*] And one thing is abundantly clear, that if any one shall have been ordained bishop contrary to the will of the metropolitan, this great synod has decreed that such an one ought not to be bishop. If however the judgment of all his own [fellows] is reasonable and according to the canons, and if two or three dissent through their own obstinacy, then let the vote of the majority prevail. For a custom has prevailed, and it is an ancient tradition, that the bishop of Jerusalem be honoured, let him have his consequent honour, but the rights of his own metropolis must be preserved."
Constantine, the secretary, read from a book handed him by Aetius, the archdeacon; Canon Six of the 318 holy Fathers. "Let the ancient customs prevail, those of Egypt,

Aetius, the archdeacon of the most holy Church of Constantinople, said: If on this subject they had received any commands, let them be brought forward.
Bonifacius, a presbyter and vicar of the Apostolic See, said: The most blessed and Apostolic Pope, among other things, gave us this commandment. And he read from the chart, "The rulings of the holy fathers shall with no rashness be violated or diminished. Let the dignity of our person in all ways be guarded by you. And if any, influenced by the power of his own city, should undertake to make usurpations, withstand this with suitable firmness."
The most glorious judges said: Let each party quote the canons.

NOTES.

An attempt has been made to shew that this statement of the acts is a mere blunder. That no correct copy of the Nicene canons was read, and that the council accepted the version produced by the Roman legate as genuine. The proposition appears to me in itself ridiculous, and taken in connexion with the fact that the acts shew that the true canon of Nice was read immediately afterwards I cannot think the hypothesis really worthy of serious consideration. But it is most ably defended by the Ballerini in their edition of St. Leo's works (Tom. iii., p. xxxvij. *et seqq*). and Hefele seems to have accepted their conclusions (Vol. III., p. 435). Bright, however, I think, takes a most just view of the case, whom I therefore quote.

BRIGHT.

If we place ourselves for a moment in the position of the ecclesiastics of Constantinople when they heard Paschasinus read his "version," which the Ballerini gently describe as "differing a little" from the Greek text, we shall see that it was simply impossible for them not to quote that text as it was preserved in their archives, and had been correctly translated by Philo and Evarestus in their version beginning "Antiqui mores obtineant." No comment on the difference between it and the Roman "version" is recorded to have been made: and, in truth, none was necessary. Simply to confront the two, and pass on to the next point, was to confute so that the bishop of Alexandria shall have jurisdiction over all, since this also is the custom at Rome.   Likewise at Antioch and in the rest of the provinces, let the rank (πρεσβεῖα) be preserved to the churches. For this is absolutely clear that if anyone contrary to the will of the metropolitan be ordained bishop, such an one the great synod decreed should not be a bishop. If however by the common vote of all, founded upon reason, and according to the canons, two or three moved by their own obstinacy, make opposition, let the vote of the majority stand.''

The same secretary read from the same codex the determination of the Second Synod. "These things the bishops decreed who assembled by the grace of God in Constantinople from far separated provinces, . . . and bishops are not to go to churches which are outside the bounds of their dioceses, nor to confound the churches, but according to the canons the bishop of Alexandria shall take the charge of the affairs of Egypt only, and the bishops of Orient shall govern the Oriental diocese only, the honours due to the Church of Antioch being guarded according to the Nicene canons, and the Asiatic bishops shall care for the diocese of Asia only, and those of Pontus the affairs of Pontus only, and those of Thrace the affairs of Thrace only. But bishops shall not enter uncalled another diocese for ordination, or any other ecclesiastical function.   And the aforesaid canon concerning dioceses being observed, it is evident that the synod of every province will administer the affairs of that particular province as was decreed at Nice.   But the churches of God in heathen nations must be governed according to the custom which has prevailed from the times of the Fathers. The bishop of Constantinople however shall have the prerogative of honour next after the bishop of Rome, because Constantinople is new Rome.''

Paschasinus at once most respectfully and most expressively.

It should be added that the Ballerini ground their theory chiefly upon the authority of a Latin MS., the *Codex Julianus,* now called *Parisiensis,* in which this reading of the true text of the canon of Nice is not contained, as Baluzius was the first to point out.

The most glorious judges said : Let the most holy Asiatic and Pontic bishops who have signed the tome just read say whether they gave their signatures of their own judgment or compelled by any necessity.   And when these were come into the midst, the most reverend Diogenes, the bishop of Cyzicum, said : I call God to witness that I signed of my own judgment.   [*And so on, one after the other.*]

The rest cried out : We signed willingly.

The most glorious judges said : As it is manifest that the subscription of each one of the bishops was given without any necessity but of his own will, let the most holy bishops who have not signed say something.

Eusebius, the bishop of Ancyra, said : I am about to speak but for myself alone.

[*His speech is a personal explanation of his own action with regard to consecrating a bishop for Gangra.*]

The most glorious judges said : From what has been done and brought forward on each side, we perceive that the primacy of all (πρὸ πάντων τὰ πρωτεῖα) and the chief honour (τὴν ἐξαίρετον τιμὴν) according to the canons, is to be kept for the most God-beloved archbishop of Old Rome, but that the most reverend archbishop of the royal city Constantinople, which is new Rome, is to enjoy the honour of the same primacy, and to have the power to ordain the metropolitans in the Asiatic, Pontic, and Thracian dioceses, in this manner : that there be elected by the clergy, and substantial (κτη-τόρων) and most distinguished men of each metropolis and moreover by all the most reverend bishops of the province, or a majority of them, and that he be elected whom those afore mentioned shall deem worthy of the metropolitan episcopate and that he should be presented by all those who had elected him to the most holy archbishop of royal Constantinople, that he might be asked whether he [i.e., the Patriarch of Constantinople] willed that he should there be ordained, or by his commission in the province where he received the vote to the episcopate. The most reverend bishops of the ordinary towns should be ordained by all the most reverend bishops of the province or by a majority of them, the metro-politan having his power according to the established canon of the fathers, and making with regard to such ordinations no communications to the most holy archbishop of royal Constantinople. Thus the matter appears to us to stand. Let the holy Synod vouchsafe to teach its view of the case.

The most reverend bishops cried out : This is a just sentence. So we all say. These things please us all. This is a just determination. Establish the proposed form of decree. This is a just vote. All has been decreed as should be. We beg you to let us go. By the safety of the Emperor let us go. We all will remain in this opinion, we all say the same things.

Lucentius, the bishop, said : The Apostolic See gave orders that all things should be done in our presence [*This sentence reads in the Latin :* The Apostolic See ought not to be humiliated in our presence. *I do not know why Canon Bright in his notes on Canon XXVIII. has followed this reading*]; and therefore whatever yesterday was done to the prejudice of the canons during our absence, we beseech your highness to command to be rescinded. But if not, let our opposition be placed in the minutes, and pray let us know clearly [*Lat.* that we may know] what we are to report to that most apostolic bishop who is the ruler of the whole church, so that he may be able to take action with regard to the indignity done to his See and to the setting at naught of the canons.

[John, the most reverend bishop of Sebaste, said : We all will remain of the opinion expressed by your magnificence.[1]]

The most glorious judges said : The whole synod has approved what we proposed.

NOTES.

HEFELE.

(*Hist. Counc.*, Vol. III., p. 428.)

That is, the prerogative assigned to the Church of Constantinople is, in spite of the opposition of the Roman legate decreed by the Synod. Thus ended the Council of Chalcedon after it had lasted three weeks.

How it is possible after reading the foregoing proceedings to imagine for an instant that the bishops of this Council considered the rights they were discussing to be of Divine origin, and that the occupant of the See of Rome was, *jure divino*, supreme over all pontiffs I cannot understand. It is quite possible, of course, to affirm, as some have done, that the acts, as we have them, have been mutilated, but the contention involves not only many difficulties but also no few absurdities ; and yet I cannot but think that even this extreme hypothesis is to be preferred to any attempt to reconcile the acts as we now have them with the acceptance on the part of the members of the council of the doctrine of a *jure divino* Papal Supremacy as it is now held by the Latin Church.

[1] These words are found only in the Latin.

THE FIFTH ECUMENICAL COUNCIL.

THE SECOND COUNCIL OF CONSTANTINOPLE.

A.D. 553.

Emperor.—JUSTINIAN I.
Pope.—VIGILIUS.

Elenchus.

HISTORICAL INTRODUCTION.

(Hefele, *History of the Councils*, Vol. IV., p. 289.)

In accordance with the imperial command, but without the assent of the Pope, the synod was opened on the 5th of May A.D. 553, in the Secretarium of the Cathedral Church at Constantinople. Among those present were the Patriarchs, Eutychius of Constantinople, who presided, Apollinaris of Alexandria, Domninus of Antioch, three bishops as representatives of the Patriarch Eustochius of Jerusalem, and 145 other metropolitans and bishops, of whom many came also in the place of absent colleagues.

(Bossuet, *Def. Cleri Gall.*, Lib. vij., cap. xix. Abridged. Translation by Allies.)

The three chapters were the point in question; that is, respecting Theodore of Mopsuestia, Theodoret's writings against Cyril, and the letter of Ibas of Edessa to Maris the Persian. They examined whether that letter had been approved in the Council of Chalcedon. So much was admitted that it had been read there, and that Ibas, after anathematizing Nestorius, had been received by the holy Council. Some contended that his person only was spared; others that his letter also was approved. Thus inquiry was made at the fifth Council how the writings on the Faith were wont to be approved in former Councils. The Acts of the third and fourth Council, those which we have mentioned above respecting the letter of St. Cyril and of St. Leo, were set forth. Then the holy Council declared: "It is plain, from what has been recited, in what manner the holy Councils are wont to approve what is brought before them. For great as was the dignity of those holy men who wrote the letters recited, yet they did not approve their letters simply or without inquiry, nor without taking cognizance that they were in all things agreeable to the exposition and doctrine of the holy Fathers, with which they were compared." But the Acts proved that this course was not pursued in the case of the letter of Ibas; they inferred, therefore, most justly, that that letter had not been approved. So, then, it is certain from the third and fourth Councils, the fifth so declaring and understanding it, that letters approved by the Apostolic See, such as was that of Cyril, or even proceeding from it, as that of Leo, were received by the holy Councils not simply, nor without inquiry. The holy Fathers proceed to do what the Bishops at Chalcedon would have done, had they undertaken the examination of Ibas's letter. They compare the letter with the Acts of Ephesus and Chalcedon. Which done, the holy Council declared—"The comparison made proves, beyond a doubt, that the letter which Ibas is said to have written is, in all respects, opposed to the definition of the right Faith, which the Council of Chalcedon set forth." All the Bishops cried out, "We all say this; the letter is heretical." Thus, therefore, is it proved by the fifth Council, that our holy Fathers in Ecumenical Councils pronounce the letters read, whether of Catholics or heretics, or even of Roman Pontiffs, and that on matter of Faith, to be orthodox or heretical, according to the same procedure, after legitimate cognizance, the truth being inquired into, and then cleared up; and upon these premises judgment given.

What! you will say, with no distinction, and with minds equally inclined to both parties? Indeed, we have said, and shall often repeat, that there was a presumption in favour of the decrees of orthodox Pontiffs; but in Ecumenical Councils, where judgment is to be passed in matter of Faith, that they were bound no longer to act upon presumption, but on the truth clearly and thoroughly ascertained.

Such were the Acts of the fifth Council. This it learnt from the third and fourth Councils, and approved; and in this argument we have brought at once in favour of our opinion the decrees of three Ecumenical Councils, of Ephesus, of Chalcedon, and the second Constantinopolitan. The Emperor Justinian desired that the question concerning the above-mentioned Three Chapters should be considered in the Church. He therefore sent for Pope Vigilius to Constantinople. There he not long after assembled a council. He and the Orientals thought it of great moment that these Chapters should be condemned, against the Nestorians, who were raising their heads to defend them; Vigilius, with the Occidentals, feared let this occasion should be taken to destroy the authority of the Council of Chalcedon: because it was admitted that Theodoret and Ibas had been received in that Council, whilst Theodore, though named, was let go without any mark of censure. Though then both parties easily agreed as to the substance of the Faith, yet the question had entirely respect to the Faith, it being feared by the one party lest the Nestorian, by the other lest the Eutychian, enemies of the Council of Chalcedon should prevail. Vigilius on the 11th of April, 548, issues his "Judicatum" against the Three Chapters, saving the authority of the Council of Chalcedon. Thereupon the Bishops of Africa, Illyria, and Dalmatia, with two of his own confidential Deacons, withdraw from his communion. In the year 550 the African Bishops, under Reparatus of Carthage, not only reject the Judicatum, but anathematize Vigilius himself, and sever him from Catholic Communion, reserving to him a place for repentance. At length the Pope publicly withdraws his "Judicatum." While the Council is sitting at Constantinople he publishes his "Constitutum," in which he condemns certain propositions of Theodore, but spares his person; the same respecting Theodoret; but with respect to Ibas, he declares that his letter was pronounced orthodox by the Council of Chalcedon. However this may be, so much is clear, that Vigilius, though invited, declined being present at the council: that nevertheless the council was held without him; that he published a "Constitutum," in which he disapproved of what Theodore, Theodoret, and Ibas were said to have written against the Faith; but decreed that their names should be spared because they were considered to have been received by the fourth Council, or to have died in the communion of the Church, and to be reserved to the judgment of God. Concerning the letter of Ibas, he published the following, that, "understood in the best and most pious sense," it was blameless; and concerning the three Chapters generally, he ordered that after his present declaration ecclesiastics should move no further question.

Such was the decree of Vigilius, issued upon the authority with which he was invested. But the council, after his Constitution, both raised a question about the Three Chapters, and decided that question was properly raised concerning the dead, and that the letter of Ibas was manifestly heretical and Nestorian, and contrary in all things to the Faith of Chalcedon, and that they were altogether accursed, who defended the impious Theodore of Mopsuestia, or the writings of Theodoret against Cyril, or the impious letter of Ibas defending the tenets of Nestorius: and all such as did not anathematize it, but said it was correct.

In these latter words they seemed not even to spare Vigilius, although they did not mention his name. And it is certain their decree was confirmed by Pelagius the Second, Gregory the Great, and other Roman Pontiffs. . . . These things prove, that in a matter of the utmost importance, disturbing the whole Church, and seeming to belong to the Faith, the decrees of sacred councils prevail over the decrees of Pontiffs, and that the letter of Ibas, though defended by a judgment of the Roman Pontiff, could nevertheless be proscribed as heretical.

EXCURSUS ON THE GENUINENESS OF THE ACTS OF THE FIFTH COUNCIL.

Some suspicion has arisen with regard to how far the acts of the Fifth Ecumenical Council may be relied upon. Between the Roman Manuscript printed by Labbe and the Paris manuscript found in Mansi there are considerable variations and, strange to say, some of the most injurious things to the memory of Pope Vigilius are found only in the Paris manuscript. Moreover we know that the manuscript kept in the patriarchal archives at Constantinople had been tampered with during the century that elapsed before the next Ecumenical Synod, for at that council the forgeries and interpolations were exposed by the Papal Legates.

At the XIVth Session of that synod the examination of the genuineness of the acts of the Second Council of Constantinople was resumed. It had been begun at the XIIth Session. Up to this time only two MSS. had been used, now the librarian of the patriarchate presented a third MS. which he had found in the archives, and swore that neither himself nor any other so far as he knew had made any change in these MSS. These were then compared and it was found that the two first agreed in containing the pretended letter of Mennas to Pope Vigilius, and the two writings addressed by Vigilius to Justinian and Theodora ; but that none of these were found in the third MS. It was further found that the documents in dispute were in a different hand from the rest of the MS., and that in the first book of the parchment MS., three quarternions had been inserted, and in the second book between quarternions 15 and 16, four unpaged leaves had been placed. So too the second MS. had been tampered with. The council inserted these particulars in a decree, and ordered that "these additions must be quashed in both MSS., and marked with an obelus, and the falsifiers must be smitten with anathema." Finally the council cried out, "Anathema to the pretended letters of Mennas and Vigilius ! Anathema to the forger of Acts ! Anathema to all who teach, etc."

From all this it would seem that the substantial accuracy of the rest of the acts have been established by the authority of the Sixth Synod, and Hefele and all recent scholars follow Mansi's Paris MS.

It may be well here to add that a most thorough-going attack upon the acts has been made in late years by Professor Vincenzi, in defence of Pope Vigilius and of Origen. The reader is referred to his writings on the subject : *In Sancti Gregorii Nysseni et Originis scripta et doctrinam nova defensio; Vigil., Orig., Justin. triumph., in Synod V.* (Romæ, 1865.) The *Catholic Dictionary* frankly says that this is " an attempt to deny the most patent facts, and treat some of the chief documents as forgeries," and "unworthy of serious notice." [1]

---

[1] Addis and Arnold. *A Catholic Dictionary.* Sixth Ed. with *imprimatur* signed by Cards. Manning and McCloskey, *s.v.* Three Chapters.

EXTRACTS FROM THE ACTS.

SESSION I.

(Labbe and Cossart, *Concilia*, Tom. V., col. 419.)

[*The Emperor's Letter which was read to the Fathers.*]

In the Name of our Lord God Jesus Christ. The Emperor Flavius Justinian, German, Gothic, etc., and always Augustus, to the most blessed bishops and patriarchs, Eutychius of Constantinople, Apollinarius of Alexandria, Domninus of Theopolis, Stephen, George, and Damian, the most religious bishops taking the place of that man of singular blessedness, Eustochius, the Archbishop and Patriarch of Jerusalem, and the other most religious bishops stopping in this royal city from the different provinces.

[*The following is the letter condensed, including Hefele's digest.* History of the Councils, *Vol. IV., p.* 298.]

The effort of my predecessors, the orthodox Emperors, ever aimed at the settling of controversies which had arisen respecting the faith by the calling of Synods. For this cause Constantine assembled 318 Fathers at Nice, and was himself present at the Council, and assisted those who confessed the Son to be consubstantial with the Father. Theodosius, 150 at Constantinople, Theodosius the younger, the Synod of Ephesus, the Emperor Marcian, the bishops at Chalcedon. As, however, after Marcian's death, controversies respecting the Synod of Chalcedon had broken out in several places, the Emperor Leo wrote to all bishops of all places, in order that everyone might declare his opinion in writing with regard to this holy Council. Soon afterwards, however, had arisen again the adherents of Nestorius and Eutyches, and caused great divisions, so that many Churches had broken off communion with one another. When, now, the grace of God raised us to the throne, we regarded it as our chief business to unite the Churches again, and to bring the Synod of Chalcedon, together with the three earlier, to universal acceptance. We have won many who previously opposed that Synod; others, who persevered in their opposition, we banished, and so restored the unity of the Church again. But the Nestorians want to impose their heresy upon the Church; and, as they could not use Nestorius for that purpose, they made haste to introduce their errors through Theodore of Mopsuestia, the teacher of Nestorius, who taught still more grievous blasphemies than his. He maintained, *e.g.*, that God the Word was one, and Christ another. For the same purpose they made use of those impious writings of Theodoret which were directed against the first Synod of Ephesus, against Cyril and his Twelve Chapters, and also the shameful letter which Ibas is said to have written. They maintain that this letter was accepted by the Synod of Chalcedon, and so would free from condemnation Nestorius and Theodore who were commended in the letter. If they were to succeed, the Logos could no longer be said to be "made man," nor Mary called the Mother (*genetrix*) of God. We, therefore, following the holy Fathers, have first asked you in writing to give your judgment on the three impious chapters named, and you have answered, and have joyfully confessed the true faith. Because, however, after the condemnation proceeding from you, there are still some who defend the Three Chapters, therefore we have summoned you to the capital, that you may here, in common assembly, place again your view in the light of day. When, for example, Vigilius, Pope of Old Rome, came hither, he, in answer to our questions, repeatedly anathematised in writing the Three Chapters, and confirmed his steadfastness in this view by much, even by the condemnation of his deacons, Rusticus and Sebastian. We possess still his declarations in his own hand. Then he issued his *Judicatum*, in which he anathematised the Three Chapters, with the words, *Et quoniam*, etc. You know that he not only deposed Rusticus and Sebastian because they defended the Three Chapters, but also wrote to Valentinian, bishop of Scythia, and Aurelian, bishop of Arles, that nothing might be undertaken against the *Judicatum*. When you afterwards came hither at my invitation, letters were exchanged between you and Vigilius in order to a common assembly.[1] But now he had altered his view, would no longer have a synod, but required that only the three patriarchs and one other bishop (in communion with the Pope and the three bishops about him) should decide the matter. In vain we sent several commands to him to take part in the synod. He rejected also our two proposals, either to call a tribunal for decision, or to hold a smaller assembly, at which, besides him and his three bishops, every other patriarch should have place and voice, with from three to five bishops of his diocese.* We further declare that we hold fast to the decrees of the four Councils, and in every way follow the holy Fathers, Athanasius, Hilary, Basil, Gregory the Theologian, Gregory of Nyssa, Ambrose, Theophilus, John (Chrysostom) of Constantinople, Cyril, Augustine, Proclus, Leo and their writings on the true faith. As, however, the heretics are resolved to defend Theodore of Mopsuestia and Nestorius with their impieties, and maintain that that letter of Ibas was received by the Synod of Chalcedon, so do we exhort you to direct your attention to the impious writings of Theodore, and especially to his Jewish Creed which was brought forward at Ephesus and Chalcedon, and anathematized by each synod with those who had so held or did so hold ; and we further exhort you to consider what the holy Fathers have written concerning him and his blasphemies, as well as what our predecessors have promulgated, as also what the Church historians have set forth

concerning him.[2] You will thence see that he and his heresies have since been condemned and that therefore his name has long since been struck from the diptychs of the Church of Mopsuestia. Consider the absurd assertion that heretics ought not to be anathematized after their deaths ; and we exhort you further to follow in this matter the doctrine of the holy Fathers, who condemned not only living heretics but also anathematized after their death those who had died in their iniquity, just as those who had been unjustly condemned they restored after their death and wrote their names in the sacred diptychs ; which took place in the case of John and of Flavian of pious memory, both of them bishops of Constantinople.[3] Moreover we exhort you to examine the writing of Theodoret and the supposed letter of Ibas, in which the incarnation of the Word is denied, the expression "Mother of God" and the holy Synod of Ephesus rejected, Cyril called a heretic, and Theodore and Nestorius defended and praised. And as they say that the Council of Chalcedon has received this letter, you must compare the declarations of this Council relating to the faith with the contents of the impious letter. Finally, we entreat you to accelerate the matter. For he who when asked concerning the right faith, puts off his answer for a long while, does nothing else but deny the right faith. For in questioning and answering on things which are of faith, it is not he who is found first or second, but he who is the more ready with a right confession, that is acceptable to God. May God keep you, most holy and religious fathers, for many years. Given IV. Nones of May, at Constantinople, in the xxviith year of the reign of the imperial lord Justinian, the perpetual Augustus, and in the xiith year after the consulate of the most illustrious Basil.

---

[1] From here to the next asterisk, the text varies. Hefele says he follows the Paris codex with " abridgments."
[2] The emperor could say that the letter was condemned at Chalcedon, because the Acts of Ephesus were read in the first session of Chalcedon. Garnier is in error with regard to this, as Hefele points out.
[3] This I have given in full.

EXTRACTS FROM THE ACTS.

SESSION VII.

(From the Paris manuscript found in Hardouin Concilia, *Tom. III., 171 et seqq.;* Mansi, *Tom. ix., 346 et seqq. This speech is not found in full in any other MS. The Ballerini [Hefele notes] raise objections to the genuineness of the additions [in* Noris. Opp., *Tom. IV., 1037], but Hefele does not consider the objections of serious moment.* [Hist. of the Councils, *Vol. IV., p. 323, note 2.] All the MSS. agree that* The most glorious quæstor of the sacred palace, Constantine, was sent by the most pious Emperor, and when he had entered the Council spake as follows : " Certum est vestræ beatitudini, quantum, etc." *The rest of the speech differs in the different manuscripts. I follow that of Paris.)*

You know how much care the most invincible Emperor has always had that the contention raised up by certain persons with regard to the Three Chapters should have a termination. . . . For this intent he has required the most religious Vigilius to assemble with you and draw up a decree on this matter in accordance with the Orthodox faith. Although therefore, Vigilius has already frequently condemned the Three Chapters in writing, and has done this also by word of mouth in the presence of the Emperor, and of the most glorious judges and of many members of this synod, and has always been ready to smite with anathema the defenders of Theodore of Mopsuestia, and the letter which was attributed to Ibas, and the writings of Theodoret which he set forth against the orthodox faith and against the twelve capitula of the holy Cyril : [1] yet he has refused to do this in communion with you and your synod.

Yesterday Vigilius sent Servus Dei, a most reverend Subdeacon of the Roman Church, and invited Belisarius,[2] Cethegus, as also Justinus and Constantine the most glorious consuls, as well as bishops Theodore, Ascidas, Benignus, and Phocas, to come to him as he wished to give through them an answer to the Emperor. They came, but speedily returned and informed the most pious lord, that we had visited Vigilius, the most religious bishop, and that he had said to us : "We have called you for this reason, that you may know what things have been done in the past days. To this end I have written a document about the disputed

Three Chapters, addressed to the most pious Emperor,[3] pray be good enough to read it, and to carry it to his Serenity." But when we had heard this and had seen the document written to your serenity, we said to him that we could not by any means receive any document written to the most pious Emperor without his bidding. "But you have deacons for running with messages, by whom you can send it." He, however, said to us : "You now know that I have made the document." But we, bishops, answered him : "If your blessedness is willing to meet together with us and the most holy Patriarchs, and the most religious bishops, and to treat of the Three Chapters and to give, in unison with us all, a suitable form of the orthodox faith, as the Holy Apostles and the holy Fathers and the four Councils have done, we will hold thee as our head, as a father and primate. But if your holiness has drawn up a document for the Emperor, you have errand-runners, as we have said; send it by them." And when he had heard these things from us, he sent Servus Dei the Subdeacon, who now awaits the answer of your serenity. And when his Piety had heard this, he commanded through the aforesaid most religious and glorious men, the before-named subdeacon to carry back this message to the most religious Vigilius : "We invited him (*you*) to meet together with the most blessed patriarchs and other religious bishops, and with them in common to examine and judge the Three Chapters. But since you have refused to do this, and you say that you alone have written by yourself somewhat on

---

[1] Thus far the MSS. agree almost word for word. The divergence for the rest is most marked.

[2] There is some doubt about this name.
[3] This was the "Constitutum."

the Three Chapters; if you have condemned them, in accordance with those things which you did before, we have already many such statements and need no more; but if you have written now something contrary to these things which were done by you before, you have condemned yourself by your own writing, since you have departed from orthodox doctrine and have defended impiety. And how can you expect us to receive such a document from you?"

And when this answer was given by the most pious Emperor, he did not send through the same deacon any document in writing from himself. And all this was done without writing as also to your blessedness.

[*He then, according to all the MSS., presented certain documents to be read, in the MS. printed by Labbe and Cossart, Tom. V., col. 549 et seqq. These are fewer than in the Paris MS., which last also contains the following just after the reading of the documents and after the Council had declared that they proved the Emperor's zeal for the faith.*]

Constantine, the most glorious Quæstor, said: While I am still present at your holy council by reason of the reading of the documents which have been presented to you, I would say that the most pious Emperor has sent a minute (*formam*), to your Holy Synod, concerning the name of Vigilius, that it be no more inserted in the holy diptychs of the Church, on account of the impiety which he defended. Neither let it be recited by you, nor retained, either in the church of the royal city, or in other churches which are intrusted to you and to the other bishops in the State committed by God to

his rule. And when you hear this minute, again you will perceive by it how much the most serene Emperor cares for the unity of the holy churches and for the purity of the holy mysteries.

[The letter was then read.]

The holy Synod said: What has seemed good to the most pious Emperor is congruous to the labours which he bears for the unity of the churches. Let us preserve unity to (*ad*) the Apostolic See of the most holy Church of ancient Rome, carrying out all things according to the tenor of what has been read. De proposita vero quæstione quod jam promisimus procedat.

NOTES.

Hefele understands that the Council heard and approved this letter of the Emperor's, but that the "Emperor did not mean entirely to break off communion with the Apostolic see, neither did he wish the Synod to do so" (*Hist. Councils*, Vol. IV., p. 326), as indeed he says in his letter.

The Ballerini consider this letter of the Emperor's to be spurious, but (says Hefele) "on insufficient grounds" (*l. c.*, p. 326, note 3). The expressions used by the Emperor may not unnaturally be somewhat startling to those holding the theological position of the Ballerini: "We will not endure to receive the spotless communion from him nor from any one else who does not condemn this impiety . . . lest we be found thus communicating with the impiety of Nestorius and Theodore."

It is noteworthy that the Fifth Ecumenical Council should strike the name of the reigning Pope from the diptychs as a father of heresy; and that the Sixth Ecumenical Synod should anathematize another Pope as a heretic!

THE SENTENCE OF THE SYNOD.

(*From the Acts.* Collation VIII., L. and C., *Conc.*, Tom. V., col. 562.)

Our Great God and Saviour Jesus Christ, as we learn from the parable in the Gospel, distributes talents to each man according to his ability, and at the fitting time demands an account of the work done by every man. And if he to whom but one talent has been committed is condemned because he has not worked with it but only kept it without loss, to how much greater and more horrible judgment must he be subject who not only is negligent concerning himself, but even places a stumbling-block and cause of offence in the way of others? Since it is manifest to all the faithful that whenever any question arises concerning the faith, not only the impious man himself is condemned, but also he who when he has the power to correct impiety in others, neglects to do so.[1]

We therefore, to whom it has been committed to rule the church of the Lord, fearing the curse which hangs over those who negligently perform the Lord's work, hasten to preserve the good seed of faith pure from the tares of impiety which are being sown by the enemy.

When, therefore, we saw that the followers of Nestorius were attempting to introduce their impiety into the church of God through the impious Theodore, who was bishop of Mopsuestia, and through his impious writings; and moreover through those things which Theodoret impiously wrote, and through the wicked epistle which is said to have been written by Ibas to Maris the Persian, moved by all these sights we rose up for the correction of what was going on, and assembled in this royal city called thither by the will of God and the bidding of the most religious Emperor.

And because it happened that the most religious Vigilius stopping in this royal city, was present at all the discussions with regard to the Three Chapters, and had often condemned them orally and in writing, nevertheless afterwards he gave his consent in writing to be present at the Council and examine together with us the Three Chapters, that a suitable definition of the right faith might be set forth by us all. Moreover the most pious Emperor, according to what had seemed good between us, exhorted both him and us to meet together, because it is comely that the priesthood should after common discussion impose a common faith. On this account we besought his reverence to fulfil his written promises; for it was not right that the scandal with regard to these Three Chapters should go any further, and the Church of God be disturbed thereby. And to this end we brought to his remembrance the great examples left us by the Apostles, and the traditions of the Fathers. For although the grace of the Holy Spirit abounded in each one of the Apostles, so that no one of them needed the counsel of another in the execution of his work, yet they were not willing to define on the question then raised touching the circumcision of the Gentiles, until being gathered together they had confirmed their own several sayings by the testimony of the divine Scriptures.

And thus they arrived unanimously at this sentence, which they wrote to the Gentiles: "It has seemed good to the Holy Ghost and to us, to lay upon you no other burden than these necessary things, that ye abstain from things offered to idols, and from blood, and from things strangled, and from fornication."

But also the Holy Fathers, who from time to time have met in the four holy councils, following the example of the ancients, have by a common discussion, disposed of by a fixed decree the heresies and questions which had sprung up, as it was certainly known, that by common discussion when the matter in dispute was presented by each side, the light of truth expels the darkness of falsehood.

Nor is there any other way in which the truth can be made manifest when there are discussions concerning the faith, since each one needs the help of his neighbour, as we read in the Proverbs of Solomon: "A brother helping his brother shall be exalted like a walled city; and he shall be strong

---

[1] This, of course, refers to Pope Vigilius.

as a well-founded kingdom;" and again in Ecclesiastes he says: "Two are better than one; because they have a good reward for their labour."

So also the Lord himself says: "Verily I say unto you that if two of you shall agree upon earth as touching anything they shall seek for, they shall have it from my Father which is in heaven. For wheresoever two or three are gathered together in my name, there am I in the midst of them."

But when often he had been invited by us all, and when the most glorious judges had been sent to him by the most religious Emperor, he promised to give sentence himself on the Three Chapters (*sententiam proferre*): And when we heard this answer, having the Apostle's admonition in mind, that "each one must give an account of himself to God," and fearing the judgment that hangs over those who scandalize one even of the least important, and knowing how much sorer it must be to give offence to so entirely Christian an Emperor, and to the people, and to all the Churches; and further recalling what was said by God to Paul: "Fear not, but speak, and be not silent, for I am with thee, and no one can harm thee.". Therefore, being gathered together, before all things we have briefly confessed that we hold that faith which our Lord Jesus Christ, the true God, delivered to his holy Apostles, and through them to the holy churches, and which they who after them were holy fathers and doctors, handed down to the people credited to them.

We confessed that we hold, preserve, and declare to the holy churches that confession of faith which the 318 holy Fathers more at length set forth, who were gathered together at Nice, who handed down the holy *mathema* or creed. Moreover, the 150 gathered together at Constantinople set forth our faith, who followed that same confession of faith and explained it. And the consent of the 200 holy fathers gathered for the same faith in the first Council of Ephesus. And what things were defined by the 630 gathered at Chalcedon for the one and the same faith, which they both followed and taught. And all those who from time to time have been condemned or anathematized by the Catholic Church, and by the aforesaid four Councils, we confessed that we hold them condemned and anathematized. And when we had thus made profession of our faith we

began the examination of the Three Chapters, and first we brought into review the matter of Theodore of Mopsuestia; and when all the blasphemies contained in his writings were made manifest, we marvelled at the long-suffering of God, that the tongue and mind which had framed such blasphemies were not immediately consumed by the divine fire; and we never would have suffered the reader of the aforenamed blasphemies to proceed, fearing [as we did] the indignation of God for their record alone (as each blasphemy surpassed its predecessor in the magnitude of its impiety and moved from its foundation the mind of the hearer) had it not been that we saw they who gloried in such blasphemies stood in need of the confusion which would come upon them through their manifestation. So that all of us, moved with indignation by these blasphemies against God, both during and after the reading, broke forth into denunciations and anathematisms against Theodore, as if he had been living and present. O Lord be merciful, we cried, not even devils have dared to utter such things against thee.

O intolerable tongue! O the depravity of the man! O that high hand he lifted up against his Creator! For the wretched man who had promised to know the Scriptures, had no recollection of the words of the Prophet Hosea, "Woe unto them! for they have fled from me: they are become famous because they were impious as touching me; they spake iniquities against me, and when they had thought them out, they spake the violent things against me. Therefore shall they fall in the snare by reason of the wickedness of their own tongues. Their contempt shall turn into their own bosom: because they have transgressed my covenant and have acted impiously against my laws."

To these curses the impious Theodore is justly subject. For the prophecies concerning Christ he rejected and hastened to destroy, so far as he had the power, the great mystery of the dispensation for our salvation; attempting in many ways to shew the divine words to be nothing but fables, for the mirth of the gentiles, and spurned the other prophetic announcements made against the impious, especially that which the divine Habacuc said of those who teach falsely, "Woe unto him that giveth his neighbour drink, that puttest thy bottle to him and makest him drunken that thou mayest look on their nakedness," that is, their doctrines full of darkness and altogether foreign to the light.

And why should we add anything further? For anyone can take in his hands the writings of the impious Theodore or the impious chapters which from his impious writings were inserted by us in our acts, and find the incredible foolishness and the detestable things which he said. For we are afraid to proceed further and again to remember these infamies.

There was also read to us what had been written by the holy Fathers against him, and his foolishness which exceeded that of all heretics, and moreover the histories and the imperial laws, setting forth his impiety from the beginning, and since after all these things the defenders of his impiety, glorying in the injuries uttered by him against his Creator, said that it was not right to anathematize him after death, although we knew the ecclesiastical tradition concerning the impious, that even after death, heretics are anathematized; nevertheless we thought it necessary concerning this also to make examination, and there were found in the acts how divers heretics had been anathematized after death; and in many ways it was manifest to us that those who were saying this cared nothing for the judgment of God, nor for the Apostolic announcements, nor for the tradition of the Fathers. And we would like to ask them what they have to say to the Lord's having said of himself: "Whosoever should have believed in him, is not judged: but who should not have believed in him is judged already, because he hath not believed in the name of the only begotten Son of God," and of that exclamation of the Apostle: Although we or an angel from heaven were to preach to you another gospel than that we have preached unto you, let him be anathema: as we have said, so now I say again, If anyone preach to you another gospel than that you have received, let him be anathema."

For when the Lord says: "he is judged already," and when the Apostle anathematizes even angels, if they teach anything different from what we have preached, how can even those who dare all things, presume to say that these words refer only to

the living? or are they ignorant, or is it not rather that they feign to be ignorant, that the judgment of anathema is nothing else than that of separation from God? For the impious person, although he may not have been verbally anathematized by anyone, nevertheless he really is anathematized, having separated himself from the true life by his impiety.

For what have they to answer to the Apostle again when he says, "A man that is an heretic reject after the first and second corrections. Knowing that such a man is perverse, and sins, and is condemned by himself."

In accordance with which words Cyril of blessed memory, in the books which he wrote against Theodore, says as follows: They are to be avoided who are in the grasp of such awful crimes whether they be among the quick or not. For it is necessary always to flee from that which is hurtful, and not to have respect of persons, but to consider what is pleasing to God. And again the same Cyril of holy memory, writing to John, bishop of Antioch, and to the synod assembled in that city concerning Theodore who was anathematized together with Nestorius, says thus: It was therefore necessary to keep a brilliant festival, since every voice which agreed with the blasphemies of Nestorius had been cast out no matter whose. For it proceeded against all those who held these same opinions or had at one time held them, which is exactly what we and your holiness have said: We anathematize those who say that there are two Sons and two Christs. For one is he who is preached by us and you, as we have said, Christ, the Son and Lord, only begotten as man, according to the saying of the most learned Paul. And also in his letter to Alexander and Martinian and John and Paregorius and Maximus, presbyters and monastic fathers, and those who with them were leading the solitary life, he so says: The holy synod of Ephesus, gathered together according to the will of God against the Nestorian perfidy with a just and keen sentence condemned together with him the empty words of those who afterwards should embrace or who had in time past embraced the same opinions with him, and who presumed to say or write any such thing, laying upon them an equal condemnation. For it followed naturally that when one was condemned for such profane emptiness of speech, the sentence should not come against one only, but (so to speak) against every one of their heresies or calumnies, which they utter against the pious doctrines of the Christ, worshipping two Sons, and dividing the indivisible, and bringing in the crime of man-worship (*anthropolatry*), both into heaven and earth. For with us the holy multitude of the supernal spirits adore one Lord Jesus Christ. Moreover several letters of Augustine, of most religious memory, who shone forth resplendent among the African bishops, were read, shewing that it was quite right that heretics should be anathematized after death. And this ecclesiastical tradition, the other most reverend bishops of Africa have preserved: and the holy Roman Church as well had anathematized certain bishops after their death, although they had not been accused of any falling from the faith during their lives: and of each we have the evidence in our hands.

But since the disciples of Theodore and of his impiety, who are so manifestly enemies of the truth, have attempted to bring forward certain passages of Cyril of holy memory and of Proclus, as though they had been written in favour of Theodore, it is opportune to fit to them the words of the prophet when he says: "The ways of the Lord are right and the just walk therein; but the wicked shall be weak in them." For these, evilly receiving the things which have been well and opportunely written by the holy Fathers, and making excuses in their sins, quote these words. The fathers do not appear as delivering Theodore from anathema, but rather as economically using certain expressions on account of those who defended Nestorius and his impiety, in order to draw them away from this error, and to lead them to perfection and to teach them to condemn not only Nestorius, the disciple of the impiety, but also his teacher Theodore. So in these very words of economy the Fathers shew their intention on this point, that Theodore should be anathematized, as has been abundantly demonstrated by us in our acts from the writings of Cyril and Proclus of holy memory with regard to the condemnation of Theodore and his impiety. And such economy is found in divine Scripture:

and it is evident that Paul the Apostle made use of this in the beginning of his ministry, in relation to those who had been brought up as Jews, and circumcised Timothy, that by this economy and condescension he might lead them on to perfection. But afterwards he forbade circumcision, writing thus to the Galatians: "Behold, I Paul say to you, that if ye be circumcised Christ profiteth you nothing." But we found that that which heretics were wont to do, the defenders of Theodore had done also. For cutting out certain of the things which the holy Fathers had written, and placing with them and mixing up certain false things of their own, they have tried by a letter of Cyril of holy memory as though from a testimony of the Fathers, to free from anathema the aforesaid impious Theodore: in which very passages the truth was demonstrated, when the parts which had been cut off were read in their proper order, and the falsehood was thoroughly evinced by the collation of the true. But in all these things, they who spake such vanities, "trusted in falsehood," as it is written, "they trust in falsehood, and speak vanity; they conceive grief and bring forth iniquity, weaving the spider's web." When we had thus considered Theodore and his impiety, we took care to have recited and inserted in our acts a few of these things which had been impiously written by Theodoret against the right faith and against the Twelve Chapters of St. Cyril and against the First Council of Ephesus, also certain things written by him in defence of those impious ones Theodore and Nestorius, for the satisfaction of the reader; that all might know that these had been justly cast out and anathematized. In the third place the letter which is said to have been written by Ibas to Maris the Persian, was brought forward for examination, and we found that it, too, should be read. When it was read immediately its impiety was manifest to all. And it was right to make the condemnation and anathematism of the aforesaid Three Chapters, as even to this time there had been some question on the subject. But because the defenders of these impious ones, Theodore and Nestorius, were scheming in some way or other to confirm these persons and their impiety, and were saying that this impious letter, which praised and defended Theodore and

Nestorius and their impiety, had been received by the holy Council of Chalcedon; we thought it necessary to shew that the holy synod was free of the impiety which was contained in that letter, that it might be clear that they who say such things do not do so with the favour of this holy council, but that through its name they may confirm their own impiety. And it was shewn in the acts that in former times Ibas had been accused because of the very impiety which is contained in this letter; at first by Proclus, of holy memory, the bishop of Constantinople, and afterwards by Theodosius, of pious memory, and by Flavian, who was ordained bishop in succession to Proclus, who delegated the examination of the matter to Photius, bishop of Tyre, and to Eustathius, bishop of the city of Beyroot. Afterwards the same Ibas, being found guilty, was cast out of his bishopric. Such was the state of the case, how could anyone presume to say that that impious letter was received by the holy council of Chalcedon, and that the holy council of Chalcedon agreed with it throughout? Nevertheless, in order that they who thus calumniate the holy council of Chalcedon may have no further opportunity of doing so, we ordered to be recited the decisions of the holy Synods, to wit, of first Ephesus, and of Chalcedon, with regard to the Epistles of Cyril of blessed memory and of Leo, of pious memory, sometime Pope of Old Rome. And since we had learned from these that nothing written by anyone else ought to be received unless it had been proved to agree with the orthodox faith of the holy Fathers, we interrupted our proceedings so as to recite also the definition of the faith which was set forth by the holy council of Chalcedon, so that we might compare the things in the epistle with this decree. And when this was done it was perfectly clear that the contents of the epistle were wholly opposite to those of the definition.

For the definition agreed with the one and unchanging faith set forth as well by the 318 holy Fathers as by the 150 and by those who assembled at the first synod at Ephesus. But that impious letter, on the other hand, contained the blasphemies of the heretics Theodore and Nestorius, and defended them, and calls them doctors, while it calls the holy Fathers heretics.

And this we made manifest to all, that we did not have any intention of omitting the Fathers of the first and second interlocutions, which the followers of Theodore and Nestorius cited on their side, but these and all the others having been read and their contents examined, we found that the aforesaid Ibas was not allowed to be received without being compelled to anathematize Nestorius and his impious teachings, which were defended in that epistle. And this the rest of the religious bishops of the aforesaid holy Council did as well as those two whose interlocutions certain tried to use.

For this they observed in the case of Theodoret, and required him to anathematize those things of which he was accused. If therefore they were willing to allow the reception of Ibas in no other manner unless he condemned the impiety which was contained in his letters, and subscribed the definition of faith adopted by the Council, how can they attempt to make out that this impious letter was received by the same holy council? For we are taught, "What fellowship hath righteousness with unrighteousness? and what communion hath light with darkness? And what concord hath Christ with Belial? Or what part hath he that believeth with an infidel? And what agreement hath the temple of God with idols."

Having thus detailed all that has been done by us, we again confess that we receive the four holy Synods, that is, the Nicene, the Constantinopolitan, the first of Ephesus, and that of Chalcedon, and we have taught, and do teach all that they defined respecting the one faith. And we account those who do not receive these things aliens from the Catholic Church. Moreover we condemn and anathematize, together with all the other heretics who have been condemned and anathematized by the before-mentioned four holy Synods, and by the holy Catholic and Apostolic Church, Theodore who was Bishop of Mopsuestia, and his impious writings, and also those things which Theodoret impiously wrote against the right faith, and against the Twelve Chapters of the holy Cyril, and against the first Synod of Ephesus, and also those which he wrote in defence of Theodore and Nestorius. In addition to these we also anathematize the impious Epistle which Ibas is said to have written to Maris, the Persian, which denies that God the Word was incarnate of the holy Mother of God, and ever Virgin Mary, and accuses Cyril of holy memory, who taught the truth, as an heretic, and of the same sentiments with Apollinaris, and blames the first Synod of Ephesus as deposing Nestorius without examination and inquiry, and calls the Twelve Chapters of the holy Cyril impious, and contrary to the right faith, and defends Theodorus and Nestorius, and their impious dogmas and writings. We therefore anathematize the Three Chapters before-mentioned, that is, the impious Theodore of Mopsuestia, with his execrable writings, and those things which Theodoret impiously wrote, and the impious letter which is said to be of Ibas, and their defenders, and those who have written or do write in defence of them, or who dare to say that they are correct, and who have defended or attempt to defend their impiety with the names of the holy Fathers, or of the holy Council of Chalcedon. These things therefore being settled with all accuracy, we, bearing in remembrance the promises made respecting the holy Church, and who it was that said that the gates of hell should not prevail against her, that is, the deadly tongues of heretics; remembering also what was prophesied respecting it by Hosea, saying, "I will betroth thee unto me in faithfulness, and thou shalt know the Lord," and numbering together with the devil, the father of lies, the unbridled tongues of heretics who persevered in their impiety unto death, and their most impious writings, will say to them, "Behold, all ye kindle a fire, and cause the flame of the fire to grow strong, ye shall walk in the light of your fire, and the flame which ye kindle." But we, having a commandment to exhort the people with right doctrine, and to speak to the heart of Jerusalem, that is, the Church of God, do rightly make haste to sow in righteousness, and to reap the fruit of life; and kindling for ourselves the light of knowledge from the holy Scriptures, and the doctrine of the Fathers, we have considered it necessary to comprehend in certain Capitula, both the declaration of the truth, and the condemnation of heretics, and of their wickedness.

THE CAPITULA OF THE COUNCIL.

(Labbe and Cossart, *Concilia*, Tom. V., col. 568.)

I.

IF anyone shall not confess that the nature or essence of the Father, of the Son, and of the Holy Ghost is one, as also the force and the power ; [if anyone does not confess] a consubstantial Trinity, one Godhead to be worshipped in three subsistences or Persons : let him be anathema. For there is but one God even the Father of whom are all things, and one Lord Jesus Christ through whom are all things, and one Holy Spirit in whom are all things.

II.

IF anyone shall not confess that the Word of God has two nativities, the one from all eternity of the Father, without time and without body ; the other in these last days, coming down from heaven and being made flesh of the holy and glorious Mary, Mother of God and always a virgin, and born of her : let him be anathema.

III.

IF anyone shall say that the wonder-working Word of God is one [Person] and the Christ that suffered another ; or shall say that God the Word was with the woman-born Christ, or was in him as one person in another, but that he was not one and the same our Lord Jesus Christ, the Word of God, incarnate and made man, and that his miracles and the sufferings which of his own will he endured in the flesh were not of the same [Person] : let him be anathema.

IV.

IF anyone shall say that the union of the Word of God to man was only according to grace or energy, *or dignity*, or equality of honour, or authority, or relation, or effect, or power, or according to good pleasure in this sense that God the Word was pleased with a man, that is to say, that he loved him for his own sake, as says the senseless Theodorus, or [if anyone pretends that this union exists only] so far as likeness of name is concerned, as the Nestorians understand, who call also the Word of God Jesus and Christ, and even accord to the man the names of Christ and of Son, speaking thus clearly of two persons, and only designating disingenuously one Person and one Christ when the reference is to his honour, or his dignity, or his worship ; if anyone shall not acknowledge as the Holy Fathers teach, that the union of God the Word is made with the flesh animated by a reasonable and living soul, and that such union is made synthetically and hypostatically, and that therefore there is only one Person, to wit : our Lord Jesus Christ, one of the Holy Trinity : let him be anathema. As a matter of fact the word "union" (τῆς ἑνώσεως) has many meanings, and the partisans of Apollinaris and Eutyches have affirmed that these natures are confounded *inter se*, and have asserted a union produced by the mixture of both. On the other hand the followers of Theodorus and of Nestorius rejoicing in the division of the natures, have taught only a relative union. Meanwhile the Holy Church of God, condemning equally the impiety of both sorts of heresies, recognises the union of God the Word with the flesh synthetically, that is to say, hypostatically. For in the mystery of Christ the synthetical union not only preserves unconfusedly the natures which are united, but also allows no separation.

V.

IF anyone understands the expression "one only Person of our Lord Jesus Christ" in this sense, that it is the union of many hypostases, and if he attempts thus to introduce into the mystery of Christ two hypostases, or two Persons, and, after having introduced two persons, speaks of one Person only out of dignity, honour or worship, as both Theodorus and Nestorius insanely have written; if anyone shall calumniate the holy Council of Chalcedon, pretending that it made use of this expression [one hypostasis] in this impious sense, and if he will not recognize rather that the Word of God is united with the flesh hypostatically, and that therefore there is but one hypostasis or one only Person, and that the holy Council of Chalcedon has professed in this sense the one Person of our Lord Jesus Christ: let him be anathema. For since one of the Holy Trinity has been made man, viz.: God the Word, the Holy Trinity has not been increased by the addition of another person or hypostasis.

VI.

IF anyone shall not call in a true acceptation, but only in a false acceptation, the holy, glorious, and ever-virgin Mary, the Mother of God, or shall call her so only in a relative sense, believing that she bare only a simple man and that God the word was not incarnate of her, but that the incarnation of God the Word resulted only from the fact that he united himself to that man who was born [of her]; [1] if he shall calumniate the Holy Synod of Chalcedon as though it had asserted the Virgin to be Mother of God according to the impious sense of Theodore; or if anyone shall call her the mother of a man (ἀνθρωποτόκον) or the Mother of Christ (Χριστοτόκον), as if Christ were not God, and shall not confess that she is exactly and truly the Mother of God, because that God the Word who before all ages was begotten of the Father was in these last days made flesh and born of her, and if anyone shall not confess that in this sense the holy Synod of Chalcedon acknowledged her to be the Mother of God: let him be anathema.

VII.

IF anyone using the expression, " in two natures," does not confess that our one Lord Jesus Christ has been revealed in the divinity and in the humanity, so as to designate by that expression a difference of the natures of which an ineffable union is unconfusedly made, [a union] in which neither the nature of the Word was changed into that of the flesh, nor that of the flesh into that of the Word, for each remained that it was by nature, the union being hypostatic; but shall take the expression with regard to the mystery of Christ in a sense so as to divide the parties, or recognising the two natures in the only Lord Jesus, God the Word made man, does not content himself with taking in a theoretical manner [2] the difference of the natures which compose him, which difference is not destroyed by the union between them, for one is composed of the two and the two are in one, but shall make use of the number [two] to divide the natures or to make of them Persons properly so called : let him be anathema. [3]

VIII.

IF anyone uses the expression " of two natures," confessing that a union was made of the Godhead and of the humanity, or the expression "the one nature made flesh of God the Word," and shall not so understand those expressions as the holy Fathers have taught, to wit : that of the divine and human nature there was made an hypostatic union, whereof is one Christ; but from these expressions shall try to introduce one nature or substance [made by a mixture] of the Godhead and manhood of Christ; let him be anathema. For in teaching that the only-begotten Word was united hypostatically [to humanity] we do not mean to say that there was made a mutual confusion of natures, but rather each [nature] remaining what it was, we understand that the Word was united to the flesh. Wherefore there is one Christ, both God and man, consubstantial with the Father as touching his Godhead, and consubstantial with us as touching his

---

[1] The text here is uncertain, and the Latin and Greek do not agree. *Vide* Hefele.

[2] *I. e.*, " as an abstraction (τῇ θεωρίᾳ μόνῃ)."
[3] The text here is uncertain.

manhood.   Therefore they are equally condemned and anathematized by the Church of God, who divide or part the mystery of the divine dispensation of Christ, or who introduce confusion into that mystery.

IX.

IF anyone shall take the expression, Christ ought to be worshipped in his two natures, in the sense that he wishes to introduce thus two adorations, the one in special relation to God the Word and the other as pertaining to the man ; or if anyone to get rid of the flesh, [that is of the humanity of Christ,] or to mix together the divinity and the humanity, shall speak monstrously of one only nature or essence (φύσιν ἤγουν οὐσίαν) of the united (natures), and so worship Christ, and does not venerate, by one adoration, God the Word made man, together with his flesh, as the Holy Church has taught from the beginning : let him be anathema.

X.

IF anyone does not confess that our Lord Jesus Christ who was crucified in the flesh is true God and the Lord of Glory and one of the Holy Trinity : let him be anathema.

XI.

IF anyone does not anathematize Arius, Eunomius, Macedonius, Apollinaris, Nestorius, Eutyches and Origen, as well as their impious writings, as also all other heretics already condemned and anathematized by the Holy Catholic and Apostolic Church, and by the aforesaid four Holy Synods and [if anyone does not equally anathematize] all those who have held and hold or who in their impiety persist in holding to the end the same opinion as those heretics just mentioned : let him be anathema.

NOTES.

HEFELE.

(*Hist. Councils*, Vol. iv., p. 336.)

Halloix, Garnier, Basnage, Walch and others suppose, and Vincenzi maintains with great zeal, that the name of Origen is a later insertion in this anathematism, because (*a*) Theodore Ascidas, the Origenist, was one of the most influential members of the Synod, and would certainly have prevented a condemnation of Origen ; further, (*b*) because in this anathematism only such heretics would be named as had been condemned by one of the first four Ecumenical Synods, which was not the case with Origen ; (*c*) because this anathematism is identical with the tenth in the ὁμολογία of the Emperor, but in the latter the name of Origen is lacking ; and, finally, (*d*) because Origen does not belong to the group of heretics to whom this anathematism refers.   His errors were quite different.

All these considerations seem to me of insufficient strength, or mere conjecture, to make an alteration in the text, and arbitrarily to remove the name of Origen.   As regards the objection in connection with Theodore Ascidas, it is known that the latter had already pronounced a formal anathema on Origen, and certainly he did the same this time, if the Emperor wished it or if it seemed advisable.   The second and fourth objections have little weight.   In regard to the third (*c*) it is quite possible that either the Emperor subsequently went further than in his ὁμολογία, or that the bishops at the fifth Synod, of their own accord, added Origen, led on perhaps by one or another anti-Origenist of their number.   What, however, chiefly determines us to the retention of the text is : (*a*) that the copy of the synodal Acts extant in the Roman archives, which has the highest credibility, and was probably prepared for Vigilius himself, contains the name of Origen in the eleventh anathematism ; and (*b*) that the monks of the new Lama in Palestine, who are known to have been zealous Origenists, withdrew Church communion from the bishops of Palestine after these had subscribed the Acts of the fifth Synod.   In the anathema on the Three Chapters these Origenists could find as little ground for such a rupture as their friends and former colleague Ascidas ; it could only be by the synod attacking their darling Origen.   (*c*) Finally, only on the ground that the name of Origen really stood in the eleventh anathematism, can we explain the widely-circulated ancient rumour that our Synod anathematized Origen and the Origenists.

XII.

IF anyone defends the impious Theodore of Mopsuestia, who has said that the Word of God is one person, but that another person is Christ, vexed by the sufferings of the soul and the desires of the flesh, and separated little by little above that which is inferior, and become better by the progress in good works and irreproachable in his manner of life, as a mere man was baptized in the name of the Father, and of the Son, and of the Holy Ghost, and obtained by this baptism the grace of the Holy Spirit, and became worthy of Sonship, and to be worshipped out of regard to the Person of God the Word (just as one worships the image of an emperor) and that he is become, after the resurrection, unchangeable in his thoughts and altogether without sin. And, again, this same impious Theodore has also said that the union of God the Word with Christ is like to that which, according to the doctrine of the Apostle, exists between a man and his wife, "They twain shall be in one flesh." The same [Theodore] has dared, among numerous other blasphemies, to say that when after the resurrection the Lord breathed upon his disciples, saying, "Receive the Holy Ghost," he did not really give them the Holy Spirit, but that he breathed upon them only as a sign. He likewise has said that the profession of faith made by Thomas when he had, after the resurrection, touched the hands and the side of the Lord, viz.: "My Lord and my God," was not said in reference to Christ, but that Thomas, filled with wonder at the miracle of the resurrection, thus thanked God who had raised up Christ. And moreover (which is still more scandalous) this same Theodore in his *Commentary on the Acts of the Apostles* compares Christ to Plato, Manichæus, Epicurus and Marcion, and says that as each of these men having discovered his own doctrine, had given his name to his disciples, who were called Platonists, Manicheans, Epicureans and Marcionites, just so Christ, having discovered his doctrine, had given the name Christians to his disciples. If, then, anyone shall defend this most impious Theodore and his impious writings, in which he vomits the blasphemies mentioned above, and countless others besides against our Great God and Saviour Jesus Christ, and if anyone does not anathematize him or his impious writings, as well as all those who protect or defend him, or who assert that his exegesis is orthodox, or who write in favour of him and of his impious works, or those who share the same opinions, or those who have shared them and still continue unto the end in this heresy: let him be anathema.

XIII.

IF anyone shall defend the impious writings of Theodoret, directed against the true faith and against the first holy Synod of Ephesus and against St. Cyril and his XII. Anathemas, and [defends] that which he has written in defence of the impious Theodore and Nestorius, and of others having the same opinions as the aforesaid Theodore and Nestorius, if anyone admits them or their impiety, or shall give the name of impious to the doctors of the Church who profess the hypostatic union of God the Word; and if anyone does not anathematize these impious writings and those who have held or who hold these sentiments, and all those who have written contrary to the true faith or against St. Cyril and his XII. Chapters, and who die in their impiety: let him be anathema.

XIV.

IF anyone shall defend that letter which Ibas is said to have written to Maris the Persian, in which he denies that the Word of God incarnate of Mary, the Holy Mother of God and ever-virgin, was made man, but says that a mere man was born of her, whom he styles a Temple, as though the Word of God was one Person and the man another person; in which letter also he reprehends St. Cyril as a heretic, when he teaches the right faith of Christians, and charges him with writing things like to the wicked Apollinaris. In addition to this he vituperates the First Holy Council of Ephesus, affirming that it deposed Nestorius without discrimination and without examination. The aforesaid impious epistle styles the XII. Chapters of Cyril of blessed memory, impious and contrary to the right faith and defends Theodore and Nestorius and their impious teachings and writings. If anyone therefore shall defend the aforementioned epistle and shall not anathematize it and those who defend it and say that it is right or that a part of it is right, or if anyone shall defend those who have written or shall write in its favour, or in defence of the impieties which are contained in it, as well as those who shall presume to defend it or the impieties which it contains in the name of the Holy Fathers or of the Holy Synod of Chalcedon, and shall remain in these offences unto the end: let him be anathema.

EXCURSUS ON THE XV. ANATHEMAS AGAINST ORIGEN.

That Origen was condemned by name in the Eleventh Canon of this council there seems no possible reason to doubt. I have given in connexion with that canon a full discussion of the evidence upon which our present text rests. But there arises a further question, to wit, Did the Fifth Synod examine the case of Origen and finally adopt the XV. Anathemas against him which are usually found assigned to it? It would seem that with the evidence now in our possession it would be the height of rashness to give a dogmatic answer to this question. Scholars of the highest repute have taken, and do take to-day, the opposite sides of the case, and each defends his own side with marked learning and ability. To my mind the chief difficulty in supposing these anathematisms to have been adopted by the Fifth Ecumenical is that nothing whatever is said about Origen in the call of the council, nor in any of the letters written in connexion with it; all of which would seem unnatural had there been a long discussion upon the matter, and had such an important dogmatic definition been adopted as the XV. Anathemas, and yet on the other hand there is a vast amount of literature subsequent in date to the council which distinctly attributes a detailed and careful examination of the teaching of Origen and a formal condemnation of him and of it to this council.

The XV. Anathemas as we now have them were discovered by Peter Lambeck, the Librarian of Vienna, in the XVIIth century; and bear, in the Vienna MS., the heading, "Canons of the 165 holy Fathers of the holy fifth Synod, held in Constantinople." But despite this, Walch (*Ketzerhist.*, Vol. vii., p. 661 *et seqq.* and 671; Vol. viij., p. 281 *et seqq.*); Döllinger (*Church History*, Eng. Trans., Vol. v., p. 203 *et seqq.*); Hefele (*Hist. Councils*, Vol. iv., p. 221 *sq.*), and many others look upon this caption as untrustworthy. Evagrius, the historian, distinctly says that Origen was condemned with special anathemas at this Council, but his evidence is likewise (and, as it seems to me, too peremptorily) set aside.

Cardinal Noris, in his *Dissertatio Historica de Synodo Quinta*, is of opinion that Origen was twice condemned by the Fifth Synod; the first time by himself before the eight sessions of which alone the acts remain, and again after those eight sessions, in connexion with two of his chief followers, Didymus the Blind and the deacon Evagrius. The Jesuit, John Garnier wrote in opposition to Noris; but his work, while exceedingly clever, is considered by the learned to contain (as Hefele says) "many statements [which] are rash, arbitrary, and inaccurate, and on the whole it is seen to be written in a spirit of opposition to Noris."[1] In defence of Noris's main contention came forward the learned Ballerini brothers, of Verona. In their *Defensio dissertationis Norisianæ de Syn. V. adv. diss. P. Garnerii*, they expand and amend Noris's hypothesis. But after all is said the matter remains involved in the greatest obscurity, and it is far easier to bring forward objections to the arguments in defence of either view than to bring forward a theory which will satisfy all the conditions of the problem.

---

[1] Hefele, *Hist. Councils*, Vol. IV., p. 230, note.

Those who deny that the XV. Anathemas were adopted by the Fifth Synod agree in assigning them to the "Home Synod," that is a Synod at Constantinople of the bishops subject to it, in A.D. 543. Hefele takes this view and advocates it with much cogency, but confesses frankly, "We certainly possess no strong and decisive proof that the fifteen anathematisms belong to the Constantinopolitan synod of the year 543 ; but some probable grounds for the opinion may be adduced.[1] This appears to be a somewhat weak statement with which to overthrow so much evidence as there can be produced for the opposite view. For the traditional view the English reader will find a complete defence in E. B. Pusey, *What is of Faith with regard to Eternal Punishment?*

Before closing it will be well to call the attention of the reader to these words now found in the acts as we have them :

"And we found that many others had been anathematised after death, also even Origen ; and if any one were to go back to the times of Theophilus of blessed memory or further he would have found him anathematised after death ; which also now your holiness and Vigilius, the most religious Pope of Old Rome has done in his case."[2] It would seem that this cannot possibly refer to anything else than a condemnation of Origen by the Fifth Ecumenical Synod, and so strongly is Vincenzi, Origen's defender, impressed with this that he declares the passage to have been tampered with. But even if these anathemas were adopted at the Home Synod before the meeting of the Fifth Ecumenical, it is clear that by including his name among those of the heretics in the XIth Canon, it practically ratified and made its own the action of that Synod.

The reader will be glad to know Harnack's judgment in this matter. Writing of the Fifth Council, he says : "It condemned Origen, as Justinian desired ; it condemned the Three Chapters and consequently the Antiochene theology, as Justinian desired," etc., and in a foot-note he explains that he agrees with "Noris, the Ballerini, Möller (R. Encykl., xi., p. 113) and Loofs (pp. 287, 291) as against Hefele and Vincenzi."[3] A few pages before, he speaks of this last author's book as "a big work which falsifies history to justify the theses of Halloix, to rehabilitate Origen and Vigilius, and on the other hand to 'remodel' the Council and partly to bring it into contempt."[4] Further on he says : "The fifteen anathemas against Origen, on which his condemnation at the council was based, contained the following points. . . . Since the 'Three Chapters' were condemned at the same time, Origen and Theodore were both got rid of. . . . Origen's doctrines of the consummation, and of spirits and matter might no longer be maintained. The judgment was restored to its place, and got back even its literal meaning."[5]

---

[1] Hefele, *Hist. Councils*, Vol. IV., p. 223.
[2] Speech of Ascidas in the V. Session.
[3] Harnack. *Hist. of Dogma*, Vol. IV., p. 249 (Eng. Trans.).
[4] Ibid., p. 245, note 2.
[5] Ibid., p. 349.

THE ANATHEMAS AGAINST ORIGEN.

I.

IF anyone asserts the fabulous pre-existence of souls, and shall assert the monstrous restoration which follows from it: let him be anathema.

II.

IF anyone shall say that the creation (τὴν παραγωγὴν) of all reasonable things includes only intelligences (νόας) without bodies and altogether immaterial, having neither number nor name, so that there is unity between them all by identity of substance, force and energy, and by their union with and knowledge of God the Word; but that no longer desiring the sight of God, they gave themselves over to worse things, each one following his own inclinations, and that they have taken bodies more or less subtile, and have received names, for among the heavenly Powers there is a difference of names as there is also a difference of bodies; and thence some became and are called Cherubims, others Seraphims, and Principalities, and Powers, and Dominations, and Thrones, and Angels, and as many other heavenly orders as there may be: let him be anathema.

III.

IF anyone shall say that the sun, the moon and the stars are also reasonable beings, and that they have only become what they are because they turned towards evil: let him be anathema.

IV.

IF anyone shall say that the reasonable creatures in whom the divine love had grown cold have been hidden in gross bodies such as ours, and have been called men, while those who have attained the lowest degree of wickedness have shared cold and obscure bodies and are become and called demons and evil spirits: let him be anathema.

V.

IF anyone shall say that a psychic (ψυχικὴν) condition has come from an angelic or archangelic state, and moreover that a demoniac and a human condition has come from a psychic condition, and that from a human state they may become again angels and demons, and that each order of heavenly virtues is either all from those below or from those above, or from those above and below: let him be anathema.

VI.

IF anyone shall say that there is a twofold race of demons, of which the one includes the souls of men and the other the superior spirits who fell to this, and that of all the number of reasonable beings there is but one which has remained unshaken in the love and contemplation of God, and that that spirit is become Christ and the king of all reasonable beings, and that he has created[1] all the bodies which exist in heaven, on earth, and between heaven and earth; and that the world which has in itself elements more ancient than itself, and which exists by themselves, viz.: dryness, damp, heat and cold, and the image (ἰδέαν) to which it was formed, was so formed, and that the most holy and consubstantial Trinity did not create the world, but that it was created by the working intelligence (Νοῦς δημιουργός) which is more ancient than the world, and which communicates to it its being: let him be anathema.

VII.

IF anyone shall say that Christ, of whom it is said that he appeared in the form of God, and that he was united before all time with God the Word, and humbled himself in these last days even to humanity, had (according to their expression) pity upon the divers falls which had appeared in the spirits united in the same unity (of which he himself is part), and that to

---

[1] The following is Hefele's note (*Hist. Councils*, Vol. IV., p. 226, note 1):

"Παραγαγεῖν can in no way be translated, as it has hitherto been, by *prætergressus* or 'passed over': 'That Christ has gone over to all corporeity on heaven and earth,' which gives no sense. Παράγειν means here, like παραγωγή in the second anathematism, *creare, producere*, 'create,' 'bring into existence.' Suicer, in his *Thesaurus*, completely overlooked this. *Cf.* Stephani. *s. vv.* παράγω and παραγωγή."

restore them he passed through divers classes, had different bodies and different names, became all to all, an Angel among Angels, a Power among Powers, has clothed himself in the different classes of reasonable beings with a form corresponding to that class, and finally has taken flesh and blood like ours and is become man for men ; [if anyone says all this] and does not profess that God the Word humbled himself and became man: let him be anathema.

VIII.

IF anyone shall not acknowledge that God the Word, of the same substance with the Father and the Holy Ghost, and who was made flesh and became man, one of the Trinity, is Christ in every sense of the word, but [shall affirm] that he is so only in an inaccurate manner, and because of the abasement (κενώσαντα), as they call it, of the intelligence (νοῦς) ; if anyone shall affirm that this intelligence united (συνημμένον) to God the Word, is the Christ in the true sense of the word, while the Logos is only called Christ because of this union with the intelligence, and e converso that the intelligence is only called God because of the Logos : let him be anathema.

IX.

IF anyone shall say that it was not the Divine Logos made man by taking an animated body with a ψυχὴ λογικὴ and νοερὰ, that he descended into hell and ascended into heaven, but shall pretend that it is the Noῦς which has done this, that Noῦς of which they say (in an impious fashion) he is Christ properly so called, and that he is become so by the knowledge of the Monad: let him be anathema.

X.

IF anyone shall say that after the resurrection the body of the Lord was ethereal, having the form of a sphere, and that such shall be the bodies of all after the resurrection ; and that after the Lord himself shall have rejected his true body and after the others who rise shall have rejected theirs, the nature of their bodies shall be annihilated : let him be anathema.

XI.

IF anyone shall say that the future judgment signifies the destruction of the body and that the end of the story will be an immaterial ψύσις, and that thereafter there will no longer be any matter, but only spirit (νοῦς) : let him be anathema.

XII.

IF anyone shall say that the heavenly Powers and all men and the Devil and evil spirits are united with the Word of God in all respects, as the Noῦς which is by them called Christ and which is in the form of God, and which humbled itself as they say; and [if anyone shall say] that the Kingdom of Christ shall have an end : let him be anathema.

XIII.

IF anyone shall say that Christ [i.e., the Noῦς] is in no wise different from other reasonable beings, neither substantially nor by wisdom nor by his power and might over all things but that all will be placed at the right hand of God, as well as he that is called by them Christ [the Noῦς], as also they were in the feigned pre-existence of all things : let him be anathema.

XIV.

IF anyone shall say that all reasonable beings will one day be united in one, when the hypostases as well as the numbers and the bodies shall have disappeared, and that the knowledge of the world to come will carry with it the ruin of the worlds, and the rejection of bodies as also the abolition of [all] names, and that there shall be finally an identity of the γνῶσις and of the hypostasis; moreover, that in this pretended apocatastasis, spirits only will continue to exist, as it was in the feigned pre-existence : let him be anathema.

XV.

IF anyone shall say that the life of the spirits (νοῶν) shall be like to the life which was in the beginning while as yet the spirits had not come down or fallen, so that the end and the beginning shall be alike, and that the end shall be the true measure of the beginning : let him be anathema.

THE ANATHEMATISMS OF THE EMPEROR JUSTINIAN AGAINST ORIGEN.[1]

(Labbe and Cossart, *Concilia*, Tom. v., col. 677.)

I.

Whoever says or thinks that human souls pre-existed, *i.e.*, that they had previously been spirits and holy powers, but that, satiated with the vision of God, they had turned to evil, and in this way the divine love in them had died out (ἀπψυγείσας) and they had therefore become souls (ψυχάς) and had been condemned to punishment in bodies, shall be anathema.

II.

If anyone says or thinks that the soul of the Lord pre-existed and was united with God the Word before the Incarnation and Conception of the Virgin, let him be anathema.

III.

If anyone says or thinks that the body of our Lord Jesus Christ was first formed in the womb of the holy Virgin and that afterwards there was united with it God the Word and the pre-existing soul, let him be anathema.

IV.

If anyone says or thinks that the Word of God has become like to all heavenly orders, so that for the cherubim he was a cherub, for the seraphim a seraph: in short, like all the superior powers, let him be anathema.

V.

If anyone says or thinks that, at the resurrection, human bodies will rise spherical in form and unlike our present form, let him be anathema.

VI.

If anyone says that the heaven, the sun, the moon, the stars, and the waters that are above heavens, have souls, and are reasonable beings, let him be anathema.

VII.

If anyone says or thinks that Christ the Lord in a future time will be crucified for demons as he was for men, let him be anathema.

VIII.

If anyone says or thinks that the power of God is limited, and that he created as much as he was able to compass, let him be anathema.

IX.

If anyone says or thinks that the punishment of demons and of impious men is only temporary, and will one day have an end, and that a restoration (ἀποκατάστασις) will take place of demons and of impious men, let him be anathema.

Anathema to Origen and to that Adamantius, who set forth these opinions together with his nefarious and execrable and wicked doctrine,[2] and to whomsoever there is who thinks thus, or defends these opinions, or in any way hereafter at any time shall presume to protect them.

---

[1] The reader should carefully study the entire tractate of the Emperor against Origen of which these anathematisms are the conclusion. It is found in Labbe and Cossart, and in many other collections.

[2] The text is, I think corrupt, at all events the Latin and Greek do not agree.

THE DECRETAL EPISTLE OF POPE VIGILIUS IN CONFIRMATION OF THE FIFTH ECUMENICAL SYNOD.

HISTORICAL NOTE.

(Fleury. *Hist. Eccl.*, Liv. xxxiii. 52.)

At last the Pope Vigilius resigned himself to the advice of the Council, and six months afterwards wrote a letter to the Patriarch Eutychius, wherein he confesses that he has been wanting in charity in dividing from his brethren. He adds, that one ought not to be ashamed to retract, when one recognises the truth, and brings forward the example of St. Augustine. He says, that, after having better examined the matter of the Three Chapters, he finds them worthy of condemnation. "We recognize for our brethren and colleagues all those who have condemned them, and annul by this writing all that has been done by us or by others for the defence of the three chapters."

THE DECRETAL LETTER OF POPE VIGILIUS.

(The manuscript from which this letter was printed was found in the Royal Library of Paris by Peter de Marca and by him first published, with a Latin translation and with a dissertation. Both of these with the Greek text are found in Labbe and Cossart's *Concilia*, Tom. V., col. 596 *et seqq.;* also in Migne's *Patr. Lat.*, Tom. LXIX., col. 121 *et seqq.* Some doubts have been expressed about its genuineness and Harduin is of opinion that the learned Jesuit, Garnerius, in his notes on the Deacon Leberatus's *Breviary*, has proved its supposititious character. But the learned have not generally been of this mind but have accepted the letter as genuine.)

Vigilius to his beloved brother Eutychius.

No one is ignorant of the scandals which the enemy of the human race has stirred up in all the world: so that he made each one with a wicked object in view, striving in some way to fulfil his wish to destroy the Church of God spread over the whole world, not only in his own name but even in ours and in those of others to compose diverse things as well in words as in writing ; in so much that he attempted to divide us who, together with our brethren and fellow bishops, are stopping in this royal city, and who defend with equal reverence the four synods, and sincerely persist in the one and the same faith of those four synods, by his sophistries and machinations he tried to part from them ; so that we ourselves who were and are of the same opinion as they touching the faith, went apart into discord, brotherly love being despised.[1]

But since Christ our God, who is the true light, whom the darkness comprehendeth not, hath removed all confusion from our minds, and hath so recalled peace to the whole world and to the Church, so that what things should be defined by us have been healthfully fulfilled through the revelation of the Lord and through the investigation of the truth.

Therefore, my dear brothers, I do you to wit, that in common with all of you, our brethren, we receive in all respects the four synods, that is to say the Nicene, the Constantinopolitan, the first Ephesian, and the Chalcedonian ; and we venerate them with devout mind, and watch over them with all our mind. And should there be any who do not follow these holy synods in all things which they have defined concerning the faith, we judge them to be aliens to the communion of the holy and Catholic Church.

Wherefore on account of our desire that you, my brothers, should know what we have done in this matter, we make it known to you by this letter. For no one can doubt how many were the discussions raised on account of the Three Chapters, that is, concerning Theodore, sometime bishop of Mopsuestia, and his writings, as well as concerning the writings of Theodoret, and concerning that letter which is said to have been written by Ibas to Maris the Persian : and how diverse were the things spoken and written concerning these Three Chapters. Now if in every busi-

---

[1] In this sentence I have followed De Marca's Latin version, but I must confess that I am not at all satisfied with the construing of the long phrase beginning Οὖτως ὡς.

ness sound wisdom demands that there should be a retractation of what was propounded after examination, there ought to be no shame when what was at first omitted is made public after it is discovered by a further study of the truth. [And if this is the case in ordinary affairs] how much more in ecclesiastical strifes should the same dictate of sound reason be observed? Especially since it is manifest that our Fathers, and especially the blessed Augustine, who was in very sooth illustrious in the Divine Scriptures, and a master in Roman eloquence, retracted some of his own writings, and corrected some of his own sayings, and added what he had omitted and afterward found out. We, led by their example never gave over the study of the questions raised by the controversy with regard to the before-mentioned Three Chapters, nor our search for passages in the writings of our Fathers which were applicable to the matter.

As a result of this investigation it became evident that in the sayings of Theodore of Mopsuestia (which are spoken against on all hands) there are contained very many things contrary to the right faith and to the teachings of the holy Fathers; and for this very reason these same holy Fathers have left for the instruction of the Church treatises which they had written against him.

For among other blasphemies of his we find that he openly said that God the Word was one [Person] and Christ another [Person], vexed with the passions of the soul and with the desires of the flesh, and that he little by little advanced from a lower to a higher stage of excellence by the improvement (προκοπῇ, per profectum operum) of his works, and became irreprehensible in his manner of life.[1] And further he taught that it was a mere man who was baptized in the Name of the Father and of the Son and of the Holy Ghost, and that he received through his baptism the grace of the Holy Spirit, and merited his adoption; and therefore that Christ could be venerated in the same way that the image of the Emperor is venerated as being the persona (εἰς πρόσωπον) of God the Word. And he also taught that [only] after his resurrection he became immutable in his thoughts and altogether impeccable.

Moreover he said that the union of the Word of God was made with Christ as the Apostle says the union is made between a man and his wife: They twain shall be one flesh; and that after his resurrection, when the Lord breathed upon his disciples and said, Receive the Holy Ghost, he did not give to them the Holy Spirit. In like strain of profanity he dared to say that the confession which Thomas made, when he touched the hands and side of the Lord after his resurrection, saying, My Lord and my God, did not apply to Christ (for Theodore did not acknowledge Christ to be God); but that Thomas gave glory to God being filled with wonder at the miracle of the resurrection, and so said these words.

But what is still worse is this, that in interpreting the Acts of the Apostles, Theodore makes Christ like to Plato, and Manichæus, and Epicurus, and Marcian, saying: Just as each of these were the authors of their own peculiar teachings, and called their disciples after their own names, Platonists, and Manichæans, and Epicureans, and Marcionites, just so Christ invented dogmas and called his followers Christians after himself.

Let therefore the whole Catholic Church know that justly and irreproachably we have arrived at the conclusions contained in this our constitution. Wherefore we condemn and anathematize Theodore, formerly bishop of Mopsuestia, and his impious writings, together with all other heretics, who (as is manifest) have been condemned and anathematized by the four holy Synods aforesaid, and by the Catholic Church: also the writings of Theodoret which are opposed to the right faith, and are against the Twelve Chapters of St. Cyril, and against the first Council of Ephesus, which were written by him in defence of Theodore and Nestorius.

Moreover we anathematize and condemn the letter to the Persian heretic Maris, which is said to have been written by Ibas, which denies that Christ the Word was incarnate of the holy Mother of God and ever-virgin Mary, and was made man, but declares that a mere man was born of her, and this man it styles a temple, so from this we are given to understand that God the Word is one [Person] and Christ another [Person]. Moreover it calumniates Saint Cyril, the master and herald of the orthodox faith, calling him a heretic, and charging him with writing things similar to Apollinaris; and it reviles the first Synod of Ephesus, as having condemned Nestorius without deliberation or investigation; it likewise declares the twelve chapters of St. Cyril to be impious and contrary to the right faith; and further still it defends Theodore and Nestorius, and their impious teachings and writings.

Therefore we anathematize and condemn

---

[1] The reader will notice that this is hardly distinguishable from the "moral growth" and "ethical development" which the modern "kenotists" attribute to the Incarnate Son of God.

the aforesaid impious Three Chapters, to-wit, the impious Theodore of Mopsuestia and his impious writings ; And all that Theodoret impiously wrote, as well as the letter said to have been written by Ibas, in which are contained the above mentioned profane blasphemies. We likewise subject to anathema whoever shall at any time believe that these chapters should be received or defended ; or shall attempt to subvert this present condemnation.

And further we define that they are our brethren and fellow-priests who ever keep the right faith set forth by those afore-mentioned synods, and shall have condemned the above-named Three Chapters, or even do now condemn them.

And further we annul and evacuate by this present written definition of ours whatever has been said by me (a me) or by others in defence of the aforesaid Three Chapters.

Far be it from the Catholic Church that anyone should say that all the blasphemies above related or they who held and followed such things, were received by the before-mentioned four synods or by any one of them. For it is most clear, that no one was admitted by the before-mentioned holy Fathers and especially by the Council of Chalcedon, about whom there was any suspicion, unless he had first repelled the above-named blasphemies and all like to them, or else had denied and condemned the heresy or blasphemies of which he was suspected.

Subscription.

May God preserve thee in health, most honourable brother. Dated VI. Id. Dec. in the xxijd year of our lord the Emperor Justinian, eternal Augustus, the xijth year after the consulate of the illustrious Basil.[1]

HISTORICAL EXCURSUS ON THE AFTER HISTORY OF THE COUNCIL.

Pope Vigilius died on his way home, but not until, as we have seen, he had accepted and approved the action of the council in doing exactly that which he "by the authority of the Apostolic See" in his *Constitutum* had forbidden it to do.[2] He died at the end of 554 or the beginning of 555.

Pelagius I., who succeeded him in the See of Rome, likewise confirmed the Acts of the Fifth Synod. The council however was not received in all parts of the West, although it had obtained the approval of the Pope. It was bitterly opposed in the whole of the north of Italy, in England, France, and Spain, and also in Africa and Asia. The African opposition died out by 559, but Milan was in schism until 571, when Pope Justin II. published his "Henoticon." In Istria the matter was still more serious, and when in 607 the bishop of Aquileia-Grado with those of his suffragans who were subject to the Empire made their submission and were reconciled to the Church, the other bishops of his jurisdiction set up a schismatical Patriarchate at old Aquileia, and this schism continued till the Council of Aquileia in 700. But before this the II. Council of Constantinople was received all the world over as the Fifth Ecumenical Council, and was fully recognized as such by the Sixth Council in 680.

---

[1] i.e. A.D. 553.

[2] The last sentence of the *Constitutum*, the sentence which the Pope gave and which the council rejected, is as follows : " We ordain and decree that it be permitted to no one who stands in ecclesiastical order of office, to write or bring forward, or undertake, or teach anything contrary to the contents of this *Constitutum* in regard to the Three Chapters. or, after this declaration begin a new controversy about them. And if anything has already been done or spoken in regard of the Three Chapters in contradiction of this our ordinance by anyone whomsoever, this we declare void by the authority of the Apostolic See." It is perfectly clear that the Emperor is the "anyone" referred to.

THE SIXTH ECUMENICAL COUNCIL.

THE THIRD COUNCIL OF CONSTANTINOPLE.

A.D. 680–681

Emperor.—CONSTANTINE POGONATUS.
Pope.—AGATHO I.

Elenchus.

HISTORICAL INTRODUCTION.

The Sixth Ecumenical Council met on November 7, 680, for its first session, and ended its meetings, which are said to have been eighteen in number, on September 16th of the next year. The number of bishops present was under three hundred and the minutes of the last session have only 174 signatures attached to them.

When the Emperor first summoned the council he had no intention that it should be ecumenical. From the *Sacras* it appears that he had summoned all the Metropolitans and bishops of the jurisdiction of Constantinople, and had also informed the Archbishop of Antioch that he might send Metropolitans and bishops. A long time before he had written to Pope Agatho on the subject.

When the synod assembled however, it assumed at its first session the title "Ecumenical," and all the five patriarchs were represented, Alexandria and Jerusalem having sent deputies although they were at the time in the hands of the infidel.

In this Council the Emperor presided in person surrounded by high court officials. On his right sat the Patriarchs of Constantinople and Antioch and next to them the representative of the Patriarch of Alexandria. On the Emperor's left were seated the representatives of the Pope. In the midst were placed, as usual, the Holy Gospels. After the eleventh session however the Emperor was no longer able to be present, but returned and presided at the closing meeting.

The sessions of the council were held in the domed hall (or possibly chapel) in the imperial palace ; which, the Acts tell us, was called Trullo (ἐν τῷ σεκρέτῳ τοῦ θείου παλατίου, τῷ οὕτω λεγομένῳ Τρούλλῳ).

It may be interesting to remark that the *Sacras* sent to the bishops of Rome and Constantinople are addressed, the one to "The Most holy and Blessed Archbishop of Old Rome and Ecumenical Pope," and the other to "The Most holy and Blessed Archbishop of Constantinople and Ecumenical Patriarch." Some of the titles given themselves by the signers of the "Prosphoneticus" are interesting—"George, an humble presbyter of the holy Roman Church, and holding the place of the most blessed Agatho, ecumenical Pope of the City of Rome . . .," "John, an humble deacon of the holy Roman Church and holding the place of the most blessed Agatho, and ecumenical Pope of the City of Rome . . . ," "George, by the mercy of God bishop of Constantinople which is New Rome," "Peter a presbyter and holding the place of the Apostolic See of the great city Alexandria . . . ," "George, an humble presbyter of the Holy Resurrection of Christ our God, and holding the place of Theodore the presbyter, beloved of God, who holds the place of the Apostolic See of Jerusalem . . . ," "John, by the mercy of God bishop of the City of Thessalonica, and legate of the Apostolic See of Rome," "John, the unworthy bishop of Portus, legate of the whole Council of the holy Apostolic See of Rome," "Stephen, by the mercy of God, bishop of Corinth, and legate of the Apostolic See of Old Rome."

EXTRACTS FROM THE ACTS.

SESSION I.

(Labbe and Cossart, *Concilia*, Tom. VI., col. 609 *et seqq.*)

[*After a history of the assembly of the Council, the Acts begin with the Speech of the Papal Legates, as follows :*]

Most benign lord, in accordance with the Sacra to our most holy Pope[1] from your God-instructed majesty, we have been sent by him to the most holy footsteps of your God-confirmed serenity, bearing with us his suggestion (ἀναφορᾶς, *suggestione*) as well as the other suggestion of his Synod equally addressed to your divinely preserved Piety by the venerable bishops subject to it, which also we offered to your God-crowned Fortitude. Since, then, during the past forty-six years, more or less, certain novelties in expression, contrary to the Orthodox faith, have been introduced by those who were at several times bishops of this, your royal and God-preserved city, to wit: Sergius, Paul, Pyrrhus, and Peter, as also by Cyrus, at one time archbishop of the city of Alexandria, as well also as by Theodore, who was bishop of a city called Pharan, and by certain others their followers, and since these things have in no small degree brought confusion into the Church throughout the whole world, for they taught dogmatically that

---

[1] The word " our " omitted in the Latin.

there was but one will in the dispensation of the Incarnation of our Lord Jesus Christ, one of the Holy Trinity, and one operation; and since many times your servant, our apostolic see, has fought against this, and then prayed against it, and by no means been able, even up to now, to draw away from such a depraved opinion its advocates, we beseech your God-crowned fortitude, that such as share these views of the most holy church of Constantinople may tell us, what is the source of this new-fangled language.

[*Answer of the Monothelites made at the Emperor's bidding :*]

We have brought out no new method of speech, but have taught whatever we have received from the holy Ecumenical Synods, and from the holy approved Fathers, as well as from the archbishops of this imperial city, to wit: Sergius, Paul, Pyrrhus, and Peter, as also from Honorius who was Pope of Old Rome, and from Cyrus who was Pope of Alexandria, that is to say with reference to will and operation, and so we have believed, and so we believe, so we preach; and further we are ready to stand by, and defend this faith.

THE LETTER OF AGATHO, POPE OF OLD ROME, TO THE EMPEROR, AND THE LETTER OF AGATHO AND OF 125 BISHOPS OF THE ROMAN SYNOD, ADDRESSED TO THE SIXTH COUNCIL.

(Read at the Fourth Session, November 15, at the request of George, Patriarch of Constantinople and his Suffragans.)

INTRODUCTORY NOTE.

(Bossuet, *Defensio Cler. Gal.* Lib. VII., cap. xxiv.)

All the fathers spoke one by one, and only after examination were the letters of St. Agatho and the whole Western Council approved. Agatho, indeed, and the Western Bishops put forth their decrees thus ['We have directed persons from our humility to your valour protected of God, which shall offer to you the report of us all, that is, of all the Bishops in the Northern or Western Regions, in which too we have summed up the confession of our Apostolic Faith, yet[1]] not as those who wished to contend about these things as being uncertain, but, being certain and unchangeable to set them forth in a brief definition, [suppliantly beseeching you that, by the favour of your sacred majesty, you would command these same things to be preached to all, and to have force with all.'] Undoubtedly, therefore, so far as in them lay, they defined the matter. The question was, whether the other Churches throughout the world would agree, and a matter so great was only made clear after Episcopal examination. But the high, magnificent, yet true expressions, which St. Agatho had used of his See, namely, that resting on the promise of the Lord it had never turned aside from the path of truth, and that its Pontiffs, the predecessors of Agatho, who were charged in the person of Peter to strengthen their brethren, had ever discharged that office, this the Fathers of the Council hear and receive. But not the less they examine the matter, they inquire into the decrees of Roman Pontiffs, and, after inquiry held, approve Agatho's decrees, condemn those of Honorius: a certain proof that they did not understand Agatho's expressions as if it were necessary to receive without discussion every decree of Roman Pontiffs even *de fide*, inasmuch as they are subjected to the supreme and final examination of a General Council: but as if these expressions taken as a whole, in their total, hold good in the full and complete succession of Peter, as we have often said, and in its proper place shall say at greater length.

THE LETTER OF POPE AGATHO.

(Found in Migne, *Pat. Lat., Tom.* LXXXVII., *col.* 1161; L. and C., *Tom. VI., col.* 630.)

Agatho a bishop and servant of the servants of God to the most devout and serene victors and conquerors, our most beloved sons and lovers of God and of our Lord Jesus Christ, the Emperor Constantine the Great, and to Heraclius and Tiberius, Augustuses.

While contemplating the various anxieties of human life, and while groaning with vehement weeping before the one true God, in prayer that he might impart to my wavering soul the comfort of his divine mercy, and might lift me by his right hand out of the depths of grief and anxiety, I most gratefully recognize, my most illustrious lords and sons, that your purpose [i.e. of holding a Council] afforded me deep and wonderful consolation. For it was most pious and emanated from your most meek tranquillity, taught by the divine benignity for the benefit of the Christian

---

[1] The words in brackets are not quoted by Bossuet.

commonwealth divinely entrusted to your keeping, that your imperial power and clemency might have a care to enquire diligently concerning the things of God (through whom Kings do reign, who is himself King of Kings and Lord of Lords) and might seek after the truth of his spotless faith as it has been handed down by the Apostles and by the Apostolic Fathers, and be zealously affected to command that in all the churches the pure tradition be held. And that no one may be ignorant of this pious intention of yours, or suspect that we have been compelled by force, and have not freely consented to the carrying into effect of the imperial decrees touching the preaching of our evangelical faith which was addressed to our predecessor Donus, a pontiff of Apostolic memory, they have through our ministry been sent to and entirely approved by all nations and peoples; for these decrees the Holy Spirit by his grace dictated to the tongue of the imperial pen, out of the treasure of a pure heart, as the words of an adviser not of an oppressor, defending himself, not looking with contempt upon others; not afflicting, but exhorting; and inviting to those things which are of God in godly wise, because he, the Maker and Redeemer of all men, who had he come in the majesty of his Godhead into the world, might have terrified mortals, preferred to descend through his inestimable clemency and humility to the estate of us whom he had created and thus to redeem us, who also expects from us a willing confession of the true faith.

And this it is that the blessed Peter, the prince of the Apostles, teaches: "Feed the flock of Christ which is among you, not by constraint, but willingly, exhorting it according to God." Therefore, encouraged by these imperial decrees, O most meek lords of all things, and relieved from the depths of affliction and raised to the hope of consolation, I have begun, refreshed somewhat by a better confidence, to comply with promptness with the things which were sometime ago bidden by the Sacra of your gentlest fortitude, and am endeavouring in obedience therewith to find persons, such as our deficient times and the quality of this obedient province permit, and taking advice with my fellow-servant bishops, as well concerning the approaching synod of this Apostolic See, as concerning our own clergy, the lovers of the Christian Empire, and, afterwards concerning the religious servants of God, that I might exhort them to follow in haste the footsteps of your most pious Tranquillity. And, were it not that the great compass of the provinces, in which our humility's council is situated had caused so great a loss of time, our servitude a while ago could have fulfilled with studious obedience what even now has scarcely been done. For while from the various provinces a council has been gathering about us, and while we have been able to select some persons of those from this very Roman city immediately subject to your most serene power, or from those near by, others again we have been obliged to wait for from far distant provinces, in which the word of Christian faith was preached by those sent by the predecessors of my littleness; and thus quite a space of time has elapsed: and I pass over my bodily pains in consequence of which life to a perpetually suffering person is neither possible nor pleasant. Therefore, most Christian lords and sons, in accordance with the most pious jussio of your God-protected clemency, we have had a care to send, with the devotion of a prayerful heart (from the obedience we owe you, not because we relied on the [superabundant] knowledge of those whom we send to you), our fellow-servants here present, Abundantius, John, and John, our most reverend brother bishops, Theodore and George our most beloved sons and presbyters, with our most beloved son John, a deacon, and with Constantine, a subdeacon of this holy spiritual mother, the Apostolic See, as well as Theodore, the presbyter legate of the holy Church of Ravenna and the religious servants of God the monks. For, among men placed amid the Gentiles, and earning their daily bread by bodily labour with considerable distraction, how could a knowledge of the Scriptures, in its fulness, be found unless what has been canonically defined by our holy and apostolic predecessors, and by the venerable five councils, we preserve in simplicity of heart, and without any distorting keep the faith come to us from the Fathers, always desirous and endeavouring to possess that one and chiefest good, viz.: that nothing be diminished from the things canonically defined, and that nothing be changed nor added thereto, but that those same things, both in words and sense, be guarded untouched? To these same commissioners we also have given the witness of some of the holy Fathers, whom this Apostolic Church of Christ receives, together with their books, so that, having obtained from the power of your most benign Christianity the privilege of suggesting, they might out of these endeavour to give satisfaction, (when your imperial Meekness shall have so commanded) as to what this Apostolic Church of Christ, their spiritual mother and the mother of your God-sprung empire, believes and preaches, not in words of worldly eloquence, which are not at the command of ordinary men, but in the integrity of the apostolic faith, in which having been taught from the cradle, we pray that we may serve and obey the Lord of heaven, the Propagator of your Christian empire, even unto the end. Consequently, we have granted them faculty or authority with your most tranquil mightiness, to afford satisfaction with simplicity whenever your clemency shall command, it being enjoined on them as a limitation that they presume not to add to, take away, or to change anything; but that they set forth this tradition of the Apostolic See in all sincerity as it has been taught by the apostolic pontiffs, who were our predecessors. For these delegates we most humbly implore with bent knees of the mind your clemency ever full of condescension, that agreeably to the most benign and most august promise of the imperial Sacra, your Christlike Tranquillity may deem them worthy of acceptance and may deign to give a favourable hearing to their most humble suggestions. Thus may your meekest Piety find the ears of Almighty God open to your prayers, and may you order that they return to their own unharmed in their rectitude of our Apostolic faith, as well as in the integrity of their bodies. And thus may the supernal Majesty restore to the benign rule of your government through the most heroic and unconquerable labours of your God-strengthened clemency, the whole Christian commonwealth, and may he subdue hostile nations to your mighty sceptre, that there may be satisfaction from this time forth to every soul and to all nations, because what you deigned to promise solemnly by your

most august letters about the immunity and safety of those who came to the Council, you have fulfilled in all respects. It is not their wisdom that gave us confidence to make bold to send them to your pious presence; but our littleness obediently complied with what your imperial benignity, with a gracious order, exhorted to. And briefly we shall intimate to your divinely instructed Piety, what the strength of our Apostolic faith contains, which we have received through Apostolic tradition and through the tradition of the Apostolical pontiffs, and that of the five holy general synods, through which the foundations of Christ's Catholic Church have been strengthened and established; this then is the status [and the regular tradition[1]] of our Evangelical and Apostolic faith, to wit, that as we confess the holy and inseparable Trinity, that is, the Father, the Son and the Holy Ghost, to be of one deity, of one nature and substance or essence, so we will profess also that it has one natural will, power, operation, domination, majesty, potency, and glory. And whatever is said of the same Holy Trinity essentially in singular number we understand to refer to the one nature of the three consubstantial Persons, having been so taught by canonical logic. But when we make a confession concerning one of the same three Persons of that Holy Trinity, of the Son of God, or God the Word, and of the mystery of his adorable dispensation according to the flesh, we assert that all things are double in the one and the same our Lord and Saviour Jesus Christ according to the Evangelical tradition, that is to say, we confess his two natures, to wit the divine and the human, of which and in which he, even after the wonderful and inseparable union, subsists. And we confess that each of his natures has its own natural propriety, and that the divine has all things that are divine, without any sin. And we recognize that each one (of the two natures) of the one and the same incarnated, that is, humanated (*humanati*) Word of God is in him unconfusedly, inseparably and unchangeably, intelligence alone discerning a unity, to avoid the error of confusion. For we equally detest the blasphemy of division and of commixture. For when we confess two natures and

---

[1] Only in the Latin.

two natural wills, and two natural operations in our one Lord Jesus Christ, we do not assert that they are contrary or opposed one to the other (as those who err from the path of truth and accuse the apostolic tradition of doing. Far be this impiety from the hearts of the faithful!), nor as though separated (*per se* separated) in two persons or subsistences, but we say that as the same our Lord Jesus Christ has two natures so also he has two natural wills and operations, to wit, the divine and the human: the divine will and operation he has in common with the coessential Father from all eternity: the human, he has received from us, taken with our nature in time. This is the apostolic and evangelic tradition, which the spiritual mother of your most felicitous empire, the Apostolic Church of Christ, holds. This is the pure expression of piety. This is the true and immaculate profession of the Christian religion, not invented by human cunning, but which was taught by the Holy Ghost through the princes of the Apostles. This is the firm and irreprehensible doctrine of the holy Apostles, the integrity of the sincere piety of which, so long as it is preached freely, defends the empire of your Tranquillity in the Christian commonwealth, and exults [will defend it, will render it stable ; and exulting], and (as we firmly trust) will demonstrate it full of happiness. Believe your most humble [servant], my most Christian lords and sons, that I am pouring forth these prayers with my tears, for its stability and exultation [*in Greek* exaltation]. And these things I (although unworthy and insignificant) dare advise through my sincere love, because your God-granted victory is our salvation, the happiness of your Tranquillity is our joy, the harmlessness of your kindness is the security of our littleness. And therefore I beseech you with a contrite heart and rivers of tears, with prostrated mind, deign to stretch forth your most clement right hand to the Apostolic doctrine which the co-worker of your pious labours, the blessed apostle Peter, has delivered, that it be not hidden under a bushel, but that it be preached in the whole earth more shrilly than a bugle: because the true confession thereof for which Peter was pronounced blessed by the Lord of all things, was revealed by the Father of heaven, for he

received from the Redeemer of all himself, by three commendations, the duty of feeding the spiritual sheep of the Church ; under whose protecting shield, this Apostolic Church of his has never turned away from the path of truth in any direction of error, whose authority, as that of the Prince of all the Apostles, the whole Catholic Church, and the Ecumenical Synods have faithfully embraced, and followed in all things; and all the venerable Fathers have embraced its Apostolic doctrine, through which they as the most approved luminaries of the Church of Christ have shone; and the holy orthodox doctors have venerated and followed it, while the heretics have pursued it with false criminations and with derogatory hatred. This is the living tradition of the Apostles of Christ, which his Church holds everywhere, which is chiefly to be loved and fostered, and is to be preached with confidence, which conciliates with God through its truthful confession, which also renders one commendable to Christ the Lord, which keeps the Christian empire of your Clemency, which gives far-reaching victories to your most pious Fortitude from the Lord of heaven, which accompanies you in battle, and defeats your foes ; which protects on every side as an impregnable wall your God-sprung empire, which throws terror into opposing nations, and smites them with the divine wrath, which also in wars celestially gives triumphal palms over the downfall and subjection of the enemy, and ever guards your most faithful sovereignty secure and joyful in peace. For this is the rule of the true faith, which this spiritual mother of your most tranquil empire, the Apostolic Church of Christ, has both in prosperity and in adversity always held and defended with energy; which, it will be proved, by the grace of Almighty God, has never erred from the path of apostolic tradition, nor has she been depraved by yielding to heretical innovations, but from the beginning she has received the Christian faith from her founders, the princes of the Apostles of Christ, and remains undefiled unto the end, according to the divine promise of the Lord and Saviour himself, which he uttered in the holy Gospels to the prince of his disciples: saying, " Peter, Peter, behold, Satan hath desired to have you, that he might sift you as wheat; but I have prayed for thee, that (thy) faith fail not. And when thou art converted, strengthen thy brethren." Let your tranquil Clemency therefore consider, since it is the Lord and Saviour of all, whose faith it is, that promised that Peter's faith should not fail and exhorted him to strengthen his brethren, how it is known to all that the Apostolic pontiffs, the predecessors of my littleness, have always confidently done this very thing: of whom also our littleness, since I have received this ministry by divine designation, wishes to be the follower, although unequal to them and the least of all. For woe is me, if I neglect to preach the truth of my Lord, which they have sincerely preached. Woe is me, if I cover over with silence the truth which I am bidden to give to the exchangers, i.e., to teach to the Christian people and imbue it therewith. What shall I say in the future examination by Christ himself, if I blush (which God forbid!) to preach here the truth of his words? What satisfaction shall I be able to give for myself, what for the souls committed to me, when he demands a strict account of the office I have received? Who, then, my most clement and most pious lords and sons, (I speak trembling and prostrate in spirit) would not be stirred by that admirable promise, which is made to the faithful: "Whoever shall confess me before men, him also will I confess before my Father, who is in heaven"? And which one even of the infidels shall not be terrified by that most severe threat, in which he protests that he will be full of wrath, and declares that "Whoever shall deny me before men, him also will I deny before my Father, who is in heaven"? Whence also blessed Paul, the apostle of the Gentiles, gives warning and says: "But though we, or an angel from the heaven should preach to you any other Gospel from what we have evangelized to you, let him be anathema." Since, therefore, such an extremity of punishment overhangs the corruptors, or suppressors of truth by silence, would not any one flee from an attempt at curtailing the truth of the Lord's faith? Wherefore the predecessors of Apostolic memory of my littleness, learned in the doctrine of the Lord, ever since the prelates of the Church of Constantinople have been trying to introduce into the immaculate Church of

Christ an heretical innovation, have never ceased to exhort and warn them with many prayers, that they should, at least by silence, desist from the heretical error of the depraved dogma, lest from this they make the beginning of a split in the unity of the Church, by asserting one will, and one operation of the two natures in the one Jesus Christ our Lord: a thing which the Arians and the Apollinarists, the Eutychians, the Timotheans, the Acephali, the Theodosians and the Gaianitæ taught, and every heretical madness, whether of those who confound, or of those who divide the mystery of the Incarnation of Christ. Those that confound the mystery of the holy Incarnation, inasmuch as they say that there is one nature of the deity and humanity of Christ, contend that he has one will, as of one, and (one) personal operation. But they who divide, on the other hand, the inseparable union, unite the two natures which they acknowledge that the Saviour possesses, not however in an union which is recognized to be hypostatic; but blasphemously join them by concord, through the affection of the will, like two subsistences, i.e., two somebodies. Moreover, the Apostolic Church of Christ, the spiritual mother of your God-founded empire, confesses one Jesus Christ our Lord existing of and in two natures, and she maintains that his two natures, to wit, the divine and the human, exist in him unconfused even after their inseparable union, and she acknowledges that each of these natures of Christ is perfect in the proprieties of its nature, and she confesses that all things belonging to the proprieties of the natures are double, because the same our Lord Jesus Christ himself is both perfect God and perfect man, of two and in two natures: and after his wonderful Incarnation, his deity cannot be thought of without his humanity, nor his humanity without his deity. Consequently, therefore, according to the rule of the holy Catholic and Apostolic Church of Christ, she also confesses and preaches that there are in him two natural wills and two natural operations. For if anybody should mean a personal will, when in the holy Trinity there are said to be three Persons, it would be necessary that there should be asserted three personal wills, and three personal operations (which is absurd and truly profane). Since, as the truth of the Christian faith holds, the will is natural, where the one nature of the holy and inseparable Trinity is spoken of, it must be consistently understood that there is one natural will, and one natural operation. But when in truth we confess that in the one person of our Lord Jesus Christ the mediator between God and men, there are two natures (that is to say the divine and the human), even after his admirable union, just as we canonically confess the two natures of one and the same person, so too we confess his two natural wills and two natural operations. But that the understanding of this truthful confession may become clear to your Piety's mind from the God-inspired doctrine of the Old and the New Testament, (for your Clemency is incomparably more able to penetrate the meaning of the sacred Scriptures, than our littleness to set it forth in flowing words), our Lord Jesus Christ himself, who is true and perfect God, and true and perfect man, in his holy Gospels shews forth in some instances human things, in others . divine, and still in others both together, making a manifestation concerning himself in order that he might instruct his faithful to believe and preach that he is both true God and true man. Thus as man he prays to the Father to take away the cup of suffering, because in him our human nature was complete, sin only excepted, "Father, if it be possible, let this cup pass from me; nevertheless not as I will, but as thou wilt." And in another passage: "Not my will, but thine be done." If we wish to know the meaning of which testimony as explained by the holy and approved Fathers, and truly to understand what "my will," what "thine" signify, the blessed Ambrose in his second book to the Emperor Gratian, of blessed memory, teaches us the meaning of this passage in these words, saying: "He then, receives my will, he takes my sorrow, I confidently call it sorrow as I am speaking of the cross, mine is the will, which he calls his, because he bears my sorrow as man, he spoke as a man, and therefore he says: 'Not as I will but as thou wilt.'" Mine is the sadness which he has received according to my affection.[1]

See, most pious of princes, how clearly here this holy Father sets forth that the words our Lord used in his prayer, "Not my will," pertain to his humanity; through which also he is said, according to the teaching of Blessed Paul the Apostle of the Gentiles, to have "become obedient unto death, even the death of the Cross." Wherefore also it is taught us that he was obedient to his parents, which must piously be understood to refer to his voluntary obedience, not according to his divinity (by which he governs all things), but according to his humanity, by which he spontaneously submitted himself to his parents. St. Luke the Evangelist likewise bears witness to the same thing, telling how the same our Lord Jesus Christ prayed according to his humanity to his Father, and said, "Father, if it be possible let the cup pass from me; nevertheless not my will but thine be done,"—which passage Athanasius, the Confessor of Christ, and Archbishop of the Church of Alexandria, in his book against Apollinaris the heretic, concerning the Trinity and the Incarnation, also understanding the wills to be two, thus explains: And when he says, "Father, if it be possible, let this cup pass from me, nevertheless not my will but thine be done," and again, "The spirit is willing, but the flesh is weak;" he shews that there are two wills, the one human which is the will of the flesh, but the other divine. For his human will, out of the weakness of the flesh was fleeing away from the passion, but his divine will was ready for it. What truer explanation could be found? For how is it possible not to acknowledge in him two wills, to wit, a human and a divine, when in him, even after the inseparable union, there are two natures according to the definitions of the synods? For John also, who leaned upon the Lord's breast, his beloved disciple, shews forth the same self-restraint in these words: "I came down from heaven not to do mine own wi but the will of the Father that sent me." And again: "This is the will of him that sent me, that of all that he gave me I should lose nothing, but should raise it up again at the last day." Again he introduces the Lord as disputing with the Jews, and saying among other things: "I seek not mine own will, but the will of him that sent me." On the meaning of which divine words

---

[1] Meo affectu : κατ' ἐμὴν διάθεσιν.

blessed Augustine, a most illustrious doctor, thus writes in his book against Maximinus the Arian. He says, "When the Son says to the Father 'Not what I will, but what thou wilt,' what doth it profit thee, that thou broughtest thy words into subjection and sayest, It shews truly that his will was subject to his Father, as though we would deny that the will of man should be subject to the will of God? For that the Lord said this in his human nature, anyone will quickly see who studies attentively this place of the Gospel. For therein he says, 'My soul is exceeding sorrowful even unto death.' Can this possibly be said of the nature of the One Word? But, O man, who thinkest to make the nature of the Holy Ghost to groan, why do you say that the nature of the Only-begotten Word of God cannot be sad? But to prevent anyone arguing in this way, he does not say 'I am sad;' (and even if he had so said, it could properly only have been understood of his human nature) but he says 'My soul is sad,' which soul he has as man; however in this also which he said, 'Not what I will' he shewed that he willed something different from what the Father did, which he could not have done except in his human nature, since he did not introduce our infirmity into his divine nature, but would transfigure human affection. For had he not been made man, the Only Word could in no way have said to the Father, 'Not what I will.' For it could never be possible for that immutable nature to will anything different from what the Father willed. If you would but make this distinction, O ye Arians, ye would not be heretics."

In this disputation this venerable Father shews that when the Lord says "his own" he means the will of his humanity, and when he says not to do "his own will," he teaches us not chiefly to seek our own wills but that through obedience we should submit our wills to the Divine Will. From all which it is evident that he had a human will by which he obeyed his Father, and that he had in himself this same human will immaculate from all sin, as true God and man. Which thing St. Ambrose also thus treats of in his explanation of St. Luke the Evangelist.

*   *   *   *   *

[*After this follows a catena of Patristic quotations which I have not thought worth while to produce in full. After St. Ambrose he cites St. Leo, then St. Gregory Nazianzen, then St. Augustine.   (L. & C., col. 647.)*]

From which testimonies it is clear that each of those natures which the spiritual Doctor has here enumerated has its own natural property, and that to each one a will ought to be assigned. For an angelic nature cannot have a divine or a human will, neither can a human nature have a divine or an angelic will. For no nature can have anything or any motion which pertains to another nature but only that which is naturally given by creation. And as this is the truth of the matter it is most certainly clear that we must needs confess that in our Lord Jesus Christ there are two natures and substances, to wit, the Divine and human, united in his one subsistence or person, and that we further confess that there are in him two natural wills, viz.: the divine and the human, for his divinity so far as its nature is concerned could not be said to possess a human will, nor should his humanity be believed to have naturally a divine will: And again, neither of these two substances of Christ must be confessed as being without a natural will; but his human will was lifted up by the omnipotency of his divinity, and his divine will was revealed to men through his humanity. Therefore it is necessary to refer to him as God such things as are divine, and as man such things as are human; and each must be truly recognized through the hypostatic union of the one and the same our Lord Jesus Christ, which the most true decree of the Council of Chalcedon sets forth—[*Here follows citation.*] This same thing also the holy synod which was gathered together in Constantinople in the time of the Emperor Justinian of august memory, teaches in the viith. chapter of its definitions. [*Here follows the citation.*] Moreover it is necessary that we should faithfully keep what those Venerable Synods taught, so that we never take away the difference of natures as a result of the union, but confess one Christ, true and perfect God and also true and perfect man, the propriety of each nature being kept intact. Wherefore, if in no respect the difference of the natures of our Lord

Jesus Christ has been taken away, it is necessary that we preserve this same difference in all its proprieties.   For whoso teaches that the difference is in no respect to be taken away, declares that it must be preserved in all things.   But when the heretics and the followers of heretics say that there is but one will and one operation, how is this difference recognized?   Or where is the difference which has been defined by this holy Synod preserved?   While if it is asserted that there is but one will in him (which is absurd), those who make this assertion must needs say that that will is either human or divine, or else composite from both, mixed and confused, or (according to the teaching of all heretics) that Christ has one will and one operation, proceeding from his one composite nature (as they hold).   And thus, without any doubt, the difference of nature is destroyed, which the holy synods declared to be preserved in all respects even after the admirable union. Because, though they taught that Christ was one, his person and substance one, yet on account of the union of the natures which was made hypostatically, they likewise decreed that we should clearly acknowledge and teach the difference of those natures which were united in him, after the admirable union.   Therefore if the proprieties of the natures in the same our one Lord Jesus Christ were preserved on account of the difference [of the natures], it is congruous that we should with full faith confess also the difference of his natural wills and operations, in order that we may be shewn to have followed in all respects their doctrine, and may admit into the Church of Christ no heretical novelty.

And although there exist numerous works of the other holy Fathers, nevertheless we subjoin to this our humble exposition a few testimonies out of the books which are in Greek, for the sake of fastidiousness.[1]

[*Here follows a catena of passages from the Greek fathers, viz.:* St. Gregory Theologus, St. Gregory Nyssen, St. John bishop of Constantinople, St. Cyril, bishop of Alexandria.   (L. & C., col. 654.)]

From these truthful testimonies it is also demonstrated that these venerable fathers predicated in the one and the same Lord Jesus Christ two natural wills, viz. : a divine and a human, for when St. Gregory Nazianzen says, " The willing of that man who is understood to be the Saviour," he shews that the human will of the Saviour was deified through its union with the Word, and therefore it is not contrary to God.   So likewise he proves that he had a human, although deified will, and this same he had (as he teaches in what follows) as well as his divine will, which was one and the same with that of the Father.   If therefore he had a divine and a deified will, he had also two wills.   For what is divine by nature has no need of being deified ; and what is deified is not truly divine by nature.   And when St. Gregory Nyssen, a great bishop, says that the true confession of the mystery is, that there should be understood one human will and another a divine will in Christ, what does he bid us understand when he says one and another will, except that there are manifestly two wills?

[*He next proceeds to comment upon the passage cited from* St. John, *then upon that from* St. Cyril of Alexandria. *After this follow quotations from* St. Hilary, St. Athanasius, St. Denys the Areopagite, St. Ambrose, St. Leo, St. Gregory Nyssen, St. Cyril of Alexandria, *which are next commented on in their order.   He then proceeds :* (L. & C., col. 662.)]

There are not lacking most telling passages in other of the venerable fathers, who speak clearly of the two natural operations in Christ, not to mention St. Cyril of Jerusalem, St. John of Constantinople, or those who afterwards conducted the laborious conflicts in defence of the venerable council of Chalcedon and of the Tome of St. Leo against the heretics from whose error the assertion of this new dogma has arisen : that is to say, John, bishop of Scythopolis, Eulogius, bishop of Alexandria, Euphræmius and Anastasius the elder, most worthy rulers of the church of Theopolis, and above all that emulator of the true and apostolic faith, the Emperor Justinian of pious memory, whose uprightness of faith exalted the Christian State as much as his sincere confession pleased God. And his pious memory is esteemed worthy

---

[1] Propter fastidium, what this may mean I have no idea; the Greek is still more extraordinary : ῥᾳθυμίας (vel. βαρυθυμίας) χάριν.

of veneration by all nations, whose uprightness of faith was disseminated with praise throughout the whole world by his most august edicts: one of these, to wit, that addressed to Zoilus, the patriarch of Alexandria, against the heresy of the Acephali to satisfy them of the rectitude of the apostolic faith, we offer to your most tranquil Christianity, sending it together with this paper of our lowliness through the same carriers. But lest this declaration should be thought burdensome on account of its length, we have inserted in this declaration of our humility only a few of the testimonies of the Holy Fathers, especially [when writing to those] on whom the care and arrangement of the whole world as on a firm foundation are recognized to rest ; since this is altogether incomparable and great, that the care of the whole Christian State being laid aside for a little out of love and zeal for true religion, your august and most religious clemency should desire to understand more clearly the doctrine of apostolical preaching. For from the different approved fathers the truth of the Orthodox faith has become clear although the treatment is short. For the approved fathers thought it to be superfluous to discourse at length upon what was evident and clear to all ; for who, even if he be dull of wit, does not perceive what is evident to all ? For it is impossible and contrary to the order of nature that there should be a nature without a natural operation : and even the heretics did not dare to say this, although they were, all of them, hunting for human craftiness and cunning questions against the orthodoxy of the faith, and arguments agreeable to their depravities.

How then can that now be asserted which never was said by the holy orthodox fathers, nor even was presumptuously invented by the profane heretics, viz.: that of the two natures of Christ, the divine and the human, the proprieties of each of which are recognized as being preserved in Christ, that anyone in sound mind should declare there was but one operation? Since if there is one, let them say whether it be temporal or eternal, divine or human, uncreated or created : the same as that of the Father or different from that of the Father. If therefore it is one, that one and the same must be common to the divinity and to the humanity (which is absurd), there-

fore while the Son of God, who is both God and man, wrought human things on earth, likewise also the Father worked with him according to his nature (naturaliter, φυσικῶς) ; for what things the Father doeth these the Son also doeth likewise. But if (as is the truth) the human acts which Christ did are to be referred to his person alone as the Son, which is not the same as that of the Father; in one nature Christ worked one set of works, and in the other another, so that according to his divinity the Son does the same things that the Father does ; and likewise according to his humanity, what things are proper to the manhood, those same, he as man, did because he is truly both God and man. For which reason we rightly believe that that same person, since he is one, has two natural operations, to wit, the divine and the human, one uncreated, and the other created, as true and perfect God and as true and perfect man, the one and the same, the mediator between God and men, the Lord Jesus Christ. Wherefore from the quality of the operations there is recognized a difference void of offence (ἀπρόσκοπος) of the natures which are joined in Christ through the hypostatic union. We now proceed to cite some passages from the execrable writings of the heretics hated of God,[1] whose words and sayings we equally abominate, for the demonstration of those things which our inventors of new dogma have followed teaching that in Christ there is but one will and one operation.

[*Then follow quotations from* Apollinaris, Severus, Theodosius of Alexandria. (L. & C., col. 667.)]

Behold, most pious lords and sons, by the testimonies of the holy Fathers, as by spiritual rays, the doctrine of the Catholic and Apostolic Church has been illustrated and the darkness of heretical blindness, which is offering error to men for imitation, has been revealed. Now it is necessary that the new doctrine should follow somebody, and by whose authority it is supported, we shall note.

[*Here follow quotations from* Cyrus of Alexandria, Theodore of Pharon, Sergius of Constantinople, Pyrrhus, Paulus *his* succes-

---

[1] The meaning of this passage is clear enough but the text is slightly corrupt.

sor, Peter *his successor*. (L. & C., col. 670.)]

Let then your God-founded clemency with the internal eye of discrimination, which for the guidance of the Christian people you have been deemed worthy to receive by the Grace of God, take heed which one of such doctors you think the Christian people should follow, the doctrine of which one of these they should embrace so as to be saved; for they condemn all, and each one of them the other, according as the various and unstable definitions in their writings assert sometimes that there is one will and one operation, sometimes that there is neither one nor two operations, sometimes one will and operation, and again two wills and two operations, likewise one will and one operation, and again neither one, nor two, and somebody else one and two.

Who does not hate, and rage against, and avoid such blind errors, if he have any desire to be saved and seek to offer to the Lord at his coming a right faith? Therefore the Holy Church of God, the mother of your most Christian power, should be delivered and liberated with all your might (through the help of God) from the errors of such teachers, and the evangelical and apostolic uprightness of the orthodox faith, which has been established upon the firm rock of this Church of blessed Peter, the Prince of the Apostles, which by his grace and guardianship remains free from all error, [that faith I say] the whole number of rulers and priests, of the clergy and of the people, unanimously should confess and preach with us as the true declaration of the Apostolic tradition, in order to please God and to save their own souls.

And these things we have taken pains to insert in the tractate of our humility, for we have been afflicted and have groaned without ceasing that such grievous errors should be entertained by bishops of the Church, who are zealous to establish their own peculiar views rather than the truth of the faith, and think that our sincere fraternal admonition has its spring in a contempt for them. And indeed the apostolic predecessors of my humility admonished, begged, upbraided, besought, reproved, and exercised every kind of exhortation that the recent wound might receive a remedy, moved thereto not by a mind filled with hatred (God is my witness) nor through the elation of boasting, nor through the opposition of contention, nor through an inane desire to find some fault with their teachings, nor through anything akin to the love of arrogance, but out of zeal for the uprightness of the truth, and for the rule of the confession of the pure Gospel, and for the salvation of souls, and for the stability of the Christian state, and for the safety of those who rule the Roman Empire. Nor did they cease from their admonitions after the long duration of this domesticated error, but always exhorted and bore record, and that with fraternal charity, not through malice or pertinacious hatred (far be it from the Christian heart to rejoice at another's fall, when the Lord of all teaches, " I desire not the death of a sinner, but that he be converted and live ;" and who rejoiceth over one sinner that repenteth more than over ninety-and-nine just persons : who came down from heaven to earth to deliver the lost sheep, inclining the power of his majesty), but desiring them with outstretched spiritual arms, and exhorting to embrace them returning to the unity of the orthodox faith, and awaiting their conversion to the full rectitude of the orthodox faith : that they might not make themselves aliens from our communion, that is from the communion of blessed Peter the Apostle, whose ministry, we (though unworthy) exercise, and preach the faith he has handed down, but that they should together with us pray Christ the Lord, the spotless sacrifice, for the stability of your most strong and serene Empire.

We believe, most pious lords [singular in the Latin] of all things, that there has been left no possible ambiguity which can prevent the recognizing of those who have followed the inventors of new dogma. For the sweetness of spiritual understanding with which the sayings of the Fathers are full has become evident to the eyes of all ; and the stench of the heretics, to be avoided by all the faithful, has been made notorious. Nor has it remained unknown that the inventors of new dogma have been shewn to be the followers of heretics, and not the walkers in the footsteps of the holy Fathers : therefore whoever wishes to colour any error of his whatever, is condemned by the light of truth, as the Apostle of the Gentiles says, "For everything that doth make manifest is light," for the truth ever remains constant and the same, but falsehood is ever varying, and in its wanderings adopting things mutually contradictory. On this account the inventors of the new dogma have been shewn to have taught things mutually contradictory, because they were not willing to be followers of the Evangelical and Apostolic faith. Wherefore since the truth has shone forth by the observations of your God-inspired piety, and falsity which has been exposed has attained the contempt which it deserved, it remains that the crowned truth may shine forth victoriously through the pious favours of your God-crowned clemency ; and that the error of novelty with it inventors and with those who follow their doctrine, may receive the punishment due their presumption, and be cast forth from the midst of the orthodox prelates for the heretical pravity of their innovation, which into the holy, Catholic and Apostolic Church of Christ they have endeavoured to introduce, and to stain with the contagion of heretical pravity the indivisible and unspotted body of the Church [of Christ]. For it is not just that the injurious should injure the innocent, nor that the offences of some should be visited upon the inoffensive, for even if in this world to the condemned mercy is extended, yet they who are thus spared reap for that sparing no benefit in the judgment of God, and by those thus sparing them there is incurred no little danger for their unlawful compassion.

But we believe that Almighty God has reserved for the happy days of your gentleness the amending of these things, that filling on earth the place and zeal of our Lord Jesus Christ himself, who has vouchsafed to crown your rule, ye may judge just judgment for his Evangelical and Apostolical truth : for although he be the Redeemer and Saviour of the human race yet he suffered injury, and bore it even until now, and inspired the empire of your fortitude, so that you should be worthy to follow the cause of his faith (as equity demanded, and as the determination of the Holy Fathers and of the Five General Synods decreed), and that you should avenge, through his guardianship, on the spurners of his faith, the injury done your Redeemer and Colleague in reigning, thus fulfilling magnanimously with imperial clemency that prophetic utterance with

which David the King and Prophet, spake to God, saying, "The zeal of thine house hath eaten me up." Wherefore having been extolled for so God-pleasing a zeal, he was deemed fit to hear that blessed word spoken by the Creator of all men, "I have found David, a man after my heart, who will do all my will." And to him also it was promised in the Psalms, "I have found David, my servant, with my holy oil have I anointed him : My hand shall aid him and my arm shall comfort him," so that the most pious majesty of your Christian clemency may work to further the cause of Christ with burning zeal for the sake of remuneration, and may he make all the acts of your most powerful empire both happy and prosperous, who hath stored up his promise in the Holy Gospels, saying, "Seek ye first the kingdom of God and all these things shall be added unto you." For all, to whom has come the knowledge of the sacred heads,[1] have been offering innumerable thanksgivings and unceasing praises to the defender of your most powerful dominion, being filled with admiration for the greatness of your clemency, in that you have so benignly set forth the kind intention of your august magnanimity ; for in truth, as most pious and most just princes, you have deigned to treat divine things with the fear of God, having promised every immunity to those persons sent to you from our littleness.

And we are confident that what your pious clemency has promised, you are powerful to carry out, in order that what has been vowed and promised to God by the religious philanthropy beyond your Christian power, may nevertheless be fulfilled by the aid of his omnipotency.

Wherefore let praise by all Christian nations, and eternal memory, and frequent prayer be poured forth before the Lord Christ, whose is the cause, for your safety, and your triumphs, and your complete victory, that the nations of the Gentiles, being impressed by the terror of the supernal majesty, may lay down most humbly their necks beneath the sceptre of your most powerful rule, that the power of your most pious kingdom may continue until the ceaseless joy of the eternal kingdom succeeds to this temporal reign. Nor could

---

[1] I. e., the imperial edicts.

anything be found more likely to commend the clemency of your unconquerable fortitude to the divine majesty, than that those who err from the rule of truth should be repelled and the integrity of our Evangelical and Apostolic faith should be everywhere set forth and preached.

Moreover, most pious and God-instructed sons and lords, if the Archbishop of the Church of Constantinople shall choose to hold and to preach with us this most unblameable rule of Apostolic doctrine of the Sacred Scriptures, of the venerable synods, of the spiritual Fathers, according to their evangelical understanding, through which the form of the truth has been set forth by us through the assistance of the Spirit, there will ensue great peace to them that love the name of God, and there will remain no scandal of dissension, and that will come to pass which is recorded in the Acts of the Apostles, when through the grace of the Holy Spirit the people had come to the acknowledging of Christianity, all of us will be of one heart and of one mind. But if (which God forbid!) he shall prefer to embrace the novelty but lately introduced by others; and shall ensnare himself with doctrines which are alien to the rule of orthodox truth and of our Apostolic faith, to decline which as injurious to souls these have put off, despite the exhortation and admonitions of our predecessors in the Apostolic See, down to this day, he himself should know what kind of an answer he will have to give for such contempt in the divine examination of Christ before the judge of all, who is in heaven, to whom when he cometh to judgment also we ourselves are about to give an account of the ministry of preaching the truth which has been committed to us, or for the toleration of things contrary to the Christian religion: and may we (as I humbly pray) preserve unconfusedly and freely, with simplicity and purity, whole and undefiled, the Apostolic and Evangelical rule of the right faith as

we have received it from the beginning. And may your most august serenity, for the affection and reverence which you bear to the Catholic and Apostolic right faith, receive the perfect reward of your pious labours from our Lord Jesus Christ himself, the ruler with you of your Christian empire, whose true confession you desire to preserve undefiled, because nothing in any respect has been neglected or omitted by your God-crowned clemency, which could minister to the peace of the churches, provided always that the integrity of the true faith was maintained: since God, the Judge of all, who disposes the ending of all matters as he deems most expedient, seeks out the intent of the heart, and will accept a zeal for piety. Therefore I exhort you, O most pious and clement Emperor, and together with my littleness every Christian man exhorts you on bended knee with all humility, that to all the God-pleasing goodnesses and admirable imperial benefits which the heavenly condescension has vouchsafed to grant to the human race through your God-accepted care, this also you would order, for the redintegration of perfect piety, to offer an acceptable sacrifice to Christ the Lord your fellow-ruler, granting entire impunity, and free faculty of speech to each one wishing to speak, and to urge a word in defence of the faith which he believes and holds, so that it may most manifestly be recognized by all that by no terror, by no force, by no threat or aversion any one wishing to speak for the truth of the Catholic and Apostolic faith, has been prohibited or repulsed, and that all unanimously may glorify your imperial (*divinam*) majesty, throughout the whole space of their lives for so great and so inestimable a good, and may pour forth unceasing prayers to Christ the Lord that your most strong empire may be preserved untouched and exalted. The Subscription. May the grace from above keep your empire, most pious lords, and place beneath its feet the neck of all the nations.

THE LETTER OF AGATHO AND OF THE ROMAN SYNOD OF 125 BISHOPS WHICH WAS TO SERVE AS AN INSTRUCTION TO THE LEGATES SENT TO ATTEND THE SIXTH SYNOD.

(*Found in Labbe and Cossart*, Concilia, *Tom. VI., col.* 677 *et seqq., and in Migne*, Pat. Lat., *Tom. LXXXVII., col.* 1215 *et seqq.* [*This last text, which is Mansi's, I have followed*].)

To the most pious Lords and most serene victors and conquerors, our own sons beloved of God and of our Lord Jesus Christ, Constantine, the great Emperor, and Heraclius and Tiberius, Augustuses, Agatho, the bishop and servant of the servants of God, together with all the synods subject to the council of the Apostolic See.

[*The Letter opens with a number of compliments to the Emperor, much in style and matter like the introduction of the preceding letter. I have not thought it worth while to translate this, but have begun at the doctrinal part, which is given to the reader in full.* (Labbe and Cossart, col. 682.)]

We believe in God the Father Almighty, maker of heaven and earth, and of all things visible and invisible; and in his only-begotten Son, who was begotten of him before all worlds; very God of Very God, Light of Light, begotten not made, being of one substance with the Father, that is of the same substance as the Father; by him were all things made which are in heaven and which are in earth; and in the Holy Ghost, the Lord and giver of life, who proceedeth from the Father, and with the Father and the Son together is worshipped and glorified; the Trinity in unity and Unity in trinity; a unity so far as essence is concerned, but a trinity of persons or subsistences; and so we confess God the Father, God the Son, and God the Holy Ghost; not three gods, but one God, the Father, the Son, and the Holy Ghost: not a subsistency of three names, but one substance of three subsistences; and of these persons one is the essence, or substance or nature, that is to say one is the godhead, one the eternity, one the power, one the kingdom, one the glory, one the adoration, one the essential will and operation of the same Holy and inseparable Trinity, which hath created all things, hath made disposition of them, and still contains them.

Moreover we confess that one of the same holy consubstantial Trinity, God the Word, who was begotten of the Father before the worlds, in the last days of the world for us and for our salvation came down from heaven, and was incarnate of the Holy Ghost, and of our Lady, the holy, immaculate, ever-virgin and glorious Mary, truly and properly the Mother of God, that is to say according to the flesh which was born of her; and was truly made man, the same being very God and very man. God of God his Father, but man of his Virgin Mother, incarnate of her flesh with a reasonable and intelligent soul: of one substance with God the Father, as touching his godhead, and consubstantial with us as touching his manhood, and in all points like unto us, but without sin. He was crucified for us under Pontius Pilate, he suffered, was buried and rose again; ascended into heaven, and sitteth at the right hand of the Father, and he shall come again to judge both the quick and the dead, and of his kingdom there shall be no end.

And this same one Lord of ours, Jesus Christ, the only-begotten Son of God, we acknowledge to subsist of and in two substances unconfusedly, unchangeably, indivisibly, inseparably, the difference of the natures being by no means taken away by the union, but rather the proprieties of each nature being preserved and concurring in one Person and one Subsistence, not scattered or divided into two Persons, nor confused into one composite nature; but we confess one and the same only-begotten Son, God the Word, our Lord Jesus Christ, not one in another, nor one added to another, but himself the same in two natures—that is to say in the Godhead and in the manhood even after the hypostatic union : for neither was the Word changed into the nature of flesh, nor was the flesh transformed into the nature of the Word, for each remained what it was by nature. We discern by contemplation alone the distinction between the natures united in him of which inconfusedly, inseparably and unchangeably he is composed ; for one is of both, and through one both, because there are together both the height of the deity and the humility of the flesh, each nature preserving after the union its own proper character without any defect ; and each form acting in communion with the other what is proper to itself. The Word working what is proper to the Word, and the flesh what is proper to the flesh ; of which the one shines with miracles, the other bows down beneath injuries. Wherefore, as we confess that he truly has two natures or substances, viz. : the Godhead and the manhood, inconfusedly, indivisibly and unchangeably [united], so also the rule of piety instructs us that he has two natural wills and two natural operations, as perfect God and perfect man, one and the same our Lord Jesus Christ. And this the apostolic and evangelical tradition and the authority of the Holy Fathers (whom the Holy Apostolic and Catholic Church and the venerable Synods receive), has plainly taught us.

[*The letter goes on to say that this is the traditional faith, and is that which was set forth in a council over which Pope Martin presided, and that those opposed to this faith have erred from the truth, some in one way, and some in another. It next apologizes for the delay in sending the persons ordered by the imperial Sacra, and proceeds thus :* (Labbe and Cossart, col. 686 ; Migne, col. 1224).]

In the first place, a great number of us are spread over a vast extent of country even to the sea coast, and the length of their journey necessarily took much time. Moreover we were in hopes of being able to join to our humility our fellow-servant and brother bishop, Theodore, the archbishop and philosopher of the island of Great Britain, with others who have been kept there even till to-day ; and to add to these divers bishops of this council who have their sees in different parts, that our humble suggestion [i.e., the doctrinal definition contained in the letters] might proceed from a council of wide-spread influence, lest if only a part were cognizant of what was being done, it might escape the notice of a part ; and especially because among the Gentiles, as the Longobards, and the Sclavi, as also the Franks, the French, the Goths, and the Britains, there are known to be very many of our fellow-servants who do not cease curiously to enquire on the subject, that they may know what is being done in the cause of the Apostolic faith : who as they can be of advantage so long as they hold the true faith with us, and think in unison with us, so are they found troublesome and contrary, if (which may God forbid !) they stumble at any article of the faith. But we, although most humble, yet strive with all our might that the commonwealth of your Christian empire may be shown to be more sublime than all the nations, for in it has been founded the See of Blessed Peter, the prince of the Apostles, by the authority of which, all Christian nations venerate and worship with us, through the reverence of the blessed Apostle Peter himself. (*This is the Latin, which appears to me to be corrupt, the Greek reads as follows :* " The authority of which for the truth, all the Christian nations together with us worship and revere, according to the honour of the blessed Peter the Apostle himself.")

[*The letter ends with prayers for constancy, and blessings on the State and Emperor, and hopes for the universal diffusion and acceptance of the truth.*]

EXTRACTS FROM THE ACTS.

SESSION VIII.

(Labbe and Cossart, *Concilia*, Tom. VI., col. 730.)

[*The Emperor said*]

Let George, the most holy archbishop of this our God-preserved city, and let Macarius, the venerable archbishop of Antioch, and let the synod subject to them [i.e., their suffragans] say, if they submit to the force (εἰ στοιχοῦσι τῇ δυνάμει) of the suggestions sent by the most holy Agatho Pope of Old[1] Rome and by his Synod.

[*The answer of George, with which all his bishops, many of them speaking one by one, agreed except Theodore of Metilene (who handed in his assent at the end of the Tenth Session).*]

I have diligently examined the whole force of the suggestions sent to your most pious Fortitude, as well by Agatho, the most holy Pope of Old[1] Rome, as by his synod, and I have scrutinized the works of the holy and approved Fathers, which are laid up in my venerable patriarchate, and I have found that all the testimonies of the holy and accepted Fathers, which are contained in those suggestions agree with, and in no particular differ from, the holy and accepted Fathers. Therefore I give my submission to them and thus I profess and believe.

[*The answer of all the rest of the Bishops subject to the See of Constantinople.* (Col. 735.)]

And we, most pious Lord, accepting the teaching of the suggestion sent to your most gentle Fortitude by the most holy and blessed Agatho, Pope of Old Rome, and of that other suggestion which was adopted by the council subject to him, and following the sense therein contained, so we are minded, so we profess, and so we believe that in our one Lord Jesus Christ, our true God, there are two natures unconfusedly, unchangeably, undividedly, and two natural wills and two natural operations; and all who have taught, and who now say, that there is but one will and one operation in the two natures of our one Lord Jesus Christ our true God, we anathematize.

[*The Emperor's demand to Macarius.* (Col. 739.)]

Let Macarius, the Venerable Archbishop of Antioch, who has now heard what has been said by this holy and Ecumenical Synod [demanding the expression of his faith], answer what seemeth him good.

[*The answer of Macarius.*]

I do not say that there are two wills or two operations in the dispensation of the incarnation of our Lord Jesus Christ, but one will and one theandric operation.

THE SENTENCE AGAINST THE MONOTHELITES.

SESSION XIII.

(L. and C., *Concilia*, Tom. VI., col. 943.)

The holy council said: After we had reconsidered, according to our promise which we had made to your highness, the doctrinal letters of Sergius, at one time patriarch of this royal god-protected city to Cyrus, who was then bishop of Phasis and to Honorius some time Pope of Old Rome, as well as the letter of the latter to the same Sergius, we find that these documents are quite foreign to the apostolic dogmas, to the declarations

---

[1] " Old " omitted in Latin.

of the holy Councils, and to all the accepted Fathers, and that they follow the false teachings of the heretics; therefore we entirely reject them, and execrate them as hurtful to the soul. But the names of those men whose doctrines we execrate must also be thrust forth from the holy Church of God, namely, that of Sergius some time bishop of this God-preserved royal city who was the first to write on this impious doctrine; also that of Cyrus of Alexandria, of Pyrrhus, Paul, and Peter, who died bishops of this God-preserved city, and were like-minded with them; and that of Theodore sometime bishop of Pharan, all of whom the most holy and thrice blessed Agatho, Pope of Old Rome, in his suggestion to our most pious and God-preserved lord and mighty Emperor, rejected, because they were minded contrary to our orthodox faith, all of whom we define are to be subjected to anathema. And with these we define that there shall be expelled from the holy Church of God and anathematized Honorius who was some time Pope of Old Rome, because of what we found written by him to Sergius, that in all respects he followed his view and confirmed his impious doctrines. We have also examined the synodal letter of Sophronius of holy memory, some time Patriarch of the Holy City of Christ our God, Jerusalem, and have found it in accordance with the true faith and with the Apostolic teachings, and with those of the holy approved Fathers. Therefore we have received it as orthodox and as salutary to the holy Catholic and Apostolic Church, and have decreed that it is right that his name be inserted in the diptychs of the Holy Churches.

SESSION XVI.

(Labbe and Cossart, *Concilia*, Tom. VI., col. 1010.)

[*The Acclamations of the Fathers.*]

Many years to the Emperor! Many years to Constantine, our great Emperor! Many years to the Orthodox King! Many years to our Emperor that maketh peace! Many years to Constantine, a second Martian! Many years to Constantine, a new Theodosius! Many years to Constantine, a new Justinian! Many years to the keeper of the orthodox faith! O Lord preserve the foundation of the Churches! O Lord preserve the keeper of the faith! Many years to Agatho, Pope of Rome! Many years to George, Patriarch of Constantinople! Many years to Theophanus, Patriarch of Antioch! Many years to the orthodox council! Many years to the orthodox Senate!

To Theodore of Pharan, the heretic, anathema! To Sergius, the heretic, anathema! To Cyrus, the heretic, anathema! To Honorius, the heretic, anathema! To Pyrrhus, the heretic, anathema!

To Paul
To Peter
To Macarius } the heretic, anathema!
To Stephen
To Polychronius
To Apergius of Perga

To all heretics, anathema! To all who side with heretics, anathema!

May the faith of the Christians increase, and long years to the orthodox and Ecumenical Council!

THE DEFINITION OF FAITH.

(Found in the Acts, Session XVIII., L. and C., *Concilia,* Tom. VI., col. 1019.)

The holy, great, and Ecumenical Synod which has been assembled by the grace of God, and the religious decree of the most religious and faithful and mighty Sovereign Constantine, in this God-protected and royal city of Constantinople, New Rome, in the Hall of the imperial Palace, called Trullus, has decreed as follows.

The only-begotten Son, and Word of God the Father, who was made man in all things like unto us without sin, Christ our true God, has declared expressly in the words of the Gospel, "I am the light of the world; he that followeth me shall not walk in darkness, but shall have the light of life." And again, "My peace I leave with you, my peace I give unto you." Our most gentle Sovereign, the champion of orthodoxy, and opponent of evil doctrine, being reverentially led by this divinely uttered doctrine of peace, and having convened this our holy and Ecumenical assembly, has united the judgment of the whole Church. Wherefore this our holy and Ecumenical Synod having driven away the impious error which had prevailed for a certain time until now, and following closely the straight path of the holy and approved Fathers, has piously given its full assent to the five holy and Ecumenical Synods (that is to say, to that of the 318 holy Fathers who assembled in Nice against the raging Arius; and the next in Constantinople of the 150 God-inspired men against Macedonius the adversary of the Spirit, and the impious Apollinaris; and also the first in Ephesus of 200 venerable men convened against Nestorius the Judaizer; and that in Chalcedon of 630 God-inspired Fathers against Eutyches and Dioscorus hated of God; and in addition to these, to the last, that is the Fifth holy Synod assembled in this place, against Theodore of Mopsuestia, Origen, Didymus, and Evagrius, and the writings of Theodoret against the Twelve Chapters of the celebrated Cyril, and the Epistle which was said to be written by Ibas to Maris the Persian), renewing in all things the ancient decrees of religion, and chasing away the impious doctrines of irreligion. And this

our holy and Ecumenical Synod inspired of God has set its seal to the Creed which was put forth by the 318 Fathers, and again religiously confirmed by the 150, which also the other holy synods cordially received and ratified for the taking away of every soul-destroying heresy.

The Nicene Creed of the 318 holy Fathers.

We believe, etc.

The Creed of the 150 holy Fathers assembled at Constantinople.

We believe, etc.

The holy and Ecumenical Synod further says, this pious and orthodox Creed of the Divine grace would be sufficient for the full knowledge and confirmation of the orthodox faith. But as the author of evil, who, in the beginning, availed himself of the aid of the serpent, and by it brought the poison of death upon the human race, has not desisted, but in like manner now, having found suitable instruments for working out his will (we mean Theodorus, who was Bishop of Pharan, Sergius, Pyrrhus, Paul and Peter, who were Archbishops of this royal city, and moreover, Honorius who was Pope of the elder Rome, Cyrus Bishop of Alexandria, Macarius who was lately bishop of Antioch, and Stephen his disciple), has actively employed them in raising up for the whole Church the stumblingblocks of one will and one operation in the two natures of Christ our true God, one of the Holy Trinity; thus disseminating, in novel terms, amongst the orthodox people, an heresy similar to the mad and wicked doctrine of the impious Apollinaris, Severus, and Themistius, and endeavouring craftily to destroy the perfection of the incarnation of the same our Lord Jesus Christ, our God, by blasphemously representing his flesh endowed with a rational soul as devoid of will or operation. Christ, therefore, our God, has raised up our faithful Sovereign, a new David, having found him a man after his own heart, who as it is written, "has not suffered his eyes to sleep nor his eyelids to slumber," until he has found a perfect declaration of orthodoxy by this our God-collected and holy Synod; for, according to the sentence spoken of God, "Where two or three are gathered together in my name, there am I in the midst of them," the present holy and Ecumenical Synod faithfully receiving and saluting with uplifted hands as well the suggestion which by the most holy and blessed Agatho, Pope of ancient Rome, was sent to our most pious and faithful Emperor Constantine, which rejected by name those who taught or preached one will and one operation in the dispensation of the incarnation of our Lord Jesus Christ who is our very God, has likewise adopted that other synodal suggestion which was sent by the Council holden under the same most holy Pope, composed of 125 Bishops, beloved of God, to his God-instructed tranquillity, as consonant to the holy Council of Chalcedon and to the Tome of the most holy and blessed Leo, Pope of the same old Rome, which was directed to St. Flavian, which also this Council called the Pillar of the right faith; and also agrees with the Synodal Epistles which were written by Blessed Cyril against the impious Nestorius and addressed to the Oriental Bishops. Following the five holy Ecumenical Councils and the holy and approved Fathers, with one voice defining that our Lord Jesus Christ must be confessed to be very God and very man, one of the holy and consubstantial and life - giving Trinity, perfect in Deity and perfect in humanity, very God and very man, of a reasonable soul and human body subsisting; consubstantial with the Father as touching his Godhead and consubstantial with us as touching his manhood; in all things like unto us, sin only excepted; begotten of his Father before all ages according to his Godhead, but in these last days for us men and for our salvation made man of the Holy Ghost and of the Virgin Mary, strictly and properly the Mother of God according to the flesh; one and the same Christ our Lord the only-begotten Son of two natures unconfusedly, unchangeably, inseparably, indivisibly to be recognized, the peculiarities of neither nature being lost by the union but rather the proprieties of each nature being preserved, concurring in one Person and in one subsistence, not parted or divided into two persons but one and the same only-begotten Son of God, the Word, our Lord Jesus Christ, according as the

Prophets of old have taught us and as our Lord Jesus Christ himself hath instructed us, and the Creed of the holy Fathers hath delivered to us; defining all this we likewise declare that in him are two natural wills and two natural operations indivisibly, inconvertibly, inseparably, inconfusedly, according to the teaching of the holy Fathers. And these two natural wills are not contrary the one to the other (God forbid!) as the impious heretics assert, but his human will follows and that not as resisting and reluctant, but rather as subject to his divine and omnipotent will. For it was right that the flesh should be moved but subject to the divine will, according to the most wise Athanasius. For as his flesh is called and is the flesh of God the Word, so also the natural will of his flesh is called and is the proper will of God the Word, as he himself says: "I came down from heaven, not that I might do mine own will but the will of the Father which sent me!" where he calls his own will the will of his flesh, inasmuch as his flesh was also his own. For as his most holy and immaculate animated flesh was not destroyed because it was deified but continued in its own state and nature ($\ddot{o}\rho\omega$ $\tau\epsilon$ $\kappa\alpha\grave{\imath}$ $\lambda\acute{o}\gamma\omega$), so also his human will, although deified, was not suppressed, but was rather preserved according to the saying of Gregory Theologus: "His will [i.e., the Saviour's] is not contrary to God but altogether deified."

We glorify two natural operations indivisibly, immutably, inconfusedly, inseparably in the same our Lord Jesus Christ our true God, that is to say a divine operation and a human operation, according to the divine preacher Leo, who most distinctly asserts as follows: "For each form ($\mu o\rho\phi\acute{\eta}$) does in communion with the other what pertains properly to it, the Word, namely, doing that which pertains to the Word, and the flesh that which pertains to the flesh."

For we will not admit one natural operation in God and in the creature, as we will not exalt into the divine essence what is created, nor will we bring down the glory of the divine nature to the place suited to the creature.

We recognize the miracles and the sufferings as of one and the same [Person], but of one or of the other nature of which he is and in which he exists, as Cyril admirably says. Preserving therefore the inconfusedness and indivisibility, we make briefly this whole confession, believing our Lord Jesus Christ to be one of the Trinity and after the incarnation our true God, we say that his two natures shone forth in his one subsistence in which he both performed the miracles and endured the sufferings through the whole of his economic conversation (δι ὅλης αὐτοῦ τῆς οἰκονομκῆς ἀναστροφῆς), and that not in appearance only but in very deed, and this by reason of the difference of nature which must be recognized in the same Person, for although joined together yet each nature wills and does the things proper to it and that indivisibly and inconfusedly. Wherefore we confess two wills and two operations, concurring most fitly in him for the salvation of the human race.

These things, therefore, with all diligence and care having been formulated by us, we define that it be permitted to no one to bring forward, or to write, or to compose, or to think, or to teach a different faith. Whosoever shall presume to compose a different faith, or to propose, or teach, or hand to those wishing to be converted to the knowledge of the truth, from the Gentiles or Jews, or from any heresy, any different Creed; or to introduce a new voice or invention of speech to subvert these things which now have been determined by us, all these, if they be Bishops or clerics let them be deposed, the Bishops from the Episcopate, the clerics from the clergy; but if they be monks or laymen: let them be anathematized.

THE PROSPHONETICUS TO THE EMPEROR.

(Labbe and Cossart, *Concilia*, Tom. VI., col. 1047 *et seqq.*)

[*This address begins with many compli-ments to the Emperor, especially for his zeal for the true faith.*]

But because the adversary Satan allows no rest, he has raised up the very ministers of Christ against him, as if armed and carry-ing weapons, etc.

[*The various heretics are then named and how they were condemned by the preceding five councils is set forth.*]

Things being so, it was necessary that your beloved of Christ majesty should gath-er together this all holy, and numerous as-sembly.

. . . .

Thereafter being inspired by the Holy Ghost, and all agreeing and consenting to-gether, and giving our approval to the doc-trinal letter of our most blessed and exalted pope, Agatho, which he sent to your mighti-ness, as also agreeing to the suggestion of the holy synod of one hundred and twenty-five fathers held under him, we teach that one of the Holy Trinity, our Lord Jesus Christ, was incarnate, and must be cele-brated in two perfect natures without divis-ion and without confusion. For as the Word, he is consubstantial and eternal with God his father; but as taking flesh of the immaculate Virgin Mary, the Mother of God, he is perfect man, consubstantial with us and made in time. We declare therefore that he is perfect in Godhead and that the same is perfect likewise in manhood, ac-cording to the pristine tradition of the fathers and the divine definition of Chalce-don.

And as we recognize two natures, so also we recognize two natural wills and two natural operations. For we dare not say that either of the natures which are in Christ in his incarnation is without a will and operation: lest in taking away the pro-prieties of those natures, we likewise take away the natures of which they are the proprieties. For we neither deny the natural will of his humanity, or its natural

operation: lest we also deny what is the chief thing of the dispensation for our sal-vation, and lest we attribute passions to the Godhead. For this they were attempting who have recently introduced the detestable novelty that in him there is but one will and one operation, renewing the malignancy of Arius, Apollinaris, Eutyches and Severus. For should we say that the human nature of our Lord is without will and operation, how could we affirm in safety the perfect humanity? For nothing else constitutes the integrity of human nature except the essential will, through which the strength of free-will is marked in us; and this is also the case with the substantial operation. For how shall we call him perfect in hu-manity if he in no wise suffered and acted as a man? For like as the union of two natures preserves for us one subsistence without confusion and without division; so this one subsistence, shewing itself in two natures, demonstrates as its own what things belong to each.

Therefore we declare that in him there are two natural wills and two natural opera-tions, proceeding commonly and without division: but we cast out of the Church and rightly subject to anathema all superfluous novelties as well as their inventors: to wit, Theodore of Pharan, Sergius and Paul, Pyr-rhus, and Peter (who were archbishops of Constantinople), moreover Cyrus, who bore the priesthood of Alexandria, and with them Honorius, who was the ruler ($\pi\rho\acute{o}\epsilon\delta\rho o\nu$) of Rome, as he followed them in these things. Besides these, with the best of cause we anathematize and depose Maca-rius, who was bishop of Antioch, and his disciple Stephen (or rather we should say master), who tried to defend the impiety of their predecessors, and in short stirred up the whole world, and by their pestilential letters and by their fraudulent institutions devastated multitudes in every direction. Likewise also that old man Polychronius, with an infantile intelligence, who promised he would raise the dead and who when they did not rise, was laughed at; and all who have taught, or do teach, or shall presume to teach one will and one operation in the incarnate Christ. . . . But the highest prince of the Apostles fought with us: for we had on our side his imitator and the successor in his see, who also had set forth in his letter the mystery of the divine word (θεολογίας). For the ancient city of Rome handed thee a confession of divine character, and a chart from the sunsetting raised up the day of dogmas, and made the darkness manifest, and Peter spoke through Agatho, and thou, O autocratic King, according to the divine decree, with the Omnipotent Sharer of thy throne, didst judge.

. . . .

But, O benign and justice-loving Lord, do thou in return do this favour to him who hath bestowed thy power upon thee; and give, as a seal to what has been defined by us, thy imperial ratification in writing, and so confirm them with the customary pious edicts and constitutions, that no one may contradict the things which have been done, nor raise any fresh question. For rest assured, O serene majesty, that we have not falsified anything defined by the Ecumenical Councils and by the approved fathers, but we have confirmed them. And now we all cry out with one mind and one voice, "O God, save the King! etc., etc."

[*Then follow numerous compliments to the Emperor and prayers for his preservation.*]

LETTER OF THE COUNCIL TO ST. AGATHO.

(*Found in Migne*, Pat. Lat., *Tom. LXXXVII.*, col. *1247 et seqq.*; *and Labbe and Cossart*, Concilia, *Tom. VI.*, col. *1071 et seqq.*)

A copy of the letter sent by the holy and Ecumenical Sixth Council to Agatho, the most blessed and most holy pope of Old Rome.

The holy and ecumenical council which by the grace of God and the pious sanction of the most pious and faithful Constantine, the great Emperor, has been gathered together in this God-preserved and royal city, Constantinople, the new Rome, in the *Secretum* of the imperial (θείον, sacri) palace called Trullus, to the most holy and most blessed pope of Old Rome, Agatho, health in the Lord.

Serious illnesses call for greater helps, as you know, most blessed [father]; and therefore Christ our true God, who is the creator and governing power of all things, gave a wise physician, namely your God-honoured sanctity, to drive away by force the contagion of heretical pestilence by the remedies of orthodoxy, and to give the strength of health to the members of the church. Therefore to thee, as to the bishop of the first see of the Universal Church, we leave what must be done, since you willingly take for your standing ground the firm rock of the faith, as we know from having read your true confession in the letter sent by your fatherly beatitude to the most pious emperor: and we acknowledge that this letter was divinely written (*perscriptas*) as by the Chief of the Apostles, and through it we have cast out the heretical sect of many errors which had recently sprung up, having been urged to making a decree by Constantine who divinely reigns, and wields a most clement sceptre. And by his help we have overthrown the error of impiety, having as it were laid siege to the nefarious doctrine of the heretics. And then tearing to pieces the foundations of their execrable heresy, and attacking them with spiritual and paternal arms, and confounding their tongues that they might not speak consistently with each other, we overturned the tower built up by these followers of this most impious heresy; and we slew them with anathema, as lapsed concerning the faith and as sinners, in the morning outside the camp of the tabernacle of God, that we may express ourselves after the manner of David,[1] in accordance with the sentence already given concerning them in your letter, and their names are these: Theodore, bishop of Pharan, Sergius, Honorius, Cyrus, Paul, Pyrrhus and Peter. Moreover, in addition to these, we justly subjected to the anathema of heretics those also who live in their impiety which they have received, or, to speak more accurately, in the impiety of these God-hated persons, Apollinaris, Severus and Themestius, to wit, Macarius, who was the bishop of the great city of Antioch (and him we also stripped deservedly of his pastor's robes on account of his impenitence concerning the orthodox faith and his obstinate stubbornness), and Stephen, his disciple in craziness and his teacher in impiety, also Polychronius, who was inveterate in his heretical doctrines, thus answering to his name; and finally all those who impenitently have taught or do teach, or now hold or have held similar doctrines.

Up to now grief, sorrow, and many tears have been our portion. For we cannot laugh at the fall of our neighbours, nor exult with joy at their unbridled madness, nor have we been elated that we might fall all the more grievously because of this thing; not thus, O venerable and sacred head, have we been taught, we who hold Christ, the Lord of the universe, to be both benign and man-loving in the highest degree; for he exhorts us to be imitators of him in his priesthood so far as is possible, as becometh the good, and to obtain the pattern of his pastoral and conciliatory government. But also to true repentance the most Serene Emperor and ourselves have exhorted them in various ways, and we have conducted the whole matter with great religiousness and care. Nor

---

[1] Psalm C., verse 8 (Heb. ci., *ult.*) neither LXX. nor Vulgate version.

have we been moved to do so for the sake of gain, nor by hatred, as you can easily see from what things have been done in each session, and related in the minutes, which are herewith sent to your blessedness: and you will understand from your holiness's vicars, Theodore and George, presbyters beloved of God, and from John, the most religious deacon, and from Constantine, the most venerable sub-deacon, all of them your spiritual children and our well-loved brethren. So too you will hear the same things from those sent by your holy synod, the holy bishops who rightly and uprightly, in accordance with your discipline, decreed with us in the first chapter of the faith.

Thus, illuminated by the Holy Spirit, and instructed by your doctrine, we have cast forth the vile doctrines of impiety, making smooth the right path of orthodoxy, being in every way encouraged and helped in so doing by the wisdom and power of our most pious and serene Emperor Constantine. And then one of our number, the most holy præsul of this reigning Constantinople, in the first place assenting to the orthodox compositions sent by you to the most pious emperor as in all respects agreeable to the teaching of the approved Fathers and of the God-instructed Fathers, and of the holy five universal councils, we all, by the help of Christ our God, easily accomplished what we were striving after. For as God was the mover, so God also he crowned our council.

Thereupon, therefore, the grace of the Holy Spirit shone upon us, displaying his power, through your assiduous prayers, for the uprooting of all weeds and every tree which brought not forth good fruit, and giving command that they should be consumed by fire. And we all agree both in heart and tongue, and hand, and have put forth, by the assistance of the life-giving Spirit, a definition, clean from all error, certain, and infallible; not 'removing the ancient landmarks, as it is written (God forbid !), but remaining steadfast in the testimonies and authority of the holy and approved fathers, and defining that, as of two and in two natures (to wit, the divinity and the humanity) of which he is composed and in which he exists, Christ our true God is preached by us, and is glorified inseparably, unchangeably, unconfusedly, and undividedly; just so also we predicate of him two natural operations, undividedly, incontrovertibly, unconfusedly, inseparably, as has been declared in our synodal definition. These decrees the majesty of our God-copying Emperor assented to, and subscribed them with his own hand. And, as has been said, we rejected and condemned that most impious and unsubstantial heresy which affirmed but one will and one operation in the incarnate Christ our true God, and by so doing we have pressed sore upon the crowd who confound and who divide, and have extinguished the inflamed storm of other heresies, but we have set forth clearly with you the shining light of the orthodox faith, and we pray your paternal sanctity to confirm our decree by your honourable rescript; through which we confide in good hope in Christ that his merciful kindness will grant freely to the Roman State, committed to the care of our most clement Emperor, stability; and will adorn with daily yokes and victories his most serene clemency; and that in addition to the good things he has here bestowed upon us, he will set your God-honoured holiness before his tremendous tribunal as one who has sincerely confessed the true faith, preserving it unsullied and keeping good ward over the orthodox flocks committed to him by God.

We and all who are with us salute all the brethren in Christ who are with your blessedness.

EXCURSUS ON THE CONDEMNATION OF POPE HONORIUS.

To this decree attaches not only the necessary importance and interest which belongs to any ecumenical decision upon a disputed doctrinal question with regard to the incarnation of the Son of God, but an altogether accidental interest, arising from the fact that by this decree a Pope of Rome is stricken with anathema in the person of Honorius.   I need hardly remind the reader how many interesting and difficult questions in theology such an action on the part of an Ecumenical Council raises, and how all important, not to say vital, to such as accept the ruling of the recent Vatican Council, it is that some explanation of this fact should be arrived at which will be satisfactory.   It would be highly improper for me in these pages to discuss the matter theologically.   Volumes on each side have been written on this subject, and to these I must refer the reader, but in doing so I hope I may be pardoned if I add a word of counsel—to read both sides.   If one's knowledge is derived only from modern Eastern, Anglican, or Protestant writers, such as " Janus and the Council," the Père Gratry's " Letters," or Littledale's controversial books against Rome, one is apt to be as much one-sided as if he took his information from Cardinal Baronius, Cardinal Bellarmine, Rohrbacher's *History*, or from the recent work on the subject by Pennacchi.[1]   Perhaps the average reader will hardly find a more satisfactory treatment than that by Bossuet in the *Defensio*.   (*Liber VII.*, *cap. xxi*, etc.)

It will be sufficient for the purposes of this volume to state that Roman Catholic Curialist writers are not at one as to how the matter is to be treated.   Pennacchi, in his work referred to above, is of opinion that Honorius's letters were strictly speaking Papal decrees, set forth *auctoritate apostolica*, and therefore irreformable, but he declares, contrary to the opinion of almost all theologians and to the decree of this Council, that they are orthodox, and that the Council erred in condemning them ; as he expresses it, the decree rests upon an *error in facto dogmatico*.   To save an Ecumenical Synod from error, he thinks the synod ceased to be ecumenical before it took this action, and was at that time only a synod of a number of Orientals !   Cardinal Baronius has another way out of the difficulty.   He says that the name of Honorius was forged and put in the decree by an erasure in the place of the name of Theodore, the quondam Patriarch, who soon after the Council got himself restored to the Patriarchal position.   Baronius moreover holds that Honorius's letters have been corrupted, that the Acts of the Council have been corrupted, and, in short, that everything which declares or proves that Honorius was a heretic or was condemned by an Ecumenical Council as such, is untrustworthy and false.   The groundlessness, not to say absurdity, of Baronius's view has been often exposed by those of his own communion, a brief but sufficient summary of the refutation will be found in Hefele, who while taking a very halting and unsatisfactory position himself, yet is perfectly clear that Baronius's contention is utterly indefensible.[2]

Most Roman controversialists of recent years have admitted both the fact of Pope Honorius's condemnation (which Baronius denies), and the monothelite (and therefore heretical) character of his epistles, but they are of opinion that these letters were not his *ex cathedrâ* utterances as Doctor Universalis, but mere expressions of the private opinion of the Pontiff as a theologian.   With this matter we have no concern in this connexion.

I shall therefore say nothing further on this point but shall simply supply the leading proofs that Honorius was as a matter of fact condemned by the Sixth Ecumenical Council.

1. His condemnation is found in the Acts in the xiiith Session, near the beginning.

2. His two letters were ordered to be burned at the same session.

---

[1] Pennacchi.   *De Honorii I., Romani Pontificis, causa in Concilio VI.*
[2] Hefele.   *History of the Councils.*   Vol. V., p. 190 *et seqq.*

3. In the xvith Session the bishops exclaimed " Anathema to the heretic Sergius, to the heretic Cyrus, to the heretic Honorius, etc."

4. In the decree of faith published at the xviijth Session it is stated that " the originator of all evil . . . found a fit tool for his will in . . . Honorius, Pope of Old Rome, etc."

5. The report of the Council to the Emperor says that " Honorius, formerly bishop of Rome " they had " punished with exclusion and anathema " because he followed the mono- thelites.

6. In its letter to Pope Agatho the Council says it " has slain with anathema Honorius."

7. The imperial decree speaks of the " unholy priests who infected the Church and falsely governed " and mentions among them " Honorius, the Pope of Old Rome, the confirmer of heresy who contradicted himself."   The Emperor goes on to anathematize " Honorius who was Pope of Old Rome, who in everything agreed with them, went with them, and strength- ened the heresy."

8. Pope Leo II. confirmed the decrees of the Council and expressly says that he too anathematized Honorius.[1]

9. That Honorius was anathematized by the Sixth Council is mentioned in the Trullan Canons (No. j.).

10. So too the Seventh Council declares its adhesion to the anathema in its decree of faith, and in several places in the acts the same is said.

11. Honorius's name was found in the Roman copy of the Acts.   This is evident from Anastasius's life of Leo II.   (*Vita Leonis II.*)

12. The Papal Oath as found in the *Liber Diurnus* [2] taken by each new Pope from the fifth to the eleventh century, in the form probably prescribed by Gregory II., " smites with eternal anathema the originators of the new heresy, Sergius, etc., together with Honorius, because he assisted the base assertion of the heretics."

13. In the lesson for the feast of St. Leo II. in the Roman Breviary the name of Pope Honorius occurs among those excommunicated by the Sixth Synod.   Upon this we may well hear Bossuet : " They suppress as far as they can, the Liber Diurnus : they have erased this from the Roman Breviary.   Have they therefore hidden it ?   Truth breaks out from all sides, and these things become so much the more evident, as they are the more studiously put out of sight." [3]

With such an array of proof no conservative historian, it would seem, can question the fact that Honorius, the Pope of Rome, was condemned and anathematized as a heretic by the Sixth Ecumenical Council.

---

[1] " Also Honorius, qui hanc apostolicam sedem non apostolicæ traditionis doctrina lustravit, sed profana proditione immacula- tam fidem subvertere conatus est, et omnes, qui in suo errore de- functi sunt."

[2] Ed. Eugène de Rozière.   Paris, 1869, No. 84.
[3] Bossuet.   *Def. Cleri Gal.*, Lib. vij., cap. xxvj.

THE IMPERIAL EDICT POSTED IN THE THIRD ATRIUM OF THE GREAT CHURCH NEAR WHAT IS CALLED DICYMBALA.

In the name of our Lord and Master Jesus Christ, our God and Saviour, the most pious Emperor, the peaceful and Christ-loving Constantine, an Emperor faithful to God in Jesus Christ, to all our Christ-loving people living in this God-preserved and royal city.

[*The document is very long, Hefele gives the following epitome, which is all sufficient for the ordinary reader, who will remember that it is an Edict of the Emperor and not anything proceeding from the council.*]

Hefele's Epitome (Hist. of the Councils, Vol. v., p. 178).

"The heresy of Apollinaris, etc., has been renewed by Theodore of Pharan and confirmed by Honorius, sometime Pope of Old Rome, who also contradicted himself. Also Cyrus, Pyrrhus, Paul, Peter; more recently. Macarius, Stephen, and Polychronius had diffused Monothelitism. He, the Emperor, had therefore convoked this holy and Ecumenical Synod, and published the present edict with the confession of faith, in order to confirm and establish its decrees. (There follows here an extended confession of faith, with proofs for the doctrine of two wills and operations.) As he recognized the five earlier Ecumenical Synods, so he anathematized all heretics from Simon Magus, but especially the originator and patrons of the new heresy, Theodore and Sergius ; also Pope Honorius, who was their adherent and patron in everything, and confirmed the heresy (τὸν κατὰ πάντα τούτοις συναιρέτην καὶ σύνδρομον καὶ βεβαιωτὴν τῆς αἱρέσεως), further, Cyrus, etc., and ordained that no one henceforth should hold a different faith, or venture to teach one will and one energy. In no other than the orthodox faith could men be saved. Whoever did not obey the imperial edict should, if he were a bishop or cleric be deposed ; if an official, punished with confiscation of property and loss of the girdle (ζώνη) ; if a private person, banished from the residence and all other cities."

THE CANONS OF THE COUNCIL IN TRULLO;

OFTEN CALLED

THE QUINISEXT COUNCIL,

A.D. 692.

Elenchus.

INTRODUCTORY NOTE.

From the fact that the canons of the Council in Trullo are included in this volume of the Decrees and Canons of the Seven Ecumenical Councils it must not for an instant be supposed that it is intended thereby to affirm that these canons have any ecumenical authority, or that the council by which they were adopted can lay any claim to being ecumenical either in view of its constitution or of the subsequent treatment by the Church of its enactments.

It is true that it claimed at the time an ecumenical character, and styled itself such in several of its canons, it is true that in the mind of the Emperor Justinian II., who summoned it, it was intended to have been ecumenical. It is true that the Greeks at first declared it to be a continuation of the Sixth Synod and that by this name they frequently denominate and quote its canons. But it is also true that the West was not really represented at it at all (as we shall see presently) ; that when the Emperor afterwards sent the canons to the Pope to receive his signature, he absolutely refused to have anything to do with them ; and it is further true that they were never practically observed by the West at all, and that even in the East their authority was rather theoretical than real.

(Fleury. *Histoire Ecclesiastique*, Livre XL., Chap. xlix.)

As the two last General Councils (in 553 and in 681) had not made any Canons, the Orientals judged it suitable to supply them eleven years after the Sixth Council, that is to say, the year 692, fifth indiction. For that purpose the Emperor Justinian convoked a Council, at which 211 Bishops attended, of whom the principal were the four Patriarchs, Paul of Constantinople, Peter of Alexandria, Anastasius of Jerusalem, George of Antioch. Next in the subscriptions are named John of Justinianopolis, Cyriacus of Cesarea in Cappadocia, Basil of Gortyna in Crete, who says that he represents the whole Council of the Roman Church, as he had said in subscribing the Sixth Council. But it is certain otherwise that in this latter council there were present Legates of the Holy See. This council, like the Sixth,[1] assembled in the dome of the palace called in Latin *Trullus*, which name it has kept. It is also named in Latin Quinisextum, in Greek Penthecton, as one might say, the fifth-sixth, to mark that it is only the supplement of the two preceding Councils, though properly it is a distinct one.

The intention was to make a body of discipline to serve thenceforth for the whole Church, and it was distributed into 102 Canons.

To this statement by Fleury some additions must be made. First, with regard to the date of the synod. This is not so certain as would appear at first sight. At the Seventh Ecumenical Council, the patriarch Tarasius of Constantinople asserted that, " four or five years after the sixth Ecumenical Council the same bishops, in a new assembly under Justinian II. had published the [Trullan] Canons mentioned," and this assertion the Seventh Council appears to have accepted as true, if we understand the sixth session aright. Now were this statement true, the date would be probably 686, but this is impossible by the words of the council itself, where we find mention made of the fifteenth of January of the past 4th indiction, or the year of the world, 6109. To make this agree at all, scholars tell us that for iv. must be read xiv. But the rest of the statement is equally erroneous, the bishops were not the same, as can readily be seen by comparing the subscriptions to the Acts.

The year of the world 6109 is certainly wrong, and so other scholars would read 6199,

---

[1] This statement of Fleury's is contested by those who agree with Asseman in thinking that the Sixth Synod was held in Santa Sophia, *vide Biblioth. Jur., Orient.* Tom. v., p. 85.

but here a division takes place, for some reckon by the Constantinopolitan era, and so fix the date at 691, and others following the Alexandrian era fix it at 706. But this last is certainly wrong, for the canons were sent for signature to Pope Sergius, who died as early as 701. Hefele's conclusion is as follows :

(Hefele. *Hist. of the Councils*, Vol. V., p. 222.)

The year 6199 of the Constantinopolitan era coincides with the year 691 after Christ and the IVth Indiction ran from September 1, 690, to August 31, 691. If then, our Synod, in canon iij., speaks of the 15th of January in the *past* Indiction IV., it means January 691; but it belongs itself, to the Vth Indiction, i.e., it was opened after September 1, 691, and before September 1, 692.

As this is not a history of the Councils but a collection of their decrees and canons with illustrative notes, the only other point to be considered is the reception these canons met with.

The decrees were signed first by the Emperor, the next place was left vacant for the Pope, then followed the subscriptions of the Patriarchs of Constantinople, Alexandria, Jerusalem, and Antioch, the whole number being 211, bishops or representatives of bishops. It is not quite certain whether any of the Patriarchs were present except Paul of Constantinople ; but taking it all in all the probability is in favour of their presence.[1] Blank places were left for the bishops of Thessalonica, Sardinia, Ravenna and Corinth. The Archbishop of Gortyna in Crete added to his signature the phrase " Holding the place of the holy Church of Rome in every synod." He had in the same way signed the decrees of III. Constantinople, Crete belonging to the Roman Patriarchate ; as to whether his delegation on the part of the Roman Synod continued or was merely made to continue by his own volition we have no information. The ridiculous blunder of Balsamon must be noted here, who asserts that the bishops whose names are missing and for which blank places were left, had actually signed.

Pope Sergius refused to sign the decrees when they were sent to him, rejected them as "lacking authority" (*invalidi*) and described them as containing "novel errors." With the efforts to extort his signature we have no concern further than to state that they signally failed. Later on, in the time of Pope Constantine, a middle course seems to have been adopted, a course subsequently in the ninth century thus expressed by Pope John VIII., " he accepted all those canons which did not contradict the true faith, good morals, and the decrees of Rome," a truly notable statement ! Nearly a century later Pope Hadrian I. distinctly recognizes all the Trullan decrees in his letter to Tenasius of Constantinople and attributes them to the Sixth Synod. "All the holy six synods I receive with all their canons, which rightly and divinely were promulgated by them, among which is contained that in which reference is made to a Lamb being pointed to by the Precursor as being found in certain of the venerable images." Here the reference is unmistakably to the Trullan Canon LXXXII.

Hefele's summing up of the whole matter is as follows :

(Hefele, *Hist. of the Councils*, Vol. V., p. 242.)

That the Seventh Ecumenical Council at Nice ascribed the Trullan canons to the Sixth Ecumenical Council, and spoke of them entirely in the Greek spirit, cannot astonish us, as it was attended almost solely by Greeks. They specially pronounced the recognition of the canons in question in their own first canon ; but their own canons have never received the ratification of the Holy See.

---

[1] *Cf.* Hefele, l.c., Vol. V., 237. On the other hand *vide* Asseman (l.c. Tom. V., pp. 30, 69), who thinks Alexandria and Jerusalem were vacant at the time !

Thus far Hefele, but it seems that Gratian's statement on the subject in the *Decretum* should not be omitted here. (Pars I., Dist. XVI., c. v.)

"Canon V. *The Sixth Synod is confirmed by the authority of Hadrian.*

"I receive the Sixth Synod with all its canons.

"Gratian. *There is a doubt whether it set forth canons but this is easily removed by examining the fourth session of the VIIth* [VIth by mistake, *vide* Roman Correctors' note] *Synod.*

"*For Peter the Bp. of Nicomedia says:*

"C. VI. *The Sixth Synod wrote canons.*

"I have a book containing the canons of the holy Sixth Synod. The Patriarch said: § 1. Some are scandalized through their ignorance of these canons, saying: Did the Sixth Synod make any canons? Let them know then that the Sixth Holy Synod was gathered together under Constantine against those who said there is one operation and one will in Christ, in which the holy Fathers anathematized these as heretics and explained the orthodox faith.

"II. Pars § 2. And the synod was dissolved in the XIVth year of Constantine. After four or five years the same holy Fathers met together under Justinian, the son of Constantine, and promulgated the aforementioned canons, of which let no one have any doubt. For they who under Constantine were in synod, these same bishops under Justinian subscribed to all these canons. For it was fitting that a Universal Synod should promulgate ecclesiastical canons. *Item:* § 3. The Holy Sixth Synod after it promulgated its definition against the Monothelites, the emperor Constantine who had summoned it, dying soon after, and Justinian his son reigning in his stead, § the same holy synod divinely inspired again met at Constantinople four or five years afterwards, and promulgated one hundred and two canons for the correction of the Church.

"Gratian. *From this therefore it may be gathered that the Sixth Synod was twice assembled: the first time under Constantine and then passed no canons; the second time under Justinian his son, and promulgated the aforesaid canons.*"

Upon this passage of Gratian's the Roman Correctors have a long and interesting note, with quotations from Anastasius, which should be read with care by the student but is too long to cite here.

I close with some eminently wise remarks by Prof. Michaud.

(E. Michaud, Discussion sur les Sept Conciles Œcuméniques, p. 272.)

Upon the canons of this council we must remark:

1. That save its acceptance of the dogmatic decisions of the six Ecumenical Councils, which is contained in the first canon, this council had an exclusively disciplinary character; and consequently if it should be admitted by the particular churches, these would always remain, on account of their autonomy, judges of the fitness or non-suitability of the practical application of these decisions.

2. That the Easterns have never pretended to impose this code upon the practice of the Western Churches, especially as they themselves do not practise everywhere the hundred and two canons mentioned. All they wished to do was to maintain the ancient discipline against the abuses and evil innovations of the Roman Church, and to make her pause upon the dangerous course in which she was already beginning to enter.

3. That if among these canons, some do not apply to the actual present state of society, e.g., the 8th, 10th, 11th, etc.; if others, framed in a spirit of transition between the then Eastern customs and those of Rome, do not appear as logical nor as wise as one might desire, e.g., the 6th, 12th, 48th, etc., nevertheless on the other hand, many of them are marked with the most profound sagacity.

THE CANONS OF THE COUNCIL IN TRULLO.

(Labbe and Cossart, *Concilia*, Tom. VI., col. 1135 *et seqq.*)

CANON I.

THAT order is best of all which makes every word and act begin and end in God. Wherefore that piety may be clearly set forth by us and that the Church of which Christ is the foundation may be continually increased and advanced, and that it may be exalted above the cedars of Lebanon ; now therefore we, by divine grace at the beginning of our decrees, define that the faith set forth by the God-chosen Apostles who themselves had both seen and were ministers of the Word, shall be preserved without any innovation, unchanged and inviolate.

Moreover the faith of the three hundred and eighteen holy and blessed fathers who were assembled at Nice under Constantine our Emperor, against the impious Arius, and the gentile diversity of deity or rather (to speak accurately) multitude of gods taught by him, who by the unanimous acknowledgment of the faithful revealed and declared to us the consubstantiality of the Three Persons comprehended in the Divine Nature, not suffering this faith to lie hidden under the bushel of ignorance, but openly teaching the faithful to adore with one worship the Father, the Son, and the Holy Ghost, confuting and scattering to the winds the opinion of different grades, and demolishing and overturning the puerile toyings fabricated out of sand by the heretics against orthodoxy.

Likewise also we confirm that faith which was set forth by the one hundred and fifty fathers who in the time of Theodosius the Elder, our Emperor, assembled in this imperial city, accepting their decisions with regard to the Holy Ghost in assertion of his godhead, and expelling the profane Macedonius (together with all previous enemies of the truth) as one who dared to judge Him to be a servant who is Lord, and who wished to divide, like a robber, the inseparable unity, so that there might be no perfect mystery of our faith.

And together with this odious and detestable contender against the truth, we condemn Apollinaris, priest of the same iniquity, who impiously belched forth that the Lord assumed a body unendowed with a soul,[1] thence also inferring that his salvation wrought for us was imperfect.

Moreover what things were set forth by the two hundred God-bearing fathers in the city of Ephesus in the days of Theodosius our Emperor, the son of Arcadius ; these doctrines we assent to as the unbroken strength of piety, teaching that Christ the incarnate Son of God is one ; and declaring that she who bare him without human seed was the immaculate Ever-Virgin, glorifying her as literally and in very truth the Mother of God. We condemn as foreign to the divine scheme the absurd division of Nestorius, who teaches that the one Christ consists of a man separately and of the Godhead separately and renews the Jewish impiety.

Moreover we confirm that faith which at Chalcedon, the Metropolis, was set forth in accordance with orthodoxy by the six hundred and thirty God-approved fathers in the time of Marcian, who was our Emperor, which handed down with a great and mighty voice, even unto the ends of the earth, that the one Christ, the son of God, is of two natures, and must be glorified[2] in these two natures, and which cast forth from the sacred precincts of the Church as a black pestilence to be avoided, Eutyches, babbling stupidly and inanely, and teaching that the great mystery of the incarnation (οἰκονωμίας) was perfected in thought only. And together with him also Nestorius and Dioscorus of whom the former was the defender and champion of the division, the latter of the confusion [of the two natures in the one Christ], both of whom fell away from the divergence of their impiety to a common depth of perdition and denial of God.

---

[1] Latin reads "mind or soul."   [2] Latin, "believed in."

Also we recognize as inspired by the Spirit the pious voices of the one hundred and sixty-five God-bearing fathers who assembled in this imperial city in the time of our Emperor Justinian of blessed memory, and we teach them to those who come after us; for these synodically anathematized and execrated Theodore of Mopsuestia (the teacher of Nestorius), and Origen, and Didymus, and Evagrius, all of whom reintroduced feigned Greek myths, and brought back again the circlings of certain bodies and souls, and deranged turnings [or transmigrations] to the wanderings or dreamings of their minds, and impiously insulting the resurrection of the dead. Moreover [they condemned] what things were written by Theodoret against the right faith and against the Twelve Chapters of blessed Cyril, and that letter which is said to have been written by Ibas.

Also we agree to guard untouched the faith of the Sixth Holy Synod, which first assembled in this imperial city in the time of Constantine, our Emperor, of blessed memory, which faith received still greater confirmation from the fact that the pious Emperor ratified with his own signet that which was written for the security of future generations. This council taught that we should openly profess our faith that in the incarnation of Jesus Christ, our true God, there are two natural wills or volitions and two natural operations; and condemned by a just sentence those who adulterated the true doctrine and taught the people that in the one Lord Jesus Christ there is but one will and one operation; to wit, Theodore of Pharan, Cyrus of Alexandria, Honorius of Rome, Sergius, Pyrrhus, Paul and Peter, who were bishops of this God-preserved city; Macarius, who was bishop of Antioch; Stephen, who was his disciple, and the insane Polychronius, depriving them henceforth from the communion of the body of Christ our God.

And, to say so once for all, we decree that the faith shall stand firm and remain unsullied until the end of the world as well as the writings divinely handed down and the teachings of all those who have beautified and adorned the Church of God and were lights in the world, having embraced the word of life. And we reject and anathematize those whom they rejected and anathematized, as being enemies of the truth, and as insane ragers against God, and as lifters up of iniquity.

But if any one at all shall not observe and embrace the aforesaid pious decrees, and teach and preach in accordance therewith, but shall attempt to set himself in opposition thereto, let him be anathema, according to the decree already promulgated by the approved holy and blessed Fathers, and let him be cast out and stricken off as an alien from the number of Christians. For our decrees add nothing to the things previously defined, nor do they take anything away, nor have we any such power.

NOTES.

ANCIENT EPITOME OF CANON I.

No innovation upon the faith of the Apostles is to be allowed. The faith of the Nicene fathers is perfect, which overthrows through the homousion the doctrines of Arius who introduced degrees into the Godhead.

The Synod held under Theodosius the great shall be held inviolate, which deposed Macedonius who asserted that the Holy Ghost was a servant.

The two hundred who under Theodosius the Younger assembled at Ephesus are to be revered for they expelled Nestorius who asserted that the Lord was man and God separately (ἰδικῶς).

Those who assembled at Chalcedon in the time

of Marcion are to be celebrated with eternal remembrance, who deposed Eutyches, who dared to say that the great mystery was accomplished only in image, as well as Nestorius and Dioscorus, observing equal things in an opposite direction.

One hundred and sixty-five were assembled in the imperial city by Justinian, who anathematized Origen, for teaching periods (περιόδους) of bodies and souls, and Theodoret who dared to set himself up to oppose the Twelve Chapters of Cyril.

At Constantinople a Synod was collected under Constantine which rejected Honorius of Rome and Sergius, prelate of Constantinople, for teaching one will and one operation.

ARISTENUS.

The fifth was held in the time of Justinian the Great at Constantinople against the crazy (παράφρονς) Origen, Evagrius and Didymus, who remodelled the Greek figments, and stupidly said that the same bodies they had joined with them would not rise again; and that Paradise was not subject to the appreciation of the sense, and that it was not from God, and that Adam was not formed in flesh, and that there would be an end of punishment, and a restitution of the devils to their pristine state, and other innumerable insane blasphemies.

CANON II.

It has also seemed good to this holy Council, that the eighty-five canons, received and ratified by the holy and blessed Fathers before us, and also handed down to us in the name of the holy and glorious Apostles should from this time forth remain firm and unshaken for the cure of souls and the healing of disorders. And in these canons we are bidden to receive the Constitutions of the Holy Apostles [written] by Clement. But formerly through the agency of those who erred from the faith certain adulterous matter was introduced, clean contrary to piety, for the polluting of the Church, which obscures the elegance and beauty of the divine decrees in their present form. We therefore reject these Constitutions so as the better to make sure of the edification and security of the most Christian flock; by no means admitting the offspring of heretical error, and cleaving to the pure and perfect doctrine of the Apostles. But we set our seal likewise upon all the other holy canons set forth by our holy and blessed Fathers, that is, by the 318 holy God-bearing Fathers assembled at Nice, and those at Ancyra, further those at Neocæsarea and likewise those at Gangra, and besides, those at Antioch in Syria: those too at Laodicea in Phrygia: and likewise the 150 who assembled in this heaven-protected royal city: and the 200 who assembled the first time in the metropolis of the Ephesians, and the 630 holy and blessed Fathers at Chalcedon. In like manner those of Sardica, and those of Carthage: those also who again assembled in this heaven-protected royal city under its bishop Nectarius and Theophilus Archbishop of Alexandria. Likewise too the Canons [i.e. the decretal letters] of Dionysius, formerly Archbishop of the great city of Alexandria; and of Peter, Archbishop of Alexandria and Martyr; of Gregory the Wonder-worker, Bishop of Neocæsarea; of Athanasius, Archbishop of Alexandria; of Basil, Archbishop of Cæsarea in Cappadocia; of Gregory, Bishop of Nyssa; of Gregory Theologus; of Amphilochius of Iconium; of Timothy, Archbishop of Alexandria; of Theophilus, Archbishop of the same great city of Alexandria; of Cyril, Archbishop of the same Alexandria; of Gennadius, Patriarch of this heaven-protected royal city. Moreover the Canon set forth by Cyprian, Archbishop of the country of the Africans and Martyr, and by the Synod under him, which has been kept only in the country of the aforesaid Bishops, according to the custom delivered down to them. And that no one be allowed to transgress or disregard the aforesaid canons, or to receive others beside them, supposititiously set forth by certain who have attempted to make a traffic of the truth. But should any one be convicted of innovating upon, or attempting to overturn, any of the afore-mentioned canons, he shall be subject to receive the penalty which that canon imposes, and to be cured by it of his transgression.

NOTES.

ANCIENT EPITOME OF CANON II.

Whatever additions have been made through guile by the heterodox in the Apostolic Constitutions edited by Clement, shall be cut out.

This canon defines what canons are to be understood as having received the sanction of ecumenical authority, and since these canons of the Council in Trullo were received at the Seventh Ecumenical Council in its first canon as the canons of the Sixth Ecumenical (of which the Quinisext claimed to be a legitimate continuation) there can be no doubt that all these canons enumerated in this canon are set forth for the guidance of the Church.

With regard to what councils are intended: there is difficulty only in two particulars, viz., the "Council of Constantinople under Nectarius and Theophilus," [1] and the "Council under Cyprian;" the former must be the Council of 394, and the latter is usually considered to be the III. Synod of Carthage, A.D. 257.

FLEURY.

(*H. E.* Liv. xl., chap. xlix.)

The Council of Constantinople under Nectarius and Theophilus of Alexandria must be that held in 394, at the dedication of Ruffinus's Church; but we have not its canons. . . . . "The canon published by St. Cyprian for the African Church alone." It is difficult to understand what canon is referred to unless it is the preface to the council of St. Cyprian where he says that no one should pretend to be bishop of bishops, or to oblige his colleagues to obey him by tyrannical fear.

It will be noticed that while the canon is most careful to mention the exact number of Apostolic canons it received, thus deciding in favour of the larger code, it is equally careful not to assign them an Apostolic origin, but merely to say that they had come down to them "in the name of" the Apostles. In the face of this it is strange to find Balsamon saying, "Through this canon their mouth is stopped who say that 85 canons were not set forth by the holy Apostles;" what the council did settle, so far as its authority went, was the number not the authorship of the canons. This, I think, is all that Balsamon intended to assert, but his words might easily be quoted as having a different meaning.

This canon is found, in part, in the *Corpus Juris Canonici*, Gratian's *Decretum*, Pars I., Dist. XVI., c. VII.

CANON III.

SINCE our pious and Christian Emperor has addressed this holy and ecumenical council, in order that it might provide for the purity of those who are in the list of the clergy, and who transmit divine things to others, and that they may be blameless ministrants, and worthy of the sacrifice of the great God, who is both Offering and High Priest, a sacrifice apprehended by the intelligence: and that it might cleanse away the pollutions wherewith these have been branded by unlawful marriages: now whereas they of the most holy Roman Church purpose to keep the rule of exact perfection, but those who are under the throne of this heaven-protected and royal city keep that of kindness and consideration, so blending both together as our fathers have done, and as the love of God requires, that neither gentleness fall into licence, nor severity into harshness; especially as the fault of ignorance has reached no small number of men, we decree, that those who are involved in a second marriage, and have been slaves to sin up to the fifteenth of the past month of January, in the past fourth Indiction, the 6109th year, and have not resolved to repent of it, be subjected to canonical deposition: but that they who are involved in this disorder of a second marriage, but before our decree have acknowledged what is fitting, and have cut off their sin, and have put far from them this strange and illegitimate connexion, or they whose wives by second marriage are already dead, or who have turned to repentance of their own accord, having learnt continence, and having quickly forgotten their former iniquities, whether they be presbyters or deacons, these we have determined should cease from all priestly ministrations or exercise, being under punishment for a certain time, but should retain the honour of their seat and station, being satisfied with their seat before the laity and begging with tears from the Lord that the transgression of their ignorance be pardoned them: for unfitting it were that he should bless another who has to tend his own wounds. But those who have been married to one wife, if she was a widow, and likewise those who after their ordination have unlawfully entered into one marriage that is, presbyters, and deacons, and subdeacons, being debarred for some short time from sacred ministration, and censured, shall be restored again to their proper rank, never advancing to any further rank, their unlawful marriage being openly dissolved. This we decree to hold good only in the case of those that are involved in the aforesaid

---

[1] The Ultramontane Roisselet de Sauclières, in his *Histoire chronologique et dogmatique des Conciles de la Chrétienté*, Tome III., p. 131, curiously divides this into two councils. This blun-der is also made by Ivo, cf. Gratian's *Dec.*, P. I., Dist. xvi., c. vii., note by correctors.

faults up to the fifteenth (as was said) of the month of January, of the fourth Indiction, decreeing from the present time, and renewing the Canon which declares, that he who has been joined in two marriages after his baptism, or has had a concubine, cannot be bishop, or presbyter, or deacon, or at all on the sacerdotal list; in like manner, that he who has taken a widow, or a divorced person, or a harlot, or a servant, or an actress, cannot be bishop, or presbyter, or deacon, or at all on the sacerdotal list.

NOTES.

Ancient Epitome of Canon III.

Priests who shall have contracted second marriages and will not give them up are to be deposed. But those who leave off the wickedness, let them cease for a fixed period. For he that is himself wounded does not bless. But who are implicated in nefarious marriage and who after ordination have contracted marriage, after a definite time they shall be restored to their grade, provided they remain without offence, having plainly broken off the marriage. But if after it shall have been prohibited by this decree they attempt to do so they shall remain deposed.

Zonaras.

What things pertain to this third canon are only adapted to the time in which the canon was passed; and afterwards are of no force at all. But what things the Fathers wished to be binding on posterity are contained in the seventeenth and eighteenth canons of the holy Apostles, which as having been neglected during the course of time this synod wished to renew.

Van Espen.

It is clear from this canon that the Emperor very especially intended that the indulgence which the Church of Constantinople extended to its presbyters and deacons in allowing them the use of marriage entered into before ordination, should not be allowed to go any further, nor to be an occasion for the violation of that truly Apostolic canon, "The bishop, the presbyter, and the deacon must be the husband of one wife." I. Tim. iii. 2.

For never did the Constantinopolitan nor any other Eastern Church allow by canon a digamist (or a man successively the husband of many wives) to be advanced to the order of presbyter or deacon, or to use any second marriage.

Antonio Pereira.

(*Tentativa Theologica.* [Eng. trans.] III. Principle, p. 79.)

In the same manner a second marriage always, and everywhere, incapacitated the clergy for Holy Orders and the Episcopate. This appears from St. Paul, 1 Tim. Chap. iii., and Titus, Chap. i., and it was expressly enacted by the sixteenth of the Apostolical Canons, renewed by the Popes Siricius, Innocent and Leo the Great, and may be gathered from the ancient fathers and councils generally received in the Church.

Nevertheless we know from Theodoret, Bishop of Cyrus, that many bishops remarkable for their learning and sanctity, frequently dispensed with this Apostolical law; as Alexander of Antioch, Acacius of Berea, Praylius of Jerusalem, Proclus of Constantinople, and others, by whose example Theodoret defends his own conduct in the case of Irenæus, in ordaining him Archbishop of Tyre, although he had been twice married. But what is more surprising in this matter is that, notwithstanding the eleventh Decretal of Siricius, and the twelfth of Innocentius the First, that they who had either been twice married, or had married widows, were incapable of ordination, and ought to be deposed; the Council of Toledo, Canon 3, and the First Council of Orange, Canon 25, both dispensed with these Pontifical laws. The first, in order that those who had married widows might remain in holy orders; the second, that such as had twice married might be promoted to the order of subdeacon. Socrates also observes that although it was a general law not to admit catechumens to orders, the bishops of Alexandria were in the habit of promoting such to the order of readers and singers.

Fleury.

(*H. E.,* Liv. XL., chap. l.)

These canons of the Council of Trullo have served ever since to the Greeks and to all the Christians of the East as the universal rule with regard to clerical continence, and they have been now in full force for a thousand years. That is to say, It is not permitted to men who are clerics in Holy Orders to marry after their ordination. Bishops must keep perfect continence, whether before their consecration they are married or not. Priests, deacons, and subdeacons already married can keep their wives and live with them, except on the days they are to approach the holy mysteries.

CANON IV.

IF any bishop, presbyter, deacon, sub-deacon, lector, cantor, or door-keeper has had intercourse with a woman dedicated to God, let him be deposed, as one who has corrupted a spouse of Christ, but if a layman let him be cut off.

NOTES.

ANCIENT EPITOME OF CANON IV.

A cleric coupled to a spouse of God shall be deposed   In the case of a layman he shall be cut off.

This canon is found in the *Corpus Juris*

Canonici, Gratian's *Decretum*, Pars II., Causa XXVII., Q. I., c. vj.

A layman ravishing a nun, by secular law was punished by death. Balsamon gives the reference thus : V Cap. primi tit. iiij. lib. Basilic. or cxxiij. Novel.

CANON V.

LET none of those who are on the priestly list possess any woman or maid servant, beyond those who are enumerated in the canon as being persons free from suspicion, preserving himself hereby from being implicated in any blame.   But if anyone transgresses our decree let him be deposed.   And let eunuchs also observe the same rule, that by foresight they may be free of censure.   But those who transgress, let them be deposed, if indeed they are clerics ; but if laymen let them be excommunicated.

NOTES.

ANCIENT EPITOME OF CANON V.

A priest, even if a eunuch, shall not have in his house a maid or other woman except those on whom no suspicion can light.

See Canon III., of First Ecumenical Council at Nice.   This canon adds Eunuchs.

CANON VI.

SINCE it is declared in the apostolic canons that of those who are advanced to the clergy unmarried, only lectors and cantors are able to marry ; we also, maintaining this, determine that henceforth it is in nowise lawful for any subdeacon, deacon or presbyter after his ordination to contract matrimony but if he shall have dared to do so, let him be deposed.   And if any of those who enter the clergy, wishes to be joined to a wife in lawful marriage before he is ordained subdeacon, deacon, or presbyter, let it be done.

NOTES.

ANCIENT EPITOME OF CANON VI.

If any ordained person contracts matrimony, let him be deposed.   If he wishes to be married he should become so before his ordination.

Aristenus points out how this canon annuls the tenth canon of Ancyra, which allows a deacon and even a presbyter to marry after ordination and continue in his ministry, pro-

vided at the time of his ordination he had in the presence of witnesses declared his inability to remain chaste or his desire to marry. This present canon follows the XXVIth of the Apostolic canons.

The last clause of this canon, limited in its application to subdeacons, is found in the *Corpus Juris Canonici*, Gratian's *Decretum*, Pars I., Dist. XXXII., c. vi.

EXCURSUS ON THE MARRIAGE OF THE CLERGY.

On this subject there is a popular misconception which must first be removed. In the popular mind to-day there is no distinction between "a married clergy" being allowed, and "the marriage of the clergy" being allowed; even theological writers who have attained some repute have confused these two things in the most unfortunate and perplexing fashion. It will suffice to mention as an instance of this Bp. Harold Browne in his book on the XXXIX. Articles, in which not only is the confusion above spoken of made, but the very blunder is used for controversial purposes, to back up and support by the authority of the ancient Church in the East (which allowed a married clergy) the practice of the Nestorians and of the modern Church of England, both of which tolerate the marriage of the clergy, a thing which the ancient Church abhorred and punished with deposition.

I cannot better express the doctrine and practice of the ancient Church in the East than by quoting the words of the Rev. John Fulton in the Introduction to the Third Edition of his *Index Canonum*.[1] He says: "Marriage was no impediment to ordination even as a Bishop; and Bishops, Priests, and Deacons, equally with other men, were forbidden to put away their wives under pretext of religion. The case was different when a man was unmarried at the time of his ordination. Then he was held to have given himself wholly to God in the office of the Holy Ministry, and he was forbidden to take back from his offering that measure of his cares and his affections which must necessarily be given to the maintenance and nurture of his family. In short, the married man might be ordained, but with a few exceptions no man was allowed to marry after ordination." In his "Digest" *sub voce* "Celibacy" he gives the earliest canon law on the subject as follows: "None of the clergy, except readers and singers may marry after ordination (Ap. Can. xxvi.); but deacons may marry, if at their ordination they have declared an intention to do so (Ancyra x.). A priest who marries is to be deposed (Neocæsarea i.). A deaconess who marries is to be anathematized (Chal. xv.); a monk or dedicated virgin who marries, is to be excommunicated (Chal. xvi.). Those who break their vows of celibacy are to fulfil the penance of digamists (Ancyra xix.)."[2]

We may then take it for a general principle that in no part of the ancient Church was a priest allowed to contract holy matrimony; and in no place was he allowed to exercise his priesthood afterwards, if he should dare to enter into such a relation with a woman. As I have so often remarked it is not my place to approve or disapprove this law of the Church, my duty is the much simpler one of tracing historically what the law was and what it is in the East and West to-day. The Reformers considered that in this, as in most other matters, these venerable churches had made a mistake, but neither the maintenance nor the disproof of this opinion in any way concerns me, so far as this volume is concerned. All that is necessary for me to do is to affirm that if a priest were at any time to attempt to marry, he would be attempting to do that which from the earliest times of which we have any record, no priest has ever been allowed to do, but which always has been punished as a gross sin of immorality.

In tracing the history of this subject, the only time during which any real difficulty presents itself is the first three centuries, after that all is much clearer, and my duty is simply to lay the undisputed facts of the case before the reader.

We begin then with the debatable ground. And first with regard to the Lord, "the great High Priest of our profession," of course there can be no doubt that he set the example, or—if any think that he was not a pattern for the priests of his Church to follow—at least lived the life, of celibacy. When we come to the question of what was the practice of his first followers in this matter, there would likewise seem to be but little if any reasonable

[1] John Fulton, *Index Canonum*, p. 29 (N. Y., 1892.)　　　　[2] Ibid., p. 294.

doubt. For while of the Apostles we have it recorded only of Peter that he was a married man, we have it also expressly recorded that in his case, as in that of all the rest who had "forsaken all" to follow him, the Lord himself said, "Every one that hath forsaken houses, or brethren, or sisters, or father, or mother, or wife, or children, or lands, for my name's sake shall receive an hundred fold and shall inherit eternal life." [1]

There can be no doubt that St. Paul in his epistles allows and even contemplates the probability that those admitted to the ranks of the clergy will have been already married, but distinctly says that they must have been the "husband of one wife," [2] by which all antiquity and every commentator of gravity recognizes that digamists are cut off from the possibility of ordination, but there is nothing to imply that the marital connexion was to be continued after ordination. For a thorough treatment of this whole subject from the ancient and Patristic point of view, the reader is referred to St. Jerome. [3]

The next stage in our progress is marked by the so-called Apostolical Canons. Now for those who hold that these canons had directly or indirectly the Apostles for their author, or that as we have them now they are all of even sub-Apostolic date, the matter becomes more simple, for while indeed these canons do not expressly set forth the law subsequently formulated for the East, they certainly seem to be not inconsistent therewith, but rather to look that way, especially Canons V. and LI. But few will be found willing to support so extreme an hypothesis, and while indeed many scholars are of opinion that most of the canons of the collection we style "Apostolical," are ante-Nicene, yet they will not be recognized as of more value than as so many mirrors, displaying what was at their date considered pure discipline. It is abundantly clear that the fathers in council *in Trullo* thought the discipline they were setting forth to be the original discipline of the Church in the matter, and the discipline of the West an innovation, but that such was really the case seems far from certain. Thomassinus treats this point with much learning, and I shall cite some of the authorities he brings forward. Of these the most important is Epiphanius, who as a Greek would be certain to give the tradition of the East, had there been any such tradition known in his time. I give the three great passages.

"It is evident that those from the priesthood are chiefly taken from the order of virgins, or if not from virgins, at least from monks ; or if not from the order of monks, then they are wont to be made priests who keep themselves from their wives, or who are widows after a single marriage. But he that has been entangled by a second marriage is not admitted to priesthood in the Church, even if he be continent from his wife, or be a widower. Anyone of this sort is rejected from the grade of bishop, presbyter, deacon, or subdeacon. The order of reader, however, can be chosen from all the orders these grades can be chosen from, that is to say from virgins, monks, the continent, widowers, and they who are bound by honest marriage. Moreover, if necessity so compel, even digamists may be lectors, for such is not a priest, etc., etc." [4]

"Christ taught us by an example that the priestly work and ornaments should be communicated to those who shall have preserved their continency after a single marriage, or shall have persevered in virginity. And this the Apostles thereafter honestly and piously decreed, through the ecclesiastical canon of the priesthood." [5]

"Nay, moreover, he that still uses marriage, and begets children, even though the husband of but one wife, is by no means admitted by the Church to the order of deacon, presbyter, bishop, or subdeacon. But for all this, he who shall have kept himself from the commerce of his one wife, or has been deprived of her, may be ordained, and this is

---

[1] Matt. xix. 29 ; Lk. xviii. 29. In Mark x. 29 is found the same incident recorded. but while "wife" is mentioned among the things "left," no "wife" is found among the things gained.
[2] 1 Tim. iii., 2 and 12 ; Titus i., 6.

[3] Hieron. *Adv. Jovin.* Lib. I. *Confer* also the *In Apolog. pro libris Adv. Jovin.*
[4] Epiph. *Exposit. Fid. Cath.*, c. xxi.
[5] Ibid. *Hæresi.* 48, n. 7.

most usually the case in those places where the ecclesiastical canons are most accurately observed." [1]

Nor is the weight of this evidence lessened, but much increased, by the acknowledgment of the same father that in some places in his days the celibate life was not observed by such priests as had wives, for he explains that such a state of things had come about "not from following the authority of the canons, but through the neglect of men, which is wont at certain periods to be the case." [2]

The witness of the Western Fathers although so absolutely and indisputably clear is not so conclusive as to the East, and yet one passage from St. Jerome should be quoted. "The Virgin Christ and the Virgin Mary dedicated the virginity of both sexes. The Apostles were chosen when either virgins or continent after marriage, and bishops, presbyters, and deacons are chosen either when virgins, or widowers, or at least continent forever after the priesthood." [3]

It would be out of place to enter into any detailed argument upon the force of these passages, but I shall lay before the reader the summing up of the whole matter by a weighty recent writer of the Ultramontane Roman School.

"Is the celibate an Apostolic ordinance? Bickel affirmed that it is, and Funk denied it in 1878. To-day [1896] canonists commonly admit that one cannot prove the existence of any formal precept, either divine or apostolic, which imposes the celibate upon the clergy, and that all the texts, whether taken out of Holy Scripture or from the Fathers, on this subject contain merely a counsel, and not a command." "In the Fourth Century a great number of councils forbade bishops, priests, and deacons to live in the use of marriage with their lawful wives. . . . But there does not appear to have been any disposition to declare by law as invalid the marriages of clerics in Holy Orders. In the Fifth and Sixth Centuries the law of the celibate was observed by all the Churches of the West, thanks to the Councils and to the Popes." "In the Seventh and down to the end of the Tenth Century,[4] as a matter of fact the law of celibacy was little observed in a great part of the Western Church, but as a matter of law the Roman Pontiffs and the Councils were constant in their proclamation of its obligation." By the canonical practice of the unreformed West, the reception of Holy Orders is an *impedimentum dirimens matrimonii*, which renders any marriage subsequently contracted not only illicit but absolutely null. On this diriment impediment the same Roman Catholic writer says: "The diriment impediment of Holy Orders is of ecclesiastical obligation and not of divine, and consequently the Church can dispense it. This is the present teaching which is in opposition to that of the old schools."

"There is no question of the nullity of the marriages contracted by clerics before 1139. At the Council of the Lateran of that year, Innocent II. declared that these marriages contracted in contempt of the ecclesiastical law are not true marriages in his eyes. His successors do not seem to have insisted much upon this new diriment impediment, although it was attacked most vigorously by the offending clergymen; but the School of Bologna, the authority of which was then undisputed, openly declared for the nullity of the marriages contracted by clerics in Holy Orders. Thus it is that this point of law has been settled rather by teaching, than by any precise text, or by any law of a known date." [5]

It should not, however, be forgotten that although this is true with regard to Pope Innocent II. in 1139, it is also true that in 530 the Emperor Justinian declared null and void all marriages contracted by clerics in Holy Orders, and the children of such marriages to be spurious (*spurii*).

The reader will be interested in reading the answer on this point made by King Henry

[1] Epiph. *Hæresi.* 59, n. 4.
[2] Ibid. ut supra.
[3] Hieron. *Apolog. pro. lib. adv. Jovin.*
[4] It is curious that this is just four centuries. the same length of time as from the Reformation.
[5] *L'Ami du Clergé*, 6 Août, 1896, pp. 677 and 678.

VIII. to the letter sent him by the German ambassadors.[1] I can here give but a part translated into English. "Although the Church from the beginning admitted married men, as priests and bishops, who were without crime, the husband of one wife, (out of the necessity of the times, as sufficient other suitable men could not be found as would suffice for the teaching of the world) yet Paul himself chose the celibate Timothy; but if anyone came unmarried to the priesthood and afterwards took a wife, he was always deposed from the priesthood, according to the canon of the Council of Neocæsarea which was before that of Nice. So, too, in the Council of Chalcedon, in the first canon of which all former canons are confirmed, it is established that a deaconess, if she give herself over to marriage, shall remain under anathema, and a virgin who had dedicated herself to God and a monk who join themselves in marriage, shall remain excommunicated. . . . No Apostolic canon nor the Council of Nice contain anything similar to what you assert, viz.: that priests once ordained can marry afterwards. And with this statement agrees the Sixth Synod, in which it was decreed that if any of the clergy should wish to lead a wife, he should do so before receiving the Subdiaconate, since afterwards it was by no means lawful; nor was there given in the Sixth Synod any liberty to priests of leading wives after their priesting, as you assert. Therefore from the beginning of the newborn Church it is clearly seen that at no time it was permitted to a priest to lead a wife after his priesting, and nowhere, where this was attempted, was it done with impunity, but the culprit was deposed from his priesthood."

CANON VII.

SINCE we have learned that in some churches deacons hold ecclesiastical offices, and that hereby some of them with arrogancy and license sit daringly before the presbyters: we have determined that a deacon, even if in an office of dignity, that is to say, in whatever ecclesiastical office he may be, is not to have his seat before a presbyter, except he is acting as representative of his own patriarch or metropolitan in another city under another superior, for then he shall be honoured as filling his place. But if anyone, possessed with a tyrannical audacity, shall have dared to do such a thing, let him be ejected from his peculiar rank and be last of all of the order in whose list he is in his own church; our Lord admonishing us that we are not to delight in taking the chief seats, according to the doctrine which is found in the holy Evangelist Luke, as put forth by our Lord and God himself. For to those who were called he taught this parable: "When ye are bidden by anyone to a marriage sit not down in the highest room lest a more honourable man than thou shall have been bidden by him; and he who bade thee and him come and say to thee: Give this man place, and thou begin with shame to take the lowest room. But when thou art bidden, sit down in the lowest place, so that when he who bade thee cometh he may say to thee, Friend go up higher: then thou shalt have worship in the presence of them that sit with thee. For whosoever exalteth himself shall be abased, and he that humbleth himself shall be exalted." But the same thing also shall be observed in the remaining sacred orders; seeing that we know that spiritual things are to be preferred to worldly dignity.

NOTES.

ANCIENT EPITOME OF CANON VII.

A deacon in the execution of his office, if he shall have occasion to sit in the presence of presbyters, shall take the lowest place unless he be the representative of the Patriarch or bishop.

Balsamon, Zonaras, and following them

Van Espen point out that this canon is a relaxation of the XVIII. Canon of Nice which punishes presumptuous deacons not only with loss of rank in their grade, but also with expulsion from their ministry.

Van Espen well remarks that the Fathers of this synod had in mind not only the pres-

---

[1] This letter is found in full in the Addenda to the Appendix at the end of the seventh volume of Burnet's *History of the Reformation* (London. Orr & Co., 1850, p. cxlviij.).

ervation of the distinction between deacons and presbyters, but also between those in ecclesiastical orders and those enjoying secular dignities with regard to ecclesiastical matters, but who were not to gain therefrom ecclesiastical precedence. This is what is meant by the last clause of the canon.

Beveridge gives a list of these *quasi* ecclesiastical dignitaries as follows: Magnus Œconomus, Magno Sacello Præpositus, Magnus Vasorum Custos, Chartophylax, Parvo Sacello Præpositus, Primus Defensor.

CANON VIII.

SINCE we desire that in every point the things which have been decreed by our holy fathers may also be established and confirmed, we hereby renew the canon which orders that synods of the bishops of each province be held every year where the bishop of the metropolis shall deem best. But since on account of the incursions of barbarians and certain other incidental causes, those who preside over the churches cannot hold synods twice a year, it seems right that by all means once a year—on account of ecclesiastical questions which are likely to arise—a synod of the aforesaid bishops should be holden in every province, between the holy feast of Easter and October, as has been said above, in the place which the Metropolitan shall have deemed most fitting. And let such bishops as do not attend, when they are at home in their own cities and are in good health, and free from all unavoidable and necessary business, be fraternally reproved.

NOTES.

ANCIENT EPITOME OF CANON VIII.

Whenever it is impossible to hold two synods a year, one at least shall be celebrated, between Easter and the month of October.

This canon under the name of the "Sixth Synod" is referred to in Canon VI. of the Seventh Ecumenical Council (II. Nice), and

the bishops of Quinisext are called "Fathers."

VAN ESPEN.

What at first was only allowed on account of necessity, little by little passed into general law, and at last was received as law, that once a year there was to be a meeting of the provincial synod.

CANON IX.

LET no cleric be permitted to keep a "public house." For if it be not permitted to enter a tavern, much more is it forbidden to serve others in it and to carry on a trade which is unlawful for him. But if he shall have done any such thing, either let him desist or be deposed.

NOTES.

ANCIENT EPITOME OF CANON IX.

If clerics are forbidden to enter public houses, much more are they forbidden to keep them. Let them either give them up or be deposed.

Compare with this canon liv. of the Apostolic Canons; xxiv. of Laodicea; and xliij. of the Synod of Carthage.[1]

CANON X.

A BISHOP, or presbyter, or deacon who receives usury, or what is called *hecatostæ*, let him desist or be deposed.

NOTES.

ANCIENT EPITOME OF CANON X.

A bishop, presbyter, or deacon who takes usury shall be deposed unless he stops doing so.

See notes on canon XVI. of Nice, and the Excursus thereto appended.

---

[1] It is curious that Balsamon quotes this canon at xl., i.e., the Latin numbering and not the Greek which he himself uses in his scholia.

CANON XI.

LET no one in the priestly order nor any layman eat the unleavened bread of the Jews, nor have any familiar intercourse with them, nor summon them in illness, nor receive medicines from them, nor bathe with them ; but if anyone shall take in hand to do so, if he is a cleric, let him be deposed, but if a layman let him be cut off.

NOTES.

ANCIENT EPITOME OF CANON XI.

Jewish unleavened bread is to be refused. Whoever even calls in Jews as physicians or bathes with them is to be deposed.

VAN ESPEN.

Theodore Balsamon is of opinion that this canon does not forbid the eating of unleavened bread ; but that what is intended is the keeping of feasts in a Jewish fashion, or in sacrifices to use unleavened bread (*azymes*), and this, says Balsamon, on account of the Latins who celebrate their feasts with azymes.

Canon lxix. [*i.e.*, lxx.] of those commonly called Apostolic forbids the observance of festivals with the Jews ; and declares it to be unlawful to receive manuscula from them, but by this canon all familiar intercourse with them is forbidden.

While there can be no doubt that in all the Trullan canons there is an undercurrent of hostility to the West, yet in this canon I can see no such spirit, and I think it has been read into it by the greater bitterness of later times. This seems the more certain from the fact that there is nothing new whatever in the provision with respect to the passover bread, *vide* canons of Laodicea xxxvij. and xxxviij.

This canon is found in the *Corpus Juris Canonici*, Gratian's *Decretum*, Pars II., Causa xxviij., can. xiii.[1]

CANON XII.

MOREOVER this also has come to our knowledge, that in Africa and Libya and in other places the most God-beloved bishops in those parts do not refuse to live with their wives, even after consecration, thereby giving scandal and offence to the people. Since, therefore, it is our particular care that all things tend to the good of the flock placed in our hands and committed to us,—it has seemed good that henceforth nothing of the kind shall in any way occur. And we say this, not to abolish and overthrow what things were established of old by Apostolic authority, but as caring for the health of the people and their advance to better things, and lest the ecclesiastical state should suffer any reproach. For the divine Apostle says : "Do all to the glory of God, give none offence, neither to the Jews, nor to the Greeks, nor to the Church of God, even as I please all men in all things, not seeking mine own profit but the profit of many, that they may be saved. Be ye imitators of me even as I also am of Christ." But if any shall have been observed to do such a thing, let him be deposed.

NOTES.

ANCIENT EPITOME OF CANON XII.

Although it has been decreed that wives are not to be cast forth, nevertheless that we may counsel for the better, we give command that no one ordained a bishop shall any longer live with his wife.

ARISTENUS.

The fifth Apostolic canon allows neither bishop, presbyter, nor deacon to cast forth his wife under pretext of piety ; and assigns penalties for any that shall do so, and if he will not amend he is to be deposed. But this canon on the other hand does not permit a bishop even to live with his wife after his consecration. But by this change no contempt is meant to be poured out upon what had been established by Apostolic authority, but it was made through care for the people's health and for leading on to better things, and for fear

---

[1] Van Espen says that in his copy of Gratian this canon is assigned to the VIIth Synod. Such is not the case in the edition in Migne's Patrologia Latina, where the reference is given as *ex VI. Synodo. c. II.*, and *Judæorum* is found in the text instead of the *eorum* of which Van Espen complains.

that the sacerdotal estate might suffer some wrong.

Van Espen.
(*In Can. vi. Apost.*)

In the time of this canon [of the Apostles so called] not only presbyters and deacons, but bishops also, it is clear, were allowed by Eastern custom to have their wives; and Zonaras and Balsamon note that even until the Sixth Council, commonly called in Trullo, bishops were allowed to have their wives.

(*The same on this canon.*)

But not only do they command [in this canon] that bishops after their consecration no longer have commerce with their own wives, but further, they prohibit them even to presume to live with them.

Zonaras.

When the faith first was born and came forth into the world, the Apostles treated with greater softness and indulgence those who embraced the truth, which as yet was not scattered far and wide, nor did they exact from them perfection in all respects, but made great allowances for their weakness and for the inveterate force of the customs with which they were surrounded, both among the heathen and among the Jews. But now, when far and wide our religion has been propagated, more strenuous efforts were made to enforce those things which pertain to a higher and holier life, as our angelical worship increased day by day, and to insist on by law a life of continence to those who were elevated to the episcopate, so that not only they should abstain from their wives, but that they should have them no longer as bed-fellows; and not only that they no longer admit them as sharers of their bed, but they do not allow them even to stop under the same roof or in the house.

CANON XIII.

SINCE we know it to be handed down as a rule of the Roman Church that those who are deemed worthy to be advanced to the diaconate or presbyterate should promise no longer to cohabit with their wives, we, preserving the ancient rule and apostolic perfection and order, will that the lawful marriages of men who are in holy orders be from this time forward firm, by no means dissolving their union with their wives nor depriving them of their mutual intercourse at a convenient time. Wherefore, if anyone shall have been found worthy to be ordained subdeacon, or deacon, or presbyter, he is by no means to be prohibited from admittance to such a rank, even if he shall live with a lawful wife. Nor shall it be demanded of him at the time of his ordination that he promise to abstain from lawful intercourse with his wife: lest we should affect injuriously marriage constituted by God and blessed by his presence, as the Gospel saith: "What God hath joined together let no man put asunder;" and the Apostle saith, "Marriage is honourable and the bed undefiled;" and again, "Art thou bound to a wife? seek not to be loosed." But we know, as they who assembled at Carthage (with a care for the honest life of the clergy) said, that subdeacons, who handle the Holy Mysteries, and deacons, and presbyters should abstain from their consorts according to their own course [of ministration]. So that what has been handed down through the Apostles and preserved by ancient custom, we too likewise maintain, knowing that there is a time for all things and especially for fasting and prayer. For it is meet that they who assist at the divine altar should be absolutely continent when they are handling holy things, in order that they may be able to obtain from God what they ask in sincerity.

If therefore anyone shall have dared, contrary to the Apostolic Canons, to deprive any of those who are in holy orders, presbyter, or deacon, or subdeacon of cohabitation and intercourse with his lawful wife, let him be deposed. In like manner also if any presbyter or deacon on pretence of piety has dismissed his wife, let him be excluded from communion; and if he persevere in this let him be deposed.

NOTES.

ANCIENT EPITOME OF CANON XIII.

Although the Romans wish that everyone *ordained deacon or presbyter should put away his wife, we wish the marriages of deacons and presbyters to continue valid and firm.*

FLEURY.

(*H.E.*, Livre XL., chap. 1.)

What is said in this canon, that the council of Carthage orders priests to abstain from their wives at prescribed periods, is a misunderstanding of the decree, caused either by malice or by ignorance. This canon is one of those adopted by the Fifth Council of Carthage held in the year 400, and it is decreed that subdeacons, deacons, priests, and bishops shall abstain from their wives, following the ancient statutes, and shall be as though they had them not. The Greek version of this canon has rendered the Latin words *priora statuta* by these, *idious horous*, which may mean "fixed times": for the translator read, following another codex, *propria* for *priora*. Be this as it may, the Fathers of the Trullan council supposed that this obliged the clergy only to continence at certain fixed times, and were not willing to see that it included bishops as well.

VAN ESPEN.

Although the Latin Church does not disapprove,[1] as contrary to the law of the Gospel the discipline of the Greeks which allows the use of marriage to presbyters and deacons, provided it was contracted before ordination; yet never has it approved this canon which with too great zeal condemns the opposite custom, and rashly assigns great errors to the Roman Church.

This canon is found in the *Corpus Juris Canonici*, Gratian's *Decretum*, Pars I., Dist. XXXI., c. xiij.

Antonius Augustinus in his proposed emendations of Gratian says (*Lib.* I. *dial. de emend. Grat.*, c. 8.): "This canon can in no way be received; for it is written in opposition to the celibacy of the Latin priests, and openly is against the Roman Church." But to me the note which Gratian appends seems much more learned and true: "This however must be understood as of local application; for the Eastern Church, to which the VI. Synod prescribed this rule, did not receive a vow of chastity from the ministers of the altar." It may be well to note here that by the opinion of most Latin casuists the obligation to chastity among the Roman clergy rests upon the vow and not upon any law of the Church binding thereto. This evidently was the opinion of Gratian.

CANON XIV.

LET the canon of our holy God-bearing Fathers be confirmed in this particular also; that a presbyter be not ordained before he is thirty years of age, even if he be a very worthy man, but let him be kept back. For our Lord Jesus Christ was baptized and began to teach when he was thirty. In like manner let no deacon be ordained before he is twenty-five, nor a deaconess before she is forty.

NOTES.

ANCIENT EPITOME OF CANON XIV.

A presbyter thirty years of age, a deacon twenty-five, and a deaconess forty.

Compare Canon XI. of Neocæsarea.

It may be interesting to note here that by the law of the Roman Communion the canonical ages are as follows:

A subdeacon must have completed his twenty-first year, a deacon his twenty-second, a priest his twenty-fourth, and a bishop his thirtieth. None of the inferior clergy can hold a simple benefice before he has begun his fourteenth year. Ecclesiastical dignities, such as Cathedral canonries, cannot be conferred on any who have not finished the twenty-second year. A benefice to which is attached a cure of souls can be given only to one who is over twenty-four, and a diocese only to one who has completed his thirtieth year. (*Vide* Ferraris, *Bibliotheca Prompta*.)

In the Anglican Communion the ages are, in England, for a bishop "fully thirty years of age," for a priest twenty-four, and for a deacon twenty-three:[2] and in the United States, for a bishop thirty years of age, for a priest twenty-four, and for a deacon twenty-one.

---

[1] Clement VIII. made a decree in conformity with this canon that a Greek presbyter who was married shall abstain from his wife for a week or three days before he offered the sacrifice of the mass. *Const.* 33, *in Bull. Rom.* (*cit.* Van Espen *l. c.*)

[2] A faculty is allowed for earlier ordination, but since 1804 only to be granted by the Archbishop of Canterbury. This limitation is, however, only of Parliamentary sanction (44 Geo. III., ch. 43).

CANON XV.

A SUBDEACON is not to be ordained under twenty years of age. And if any one in any grade of the priesthood shall have been ordained contrary to the prescribed time let him be deposed.

NOTES.

ANCIENT EPITOME OF CANON XV.

Those shall be chosen as Subdeacons who are twenty years of age.

This age seems first to have been fixed by the Second Council of Toledo[1] (*circa*, A.D. 535) in its first canon.

CANON XVI.

SINCE the book of the Acts tells us that seven deacons were appointed by the Apostles, and the synod of Neocæsarea in the canons which it put forth determined that there ought to be canonically only seven deacons, even if the city be very large, in accordance with the book of the Acts; we, having fitted the mind of the fathers to the Apostles' words, find that they spoke not of those men who ministered at the Mysteries but in the administration which pertains to the serving of tables. For the book of the Acts reads as follows : "In those days, when the number of the disciples was multiplied, there arose a murmuring dissension of the Grecians against the Hebrews, because their widows were neglected in the daily ministrations. And the Twelve called the multitude of the disciples with them and said, It is not meet for us to leave the word of God and serve tables. Look ye out therefore, brethren, from among you seven men of good report full of the Holy Ghost and of wisdom, whom we may appoint over this business. But we will give ourselves continually unto prayer and unto the ministry of the word. And the saying pleased the whole multitude : and they chose Stephen a man full of faith and of the Holy Ghost, and Philip, and Prochorus, and Nicanor, and Timon, and Parmenas, and Nicolas a proselyte of Antioch : whom they set before the Apostles."

John Chrysostom, a Doctor of the Church, interpreting these words, proceeds thus : "It is a remarkable fact that the multitude was not divided in its choice of the men, and that the Apostles were not rejected by them. But we must learn what sort of rank they had, and what ordination they received. Was it that of deacons? But this office did not yet exist in the churches. But was it the dispensation of a presbyter? But there was not as yet any bishop, but only Apostles, whence I think it is clear and manifest that neither of deacons nor of presbyters was there then the name."[2]

But on this account therefore we also announce that the aforesaid seven deacons are not to be understood as deacons who served at the Mysteries, according to the teaching before set forth, but that they were those to whom a dispensation was entrusted for the common benefit of those that were gathered together, who to us in this also were a type of philanthropy and zeal towards those who are in need.

NOTES.

ANCIENT EPITOME OF CANON XVI.

Whoever affirms that the number of deacons should be seven according to the saying of the Acts, should know that the reference in that passage is not to Deacons of the Mysteries but to such as serve tables.

Van Espen here reminds us that this is, as

Zonaras calls attention to in his scholion on this place, a correction rather than an interpretation of the XVth Canon of Neocæsarea, and Balsamon also says the same. The only interest that the matter possesses is that a canon which had been received by the Fourth Ecumenical Council (Chalcedon) should receive such treatment from such an assembly as the Synod in Trullo.

[1] It is curious that so learned a scholar as the late Henry Bradshaw in his article " Subdeacon " in Smith & Cheetham's *Dictionary of Christ. Antiq.* should give the date of this synod as 447. Hefele fixes it at 527 or 531. Baronius, Binius, Labbe, and many others at 531. A very ancient MS. assigns it to the year 565 of the Spanish era, i.e. 527, and this is the date Cardinal de Aguirre adopts, and is also the one given to the council by the editors of *L'Art de Vérifier les dates.*

[2] I have not followed the Oxford translation, which seems to me to have reversed the point. In a foot-note to that translation (Chrysostom on Acts, Part I., p. 199) will be found a translation of this canon.

CANON XVII.

Since clerics of different churches have left their own churches in which they were ordained and betaken themselves to other bishops, and without the consent of their own bishop have been settled in other churches, and thus they have proved themselves to be insolent and disobedient; we decree that from the month of January of the past IVth Indiction no cleric, of whatsoever grade he be, shall have power, without letters dimissory of his own bishop, to be registered in the clergy list of another church. Whoever in future shall not have observed this rule, but shall have brought disgrace upon himself as well as on the bishop who ordained him, let him be deposed together with him who also received him.

NOTES.

Ancient Epitome of Canon XVII.

Whoever receives and ordains a wandering cleric shall be deposed together with him thus wickedly ordained.

This canon is found in the *Corpus Juris Canonici*, Gratian's *Decretum*, Pars II., Causa XXI., Quæst., ii. can. j.

CANON XVIII.

Those clerics who in consequence of a barbaric incursion or on account of any other circumstance have gone abroad, we order to return again to their churches after the cause has passed away, or when the incursion of the barbarians is at an end. Nor are they to leave them for long without cause. If anyone shall not have returned according to the direction of this present canon—let him be cut off until he shall return to his own church. And the same shall be the punishment of the bishop who received him.

NOTES.

Ancient Epitome of Canon XVIII.

Whoever has emigrated on account of an invasion of the barbarians, shall return to the Church to whose clergy he belongs as soon as the incursion ceases. But if he shall not do so, he shall be cut off together with him to whom he has gone.

Balsamon.

The Fathers are worthy of great praise. For having regard to the honour of the ecclesiastical order and of each bishop, they have decreed that clergymen, who from just and valid causes have gone forth without letters dimissory from those who ordained them, should return to their own clergy as soon as the cause which drove them forth ceases; and that they should not be enrolled on the clergy list of any other church. But whosoever cannot be persuaded to return is to be cut off, as well as the bishop who detains him. But someone will say, If a bishop who does such a thing is cut off by his Metropolitan; and likewise if a Metropolitan spurns this canon he is punished by the Patriarch. But if an autocephalous archbishop or a Patriarch other than the Patriarch of Constantinople (for he has a faculty for doing so) should be convicted of a breach of this Canon, by whom would he be cut off? I suppose by the Supreme Pontiff [1] (οἴομαι οὖν παρά τοῦ μείζονος ἀρχιερέως).

CANON XIX.

It behoves those who preside over the churches, every day but especially on Lord's days, to teach all the clergy and people words of piety and of right religion, gathering out of holy Scripture meditations and determinations of the truth, and not going beyond the limits now fixed, nor varying from the tradition of the God-bearing fathers. And if any controversy in regard to Scripture shall have been raised, let them not interpret it otherwise than as the lights and doctors of the church in their writings have expounded it, and in these let them glory rather than in composing things out of their own heads, lest through their lack of skill [2] they may have departed from what was fitting. For

---

[1] Can this mean the Pope?　　　[2] I have followed the reading ἀπείρως.

through the doctrine of the aforesaid fathers, the people coming to the knowledge of what is good and desirable, as well as what is useless and to be rejected, will remodel their life for the better, and not be led by ignorance, but applying their minds to the doctrine, they will take heed that no evil befall them and work out their salvation in fear of impending punishment.

NOTES.

ANCIENT EPITOME OF CANON XIX.

The prelates of the Church, especially upon Lord's days, shall teach doctrine.

VAN ESPEN.

How great an obligation of preaching rests upon bishops, the successors of the Apostles, is evident from the words of St. Paul, "Christ sent me not to baptize but to preach" (1 Cor. i., 17), and his chief adjuration to Timothy though Jesus Christ and his coming, was "Preach the Word" (2 Tim. ii. 4.) For this reason the fathers formerly called the episcopate the preaching-office (*officium predicationis*), as is evident from the profession of Adelbert Morinensis, and the form of profession of a future Archbishop. Both of these will be found in Labbe, appendix to Tom. VIII., of his *Concilia*.

COUNCIL OF TRENT.

(*Sess.* V., c. 2.)

The preaching of the Gospel is the chief work of bishops.

CONVOCATION OF CANTERBURY, A.D. 1571.

(Cardwell. *Synodalia*, Vol. I., p. 126.)

The clergy will be careful to teach nothing in their sermons to be religiously held and believed by the people except what is agreeable to the doctrine of the Old and New Testament, and what the Catholic Fathers and Ancient Bishops have collected out of the same.[1]

COUNCIL OF TRENT.

(*Sess.* IV.)

No one shall dare to interpret the Holy Scripture contrary to the unanimous consent of the fathers.

CANON XX.

IT shall not be lawful for a bishop to teach publicly in any city which does not belong to him. If any shall have been observed doing this, let him cease from his episcopate, but let him discharge the office of a presbyter.

NOTES.

ANCIENT EPITOME OF CANON XX.

The bishop of one city shall not teach publicly in another. If he shall be shown to have done so he shall be deprived of the episcopate and shall perform the functions of a presbyter.

The meaning of this canon is most obscure.

Balsamon and Zonaras think that the Bishop is not to be deposed from his Episcopate, but only shorn of his right of executing the Episcopal functions, so that he will virtually be reduced to a presbyter. Aristenus, on the other hand, considers the deposition to be real and that this canon creates an exception to Canon XXIX. of Chalcedon.

CANON XXI.

THOSE who have become guilty of crimes against the canons, and on this account subject to complete and perpetual deposition, are degraded to the condition of laymen. If, however, keeping conversion continually before their eyes, they willingly deplore the sin on account of which they fell from grace, and made themselves aliens therefrom, they may still cut their hair after the manner of clerics. But if they are not willing to submit themselves to this canon, they must wear their hair as laymen, as being those who have preferred the communion of the world to the celestial life.

---

[1] It is not generally known that this evident citation of Canon XIX. of the Quinisext Council forms part of the action enforcing the XXXIX. Articles of the Church of England.

NOTES.

Whoever is already deposed and reduced to the lay estate, if he shall repent, let him continue deposed but be shorn. But if otherwise, he must let his hair grow.

Beveridge wishes to read who have become canonically guilty of crimes," substituting κανονικῶς for κανονικοῖς, in accordance with the Bodleian and Amerbachian codices.

CANON XXII.

THOSE who are ordained for money, whether bishops or of any rank whatever, and not by examination and choice of life, we order to be deposed as well as those also who ordained them.

NOTES.

ANCIENT EPITOME OF CANON XXII.

Whoever is ordained for pay shall be deposed together with his ordainer.

VAN ESPEN.

The present canon orders to be deposed not only the one simoniacally ordained, but also his ordainer, ordering that ordinations should take place on account, not of money, but of the excellence of the examination stood by the candidate and on account of his uprightness of life. And it evidently takes it for granted that, where money has been used, examination, excellence of life, and consideration of merit enter but little into the matter, or at least are paid no attention to.

CANON XXIII.

THAT no one, whether bishop, presbyter, or deacon, when giving the immaculate Communion, shall exact from him who communicates fees of any kind. For grace is not to be sold, nor do we give the sanctification of the Holy Spirit for money ; but to those who are worthy of the gift it is to be communicated in all simplicity. But if any of those enrolled among the clergy make demands on those he communicates let him be deposed, as an imitator of the error and wickedness of Simon.

NOTES.

ANCIENT EPITOME OF CANON XXIII.

Whoever shall demand an obolus or anything else for giving the spotless communion shall be deposed.

This canon is found in the *Corpus Juris Canonici*, Gratian's *Decretum*, Pars. II., Causa I., Quæst. I., can. 100, attributed to the VI. Synod. Ivo reads, "From the Sixth Synod, III. Constantinople."

CANON XXIV.

No one who is on the priestly catalogue nor any monk is allowed to take part in horse-races or to assist at theatrical representations. But if any clergyman be called to a marriage, as soon as the games begin let him rise up and go out, for so it is ordered by the doctrine of our fathers. And if any one shall be convicted of such an offence let him cease therefrom or be deposed.

NOTES.

ANCIENT EPITOME OF CANON XXIV.

A clergyman or monk shall be deposed who goes to horse-races, or does not leave nuptials before the players are brought in.

VAN ESPEN.

Scarcely ever were these plays exhibited without the introduction of something contrary to honesty and chastity. As Lupus here notes, the word "obscene" has its derivation from these "scenic" representations.

Rightly therefore has it been forbidden by the sacred canons that the clergy should witness any such plays.

In the second part of this canon by the words "ordered by the doctrine of our fathers," the Synod understands the doctrine of the fathers of the synod of Laodicea, which in its canon liv. condemned the same abuse.

Compare the canon given in the *Corpus Juris Canonici*, Gratian's *Decretum*, Pars I., Dist. XXXIV., can. xix.

CANON XXV.

MOREOVER we renew the canon which orders that country (ἀγροικικὰς) parishes and those which are in the provinces (ἐγχωρίους) shall remain subject to the bishops who had possession of them; especially if for thirty years they had administered them without opposition. But if within thirty years there had been or should be any controversy on the point, it is lawful for those who think themselves injured to refer the matter to the provincial synod.

NOTES.

ANCIENT EPITOME OF CANON XXV.

Rural and out of town parishes held for thirty years may be retained. But within that time there may be a controversy.

Compare notes on Canon XVII. of Chalcedon.

CANON XXVI.

IF a presbyter has through ignorance contracted an illegal marriage, while he still retains the right to his place, as we have defined in the sacred canons, yet he must abstain from all sacerdotal work. For it is sufficient if to such an one indulgence is granted. For he is unfit to bless another who needs to take care of his own wounds, for blessing is the imparting of sanctification. But how can he impart this to another who does not possess it himself through a sin of ignorance? Neither then in public nor in private can he bless nor distribute to others the body of Christ, [nor perform any other ministry]; but being content with his seat of honour let him lament to the Lord that his sin of ignorance may be remitted. For it is manifest that the nefarious marriage must be dissolved, neither can the man have any intercourse with her on account of whom he is deprived of the execution of his priesthood.

NOTES.

ANCIENT EPITOME OF CANON XXVI.

A priest who has fallen into an illicit marriage and been deposed, may still have his seat, but only when he abstains for the future from his wickedness.

ARISTENUS.

If any presbyter before his ordination had married a widow, or a harlot, or an actress, or any other woman such as are forbidden, in ignorance, he shall cease from his priesthood but shall still have his place among the presbyters. But such an illegitimate marriage, on account of which he was deprived of the Sacred Ministry, must be dissolved.

VAN ESPEN.

The sacred canon to which the Synod here refers is number xxvij. of St. Basil in his Canonical Epistle to Amphilochius.

CANON XXVII.

NONE of those who are in the catalogue of the clergy shall wear clothes unsuited to them, either while still living in town or when on a journey: but they shall wear such clothes as are assigned to those who belong to the clergy. And if any one shall violate this canon, he shall be cut off for one week.

ANCIENT EPITOME OF CANON XXVII.

A clergyman must not wear an unsuitable dress either when travelling or when at home. Should he do so, he shall be cut off for one week.

CANON XXVIII.

SINCE we understand that in several churches grapes are brought to the altar, according to a custom which has long prevailed, and the ministers joined this with the unbloody sacrifice of the oblation, and distributed both to the people at the same time, we decree that no priest shall do this for the future, but shall administer the oblation alone to the people for the quickening of their souls and for the remission of their sins. But with regard to the offering of grapes as first fruits, the priests may bless them apart [from the offering of the oblation] and distribute them to such as seek them as an act of thanksgiving to him who is the Giver of the fruits by which our bodies are increased and fed according to his divine decree. And if any cleric shall violate this decree let him be deposed.

NOTES.

ANCIENT EPITOME OF CANON XXVIII.

Grapes are by some joined with the unbloody sacrifice. It is hereby decreed that no one shall for the future dare to do this.

VAN ESPEN.

Similar blessings of fruit, and particularly of grapes, are found in more recent rituals as well as in the ancient Greek Euchologions and the Latin Rituales. In the Sacramentary of St. Gregory will be found a benediction of grapes on the feast of St. Sixtus.

Cardinal Bona says (*De Reb. Liturg.*, Lib. II., cap. xiv.), that immediately before the words *Semper bona creas, sanctificas, etc.*, if new fruits or any other things adapted to human use were to be blessed, they were wont in former times to be placed before the altar, and there to be blessed by the priest; and when the benediction was ended with the accustomed words "Through Christ our Lord," there was added the following prayer: "Perquem hæc omnia, etc.," which words are not so much to be referred to the body and blood of Christ, as to the things to be blessed, which God continually creates by renewing, and we ask that they may be sanctified by his benediction to our use.

But in after ages when the fervour of the faithful had grown cold, that the mass might not be too long, they were separated and yet the prayer remained which, as said to-day over the consecrated species alone, can hardly be understood.

This canon is found in a shortened form in the *Corpus Juris Canonici*, Pars. III., De Consecrat., Dist. II., can. vj.

Compare Canon of the Apostles number iv.

CANON XXIX.

A CANON of the Synod of Carthage says that the holy mysteries of the altar are not to be performed but by men who are fasting, except on one day in the year on which the Supper of the Lord is celebrated. At that time, on account perhaps of certain occasions in those places useful to the Church, even the holy Fathers themselves made use of this dispensation. But since nothing leads us to abandon exact observance, we decree that the Apostolic and Patristic tradition shall be followed; and define that it is not right to break the fast on the fifth feria of the last week of Lent, and thus to do dishonour to the whole of Lent.

NOTES.

ANCIENT EPITOME OF CANON XXIX.

Some of the Fathers after they had supped on the day of the Divine Supper made the offering.[1]
However, it has seemed good to the synod that this should not be done, and that the fast should not be broken upon the fifth feria[2] *of the last*

---

[1] I.e., of the Mass. [2] Maundy Thursday.

week of Lent, and so the whole of Lent be dishonoured.

Zonaras remarks that the "Apostolic and Patristic tradition" is a reference to canon lxix. of the Apostolic Canons and to canon l. of Laodicea. See notes on this last canon.

CANON XXX.

WILLING to do all things for the edification of the Church, we have determined to take care even of priests who are in barbarian churches. Wherefore if they think that they ought to exceed the Apostolic Canon concerning the not putting away of a wife on the pretext of piety and religion, and to do beyond that which is commanded, and therefore abstain by agreement with their wives from cohabitation, we decree they ought no longer to live with them in any way, so that hereby they may afford us a perfect demonstration of their promise. But we have conceded this to them on no other ground than their narrowness, and foreign and unsettled manners.

NOTES.

ANCIENT EPITOME OF CANON XXX.

Those priests who are in churches among the barbarians, if with consent they have abstained from commerce with their wives shall never afterwards have any commerce with them in any way.

FLEURY.

(*Hist. Eccl.*, Liv. XL., chap. 1.)

"Priests who are among the barbarians," that is to say, it would seem, in Italy and in the other countries of the Latin rite. "Their narrowness and foreign and unsettled manners," that is to say that according to them it is an imperfection to aspire after perfect continence.

I do not think that this explanation of Fleury's can be sustained, and it would seem that Van Espen is more near the truth when he says: "Some priests in barbarous countries thought they should abstain after the Latin custom even from wives taken before ordination. And although this was contrary to the discipline of the Greeks, and also to Canon V. of the Apostles, nevertheless the Fathers thought it might be tolerated, provided such priests should also not live any longer with their wives." There seems no reason to introduce anti-Roman bitterness where it is not already found.

CANON XXXI.

CLERICS who in oratories which are in houses offer the Holy Mysteries or baptize, we decree ought to do this with the consent of the bishop of the place. Wherefore if any cleric shall not have so done, let him be deposed.

NOTES.

ANCIENT EPITOME OF CANON XXXI.

Thou mayest not offer in an oratory in a private house without the consent of the bishop.

On this whole subject the reader is referred to the curious and most interesting volume published by Venantius Monaldini of Venice, in 1765. I cannot better give its scope than by copying out its title in full.

Commentarius Theologico - canonico - criticus *De ecclesiis, earum reverentia, et asylo atque concordia sacerdotii, et imperii,* auctore Josepho Aloysio Assemani. Accesserunt tractatus cl. virorum D. Josephi de Bonis, *De Oratoriis Publicis ;* ac. R. P. Fortunati a Brixia *De Oratoriis Domesticis,* in supplementum celeberrimi operis Joannis Baptistæ Gattico *De Oratoriis Domesticis, et usu altaris portatilis.*

CANON XXXII.

SINCE it has come to our knowledge that in the region of Armenia they offer wine only on the Holy Table, those who celebrate the unbloody sacrifice not mixing water with it, adducing, as authority thereof, John Chrysostom, a doctor of the Church, who says in his interpretation of the Gospel according to St. Matthew :

"And wherefore did he not drink water after he was risen again, but wine? To pluck up by the roots another wicked heresy. For since there are certain who use water in the Mysteries to shew that both when he delivered the mysteries he had given wine and that when he had risen and was setting before them a mere meal without mysteries, he used wine, 'of the fruit,' saith he, 'of the vine.'   But a vine produces wine, not water."[1]   And from this they think the doctor overthrows the admixture of water in the holy sacrifice.   Now, lest on the point from this time forward they be held in ignorance, we open out the orthodox opinion of the Father.   For since there was an ancient and wicked heresy of the Hydroparastatæ (i.e., of those who offered water), who instead of wine used water in their sacrifice, this divine, confuting the detestable teaching of such a heresy, and showing that it is directly opposed to Apostolic tradition, asserted that which has just been quoted.   For to his own church, where the pastoral administration had been given him, he ordered that water mixed with wine should be used at the unbloody sacrifice, so as to shew forth the mingling of the blood and water which for the life of the whole world and for the redemption of its sins, was poured forth from the precious side of Christ our Redeemer; and moreover in every church where spiritual light has shined this divinely given order is observed.

For also James, the brother, according to the flesh, of Christ our God, to whom the throne of the church of Jerusalem first was entrusted, and Basil, the Archbishop of the Church of Cæsarea, whose glory has spread through all the world, when they delivered to us directions for the mystical sacrifice in writing, declared that the holy chalice is consecrated in the Divine Liturgy with water and wine.   And the holy Fathers who assembled at Carthage provided in these express terms: "That in the holy Mysteries nothing besides the body and blood of the Lord be offered, as the Lord himself laid down, that is bread and wine mixed with water."   Therefore if any bishop or presbyter shall not perform the holy action according to what has been handed down by the Apostles, and shall not offer the sacrifice with wine mixed with water, let him be deposed, as imperfectly shewing forth the mystery and innovating on the things which have been handed down.

NOTES.

ANCIENT EPITOME OF CANON XXXII.

Chrysostom, when overthrowing the heresy of the Hydroparastatæ, says: "When the Lord suffered and rose again he used wine."   The Armenians, laying hold on this, offer wine alone, not understanding that Chrysostom himself, and Basil, and James used wine mixed with water; and left the tradition that we should so make the offering.   If, therefore, any one shall offer wine alone, or water alone, and not the mixed [chalice] let him be deposed.

VAN ESPEN.

Justin Martyr in his Second Apology, Ambrose, or whoever was the author of the books on the Sacraments (Lib. v., cap. i.), Augustine and many others make mention of this rite, and above all St. Cyprian, who wrote a long epistle on the subject to Cecilius, and seeking the reason of the ceremony as a setting forth of the union of the people, represented by the water, with Christ, figured by the wine.

Another signification of this rite St. Augustine indicates in his sermon to Neophytes, saying: "Take this in bread, which hung upon the Cross: Take this in the cup which poured forth from the side," that is to say blood and water.

Cardinal Bona (*De Rebus Liturgicis*, Lib. II.,

cap. ix., n. 3 and 4) refers to many ancient rituals in which a similar prayer is used to that found in the Ambrosian rite, which says as the water is poured in : "Out of the side of Christ there flowed forth blood and water together.   In the name of the Father, etc." Bona further notes that "The Greeks twice mingle water with the wine, once cold water, when in the prothesis they are preparing the Holy Gifts, and the Priest pierces the bread with the holy spear, and says, "One of the soldiers with a lance opened his side, and immediately there flowed forth blood and water," and the deacon pours in wine and water. From this it is evident that the Greeks agree with St. Augustine's explanation.

For the second time the Greeks mix "hot water after consecration and immediately before communion, the deacon begging from the priest a blessing upon the warm water ; and he blesses it in these words : 'Blessed be the fervour of thy Saints, now and ever and to the ages of ages.   Amen.'   Then the deacon pours the water into the chalice, saying : 'The fervour of faith, full of the Holy Spirit.'" So Cardinal Bona as above.

The third reason of this rite is assumed by some from the fact that Christ is believed thus to have instituted this sacrament at the

---

[1] Chrysos. *In Matt.* XXVI. 29—I have taken the Oxford translation, "Library of the Fathers."

last supper; and this the synod seems to intimate in the present canon when it says "as the Lord himself delivered."

In this case the Greeks suppose that this rite was also handed down by the Apostles, and this is evident from their citing the Liturgy of St. James, which they believed to be a genuine work of his.

CANON XXXIII.

SINCE we know that, in the region of the Armenians, only those are appointed to the clerical orders who are of priestly descent (following in this Jewish customs); and some of those who are even untonsured are appointed to succeed cantors and readers of the divine law, we decree that henceforth it shall not be lawful for those who wish to bring any one into the clergy, to pay regard to the descent of him who is to be ordained; but let them examine whether they are worthy (according to the decrees set forth in the holy canons) to be placed on the list of the clergy, so that they may be ecclesiastically promoted, whether they are of priestly descent or not; moreover, let them not permit any one at all to read in the ambo, according to the order of those enrolled in the clergy, unless such an one have received the priestly tonsure and the canonical benediction of his own pastor; but if any one shall have been observed to act contrary to these directions, let him be cut off.

NOTES.

ANCIENT EPITOME OF CANON XXXIII.

Whoever is worthy of the priesthood should be ordained whether he is sprung of a priestly line or no. And he that has been blessed untonsured shall not read the Holy Scriptures at the ambo.

VAN ESPEN.

Here not obscurely does the canon join the clerical tonsure received from the bishop with the office of Reader, so much so that he that has been tonsured by the bishop is thought to have received at the same time the tonsure and the order of lector.

CANON XXXIV.

BUT in future, since the priestly canon openly sets this forth, that the crime of conspiracy or secret society is forbidden by external laws, but much more ought it to be prohibited in the Church; we also hasten to observe that if any clerics or monks are found either conspiring or entering secret societies, or devising anything against bishops or clergymen, they shall be altogether deprived of their rank.

NOTES.

ANCIENT EPITOME OF CANON XXXIV.

If clerics or monks enter into conspiracies or fraternities, or plots against the bishop or their fellow clerics, they shall be cast out of their grade.

This is but a renewal of Canon xviij. of Chalcedon, which see with the notes.

CANON XXXV.

IT shall be lawful for no Metropolitan on the death of a bishop of his province to appropriate or sell the private property of the deceased, or that of the widowed church: but these are to be in the custody of the clergy of the diocese over which he presided until the election of another bishop, unless in the said church there are no clergymen left. For then the Metropolitan shall protect the property without diminution, handing over everything to the bishop when he is appointed.

NOTES.

ANCIENT EPITOME OF CANON XXXV.

When the bishop is dead the clergy shall

guard his goods. If, however, no clergyman remains, the Metropolitan shall take charge of them until another be ordained.

Compare Canon xxii. of Chalcedon. This canon extends the prohibition to Metropolitans as well.

ARISTENUS.

Neither the clergy nor metropolitan after the death of the bishop are allowed to carry off his goods, but all should be guarded by the clergy themselves, until another bishop is chosen. But if by chance no clergyman is left in that church, the metropolitan is to keep all the possessions undiminished and to return them to the future bishop.

CANON XXXVI.

RENEWING the enactments by the 150 Fathers assembled at the God-protected and imperial city, and those of the 630 who met at Chalcedon; we decree that the see of Constantinople shall have equal privileges with the see of Old Rome, and shall be highly regarded in ecclesiastical matters as that is, and shall be second after it. After Constantinople shall be ranked the See of Alexandria, then that of Antioch, and afterwards the See of Jerusalem.

NOTES.

ANCIENT EPITOME OF CANON XXXVI.

Let the throne of Constantinople be next after that of Rome, and enjoy equal privileges. After it Alexandria, then Antioch, and then Jerusalem.

BALSAMON.

The Fathers here speak of the Second and Third canons of the Second Synod [i.e. I. Constantinople] and of canon xxviij. of the Fourth Synod [i.e. Chalcedon]. And read what we have said on these canons.

ARISTENUS.

We have explained the third canon of the Synod of Constantinople and the twenty-eighth canon of the Synod of Chalcedon as meaning, when asserting that the bishop of Constantinople should enjoy equal privileges after the Roman bishop, that he should be placed second from the Roman in point of time. So here too this preposition "after" denotes time but not honour. For after many years this throne of Constantinople obtained equal privileges with the Roman Church; because it was honoured by the presence of the Emperor and of the Senate.

On this opinion of Aristenus's the reader is referred to the notes on Canon iij. of I. Constantinople.

JUSTINIAN.

(*Novella* CXXXI., *Cap.* ij.)

We command that according to the definitions of the Four Councils the most holy Pope of Old Rome shall be first of all the priests. But the most blessed Archbishop of Constantinople, which is New Rome, shall have the second place after the Holy Apostolic See of Old Rome.

This canon, in a mutilated form, is found in the *Corpus Juris Canonici*, Gratian's *Decretum*, Pars I., Dist. XXII., c. vj.

CANON XXXVII.

SINCE at different times there have been invasions of barbarians, and therefore very many cities have been subjected to the infidels, so that the bishop of a city may not be able, after he has been ordained, to take possession of his see, and to be settled in it in sacerdotal order, and so to perform and manage for it the ordinations and all things which by custom appertain to the bishop: we, preserving honour and veneration for the priesthood, and in no wise wishing to employ the Gentile injury to the ruin of ecclesiastical rights, have decreed that those who have been ordained thus, and on account of the aforesaid cause have not been settled in their sees, without any prejudice from this thing may be kept [in good standing] and that they may canonically perform the ordination of the different clerics and use the authority of their office according to the defined limits, and that whatever administration proceeds from them may be valid and legitimate. For the exercise of his office shall not be circumscribed by a season of necessity when the exact observance of law is circumscribed.

NOTES.

ANCIENT EPITOME OF CANON XXXVII.

A bishop who, on account of the incursions of the barbarians, is not set in his throne, shall have his own chair of state, and shall ordain, and shall enjoy most firmly all the rights of the priesthood.

By Canon XVIII. of Antioch the principle of this canon was enunciated, that when a bishop did not take possession of his see because he could not do so, he was not to be held responsible or to lose any of his episcopal rights and powers, in that case the impossibility arose from the insubordination of the people, in this from the diocese being in the hands of the barbarians.

It has been commonly thought that the Bishops *in partibus infidelium* had their origin in the state of things calling for this canon.

CANON XXXVIII.

THE canon which was made by the Fathers we also observe, which thus decreed: If any city be renewed by imperial authority, or shall have been renewed, let the order of things ecclesiastical follow the civil and public models.

NOTES.

ANCIENT EPITOME OF CANON XXXVIII.

If any city is or shall be renewed by the Emperor, the ecclesiastical order shall follow the political and public example.

VAN ESPEN.

The canon of the Fathers which the Synod wishes observed is XVII of Chalcedon, the notes on which see.

Here it must be noted that by "civil and public models" is signified the "pragmatic" or imperial letters, by which the emperors granted to newly raised up or re-edified towns the privilege of other cities, or else annexed them to some Province.

CANON XXXIX.

SINCE our brother and fellow-worker, John, bishop of the island of Cyprus, together with his people in the province of the Hellespont, both on account of barbarian incursions, and that they may be freed from servitude of the heathen, and may be subject alone to the sceptres of most Christian rule, have emigrated from the said island, by the providence of the philanthropic God, and the labour of our Christ-loving and pious Empress; we determine that the privileges which were conceded by the divine fathers who first at Ephesus assembled, are to be preserved without any innovations, viz.: that new Justinianopolis shall have the rights of Constantinople and whoever is constituted the pious and most religious bishop thereof shall take precedence of all the bishops of the province of the Hellespont, and be elected [?] by his own bishops according to ancient custom. For the customs which obtain in each church our divine Fathers also took pains should be maintained, the existing bishop of the city of Cyzicus being subject to the metropolitan of the aforesaid Justinianopolis, for the imitation of all the rest of the bishops who are under the aforesaid beloved of God metropolitan John, by whom, as custom demands, even the bishop of the very city of Cyzicus shall be ordained.

NOTES.

ANCIENT EPITOME OF CANON XXXIX.

The new Justinianopolis shall have the rights of Constantinople, and its prelate shall rule over all the bishops of the Hellespont to whom he has gone, and he shall be ordained by his own bishop: as the fathers of Ephesus decreed.

HEFELE.

Hitherto the bishop of Cyzicus was metropolitan of the province of the Hellespont. Now he too is to be subject to the bishop of New-Justinianopolis. What, however, is meant by "the right of Constantinople"? It was impossible that the Synod should place the bishop of Justinianopolis in equal dignity with the patriarch of Constantinople. But they probably meant to say: "The rights which the bishop of Constantinople has hitherto exercised over the province of the Hellespont, as chief metropolitan, fall now to the bishop of New-Justinianopolis." Or perhaps we should read, instead of Constantinople Κωνσταντινέων πόλεως, as the Amerbachian MS. has it, and translate: "The same rights which

Constantia (the metropolis of Cyprus) possessed, New Justinianopolis shall henceforth have." The latter is the more probable.

VAN ESPEN.

To understand this canon it must be remembered that the Metropolis of Cyprus, which was formerly called Constantia, when restored by the Emperor Justinian was called by his name, New Justinianopolis.

CANON XL.

SINCE to cleave to God by retiring from the noise and turmoil of life is very beneficial, it behoves us not without examination to admit before the proper time those who choose the monastic life, but to observe respecting them the limit handed down by our fathers, in order that we may then admit a profession of the life according to God as for ever firm, and the result of knowledge and judgment after years of discretion have been reached. He therefore who is about to submit to the yoke of monastic life should not be less than ten years of age, the examination of the matter depending on the decision of the bishop, whether he considers a longer time more conducive for his entrance and establishment in the monastic life. For although the great Basil in his holy canons decreed that she who willingly offers to God and embraces virginity, if she has completed her seventeenth year, is to be entered in the order of virgins: nevertheless, having followed the example respecting widows and deaconesses, analogy and proportion being considered, we have admitted at the said time those who have chosen the monastic life. For it is written in the divine Apostle that a widow is to be elected in the church at sixty years old: but the sacred canons have decreed that a deaconess shall be ordained at forty, since they saw that the Church by divine grace had gone forth more powerful and robust and was advancing still further, and they saw the firmness and stability of the faithful in observing the divine commandments. Wherefore we also, since we most rightly comprehend the matter, appoint the benediction of grace to him who is about to enter the struggle according to God, even as impressing speedily a certain seal upon him, hereupon introducing him to the not-long-to-be-hesitated-over and declined, or rather inciting him even to the choice and determination of good.

NOTES.

ANCIENT EPITOME OF CANON XL.

A monk must be ten years old. Even if the Divine Basil thought the one shorn should be over seventeen. But although the Apostle ordains that a widow to be espoused to the Church must be sixty, yet the Fathers say a Deaconess is to be ordained at forty, the Church in the meanwhile having become stronger ; so we place the seal on a monk at an earlier age.

ARISTENUS.

The eighteenth canon of Basil the Great orders that she who offers herself to the Lord and renounces marriage, ought to be over sixteen or even seventeen years of age : so that her promise may be firm and that if she violates it she may suffer the due penalties. For, says he, children's voices are not to be thought of any value in such matters. But the pres-

ent canon admits him who is not less than ten years and desires to be a monk, but entrusts the determination of the exact time to the judgment of the hegumenos, whether he thinks it more advantageous to increase the age-requirement for the entering and being established in the married life. But the canon lessens the time defined by Basil the Great, because the Fathers thought that the Church by divine grace had grown stronger since then, and was going on more and more, and that the faithful seemed firmer and more stable for the observance of the divine commandments. And for the same reason, viz , that the Church was growing better, the sacred canons had lessened the age of deaconesses, and fixed it at forty years, although the Apostle himself orders that no widow is to be chosen into the Church under sixty years of age.

CANON XLI.

THOSE who in town or in villages wish to go away into cloisters, and take heed for themselves apart, before they enter a monastery and practise the anchorite's life,[1] should for the space of three years in the fear of God submit to the Superior of the house, and fulfil obedience in all things, as is right, thus shewing forth their choice of this life and that they embrace it willingly and with their whole hearts; they are then to be examined by the superior (προέδρος) of the place; and then to bear bravely outside the cloister one year more, so that their purpose may be fully manifested. For by this they will shew fully and perfectly that they are not catching at vain glory, but that they are pursuing the life of solitude because of its inherent beauty and honour. After the completion of such a period, if they remain in the same intention in their choice of the life, they are to be enclosed, and no longer is it lawful for them to go out of such a house when they so desire, unless they be induced to do so for the common advantage, or other pressing necessity urging on to death; and then only with the blessing of the bishop of that place.

And those who, without the above-mentioned causes, venture forth of their convents, are first of all to be shut up in the said convent even against their wills, and then are to cure themselves with fasting and other afflictions, knowing how it is written that "no one who has put his hand to the plough and has looked back, is fit for the kingdom of heaven."

NOTES.

ANCIENT EPITOME OF CANON XLI.

Whoever is about to enter a cloister, let him live for three years in a monastery, and before he is shut up let him spend one year more, and so let him be shut up. And he shall not then go forth unless death or the common good demands.

VAN ESPEN.

This canon, so far as it sets forth the necessity of probation before admission to the Anchorite life, synods in after-years frequently approved, taught as they were by experience how perilous a matter it is to admit without sufficient probation to this solitary life and state of separation from the common intercourse with his fellow men. Vide the Synod of Vannes (about A.D. 465) canon vij., of Agde chap. lxxviij., of Orleans the First can. xxij., of Frankfort can. xij., of Toledo the Seventh can. v., and the *Capitular* of Charlemagne *To monks*, Chap. ij.

CANON XLII.

THOSE who are called Eremites and are clothed in black robes, and with long hair go about cities and associate with the worldly both men and women and bring odium upon their profession—we decree that if they will receive the habit of other monks and wear their hair cut short, they may be shut up in a monastery and numbered among the brothers; but if they do not choose to do this, they are to be expelled from the cities and forced to live in the desert (ἐρήμους) from whence also they derive their name.

NOTES.

ANCIENT EPITOME OF CANON XLII.

An eremite dressed in black vesture and not having his hair cut, unless he has his hair cut shall be expelled the city and be shut up in his monastery.

It may not be irreverent to remark that this species of impostors always has been common in the East, and many examples will be found of the dervishes in the *Arabian Nights* and other Eastern tales. The "vagabond" monks of the West also became a great nuisance as well as a scandal in the Middle Ages. The reader will find interesting instances of Spanish deceivers of the same sort in "Gil Blas" and other Spanish romances.

---

[1] The Latin adds, "That is, separate and remote from others."

CANON XLIII.

It is lawful for every Christian to choose the life of religious discipline, and setting aside the troublous surgings of the affairs of this life to enter a monastery, and to be shaven in the fashion of a monk, without regard to what faults he may have previously committed. For God our Saviour says: "Whoso cometh to me, I will in no wise cast out."

As therefore the monastic method of life engraves upon us as on a tablet the life of penitence, we receive[1] whoever approaches it[2] sincerely; nor is any custom to be allowed to hinder him from fulfilling his intention.

NOTES.

Ancient Epitome of Canon XLIII.

Whoever flees from the surging billows of life and desires to enter a monastery, shall be allowed to do so.

Zonaras.

The greatness or the number of a man's sins ought not to make him lose hope of propitiating the divinity by his penitence, if he turns his eyes to the divine mercy. This is what the canon asserts, and affirms that everyone, no matter how wicked and nefarious his life may have been, may embrace monastic discipline, which inscribes, as on a tablet,[3] to us a life of penitence. For as a tablet describes to us what is inscribed upon it, so the monastic profession writes and inscribes upon us penitence, so that it remains for ever.

CANON XLIV.

A monk convicted of fornication, or who takes a wife for the communion of matrimony and for society, is to be subjected to the penalties of fornicators, according to the canons.

NOTES.

Ancient Epitome of Canon XLIV.

A monk joined in marriage or committing fornication shall pay the penalty of a fornicator.

The punishment here seems too light, so that Balsamon thinks that this canon only refers to such monks as freely confess their sin and desist from it, remaining in their monasteries; and that the sterner penalties assigned to unchaste religious by other synods (notably Chalcedon, can. xvj., and Ancyra, can. xix.) are for such as do not confess their faults but are after some time convicted of them.

Aristenus.

The monk will receive the same punishment whether he be a fornicator or has joined himself with a woman for the communion of marriage.

Van Espen.

It is very likely from this canon that the Monastic vow at the time of this Synod was not yet an *impedimentum dirimens* of matrimony, for nothing is said about the dissolution of the marriage contracted by a monk although he had gravely sinned in violating his faith pledged to God.

CANON XLV.

Whereas we understand that in some monasteries of women those who are about to be clothed with the sacred habit are first adorned in silks and garments of all kinds, and also with gold and jewels, by those who bring them thither, and that they thus approach the altar and are there stripped of such a display of wealth, and that immediately thereafter the blessing of their habit takes place, and they are clothed with the black robe; we decree that henceforth this shall not be done.

For it is not lawful for her who has already of her own free will put away every

---

[1] Latin adds "and favour."
[2] Latin reads, "germanely and sincerely."
[3] Beveridge translates στύλη by *columna* but I think incorrectly. *Cf.* Liddell and Scott.

delight of life, and has embraced that method of life which is according to God, and has confirmed it with strong and stable reasons, and so has come to the monastery, to recall to memory the things which they had already forgotten, things of this world which perisheth and passeth away. For thus they raise in themselves doubts, and are disturbed in their souls, like the tossing waves, turning hither and thither. Moreover, they should not give bodily evidence of heaviness of heart by weeping, but if a few tears drop from their eyes, as is like enough to be the case, they may be supposed by those who see them to have flowed μὴ μᾶλλον on account of their affection (διαθέσεως, affectionem) for the ascetic struggle rather than (ἢ) because they are quitting the world and worldly things.

NOTES.

ANCIENT EPITOME OF CANON XLV.

Parents shall not deck out in silks a daughter who has chosen the monastic life, and thus clothe her, *for this is a recalling to her mind the world she is leaving.*

This canon is at the present day constantly broken at the profession of Carmelites.

CANON XLVI.

THOSE women who choose the ascetic life and are settled in monasteries may by no means go forth of them. If, however, any inexorable necessity compels them, let them do so with the blessing and permission of her who is mother superior; and even then they must not go forth alone, but with some old women who are eminent in the monastery, and at the command of the lady superior. But it is not at all permitted that they should stop outside.

And men also who follow the monastic life let them on urgent necessity go forth with the blessing of him to whom the rule is entrusted.

Wherefore, those who transgress that which is now decreed by us, whether they be men or women, are to be subjected to suitable punishments.

NOTES.

ANCIENT EPITOME OF CANON XLVI.

A nun shall not go out of her convent without the consent of her superior, nor shall she go alone but with an older one of the order. It is in *no case permitted to her to spend the night outside. The same is the case with a monk; he cannot go out of the monastery without the consent of the superior.*

CANON XLVII.

No woman may sleep in a monastery of men, nor any man in a monastery of women. For it behoves the faithful to be without offence and to give no scandal, and to order their lives decorously and honestly and acceptably to God. But if any one shall have done this, whether he be cleric or layman, let him be cut off.

NOTES.

ANCIENT EPITOME OF CANON XLVII.

It is not allowed that a woman should sleep in a convent of men, nor a man in a monastery of women.

The ground covered by this canon is also found in Justinian's Code, Book xliv., *Of Bishops and Clergy. Vide* also *Novella cxxxiii.,* chap. v.

VAN ESPEN.

From the whole context of Justinian's law it is manifest that Justinian here is condemning "double monasteries," in which both men and women dwelt. And he wishes such to be separated, the men from the women, and *e contra* the women from the men, and that each should dwell in separate monasteries.

The reader may be reminded of some curious double religious houses in England for men and women, of which sometimes a woman was the superior of both.

CANON XLVIII.

THE wife of him who is advanced to the Episcopal dignity, shall be separated from her husband by their mutual consent, and after his ordination and consecration to the episcopate she shall enter a monastery situated at a distance from the abode of the bishop, and there let her enjoy the bishop's provision.   And if she is deemed worthy she may be advanced to the dignity of a deaconess.

NOTES.

ANCIENT EPITOME OF CANON XLVIII.
She who is separated from one about to be consecrated bishop, shall enter a monastery after his ordination, *situated at a distance from the See city, and she shall be provided for by the bishop.*

CANON XLIX.

RENEWING also the holy canon, we decree that the monasteries which have been once consecrated by the Episcopal will, are always to remain monasteries, and the things which belong to them are to be preserved to the monastery, and they cannot any more be secular abodes nor be given by any one to seculars.   But if anything of this kind has been done already, we declare it to be null ; and those who hereafter attempt to do so are to be subjected to canonical penalties.

NOTES.

ANCIENT EPITOME OF CANON XLIX.
Monasteries built with the consent of the bishop shall not afterwards be turned into secular houses, nor shall they pass into the hands of seculars.

VAN ESPEN.
This canon renews canon xxiv. of Chalcedon.   And here it may be observed that the canons even of Ecumenical Synods fall into desuetude little by little, unless the care of bishops and pastors keeps them alive, and from the example of this synod it may be seen how often they need calling back again into observance.

Nor can there be any doubt that frequently it would be more advantageous to renew the canons already set forth by the Fathers, rather than to frame new ones.

CANON L.

No one at all, whether cleric or layman, is from this time forward to play at dice. And if any one hereafter shall be found doing so, if he be a cleric he is to be deposed, if a layman let him be cut off.

NOTES.

ANCIENT EPITOME OF CANON L.
A layman should not play at dice.

This renews canons xlii. and xliij. of the Apostolic canons.

CANON LI.

THIS holy and ecumenical synod altogether forbids those who are called "players," and their "spectacles," as well as the exhibition of hunts, and the theatrical dances.   If any one despises the present canon, and gives himself to any of the things which are forbidden, if he be a cleric he shall be deposed, but if a layman let him be cut off.

NOTES.

ANCIENT EPITOME OF CANON LI.
Whoso shall play as an actor or shall attend theatrical representations or hunts shall be cut off.   Should he be a cleric he shall be deposed.

BALSAMON.
Some one will enquire why canon xxiiij. decrees that those in holy orders and monks, who are constantly attending horse-races, and

scenic plays, are to cease or be deposed : but the present canon says without discrimination, that those who give themselves over to such things if clergymen are to be deposed, and if laymen to be cut off. The solution is this. It is one thing and more easily to be endured, that a man should be present at a horse-race, or be convicted of going to see a play ; and another thing, and one that cannot be pardoned, that he should give himself over to such things, and to exercise this continually as his business. Wherefore those who have once sinned deliberately, are admonished to cease. If they are not willing to obey, they are to be deposed. But those who are constantly engaged in this wickedness, if they are clerics, they must be deposed from their clerical place, if laymen they must be cut off.

CANON LII.

ON all days of the holy fast of Lent, except on the Sabbath, the Lord's day and the holy day of the Annunciation, the Liturgy of the Presanctified is to be said.

NOTES.

ANCIENT EPITOME OF CANON LII.

Throughout the whole of Lent except upon the Lord's day, the Sabbath, and upon the day of the Annunciation, the presanctified gifts shall be offered.

BALSAMON.

We do not call the service of the Presanctified the unbloody sacrifice, but the offering of the previously offered, and of the perfected sacrifice, and of the completed priestly act.

VAN ESPEN.

The Greeks therefore confess that the bread once offered and consecrated, is not to be consecrated anew on another day ; but a new offering is made of what was before consecrated and presanctified : just as in the Latin Church the consecrated or presanctified bread of Maundy Thursday is offered on Good Friday.

The Patriarch Michael of Constantinople is quoted by Leo Allatius as saying that "none of the mystic consecratory prayers are said over the presanctified gifts, but the priest only recites the prayer that he may be a worthy communicant."

Some among the later Greeks have been of opinion that the unconsecrated wine was consecrated by the commixture with the consecrated bread, and (without any words of consecration) was transmuted into the sacred blood,[1] and with this seems to agree the already quoted Michael, Patriarch of Constantinople, who is cited by Leo Allatius in his treatise on the rite of the presanctified. "The presanctified is put into the mystic chalice, and so the wine which was then in it, is changed into the holy blood of the Lord." And with this agrees Simeon, Archbishop of Thessalonica, in his answer to Gabriel of Pentapolis, when he writes : "In the mass of the Presanctified no consecration of what is in the chalice is made by the invocation of the Holy Spirit and of his sign, but by the participation and union of the life-giving bread, which is truly the body of Christ."

From this opinion, which was held by some of the Greeks, it gradually became the practice at Constantinople not to dip the bread in the Sacred Blood, as Michael the patriarch of this very church testifies. But in the ordinary *Euchologion* of the Greeks it is expressly set forth that the presanctified bread before it is reserved, should be dipped in the sacred blood, and for this a rite is provided.

Leo Allatius's *Dissertatio de Missa Præsanctificatorum* should be read ; an outline of the service as found in the *Euchologion*, and as reprinted by Renaudotius is as follows.

First of all vespers is said. After some lessons and prayers, including the "Great Ectenia" and that for the Catechumens, these are dismissed.

After the Catechumens have departed there follows the Ectenia of the Faithful. After which, "Now the heavenly Powers invisibly minister with us ; for, behold, the King of Glory is borne in. Behold the mystic sacrifice having been perfected is borne aloft by angels.

"Let us draw near with faith and love, that we may become partakers of life eternal. Alleluia, Alleluia, Alleluia.

"*Deacon.* Let us accomplish our evening prayer to the Lord.

"For the precious and presanctified gifts that are offered, let us pray to the Lord.

"That our man-loving God, etc." as in the

---

[1] Gerbert makes it quite evident that from about 850 until 1200, that is from Amalarius until Durand, the same view was held in the West. *Vide* Gerbertus. *Vetus Liturgia Allomanica,* p. 855 *et seqq.*

ordinary liturgy past the Lord's prayer, and down to the *Sancta Sanctis*, which reads as follows :

Priest. Holy things presanctified for holy persons.

Choir. One holy, one Lord Jesus Christ, to the Glory of God the Father—Amen.

Then the Communion Hymn and the Communion, and the rest as in the ordinary liturgy, except " this whole evening," is said for "this whole day," and another prayer is provided in the room of that beginning " Lord, who blessest them, etc." [1]

It is curious to note that on Good Friday, the only day on which the Mass of the Presanctified is celebrated in the West, its use has died out in the East, and now it is used " on the Wednesdays and Fridays of the first six weeks of the Great Quadragesima, on the Thursday of the fifth week, and on the Monday, Tuesday, and Wednesday of Holy Passion Week. It may also be said, excepting on Saturdays and Sundays, and on the Festival of the Annunciation, on other days during the Fast, to wit, on those of festivals and their Vigils, and on the Commemoration of the Dedication of the Church."

Symeon, who was bishop of Thessalonica, and flourished in the early part of the XVth Century, complains of the general neglect of the Mass of the Presanctified on Good Friday in his time, and says that his church was the only one in the Exarchate that then retained it. He ascribes the disuse to the example of the Church of Jerusalem. See the matter treated at length in his *Quæstiones*, lv–lix. Migne's *Pat. Græc.*

Cf. J. M. Neale *Essays on Liturgiology*, p. 109.

CANON LIII.

WHEREAS the spiritual relationship is greater than fleshly affinity ; and since it has come to our knowledge that in some places certain persons who become sponsors to children in holy salvation-bearing baptism, afterwards contract matrimony with their mothers (being widows), we decree that for the future nothing of this sort is to be done. But if any, after the present canon, shall be observed to do this, they must, in the first place, desist from this unlawful marriage, and then be subjected to the penalties of fornicators.

NOTES.

ANCIENT EPITOME OF CANON LIII.

Godfathers cannot be permitted to be married with the mother of their godchildren. If any one is so joined, let him do penance after separation.

JOHNSON.

(*Clergyman's Vade Mecum.*)

The imperial law forbade the adopter parent to marry his or her adopted son or daughter ; for the godchild was thought a sort of an adopted child. See Justin., *Institut.*, Lib. I., Tit. x.

Van Espen however refers, and to my mind with greater truth, to Justinian's law (xxvj of the *Cod. de Nuptiis*) which forbids the marriage of a man with his nurse or with whoever received him from the font, " because," says the law, "nothing can so incite to parental affection, and therefore induce a just prohibition of marriage, than a bond of this sort by which, through God's meditation, their souls are bound together."

CANON LIV.

THE divine scriptures plainly teach us as follows, " Thou shalt not approach to any that is near of kin to thee to uncover their nakedness." Basil, the bearer-of-God, has enumerated in his canons some marriages which are prohibited and has passed over the greater part in silence, and in both these ways has done us good service. For by avoiding a number of disgraceful names (lest by such words he should pollute his discourse) he included impurities under general terms, by which course he shewed to us in a general way the marriages which are forbidden. But since by such silence, and because of the difficulty of understanding what marriages are prohibited, the matter has become confused ; it seemed good to us to set it forth a little more clearly, decreeing that from this time forth he who shall marry with the daughter of his father ; or a father or son with a mother and daughter ; or a father and son with two girls who are

---

[1] The English reader is referred to G. V. Shann, *Euchology*, and *The Book of Needs*, for excellent translations of the Greek offices ; J. M. Neale's *Introduction to the History of the Holy Orthodox Eastern Church* will, of course, be consulted.

sisters; or a mother and daughter with two brothers; or two brothers with two sisters, fall under the canon of seven years, provided they openly separate from this unlawful union.

ANCIENT EPITOME OF CANON LIV.	riage of a son and his father; neither a mother

ANCIENT EPITOME OF CANON LIV.

Thou shalt not permit the marriage of a son of a brother to the daughter of a brother; nor with a daughter and her mother shall there be the mar-

riage of a son and his father; neither a mother and a daughter with two brothers; nor brothers with two sisters. But should anything of this sort have been done, together with separation, penance shall be done for seven years.

CANON LV.

SINCE we understand that in the city of the Romans, in the holy fast of Lent they fast on the Saturdays, contrary to the ecclesiastical observance which is traditional, it seemed good to the holy synod that also in the Church of the Romans the canon shall immovably stand fast which says: "If any cleric shall be found to fast on a Sunday or Saturday (except on one occasion only) he is to be deposed; and if he is a layman he shall be cut off."

NOTES.

ANCIENT EPITOME OF CANON LV.

The Romans fast the Sabbaths of Lent. Therefore this Synod admonishes that upon these days the Apostolical canon is of force.

The canon quoted is LXVI. of the Apostolic Canons.

VAN ESPEN.

The Fathers of this Synod thought that this canon of the Apostles was edited by the Apostles themselves, and therefore they seem to have reprobated the custom of the Roman Church of fasting on the Sabbath more bitterly than was right. Whence it happens

this is one of those canons which the Roman Church never received.

ZONARAS.

The synod took in hand to correct this failing (σφάλμα) of the Latins; but until this time they have arrogantly remained in their pertinacity, and so remain to-day. Nor do they heed the ancient canons which forbid fasting on the Sabbath except that one, to wit the great Sabbath, nor are they affected by the authority of this canon. Moreover the clerics have no regard for the threatened deposition, nor the laymen for their being cut off.

CANON LVI.

WE have likewise learned that in the regions of Armenia and in other places certain people eat eggs and cheese on the Sabbaths and Lord's days of the holy lent. It seems good therefore that the whole Church of God which is in all the world should follow one rule and keep the fast perfectly, and as they abstain from everything which is killed, so also should they from eggs and cheese, which are the fruit and produce of those animals from which we abstain. But if any shall not observe this law, if they be clerics, let them be deposed; but if laymen, let them be cut off.

NOTES.

ANCIENT EPITOME OF CANON LVI.

Armenians eat eggs and cheese on the Sabbaths in Lent. It is determined that the whole world should abstain from these. If not let the offender be cast out.

VAN ESPEN.

This canon shows that the ancient Greeks,

although they did not fast on the Sabbaths and Lord's days of Lent, nevertheless they abstained on them from flesh food; and it was believed by them that abstinence from flesh food involved also necessarily abstinence from all those things which have their origin from flesh. This also formerly was observed by the Latins in Lent, and in certain regions is known still to be the usage.

CANON LVII.

IT is not right to offer honey and milk on the altar.

NOTES.

ANCIENT EPITOME OF CANON LVII.

No one should offer honey or milk at the altar.

See canon iij. of the Apostles, canon xxviij.

of the African code, also canon xxviij. of this synod. The Greeks apparently do not recognize the exception specified in the canon of the African Code.

CANON LVIII.

NONE of those who are in the order of laymen may distribute the Divine Mysteries to himself if a bishop, presbyter, or deacon be present. But whoso shall dare to do such a thing, as acting contrary to what has been determined shall be cut off for a week and thenceforth let him learn not to think of himself more highly than he ought to think.

NOTES.

ANCIENT EPITOME OF CANON LVIII.

A layman shall not communicate himself. Should he do so, let him be cut off for a week.

VAN ESPEN.

It is well known that in the first centuries it was customary that the Holy Eucharist should be taken back by the faithful to their houses; and that at home they received it at their own hands. It is evident that this was what was done by the Anchorites and monks who lived in the deserts, as may be seen proved by Cardinal Bona. (*De Rebus Liturg.*, Lib. II., cap. xvij.). From this domestic communion it is easily seen how the abuse arose which is condemned in this canon.

CANON LIX.

BAPTISM is by no means to be administered in an oratory which is within a house; but they who are about to be held worthy of the spotless illumination are to go to a Catholic Church and there to enjoy this gift. But if any one shall be convicted of not observing what we have determined, if he be a cleric let him be deposed, if a layman let him be cut off.

ANCIENT EPITOME OF CANON LIX.

In oratories built in houses they shall not cele-brate baptism. Whoever shall not observe this, if a cleric he shall be deposed, if a layman he shall be cut off.

CANON LX.

SINCE the Apostle exclaims that he who cleaves to the Lord is one spirit, it is clear that he who is intimate with his [i.e. the Lord's] enemy becomes one by his affinity with him. Therefore, those who pretend they are possessed by a devil and by their depravity of manners feign to manifest their form and appearance; it seems good by all means that they should be punished and that they should be subjected to afflictions and hardships of the same kind as those to which they who are truly demoniacally possessed are justly subjected with the intent of delivering them from the [work or rather] energy of the devil.

NOTES.

ANCIENT EPITOME OF CANON LX.

Whoever shall pretend to be possessed by a devil, shall endure the penance of demoniacs.

Zonaras says in his scholion that even in his day people made the same claim to diabolical possession.

CANON LXI.

THOSE who give themselves up to soothsayers or to those who are called hecaton-tarchs or to any such, in order that they may learn from them what things[1] they wish to have revealed to them, let all such, according to the decrees lately made by the Fathers concerning them, be subjected to the canon of six years. And to this [penalty] they also should be subjected who carry about[2] she-bears or animals of the kind for the diversion and injury of the simple; as well as those who tell fortunes and fates, and genealogy, and a multitude of words of this kind from the nonsense of deceit and imposture. Also those who are called expellers of clouds, enchanters, amulet-givers, and soothsayers.

And those who persist in these things, and do not turn away and flee from pernicious and Greek pursuits of this kind, we declare are to be thrust out of the Church, as also the sacred canons say. "For what fellowship hath light with darkness?" as saith the Apostle, "or what agreement is there between the temple of God and idols? or what part hath he that believeth with an infidel? And what concord hath Christ with Belial?"

NOTES.

ANCIENT EPITOME OF CANON LXI.

Whoever shall deliver himself over to a heca-tontarch or to devils, so as to learn some secret, he shall be put under penance for six years. So too those who take around a bear, who join themselves with those who seek incantations and drive away the clouds, and have faith in fortune and fate, shall be cast out of the assembly of the Church.

HEFELE.

According to Balsamon (in Beveridge, *Synod.*, Tom. I., p. 228) old people who had the reputation of special knowledge [were called "hecatontarchs"]. They sold the hair [of these she bears and other animals] as medicine or for an amulet. *Cf.* Balsamon and Zonaras *ut supra*.

St. Chrysostom in his *Homilies on the Statutes* explains, in answer to certain who defended them on this ground, that if these incanta-tions are made in the name of Christ they are so much the worse. The Saint says, "More-over I think that she is to be hated all the more who abuses the name of God for this purpose, because while professing to be a Christian, she shows by her actions that she is a heathen."

CANON LXII.

THE so-called Calends, and what are called Bota and Brumalia, and the full assembly which takes place on the first of March, we wish to be abolished from the life of the faithful. And also the public dances of women, which may do much harm and mis-chief. Moreover we drive away from the life of Christians the dances given in the names of those falsely called gods by the Greeks whether of men or women, and which are performed after an ancient and un-Christian fashion; decreeing that no man from this time forth shall be dressed as a woman, nor any woman in the garb suitable to men. Nor shall he assume comic, satyric, or tragic masks; nor may men invoke the name of the execrable Bacchus when they squeeze out the wine in the presses; nor when pour-ing out wine into jars [to cause a laugh[3]], practising in ignorance and vanity the things which proceed from the deceit of insanity. Therefore those who in the future attempt any of these things which are written, having obtained a knowledge of them, if they be clerics we order them to be deposed, and if laymen to be cut off.

NOTES.

ANCIENT EPITOME OF CANON LXII.

Let these be taken away from the lives of the faithful, viz.: the Bota, and the Calends, and the Brumalia, and salutations in honour of the gods, and comic, satyric and tragic masks, and the in-vocation of Bacchus at the wine press, and the laughing at the wine jars. Whoever shall persist in these after this canon shall be liable to give an account.

---

[1] Bev. reads ὅτι. [2] Bev. reads ἐπιφερομένως. [3] Not found in Mansi.

On the *Calends* see Du Cange (*Glossarium* in loc.). The *Bota* were feasts in honour of Pan, the *Brumalia* feasts in honour of Bacchus. Many particulars with regard to these superstitions will be found in Balsamon's scholion, to which the curious reader is referred. Van Espen also has some valuable notes on the Kalends of January.

CANON LXIII.

WE forbid to be publicly read in Church, histories of the martyrs which have been falsely put together by the enemies of the truth, in order to dishonour the martyrs of Christ and induce unbelief among those who hear them, but we order that such books be given to the flames. But those who accept them or apply their mind to them as true we anathematize.

NOTES.

ANCIENT EPITOME OF CANON LXIII.

Martyrologies made up by the ethnics (Ἑλληνων) *shall not be published in church.*

What is condemned is false histories of true martyrs, not (as Johnson erroneously supposes) "false legends of pretended martyrs." There have been martyrs, both royal and plebeian, in much later times whose lives have been made ridiculous and whose memory has been rendered hateful to the ignorant people by so-called "histories" which might well have received the treatment ordered by the canon.

CANON LXIV.

IT does not befit a layman to dispute or teach publicly, thus claiming for himself authority to teach, but he should yield to the order appointed by the Lord, and to open his ears to those who have received the grace to teach, and be taught by them divine things; for in one Church God has made "different members," according to the word of the Apostle: and Gregory the Theologian, wisely interpreting this passage, commends the order in vogue with them saying:[1] "This order brethren we revere, this we guard. Let this one be the ear; that one the tongue, the hand or any other member. Let this one teach, but let that one learn." And a little further on: "Learning in docility and abounding in cheerfulness, and ministering with alacrity, we shall not all be the tongue which is the more active member, not all of us Apostles, not all prophets, nor shall we all interpret." And again: "Why dost thou make thyself a shepherd when thou art a sheep? Why become the head when thou art a foot? Why dost thou try to be a commander when thou art enrolled in the number of the soldiers?" And elsewhere: "Wisdom orders, Be not swift in words; nor compare thyself with the rich, being poor; nor seek to be wiser than the wise." But if any one be found weakening the present canon, he is to be cut off for forty days.

NOTES.

ANCIENT EPITOME OF CANON LXIV.

A layman shall not teach, for all are not prophets, nor all apostles.

Zonaras points out that this canon refers only to public instruction and not to private. Van Espen further notes that in the West this restriction is limited to the solemn and public preaching and announcing of the Word of God, which is restricted to bishops, and only by special and express license given to the other clergy, and refers to his own treatment of the subject *In jure Eccles.*, Tom I., part 1, tit. xvj., cap. viij.

CANON LXV.

THE fires which are lighted on the new moons by some before their shops and houses, upon which (according to a certain ancient custom) they are wont foolishly and crazily to leap, we order henceforth to cease. Therefore, whosoever shall do such a thing, if he be a cleric, let him be deposed; but if he be a layman, let him be cut off.

---

[1] λέγων in Beveridge's text.

For it is written in the Fourth Book of the Kings "And Manasses built an altar to the whole host of heaven, in the two courts of the Lord, and made his sons to pass through the fire, he used lots and augurs and divinations by birds and made ventriloquists [or pythons[1]] and multiplied diviners, that he might do evil before the Lord and provoke him to anger." [2]

NOTES.

ANCIENT EPITOME OF CANON LXV.

The fires which were made upon the new moons at the workshops are condemned and those who leaped upon them.

Lupin remarks that the fires kindled on certain Saints' days are almost certainly remains of this heathen practice. These fires are often accompanied with leaping, drinking, and the wrestling of young men.

CANON LXVI.

FROM the holy day of the Resurrection of Christ our God until the next Lord's day, for a whole week, in the holy churches the faithful ought to be free from labour, rejoicing in Christ with psalms and hymns and spiritual songs; and celebrating the feast, and applying their minds to the reading of the holy Scriptures, and delighting in the Holy Mysteries; for thus shall we be exalted with Christ and together with him be raised up. Therefore, on the aforesaid days there must not be any horse races or any public spectacle.

NOTES.

ANCIENT EPITOME OF CANON LXVI.

The faithful shall every one of them go to church during the whole week after Easter.

VAN ESPEN.

It is certain that the whole of Easter week was kept as a feast by the whole Church both East and West; and this Synod did not introduce this custom by its canon, but adopted this canon to ensure its continuance.

Here we have clearly set forth the Christian

manner of passing a feast-day, viz., that the faithful on those days did give themselves up to "Psalms and Hymns and Spiritual Songs," from which the divine office which we call to-day canonical [i.e., chiefly Mattins and Vespers] are made up ; and hence we understand that all the faithful ought to attend the choir-offices, which was indeed observed for many centuries, as I have shewn in my *Dissertation on the Canonical Hours*, cap. III., § 1, and therefore it was called "public" [or common] prayer.

CANON LXVII.

THE divine Scripture commands us to abstain from blood, from things strangled, and from fornication. Those therefore who on account of a dainty stomach prepare by any art for food the blood of any animal, and so eat it, we punish suitably. If anyone henceforth venture to eat in any way the blood of an animal, if he be a clergyman, let him be deposed; if a layman, let him be cut off.

NOTES.

ANCIENT EPITOME OF CANON LXVII.

A cleric eating blood shall be deposed, but a layman shall be cut off.

VAN ESPEN.

The apostolic precept of abstaining "from blood and from things strangled" for some ages, not only among the Greeks but also among the Latins, was observed in many churches, but little by little and step by step

it died out in the whole Church, at least in the Latin Church, altogether.

In this the Latin Church followed the opinion of St. Augustine, *Contra Faustum Manichœum*, Lib. XXXII., cap. xiij., where he teaches at great length that the precept was given to Christians only while the Gentile Church was not yet settled. This passage of Augustine also proves that at that time Africa did not observe this precept of the Apostles.

---

[1] Only in the Latin. [2] II. Kgs. xxi. 5 & 6.

CANON LXVIII.

IT is unlawful for anyone to corrupt or cut up a book of the Old or New Testament or of our holy and approved preachers and teachers, or to give them up to the traders in books or to those who are called perfumers, or to hand it over for destruction to any other like persons: unless to be sure it has been rendered useless either by bookworms, or by water, or in some other way. He who henceforth shall be observed to do such a thing shall be cut off for one year. Likewise also he who buys such books (unless he keeps them for his own use, or gives them to another for his benefit to be preserved) and has attempted to corrupt them, let him be cut off.

NOTES.

ANCIENT EPITOME OF CANON LXVIII.

Thou shalt not destroy nor hand over copies of the Divine Scriptures to be destroyed unless they are absolutely useless.

VAN ESPEN.
(Foot-note.)

I think that this canon was directed against certain Nestorian and Eutychian heretics, who, that they might find some patronage of their errors from the Holy Scriptures, dared in the sixth century most infamously to corrupt certain passages of the New Testament.

CANON LXIX.

IT is not permitted to a layman to enter the sanctuary (Holy Altar, Gk.), though, in accordance with a certain ancient tradition, the imperial power and authority is by no means prohibited from this when he wishes to offer his gifts to the Creator.

NOTES.

ANCIENT EPITOME OF CANON LXIX.
No layman except the Emperor shall go up to the altar.

VAN ESPEN.

That in the Latin Church as well as in the Greek for many centuries it was the constant custom, ratified by various councils, that laymen are to be excluded from the sanctuary and from the place marked off for the priests who are celebrating the divine mysteries, is so notorious as to need no proof, and the present canon shows that among the Greeks the laity were not admitted to the *sacrarium* even to make offerings.

The Synod makes but one exception, to wit, the Emperor, who can enter the rails of the holy altar by its permission "when he wishes to offer his gifts to the Creator, according to ancient custom."

Not without foundation does the Synod claim "ancient custom" for this; for long

before, it is evident, it was the case from the words of the Emperor Theodosius the Younger. See also Theodoret (*H. E.*, lib. v., cap. xvij.).

In the Latin Church, not only to emperors, kings, and great princes but also to patrons of churches, to toparchs of places, and even to magistrates, seats have been wont to be assigned *honoris causâ* within the sanctuary or choir, and it has been contended that these are properly due to such persons.

It is evident from Balsamon's note that the later Greeks at least looked upon the Emperor as being (like the kings of England and France) a *persona mixta*, sharing in some degree the sacerdotal character, as being anointed not merely with oil, but with the sacred chrism. *Vide* in this connexion J. Wickham Legg, *The Sacring of the English Kings*, in "The Archæological Journal," March, 1894.

CANON LXX.

WOMEN are not permitted to speak at the time of the Divine Liturgy; but, according to the word of Paul the Apostle, "let them be silent. For it is not permitted to them to speak, but to be in subjection, as the law also saith. But if they wish to learn anything let them ask their own husbands at home."

NOTES.

ANCIENT EPITOME OF CANON LXX.

Women are not permitted to speak in church.

"Let your women keep silence in the churches; for it is not permitted unto them to speak," is the passage referred to. I. Cor. xiv. 34.

CANON LXXI.

THOSE who are taught the civil laws must not adopt the customs of the Gentiles, nor be induced to go to the theatre, nor to keep what are called *Cylestras*, nor to wear clothing contrary to the general custom; and this holds good when they begin their training, when they reach its end, and, in short, all the time of its duration. If any one from this time shall dare to do contrary to this canon he is to be cut off.

NOTES.

ANCIENT EPITOME OF CANON LXXI.

Whoever devotes himself to the study of law, uses the manner of the Gentiles, going to the theatre, and rolling in the dust, or dressing differently to custom, shall be cut off.

Liddell and Scott identify καλίστρα with καλινδήθρα, which they define as "a place for horses to roll after exercise," and note that it is a synonym of ἀλινδήθρα. But it is interesting to note that ἀλίνησις is "a rolling in the dust, an exercise in which wrestlers rolled on the ground."

Hefele says that Balsamon and Zonaras have not been able rightly to explain what we are to understand by the forbidden "Cylestras," but I think Johnson is not far out of the way when he translates "nor to meddle with athletic exercises."

CANON LXXII.

AN orthodox man is not permitted to marry an heretical woman, nor an orthodox woman to be joined to an heretical man. But if anything of this kind appear to have been done by any [we require them] to consider the marriage null, and that the marriage be dissolved. For it is not fitting to mingle together what should not be mingled, nor is it right that the sheep be joined with the wolf, nor the lot of sinners with the portion of Christ. But if any one shall transgress the things which we have decreed let him be cut off. But if any who up to this time are unbelievers and are not yet numbered in the flock of the orthodox have contracted lawful marriage between themselves, and if then, one choosing the right and coming to the light of truth and the other remaining still detained by the bond of error and not willing to behold with steady eye the divine rays, the unbelieving woman is pleased to cohabit with the believing man, or the unbelieving man with the believing woman, let them not be separated, according to the divine Apostle, "for the unbelieving husband is sanctified by the wife, and the unbelieving wife by her husband."

NOTES.

ANCIENT EPITOME OF CANON LXXII.

A marriage contracted with heretics is void. But if they have made the contract before [conversion] let them remain [united] if they so desire.

Perhaps none of the canons of this synod present greater and more insolvable difficulties than the present. It has been for long centuries the tradition of the Church that the marriage of a baptized Christian with an unbaptized person is null, but this canon seems to say that the same is the case if the one party be a heretic even though baptized. If this is what the canon means it elevates heresy into an *impedimentum dirimens*. Such is not and never has been the law of the West, and such is not to-day the practice of the Eastern church, which allows the marriage of its people with Lutherans and with Roman Catholics and never questions the validity of their marriages. Van Espen thinks "the Greek commentators seem" to think that the heretics referred to are unbaptized; I do not know exactly why he thinks so.

CANON LXXIII.

Since the life-giving cross has shewn to us Salvation, we should be careful that we render due honour to that by which we were saved from the ancient fall. Wherefore, in mind, in word, in feeling giving veneration (προσκύνησιν) to it, we command that the figure of the cross, which some have placed on the floor, be entirely removed therefrom, lest the trophy of the victory won for us be desecrated by the trampling under foot of those who walk over it. Therefore those who from this present represent on the pavement the sign of the cross, we decree are to be cut off.

NOTES.

Ancient Epitome of Canon LXXIII.

If there is a cross upon a pavement it must be removed.

This canon defines that to the image of the cross is to be "given veneration (προσκύνησις) of the intellect, of the words, and of the sense," i.e., the cross is to be venerated with the interior cultus of the soul, is to be venerated with the exterior culture of praise, and also with sensible acts, such as kissings, bowings, etc.

CANON LXXIV.

It is not permitted to hold what are called agapæ, that is love-feasts, in the Lord's houses or churches, nor to eat within the house, nor to spread couches. If any dare to do so let him cease therefrom or be cut off.

NOTES.

Ancient Epitome of Canon LXXIV.

Agapæ are not to be held in the churches, nor shall beds be put up. Whoso refuse to give up these, let them be cut off.

This is a renewal of canon xxviij., of Laodicea, on which canon see the notes.

CANON LXXV.

We will that those whose office it is to sing in the churches do not use undisciplined vociferations, nor force nature to shouting, nor adopt any of those modes which are incongruous and unsuitable for the church : but that they offer the psalmody to God, who is the observer of secrets, with great attention and compunction. For the Sacred Oracle taught that the Sons of Israel were to be pious.[1]

NOTES.

Ancient Epitome of Canon LXXV.

Inordinate vociferation of the psalms is not allowed, nor he that adopts things unsuited to the churches.

This question of the character of church-music was one early discussed among Christians, and (long before the time of this synod), St. Augustine, in debating as to whether the chanting or the reading of the psalter was the more edifying, concludes, "when the psalms are chanted with a voice and most suitable modulation (*liquida voce et convenientissima modulatione*), I recognize that there is great utility in the practice," and further on he adds that singing is to be the rather approved, because "by the delight given to the ears the infirm soul is worked up to pious aspirations." (*Confess.*, Lib. x., cap. xxxiij.).

CANON LXXVI.

It is not right that those who are responsible for reverence to churches should place within the sacred bounds an eating place, nor offer food there, nor make other sales. For God our Saviour teaching us when he was tabernacling in the flesh commanded not

---

[1] The Latin adds, " and holy."

to make his Father's house a house of merchandize. He also poured out the small coins of the money-changers, and drave out all those who made common the temple. If, therefore, anyone shall be taken in the aforesaid fault let him be cut off.

NOTES.

ANCIENT EPITOME OF CANON LXXVI.

A public house should not be established within the sacred precincts ; and it is wrong to sell food there ; and whosoever shall do so shall be cut off.

Both Balsamon and Zonaras remark that this canon refers to the vestibule of the church and to the rest of the sacred inclosure, and not to the interior of the church proper, for there no one would ever think of having a shop.

CANON LXXVII.

IT is not right that those who are dedicated to religion, whether clerics or ascetics,[1] should wash in the bath with women, nor should any Christian man or layman do so. For this is severely condemned by the heathens. But if any one is caught in this thing, if he is a cleric let him be deposed; if a layman, let him be cut off.

NOTES.

ANCIENT EPITOME OF CANON LXXVII.

A Christian man shall not bathe with women. Should a cleric do so he is to be deposed, and a layman cut off.

This is a renewal of the XXXth canon of Laodicea. It will be noted, as Zonaras remarks, that the monks must be counted among the laymen who are to be cut off, since they have no clerical character or tonsure.

CANON LXXVIII.

IT behoves those who are illuminated to learn the Creed by heart and to recite it to the bishop or presbyters on the Fifth Feria of the Week.

NOTES.

ANCIENT EPITOME OF CANON LXXVIII.
He that is illuminated is to recite (ἀπαγγελλέτω) the faith on the fifth feria of the week.

This is a renewal of canon xlvi. of Laodicea.

CANON LXXIX.

AS we confess the divine birth of the Virgin to be without any childbed, since it came to pass without seed, and as we preach this to the entire flock, so we subject to correction those who through ignorance do anything which is inconsistent therewith. Wherefore since some on the day after the holy Nativity of Christ our God are seen cooking σεμίδαλιν, and distributing it to each other, on pretext of doing honour to the *puerperia* of the spotless Virgin Maternity, we decree that henceforth nothing of the kind be done by the faithful. For this is not honouring the Virgin (who above thought and speech bare in the flesh the incomprehensible Word) when we define[2] and describe, from ordinary things and from such as occur with ourselves, her ineffable parturition. If therefore anyone henceforth be discovered doing any such thing, if he be a cleric let him be deposed, but if a layman let him be cut off.

NOTES.

ANCIENT EPITOME OF CANON LXXIX.

Whoever after the feast of the Mother of God

shall prepare σεμίδιλιν (semilam) or anything else on account of what is called puerperia, let him be cut off.

---

[1] The Latin adds "that is to say 'Exercisers,' (*Exercitatores*) or monks."   [2] The Latin adds "and measure."

As the Catholic Church has always taught the Virgin-birth as well as the Virgin-conception of our Blessed Lord, and has affirmed that Mary was ever-virgin, even after she had brought forth the incarnate Son, so it follows necessarily that there could be no childbed nor puerperal flux. It need hardly be remarked here that besides other texts that of the prophet is considered as teaching thus much, "Behold the Virgin (*ha alma*) shall conceive and bear a son," she that "bare" as well as she that "conceived" being a virgin. Some commentators have taken ἐπιλόχεια for the afterbirth, but Christian Lupus, as Van Espen notes, has pointed out that the early fathers seem to have recognized that the Virgin did have the "afterbirth," and this St. Jerome expressly teaches in his book, *Contra Helvidium.*

The Greeks, however, understood it as I have translated, and the witness of Zonaras will be sufficient. The words λοχος, λοχαιος and the like all signify "lying in," "a place of lying in," and Liddell and Scott say that the latter word is used of "bearing down like heavy ears of corn," which would well express the labour pains.

ZONARAS.

This canon teaches that the parturition of the holy Virgin was without any childbed. For childbed (*puerperium*) is the emission of the fœtus accompanied by pain and a flux of blood : but none of us ever believed that the Mother of God was subjected to sufferings of this sort, for these are the consequents of natural conception, but her conception was supernatural ; and by the Holy Spirit it was brought to pass that she was not subjected to those evils which rightly are attached to natural parturition.

On this canon should be read the extensive treatment of Asseman (*Bib. Juris Orient.*, Tom. v., pp. 193 *et seqq.*)

CANON LXXX.

IF any bishop, or presbyter, or deacon, or any of those who are enumerated in the list of the clergy, or a layman, has no very grave necessity nor difficult business so as to keep him from church for a very long time, but being in town does not go to church on three consecutive Sundays—three weeks—if he is a cleric let him be deposed, but if a layman let him be cut off.

NOTES.

ANCIENT EPITOME OF CANON LXXX.

If anyone without the constraint of necessity leaves his church for three Lord's days, he shall be deprived of communion.

This is a renewal of canon xi. of Sardica (xiv. according to the numbering of Dionysius Exiguus.)

CANON LXXXI.

WHEREAS we have heard that in some places in the hymn Trisagion there is added after " Holy and Immortal," " Who was crucified for us, have mercy upon us," and since this as being alien to piety was by the ancient and holy Fathers cast out of the hymn, as also the violent heretics who inserted these new words were cast out of the Church ; we also, confirming the things which were formerly piously established by our holy Fathers, anathematize those who after this present decree allow in church this or any other addition to the most sacred hymn; but if indeed he who has transgressed is of the sacerdotal order, we command that he be deprived of his priestly dignity, but if he be a layman or monk let him be cut off.

NOTES.

ANCIENT EPITOME OF CANON LXXXI.

Whoever adds to the hymn Trisagion these words " Who wast crucified" shall be deemed heterodox.

The addition of the phrase condemned by this canon was probably made first by Peter Fullo, and although indeed it was capable of a good meaning, if the whole hymn was understood as being addressed to Christ, and although this was admitted by very many of the orthodox, yet as it was chiefly used by the Monophysites and with an undoubtedly heretical intention, it was finally ousted from this position and its adherents were styled Theo-paschites. From all this it came about that by 518 it was a source of disagreement among the Catholics, some affirming the expression, as looked at by itself, to be a touchstone of orthodoxy. The Emperor Justinian tried to have it approved by Pope Hormisdas, but un-successfully, the pontiff only declaring that it was unnecessary, and even dangerous. Ful-gentius of Ruspe and Dionysius Exiguus had declared it orthodox. Pope John II. almost came to the point of approving the phrase " one of the Trinity suffered," nor did his suc-cessor Agapetus I. speak any more definitely on the point, but the Fifth Ecumenical Coun-cil directly approved the formula.

But this, of course. did not touch the point

of its introduction into the Trisagion or, more accurately, of the introduction of the words " who was crucified for us."

It should have been noted that at a Home Synod in 478, Peter Fullo had been deposed for the insertion of this clause, because he in-tended to imply that the true God had suf-fered death upon the cross. This sentence was a confirmation of one already pronounced against him by a synod held at Antioch which had raised a man, Stephen by name, to its episcopal throne.

Such is the history of a matter which, while it seemed at first as of little moment, yet for many years was a source of trouble in the Church. (*Vide* Hefele, *History of the Councils*, Vol. III., pp. 454, 457 ; Vol. IV., p. 26.)

CANON LXXXII.

IN some pictures of the venerable icons, a lamb is painted to which the Precursor points his finger, which is received as a type of grace, indicating beforehand through the Law, our true Lamb, Christ our God. Embracing therefore the ancient types and shadows as symbols of the truth, and patterns given to the Church, we prefer " grace and truth," receiving it as the fulfilment of the Law. In order therefore that " that which is perfect " may be delineated to the eyes of all, at least in coloured expression, we decree that the figure in human form of the Lamb who taketh away the sin of the world, Christ our God, be henceforth exhibited in images, instead of the ancient lamb, so that all may understand by means of it the depths of the humiliation of the Word of God, and that we may recall to our memory his conversation in the flesh, his passion and salutary death, and his redemption which was wrought for the whole world.

NOTES.

ANCIENT EPITOME OF CANON LXXXII.

Thou shalt not paint a lamb for the type of Christ, but himself.

As from this canon, a century earlier than the iconoclastic controversy, the prevalence of pictures is evident, so from the canon of the same synod with regard to the venera-tion due to the image of the cross (number lxxiii.), we learn that the teaching of the Church with regard to relative worship was the same as was subsequently set forth, so that the charge of innovating, sometimes rash-ly brought against the Seventh Ecumenical Council, has no foundation in fact whatever.

This canon is further interesting as being the one cited by more than one Pope and Western Authority as belonging to " the Sixth Synod."

CANON LXXXIII.

No one may give the Eucharist to the bodies of the dead ; for it is written " Take and eat." But the bodies of the dead can neither " take " nor " eat."

NOTES.

ANCIENT EPITOME OF CANON LXXXIII.

The Sacraments must not be given to a dead body.

This is canon iv. of the Council of Hippo,

in the year 393. (*Vide* Hefele, Vol. II , p. 397.) The earlier canon includes baptism also, in its prohibition. This is canons xviii. and xx. of the African code, according to the Greek numbering.

CANON LXXXIV.

FOLLOWING the canonical laws of the Fathers, we decree concerning infants, as often as they are found without trusty witnesses who say that they are undoubtedly baptized; and as often as they are themselves unable on account of their age to answer satisfactorily in respect to the initiatory mystery given to them; that they ought without any offence to be baptized, lest such a doubt might deprive them of the sanctification of such a purification.

NOTES.

ANCIENT EPITOME OF CANON LXXXIV.

Whoever do not know nor can prove by documents that they have been baptized, let them be christened.

This is canon VII., of the Sixth Council of Carthage, (*Vide* Hefele, *Hist. of the Councils*, Vol. II., p. 424); and Canon lxxv., of the African code (to which Balsamon attributes this canon), by the Greek numbering, (lxxii. by the Latin).

CANON LXXXV.

WE have received from the Scriptures that in the mouth of two or three witnesses every word shall be established. Therefore we decree that slaves who are manumitted by their masters in the presence of three witnesses shall enjoy that honour; for they being present at the time will add strength and stability to the liberty given, and they will bring it to pass that faith will be kept in those things which they now witness were done in their presence.

ANCIENT EPITOME OF CANON LXXXV.

A slave manumitted by his master before two witnesses shall be free.

CANON LXXXVI.

THOSE who to the destruction of their own souls procure and bring up harlots, if they be clerics, they are to be [cut off and] deposed, if laymen to be cut off.

NOTES.

ANCIENT EPITOME OF CANON LXXXVI.

Whoever gathers together harlots to the ruin of souls, shall be cut off.

The brackets enclose the reading of Hervetus. But Zonaras had this same text, and therefore it may be safely followed instead of that of Balsamon, as edited by Beveridge.

CANON LXXXVII.

SHE who has left her husband is an adulteress if she has come to another, according to the holy and divine Basil, who has gathered this most excellently from the prophet Jeremiah: "If a woman has become another man's, her husband shall not return to her, but being defiled she shall remain defiled;" and again, "He who has an adulteress is senseless and impious." If therefore she appears to have departed from her husband without reason, he is deserving of pardon and she of punishment. And pardon shall be given to him that he may be in communion with the Church. But he who leaves the wife lawfully given him, and shall take another is guilty of adultery by the sentence of the Lord. And it has been decreed by our Fathers that they who are such must be "weepers" for a year, "hearers" for two years, "prostrators" for three years, and in the seventh year to stand with the faithful and thus be counted worthy of the Oblation [if with tears they do penance.]

NOTES.

She who goes from her husband to another man is an adulteress. And he who from his wife goes to another woman is an adulterer according to the word of the Lord.

Compare with this canon lviij. of St. Basil.

The words in brackets are found in Beveridge, but were lacking in Hervetus's text.

JOHNSON.

Here discipline is relaxed ; formerly an adulteress did fifteen years' penance. See *Can. Bas.*, 58. No wonder if in 200 years' time from St. Basil, the severity of discipline was abated.

CANON LXXXVIII.

No one may drive any beast into a church except perchance a traveller, urged thereto by the greatest necessity, in default of a shed or resting-place, may have turned aside into said church. For unless the beast had been taken inside, it would have perished, and he, by the loss of his beast of burden, and thus without means of continuing his journey, would be in peril of death. And we are taught that the Sabbath was made for man : wherefore also the safety and comfort of man are by all means to be placed first. But should anyone be detected without any necessity such as we have just mentioned, leading his beast into a church, if he be a cleric let him be deposed, and if a layman let him be cut off.

ANCIENT EPITOME OF CANON LXXXVIIᵀ.

Cattle shall not be led into the holy halls, unless the greatest necessity compels it.

CANON LXXXIX.

THE faithful spending the days of the Salutatory Passion in fasting, praying and compunction of heart, ought to fast until the midnight of the Great Sabbath : since the divine Evangelists, Matthew and Luke, have shewn us how late at night it was [that the resurrection took place], the one by using the words ὀψὲ σαββάτων, and the other by the words ὄρθρου βαθέος.

ANCIENT EPITOME OF CANON LXXXIX.

On the Great Sabbath the fast must be continued until midnight.

CANON XC.

WE have received from our divine Fathers the canon law that in honour of Christ's resurrection, we are not to kneel on Sundays. Lest therefore we should ignore the fulness of this observance we make it plain to the faithful that after the priests have gone to the Altar for Vespers on Saturdays (according to the prevailing custom) no one shall kneel in prayer until the evening of Sunday, at which time after the entrance for compline, again with bended knees we offer our prayers to the Lord. For taking the night after the Sabbath, which was the forerunner of our Lord's resurrection, we begin from it to sing in the spirit hymns to God, leading our feast out of darkness into light, and thus during an entire day and night we celebrate the Resurrection.

NOTES.

ANCIENT EPITOME OF CANON XC.

From the evening entrance of the Sabbath until the evening entrance of the Lord's day there must be no kneeling.

VAN ESPEN.

No doubt the synod by the words "we have received from the divine Fathers," referred to canon xx. of the Council of Nice.

For many centuries this custom was preserved even in the Latin Church; and the custom of keeping feasts and whole days generally from evening to evening is believed to have been an Apostolic tradition, received by them from the Jews. At the end of the VIIIth Century the Synod of Frankfort declared in its xxj. canon, that "the Lord's day should be kept from evening to evening."[1]

CANON XCI.

THOSE who give drugs for procuring abortion, and those who receive poisons to kill the fœtus, are subjected to the penalty of murder.

NOTES.

ANCIENT EPITOME OF CANON XCI.

Whoever gives or receives medicine to produce abortion is a homicide.

See Canon XXI. of Ancyra, and Canon II. of St. Basil; to wit, "She who purposely destroys the fœtus, shall suffer the punishment of murder. And we pay no attention to the subtile distinction as to whether the fœtus was formed or unformed. And by this not only is justice satisfied for the child that should have been born, but also for her who prepared for herself the snares, since the women very often die who make such experiments."

CANON XCII.

THE holy synod decrees that those who in the name of marriage carry off women and those who in any way assist the ravishers, if they be clerics, they shall lose their rank, but if they be laymen they shall be anathematized.

NOTES.

ANCIENT EPITOME OF CANON XCII.

Those who run away with women, and those who assist and give a hand, if they be clerics they shall be deposed, if laymen they shall be anathematized.

VAN ESPEN.

This canon simply renews and confirms Canon xxvij of Chalcedon.

CANON XCIII.

IF the wife of a man who has gone away and does not appear, cohabit with another before she is assured of the death of the first, she is an adulteress. The wives of soldiers who have married husbands who do not appear are in the same case; as are also they who on account of the wanderings of their husbands do not wait for their return. But the circumstance here has some excuse, in that the suspicion of his death becomes very great. But she who in ignorance has married a man who at the time was deserted by his wife, and then is dismissed because his first wife returns to him, has indeed committed fornication, but through ignorance; therefore she is not prevented from marrying, but it is better if she remain as she is. If a soldier shall return after a long time, and find his wife on account of his long absence has been united to another man, if he so wishes, he may receive his own wife [back again], pardon being extended in consideration of their ignorance both to her and to the man who took her home in second marriage.

NOTES.

ANCIENT EPITOME OF CANON XCIII.

A woman who when her husband does not turn up, before she is certain he is dead, takes another commits adultery. But when the man returns he may receive her again, if he so elects.

Compare in the *Corpus Juris Canonici*, Gratian's *Decretum*, Pars II., Causa xxxiv., Quæst. I. and II. Epistle of St. Leo to Nicetas. Also compare of St. Basil's canons xxxj., xxxvj., and xlvj.

---

[1] "The evening and the morning were the first day."—Gen. i. 5.

CANON XCIV.

THE canon subjects to penalties those who take heathen oaths, and we decree to them excommunication.

NOTES.

Whoever uses Gentile oaths, is worthy of punishment, for he is cut off.

The reference is to canon lxxxj. of St. Basil's canons.

VAN ESPEN.

Tertullian (*De Idolatria*, cap. xx.) supposes that to swear by the false gods of the Gentiles, contains in itself some idolatry, an opinion shared by St. Basil, comparing those using such oaths with them who betrayed Christ, and who are partakers of the talk of devils.

CANON XCV.

THOSE who from the heretics come over to orthodoxy, and to the number of those who should be saved, we receive according to the following order and custom. Arians, Macedonians, Novatians, who call themselves Cathari, Aristeri, and Testareskaidecatitæ, or Tetraditæ, and Apollinarians, we receive on their presentation of certificates and on their anathematizing every heresy which does not hold as does the holy Apostolic Church of God: then first of all we anoint them with the holy chrism on their foreheads, eyes, nostrils, mouth and ears; and as we seal them we say—"The seal of the gift of the Holy Ghost."

But concerning the Paulianists it has been determined by the Catholic Church that they shall by all means be rebaptized. The Eunomeans also, who baptize with one immersion; and the Montanists, who here are called Phrygians; and the Sabellians, who consider the Son to be the same as the Father, and are guilty in certain other grave matters, and all the other heresies—for there are many heretics here, especially those who come from the region of the Galatians—all of their number who are desirous of coming to the Orthodox faith, we receive as Gentiles. And on the first day we make them Christians, on the second Catechumens, then on the third day we exorcise them, at the same time also breathing thrice upon their faces and ears; and thus we initiate them, and we make them spend time in church and hear the Scriptures; and then we baptize them.

And the Manichæans, and Valentinians and Marcionites and all of similar heresies must give certificates and anathematize each his own heresy, and also Nestorius, Eutyches, Dioscorus, Severus, and the other chiefs of such heresies, and those who think with them, and all the aforesaid heresies; and so they become partakers of the holy Communion.

NOTES.

Thus we admit those converted from the heretics. We anoint with the holy chrism, upon the brow, eyes, nostrils, mouth, and ears, Arians, Macedonians, Novatians (who are called Cathari), Aristerians (who are called Quartadecimans or Tetraditæ), and Apollinarians when they anathematize every heresy; and sign them with the cross as we say, "The Seal of the gift of the Holy Ghost. Amen."

Compare with this Canon vij. of Laodicea, and the so-called vijth. canon of the First Council of Constantinople.

The text I have translated is that ordinarily given, I now present to the reader Hefele's argument for its worthlessness.

HEFELE.

This text is undoubtedly false, for (*a*) the baptism of the Gnostics was, according to the recognized ecclesiastical principle, invalid, and a Gnostic coming into the Church was required to be baptized anew; (*b*) besides, it would have us first to require of a Gnostic an anathema on Nestorius, Eutyches, etc. More accurate, therefore, is the text, as it is given by Beveridge, and as Balsamon had it, to the effect that: "In the same way (as the preceding) are the Manichæans, Valentinians, Marcionites, and similar heretics to be treated (*i.e.*, to be baptized anew); but the Nestorians must (merely) present certificates, and anathematize their heresy, Nestorius, Eutyches, etc." Here we have only this mistake, that the Nestorians must anathematize, among others, also Eutyches, which they would certainly have done very willingly. At the best, we must suppose that there is a gap in the text, and that after, " all of similar heresies," we must add " the later heretics must present certificates and anathematize Nestorius, Eutyches, etc."

There seems but little doubt that whatever may be the truth in the matter, the early theologians and fathers held that even though the external rite of Holy Baptism might be validly performed by schismatics and heretics, yet that by it the person so baptized did not receive the Holy Ghost, and this opinion was not confined to the East, but was also prevalent in the West.   *Vide* Rupertus, *De Divinis Officiis*, Lib. X., Cap. xxv.

CANON XCVI.

THOSE who by baptism have put on Christ have professed that they will copy his manner of life which he led in the flesh.   Those therefore who adorn and arrange their hair to the detriment of those who see them, that is by cunningly devised intertwinings, and by this means put a bait in the way of unstable souls, we take in hand to cure paternally with a suitable punishment : training them and teaching them to live soberly, in order that having laid aside the deceit and vanity of material things, they may give their minds continually to a life which is blessed and free from mischief, and have their conversation in fear, pure, [and holy[1]] ; and thus come as near as possible to God through their purity of life; and adorn the inner man rather than the outer, and that with virtues, and good and blameless manners, so that they leave in themselves no remains of the left-handedness of the adversary.   But if any shall act contrary to the present canon let him be cut off.

NOTES.

ANCIENT EPITOME OF CANON XCVI.

Whoever twist up their hair into artistic plaits for the destruction of the beholders are to be cut off.

For the intricate manner of dressing the hair used in the East, and for a description of the golden dye, see the scholion of Zonaras. Van Espen remarks that the curious care for somebody else's hair in the form of wigs, so prevalent with many laymen and ecclesiastics of his day, is the same vice condemned by the canon in another shape.[2]

CANON XCVII.

THOSE who have commerce with a wife or in any other manner without regard thereto make sacred places common, and treat them with contempt and thus remain in them, we order all such to be expelled, even from the dwellings of the catechumens which are in the venerable temples.   And if any one shall not observe these directions, if he be a cleric let him be deposed, but if a layman let him be cut off.

NOTES.

ANCIENT EPITOME OF CANON XCVII.

Whoever in a temple has commerce with his wife and remains there out of contempt, shall be expelled even from the Catechumens.   If any one shall not observe this he shall be deposed or cut off.

ZONARAS.

In the name of holy places, not the church itself but the adjoining and dependent buildings are intended such as those which are called the " Catechumena." For no one would be audacious enough to wish to cohabit with his wife in the very temple itself.

CANON XCVIII.

HE who brings to the intercourse of marriage a woman who is betrothed to another man who is still alive, is to lie under the charge of adultery.

---

[1] These words only in the Latin.
[2] It is curious to note that so great was the care of the clergy for their wigs that the very shape of the vestments was changed so as not to disturb them, and the surplices were slit all the way down the front, as they continue in some places even down to our own days, after the original cause had long passed away.

NOTES.

ANCIENT EPITOME OF CANON XCVIII.

He is an adulterer who takes one espoused to some one else.

Aristenus's commentary on this canon is Σαφής. A more extraordinary estimate of it could hardly be made. So far from the meaning being "perspicuous," as the Latin translation has it, the meaning seems to be past finding out; for, as Van Espen remarks, a man who sins with a betrothed woman is certainly

not an "adulterer." He tries therefore to introduce the idea that though he is not an adulterer, yet he is to be punished as if he were. But the Greek hardly seems patient of this meaning, and the Ancient Epitome says in so many words that he is an adulterer.

On account of this difficulty some have supposed that the espousals here mentioned were not *de futuro* but *de præsenti*, and that therefore it was the case of stealing a real wife of another man. But this explanation also is involved in many difficulties.

CANON XCIX.

WE have further learned that, in the regions of the Armenians, certain persons boil joints of meat within the sanctuary and offer portions to the priests, distributing it after the Jewish fashion. Wherefore, that we may keep the church undefiled, we decree that it is not lawful for any priest to seize the separate portions of flesh meat from those who offer them, but they are to be content with what he that offers pleases to give them; and further we decree that such offering be made outside the church. And if any one does not thus, let him be cut off.

NOTES.

ANCIENT EPITOME OF CANON XCIX.

There are some who like the Jews cook meat in the holy places. Whoever permits this, or receives aught from them, is not fit to be priest. But if any one should of his own free choice offer it, then he might receive as much as the

offerer chose to give him, provided the offer were made outside the church.

A similar Judaizing superstitious custom was also found in the West, of which Walafrid Strabo gives an account in the IX. Century (*De Rebus Ecclesiasticis,* cap. xviii.).

CANON C.

"LET thine eyes behold the thing which is right," orders Wisdom, "and keep thine heart with all care." For the bodily senses easily bring their own impressions into the soul. Therefore we order that henceforth there shall in no way be made pictures, whether they are in paintings or in what way so ever, which attract the eye and corrupt the mind, and incite it to the enkindling of base pleasures. And if any one shall attempt to do this he is to be cut off.

ANCIENT EPITOME OF CANON C.

Pictures which induce impurity are not to be painted. Whoso shall transgress shall be cut off.

CANON CI.

THE great and divine Apostle Paul with loud voice calls man created in the image of God, the body and temple of Christ. Excelling, therefore, every sensible creature, he who by the saving Passion has attained to the celestial dignity, eating and drinking Christ, is fitted in all respects for eternal life, sanctifying his soul and body by the participation of divine grace. Wherefore, if any one wishes to be a participator of the immaculate Body in the time of the Synaxis, and to offer himself for the communion, let him draw near, arranging his hands in the form of a cross, and so let him receive the communion of grace.   But such as, instead of their hands, make vessels of gold or other materials for the reception of the divine gift, and by these receive the immaculate communion, we by no means allow to come, as preferring inanimate and inferior matter to the image of God.   But if any one shall be found imparting the immaculate Communion to those who bring vessels of this kind, let him be cut off as well as the one who brings them.

NOTES.

Ancient Epitome of Canon CI.

Whoever comes to receive the Eucharist holds his hands in the form of a cross, and takes it with his mouth; whoever shall prepare a receptacle of gold or of any other material instead of his hand, shall be cut off.

Balsamon.

At first, perchance, this was invented from pious feelings, because the hand which came in contact with base and unworthy things was not worthy to receive the Lord's body, but, as time went on, piety was turned to the injury of the soul, so that those who did this when they came to receive with an arrogant and insolent bearing, were preferred to the poor.

St. Cyril of Jerusalem.

(Cateches. Mystagog. v. [1])

When thou goest to receive communion go not with thy wrists extended, nor with thy fingers separated, but placing thy left hand as a throne for thy right, which is to receive so great a King, and in the hollow of the palm receive the body of Christ, saying, Amen.

Vide also St. John Damascene, *De Fide Orthodoxa,* lib. iv., cap. xiv.   On the whole matter cf. Card. Bona, *De Rebus Lit.,* lib. ii., cap. xvij., n. 3.

CANON CII.

It behoves those who have received from God the power to loose and bind, to consider the quality of the sin and the readiness of the sinner for conversion, and to apply medicine suitable for the disease, lest if he is injudicious in each of these respects he should fail in regard to the healing of the sick man.   For the disease of sin is not simple, but various and multiform, and it germinates many mischievous offshoots, from which much evil is diffused, and it proceeds further until it is checked by the power of the physician.   Wherefore he who professes the science of spiritual medicine ought first of all to consider the disposition of him who has sinned, and to see whether he tends to health or (on the contrary) provokes to himself disease by his own behaviour, and to look how he can care for his manner of life during the interval.   And if he does not resist the physician, and if the ulcer of the soul is increased by the application of the imposed medicaments, then let him mete out mercy to him according as he is worthy of it.   For the whole account is between God and him to whom the pastoral rule has been delivered, to lead back the wandering sheep and to cure that which is wounded by the serpent; and that he may neither cast them down into the precipices of despair, nor loosen the bridle towards dissolution or contempt of life; but in some way or other, either by means of sternness and astringency, or by greater softness and mild medicines, to resist this sickness and exert himself for the healing of the ulcer, now examining the fruits of his repentance and wisely managing the man who is called to higher illumination.   For we ought to know two things, to wit, the things which belong to strictness and those which belong to custom, and to follow the traditional form in the case of those who are not fitted for the highest things, as holy Basil teaches us.

Ancient Epitome of Canon CII.

The character of a sin must be considered from all points and conversion expected.   And so let mercy be meted out.

---

[1] Oxford Translation, p. 279.

THE CANONS OF THE SYNODS OF SARDICA, CARTHAGE, CONSTANTINOPLE, AND CARTHAGE UNDER ST. CYPRIAN, WHICH CANONS WERE RECEIVED BY THE COUNCIL IN TRULLO AND RATIFIED BY II. NICE.

INTRODUCTORY NOTE.

I have placed the canons of Sardica and those of Carthage and those of the Council held at Constantinople under Nectarius and Theophilus, and that of the Council of Carthage under St. Cyprian, immediately after the Council in Trullo, because in the second canon of that synod they are for the first time mentioned by name as being accepted by the Universal Church.

THE COUNCIL OF SARDICA.

A.D. 343 OR 344.

Emperors.—CONSTANTIUS AND CONTANS.
Pope.—JULIUS I.

Elenchus.

INTRODUCTION ON THE DATE OF THE COUNCIL.

(Hefele, *Hist. Councils*, Vol. II., pp. 86 *et seqq.*)

Our inquiries concerning the Synod of Sardica must begin with a chronological examination of the date of this assembly. Socrates and Sozomen place it expressly in the year 347 A.D., with the more precise statement that it was held under the Consuls Rufinus and Eusebius in the eleventh year after the death of Constantine the Great, therefore after the 22d of May, 347, according to our way of reckoning.

This was the most general view until, rather more than a hundred years ago, the learned Scipio Maffei discovered at Verona, the fragment of a Latin translation of an old Alexandrian chronicle (the *Historia Acephala*), and edited it in the third volume of the *Osservazioni Litterarii* in 1738. This fragment contains the information that on the 24th Phaophi (October 21), under the Consuls Constantius IV. and Constans II., in the year 346, Athanasius had returned to Alexandria from his second exile. As it is universally allowed, however, as we shall presently show more clearly, that this return certainly only took place about two years after the Synod of Sardica, Mansi hence saw the necessity of dating this synod as early as the year 344. In this he is confirmed by St. Jerome, in the continuation of the Eusebian chronicle, who, in accordance with the *Historia Acephala*, has assigned the return of St. Athanasius to the tenth year of the reign of the Emperor Constantius, in 346.

Many learned men now followed Mansi, the greater number blindly ; others, again, sought to contradict him, at first the learned Dominican, Mamachi ; then Dr. Wetzer (Professor at Freiburg) ; and latterly, we ourselves in a treatise, "Controversen über die Synode von Sardika," in the *Tübinger Theol. Quartalschrift*, 1852. Soon after there was a fresh discovery. Some of the *Paschal Letters* of St. Athanasius, which until then were supposed to be lost, were discovered in an Egyptian monastery, with a very ancient preface translated into Syriac, and were published in that language by Cureton in London, and in the year 1852 in German by Professor Larsow, at the Grey Friars Convent, in Berlin.

Among these *Festal Letters*, the nineteenth, intended for Easter 347, and therefore composed in the beginning of that year, had been re-written in Alexandria, as the introduction expressly states. This confirms the statement of the *Historia Acephala*, that Athanasius was already returned to Alexandria in October, 346, and confirms the chief points of Mansi's hypothesis ; while, on the other hand, it unanswerably refutes, by Athanasius' own testimony, the statements of Socrates and Sozomen (which, from their dependence on each other, only count as one), with reference to the date 347.

As we said, Mansi placed this Synod in the year 344 ; but the old preface to the Festal Letters of St. Athanasius dates it in the year 343, and in fact we can now only hesitate between the dates 343 and 344. If the preface were as ancient and as powerfully convincing as the *Festal Letters* themselves, then the question concerning the date of the Council of Sardica would be most accurately decided. As, however, this preface contains mistakes in several places, especially chronological errors—for instance, regarding the death of Constantine the Great—we cannot unconditionally accept its statement as to the date 344, but can only do so when it corresponds with other dates concerning that time.

Let us, at all events, assume that Athanasius came to Rome about Easter, 340. As is known, he was there for three whole years, and in the beginning of the fourth year was summoned to the Emperor Constans at Milan. This points to the summer of 343. From thence he went through Gaul to Sardica, and thus it is quite possible that that Synod might have begun in the autumn of 343. It probably lasted, however, until the spring ; for when the two envoys, Euphrates of Cologne, and Vincent of Capua, who were sent by the Synod to the Emperor Constans, arrived in Antioch, it was already Easter 344. Stephen, the bishop of the latter city, treated them in a truly diabolical manner ; but his wickedness soon became notorious, and a synod was established, which deposed him after Easter 344. Its members were Eusebians, who therefore appointed Leontius Castratus as Stephen's successor, and it is indeed no other than this assembly which Athanasius has in mind, when he says it took place three years after the *Synod in Encœniis*, and drew up a very explicit Eusebian confession of faith, the μακρόστιχος.

The disgraceful behaviour of Bishop Stephen of Antioch for some time inclined the Emperor to place less confidence in the Arian party, and to allow Athanasius's exiled clergy to return home in the summer of 344. Ten months later, the pseudo-bishop, Gregory of Alexandria, died (in June, 345), and Constantius did not permit any fresh appointment to the see of Alexandria, but recalled St. Athanasius by three letters, and waited for him more than a year. Thus the see of Alexandria remained unoccupied for more than a year, until the last six months of 346. At length, in October, 346, Athanasius returned to his bishopric.

We see then that by accepting the distinct statements of the *Paschal Letters* of St. Athanasius and the preface, we obtain a satisfactory chronological system in which the separate details cohere well together, and which thus recommends itself. One great objection which we formerly raised ourselves against the date 344 can now be solved. It is certainly true that in 353 or 354 Pope Librius wrote thus : "Eight years ago the Eusebian deputies, Eudoxius and Martyrius (who came to the West with the formula μακρόστικος), refused to anathematize the Arian doctrine at Milan." But the Synod of Milan here alluded to, and placed about the year 345, was not, as we before erroneously supposed, held before the Synod of Sardica, but after it. We are somewhat less fortunate as regards another difficulty. The Eusebians assembled at Philippopolis (the pseudo-synod of Sardica) say, in their synodal letter : "Bishop Asclepas of Gaza was deposed from his bishopric seventeen years ago." This deposition occurred at an Antiochian synod. If we identified this synod with the well-known one of 330, by which Eustathius of Antioch also was overthrown, we should, reckoning the seventeen years, have the year 346 or 347, in which to place the writing of the Synodal Letter of Philippopolis, and therefore the Synod of Sardica. There are, however, two ways of avoiding this conclusion, either we must suppose that Asclepas has been already deposed a year or so before the Antiochian Synod of 330 ; or that the statement as to the number seventeen in the Latin translation of the Synodal Letter of Philippopolis (for we no longer possess the original text) is an error or slip of the pen. But in no case can this Synodal Letter alter the fact that Athanasius was again in Alexandria when he composed his Paschal Letter for the year 347, and that the Synod of Sardica must therefore have been held several years before.

NOTE ON THE TEXT OF THE CANONS.

The Canons of Sardica have come down to us both in Greek and Latin, and some writers such as Richer (*Histoire Conc. Générale*, Tom. i., p. 98), have been of opinion that the Latin text alone was the original, while others, such as Walch (*Gesch. der Kirchenvers.*, p. 179), have arrived at a directly opposite conclusion. Now, however, chiefly owing to the investigations of the Ballerini and of Spittler, the unanimous opinion of scholars—so says Hefele—is that the canons were originally drawn up in both languages, intended as they were for both Latins and Greeks. I may perhaps remind the reader that in many Western collections of canons the canons of Sardica immediately follow those of Nice without any break, or note that they were not enacted at that council. It will also be well to bear in mind that they were received by the Greeks as of Ecumenical authority by the Council in Trullo, and as such are contained in the body of the Greek Canon Law.

I have provided the reader with a very accurate translation of each text.

THE CANONS OF THE COUNCIL OF SARDICA.

The holy synod assembled in Sardica from various provinces decreed as follows.

(Found in Greek in John of Constantinople's collection of the sixth century and several other MSS. Found also in the works of the Greek scholiasts. Found in Latin in the Prisca, in Dionysius Exiguus, and in Isidore, genuine and false.)

CANON I.

(Greek.)

HOSIUS, bishop of the city of Corduba, said: A prevalent evil, or rather most mischievous corruption must be done away with from its very foundations. Let no bishop be allowed to remove from a small city to a different one: as there is an obvious reason for this fault, accounting for such attempts; since no bishop could ever yet be found who endeavoured to be translated from a larger city to a smaller one. It is therefore evident that such persons are inflamed with excessive covetousness and are only serving ambition in order to have the repute of possessing greater authority. Is it then the pleasure of all that so grave an abuse be punished with great severity? For I think that men of this sort should not be admitted even to lay communion. All the bishops said: It is the pleasure of all.

(Latin.)

BISHOP HOSIUS said: A prevalent evil and mischievous corruption must be done away with from its foundation. Let no bishop be allowed to remove from his own city to another. For the reason of such attempts is manifest, since in this matter no bishop has been found who would remove from a larger city to a smaller one. It is therefore evident that these men are inflamed with excess of covetousness, and are serving ambition and aiming at the possession of power. If it be the pleasure of all, let so great an evil be punished right harshly and sternly, so that he who is such shall not even be admitted to lay communion. All with one accord answered: Such is our pleasure.

NOTES.

ANCIENT EPITOME OF CANON I.

No bishop is to be found passing from a smaller to a greater city. If anyone should move from an humble to a more important see, he shall be excommunicated through his whole life as proud and grasping.

VAN ESPEN.

(Dissert. in Synod. Sard., § II.[1])

What Peter de Marca says (*De Concordia Sacerdotii et Imp.*, Lib. V., cap. iv.), "Hosius presided over" this council as legate of the Roman bishop, rests upon no solid foundation, and no trace of any such legation is found in Athanasius or in any of the other writers who treated of this synod. Moreover such a thing is contrary to the form of subscription used. For of those who signed the first is Hosius, and Athanasius designates him simply as "from Spain," without any addition; and then next he mentions "Julius of Rome, by Archidamus and Philoxenus, his presbyters," etc. What is clearer than that, by the testimony of Athanasius, Julius was present by these two presbyters only, and that they only were his legates or vicars, who in his room were present at this synod?

The first part of this canon is found in the *Corpus Juris Canonici*; Raymund's *Decretales*, *De Clericis non residentibus*, Cap. ii.

CANON II.

(Greek.)

BISHOP HOSIUS said: But if any such person should be found so mad or audacious as to think to advance by way of excuse an affirmation that he had brought letters from

---

[1] The whole of this *Dissertation* is worthy of careful study.

the people [laity], it is plain that some few persons, corrupted by bribes and rewards, could have got up an uproar in the church, demanding, forsooth, the said man for bishop. I think then that practices and devices of such sort absolutely must be punished, so that a man of this kind be deemed unworthy even of lay communion *in extremis*. Do ye therefore make answer whether this sentence is approved by you. They [the bishops] answered : What has been said is approved of.

(*Latin.*)

BISHOP HOSIUS said : Even if any such person should show himself so rash as perhaps to allege as an excuse and affirm that he has received letters from the people, inasmuch as it is evident that a few persons could have been corrupted by rewards and bribes—[namely] persons who do not hold the pure faith—to raise an uproar in the church, and seem to ask for the said man as bishop ; I judge that these frauds must be condemned, so that such an one should not receive even lay communion at the last. If ye all approve, do ye decree it. The synod answered : We approve.

NOTES.

ANCIENT EPITOME OF CANON II.

If anyone shall pass from one city to another, and shall raise up seditions, tickling the people and be assisted by them in raising a disturbance, he shall not be allowed communion even when dying.

VAN ESPEN.

To understand this canon aright it must be remembered that in the first ages of the Church the people were accustomed to have a share in the election of their bishop ; and he whom the people demanded was usually ordained their bishop.

ARISTENUS.

This [penalty] is something unheard of and horrible, that he should not be deemed worthy of communion even at the hour of death ; for it is a provision found nowhere else imposed by any canon, nor inflicted upon any sin.

VAN ESPEN.

The Greek author Aristenus [in the above remarks] probably has not erred from the truth when he asserts that to no crime was this penalty attached, if he refers to the Eastern Churches ; for Morinus himself (in the xixth chapter of the ixth book, *De Penitentia*), confesses that this penalty was never attached to any crime among the Easterns : nevertheless in some Churches in the first ages the three crimes of idolatry, murder, and adultery were thus punished : that is, that to those who admitted any one of these, reconciliation was denied even at his death, "and this," says Morinus, " I think no one can deny, who is at all versed in the testimony of the ancients on this point."

HEFELE.

The addition in the Latin text, *qui sinceram fidem non habent*, is found both in Dionysius Exiguus and in Isidore and the *Prisca*, and its meaning is as follows : " In a town, some few, especially those who have not the true faith, can be easily bribed to demand this or that person as bishop." The Fathers of Sardica plainly had here in view the Arians and their adherents, who, through such like machinations, when they had gained over, if only a small party in a town, sought to press into the bishoprics. The Synod of Antioch moreover, in 341, although the Eusebians, properly speaking, were dominant there, had laid down in the twenty-first canon a similar, only less severe, rule.

This canon is found in the *Corpus Juris Canonici*, Raymond's *Decretales*, cap. ii., *De electione*, but with the noteworthy addition "unless he shall have repented." These words do not occur in the other Latin versions, and Hefele thinks them to have been added by Raymond of Pennaforte.

CANON III.

(*Greek.*)

BISHOP HOSIUS said : This also it is necessary to add,—that no bishop pass from his own province to another province in which there are bishops, unless indeed he be called by his brethren, that we seem not to close the gates of charity.

And this case likewise is to be provided for, that if in any province a bishop has some matter against his brother and fellow-bishop, neither of the two should call in as arbiters bishops from another province.

But if perchance sentence be given against a bishop in any matter and he supposes his case to be not unsound but good, in order that the question may be reopened, let us, if it seem good to your charity, honour the memory of Peter the Apostle, and let those who gave judgment write to Julius, the bishop of Rome, so that, if necessary, the case may be retried by the bishops of the neighbouring provinces and let him appoint arbiters; but if it cannot be shown that his case is of such a sort as to need a new trial, let the judgment once given not be annulled, but stand good as before.

(*Latin.*)

BISHOP HOSIUS said: This also it is necessary to add,—that bishops shall not pass from their own province to another province in which there are bishops, unless perchance upon invitation from their brethren, that we seem not to close the door of charity.

But if in any province a bishop have a matter in dispute against his brother bishop, one of the two shall not call in as judge a bishop from another province.

But if judgment have gone against a bishop in any cause, and he think that he has a good case, in order that the question may be reopened, let us, if it be your pleasure, honour the memory of St. Peter the Apostle, and let those who tried the case write to Julius, the bishop of Rome, and if he shall judge that the case should be retried, let that be done, and let him appoint judges; but if he shall find that the case is of such a sort that the former decision need not be disturbed, what he has decreed shall be confirmed.

Is this the pleasure of all? The synod answered, It is our pleasure.

NOTES.

ANCIENT EPITOME OF CANON III.

No bishop, unless called thereto, shall pass to another city. Moreover a bishop of the province who is engaged in any litigation shall not appeal to outside bishops. But if Rome hears the cause, even outsiders may be present.

VAN ESPEN.

According to the reading of Dionysius and Isidore, as well as of the Greeks, Balsamon, Zonaras and Aristenus, as also of Hervetus the provision is that bishops of one province shall not pass to another in which there are NOT bishops.

ZONARAS.

Not only are bishops prohibited from changing their cities, and passing from a smaller to a larger one, but also from passing from one province to another in which there are bishops, for the sake of doing any ecclesiastical work there unless they are called by the bishops of that province.

On the phrase "if it pleases you" the following from St. Athanasius is much to the point (cit. by Pusey, *Councils*, p. 143). "They [i.e., the Council of Nice] wrote concerning Easter, 'It seemed good' as follows: for it did *then* seem good, that there should be a general compliance; but about the faith they wrote not 'It seemed good,' but 'Thus believes the Catholic Church'; and thereupon they confessed how the faith lay, in order to shew that their sentiments were not novel, but apostolic."

TILLEMONT.

This form is very strong to shew that it was a right which the Pope had not had hitherto.

VAN ESPEN.

Peter de Marca (*De Concordia Sacerdotii et Imperii*, Lib. VII., Cap. iij., § 8) says that Hosius here proposed to the fathers to honour the memory of St. Peter that he might the more easily lead them to consent to this new privilege; for, as De Marca has proved, the right here bestowed upon the Roman Pontiff was clearly unknown before.

It has been urged that the mention of the pope by name, intimates clearly that the provision of these canons of an appeal to Rome was of a purely temporary character; and some famous authors such as Edmund Richer, of the Sorbonne, have written in defence of this view, but Hefele quotes with great force the words of the learned Protestant, Spittler (*Critical Examination of the Sardican Decisions*. Spittler, *Sämmtlichen Werken*, P. viij., p. 129 sq.).

SPITTLER.

It is said that these Sardican decisions were simply provisional, and intended for the present necessity; because Athanasius, so hardly pressed by the Arians, could only be rescued by authorizing an appeal to the Bishop of Rome for a final judgment. Richer, in his *History of the General Councils*, has elaborately defended this opinion, and Horix also has declared in its favour. But would not all secure use of the canons of the councils be done away with if this distinction between provisional and permanent synodal decisions were admitted? Is there any sure criterion for distinguishing those canons which were only to be provisional, from the others which were made for all future centuries? The Fathers of the Synod of Sardica express themselves quite generally; is it not therefore most arbitrary on our part to insert limitations? It is beyond question that these decisions were occasioned by the very critical state of the affairs of Athanasius; but is everything only provisional that is occasioned by the circumstances of individuals? In this way the most important of the ancient canons might be set aside.

HEFELE.

According to the Greek text, and that of Dionysius, those who had pronounced the first judgment were to write to Rome; and Fuchs rightly adds, that they were to do this at the desire of the condemned. But, according to Isidore and the *Prisca*, the right or the duty of bringing the affair before Rome, also belonged to the neighbouring bishops. I believe that the last interpretation has only arisen through a mistake, from a comment belonging to the next sentence being inserted in the wrong place. It only remains to be remarked here, that Isidore and the *Prisca* have not the name *Julio*, . . . But Hardouin's conjecture, that instead of *Julio*, perhaps *illi* may be read, is entirely gratuitous, contrary to the Greek text, and plainly only a stratagem against the Gallicans.

This canon is found in the *Corpus Juris Canonici*, Gratian's *Decretum*, Pars II., Causa VI., Quæst. iv., Canon j. 7, in Isidore's version. Dionysius's version is quite wrong as given by Justellus and in the Munich edition, changing the negative into the affirmative in the phrase *ne unus de duobus*.

CANON IV.

(*Greek.*)

BISHOP GAUDENTIUS said: If it seems good to you, it is necessary to add to this decision full of sincere charity which thou hast pronounced, that[1] if any bishop be deposed by the sentence of these neighbouring bishops, and assert that he has fresh matter in defence, a new bishop be not settled in his see, unless the bishop of Rome judge and render a decision as to this.

(*Latin.*)

BISHOP GAUDENTIUS said: It ought to be added, if it be your pleasure, to this sentence full of sanctity which thou hast pronounced, that—when any bishop has been deposed by the judgment of those bishops who have sees in neighbouring places, and he [the bishop deposed] shall announce that his case is to be examined in the city of Rome—that no other bishop shall in any wise be ordained to his see, after the appeal of him who is apparently deposed, unless the case shall have been determined in the judgment of the Roman bishop.

NOTES.

ANCIENT EPITOME OF CANON IV.

If a bishop has been deposed and affirms that he has an excuse to urge, unless Rome has judged the case, no bishop shall be appointed in his room. For he might treat the decree with scorn either through his nuncios or by his letters.

There are two distinct understandings of this canon. The one view is that the

"neighbours" of this canon are the same as the "neighbours" of the preceding canon (number iij.) and that the meaning of this canon therefore is—If the court of second instance, consisting of the bishops of the neighbouring province, has pronounced the accused guilty, he still has one more appeal to a third court, viz., Rome. This is the view taken by the Greeks, Zonaras and Balsamon, by the

---

[1] At this point begins the Greek text as given in Bev.

Ballerini, Van Espen, Palma, Walter, Natalis Alexander and many others.

In direct opposition to this is the view that there is no third but only a second appeal mentioned by the canon. The supporters of this interpretation are Peter de Marca, Tillemont, Dupin, Fleury, Remi Ceillier, Neander, Stolberg, Echhorn, Kober, and with these Hefele sides and states his reasons for doing so.

HEFELE.

There must be added to the reasons of the connexion of this canon with the preceding, the course of events, etc.:

1. That it certainly would be very curious if in the third canon mention was made of the appeal to Rome as following the judgment of the court of first instance; in the fourth, after that of the court of second instance; and again in the fifth, after the judgment of the court of first instance.

2. That if the Synod had really intended to institute a court of third instance, it would have done so in clearer and more express terms, and not only have, as it were, smuggled in the whole point with the secondary question, as to "what was to be done with the bishop's see."

3. Farther, that it is quite devoid of proof that the expression "neighbouring bishops" is identical with "Bishops in the neighbourhood of the said Province," that, indeed this identification is throughout unwarrantable and wrong, and it is far more natural to understand by the neighbouring bishops, the comprovincials, therefore the court of first instance.

4. That by this interpretation we obtain clearness, consistency, and harmony in all three canons.

5. That the word πάλιν in the fourth canon presents no difficulty; for even one who has only been heard in the court of first instance may say he desires again to defend himself, because he has already made his first defence in the court of first instance.

CANON V.

(*Greek*.)

BISHOP HOSIUS said: Decreed, that if any bishop is accused, and the bishops of the same region assemble and depose him from his office, and he appealing, so to speak, takes refuge with the most blessed bishop of the Roman church, and he be willing to give him a hearing, and think it right to renew the examination of his case, let him be pleased to write to those fellow-bishops who are nearest the province that they may examine the particulars with care and accuracy and give their votes on the matter in accordance with the word of truth. And if any one require that his case be heard yet again, and at his request it seem good to move the bishop of Rome to send presbyters *a latere*, let it be in the power of that bishop, according as he judges it to be good and decides it to be right—that some be sent to be judges with the bishops and invested with his authority by whom they were sent. And be this also ordained. But if he think that the bishops are sufficient for the examination and decision of the matter let him do what shall seem good in his most prudent judgment.

The bishops answered: What has been said is approved.

(*Latin*.)

BISHOP HOSIUS said: Further decreed, that if a bishop is accused, and the bishops of that region assemble and depose him from his office, if he who has been deposed shall appeal and take refuge with the bishop of the Roman church and wishes to be given a hearing, if he think it right that the trial or examination of his case be renewed, let him be pleased to write to those bishops who are in an adjacent and neighbouring province, that they may diligently inquire into all the particulars and decide according to the word of truth. But if he who asks to have his case re-heard, shall by his entreaty move the Bishop of Rome to send a presbyter *a latere* it shall be in the power of that bishop to do what he shall resolve and determine upon; and if he shall decide that some be sent, who shall be present and be judges with the bishops invested with his authority by whom they were appointed, it shall be as he shall choose. But if he believe that the bishops suffice to give a final decision, he shall do what he shall determine upon in his most wise judgment.

NOTES.

[Lacking.]

This Canon is vij. of Isidore's collection.

VAN ESPEN.

Here there is properly speaking no provision for "appeal," which entirely suspends [i.e. by the canon law] the execution and effect of the first sentence ; but rather for a revision of judgment . . . . ; those who were sent by the Roman bishop from his side (*a latere*) or the bishops who were appointed, ought, together with the bishops of the province who had given the former sentence, to give a fresh judgment and declare their sentence.   And this Hincmar of Rheims was the first to notice in his letters in the name of Charles the Bald sent to John VIII.

This view is supported with his accustomed learning and acumen by Du Pin, *De Antiqua Eccl. Disciplina*, Diss. II., Cap. I., Sec. 3.

CANON VI.

(*Greek.*)

BISHOP HOSIUS said : If it happen that in a province in which there are very many bishops one bishop should stay away and by some negligence should not come to the council and assent to the appointment made by the bishops, but the people assemble and pray that the ordination of the bishop desired by them take place—it is necessary that the bishop who stayed away should first be reminded by letters from the exarch of the province (I mean, of course, the bishop of the metropolis), that the people demand a pastor to be given them.   I think that it is well to await his [the absent bishop's] arrival also.   But if after summons by letter he does not come, nor even write in reply, the wish of the people ought to be complied with.

The bishops from the neighbouring provinces also should be invited to the ordination of the bishop of the metropolis.

It is positively not permitted to ordain a bishop in a village or petty town, for which even one single presbyter is sufficient (for there is no necessity to ordain a bishop there) lest the name and authority of bishop should be made of small account, but the bishops of the province ought, as before said, to ordain bishops in those cities in which there were bishops previously ; and if a city should be found with a population so large as to be thought worthy of an episcopal see, let it receive one.

Is this the pleasure of all ?   All answered : It is our pleasure.

(*Latin.*)

BISHOP HOSIUS said : If it shall have happened, that in a province in which there have been very many bishops, one [i.e., but one] bishop remains, but that he by negligence has not chosen [to ordain] a bishop, and the people have made application, the bishops of the neighbouring province ought first to address [by letter] the bishop who resides in that province, and show that the people seek a ruler [i.e., pastor] for themselves and that this is right, so that they also may come and with him ordain a bishop. But if he refuses to acknowledge their written communication, and leaves it unnoticed, and writes no reply, the people's request should be satisfied, so that bishops should come from the neighbouring province and ordain a bishop.

But permission is not to be given to ordain a bishop either in any village, or in an unimportant city, for which one presbyter suffices, lest the name and authority of bishop grow cheap.   Those [bishops] who are invited from another province ought not to ordain a bishop unless in the cities which have [previously] had bishops, or in a city which is so important or so populous as to be entitled to have a bishop.

Is this the pleasure of all ?   The synod replied : It is our pleasure.

NOTES.

ANCIENT EPITOME OF CANON VI.

If the bishops were present when the people were seeking for a bishop, and one was away, let that one be called. But if he is willing to answer the call neither by letter nor in person, let him be ordained whom they desire.

When a Metropolitan is appointed the neighbouring bishops are to be sent for.

In a little city and town, for which one presbyter suffices, a bishop is not to be appointed. But if the city be very populous, it is not unfitting to do so.

The second portion of this canon is entirely lacking in the Latin. The Greek scholiasts, Zonaras, Balsamon, and Aristenus, understand this to mean "that 'at the appointment of a metropolitan the bishops of the neighbouring provinces shall also be invited,' probably to give greater solemnity to the act," so says Hefele. And to this agree Van Espen, Tillemont, and Herbst.

The first part in the Greek and Latin have different meanings; the Greek text contemplating the case of one bishop stopping away from a meeting of bishops for an election to fill a vacancy; the Latin text the case of there being only one bishop left in a province (after war, pestilence, or the like). This second meaning is accepted by Van Espen, Christian Lupus and others. Moreover, it would seem from Flodoard's *History of the Church of Rheims (Geschichte der Rheimser Kirche*, Lib. III., c. 20 [a book I have never seen]) that the Gallican Church acted upon this understanding of this canon. It is that also of Gratian.

Between the Latin and the Greek text stands the interpretation of Zonaras, which is that if a province once having many bishops has by any contingency only one left besides the Metropolitan, and he neglects to be present at the consecration of the new bishops, he is to be summoned by letter of the Metropolitan, and if he does not then come, the consecrations are to go on without him. With this explanation Harmenopulus also agrees, adding further that the Metropolitan might alone consecrate the bishops, resting his argument on the words τὸ ἱκανὸν κ.τ.λ.

Some scholars have supposed that neither the present Greek nor the present Latin text represent the original, but that the Greek text is nearest to it, but must be corrected by an ancient Latin version found by Maffei in a codex at Verona. The Ballerini have devoted careful attention to this point in their notes to the Works of St. Leo the Great (Tom. iii., p. xxxij. 4). It would seem that this might be the canon quoted by the fathers of Constantinople in 382, and if so, it would seem that they had a Greek text like that from which the Verona version was made.

VAN ESPEN.

The fathers of Sardica [in the second part of this canon, which is Canon VII. by the Latin computation] decreed two things: first, that where the people justly asked for a Pastor to be ordained for them, their demand should be complied with; but where the people insisted upon having a bishop ordained for a village or little city, for which one presbyter was all that was needed, no attention should be paid to their demands, lest the name and authority of a bishop should become despicable.

This canon is found in the *Corpus Juris Canonici,* Gratian's *Decretum*, P. I., Distinc. lxv., c. ix.

CANON VII.

(*Greek.*)

BISHOP HOSIUS said: Our importunity and great pertinacity and unjust petitions have brought it about that we do not have as much favour and confidence as we ought to enjoy. For many of the bishops do not intermit resorting to the imperial Court, especially the Africans, who, as we have learned from our beloved brother and fellow-bishop, Gratus, do not accept salutary counsels, but so despise them that one man carries to the Court petitions many and diverse and of no possible benefit to the Church, and does not (as ought to be done and as is fitting) assist and help the poor and the laity or the widows, but is intriguing to obtain worldly dignities and offices for certain persons. This evil then causes enfeeblement [*better*, murmuring (*read* τονθρυσμόν or τονθορυσμόν)], not without some scandal and blame to us. But I account it quite proper for a bishop to give assistance to one oppressed by some one, or to a widow suffering injustice, or, again, an orphan robbed of his estate, always provided that these persons have a just cause of petition.

If, then, beloved brethren, this seems good to all, do ye decree that no bishop shall go to the imperial Court except those whom our most pious emperor may summon by his own letters. Yet since it often happens that persons condemned for their offences to deportation or banishment to an island, or who have received some sentence or other, beg for mercy and seek refuge with the Church [*i.e.*, take sanctuary], such persons are not to be refused assistance, but pardon should be asked for them without delay and without hesitation. If this, then, is also your pleasure, do ye all vote assent.

All gave answer: Be this also decreed.

(*Latin.*)

BISHOP HOSIUS said: Importunities and excessive pertinacity and unjust petitions have caused us to have too little favour or confidence, while certain bishops cease not to go to the Court, especially the Africans, who (as we have learned) spurn and contemn the salutary counsels of our most holy brother and fellow-bishop, Gratus, so that they not only bring to the Court many and diverse petitions (not for the good of the Church nor, as is usual and right, to succour the poor or widows or orphans), but even seek to obtain worldly dignities and offices for certain persons. This evil therefore stirs up at times not only murmurings, but even scandals. But it is proper that bishops should intercede for persons suffering from violence and oppression, afflicted widows and defrauded orphans, provided, nevertheless, that these persons have a just cause or petition.

If, then, brethren dearly beloved, such be your pleasure, do we decree that no bishops go to the Court except those who may have been invited or summoned by letters of the God-fearing emperor. But since it often happens that those who are suffering from injustice or who are condemned for their offences to deportation or banishment to an island, or, in short, have received some sentence or other, seek refuge with the mercy of the Church, such persons should be succoured and pardon be begged for them without hesitation. Decree this, therefore, if it be your pleasure.

All said: It is our pleasure and be it decreed.

NOTES.

ANCIENT EPITOME OF CANON VII.

When an orphan, widow, and other desolate persons are oppressed by force let the bishop give them succour and approach the Emperor; but through a pretext of this kind let him not be a hanger on of the camp, but rather let him send a deacon.

VAN ESPEN.

The "salutary counsels" (*salutaria consilia*) here seem to be synodical admonitions, as Zonaras notes; and these might well be ascribed to Gratus, the bishop of Carthage, because many of the African synods were held under his presidency and direction.

* * * * * * *

Nothing is more noteworthy than how from the first princes summoned bishops in counsel with regard to affairs touching either the estate of the Church or of the Realm; and called them to their presence in urgent and momentous cases, and kept them with them.

Justinian, the emperor, in his *Novels* (Chapter II.) defines that no one of the God-beloved bishops shall dare to be absent any more from his diocese for a whole year, and adds this exception, "unless he does so on account of an imperial *jussio*; in this case alone he shall be held to be without blame."

On this whole matter of bishops interceding for culprits, and especially for those condemned to death, see St. Augustine (*Epist.* 153 ad Macedonium).

With this canon may be compared Canon VII. of the Council of Rheims in A.D. 630.

This canon is found in part in the *Corpus Juris Canonici*, Gratian's *Decretum*, P. II., Causa xxiij., Quæst. viij., c. xxviij.

CANON VIII.

(*Greek.*)

BISHOP HOSIUS said : This also let your sagacity determine, that [1]—inasmuch as this was decreed in order that a bishop might not fall under censure by going to the Court—that if any have such petitions as we mentioned above, they should send these by one of their deacons. For the person of a subordinate does not excite jealousy, and what shall be granted [by the Emperor] can thus be reported more quickly.

All answered: Be this also decreed.

(*Latin.*)

BISHOP HOSIUS said : This also your forethought should provide for—inasmuch as ye have made this decree in order that the audacity of bishops might not labour [*or*, be observed] to go to Court. Whosoever therefore shall have or receive petitions such as we have mentioned above, let them send these [each] by a deacon of his, because the person of a minister is not an object of jealousy, and he will be able to report more quickly what he has obtained.

NOTES.

ANCIENT EPITOME OF CANON VIII.

[Lacking.]

VAN ESPEN.

This decree is threefold. First, that the bishop in going to Court should not fall under suspicion either at Court or of his own people that he was approaching the Prince to obtain some cause of his own. Second, according to the interpretation of Zonaras, "that no one should be angry with the Minister or Deacon who tarried in camp, as the bishop had departed thence." And third, that the Minister could carry away what he had asked for, that is (according to Zonaras), the letters of the Emperor pardoning the fault, or such like other matters.

CANON IX.

(*Greek.*)

BISHOP HOSIUS said : This also, I think, follows, that,[2] if in any province whatever, bishops send petitions to one of their brothers and fellow-bishops, he that is in the largest city, that is, the metropolis, should himself send his deacon and the petitions, providing him also with letters commendatory, writing also of course in succession to our brethren and fellow-bishops, if any of them should be staying at that time in the places or cities in which the most pious Emperor is administering public affairs.

But if any of the bishops should have friends at the Court and should wish to make requests of them as to some proper object, let him not be forbidden to make such requests through his deacon and move these [friends] to give their kind assistance as his desire.

But those who come to Rome ought, as I said before, to deliver to our beloved brother and fellow-bishop, Julius, the petitions which they have to give, in order that he may first examine them, lest some of them should be improper, and so, giving them his own advocacy and care, shall send them to the Court.

All the Bishops made answer that such was their pleasure and that the regulation was most proper.

(*Latin.*)

THIS also seems to follow, that from whatever province bishops shall send petitions to that brother and fellow-bishop of ours who has his see in the metropolis, he [the metropolitan] should dispatch his deacon with the petitions, providing him with commendatory letters of like tenour to our brethren and fellow-bishops at that time resi-

---

[1] Here the Greek text begins as given by Bev.   [2] Here the Greek text in Bev. begins.

dent in those regions and cities in which the fortunate and blessed Emperor is ruling the State.

If however a bishop who seeks to obtain some petition (a worthy one, that is) has friends in the palace, he is not forbidden to make his request through his deacon and to advise those who, he knows, can kindly intercede for him in his absence.

X. But let those who come to Rome, deliver, as before said, to our most holy brother and fellow-bishop, the bishop of the Roman church, the petitions which they bear, that he also may examine whether they are worthy and just, and let him give diligence and care that they be forwarded to the Court.

All said that such was their pleasure and that the regulation was proper.

Bishop Alypius said : If they have incurred the discomforts of travel for the sake of orphans and widows or any in distress and having cases that are not unjust, they will have some good reason [for their journey] ; but now since they chiefly make requests which cannot be granted without envy and reproach, it is not necessary for them to go to Court.

NOTE.

Ancient Epitome of Canon IX.

If one brother sends to another, let the Metropolitan fortify the nuncio with letters ; and let him write to the bishops, who have the matter in hand, to protect the nuncio.

Here the Latin is not only a translation but an interpretation of the Greek text, for it distinctly says that every bishop shall send the petition he intends to present at court first to his Metropolitan, who shall send it in. This is not clearly in the Greek, and yet the Greek Commentators find it there.

Christian Lupus.

The authority of the bishop alone is not sufficient to send a deacon to Court, there must be added the judgment of the Metropolitan who shall examine the petition, approve, sign, and commend it, not only to the Prince, but also to the bishop in whose diocese he may happen to be.

Hefele.

Zonaras, Balsamon, and Aristenus explained this canon somewhat differently, thus : "If a bishop desires to send his petitions addressed to the Emperor to the bishop of the town where the Emperor is staying, he shall first send them to the Metropolitan of that province (according to Aristenus, his own Metropolitan) and the latter shall send his own deacon with letters of recommendation to the bishop or bishops who may be at court." This difference rests upon the various meanings of " to the brother and fellow-bishop " in the beginning of the canon. We understand by this his own Metropolitan, and treat the words : ὁ ἐν τῇ μείζονι κ. τ. λ., as a more exact definition of " fellow-bishop," and the participle τυγχάνων as equivalent to τυγχάνει, and make the principal clause begin at αὐτὸς καὶ τὸν διάκονον. Beveridge translated the canon in the same way. Zonaras and others, on the contrary, understood by " fellow-bishop," the bishop of the Emperor's residence for the time being, and regarded the words ὁ ἐν τῇ μείζῃ κ.τ.λ. not as a clearer definition of what had gone before, but as the principal clause, in the sense of " then the Metropolitan shall," etc. According to this interpretation, the words conveying the idea that the bishop must have recourse to the Metropolitan are entirely wanting in the canon.

The first part of this Canon is the last part of Canon IX. of the Latin. The last part is Canon X. of the Latin, but the personal part about *Alypius* is omitted from the Greek.

CANON X.

(*Greek.*)

Bishop Hosius said : This also I think necessary.[1] Ye should consider with all thoroughness and care, that if some rich man or professional advocate be desired for bishop, he be not ordained until he have fulfilled the ministry of reader, deacon, and presbyter, in order that, passing by promotion through the several grades, he may

---

[1] Here the Greek begins (reading ἀεί for ἵνα and ἐξετάζεσθαι for ἐξετάζοιτο) according to Beveridge.

advance (if, that is, he be found worthy) to the height of the episcopate. And he shall remain in each order assuredly for no brief time, that so his faith, his reputable life, his steadfastness of character and considerateness of demeanour may be well-known, and that he, being deemed worthy of the divine sacerdotal office [*sacerdotium*, i.e., the episcopate], may enjoy the highest honour. For it is not fitting, nor does discipline or good conversation allow to proceed to this act rashly or lightly, so as to ordain a bishop or presbyter or deacon hastily; as thus he would rightly be accounted a novice, especially since also the most blessed Apostle, he who was the teacher of the Gentiles, is seen to have forbidden hasty ordinations; for the test of [even] the longest period will not unreasonably be required to exemplify the conversation and character of each [candidate].

All said that this was their pleasure and that it must be absolutely irreversible.

(*Latin.*)

BISHOP HOSIUS said: This also I think it necessary for you to consider most carefully, that if perchance some rich man or professional advocate or ex-official be desired for bishop, he be not ordained until he have fulfilled the ministry of a reader and the office of deacon and presbyter, and so ascend, if he have shown himself worthy, through the several grades to the height of the episcopate. For by these promotions which in any case take a considerable length of time can be tested his faith, his discretion, his gravity and modesty. And if he be found worthy, let him be honoured with the divine sacerdotal office [i.e. the episcopate]. For it is not fitting, nor does order or discipline allow, that one be rashly or lightly ordained bishop, presbyter or deacon, who is a novice, especially since also the blessed Apostle, the teacher of the Gentiles, is seen to have expressly forbidden it. But those [should be ordained] whose life has been tested and their merit approved by length of time.

All said that this was their pleasure.

NOTES.

ANCIENT EPITOME OF CANON X.

No lawyer, teacher, or gentleman (πλούσιος) *shall be made a bishop without passing through the holy orders. Nor shall the space of time between the orders be made too brief, that there may be a better proof of his faith and good conversation. For otherwise he is a neophyte.*

This is Canon XIII. of Dionysius, Isidore, and the *Prisca*.

VAN ESPEN.

By *Scholasticus de foro* ["professional advocate"] must be understood an eloquent pleader of difficult causes, who being bound up in forensic disputes and strifes, may be presumed to be little fitted for the priesthood, and therefore to need a more strict examination.

The Synodal approbation is lacking in Dionysius as given by Justellus, as well as in that of the Roman Code, but is found in Labbe's reprint of Dionysius and Isidore.

This Canon is found in the *Corpus Juris Canonici*, Gratian's *Decretum*, P. I., Dist. lxj., c. x.

CANON XI.

(*Greek.*)

BISHOP HOSIUS said: This also we ought to decree, that[1] when a bishop comes from one city to another city, or from one province to another province, to indulge boastfulness, ministering to his own praises rather than serving religious devotion, and wishes to prolong his stay [in a city], and the bishop of that city is not skilled in teaching, let him [the visiting bishop] not do despite to the bishop of the place and attempt by frequent discourses to disparage him and lessen his repute (for this device is wont to cause tumults), and strive by such arts to solicit and wrest to himself another's throne,

---

[1] Here begins the Greek text, according to Bev.

not scrupling to abandon the church committed to him and to procure translation to another. A definite limit of time should therefore be set in such a case, especially since not to receive a bishop is accounted the part of rude and discourteous persons. Ye remember that in former times our fathers decreed that if a layman were staying in a city and should not come to divine worship for three [successive] Sundays [that is], for three [full] weeks, he should be repelled from communion. If then this has been decreed in the case of laymen, it is neither needful, nor fitting, nor yet even expedient that a bishop, unless he has some grave necessity or difficult business, should be very long absent from his own church and distress the people committed to him.

All the bishops said : We decide that this decree also is most proper.

(*Latin.*)

BISHOP HOSIUS said : This also ye ought to determine. If a bishop comes from one city to another city, or from his own province to another province, and serving ambition rather than devotion, wishes to remain resident for a long time in a strange city, and then (as it perchance happens that the bishop of the place is not so practised or so learned as himself) he, the stranger, should begin to do him despite and deliver frequent discourses to disparage him and lessen his repute, not hesitating by this device to leave the church assigned him and remove to that which is another's—do ye then [in such a case] set a limit of time [for his stay in the city], because on the one hand to refuse to receive a bishop is discourteous, and on the other his too long stay is mischievous. Provision must be made against this. I remember that in a former council our brethren decreed that if any layman did not attend divine service in a city in which he was staying three Sundays, that is, for three weeks, he should be deprived of communion. If then this has been decreed in the case of laymen, it is far less lawful and fitting that a bishop, if there be no grave necessity detaining him, should be absent from his church longer than the time above written.

All said that such was their pleasure.

NOTES.

ANCIENT EPITOME OF CANON XI.

A bishop when called in by another bishop, if he that called him is unskilled, must not be too assiduous in preaching, for this would be indecorous to the unlearned bishop, and an attack upon his bishopric. And both improper. Without grave necessity it is undesirable for a bishop to be absent from his church.

This is Canon XIV. of the Latin.

VAN ESPEN.

To understand this canon it must be again remembered that in the first ages of the Church bishops were wont to be appointed at the demand of the people ; wherefore whoever were going around after the episcopate, were accustomed to solicit the hearts of the people, and to make it their study to win their affections.

CANON XII.

(*Greek.*)

BISHOP HOSIUS said : Since no case should be left unprovided for, let this also be decreed.[1] Some of our brethren and fellow-bishops are known to possess very little private property in the cities in which they are placed as bishops, but have great possessions in other places, with which they are, moreover, able to help the poor. I think then permission should be given them, if they are to visit their estates and attend to the gathering of the harvest, to pass three Sundays, that is, to stay for three weeks, on their estates, and to assist at divine worship and celebrate the liturgy in the nearest church in which a presbyter holds service, in order that they may not be seen to be absent from worship, and in order that they may not come too frequently to the

---

[1] Here begins the Greek text according to Bev.

city in which there is a bishop. In this way their private affairs will suffer no loss from their absence and they will be seen to be clear from the charge of ambition and arrogance.

All the bishops said : This decree also is approved by us.

(Latin.)

BISHOP HOSIUS said : Since no case should be left unprovided for [let this also be decreed]. There are some of our brother-bishops, who do not reside in the city in which they are appointed bishops, either because they have but little property there, while they are known to have considerable estates elsewhere, or, it may be, through affection for kith and kin and in complaisance to these. Let this much be permitted them, to go to their estates to superintend and dispose of their harvest, and [for this purpose] to remain over three Sundays, that is, for three weeks, if it be necessary, on their estates ; or else, if there is a neighbouring city in which there is a presbyter, in order that they may not be seen to pass Sunday without church, let them go thither, so that [in this way] neither will their private affairs suffer loss from their absence, nor will they, by frequent going to the city in which a bishop is resident, incur the suspicion of ambition and place-seeking. All said that this was approved by them.

NOTES.

ANCIENT EPITOME OF CANON XII.

If a bishop has possessions outside his diocese, and visits them, let him be careful not to remain there more than three Lord's days. For thus his own flock will be enriched by him, and he himself will avoid the charge of arrogance.

This is Canon XV. of the Latin.

VAN ESPEN.

As Balsamon notes, this canon is an appendix to that which goes before, and the context of the canon indicates this clearly enough ;

for while the last canon decrees that no bishop is to be absent from his diocese for more than three Lord's days, without grave necessity, in this canon a certain modification is introduced with regard to certain bishops.

HEFELE.

According to the Latin text of Dionysius, it is : "Some bishops do not reside in their Cathedral town, etc." Isidore and the *Prisca*, however, are nearer the Greek text, as instead of *resident* they more rightly read *possident*.

CANON XIII.

(Greek.)

BISHOP HOSIUS said : Be this also the pleasure of all. 'If any deacon or presbyter or any of the clergy be excommunicated and take refuge with another bishop who knows him and who is aware that he has been removed from communion by his own bishop, [that other bishop] must not offend against his brother bishop by admitting him to communion.[1] And if any dare to do this, let him know that he must present himself before an assembly of bishops and give account.

All the bishops said : This decision will assure peace at all times and preserve the concord of all.

(Latin.)

BISHOP HOSIUS said : Be this also the pleasure of all. If a deacon or presbyter or any of the clergy be refused communion by his own bishop and go to another bishop, and he with whom he has taken refuge shall know that he has been repelled by his own bishop, then must he not grant him communion. But if he shall do so, let him know that he must give account before an assembly of bishops.

All said : This decision will preserve peace and maintain concord.

---

[1] Here begins the Greek text according to Bev., and ends at the asterisk.

NOTES.

Whoso knowingly admits to communion one excommunicated by his own bishop is not without blame.

This is Canon XVI. of the Latin.

VAN ESPEN.

The present canon agrees with Canon V. of Nice and with Canon IV. of Antioch, on which canons see the notes. The Synod's approbation of this canon is found in Dionysius, Isidore, and in the Roman Codex *apud* Hervetus; but it is lacking from Balsamon and Zonaras.

CANON XIV.

(*Greek.*)

BISHOP HOSIUS said: I must not fail to speak of a matter which constantly urgeth me.[1] If a bishop be found quick to anger (which ought not to sway such a man), and he, suddenly moved against a presbyter or deacon, be minded to cast him out of the Church, provision must be made that such a one be not condemned too hastily [*or read ἀθῶον*, if innocent] and deprived of communion.

All said: Let him that is cast out be authorized to take refuge with the bishop of the metropolis of the same province. And if the bishop of the metropolis is absent, let him hasten to the bishop that is nearest, and ask to have his case carefully examined. For a hearing ought not to be denied those who ask it.

And that bishop who cast out such a one, justly or unjustly, ought not to take it ill that examination of the case be made, and his decision confirmed or revised. But, until all the particulars have been examined with care and fidelity, he who is excluded from communion ought not to demand communion in advance of the decision of his case. And if any of the clergy who have met [to hear the case] clearly discern arrogance and pretentiousness in him, inasmuch as it is not fitting to suffer insolence or unjust censure, they ought to correct such an one with somewhat harsh and grievous language, that men may submit to and obey commands that are proper and right. For as the bishop ought to manifest sincere love and regard to his subordinates, so those who are subject to him ought in like manner to perform the duties of their ministry in sincerity towards their bishops.

(*Latin.*)

BISHOP HOSIUS said: I must not fail to speak of a matter which further moveth me. If some bishop is perchance quick to anger (which ought not to be the case) and, moved hastily and violently against one of his presbyters or deacons, be minded to cast him out of the Church, provision must be made that an innocent man be not condemned or deprived of communion.

Therefore let him that is cast out be authorized to appeal to the neighbouring bishops and let his case be heard and examined into more diligently. For a hearing ought not to be denied one who asks it.

And let that bishop who cast him out, justly or unjustly, take it patiently that the matter is discussed, so that his sentence may either be approved by a number [of judges] or else revised. Nevertheless, until all the particulars shall be examined with care and fidelity, no one else ought to presume to admit to communion him who was excluded therefrom in advance of the decision of his case. If, however, those who meet to hear it observe arrogance and pride in [such] clergy, inasmuch as it surely is not fitting for a bishop to suffer wrong or insult, let them correct them with some severity of language, that they may obey a bishop whose commands are proper and right. For as he [the bishop] ought to manifest sincere love and charity to his clergy, so his ministers ought for their part to render unfeigned obedience to their bishop.

---

[1] The Greek text of Bev. begins here.

NOTES.

ANCIENT EPITOME OF CANON XIV.

One condemned out of anger, if he asks for assistance, should be heard. But until [he shall have asked for [1]] the assistance let him remain excommunicated.

This is Canon XVII. of the Latin version.

VAN ESPEN.

This canon is intended especially to aid presbyters, deacons, and other clerics, who have been excommunicated precipitately and without just cause, or suspended by their own bishop in his anger and fury. . . . The canon, moreover, admonishes that the bishop with regard to whose sentence the dispute has arisen shall patiently consent to the discussion of the matter *de novo*, whether his decision be sustained by the majority or emended.

And let bishops and other prelates who have spiritual jurisdiction over the clergy note this, who cannot bear with equanimity that a word should be said against their decisions, but exact a kind of blind obedience, even frequently with great conscientious suffering to their very best ecclesiastics; and in such cases as do not promptly and blindly obey them, the clergy are traduced as rebels and even a patient hearing is refused to them.

This canon is found in the *Corpus Juris Canonici*, Gratian's *Decretum*, P. II., Causa XI., Q. iij., c. iv.

[AFTER CANON XIV.]

CANON XVIII. (*Of the Latin.*)

BISHOP JANUARIUS said: Let your holiness also decree this, that no bishop be allowed to try to gain for himself a minister in the church of a bishop of another city and ordain him to one of his own parishes.

All said: Such is our pleasure, inasmuch as discord is apt to spring from contentions in this matter, and therefore the sentence of us all forbids anyone to presume to do

NOTE.

VAN ESPEN.

It is manifest that these two canons [xviii. of the Latin and xv. of the Greek], contain the resolution of the same case, and therefore it is that the Greeks keep only the former which contains the decree of the synod, made on Hosius's motion, the suggestion having been made by Januarius the bishop: which suggestion makes the first of these canons. [I.e. Latin canon xviij.]

CANON XV.

(*Greek.*)

BISHOP HOSIUS said: And let us all decree this also, that [2] if any bishop should ordain to any order the minister of another from another diocese without the consent of his own bishop, such an ordination should be accounted invalid and not confirmed. And if any take upon themselves to do this they ought to be admonished and corrected by our brethren and fellow-bishops.

All said: Let this decree also stand unalterable.

(*Latin.*)

BISHOP HOSIUS said: This also we all decree, that if any [bishop] should ordain the minister of another from another diocese without the consent and will of his own bishop, his ordination be not ratified. And whoever shall have taken upon himself to do this ought to be admonished and corrected by our brethren and fellow-bishops.

---

[1] This is the understanding of Beveridge's Latin. I should have supposed the words to be supplied were "the reception of."

[2] The Greek text of Bev. begins here.

NOTES.

ANCIENT EPITOME OF CANON XV.

If one places a foreign minister without the knowledge of his own bishop in any grade (ἐμβαθ-μον, in aliquo gradu), he has indeed made the appointment, but it is without force.

This is Canon XIX. in the Latin.

HEFELE.

Fuchs, in his *Bibliothek der Kirchenversamm-lungen* (Pt. II., p. 123, note 125), thinks he has discovered a difference between this can-on and the exclusively Latin one preceding it, in that the latter supposes the case of a bishop ordaining a foreign cleric, over whom he has no jurisdiction, to a higher grade, with the view of retaining him for his own diocese ; while the other—fifteenth or nine-teenth canon—treats of a case where such an ordination takes place without the ordaining bishop intending to keep the person ordained for his own diocese. Van Espen is of another opinion, and maintains that both canons ob-viously refer to one and the same case, for which reason the Greek text has only inserted one of them. It is certain that the text of both canons, as we have it, does not clearly indicate the difference conjectured by Fuchs, but that it may easily be found there.

VAN ESPEN.

If the reading of all the Latins and Greeks is decisive, this canon only treats of the ordi-nation of those already ministers or clerics, and so the Greek commentators Balsamon, Zonaras, and Aristenus understood it, as is evident from their annotations. But Gratus, Bishop of Carthage, and Primate of Africa, in the First Synod of Carthage testified that in this canon it was decreed, that without the licence of his own bishop, a layman of another diocese was not to be ordained, and this inter-pretation or rather extension of the Canon, was received everywhere, as is demonstrated by the fifty-sixth of the African Code.

This together with Canon XIX. of the Latin text are found as one in the *Corpus Juris Canonici* (Gratian's *Decretum*, P. I., Dist. lxxj.), c. j.

CANON XVI.

(*Greek.*)

BISHOP AËTIUS said : Ye are not ignorant how important and how large is the metro-politan city of Thessalonica. Accordingly presbyters and deacons often come to it from other provinces and, not content with staying a short time, remain and make it their permanent place of residence, or are compelled with difficulty and after a very long de-lay to return to their own churches. A decree should be made bearing on this matter.

Bishop Hosius said : Let those decrees which have been made in the case of bishops, be observed as to these persons also.

(*Latin.*)

BISHOP AËTIUS said : Ye are not ignorant how large and important is the city of Thes-salonica. Presbyters and deacons often come to it from other regions, and are not con-tent to remain a short time, but either make their residence there or at least are with difficulty compelled to return after a long interval to their own place.

All said : Those limits of time which have been decreed in the case of bishops ought to be observed as to these persons also.

NOTES.

ANCIENT EPITOME OF CANON XVI.

What things have been decreed for bishops with regard to the length of their absence, applies also to presbyters and deacons.

VAN ESPEN.

This canon needs no explanation.

---

[1] The reference is given incorrectly in the English Hefele.

CANON XVII.

(*Greek.*)

AT the suggestion moreover of our brother Olympius, [1] we are pleased to decree this also: That if a bishop suffer violence and is unjustly cast out either on account of his discipline or for his confession of [the faith of] the Catholic Church or for his defence of the truth, and, fleeing from danger, although innocent and devout [*or*, innocent and being under charge of high treason], comes to another city, let him not be forbidden to stay there until he is restored or until deliverance can be found from the violence and injustice that have been done him. For it would be harsh indeed and most oppressive that one who has suffered unjust expulsion should not be harboured by us; as such a man ought to be received with the greatest consideration and cordiality.*

All said: This also is our pleasure.

(*Latin.*)

AT the suggestion of our brother Olympius, we are pleased to decree this also: That if any suffer violence and is unjustly cast out on account of his discipline and his Catholic confession or for his defence of the truth, and, fleeing from dangers, although innocent and devout, comes to another city, let him not be forbidden to stay there until he can return or his wrong has been redressed. For it is harsh and unfeeling that he who is suffering persecution should not be received; indeed, great cordiality and abundant consideration should be shown him.

All the synod said: All that has been decreed the Catholic Church spread abroad throughout all the world will preserve and maintain.

And all the bishops of the various provinces who had assembled subscribed thus:

I, N., bishop of the city of N. and the province of N., so believe as above is written.

NOTES.

ANCIENT EPITOME OF CANON XVII.

If a bishop goes into another province after he has been unjustly expelled from his own, he should be received, until he has been delivered from his injury.

This is Canon XXI. of the Latin and the last.

VAN ESPEN.

St. Gregory seems to have had this canon in mind when he wrote to the bishops of Illyria (Lib. III., *Epist.* xliij.), who had been cast out by the hostility of the barbarians.

CANON XVIII.

(*Greek.*)

BISHOP GAUDENTIUS said: Thou knowest, brother Aëtius, that since thou wast made bishop, peace hath continued to rule [in thy diocese]. In order that no remnants of discord concerning ecclesiastics remain, it seems good that those who were ordained by Musæus and by Eutychianus, provided no fault be found in them, should all be received.

(This canon is wanting in the *Latin.*)

CANON XIX.

(*Greek.*)

BISHOP HOSIUS said: This is the sentence of my mediocrity [i.e., unworthiness]— that, since we ought to be gentle and patient and to be constant in compassion towards all, those who were once advanced to clerical office in the Church by certain of our

---

[1] The Greek text of Bev. begins here and ends at the asterisk.

brethren, if they are not willing to return to the churches to which they were nominated [or, espoused], should for the future not be received, and that neither Eutychianus should continue to vindicate to himself the name of bishop, nor yet that Musæus be accounted a bishop; but that if they should seek for lay communion, it should not be denied them.

All said: Such is our pleasure.

(This canon is wanting in the *Latin*.)

NOTES.

ANCIENT EPITOME OF CANONS XVIII. AND XIX.

A clergyman who does not live in the Church among whose clergy he is enrolled should not be received. Eutychian and Musæus shall not have the name of bishops. But let them be admitted to communion with the laity, if they wish.

Both of these canons are lacking in the Latin.

HEFELE.

It is clear that the reason why these two canons do not exist in the Latin text is that they did not apply to the Latin Church and only contained a special rule for Thessalonica.

CANON XX.

(*Greek.*)

BISHOP GAUDENTIUS said: These things wholesomely, duly, and fitly decreed, in the estimation of us the bishops [τῶν ἱερέων] such as are pleasing both to God and to man will not be able to obtain due force and validity, unless fear [of a penalty] be added to the decrees proclaimed. For we ourselves know that through the shamelessness of a few, the divine and right reverend title of bishop [of the τῆς ἱερωσύνης] hath often come into condemnation. If therefore any one, moved by arrogance and ambition rather than seeking to please God, should have the hardihood to pursue a different course of action, contrary to the decree of all, let him know beforehand that he must give account and defend himself on this charge, and lose the honour and dignity of the episcopate.

All answered: This sentence is proper and right, and such is our pleasure.[1]

And this decree will be most widely known and best carried into effect, if each of those bishops among us who have sees on the thoroughfares or highway, on seeing a bishop [pass by] shall inquire into the cause of his passage and his place of destination. And if at his departure he shall find that he is going to the Court, he will direct his inquiries with reference to the objects [of a resort to the Court] above mentioned. And if he come by invitation let no obstacle be put in the way of his departure. But if he is trying to go to the Court out of ostentation, as hath afore been said by your charity, or to urge the petitions of certain persons, let neither his letters be signed nor let such an one be received to communion.

All said: Be this also decreed

(*Latin.*)

BISHOP GAUDENTIUS said: These things which you have wholesomely and suitably provided [in your decrees] pleasing in [or, to] the estimation of all both [or, and] to God and to men, can obtain force and validity only in case fear [of a penalty] be added to this your action. For we ourselves know that through the shamelessness of a few the sacred and venerable sacerdotal [—episcopal] name hath been many times and oft brought to blame. If therefore anyone attempts to oppose the judgment of all and seeks to serve ambition rather than please God, he must be given to know that he will have to render an account and lose office and rank.

This can be carried into effect only provided each of us whose see is on the highway shall, if he sees a bishop pass, inquire into the cause of his journey, ascertain his desti-

---

[1] Here begins Canon xxj., according to the Greek text of Bev.

nation, and if he finds that he is on his way to the Court, satisfy himself as to what is contained above [i.e., as to his objects at Court], lest perhaps he has come by invitation, that permission may be given him to proceed. If, however, as your holiness mentioned above, he is going to Court to urge petitions and applications for office, let neither his letters be signed nor let him be received to communion.

All said that this was proper and right and that this regulation was approved by them.

NOTES.

Ancient Epitome of Canon XX. [the last part of which in Beveridge, *Synod.*, is numbered xxj.]

If any bishop tries out of pride to do away with what has been decreed admirably, and in a manner pleasing to God, he shall lose his episcopate. A bishop who shall see a bishop on his way to the camp, if he shall know that he goes there for any of the before-mentioned causes, let him not trouble him, but if otherwise let him pronounce excommunication against him.

This is Canon XI. of the Latin.

Van Espen.

After the words ["honour and dignity"] according to Balsamon and Zonaras, as also Gentian Hervetus, there follows the approbation of the synod in these words : "All answered, This opinion is becoming and well-pleasing to us," which indicate this to be the end of the canon ; and therefore the Greeks make of this two distinct canons.

Dionysius and Isidore make but one canon, . . . and this appears to be more congruous on account of the subject-matter of the first part, and will be manifest by connecting the two parts together.

Van Espen follows Zonaras and Balsamon in understanding "Bishops in Canali," as such as were set on the public roads and public highways, or rather "in cities which are on the public highways, or 'Canals,' by which they that pass go without labour, as in a canal or aqueduct the water flows, for aqueduct and canal are the same thing in the Roman tongue."

[AFTER CANON XX.]

CANON XII. (*Of the Latin Texts.*)

BISHOP HOSIUS said : But some discretion is here requisite, brethren dearly beloved, in case some should come to those cities which are on the highway still ignorant of what has been decreed in the council. The bishop of such a city ought therefore to admonish him [a bishop so arriving], and instruct him to send his deacon from that place. Upon this admonition he must, however, himself return to his diocese.

NOTES.

Van Espen.

This proposition of Hosius in the Roman Codex is joined as an appendix to the preceding canon. The Greeks omit it altogether, very likely either because it seemed to be a proposition of Hosius's rather than a synodal canon, for no adoption by the synod is recorded : or else because, even if it were a decree, it was only of temporary character, that is to say, until the canons had been sufficiently promulgated, and therefore some on the ground of ignorance might be exempt from the threatened penalties.

EXCURSUS ON THE OTHER ACTS OF THE COUNCIL.

As only the Canons have any real connexion with the Ecumenical Synods, they alone have properly a place in this volume, and yet it may not be amiss to give a brief account of the other acts of the council, so far as we know them.

(a) *The Rule for Keeping Easter.*—The Anglican Scholar, the Rev. William Cureton, of the British Museum, first edited the then recently discovered Preface to the *Paschal Letters* of St. Athanasius, together with the Letters themselves.   The MS. which he then published was in Syriac and was discovered in Egypt.   In the preface just referred to, it is expressly stated that "a plan was agreed upon at Sardica with regard to the feast of Easter."   But this new plan, which was only expected to hold good for fifty years, failed, and although in A.D. 346 Easter should have fallen on March 23d, yet the Council (so says St. Athanasius) agreed to observe it on March 30th.   Another divergence fell in A.D. 349.   Easter, by the Alexandrian calculation, would have been April 23d.   But by Roman count, the origin of which was attributed to St. Peter, Easter was never to be later than April 21st, and for the sake of peace the Alexandrians yielded to the Romans and kept Easter on March 26th; but in 350, 360, and 368 the Alexandrian and Roman methods again disagreed, and even the fifty years which Sardica had thought to ensure uniformity were marked by diverse usages.

(b) *The Encyclical Letter.*—The Council addressed a long Encyclical letter to all the bishops of the world; it is found in St. Athanasius[1] in Greek, in St. Hilary of Poictiers[2] in Latin, and in Theodoret's *Ecclesiastical History.*[3]   In this last there occurs at the end the so-called "Creed of Sardica," which is now considered by scholars to be undoubtedly spurious.

(c) *A Letter to the Diocese of Alexandria.*—St. Athanasius[4] gives us the Greek text of a letter sent by the council to the diocese of Alexandria to the bishops of Egypt and Libya.

(d) *A Letter to Pope Julius.*—Among the *Fragments* of St. Hilary[5] is found a letter from the synod to Pope Julius.   Hefele says that the text is "considerably injured."   One clause of this letter above all others has given occasion to much controversy.   The passage runs as follows: "It was best and fittest that the priests [i.e., bishops] from all the provinces should make their reports to the head, that is, the chair of St. Peter."   Blondell declares the passage to be an interpolation, resting his opinion upon the barbarous Latin of the expression *valde congruentissimum.*   And even Remi Ceillier, while explaining this by the supposition, which is wholly gratuitous, that the original was Greek, yet is forced to confess that the sentence interrupts the flow of thought and looks like an insertion.   Bower,[6] in his *History of the Popes*, and Fuchs[7] have urged still more strongly the spurious character of the phrase, the latter using the convenient "marginal comment" explanation.

Besides these there are three documents which Scipio Maffei discovered in MS. at Verona, which by some are supposed to belong to the Council of Sardica.

(*a*) A Letter to the Christians of Mareotis.

(*b*) A Letter of St. Athanasius to the same Mareotic Churches.   This letter is signed not only by Athanasius, but also by a great number of the bishops composing the synod.

(*c*) A Letter from St. Athanasius to the Church of Alexandria.

On the authority to be attributed to these three documents I can do no better than quote the closing words of Hefele,[8] whom I have followed in this whole excursus.

"These extracts shew, I think, quite sufficiently the spuriousness of these documents. Is it possible that the Eusebians would have said of themselves: 'We are enemies of Christ?' But apart from this, the whole contents of these three letters are lame and feeble.   The constant repetition of the same words is intolerable, and the whole style pointless and trivial. To this it must be added that the whole of Christian antiquity knew nothing of these three documents, which only exist in the codex at Verona, so that we cannot acknowledge them as genuine."

---

[1] Athanas. *Apol. contra Arian.*, c. 44.
[2] Hilar. *Fragm.*, t ii., 1283.
[3] Theodoret. *Hist. Eccl.*, Lib. II., cap. 6.
[4] Athanas. *Apol. ctr. Arian.*, c. 37, and again in chapter 41 (this last, which is really the same, is addressed to the bishops of Egypt and Libya).

[5] Hilar. *Fragment.*, Tom. ii.
[6] Bower. *Hist. Popes, in loc.*
[7] Fuchs' *Bibliothe der Kirchen vers.*, vol. ii., p. 128 (cit. by Hef.)
[8] Hefele, *History Councils*, vol. ii., p. 166.

EXCURSUS AS TO WHETHER THE SARDICAN COUNCIL WAS ECUMENICAL.

Some theologians and canonists have been of opinion that the Council of Sardica was Ecumenical and would reckon it as the Second. But besides the fact that such a numbering is absolutely in contrariety to all history it also labours under the difficulty, as we shall see presently, that the Westerns by insisting that St. Athanasius should have a seat caused a division of the synod at the very outset, so that the Easterns met at Philippopolis and confirmed the deposition of the Saint. It is also interesting to remember that when Alexander Natalis in his history expressly called this synod ecumenical, the passage was marked with disapproval by the Roman censors.

(Hefele. *Hist. Councils.* Vol. II., pp. 172 *et seqq.*)

The ecumenical character of this Synod certainly cannot be proved.[1] It is indeed true that it was the design of Pope Julius, as well as of the two Emperors, Constantius and Constans, to summon a General Council at Sardica ; but we do not find that any such actually took place : and the history of the Church points to many like cases, where a synod was probably intended to be ecumenical, and yet did not attain that character. In the present case, the Eastern and Western bishops were indeed summoned, but by far the greater number of the Eastern bishops were Eusebians, and therefore Semi-Arians, and instead of acting in a better mind in union with the orthodox, they separated themselves and formed a cabal of their own at Philippopolis.

We cannot indeed agree with those who maintain that the departure of the Eusebians in itself rendered it impossible for the synod to be ecumenical, or it would be in the power of heretics to make an Ecumenical Council possible or not. We cannot, however, overlook the fact that, in consequence of this withdrawal, the great Eastern Church was far more poorly represented at Sardica, and that the entire number of bishops present did not even amount to a hundred ! So small a number of bishops can only form a General Council if the great body of their absent colleagues subsequently give their express consent to what has been decided. This was not, however, the case at the Synod of Sardica. The decrees were no doubt at once sent for acceptance and signature to the whole of Christendom, but not more than about two hundred of those bishops who had been absent signed, and of these, ninety-four, or nearly half, were Egyptians. Out of the whole of Asia only a few bishops from the provinces of Cyprus and Palestine signed, not one from the other Eastern provinces ; and even from the Latin Church in Africa, which at that time numbered at least three hundred bishops, we meet with very few names. We cannot give much weight to the fact that the Emperor Constantius refused to acknowledge the decrees of Sardica : it is of much greater importance that no single later authority declared it to be a General Council. Natalis Alexander[2] is indeed of opinion that because Pope Zosimus, in the year 417 or 418, cited the fifth canon of Sardica as Nicene, and a synod held at Constantinople in 382 cited the sixth as Nicene, the synod must evidently have been considered as an appendix to that of Nicea, and therefore its equal, that is, must have been honoured as ecumenical. But we have already shown how Zosimus and the bishops of Constantinople had been led into this confusion from the defects of their manuscript collections of the canons. Athanasius, Sulpicius Severus, Socrates, and the Emperor Justinian were cited in later times for the ecumenical character of this synod. Athanasius calls it a μεγάλη σύνοδος ; Sulpicius Severus says it was *ex toto orbe convocata ;* and Socrates relates that "Athanasius and other bishops had demanded an Ecumenical Synod, and that of Sardica had been then summoned.[3] It is clear at the first

---

[1] Hefele refers to his having himself treated this matter fully in the *Theologischer Quartalschrift* of Tübingen, 1852.

[2] Nat Alex. *H. E.*, sec. iv., Diss. xxvij., Art. 3.
[3] Socrates. *H. E.*, Lib. ii., cap. 20.

glance that the two last authorities only prove that the Synod had been intended to be a general one, and the expression "Great Synod," used by Athanasius, cannot be taken as simply identical with ecumenical.   While, however, the Emperor Justinian, in his edict of 346, on the Three Chapters, calls the Synod of Sardica ecumenical, he yet, in the same edict, as well as in other places, does not reckon it among the General Councils, of which he counts four.   To this must be added, first, that the Emperor is not the authority entitled to decide as to the character of an Ecumenical Synod ; and secondly, that the expression *Universale Concilium* was employed in a wider sense in speaking of those synods which, without being general, represented a whole patriarchate.

The Trullan Synod and Pope Nicholas I. are further appealed to.   The former in its second canon approved of the Sardican canons, and Pope Nicholas said of them: "*omnis Ecclesia recepit eos.*"   But this in no way contains a declaration that the Synod of Sardica was ecumenical, for the canons of many other councils also—for instance, Ancyra, Neocæsarea, and others—were generally received without those synods themselves being therefore esteemed ecumenical.   Nay, the Trullan Synod itself speaks for us ; for had it held the Synod of Sardica to be the second General Council, it would have placed its canons immediately after those of Nice, whereas they are placed after the four ancient General Councils, and from this we see that the Trullan Synod did not reckon the Sardican among those councils, but after them.   To this it must be added that the highest Church authorities speak most decidedly against the synod being ecumenical.   We may appeal first to Augustine, who only knew of the Eusebian assembly at Sardica, and nothing at all of an orthodox synod in that place ; which would have been clearly impossible, if .it had at that time been counted among the ecumenical synods.   Pope Gregory the Great [1] and St. Isidore of Seville[2] speak still more plainly.   They only know of four ancient General Councils—those of Nice, Constantinople, Ephesus, and Chalcedon.   The objection of the Ballerini that Gregory and Isidore did not intend to enumerate the most ancient general synods as such, but only those which issued important dogmatic decrees, is plainly quite arbitrary, and therefore without force.   Under such circumstances it is natural that among the later scholars by far the great majority should have answered the question, whether the Synod of Sardica is ecumenical, in the negative, as have Cardinal Bellarmin, Peter de Marca, Edmund Richer, Fleury, Orsi, Sacharelli, Tillemont, Du Pin, Berti, Ruttenstock, Rohrbacher, Remi Ceillier, Stolberg, Neander, and others.   On the other hand, Baronius, Natalis Alexander, the brothers Ballerini, Mansi, and Palma[3] have sought to maintain the ecumenical character of the synod, but as early as the seventeenth century the Roman censors condemned the direct assertions of Natalis Alexander on the subject.

---

[1] Greg. M.   Lib. ii., *Epist.* 10.
[2] Isidor.   Hispal.   *Etymolog.*, Lib. vi., cap. 16.

[3] Jno. Bapt. Palma.   *Prælectiones Hist. Eccl. quas in Collegio Urbano habuit.*   Rome, 1838.   Tom. i., P. ii., p. 85.

THE CANONS OF THE CCXVII BLESSED FATHERS WHO ASSEMBLED AT CARTHAGE.

COMMONLY CALLED

THE CODE OF CANONS OF THE AFRICAN CHURCH.

A.D. 419

Elenchus.

Introductory Note.   *The Canons with the Ancient Epitome and Notes.*

INTRODUCTORY NOTE.

An attempt to write a commentary upon all the canons of the African Code, would have meant nothing less than the preparation of one volume or more on the canon law of the West. This is impossible and therefore, interesting as the field would be, I have been compelled to restrain my pen, and rather than give a scant and insufficient annotation, I have contented myself with providing the reader with as good a translation as I have been able to make of the very corrupt Latin (correcting it at times by the Greek), and have added the Ancient Epitome and the quaint notes in full of John Johnson from the Second Edition, of 1714, of his "Clergyman's Vade-mecum," Pt. II., which occupy little space, but may not be easily reached by the ordinary reader. The student will find full scholia on these Canons in Van Espen in the Latin, and in Zonaras and Balsamon in the Greek. These latter are in Beveridge's *Synodicon*.

Johnson writes an excellent Introduction to his Epitome of these Canons, as follows:

"Councils were nowhere more frequently called in the Primitive Times than in Africa. In the year 418–19, all canons formerly made in sixteen councils held at Carthage, one at Milevis, one at Hippo, that were approved of, were read, and received a new sanction from a great number of bishops, then met in synod at Carthage. This Collection is the Code of the African Church, which was always in greatest repute in all Churches next after the Code of the Universal Church. This code was of very great authority in the old English Churches, for many of the Excerptions of Egbert were transcribed from it. And though the Code of the Universal Church ends with the canons of Chalcedon,[1] yet these African Canons are inserted into the Ancient Code both of the Eastern and Western Churches. These canons though ratified and approved by a synod, yet seem to have been divided or numbered by some private and unlearned hand, and have probably met with very unskilful transcribers, by which means some of them are much confounded and obscured, as to their sense and coherence. They are by Dionysius Exiguus and others entituled *The Canons of the Synod of Africa*. And though all were not originally made at one time, yet they were all confirmed by one synod of African bishops, who, after they had recited the Creed and the twenty canons of the Council of Nice, proceeded to make new canons, and re-enforce old ones."

In his "Library of Canon Law" (*Bibliotheca Juris Canonici*) Justellus gives these canons, and, in my opinion, gives them rightly, the title "The Code of Canons of the African Church" (*Codex Canonum Ecclesiæ Africanæ*), although Hefele[2] describes them as "the collection of those African Canons put together in 419 by Dionysius Exiguus." Hefele says that the title Dionysius gave them in his collection was "The Statutes of an African Council" (*Statuta Concilii Africani*) which would certainly be wholly inadequate and misleading ; but in the edition of Dionysius in Migne's *Patrologia Latina* (Tom. LXVII., col. 181) in the *Codex Canonum Ecclesiasticorum* no such title occurs, but the perfectly accurate one, " A Synod at Carthage in Africa, which adopted one hundred and thirty-eight canons." This is an exact description of what took place and of the origin of these most important dogmatic and disciplinary enactments. Hefele must have been thinking of Dionysius's *Preface* where the expression does occur but not as a title.

(Beveridge. *Synodicon*, Tom. II., p. 202.)

Carthage was formerly the head of the whole of Africa, as St. Augustine tells us in his Epistle CLXII. From this cause it happened that a great number of councils were held

---

[1] I do not understand what Johnson means by this statement. Vide Can. j. of Chalcedon.
[2] Hefele. *Hist. of the Councils*, vol. ii., p. 468, Note 1.

there, gathered from all the provinces of Africa. Especially while Aurelius as Archbishop was occupying the throne were these meetings of bishops frequently holden; and by these, for the establishing of ecclesiastical discipline in Africa, many canons were enacted. At last, after the consulate of Honorius (XII.) and Theodosius (VIII.), Augustuses, on the eighth day before the Calends of June, that is to say, on May 25, in the year of our Lord 419, another Council was held in the same city at which all the canons previously adopted were considered, and the greater part of them were again confirmed by the authority of the synod. These canons, thus confirmed by this council, merited to be called from that day to this " The Code of Canons of the African Church." These canons were not at first adopted in Greek but in Latin, and they were confirmed in the same language. This Dionysius Exiguus distinctly testifies to in his preface to the " Code of Ecclesiastical Canons," in which they are included. It is uncertain when the canons of this Carthaginian synod were done into Greek. This only is certain, that they had been translated into Greek before the Council in Trullo by which, in its Second Canon, they were received into the Greek Nomocanon, and were confirmed by the authority of this synod; so that from that time these canons stand in the Eastern Church on an equality with all the rest.

An extremely interesting point arises as to what was the authority of the collection as a collection, and how this collection was made? There seems no doubt that the collection substantially as we know it was the code accepted by the Council of Trullo, the canons of which received a quasi-ecumenical authority from the subsequent general imprimatur given them by the Seventh Ecumenical Council, the Second of Nice. Van Espen has considered this point at great length in Dissertation VIII. of the First Part of his *Commentaries*, and to his pages I must refer the reader for anything like an adequate presentation of the matter. He concludes (§ I.) that the " Code owes its origin to this synod," and argues against De Marca in proof of the proposition that the collection was not the private work of Dionysius, but the official work of the council by one of its officials, concluding with the remark (§ II.) that " this was the persuasion both of Greeks and Latins, . . . and these canons are set forth by Balsamon with the title, 'The Canons of the CCXVII. Blessed Fathers who met together at Carthage.'"

In the notes on each canon I shall give the source, following Hefele in all respects (*Hist. of the Councils*, vol. ii., pp. 468 *et seqq.*), and content myself here with setting down a list of the various councils which made the enactments, with their dates.

The numbering of the African councils differs very widely between the different writers, and Cave reckons nine between 401 and 608, and thirty-five Carthaginian between 215 and 533.[1] Very useful tables, shewing the conclusions of Fuchs, are found at the end of Bruns, *Canones Apostolorum et Conciliorum Veterum Selecti.*

I need only add that I have frequently used Dr. Bruns's text, but have not confined myself to it exclusively. Evidently in the Latin, as we now have it, there are many corrupt passages. In strange contradistinction to this, the Greek is apparently pure and is clear throughout. Possibly the Greek translation was made from a purer Latin text than we now possess.

AN ANCIENT INTRODUCTION.

(Found in Dionysius Exiguus, Codex Can. *Migne,* Pat. Lat., Tom. lxvii., col. 182.)

After the consulate of the most glorious emperors, Honorus for the twelfth time and Theodosius for the eighth time, Augustuses, on the VIII. before the Calends of June at Carthage, in the Secretarium of the basilica of Faustus, when Pope Aurelius had sat down, together with Valentine of the primatial see of the province of Numidia, and Faustinus of the Potentine Church, of the Italian province Picenum, a legate of the Roman Church, and also with legates of the different African provinces, that is to say, of the two Numidias, of Byzacena, of Mauritania Cæsariensis, as well as of Tripoli, and with Vincent Colositanus, Fortunatian, and other bishops of the proconsular province, in all two hundred and seventeen, also with Philip and Asellus, presbyters and legates of the Roman Church, and while the deacons were standing by, Aurelius the bishop said, etc., *ut infra.*

---

[1] For this statement I am indebted to Mr. Ffoulkes in art. "African Councils." Smith and Cheetham, *Dict. Christ. Antiq.*

THE CANONS OF THE 217 BLESSED FATHERS WHO ASSEMBLED AT CARTHAGE.

(Labbe and Cossart: *Concilia*, Tom. II., Col. 1041; Dionysius Ex., *Codex Can. Eccles.* [Migne, *Pat. Lat.*, Tom. LXVII.]; Beveridge, *Synodicon* in loc.)

AURELIUS THE BISHOP said:[1] You, most blessed brethren, remember that after the day fixed for the synod we discussed many things while we were waiting for our brethren who now have been sent as delegates and have arrived at the present synod, which must be placed in the acts. Wherefore let us render thanks to our Lord for the gathering together of so great an assembly. It remains that the acts of the Nicene Synod which we now have, and have been determined by the fathers, as well as those things enacted by our predecessors here, who confirmed that same Synod, or which according to the same form have been usefully enacted by all grades of the clergy, from the highest even to the lowest, should be brought forward. The whole Council said: Let them be brought forward.

Daniel the Notary read: The profession of faith or statutes of the Nicene Synod are as follows.

And while he was speaking, Faustinus, a bishop of the people of Potentia, of the Italian province of Picenum, a legate of the Roman Church said: There have been entrusted to us by the Apostolic See certain things in writings, and certain other things as in ordinances to be treated of with your blessedness as we have called to memory in the acts above, that is to say, concerning the canons made at Nice, that their decrees and customs be observed; for some things are observed out of decree and canon, but some from custom. Concerning these things therefore in the first place let us make enquiry, if it please your blessedness; and afterwards let the other ordinances which have been adopted or proposed be confirmed; so that you may be able to show by your rescripts to the Apostolic See, and that you may declare to the same venerable Pope, that we have diligently remembered these things; although the headings of action taken had been already inserted in the acts.[2] In this matter we should act, as I have said above, as shall please your beloved blessedness. Let, therefore the commonitorium come into the midst, that ye may be able to recognize what is contained in it, so that an answer can be given to each point.

Aurelius said: Let the commonitorium be brought forward, which our brethren and fellow-ministers lately placed in the acts, and let the rest of the things done or to be done, follow in order.

Daniel the Notary read the Commonitorium. To our brother Faustinus and to our sons, the presbyters Philip and Asellus, Zosimus, the bishop. You well remember that we committed to you certain businesses, and now [we bid you] carry out all things as if we ourselves were there (for), indeed, our presence is there with you; especially since ye have this our commandment, and the words of the canons which for greater certainty we have inserted in this our commonitory. For thus said our brethren in the Council of Nice when they made these decrees concerning the appeals of bishops:

" But it seemed good that if a bishop had been accused, etc." [*Here follows* verbatim *Canon v. of Sardica.*]

ANCIENT EPITOME.	benignantly heard, the Roman bishop writing or ordering.
If bishops shall have deposed a bishop, and if he appeal to the Roman bishop, he should be	

And when this had been read, Alypius, bishop of the Tagastine Church, and legate of the province of Numidia, said: On this matter there has been some legislation in

---

[1] The reader must not complain if he finds the meaning of the translation often obscure. So great a scholar as Hefele says of one of these speeches, " This, I believe, must be the meaning of the somewhat unintelligible text, etc.," and again of another passage he says that it " is even more obscure," and that " the text is undoubtedly corrupt. The sense is probably, etc."

[2] I have followed in this passage the Greek text as a trifle less incomprehensible.

former sessions of our council, and we profess that we shall ever observe what was de-creed by the Nicene Council ; yet I remember that when we examined the Greek copies of this Nicene Synod, we did not find these the words quoted—Why this was the case, I am sure I do not know.   For this reason we beg your reverence, holy Pope Aurelius, that, as the authentic record of the decrees of the Council of Nice are said to be preserved in the city of Constantinople, you would deign to send messengers with letters from your Holiness, and not only to our most holy brother the bishop of Con-stantinople, but also to the venerable bishops of Alexandria and Antioch, who shall send to us the decrees of that council with the authentification of their signatures, so that hereafter all ambiguity should be taken away, for we failed to find the words cited by our brother Faustinus ; notwithstanding this however we promise to be ruled by them for a short time, as I have already said, until reliable copies come to hand. Moreover the venerable bishop of the Roman Church, Boniface, should be asked like-wise to be good enough to send messengers to the aforementioned churches, who should have the same copies according to his rescript, but the copies of the aforementioned Nicene Council which we have, we place in these Acts.

Faustinus the bishop, legate of the Roman Church, said : Let not your holiness do dishonour to the Roman Church, either in this matter or in any other, by saying the canons are doubtful, as our brother and fellow-bishop Alypius has vouchsafed to say : but do you deign to write these things to our holy and most blessed pope, so that he seeking out the genuine canons, can treat with your holiness on all matters decreed. But it suffices that the most blessed bishop of the city of Rome should make enquiry just as your holiness proposes doing on your part, that there may not seem to have arisen any contention between the Churches, but that ye may the rather be enabled to deliberate with fraternal charity, when he has been heard from, what is best should be observed.

Aurelius the bishop said : In addition to what is set down in the acts, we, by the letters from our insignificance, must more fully inform our holy brother and fellow-bishop Boniface of everything which we have considered.   Therefore if our plan pleases all, let us be informed of this by the mouth of all.   And the whole council said : It seems good to us.

Novatus the bishop, legate of Mauritania Sitifensis, said : We now call to mind that there is contained in this commonitory something about presbyters and deacons, how they should be tried by their own bishops or by those adjoining, a provision which we find nothing of in the Nicene Council.   For this cause let your holiness order this part to be read.

Aurelius the bishop said : Let the place asked for be read.   Daniel the notary read as follows : Concerning the appeals of clergymen, that is of those of inferior rank, there is a sure answer of this very synod, concerning which thing what ye should do, we think should be inserted, as follows :

" Hosius the bishop said : I should not conceal what has come into my mind up to this time.   If any bishop perchance has been quickly angered (a thing what should not happen) and has acted quickly or sharply against a presbyter or a deacon of his, and has wished to drive him out of the Church, provision should be made that the innocent be not condemned, or be deprived of communion : he that has been ejected should have the right of appeal to the bishops of the bordering dioceses, that his case should be heard, and it should be carried on all the more diligently because to him who asks a hearing it should not be denied.   And the bishop who either justly or unjustly rejected him, should patiently allow the affair to be discussed, so that his sentence be either ap-proved or else emended, etc."

NOTES.

ANCIENT EPITOME.

A presbyter or deacon who has been cut off, has the privilege of appealing to the neighbouring bishops.   Moreover, he who cut him off should bear with equanimity the conclusion arrived at.

This is the first part of Canon xiv. of Sardica, as the canon previously quoted is Canon v. of the same synod.

And when this had been read, Augustine, the bishop of the Church of Hippo of the province of Numidia, said: We promise that this shall be observed by us, provided that upon more careful examination it be found to be of the Council of Nice. Aurelius the bishop said. If this also is pleasing to the charity of you all, give it the confirmation of your vote. The whole Council said: Everything that has been ordained by the Nicene Council pleases us all. Jocundus, the bishop of the Church of Suffitula, legate of the province of Byzacena, said: What was decreed by the Nicene Council cannot in any particular be violated.

Faustinus the bishop, legate of the Roman Church, said: So far as has developed by the confession of your holiness as well as of the holy Alypius, and of our brother Jocundus, I believe that some of the points have been made weak and others confirmed, which should not be the case, since even the very canons themselves have been brought into question. Therefore, that there may be harmony between us and your blessedness, let your holiness deign to refer the matter to the holy and venerable bishop of the Roman Church, that he may be able to consider whether what St. Augustine vouchsafed to enact, should be conceded or not, I mean in the matter of appeals of the inferior grade. If therefore there still is doubt, on this head it is right that the bishop of the most blessed see be informed, if this can be found in the canons which have been approved.

ANCIENT EPITOME.

Since the written decrees of the Nicene Council have not been found, let the Roman bishop deign to write to the bishop of Constantinople and to him of Alexandria, and let us know what he receives from them.

Aurelius the bishop said: As we have suggested to your charity, pray allow the copies of the statutes of the Nicene Council to be read and inserted in the acts, as well as those things what have been most healthfully defined in this city by our predecessors, according to the rule of that council, and those which now have been ordained by us. And the whole council said: The copies of the Creed, and the statutes of the Nicene Synod which formerly were brought to our council through Cæcilean of blessed memory, the predecessor of your holiness (who was present at it), as well as the copies of the decrees made by the Fathers in this city following them, or which now we have decreed by our common consultation, shall remain inserted in these ecclesiastical acts, so that (as has been already said) your blessedness may vouchsafe to write to those most venerable men of the Church of Antioch, and of that of Alexandria, and also of that of Constantinople, that they would send most accurate copies of the decrees of the Council of Nice under the authentification of their signatures, by which, the truth of the matter having become evident, those chapters which in the commonitory our brother who is present, and fellow-bishop Faustinus, as well as our fellow-presbyters Philip and Asellus brought with them, if they be found therein, may be confirmed by us; or if they be not found, we will hold a synod and consider the matter further. Daniel the notary read the profession of faith of the Council of Nice and its statutes to the African Council.

The Profession of Faith of the Nicene Council.

We believe in one God, etc., . . . and in the Holy Ghost. But those who say, etc., . . . anathematize them.

The statutes also of the Nicene Council in twenty heads were likewise read, as are found written before. Then what things were promulgated in the African Synods, were inserted in the present acts.

CANON I.

That the statutes of the Nicene Council are to be scrupulously observed.

AURELIUS the bishop said: Such are the statutes of the Nicene Council, which our fathers at that time brought back with them: and preserving this form, let these things which follow, adopted and confirmed by us, be kept firm.

NOTES.

ANCIENT EPITOME OF CANON I.

Let the copies of the decrees of the Nicene Council which our fathers brought back with them from that synod, be observed.

JOHNSON.

It is certain that Cæcilian, then Bishop of Carthage, was present at the Council of Nice; that any other African bishop was there does not appear; but probably he was attended with several clergyman, who were afterwards ordained bishops.

CANON II.

Of Preaching the Trinity.

THE whole Council said: By the favour of God, by a unanimous confession the Church's faith which through us is handed down should be confessed in this glorious assembly before anything else; then the ecclesiastical order of each is to be built up and strengthened by the consent of all. That the minds of our brethren and fellow bishops lately elevated may be strengthened, those things should be propounded which we have certainly received from our fathers, as the unity of the Trinity, which we retain consecrated in our senses, of the Father, and of the Son, and of the Holy Ghost, which has no difference, as we say,[2] so we shall instruct the people of God. Moreover by all the bishops lately promoted it was said: So we openly confess, so we hold, so we teach, following the Evangelic faith and your teaching.

NOTES.

ANCIENT EPITOME OF CANON II.
No difference is recognised or taught by the decrees of the Council of Nice between the Persons of the Holy Trinity.

This canon, or rather introduction, is taken from Canon j., of the Council of Carthage held under Genethlius, A.D. 387 or 390.[1]

CANON III.

Of Continence.

AURELIUS the bishop said: When at the past council the matter on continency and chastity was considered, those three grades, which by a sort of bond are joined to chastity by their consecration, to wit bishops, presbyters, and deacons, so it seemed that it was becoming that the sacred rulers and priests of God as well as the Levites, or those who served at the divine sacraments, should be continent altogether, by which they would be able with singleness of heart to ask what they sought from the Lord: so that what the apostles taught and antiquity kept, that we might also keep.

NOTES.

ANCIENT EPITOME OF CANON III.
Let a bishop, a presbyter, and a deacon be chaste and continent.

This canon is taken from Canon ij., of Carthage 387 or 390.

---

[1] In assigning these canons to the several synods that adopted them, I have simply followed Hefele.   [2] Or "have learned."

CANON IV.

Of the different orders that should abstain from their wives.

Faustinus, the bishop of the Potentine Church, in the province of Picenum, a legate of the Roman Church, said: It seems good that a bishop, a presbyter, and a deacon, or whoever perform the sacraments, should be keepers of modesty and should abstain from their wives.

By all the bishops it was said: It is right that all who serve the altar should keep pudicity from all women.

NOTES.

Ancient Epitome of Canon IV.

Let those who pray abstain from their wives that they may obtain their petitions.

This canon is taken from Canon ij., of Carthage 387 or 390, last mentioned.

Johnson.

See Canon XXV. "Abstain from their wives," i.e. Some time before and after the Eucharist, as the old Scholiasts understand it. [*i.e.* the Greek scholiasts, but see notes to Canon xiij. of Quinisext.]

CANON V.

Of Avarice.

Aurelius, the bishop, said: The cupidity of avarice (which, let no one doubt, is the mother of all evil things), is to be henceforth prohibited, lest anyone should usurp another's limits, or for gain should pass beyond the limits fixed by the fathers, nor shall it be at all lawful for any of the clergy to receive usury of any kind. And those new edicts (*suggestiones*) which are obscure and generally ambiguous, after they have been examined by us, will have their value fixed (*formam accipiunt*); but with regard to those upon which the Divine Scripture hath already most plainly given judgment, it is unnecessary that further sentence should be pronounced, but what is already laid down is to be carried out. And what is reprehensible in laymen is worthy of still more severe censure in the clergy. The whole synod said: No one hath gone contrary to what is said in the Prophets and in the Gospels with impunity.

NOTES.

Ancient Epitome of Canon V.

As the taking of any kind of usury is condemned in laymen, much more is it condemned in clergymen.

This canon is made up of Canons x. and xiij. of the Synod of Carthage held under Gratus in A.D. 345–348. This synod was held to return thanks for the ending of the Donatist schism; and indeed for some time the evil did seem to have been removed. Donatist worship was prohibited by the imperial law and it was not until the times of Constans and Constantius that it again openly asserted itself. The synod while in session also took advantage of the opportunity of passing some useful general canons on discipline.

Johnson.

See Canon of the Apostles 36 (44); Nic., 17.

CANON VI.

That the chrism should not be made by presbyters.

Fortunatus the bishop, said: In former councils we remember that it was decreed that the chrism or the reconciliation of penitents, as also the consecration of virgins be not done by presbyters: but should anyone be discovered to have done this, what ought we to decree with regard to him?

Aurelius the bishop said: Your worthiness has heard the suggestion of our brother and fellow-bishop Fortunatus; What answer will you give?

And all the bishops replied: Neither the making of the chrism, nor the consecration of virgins, is to be done by presbyters, nor is it permitted to a presbyter to reconcile anyone in the public mass (*in publica missa*), this is the pleasure of all of us.

NOTES.

Ancient Epitome of Canon VI.

Let no presbyter make the chrism, nor prepare the unction, nor consecrate virgins, nor publicly reconcile anyone to communion.

This is Canon iij. of the Carthaginian Synod under Genethlius, A.D. 387 or 390.

Johnson.

Not the chrism used upon persons at their baptism, says the scholion in Bishop Beveridge's *Annotation*, but the Mystical Chrism, viz., that used at Confirmation; though neither was the chrism used at baptism to be consecrated by Priests. See Decr. of Gelasius 6.

Du Pin observes, That this is one of the first monuments where the name of "mass" occurs to signify the public prayers, which the church made at offering the Eucharist. And let the reader observe, that there is no mention of the "mass" in the copies which the Greeks made use of. And further, he restrains the meaning of the word "mass" too much, when he supposes that it denoted the Communion Office only.

CANON VII.

Concerning those who are reconciled in peril of death.

AURELIUS the bishop said: If anyone had fallen into peril of death during the absence of the bishop, and had sought to reconcile himself to the divine altars, the presbyter should consult the bishop, and so reconcile the sick man at his bidding, which thing we should strengthen with healthy counsel. By all the bishops it was said: Whatever your holiness has taught us to be necessary, that is our pleasure.

NOTES.

Ancient Epitome of Canon VII.

A priest desiring to reconcile anyone in peril to the sacred altars must consult the bishop and do what seems good to him.

This is Canon iv. of the Synod of 387 or 390.

Johnson.

See Canon 43.

CANON VIII.

Of those who make accusation against an elder; and that no criminal is to be suffered to bring a charge against a bishop.

NUMIDIUS, the bishop of Maxula, said: Moreover, there are very many, not of good life, who think that their elders or bishops should be the butt for accusation; ought such to be easily admitted or no? Aurelius the bishop said: Is it the pleasure of your charity that he who is ensnared by divers wickednesses should have no voice of accusation against these?

All the bishops said: If he is criminous, his accusation is not to be received.

NOTES.

Ancient Epitome of Canon VIII.

It has seemed good that they who are themselves defendants for crimes should not bring accusations; nor should they be allowed to lay crimes to anyone's charge.

This is Canon vi. of Genethlius's Synod at Carthage, A.D. 387 or 390.

Johnson.

See Canons 132 and 133 and Constantinople Canon 6.

[The "elders" mentioned in this canon are] probably the same with *senes* in other canons, viz., Metropolitans, as is generally believed. The Latin here calls them *Majores natu*, the Greek πατέρας. Bishop Beveridge supposes that the word denotes bishop, though perhaps *Majores natu* may signify presbyters.

Justellus on the canon produces some seeming authorities for this.

CANON IX.

Of those who on account of their deeds are justly cast forth from the congregation of the Church.

AUGUSTINE the bishop, the legate of the Numidian province, said: Deign to enact that if any perchance have been rightly on account of their crimes cast forth from the Church, and shall have been received into communion by some bishop or presbyter, such shall be considered as guilty of an equal crime with them who flee away from the judgment of their own bishop. And all the bishops said: This is the pleasure of all of us.

NOTES.

ANCIENT EPITOME OF CANON IX.

Let him be excommunicated who communicates with one excommunicated.

This is Canon vii. of the same synod of 387 or 390.

CANON X.

Of presbyters who are corrected by their own bishops.

ALYPIUS the bishop, a legate of the province of Numidia, said: Nor should this be passed over; if by chance any presbyter when corrected by his bishop, inflamed by self-conceit or pride, has thought fit to offer sacrifices to God separately [from the authority of the bishop] or has believed it right to erect another altar, contrary to ecclesiastical faith and discipline, such should not get off with impunity. Valentine, of the primatial see of the province of Numidia, said: The propositions made by our brother Alypius are of necessity congruous to ecclesiastical discipline and faith; therefore enact what seems good to your belovedness.

NOTES.

ANCIENT EPITOME OF CANON X.

If one condemned by his bishop shall separate himself and set up an altar or make the offering he should be punished.

ARISTENUS.

Whoever has been cut off by his own bishop and does not go to the synod to which his bishop is subject, that an examination may be made of the grounds of his cutting off, and that whatever is contrary to justice may be corrected; but, puffed up with pride and conceit, shall despise the synod and separate himself from the Church, and shall set up another altar, and shall offer to God the holy gifts; such an one shall not be allowed to go on with impunity, since he is acting contrary to the faith and constitution of the Church; but he is to be stricken with anathema.

This and the following canon are Canon viii. of the so often mentioned synod of 387 or 390.

JOHNSON.

See Canon of the Apostles 24 (or 32) and that of Gangra 6.

CANON XI.

If any presbyter, inflated against his bishop, makes a schism, let him be anathema.

ALL the bishops said: If any presbyter shall have been corrected by his superior, he should ask the neighbouring bishops that his cause be heard by them and that through them he may be reconciled to his bishop: but if he shall not have done this, but, puffed up with pride, (which may God forbid!) he shall have thought it proper to separate himself from the communion of his bishop, and separately shall have offered the sacrifice to

God, and made a schism with certain accomplices, let him be anathema, and let him lose his place; and if the complaint which he brought against his bishop shall [not] have been found to be well founded, an enquiry should be instituted.

NOTES.

ANCIENT EPITOME OF CANON XI.

A Presbyter condemned by his bishop, is allowed to appeal to the neighbouring bishops: but if he shall not make any appeal, but shall make a schism, and be elated with conceit and shall offer the Holy Gifts to God, let him be anathema.

See note to last canon. The last clause is certainly corrupt; in the council of Carthage at which it was first adopted there is no "non," making the meaning clear.

CANON XII.

If any bishop out of Synod time shall have fallen under accusation, let his cause be heard by 12 bishops.

FELIX the bishop, said: I suggest, according to the statutes of the ancient councils, that if any bishop (which may God forbid!) shall have fallen under any accusation, and there shall have been too great necessity to wait for the summoning of a majority of the bishops, that he may not rest under accusation, let his cause be heard by 12 bishops; and let a presbyter be heard by six bishops with his own bishop, and a deacon shall be heard by three.

NOTES.

ANCIENT EPITOME OF CANON XII.

When a bishop is to be tried, if the whole synod does not sit, let at least twelve bishops take up the matter; and for the case of a presbyter, six and his own diocesan; and for the case of a deacon, three.

This is Canon x. of the Synod of Genethlius.

JOHNSON.

Hereby must be meant African canons; that under Gratus [A.D. 348] had decreed the same thing.

Who was the bishop's judge at the first instance does not appear by this canon; but it is natural to suppose it was the Primate. It is probable that this canon is to be understood of hearing upon an appeal, because it is certain that a priest's cause, at the first instance, was to be tried before the bishop (see Can. 10, 11). And therefore the latter part of the canon can be understood of no hearing but by way of appeal, nor by consequence the former. And this seems more clear by Can. Afr. 29.

CANON XIII.

That a bishop should not be ordained except by many bishops, but if there should be necessity he may be ordained by three.

BISHOP AURELIUS said: What says your holiness on this matter? By all the bishops it was answered: The decrees of the ancients must be observed by us, to wit, that without the consent of the Primate of any province even many bishops assembled together should not lightly presume to ordain a bishop. But should there be a necessity, at his bidding, three bishops should ordain him in any place they happen to be, and if anyone contrary to his profession and subscription shall come into any place he shall thereby deprive himself of his honour.

NOTES.

ANCIENT EPITOME OF CANON XIII.

At the bidding of the Primate even three bishops can make a bishop. But whoever goes counter to his profession and subscription, is deprived of his honour by his own judgment.

This is Canon xij. of the before mentioned Synod of 387 or 390.

JOHNSON.

See Can. Ap. 1, Nic. 1.

He that was called a Metropolitan in other Churches was a Primate in Africa.

CANON XIV.

That one of the bishops of Tripoli should come as legate, and that a presbyter might be heard there by five bishops.

IT also seemed good that one bishop from Tripoli, on account of the poverty of the province, should come as a legation, and that there a presbyter might be heard by five bishops, and a deacon by three, as has been noted above, his own bishop presiding.

NOTES.

ANCIENT EPITOME OF CANON XIV.

On account of the scarcity of bishops in Tripoli, one bishop shall suffice for a legation.

This canon is made up of two parts. The first part is Canon v. of the synod of Hippo,

A. D. 393, and was repeated at the Carthaginian synod of 397. The second half is from Canon viij. of the same council.

JOHNSON (*See Canon* 12).

" Legate," *i. e.*, to a Synod, there being few bishops in that province.

CANON XV.

Of the divers orders who serve the Church, that if any one fall into a criminal business and refused to be tried by the ecclesiastical court, he ought to be in danger therefor ; and that the sons of bishops (sacerdotum) are not to attend worldly shows.

MOREOVER it seemed good that if any bishop, presbyter, or deacon, who had a criminal charge brought against him or who had a civil cause, refused to be tried by the ecclesiastical tribunal, but wished to be judged by the secular courts, even if he won his suit, nevertheless he should lose his office.

This is the law in a criminal suit ; but in a civil suit he shall lose that for the recovery of which he instituted the proceedings, if he wishes to retain his office.

This also seemed good, that if from some ecclesiastical judges an appeal was taken to other ecclesiastical judges who had a superior jurisdiction, this should in no way injure the reputation of those from whom the appeal was taken, unless it could be shown that they had given sentence moved by hatred or some other mental bias, or that they had been in some way corrupted. But if by the consent of both parties judges had been chosen, even if they were fewer in number than is specified, no appeal can be taken.

And [it seemed good] that the sons of bishops should not take part in nor witness secular spectacles. For this has always been forbidden to all Christians, so let them abstain from them, that they may not go where cursing and blasphemy are to be found.

NOTES.

ANCIENT EPITOME OF CANON XV.

A bishop or cleric who has a criminal suit brought against him, if he leaves the Church and betakes himself to secular judges, even if he had been unjustly used, shall lose his rank. And if he was successful in his political affairs, if he follows this, he shall lose his own grade. No appeal can be taken from the ecclesiastical judges, except they be proved to have given their decision beforehand moved thereto by a bribe or by hatred.

No appeal can be taken from the decision of judges chosen by each side.

This canon is made up of Canons ix., x., and xj. of the Council of Hippo, A. D. 393.

JOHNSON.

In this canon the African bishops made bold with the Civil Courts. To lay such restraints on bishops and clergymen is, I am sure, very proper, to say no more.

CANON XVI.

That no bishop, presbyter or deacon should be a "conductor;" and that Readers should take wives; and that the clergy should abstain from usury; and at what age they or virgins should be consecrated.

LIKEWISE it seemed good that bishops, presbyters, and deacons should not be "conductors" or "procurators;" nor seek their food by any base and vile business, for they should remember how it is written, "No man fighting for God cumbereth himself with worldly affairs."

Also it seemed good that Readers when they come to years of puberty, should be compelled either to take wives or else to profess continence.

Likewise it seemed good that if a clergyman had lent money he should get it back again, but if kind (*speciem*) he should receive back the same kind as he gave.

And that younger than twenty-five years deacons should not be ordained, nor virgins consecrated.

And that readers should not salute the people.

NOTES.

ANCIENT EPITOME OF CANON XVI.

A bishop, presbyter, and deacon may not be a "conductor" or a "procurator." A reader when he comes to puberty must contract marriage or profess continence.

A cleric who has lent to someone, what he gave let him receive, or as much.

Let not him be a deacon, who is made a deacon being under twenty-five.

And let not readers salute the people.

This canon is made up of Canons xv., xviij., and xxj., and added to these Canon j. of the same Second Series of the synod of Hippo, A.D. 393.

JOHNSON.

Zonaras says this was never observed anywhere but in Africa. See Can. Afr. 19 (27).

Du Pin turns the Latin, *saluto*, by "addressing his speech to the people."

CANON XVII.

That any province on account of its distance, may have its own Primate.

IT seemed good that Mauretania Sitiphensis, as it asked, should have a Primate of its own, with the consent of the Primate of Numidia from whose synod it had been separated.[1] And with the consent of all the primates of the African Provinces and of all the bishops permission was given, by reason of the great distance between them.

NOTES.

ANCIENT EPITOME OF CANON XVII.

Mauretania Sitiphensis, on account of the great distance, is permitted to have its own Primate.

This canon is Canon iij. of the first series of canons enacted at Hippo in 393.

JOHNSON.

N.B. From this place forward the Latin and Greek numeration varies; but Justellus's Edition in Greek and Latin follows the Latin division.

CANON XVIII. (Gk. xviii. *The Latin caption is the canon of the Greek.*)

If any cleric is ordained he ought to be admonished to observe the constitutions.
And that neither the Eucharist nor Baptism should be given to the bodies of the dead.
And that every year in every province the Metropolitans come together in synod.

(Gk. Canon xix.)

It seemed good that before bishops, or clerics were ordained, the provisions of the canons should be brought to their notice, lest they might afterwards repent of having through ignorance acted contrary to law.

---

[1] The text here is corrupt.

ANCIENT EPITOME OF GREEK CANON XIX. | *synods should be made known to him who is to*
The things which have been adopted by the | *be ordained.*

(Gk. Canon xx.)

It also seemed good that the Eucharist should not be given to the bodies of the dead. For it is written : " Take, Eat," but the bodies of the dead can neither "take" nor " eat." Nor let the ignorance of the presbyters baptize those who are dead.

ANCIENT EPITOME OF GREEK CANON XX.

The Eucharist is not to be given to the body | *The ignorance of a presbyter shall not bap-*
of one dead for it neither eats nor drinks. | *tize a dead man.*

(Gk. Canon xxi.)

And therefore in this holy synod should be confirmed in accordance with the Nicene decrees, on account of Ecclesiastical causes, which often are delayed to the injury of the people, that every year there should be a synod, to which all, who are primates of the provinces, should send bishops as legates, from their own synods, two or as many as they choose ; so that when the synod meets it may have full power to act.

NOTES.

ANCIENT EPITOME OF GREEK CANON XXI.

According to the decrees of the Nicene Fathers a yearly synod shall be assembled, and two legates or as many as they shall choose, shall be sent by the primates of every province.

This is composed of Canons II., IV., and V. of the second series of enactments of Hippo, A.D. 393.

JOHNSON.

The 18th canon in the Edition of Tilius and Bishop Beveridge runs thus ; viz. [If any clergyman be ordained he ought to be reminded to keep the canons ; and that the Eucharist or Baptism be not given to dead corpses ; and that the Metropolitans in every province meet in synod yearly.] They speak their own language, and call him a Metropolitan, whom the Africans called a Primate ; but then they have also the entire 18th canon, as it here stands according to the Latin, which they divide into three, and number them 19, 20, 21.

See Can. Nic. 5. It seems very odd that they should allege the authority of the Nicene Synod upon this occasion ; for that orders a synod twice a year, this but once ; that intends a provincial synod, this a diocesan or national one.

CANON XIX. (Greek xxii.) [1]

That if any bishop is accused the cause should be brought before the primate of his own province.

AURELIUS, the bishop, said : Whatever bishop is accused the accuser shall bring the case before the primates of the province to which the accused belongs, and he shall not be suspended from communion by reason of the crime laid to his charge unless he fails to put in an appearance on the appointed day for arguing his cause before the chosen judges, having been duly summoned by the letters ; that is, within the space of one month from the day in which he is found to have received the letters. But should he be able to prove any true necessity which manifestly rendered it impossible for him to appear, he shall have the opportunity of arguing his case within

---

[1] For Greek xx. and xxi. see Latin Canon XVIII.

another full month; but after the second month he shall not communicate until he is acquitted.

But if he is not willing to come to the annual general council, so that his cause may there be terminated, he himself shall be judged to have pronounced the sentence of his own condemnation at the time in which he does not communicate, nor shall he communicate either in his own church or diocese.

But his accuser, if he has not missed any of the days for pleading the cause, shall not be shut out from communion; but if he has missed some of them, withdrawing himself, then the bishop shall be restored to communion and the accuser shall be removed from communion; so, nevertheless, that the possibility of going on with the case be not taken from him, if he shall prove that his absence was caused by lack of power and not by lack of will.

And this is enacted, that if the accuser turn out to be himself a criminal when the case against the bishop has come to argument, he shall not be allowed to testify unless he asserts that the causes are personal and not ecclesiastical.

NOTES.

ANCIENT EPITOME OF CANON XIX.

A bishop accused and haled to judgment shall have the space of two months; if there is any excuse [1] for his delay from the other side. But after this he shall be excommunicated if he does not appear. But if when the accused is present the accuser flees, then the accuser shall be deprived of communion. But the accuser who is infamous shall not be an accuser at all.

This canon is made up from Canons VI. and VII. of the last mentioned second series of the enactments of Hippo, 393.

JOHNSON.

See *Can. Afr.* 28 and *Can. Ap.* 11 (14).

By this ["Universal Synod"] is meant a National Synod of Africa.

See Can. Constantinople 6.

CANON XX. (Greek xxiii.)

Of accused presbyters or clerks.

BUT if presbyters or deacons shall have been accused, there shall be joined together from the neighbouring places with the bishop of the diocese, the legitimate number of colleagues, whom the accused shall seek from the same; that is together with himself six in the case against a presbyter, in that against a deacon three. They shall discuss the causes, and the same form shall be kept with regard to days and postponements and removals from communion, and in the discussion of persons between the accusers and the accused.

But the causes of the rest of the clergy, the bishop of the place shall take cognizance of and determine alone.

NOTES.

ANCIENT EPITOME OF CANON XX.

When a presbyter is accused, six of the neighbouring bishops together with the bishop of that region shall judge the matter. But for a deacon, three. What things concern the other clerics even one bishop shall examine.

This is Canon viij. of Hippo, 393.

JOHNSON.

See Canon 12.

CANON XXI. (Greek xxiv.)

That the sons of clergymen are not to be joined in marriage with heretics.

LIKEWISE it seemed good that the sons of clergymen should not be joined in matrimony with gentiles and heretics.

[1] It would seem that this must be the meaning.

NOTES.

ANCIENT EPITOME OF CANON XXI.
[The same as the canon.]

This is Canon xij. of Hippo, 393.

CANON XXII. (Greek xxv.)

That bishops or other clergymen shall give nothing to those who are not Catholics.

AND that to those who are not Catholic Christians, even if they be blood relations, neither bishops nor clergymen shall give anything at all by way of donation of their possessions.

NOTES.

ANCIENT EPITOME OF CANON XXII.

Bishops and clergymen shall give nothing of their goods to heretics, nor confer aught upon them even if they be their relatives.

This is Canon xiv. of Hippo, 393.

CANON XXIII. (Greek xxvi.)

That bishops shall not go across seas.

ITEM, That bishops shall not go beyond seas without consulting the bishop of the primatial see of his own province: so that from him they may be able to receive a formed or commendatory letter.

NOTES.

ANCIENT EPITOME OF CANON XXIII.

A bishop is not to cross the seas unless he has received from the Primate of his region a letter dimissory.

This is Canon xxvij. of Hippo, 393.

JOHNSON.

See note on Canons of the Apostles, 10 (13). [viz:]

[The use of Letters Commendatory was very early in the Church; St. Paul mentions them II. Cor. iij. 1. And it is not easy to be conceived how discipline can be restored but by the reviving of this practice. It is surely irregular to admit all chance comers to the Communion, who, for aught we know, may stand excommunicated by their own bishop. Of the difference between Commendatory and Pacific and Formal Letters, see Can. Chalc., 11; Apost., 25, 26; Ant., 6; Sardic., 13].

CANON XXIV. (Greek xxvii.)

That nothing be read in church besides the Canonical Scripture.

ITEM, that besides the Canonical Scriptures nothing be read in church under the name of divine Scripture.
But the Canonical Scriptures are as follows:
Genesis.
Exodus.
Leviticus.
Numbers.
Deuteronomy.
Joshua the Son of Nun.
The Judges.
Ruth.
The Kings, iv. books.

The Chronicles, ij. books.
Job.
The Psalter.
The Five books of Solomon.
The Twelve Books of the Prophets.
Isaiah.
Jeremiah.
Ezechiel.
Daniel.
Tobit.
Judith.
Esther.
Ezra, ij. books.
Macchabees, ij. books.

THE NEW TESTAMENT.

The Gospels, iv. books.
The Acts of the Apostles, j. book.
The Epistles of Paul, xiv.
The Epistles of Peter, the Apostle, ij.
The Epistles of John the Apostle, iij.
The Epistles of James the Apostle, j.
The Epistle of Jude the Apostle, j.
The Revelation of John, j. book.

Let this be sent to our brother and fellow bishop, Boniface, and to the other bishops of those parts, that they may confirm this canon, for these are the things which we have received from our fathers to be read in church.

NOTES.

ANCIENT EPITOME OF CANON XXIV.

Let nothing besides the canonical Scriptures be read in church.

This is Canon xxxvj. of Hippo., 393. The last phrase allowing the reading of the "passions of the Martyrs" on their Anniversaries is omitted from the African code.

JOHNSON.

These two books [i.e. the two Maccabees] are mentioned only in Dionysius Exiguus's copy. See *Can. Ap. ult.*, *Can. Laod. ult.* "Boniface," *i.e.*, Bishop of Rome.

CANON XXV. (Greek xxviii.)

Concerning bishops and the lower orders who wait upon the most holy mysteries. It has seemed good that these abstain from their wives.

AURELIUS, the bishop, said: We add, most dear brethren, moreover, since we have heard of the incontinency of certain clerics, even of readers, towards their wives, it seemed good that what had been enacted in divers councils should be confirmed, to wit, that subdeacons who wait upon the holy mysteries, and deacons, and presbyters, as well as bishops according to former statutes,[1] should contain from their wives, so that they should be as though they had them not : and unless they so act, let them be removed from office. But the rest of the clergy are not to be compelled to this, unless they be of mature age. And by the whole council it was said : What your holiness has said is just, holy, and pleasing to God, and we confirm it.

---

[1] The Greek reads "κατὰ τοὺς ἰδίους ὅρους," and so it was understood at the Council of Trullo, as is evident from Canon XIII. of that synod. The Latin is "secundum propria statuta," but Bruns reads "priora."

NOTES.

ANCIENT EPITOME OF CANON XXV.

Those who handle holy things should abstain even from their own wives at the times of their ministration.

This is founded upon Canon iv. of the Council of Carthage, which met September 13th, 401, but the provisions are more stringent here, subdeacons as well as deacons being constrained to continence.

JOHNSON.

"Times of ministration," so it is explained,

Can. Trull., 13, where there were several African Bishops present, and allowed of that explication; yet Dion. Exig. is not clear, viz., *Secundum propria statuta.*

By *Can. Laod., 23.* Ministers, i.e., subdeacons, are forbid to touch the Holy Vessels, yet here they are said to handle the Mysteries; I suppose they might handle the Holy Vessels, etc. before and after the celebration, but not during the solemnity; or else the customs of several ages and countries differed as to this particular.

CANON XXVI. (Greek xxix.)

That no one should take from the possessions of the Church.[1]

LIKEWISE it seemed good that no one should sell anything belonging to the Church: that if there was no revenue, and other great necessity urged thereto, this might be brought before the Metropolitan of the province that he might deliberate with the appointed number of bishops whether this should be done: that if such urgent necessity lay upon any church that it could not take counsel beforehand, at least let it call together the neighbouring bishops as witnesses, taking care to refer all the necessities of his church to the council: and that if he shall not do this, he shall be held as responsible toward God, and as a seller in the eye of the council, and he shall have lost thereby his honour.

NOTES.

ANCIENT EPITOME OF CANON XXVI.

Church goods must not be sold. If they bring in no revenue they may be sold at the will of the bishops. If the necessity does not allow that consultation should take place, he who sells shall call together the neighbouring bishops. If

he does not do so he shall be held responsible to God and to the Synod.

This is Canon v. of the Synod of Carthage, Sept. 13th, 401.

JOHNSON.

"Appointed number," i.e., Twelve, see Canon 12.

CANON XXVII. (Greek xxx.)

Presbyters and deacons convicted of the graver crimes shall not receive laying on of hands, like laymen.[2]

IT also was confirmed that if presbyters or deacons were convicted of any of the greater crimes on account of which it was necessary that they should be removed from the ministry, that hands should not be laid upon them as upon penitents, or as upon faithful laymen, nor should it be permitted that they be baptized over again and then advanced to the clerical grade.

NOTES.

ANCIENT EPITOME OF CANON XXVII.

A presbyter convicted and repenting, is not to be rebaptized as one to be advanced, neither as a layman is he to be reordained.

This is Canon xij. of the before-mentioned Council of Carthage, Sept. 13th, 401.

JOHNSON.

This canon seems to have been designed to preclude deposed clergymen from all possibility of being restored, directly or indirectly.

---

[1] Not found in the Greek of Beveridge, but in that given by Labbe.   [2] This found only in Latin.

CANON XXVIII. (Greek xxxi.)

Presbyters, deacons, or clerics, who shall think good to carry appeals in their causes across the water shall not at all be admitted to communion.[1]

IT also seemed good that presbyters, deacons, and others of the inferior clergy in the causes which they had, if they were dissatisfied with the judgments of their bishops, let the neighbouring bishops with the consent of their own bishop hear them, and let the bishops who have been called in judge between them : but if they think they have cause of appeal from these, they shall not betake themselves to judgments from beyond seas, but to the primates of their own provinces, or else to an universal council, as has also been decreed concerning bishops. But whoso shall think good to carry an appeal across the water shall be received to communion by no one within the boundaries of Africa.

NOTES.

ANCIENT EPITOME OF CANON XXVIII.

Clerics who have been condemned, if they take exception to the judgment, shall not appeal beyond seas, but to the neighbouring bishops, and to their own ; if they do otherwise let them be excommunicated in Africa.

This canon is the same as Canon xvij. of the Synod of Carthage of 418, but it has some words with regard to appeals which that canon does not contain, viz.: "*Aut ad universale conciliam, sicut et de episcopis sæpe constitutum est.*" This clause, affirming that bishops have often been forbidden to appeal across the water from the decisions of the African bishops, has caused great perplexity as no such decrees are extant. The Ballerini, to avoid this difficulty, and possibly for other reasons, suggest an entirely

different meaning to the passage, and suppose that it means that "bishops have often been allowed to appeal to the Universal Council and now this privilege is extended to priests."[2] But this would seem to be a rather unnatural interpretation and Van Espen in his *Commentary* shews good reason for adopting the more evident view.

JOHNSON.

See *Can. Afr.*, 19.

Clearly the See of Rome is here aimed at, as if Carthage were the place designed by Providence to put a stop to the growth of power in Christian Rome, as well as heathen. It is strange, that this canon should be received by the Church of Rome in former ages.

CANON XXIX. (Greek xxxii.)

If anyone who is excommunicated shall receive communion before his cause is heard he brings damnation on himself.[3]

LIKEWISE it pleased the whole Council that he who shall have been excommunicated for any neglect, whether he be bishop, or any other cleric, and shall have presumed while still under sentence, and his cause not yet heard, to receive communion, he shall be considered by so doing to have given sentence against himself.

NOTES.

ANCIENT EPITOME OF CANON XXIX.

One excommunicate who shall communicate before absolution sentences himself.

This canon seems to be founded upon Canon iv. of Antioch.

JOHNSON.

See *Can. Ap.*, 21 (29), *Antioch*, 4.

By this canon the criminous bishop is supposed to be excommunicated before he comes to have his cause heard by a Synod, or by 12 neighbouring bishops : and it is therefore most rational to believe that he was thus censured by his Primate. See *Can. Afr.*, 12.

---

[1] This is not found in the Greek of Beveridge.
[2] Ballerini, edit. *S. Leon M.*, Tom. II., p. 966.

[3] Not found in the Greek of Beveridge.

CANON XXX. (Greek xxxiii.)

Concerning the accused or accuser.[1]

LIKEWISE it seemed good that the accused, or the accusor, if (living in the same place as the accused) he fears some evil may be done him by the tumultuous multitude, may choose for himself a place near by, where the cause may be determined, and where there will be no difficulty in producing the witnesses.

ANCIENT EPITOME OF CANON XXX.

Accuser or accused may select for himself a safe place if he fears violence.

CANON XXXI. (Greek xxxiv.)

If certain clerics advanced by their own bishops are supercilious, let them not remain whence they are unwilling to come forth.

IT also seemed good that whoever of the clergy or of the deacons would not help the bishop in the necessities of the churches, when he wished to lift them to a higher position in his diocese, should no longer be allowed to exercise the functions of that grade from which they were not willing to be removed.

NOTES.

ANCIENT EPITOME OF CANON XXXI.

Who despises a greater honour shall lose what he hath.

JOHNSON.

It is most probable that this canon is to be understood of deacons designed by the bishop to be ordained priests, for the deacons, at least in some Churches, were provided of a better maintenance than priests; or it may be understood of inferior clergymen, who were permitted to marry in the degree they were now in, but would not willingly take the order of priest or deacon, because then they were prohibited marriage.

CANON XXXII. (Greek xxxv.)

If any poor cleric, no matter what his rank may be, shall acquire any property, it shall be subject to the power of the bishop.[2]

IT also seemed good that bishops, presbyters, deacons and any other of the clergy, who when they were ordained had no possessions, and in the time of their episcopate or after they became clerics, shall purchase in their own names lands or any other property, shall be held guilty of the crime of intrenching upon the Lord's goods, unless, when they are admonished to do so, they place the same at the disposal of the Church. But should anything come to them personally by the liberality of anyone, or by succession from some relative, let them do what they will with it; if, however, they demand it back again, contrary to what they proposed, they shall be judged unworthy of ecclesiastical honour as back-sliders.

NOTES.

ANCIENT EPITOME OF CANON XXXII.

Whoso after his ordination although he has nothing yet buys a field, shall give it to the Church, unless he got it by succession from a relation or by pure liberality.

In this canon there is difficulty about the meaning of the phrase "quod eorum proposito congruat." Hardouin suggests that "propo- situm" is the same as "profession," or "call-ing," and the meaning, were this the case, would be that he must employ it as befits his clerical calling. Van Espen follows Balsamon and Zonaras in understanding it to mean that if he has proposed to employ a part for the Church or for the poor, and changes his mind, he is to be deposed; and this meaning I have followed.

---

[1] Found only in Latin.   [2] "Of the Church" in Dion. Exig.

CANON XXXIII. (Greek xxxvi.)

That presbyters should not sell the goods of the Church in which they are constituted; and that no bishop can rightly use anything the title to which vests in the ecclesiastical maternal centre (μάτρικος).

IT also seemed good that presbyters should not sell the ecclesiastical property where they are settled without their bishop's knowledge; and it is not lawful for bishops to sell the goods of the Church without the council or their presbyters being aware of it. Nor should the bishop without necessity usurp the property of the maternal (*matricis*) Church [nor should a presbyter usurp the property of his own cure (*tituli*)].[1]

NOTES.

ANCIENT EPITOME OF CANON XXXIII.

A presbyter is not to sell ecclesiastical property without the consent of the bishop. A bishop is not to sell without the approbation of his synod a country property.

Fuchs (*Biblioth. der Kirchenvers.*, vol. iij., p. 5) thinks the text is corrupt in the last sentence and should be corrected by Canon x. of the Council of Carthage of 421, so as to read, "that which is left by will to a rural church in the diocese must not be applied to the Mother Church through the usurpation of the bishop."

JOHNSON.

"Or title." So I turn the Lat. *Titulus* for want of a proper English word. It denotes a lesser church in any city or diocese, served by a priest.

"The Mother Church," i.e., The cathedral, the Church in which the bishop resides.

Moreover at this Synod we read all the conciliar decrees of all the Province of Africa in the different synods held in the time of Bishop Aurelius.[2]

Concerning the Synod which assembled in Hippo Regio.

Under the most illustrious consuls, the most glorious Emperor Theodosius Augustus for the third time, and Abundantius, on the viij. Ides of October, at Hippo Regio, in the *secretarium* of the Church of Peace. And the rest of the acts of this Synod have not been written down here because these constitutions are found set forth above.

Of the Council of Carthage at which the proconsular bishops were appointed legates to the Council at Adrumetum.

In the consulate of the most glorious emperors—Arcadius for the third time and Honorius for the second time, Augustuses, on the vith[3] day before the Calends of July, at Carthage. In this council the proconsular bishops were chosen as legates to the Council of Adrumetum.

Of a Council of Carthage at which many statutes were made.

In the consulate of those most illustrious men, Cæsarius and Atticus, on the vth day before the Calends of September in the secretarium of the restored basilica, when Aurelius the bishop, together with the bishops, had taken his seat, the deacons also standing by, and Victor the old man of Puppiana, Tutus of Migirpa and Evangel of Assuri.

The Allocution of Aurelius the bishop of Carthage to the bishops.

Aurelius, the bishop, said:[4] After the day fixed for the council, as ye remember, most blessed brethren, we sat and waited for the legations of all the African provinces to assemble upon the day, as I have said, set by our missive; but when the letter of our

---

[1] Only found in the Latin.
[2] These interludes or "Digressions," as Van Espen calls them, are found in Dionysius and in the Greek texts.
[3] In the Greek this reads xvith.
[4] The text here I suspect is much corrupted. The Greek and Latin do not agree.

Byzacene bishops had been read, that was read to your charity, which they had discussed with me who had anticipated the time and day of the council; also it was read by our brethren Honoratus and Urban, who are to-day present with us in this council, sent as the legation of the Sitifensine Province. For our brother Reginus of the Vege[t]selitane [1] Church,[2] the letters sent to my littleness by Crescentian and Aurelius, our fellow-bishops, of the first sees of the [two] Numidias, in which writings your charity will see with me how they promised that either they themselves would be good enough to come or else that they would send legates according to custom to this council; but this it seems they did not do at all, the legates of Mauritania Sitifensis, who had come so great a distance gave notice that they could stay no longer; and, therefore, brethren, if it seem good to your charity, let the letters of our Byzacene brethren, as also the breviary, which they joined to the same letter, be read to this assembly, so that if by any chance they are not entirely satisfactory to your charity, such things in the breviary may be changed for the better after diligent examination. For this very thing our brother and fellow-bishop of the primatial see, a man justly conspicuous for his gravity and prudence, Mizonius, demanded in a letter he addressed to my littleness. If therefore it meets with your approval, let there be read the things which have been adopted and let each by itself be considered by your charity.

CANON XXXIV. (Greek xxxvii.)

That nothing of those things enacted in the Synod of Hippo is to be corrected.

BISHOP EPIGONIUS said: In this summary (*Breviarium*) which was adopted at the Synod of Hippo, we think nothing should be amended, nor anything added thereto except that the day on which the holy Feast of Easter falls should be announced in Synod.

NOTES.

ANCIENT EPITOME OF CANON XXXIV.

Nothing is to be corrected in the synod of Hippo, nor anything added thereto, except that the time of celebrating Easter should be announced in time of synod.

The first of these introductions is that of the Synod of Hippo in A.D. 393; the next that of Carthage in A.D. 394, and the third that of the same place, held August 28th, A.D. 397.

This canon (number xxxiv. of the code) is the beginning of Canon v. of the last named Synod.

JOHNSON.

See Canons 51 and 73.

CANON XXXV. (Greek xxxviii.)

That bishops or clergymen should not easily set free their sons.

That bishops or clerics should not easily let their children pass out of their power; unless they were secure of their morals and age, that their own sins may pertain to them.

NOTES.

ANCIENT EPITOME OF CANON XXXV.

Bishops and clergy shall not set their children free until their morals are established.

This canon is Canon xiij. of the Synod of Hippo, A.D. 393.

---

[1] In Gustavus Willmann's *Corpus Inscriptionum Latinarum*, Vol. viii., p. 47, the reading is given as *Vegeselitanæ*, in one word. The town was Vegesela, and unfortunately there were two towns having the same name and not far one from the other. *Cf.* map 20, Spruner-Sieglin, *Atlas Antiquus*.

[2] The verb is lacking. The Ed. of Migne's Dion. Exig. suggests *legit*.

CANON XXXVI. (Greek xxxix.)

That bishops or clergymen are not to be ordained unless they have made all their family Christians.

NONE shall be ordained bishop, presbyters, or deacons before all the inmates of their houses shall have become Catholic Christians.

NOTES.

ANCIENT EPITOME OF CANON XXXVI.

He shall not be ordained who hath not made all his household orthodox.

This canon is Canon xvij. of the Synod of Hippo, A.D. 393.

CANON XXXVII. (Greek xl.)

It is not lawful to offer anything in the Holy Mysteries except bread and wine mixed with water.

IN the sacraments of the body and blood of the Lord nothing else shall be offered than that which the Lord himself ordained, that is to say, bread and wine mixed with water. But let the first-fruits, whether honey or milk, be offered on that one most solemn day, as is wont, in the mystery of the infants. For although they are offered on the altar, let them have nevertheless their own benediction, that they may be distinguished from the sacraments of the Lord's body and blood; neither let there be offered as first-fruits anything other than grapes and corns.

NOTES.

ANCIENT EPITOME OF CANON XXXVII.

Let bread and wine mixed with water only be offered.

The text of the Greek here does not exactly agree with the Latin. The Greek reads as follows: "That in the Holy Mysteries nothing else be offered than the body and blood of the Lord, even as the Lord himself delivered, that is bread and wine mixed with water."

Further down with regard to the first-fruits I have followed the Greek text which seems decidedly preferable, in fact the Latin is so corrupt that Van Espen notes that for the ordinary " *offerantur* " some MSS. read " *non offerantur.* "

This canon is Canon xxiij. of the Synod of Hippo, A.D. 393.

JOHNSON.

See Can. Ap. 2 (3).

"The Mystery of Infants" of this *Quære*, all that I have met with are in the dark as to this matter. Dionysius Exiguus's Latin is *Lac*, etc. The Greek stands thus, Ἔιτε ·γάλα κ. τ. λ.

CANON XXXVIII. (Greek xli.)

That clerics or those who are continent shall not visit virgins or widows.

NEITHER clerics nor those who profess continence should enter the houses of widows or virgins without the bidding or consent of the bishops or presbyters: and then let them not go alone, but with some other of the clergy, or with those assigned by the bishop or presbyter for this purpose; not even bishops and presbyters shall go alone to women of this sort, except some of the clergy are present or some other grave Christian men.

NOTES.

ANCIENT EPITOME OF CANON XXXVIII.

Clerics and those who are continent shall not go to widows or virgins, unless at the bidding of the bishop and presbyter: and even then not alone, but with those with whom presbyters and deacons visit them.

This canon is canon xxiv. of the Synod of Hippo, A.D. 393.

CANON XXXIX. (Greek xlii.)

That a bishop should not be called the chief of the priests.[1]

THAT the bishop of the first see shall not be called Prince of the Priests or High Priest (*Summus Sacerdos*) or any other name of this kind, but only Bishop of the First See.

NOTES.

ANCIENT EPITOME OF CANON XXXIX.

The first bishop shall not be called Prince of the Priests, nor High Priest, but Bishop of the first see.

This canon is Canon xxv. of the Synod of Hippo, A.D. 393.

JOHNSON.

"The bishop of the Prime See," i.e., The primate. So Xantippus is called bishop of the Prime. So in Numidia, Nicetius in Mauritania, in the original Latin between Can. 85, and Can. 86, and see Can. 86.

N. B. Justellus on this canon shews, that Tertullian, Optatus, and Augustine, did apply these titles to their own African bishops; and therefore supposes, that the meaning of the canon was to suppress the flame of vain glory, which proceeded from these sparks of lofty titles.

CANON XL. (Greek xliii.)

Concerning the non-frequenting of taverns by the clergy, except when travelling.

THAT the clergy are not to enter taverns for eating or drinking, nor unless compelled to do so by the necessity of their journey.

NOTES.

ANCIENT EPITOME OF CANON XL.

A cleric on a journey may enter a tavern, otherwise not.

This canon is Canon xxvj. of the Synod of Hippo, A.D. 393.

CANON XLI. (Greek xliv.)

That by men who are fasting sacrifices are to be offered to God.

THAT the Sacraments of the Altar are not to be celebrated except by those who are fasting, except on the one anniversary of the celebration of the Lord's Supper; for if the commemoration of some of the dead, whether bishops or others, is to be made in the afternoon, let it be only with prayers, if those who officiate have already breakfasted.

NOTES.

ANCIENT EPITOME OF CANON XLI.

The holy mysteries are not offered except by those who are fasting.

This canon is Canon xxviij. of the Synod of Hippo, A.D. 393.

JOHNSON.

From this canon and the 29th of Trullo, it is evident that by the Lord's Supper, the ancients understood the supper going before the Eucharist, and not the Eucharist itself, and that on Maunday-Thursday[2] yearly, before the Eucharist, they had such a public entertainment in imitation of our Saviour's last Paschal Supper. I refer it to the consideration of the learned reader, whether St. Paul, by the Δεῖπνον κυριακὸν, 1 Cor. xi. 20, does not mean this entertainment. For the obvious translation of that verse is, "It is not your [duty or business] when you meet together [in the church] to eat the Lord's Supper."

---

[1] The Greek reads for "bishop," "a Primate."

[2] This is Johnson's spelling here, but not in the last phrase of this same note.

He would not have them to eat this supper in the public assembly: "For" (says he) "have ye not houses to eat and drink in, or despise ye the Church of God?" From the 4th age forward, the Eucharist was sometimes called the Lord's Supper; but from the beginning it was not so. And even after it did sometimes pass by this name, yet at other times this name was strictly used for the previous entertainment, as may be seen by this canon, which was made in the 4th century. Further it seems probable, that the Lord's Supper and the Love-feast was the same, though it was not usually called the Lord's Supper; but only (perhaps) that love-feast, which was made on the day of the institution of the Eucharist, which we now call Maundy-Thursday.

CANON XLII. (Greek xlv.)

Concerning the not having feasts under any circumstances in churches.

THAT no bishops or clerics are to hold feasts in churches, unless perchance they are forced thereto by the necessity of hospitality as they pass by. The people, too, as far as possible, are to be prohibited from attending such feasts.

NOTES.

ANCIENT EPITOME OF CANON XLII.

A cleric is not to feast in a church, unless perchance he is driven thereto by the necessity of hospitality. This also is forbidden to the laity.

This canon is Canon xxix. of the Synod of Hippo, A.D. 393.

CANON XLIII. (Greek xlvi.)

Concerning penitents.

THAT to penitents the times of their penance shall be assigned by the will of the bishop according to the difference of their sins; and that a presbyter shall not reconcile a penitent without consulting the bishop, unless the absence of the bishop urges him necessarily thereto. But when of any penitent the offence has been public and commonly known, so as to have scandalized the whole Church, he shall receive imposition of the hand before the altar (Lat. " before the apse ").

NOTES.

ANCIENT EPITOME OF CANON XLIII.

The bishops shall fix the time of penance for those doing penance according to their sins. A presbyter without his knowledge shall not reconcile one doing penance, even when necessity impels him thereto.[1]

This canon is canon xxx. of the Synod of Hippo, A.D. 393.

JOHNSON.

Here [i. e., in translating *absidem* church-porch] I follow Zonoras; see Can. Nic., 11. Du Pin renders *absidem*, a high place near the bishop's throne.

CANON XLIV. (Greek xlvii.)

Concerning Virgins.

THAT holy virgins when they are separated from their parents by whom they have been wont to be guarded, are to be commended by the care of the bishop, or presbyter where the bishop is absent, to women of graver age, so that[2] living with them they may take care of them, lest they hurt the reputation of the Church by wandering about.

---

[1] This last clause seems manifestly to be corrupt and should read "unless when, etc."

[2] The Latin is *aut*.

NOTES.

ANCIENT EPITOME OF CANON XLIV.
She who leaves her father for the sake of virginity is to be commended to grave women.

This canon is Canon xxxj. of the Synod of Hippo, A.D. 393.

CANON XLV. (Greek xlviii.)

Concerning those who are sick and cannot answer for themselves.

THAT the sick are to be baptized who cannot answer for themselves if their [servants] shall have spoken at their own proper peril a testimony of the good will [of the sick man.]

(Greek Canon xlix.)

Concerning players who are doing penance and are converted to the Lord.[1]

THAT to players and actors and other persons of that kind, as also to apostates when they are converted[2] and return to God, grace or reconciliation is not to be denied.

NOTES.

ANCIENT EPITOME OF CANON XLV.
That he who cannot answer for himself on account of illness is to be baptized when he shall have given evidence of his desire.

A repentant actor is to be received to penance.

This canon is made up of Canons xxxij. and xxxiij. of the Synod of Hippo, A.D. 393.

JOHNSON.

"Apostates," i.e., those who elsewhere are called *Lapsi;* those who had done sacrifice through the violence of torment in time of persecution, professing in the meantime that their consciences did not consent to what their hands did.

CANON XLVI. (Greek l.)

Concerning the passions of the martyrs.

THE passions of the Martyrs may be read when their anniversary days are celebrated.

NOTE.

ANCIENT EPITOME OF CANON XLVI.
The passions of the martyrs are to be read on their commemorations.

This canon is the last part of Canon xxxvj. of the Synod of Hippo, A.D. 393.

CANON XLVII. (Greek li.)

Concerning [the Donatists and [3]] the children baptized by the Donatists.

CONCERNING the Donatists[4] it seemed good that we should hold counsel with our brethren and fellow priests Siricius and Simplician concerning those infants alone who are baptized by Donatists:[5] lest what they did not do of their own will, when they should be converted to the Church of God with a salutary determination, the error of their parents might prevent their promotion to the ministry of the holy altar.

But when these things had been begun, Honoratus and Urbanus, bishops of Mauri-

---

[1] Found only in the Greek.
[2] In the Greek "doing penance."
[3] Found only in the Greek.

[4] Not in the Greek.
[5] Latin reads "among them" instead of "by Donatists."

tania Sitifensis, said : When some time ago we were sent to your holiness, we laid aside what things had been written on this account, that we might wait for the arrival of our brethren the legates from Numidia.   But because not a few days have passed in which they have been looked for and as yet they are not arrived, it is not fitting that we should delay any longer the commands we received from our brother-bishops ; and therefore, brethren, receive our story with alacrity of mind.   We have heard concerning the faith of the Nicene tractate : True it is that sacrifices are to be forbidden after breakfast, so that they may be offered as is right by those who are fasting, and this has been confirmed then and now.

NOTES.

ANCIENT EPITOME OF CANON XLVII.

When those in infancy baptized by Donatists are converted, this shall be no impediment to them. And the Holy Mysteries, as is right, are to be celebrated only by them fasting.

This canon is made from Canon xxxvij. of the Synod of Hippo, A.D. 393, and from Canon j. of the Synod of Carthage of August 28th, A.D. 397.

JOHNSON.

See Can. 41.

The pretence that the Donatists had for making a schism was, that Cæcilian, Bishop of Carthage, had, in the time of persecution, been a *Traditor*, i.e., given up the Bible to the heathen inquisitors ; this was denied by the Orthodox, who charged them with the same crime in effect, viz. of being too favourable to the *Traditors*, and those that had lapsed. They likewise are charged with Arianism.

I have omitted what is here mentioned concerning the Council of Nice ; because I do not find that any one has been able to penetrate into the meaning of the Fathers as to that particular.

CANON XLVIII.   (Greek lii.)

Of rebaptisms, reordinations, and translations of bishops.

BUT we suggest that we decree what was set forth by the wisdom of the plenary synod at Capua, that no rebaptisings, nor reordinations should take place, and that bishops should not be translated.   For Cresconius, bishop of Villa Regis, left his own people and invaded the Church of Tubinia and having been admonished down to this very day, to leave, according to the decree, the diocese he had invaded, he treated the admonition with disdain.   We have heard that the sentence pronounced against him has been confirmed ; but we seek, according to our decree, that ye deign to grant that being driven thereto by necessity, it be free to us to address the rector of the province against him, according to the statutes of the most glorious princes, so that whoever is not willing to acquiesce in the mild admonition of your holiness and to amend his lawlessness, shall be immediately cast out by judicial authority.   Aurelius the bishop said : By the observance of the constituted form, let him not be judged to be a member of the synod, if he has been asked by you, dear brethren, to depart and has refused : for out of his own contempt and contumacy he has fallen to the power of the secular magistrate.[1]   Honoratus and Urban the bishops said : This pleases us all, does it not ?   And all the bishops answered : It is just, it pleases us.

NOTES.

ANCIENT EPITOME OF CANON XLVIII.

Let there be no rebaptisms, nor reordinations nor translations of bishops. Therefore let Cresconius be forbidden by judicial authority, for he has left his own people, and has taken possession of the diocese of Ceneum, although ecclesiastically admonished that he was not to change.

This canon is Canon j., of the Synod of Carthage of August 28th, A.D. 397.   The acts of this synod were first accurately edited by the Ballerini (in their edition of the works of St. Leo) and were printed by Mansi, in an amended form, in his *Concilia*.

[1] I have followed the Greek text here, the Latin is very confused.

CANON XLIX. (Greek liii.)

How many bishops there should be to ordain a bishop.

HONORATUS and Urban, the bishops, said: We have issued this command, that (because lately two of our brethren, bishops of Numidia, presumed to ordain a pontiff,) only by the concurrence of twelve bishops the ordination of bishops be celebrated. Aurelius, the bishop, said: The ancient form shall be preserved, that not less than three suffice who shall have been designated for ordaining the bishop. Moreover, because in Tripoli, and in Arzug the barbarians are so near, for it is asserted that in Tripoli there are but five bishops, and out of that number two may be occupied by some necessity; but it is difficult that all of the number should come together at any place whatever; ought this circumstance to be an impediment to the doing of what is of utility to the Church? For in this Church, to which your holiness has deigned to assemble[1] we frequently have ordinations and nearly every Lord's day; could I frequently summon twelve, or ten, or about that number of bishops? But it is an easy thing for me to join a couple of neighbours to my littleness. Wherefore your charity will agree with me that this cannot be observed.

NOTES.

ANCIENT EPITOME OF CANON XLIX.

Fewer than three bishops do not suffice for the ordination of a bishop.

This is Canon ij., of the Synod of Carthage, August 28th, 397.

JOHNSON.

See Can. 13.

The occasion of this canon was a complaint that two bishops in Numidia had presumed to ordain a third; upon which it was proposed that not less than twelve should perform this office: But Aurelius, Bishop of Carthage, desires that the old form might be observed, and three bishops be sufficient; especially, because in Tripoli, where there were but five bishops in all, it would be hard to get more than three together. And he adds, that though it were no hard matter for him to get two bishops to assist him in his ordinations at Carthage, yet it would not be practicable for him to get twelve: "For," says he, "we have frequently, and almost every Sunday, men to be ordained." He must mean bishops for otherwise it had been nothing to his purpose, because he could ordain priests or deacons by himself, without the assistance of other bishops: and yet it is very strange, that ordinations of bishops should be so frequent as to bear that expression of "almost every Sunday." There were indeed above one hundred bishoprics in his Province; but these could not occasion above six or eight ordinations in a year; but it is probable that the privilege belonging to him, Can. 55, brought very many ordinations to the church of Carthage; for it is evident, there was a great scarcity of men fit for the Episcopal office in Africa. It is further evident from this canon, that bishops were not ordained in the church of their own see, but in that of the Primate. See Can. Ant., 19.

CANON L. (Greek liv.)

How many bishops should be added to the number of those ordaining, if any opposition had been made to the one to be ordained.

BUT this should be decreed, that when we shall have met together to choose a bishop, if any opposition shall arise, because such things have been treated by us, the three shall not presume to purge[2] him who was to be ordained, but one or two more shall be asked to be added to the aforesaid number, and the persons of those objecting shall first be discussed in the same place (*plebe*) for which he was to be ordained. And last of all the objections shall be considered; and only after he has been cleared in the

---

[1] Notice the African use of the phrase *convenire ad.*
[2] The Greek reads "to depose him," and varies considerably from the Latin. I have followed the Latin but confess that in part I have failed to catch a meaning. The Greek is perfectly clear, as usual.

public sight shall he at last be ordained. If this agrees with the mind of your holiness, let it be confirmed by the answer of your worthiness. All the bishops said, We are well pleased.

NOTES.

ANCIENT EPITOME OF CANON L.

If any controversy arise concerning a bishop who has been elected by three bishops, let two others be coöpted, and so let there be an examination made of his affairs; and if it shall appear that he is pure, let him be ordained.

This canon is Canon iij., of the Synod of Carthage, Aug. 28th, 397.

JOHNSON.

Here the bishops meet to choose a new one,

and it is evident by the foregoing canon, that they met not in the vacant church, but in that of the Primate; and that therefore not the people, but the bishops had the chief share in the election. The people might make their objections, which supposes they knew who their intended bishop was; but the bishops were the judges of the cause. And it seems probable, that if there were any dispute, some of the bishops went to the vacant church to hear the allegations against the person that was elected, or proposed.

CANON LI. (Greek lv.)

That the date of Easter is to be announced by the Church of Carthage.

HONORATUS and Urban, the bishops, said: Since all things treated by our commonitory are known,[1] we add also what has been ordered concerning the day of Easter, that we be informed of the date always by the Church of Carthage, as has been accustomed and that no short time before. Aurelius, the bishop, said: If it seems good to your holiness, since we remember that we pledged ourselves sometime ago that every year we would come together for discussion, when we assemble, then let the date of the holy Easter be announced through the legates present at the Council. Honoratus and Urban, the bishops, said: Now we seek of the present assembly that ye deign to inform our province of that day by letters. Aurelius, the bishop, said: It is necessary it should be so.

NOTES.

ANCIENT EPITOME OF CANON LI.

Let the day on which Easter is to be kept be announced by the Church of Carthage in the annual synod.

This canon is the first part of Canon iv. of the Synod of Carthage, August 28th, 397.

JOHNSON.

The synod met in August. See Can. 73.

CANON LII. (Greek lvi.)

Of visiting provinces.

HONORATUS and Urban, the bishops, said: This was commanded to us in word, that because it had been decreed in the Council of Hippo that each province should be visited in the time of the council, that ye also deign that this year or next, according to the order ye have drawn up, you should visit the province of Mauritania.

Aurelius, the bishop, said: Of the province of Mauritania because it is situated in the confines of Africa, we have made no decree, for they are neighbours of the barbarians; but God grant (not however that I make any rash promise of doing so), we may be able to come to your province. For ye should consider, brethren, that this same thing our brethren of Tripoli and of the Arzuges region [2] could demand also, if occasion offered

---

[1] The Latin "noscuntur" is almost certainly corrupt, Van Espen suggests "absoluta sunt" as the meaning.
[2] Vide Corripus (Partsch's ed.) *Johannid* in *Mon. Germ. Hist.* (in the Series *Auctores Antiquissimi*), Proem, p. xiv. It seems from Orosius that the same province was called Tripolitana and Regio Arzugum, and that *Arzuges* was a race name of wider application.

NOTES.

ANCIENT EPITOME OF CANON LII.

As the Synod at Hippo decreed, every province should be visited in an annual Synod.

This canon is the last part of canon iv of the Council of Carthage, August 28th, A.D. 397.

JOHNSON.

The manner of visiting provinces, and that annually; and the persons by whom this visitation was performed, can scarce now be discovered; only it appears, by the words of Aurelius, that the Bishop of Carthage was one, if not the only visitor; but it was impossible that he could visit all the provinces in Africa personally every year, he must use delegates.

CANON LIII.   (Greek lvii.)

That dioceses should not receive a bishop except by the consent of its own bishop.

EPIGONIUS, the bishop, said: In many councils it has been decreed by the sacerdotal assembly that such communities as are contained in other dioceses and ruled by their bishops, and which never had any bishops of their own, should not receive rulers, that is bishops, for themselves except with the consent of the bishop under whose jurisdiction they have been. But because some who have attained a certain domination abhor the communion of the brethren, or at least, having become depraved, claim for themselves domination with what is really tyranny, for the most part tumid and stolid presbyters, who lift up their heads against their own bishops or else win the people to themselves by feasting them or by malignant persuasion, that they may by unlawful favour wish to place themselves as rulers over them; we indeed hold fast that glorious desire of your mind, most pious brother Aurelius, for thou hast often opposed these things, paying no heed to such petitioners; but on account of their evil thoughts and basely conceived designs this I say, that such a community, which has always been subject in a diocese, ought not to receive a rector, nor should it ever have a bishop of its own. Therefore if this which I have proposed seems good to the whole most holy council, let it be confirmed.

Aurelius, the bishop, said: I am not in opposition to the proposition of our brother and fellow bishop: but I confess that this has been and shall be my practice concerning those who were truly of one mind, not only with regard to the Church of Carthage, but concerning every sacerdotal assemblage. For there are many who, as has been said, conspire with the people whom they deceive, tickling their ears and blandly seducing them, men of vicious lives, or at least puffed up and separated from this meeting, who think to watch over their own people, and never come to our council for fear that their wickedness should be discussed. I say, if it seems good, that not only should these not keep their dioceses, but that every effort should be made to have them expelled by public authority from that church of theirs which has evilly favoured them, and that they be removed even from the chief sees. For it is right that he who cleaves to all the brethren and the whole council, should possess with full right not only his church but also the dioceses. But they who think that the people suffice them and spurn the love of the brethren, shall not only lose their dioceses, but (as I have said,) they shall be deprived by public authority of their own cures as rebels. Honoratus and Urban, the bishops, said: The lofty provision of your holiness obtains the adherence of the minds of all of us, and I think that by the answer of all what you have deigned to propose will be confirmed. All the bishops said: Placet, placet.

NOTES.

ANCIENT EPITOME OF CANON LIII.

Whoso shall neglect his call to a synod, and shall despise the charity of his brethren, putting his trust in the multitude who are with him, let him be deprived of them by the imperial authority.

This canon is Canon v. of the Synod of Carthage of August 28th, A.D. 397, beginning with the second clause.

JOHNSON.

It is very evident that a diocese here signi-fies some town or village lying remote from the Bishop's City, but belonging to his jurisdiction ; and is to be understood to be a place distinct from the bishop's church or cathedral.

See also Can. 56 and Decr. Anast., 6.

<h2 style="text-align:center">CANON LIV. (Greek lviii.)</h2>

That a strange cleric is under no circumstances to be received by another.

EPIGONIUS, the bishop, said : This has been decreed in many councils, also just now it has been confirmed by your prudence, most blessed brethren, that no bishop should receive a strange cleric into his diocese without the consent of the bishop to whose jurisdiction the cleric belongs. But I say that Julian, who is ungrateful for the favours bestowed upon him by God through my littleness, is so rash and audacious, that a certain man who was baptized by me, when he was a most needy boy, commended to me by the same, and when for many years he had been fed and reared by me, it is certain that this one, as I have said, was baptized in my church, by my own unworthy hands ; this same man began to exercise the office of reader in the Mappalien diocese, and read there for nearly two years, with a most incomprehensible contempt of my littleness, the aforenamed Julian took this man, whom he declared to be a citizen of his own city Vazarita, and without consulting me ordained him deacon. If, most blessed brethren, that is permissible, let it be declared to us ; but if not, let such an impudent one be restrained that he may in no way mix himself in someone's communion.

Numidius, the bishop, said : If, as it seems, Julian did this without your worthiness being asked for his consent, nor even consulted, we all judge that this was done iniquitously and unworthily. Wherefore unless Julian shall correct his error, and shall return the cleric to your people with proper satisfaction, since what he did was contrary to the decrees of the council, let him be condemned and separated from us on account of his contumacy. Epigonius, the bishop, said: Our father in age, and most ancient by his promotion, that laudable man, our brother and colleague Victor wishes that this petition should be made general to all.

<h3 style="text-align:center">NOTES.</h3>

ANCIENT EPITOME OF CANON LIV.

Since Julian has ordained a reader of Epigonius's to the diaconate, unless he shall shew authority received from him to do so, he shall increase the penalty of his contumacy.

This canon is Canon vj. of the Synod of Carthage, August 28th, A.D. 397.

JOHNSON.

See Canon of the Apostles, 12 (15, 16), and Chalcedon, 10.

<h2 style="text-align:center">CANON LV. (Greek lix.)</h2>

That it be lawful for the bishop of Carthage to ordain a cleric whenever he wishes.

AURELIUS, the bishop, said : My brethren, pray allow me to speak. It often happens that ecclesiastics who are in need seek deacons [*præpositis* in the Latin], or presbyters or bishops from me : and I, bearing in mind what things have been ordained these I observe, to wit, I summon the bishop of the cleric who is sought for, and I shew him the state of affairs, how that they of a certain church ask for a certain one of his clergy. Perchance then they make no objection, but lest it happen that afterwards they might object when in this case they shall have been demanded (*postulati*) by me, who (as you know) have the care of many churches and of the ordinands. It is right therefore that I should summon a fellow bishop with two or three witnesses from our number. But if he be found *indevotus* [ἀκαθοσίωτος], what does your charity think should be done? For I, as ye know, brethren, by the condescension of God have the care of all the churches.

Numidius, the bishop, said:[1] This see always had the power of ordaining a bishop according to the desire of each Church as he wills and on whose name there was agreement (*fuisset conventus*). Epigonius, the bishop, said: Your good nature makes small use of your powers, for you make much less use of them than you might, since, my brother, you are good and gentle to all; for you have the power, but it is far from your practice to satisfy the person of each bishop in prima tantummodo conventione. But if it should be thought that the rights of this see ought to be vindicated, you have the duty of supporting all the churches, wherefore we do not give thee power, but we confirm that power thou hast, viz.: that thou hast the right at thy will always to choose whom thou wilt, to constitute[2] prelates over peoples and churches who shall have asked thee to do so, and when thou so desirest. Posthumianus, the bishop, said: Would it be right that he who had only one presbyter should have that one taken away from him? Aurelius, the bishop, said: But there may be one bishop by whom many presbyters can be made through the divine goodness, but one fit to be made bishop is found with difficulty. Wherefore if any bishop has a presbyter necessary for the episcopate and has one only, my brother, as you have said, even that one he ought to give up for promotion. Posthumianus, the bishop, said: If some other bishop has plenty of clergy, should that other diocese come to my help? Aurelius, the bishop, said: Of course, when you have come to the help of another Church, he who has many clerics should be persuaded to make one over to you for ordination.

NOTES.

ANCIENT EPITOME OF CANON LV.

It is lawful for the bishop of Carthage, whenever he wills, to choose those who are to be set over the churches: even if there were only one presbyter worthy of rule. For one bishop can ordain many presbyters, but one fit for the episcopate is hard to find.

This canon is the first half of Canon vij. of the Council of Carthage held August 28th A.D. 397.

JOHNSON.

It is evident, that this privilege of the Bishop of Carthage extended to the whole African diocese or the six provinces of Africa, which contained near five hundred bishoprics. This was what caused such frequent ordinations of bishops in the Church of Carthage (See Can. Afr. 49, and the Note) And it is further apparent, that the Bishop of Carthage had some power over the whole African church, and was probably their visitor (See Can. 52). But that he had the sole power of ordaining bishops for every church, with the assistance of any two bishops, does not appear, though Justellus is of this opinion; nay, the 49th canon proves that he had it not.

CANON LVI. (Greek lx.)

That bishops who were ordained for dioceses shall not choose for themselves dioceses [in the Greek *provinces*].

HONORATUS and Urban, the bishops, said: We have heard that it has been decreed that dioceses should not be deemed fit to receive bishops, unless with the consent of their founder: but in our province since some have been ordained bishops in the diocese, by the consent of that bishop by whose power they were established, have even seized dioceses for themselves, this should be corrected by the judgment of your charity, and prohibited for the future. Epigonius, the bishop, said: To every bishop should be reserved what is right, so that from the mass of dioceses no part should be snatched away, so as to have its own bishop, without consent from the proper authority. For it shall suffice, if the consent be given, that the diocese thus set apart have its own bishop

---

[1] The meaning of this whole canon is very obscure, the text is almost certainly corrupt; and the Greek in many places in no way corresponds to the Latin.

[2] Migne's text reads this negatively " ut non constituas," but I have followed Labbe and Cossart and have omitted the " non."

only, and let him[1] not seize other dioceses, for only the one cut off from the many merited the honour of receiving a bishop.   Aurelius, the bishop, said : I do not doubt that it is pleasing to the charity of you all, that he who was ordained for a diocese by the consent of the bishop who held the mother see, should retain only the people for whom he was ordained.   Since therefore I think that everything has been treated of, if all things are agreeable to your mind, pray confirm them all by your suffrage.   All the bishops said : We all are well pleased, and we have confirmed them with our subscription.   And they signed their names.

I, Aurelius, bishop of the Church of Carthage, have consented to this decree, and have subscribed what has been read.   So too did all the other bishops in like fashion sign.

NOTES.

Ancient Epitome of Canon LVI.

If any diocese has received consent to have a bishop of its own from him who has the right, that one shall not invade the rest of the dioceses.

This is the last part of Canon vij. of the Synod of Carthage, August 28, A.D. 397.

Johnson.

It had scarce been worth while to give so much of this canon in English if I had not thought it proper, in order to confirm the sense of the word diocese, mentioned in note on Can. 53, viz., a town or village, where there is a church subject to the bishop of the city.

Between this canon and the following, there is a reference to a former council at Carthage forbidding bishops to sail, without a formal letter from the Primate ; and this said to be done when Cæsarius and Atticus were consuls, anno æræ vulg. 397, and there is mention of an embassy of two bishops from a council of Carthage to the Emperors, to procure the privilege of sanctuary to all impeached for any crime, if they fled to the Church.   This is said to be done when Honorius and Eutychianus were consuls, anno æræ vulg. 398.   And further, here is an account of a bishop sent legate to Anastasius, Bishop of the Apostolical see, and Venerius of Milan, to supply the African Church with men fit to be ordained. For Aurelius complains that many Churches have not so much as one man, not so much as an illiterate one, in deacon's orders, much less had they a competent number of men for the superior dignities.   He speaks of the importunate clamours of many people, that were themselves almost killed, I suppose, by some common pestilence.

In this council it was decreed that bishops should not travel by sea without formed letters.

During the consulate of those illustrious men, Cæsar and Atticus, on the sixth before the Calends of July, at Carthage, it seemed good that no bishop should travel by water without "formed letters" from the Primate.   The authentic acts will be found by him who seeks them.

In this council, bishops whose names are set down hereafter were sent as legates to the Emperor.

After the consulate of the most glorious Emperor Honorius Augustus for the fourth time, and of the renowned Eutychian, on the fifth of the calends of May, at Carthage in the secretarium of the restored basilica.   In this council Epigonius and Vincent, the bishops, received a legation, in order that they might obtain a law from the most glorious princes in behalf of those taking refuge in the Church, whatever might be the crime of which they were accused, that no one should dare to force them away.

In this council a legation was sent to the Bishops of Rome and Milan with regard to children baptized by heretics, and to the Emperor with regard to having such idols as still remained taken away, and also with regard to many other matters.

After the consulate of the renowned Flabius Stilico, on the sixteenth of the calends of July, at Carthage in the secretarium of the restored basilica.

When Aurelius, the Bishop, together with his fellow-bishops had taken their seats,

---

[1] The common reading " vinaicent " is almost certainly wrong, and is not even mentioned by Bruns.

the deacons standing by, Aurelius, the Bishop, said: Your charity, most holy brethren, knows fully as well as I do the necessities of the churches of God throughout Africa. And since the Lord has vouchsafed that from a part of your holy company this present assembly should be convened, it seems to me that these necessities which in the discharge of our solicitude we have discovered, we ought to consider together. And afterwards, that there should be chosen a bishop from our number who may, with the help of the Lord and your prayers, assume the burden of these necessities, and zealously accomplish whatever ought to be done in the premises, going to the parts of Italy across seas, that he may acquaint our holy brethren and fellow-bishops, the venerable and holy brother Anastasius, bishop of the Apostolic see, and also our holy brother Venerius the Bishop of Milan, with our necessity and grief, and helplessness. For there has been withheld from these sees the knowledge of what was necessary to provide against the common peril, especially that the need of clergy is so great that many churches are in such destitution as that not so much as a single deacon or even an unlettered clerk is to be found. I say nothing of the superior orders and offices, because if, as I have said, the ministry of a deacon is not easily to be had, it is certainly much more difficult to find one of the superior orders. [And let them also tell these bishops] that we can no longer bear to hear the daily lamentations of the different peoples almost ready to die, and unless we do our best to help them, the grievous and inexcusable cause of the destruction of innumerable souls will be laid at our door before God.

CANON LVII. (Greek lxi.)

That persons baptized when children by the Donatists may be ordained clergymen in the Catholic Church.

SINCE in the former council it was decreed, as your unanimity remembers as well as I do, that those who as children were baptized by the Donatists, and not yet being able to know the pernicious character of their error, and afterward when they had come to the use of reason, had received the knowledge of the truth, abhorred their former error, and were received, (in accordance with the ancient order) by the imposition of the hand, into the Catholic Church of God spread throughout the world, that to such the remembrance of the error ought to be no impediment to the reception of the clerical office. For in coming to faith they thought the true Church to be their own and there they believed in Christ, and received the sacraments of the Trinity. And that all these sacraments are altogether true and holy and divine is most certain, and in them the whole hope of the soul is placed, although the presumptuous audacity of heretics, taking to itself the name of the truth, dares to administer them. They are but one after all, as the blessed Apostle tells us, saying: "One God, one faith, one baptism," and it is not lawful to reiterate what once only ought to be administered. [Those therefore who have been so baptized] having anathematized their error may be received by the imposition of the hand into the one Church, the pillar as it is called, and the one mother of all Christians, where all these Sacraments are received unto salvation and everlasting life; even the same sacraments which obtain for those persevering in heresy the heavy penalty of damnation. So that which to those who are in the truth lighteneth to the obtaining of eternal life, the same to them who are in error tends but to darkness and damnation. With regard then to those who, having fled from error, acknowledge the breasts of their mother the Catholic Church, who believe and receive all these holy mysteries with the love of the truth, and besides the Sacraments have the testimony of a good life, there is no one who would not grant that without doubt such persons may be raised to the clerical office, especially in such necessity as the present. But there are others of this sect, who being already clergymen, desire to pass to us with their peoples and also with their honours, such as for the sake of office are converts to life, and that they may retain them seek for salvation [i.e., enter the Church]. I think that the question concerning such may be left to the graver consideration of our aforesaid brothers, and that when they have considered by their more prudent counsel the matter referred to them, they may vouchsafe to advise us what approves itself to them with regard to this question. Only concerning those who as children were baptized by heretics we decree that they consent, if it seems good, to our decision concerning the ordination of the same. All things, therefore, which we have set forth above with the holy bishops, let your honourable fraternity with me adjudge to be done.

NOTES.

ANCIENT EPITOME OF CANON LVII.

Such as have been while children baptized by the Donatists may be ordained should they repent, anathematize their heresy, and be otherwise worthy.

Of the three Introductions to Carthaginian Councils which precede this canon, the first refers to the synod held June 26, A.D. 397; the second to that held April 27, A.D. 399; and the third to that of June 15 (or 16), A.D. 401.

The canon is Canon j. of the Synod of Carthage of June 15 (or 16), A.D. 401. The eight other canons of this synod follow in the African Code in their own order.

JOHNSON.

See Can. 47, which was made in a former synod.

CANON LVIII. (Greek lxii.)

Of the remaining idols or temples which should be done away by the Emperors.

WHEREFORE the most religious Emperors should be asked[1] that they order the remaining idols to be taken entirely away throughout all Africa; for in many maritime places and in divers possessions the iniquity of this error still flourishes: that they command them to be taken away and their temples, (such as are no ornament, being set up in fields or out of the way places) be ordered to be altogether destroyed.

NOTES.

ANCIENT EPITOME OF CANON LVIII.

The remains of the idols should be abolished altogether.

This is Canon ij. of the Synod of Carthage of June 15 (16), A.D. 401.

CANON LIX. (Greek lxiii.)

That clerics be not compelled to give testimony in public concerning the cognizance of their own judgment.

IT should be petitioned also that they deign to decree, that if perchance any shall have been willing to plead their cause in any church according to the Apostolic law imposed upon the Churches, and it happens that the decision of the clergy does not satisfy one of the parties, it be not lawful to summon that clergyman who had been cognitor or present,[2] into judgment as a witness, and that no person attached to any ecclesiastic be compelled to give testimony.

NOTES.

ANCIENT EPITOME OF CANON LIX.

A cleric who has decided a case shall not, if it be displeasing, be summoned to a tribunal to give evidence concerning it; and no ecclesiastical person shall be forced to give testimony.

This is Canon iij. of the Synod of Carthage, June 15 (or 16), A.D. 401.

JOHNSON.

"According to the Apostolic law," viz., that of St. Paul, 1 Cor. vi. 1, 2, etc. I follow the Greek scholia in rendering this canon. In Latin *cognitor* is he that is solicitor, or advocate, rather than the judge who takes cognizance.

---

[1] I have followed the Greek text. The Latin reads: "Instant etiam aliæ necessitates religiosis imperitoribus postulandæ."

[2] This must mean "who had heard the cause or been present at the hearing," and so the Greek has it.

CANON LX. (Greek lxiii.)

Of heathen feasts.

THIS also must be sought, that (since contrary to the divine precepts feasts are held in many places, which have been induced by the heathen error, so that now Christians are forced to celebrate these by heathens, from which state of things it happens that in the times of the Christian Emperors a new persecution seems to have secretly arisen :) they order such things to be forbidden and prohibit them from cities and possessions under pain of punishment; especially should this be done since they do not fear to commit such iniquities in some cities even upon the natal days of most blessed martyrs, and in the very sacred places themselves. For upon these days, shame to say, they perform the most wicked leapings throughout the fields and open places, so that matronal honour and the modesty of innumerable women who have come out of devotion for the most holy day are assaulted by lascivious injuries, so that all approach to holy religion itself is almost fled from.

NOTES.

ANCIENT EPITOME OF CANON LX.

The Greek feasts must cease to be kept, because of their impropriety, and because they seduce many Christians, moreover they are celebrated on the commemorations of the martyrs.

This is Canon iv. of the Synod of Carthage, Aug. 15 (or 16), A.D. 401.

JOHNSON.

Bishop Beveridge and Tilius's edition of these canons, in Greek and Latin, number the two preceding canons as I have done in the margin, with the same figures [viz : 63]. I follow them in this error because by this means the reader may more readily be referred from the Latin original and from this English translation to the Greek.

CANON LXI. (Greek lxiv.)

Of spectacles, that they be not celebrated on Lord's days nor on the festivals of the Saints.

FURTHERMORE, it must be sought that theatrical spectacles and the exhibition of other plays be removed from the Lord's day and the other most sacred days of the Christian religion, especially because on the octave day of the holy Easter [i.e., Low Sunday] the people assemble rather at the circus than at church, and they should be transferred to some other day when they happen to fall upon a day of devotion, nor shall any Christian be compelled to witness these spectacles,[1] especially because in the performance of things contrary to the precepts of God there should be no persecution made by anyone, but (as is right) a man should exercise the free will given him by God. Especially also should be considered the peril of the coöperators who, contrary to the precepts of God, are forced by great fear to attend the shews.

NOTES.

ANCIENT EPITOME OF CANON LXI.
There shall be no theatrical representations upon Lord's days or feast days.

This is Canon V. of the Synod of Carthage, June 15th (16), A.D. 401.

CANON LXII. (Greek lxv.)

Of condemned clerics.

AND this should be sought, that they deign to decree that if any clergyman of whatever rank shall have been condemned by the judgment of the bishops for any crime, he may not be defended either by the churches over which he presided, nor by anyone what-

---

[1] Here ends the Greek text.

ever, under pain of loss both of money and office, and let them order that neither age nor sex be received as an excuse.

NOTES.

<small>ANCIENT EPITOME OF CANON LXII.</small>

No one shall justify a clergyman condemned by his own bishop.

This is Canon vj. of the Synod of Carthage, June 15 (or 16), A.D. 401.

CANON LXIII. (Greek lxvi.)

Of players who have become Christians.

AND of them also it must be sought that if anyone wishes to come to the grace of Christianity from any ludicrous art (*ludicra arte*) and to remain free of that stain, it be not lawful for anyone to induce him or compel him to return to the performance of the same things again.

NOTES.

<small>ANCIENT EPITOME OF CANON LXIII.</small>

Whoever has turned away from the stage to adopt an honest life, shall not be led back thereto

This is Canon vij. of the Synod of Carthage, June 15 (or 16), A. D. 401.

<small>JOHNSON.</small>

This canon is probably to be understood of slaves bought by their masters for the service of the Circ, or Theatre.

CANON LXIV. (Greek lxvii.)

Of celebrating manumissions in church, that permission be asked from the Emperor.

CONCERNING the publishing of manumissions in church, if our fellow bishops throughout Italy shall be found to do this, it will be a mark of our confidence to follow their order [of proceedings], full power being given to the legate we send, that whatever he can accomplish worthy of the faith, for the state of the Church and the salvation of souls, we shall laudably accept in the sight of the Lord. All which things, if they please your sanctity, pray set forth, that I may be assured that my suggestion has been ratified by you and that their sincerity may freely accept our unanimous action. And all the bishops said : The things which have been enjoined to be done and have been wisely set forth by your holiness are pleasing to all.

NOTES.

<small>ANCIENT EPITOME OF CANON LXIV.</small>

The Emperor's permission should be sought to allow the public manumission of slaves in church.

This is Canon viij. of the Synod of Carthage, June 15 (or 16), A. D. 401.

<small>JOHNSON.</small>

It is certain, that in Italy, and some other parts of the Empire, slaves were solemnly set at liberty by their masters, in the church and presence of the bishop, from the time of Constantine, but it should seem this custom had not yet obtained in Africa.

CANON LXV. (Greek lxviii.)

Concerning the condemned bishop Equitius.

AURELIUS, the bishop, said : I do not think that the case of Equitius should be passed over in the legation, who some time ago for his crimes was condemned by an Episcopal sentence; that if by any chance our legate should meet him in those parts, our brother should take care for the state of the Church, as opportunity offered or where he could, to act against him. And all the bishops said: This prosecution is exceedingly agreeable to us, especially as Equitius was condemned some time ago, his impudent unrest ought to be repelled everywhere more and more for the good estate and health of the Church. And they subscribed, I, Aurelius, the bishop of the Church of Carthage, have consented to this decree, and after having read it have signed my name. Likewise also signed all the other bishops.

NOTES.

ANCIENT EPITOME OF CANON LXV.

Equitius, who had been condemned by the judgment of the bishops, and had behaved impudently against the ecclesiastical authority, ought to be opposed.

This is Canon ix. of the Synod of Carthage, June 15 (or 16), A.D. 401.

JOHNSON.

See Can. Afr., 78.

In this council the letters of Anastasius the Roman Pontiff were read, admonishing the Catholic bishops concerning the Donatists.

In the consulship of those most illustrious men Vencentius and Flavius, on the Ides of September, at Carthage, in the secretarium of the restored basilica. When we had been gathered together in council in the church at Carthage and had taken our seats, bishops from all the African Provinces, that is to say, Aurelius, the bishop of that see with his colleagues (just who they were is made evident by their signatures) [the same bishop Aurelius said]: When the letters of our most blessed brother and fellow priest, Anastasius, bishop of the Church of Rome, had been read, in which he exhorted us out of the solicitude and sincerity of his paternal and brotherly love, that we should in no way dissimulate with regard to the wiles and wickednesses of the Donatist heretics and schismatics, by which they gravely vex the Catholic Church of Africa, we thank our Lord that he hath vouchsafed to inspire that best and holy archbishop with such a pious care for the members of Christ, although in divers lands, yet builded together into the one body of Christ.

CANON LXVI. (Greek lxix.)

That the Donatists are to be treated leniently.

THEN when all things had been considered and treated of which seem to conduce to the advantage of the church, the Spirit of God suggesting and admonishing us, we determined to act leniently and pacifically with the before-mentioned men, although they were cut off from the unity of the Lord's body by an unruly dissent, so that (as much as in us lies) to all those who have been caught in the net of their communion and society, it might be known throughout all the provinces of Africa, how they have been overcome by miserable error, holding different opinions, "that perchance," as the Apostle says, when we have corrected [1] them with gentleness, "God should grant them repentance for the acknowledging of the truth, and that they might be snatched out of the snares of the devil, who are led captive of him at his will."

NOTES.

ANCIENT EPITOME OF CANON LXVI.

It seemed good that the Donatists should be treated kindly and with leniency, even if they should separate themselves from the Church, so that perchance through their respect for our great gentleness they may be loosed from their captivity.

The introduction refers to the Synod of Carthage of September 13, 401, and this canon is part of Canon j. of that Synod. We are indebted to the Ballerini for collecting the acts of this Synod by a comparison of the pseudo-Isidore, Dionysius, Ferrandus and the quotations contained in the acts of the Synod of Carthage of 525.

---

[1] The Greek reads "when we have gathered them together."

CANON LXVII.   (Greek lxx.)

Of the letters to be sent to the judges, that they may take note of the things done between the Donatists and the Maximianists.

THEREFORE it seemed good that letters should be given from our council to the African judges, from whom it would seem suitable that this should be sought, that in this matter they would aid the common mother, the Catholic Church, that the episcopal authority may be fortified[1] in the cities; that is to say that by their judicial power and with diligence out of their Christian faith, they enquire and record in the public acts, that all may have a firm notion of it, what has taken place in all those places in which the Maximianists, who made a schism from them, have obtained basilicas.

NOTES.

ANCIENT EPITOME OF CANON LXVII.

The secular arm must be implored by synodal letters to assist our common Mother the Catholic Church against those by whom the authority of the bishop is despised.

This canon is the other half of Canon j. of the Synod of Carthage, September 13, A.D. 401.

JOHNSON.

Maximianists were a sect bred out of the Donatists, and separating from them.

CANON LXVIII.   (Greek lxxi.)

That the Donatist clergy are to be received into the Catholic Church as clergymen.

IT moreover seemed good that letters be sent to our brethren and fellow-bishops, and especially to the Apostolic See, over which our aforesaid venerable brother and colleague Anastasius, presides, that [ἐπειδὴ in the Greek, *quo* in the Latin] he may know that Africa is in great need, for the peace and prosperity of the Church, that those Donatists who were clergymen and who by good advice had desired to return to Catholic unity, should be treated according to the will and judgment of each Catholic bishop who governs the Church in that place; and, if it seem good for Christian peace, they be received with their honours, as it is clear was done in the former times of this same division. And that this was the case the example of the majority, yea, of nearly all the African Churches in which this error had sprung up, testify; not that the Council which met about this matter in foreign parts should be done away, but that it may remain in force with regard to those who so will to come over to the Catholic Church that there be procured by them no breaking of unity.   But those through whom Catholic unity was seen to have been altogether perfected or assisted by the manifest winning of the souls of their brethren in the places where they live, there shall not be objected to them the decree contrary to their honour adopted by a foreign council, for salvation is shut off to no one, that is to say, that those ordained by the Donatist party, if having been corrected they have been willing to return to the Catholic Church, are not to be[2] received in their grades, according to the foreign council; but they are to be excepted through whom they received the advice to return to Catholic unity.

NOTES.

ANCIENT EPITOME OF CANON LXVIII.

Those ordained by the Donatists, even though their reception has been forbidden by a foreign synod, since it is truly good that all should be saved, if they correct themselves, let them be received.

BALSAMON.

This canon is special, for it seemed good to the fathers that such of the Donatists as came to the orthodox faith should be so received as to hold the grade of their holy orders, even though a transmarine, that is to say an Italian, council had decreed otherwise.

---

[1] In the Greek, "since the episcopal authority is spurned."   [2] The Greek and Beveridge introduce a second "not."

ARISTENUS.

Those Donatists who are penitent and anathematize their heresy are to be allowed to remain in their proper rank, and be numbered among the clergy of the Catholic Church, because Africa was labouring under a great shortness of clergy.

This canon is Canon ij. of Carthage, Sept., A.D. 401.

JOHNSON.

Whether the Donatists' clergy should be re-ordained was only a point of discipline; for the Donatists retained Episcopacy. Therefore the African fathers, as they leave other churches to their liberty, so at the same time they declare that they would continue their old practice, and leave every bishop to act according to his own discretion in this matter. Probably, one great motive, besides that of peace, which they had to this, was the great scarcity of clergymen in Africa, of which Aurelius complains in his speech, inserted into the Acts before Canon 77 (61), and proposes that they send to the bishops of Rome and Milan for a supply. And that this was the true reason, does in some measure appear from the words of the Latin canon at large, in which the occasion of this decree is said to be *propter necessitatem*. And this is the most probable reason why it is left to the discretion of the bishop, whether to admit Donatist clergymen as such, if he had occasion for their service. And after all it is clear from this very canon, that other churches had determined this point the contrary way. Therefore Mr. Calamy exceeds when he says: "As for the Donatists, all agree that their orders were acknowledged." Further, he would have it thought probable, that orders were not always conferred among the Donatists by persons superior to presbyters. This he would infer from the great number of the bishops of that faction in Africa, viz., 278, many of which (says he) could be no more than parish ministers. But why so? Were there not above four hundred Catholic bishops? And why not as many of one side as the other? If our dissenters of any sort had fallen into the Episcopal form of government, no question but they would have had a bishop in every city at least, and equalled our church in the number of prelates.

CANON LXIX. (Greek lxxii.)

That a legation be sent to the Donatists for the sake of making peace.

IT further seemed good, that when these things were done, legates should be sent from our number to those of the Donatists whom they hold as bishops, or to the people, for the sake of preaching peace and unity, without which Christian salvation cannot be attained; and that these legates should direct the attention of all to the fact that they have no just objection to urge against the Catholic Church. And especially that this be made manifest to all by the municipal acts (on account of the weight of their documents) what they themselves had done in the case of the Maximianists, their own schismatics. For in this case it is shewn them by divine grace, if they will but heed it, that their separation from the unity of the Church is as iniquitous as they now proclaim the schism of the Maximianists from themselves to be. Nevertheless from the number, those whom they condemned by the authority of their plenary council, they received back with their honours, and accepted the baptism which they had given while condemned and cut off. And thus let them see how with stupid heart they resist the peace of the Church scattered throughout the whole world, when they do these things on the part of Donatus, neither do they say that they are contaminated by communion with those whom they so receive for the making of peace, and yet they despise us, that is the Catholic Church, which is established even in the extreme parts of the earth, as being defiled by the communion of those whom the accusers have not been able to win over to themselves.[1]

NOTES.

ANCIENT EPITOME OF CANON LXIX.

It seemed good that legates be sent to preach peace and unity to the Donatists who had been converted to the orthodox faith.

This canon is Canon iij. of Carthage, September, A.D. 401.

---

[1] I think this is the probable meaning of the canon.

CANON LXX. (Greek lxxiii.)

What clerics should abstain from their wives.

MOREOVER since incontinence has been charged against some clergymen with regard to their own wives it has seemed good that bishops, presbyters, and deacons should according to the statutes already made abstain even from their own wives; and unless they do so that they should be removed from the clerical office. But the rest of the clergy shall not be forced to this but the custom of each church in this matter shall be followed.

NOTES.

ANCIENT EPITOME OF CANON LXX.

Bishops, presbyters and deacons shall abstain for their wives or else be removed from the ecclesiastical order. But the rest of the clergy shall not be forced to the same: but let the custom be observed.

This is Canon iv. of Carthage, September, A.D. 401.

JOHNSON.

A repetition of Canon 25 (28).

CANON LXXI. (Greek lxxiv.)

Of those who leave in neglect their own people.

MOREOVER it seemed good that no one should be allowed to leave his chief cathedral and go to another church built in the diocese, or to neglect the care and frequent attendance upon his own cathedral by reason of too great care for his own affairs.

NOTES.

ANCIENT EPITOME OF CANON LXXI.

It seemed good that no bishop shall translate himself to another see, leaving his own, nor that through a care for his own affairs he should neglect his diocese.

This is Canon vj. of Carthage, September, A.D. 401.

JOHNSON.

See Canons 53 (57), 56 (60).
"Principalis Cathedra," his own Cathedral.

CANON LXXII. (Greek lxxv.)

Of the baptism of infants when there is some doubt of their being already baptized.

ITEM, it seemed good that whenever there were not found reliable witnesses who could testify that without any doubt they were baptized and when the children themselves were not, on account of their tender age, able to answer concerning the giving of the sacraments to them, all such children should be baptized without scruple, lest a hesitation should deprive them of the cleansing of the sacraments. This was urged by the Moorish Legates, our brethren, since they redeem many such from the barbarians.

NOTES.

ANCIENT EPITOME OF CANON LXXII.

It seemed good that they should be baptized about whom there was an ambiguity whether they had been baptized or no; *lest they might through that doubt lose the divine ablution.*

This is Canon vij. of Carthage, September, A.D. 401.

CANON LXXIII. (Greek lxxvi.)

The date of Easter and the date of the Council should be announced.

ITEM, it seemed good that the day of the venerable Easter should be intimated to all by the subscription of formed letters; and that the same should be observed with regard to the date of the Council, according to the decree of the Council of Hippo, that is to say the X. Calends of September, and that it should be written to the primates of each province so that when they summon their councils they do not impede this day.

NOTES.

ANCIENT EPITOME OF CANON LXXIII.

It seemed good that the day of the Holy Easter should be announced on the day of the annual Synod, or on the tenth day before the calends of September.

This is Canon viij. of Carthage, September, A.D. 401.

JOHNSON.

See Can. 51 (55).

"The time of council," i.e., of the national council at Carthage.

The Greek canon says ἡ πρὸ δέκα καλανδῶν Σεπτεμβρίων, and Zonaras makes this the 21st of August, but he mistakes in his calculation.

CANON LXXIV. (Greek lxxvii.)

That no bishop who is an intercessor is to hold the see where he is intercessor.

ITEM, it has been decreed that it is not lawful to any intercessor to retain the see to which he has been appointed as intercessor, by any popular movements and seditions; but let him take care that within a year he provide them with a bishop: but if he shall neglect to do so, when the year is done, another intercessor shall be appointed.

NOTES.

ANCIENT EPITOME OF CANON LXXIV.

It seemed good that the bishop who had been called in as an intercessor, by the zeal and dissensions of the people, should not be allowed to become the occupant of its throne: but let a bishop be provided within a year, or else in the next year let another intercessor be appointed.

This is Canon IX. of Carthage, September, A.D. 401.

JOHNSON.

We here call this officer "Guardian of the spiritualities" in the vacancy of the see.

CANON LXXV. (Greek lxxviii.)

Of asking from the Emperors defenders of the Churches.

ON account of the afflictions of the poor by whose troubles the Church is worn out without any intermission, it seemed good to all that the Emperors be asked to allow defenders for them against the power of the rich to be chosen under the supervision of the bishops.

NOTES.

ANCIENT EPITOME OF CANON LXXV.

That the bishop be not annoyed, let Defensors be appointed.

This is Canon X. of Carthage, September, 401.

JOHNSON.

See note on Can. Chalcedon, 23.

CANON LXXVI. (Greek lxxix.)

Of bishops who do not put in an appearance at Council.

ITEM, it seemed good that as often as the council is to be assembled, the bishops who are impeded neither by age, sickness, or other grave necessity, come together, and that notice be given to the primates of their several provinces, that from all the bishops there be made two or three squads, and of each of these squads there be elected some who shall be promptly ready on the council day: but should they not be able to attend, let them write their excuses in the tractory,[1] or if after the coming of the tractory certain necessities suddenly arise by chance, unless they send to their own primate an account of their impediment, they ought to be content with the communion of their own Church.

NOTES.

ANCIENT EPITOME OF CANON LXXVI.

Those who do not attend the annual synod, unless they be involuntarily prevented, must be satisfied with the communion of their own churches.

This is Canon xj., of Carthage, September, 401.

JOHNSON.

"Tractory" has several significations; here it seems to denote the written return made by the Primate of the province to the synodical letter sent by the Bishop of Carthage. In the acts inserted between canon 90th and 91st "Tractoria" seems to denote the letter of the Primate to the inferior bishops for choosing legates, if it do not rather denote the Bishop of Carthage's circular-letter to all the primates, as it does in the next paragraph.

[The penalty in the last clause is] a very singular sort of censure, and very moderate. See Can. 80 (83).

CANON LXXVII. (Greek lxxx.)

Of Cresconius.

CONCERNING Cresconius of Villa Regis this seemed good to all, that the Primate of Numidia should be informed on this matter so that he should by his letters summon the aforementioned Cresconius in order that at the next plenary Council of Africa he should not put off making an appearance. But if he contemns the summons and does not come, let him recognize the fact that sentence should be pronounced against him.

NOTES.

ANCIENT EPITOME OF CANON LXXVII.

Unless Cresconius who has been summoned by letter to the Synod, shall appear, let him know that he will have sentence given against him.

This canon was probably formerly an appendix (so Hefele thinks) to Canon xj., of the Synod of Carthage of September 13, 401.

CANON LXXVIII. (Greek lxxxi.)

Of the Church of Hippo-Diarrhytus.

IT further seemed good that since the destitution of the Church of Hippo-Diarrhytus should no longer be neglected, and the churches there are retained by those who have declined the infamous communion of Equitius, that certain bishops be sent from the present council, viz.: Reginus, Alypius, Augustine, Maternus, Theasius, Evodius, Placian, Urban, Valerius, Ambivius, Fortunatus, Quodvultdeus, Honoratus, Januarius, Aptus, Honoratus, Ampelius, Victorian, Evangelus and Rogation; and when those had been gathered together, and those had been corrected who with culpable pertinacity were of opinion that this flight of the same Equitius should be waited for, let a bishop be ordained for them by the vote of all. But if these should not be willing to consider peace, let them not prevent the choosing for ordination of a bishop, for the advantage of the church which has been so long destitute.

NOTES.

ANCIENT EPITOME OF CANON LXXVIII.

It seemed good that, after Equitius had been condemned by the universal vote, a bishop of Hippo should be elected, and that they should in no way impede the ordination of a prelate for that church.

---

[1] All mention of the "tractory" is omitted in the Greek version.

This canon was likewise probably an appendix, to Canon xiij, of the Synod of Carthage of September 13th, 401, according to Hefele.

See Can. Afr., 65.

Here the place of election and consecration seems to be the vacant see.

CANON LXXIX. (Greek lxxxii.)

Of clerics who do not take care to have their causes argued within a year.

IT was further decreed that as often as clergymen convicted and confessed [1] of any crime either on account of eorum, quorum verecundiæ parcitur, or on account of the opprobrium to the Church, and of the insolent glorying of heretics and Gentiles, if perchance they are willing to be present at their cause and to assert their innocence, let them do so within one year of their excommunication ; if in truth they neglect during a year to purge their cause, their voice shall not be heard afterwards.

NOTES.

ANCIENT EPITOME OF CANON LXXIX.

When a cleric has been convicted of a crime, if he says his cause should be heard upon appeal, let the appeal be made within a year ; after that the appeal shall not be admitted.

This is Canon xiij. of Carthage, September, A.D. 401.

JOHNSON.

Though the Latin syntax of this canon is very confused, and, I am apt to think, corrupted, yet it is evident enough, that this is the intention of it.

CANON LXXX. (Greek lxxxiii.)

That it is not permitted to make superiors of monasteries nor to ordain as clerics those who are received from a monastery not one's own.

ITEM, it seemed good that if any bishop wished to advance to the clericature a monk received from a monastery not under his jurisdiction, or shall have appointed him superior of a monastery of his own, the bishop who shall have thus acted shall be separated from the communion of others and shall rest content with the communion of his own people alone, but the monk shall continue neither as cleric nor superior.

NOTES.

ANCIENT EPITOME OF CANON LXXX.

Whoever shall receive a monk from a monastery not subject to his jurisdiction, and if he shall ordain him to the clerical estate or shall appoint him prior of his monastery, such an one shall be cut off from communion.

This is Canon xiv. of Carthage, September, A.D. 401.

JOHNSON.

See Canons 76 (79) and 122 (123).

CANON LXXXI. (Greek lxxxiv.)

Of bishops who appoint heretics or heathens as their heirs.

ITEM, it was ordained that if any bishop should prefer to his Church strangers to blood relationship with him, or his heretical relatives, or pagans as his heirs, he shall be anathematized even after his death, and his name shall by no means be recited among those of the priests of God. Nor can he be excused if he die intestate, because being a bishop he was bound not to postpone making such a disposition of his goods as was befitting his profession.

---

[1] Bruns says, *Locus corruptus.*

NOTES.

ANCIENT EPITOME OF CANON LXXXI.

Let a bishop be anathema if he make heretics and heathen his heirs.

This is Canon xv. of Carthage, September, A.D. 401.

JOHNSON.

There were in this age two written tables kept in every church, whereof one contained the names of all eminent bishops and clergy-men now living, with whom that church held communion and correspondence; the other, the names of all eminent bishops, and other men of their own or other churches, now dead. The deacon rehearsed all the names, in both tables at the altar, whenever the Eucharist was celebrated. These tables were by the Greeks called Δίπτυχα, and by some English writers "diptychs." See Can. of Peter of Alex., 14.

CANON LXXXII. (Greek lxxxv.)

Of manumissions.

ITEM, it seemed good that the Emperor be petitioned with regard to announcing manumissions in church.

NOTES.

ANCIENT EPITOME OF CANON LXXXII.

The imperial permission must be asked for the making of the manumission of slaves in churches.

ARISTENUS.

This is the same as the sixty-fourth [Greek numbering] canon, and is there explained.

This is Canon xvj. of Carthage, September, A.D. 401.

JOHNSON.

A repetition of Canon 64 (67).

CANON LXXXIII. (Greek lxxxvi.)

Of false Memories of Martyrs.

ITEM, it seemed good that the altars which have been set up here and there, in fields and by the wayside as Memories of Martyrs, in which no body nor reliques of martyrs can be proved to have been laid up, should be overturned by the bishops who rule over such places, if such a thing can be done. But should this be impossible on account of the popular tumult it would arouse, the people should none the less be admonished not to frequent such places, and that those who believe rightly should be held bound by no superstition of the place. And no memory of martyrs should at all be accepted, unless where there is found the body or some reliques, or which is declared traditionally and by good authority to have been originally his habitation, or possession, or the scene of his passion. For altars which have been erected anywhere on account of dreams or inane *quasi*-revelations of certain people, should be in every way disapproved of.

NOTES.

ANCIENT EPITOME OF CANON LXXXIII.

An altar in the fields or in a vineyard which lacks the reliques of the martyrs should be thrown down unless it would cause a public tumult to do so: and the same is the case with such as have been set up on account of dreams and false revelations.

This is Canon xvij. of Carthage, September, A.D. 401.

CANON LXXXIV. (Greek lxxxvii.)

Of extirpating the remains of the idols.

ITEM, it seemed good to petition the most glorious Emperors that the remains of idolatry not only in images, but in any places whatever or groves or trees, should altogether be taken away.

NOTES.

ANCIENT EPITOME OF CANON LXXXIV.

Let all remains of idolatry be abolished whether in statues, or in places, or groves or trees.

This is Canon xviij. of Carthage, September, A.D. 401.

JOHNSON.

See Canon 58 (62.)

CANON LXXXV. (Greek lxxxviii.)

That by the bishop of Carthage, when there shall be need, letters shall be written and subscribed in the name of all the bishops.

IT was said by all the bishops: If any letters are to be composed in the name of the council it seemed good that the venerable bishop who presides over this See should vouchsafe to dictate and sign them in the name of all, among which also are those to the episcopal legates, who are to be sent throughout the African provinces, in the matter of the Donatists; and it seemed good that the letters given them should contain the tenor of the mandate which they are not to go beyond. And they subscribed: I, Aurelius, bishop of the church of Carthage have consented to this decree and having read it have signed it. Likewise all the rest of the bishops subscribed.

NOTES.

ANCIENT EPITOME OF CANON LXXXV.

It seemed good that whatever letters were to be sent from the Synod should be written and subscribed by the bishop of Carthage in the name of all.

This is Canon xix. of Carthage, September, A.D. 401.

In this Council previous decrees are confirmed.

In the fifth consulate of the most glorious Emperors Arcadius and Honorius, Augusti, the VI Calends of September, in the City of Milevis, in the secretarium of the basilica, when Aurelius the bishop of Carthage had taken his seat in plenary council, the deacons standing by, Aurelius, the bishop, said: Since the body of the holy Church is one, and there is one head of all the members, it has come to pass by the divine permission and assistance given to our weakness, that we, invited out of brotherly love, have come to this church. Wherefore I beg your charity to believe that our coming to you is neither superfluous, nor unacceptable to all; and that the consent of all of us may make it manifest that we agree with the decrees already confirmed by the Council at Hippo or which were defined afterwards by a larger synod at Carthage, these shall now be read to us in order. Then at last the agreement of your holiness will appear clearer than light, if they know that the things lawfully defined by us in former councils, ye have set forth, not only by your consent to these acts, but also by your subscriptions.

Xantippus, bishop of the first see of Numidia said: I believe what pleased all the brethren and the statutes they confirmed with their hands; we by our subscribing our names shew that it pleases us also, and have confirmed them with our superscription.

Nicetius, the bishop of the first see of Mauritania Sitifensis said: The decrees which have been read, since they do not lack reason, and have been approved by all, these also are pleasing to my littleness, and I will confirm them with my subscription.

CANON LXXXVI. (Greek lxxxix.)

Of the order of bishops, that those ordained more recently do not dare to take precedence of those ordained before them.

VALENTINE, the bishop, said: If your good patience will permit, I follow the things which were done in time past in the Church of Carthage, and which were illustrious having been confirmed by the subscriptions of the brethren, and I profess that we intend to preserve this. For this we know, that ecclesiastical discipline has always remained inviolate: therefore let none of the brethren dare to place himself before those ordained earlier than himself; but by the offices of charity this has always been shewn to those ordained earlier, which always should be accepted joyfully by those ordained more recently. Let your holiness give command that this order be strengthened by your interlocutions. Aurelius, the bishop, said: It would not be fitting that we should repeat these things, were it not for the existence of certain inconsiderate minds, which would induce us to making such statutes; but this is a common cause about which our brother and fellow bishop has spoken, that each one of us should recognize the order decreed to him by God, and that the more recent should defer to the earlier ordained, and they should presume to do nothing when these have not been consulted. Wherefore I say, now that I think of it, that they who think they may presume to take precedence over those ordained before them, should be coerced suitably by the great council. Xantippus, bishop of the first see of Numidia, said: All the brethren present have heard what our brother and fellow bishop Aurelius has said, what answer do we make? Datian, the bishop, said: The decrees made by our ancestors should be strengthened by our assent, so that the action taken by the Church of Carthage in past synods should hold fast, being confirmed by the full assent of all of us. And all the bishops said: This order has been preserved by our fathers and by our ancestors, and shall be preserved by us through the help of God, the rights of the primacy of Numidia and of Mauritania being kept intact.

Of the archives and matricula of Numidia.

Moreover it seemed good to all the bishops who subscribed in this council that the matricula and the archives of Numidia should be at the first see and in the Metropolis, that is Constantina.

NOTES.

ANCIENT EPITOME OF CANON LXXXVI.

Thou shalt not prefer thyself to thine elders, but shalt follow them. For he that spurns those who were before him should be frowned down upon.

The introduction belongs to the Synod of Milevis, of August 27, A.D. 402.

This canon (lxxxvj.) is Canon j., of the above named Synod.

JOHNSON.

From this canon it appears that the primacy in Africa was ambulatory, and belonged to the senior bishop of the province. If the primacy had been fixed to the bishop of any certain city, as in other countries, there would have been a salvo or exception for that bishop, as there is in the 24th canon of the Synod of Bracara [Braga] in Spain, which orders that all bishops take place according to their seniority, with a reserve to the bishop of the metropolis. The bishop of Carthage was not included in this canon; for it is evident that he had a precedence annexed to his see, and that he was in reality a sort of patriarch. The reason why Numidia and Mauritania are particularly mentioned is, that some disputes had been started there on that subject.

CANON LXXXVII. (Greek xc.)

Concerning Quodvultdeus, the bishop.

IN the case of Quodvultdeus of Centuria, it pleased all the bishops that no one should communicate with him until his cause should be brought to a conclusion, for his accuser when he sought to bring the cause before our council, upon being asked whether he was willing with him to be tried before the bishops, at first said that he was, but on another day answered that he was not willing, and went away. Under these circumstances to deprive him of his bishoprick, before the conclusion of his cause was known, could commend itself to no Christian as a just act.

NOTES.

ANCIENT EPITOME OF CANON LXXXVII.

Since Quodvultdeus at first promised to come to our synod when his opposer had asked that he be admitted, and afterwards withdrew, saying that that was displeasing to him, he should be excom- municated, *until the cause is finished. But it is not just that he be deposed before sentence is given.*

This canon is part of Canon ij. of Synod of Milevis, A.D. 402.

CANON LXXXVIII. (Greek xci.)

Of Maximian, the bishop.

BUT in the case of Maximian of Vagai [1] it seemed good that letters be sent from the council both to him and to his people ; that he should vacate the bishoprick, and that they should request another to be appointed for them.

NOTES.

ANCIENT EPITOME OF CANON LXXXVIII.
Let Maximian of Bagai be expelled from his church, and another be set in his room.

This canon is remaining part of Canon ij., of the Synod of Milevis, A.D. 402.

CANON LXXXIX. (Greek xcii.)

That bishops who are ordained shall receive letters from their ordainers bearing the date and the name of the consul.

IT further seemed good that whoever thereafter should be ordained by the bishops throughout the African provinces, should receive from their ordainers letters, written in their own hands, containing the name of the consul and the date, that no altercation might arise concerning which were ordained first and which afterwards.

NOTES.

ANCIENT EPITOME OF CANON LXXXIX.
Whoever is ordained in Africa let him have letters signed by the proper hand of him that ordained him, containing the date and the name of the Consul.

This is Canon iij. of Milevis, A.D. 402.

JOHNSON.

It is evident from this canon that the church in this age followed the date of the civil government, which was in the consulship of Caius and Titius, as our civil date is in the 1st, 2d, 3d, etc., year of the reign of our King or Queen.

CANON XC. (Greek xciii.)

Of those who have once read in church, that they cannot be advanced by others.

ITEM, it seemed good that whoever in church even once had read should not be admitted to the ministry (*clericatum*) by another church.

And they subscribed : I, Aurelius, bishop of the Church of Carthage, have consented to this decree, and, having read it, have signed it. Likewise also the rest of the bishops signed.

ANCIENT EPITOME OF CANON XC.

He who has only once read in a Church [i.e., diocese] *shall not be admitted into the clergy by another Church.*

This is Canon iv. of Milevis, 402.

---

[1] Hefele says (*Hist. Councils.* Vol. II., p. 428) that *Vagiensem* not *Bagajensem* is the true reading.

There is set forth in this council what the bishops did who were sent as legates across seas.

In the consulship of those most illustrious men, the most glorious Emperor Theodosius Augustus, and Rumoridus, the VIII. [1] Calends of September, at Carthage, in the basilica of the second region, when Aurelius the bishop had taken his seat in plenary council, the deacons standing by, Aurelius, the bishop, said : From stress of circumstances, venerable brethren, I, although so small, have been led to assemble you in council.   For a while ago, as your holinesses will remember, while holding a council we sent our brothers as legates to the regions beyond seas.   It is right that these should at this meeting of your holinesses narrate the course of their now finished legation, and although yesterday when we were in session concerning this matter, besides ecclesiastical matters, we paid some prolonged attention to what they had done, nevertheless it is right that to-day the discussion of yesterday should be confirmed by ecclesiastical action.

Of the bishops of the African provinces who were not present at this council.[2]

The right order of things demands that first of all we should enquire concerning our brethren and fellow bishops, who were to come to this council either from Byzacena or at least from Mauritania, like as they decreed that they would be present in this council. And when Philologius, Geta, Venustianus, and Felician, bishops of the province of Byzacena had presented and read their letters of legation, and Lucian and Silvanus, legates of the province of Mauritania Sitiphensis, had done the same, the bishop Aurelius said : Let the text of these writings be placed in the acts.

Of the Byzacene bishops.

Numidius, the bishop, said : We observe that our brethren and fellow bishops of the province of Byzacena and of the province of Mauritania Sitiphensis have sent legates to the council ; we now seek whether the legates of Numidia have come, or at least of the province of Tripoli or of Mauritania-Cæsariensis.

Of the bishops of Mauritania Sitiphensis.

Lucian and Silvanus, the bishops, legates of the Province of Mauritania Sitiphensis said : The tractory came late to our Cæsarian brethren or they would have been here ; and they will certainly come, and we are confident of their attitude of mind that whatever shall be determined by this council, they without doubt will assent unto.

Of the bishops of Numidia.

Alypius, bishop of the church of Tagaste said : We have come from Numidia, I and the holy brethren Augustine and Possidius, but a legation could not be sent from Numidia, because by the tumult of the recruits the bishops have either been prevented from coming or fully occupied by their own necessary affairs in their sees.   For after I had brought to the holy Senex Xantippus your holiness's tractory, this seemed good in the present business that a council should be appointed, to which a delegation with instructions should be sent, but when I reported to him in later letters the impediment of the recruits, of which I have just spoken, he excused them by his own rescripts.   Aurelius, the bishop, said : There is no doubt that the aforesaid brethren and bishops of Numidia, when they shall have received the acts of the council, will give their consent and will take pains to carry into effect whatever shall have been adopted.   It is therefore necessary that by the solicitude of this see what we shall have determined be communicated to them.

---

[1] Nine, in some MSS.
[2] In the Greek this is made part of the last sentence, and for " Of " it reads " for the sake of " (διὰ).

Of the bishops of Tripoli.

This is what I could learn concerning our brethren of Tripoli, that they appointed our brother Dulcicius as a legate: but because he could not come, certain of our sons coming from the aforesaid province asserted that the aforesaid had taken shipping, and that it was thought that his arrival had been delayed by storms; nevertheless also concerning these matters, if your charity is willing, this form shall be preserved, that the placets of the council be sent to them. And all the bishops said: What your holiness has decreed pleases us all.

CANON XCI. (Greek xciv.)

Of holding meetings with the Donatists.

Aurelius, the bishop, said: What has come out in the handling of your charity, I think this should be confirmed by ecclesiastical acts. For the profession of all of you shews that each one of us should call together in his city the chiefs of the Donatists either alone and with one of his neighbour bishops, so that in like manner in the different cities and places there should be meetings of them assembled by the magistrates or seniors of the places. And let this be made an edict if it seems good to all. And all the bishops said: It seems good to all, and we all have confirmed this with our subscription. Also we desire that your holiness sign the letters to be sent from the council to the judges. Aurelius, the bishop, said: If it seems good to your charity, let the form of summoning them be read, in order that we all may hold the same tenour•of proceeding. All the bishops said: Let it be read. Lætus the Notary read.

NOTES.

ANCIENT EPITOME OF CANON XCI.

Let each of the bishops meet with the leaders of the Donatists in his own city; or let him associate with himself a neighbouring bishop, that they together may meet them.

This introduction together with the propositions of the different bishops belongs to the Synod of Carthage of August, 403.

This canon (xcj.) is Canon j. of that synod.

CANON XCII. (Greek xcv.)

Form of convening the Donatists.

THAT bishop of that church said: What by the authority of that most ample see we shall have impetrated, we ask your gravity to have read, and that you order it to be joined to the acts and carried into effect. When the jussio had been read and joined to the acts, the bishop of the Catholic Church,[1] said: Vouchsafe to listen to the mandate to be sent through your gravity to the Donatists, and to insert it in the acts, and to carry it to them, and informs us in your acts of their answer. "We, sent by the authority of our Catholic Council, have called you together, desiring to rejoice in your correction, bearing in mind the charity of the Lord who said: Blessed are the peacemakers, for they shall be called the children of God; and moreover he admonished through the prophet those who say they are not our brothers, that we ought to say: Ye are our brethren. Therefore you ought not to despise this pacific commonitory coming of love, so that if ye think we have any part of the truth, ye do not hesitate to say so: that is, when your council is gathered together, ye delegate of your number certain to whom you intrust the statement of your case; so that we may be able to do this also, that there shall be delegated from our Council who with them delegated by you may discuss peacefully, at a determined place and time, whatever question there is which separates your communion from us; and that at length the old error may receive an end through the assistance of our Lord God, lest through the animosity of men, weak souls, and ignorant

---

[1] i.e. Carthage. Migne reads "of that Church" and differs in what follows.

people should perish by sacrilegious dissension.　But if ye shall accept this proposition in a fraternal spirit, the truth will easily shine forth, but if ye are not willing to do this, your distrust will be easily known."　And when this had been read, all the bishops said: This pleases us well, so let it be.　And they subscribed: I, Aurelius, bishop of the Carthaginian Church, have consented to this decree, and having read it, have subscribed it.　Likewise also the rest of the bishops signed.

This synod sent a legation to the Princes against the Donatists.

The most glorious emperor Honorius Augustus, being consul for the sixth time, on the Calends of July, at Carthage in the basilica of the second region.　In this council Theasius and Euodius received a legation against the Donatists.　In this council was inserted the commonitorium which follows.

NOTES.

Ancient Epitome of Canon XCII.

What things should be said to the Donatists are these: "We greatly desire to rejoice in your conversion; for we have been commanded to say even to those not desiring to be our brethren, 'Ye are our brothers.'　We come therefore to you and we exhort you that if you have any defence to make, *ye should appoint certain persons to whom this should be entrusted, who, at a fixed time and place, shall urge your case; otherwise your distrust will be thenceforward patent."*

This canon is Canon ij. of the Synod of Carthage of August 25, A.D. 403.

CANON XCIII.　(Greek xcvi.)

The character of the Commonitory which the legates received against the Donatists.

The Commonitorium for our brothers Theasius and Evodius, sent as legates from the Council of Carthage to the most glorious and most religious princes.　When by the help of the Lord they are come into the presence of the most pious princes, they shall declare to them with what fulness of confidence, according to the direction of the council of the year before, the prelates of the Donatists had been urged by the municipal authority to assemble, in order that if they really meant their professions, they might by fit persons chosen from their number, enter into a peaceful conference with us in Christian meekness, and whatever they held as truth they might not hesitate to declare it frankly; so that from such conference the sincerity of the Catholic position, which has been conspicuous for so long a time, might be perceived even by those who from ignorance or obstinacy were opposing themselves to it.　But deterred by their want of confidence they scarcely ventured to reply.　And forsooth, because we had discharged toward them the offices which become bishops and peacemakers, and they had no answer to make to the truth, they betook themselves to unreasonable acts of brute force, and treacherously oppressed many of the bishops and clergy, to say nothing of the laity.　And some of the churches they actually invaded, and tried to assault still others.

And now, it behoves the gracious clemency of their Majesties to take measures that the Catholic Church, which has begotten them as worshippers of Christ in her womb, and has nourished them with the strong meat of the faith, should by their forethought, be defended, lest violent men, taking advantage of the times of religious excitement, should by fear overcome a weak people, whom by argument they were not able to pervert.　It is well known how often the vile gatherings (*detestabilis manus*) of the Circumcelliones [1] have been forbidden by the laws, and also condemned by many decrees of the Emperors, their majesties most religious predecessors.　Against the madness of these people it is not unusual nor contrary to the holy Scriptures to ask for secular [θείας in the Greek] protection, since Paul the Apostle, as is related in the authentic Acts of the Apostles, warded off a conspiracy of certain lawless men by the help of the mili-

---

[1] Vide Kraus.　*Real. Encyclopædie.*

tary. Now then we ask that there be extended to the Catholic Churches, without any dissimulation, the protection of the ordinum [*i.e.* companies of soldiers, stationed] in each city, and of the holders of the suburban estates in the various places.[1] At the same time it will be necessary to ask that they give commandment that the law, set forth by their father Theodosius, of pious memory, which imposed a fine of ten pounds of gold upon both the ordainers and the ordained among heretics, and which was also directed against proprietors at whose houses conventicles were held, be confirmed anew; so that it may be effective with persons of this sort when Catholics, provoked by their wiles, shall lay complaint against them; so that through fear at least, they may cease from making schisms and from the wickedness of the heretics, since they refuse to be cleansed and corrected by the thought of the eternal punishment.

Let request be also made that the law depriving heretics of the power of being able to receive or bequeath by gift or by will, be straightway renewed by their Piety, so that all right of giving or receiving may be taken away from those who, blinded by the madness of obstinacy, are determined to continue in the error of the Donatists.

With regard to those who by considerations of unity and peace are willing to correct themselves, let permission be granted to them to receive their inheritance, the law notwithstanding, even though the bequest by gift or inheritance was made while they were yet living in the error of the heretics; those of course being excepted, who under the stress of legal proceedings have sought to enter the Catholic Church; for it may well be supposed, that persons of this latter sort desired Catholic unity, not so much from fear of the judgment of heaven, as from the greed of earthly gain.

For the furtherance of all these things the help of the Powers (*Potestatum*) of each one of the provinces is needed. With regard to other matters, whatever they shall perceive is for the Church's interests, this we have resolved that the legation have full authority to do and to carry into effect. Moreover it seemed good to us all, that letters from our assembly should be sent to the most glorious Emperors and most Excellent Worthinesses, whereby they may be assured of the agreement of us all that the legates should be sent by us to their most blessed court.

Since it is a very slow business for us all to set our names to these letters, and in order that they may not be burdened with the signature of each one of us, we desire thee, brother Aurelius, that thy charity be good enough to sign them in the name of us all. And to this they all agreed.

I, Aurelius, Bishop of the Church of Carthage have consented to this decree and have subscribed my name. And so all the other bishops subscribed.

Letters ought likewise to be sent to the judges that, until the lord permit the legates to return to us, they give protection through the soldiers of the cities, and through the holders of the farms of the Catholic Church. It ought also to be added concerning the dishonest Equitius, which he had shewn by laying claim to the jus sacerdotum, that he be rejected from the diocese of Hippo according to the statutes of the Emperors. Letters ought also to be sent to the Bishop of the Church of Rome in commendation of the legates, and to the other Bishops who may be where the Emperor is. To this they assented.

Likewise I, Aurelius, Bishop of the Church of Carthage, have consented to this decree, and having read it, have set my name to it.

And all the other bishops likewise subscribed.

NOTES.

ANCIENT EPITOME OF CANON XCIII.

The Emperors who were born in the true religion and were educated in the faith, ought to stretch forth a helping hand to the Churches. For the military band overthrew the dire conspiracy which was threatening Paul.

---

[1] The text is corrupt and the Greek and Latin do not agree in many places.

Here follows a brief declaration of what things were decreed in this Synod.

When Stilico a second time and Anthemius, those illustrious men, were consuls, on the tenth before the calends of September, at Carthage in the basilica of the second region. I have not written out in full the acts of this council[1] because they treat of the necessities of the time rather than of matters of general interest, but for the instruction of the studious I have added a brief digest of the same council.[2]

CANON XCIV. (Greek xcvii.)

Summary of Chapters.

THAT a free delegation be sent to the council from all the provinces to Mizoneum. Legates[3] and letters were ordered to be sent for the purpose of directing the free legation : that became the unity had been made only at Carthage, letters should also be given to the judges, that they might order in the other provinces and cities the work of union to be proceeded with, and the thanksgivings of the Church of Carthage for the whole of Africa concerning the exclusion of the Donatists should be sent with the letters of the bishops to Court (*ad Comitatum*).

The letters of Pope Innocent were read : that bishops ought not readily to carry causes across seas, and this very thing was confirmed by the judgment of the bishops themselves; that on account of thanksgiving and the exclusion of the Donatists, two clerics of the Church of Carthage should be sent to Court.

NOTES.

ANCIENT EPITOME OF CANON XCIV.

It seemed good that letters be sent to the Magistrates that the Donatists be expelled.[4]

This introduction is taken from the Synod of Carthage of August 23, 405. There is also added the introduction of the Synod of Carthage of June 13, 407.

In this synod certain things already decreed are corrected.

Under the most illustrious emperors Honorius for the VIIth time, and Theodosius for the second time, the consuls being the Augusti, on the Ides of July in Carthage in the basilica of the second region, when bishop Aurelius together with his other bishops had taken his seat, and while the deacons stood by, he said : Since it was decreed in the council of Hippo, that each year there should assemble a plenary council of Africa, not only here in Carthage but also in the different provinces in their order, and this was reserved that we should determine its place of meeting sometimes in Numidia and sometimes in Byzacium. But this seemed laborious to all the brethren.

CANON XCV. (Greek xcviii.)

An universal council to be held only when necessary.

IT seemed good that there should be no more the yearly necessity of fatiguing the brethren; but as often as common cause, that is of the whole of Africa, demands, that letters shall be given on every side to that see in this matter, that a synod should be gathered in that province, where the desirability of it induces; but let the causes which are not of general interest be judged in their own provinces.

---

[1] In the Greek, "The acts of the present synod have not been written out here in full, etc."
[2] The Greek text here is much to be preferred, "wherefore a brief synopsis of what was studiously enacted in this synod is here set forth."
[3] The Latin text here is certainly corrupt.
[4] This is placed by Beveridge under Greek canon xcviij.

NOTES.

ANCIENT EPITOME OF CANON XCV.

When general necessity so urges, letters are to be sent to the chief see, and a synod held in a convenient place. But let ordinary causes be settled in their own provinces.

This canon is Canon j. of the Synod of Carthage, A.D. 407.

JOHNSON.

This canon is a tacit revocation of that clause for annual synods in the 18th canon, which was made in a former council.

CANON XCVI. (Greek xcix.)

That from judges who have been chosen, no appeals may be taken.

IF an appeal be taken, let him who makes it choose the judges, and with him he also against whom the appeal is taken; and from their decision no appeal may be made.

Concerning the delegates of the different provinces.

When all the delegates of the different provinces came together, they have been most graciously received, that is those of the Numidians, Byzacenes, Stifensian Moors, as well as Cæsarians and Tripolitans.

Concerning the executors of Churches.

It has seemed good moreover that the appointment of five executors should be asked for in all matters pertaining to the necessities of the Church, who shall be portioned off in the different provinces.

NOTES.

ANCIENT EPITOME OF CANON XCVI.

If one party to a suit takes an appeal, and if both choose together a judge, no further appeal shall be allowed.

This canon is Canon ij. of Carthage, A.D. 407.

CANON XCVII. (Greek c.)

That there be sought from the Emperor the protection of Advocates in causes ecclesiastical.

IT seemed good that the legates who were about leaving, viz., Vincent and Fortunatian, should in the name of all the provinces ask from the most glorious Emperors to give a faculty for the establishment of scholastic defensors, whose shall be the care of this very kind of business : so that as the priests [1] of the province, they who have received the faculty as defensors of the Churches in ecclesiastical affairs, as often as necessity arises, may be able to enter the private apartments of the judges, so as to resist what is urged on the other side, or to make necessary explanations.

NOTES.

ANCIENT EPITOME OF CANON XCVII.

That there be asked of the Emperor the appointment of Patrons for ecclesiastical heads, whose care it should be to defend the Church in its affairs, and who as priests could easily refer what things were urgent.

(Greek ci.)

That the legation be free.

IT seemed good that the chosen legates should have at the meeting freedom of action (*legationem liberam*).

---

[1] Mansi notes that this refers to the heathen priests, and quotes Cod. Theod. 47, *de decurionibus.*

The protest of the Mauritanian bishops against Primosus.

It is evident that those of Mauritania Cæsariensis gave evidence in their own writings that Primosus had been summoned by the chiefs of the Thiganensian city, that he should present himself to the plenary council according to the imperial constitutions, and, when sought for, as was right, Primosus was not found, at least so the deacons reported. But since the same Mauritanians petitioned that letters be sent from the whole synod to the venerable brother, the aged Innocent, it seemed good that they should be sent, that he might know that Primosus had been sought at the council and not found at all.

NOTES.

ANCIENT EPITOME.

[Lacking.]

BALSAMON.

The contents of this canon being special are useless, therefore no explanation has been given.

This Canon is Canon iij. of Carthage, A.D. 407.

JOHNSON.

See can. 75 (78) and note on Can. Chalced., 23.

These officers [i.e. "defensors"] seem to be called "executores" in the acts of synod just before this canon.

The "priest of the province" was one chosen out of the body of advocates to be counsel to the province, to act and plead in their behalf; and that he might do it more effectually he was allowed to have private conference with the judge.

CANON XCVIII. (Greek cii.)

Of the peoples which never had bishops.

It seemed good that such peoples as had never had bishops of their own should in no way receive such unless it had been decreed in a plenary council of each province and by the primates, and with the consent of the bishop of that diocese to which the church belonged.

NOTES.

ANCIENT EPITOME OF CANON XCVIII.

Whoso never heretofore had a bishop of their own, unless the general synod of the Province shall agree to it, and the Primate, in agreement with him to whom the province in which the

Church is, is subject, shall not have bishops of their own.

This canon is Canon iv. of the Synod of Carthage, A.D. 407.

CANON XCIX. (Greek ciii.)

Of people or dioceses returned from the Donatists.

Such communities as have returned from the Donatists and have had bishops, without doubt may continue to have them even without any action of the councils, but such a community as had a bishop and when he dies wish no longer to have a bishop of their own, but to belong to the diocese of some other bishop, this is not to be denied them. Also such bishops as before the promulgation of the imperial law concerning unity as brought back their people to the Catholic Church, they ought to be allowed still to rule them : but from the time of that law of unity, all the Churches, and their dioceses, and if perchance there be any instruments of the Church or things pertaining to its rights should belong to the Catholic bishops of those places to whom the places pertained while under the heretics, whether they be converted to the Catholic Church or remain unconverted heretics. Whoever after this law shall make any such usurpation, shall restore as is meet the usurped possessions.

NOTES.

ANCIENT EPITOME OF CANON XCIX.

Whoever are converted from the Donatists may retain their own bishops, although they had them without the consent of the synod ; and when the bishop is dead, if they do not wish another to be substituted in his room, but desire to place themselves under some other bishop, they shall be allowed to do so. And such bishops as before the union have brought back the people they ruled, let

them still rule them. After the imperial Edict on Unity every church must defend its own rights.

This canon is Canon v. of Carthage, A.D. 407.

JOHNSON.

"An imperial law concerning unity" i.e. For uniting all in the catholic faith, and ejecting the donatistical bishops.

CANON C. (Greek civ.)

Of the suggestion of Bishop Maurentius.

[*Hefele says " The text of this canon is much corrupted and very difficult to be understood." He gives as a synopsis, " The council appoints judges in the affair of Bishop Maurentius." (Hefele, Vol. II., p. 443.)*]
Johnson thus condenses and translates.

Bishop Maurentius having an information against him, lying before the council, moves for a hearing ; but the informers don't appear upon three calls made by the deacons on the day appointed. The cause is referred to Senex Xantippus, Augustinus, and five more summoned by the council, the informers were to make up the number twelve.

NOTES.

ANCIENT EPITOME OF CANON C.

It is right that sentence be given on the subdeacons who are said to be present from Nova Germania, who have thrice been sought and not found. But out of regard to ecclesiastical gentleness, let some be sent to look into the matter.

BALSAMON.

The contents of this canon are of a private

character, and therefore have not been commented on.

This canon is Canon vj. of Carthage, A.D. 407.

JOHNSON.

"Senex" i.e. Primate Xantippus, as is commonly believed. He and others have this title frequently given them in the acts of these councils. See can. 8.

CANON CI. (Greek civ. *bis*)

Of making peace between the Churches of Rome and Alexandria.

IT seemed good that a letter be written to the holy Pope Innocent concerning the dissension between the Churches of Rome and Alexandria, so that each Church might keep peace with the other as the Lord commanded.

NOTES.

ANCIENT EPITOME OF CANON CI.

It seemed good to write to Innocent that the Roman and Alexandrian churches might be at peace between themselves.

This canon is Canon vij. of Carthage, A.D. 407.

CANON CII. (Greek cv.)

Of those who put away their wives or husbands, that so they remain.

IT seemed good that according to evangelical and apostolical discipline a man who had been put away from his wife, and a woman put away from her husband should not be married to another, but so should remain, or else be reconciled the one to the other ;

but if they spurn this law, they shall be forced to do penance, covering which case we must petition that an imperial law be promulgated.

NOTES.

Married people who are loosed must remain unmarried or else be reconciled, otherwise they shall be forced to do penance.

This canon is Canon viij. of Carthage, A.D. 407, and is found in the *Corpus Juris Canonici*, Gratian's *Decretum*, P. II., Causa xxxij., Quæst. vij., can. v.

CANON CIII. (Greek cvi.)

Of the prayers to be said at the Altar.

THIS also seemed good, that the prayers which had been approved in synod should be used by all, whether prefaces, commendations, or laying on of the hand, and that others contrary to the faith should not be used by any means, but that those only should be said which had been collected by the learned.

NOTES.

[*The same as the canon, but omits the last phrase.*]

This canon is Canon ix. of Carthage, A.D. 407.

JOHNSON.

That is, such forms fitted for the present time or occasion, as our Church uses in her Communion Office before the trisagium, on Christmas, Easter, etc. These prefaces were very ancient in the Christian church. Prayers used to recommend the catechumens, penitents, and dying souls to God's protection were styled "Commendations."

CANON CIV. (Greek cvii.)

Of these who ask from the Emperor that secular judges may take cognizance of their causes.

IT seemed good that whoever should seek from the Emperor, that secular judges should take cognizance of his business, should be deprived of his office; if however, he had asked from the Emperor an episcopal trial, no objection should be made.

NOTES.

Let not him be a bishop who from the Emperor seeks a public judgment.

This canon is Canon X. of Carthage, A.D. 407.

JOHNSON.

See Canon Ant., 12.

CANON CV. (Greek cviii.)

Of those who do not communicate in Africa and would go across seas.

WHOEVER does not communicate in Africa, and goes to communicate across seas, let him be cast out of the clergy.

NOTES.

Whoever is cut off from communion in Africa, and goes to parts across seas that he may there communicate, is to be cast out of the clergy.

This canon is Canon j. of Carthage, A.D. 407.

CANON CVI. (Greek cix.)

That those who are going to carry their case to court should be careful to inform either the bishop of Carthage or [1] the bishop of Rome.

IT seemed good that whoever wished to go to court, should give notice in the form which is sent to the Church of the city of Rome, that from thence also he should receive a formed letter to court. But if receiving only a formed letter to Rome, and saying nothing about the necessity which he had of going to court, he willed immediately to go thither, let him be cut off from communion. But if while at Rome the necessity of going to court suddenly arose, let him state his necessity to the bishop of Rome and let him carry with him a rescript of the same Roman bishop. But let the formed letters which are issued by primates and by certain bishops to their own clergy have the date of Easter; but if it be yet uncertain what is the date of Easter of that year, let the preceding Easter's date be set down, as it is customary to date public acts after the consulship.

It further seemed good that those who were sent as delegates from this glorious council should ask of the most glorious princes whatever they saw would be useful against the Donatists and Pagans, and their superstitions.

It also seemed good to all the bishops that all conciliar letters be signed by your holiness alone. And they subscribed : I, Aurelius, Bishop of Carthage, have consented to this decree, and having read it, now subscribe my name. Likewise also the rest of the bishops subscribed.

ANCIENT EPITOME OF CANON CVI.

Whoever from any necessity was going to court, must declare his intention to the bishop of Carthage and to the bishop of Rome, and receive a letter dimissory, and otherwise he shall be excommunicated.

Whatever shall seem to the legates useful against the Donatists and Greeks, and their superstitions, that shall be sought from the Emperor.

(Greek cx.)
Synod against the pagans and heretics.

In the consulship of those most illustrious men Bassus and Philip, the xvith Calends of July, at Carthage, in the secretarium of the restored basilica.* In this council the bishop Fortunatian received a second appointment as legate against the pagans and heretics.

Item, a council against the pagans and heretics.

In the consulship of those most illustrious men Bassus and Philip, the iii. Ides of October at Carthage, in the Secretarium of the restored basilica *. In this council the bishops Restitutus and Florentius received a legation against the pagans and heretics, at the time Severus and Macarius were slain, and on their account the bishops Euodius, Theasius and Victor were put to death.

NOTES.

This canon is Canon xij. of Carthage, A.D. 407.

JOHNSON.

Of "Formal Letters" see Can. Ap., 10 (13).

CANON CVII. (Greek cx. continued.)

A Council concerning a bishop taking cognizance.

IN the consulate of the most glorious Emperors Honorius for the VIIth time and Theodosius for the IIId, Augusti, xvii. Calends of July, a synod was held at Carthage in the basilica of the second region. In this council it seemed good that no one bishop

---

[1] "And" in the Greek. which omits the preceding "either."   ** Between these asterisks all is missing in the Greek.

should claim the right to take cognizance of a cause. The acts of this council I have not here written down, because it was only provincial and not general.

ANCIENT EPITOME OF CANON CVII.

One bishop shall not claim for himself to take cognizance of a cause alone.

(Greek cxi.)

Synod against the Donatists.

After the consulate of the most illustrious Emperors Honorius for the VIIIth time and Theodosius for the IVth time, Augusti, xviii. Calends of July, at Carthage in the basilica of the second region. In this council the bishops, Florentius, Possidius, Præsidius and Benenatus received legation against the Donatists, at that time at which a law was given that anyone might practice the Christian worship at his own will.

NOTES.

ANCIENT EPITOME OF CANON CVII.

Let each one receive the practice of piety of his own free will.

The two first introductions belong respectively to the Synods of Carthage of June 16 and of October 13, A.D. 408.

Canon cvij. of the African code and that which follows it are the introductions to the Synods of Carthage of June 15, A.D. 409, and of June 14, A.D. 410.

JOHNSON.

See can. 10, 11, 12, 28 (31), 79 (80). Recognises, a law of the Empire, that everyone receive christianity at his own free choice.

CANON CVIII.   (Greek cxii.)

Synod against the heresy of Pelagius and Celestius.

IN the consulate of the most glorious Emperors, Honorius for the XIIth time and Theodosius for the VIIIth, Augusti most exalted, on the Calends of May, at Carthage in the secretarium of the Basilica of Faustus.   When Aurelius the bishop presided over the whole council, the deacons standing by, it pleased all the bishops, whose names and subscriptions are indicated,[1] met together in the holy synod of the Church of Carthage to define—[2]

CANON CIX.   (Greek cxij. continued.)

That Adam was not created by God subject to death.

THAT whosoever says that Adam, the first man, was created mortal, so that whether he had sinned or not, he would have died in body—that is, he would have gone forth of the body, not because his sin merited this, but by natural necessity, let him be anathema.

NOTES.

ANCIENT EPITOME OF CANON CIX.

Whoso shall assert that the protoplast would have died without sin and through natural necessity, let him be anathema.

Canon CVIII. is the introduction to the Synod of Carthage of May 1, A.D. 418; and Canon CIX. is Canon j. of that synod.

CANON CX. (Greek cxii. *bis*)

That infants are baptized for the remission of sins.

LIKEWISE it seemed good that whosoever denies that infants newly from their mother's wombs should be baptized, or says that baptism is for remission of sins, but that they derive from Adam no original sin, which needs to be removed by the laver of

---

[1] The Latin here is corrupt.　　　[2] Here begins Canon CIX. of the Latin text.

regeneration, from whence the conclusion follows, that in them the form of baptism for the remission of sins, is to be understood as false and not true, let him be anathema.

For no otherwise can be understood what the Apostle says, " By one man sin is come into the world, and death through sin, and so death passed upon all men in that all have " sinned," than the Catholic Church everywhere diffused has always understood it. For on account of this rule of faith (*regulam fidei*) even infants, who could have committed as yet no sin themselves, therefore are truly baptized for the remission of sins, in order that what in them is the result of generation may be cleansed by regeneration.

NOTES.

ANCIENT EPITOME OF CANON CX.

Whoso affirms that those newly born and baptized contract nothing from Adam's transgression, which needs to be washed away by baptism, is to be execrated: for through one both death and sin invaded the whole world.

This is Canon ij. of Carthage, A.D. 418 [Greek Canon 112].

JOHNSON.

See Can. 63, 104, both which are double, as this likewise is in the old Greek scholiasts.

[Also it seemed good, that if anyone should say that the saying of the Lord, " In my Father's house are many mansions " is to be understood as meaning that in the kingdom of heaven there will be a certain middle place, or some place somewhere, in which infants live in happiness who have gone forth from this life without baptism, without which they cannot enter the kingdom of heaven, which is eternal life, let him be anathema. For after our Lord has said : " Except a man be born again of water and of the Holy Spirit he shall not enter the kingdom of heaven," what Catholic can doubt that he who has not merited to be coheir with Christ shall become a sharer with the devil : for he who fails of the right hand without doubt shall receive the left hand portion.]

NOTES.

The foregoing, says Surius, is found in this place in a very ancient codex. It does not occur in the Greek, nor in Dionysius. Bruns relegates it to a foot-note.

CANON CXI. (Greek cxiij.)

That the grace of God not only gives remission of sins, but also affords aid that we sin no more.

LIKEWISE it seemed good, that whoever should say that the grace of God, by which a man is justified through Jesus Christ our Lord, avails only for the remission of past sins, and not for assistance against committing sins in the future, let him be anathema.

ANCIENT EPITOME OF CANON CXI.

Whoever is of opinion that the grace of God only gives remission of those sins we have already committed, and does not afford aid against sin in the future, is to be twice execrated.

CANON CXII. (Greek cxiij. continued.)

That the grace of Christ gives not only the knowledge of our duty, but also inspires us with a desire that we may be able to accomplish what we know.

ALSO, whoever shall say that the same grace of God through Jesus Christ our Lord helps us only in not sinning by revealing to us and opening to our understanding the commandments, so that we may know what to seek, what we ought to avoid, and also that we should love to do so, but that through it we are not helped so that we are able to do what we know we should do, let him be anathema. For when the Apostle says : " Wisdom puffeth up, but charity edifieth " it were truly infamous were we to believe that we have the grace of Christ for that which puffeth us up, but have it not for that which edifieth, since in each case it is the gift of God, both to know what we ought to do, and to love to do it; so that wisdom cannot puff us up while charity is edifying us. For as of God it is written, "Who teacheth man knowledge," so also it is written, "Love is of God."

NOTES.

ANCIENT EPITOME OF CANON CXII.

Whoever says that the grace of God is given to us only that we may know what we ought to do and what to flee from, but not also that we may love the thing known, and be able to accomplish it, let him be anathema.

Canon cxi. is Canon iij. of Carthage, A.D. 418, and Canon cxii. is Canon iv. of the same synod.

CANON CXIII. (Greek cxiiii.)

That without the grace of God we can do no good thing.

IT seemed good that whosoever should say that the grace of justification was given to us only that we might be able more readily by grace to perform what we were ordered to do through our free will; as if though grace was not given, although not easily, yet nevertheless we could even without grace fulfil the divine commandments, let him be anathema. For the Lord spake concerning the fruits of the commandments, when he said: "Without me ye can do nothing," and not "Without me ye could do it but with difficulty."

NOTES.

ANCIENT EPITOME OF CANON CXIII.

Whoso preaches that without grace we could keep the commandments although with

difficulty, is to be thrice execrated. For the Lord says, "Without me ye can do nothing."

This is Canon V. of Carthage, A.D. 418.

CANON CXIV. (Greek cxv.)

That not only humble but also true is that voice of the Saints: "If we say that we have no sin we deceive ourselves."

IT also seemed good that as St. John the Apostle says, "If we shall say that we have no sin we deceive ourselves and the truth is not in us," whosoever thinks that this should be so understood as to mean that out of humility, we ought to say that we have sin, and not because it is really so, let him be anathema. For the Apostle goes on to add, "But if we confess our sins, he is faithful and just to forgive us our sins and to cleanse us from all iniquity," where it is sufficiently clear that this is said not only of humility but also truly. For the Apostle might have said, "If we shall say we have no sins we shall extoll ourselves, and humility shall have no place in us;" but when he says, "we deceive ourselves and the truth is not in us" he sufficiently intimates that he who affirmed that he had no sin would speak not that which is true but that which is false.

NOTES.

ANCIENT EPITOME OF CANON CXIV.

Whosoever shall interpret the saying of the Divine [i.e. St. John]: "If we shall say that we have no sin, we deceive ourselves" as not being

really true but as spoken out of humility, let him be anathema.

This is Canon vj. of Carthage, A.D. 418.

CANON CXV. (Greek cxvi.)

That in the Lord's Prayer the Saints say for themselves: "Forgive us our trespasses."

IT has seemed good that whoever should say that when in the Lord's prayer, the saints say, "forgive us our trespasses," they say this not for themselves, because they have no need of this petition, but for the rest who are sinners of the people; and that therefore no one of the saints can say, "Forgive me my trespasses," but "Forgive us our trespasses;" so that the just is understood to seek this for others rather than for himself; let him be anathema. For holy and just was the Apostle James, when he said, "For in many things we offend all." For why was it added "all," unless that this sentence might agree also with the psalm, where we read, "Enter not into judgment with thy servant, O Lord, for in thy sight shall no man living be justified;" and in the prayer of the most wise Solomon: "There is no man that sinneth not;" and in the book of the holy Job: "He sealeth in the hand of every man, that every man may know his own infirmity;" wherefore even the holy and just Daniel when in prayer said several times: "We have sinned, we have done iniquity," and other things which there truly and humbly he confessed; nor let it be thought (as some have thought) that this was said not of his own but rather of the people's sins, for he said further on: "When I shall pray and confess my sins and the sins of my people to the Lord my God;" he did not wish to say our sins, but he said the sins of his people and his own sins, since he as a prophet foresaw that those who were to come would thus misunderstand his words.

NOTES.

Ancient Epitome of Canon CXV.

Whoso expounds this, "forgive us our trespasses" as speaking only of the multitude and not of individuals let him be anathema: Since

Daniel even he can behold saying with the multitude "I confessed my sins and the sins of my people."

This is Canon vij. of Carthage, A.D. 418.

CANON CXVI. (Greek cxvii.)

That the Saints say with accuracy, "Forgive us our trespasses."

LIKEWISE also it seemed good, that whoever wished that these words of the Lord's prayer, when we say, "Forgive us our trespasses" are said by the saints out of humility and not in truth let them be anathema. For who would make a lying prayer, not to men but to God? Who would say with his lips that he wished his sins forgiven him, but in his heart that he had no sins to be forgiven.

NOTES.

Ancient Epitome of Canon CXVI.
(Lacking.)

This is Canon viij. of Carthage, A.D. 418.

CANON CXVII. (Greek cxviii.)

Of peoples converted from the Donatists.

ITEM, it seemed good, since it was so decreed some years ago by a plenary council, that whatever churches were erected in a diocese before the laws were made concerning Donatists when they became Catholic, should pertain to the sees of those bishops through whom their return to Catholic unity was brought about; but after the laws whatever churches communicated were to belong there where they belonged when they were Donatists. But because many controversies afterward arose and are still springing up between bishops concerning dioceses, which were not then at all in prospect, now it has seemed good to this council, that wherever there was a Catholic and a Donatist party, pertaining to different sees, at whatever time unity has been or shall be made, whether before or after the laws, the churches shall belong to that see to which the Catholic church which was already there belonged.

NOTES.

Ancient Epitome of Canon CXVII.

Whenever conversions and unions of Donatists are effected, let them be subject to that throne to

which the Catholic Church which was formerly there was subject.

This is Canon ix. of Carthage, A.D. 418.

CANON CXVIII. (Greek cxix.)

How bishops as well Catholic as those who have been converted from the Donatists are to divide between themselves the dioceses.

So, too, it has seemed good that if a bishop has been converted from the Donatists to Catholic unity, that equally there should be divided what shall have been so found where there were two parties; that is, that some places should pertain to one and some to the other; and let the division be made by him who has been the longest time in the episcopate, and let the younger choose. But should there be only one place let it belong to him who is found to be the nearer. But should the distance be equal to each of the two cathedrals let it belong to the one the people may choose. But should the old Catholics wish their own bishop, and if the same be the case with the converted Donatists, let the will of the greater number prevail, but should the parties be equal, let it belong to him who has been longest bishop. But if so many places be found in which there were both parties, that an equal division is impossible, as for example, if they are unequal in number, after those places have been distributed which have an equal number, the place that remains over shall be disposed of as is provided above in the case where there is but one place to be treated.

NOTES.

ANCIENT EPITOME OF CANON CXVIII.

Those who have been converted from Donatus, let them divide the dioceses; and let the senior bishop *make the division, and the junior choose which he will.*

This is Canon x. of Carthage, A.D. 418.

CANON CXIX. (Greek cxx.)

That if a bishop shall possess a diocese which he has snatched from heresy for three years, no one may take it from him.

ITEM, it seemed good that if anyone after the laws should convert any place to Catholic unity and retain it for three years without opposition, it should not be taken away from him afterwards. If however there was during those three years a bishop who could claim it and was silent, he shall lose the opportunity. But if there was no bishop, no prejudice shall happen to the see,[1] but it shall be lawful when the place that had none shall receive a bishop, to make the claim within three years of that day. Item, if a Donatist bishop shall be converted to the Catholic party, the time that has elapsed shall not count against him, but from the day of his conversion for three years he shall have the right of making a claim on the places which belonged to his See.

NOTES.

ANCIENT EPITOME OF CANON CXIX.

Whosoever shall convert a region to Orthodoxy and shall keep it converted for three years, let him be without blame. But if the bishop converted from Donatus within three years of its conversion seeks his diocese again, let it be returned to him (εἰ ἐνάγει, ἐναγέτω.)

This is Canon xj. of Carthage, A.D. 418.

CANON CXX. (Greek cxxi.)

Of those who intrude upon peoples which they think belong to them, without the consent of those by whom they are held.

ITEM, it seemed good that whatever bishops seek the peoples whom they consider to pertain to their see, not by bringing their causes before the episcopal judges, but rush in while another is holding the place, all such, (whether said people are willing to receive

---

[1] In the Latin " Matrici."

them or no) shall lose their case. And whoever have done this, if the contention between the two bishops is not yet finished but still going on, let him depart who intruded without the decree of the ecclesiastical judges; nor let anyone flatter himself that he will retain [what he has seized] if he shall obtain letters from the primate, but whether he has such letters or has them not, it is suitable that he who holds and receives his letters should make it appear then that he has held the church pertaining to him peaceably. But if he has referred any question, let the cause be decided by the episcopal judges, whether those whom the primates have appointed for them, or the neighbouring bishops whom they have chosen by common consent.

NOTES.

ANCIENT EPITOME OF CANON CXX.

Let no one seize for himself what he thinks belongs to him: but let the bishops judge or whom the Primate will give, or whom the neighbouring bishops shall give with his consent. But

whosoever has received letters from the primate concerning the keeping [of such regions and churches] merely deceives himself.

This is Canon xij. of Carthage, A.D. 418.

CANON CXXI. (Greek cxxii.)

Of those who neglect the peoples belonging to them.

ITEM, it seemed good that whoever neglect to bring the places belonging to their see into Catholic unity should be admonished by the neighbouring diligent bishops, that they delay no longer to do this; but if within six months from the day of the convention they do nothing, let them pertain to him who can win them: but with this proviso however, that if he to whom it seemed they naturally belonged can prove that this neglect was intentional and more efficacious in winning them than the greater apparent diligence of others; when the episcopal judges shall be convinced that this is the case, they shall restore the places to his see. If the bishops between whom the cause lies are of different provinces, let the Primate in whose province the place is situated about which there is the dispute, appoint judges; but if by mutual consent they have chosen as judges the neighbouring bishops, let one or three be chosen: so that if they choose three they may follow the sentence of all or of two.

NOTES.

ANCIENT EPITOME OF CANON CXXI.

If any neglect what belongs to their jurisdiction, let them be admonished; and if they shall do nothing within a six month, let them be adjudged to him who can win them. But if they have committed the neglect out of policy so as not to irri-

tate the heretics, and this shall appear to have been the case, their sees shall be restored to them, by the judgment of the bishops either appointed or elected.

This is Canon xiij. of Carthage, A.D. 418.

CANON CXXII. (Greek cxxiii.)

The sentence of the elected judges ought not to be spurned.

FROM the judges chosen by common consent of the parties, no appeal can be taken; and whoever shall be found to have carried such an appeal and contumaciously to be unwilling to submit to the judges, when this has been proved to the primate, let him give letters, that no one of the bishops should communicate with him until he yield.

NOTES.

ANCIENT EPITOME OF CANON CXXII.

A judge chosen by both parties cannot be repudiated.

This is Canon xiv. of Carthage, A.D. 418.

JOHNSON.

See Canons 76 (79) and 80 (83).

CANON CXXIII. (Greek cxxiv.)

That if a bishop neglects his diocese he is to be deprived of communion.

IF in the mother cathedrals a bishop should have been negligent against the heretics, let a meeting be held of the neighbouring diligent bishops, and let his negligence be pointed out to him, so that he can have no excuse. But if within six months after this meeting, if an execution was in his own province, and he had taken no care to convert them to Catholic unity, no one shall communicate with him till he does his duty. But if no executor shall have come to the places, then the fault shall not be laid to the bishop.

NOTES.

ANCIENT EPITOME OF CANON **CXXIII.**

A bishop who spurns the care of heretics, and if after being warned he continues for six months in his contempt, and has no care for their conversion, is to be excommunicated.

This is Canon xv. of Carthage, A.D. 418.

JOHNSON.

So [*i.e.* "Metropoles"] I turn matrices cathedræ. I know indeed there were no fixed ecclesiastical metropoles, in Africa ; but they had civil metropoles called by that name, can. 86, (89) which see.

Of these officers [*i.e.* "Executors"] see can. 97 (100).

CANON CXXIV. (Greek cxxv.)

Of bishops who shall lie with regard to Donatists' communions.

IF it shall be proven that any bishop has lied concerning the communion of those [who had been Donatists], and had said that they had communicated when he knew it was an established fact that they had not done so, let him lose his bishoprick.

NOTES.

ANCIENT EPITOME OF CANON **CXXIV.**

Whoso says that a man, whom he knows does not communicate, does communicate is to be deprived of his episcopate.

This is Canon xvj. of Carthage, A.D. 418.

CANON CXXV. (Greek cxxvi.)

That presbyters and clerics are not to appeal except to African Synods.

ITEM, it seemed good that presbyters, deacons, or other of the lower clergy who are to be tried, if they question the decision of their bishops, the neighbouring bishops having been invited by them with the consent of their bishops, shall hear them and determine whatever separates them. But should they think an appeal should be carried from them, let them not carry the appeal except to African councils or to the primates of their provinces. But whoso shall think of carrying an appeal across seas he shall be admitted to communion by no one in Africa.

NOTES.

ANCIENT EPITOME OF CANON **CXXV.**

A presbyter and deacon, who has been condemned by his own bishop, let him appeal to the neighbouring bishops: but let them not cross the sea. In Africa they shall be excommunicated.

This is Canon xvij. of Carthage, A.D. 418.

JOHNSON.

A repetition of Canon 28 (31).

CANON CXXVI. (Greek cxxvii.)

That Virgins, even when minors, should be given the veil.

ITEM, it seemed good that whatever bishop, by the necessity of the dangers of virginal purity, when either a powerful suitor or some ravisher is feared, or if she shall be pricked with some scruple of death that she might die unveiled, at the demand either of her parents or of those to whose care she has been entrusted, shall give the veil to a virgin, or shall have given it while she was under twenty-five years of age, the council which has appointed that number of years shall not oppose him.

NOTES.

ANCIENT EPITOME OF CANON CXXVI.

Whosoever has veiled or shall veil a virgin before she is twenty-five years of age (that is give her the habit, or clothe her), being forced thereto on account of a powerful lover, or a ravisher, or deadly disease, provided those who have the charge of her so exhort, shall receive no damage from the synod concerning that age.

This is Canon xviij. of Carthage, A.D. 418. The reference to a former canon is to Canon j. of the second series of the canons of the Synod of Hippo in A.D. 393.

CANON CXXVII. (Greek cxxviii.)

That bishops be not detained too long in council, let them choose three judges from themselves of the singular provinces.

ITEM, it seemed good, lest all the bishops who are assembled at a council be kept too long, that the whole synod should choose three judges of the several provinces; and they elected for the province of Carthage Vincent, Fortunatian, and Clarus; for the province of Numidia Alypius, Augustine, and Restitutus; for the province of Byzacena, with the holy Senex Donatian the Primate, Cresconius, Jocundus, and Æmilian; for Mauritania Sitephensis Severian, Asiaticus, and Donatus; for the Tripolitan province Plautius, who alone was sent as legate according to custom; all these were to take cognizance of all things with the holy senex Aurelius, from whom the whole council sought that he should subscribe all things done by the council whether acts or letters. And they subscribed: I, Aurelius, bishop of the church of Carthage consent to this decree and having read it sign my name. Likewise also signed they all.

ANCIENT EPITOME OF CANON CXXVII.

Whenever the bishops who come to synod can remain no longer in attendance, let three be chosen from each province.

This is Canon xix. of Carthage, A.D. 418.

JOHNSON.

Two Sancti Senes mentioned, who we are sure were both primates. See can. 100 (104). See can. 14.

And here we have an ancient precedent for synods delegating their authority to a committee, with the primate of all Africa at the head of it.

Item, at this council there was present a legation from the Roman Church.

After the consulate of the most glorious emperors Honorius for the XIIth. time and Theodosius for the VIIIth., Augusti, on the III. Calends of June, at Carthage, in the Secretarium of the restored basilica, when Aurelius the bishop together with Faustinus of the church of Potentia in the Italian province of Picenum, a legate of the Roman Church, Vincent of Calvita[1] (Culositanus), Fortunatian of Naples, Marianus Uzipparen-

---

[1] Not Calusita.

sis, Adeodatus of Simidica, Pentadius of Carpi, Rufinian of Muzuba, Prætextatus of Sicily, Quodvultdeus of Veri (Verensis), Candidus of Abbirita, Gallonian of Utica, legates of the proconsular province; Alypius of Tagaste, Augustine of Hippo Regia and Posidonius of Calama, legates of the province of Numidia; Maximian of Aquae, Jocundus of Sufetula, and Hilary of Horrea-Cascilia, legates of the province of Byzacena; Novatus of Sitifi and Leo of Mocta, legates of the province of Mauritania Sitiphensis; Ninellus of Rusucarrum, Laurence of Icosium and Numerian of Rusgunium, legates of the Province of Mauritania Cæsariensis, the judges chosen by the plenary council, had taken their seats, the deacons standing by, and when, after certain things had been accomplished, many bishops complained that it was not possible for them to wait for the completion of the rest of the business to be treated of, and that they must hasten to their own churches; it seemed good to the whole council, that by all some should be chosen from each province who should remain to finish up what was left to be done. And it came about that those were present whose subscriptions testify that they were present.

CANON CXXVIII. (Greek cxxix.)

That those out of communion should not be allowed to bring accusation.

It seemed good to all, as it had been decreed by the former councils, concerning what persons were to be admitted to bring accusations against clerics; and since it had not been expressed what persons should not be admitted, therefore we define, that he cannot properly be admitted to bring an accusation, who had been already excommunicated, and was still lying under that censure, whether he that wished to be the accuser were cleric or layman.

NOTES.

Ancient Epitome of Canon CXXVIII.

One excommunicated is not to give witness.

The Council of Carthage of 419 had at its first session on May 25th done thus much.

But when it met again on the 30th of the same month, it continued the code. The introduction in regard to this new session is this introduction. The Canons then enacted were original, viz. numbers 128, 129, 130, 131, 132 and 133.

CANON CXXIX. (Greek cxxx.)

That slaves and freedmen and all infamous persons ought not to bring accusation.

To all it seemed good that no slaves or freedmen, properly so called, be admitted to accusation nor any of those who by the public laws are debarred from bringing accusation in criminal proceedings. This also is the case with all those who have the stain of infamy, that is actors, and persons subject to turpitudes, also heretics, or heathen, or Jews; but even all those to whom the right of bringing accusation is denied, are not forbidden to bring accusation in their own suits.

NOTES.

Ancient Epitome of Canon CXXIX.

A slave, and a freedman, and he who before was accused of any of these crimes on account of which he is not admitted in court, and a player, and a heathen, and a heretic, and a Jew

[There is no verb to finish the sentence.

However, this is intended as a continuation of the epitome of the former canon, the words to be supplied being "are not to give witness."]

Johnson.

See Can., Const., 6.

CANON CXXX. (Greek cxxxi.)

That he who has failed to prove one charge shall not be allowed to give evidence to another.

So, too, it seemed good that as often as many crimes were laid to clerics by their accusers, and one of the first examined could not be proved,[1] they should not be allowed to go on giving evidence on the other counts.

ANCIENT EPITOME OF CANON CXXX.

He who makes many accusations and proves nothing [is not to give witness].

CANON CXXXI. (Greek cxxxii.)

Who should be allowed to give evidence.

THEY who are forbidden to be admitted as accusers are not to be allowed to appear as witnesses, nor any that the accuser may bring from his own household. And none shall be admitted to give witness under fourteen years of age.

NOTES.

ANCIENT EPITOME OF CANON CXXXI.

And whoso is not past fourteen years of age [is not to give witness]. An accuser is not to produce witnesses from his own house.

JOHNSON.

See Can. 129.

CANON CXXXII. (Greek cxxxiii.)

Concerning a bishop who removes a man from communion who says he has confessed to the bishop alone his crime.

IT also seemed good that if on any occasion a bishop said that someone had confessed to him alone a personal crime, and that the man now denies it; let not the bishop think that any slight is laid upon him if he is not believed on his own word alone, although he says he is not willing to communicate with the man so denying through a scruple of his own conscience.

NOTES.

ANCIENT EPITOME OF CANON CXXXII.

If a bishop says "someone has confessed to me alone a crime," if the someone denies it, he [i.e. the bishop] is not easily to be believed.

N.B. The word used for "someone" in the Epitome is πέλας, which ordinarily means a "neighbour" but may mean "any one." *Vide* Liddell and Scott.

CANON CXXXIII. (Greek cxxxiv.)

That a bishop should not rashly deprive anyone of communion.

As long as his own bishop will not communicate with one excommunicated, the other bishops should have no communion with that bishop, that the bishop may be more careful not to charge anyone with what he cannot prove by documentary evidence to others.

(Greek cxxxv.)

BISHOP AURELIUS said: According to the statutes of this whole assembled council, and the opinion of my littleness, it seems good to make an end of all the matters of the whole of the before-manifested title, and let the ecclesiastical acts receive the discussion of the present day's constitution.

---

[1] The Latin here is evidently corrupt.

And what things have not yet been expressed ("treated of" in the Greek) we shall write on the next day through our brethren, Bishop Faustinus and the Presbyters Philip and Asellus to our venerable brother and fellow-bishop Boniface; and they gave their assent in writing.

NOTES.

ANCIENT EPITOME OF CANON CXXXIII.

If a bishop deprives of communion an unconvicted man, he shall likewise be deprived of communion with his fellows.

JOHNSON.

Never was a more impartial law made, especially when all the legislators were bishops except two. There were 217 bishops, and two priests, being legates from the bishop of Rome.

The Greeks make a canon of the ratifications, and reckon no more than 135. Aurelius, Bishop of Carthage, subscribes first, and after him 217 bishops, then Asellus and Philippus, priests, legates of the church of Rome. And it does not appear that any other priests were present in any of the councils, mentioned in the body of this code; but there is several times notice taken of the deacons who stood by.

CANON CXXXIV. (Continuation of cxxxv. in the Greek.)

Here beginneth the letter directed from the whole African Council to Boniface, bishop of the City of Rome, by Faustinus the bishop, and Philip and Asellus the presbyters, legates of the Roman Church.

To the most blessed lord, and our honourable brother Boniface, Aurelius, Valentine of the primatial See of Numidia, and others present with us to the number of 217 from the whole council in Africa.

Since it has pleased the Lord that our humility should write concerning those things which with us our holy brethren, Faustinus a fellow-bishop and Philip and Asellus, fellow presbyters, have done, not to the bishop Zosimus of blessed memory, from whom they brought commands and letters to us, but to your holiness, who art constituted in his room by divine authority, we ought briefly to set forth what has been determined upon by mutual consent; not indeed those things which are contained in the prolix volumes of the acts, in which, while charity was preserved, yet we loitered not without some little labour of altercation, deliberating those things in the acts which now pertain to the cause. However the more gratefully would he have received this news as he would have seen a more peaceful ending of the matter, my lord and brother, had he been still in the body! Apiarius the presbyter, concerning whose ordination, excommunication, and appeal no small scandal arose not only at Sicca but also in the whole African Church, has been restored to communion upon his seeking pardon for all his sins. First our fellow bishop Urban of Sicca doubtless corrected whatever in him seemed to need correction. For there should have been kept in mind the peace and quiet of the Church not only in the present but also in the future, since so many evils of such a kind had gone before, that it was incumbent to take care that like or even graver evils should be prevented thereafter. It seemed good to us that the presbyter Apiarius should be removed from the church of Sicca, retaining only the honour of his grade, and that he should exercise the office of the presbyterate wherever else he wished and could, having received a letter to this effect. This we granted without difficulty at his own petition made in a letter. But truly before this case should be thus closed, among other things which we were treating of in daily discussions, the nature of the case demanded that we should ask our brothers, Faustinus our fellow bishop, and Philip and Asellus our fellow presbyters, to set forth what they had been enjoined to treat of with us that they might be inserted in the ecclesiastical acts. And they proceeded to make a verbal statement, but when we earnestly asked that they would present it rather in writing, then they produced the Commonitory. This was read to us and also set down in the acts, which they are bringing with them to you. In this they were bidden to treat of four things with us, first concerning the appeal of bishops to the Pontiff of the Roman Church, second that bishops should not unbecomingly be sailing to court, thirdly concerning the treating the causes of presbyters and deacons by contiguous bishops, if they had been wrongly excommunicated by their own, and fourthly concerning the bishop Urban who should be excommunicated or even sent to Rome, unless he should have corrected what seemed to need correction. Of all which things concerning the first and third, that is that it is allowed to bishops to appeal to Rome and that the causes of clerics should be settled by the bishops of their own provinces, already last year we have taken pains to insinuate, in our letter to the same bishop Zosimus of venerable memory, that we were willing to observe these provisions for a little while without any injury to him, until the search for the statutes of the Council of Nice had been finished. And now we ask of your holiness that you would cause to be observed by us the acts and constitutions of our fathers at the Council of Nice, and that you cause to be exercised by you there, those things which they brought in the commonitory : that is to say, If a bishop shall have been accused, etc. [*Here follows Canon vii. of Sardica.*]

Item concerning presbyters and deacons. If any bishop has been quickly angered, etc. [*Here follows Canon xvii. of Sardica.*]

These are the things which have been inserted in the acts until the arrival of the most accurate copies of the Nicene Council, which things,[1] if they are contained there (as in the Commonitory, which our brethren directed to us from the Apostolic See alleged) and be even kept according to that order by you in Italy, in no way could we be compelled either to endure such treatment as we are unwilling to mention or could suffer what is unbearable :[2] but we believe, through the mercy of our Lord God, while your holiness presides over the Roman Church, we shall not have to suffer that pride (*istum typhum passuri*). And there will be kept toward us, what should be kept with brotherly love to us who are making no dispute. You will also perceive according to the wisdom and the justice which the most Highest has given thee, what should be observed,[3] if perchance the canons of the Council of Nice are other [than you suppose]. For although we have read very many copies, yet never have we read in the Latin copies that there were any such decrees as are contained in the commonitory before mentioned. So too, because we can find them in no Greek text here, we have desired that there should be brought to us from the Eastern Churches copies of the decrees, for it is said that there correct copies of the decrees are to be found. For which end we beg your reverence, that you would deign yourself also to write to the pontiffs of these parts, that is of the churches of Antioch, Alexandria, and Constantinople,[4] and to any others also if it shall please your holiness, that thence there may come to us the same canons decreed by the Fathers in the city of Nice, and thus you would confer by the help of the Lord this most great benefit upon all the churches of the West. For who can doubt that the copies of the Nicene Council gathered in the Greek empire are most accurate, which although brought together from so diverse and from such noble Greek churches are found to agree when compared together ? And until this be done, the provisions laid down to us in the Commonitory aforesaid, concerning the appeals of bishops to the pontiff of the Roman Church and concerning the causes of clerics which should be terminated by the bishops of their own provinces, we are willing to allow to be observed until the proof arrives and we trust your blessedness will help us in this according to the will of God. The rest of the matters treated and defined in our synod, since the aforesaid brethren, our fellow bishop Faustinus, and the presbyters Philip and Asellus are carrying the acts with them, if you deign to receive them, will make known to your holiness. And they signed.[5] Our Lord keep thee to us for many years, most blessed brother. Alypius, Augustine, Possidius, Marinus and the rest of the bishops [217] also signed.

---

[1] The text here is very uncertain. I follow Allies.

[2] It is evident that the Latin text here is corrupt in more places than one. There would seem to be no doubt that for Migne's reading *quæ sibi*, the Greek translators had *quæ si ibi* and accordingly rendered it ἅτινα ἐὰν ἐκεῖ, and so the text stands in Labbe and Cossart. The following sentence is also clearly in a somewhat altered form from its original.

[3] L. and C. insert here wrongly a *nisi*.

[4] This order of naming the sees is worthy of note.

[5] So in the Greek ; the Latin reads *Et alia manu.*

ANCIENT EPITOME OF CANON CXXXIV.

Urban, the bishop of Siccas, is either to be ex-
communicated or else summoned to Rome unless he corrects what should be corrected by him.

CANON CXXXV.   (Not numbered in the Greek.)

Here begin the rescripts to the African Council from Cyril bishop of Alexandria in which he sends the authentic proceedings of the Nicene Council,[1] translated from the Greek by Innocent the presbyter: these letters with the same Nicene council were also sent through the aforementioned presbyter Innocent and by Marcellus a subdeacon of the Church of Carthage, to the holy Boniface, bishop of the Roman Church, on the sixth day before the calends of December in the year 419.[2]

To the most honourable, lords, our holy brethren and fellow bishops, Aurelius, Valentinus, as well as to the whole holy synod met in Carthage, Cyril salutes your holiness in God.

I have received with all joy at the hands of our son, the presbyter Innocent, the letters of your reverence so full of piety, in which you express the hope that we will send you most accurate copies of the decrees of the holy Fathers at the Synod held at Nice the metropolis of Bithynia from the archives of our church; with our own certificate of accuracy attached thereto.   In answer to which request, most honourable lords and brethren, I have thought it necessary to send to you, with our compliments, by our son, Innocent the presbyter, the bearer of these, most faithful copies of the decisions of the synod held at Nice in Bithynia.   And when ye have sought in the history of the church, you will find them there also.   Concerning Easter, as you have written, we announce to you that we shall celebrate it on the xviiiith [3] before the calends of May of the next indiction.   The subscription.   May God and our Lord preserve your holy synod as we desire, dear brethren.

ANCIENT EPITOME OF CANON CXXXV.

According to your written request, we have sent *to your charity most faithful copies of the authentic decrees of the Synod which was held at Nice, a city of Bithynia.*

CANON CXXXVI.   (Not numbered in the Greek but with a new heading.)

Here beginneth the letter of Atticus, bishop of Constantinople to the same.

To our holy lords, and rightly most blessed brethren and fellow bishops, Aurelius, Valentine, and [4] to the other beloved ones met together in the Synod held at Carthage, Atticus the bishop.

By our son Marcellus the subdeacon, I have received with all thanksgiving the writings of your holiness, praising the Lord that I enjoyed the blessing of so many of my brethren.   O my lords and most blessed brethren, ye have written asking me to send you most accurate copies of the canons enacted at the city of Nice, the metropolis of Bithynia, by the Fathers for the exposition of the faith.   And who is there that would deny to his brethren the common faith, or the statutes decreed by the Fathers.   Wherefore by the same son of mine, Marcellus, your subdeacon, who was in great haste, I have sent to you the canons in full as they were adopted by the Fathers in the city of Nice; and I ask of you that your holy synod would have me much in your prayers. The subscription.   May our God keep your sanctity, as we desire, most holy brethren.

---

[1] The Greek adds "and the canons."
[2] No year is given in the Greek nor in Migne's Latin.

[3] Bruns says "all the books" read "xvij. Kal.," but, as a fact, Easter was "xiv. Kal." that year.
[4] So in the Greek, *vel* in Latin.

CANON CXXXVII.   (Continuation of the last in the Greek.)

Here begin the examples of the Nicene Council, sent on the sixth day before the calends of December in the year 419,[1] after the consulate of the most glorious emperor Honorius for the XIIth time, and Theodosius for the IXth time,[2] Augustuses, to Boniface the bishop of the City of Rome.

WE believe in one God etc.   .   .   .   the Catholic and Apostolic Church anathematizes them.[3]

To this symbol of the faith there were also annexed copies of the statutes of the same Nicene Councils from the aforenamed pontiffs, in all respects as are contained above ; which we do not think it necessary to write out here again.

NOTES.

ANCIENT EPITOME OF CANON CXXXVII.

The Canons of the Synod of Nice are sent, as they were decreed by the Fathers, in accordance with your letters.

[Here follows the Nicene Creed in full.]

CANON CXXXVIII.   (Not numbered in the Greek.)

Here beginneth the epistle of the African synod to Pope Celestine, bishop of the City of Rome.

To the lord and most beloved and our honourable brother Celestine, Aurelius, Palatinus, Antony, Totus, Servusdei, Terentius, Fortunatus, Martin, Januarius, Optatus, Ceticius, Donatus, Theasius, Vincent, Fortunatian, and the rest of us, assembled at Carthage in the General Council of Africa.

We could wish that, like as your Holiness intimated to us, in your letter sent by our fellow presbyter Leo, your pleasure at the arrival of Apiarius, so we also could send to you these writings with pleasure respecting his clearing.   Then in truth both our own satisfaction, and yours of late would be more reasonable ; nor would that lately expressed by you concerning the hearing of him then to come, as well as that already past, seem hasty and inconsiderate.   Upon the arrival, then, of our holy Brother and fellow-Bishop Faustinus, we assembled a council, and believed that he was sent with that man, in order that, as he [Apiarius] had before been restored to the presbyterate by his assistance, so now he might with his exertions be cleared of the very great crimes charged against him by the inhabitants of Tabraca.   But the due course of examination in our council discovered in him such great and monstrous crimes as to overbear even Faustinus, who acted rather as an advocate of the aforementioned person than as a judge, and to prevail against what was more the zeal of a defender, than the justice of an inquirer.   For first he vehemently opposed the whole assembly, inflicting on us many injuries, under pretence of asserting the privileges of the Roman Church, and wishing that he should be received into communion by us, on the ground that your Holiness, believing him to have appealed, though unable to prove it, had restored him to communion.   But this we by no means allowed, as you will also better see by reading the acts.   After however, a most laborious inquiry carried on for three days, during which in the greatest affliction we took cognizance of various charges against him, God the just Judge, strong and long suffering, cut short by a sudden stroke both the delays of our fellow-bishop Faustinus and the evasions of Apiarius himself, by which he was endeavouring to veil his foul enormities.   For his strong and shameless obstinacy was

---

[1] No year in the Greek nor in Migne's Latin.
[2] Bruns notes with Justellus and Hardouin and the Codd. Hisp. this should read viii. for ix.

[3] In the Greek the creed is not given here in full, but as follows : " We believe in one God the Father ; and then the holy creed as written in the first synod."

overcome, by which he endeavoured to cover, through an impudent denial, the mire of his lusts, and God so wrought upon his conscience and published, even to the eyes of men, the secret crimes which he was already condemning in that man's heart, a very sty of wickedness, that, after his false denial he suddenly burst forth into a confession of all the crimes he was charged with, and at length convicted himself of his own accord of all infamies beyond belief, and changed to groans even the hope we had entertained, believing and desiring that he might be cleared from such shameful blots, except indeed that it was so far a relief to our sorrow, that he had delivered us from the labour of a longer inquiry, and by confession had applied some sort of remedy to his own wounds, though, lord and brother, it was unwilling, and done with a struggling conscience. Premising, therefore, our due regards to you, we earnestly conjure you, that for the future you do not readily admit to a hearing persons coming hence, nor choose to receive to your communion those who have been excommunicated by us, because you, venerable Sir, will readily perceive that this has been prescribed even by the Nicene council. For though this seems to be there forbidden in respect of the inferior clergy, or the laity, how much more did it will this to be observed in the case of bishops, lest those who had been suspended from communion in their own Province might seem to be restored to communion hastily or unfitly by your Holiness. Let your Holiness reject, as is worthy of you, that unprincipled taking shelter with you of presbyters likewise, and the inferior clergy, both because by no ordinance of the Fathers hath the Church of Africa been deprived of this authority, and the Nicene decrees have most plainly committed not only the clergy of inferior rank, but the bishops themselves to their own Metropolitans. For they have ordained with great wisdom and justice, that all matters should be terminated in the places where they arise; and did not think that the grace of the Holy Spirit would be wanting to any Province, for the bishops of Christ (*Sacerdotibus*) wisely to discern, and firmly to maintain the right: especially since whosoever thinks himself wronged by any judgment may appeal to the council of his Province, or even to a General Council [i.e. of Africa] unless it be imagined that God can inspire a single individual with justice, and refuse it to an innumerable multitude of bishops (*sacerdotum*) assembled in council. And how shall we be able to rely on a sentence passed beyond the sea, since it will not be possible to send thither the necessary witnesses, whether from the weakness of sex, or advanced age, or any other impediment? For that your Holiness should send any on your part we can find ordained by no council of Fathers. Because with regard to what you have sent us by the same our brother bishop Faustinus, as being contained in the Nicene Council, we can find nothing of the kind in the more authentic copies of that council, which we have received from the holy Cyril our brother, Bishop of the Alexandrine Church, and from the venerable Atticus the Prelate of Constantinople, and which we formerly sent by Innocent the presbyter, and Marcellus the subdeacon through whom we received them, to Boniface the Bishop, your predecessor of venerable memory. Moreover whoever desires you to delegate any of your clergy to execute your orders, do not comply, lest it seem that we are introducing the pride of secular dominion into the Church of Christ which exhibiteth to all that desire to see God the light of simplicity and the day of humility. For now that the miserable Apiarius has been removed out of the Church of Christ for his horrible crimes, we feel confident respecting our brother Faustinus, that through the uprightness and moderation of your Holiness, Africa, without violating brotherly charity, will by no means have to endure him any longer. Lord and brother, may our Lord long preserve your Holiness to pray for us.[1]

ANCIENT EPITOME OF CANON CXXXVIII.

Those excommunicated by us, ye are not to be willing to admit afterwards to communion, according to the decree of the Nicene Synod.

For Apiarius, who was restored by you, has resisted the Synod, and treated it with scorn, and at length has been converted and confessed himself guilty with sighs and tears.

---

[1] This translation is by Allies.

COUNCIL OF CONSTANTINOPLE HELD UNDER NECTARIUS.

A.D. 394.

Elenchus.

Introductory Note.
Extracts from the Acts.

Ancient Epitome and Notes.

INTRODUCTORY NOTE.

The acts of this Council are found in Balsamon, page 761 of the Paris edition, with Hervetus's translation. Labbe [1] has taken Balsamon's text and inserted it into his Collection, from which the following translation is made. There is another version extant in Leunclavius, *Jus Græco-Roman.* p. 247.

On September the twenty-ninth of the year 394, a magnificent church, dedicated to SS. Peter and Paul, built by the munificence of Rufinus the Prætoreal prefect, and situated at a place called "the Oaks," a suburb of Chalcedon, was consecrated. Most scholars have adopted Tillemont's suggestion that this was the occasion which brought the patriarchs of Alexandria and Antioch to Constantinople, and that occasion was taken advantage of to hold a synod with regard to the dispute as to the see of Bostra. At this council, in accordance with the canon of the Second Ecumenical Council, adopted only a dozen years before, Constantinople took the first place and its bishop presided, but so strong was the hold of Alexandria that three centuries afterwards the Quinisext Synod speaks of this council as held "under Nectarius and Theophilus." In passing it may not be amiss to remark that St. Gregory of Nyssa and Theodore of Mopsuestia, and Flavian were present at this council! Well may Tillemont [2] exclaim, "It is remarkable to see Theophilus there with Flavian, although they were not in communion with each other."

---

[1] Labbe and Cossart, *Concilia*, Tom. II., col. 1151.   [2] Tillemont. *Memoires*, ix., 592.

COUNCIL OF CONSTANTINOPLE UNDER NECTARIUS OF CONSTANTINOPLE AND THEOPHILUS OF ALEXANDRIA.

A.D. 394.

(*Found in Beveridge*, Synodicon. *Tom. I.*, p. 678; *Labbe and Cossart*, Concilia, *Tom. II.*, col. 1151. *Both taken from Balsamon.*)

IN the consulate of our most religious and beloved-of-God Emperors, Flavius Arcadius Augustus, for the third time, and Honorius for the second time, on the third day before the calends of October, in the baptistery of the most holy church of Constantinople, when the most holy bishops had taken their seats [*here follow the names*], Nectarius, the bishop of Constantinople, said: Since by the grace of God this synod has met in this holy place, if the synod of my holy brethren and fellow ministers in holy things thinks good, since I see our brothers Bagadius and Agapius, who contend between themselves about the bishopric of Bostra, are also present, let these begin to set forth their mutual rights. And after some things had been done by them for the sake of this cause, and it had been shewn that the afore-named Bagadius was deposed by only two bishops, both of whom were dead, Arabianus, bishop of Ancyra, said: Not on account of this judgment, but fearing henceforth for my whole life, I desire the holy Synod to make a decree, whether or no, a bishop can be deposed by only two bishops, and whether the Metropolitan is absent or not, without prejudice to the present cause. For I fear that some, taking their power from these acts, may dare to attempt such things. I wish therefore your response.

Nectarius, the bishop of Constantinople, said: The most religious bishop Arabianus hath spoken most laudably. But since it is impossible to go backward in judgment, let us, without condemning that which is past, establish things for the future. Arabianus, bishop of Ancyra, said: The synod of blessed fathers who met at Nice condemns what has taken place, for it orders that not less than three shall ordain, nor even so without the metropolitan. But of the future I, full of fear, have made this question. I would wish therefore that you would say clearly and without delay or doubt, that a bishop could not, according to the decree of the Synod of Nice, lawfully be ordained or deposed by two men.

And, after some further debate, Theophilus, the bishop of Alexandria, said: Against those who have gone forth, no sentence of indignation can be pronounced, since those to be condemned were not present. But if any one were to consider those who are to be deposed in future, it seems to me that not only these ought to assemble, but so far as possible all the other provincials, that by the sentence of many there may be rendered a more accurate condemnation of him who is present and is being judged, and who deserves deposition. Nectarius, the bishop of Constantinople, said: Since, the controversy is concerning legitimate institutions and decrees, it follows that nothing must be decreed on account of personal causes. Wherefore as the most holy bishop Arabianus has said, wishing to make the future certain, the sentence of the most holy bishop Theophilus hath consistently and considerately decreed that for the future it shall be lawful not even for three, far less for two bishops to depose him who is examined as a defendant: but by the sentence of the greater synod and of the bishops of the province, according to the Apostolic Canons. Flavian, the bishop of Antioch, said: What things the most holy bishop Nectarius, and the most holy bishop Theophilus have set forth are clearly right. And all the ecclesiastics agreed with these.

NOTES.

ANCIENT EPITOME.

In future when a defendant is examined, he ought not to be deposed by two or three bishops: but by the sentence of the greater Synod and of his own provincials, as also the Apostolic Canons provide.

BALSAMON.

As Bagadius, the bishop of Bostra, had been deposed by only two bishops, the matter was considered in the synod at Constantinople, whether that deposition had been rightly decreed. Agapius, the elect, laying claim to it under the decision. And it was decreed that the deposition was not canonical, since not two but a number should judge of those accusations which are made against bishops. But know that this constitution has no force to-day, for by the twelfth canon of the synod of Carthage, which is much later, crimes charged against bishops are to be judged of by twelve bishops. Read that canon, and know that this synod was held in the time of the Emperor Arcadius, while that of Carthage was in the days of Theodosius the younger.

Zonaras explains that by the words " have gone forth " in the speech of Theophilus of Alexandria is to be understood have died.

THE COUNCIL OF CARTHAGE HELD UNDER CYPRIAN.

A.D. 257.

Elenchus.

Introductory Note.	*Notes, with St. Cyprian's Epistle to Janu-*
The remains of the Acts.	*arius et al.*

INTRODUCTORY NOTE.

It is commonly supposed by the commentators that what follows is the "Canon of St. Cyprian" referred to in the Second canon of the Synod in Trullo. Johnson [1] thinks that that canon comes down to us as Canon XXXIX. of the Apostolic Canons. Baronius [2] agrees with Asseman [3] in thinking that from hatred to Rome the Greeks adopted the theory of the non-validity of heretical baptism. "But," as Hefele [4] well remarks, "in that case they would have contradicted themselves."

Zonaras remarks : " This is the most ancient of all the synods. For that which was held at Antioch in Syria concerning Paul of Samorata was more ancient than the others, being holden in the time of the Roman Emperor Aurelius, but this one is still earlier. For the great Cyprian finished his martyr course in the time of the Emperor Decius : but there was a long interval between Aurelian and Decius. For many emperors reigned after the death of Decius, to whom at last Aurelian succeeded on the throne. Therefore this is by far the most ancient of all synods. In it moreover above eighty-four bishops were gathered together, and considered the question as to what was to be done about the baptism of those who came to the Church after abandoning their heresies, and of schismatics who returned to the Church."

---

[1] Johnson. *Clergyman's Vade Mecum.* Notes *in loc.*
[2] Baronius. *Annal. ad ann.*, 692.

[3] Asseman. *Bib. Jur. Orient.* Tom. I., p. 414.
[4] Hefele. *Hist. Councils*, Vol. V., p. 224, note 2.

THE SYNOD HELD AT CARTHAGE OVER WHICH PRESIDED THE GREAT AND HOLY MARTYR CYPRIAN, BISHOP OF CARTHAGE.

A.D. 257.

(Found in Beveridge, Synodicon, Tom. I., p. 365, and in Labbe and Cossart, Concilia, Tom. I., col. 786.)

When very many bishops were met together at Carthage on the Calends of September from the province of Africa, Numidia and Mauritania, with the presbyters and deacons (the greater part of the people being likewise present) and when the holy letters of Jubaianus to Cyprian had been read, and Cyprian's answers to Jubaianus, concerning heretical baptisms, as well as what the same Jubaianus afterwards wrote to Cyprian,

Cyprian said: Ye have heard, my dearly beloved colleagues, what our fellow bishop Jubaianus has written to me, taking counsel of my littleness concerning the illicit and profane baptisms of heretics, and the answer which I made him; being of the same opinion as we have been on former occasions, that heretics coming to the Church should be baptized and sanctified with the Church's baptism. Moreover there has been read to you also the other letter of Jubaianus, in which answering for his sincere and pious devotion to our letter, not only he agrees therewith but offered thanks that he has been so instructed by it. It only remains therefore that we, each one of us, one by one, say what our mind is in this matter, without condemning any one or removing any one from the right of communion who does not agree with us.

For no one [of us [1]] has set himself up [to be] bishop [of bishops],[1] or attempted with tyrannical dread to force his colleagues to obedience to him, since every bishop has, for the license of liberty and power, his own will, and as he cannot be judged by another, so neither can he judge another. But we await the judgment of our universal Lord, our Lord Jesus Christ, who one and alone hath the power, both of advancing us in the governance of his Church, and of judging of our actions [in that position].

[*The bishops then one by one declared against heretical baptism.*[2] *Last of all* (col. 796)] :

Cyprian, the Confessor and Martyr of Carthage, said: The letter which was written to Jubaianus, my colleague, most fully set forth my opinion, that heretics who, according to the evangelical and apostolic witness, are called adversaries of Christ's and anti-Christs, when they come to the Church, should be baptized with the one (*unico*) baptism of the Church, that they may become instead of adversaries friends, and Christians instead of Antichrists.

NOTES.

ZONARAS.

These are the opinions therefore of the fathers, which assembled in council with the great Cyprian: but they do not apply to all heretics nor to all schismatics. For the Second Ecumenical Council, as we have just said [i.e. in the Preface he has placed to the acts of the synod. *Vide* L. and C., *Conc.*, Tom. i., col. 801] makes an exception of some heretics, and give its sanction to their reception without baptism, only requiring their anointing with the holy chrism, and then anathematizing at the same time their own and all heresies.

Balsamon does not print the acts of the Council at all but only the letter of St. Cyprian (Labbe and Cossart, *Concilia*, Tom. I., col. 799.) I have not thought it worth while to place here the remarks of the eighty-six bishops, ὡς μὴ ἀναγκαῖαι, οἷα μὴδε ἐνεργοῦσαι, to quote Zonaras's words.

BINIUS.

The allusion here is to the decree of Stephen, who was wont, according to the custom of his elders, to be styled "Bishop of bishops," and because he had acrimoniously threatened excommunication to all not agreeing with him.

---

[1] These words are omitted in Zonaras's Greek! The very gist of the matter for the Easterns.
[2] These will be found translated in full in the Oxford "Library of the Fathers," Vol. 17. "St. Cyprian's Epistles," p. 286; also in the American reprint of the "Ante-Nicene Fathers," Vol. V. "Hippolitus, Cyprian, etc.," p. 565.

On the disputed historical fact as to whether St. Cyprian died in or out of the communion of the See of Rome the reader will do well to consult Puller, *The Primitive Saints and the See of Rome.*

I place here St. Cyprian's Seventieth Epistle in the Oxford Translation (*Epistle of St. Cyprian*, pp. 232 *et seqq.*). This letter is addressed to Januarius, Satterninus, etc., and is headed in Beveridge's *Synodicon* "Canon I."

EPISTLE LXX.

Cyprian, Liberalis, Caldonius, etc., to their brethren Januarius, etc. Greeting.

WHEN we were together in council, dearest brethren, we read the letter which you addressed to us respecting those who are thought to be baptized by heretics and schismatics, whether, when they come to the one true Catholic Church, they ought to be baptized. Wherein, although ye yourselves also hold the Catholic rule in its truth and fixedness, yet since, out of our mutual affection, ye have thought good to consult us, we deliver not our sentence as though new but, by a kindred harmony, we unite with you in that long since settled by our predecessors, and observed by us; thinking, namely, and holding for certain, that no one can be baptized without the Church, in that there is one Baptism appointed in the holy Church, and it is written, the Lord himself speaking, "They have forsaken me, the Fountain of living water, and hewed them out broken cisterns that can hold no water." Again, holy Scripture admonishes us, and says, "Keep thee from the strange water, and drink not from a fountain of strange water." The water then must first be cleansed and sanctified by the priest, that it may be able, by Baptism therein, to wash away the sins of the baptized, for the Lord says by the prophet Ezekiel, "Then will I sprinkle clean water upon you, and ye shall be cleansed from all your filthiness, and from all your idols will I cleanse you; a new heart also will I give you, and a new spirit will I put within you." But how can he cleanse and sanctify the water, who is himself unclean, and with whom the Spirit is not? whereas the Lord says in Numbers, "And whatsoever the unclean person toucheth shall be unclean." Or how can he that baptizeth give remission of sins to another, who cannot himself free himself from his own sins, out of the Church?

Moreover, the very interrogatory which is put in Baptism, is a witness of the truth. For when we say, "Dost thou believe in eternal life, and remission of sins through the holy Church?" we mean, that remission of sins is not given, except in the Church; but that, with heretics, where the Church is not, sins cannot be remitted. They, therefore, who claim that heretics can baptize, let them either change the interrogatory, or maintain the truth; unless indeed they ascribe a Church also to those who they contend have Baptism.

Anointed also must he of necessity be, who is baptized, that having received the chrism—that is, unction, he may be the anointed of God, and have within him the grace of Christ. Moreover, it is the Eucharist through which the baptized are anointed, the oil sanctified on the altar. But he cannot sanctify the creature of oil, who has neither altar nor church. Whence neither can the spiritual unction be with heretics, since it is acknowledged that the oil cannot be sanctified nor the Eucharist celebrated among them. But we ought to know and remember that it is written, "Let not the oil of a sinner anoint my head;" which the Holy Ghost forewarned in the Psalms, lest any, quitting the track, and wandering out of the path of truth, be anointed by heretics and adversaries of Christ. Moreover, when baptized, what kind of prayer can a profane priest and a sinner offer? in that it is written, "God heareth not a sinner; but if any man be a worshipper of God, and doeth his will, him he heareth."

But who can give what himself hath not? or how can he perform spiritual acts, who hath himself lost the Holy Spirit? Wherefore he is to be baptized and received, who comes uninitiated to the Church, that within he may be hallowed through the holy; for it is written, "Be ye holy, for I am holy, saith the Lord." So that he who has been seduced into error and washed without should, in the true Baptism of the Church, put off this very thing also; that he, a man coming to God, while seeking for a priest, fell, through the deceit of error, upon one profane. But to acknowledge any case where they have baptized, is to approve the baptism of heretics and schismatics.

For neither can part of what they do be void and part avail. If he could baptize, he could also give the Holy Ghost. But if he cannot give the Holy Ghost because, being set without, he is not with the Holy Ghost, neither can he baptize any that cometh: for that there is both one Baptism, and one Holy Ghost, and one Church, founded by Christ the Lord upon Peter, through an original and principle of unity; so it results, that since all among them is void and false, nothing that they have done ought to be approved by us. For what can be ratified and confirmed by God, which they do whom the Lord calls his enemies and adversaries, propounding in his Gospel, "He that is not with me, is against me; and he that gathereth not with me, scattereth." And the blessed Apostle John also, keeping the commandments and precepts of the Lord, has written in his Epistle, "Ye have heard that Antichrist shall come; even now are there many Antichrists, whereby we know that it is the last time. They went out from us, but were not of us; for if they had been of us, they would no doubt have continued with us." Whence we, too, ought to infer and consider, whether they who are the adversaries of the Lord, and are called Antichrists, can give the grace of Christ. Wherefore we who are with the Lord, and who hold the unity of the Lord, and according to this vouchsafement administer his priesthood in the Church, ought to repudiate and reject and account as profane, whatever his adversaries and Antichrists do; and to those who, coming from error and wickedness, acknowledge the true faith of the one Church, we should impart the reality of unity and faith by all the sacraments of Divine grace.

We bid you, dearest brethren, ever heartily farewell.

THE SEVENTH ECUMENICAL COUNCIL.

THE SECOND COUNCIL OF NICE.

A.D. 787.

Emperors.—Constantine VI. and Irene.
Pope.—Hadrian.

Elenchus.

INTRODUCTION.

Gibbon thus describes the Seventh Ecumenical Council of the Christian Church: "The decrees were framed by the president[1] Tarasius, and ratified by the acclamations and subscriptions of three hundred and fifty bishops. They unanimously pronounced that the worship of images is agreeable to Scripture and reason, to the Fathers and councils of the Church; but they hesitated whether that worship be relative or direct; whether the godhead and the figure of Christ be entitled to the same mode of adoration.[2] Of this second Nicene Council the acts are still extant; a curious monument of superstition and ignorance, of falsehood and folly." (*Decline and Fall*, chapter xlix.)

And this has been read as history, and has passed as such in the estimation of the overwhelming majority of educated English-speaking people for several generations, and yet it is a statement as full of absolute and inexcusable errors as the passage in another part of the same work which the late Bishop Lightfoot so unmercifully exposed, and which the most recent editor, Bury, has taken pains to correct.

I do not know whether it is worth while to do so, but perhaps it may be as well to state, that whatever may be his opinion of the truths of the conclusions arrived at by the council, no impartial reader can fail to recognize the profound learning[3] of the assembly, the singular acumen displayed in the arguments employed, and the remarkable freedom from what Gibbon and many others would consider "superstition." So radical is this that Gibbon would have noticed it had he read the acts of the synod he is criticising (which we have good reason for believing that he never did). There he would have found the Patriarch declaring that at that time the venerable images worked no miracles, a statement that would be made by no prelate of the Latin or Greek Church to-day, even in the light of the nineteenth century.

As I have noted in the previous pages my task is not that of a controversialist. To me at present it is a matter of no concern whether the decision of the council is true or false. I shall therefore strictly confine myself to two points : 1. That the Council was Ecumenical. 2. What its decision was; explaining the technical meaning of the Greek words employed during this controversy and finally incorporated in the decree.

1. *This Council was certainly Ecumenical.*

It seems strange that any person familiar with the facts of the case could for a moment entertain a doubt as to the ecumenical character of the council which met at Nice in 787.

(*a*) It was called by the Roman Emperors to be an Ecumenical Council. *Vide* letter of Tarasius.

(*b*) It was called with the approval of the Pope (not like I. Constantinople, without his knowledge; or like Chalcedon, contrary to his expressed wish), and two papal legates were present at its deliberations and signed its decrees.

(*c*) The Patriarch of Constantinople was present in person.

(*d*) The other Patriarchates were represented, although on account of the Moslem tyranny the Patriarchs could not attend in person, nor could they even send proctors.

(*e*) The decrees were adopted by an unanimous vote of the three hundred and fifty bishops.

---

[1] Who was possibly at least not the president, vide Michaud, *Sept. Conc. Œcuméniques*, p. 330.

[2] Worship is "relative" or "absolute," what Gibbon means by "direct" would be hard to say. How entirely false the whole statement is, Gibbon himself would have recognized had he read the acts.

[3] Dr. Neale complains that the acts display a painful lack of critical knowledge and that several spurious passages are attributed to the Fathers. But I confess this does not seem to me either surprising or disgraceful. The attributing of books, even in our critical days, to persons who were not their authors is not so uncommon as to make us wonder such a thing might have occurred in such stormy times, when learning of this sort must have suffered by the adversities of the Church and State, the Iconoclastic persecutions and the Moslem incursions.

(*f*) They were immediately received in all the four Eastern Patriarchates.[1]

(*g*) They were immediately accepted by the Pope.

(*h*) For a full thousand years they have been received by the Latin and Greek Churches with but a few exceptions altogether insignificant, save the Frankish kingdom.

In the face of such undisputed facts, it would be strange were anyone to doubt the historical fact that the Second Council of Nice is one of the Ecumenical Councils of the Catholic Church, and indeed so far as I am aware none have done so except such as have been forced into this position for doctrinal consistency.

Nor have all Protestants allowed their judgment to be warped in this matter. As a sample I may quote from that stanch Protestant whom Queen Elizabeth appointed a chaplain in ordinary in 1598, and who in 1610 was made Dean of Gloucester, the profoundly learned Richard Field. In his famous "Book of the Church" (Book V. chap. lj.), he says: "These" [six, which he had just described] " were all the lawful General Councils (lawful, I say, both in their beginning and proceeding and continuance) that ever were holden in the Christian Church, touching matters of faith. For the Seventh, which is the Second of Nice, was not called about any question of faith but of manners. . . . So that there are but Seven General Councils that the whole Church acknowledgeth, called to determine matters of faith and manners. For the rest that were holden afterwards, which our adversaries [the Roman Catholics] would have to be acknowledged general, they are not only rejected by us but by the Grecians also, as not general, but patriarchal only, etc."

Of course there are a number of writers (principally of the Anglican Communion), who have argued thus: "The doctrine taught by the Second Council of Nice we reject, *ergo* it cannot have been an Ecumenical Council of the Catholic Church." And they have then gone on to prove their conclusion. With such writers I have no concern. My simple contention is that the Council is admitted by all to have been representative of East and West, and to have been accepted for a thousand years as such, and to be to-day accepted as Ecumenical by the Latin and Greek Churches. If its doctrines are false, then one of the Ecumenical Synods set forth false doctrine, a statement which should give no trouble, so far as I can understand, to anyone who does not hold the necessary infallibility of Ecumenical Synods.[2]

Among those who have argued against the ecumenical character of the Seventh Council there are, however, two whose eminent learning and high standing demand a consideration of anything they may advance on any subject they treat of, these are the Rev. John Mason Neale and the Rev. Sir William Palmer.

Dr. Neale considers the matter at some length in a foot-note to his *History of the Eastern Church* (Vol. II., pp. 132–135), but I think it not improper to remark that the author ingenuously confesses in this very note that if he came to the conclusion that the council was ecumenical, " it would be difficult to clear our own Church from the charge of heresy." Entertaining such an opinion at the start, his conclusion could hardly be unbiassed.

The only argument which is advanced in this note which is different from those of other opponents of the Council, is that it had not the authentication of a subsequent Ecumenical Synod. The argument seems to me so extraordinary that I think Dr. Neale's exact words should be cited : " In the first place, we may remark that the Second Council of Nicæa wants one mark of authority, shared according to the more general belief by the six—according to the opinions which an English Churchman must necessarily embrace by the first five Coun-

[1] " It is certain," confesses Dr. Neale (*History of the Holy Eastern Church*, Vol. II., p. 133 ; in his attempt to overthrow the authority of this council) " that Politian approved (S. Theod. Stud. Ep. xviij.) although he was not present at the Council of Nicæa ; and the controversy, which had never much disturbed Africa, may henceforth be considered as terminated in the Diocese of Alexandria."

[2] As a sample of all that bigotry and dishonesty can do when writing on such a subject, the reader is referred to a little book by the Rev. F. Meyrick (a canon of the Church of England) published in Paris for the Anglo-Continental Society, 1877, entitled, *Du Schisme d'Orient et de l'authorité du prétendu septième concile*.

cils—its recognition as Ecumenical by a later Council undoubtedly so." But surely this involves an absurdity, for if it is not known whether the last one is ecumenical or no, how will its approval of the next to the last give that council any certainty? If III. Constantinople is doubtful being the sixth, because there is no seventh to have confirmed it; then II. Constantinople, the fifth, is doubtful because it has only been confirmed by a synod itself doubtful and so on, which is absurd. The test of the ecumenicity of a council is not its acceptance by a subsequent synod, but its acceptance by the whole Church, and this Dr. Neale frankly confesses is the case with regard to II. Nice: "It cannot be denied," he admits, "that at the present day both the Eastern and the Latin Churches receive it as Ecumenical" (p. 132). He might have added, "and have done so without any controversy on the subject for nearly a thousand years."

I do not think there is any need of my delaying longer over Dr. Neale's note, which I have noticed at all only because of his profound scholarship, and not because on this particular point I thought he had thrown any new light upon the matter, nor urged any argument really calling for an answer.

Sir William Palmer's argument (*A Treatise on the Church of Christ*, Pt. IV., Chapter X., Sect. IV.) is one of much greater force, and needs an answer. He points out how, long after the Council of Nice, the number of the General Councils was still spoken of as being Six, and that in some instances this council is referred to as the "pseudo" General Council of Nice. Now at first sight this argument seems to be of great force. But upon further consideration it will be seen to be after all of no great weight. We may not be able to explain, nor are we called upon to do so, why in certain cases writers chose still to speak of Six instead of Seven General Councils, but we would point out that the same continuance of the old expression can be found with regard to others of the General Councils. For example, St. Gregory the Great says that he "revered the four Ecumenical Councils as he did the four Gospels," but the fifth Ecumenical Synod had been held a number of years before. Will anyone pretend from this to draw the conclusion that at that time the Ecumenical character of the Fifth Synod (II. Constantinople) was not recognized at Rome? Moreover, among the instances cited (and there are but a very few all told) one of them is fatal to the argument. For if Pope Hadrian in 871 still speaks of only six Ecumenical Synods, he omits two (according to Roman count), for this date is after the synod which deposed Photius—a synod rejected indeed afterwards by the Greeks, but always accepted by the Latins as the Eighth of the Ecumenical Councils. Would Sir William pretend for an instant that Hadrian and the Church of Rome did not recognize that Council as Ecumenical and as the Eighth Synod? He could not, for on page 208 he ingenuously confesses that that Council "had been approved and confirmed by that Pope."

But after all, the contention fails in its very beginning, for Sir William frankly recognizes that the Popes from the first espoused the cause of the council and were ready to defend it. Now this involved the acknowledgment of its ecumenical character, for it was called as an Ecumenical Synod, this we expressly learn from the letter of Tarasius to the other Eastern Patriarchs (Labbe, *Conc.*, Tom. VII., col. 165), from the letter of the Emperor and Empress to the bishops throughout the empire (L. and C., *Conc.*, Tom. VII., col. 53), and (above all) from the witness of the Council itself, assuming the style of the "Holy Ecumenical Synod." In the face of such evidence any further proof is surely uncalled for.

We come now to the only other argument brought against the ecumenical character of this council—to wit, that many writers, even until after the beginning of the XVIth century, call the Seventh a "pseudo-Council." But surely this proves too much, for it would seem to imply that even down to that time the cultus of images was not established in the West, a proposition too ridiculous to be defended by anyone. It is indeed worthy of notice that all the authors cited are Frankish, (1) the *Annales Francorum* (A.D. 808) in the continuation of the same (A.D. 814), in an anonymous life of Charlemagne, and the *Annales* written after 819 ; (2) Eginhard in his *Annales Francorum* (A.D. 829) ; (3) the Gallican bishops at Paris, 824 ;[1] (4) Hincmar of Rheims ; (5) Ado, bishop of Vienne (died 875) ; (6) Anastasius acknowledges that the French had not accepted the veneration of the sacred images ; (7) The *Chronicle of St. Bertinus* (after 884) ; (8) The *Annales Francorum* after the council still speak of it as pseudo ; (9) Regino, Abbot of Prum (circa 910) ; (10) the *Chronicle of St. Bertinus*, of the Xth Century. (11) Hermanus Contractus : (12) the author who continued the Gestes Francorum to A.D. 1165 ; (13) Roger Hoverden (A.D. 1204) ; (14) Conrade à Lichtenau, Abbot of Urspurg (circa 1230) ; (15) Matthew of Westminster.

No doubt to these, given in Palmer, who has made much use of Lannoy, others could be added ; but they are enough to shew that the council was very little known, and that none of these writers had ever seen its acts.

Sir William is of opinion that by what precedes in his book he has "proved that for at least five centuries and a half the Council of Nice remained rejected in the Western Church." I venture to think that the most he has proved is that during that period of time he has been able to find fifteen individuals who for one reason or another wrote rejecting that council, that is to say three in a century, a number which does not seem quite sufficient to make the foundation of so considerable a generalization as "the Western Church." The further conclusion of Sir William, I think, every scholar will reject as simply preposterous, viz. : "In fact the doctrine of the adoration of images [by which he means the doctrine taught by the II. Council of Nice] was never received in the West, except where the influence of the Roman See was predominant" (p. 211).

Sir William is always, however, honest, and the following quotation which he himself makes from Cardinal Bellarmine may well go far toward explaining the erroneous or imperfect statements he has so learnedly and laboriously gathered together. "Bellarmine says : 'It is very credible that St. Thomas, Alexander of Hales, and other scholastic doctors had not seen the second synod of Nice, nor the eighth general synod ;' he adds that they 'were long in obscurity, and were first published in our own age, as may be known from their not being extant in the older volumes of the councils ; and St. Thomas and the other ancient schoolmen never make any mention of this Nicene Synod.' (Bell. *De Imag. Sanct.* Lib. II. cap. xxij.)"

2. *What the Council decreed.*

The council decreed that similar veneration and honour should be paid to the representations of the Lord and of the Saints as was accustomed to be paid to the "laurata" and tablets representing the Christian emperors, to wit, that they should be bowed to, and saluted with kisses, and attended with lights and the offering of incense.[2] But the Council was most explicit in declaring that this was merely a veneration of honour and affection, such as can be given to the creature, and that under no circumstances could the adoration of divine worship be given to them but to God alone.

The Greek language has in this respect a great advantage over the Hebrew, the Latin and the English ; it has a word which is a general word and is properly used of the affectionate regard and veneration shown to any person or thing, whether to the divine Creator or to any of his creatures, this word is προσκύνησις ; it has also another word which can properly be used to denote only the worship due to the most high God, this word is λατρεία. When then the Council defined that the worship of "latria" was never to be given to any but God alone,

---

[1] The true date is 825.   [2] Vide Labbe and Cossart, *Concilia*, tom. vii., col. 59.

it cut off all possibility for ido*latry*, mario*latry*, icono*latry*, or any other "latry" except "theo-latry." If therefore any of these other "latries" exist or ever have existed, they exist or have existed not in accordance with, but in defiance of, the decree of the Second Council of Nice.

But unfortunately, as I have said, we have neither in Hebrew, Latin, nor English any word with this restricted meaning, and therefore when it became necessary to translate the Greek acts and the decree, great difficulty was experienced, and by the use of "adoro" as the equivalent of προσκυνέω many were scandalized, thinking that it was divine adoration which they were to give to the sacred images, which they knew would be idolatry. The same trouble is found in rendering into English the acts and decrees; for while indeed properly speaking "worship" no more means necessarily divine worship in English than "adoratio" does in Latin (e.g. I. Chr. xxix. 20, "All the congregation bowed down their heads and worshipped the Lord and the King" [i.e. Solomon]; Luke xiv. 10, "Then shalt thou have worship in the presence of them that sit at meat with thee"), yet to the popular mind "the worship of images" is the equivalent of idolatry. In the following translations I have uni-formly translated as follows and the reader from the English will know what the word is in the original.

Προσκυνέω, to venerate; τιμάω, to honour; λατρεύω, to adore; ἀσπάζομαι, to salute; δουλεύω, to serve; εἰκών, an image.

The relative force of προσκύνησις and λατρεία cannot better be set forth than by Archbishop Trench's illustration of two circles having the same centre, the larger including the less (*New Testament Synonyms, sub voce* Λατρεύω).

To make this matter still clearer I must ask the reader's attention to the use of the words *abadh* and *shachah* in the Hebrew; the one *abadh*, which finds, when used with reference to God or to false gods its equivalent in λατρεύω; the other *shachah*, which is represented by προσκυνέω. Now in the Old Testament no distinction in the Hebrew is drawn between these words when applied to creator or creature. The one denotes service primarily for hire; the other bowing down and kissing the hand to any in salutation. Both words are constantly used and sometimes refer to the Creator and sometimes to the creature—*e.g.*, we read that Jacob served (*abadh*) Laban (Gen. xxix. 20); and that Joshua commanded the people not to serve the gods of their fathers but to serve (*abadh*) the Lord (Josh. xxiv. 14). And for the use of *shachah* the following may suffice: "And all the congregation blessed the Lord God of their fathers and bowed down their heads and worshipped (Hebrew, *shachah*; Greek, προσ-κυνέω; Latin, *adoro*) the Lord and the King" (I. Chr. xxix. 20). But while it is true of the Hebrew of the Old Testament that there is no word which refers alone to Divine Worship this is not true of the Septuagint Greek nor of the Greek of the New Testament, for in both προσκυνέω has always its general meaning, sometimes applying to the creature and sometimes to the Creator; but λατρεύω is used to denote divine worship alone, as St. Augustine pointed out long ago.

This distinction comes out very clearly in the inspired translation of the Hebrew found in Matthew iv. 10, "Thou shalt worship (προσκυνήσεις) the Lord thy God, and him only shalt thou serve (λατρεύσεις)." "Worship" was due indeed to God above all but not exclusively to him, but latria is to be given to "him only."[1]

I think I have now said enough to let the reader understand the doctrine taught by the council and to prove that in its decree it simply adopted the technical use of words found in the Greek of the Septuagint and of the New Testament. I may then close this introduction with a few remarks upon outward acts of veneration in general.

---

[1] Vide the Synod's Letter to the Emperor and Empress.

Of course, the outward manifestation in bodily acts of reverence will vary with times and with the habits of peoples. To those accustomed to kiss the earth on which the Emperor had trodden, it would be natural to kiss the feet of the image of the King of Kings. The same is manifestly true of any outward acts whatever, such as bowing, kneeling, burning of lights, and offering of incense. All these when offered before an image are, according to the mind of the Council, but outward signs of the reverence due to that which the image represents and pass backward to the prototype, and thus it defined, citing the example of the serpent in the wilderness, of which we read, "For he that turned himself toward it was not saved by the thing that he saw, but by thee, that art the Saviour of all" (Wisdom xvi. 17). If anyone feels disposed to attribute to outward acts any necessary religious value he is falling back into Judaism, and it were well for him to remember that the nod which the Quakers adopted out of protest to the bow of Christians was once the expression of divine worship to the most sacred idols; that in the Eastern Church the priest only bows before the Lord believed to be present in the Holy Sacrament while he prostrates himself before the infidel Sultan; and that throughout the Latin communion the acolytes genuflect before the Bishop, as they pass him, with the same genuflection that they give to the Holy Sacrament upon the Altar. In this connexion I quote in closing the fine satire in the letter of this very council to the Emperor and Empress. St. Paul "says of Jacob (Heb. xi. 21), 'He worshipped the top of his staff,' and like to this is that said by Gregory, surnamed the theologian, 'Revere Bethlehem and worship the manger.' But who of those truly understanding the Divine Scriptures would suppose that here was intended the Divine worship of latria? Such an opinion could only be entertained by an idiot or one ignorant of Scriptural and Patristic knowledge. Would Jacob give divine worship to his staff? Or would Gregory, the theologian, give command to worship as God a manger!"[1]

---

[1] The treatise of St. John Damascene on *The Holy Images* has very recently been published in an English translation by M. H. Allies. (London. Thos. Baker, 1898.)

THE DIVINE[1] SACRA[2] SENT BY THE EMPERORS CONSTANTINE AND IRENE TO THE MOST HOLY AND MOST BLESSED HADRIAN, POPE OF OLD ROME.

(Found in Labbe and Cossart, Concilia, Tom. VII., col. 32.)

They who receive the dignity of the empire, or the honour of the principal priesthood from our Lord Jesus Christ, ought to provide and to care for those things which please him, and rule and govern the people committed to their care according to his will and good pleasure.

Therefore, O most holy Head (Caput), it is incumbent upon us and you, that irreprehensibly we know the things which be his, and that in these we exercise ourselves, since from him we have received the imperatorial dignity, and you the dignity of the chief priesthood.

But now to speak more to the point. Your paternal blessedness knows what hath been done in times past in this our royal city against the venerable images, how those who reigned immediately before us destroyed them and subjected them to disgrace and injury : (O may it not be imputed to them, for it had been better for them had they not laid their hands upon the Church !) — and how they seduced and brought over to their own opinion all the people who live in these parts—yea, even the whole of the East, in like manner, up to the time in which God hath exalted us to this kingdom, who seek his glory in truth, and hold that which has been handed down by his Apostles together with all other teachers. Whence now with pure heart and unfeigned religion we have, together with all our subjects and our most learned divines, had constant conferences respecting the things which relate to God, and by their advice have determined to summon a General Council. And we entreat your paternal blessedness, or rather the Lord God entreats, " who will have all men to be saved and to come to the knowledge of the truth," that you will give yourself to us and make no delay, but come up hither to aid us in the confirmation and establishment of the ancient tradition of venerable images. It is, indeed, incumbent on your holiness to do this, since you know how it is written—" Comfort ye, comfort ye, my people, ye priests, saith the Lord," and " the lips of the priest shall keep knowledge, and the law shall go forth out of his mouth, for he is the angel of the Lord of Hosts." And again, the divine Apostle, the preacher of the truth, who, " from Jerusalem and round about unto Illyricum, preached the Gospel," hath thus commanded — " Feed with discipline the flock of Christ which he purchased with his own blood." As then you are the veritable chief priest (primus sacerdos) who presides in the place and in the see of the holy and superlaudable Apostle Peter, let your paternal blessedness come to us, as we have said before, and add your presence to all those other priests who shall be assembled together here, that thus the will of the Lord may be accomplished. For as we are taught in the Gospels our Lord saith— " When two or three are met together in my name, there am I in the midst of them " —let your paternal and sacred blessedness be certified and confirmed by the great God and King of all, our Lord Jesus Christ, and by us his servants, that if you come up hither you shall be received with all honour and glory, and that everything necessary for you shall be granted. And again, when the definition (capitulum) shall be completed, which by the good pleasure of Christ our God we hope shall be done, we take upon us to provide for you every facility of returning with honour and distinction. If, however, your blessedness cannot attend upon us (which we can scarcely imagine, knowing what is your zeal about divine things), at least, pray select for us men of understanding, having with them letters from your holiness, that they may be present here in the person of your sacred and paternal blessedness. So, when they meet

---

[1] " Divine" here, as usually in such connections, means " imperial."

[2] Mendham (*The Seventh General Council, the Second of Nicæa.* London, s.d.) by a curious blunder takes the adjective for the substantive, and translates " The Sacred Divalis." This is a mere trip, for he knows the word " sacra," as appears a few pages further on.

with the other priests who are here, the ancient tradition of our holy fathers may be synodically confirmed, and every evil plant of tares may be rooted out, and the words of our Lord and Saviour Jesus Christ may be fulfilled, that "the gates of hell shall not prevail against her." And after this, may there be no further schism and separation in the one holy Catholic and Apostolic Church, of which Christ our true God is the Head.

We have had Constantine, beloved in Christ, most holy Bishop of Leontina in our beloved Sicily, with whom your paternal blessedness is well acquainted, into our presence; and, having spoken with him face to face, have sent him with this our present venerable jussio to you. Whom,

after that he hath seen you, forthwith dismiss, that he may come back to us, and write us by him concerning your coming—what time we may expect will be spent in your journeying thence and coming to us. Moreover, he can retain with him the most holy Bishop of Naples, and come up hither together with him. And, as your journey will be by way of Naples and Sicily we have given orders to the Governor of Sicily about this, that he take due care to have every needful preparation made for your honour and rest, which is necessary in order that your paternal blessedness may come to us. Given on the ivth before the calends of September, the seventh indiction, from the Royal City.

THE IMPERIAL SACRA.

READ AT THE FIRST SESSION.

(Found in Labbe and Cossart, Concilia, Tom. VII., col. 49.)

CONSTANTINE and Irene—Sovereigns of the Romans in the Faith, to the most holy Bishops, who, by the grace of God and by the command of our pious Sovereignty, have met together in the Council of Nice.

The Wisdom which is truly according to the nature of God and the Father—our Lord Jesus Christ, our true God—who, by his most divine and wonderful dispensation in the flesh, hath delivered us from all idolatrous error: and, by taking on him our nature, hath renewed the same by the co-operation of the Spirit, which is of the same nature with himself; and having himself become the first High Priest, hath accounted you holy men, worthy of the same dignity.

He is that good Shepherd who, bearing on his own shoulders that wandering sheep —fallen man, hath brought him back to his own peculiar fold—that is, the company of angelic and ministering powers (Eph. ii. 14, 15), and hath reconciled us in himself and having taken away the wall of partition, hath broken down the enmity through his flesh, and hath bestowed upon us a rule of conduct tending to peace; wherefore, preaching to all, he saith in the Gospel, Blessed are the peacemakers, for they shall be called the children of God

(Matt. v. 9). Of which blessedness, confirming as it does the exaltation of the adoption of sons, our pious Sovereignty desiring above all things to be made partakers, hath ever applied the utmost diligence to direct all our Roman Commonwealth into the ways of unity and concord; and more especially have we been solicitous concerning the right regulation of the Church of God, and most anxious in every way to promote the unity of the priesthood. For which cause the Chiefs of the Sacerdotal Order of the East and of the North, of the West and of the South, are present in the person of their Representative Bishops, who have with them respectively the replies written in answers to the Synodical Epistle sent from the most holy Patriarch; for such was from the beginning the synodical regulation of the Church Catholic, which, from the one end of the earth to the other, hath received the Gospel. On this account we have, by the good will and permission of God, caused you, his most holy Priests, to meet together —you who are accustomed to dispense his Testimony in the unbloody sacrifice—that your decision may be in accordance with the definitions of former councils who decreed rightly, and that the splendour of the

Spirit may illumine you in all things, for, as our Lord teaches, No man lighteth a candle and putteth it under a bushel, but on a candlestick, that it may give light to all that are in the house; even so, should ye make such use of the various regulations which have been piously handed down to us of old by our Fathers, that all the Holy Churches of God may remain in peaceful order.

As for us, such was our zeal for the truth—such our earnest desire for the interests of religion, our care for ecclesiastical order, our anxiety that the ancient rules and orders should maintain their ground—that though fully engaged in military councils—though all our attention was occupied in political cares—yet, treating all these affairs as but of minor importance, we would allow nothing whatever to interfere with the convocation of your most holy council. To every one is given the utmost freedom of expressing his sentiments without the least hesitation, that thus the subject under enquiry may be most fully discussed and truth may be the more boldly spoken, that so all dissensions may be banished from the Church and we all may be united in the bonds of peace.

For, when the most holy Patriarch Paul, by the divine will, was about to be liberated from the bands of mortality and to exchange his earthly pilgrimage for a heavenly home with his Master Christ, he abdicated the Patriarchate and took upon him the monastic life, and when we asked him, Why hast thou done this? he answered, Because I fear that, if death should surprise me still in the episcopate of this royal and heaven-defended city, I should have to carry with me the anathema of the whole Catholic Church, which consigns me to that outer darkness which is prepared for the devil and his angels; for they say that a certain synod hath been held here in order to the subversion of pictures and images which the Catholic Church holds, embraces, and receives, in memory of the persons whom they represent. This is that which distracts my soul—this is that which makes me anxiously to enquire how I may escape the judgment of God—since among such men I have been brought up and with such am I numbered. No sooner had he thus spoken in the presence of some of our most illustrious nobles than he expired.

When our Pious Sovereignty reflected on this awful declaration (and truly, even before this event, we had heard of similar questionings from many around), we took counsel with ourselves as to what ought to be done; and we determined, after mature deliberation, that when a new Patriarch had been elected, we should endeavour to bring this subject to some decisive conclusion. Wherefore, having summoned those whom we knew to be most experienced in ecclesiastical matters, and having called upon Christ our God, we consulted with them who was worthy to be exalted to the chair of the Priesthood of this Royal and God-preserved city; and they all with one heart and soul gave their vote in favour of Tarasius—he who now occupies the Pontifical Presidency. Having, therefore, sent for him, we laid before him our deliberations and our vote; but he would by no means consent, nor at all yield to that which had been determined. And when we enquired, Wherefore he thus refused his consent?—at first he answered evasively, That the yoke of the Chief Priesthood was too much for him. But we, knowing this to be a mere pretext covering his unwillingness to obey us, would not desist from our importunity, but persisted in pressing the acceptance of the dignity of the Chief Priesthood upon him. When he found how urgent we were with him, he told us the cause of his refusal. It is (said he) because I perceive that the Church which has been founded on the rock, Christ our God, is rent and torn asunder by schisms, and that we are unstable in our confession, and that Christians in the East, of the same faith with ourselves, decline communion with us, and unite themselves with those of the West; and so we are estranged from all, and each day are anathematized by all: and, moreover, I should demand that an Ecumenical Council should be held, at which should be found Legates from the Pope of Rome and from the Chief Priests of the East. We, therefore, fully understanding these things, introduced him to the assembled company of the Priests—of our most illustrious Princes—and of all our Christian people; and then, in their presence, he repeated to them all that he had before said to us; which, when they heard, they received him joyfully, and earnestly entreated our peace-making and pious Sovereignty that an Ecumenical Council might be assembled.   To this their request, we gave our hearty consent; for, to speak the truth, it is by the good will and under the direction of our God that we have assembled you together.   Wherefore as God, willing to establish his own counsel, hath for this purpose brought you together from all parts of the world, behold the Gospels now lying before you, and plainly crying aloud, "Judge justly;" stand firm as champions of religion, and be ready with unsparing hand to cut away all innovations and new fangled inventions.   And, as Peter the Chief of the Apostolic College, struck the mad slave and cut off his Jewish ear with the sword, so in like manner do ye wield the axe of the Spirit, and every tree which bears the fruit of contention, of strife, or newly-imported innovation, either renew by transplanting through the words of sound doctrine, or lay it low with canonical censure, and send it to the fires of the future Gehenna, so that the peace of the Spirit may evermore protect the whole body of the Church, compacted and united in one, and confirmed by the traditions of the Fathers; and so may all our Roman State enjoy peace as well as the Church.

We have received letters from Hadrian, most Holy Pope of old Rome, by his Legates — namely, Peter, the God-beloved Archpresbyter, and Peter, the God-beloved Presbyter and Abbot—who will be present in council with you; and we command that, according to synodical custom, these be read in the hearing of you all; and that, having heard these with becoming silence, and moreover the Epistles contained in two octavos sent by the Chief Priest and other Priests of the Eastern dioceses by John, most pious Monk and Chancellor of the Patriarchal throne of Antioch, and Thomas, Priest and Abbot, who also are present together with you, ye may by these understand what are the sentiments of the Church Catholic on this point.

EXTRACTS FROM THE ACTS.

SESSION I.

(Labbe and Cossart, *Concilia*, Tom. VII., col. 53.)

[Certain bishops who had been led astray by the Iconoclasts came, asking to be received back. The first of these was Basil of Ancyra.]

The bishop Basil of Ancyra read as follows from a book; Inasmuch as ecclesiastical legislation has canonically been handed down from past time, even from the beginning from the holy Apostles, and from their successors, who were our holy fathers and teachers, and also from the six holy and ecumenical synods, and from the local synods which were gathered in the interests of orthodoxy, that those returning from any heresy whatever to the orthodox faith and to the tradition of the Catholic Church, might deny their own heresy, and confess the orthodox faith,

Wherefore I, Basil, bishop of the city of Ancyra, proposing to be united to the Catholic Church, and to Hadrian the most holy Pope of Old Rome, and to Tarasius the most blessed Patriarch, and to the most holy apostolic sees, to wit, Alexandria, Antioch, and the Holy City, as well as to all orthodox high-priests and priests, make this written confession of my faith, and I offer it to you as to those who have received power by apostolic authority. And in this also I beg pardon from your divinely gathered holiness for my tardiness in this matter. For it was not right that I should have fallen behind in the confession of orthodoxy, but it arose from my entire lack of knowledge, and slothful and negligent mind in the matter. Wherefore the rather I ask your blessedness to grant me indulgence in God's sight.

I believe, therefore, and make my confession in one God, the Father Almighty, and in one Lord Jesus Christ, his only begotten Son, and in the Holy Ghost, the Lord and Giver of Life. The Trinity, one in essence and one in majesty, must be worshipped and glorified in one godhead, power, and authority. I confess all things pertaining to the incarnation of one of the Holy Trinity, our Lord and God, Jesus Christ, as the Saints and the six Ecumenical Synods have handed down. And I reject and anathematize every heretical babbling, as they also have rejected them. I ask for the intercessions ($\pi\rho\epsilon\sigma\beta\epsilon\iota\alpha\varsigma$) of our spotless Lady the Holy Mother of God, and those of the holy and heavenly powers, and those of all the Saints.[1]

And receiving their holy and honourable reliques with all honour ($\tau\iota\mu\hat{\eta}\varsigma$), I salute and venerate these with honour ($\tau\iota\mu\eta\tau\iota\kappa\hat{\omega}\varsigma\ \pi\rho\sigma\kappa\upsilon\nu\epsilon\omega$), hoping to have a share in their holiness. Likewise also the venerable images ($\epsilon\iota\kappa\delta\nu\alpha\varsigma$) of the incarnation of our Lord Jesus Christ, in the humanity he assumed for our salvation; and of our spotless Lady, the holy Mother of God; and of the angels like unto God; and of the holy Apostles, Prophets, Martyrs, and of all the Saints—the sacred images of all these, I salute and venerate—rejecting and anathematizing with my whole soul and mind the synod which was gathered together out of stubbornness and madness, and which styled itself the Seventh Synod, but which by those who think accurately was called lawfully and canonically a pseudo-synod, as being contrary to all truth and piety, and audaciously and temerariously against the divinely handed down ecclesiastical legislation, yea, even impiously having yelped at and scoffed at the holy and venerable images, and having ordered these to be taken away out of the holy churches of God; over which assembly presided Theodosius with the pseudonym of Ephesius, Sisinnius of Perga, with the surname Pastillas, Basilius of Pisidia, falsely

---

[1] Thus far there was no expression of opinion from which the Iconoclasts would have dissented, for in all that regarded the Blessed Virgin and the Saints and their invocation and patronage, the heretics agreed with the orthodox. Protestants have been in the habit of treating the Iconoclasts as if they were substantially agreed with them with regard to the cultus of the Blessed Virgin and of the other Saints. What an error this is, is easily proved by citing two of the anathematisms of their Conciliabulum.

"If anyone shall not confess that the Ever-virgin Mary is properly and truly the Mother of God, and more exalted than every creature, whether visible or invisible, and does not seek her intercessions with sincere faith, because she has confidence in approaching our God, who was born of her, let him be anathema." (L. and C., *Conc.*, Tom. VII., col. 524.)

"If anyone does not confess that all the Saints from the beginning down to now, who whether before the Law, or under the Law, or in grace pleased God, should be honoured in his presence both with soul and body; and does not seek their prayers, according to the tradition of the Church as of those having confidence to plead for the world, let him be anathema." (*Ibid.* col. 528.)

called "tricaccabus;" with whom the wretched Constantine, the then Patriarch, was led (ἐματαιώϑη) astray.

These things thus I confess and to these I assent, and therefore in simplicity of heart and in uprightness of mind, in the presence of God, I have made the subjoined anathematisms.

Anathema to the calumniators of the Christians, that is to the image breakers.

Anathema to those who apply the words of Holy Scripture which were spoken against idols, to the venerable images.

Anathema to those who do not salute the holy and venerable images.

Anathema to those who say that Christians have recourse to the images as to gods.

Anathema to those who call the sacred images idols.

Anathema to those who knowingly communicate with those who revile and dishonour the venerable images.

Anathema to those who say that another than Christ our Lord hath delivered us from idols.

Anathema to those who spurn the teachings of the holy Fathers and the tradition of the Catholic Church, taking as a pretext and making their own the arguments of Arius, Nestorius, Eutyches, and Dioscorus, that unless we were evidently taught by the Old and New Testaments, we should not follow the teachings of the holy Fathers and of the holy Ecumenical Synods, and the tradition of the Catholic Church.

Anathema to those who dare to say that the Catholic Church hath at any time sanctioned idols.

Anathema to those who say that the making of images is a diabolical invention and not a tradition of our holy Fathers.

This is my confession [of faith] and to these propositions I give my assent. And I pronounce this with my whole heart, and soul, and mind.

And if at any time by the fraud of the devil (which may God forbid!) I voluntarily or involuntarily shall be opposed to what I have now professed, may I be anathema from the Father, the Son and the Holy Ghost, and from the Catholic Church and every hierarchical order a stranger.

I will keep myself from every acceptance of a bribe and from filthy lucre in accordance with the divine canons of the holy Apostles and of the approved Fathers.

Tarasius, the most holy Patriarch, said: This whole sacred gathering yields glory and thanks to God for this confession of yours, which you have made to the Catholic Church.

The Holy Synod said: Glory to God which maketh one that which was severed.

[*Theodore, bishop of Myra, then read the same confession, and was received. The next bishop who asked to be received read as follows: (col.* 60)]

Theodosius, the humble Christian, to the holy and Ecumenical Synod: I confess and I agree to (συντίϑεμαι) and I receive and I salute and I venerate in the first place the spotless image of our Lord Jesus Christ, our true God, and the holy image of her who bore him without seed, the holy Mother of God, and her help and protection and intercessions each day and night as a sinner to my aid I call for, since she has confidence with Christ our God, as he was born of her. Likewise also I receive and venerate the images of the holy and most laudable Apostles, prophets, and martyrs and the fathers and cultivators of the desert. Not indeed as gods (God forbid!) do I ask all these with my whole heart to pray for me to God, that he may grant me through their intercessions to find mercy at his hands at the day of judgment, for in this I am but showing forth more clearly the affection and love of my soul which I have borne them from the first. Likewise also I venerate and honour and salute the reliques of the Saints as of those who fought for Christ and who have received grace from him for the healing of diseases and the curing of sicknesses and the casting out of devils, as the Christian Church has received from the holy Apostles and Fathers even down to us to-day.

Moreover, I am well pleased that there should be images in the churches of the faithful, especially the image of our Lord Jesus Christ and of the holy Mother of God, of every kind of material, both gold and silver and of every colour, so that his incarnation may be set forth to all men. Likewise there may be painted the lives of the Saints and Prophets and Martyrs, so that their struggles and agonies may be set forth in brief, for the stirring up and teaching of the people, especially of the unlearned.

For if the people go forth with lights and incense to meet the "laurata" and images of the Emperors when they are sent to cities or rural districts, they honour surely not the tablet covered over with wax, but the Emperor himself. How much more is it necessary that in the churches of Christ our God, the image of God our Saviour and of his spotless Mother and of all the holy and blessed fathers and ascetics should be painted? Even as also St. Basil says: "Writers and painters set forth the great deeds of war; the one by word, the other by their pencils; and each stirs many to courage." And again the same author, "How much pains have you ever taken that you might find one of the Saints who was willing to be your importunate intercessor to the Lord?"[1] And Chrysostom says, "The charity of the Saints is not diminished by their death, nor does it come to an end with their exit from life, but after their death they are still more powerful than when they were alive," and many other things without measure. Therefore I ask you, O ye Saints! I call out to you. I have sinned against heaven and in your sight. Receive me as God received the luxurious man, and the harlot, and the thief. Seek me out, as Christ sought out the sheep that was lost, which he carried on his shoulders; so that there may be joy in the presence of God and of his angels over my salvation and repentance, through your intervention, O all-holy lords! Let them who do not venerate the holy and venerable images be anathema! Anathema to those who blaspheme against the honourable and venerable images! To those who dare to attack and blaspheme the venerable images and call them idols, anathema! To the calumniators of Christianity, that is to say the Iconoclasts, anathema! To those who do not diligently teach all the Christ-loving people to venerate and salute the venerable and sacred and honourable images of all the Saints who pleased God in their several generations, anathema! To those who have a doubtful mind and do not confess with their whole hearts that they venerate the sacred images, anathema!

Sabbas, the most reverend hegumenus of the monastery of the Studium, said: According to the Apostolic precepts and the Ecumenical Synods he is worthy to be received back.

Tarasius, the most holy Patriarch, said: Those who formerly were the calumniators of orthodoxy, now are become the advocates of the truth.

[*Near the end of this session,* (col. 77)]

John, the most reverend bishop and legate of the Eastern high priests said: This heresy is the worst of all heresies. Woe to the iconoclasts! It is the worst of heresies, as it subverts the incarnation ($οἰκονομίαν$) of our Saviour.[2]

---

[1] Mendham seems to have reversed the sense here altogether.

[2] In the English Hefele (Vol. V., p. 363) this appears in the following most extraordinary form. "John . . . declared that the veneration of images was the worst of all heresies 'because it detracted from the Economy (Incarnation) of the Redeemer.'" (!)

EXTRACTS FROM THE ACTS.

SESSION II.

[The Papal Letters were presented by the Legates. First was read that to Constantine and Irene, but not in its entirety, if we may trust Anastasius the Librarian, who gives what he says is the original Latin text. Here follows a translation of this and of the Greek, also a translation of the Latin passage altogether omitted, (as we are told) with the consent of the Roman Legates.]

PART OF POPE HADRIAN'S LETTER.

[As written by the Pope.]

(Migne, *Pat. Lat.*, Tom. XCVI., col. 1217.)

If you persevere in that orthodox Faith in which you have begun, and the sacred and venerable images be by your means erected again in those parts, as by the lord, the Emperor Constantine of pious memory, and the blessed Helen, who promulgated the orthodox Faith, and exalted the holy Catholic and Apostolic Roman Church your spiritual mother, and with the other orthodox Emperors venerated it as the head of all Churches, so will your Clemency, that is protected of God, receive the name of another Constantine, and another Helen, through whom at the beginning the holy Catholic and Apostolic Church derived strength, and like whom your own imperial fame is spread abroad by triumphs, so as to be brilliant and deeply fixed in the whole world. But the more, if following the traditions of the orthodox Faith, you embrace the judgment of the Church of blessed Peter, chief of the Apostles, and, as of old your predecessors the holy Emperors acted, so you, too, venerating it with honour, love with all your heart his Vicar, and if your sacred majesty follow by preference their orthodox Faith, according to our holy Roman Church. May the chief of the Apostles himself, to whom the power was given by our Lord God to bind and remit sins in heaven and earth, be often your protector, and trample all barbarous nations under your feet, and everywhere make you conquerors. For let sacred authority lay open the marks of his dignity, and how great veneration ought to be shewn to his, the highest See, by all the faithful in the world. For the Lord set him who bears the keys

[As read in Greek to the Council.]

(Migne, *Pat. Lat.*, Tom. XCVI., col. 1218.)

If the ancient orthodoxy be perfected and restored by your means in those regions, and the venerable icons be placed in their original state, you will be partakers with the Lord Constantine, Emperor of old, now in the Divine keeping, and the Empress Helena, who made conspicuous and confirmed the orthodox Faith, and exalted still more your holy mother, the Catholic and Roman and spiritual Church, and with the orthodox Emperors who ruled after them, and so your most pious and heaven-protected name likewise will be set forth as that of another Constantine and another Helena, being renowned and praised through the whole world, by whom the holy Catholic and Apostolic Church is restored. And especially if you follow the tradition of the orthodox Faith of the Church of the holy Peter and Paul, the chief Apostles, and embrace their Vicar, as the Emperors who reigned before you of old both honoured their Vicar, and loved him with all their heart: and if your sacred majesty honour the most holy Roman Church of the chief Apostles, to whom was given power by God the Word himself to loose and to bind sins in heaven and earth. For they will extend their shield over your power, and all barbarous nations shall be put under your feet: and wherever you go they will make you conquerors. For the holy and chief Apostles themselves, who set up the Catholic and orthodox Faith, have laid it down as a written law that all who after them are to be successors of their seats, should hold their Faith and remain in it to the end.

of the kingdom of heaven as chief over all, and by Him is he honoured with this privilege, by which the keys of the kingdom of heaven are entrusted to him. He, therefore, that was preferred with so exalted an honour was thought worthy to confess that Faith on which the Church of Christ is founded. A blessed reward followed that blessed confession, by the preaching of which the holy universal Church was illumined, and from it the other Churches of God have derived the proofs of Faith. For the blessed Peter himself, the chief of the Apostles, who first sat in the Apostolic See, left the chiefship of his Apostolate, and pastoral care, to his successors, who are to sit in his most holy seat for ever. And that power of authority, which he received from the Lord God our Saviour, he too bestowed and delivered by divine command to the Pontiffs, his successors, etc.

[The part which was never read to the Council at all.]

(Found in L. and C., *Concilia*, Tom. VII., col. 117.)

We greatly wondered that in your imperial commands, directed for the Patriarch of the royal city, Tarasius, we find him there called Universal: but we know not whether this was written through ignorance or schism, or the heresy of the wicked. But henceforth we advise your most merciful and imperial majesty, that he be by no means called Universal in your writings, because it appears to be contrary to the institutions of the holy Canons and the decrees of the traditions of the holy Fathers. For he never could have ranked second, save for the authority of our holy Catholic and Apostolic Church, as is plain to all.[1] Because if he be named Universal, above the holy Roman Church which has a prior rank, which is the head of all the Churches of God, it is certain that he shews himself as a rebel against the holy Councils, and a heretic. For, if he is Universal, he is recognized to have the Primacy even over the Church of our See, which appears ridiculous to all faithful Christians: because in the whole world the chief rank and power was given to the blessed Apostle Peter by the Redeemer of the world himself; and through the same Apostle, whose place we unworthily hold, the holy Catholic and Apostolic Roman Church holds the first rank, and the authority of power, now and for ever, so that if any one, which we believe not, has called him, or assents to his being called Universal, let him know that he is estranged from the orthodox Faith, and a rebel against our holy Catholic and Apostolic Church.

[After the reading was ended (col. 120)]

Tarasius the most holy patriarch said: Did you yourselves receive these letters from the most holy Pope, and did you carry them to our pious Emperor?

Peter and Peter the most beloved-of-God presbyters who held the place of Hadrian, the most holy pope of Rome, said: We ourselves received such letters from our apostolic father and delivered them to the pious lords.

John, the most magnificent Logothete, said: That this is the case is also known to the Sicilians, the beloved of God Theodore, the bishop of Catanea, and the most revered deacon Epiphanius who is with him,

[1] This statement seems somewhat open to criticism in view of the position taken by St. Leo, and of the assertion of Pope Gelasius that Constantinople was a suffragan see to Heraclea.

who holds the place of the archbishop of Sardinia.   For both of these at the bidding of our pious Emperors, went to Rome with the most reverend apocrisarius of our most holy patriarch.

Theodore the God-beloved bishop of Catanea, standing in the midst, said: The pious emperor, by his honourable jussio, bid send Leo, the most god-beloved presbyter (who together with myself is a slave of your holiness), with the precious letter of his most sacred majesty; and he who reveres our [*sic* in Greek, "your," in Latin] holiness, being the governor (στρατηγὸς) of my province of Sicily, sent me to Rome with the pious jussio of our orthodox Emperors.[1]

And when we were gone, we announced the orthodox faith of the pious emperors.

And when the most blessed Pope heard it, he said: Since this has come to pass in the days of their reign, God has magnified their pious rule above all former reigns. And this suggestion (ἀναφορὰν) which has been read he sent to our most pious kings together with a letter to your holiness and with his vicars who are here present and presiding.

Cosmas, the deacon, notary, and chamberlain (*Cubuclesius*) said: And another letter was sent by the most holy Pope of Old Rome to Tarasius, our most holy and œcumenical Patriarch.   Let it be disposed of as your holy assembly shall direct.

The Holy Synod said, Let it be read.

[*Then was read Hadrian's letter to Tarasius of Constantinople, which ends by saying that,* " our dearly-loved proto-presbyter of the Holy Church of Rome, and Peter, a monk, a presbyter, and an abbot, who have been sent by us to the most tranquil and pious emperors, we beg you will deem them worthy of all kindness and humane amenity for the sake of St. Peter, coropheus of the Apostles, and for our sakes, so that for this we may be able to offer you our sincere thanks."[2] *The letter being ended* (col. 128),]

Peter and Peter, the most reverend presbyters and representatives of the most holy

Pope of Old Rome said: Let the most holy Tarasius, Patriarch of the royal city, say whether he agrees (στοιχεῖ) with the letters of the most holy Pope of Old Rome or not.

Tarasius the most holy patriarch said: The divine Apostle Paul, who was filled with the light of Christ, and who hath begotten us through the gospel, in writing to the Romans, commending their zeal for the true faith which they had in Christ our true God, thus said: "Your faith is gone forth into all the world."   It is necessary to follow out this witness, and he that would contradict it is without good sense.   Wherefore Hadrian, the ruler of Old Rome, since he was a sharer of these things, thus borne witness to, wrote expressly and truly to our religious Emperors, and to our humility, confirming admirably and beautifully the ancient tradition of the Catholic Church. And we also ourselves, having examined both in writing,[3] and by inquisition, and syllogistically and by demonstration, and having been taught by the teachings of the Fathers, so have confessed, so do confess, and so will confess; and shall be fast, and shall remain, and shall stand firm in the sense of the letters which have just been read, receiving the imaged representations according to the ancient tradition of our holy fathers; and these we venerate with firmly-attached[4] affection, as made in the name of Christ our God, and of our Spotless Lady the Holy Mother of God, and of the Holy Angels, and of all the Saints, most clearly giving our adoration and faith to the one only true God.

And the holy Synod said: The whole holy Synod thus teaches.

messengers, two priests without any special commission, and who were disavowed on their return.   Some vagabond monks were persuaded by the Catholics to represent the Oriental patriarchs. This curious anecdote is revealed by Theodore Studites, one of the warmest Iconoclasts of the age."   And yet to this tissue of false statements Bury, in his just-published edition of Gibbon (1898), has no note of correction to make!   And this has passed, and will pass, for history among the overwhelming majority of English readers!   Nor does there seem to be any possible excuse for Gibbon in either particular, the first statement is proved to be false by the letters of Hadrian, the second statement is equally disproved by the letters of the "high priests of the East," in which it is quite clear that no claim was set up that they represented the Patriarchs, but the Patriarchates, which they did, as they proved, in a very real sense.   This letter Gibbon must have seen, if indeed he ever took the trouble to read the Acts, for it is spread out in full in Actio Secunda and was read at length to the Council.

[1] The meaning of the passage is obscure, but Mendham's translation seems clearly wrong.

[2] Compare with this the statement of the famous historian, Gibbon (Chapter XLIX., N. 79), "The pope's legates were casual

[3] Mendham here has translated "The Scriptures," following the Latin, the Greek is γραφικῶς.

[4] Mendham translates σχετικῷ "relative," which is a quite possible rendering.

Peter and Peter, the God-loved presbyters and legates of the Apostolic See, said: Let the holy Synod say whether it receives the letters of the most holy Pope of Old Rome.

The holy Synod said: We follow, we receive, we admit them.

[*The bishops then give one by one their votes all in the same sense.*]

EXTRACTS FROM THE ACTS.

SESSION III.

(Labbe and Cossart, *Concilia*, Tom. VII., col. 188.)

CONSTANTINE, the most holy bishop of Constantia in Cyprus, said: Since I, unworthy that I am, find that the letter which has just been read, which was sent from the East to Tarasius the most holy archbishop and ecumenical patriarch, is in no sense changed from that confession of faith which he himself had before made, to these I consent and become of one mind, receiving and saluting with honour the holy and venerable images. But the worship of adoration I reserve alone to the supersubstantial and life-giving Trinity. And those who are not so minded, and do not so teach I cast out of the holy Catholic and Apostolic Church, and I smite them with anathema, and I deliver them over to the lot of those who deny the incarnation and the bodily economy of Christ our true God.

NOTES.

HEFELE.

(*Hist. Councils*, Vol. V., p. 366.)

By false translation and misunderstanding the Frankish bishops subsequently at the Synod of Frankfort, A.D. 794, and also in the Carolingian books (iii. 17), understood this to mean that a demand had been made at Nicæa that the same devotion should be offered to the images as to the Most Holy Trinity.

Under these circumstances it is clear that the Franks could do nothing but reject the decrees. I have treated of this whole matter elsewhere.

EXTRACTS FROM THE ACTS.

SESSION IV.

(Labbe and Cossart, *Concilia*, Tom. VII., col. 204.)

[*Among numerous passages of the Fathers one was read from a sermon by St. Gregory Nyssen in which he describes a painting representing the sacrifice of Isaac and tells how he could not pass it "without tears."*]

The most glorious princes said: See how our father grieved at the depicted history, even so that he wept.

Basil, the most holy bishop of Ancyra, said: Many times the father had read the story, but perchance he had not wept; but when once he saw it painted, he wept.

John the most reverend monk and presbyter and representative of the Eastern high priests, said: If to such a doctor the picture was helpful and drew forth tears, how much more in the case of the ignorant and simple will it bring compunction and benefit.

The holy Synod said: We have seen in several places the history of Abraham painted as the father says.

Theodore the most holy bishop of Catanea, said: If the holy Gregory, vigilant [1] in divine cogitation, was moved to tears at the sight of the story of Abraham, how much more shall a painting of the incarnation of our Lord Christ, who for us was made man,

---

[1] It is impossible in English to reproduce the play upon the words Γρηγόριος ὁ γρηγορῶν εἰς τὰ θεῖα νοήματα, κ. τ. λ.

move the beholders to their profit and to tears?

Tarasius the most holy Patriarch said: Shall we not weep when we see an image of our crucified Lord?

The holy Synod said: We shall indeed —for in that shall be found perfectly the profundity of the abasement of the incarnate God for our sakes.

[*Post nonnulla a passage is read from St. Athanasius in which he describes the miracles worked at Berytus, after which there is found the following* (col. 224),]

Tarasius, the most holy Patriarch, said: But perhaps someone will say, Why do not the images which we have work miracles? To which we answer, that as the Apostle has said, signs are for those who do not believe, not for believers. For they who approached that image were unbelievers. Therefore God gave them a sign through the image, to draw them to our Christian faith. But "an evil and adulterous generation that seeketh after a sign and no sign shall be given it."

[*After a number of other quotations, was read the Canon of the Council in Trullo as a canon of the Sixth Synod* (col. 233).]

Tarasius, the most holy Patriarch said: There are certain affected with the sickness of ignorance who are scandalized by these canons [viz. of the Trullan Synod] and say, And do you really think they were adopted at the Sixth Synod? Now let all such know that the holy great Sixth Synod was assembled at Constantinople concerning those who said that there was but one energy and will in Christ. These anathematized the heretics, and having expounded the orthodox faith, they went to their homes in the fourteenth year of Constantine. But after four or five years the same[1] fathers came together under Justinian, the son of Constantine, and set forth the before-mentioned canons. And let no one doubt concerning them. For they who subscribed under Constantine were the same as they who under Justinian signed the present chart, as can manifestly be established from the unchangeable similarity of their own hand-

writing. For it was right that they who had appeared at an ecumenical synod should also set forth ecclesiastical canons. They said that we should be led as (by the hand) by the venerable images to the recollection of the incarnation of Christ and of his saving death, and if by them we are led to the realization of the incarnation of Christ our God, what sort of an opinion shall we have of them who break down the venerable images?

[*At the close of the Session, after a number of anathematisms had been pronounced, the following was read, to which all the bishops subscribed* (col. 317).]

Fulfilling the divine precept of our God and Saviour Jesus Christ, our holy Fathers did not hide the light of the divine knowledge given by him to them under a bushel, but they set it upon the candlestick of most useful teaching, so that it might give light to all in the house—that is to say, to those who are born in the Catholic Church; lest perchance anyone of those who piously confess the Lord might strike his foot against the stone of heretical evil doctrine. For they expelled every error of heretics and they cut off the rotten member if it was incurably sick. And with a fan they purged the floor. And the good wheat, that is to say the word which nourisheth and which maketh strong the heart of man, they laid up in the granary of the Catholic Church; but throwing outside the chaff of heretical evil opinion they burned it with unquenchable fire. Therefore also this holy and ecumenical Synod, met together for the second time in this illustrious metropolis of Nice, by the will of God and at the bidding of our pious and most faithful Emperors, Irene a new Helena, and a new Constantine, her God-protected offspring, having considered by their perusal the teachings of our approved and blessed Fathers, hath glorified God himself, from whom there was given to them wisdom for our instruction, and for the perfecting of the Catholic and Apostolic Church: and against those who do not believe as they did, but have attempted to overshadow the truth through their novelty, they have chanted the words of the psalm:[2] "Oh how much evil have thine enemies done

---

[1] We have seen that this is an error. Vide Introduction to Trullan Canons.

[2] The reference is to Ps. lxxiv. 3, but the text is quite different from ours.

in thy sanctuary; and have glorified themselves, saying, There is not a teacher any more, and they shall not know that we treated with guile the word of truth." But we, in all things holding the doctrines and precepts of the same our God-bearing Fathers, make proclamation with one mouth and one heart, neither adding anything, nor taking anything away from those things which have been delivered to us by them. But in these things we are strengthened, in these things we are confirmed. Thus we confess, thus we teach, just as the holy and ecumenical six Synods have decreed and ratified. We believe in one God the Father Almighty, maker of all things visible and invisible; and in one Lord Jesus Christ, his only-begotten Son and Word, through whom all things were made, and in the Holy Ghost, the Lord and giver of life, consubstantial and coeternal with the same Father and with his Son who hath had no beginning. The unbuilt-up, indivisible, incomprehensible, and non-circumscribed Trinity; he, wholly and alone, is to be worshipped and revered with adoration; one Godhead, one Lordship, one dominion, one realm and dynasty, which without division is apportioned to the Persons, and is fitted to the essence severally. For we confess that one of the same holy and consubstantial Trinity, our Lord Jesus Christ the true God, in these last days was incarnate and made man for our salvation, and having saved our race through his saving incarnation, and passion, and resurrection, and ascension into heaven; and having delivered us from the error of idols; as also the prophet says, Not an ambassador, not an angel, but the Lord himself hath saved us. Him we also follow, and adopt his voice, and cry aloud; No Synod, no power of kings, no God-hated agreement hath delivered the Church from the error of the idols, as the Jewdaizing conciliabulum hath madly dreamed, which raved against the venerable images; but the Lord of glory himself, the incarnate God, hath saved us and hath snatched us from idolatrous deceit. To him therefore be glory, to him be thanks, to him be eucharists, to him be praise, to him be magnificence. For his redemption and his salvation alone can perfectly save, and not that of other men who come of the earth. For he himself hath fulfilled for us, upon whom the ends of the earth are come through the economy of his incarnation, the words spoken beforehand by his prophets, for he dwelt among us, and went in and out among us, and cast out the names of idols from the earth, as it was written. But we salute the voices of the Lord and of his Apostles through which we have been taught to honour in the first place her who is properly and truly the Mother of God and exalted above all the heavenly powers; also the holy and angelic powers; and the blessed and altogether lauded Apostles, and the glorious Prophets and the triumphant Martyrs which fought for Christ, and the holy and God-bearing Doctors, and all holy men; and to seek for their intercessions, as able to render us at home with the all-royal God of all, so long as we keep his commandments, and strive to live virtuously. Moreover we salute the image of the honourable and life-giving Cross, and the holy reliques of the Saints; and we receive the holy and venerable images: and we salute them, and we embrace them, according to the ancient traditions of the holy Catholic Church of God, that is to say of our holy Fathers, who also received these things and established them in all the most holy Churches of God, and in every place of his dominion. These honourable and venerable images, as has been said, we honour and salute and reverently venerate: to wit, the image of the incarnation of our great God and Saviour Jesus Christ, and that of our spotless Lady the all-holy Mother of God, from whom he pleased to take flesh, and to save and deliver us from all impious idolatry; also the images of the holy and incorporeal Angels, who as men appeared to the just. Likewise also the figures and effigies of the divine and all-lauded Apostles, also of the God-speaking Prophets, and of the struggling Martyrs and of holy men. So that through their representations we may be able to be led back in memory and recollection to the prototype, and have a share in the holiness of some one of them.

Thus we have learned to think of these things, and we have been strengthened by our holy Fathers, and we have been strengthened by their divinely handed down teaching. And thanks be to God for his ineffable gift, that he hath not deserted us at the end nor hath the rod of the ungodly come into the lot of the righteous, lest the righteous put their hands, that is to say their actual deeds,[1] unto wickedness. But he doeth well unto those who are good and true of heart, as the psalmist David melodiously has sung; with whom also we sing the rest of the psalm: As for such as turn back unto their own wickedness, the Lord shall lead them forth with the evil doers; and peace shall be upon the Israel of God.

[*The subscriptions follow immediately and close the acts of this session (col. 321–346).*]

EXTRACTS FROM THE ACTS.

SESSION VI.

(Labbe and Cossart, *Concilia*, Tom. VII., col. 389.)

LEO the most renowned secretary said: The holy and blessed Synod know how at the last session we examined divers sayings of the God-forsaken heretics, who had brought charges against the holy and spotless Church of the Christians for the setting up of the holy images. But to-day we have in our hands the written blasphemy of those calumniators of the Christians, that is to say, the absurd, and easily answered, and self-convicting definition (ὅρον) of the pseudosyllogus, in all respects agreeing with the impious opinion of the God-hated heretics. But not only have we this, but also the artful and most drastic refutation thereof, which the Holy Spirit had supervised. For it was right that this definition should be made a triumph by wise contradictions, and should be torn to pieces with strong refutations. This also we submit so as to know your pleasure with regard to it.

The holy Synod said: Let it be read.

John, the deacon and chancellor [of the most holy great Church of Constantinople, *in Lat. only*] read.

[*John, the deacon, then read the orthodox refutation, and Gregory, the bishop of Neocæsarea, the Definition of the Mock Council, the one reading the heretical statement and the other the orthodox answer.*]

---

[1] This obscure phrase Mendham omits altogether.

EPITOME OF THE DEFINITION OF THE ICONOCLASTIC CONCILIABULUM, HELD IN CONSTANTINOPLE, A.D. 754.[1]

THE DEFINITION OF THE HOLY, GREAT, AND ECUMENICAL SEVENTH SYNOD.

The holy and Ecumenical synod, which by the grace of God and most pious command of the God-beloved and orthodox Emperors, Constantine and Leo,[2] now assembled in the imperial residence city, in the temple of the holy and inviolate Mother of God and Virgin Mary, surnamed in Blachernæ, have decreed as follows.

Satan misguided men, so that they worshipped the creature instead of the Creator. The Mosaic law and the prophets co-operated to undo this ruin ; but in order to save mankind thoroughly, God sent his own Son, who turned us away from error and the worshipping of idols, and taught us the worshipping of God in spirit and in truth. As messengers of his saving doctrine, he left us his Apostles and disciples, and these adorned the Church, his Bride, with his glorious doctrines. This ornament of the Church the holy Fathers and the six Ecumenical Councils have preserved inviolate. But the before-mentioned demiurgos of wickedness could not endure the sight of this adornment, and gradually brought back idolatry under the appearance of Christianity. As then Christ armed his Apostles against the ancient idolatry with the power of the Holy Spirit, and sent them out into all the world, so has he awakened against the new idolatry his servants our faithful Emperors, and endowed them with the same wisdom of the Holy Spirit. Impelled by the Holy Spirit they could no longer be witnesses of the Church being laid waste by the deception of demons, and summoned the sanctified assembly of the God-beloved bishops, that they might institute at a synod a scriptural examination into the deceitful colouring of the pictures (ὁμοιωμάτων) which draws down the spirit of man from the lofty adoration (λατρείας) of God to the low and material adoration (λατρείαν) of the creature, and that they, under divine guidance, might express their view on the subject. Our holy synod therefore assembled, and we, its 338 members, follow the older synodal decrees, and accept and proclaim joyfully the dogmas handed down, principally those of the six holy Ecumenical Synods. In the first place the holy and ecumenical great synod assembled at Nice, etc.

After we had carefully examined their decrees under the guidance of the Holy Spirit, we found that the unlawful art of painting living creatures blasphemed the fundamental doctrine of our salvation—namely, the Incarnation of Christ, and contradicted the six holy synods. These condemned Nestorius because he divided the one Son and Word of God into two sons, and on the other side, Arius, Dioscorus, Eutyches, and Severus, because they maintained a mingling of the two natures of the one Christ.

Wherefore we thought it right, to shew forth with all accuracy, in our present definition the error of such as make and venerate these, for it is the unanimous doctrine of all the holy Fathers and of the six Ecumenical Synods, that no one may imagine any kind of separation or mingling in opposition to the unsearchable, unspeakable, and incomprehensible union of the two natures in the one hypostasis or person. What avails, then, the folly of the painter, who from sinful love of gain depicts that which should not be depicted—that is, with his polluted hands he tries to fashion that which should only be believed in the heart and confessed with the mouth? He makes an image and calls it Christ. The name *Christ* signifies *God and man*. Consequently it is an image of God and man, and consequently he has in his foolish mind, in his representation of the created flesh, depicted the Godhead which cannot be represented, and thus mingled what should not be mingled. Thus he is guilty of a double blasphemy—the one in making an image of the Godhead, and the other by mingling the Godhead and manhood. Those fall into the same blasphemy who venerate

---

[1] In this epitome of the verbose definition of the council, I have followed for the most part Hefele. (*Hist. of the Councils*, Vol. V., p. 309 *et seqq*.)
[2] Now four years old.

the image, and the same woe rests upon both, because they err with Arius, Dioscorus, and Eutyches, and with the heresy of the Acephali. When, however, they are blamed for undertaking to depict the divine nature of Christ, which should not be depicted, they take refuge in the excuse : We represent only the flesh of Christ which we have seen and handled. But that is a Nestorian error. For it should be considered that that flesh was also the flesh of God the Word, without any separation, perfectly assumed by the divine nature and made wholly divine. How could it now be separated and represented apart ? So is it with the human soul of Christ which mediates between the Godhead of the Son and the dulness of the flesh. As the human flesh is at the same time flesh of God the Word, so is the human soul also soul of God the Word, and both at the same time, the soul being deified as well as the body, and the Godhead remained undivided even in the separation of the soul from the body in his voluntary passion. For where the soul of Christ is, there is also his Godhead ; and where the body of Christ is, there too is his Godhead. If then in his passion the divinity remained inseparable from these, how do the fools venture to separate the flesh from the Godhead, and represent it by itself as the image of a mere man ? They fall into the abyss of impiety, since they separate the flesh from the Godhead, ascribe to it a subsistence of its own, a personality of its own, which they depict, and thus introduce a fourth person into the Trinity. Moreover, they represent as not being made divine, that which has been made divine by being assumed by the Godhead. Whoever, then, makes an image of Christ, either depicts the Godhead which cannot be depicted, and mingles it with the manhood (like the Monophysites), or he represents the body of Christ as not made divine and separate and as a person apart, like the Nestorians.

The only admissible figure of the humanity of Christ, however, is bread and wine in the holy Supper. This and no other form, this and no other type, has he chosen to represent his incarnation. Bread he ordered to be brought, but not a representation of the human form, so that idolatry might not arise. And as the body of Christ is made divine, so also this figure of the body of Christ, the bread, is made divine by the descent of the Holy Spirit ; it becomes the divine body of Christ by the mediation of the priest who, separating the oblation from that which is common, sanctifies it.

The evil custom of assigning names to the images does not come down from Christ and the Apostles and the holy Fathers ; nor have these left behind them any prayer by which an image should be hallowed or made anything else than ordinary matter.

If, however, some say, we might be right in regard to the images of Christ, on account of the mysterious union of the two natures, but it is not right for us to forbid also the images of the altogether spotless and ever-glorious Mother of God, of the prophets, apostles, and martyrs, who were mere men and did not consist of two natures ; we may reply, first of all : If those fall away, there is no longer need of these. But we will also consider what may be said against these in particular. Christianity has rejected the *whole* of heathenism, and so not merely heathen sacrifices, but also the heathen worship of images. The Saints live on eternally with God, although they have died. If anyone thinks to call them back again to life by a dead art, discovered by the heathen, he makes himself guilty of blasphemy. Who dares attempt with heathenish art to paint the Mother of God, who is exalted above all heavens and the Saints ? It is not permitted to Christians, who have the hope of the resurrection, to imitate the customs of demon-worshippers, and to insult the Saints, who shine in so great glory, by common dead matter.

Moreover, we can prove our view by Holy Scripture and the Fathers. In the former it is said : "God is a Spirit : and they that worship him must worship him in spirit and in truth ;" and : "Thou shalt not make thee any graven image, or any likeness of any thing that is in heaven above, or that is in the earth beneath ;" on which account God spoke to the Israelites on the Mount, from the midst of the fire, but showed them no image. Further : "They changed the glory of the incorruptible God into an image made like to corruptible man, . . . and served the creature more than the Creator." [*Several other passages, even less to the point, are cited.*] [1]

---

[1] These are Hefele's words.

The same is taught also by the holy Fathers. [*The Synod appeals to a spurious passage from Epiphanius and to one inserted into the writings of Theodotus of Ancyra, a friend of St. Cyril's ; to utterances—in no way striking—of Gregory of Nazianzum, of SS. Chrysostom, Basil, Athanasius, of Amphilochius and of Eusebius Pamphili, from his Letter to the Empress Constantia, who had asked him for a picture of Christ.*] [1]

Supported by the Holy Scriptures and the Fathers, we declare unanimously, in the name of the Holy Trinity, that there shall be rejected and removed and cursed out of the Christian Church every likeness which is made out of any material and colour whatever by the evil art of painters.

Whoever in future dares to make such a thing, or to venerate it, or set it up in a church, or in a private house, or possesses it in secret, shall, if bishop, presbyter, or deacon, be deposed; if monk or layman, be anathematised, and become liable to be tried by the secular laws as an adversary of God and an enemy of the doctrines handed down by the Fathers. At the same time we ordain that no incumbent of a church shall venture, under pretext of destroying the error in regard to images, to lay his hands on the holy vessels in order to have them altered, because they are adorned with figures. The same is provided in regard to the vestments of churches, cloths, and all that is dedicated to divine service. If, however, the incumbent of a church wishes to have such church vessels and vestments altered, he must do this only with the assent of the holy Ecumenical patriarch and at the bidding of our pious Emperors. So also no prince or secular official shall rob the churches, as some have done in former times, under the pretext of destroying images. All this we ordain, believing that we speak as doth the Apostle, for we also believe that we have the spirit of Christ; and as our predecessors who believed the same thing spake what they had synodically defined, so we believe and therefore do we speak, and set forth a definition of what has seemed good to us following and in accordance with the definitions of our Fathers.

(1) If anyone shall not confess, according

to the tradition of the Apostles and Fathers, in the Father, the Son and the Holy Ghost one godhead, nature and substance, will and operation, virtue and dominion, kingdom and power in three subsistences, that is in their most glorious Persons, let him be anathema.

(2) If anyone does not confess that one of the Trinity was made flesh, let him be anathema.

(3) If anyone does not confess that the holy Virgin is truly the Mother of God, etc.

(4) If anyone does not confess one Christ both God and man, etc.

(5) If anyone does not confess that the flesh of the Lord is life-giving because it is the flesh of the Word of God, etc.

(6) If anyone does not confess two natures in Christ, etc.

(7) If anyone does not confess that Christ is seated with God the Father in body and soul, and so will come to judge, and that he will remain God forever without any grossness, etc.

(8) If anyone ventures to represent the divine image ($\chi\alpha\rho\alpha\kappa\tau\acute{\eta}\rho$) of the Word after the Incarnation with material colours, let him be anathema !

(9) If anyone ventures to represent in human figures, by means of material colours, by reason of the incarnation, the substance or person (*ousia* or *hypostasis*) of the Word, which cannot be depicted, and does not rather confess that even after the Incarnation he [*i.e.*, the Word] cannot be depicted, let him be anathema !

(10) If anyone ventures to represent the hypostatic union of the two natures in a picture, and calls it Christ, and thus falsely represents a union of the two natures, etc.!

(11) If anyone separates the flesh united with the person of the Word from it, and endeavours to represent it separately in a picture, etc.!

(12) If anyone separates the one Christ into two persons, and endeavours to represent Him who was born of the Virgin separately, and thus accepts only a relative ($\sigma\chi\epsilon\tau\iota\kappa\acute{\eta}$) union of the natures, etc.

(13) If anyone represents in a picture the flesh deified by its union with the Word, and thus separates it from the Godhead, etc.

(14) If anyone endeavours to represent by material colours, God the Word as a mere man, who, although bearing the form

---

[1] These are Hefele's words.

of God, yet has assumed the form of a servant in his own person, and thus endeavours to separate him from his inseparable Godhead, so that he thereby introduces a quaternity into the Holy Trinity, etc.

(15) If anyone shall not confess the holy ever-virgin Mary, truly and properly the Mother of God, to be higher than every creature whether visible or invisible, and does not with sincere faith seek her intercessions as of one having confidence in her access to our God, since she bare him, etc.

(16) If anyone shall endeavour to represent the forms of the Saints in lifeless pictures with material colours which are of no value (for this notion is vain and introduced by the devil), and does not rather represent their virtues as living images in himself, etc.

(17) If anyone denies the profit of the invocation of Saints, etc.

(18) If anyone denies the resurrection of the dead, and the judgment, and the condign retribution to everyone, endless torment and endless bliss, etc.

(19) If anyone does not accept this our Holy and Ecumenical Seventh Synod, let him be anathema from the Father and the Son and the Holy Ghost, and from the seven holy Ecumenical Synods!

[*Then follows the prohibition of the making or teaching any other faith, and the penalties for disobedience. After this follow the acclamations.*]

The divine Kings Constantine and Leo said: Let the holy and ecumenical synod say, if with the consent of all the most holy bishops the definition just read has been set forth.

The holy synod cried out: Thus we all believe, we all are of the same mind. We have all with one voice and voluntarily subscribed. This is the faith of the Apostles. Many years to the Emperors! They are the light of orthodoxy! Many years to the orthodox Emperors! God preserve your Empire! You have now more firmly proclaimed the inseparability of the two natures of Christ! You have banished all idolatry! You have destroyed the heresies of Germanus [of Constantinople], George and Mansur [μανσουρ, John Damascene]. Anathema to Germanus, the double-minded, and worshipper of wood! Anathema to George, his associate, to the falsifier of the doctrine of the Fathers! Anathema to Mansur, who has an evil name and Saracen opinions! To the betrayer of Christ and the enemy of the Empire, to the teacher of impiety, the perverter of Scripture, Mansur, anathema! The Trinity has deposed these three![1]

---

[1] These are not given in full but are sufficient to give the true gist.

EXCURSUS ON THE CONCILIABULUM STYLING ITSELF THE SEVENTH ECUMENICAL COUNCIL, BUT COMMONLY CALLED THE MOCK SYNOD OF CONSTANTINOPLE.

A.D. 754.

The reader will find all the information he desires with regard to the great iconoclastic controversy in the ordinary church-histories, and the theological side of the matter in the writings of St. John Damascene. It seems, however, that in order to render the meaning of the action of the last of the Ecumenical Councils clear it is necessary to provide an account of the synod which was held to condemn what it so shortly afterward expressly approved. I quote from Hefele *in loco*, and would only further draw the reader's attention to the fact that the main thing objected to was not (as is commonly supposed) the outward veneration of the sacred icons, but the making and setting up of them, as architectural ornaments; and that it was not only representations of the persons of the Most Holy Trinity, and of the Divine Son in his incarnate form that were denounced, but even pictures of the Blessed Virgin and of the other saints; all this is evident to anyone reading the foregoing abstract of the decree.

(Hefele, *History of the Councils*, Vol. V., p. 308 *et seqq.*)

The Emperor, after the death of the Patriarch Anastasius (A.D. 753), summoned the bishops of his Empire to a great synod in the palace Hieria, which lay opposite to Constantinople on the Asiatic side of the Bosphorus, between Chrysopolis and Chalcedon, a little to the north of the latter. The vacancy of the patriarchate facilitated his plans, since the hope of succeeding to this see kept down, in the most ambitious and aspiring of the bishops, any possible thought of opposition. The number of those present amounted to 338 bishops, and the place of president was occupied by Archbishop Theodosius of Ephesus, already known to us as son of a former Emperor—Apsimar, from the beginning an assistant in the iconoclastic movement. Nicephorus names him alone as president of the synod ; Theophanes, on the contrary, mentions Bishop Pastillas of Perga as second president, and adds, " The Patriarchates of Rome, Alexandria, Antioch, and Jerusalem were not represented [the last three were then in the hands of the Saracens], the transactions began on February 10th, and lasted until August 8th (in Hieria) ; on the latter date, however, the synod assembled in St. Mary's Church in Blachernæ, the northern suburb of Constantinople, and the Emperor now solemnly nominated Bishop Constantine of Sylæum, a monk, as patriarch of Constantinople. On August 27th, the heretical decree [of the Synod] was published."

We see from this that the last sessions of this Conciliabulum were held no longer in Hieria, but in the Blachernæ of Constantinople. We have no complete Acts of this assembly, but its very verbose ὅρος (decree), together with a short introduction, is preserved among the acts of the Seventh Ecumenical Council.

This decree was by no means suffered to remain inoperative.

(W. M. Sinclair. Smith and Wace, *Dictionary of Chr. Biog.*, *sub voce* Constantinus VI.)

The Emperor singled out the more noted monks, and required them to comply with the decrees of the synod. In A.D. 766 he exacted an oath against images from all the inhabitants of the empire. The monks refused with violent obstinacy, and Copronymus appears to have amused himself by treating them with ruthless harshness. The Emperor, indeed, seems to have contemplated the extirpation of monachism. John the Damascene he persuaded his bishops to excommunicate. Monks were forced to appear in the hippodrome at Constantinople hand in hand with harlots, while the populace spat at them. The new patriarch Constantinus, presented by the emperor to the council the last day of its session, was forced to foreswear images, to attend banquets, to eat and drink freely against his monastic vows, to wear garlands, to witness the coarse spectacles and hear the coarse language which entertained the Emperor. Monasteries were destroyed, made into barracks, or secularized. Lachanodraco, governor of the Thracian Theme, seems to have exceeded Copronymus in his ribaldry and injustice. He collected a number of monks into a plain, clothed them with white, presented them with wives, and forced them to choose between marriage and loss of eyesight. He sold the property of the monasteries, and sent the price to the Emperor. Copronymus publicly thanked him, and commended his example to other governors.

(Harnack. *History of Dogma*, Vol. V., p. 325 [Eng. Tr.].)

The clergy obeyed when the decrees were published ; but resistance was offered in the ranks of the monks. Many took to flight, some became martyrs. The imperial police stormed the churches, and destroyed those images and pictures that had not been secured. The iconoclastic zeal by no means sprang from enthusiasm for divine service in spirit and in truth. The Emperor now also directly attacked the monks ; he meant to extirpate the hated order, and to overthrow the throne of Peter. We see how the idea of an absolute military state rose powerfully in Constantinople ; how it strove to establish itself by brute force. The Emperor, according to trustworthy evidence, made the inhabitants of the city swear that they would henceforth worship no image, and give up all intercourse with monks. Cloisters were turned into arsenals and barracks, relics were hurled into the sea, and the monks, as far as possible, secularized. And the politically far-seeing Emperor, at the same time entered into correspondence with France (Synod of Gentilly, A.D. 767), and sought to win Pepin. History seemed to have suffered a violent rupture, a new era was dawning which should supersede the history of the Church.

But the Church was too powerful, and the Emperor was not even master of Oriental Christendom, but only of part of it. The orthodox Patriarchs of the East (under the rule of Islam) declared against the iconoclastic movement, and a Church without monks or pictures, in schism with the other orthodox Churches, was a nonentity. A spiritual reformer was wanting. Thus the great reaction set in after the death of the Emperor (A.D. 775), the ablest ruler Constantinople had seen for a long time. This is not the place to describe how it was inaugurated and cautiously carried out by the skilful policy of the Empress Irene ; cautiously, for a generation had already grown up that was accustomed to the cultus without images. An important part was played by the miracles performed by the re-emerging relics and pictures. But the lower classes had always been really favourable to them ; only the army and the not inconsiderable number of bishops who were of the school of Constantine had to be carefully handled. Tarasius, the new Patriarch of Constantinople and a supporter of images, succeeded, after overcoming much difficulty, and especially distrust in Rome and the East, after also removing the excited army, in bringing together a General Council of about 350 bishops at Nicæa, A.D. 787, which reversed the decrees of A.D. 754. The proceedings of the seven sittings are of great value, because very important patristic passages have been preserved in them which otherwise would have perished ; for at this synod also the discussions turned chiefly on the Fathers. The decision (ὅρος) restored orthodoxy and finally settled it.

I cannot do better than to cite in conclusion the words of the profoundly learned Archbishop of Dublin, himself a quasi-Iconoclast.

(Trench. *Lect. Medieval Ch. Hist.*, p. 93.)

It is only fair to state that the most zealous favourers and promoters of this ill-directed homage always disclaimed with indignation the charge of offering to the images any reverence which did not differ in kind, and not merely in degree, from the worship which they offered to Almighty God, designating it as they did by altogether a different name. We shall very probably feel that in these distinctions which they drew between the one and the other, between the "honour" which they gave to these icons and the "worship" which they withheld from these and gave only to God, there lay no slightest justification of that in which they allowed themselves ; but these distinctions acquit them of idolatry, and it is the merest justice to remember this.

(Trench. *Ut supra*, p. 99.)

I can close this Lecture with no better or wiser words than those with which Dean Milman reads to us the lesson of this mournful story : "There was this irremediable weakness in the cause of iconoclasm ; it was a mere negative doctrine, a proscription of those sentiments which had full possession of the popular mind, without any strong countervailing excitement. The senses were robbed of their habitual and cherished objects of devotion, but there was no awakening of an inner life of intense and passionate piety. The cold, naked walls from whence the Scriptural histories had been effaced, the despoiled shrines, the mutilated images, could not compel the mind to a more pure and immaterial conception of God and the Saviour. Hatred of images, in the process of the strife, might become, as it did, a fanaticism, it could never become a religion. Iconoclasm might proscribe idolatry ; but it had no power of kindling a purer faith."

THE DECREE OF THE HOLY, GREAT, ECUMENICAL SYNOD, THE SECOND OF NICE.

(Found in Labbe and Cossart, Concilia. Tom. VII., col. 552.)

The holy, great, and Ecumenical Synod which by the grace of God and the will of the pious and Christ-loving Emperors, Constantine and Irene, his mother, was gathered together for the second time at Nice, the illustrious metropolis of Bithynia, in the holy church of God which is named Sophia, having followed the tradition of the Catholic Church, hath defined as follows:

Christ our Lord, who hath bestowed upon us the light of the knowledge of himself, and hath redeemed us from the darkness of idolatrous madness, having espoused to himself the Holy Catholic Church without spot or defect, promised that he would so preserve her: and gave his word to this effect to his holy disciples when he said: "Lo! I am with you always, even unto the end of the world," which promise he made, not only to them, but to us also who should believe in his name through their word. But some, not considering of this gift, and having become fickle through the temptation of the wily enemy, have fallen from the right faith; for, withdrawing from the traditions of the Catholic Church, they have erred from the truth and as the proverb saith: "The husbandmen have gone astray in their own husbandry and have gathered in their hands nothingness," because certain priests, priests in name only, not in fact, had dared to speak against the God-approved ornament of the sacred monuments, of whom God cries aloud through the prophet, "Many pastors have corrupted my vineyard, they have polluted my portion."

And, forsooth, following profane men, led astray by their carnal sense, they have calumniated the Church of Christ our God, which he hath espoused to himself, and have failed to distinguish between holy and profane, styling the images of our Lord and of his Saints by the same name as the statues of diabolical idols. Seeing which things, our Lord God (not willing to behold his people corrupted by such manner of plague) hath of his good pleasure called us together, the chief of his priests, from every quarter, moved with a divine zeal and brought hither by the will of our princes, Constantine and Irene, to the end that the traditions of the Catholic Church may receive stability by our common decree. Therefore, with all diligence, making a thorough examination and analysis, and following the trend of the truth, we diminish nought, we add nought, but we preserve unchanged all things which pertain to the Catholic Church, and following the Six Ecumenical Synods, especially that which met in this illustrious metropolis of Nice, as also that which was afterwards gathered together in the God-protected Royal City.

We believe . . . life of the world to come. Amen.[1]

We detest and anathematize Arius and all the sharers of his absurd opinion; also Macedonius and those who following him are well styled "Foes of the Spirit" (Pneumatomachi). We confess that our Lady, St. Mary, is properly and truly the Mother of God, because she was the Mother after the flesh of One Person of the Holy Trinity, to wit, Christ our God, as the Council of Ephesus has already defined when it cast out of the Church the impious Nestorius with his colleagues, because he taught that there were two Persons [in Christ]. With the Fathers of this synod we confess that he who was incarnate of the immaculate Mother of God and Ever-Virgin Mary has two natures, recognizing him as perfect God and perfect man, as also the Council of Chalcedon hath promulgated, expelling from the divine Atrium [αὐλῆς] as blasphemers, Eutyches and Dioscorus; and placing in the same category Severus, Peter and a number of others, blaspheming in divers fashions. Moreover, with these we anathematize the fables of Origen, Evagrius, and

---

[1] Anastasius in his *Interpretatio* (Migne, *Pat. Lat.*, Tom. CXXIX., col. 458), gives the Creed with the words, "Filioque." Cardinal Julian in the Fifth Session of the Council of Florence gave evidence that there was then extant a very ancient codex containing these words; and this MS., which was in Greek, was actually shown. The Greek scholar Gemistius Pletho remarked that if this were so, then the Latin theologians, like St. Thomas Aquinas would long ago have appealed to the Synod. (Cf. Hefele, *Hist. Councils*, Vol. V., p. 374, Note 2.) This reasoning is not conclusive if Cardinal Bellarmine is to be believed, who says that St. Thomas had never seen the Acts of this synod. (*De Imag. Sanct.*, Lib. ii., cap. xxii.)

Didymus, in accordance with the decision of the Fifth Council held at Constantinople. We affirm that in Christ there be two wills and two operations according to the reality of each nature, as also the Sixth Synod, held at Constantinople, taught, casting out Sergius, Honorius, Cyrus, Pyrrhus, Macarius, and those who agree with them, and all those who are unwilling to be reverent.

To make our confession short, we keep unchanged all the ecclesiastical traditions handed down to us, whether in writing or verbally, one of which is the making of pictorial representations, agreeable to the history of the preaching of the Gospel, a tradition useful in many respects, but especially in this, that so the incarnation of the Word of God is shewn forth as real and not merely phantastic, for these have mutual indications and without doubt have also mutual significations.

We, therefore, following the royal pathway and the divinely inspired authority of our Holy Fathers and the traditions of the Catholic Church (for, as we all know, the Holy Spirit indwells her), define with all certitude and accuracy that just as the figure of the precious and life-giving Cross, so also the venerable and holy images, as well in painting and mosaic as of other fit materials, should be set forth in the holy churches of God, and on the sacred vessels and on the vestments and on hangings and in pictures both in houses and by the wayside, to wit, the figure of our Lord God and Saviour Jesus Christ, of our spotless Lady, the Mother of God, of the honourable Angels, of all Saints and of all pious people. For by so much more frequently as they are seen in artistic representation, by so much more readily are men lifted up to the memory of their prototypes, and to a longing after them ; and to these should be given due salutation and honourable reverence (ἀσπασμὸν καὶ τιμητικὴν προσκύνησιν), not indeed that true worship of faith (λατρείαν) which pertains alone to the divine nature ; but to these, as to the figure of the precious and life-giving Cross and to the Book of the Gospels and to the other holy objects, incense and lights may be offered according to ancient pious custom. For the honour which is paid to the image passes on to that which the image represents, and he who reveres the image reveres

in it the subject represented. For thus the teaching of our holy Fathers, that is the tradition of the Catholic Church, which from one end of the earth to the other hath received the Gospel, is strengthened. Thus we follow Paul, who spake in Christ, and the whole divine Apostolic company and the holy Fathers, holding fast the traditions which we have received. So we sing prophetically the triumphal hymns of the Church, " Rejoice greatly, O daughter of Sion ; Shout, O daughter of Jerusalem. Rejoice and be glad with all thy heart. The Lord hath taken away from thee the oppression of thy adversaries ; thou art redeemed from the hand of thine enemies. The Lord is a King in the midst of thee ; thou shalt not see evil any more, and peace be unto thee forever."

Those, therefore who dare to think or teach otherwise, or as wicked heretics to spurn the traditions of the Church and to invent some novelty, or else to reject some of those things which the Church hath received (e.g., the Book of the Gospels, or the image of the cross, or the pictorial icons, or the holy reliques of a martyr), or evilly and sharply to devise anything subversive of the lawful traditions of the Catholic Church or to turn to common uses the sacred vessels or the venerable monasteries,[1] if they be Bishops or Clerics, we command that they be deposed ; if religious or laics, that they be cut off from communion.

[After all had signed, the acclamations began (col. 576).]

The holy Synod cried out : So we all believe, we all are so minded, we all give our consent and have signed. This is the faith of the Apostles, this is the faith of the orthodox, this is the faith which hath made firm the whole world. Believing in one God, to be celebrated in Trinity, we salute the honourable images ! Those who do not so hold, let them be anathema. Those who do not thus think, let them be driven far away from the Church. For we follow the most ancient legislation of the Catholic Church. We keep the laws of the Fathers. We anathematize those who add anything to or take anything away from the Catholic

---

[1] Constantine Copronymus turned many monasteries into soldiers' barracks. In this he has been followed by other crowned enemies of Christ.

Church. We anathematize the introduced novelty of the revilers of Christians. We salute the venerable images. We place under anathema those who do not do this. Anathema to them who presume to apply to the venerable images the things said in Holy Scripture about idols. Anathema to those who do not salute the holy and venerable images. Anathema to those who call the sacred images idols. Anathema to those who say that Christians resort to the sacred images as to gods. Anathema to those who say that any other delivered us from idols except Christ our God. Anathema to those who dare to say that at any time the Catholic Church received idols.

Many years to the Emperors, etc., etc.

EXCURSUS ON THE PRESENT TEACHING OF THE LATIN AND GREEK CHURCHES ON THE SUBJECT.

To set forth the present teaching of the Latin Church upon the subject of images and the cultus which is due them, I cite the decree of the Council of Trent and a passage from the Catechism set forth by the authority of the same synod.

(*Conc. Trid.*, Sess. xxv. December 3d and 4th, 1563. [Buckley's Trans.])

The holy synod enjoins on all bishops, and others sustaining the office and charge of teaching that, according to the usage of the Catholic and Apostolic Church received from the primitive times of the Christian religion, and according to the consent of the holy Fathers, and to the decrees of sacred councils, they especially instruct the faithful diligently touching the intercession and invocation of saints ; the honour paid to relics ; and the lawful use of images—teaching them, that the saints, who reign together with Christ, offer up their own prayers to God for men ; that it is good and useful suppliantly to invoke them, and to resort to their prayers, aid and help, for obtaining benefits from God, through his Son, Jesus Christ our Lord, who alone is our Redeemer and Saviour ; but that they think impiously, who deny that the saints, who enjoy eternal happiness in heaven, are to be invoked ; or who assert either that they do not pray for men ; or, that the invocation of them to pray for each of us, even in particular, is idolatry ; or, that it is repugnant to the word of God, and is opposed to the honour of the *one mediator between God and men, Christ Jesus*, or, that it is foolish to supplicate, orally or inwardly, those who reign in heaven. Also, that the holy bodies of holy martyrs and of others now living with Christ, which were the living members of Christ, and *the temples of the Holy Ghost*, and which are by him to be raised unto eternal life, and to be glorified, are to be venerated by the faithful, through which [bodies] many benefits are bestowed by God on men ; so that they who affirm that veneration and honour are not due to the relics of saints ; or, that these, and other sacred monuments, are uselessly honoured by the faithful ; and that the places dedicated to the memories of the Saints are vainly visited for the purpose of obtaining their aid ; are wholly to be condemned, as the Church has already long since condemned, and doth now also condemn them.

Moreover, that the images of Christ, of the Virgin Mother of God and of the other Saints, are to be had and retained particularly in temples, and that due honour and veneration are to be awarded them ; not that any divinity or virtue is believed to be in them, on account of which they are to be worshipped ; or that anything is to be asked of them ; or that confidence is to be reposed in images, as was of old done by Gentiles, who placed their hope in idols ; but because the honour which is shown unto them is referred to the prototypes which they represent; in such wise that by the images which we kiss, and before which we uncover the head, and prostrate ourselves, we adore Christ, and venerate the

Saints, whose similitude they bear. And this, by the decrees of councils, and especially of the second synod of Nicæa, has been ordained against the opponents of images.

And the bishops shall carefully teach this; that, by means of the histories of the mysteries of our Redemption, depicted by paintings or other representations, the people are instructed, and strengthened in remembering, and continually reflecting on the articles of faith; as also that great profit is derived from all sacred images, not only because the people are thereby admonished of the benefits and gifts which have been bestowed upon them by Christ, but also because the miracles of God through the means of the Saints, and their salutary examples, are set before the eyes of the faithful; that so, for those things they may give God thanks; may order their own life and manners in imitation of the Saints; and may be excited to adore and love God, and to cultivate piety. But if any one shall teach or think contrary to these decrees, let him be anathema. And if any abuses have crept in amongst these holy and salutary observances, the holy synod earnestly desires that they be utterly abolished; in such wise that no images conducive to false doctrine, and furnishing occasion of dangerous error to the uneducated, be set up. And if at times, when it shall be expedient for the unlearned people, it happen that the histories and narratives of Holy Scripture are pourtrayed and represented; the people shall be taught, that not thereby is the Divinity represented, as though it could be perceived by the eyes of the body, or be depictured by colours or figures. Moreover, in the invocation of saints, the veneration of relics, and the sacred use of images, every superstition shall be removed, all filthy lucre be abolished, finally, all lasciviousness be avoided; in such wise that figures shall not be painted or adorned with a wantonness of beauty: nor shall men also pervert the celebration of the saints, and the visitation of relics, into revellings and drunkenness; as if festivals are celebrated to the honour of the saints by luxury and wantonness. Finally, let so great care and diligence be used by bishops touching these matters, as that there appear nothing disorderly, or unbecomingly or confusedly arranged, nothing profane, nothing indecorous; *since holiness becometh the house of God.*

And that these things may be the more faithfully observed, the holy synod ordains, that it be lawful for no one to place, or cause to be placed, any unusual image in any place, or church, howsoever exempted, except it shall have been approved of by the bishop: also, that no new miracles are to be admitted, or new relics received, unless the said bishop has taken cognizance and approved thereof; who, as soon as he has obtained some certain information in regard of these matters shall, after having taken advice with theologians, and other pious men, act therein as he shall judge to be agreeable to truth and piety. But if any doubtful, or difficult abuse is to be extirpated, or, in fine, if any more serious question shall arise touching these matters, the bishop, before he decides the controversy, shall await the sentence of the metropolitan and of the bishops of the same province, in a provincial council; yet so, that nothing new, or that has not previously been usual in the Church, shall be decreed, without the most holy Roman Pontiff having been first consulted.

(Catechism of the Council of Trent.[1] Pt. IV., Chap. VI. [Buckley's trans.])

Question III.

God and the Saints addressed differently.

From God and from the Saints we implore assistance not after the same manner: for we implore God to grant us the blessing which we want, or to deliver us from evils; but the Saints, because favourites with God, we solicit to undertake our advocacy with God, to obtain

---

[1] The reader will remember that while of great weight the Catechism was not set forth by the Council, nor are its statements *de fide* in the Latin Church.

of him for us those things of which we stand in need. Hence we employ two different forms of prayer: for to God, we properly say, *Have mercy on us, hear us;* to the saints, *Pray for us.*

Question IV.

In what Manner we may beseech the Saints to have mercy on us.

We may, however, also ask the saints themselves to have mercy on us, for they are most merciful; but we do so on a different principle, for we may beseech them that, touched with the misery of our condition, they would interpose, in our behalf, their favour and intercession with God. In the performance of this duty, it is most strictly incumbent on all, to beware lest they transfer to any creature the right which belongs exclusively to the Deity; and when we repeat before the image of any Saint the Lord's Prayer, our idea must then be to beg of the Saint to pray with us, and ask for us those favours that are contained in the form of the Lord's Prayer, to become, in fine, our interpreter and intercessor with God; for that this is an office which the saints discharge, St. John the apostle has taught in the Revelation.

The doctrine of the Eastern Church may be seen from the following from *The Orthodox Confession of the faith of the Catholic and Apostolic Church of the East.*

(Confes. Orthodox. P. III. Q. LII. [apud Kimmel, Libri Symbolici Ecclesiæ Orientalis[1]].)

Rightly therefore do we honour the Saints of God, as it is written (Ps. cxxxix. 17) "How dear are thy friends unto me, O God." And divine assistance we ask for through them, just as God ordered the friends of Job to go to his faithful servant, and that he should offer sacrifice and pray for them that they might obtain remission of sin through their patronage. And in the second place this [First] commandment forbids men to adore any creature with the veneration of adoration (λατρείας). For we do not honour the Saints as though adoring them, but we call upon them as our brothers, and as friends of God, and therefore we seek the divine assistance through these, our brethren. For they go between the Lord and us for our advantage. And this in no respect is opposed to this commandment of the decalogue.

Wherefore just as the Israelites did not sin when they called upon Moses to mediate between them and God, so neither do we sin, when we call for the aid and intercession of the Saints.

(Ibid.   Quæstio LIV.)

This [Second] Commandment is separate from the first. For that treated of the Unity of the true God, forbidding and taking away the multitude of gods. But the present treats of external religious ceremonies. For besides the not honouring of false gods, we ought to dedicate no carved likeness in their honour, nor to venerate with adoration such things, nor to offer the sacrifices of adoration to them. Therefore they sin against this commandment who venerate idols as gods, and offer sacrifices to them, and place their whole confidence and hope in them; as also the Psalmist says (Ps. cxxxv. 15), "The images of the heathen are silver and gold, etc." They also transgress this precept who are given up to covetousness, etc.

(Ibid.   Quæstio LV.)

There is a great distinction between idols and images (τῶν εἰδώλων καὶ τῶν εἰκόνων). For idols are the figments and inventions of men, as the Apostle testifies when he says (1 Cor.

---

[1] This is not found in Schaff's, *The Creeds of Christendom.* Vol. II., although part of the *Orthodox Confession* (viz. Pt. I.) is reprinted. The editor explains (p. 275) that he has printed "the doctrinal part in full," and has omitted the rest because it "belongs to Ethics rather than Symbolics." A somewhat extraordinary opinion to be held by anyone who has read the omitted parts.

viij. 4), "We know that an idol is nothing in the world." But an image is a representation of a true thing having a real existence in the world. Thus, for example, the image of our Saviour Jesus Christ and of the holy Virgin Mary, and of all the Saints. Moreover, the Pagans venerated their idols as gods, and offered to them sacrifices, esteeming the gold and silver to be God, as did Nebuchadnezzar.

But when we honour and venerate the images, we in no way venerate the colours or the wood of which they are made; but we glorify with the veneration of dulia (δουλείας), those holy beings of which these are the images, making them by this means present to our minds as if we could see them with our eyes. For this reason we venerate the image of the crucifixion, and place before our minds Christ hung upon the cross for our salvation, and to such like we bow the head, and bend the knee with thanksgiving. Likewise we venerate the image of the Virgin Mary, we lift up our mind to her the most holy Mother of God, bowing both head and knees before her; calling her blessed above all men and women, with the Archangel Gabriel. The veneration, moreover, of the holy images as received in the orthodox Church, in no respect transgresses this commandment.

But this is not one and the same with that we offer to God; nor do the orthodox give it to the art of the painting, but to those very Saints whom the images represent. The Cherubim which overshadowed the mercy-seat, representing the true Cherubim which stand before God in heaven, the Israelites revered and honoured without any violation of the commandment of God, and likewise the children of Israel revered the tabernacle of witness with a suitable honour (II. Sam. vi. 13), and yet in no respect sinned nor set at naught this precept, but rather the more glorified God. From these considerations it is evident that when we honour the holy images, we do not transgress the commandment of the decalogue, but we most especially praise God, who is "to be admired in his Saints" (Ps. lxviii. 35). But this only we should be careful of, that every image has a label, telling of what Saint it is, that thus the intention of him who venerates it may be the more easily fulfilled.

And for the greater establishment of the veneration of the holy images, the Church of God at the Seventh Ecumenical Synod anathematized all those who made war against the images, and set forth the veneration of the august images, and established it forever, as is evident from the ninth canon of that synod.

(*Ibid.* Quæstio LVI.)

Why was he praised in the Old Testament who broke down the brazen serpent (II. Kgs. xviii. 4) which long before Moses had set up on high? Answer: Because the Jews were beginning an apostasy from the veneration of the true God, venerating that serpent as the true God; and offering to it incense as the Scripture saith. Therefore wishing to cut off this evil, lest it might spread further, he broke up that serpent in order that the Israelites might have no longer that incentive to idolatry. But before they honoured the serpent with the veneration of adoration, no one was condemned in that respect nor was the serpent broken.

But Christians in no respect honour images as gods, neither in their veneration do they take anything from the true adoration due to God. Nay, rather they are led by the hand, as it were, by the image to God, while under their visible representations they honour the Saints with the veneration of dulia (δουλικῶς) as the friends of God; asking for their mediation (μεσιτεύουσιν) to the Lord. And if perchance some have strayed, from their lack of knowledge, in their veneration, it were better to teach such an one, rather than that the veneration of the august images should be banished from the Church.

THE CANONS OF THE HOLY AND ECUMENICAL SEVENTH COUNCIL.[1]

CANON I.

That the sacred Canons are in all things to be observed.

THE pattern for those who have received the sacerdotal dignity is found in the testimonies and instructions laid down in the canonical constitutions, which we receiving with a glad mind, sing unto the Lord God in the words of the God-inspired David, saying: "I have had as great delight in the way of thy testimonies as in all manner of riches." "Thou hast commanded righteousness as thy testimonies for ever." "Grant me understanding and I shall live." Now if the word of prophesy bids us keep the testimonies of God forever and to live by them, it is evident that they must abide unshaken and without change. Therefore Moses, the prophet of God, speaketh after this manner: "To them nothing is to be added, and from them nothing is to be taken away." And the divine Apostle glorying in them cries out, "which things the angels desire to look into," and, "if an angel preach to you anything besides that which ye have received, let him be anathema." Seeing these things are so, being thus well-testified unto us, we rejoice over them as he that hath found great spoil, and press to our bosom with gladness the divine canons, holding fast all the precepts of the same, complete and without change, whether they have been set forth by the holy trumpets of the Spirit, the renowned Apostles, or by the Six Ecumenical Councils, or by Councils locally assembled for promulgating the decrees of the said Ecumenical Councils, or by our holy Fathers. For all these, being illumined by the same Spirit, defined such things as were expedient. Accordingly those whom they placed under anathema, we likewise anathematize; those whom they deposed, we also depose; those whom they excommunicated, we also excommunicate; and those whom they delivered over to punishment, we subject to the same penalty. And now "let your conversation be without covetousness," crieth out Paul the divine Apostle, who was caught up into the third heaven and heard unspeakable words.

NOTES.

ANCIENT EPITOME OF CANON I.

We gladly embrace the Divine Canons, viz.: those of the Holy Apostles, of the Six Ecumenical Synods, as also of the local synods and of our Holy Fathers, as inspired by one and the same Holy Spirit. Whom they anathematize we also anathematize; whom they depose, we depose; whom they cut off, we cut off; and whom they subject to penalties, we also so subject.

HARNACK (*Hist. of Dogma* [Eng. Trans.], Vol. V., p. 327).

Just as at Trent, in addition to the restoration of mediæval doctrine, a series of reforming decrees was published, so this Synod promulgated twenty-two canons which can be similarly described. The attack on monachism and the constitution of the Church had been of some use. They are the best canons drawn up by an Ecumenical Synod. The bishops were enjoined to study, to live simply, and be unselfish, and to attend to the cure of souls; the monks to observe order, decorum, and also to be unselfish. With the State and the Emperor no compromise was made; on the contrary, the demands of Maximus Confessor and John of Damascus are heard, though in muffled tones, from the canons.

VAN ESPEN.

From the wording of this canon it is clearly seen that by the Fathers of this Council the canons commonly called "Apostolical" are attributed to the Apostles themselves as to their true authors, conformably to the Trullan Synod[2] and to the opinion then prevalent among the Greeks.

For since the Fathers were well persuaded that the discipline and doctrine contained in these canons could be received and confirmed, they cared but little to enquire anxiously who were their true authors, being content in this

---

[1] This is the caption as given in the Greek of Beveridge's *Synod*.   [2] But see notes to canon of that synod.

question to follow and embrace the then commonly received opinion, and to ascribe these canons to them, just as, the other day, the Tridentine Synod (Sess. XXV., cap. j., De Reform) calls these, without any explanation, the "Canons of the Apostles," because then as now they were commonly called by that name.

BEVERIDGE (*Annotat.*, p. 166, at end of Vol. II.).

Here are recognized and confirmed the canons set forth by the Six Ecumenical Councils. And although all agree that the fifth and sixth Synods adopted no canons, unless that those of the Council in Trullo be attributed to them, yet when Tarasius the

Patriarch of Constantinople claimed Canon 82 of the Trullan Canons as having been set forth by the sixth synod (as is evident from the annotations on that canon), all the canons of Trullo seem to be confirmed as having issued from the Sixth Synod. Or else, perchance, as is supposed by Balsamon and Zonaras, as also by this present synod, the Trullan was held to be Quinisext ($\pi\epsilon\nu\vartheta\epsilon\kappa\tau\eta$), and the canons decreed by it to belong to both the fifth and the sixth council. Otherwise I do not see what meaning these words ["of the Six Ecumenical Synods"] can have, for it will be remembered that the reference is to the ecclesiastical canons of the Six Ecumenical Synods, and not to their dogmatic decrees.

CANON II.

That he who is to be ordained a Bishop must be steadfastly resolved to observe the canons, otherwise he shall not be ordained.

WHEN we recite the psalter, we promise God: "I will meditate upon thy statutes, and will not forget thy words." It is a salutary thing for all Christians to observe this, but it is especially incumbent upon those who have received the sacerdotal dignity. Therefore we decree, that every one who is raised to the rank of the episcopate shall know the psalter by heart, so that from it he may admonish and instruct all the clergy who are subject to him. And diligent examination shall be made by the metropolitan whether he be zealously inclined to read diligently, and not merely now and then, the sacred canons, the holy Gospel, and the book of the divine Apostle, and all other divine Scripture; and whether he lives according to God's commandments, and also teaches the same to his people. For the special treasure ($o\dot{v}\sigma\dot{\iota}a$) of our high priesthood is the oracles which have been divinely delivered to us, that is the true science of the Divine Scriptures, as says Dionysius the Great. And if his mind be not set, and even glad, so to do and teach, let him not be ordained. For says God by the prophet, "Thou hast rejected knowledge, I will also reject thee, that thou shalt be no priest to me."

NOTES.

ANCIENT EPITOME OF CANON II.

Whoever is to be a bishop must know the Psalter by heart: he must thoroughly understand what he reads, and not merely superficially, but with diligent care, that is to say the Sacred Canons, the Holy Gospel, the book of the Apostle, and the whole of the Divine Scripture. And should he not have such knowledge, he is not to be ordained.

ARISTENUS.

Whoso is to be elevated to the grade of the episcopate should know . . . the book of the Apostle Paul, and the whole divine scripture and search out its meaning and understand the things that are written. For the very foundation and essence of the high priesthood is the true knowledge of holy

Scripture, according to Dionysius the Great. And if he has this knowledge let him be ordained, but if not, not. For God hath said by the prophet: "Thou hast put away from thee knowledge, therefore I have also put thee away from me, that thou mayest not be my priest."

FLEURY.

The persecution of the Iconoclasts had driven all the best Christians into hiding, or into far distant exile; this had made them rustic, and had taken from them their taste for study. The council therefore is forced to be content with a knowledge of only what is absolutely necessary, provided it was united with a willingness to learn. The examination with which the ceremony of the ordination of bishops begins seems to be a remains of this discipline.

The Synod teaches in this canon that "all Christians" will find it most profitable to meditate upon God's justifyings and to keep his words in remembrance, and especially is this the case with bishops.

And it should be noted that formerly not only the clergy, but also the lay people, learned the Psalms, that is the whole Psalter, by heart, and made a most sweet sound by chanting them while about their work.

But as time went on, little by little this pious custom of reciting the Psalter and of imposing its recitation and a meditation thereon at certain intervals, slipped away to the clergy only and to monks and nuns, as to those specially consecrated to the service of God and to meditation upon the divine words, as Lupus points out. And from this discipline and practice the appointment of the Ecclesiastical or Canonical Office had its rise, which imposes the necessity of reciting the Psalms at certain intervals of time.

This canon is found in the *Corpus Juris Canonici*, Gratian's *Decretum*, Pars I., Dist. xxxviij., C. vj., in Anastasius's translation.

CANON III.

That it does not pertain to princes to choose a Bishop.

LET every election of a bishop, presbyter, or deacon, made by princes stand null, according to the canon which says: If any bishop making use of the secular powers shall by their means obtain jurisdiction over any church, he shall be deposed, and also excommunicated, together with all who remain in communion with him. For he who is raised to the episcopate must be chosen by bishops, as was decreed by the holy fathers of Nice in the canon which says: It is most fitting that a bishop be ordained by all the bishops in the province; but if this is difficult to arrange, either on account of urgent necessity, or because of the length of the journey, three bishops at least having met together and given their votes, those also who are absent having signified their assent by letters, the ordination shall take place. The confirmation of what is thus done, shall in each province be given by the metropolitan thereof.

NOTES.

ANCIENT EPITOME OF CANON III.

Every election made by a secular magistrate is null.

This is a canon of a synod recognized by East and West as ecumenical! The reader can hardly resist the reflection that in this case there have been and are a great many intruding clergymen in the world, whose appointment to their several offices is "null." Van Espen, however, suggests an ingenious way out of the difficulty, which is followed with great approval by Hefele.

VAN ESPEN.

Canon xxix. of those commonly called Apostolic, and canon iv. of Nice are renewed in this canon.

From the words of this canon it is sufficiently clear that in this canon the synod is treating of the choice and intrusion of persons into ecclesiastical offices which the magistrates and Princes had arrogated to themselves under the title of Domination (*Dominatio*); and by no means of that choice or rather nomination which Catholic princes and kings have everywhere and always used.

This canon is found in the *Corpus Juris Canonici*, Gratian's *Decretum*, Pars I., Dist. xciii., C. vij.

CANON IV.

That Bishops are to abstain from all receiving of gifts.

THE Church's herald, Paul the divine Apostle, laying down a rule (κανόνα) not only for the presbyters of Ephesus but for the whole company of the priesthood, speaks thus explicitly, saying, "I have coveted no man's silver or gold, or apparel. I have shewed you all things, how that so labouring ye ought to support the weak;" for he accounted it more blessed to give. Therefore we being taught by him do decree, that under no circumstances, shall a Bishop for the sake of filthy lucre invent feigned excuses for sins, and exact gold or silver or other gifts from the bishops, clergy, or monks who are subject to him. For says the Apostle, "The unrighteous shall not possess the kingdom of God," and, "The children ought not to lay up for the parents, but the parents for the children." If then any is found, who for the sake of exacting gold or any other gift, or who from personal feeling, has suspended from the ministry, or even excommunicated, any of the clergy subject to his jurisdiction, or who has closed any of the venerable temples, so that the service of God may not be celebrated in it, pouring out his madness even upon things insensible, and thus shewing himself to be without understanding, he shall be subjected to the same punishment he devised for others, and his trouble shall return on his own head, as a transgressor of God's commandment and of the apostolic precepts. For Peter the supreme head (ἡ κερυφαία ἀκρότης) of the Apostles commands, "Feed the flock of God which is among you, taking the oversight thereof, not by constraint, but willingly; not for filthy lucre but of a ready mind; neither as being lords over the clergy (τῶν κλή-ρων [A. V. God's heritage]); but being ensamples to the flock. And when the chief shepherd shall appear, ye shall receive a crown of glory that fadeth not away."

NOTES.

Ancient Epitome of Canon IV.

We decree that no bishop shall extort gold or silver, or anything else from bishops, clerics, or monks subject to his jurisdiction. And if anyone through the power of gold or of any other thing or through his own whims, shall be found to have prevented any one of the clergy who are subject to him, from the celebration of the holy offices, or shall have shut up a venerable temple so that the sacred worship of God could not be performed in it, he shall be subject to the lex talionis. For Peter the Apostle says: Feed the flock of God, not of necessity but willingly, and according to God; not for filthy lucre's sake, but with a prompt mind; not exercising lordship over the clergy, but being an example to the flock.

Balsamon.

Note the present canon, which punishes those bishops by the *lex talionis*, who for filthy lucre's sake, or out of private affection, separate any from themselves, or close temples. Wherefore he who cuts off others thus, let him be cut off. But he who shuts off a temple shall be punished even more than by cutting off. But lest any one should say, by the argument *à contrario*, that a bishop should not be punished who neither for the sake of filthy lucre nor out of private spite, but lawfully cuts some off, or closes temples, I answer that this argument only holds good of the cutting off. For a bishop who for any reason, whether just or unjust, shuts up a temple, should be punished, so it seems to me, as I have said above.

Van Espen.

It would seem that at that time among the Greeks the use of local interdict (*interdicti localis*) was not known. But very many theologians wish to find a vestige of this interdict in the IVth century, in St. Basil's epistle cclxx. (otherwise ccxliv.), where the holy doctor teaches that the person who carries off by force a virgin, and those who are cognizant of this wickedness ought to be smitten with excommunication, and that the village or its inhabitants, to which the ravisher shall escape and where he shall be kept in safety, shall be shut out from the prayers.

This canon, or rather the first part of it, is found in the *Corpus Juris Canonici*, Gratian's *Decretum*, Pars II., Causa XVI., Q. I., Canon lxiv.; all the latter part is represented by the words "et infra."

CANON V.

That they who cast contumely upon clerics because they have been ordained in the church without bringing a gift with them, are to be punished with a fine.

IT is a sin unto death when men incorrigibly continue in their sin, but they sin more deeply, who proudly lifting themselves up oppose piety and sincerity, accounting mammon of more worth than obedience to God, and caring nothing for his canonical precepts.

The Lord God is not found among such, unless, perchance, having been humbled by their own fall, they return to a sober mind. It behoves them the rather to turn to God with a contrite heart and to pray for forgiveness and pardon of so grave a sin, and no longer to boast in an unholy gift. For the Lord is nigh unto them that are of a contrite heart. With regard, therefore, to those who pride themselves that because of their benefactions of gold they were ordained in the Church, and resting confidently in this evil custom (so alien from God and inconsistent with the whole priesthood), with a proud look and open mouth vilify with abusive words those who on account of the strictness of their life were chosen by the Holy Ghost and have been ordained without any gift of money, we decree in the first place that they take the lowest place in their order; but if they do not amend let them be subjected to a fine. But if it appear that any one has done this [i.e., given money], at any time as a price for ordination, let him be dealt with according to the Apostolic Canon which says: " If a bishop has obtained possession of his dignity by means of money (the same rule applies also to a presbyter or deacon) let him be deposed and also the one who ordained him, and let him also be altogether cut off from communion, even as Simon Magus was by me Peter." To the same effect is the second canon of our holy fathers of Chalcedon, which says: If any bishop gives ordination in return for money, and puts up for sale that which cannot be sold, and ordains for money a bishop or chorepiscopus, or presbyter, or deacon, or any other of those who are reckoned among the clergy; or who for money shall appoint anyone to the office of œconomus, advocate, or paramonarius; or, in a word, who hath done anything else contrary to the canon, for the sake of filthy lucre—he who hath undertaken to do anything of this sort, having been convicted, shall be in danger of losing his degree. And he who has been ordained shall derive no advantage from the ordination or promotion thus negotiated; but let him remain a stranger to the dignity and responsibility which he attained by means of money. And if any one shall appear to have acted as a go-between in so shameful and godless a traffic, he also, if he be a cleric, shall be removed from his degree; if he be a layman or a monk, let him be excommunicated.

NOTES.

Ancient Epitome of Canon V.

It seems that such as glory in the fact that they owe their position to their liberality in gold to the Church, and who contemn those who were chosen because of their virtue and were appointed without any largess, should receive the lowest place in their order. And should they continue in their ways, let them be punished. But those who made such gifts so as to get ordinations, let such be cast forth from communion, as Simon Magus was by Peter.

Hefele.

Zonaras and Balsamon in earlier times, and later Christian Lupus and Van Espen, remarked that the second part of this canon treats of simony, but not the first. This has in view rather those who, on account of their large expenditure on churches and the poor, have been raised, without simony, to the clerical estate as a reward and recognition of their beneficence; and being proud of this, now depreciate other clergymen who were unable or unwilling to make such foundations and the like.

CANON VI.

Concerning the holding of a local Synod at the time appointed.

Since there is a canon which says, twice a year in each province, the canonical enquiries shall be made in the gatherings of the bishops; but because of the inconveniences which those who thus came together had to undergo in travelling, the holy fathers of the Sixth Council decreed that once each year, without regard to place or excuse which might be urged, a council should be held and the things which are amiss corrected. This canon we now renew. And if any prince be found hindering this being carried out, let him be excommunicated. But if any of the metropolitans shall take no care that this be done, he being free from constraint or fear or other reasonable excuse, let him be subjected to the canonical penalties. While the council is engaged in considering the canons or matters which have regard to the Gospel, it behoves the assembled Bishops, with all attention and grave thought to guard the divine and life-giving commandments of God, for in keeping of them there is great reward; because our lamp is the commandment, and our light is the law, and trial and discipline are the way of life, and the commandment of the Lord shining afar giveth light to the eyes. It is not permitted to a metropolitan to demand any of those things which the bishops bring with them, whether it be a horse or any other gift. If he be convicted of doing anything of this sort, he shall restore fourfold.

NOTES.

Ancient Epitome of Canon VI.

Whenever it is not possible for a synod to meet according to the decree formulated long ago, twice in each year, at least let it be held once, as seemed good to the Sixth Synod. Should any magistrate forbid such meeting, let him be cast out: and a bishop who shall take no pains to assemble it, shall be subject to punishment. And when the synod is held, should it appear that the Metropolitan has taken anything away from any bishop, let him restore four-fold.

Hefele.

Anastasius remarks on this, that this ordi-nance (whether the whole canon or only its last passage must remain undecided) was not accepted by the Latins. That this canon did not forbid the so-called Synodicum, which the metropolitans had lawfully to receive from the bishops, and the bishops from the priests, is remarked by Van Espen, l. c. p. 464.

Compare with this (as Balsamon advises) the eighth canon of the Council in Trullo.

This canon is found in the *Corpus Juris Canonici*, Gratian's *Decretum*, Pars I., Dist. XVIII., C. vij.

CANON VII.

That to churches consecrated without any deposit of the reliques of the Saints, the defect should be made good.

Paul the divine Apostle says: "The sins of some are open beforehand, and some they follow after." These are their primary sins, and other sins follow these. Accordingly upon the heels of the heresy of the traducers of the Christians, there followed close other ungodliness. For as they took out of the churches the presence of the venerable images, so likewise they cast aside other customs which we must now revive and maintain in accordance with the written and unwritten law. We decree therefore that relics shall be placed with the accustomed service in as many of the sacred temples as have been consecrated without the relics of the Martyrs. And if any bishop from this time forward is found consecrating a temple without holy relics, he shall be deposed, as a transgressor of the ecclesiastical traditions.

NOTES.

Ancient Epitome of Canon VII.

Let reliques of the Holy Martyrs be placed in such churches as have been consecrated without them, and this with the accustomed prayers. But whoever shall consecrate a church without these shall be deposed as a transgressor of the traditions of the Church.

Balsamon.

But someone may be surprised that oratories to-day are consecrated without any deposition of reliques. And they may ask why the Divine Liturgy is not celebrated in them by bishops and not by priests only. The answer is that the superaltars (ἀντιμένσια) which are made by the bishops when a church is consecrated, suffice oratories in lieu of consecration or enthronement when they are sent to them, on the occasion of their dedication or opening. They are called ἀντιμένσια because they are in place of, and are antitypes of those many like tables which furnish thoroughly the holy Lord's table.

On the rite of consecrating churches with reliques see Cardinal Bona. (*De Rebus Lit.*, Lib. I., cap. xix.)

The Antimensia are consecrated at the same time as the church; a full account of the ceremony is found in the Euchologion (Goar's ed., p. 648). A piece of cloth is placed on the altar and blessed, and then subsequently, as need requires, pieces are cut off from it and sent to the various oratories, etc. The main outline of the ceremony of consecration is as follows.

J. M. NEALE. (*Int. Hist. East. Ch.*, p. 187.)

Relics being pounded up with fragrant gum, oil is poured over them by the bishop, and, distilling out to the corporals, is supposed to convey to them the mysterious virtues of the relics themselves. The holy Eucharist must then be celebrated on them for seven days, after which they are sent forth as they are wanted.

CANON VIII.

That Hebrews ought not to be received unless they have been converted in sincerity of heart.

SINCE certain, erring in the superstitions of the Hebrews, have thought to mock at Christ our God, and feigning to be converted to the religion of Christ do deny him, and in private and secretly keep the Sabbath and observe other Jewish customs, we decree that such persons be not received to communion, nor to prayers, nor into the Church; but let them be openly Hebrews according to their religion, and let them not bring their children to baptism, nor purchase or possess a slave. But if any of them, out of a sincere heart and in faith, is converted and makes profession with his whole heart, setting at naught their customs and observances, and so that others may be convinced and converted, such an one is to be received and baptized, and his children likewise; and let them be taught to take care to hold aloof from the ordinances of the Hebrews. But if they will not do this, let them in no wise be received.

NOTES.

ANCIENT EPITOME OF CANON VIII.

Hebrews must not be received unless they are manifestly converted with sincerity of heart.

HEFELE.

The Greek commentators Balsamon and Zonaras understood the words "nor to baptize their children" to mean, "these seeming Christians may not baptize their own children," because they only seem to be Christians. But parents were never allowed to baptize their own children, and the true sense of the words in question comes out clearly from the second half of the canon.

CANON IX.

That none of the books containing the heresy of the traducers of the Christians are to be hid.

ALL the childish devices and mad ravings which have been falsely written against the venerable images, must be delivered up to the Episcopium of Constantinople, that they may be locked away with other heretical books. And if anyone is found hiding such books, if he be a bishop or presbyter or deacon, let him be deposed; but if he be a monk or layman, let him be anathema.

NOTES.

ANCIENT EPITOME OF CANON IX.

If any one is found to have concealed a book written against the venerable images, if he is on the clergy list let him be deposed; if a layman or monk let him be cut off.

VAN ESPEN.

What here is styled Episcopium was the palace of the Patriarch. In this palace were the archives, and this was called the "Cartophylacium," in which the charts and episcopal laws were laid up. To this there was a pre-fect, the grand Chartophylax, one of the principal officials and of most exalted dignity of the Church of Constantinople, whose office Codinus explains as follows : "The Chartophylax has in his keeping all the charts which pertain to ecclesiastical law (that is to say the letters in which privileges and other rights of the Church are contained) and is the judge of all ecclesiastical causes, and presides over marriage controversies which are taken cog-nizance of, and proceedings for dissolution of the marriage bond ; moreover, he is judge in other clerical strifes, as the right hand of the Patriarch."

In this Cartophylaceum or Archives, therefore, under the faithful guardianship of the Chartophylax, the fathers willed that the writings of the Iconoclasts should be laid up, lest in their perusal simple Catholics might be led astray.

CANON X.

That no cleric ought to leave his diocese and go into another without the knowledge of the Bishop.

SINCE certain of the clergy, misinterpreting the canonical constitutions, leave their own diocese and run into other dioceses, especially into this God-protected royal city, and take up their abode with princes, celebrating liturgies in their oratories, it is not permitted to receive such persons into any house or church without the license of their own Bishop and also that of the Bishop of Constantinople. And if any clerk shall do this without such license, and shall so continue, let him be deposed. With regard to those who have done this with the knowledge of the aforesaid Bishops, it is not lawful for them to undertake mundane and secular responsibilities, since this is forbidden by the sacred canons. And if anyone is discovered holding the office of those who are called Meizoteroi ; let him either lay it down, or be deposed from the priesthood. Let him rather be the instructor of the children and others of the household, reading to them the Divine Scriptures, for to this end he received the priesthood.

NOTES.

ANCIENT EPITOME OF CANON X.

A clergyman who after leaving his own parish has settled in another far off from his own bishop and from the bishop of Constantinople, shall be received neither into house nor church. And if he shall persevere in his course, he shall be deposed. But if they shall do this with a knowledge of what we have said, they shall not receive a secular position; or should they have received them, they shall cease from them. And if they refuse they shall be deposed.

HEFELE.

On the office of the μειζότεροι, the Greek commentators Zonaras and Balsamon give us more exact information. We give the substance of it, viz.: they were *majores domus* stewards of the estates of high personages.

BALSAMON.

On account of this canon it seems to me that the most holy Patriarch at the time and his Chartophylax allow alien clergymen to celebrate the liturgy in this royal city, even without letters dimissory of the local bishop of each one.

CANON XI.

That Œconomi ought to be in the Episcopal palaces and in the Monasteries.

SINCE we are under obligation to guard all the divine canons, we ought by all means to maintain in its integrity that one which says œconomi are to be in each church. If the metropolitan appoints in his Church an œconomus, he does well; but if he does not, it is permitted to the Bishop of Constantinople by his own (ἰδίας) authority to choose an œconomus for the Church of the Metropolitan. A like authority belongs to the metropolitans, if the Bishops who are subject to them do not wish to appoint œconomi in their churches. The same rule is also to be observed with respect to monasteries.

NOTES.

Ancient Epitome of Canon XI.

If the Metropolitan does not elect an œconomus of the metropolis, the patriarch shall do so. If the bishop shall not do so, the Metropolitan shall; for so it seemed good to the fathers assembled at Chalcedon. The same law shall hold in monasteries.

Hefele.

The Synod of Chalcedon required the appointment of special œconomi only for all bishops' churches; but our synod extended this prescription also to monasteries.

Van Espen.

Bishops at their ordination among other things promise that they will observe the canons, and the bishops of the Synod say that among these canons they are bound to keep the one that orders them to appoint an Œconomus.

Among the officials of the Constantinopolitan Church, Codinus names first The Grand Œconomus, "who" (he says) "holds in his own power all the faculties of the Church, and all their returns; and is the dispenser in this matter as well to the Patriarch as to the Church."

Balsamon and Aristenus refer to Canon xxvj. of Chalcedon; and point out how here the power of Constantinople was added to.

This canon is found in the *Corpus Juris Canonici*, Gratian's *Decretum*, Pars. II., Causa IX., Quæst. III., Canon iij.

CANON XII.

That a Bishop or Hegumenos ought not to alienate any part of the suburban estate of the church.

If a bishop or hegumenos is found alienating any part of the farm lands of the bishoprick or monastery into the hands of secular princes, or surrendering them to any other person, such act is null according to the canon of the holy Apostles, which says: "Let the bishop take care of all the Church's goods, and let him administer the same according as in the sight of God." It is not lawful for him to appropriate any part himself, or to confer upon his relations the things which belong to God. If they are poor let them be helped among the poor; but let them not be used as a pretext for smuggling away the Church's property. And if it be urged that the land is only a loss and yields no profit, the place is not on that account to be given to the secular rulers, who are in the neighbourhood; but let it be given to clergymen or husbandmen. And if they have resorted to dishonest craft, so that the ruler has bought the land from the husbandman or cleric, such transaction shall likewise be null, and the land shall be restored to the bishoprick or monastery. And the bishop or hegumenos doing this shall be turned out, the bishop from his bishoprick and the hegumenos from his monastery, as those who wasted what they did not gather.

NOTES.

Ancient Epitome of Canon XII.

According to what seemed good to the Holy Apostles, any act of alienation of the goods of a diocese or of a monastery made by the bishop, or by the superior of the monastery, shall be null. And the Bishop or Superior who shall have done this shall be expelled.

Van Espen.

As at the time of this Synod by the favour of kings and princes the way was frequently open to ecclesiastical dignities, clergymen might easily be induced through ambition to make over to princes some part of the Church's possessions, if only by so doing they might arrive at the coveted preferment through their patronage, and then desiring to make good this simoniacal promise, they studied to transfer the church's goods to their patrons; with regard to these the present decree of the synod was made.

But because human ambition is cunning,

and solicitously seeks a way of attaining its ends, ambitious clerics tried by various colouring to give a tone to and to palliate these translations of church-goods to princes and magistrates, so that they might attain to that they aimed at by the favour of said princes and magistrates.

Two such pretexts the synod exposes and rejects in the present canon.

This canon is found in the *Corpus Juris Canonici*, Pars II., Causa XII., Quæst. II., canon xix.

CANON XIII.

That they are worthy of special condemnation who turn the monasteries into public houses.

DURING the calamity which was brought to pass in the Churches, because of our sins, some of the sacred houses, for example, bishops' palaces and monasteries, were seized by certain men and became public inns. If those who now hold them choose to give them back, so that they may be restored to their original use, well and good; but if not, and these persons are on the sacerdotal list, we command that they be deposed; if they be monks or laymen, that they be excommunicated, as those who have been condemned from the Father, and the Son, and the Holy Ghost, and assigned their place where the worm dieth not and the fire is not quenched, because they set themselves against the voice of the Lord, which says: "Make not my Father's house an house of merchandise."

NOTES.

ANCIENT EPITOME OF CANON XIII.

Those who make common diocesan or monastic goods, unless they restore to the bishop or superior the things belonging to the diocese or monastery, the whole proceeding shall be null. If they are persons in Holy Orders they shall be deposed, but if laymen or monks they shall be cast out.

VAN ESPEN.

No doubt by "the calamity" here is intended a reference to the troubles occasioned by the Iconoclasts, during whose time of domination many nefarious things were perpetrated against the orthodox, and most bitter of all was the persecution of the monks and priests by Leo the Isaurian and by his son Constantine Copronymus, both of them supporters of the Iconoclasts.

And so it came to pass that by this persecution and through the nefarious vexations of the Iconoclasts, many monks and clerics fled from their monasteries and left vacant the *Episcopia* or holy houses, and so it became easy for people to come in and occupy the empty monasteries and religious houses, and to turn them to common and profane uses, especially when the anger of the Emperors and of the Iconoclasts was known to be fierce against the monks, and such bishops and priests as were worshippers of images.

This canon is found in the *Corpus Juris Canonici*, Pars. II., Causa xix., Quæst. III., canon v., in Anastasius's version but lacking the opening words which are supplied by the Roman Correctors.

CANON XIV.

That no one without ordination ought to read in the ambo during the synaxis.

THAT there is a certain order established in the priesthood is very evident to all, and to guard diligently the promotions of the priesthood is well pleasing to God. Since therefore we see certain youths who have received the clerical tonsure, but who have not yet received ordination from the bishop, reading in the ambo during the Synaxis, and in doing this violating the canons, we forbid this to be done (from henceforth,) and let this prohibition be observed also amongst the monks. It is permitted to each hegumenos in his own monastery to ordain a reader, if he himself had received the laying on of hands by a bishop to the dignity of hegumenos, and is known to be a presbyter.   Chorepiscopi may likewise, according to ancient custom and with the bishop's authorization, appoint readers.[1]

---

[1] Bev. adds in the Latin " by imposition of hands."

NOTES.

Ancient Epitome of Canon XIV.

No one shall read from the ambon unless he has been ordained by the bishop. And this shall be in force also among monks. The superior of a monastery, if he has been ordained by the bishop, may ordain a lector but only in his own monastery. A chorepiscopus also can make a lector.

Balsamon.

I say therefore from this present canon and from canon xix. that they may properly be made superiors, who have never received holy orders; since women may be placed in such positions in our monasteries. And as these women do not hear confessions, nor make readers, so neither do superiors do this who are neither monks nor priests, nor could they do this even with the license of the bishop.

Hefele.

Van Espen (l.c. p. 469 sqq., and *Jus Canon.*, t. i. pt. xxxi. tit. 31, c. 6), professes to show (a) that at that time there was no special benediction of abbots (different from their ordination as priests), and that therefore the words, "if he (the superior of the monastery) himself is consecrated by the bishop to the office of hegumenus," and "evidently is a priest," mean the same; (b) that at the time of our Synod every superior of a monastery, a prior as well as an abbot, had the power of conferring upon the monks of his monastery the order of lector; but (c) that the way in which Anastasius translated the canon (*si dumtaxat Abbati manus impositio facta noscatur ab episcopo secundum morem præficiendorum abbatum*), and the reception of this translation into the *Corpus juris canonici*, c.l., Dist. lxix., gave occasion to concede the right in question, of ordaining lectors, only to the solemnly consecrated (and insulated) abbots.

This canon is found (as just noted) in the *Corpus Juris Canonici*, Pars I., Dist. LXIX., c. j.

CANON XV.

That a clerk ought not to be set over two churches.

From henceforth no clergyman shall be appointed over two churches, for this savours of merchandise and filthy lucre, and is altogether alien from ecclesiastical custom. We have heard by the very voice of the Lord that, "No man can serve two masters, for either he will hate the one and love the other, or else he will hold to the one and despise the other." Each one, therefore, as says the Apostle, in the calling wherein he was called, in the same he ought to abide, and in one only church to give attendance. For in the affairs of the Church, what is gained through filthy lucre is altogether separate from God. To meet the necessities of this life, there are various occupations, by means of which, if one so desire, let him procure the things needful for the body. For says the Apostle, "These hands have ministered unto my necessities, and to them that were with me." Occupations of this sort may be obtained in the God-protected city. But in the country places outside, because of the small number of people, let a dispensation be granted.

NOTES.

Ancient Epitome of Canon XV.

Hereafter at Constantinople a cleric may not serve two churches. But in the outskirts this may be permitted on account of the scarcity of men.

Van Espen.

This means that in the country or where men are so scarce that each parish cannot have its own presbyter, one presbyter should be allowed to serve two churches, not that so he may supply his own need, (as to-day is allowed by the combination of benefices), but that so the necessities of the parishioners may be provided for.

It should be noted that the synod deems it "filthy lucre" and "separate from God" if ecclesiastical ministries are performed "for the necessaries of life," and is of opinion that the clergy should seek their support from some honest employment or work by the example of Paul, rather than to turn ecclesiastical ministrations to the attaining of temporal things, and to use these as an art by which to gain bread.

This canon is found in the *Corpus Juris Canonici*, Pars. II., Causa XXI., Quæst. I., canon j., where the gloss is "because there the clergy are few."

CANON XVI.

That it does not become one in holy orders to be clad in costly apparel.

ALL buffoonery and decking of the body ill becomes the priestly rank. Therefore those bishops and clerics who array themselves in gay and showy clothing ought to correct themselves, and if they do not amend they ought to be subjected to punishment. So likewise they who anoint themselves with perfumes. When the root of bitterness sprang up, there was poured into the Catholic Church the pollution of the heresy of the traducers of the Christians. And such as were defiled by it, not only detested the pictured images, but also set at naught all decorum, being exceedingly mad against those who lived gravely and religiously; so that in them was fulfilled that which is written, "The service of God is abominable to the sinner." If therefore, any are found deriding those who are clad in poor and grave raiment, let them be corrected by punishment. For from early times every man in holy orders wore modest and grave clothing; and verily whatever is worn, not so much because of necessity, as for the sake of outward show, savours of dandyism, as says Basil the Great. Nor did anyone array himself in raiment embroidered with silk, nor put many coloured ornaments on the border of his garments ; for they had heard from the lips of God that "They that wear soft clothing are in kings' houses."

NOTES.

ANCIENT EPITOME OF CANON XVI.

Bishops and clergymen arraying themselves in splendid clothes and anointed with perfumes must be corrected. Should they persist, they must be punished.

Balsamon and Zonaras tell of the magnificence in dress assumed by some of the superior clergy among the Iconoclasts, wearing stuffs woven with threads of gold, and their loins girt with golden girdles, and sentences embroidered in gold on the edge of their raiment. It is curious to note how often heretics fall into extremes. We have seen how Eustathius wore a conspicuous garb and was not willing to appear in the ordinary dress of a clergyman of his day. His was the one extreme of ultra clerical or, I should say, ascetic clothing. These Iconoclasts went to the other extreme and dressed themselves like men of the world, giving themselves the dandy airs of the fops of the day, thus, as always, making themselves ridiculous in the eyes of the wise, and their office contemptible in the eyes of the common people.

This canon is found in the *Corpus Juris Canonici*, Gratian's *Decretum*, Pars. II., Causa XXI., Quæst. IV., canon j.

CANON XVII.

That he shall not be allowed to begin the building of an oratory, who has not the means wherewith to finish it.

CERTAIN monks having left their monasteries because they desired to rule, and, unwilling to obey, are undertaking to build oratories, but have not the means to finish them. Now whoever shall undertake to do anything of this sort, let him be forbidden by the bishop of the place. But if he have the means wherewith to finish, let what he has designed be carried on to completion. The same rule is to be observed with regard to laymen and clerics.

NOTES.

ANCIENT EPITOME OF CANON XVII.

Whoever wishes to build a monastery, if he has the wherewithal to finish it, let him begin the work, and let him bring it to a conclusion. But if not, let him be prohibited by the bishop of the place. The same law shall apply to laymen and monks.

Van Espen refers to Gratian's *Decretum*, Pars. III., De Consecrat., Dist. I., canon ix., *et seqq.*

Balsamon also refers his readers to the Fourth Book of the Basilica, title I., chapter I., which is part of Justinian's cxxiij. Novel, also to the first canon of the so-called First-and-Second Council held at Constantinople in the Church of the Holy Apostles.

CANON XVIII.

That women ought not to live in bishops' houses, nor in monasteries of men.

"Be ye without offence to those who are without," says the divine Apostle. Now for women to live in Bishops' houses or in monasteries is ground for grave offence. Whoever therefore is known to have a female slave or freewoman in the episcopal palace or in a monastery for the discharge of some service, let him be rebuked. And if he still continue to retain her, let him be deposed. If it happens that women are on the suburban estates, and the bishop or hegumenos desires to go thither, so long as the bishop or hegumenos is present, let no woman at that time continue her work, but let her betake herself to some other place until the bishop [or hegumenos[1]] has departed, so that there be no occasion of complaint.

NOTES.

Ancient Epitome of Canon XVIII.

It is not fitting that women should be kept in episcopal houses or in monasteries. If anyone shall dare to do so, he shall be reproved; but if he persists, he shall be deposed. No woman is allowed to serve or even to appear where a bishop or a superior of a monastery is present, but let her keep herself apart until he be gone.

Van Espen.

Every woman the present canon expels from the *Episcopium* or bishop's house, agreeably to Novel CXXIII, chapter 29, of the Emperor Justinian, which, (although the Nicene canon on the subject makes a mother, sister, daughter and other persons free from all suspicions, exceptions), admits no exceptions in the case of a bishop, but says, "We allow no bishop to have any woman or to live with one."

For as bishops are set in a higher grade above the rest of the clergy, and ought to be like lights set on a candlestick to give light, rightly they are ordered more than others to take care to avoid all appearance of evil, and to remove all from them that might cause suspicion.

With regard to monks and their houses see Justinian's Novel CXXXIII., Cap. IV.

CANON XIX.

That the vows of those in holy orders and of monks, and of nuns are to be made without the exaction of gifts.

The abomination of filthy lucre has made such inroads among the rulers of the churches, that certain of those who call themselves religious men and women, forgetting the commandments of the Lord have been altogether led astray, and for the sake of money have received those presenting themselves for the sacerdotal order and the monastic life. And hence the first step of those so received being unlawful, the whole proceeding is rendered null, as says Basil the Great. For it is not possible that God should be served by means of mammon.[2] If therefore, anyone is found doing anything of this kind, if he be a bishop or hegumenos, or one of the priesthood, either let him cease to do so any longer or else let him be deposed, according to the second canon of the Holy Council of Chalcedon. If the offender be an abbess, let her be sent away from her monastery, and placed in another in a subordinate position. In like manner is a hegumenos to be dealt with, who has not the ordination of a presbyter. With regard to what has been given by parents as a dowry for their children, or which persons themselves have contributed out of their own property, with the declaration that such gifts were made to God, we have decreed, that whether the persons in whose behalf the gifts were made, continue to live in the monastery or not, the gifts are to remain with the monastery in accordance with their first determination; unless indeed there be ground for complaint against the superior.

[1] Not found in Bev.   [2] Bev. "To serve God and mammon."

NOTES.

ANCIENT EPITOME OF CANON XIX.

Whoever for money admits those coming to Holy Orders or to the monastic life, if he be bishop, or superior of a monastery or any other in sacred orders, shall either cease or be deposed. And the Superior of a monastery of women shall be expelled [if she have done so] and shall be given over to subjection. The same shall be the case with a superior of monks, if he be not a priest. But the possessions brought by those who come in, let them remain, whether the persons remain or not, provided the superior be not to blame.

BALSAMON.

But someone may ask how it is that canon V., orders that he that performs an ordination for money is *eo ipso* to be deposed, whereas this canon provides that he who receives a cleric or monk on account of a pecuniary gift is to cease or else to be deposed. The answer is, that whenever anyone performs an ordination for money, according to canon V., he is to be deposed ; but when it was only a reception of a person which took place, whether into the list of the clergy or into a monastery by reason of money, who did this is only to be deposed, if after being denounced he persists in this evil. The canons therefore are diverse in their scope. The fifth treats of unlawful ordination, but this one of improper receptions.

CANON XX.

That from henceforth, no double monastery shall be erected; and concerning the double monasteries already in existence.

WE decree that from henceforth, no double monastery shall be erected; because this has become an offence and cause of complaint to many. In the case of those persons who with the members of their family propose to leave the world and follow the monastic life, let the men go into a monastery for men, and the women into a monastery for women; for this is well-pleasing to God. The double monasteries which are already in existence, shall observe the rule of our holy Father Basil, and shall be ordered by his precepts, monks and nuns shall not dwell together in the same monastery, for in thus living together adultery finds its occasion. No monk shall have access to a nunnery; nor shall a nun be permitted to enter a monastery for the sake of conversing with anyone therein. No monk shall sleep in a monastery for women, nor eat alone with a nun.[1] When food is brought by men to the canonesses, let the abbess accompanied by some one of the aged nuns, receive it outside the gates of the women's monastery. When a monk desires to see one of his kinswomen, who may be in the nunnery, let him converse with her in the presence of the abbess, and that in a very few words, and then let him speedily take his departure.

NOTES.

ANCIENT EPITOME OF CANON XX.

Monasteries shall not be double, neither shall monks and nuns live in the same building, nor shall they talk together apart. Moreover if a man takes anything to a canoness, let him wait without and hand it to her, and let him see his relative in the presence of her superior.

VAN ESPEN.

It is evident, as Zonaras remarks, that the double monasteries here referred to are not those in which men and women live together in one house, which in this canon is not tolerated at all, but those which were situated so close together that it was evident there could easily be an entrance from one to the other, these are allowed under certain cautions by this canon.

But not only the Greeks but the Latins also often disapproved of such monasteries. See decree in Gratian, Pars. II., Causa XVIII., Q. II., canon xxviij., and Pope Paschal's letter (*Epis.* X) to Didacus, Abp. of Compostella.

Despite all this St. Bridget of Sweden again instituted double monasteries in the XVth century, concerning which Thomas Walsingham, a monk of St. Alban's Abbey, in England, writes that in 1414, King Henry founded three monasteries, of which the third

---

[1] Bev.   Neither shall a nun eat alone.

was a Brigittine, professing the rule of St. Augustine, with the additions called by them the Rule of the Saviour. "These two convents had one church in common, the nuns lived in the upper part under the roof, the brothers on the ground-floor, and each convent had a separate inclosure; and after profession no one went forth, except by special licence of the Lord Pope."

With regard to the chaplains of nuns, provision is found in Justinian's Code. (Lib. xliv., *De Epis. et clericis.*)

This canon is found in the *Corpus Juris Canonici*, Gratian's *Decretum*, Pars. II., Causa XVIII., Q. II., canon xxj.

CANON XXI.

That monks are not to leave their monasteries and go into others.

A MONK or nun ought not to leave the monastery to which he or she is attached, and betake themselves to others. But if one do this, he ought to be received as a guest. It is not however proper that he be made a member of the monastery, without the consent of his hegumenos.

NOTES.

ANCIENT EPITOME OF CANON XXI.

It is not allowed to a monk or a nun to leave her own house and enter another; but if he (or she) enters let (him or her) be received as a guest; but let him (or her) not be admitted at all nor given hospitality contrary to the will of the superior.

ARISTENUS.

The present canon does not allow a monk or a nun who goes to another house to be received into, nor even to be admitted as a guest, lest by force of necessity he be led astray to worldly things and so remain. Moreover it does not permit a woman to be admitted and received and reckoned in the number of the sisters without the consent of the superior.

It seems to me that in Aristenus an οὐκ must have crept into the text and that the first sentence should read as now but omitting the "not." This makes him agree with Zonaras who says "the man must be received as a guest, lest he go to a profane tavern and be forced to associate with those who have never learned how to live decently." It is clear that the "superior" referred to is that of the house whence the monk or nun went forth.

CANON XXII.

That when it happens that monks have to eat with women they ought to observe giving of thanks, and abstemiousness, and discretion.

To surrender all things to God, and not to serve our own wills, is great gain. For says the divine Apostle, "whether ye eat or drink, do all to the glory of God." And Christ our God has bidden us in his Gospels, to cut off the beginning of sins; for not only is adultery rebuked by him, but even the movement of the mind towards the act of adultery when he says, "Whosoever looketh on a woman to lust after her, hath committed adultery with her already in his heart." . We who have been thus taught ought therefore to purify our minds. Now although all things are lawful, all things are not expedient, as we have been taught by the mouth of the Apostle. It is needful that all men should eat in order that they may live. And for those to whom life consists of marrying, and bringing forth children, and of the condition of the lay state, there is nothing unbecoming in men and women eating together, only let them give thanks to the giver of the food; but if there be the entertainments of the theatre, that is, Satanic songs accompanied with the meretricious inflections of harps, there come upon them, through these things, the curse of the prophet, who thus speaks: "Woe to them who drink wine with harp and psaltery, but they regard not the works of the Lord, and consider not the works of his hands." Whenever persons of this sort are found among

Christians, let them amend their ways; but if they will not do so, let there overtake them the penalties which have been enacted in the canons by our predecessors. With regard to those whose life is free from care and apart from men, that is, those who have resolved before the Lord God to carry the solitary yoke, they should sit down alone and in silence. Moreover it is also altogether unlawful for those who have chosen the priestly life to eat in private with women, unless it be with God-fearing and discreet men and women, so that even their feast may be turned to spiritual edification. The same rule is to be observed with relatives. Again, if it happen that a monk or priest while on a journey does not have with him what is absolutely necessary for him, and, because of his pressing needs, thinks well to turn aside into an inn or into someone's house, this he is permitted to do, seeing that need compels.

NOTES.

ANCIENT EPITOME OF CANON XXII.

There is no objection to laywomen eating with men: it is not right however for men who have chosen the lonely life, to eat privately with women; unless perchance together with them that fear God and with religious men and women. But when travelling, a monk or any-one in sacred orders, not carrying necessary provisions with him, may enter a public house.

Balsamon refers in connexion with this canon to Apostolic Canons xlij. and xliij.; lx. of the Synod of Carthage, and lxij. of the Synod in Trullo.

THE LETTER OF THE SYNOD TO THE EMPEROR AND EMPRESS.

(Labbe and Cossart, *Concilia*, Tom. VII., col. 577.)

To our most religious and most serene princes, Constantine and Irene his mother. Tarasius, the unworthy bishop of your God-protected royal city, new Rome, and all the holy Council which met at the good pleasure of God and upon the command of your Christ-loving majesty in the renowned metropolis of Nice, the second council to assemble in this city.

Christ our God (who is the head of the Church) was glorified, most noble princes, when your heart, which he holds in his hands, gave forth that good word bidding us to assemble in his name, in order that we might strengthen our hold on the sure, immovable, and God-given truth contained in the Church's dogmas. As your heads were crowned with gold and most brilliant stones, so likewise were your minds adorned with the precepts of the Gospel and the teachings of the Fathers. And being the disciples and companions, as it were, of those whose sounds went forth into all the earth, ye became the leaders in the way of piety of all who bore the name of Christ, setting forth clearly the word of truth, and giving a brilliant example of orthodoxy and piety ; so that ye were to the faithful as so many burning lamps. The Church which was ready to fall, ye upheld with your hands, strengthening it with sound doctrine, and bringing into the unity of a right judgment those who were at variance. We may therefore well say with boldness that it was through you that the good pleasure of God brought about the triumph of godliness, and filled our mouth with joy and our tongue with gladness. And these things our lips utter with a formal decree. For what is more glorious than to maintain the Church's interests ; and what else is more calculated to provoke our gladness ?

Certain men rose up, having the form of godliness, inasmuch as they were clothed with the dignity of the priesthood, but denying the power thereof; and thus deserving for themselves the charge of being but priests of Babylon. Of such the word of prophecy had before declared that "law-lessness went forth from the priests [1] of Babylon." Nay more, they banded themselves together in a sanhedrim, like to that which Caiaphas held, and became the propagators of ungodly doctrines. And having a mouth full of cursing and bitterness, they thought to win the mastery by means of abusive words. With a slanderous tongue and a pen of a like character, and objecting to the very terms used by God himself, they devised marvellous tales, and then proceeded to stigmatise as idolaters the royal priesthood and the holy nation, even those who had put on Christ, and by his grace had been kept safe from the folly of idols. And having a mind set upon evil, they took in hand unlawful deeds, thinking to suppress altogether the depicting of the venerable images. Accordingly, as many icons as were set in mosaic work they dug out, and those which were in painted waxwork, they scraped away; thus turning the comely beauty of the sacred temples into complete disorder. Among doings of this sort, it is to be specially noted that the pictures set up on tablets in memory of Christ our God and of his Saints, they gave over to the flames. Finally, in a word, having desecrated our churches, they reduced them to utter confusion. Then some bishops became the leaders of this heresy and where before was peace, they fomented strife among the people; and instead of wheat sowed tares in the Church's fields. They mingled wine with water, and gave the foul draught to those about them. Although but Arabian wolves, they hid themselves under sheeps' clothing, and by specious reasoning against the truth sought to commend their lie. But all the while " they hatched asps' eggs and wove a spider's web," as says the prophet; and " he that would eat of their eggs, having crushed one, found it to be addled, with a basilisk within it," and giving forth a deadly stench.

In such a state of affairs, with a lie busy destroying the truth, ye, most gracious and

---

[1] " Presbyters " in LXX.

most noble princes, did not idly allow so grave a plague, and such soul-destroying error long to continue in your day. But moved by the divine Spirit which abideth in you, ye set yourselves with all your strength utterly to exterminate it, and thus preserve the stability of the Church's government, and likewise concord among your subjects; so that your whole empire might be established in peace agreeably with the name [Irene] you bear. Ye rightly reasoned, that it was not to be patiently endured, that while in other matters we could be of one mind and live in concord, yet in what ought to be the chief concern of our life, the peace of the Churches, there was amongst us strife and division. And that too, when Christ being our head, we ought to be members one of another, and one body, by our mutual agreement and faith. Accordingly, ye commanded our holy and numerously-attended council to assemble in the metropolis of Nice, in order that after having rid the Church of division, we might restore to unity the separated members, and might be careful to rend and utterly destroy the coarse cloak of false doctrine, which they had woven of thorn fibre, and unfold again the fair robe of orthodoxy.

And now having carefully traced the traditions of the Apostles and Fathers, we are bold to speak. Having but one mind by the inbreathing of the most Holy Spirit, and being all knit together in one, and understanding the harmonious tradition of the Catholic Church, we are in perfect harmony with the symphonies set forth by the six, holy and ecumenical councils; and accordingly we have anathematised the madness of Arius, the frenzy of Macedonius, the senseless understanding of Appolinarius, the man-worship of Nestorius, the irreverent mingling of the natures devised by Eutyches and Dioscorus, and the many-headed hydra which is their companion. We have also anathematised the idle tales of Origen, Didymus, and Evagrius; and the doctrine of one will held by Sergius, Honorius, Cyrus, and Pyrrhus, or rather, we have anathematised their own evil will. Finally, taught by the Spirit, from whom we have drawn pure water, we have with one accord and one soul, altogether wiped out with the sponge of the divine dogmas the newly devised heresy, well-worthy to be

classed with those just mentioned, which springing up after them, uttered such empty nonsense about the sacred icons. And the contrivers of this vain, but revolutionary babbling we have cast forth far from the Church's precincts.

And as the hands and feet are moved in accordance with the directions of the mind, so likewise, we, having received the grace and strength of the Spirit, and having also the assistance and co-operation of your royal authority, have with one voice declared as piety and proclaimed as truth: that the sacred icons of our Lord Jesus Christ are to be had and retained, inasmuch as he was very man; also those which set forth what is historically narrated in the Gospels; and those which represent our undefiled Lady, the holy Mother of God; and likewise those of the Holy Angels (for they have manifested themselves in human form to those who were counted worthy of the vision of them), or of any of the Saints. [We have also decreed] that the brave deeds of the Saints be pourtrayed on tablets and on the walls, and upon the sacred vessels and vestments, as hath been the custom of the holy Catholic Church of God from ancient times; which custom was regarded as having the force of law in the teaching both of those holy leaders who lived in the first ages of the Church, and also of their successors our reverend Fathers. [We have likewise decreed] that these images are to be reverenced (προσκυνεῖν), that is, salutations are to be offered to them. The reason for using the word is, that it has a two-fold signification. For κυνεῖν in the old Greek tongue signifies both "to salute" and "to kiss." And the preposition προς gives to it the additional idea of strong desire towards the object; as for example, we have φέρω and προσφέρω, κυρῶ and προσκυρῶ, and so also we have κυνέω and προσκυνέω. Which last word implies salutation and strong love; for that which one loves he also reverences (προσκυνεῖ) and what he reverences that he greatly loves, as the everyday custom, which we observe towards those we love, bears witness, and in which both ideas are practically illustrated when two friends meet together. The word is not only made use of by us, but we also find it set down in the Divine Scriptures by the ancients. For it is written in the histories of the Kings,

" And David rose up and fell upon his face and did reverence to ($\pi\rho o\sigma\epsilon\kappa\acute{v}\nu\eta\sigma\epsilon$) Jonathan three times and kissed him " (1 Kings xx., 41). And what is it that the Lord in the Gospel says concerning the Pharisees? " They love the uppermost rooms at feasts and greetings ($\dot{a}\sigma\pi a\sigma\mu o\grave{v}\varsigma$) in the markets." It is evident that by "greetings " here, he means reverence ($\pi\rho o\sigma\kappa\acute{v}\nu\eta\sigma\iota\nu$) for the Pharisees being very high-minded and thinking themselves to be righteous were eager to be reverenced by all, but not [merely] to be kissed. For to receive salutations of this latter sort savoured too much of lowly humility, and this was not to the Pharisees' liking. We have also the example of Paul the divine Apostle, as Luke in the Acts of the Apostles relates : "When we were come to Jerusalem, the brethren received us gladly, and the day following Paul went in with us unto James, and all the presbyters were present. And when he had saluted ($\dot{a}\sigma\pi a\sigma\acute{a}\mu\epsilon\nu o\varsigma$) them, he declared particularly what things God had wrought among the Gentiles by his ministry " (Acts xxi., 17, 18, 19). By the salutation here mentioned, the Apostle evidently intended to render that reverence of honour ($\tau\iota\mu\eta\tau\iota\kappa\grave{\eta}\nu$ $\pi\rho o\sigma\kappa\acute{v}\nu\eta\sigma\iota\nu$) which we shew to one another, and of which he speaks when he says concerning Jacob, that "he reverenced ($\pi\rho o\sigma\epsilon\kappa\acute{v}\nu\eta\sigma\epsilon\nu$) the top of his staff " (Heb. xi., 21). With these examples agrees what Gregory surnamed Theologus says : "Honour Bethlehem, and reverence ($\pi\rho o\sigma$-$\kappa\upsilon\nu\acute{\eta}\sigma o\nu$) the manger."

Now who of those rightly and sincerely understanding the Divine Scriptures, has ever supposed that these examples which we have cited speak of the worship in spirit ($\tau\hat{\eta}\varsigma$ $\dot{\epsilon}\nu$ $\pi\nu\epsilon\acute{v}\mu a\tau\iota$ $\lambda a\tau\rho\epsilon\acute{\iota}a\varsigma$)? [Certainly no one has ever thought so] except perhaps some persons utterly bereft of sense and ignorant of all knowledge of the Scriptures and of the teaching of the Fathers. Surely Jacob did not adore ($\dot{\epsilon}\lambda\acute{a}\tau\rho\epsilon\upsilon\sigma\epsilon\nu$) the top of his staff; and surely Gregory Theologus does not bid us to adore ($\lambda a\tau\rho\epsilon\acute{v}\epsilon\iota\nu$) the manger? By no means. Again, when offering salutations to the life-giving Cross, we together sing : " We reverence ($\pi\rho o\sigma\kappa\upsilon\nu$-$\hat{\omega}\mu\epsilon\nu$), thy cross, O Lord, and we also reverence ($\pi\rho o\sigma\kappa\upsilon\nu\hat{\omega}\mu\epsilon\nu$) the spear which opened the life-giving side of thy goodness." This is clearly but a salutation, and

is so called, and its character is evinced by our touching the things mentioned with our lips. We grant that the word $\pi\rho o$-$\sigma\kappa\acute{v}\nu\eta\sigma\iota\varsigma$ is frequently found in the Divine Scriptures and in the writings of our learned and holy Fathers for the worship in spirit ($\dot{\epsilon}\pi\grave{\iota}$ $\tau\eta\varsigma$ $\dot{\epsilon}\nu$ $\pi\nu\epsilon\acute{v}\mu a\tau\iota$ $\lambda a\tau\rho\epsilon\acute{\iota}a\varsigma$), since, being a word of many significations, it may be used to express that kind of reverence which is service. As there is also the veneration of honour, love and fear. In this sense it is, that we venerate your glorious and most noble majesty. So also there is another veneration which comes of fear alone, thus Jacob venerated Esau. Then there is the veneration of gratitude, as Abraham reverenced the sons of Heth, for the field which he received from them for a burying place for Sarah his wife. And finally, those looking to obtain some gift, venerate those who are above them, as Jacob venerated Pharaoh. Therefore because this term has these many significations, the Divine Scriptures teaching us, "Thou shalt venerate the Lord thy God, and him only shalt thou serve," says simply that veneration is to be given to God, but does not add the word " only ; " for veneration being a word of wide meaning is an ambiguous term; but it goes on to say " thou shalt serve ($\lambda a\tau$-$\rho\epsilon\acute{v}\sigma\epsilon\iota\varsigma$) him *only*," for to God alone do we render latria.

The things which we have decreed, being thus well supported, it is confessedly and beyond all question acceptable and wellpleasing before God, that the images of our Lord Jesus Christ as man, and those of the undefiled Mother of God, the evervirgin Mary, and of the honourable Angels and of all Saints, should be venerated and saluted. And if anyone does not so believe, but undertakes to debate the matter further and is evil affected with regard to the veneration due the sacred images, such an one our holy ecumenical council (fortified by the inward working of the Spirit of God, and by the traditions of the Fathers and of the Church) anathematises. Now anathema is nothing less than complete separation from God. For if any are quarrelsome and will not obediently accept what has now been decreed, they but kick against the pricks, and injure their own souls in their fighting against Christ. And in taking pleasure at the insults which are offered to the Church, they clearly shew themselves to be of those who madly make war upon piety, and are therefore to be regarded as in the same category with the heretics of old times, and their companions and brethren in ungodliness.

We have sent our brethren and fellow priests, God-beloved Bishops, together with certain of the Hegumenoi and clergy, that they may give a full report of our proceedings to your godly-hearing ears. In proof and confirmation of what we have decreed, and also for the assurance of your most religious majesty, we have submitted proofs from the Fathers, a few of the many we have gathered together in illustration of the brightly shining truth.

And now may the Saviour of us all, who reigns with you (συμβασιλεύων ὑμῖν) and who was pleased to vouchsafe his peace to the Churches through you, preserve your kingdom for many years, and also your council, princes, and faithful army, and the whole estate of the empire; and may he also give you victory over all your enemies. For he it is, who says: "As I live, saith the Lord, they that glorify me, I will glorify." He it is also who hath girded you with strength, and will smite all your enemies, and make your people to rejoice.

And do thou, O city, the new Sion, rejoice and be glad; thou that art the wonder of the whole world. For although David hath not reigned in thee, nevertheless thy pious princes here preside over thy affairs as David would have done. The Lord is in the midst of thee; may his name be blessed forever and ever. Amen.

EXCURSUS ON THE TWO LETTERS OF GREGORY II. TO THE EMPEROR LEO.

(J. B. Bury, Appendix 14 to Vol. V. of his edition of Gibbon's *Rome*. 1898.)

It is incorrect to say that "the two epistles of Gregory II. have been preserved in the Acts of the Nicene Council" [as Gibbon does]. In modern collections of the Acts of Ecclesiastical Councils, they have been printed at the end of the Acts of the Second Nicene Council. But they first came to light at the end of the XVIth. century and were printed for the first time in the *Annales Ecclesiastici* of Baronius, who had obtained them from Fronton le Duc. This scholar had copied the text from a Greek MS. at Rheims. Since then other MSS. have been found, the earliest belonging to the XIth., if not the Xth century.

In another case we should say that the external evidence for the genuineness of the epistles was good. We know on the authority of Theophanes that Gregory wrote one or more letters to Leo (ἐπιστολὴν δογματικήν, *sub* A. M. 6172, ὅ'ι ἐπιστολῶν, *sub* A. M. 6221) ; and we should have no external reasons to suspect copies dating from about 300 years later. But the omission of these letters in the Acts of the Nicene Council, though they are stated to have been read at the council, introduces a shadow of suspicion. If they were preserved, how comes it that they were not preserved in the Acts of the Council, like the letter of Gregory to the Patriarch Germanus ? There is no trace anywhere of the Latin originals.

Turning to the contents, we find enough to convert suspicion into a practical certainty that the documents are forgeries. This is the opinion of M. l'abbé Duchesne (the editor of the *Liber Pontificalis*), M. L. Guérard (*Mélanges d'Archéologie et d'Histoire*, p. 44 *sqq.*, 1890) ; Mr. Hodgkin (*Italy and her Invaders*, Vol. vi., p. 501 *sqq.*) A false date (the beginning of Leo's reign is placed in the XIVth. instead of the XVth. indiction), and the false implication that the Imperial territory of the "Ducatus Romæ" terminated at twenty-four stadia, or three miles, from Rome, point to an author who was neither a contemporary of Leo nor a resident in Rome. But the insolent tone of the letters is enough to condemn them. Gregory II. would never have addressed to his sovereign the crude abuse with which these documents teem. Another objection (which I have never seen noticed) is that in the First Letter the famous image of Christ which was pulled down by Leo, is stated to have been in the "Chalkoprateia" (bronzesmith's quarter), whereas, according to the trustworthy sources, it was above the Chalkâ gate of the Palace.

Rejecting the letters on these grounds—which are supported by a number of smaller points—we get rid of the difficulty about a Lombard siege of Ravenna before A. D. 727 : a siege which is not mentioned elsewhere and was doubtless created by the confused knowledge of the fabricator.

EXCURSUS ON THE RECEPTION OF THE SEVENTH COUNCIL.

The reception of the Seventh Council in the East was practically universal. No historian pretends that the iconoclastic opinions had any hold over the masses of the people. It was strictly speaking a court movement, backed by the army, and whenever the images were laid low and their veneration condemned it was by the power of the State, enforcing its will upon a yielding and (as we would call them to-day) Erastian clergy. (Cf. Harnack, *History of Dogma*, Eng. tr. Vol. iv., p. 326.)

The struggle indeed was not quite put an end to by the conciliar decree After the death of the Empress in A. D. 803, several iconoclastic rulers sat on the throne of the East, among them Michael the Stammerer, who (as Michaud wittily says) "fought the images and married the nuns."[1] He sent a letter, which is still extant, to Louis le Débonnaire of France, setting forth the superstitions of the orthodox, which is most curious and interesting reading. (*Vide* Mansi.)

His successor was Theophilus, who reigned from 829 until 842, and was a fanatical iconoclast. The Patriarchs of Antioch, Alexandria, and Jerusalem wrote to him officially, several years after his accession, begging him not to imitate the bad example of the iconoclasts. At that time the only Patriarch who sided with the heretics was John the Grammarian, the Patriarch of Constantinople, the very same who in 814 had repudiated the iconoclast doctrine ! With the death of this Emperor, the power of the Iconoclasts likewise died ; and at the accession of Michael III. with his mother Theodora and his sister Thecla came the final triumph of the images. I shall quote here the words of Harnack : "Then came an Empress, Theodora, who finally restored the worship. This took place at the Synod held at Constantinople A. D. 842. This Synod decreed that a Feast of Orthodoxy (ἡ κυριακὴ τῆς ὀρθοδοξίας) should be celebrated annually, at which the victory over the iconoclasts should be regularly remembered. Thus the whole of orthodoxy was united in image-worship. In this way the Eastern Church reached the position which suited its nature. We have here the conclusion of a development, consistent in the main points. The divine and sacred, as that had descended into the sensuous world by the incarnation, had created for itself in the Church a system of material, supernatural things, which offered themselves for man's use." (*Hist. Dogma.* Vol. iv., p. 328.)

Much has been written, and truly written, of the superiority of the iconoclastic rulers ; but when all has been said that can be, the fact still remains, that they were most of them but sorry Christians, and the justice of the Protestant Archbishop of Dublin's summing up of the matter will not be disputed by any impartial student. He says, "No one will deny that with rarest exceptions, all the religious earnestness, all which constituted the quickening power of a church, was ranged upon the other [i.e. the orthodox] side. Had the Iconoclasts triumphed, when their work showed itself at last in its true colours, it would have proved to be the triumph, not of faith in an invisible God, but of frivolous unbelief in an incarnate Saviour." (Trench. *Mediæval History*, Chap. vii.)

We come now to consider what reception the Seventh of the General Councils met with in the West. And first we find that it was accepted, so far at least as its dogmatic decrees went, by the Pope, the whole Roman Church and, so far as we know, by all the West except the realm of Charlemagne and, as would naturally be expected, the English Church.

It is true that this was a large and very important exception ; so large and so important that it becomes necessary to examine in detail the causes which led to this rejection.

Some persons have supposed that the English council held at Calcuth in 787 rejected the ecumenical character of II. Nice, because in two of its canons (the 1st and the 4th) it only speaks of "the faith of the Six General Councils." But it is evident that the reason for this was that it had not yet heard of the Nicene synod ; moreover such action would have been clearly impossible, since the council was presided over by the Bishop of Ostia, the legate of Pope Hadrian.

The first opposition to the council in the West was made apparently by Charlemagne himself. Pope Hadrian sent him a translation of the acts into Latin and signified his accept-

---

[1] It was during this period that St. Theodore, writing in 826 to Arsenius, observes :

"Rome has not received it as an Ecumenical Council, but only as a provincial Synod, assembled to remedy a particular evil ; Legates of the other Patriarchs were not there ; those of Rome had come on different business : Legates, indeed, there were from the East, but they were brought by our deputies, not sent by their Patriarchs, who knew nothing of the matter till after-

wards. Our countrymen acted thus for the purpose of more easily bringing back the heretics by persuading them that it was an Ecumenical Council." "Theodore, however, it is fair to add, afterwards changed his opinion." Such is Dr. Neale's candid admission. *Hist of the East. Ch.*, Vol. II., p. 135. How often, alas ! has this passage been quoted by controversialists, and the word of warning to the reader been wholly omitted.

ance of the council.   But this translation was so badly done that not only was a large part of the acts utterly unintelligible, but also, in at least one place, a bishop of the council was made to say that the sacred images were to be adored with the same supreme worship as is paid to the Holy Trinity.

It may not be wholly charitable to suggest the possibility of such a thing having any influence in the matter.   On the other hand it would be unfair to the reader not to state that Charlemagne had, or thought that he had, serious grievances against the Empress Irene, and that he might not have been sorry to have discovered some reason for which to reject her council.   It should, moreover, be remembered how much the Pope in his struggle for independence of the Eastern Empire trusted to Charlemagne, and therefore how reluctant he might readily have been to break with so important an ally; and so might be induced to tolerate the rejection by the Frankish Emperor of what had been received by him, the Vicar of Christ and the successor of Peter, as the Seventh Ecumenical Synod of the Catholic Church.

As a result of this feeling of Charlemagne's, there were written what we call the " Caroline Books," and these exercised so mighty an influence on this whole question, and so completely misled even the learned, that I shall give a careful examination of their authorship, authority, and contents ; for there can be no doubt that it was the influence of these books (which appeared in 790) that induced the unfortunate action of the Council of Frankfort four years later (in 794) ; and that of the Convention of Paris in 825.

EXAMINATION OF THE CAROLINE BOOKS.

I. *Authorship of the Caroline Books.*

I find that many writers on the subject of what they call "image worship," speak frequently of these "Caroline Books," and refer to them with great admiration. It is also absolutely certain that many of these writers have never read, possibly never seen, the books of which they write so eloquently. I have used the reprint of Melchior Goldast's edition (Frankfort, 1608) in Migne's *Patrologia Latina*, Tom. xcviij., in this article.

The work begins thus. "In the name of our Lord and Saviour Jesus Christ beginneth the work of the most illustrious and glorious man Charles, by the will of God, king of the Franks, Gauls, Germany, etc., against the Synod which in Greek parts firmly and proudly decreed in favour of adoring (*adorandis*) images," then follows immediately what is called "Charlemagne's Preface."

Now of course nobody supposes for a moment that Charlemagne wrote these books himself. But Sir William Palmer (*Treatise on the Church*, Vol. II., p. 204) says that the prelates of the realm of France "composed a reply to this Synod," he further says that "This work was published by the authority and in the name of the Emperor Charlemagne and with the consent of his bishops, in 790" (p. 205). I am entirely at a loss to know on what authority these statements rest. The authorship of the work has, not without great show of reason, been attributed to Alcuin. Besides the English tradition that he had written such a book, there has been pointed out the remarkable similarity of his commentary on St. John (4, 5, *et seqq.*) to a passage in Liber IV., cap. vj., of these Caroline Books. (On this point see Forster, *General Preface to the Works of Alcuin* n. 10.) But after all whether Alcuin was the author or no, matters little, the statement that the "bishops of France" were in any sense responsible for it is entirely gratuitous, unless indeed some should think it may be gathered from the statement of the Preface ;

"We have undertaken this work with the priests who are prelates of the Catholic flocks in the kingdom which has been granted to us of God."[1] But this would not be the only book written at the command of, and set forth by, a secular prince and yet claiming the authority of the Church. I need only give as examples "The Institution of a Christian Man" and the Second Prayer Book of Edward the VIth.

II. *Authority of the Caroline Books.*

But be their authorship what it may, we come next to consider their authority ; and here we are met with the greatest difficulty, for it is certain that despite the statements to the contrary, these books were not those sent to Pope Hadrian by Charlemagne, those of which the Pope deigned to write a refutation. This Hefele has clearly proved, by pointing out that those sent to the Pope treated the matter in an entirely different order ; that there were in those sent only 85 chapters, while these books have 120 (or 121 if the authenticity of the last chapter is granted). Moreover the quotations made by Hadrian do not occur *verbatim* in the Caroline books, but are in some cases enlarged, in others abbreviated. (Cf. Hefele's treatment of the whole subject in the original German.) Petavius thinks that what Hadrian received were extracts from the Caroline Books, made by the Council of Frankfort.

---

[1] It is curious that Michaud (*Sept. Conciles Œcuméniques.* p. 294) should say "the title priest given to those who composed the book proves that no one of them was a bishop." The Latin is "Sacerdotum Prælatorum"!

Hefele arrives at a directly opposite conclusion, viz., that the Caroline Books are an expansion of the *Capitula* sent to the Pope, and that this expansion was made at the bidding of Charlemagne.

It should be noted here that Baronius, Bellarmine, Binius, and Surius all question the authenticity of the Caroline Books altogether. (*Vide* Baron, *Annal.*, A.D., 794.) But this extreme position seems to be refuted by the fact that certain quotations made by Hincmar are found in the books as we have them. (*Cf.* Sirmond in Mansi, Tom. XIII., 905, Labbe, Tom. VII., col. 1054.)

III.   *Contents of the Caroline Books.*

If the authorship and authority of these books are difficult subjects, the contents of the books are still more extraordinary, for it seems to be certain, past all possibility of doubt, that the authors of these books had never read the acts nor decrees of the Seventh Ecumenical Synod, of which they were writing ; and further that he or they were also completely ignorant of what took place at the Conciliabulum of 754.

One example will be sufficient to prove this point.   In Book IV., Chapter XIV., and also in chapter XX., (Migne's ed., col. 1213 and col. 1226), the charge is made that the Seventh Council, especially Gregory, the bishop of Neocæsarea, unduly flattered the Empress.   Now as a matter of fact the remarks referred to were made at the Conciliabulum of 754, and not at the Second Council of Nice ; they were not made by Gregory of Neocæsarea at all, and the reason they are attributed to him is because he read them in the proceedings of that pseudo-council to the true council of 787.

Other examples could easily be given, but this is sufficient.   *Ab uno disce omnes.*   The most famous however of all the ignorant blunders found in these books must not here be omitted.   It occurs in Book III., chapter xvij., and is no less serious than to attribute to Constantius, the bishop of Cyprus, the monstrous statement that the sacred images were to be given the supreme adoration due to the Holy Trinity.   What a complete mistake this was, we have already pointed out, and will have been evident to anyone who has read the extracts of the acts given in the foregoing pages.   I have said "mistake ;" and I have said so deliberately, because I am convinced that the Caroline books, the decree of Frankfort, and the decision of the Convention of Paris, all sprung from ignorance and blundering ; and largely through the force of this particular false statement on which I am writing.   But I must not omit the statement of Sir William Palmer, a champion of these books, that " the acts of the synod of Nice having been sent to Rome in the year 787, Pope Hadrian himself, according to Hincmar, transmitted them into France to Charlemagne, to be confirmed by the bishops of his kingdom ; and the Emperor [i.e. Charlemagne] also received the acts directly from Constantinople according to Roger Hovedon.   These prelates, thus furnished with an authentic copy and not a mere translation, composed a reply to the synod " (*Treatise on the Church*, Vol. II., p. 203).

If Sir William is right, then the author of the Caroline books is thrown into a dark shade indeed, for either he was too ignorant or too careless to read the original Greek, or else, knowing the real state of the case, deliberately misrepresented the synod.   Sir William feels this difficulty, and, a few lines below the sentence I have quoted, attributes the misstatements to a " mistranslation," viz. the false statement—upon which alone all the rest hung— attributed to the bishop of Cyprus.   But the two claims are *contraria inter se.*   If they were using an authentic copy of the original sent from Constantinople then they could not have been misled by a " mistranslation ;" if they used a mistranslation and took no pains to read the decrees, their opinion and their writings—as well as the decrees which followed from them—were evidently entirely without theological value, and this is the estimation in which they have been held by all unprejudiced scholars without exception, whether agreeing with their conclusions or no.

It will be well to set plainly before the reader the foundation upon which rests the dogmatic teaching of the Caroline Books. This is, in short, the authority of the Roman See. That there may be no possible doubt upon this point, I proceed to quote somewhat at length chapter vi., of Book I.; the heading of which reads as follows: "That the Holy Roman Catholic and Apostolic Church is placed above all other Churches, and is to be consulted at every turn when any controversy arises with regard to the faith."

"Before entering upon a discussion of the witnesses which the Easterns have absurdly brought forward in their Synod, we think well to set forth how greatly the holy Roman Church has been exalted by the Lord above the other Churches, and how she is to be consulted by the faithful: and this is especially the case since only such books as she receives as canonical and only such Fathers as she has recognized by Gelasius and the other Pontiffs, his successors, are to be accepted and followed; nor are they to be interpreted by the private will of anyone, but wisely and soberly. . . . For as the Apostolic Sees in general are to be preferred to all the other dioceses of the world, much more is that see to be preferred which is placed over all the other apostolic sees. For just as the Apostles were exalted above the other disciples, and Peter was exalted above the other Apostles, so the apostolic sees are exalted above the other sees, and the Roman See is eminent over the other apostolic sees. And this exaltation arises from no synodical action of the other Churches, but she holds the primacy (*primatum*) by the authority of the Lord himself, when he said, 'Thou art Peter, etc.' . . .

"This church, therefore, fortified with the spiritual arms of the holy faith, and satiated with the health-giving fountains which flow from the well of light and from the source of goodness, resists the horrible and atrocious monsters of heresies, and ministers the honey-sweet cups of teaching to the Catholic Churches of the whole world. . . . Whence [i.e. from St. Jerome consulting the Pope] we can understand how Saints and learned men who were shining lights in different parts of the world, not only did not depart in faith from the holy Roman Church, but also asked aid of her in time of necessity for the strengthening of the faith. And this all Catholic Churches should regularly observe, so that they may seek help from her, after Christ, for protecting the faith: which (*quæ*) having neither spot nor wrinkle, smites the portentous heads of heresies, and strengthens the minds of the faithful in the faith. And although many have separated from this holy and venerable communion, nevertheless never have the Churches of our part done so, but instructed by that apostolical erudition, and by his assistance from whom cometh every good and perfect gift, have always received the venerable charismata . . .; and are careful to follow the see of blessed Peter in all things, as they desire thither to arrive where he sits as keeper of the keys. To which blessedness may he who deigned to found his Church upon Peter bring us, and make us to persevere in the unity of the holy Church; and may we merit a place in that kingdom of heaven through the intervention of him whose See we follow and to whom have been given the keys."

Such is the doctrinal foundation of the Caroline books, viz.: the absolute authority of the Roman See in matters pertaining to the faith of the Church. It is certainly very difficult to understand how the author of these books could have known that the doctrinal decree of the Synod of Nice had received the approbation of this supreme power which it was so necessary to consult and defer to; and that the Synod which he denounces and rejects had been received by that chief of all the Apostolic Sees as the Seventh of the Ecumenical Councils of the Catholic Church.

Whether the author [or authors] had ever seen the Pope's letter or no, one thing is certain, he never read with any care even the imperfect translation with which he had been furnished, and of that translation Anastasius Bibliothetius says: "The translator both misunderstood the genius of the Greek language as well as that of the Latin, and has merely translated word for word; and in such a fashion that it is scarcely ever possible to know (*aut vix aut nunquam*) what it means; moreover nobody ever reads this translation and no copies of it are made." [1]

This being the case, when we come to examine the Caroline Books, we are not astonished to find them full of false statements.

In the Preface we are told that the Conciliabulum was "held in Bithynia;" of course as a matter of fact it met in Constantinople.

In Bk. I., chapter j., we find certain words said to occur in the letters of the Empress and her son. On this Hefele remarks: "One cannot find the words in either of the two letters of these sovereigns, which are preserved in the acts of the Council of Nice, it is the synod that uses them. [2]"

In the Second Book, chapter xxvij., the council is charged with saying "Just as the Lord's body and blood pass over from fruits of the earth to a notable mystery, so also the images, made by the skill of the artificers, pass over to the veneration of those persons whose images they bear." Now this was never said nor taught by the Nicene Synod, but something like it was taught by the Constantinopolitan conciliabulum of 754; but the very words cited occur neither in the one set of acts nor in the other! The underlying thought however was, as we have said, clearly exposed by the iconoclastic synod of 754 and as clearly refuted by the orthodox synod of 787.

In Book III., chapter V., we are told that "Tarasius said in his confession of faith that the Holy Spirit was the companion (*contribulum* in the Caroline Books) of the Father and of the Son." It was not Tarasius who said so at all, but Theodore of Jerusalem, and in using the word ὁμόφυλος he was but copying Sophronius of Jerusalem.

Chapter XVII. begins thus: "How rashly and (so to speak) like a fool, Constantine, bishop of Constantia in Cyprus, spoke when he said, with the approval of the rest of the bishops, that he would receive and honourably embrace the images; and babbled that the service of adoration which is due to the consubstantial and life-giving Trinity, should be given images, we need not here discuss, since to all who either read or hear this it will be clear that he was swamped in no small error, to wit to confess that he exhibited to creatures the service due to the Creator alone, and through his desire to favour the pictures overturned all the Holy Scriptures. For what sane man ever either said or thought of saying such an absurdity, as that different pictures should be held in the same honour as the holy, victorious Trinity, the creator of all things, etc." But as will be seen by a glance at the acts this is exactly the opposite of what Constantine did say. Now if, as Sir William Palmer asserts, the author had before him the genuine acts in the original, I do not see how his honesty can be defended, or if his honesty is kept intact, it must be at the expense of his learning or carefulness. Bower felt this so keenly that he thinks the Caroline Books attribute the words to Constantine the bishop alone and not to the council. But the subterfuge is vain, for, as we have just seen, the author affirms that Constantine's speech received "the assent of the rest of the bishops (*cœteris consentientibus*)," and further not obscurely suggests that Constantine had the courage to say what the others were content to think, but did not dare to say.

In Book IV., the third chapter distinctly states that while lights and incense were used

---

by them in their churches, yet that neither the one nor the other was placed before images. If this can be relied upon it would seem to fix the Frankish custom of that date.

Chapters XIV. and XX. are distinguished by the most glaring blunders, for they attribute to the Council of Nice the teachings of the Conciliabulum, and in particular they lay them to the door of Gregory of Neocæsarea because he it was who read them.

Finally, in chapter the twenty-eighth, the ecumenical character of II. Nice is denied, on the ground that it has not preserved the faith of the Fathers, and that it was not universal in its constitution. I beg the reader, who has fresh in his memory the Papal claims set forth in a previous chapter, to consider whether it is possible that the author of that chapter should have seen and known of the Papal acceptance of the Seventh Synod and yet have written as follows: "Among all the inanities said and done by this synod, this does not seem by any means to be the least, that they styled it ecumenical, for it neither held the purity of the ecumenical faith, nor did it obtain authority through the ecumenical action of the Churches. . . . If this synod had kept clear of novelties and had rested satisfied with the teachings of the ancient Fathers, it might have been styled ecumenical. But since it was not contented with the teachings of the ancient Fathers it cannot be styled ecumenical," etc., etc.

Such are in brief the contents and spirit of the Caroline Books. Binius indeed says that he found a twenty-ninth chapter in a French MS. of Hadrian's Epistle. It is lacking in the ordinary codices. Petavius thinks it was added by the Council of Frankfort. It is found in Migne (col. 1218) and the main point is that St. Gregory's advice is to be followed, viz.: "We permit images of the Saints to be made by whoever is so disposed, as well in churches as out of them, for the love of God and of his Saints; but never compel anyone who does not wish to do so to bow to them (*adorare eas*); nor do we permit anyone to destroy them, even if he should so desire." I cannot but think that this would be a very lame conclusion to all the denunciation of the preceding chapters.

IV. *The Chief Cause of Trouble a Logomachy.*

Now from all this one thing is abundantly clear, that the great point set forth with such learning and perspicuity by the Seventh Synod, to wit, the distinction between λατρεία and προσκύνεσις was wholly lost upon these Frankish writers; and that their translation of both words by "*adoro*" gave rise to nine-tenths of the trouble that followed. The student of ecclesiastical history will remember how a similar logomachy followed nearly every one of the Ecumenical Synods, and will not therefore be astonished to find it likewise here. The "homousion," the "theotocos," the "two natures," "the two wills," each one gave rise to heated discussion in different sections of the Church, even after it had been accepted and approved by a Synod which no one now for an instant disputes to have been ecumenical.

Moreover, that after this serious error and bungling on the part of the Caroline divines and of the French and Allemanic Churches, the Pope did not proceed to enforce the acceptance of the council will not cause astonishment to any who are familiar with what St. Athanasius said with regard to the Semi-Arians, who even after I. Nice refused to use the word "homousios;" or with the extreme gentleness and moderation of St. Cyril of Alexandria in his treatment of John of Antioch.

Perhaps before leaving the subject I should give here the chief strictures which Hefele makes upon these books (§ 400).

(1) The Caroline Books condemn passages which they quote (without saying so) from Pope Hadrian's own letter to the Empress.

(2) They blame St. Basil for teaching that the reverence done to the image passes on to the prototype.

(3) They treat St. Gregory Nyssen with contempt, and refuse to listen to him (Lib. II., c. xvij.).

(4) They are full of most careless and inexcusable blunders.

(a) They attribute to the Emperors a phrase which belongs to the Synod (I. j.).

(b) They confound Leontius with John (I. xxj.).

(c) They confound Tarasius with Theodore of Jerusalem (III. v.).

(d) They impute to the Council the opinions of the Iconoclastic Conciliabulum (IV., xiv. and xx.).

(e) They attribute to Epiphanius the deacon the propositions of others when he merely read (IV., xv.)

It had usually been supposed that these Four Books were the "quædam capitula" which Charlemagne had sent by Angelbert to Pope Hadrian "to be corrected by his judgment (*ut illius judicio corrigerentur*). Considering the nature of the contents of the Caroline Books as we now have them, such would seem *à priori* highly improbable, but this matter has been practically settled, as we have already pointed out, by Bishop Hefele, who has shown from Pope Hadrian's answer "correcting" those "capitula," that they must have been entirely different in order though no doubt their contents were similar. The differing views of Petavius and Walch will be found in full in Hefele (§ 401).

In concluding his masterly treatment of this whole matter, Hefele makes (§ 402) a remark well worthy of repetition in this place:

"The great friendship which Charles shewed to Pope Hadrian down to the hour of his death proves that their way of thinking with regard to the cultus of images was not so opposite as many suppose, and—above all—as many have tried to make out."

I shall close this matter with the admirably learned and judicious words of Michaud.

"No doubt there had been abuses in connexion with the worship of images; but the Council of Nice never approved of these. No doubt, too, certain marks of veneration used in the East were not practised in Gaul; but the Council of Nice did not go into these particulars. It merely determined the principle, to wit, the lawfulness and moral necessity of honouring the holy images; and in doing this it did not in any degree innovate. Charlemagne ought to have known this, for, already in the sixth century Fortunatus, in his Poem on St. Martin, tells how in Gaul they lighted lamps before the images.[1] The great point that Charlemagne made was that what was called in the West 'adoration,' in the strict sense (that is to say the worship of Latria) should be rendered to none other than God; now this is exactly the doctrine of the Council of Nice. Charlemagne himself admits that the learned may venerate images, meaning thereby that the veneration is really addressed to the prototypes, but that such veneration is a source of scandal to the ignorant who in the image venerate [2] nothing but the material image itself (Lib. III., cap. xvj.)." [3]

EXCURSUS ON THE COUNCIL OF FRANKFORT, A.D. 794.

It has been commonly represented that the Council of Frankfort, which was a large Synod of the West, with legates of the Pope present and composed of the bishops of Gaul, Germany, and Aquitaine, devoted its attention to a consideration of the question of the ven-

---

[1] " Here on the wall is an image of the Saint and under its feet a little window, and a lamp, in the glass bowl of which the fire burns." Fortun. (Migne., *Pat. Lat.*, Tom. LXXXVIII.) *De Vita S. Martin*, Lib. iv., 690 (col. 426).

[2] " And adore " in the Latin.
[3] Michaud. *Discussion sur les Sept Conciles Œcuméniques*, p. 300.

eration due to images and of the claims of the Second Council of Nice to being an Ecumenical Synod. I do not know upon what grounds such statements have rested, but certainly not upon anything revealed by any remains of the council we possess, for among these we find but one brief paragraph upon the subject, to wit, the Second Canon, which reads as follows (Labbe and Cossart, *Concilia*, Tom. vii., col. 1057) :

"II. The question was brought forward concerning the recent synod which the Greeks had held at Constantinople concerning the adoration of images, that all should be judged as worthy of anathema who did not pay to the images of the Saints service and adoration as to the Divine Trinity. Our most holy fathers rejected with scorn and in every way such adoration and service, and unanimously condemned it."

Now in the first place I call the reader's attention to the fact that the Conciliabulum of 754 was held at Constantinople but that the Seventh Council was held at Nice. It would seem as if the two had got mixed in the mind of the writer.[1]

In the second place neither of these synods, nor any other synod, decreed that the "service" ($\lambda\alpha\tau\rho\epsilon\acute{\iota}\alpha$) and "adoration" ($\pi\rho\sigma\sigma\kappa\acute{\nu}\nu\eta\sigma\iota\varsigma$) due to the holy Trinity was under pain of anathema to be given to "the images of the Saints."

On this second canon Hefele writes as follows :

(Hefele. *Concil.*, § 398).

The second of these canons deserves our full attention ; in it, as we have seen, the Synod of Frankfort expresses its feeling against the Second Ecumenical Council of Nice, and against the veneration of images ; Eginhard also gives us the information that it took this action, viz. : "for it was decided by all [i. e. at Frankfort] that the synod, which a few years before was gathered together in Constantinople (*sic*) under Irene and her son Constantine, and is called by them not only the Seventh but also Ecumenical, should neither be held nor declared to be the Seventh nor ecumenical but wholly without authority."

Hefele rejects the views of Baronius, Bellarmine, Surius, and Binius. I have no intention of defending the position of any one of these writers but I translate Binius's note, merely remarking that it is easier to reject his conclusion than to answer the arguments upon which it rests.

(Severinus Binius, Labbe and Cossart, *Concilia*, Tom. VII., col. 1070.)

Baronius was of opinion that the Second Council of Nice was condemned by this council ; and before him Bellarmine had taught the same thing. But two things make me dissent from their conclusion :

First. That as the history and acts of this council inform us that the legates of Pope Hadrian (whom Ado in his chronology names Theophylact and Stephen) were present at this council, it was not possible that the whole council was ignorant by what authority the true Seventh Council was assembled at Nice, and what its decrees had been. For as this Synod at Nice was assembled under the same Pontiff, the legates of that same Pontiff could not have been ignorant of its authority and teaching. Therefore even if false rumours concerning the Seventh Synod had been scattered about, as Genebrardus affirms (on what foundation I know not), the Fathers of the Council of Frankfort could have been instructed by the papal legates, and been given information and taught what were the writings of that Seventh Council. Moreover since the celebration of that Nicene Council was an event most celebrated and most widely published throughout the whole Church, it is not credible that among

---

[1] This has been explained by saying that the last meeting was in the palace at Constantinople.

the bishops of all France and Germany, assembled in this place, no single one was found who had accurate information concerning the manner in which the Council of Nice was assembled, or of how it had received the approval of the Supreme Pontiff. For as a matter of fact, that error of adoring images as gods is rather an error of the Gentiles than of any heretics or of any who profess the faith of Christ. Therefore in no way is it credible that the fathers of the Council of Frankfort should have thought this, or rashly on account of certain rumours have believed this; especially since at that time in no Church was there the suspicion of any such error; and the bishops of the council were too pious and Catholic to allow the suspicion that out of base enmity to the Orientals they were led to attribute error to the fathers of the most sacred Council of Nice, or that they would have attached an heretical sense to their decision.

Another reason is this; that the fathers of this council often made profession of acting under the obedience of the Roman Pontiffs; and in the book *Sacrosyllabus* at the end, when they gave sentence against the heretics, they subjoin these words: "The privilege of our lord and father the Supreme Pontiff, Hadrian I., Pope of the most blessed See, being in all respects maintained." And this same principle the same fathers often professed in this council, that they followed the tradition of their predecessors, and did not depart from their footsteps; and that Charlemagne, who was present at this council, in his letter to the Spanish bishops, said that in the first place he had consulted the pontiff of the Apostolic See, what he thought concerning the matter treated of in that council: and that a little further on he adds these words: "I am united to the Apostolic See, and to the ancient Catholic traditions which have come down from the beginnings of the new-born Church, with my whole mind, and with complete alacrity of heart."

Now the fathers of this council could not make such a profession if they had condemned the Sacrosant Synod of Nice, which had been confirmed by the Apostolic See. For as I have shown above they could not have been misled by false information upon this point. If therefore knowingly and through heretical pravity they did these things, so too they did them out of pertinacity and heresy; and so concerning the authority of the Apostolic See one way they had thought and another way spoken. But in my judgment such things are not to be imputed to so great and to such an assembly of bishops, for it is not likely that the fathers of this council, in the presence of the legates of the Supreme Pontiff and of a Catholic Prince, would have condemned the Seventh Synod, confirmed as it was by the authority of the Pontiff and have referred the matter to Hadrian the Supreme Pontiff.

Moreover it would have surely come to pass that if the Nicene Council had been condemned by the authority of this synod, and so the error of the Iconoclasts had been approved through erroneous information, before our days some follower of that error would have tried to back up himself and his opinion by its authority: but no one did this, and this is all the more noteworthy since, only shortly after the time of Charlemagne, Claudius of Turin sprang up in that very Gaul, and wished to introduce that error into the Western Church, and he could have confirmed his teaching in the highest manner if he could have shewn that that plenary council of the West had confirmed his error. But as a matter of fact Claudius did not quote it in his favour; nor did Jonas of Orleans, who wrote against him at that time, and overthrew his foundations, make any mention in this respect of the Council of Frankfort in his response.

Lastly I add that the Roman Church never gave its approbation and received any provincial synod, so far as one part of its action was concerned while in another part it was persistently heretical. But this provincial council so far as it defined concerning the servitude and filiation of Christ was received and approved by the Church, it is not then credible that in the same council the Nicene Synod would have been condemned.

I need only add that every proposed theory is so full of difficulties as to seem to involve more absurdities and improbabilities than it explains. The reader is referred especially to Vasquez (*De adorat. imag.*, Lib. II., Dispt. VII., cap. vij.) and to Suarez (Tom. I, Disp. LIV., Sec. iij.), for learned and instructive discussions of the whole matter.

EXCURSUS ON THE CONVENTION SAID TO HAVE BEEN HELD IN PARIS,
A.D. 825.

It is curious that besides the Caroline Books and the second canon of Frankfort, another matter of great difficulty springs up with regard to the subject of the authority of the Seventh Synod.   In 1596 there appeared what claims to be an ancient account of a convention of bishops in Paris in the year 824.[1] The point in which this interests us is that the bishops at this meeting are supposed to have condemned the Seventh Council, and to have approved the Caroline books.   The whole story was rejected by Cardinal Bellarmine and he promptly wrote a refutation.   Sismondi accepted this view of the matter, and Labbe has excluded the pretended proceedings from his " Concilia" altogether.

But while scholars are agreed that the assigned date is impossible and that it must be 825, they have usually accepted the facts as true, I need not mention others than such widely differing authors as Fleury (*Hist. Eccles.*, Lib. xlvij. iv.), Roisselet de Sauclières (*Hist. Chronol.*, Tome III., No. 792, p. 385), and Hefele (*Concilien.* § 425).

It would be the height of presumption were I to express any opinion upon this most disputed point, the reader will find the whole matter at length in Walch (Bd. XI., S. 135, 139).   I only here note that if the account be genuine, then it is an established fact that as late as 825, an assembly of bishops rejected an Ecumenical Council accepted by the pope, and further charged the Supreme Pontiff with having " commanded men to adore superstitiously images (*quod superstitiose eas adorare jussit*)," and asked the reigning Pontiff to correct the errors of his predecessors, and all this without any reproof from the Holy See !

Hefele points out also that they not only entirely misrepresent the teaching of Hadrian and the Seventh Council, but that they also cite a passage from St. Augustine, "which teaches exactly the opposite of that which this synod would make out, for the passage says that the word *colere* can be applied to men."

HISTORICAL NOTE ON THE SO-CALLED "EIGHTH GENERAL COUNCIL"
AND SUBSEQUENT COUNCILS.

Whatever may be the final verdict of history with regard to the Caroline books, to the action of this Synod of Frankfort, and to the genuineness of the account of the Convention of Paris, there can be no doubt with regard to the position held by the Seventh of the Ecumenical Synods in all subsequent conciliar action.

In 869[2] was held at Constantinople what both the Easterns and Westerns then considered to be the Eighth of the Ecumenical Synods.   Its chief concern was to restore peace and it thought to accomplish this by taking the strongest position against Photius.   At this Synod the Second Council of Nice was accepted in the most explicit manner, not only its teaching but also its rank and number.[3]

---

[1] This is reprinted in full in Mansi, and from nim in Migne's *Pat. Lat.*, Tom. XCVIII. col. 1299, *et seqq.* Cardinal Bellarmine's refutation is also found in Migne's Charlemagne, and in Labbe and Cossart, Tom. VII., of the *Concilia*.
[2] Hefele. *Concilien*, § 487, also Fleury.

[3] The definition of faith says : "also we confess that the Seventh Holy and Ecumenical synod, which met in Nice for the second time, taught in accordance with orthodoxy, etc." (Labbe and Cossart, *Concilia*, Tom. VIII., col. 1147.)

But not many years afterwards Photius again got the upper hand and another synod was held, also at Constantinople, in A.D. 879, which restored Photius and which was afterwards accepted by many Easterns as the Eighth of the Ecumenical Synods. But at this synod, as well as in that of 869, the position of Second Nice was fully acknowledged. So that after that date, roughly speaking one century after the meeting of the Seventh Synod, despite all opposition it was universally recognized and revered, even by those who were so rapidly drifting further and further apart as were the East and West in the time of Photius and his successors.

At the Council of Lyons in A.D. 1274 there was consent on all hands that all were united in accepting the Seven Synods as a basis of union.

And finally when the acts and agreements of the Council of Florence (1438) appeared in the first edition issued under papal authority, that synod was styled the "Eighth," and in this there was no accident, for during the debate the Cardinal Julian Cæsarini had asked the Greeks for the proceedings of the Eighth Synod and Mark answered: " We cannot be forced to count that synod as ecumenical, since we do not at all recognize it but in fact reject it. . . . " A few years afterwards was held a second synod which restored Photius and annulled the acts of the preceding assembly, and this synod also bears the title of the Eighth Ecumenical. But Cardinal Julian did not enter on any defence of the Ecumenical character of this so-called "Eighth Synod." [1]

For the purposes of this discussion, the matter is perfectly clear, and even if some later writers speak still of the "Six Ecumenical Councils" in doing so they are rejecting the Eighth as much as the Seventh ; in fact they are rejecting neither, but speaking as did St. Gregory, who still mentioned the Four General Councils and compared them to the Four Gospels, although the fifth had been already held. Those few Frankish writers who continued to speak of II. Nice as a *pseudo council* did so out of ignorance or else in contrariety to the teaching of the Roman Church to whose obedience they professed subjection. It is no place of mine to offer moral reflections upon their doings.

---

[1] For which Baronius condemns him in his *Annales*, A.D. 869.

APPENDIX CONTAINING CANONS AND RULINGS NOT HAVING CONCILIAR ORIGIN BUT APPROVED BY NAME IN CANON II. OF THE SYNOD IN TRULLO.

Elenchus.

[1] For some reason Beveridge does not follow, as I have done, the order of the enumeration in the Trullan Canon. Johnson has followed Beveridge's order.

PREFATORY NOTE.

As this volume only professes to contain the conciliar decrees of the Ecumenical Councils, it would seem that canons and rulings which were of private or quasi-private origin should have no place in it ; and yet a very considerable number of such determinations are expressly approved by name in the Canons of the Synod in Trullo, which canons were received, to some extent at least (as we have seen), by the Seventh Ecumenical Council. Under these circumstances I have felt that the reader might justly expect to find some mention made of these decrees, which while indeed non-conciliar in origin, yet had received such high conciliar sanction. I have therefore placed a translation of the text of the " Apostolical Canons " with a brief introduction, and have reprinted Johnson's epitome of the other decrees and canons, supplying a few omissions and adding a few notes, chiefly taken from the Greek scholiasts, Zonaras and Balsamon. It is hoped that thus the present volume has been made practically complete, and that from it any student can obtain a satisfactory knowledge of all the doctrinal definitions and of all the disciplinary enactments of the undivided Church.

THE APOSTOLICAL CANONS.

INTRODUCTION.

To affirm that the "Apostolical Canons" were a collection of canons made by the Apostles would be about as sensible as to affirm that the "Psalterium Davidicum"[1] was a collection of his own psalms made by David, or that the "Proverbs of Solomon" was a collection of proverbs made by Solomon.

Many of the Psalms had David for their composer; many of the Proverbs had Solomon for their originator; but neither the book we call "The Psalter" nor the book we call "The Proverbs" had David or Solomon for its compiler. The matter contained in the one is largely, many think chiefly, of Davidic origin, the matter contained in the other is no doubt Solomonic; and just so "The Apostolical Canons" may well be to a great extent of Apostolic origin, committed to writing, some possibly by the Apostles themselves, others by their immediate successors, who heard them at their mouth; and these at some period not far removed from the date of the Nicene Council (A.D. 325), probably earlier than the Council of Antioch, were gathered together into a code which has since then been somewhat enlarged and modified. This is the view of the matter to which the general drift of the learned seems to be moving, and it is substantially the view so ably defended by Bishop Beveridge in his *Synodicon*, and in his remarkably learned and convincing answer to his French opponent,[2] entitled *Codex Canonum Ecclesiæ Primitivæ vindicatus ac illustratus*. (This last volume, together with the "Preface to the Notes on the Apostolical Canons" has been reprinted in Vol. XII. of Bishop Beveridge's Works in the "Library of Anglo-Catholic Theology.")[3]

In thus accepting in the main the old conclusions I am far from intending to imply that more recent research has not shewn some of the details of the bishop's view to be erroneous. In brief, the proposition which

seems to be most tenable is that in the main the Apostolic Canons represent the very early canon-law of the Church, that the canons which make up the collection are of various dates, but that most of them are earlier than the year 300, and that while it is not possible to say exactly when the collection, as we now have it, was made, there is good reason for assigning it a date not later than the middle of the fourth century. With regard to the name "Apostolic Canons" there need be no more hesitation in applying it to these canons than in calling Ignatius an "Apostolic Father," the adjective necessarily meaning nothing more than that the canons set forth the disciplinary principles which were given to the early Church by the Apostles, just as we speak of the "Apostles' Creed."

While this is true there can be no question that in the East the Apostolic Canons were very generally looked upon as a genuine work prepared by the Holy Apostles. I proceed now to quote Bishop Hefele, but I have already (Cf. Council in Trullo) expressed my own opinion that there is not contained in the Quinisext decree any absolute definition of what is technically known as the "authenticity" of the Canons of the Apostles.

(Hefele. *Hist. of the Councils*, Vol. I., p. 451 *et seqq.*).

The Synod *in Trullo* being, as is well known, regarded as ecumenical by the Greek Church, the authenticity of the eighty-five canons was decided in the East for all future time. It was otherwise in the West. At the same period that Dionysius Exiguus translated the collection in question for Bishop Stephen, Pope Gelasius promulgated his celebrated decree *de libris non recipiendis*. Drey mentions it, but in a way which requires correction. Following in this the usual opinion, he says that the Synod at Rome in which Gelasius published this decree was held in 494; but we shall see hereafter that this synod was held in 496. Also Drey considers himself obliged to adopt another erroneous opinion, according to which Gelasius declared in the same decree the Apostolic Canons to be apocryphal. This opinion is to be maintained only so long as the usual text of this decree is consulted, since the original text as it is given

[1] The reader may remember that when it was proposed in a first draft to the Council of Trent to say the "Psalms of David," the Fathers refused to pass it as proposed, because the Psalter contained Psalms not by David, and substituted the expression "The Davidic Psalter" (*Psalterium Davidicum*).

[2] Matthieu de Larroque. *Observationes . . . et in Annot. Bev. in Can. Apost.* 1674.

[3] It is most unfortunate that the Rev. A. B. Grosart, LL.D.. in the article "Beveridge" in that usually accurate and learned work. the *Dictionary of English Biography*. should have written "regretting" this republication of the *Vindicatio*, on the ground that Bp Beveridge in its pages "demonstrates that he lacked the instincts of the genuine scholar as distinguished from the merely largely read man!" There seem to be a great many *soi-disant* "genuine scholars" who lack all sense of humour!

in the ancient manuscripts does not contain the passage which mentions the Apostolic Canons.[1] This passage was certainly added subsequently, with many others, probably by Pope Hormisdas (514–543) when he made a new edition of the decree of Gelasius. As Dionysius Exiguus published his collection in all probability subsequently to the publication of the decree of Gelasius, properly so called, in 496, we can understand why this decree did not mention the Apostolical Canons. Dionysius did not go to Rome while Gelasius was living, and did not know him personally, as he himself says plainly in the *Præfatio* of his collection of the papal decrees. It is hence also plain how it was that in another collection of canons subsequently made by Dionysius, of which the preface still remains to us, he does not insert the Apostolic Canons, but has simply this remark: *Quos non admisit uniniversalitas, ego quoque in hoc opere prætermisi.* Dionysius Exiguus in fact compiled this new collection at a time when Pope Hormisdas had already explicitly declared the Apostolic Canons to be apocryphal.

Notwithstanding this, these canons, and particularly the fifty mentioned by Dionysius, did not entirely fall into discredit in the West; but rather they came to be received, because the first collection of Dionysius was considered of great authority. They also passed into other collections, and particularly into that of the pseudo-Isidore; and in 1054, Humbert, legate of Pope Leo IX., made the following declaration: *Clementis liber, id est itinerarium Petri Apostoli et Canones Apostolorum numerantur inter apocrypha,* EXCEPTIS CAPITULIS QUISQUAGINTA, *quæ decreverunt regulis orthodoxis adjungenda.* Gratian also, in his decree, borrowed from the fifty Apostolic Canons, and they gradually obtained the force of laws. But many writers, especially Hincmar of Rheims, like Dionysius Exiguus, raised doubts upon the apostolical origin of these canons. From the sixteenth century the opinion has been universal that these documents are not authentic; with the exception, however, of the French Jesuit Turrianus, who endeavoured to defend their genuineness, as well as the authenticity of the pseudo-Isidorian decrees. According to the Centuriators of Magdeburg, it was especially Gabriel d' Aubespine, Bishop of Orleans, the celebrated Archbishop Peter de Marca, and the Anglican Beveridge, who proved that they were not really compiled by the Apostles, but were made partly in the second and chiefly in the third century. Beveridge considered this collection to be a repertory of ancient canons given by synods in the second and third centuries. In opposition to them, the Calvinist Dallæus (Daillé) regarded it as the work of a forger who lived in the fifth and sixth centuries; but Beveridge refuted him so convincingly, that from that time his opinion, with some few modifications, has been that of all the learned.

Beveridge begins with the principle, that the Church in the very earliest times must have had a collection of canons; and he demonstrates that from the commencement of the fourth century, bishops, synods, and other authorities often quote, as documents in common use, a κανὼν ἀποστολικὸς, or ἐκκλησιαστικὸς, or ἀρχαῖος; as was done, for instance, at the Council of Nice, by Alexander, Bishop of Alexandria, and by the Emperor Constantine, etc.[2] According to Beveridge, these quotations make allusion to the Apostolic Canons, and prove that they were already in use *before* the fourth century.

In opposition to Beveridge Dr. von Drey wrote with profound learning;[3] and Bickell, in his work just quoted, to a great degree accepts his conclusions as being well-founded.

These conclusions in short are that the so-called "Apostolic Canons" are a patchwork taken from the "Apostolic Constitutions," which are said to have been of Eastern origin and to date from the latter part of the third century, and from the canons of various synods, notably Nice, Antioch, and Chalcedon.

But this last reference to Chalcedon is too much for Bickell to stomach; and for many reasons he makes the date of the collection earlier.

Hefele points out a rather significant document which he says both "Drey and Bickell have overlooked. In 1738 Scipio Maffei published three ancient documents, the first of which was a Latin translation of a letter written on the subject of Meletius by the Egyptian bishops Hesychius, Phileas, etc. This letter was written during the persecution of Diocletian, that is, between 303 and 305: it is addressed to Meletius himself, and especially accuses him of having ordained priests in other dioceses. This conduct, they tell him, is contrary to all ecclesiastical rule (*aliena a more divino et regula ecclesiastica*), and

---

[1] Cf. Ballerini. *Opp. S. Leon. M.*, Vol. III. p. 158; Mansi. *Conc.*, Tom. VIII., 170.

[2] Cf 'for catena) Bickell, *Geschichte des Kirchenrechts*, S. 82.

[3] *Neue Untersuchungen über die Const. und Canones der Apostel.* Tübing., 1832.

Meletius himself knows very well that it is a *lex patrum et propatrum . . . in alienis paræciis non licere alicui episcoporum ordinationes celebrare.* Maffei himself supposes that the Egyptian bishops were here referring to the thirty-fifth canon (the thirty-sixth according to the enumeration of Dionysius), and this opinion can hardly be controverted."

After Bickell and Drey about ten years passed and then Bunsen and Ültzen wrote on the subject. Of these Bunsen renewed Beveridge's arguments, and considers the "Apostolic Canons" as a reflex of the customs of the Primitive Church, if not in the Johannean age, at latest in that which immediately succeeded ; and he is of opinion that the legend attributing them to the Apostles is earlier in date than the Council of Nice. Ültzen does not express himself definitely on the point, but in a note to p. xvj. of the Preface to his book regrets that Bunsen should have renewed Beveridge's argument with regard to the relative age of the Apostolic Canons and those of Antioch because in his judgment "all the more recent judges of this matter had refuted it."

I think I should here interrupt my narrative to warn the reader that Beveridge has been often misunderstood and misrepresented. For example he expressly says that according to his theory[1] "these canons were set forth by various synods, so too they seem to us to have been collected by different persons, of whom some collected more, some fewer. . . . And these canons, thus collected, some called ecclesiastical and some called them Apostolical ; not that they believed them to have been written by the very Apostles, for they had made the collection themselves, but because they were consonant to the doctrine and traditions of the Apostles, and they were persuaded that they had been originally established at least by apostolic men." This is Beveridge's position in his own words.

I come now to the most recent writings upon the subject. Harnack has developed a theory which is partly his own with regard to the Apostolical Constitutions, in his edition of the "Didache," and has also considered the question of the Apostolic Canons. The fullest

discussion however of the matter is in a work entitled, *Die Apostolischen Konstitutionem, Eine Litteran-historische Untersuchung, von Franz Zaver Funk. Rottenburg am Neckar.* 1891.

Funk gives the history of the controversy, and refuses to allow that Hefele's citation of the Letter of the Egyptian bishops throws any light upon the point. In most matters he agrees with Bickell, and declares (p. 188) that "the Synod of Antioch is certainly to be regarded as the source of the Apostolic Canons," and that thus by comparing the canons, it is manifest that the Apostolic "are certainly to be regarded as the dependent writing" (p. 185). And after considering their relation to the Apostolical Constitutions, Funk states his conclusion as follows (p. 190): "The drawing up of the canons falls therefore not earlier than the interpolation of the Didaskalia and the preparation of the two last books of the Constitution, hence not before the beginning of the fifth century. On tne other hand there is no ground for fixing the writing at a later period, not a single canon bears the mark of a later time."

Such was the state of things until Mgr. Rihmani, the Syrian Archbishop of Aleppo, gave notice that he had found in a codex at Mossul a Syrian version of the Apocryphal book known as the *Testamentum Jesu Christi.* It is stated that in the discoverer's opinion the *Testamentum* is earlier in date than the Apostolic Canons, than the Canons of Hippolytus, and than the VIIIth Book of the Apostolic Constitutions ; and further that it was the direct source of the Apostolic Canons. As I know nothing further of this matter, I must simply note it for the guidance of the reader in his further study of the subject.

Having now traced the history of the discussion, I need only add that Mr. Turner has just issued a very critical text of the version of Dionysius Exiguus, the full title of which is as follows :

Ecclesiæ Occidentalis Monvmenta Jvris Antiqvissima Canonvm et Conciliorvm Græcorum, Interpretationes Latinæ. Edidit Cvthbertvs Hamilton Turner, A.M. Fascicvli Primi Pars Prior Canones Apostolorvm Nicaenorvm Patrvm Svbscriptiones. And that I have taken, except where noted to the contrary, Hammond's translation.

---

[1] Bev. *Præfatio ad Annotat. in Can. Apost.*, § xiii.

THE CANONS OF THE HOLY AND ALTOGETHER AUGUST APOSTLES.[1]

CANON I.[2]

Let a bishop be ordained by two or three bishops.

CANON II.

Let a presbyter, deacon, and the rest of the clergy, be ordained by one bishop.

CANON III. (III. and IV.)

If any bishop or presbyter offer any other things at the altar, besides that which the Lord ordained for the sacrifice, as honey, or milk, or strong-made drink instead of wine,[3] or birds, or any living things, or vegetables, besides that which is ordained, let him be deposed. Excepting only new ears of corn, and grapes at the suitable season. Neither is it allowed to bring anything else to the altar at the time of the holy oblation, excepting oil for the lamps, and incense.

CANON IV. (V.)

Let all other fruits be sent home as first-fruits for the bishops and presbyters, but not offered at the altar. But the bishops and presbyters should of course give a share of these things to the deacons, and the rest of the clergy.

CANON V. (VI.)

Let not a bishop, presbyter, or deacon, put away his wife under pretence of religion; but if he put her away, let him be excommunicated; and if he persists, let him be deposed.

CANON VI. (VII.)

Let not a bishop, presbyter, or deacon, undertake worldly business; otherwise let him be deposed.

CANON VII. (VIII.)

If any bishop, presbyter, or deacon, shall celebrate the holy day of Easter before the vernal equinox, with the Jews, let him be deposed.

CANON VIII. (IX.)

If any bishop, presbyter, or deacon, or any one on the sacerdotal list, when the offering is made, does not partake of it, let him declare the cause; and if it be a reasonable one, let him be excused; but if he does not declare it, let him be excommunicated, as being a cause of offence to the people, and occasioning a suspicion against the offerer, as if he had not made the offering properly.

CANON IX. (X.)

All the faithful who come in and hear the Scriptures, but do not stay for the prayers and the Holy Communion, are to be excommunicated, as causing disorder in the Church.

CANON X. (XI.)

If any one shall pray, even in a private house, with an excommunicated person, let him also be excommunicated.

CANON XI. (XII.)

If any clergyman shall join in prayer with a deposed clergyman, as if he were a clergyman,[4] let him also be deposed.

CANONS XII. and XIII. (XIII.)

If any one of the clergy or laity who is excommunicated, or not to be received, shall go away, and be received in another city without commendatory letters, let both the receiver and the received be excommunicated.

But if he be excommunicated already, let the time of his excommunication be lengthened.

CANON XIV.

A bishop is not to be allowed to leave his own parish, and pass over into another, although he may be pressed by many to do so, unless there be some proper cause constraining him, as if he can confer some greater benefit upon the persons of that place in the word of godliness. And this must be done not of his own accord, but by the judgment of many bishops, and at their earnest exhortation.

CANON XV.

If any presbyter, or deacon, or any other of the list of the clergy, shall leave his own parish, and go into another, and having entirely forsaken his own, shall make his abode in the other parish without the permission of his own bishop, we ordain that he shall no longer perform divine service; more especially if his own bishop having exhorted him to return he has refused to do so, and persists in his disorderly conduct. But let him communicate there as a layman.

---

[1] The Latin caption is "The Ecclesiastical Rules of the Holy Apostles, set forth by Clement, Pontiff of the Roman Church."

[2] The numbering which I have followed is Hammond's, but, where it differs from that given by Hefele, I have placed Hefele's numbering in parenthesis. With Hefele agree Van Espen and Bruns (in his alternative numbering) and Johnson's marginal numbering. The numbering that Johnson himself follows is that of Cotelerius.

[3] The text here varies.

[4] Hammond seems to have omitted ὡς κληρικῷ, which I have supplied.

Canon XVI.

If, however, the bishop, with whom any such persons are staying, shall disregard the command that they are to cease from performing divine offices, and shall receive them as clergymen, let him be excommunicated, as a teacher of disorder.

Canon XVII.

He who has been twice married after baptism, or who has had a concubine, cannot become a bishop, presbyter, or deacon, or any other of the sacerdotal list.

Canon XVIII.

He who married a widow, or a divorced woman, or an harlot, or a servant-maid, or an actress, cannot be a bishop, presbyter, or deacon, or any other of the sacerdotal list.

Canon XIX.

He who has married two sisters, or a niece, cannot become a clergyman.

Canon XX.

If a clergyman becomes surety for any one, let him be deposed.

Canon XXI.

An eunuch, if he has been made so by the violence of men or [if his *virilia* have been amputated[1]] in times of persecution, or if he has been born so, if in other respects he is worthy, may be made a bishop.

Canon XXII.

He who has mutilated himself, cannot become a clergyman, for he is a self-murderer, and an enemy to the workmanship of God.

Canon XXIII.

If any man being a clergyman shall mutilate himself, let him be deposed, for he is a self-murderer.

Canon XXIV.

If a layman mutilate himself, let him be excommunicated for three years, as practising against his own life.

Canon XXV.   (XXV. and XXVI.)

If a bishop, presbyter, or deacon be found guilty of fornication, perjury, or theft, let him be deposed, but let him not be excommunicated; for the Scripture says, "thou shalt not punish a man twice for the same offence."

In like manner the other clergy shall be subject to the same proceeding.[2]

Canon XXVI.   (XXVII.)

Of those who have been admitted to the clergy unmarried, we ordain, that the readers and singers only may, if they will, marry.

Canon XXVII.   (XXVIII.)

If a bishop, presbyter, or deacon shall strike any of the faithful who have sinned, or of the unbelievers who have done wrong, with the intention of frightening them, we command that he be deposed.   For our Lord has by no means taught us to do so, but, on the contrary, when he was smitten he smote not again, when he was reviled he reviled not again, when he suffered he threatened not.

Canon XXVIII.   (XXIX.)

If any bishop, presbyter, or deacon, having been justly deposed upon open accusations, shall dare to meddle with any of the divine offices which had been intrusted to him, let him be altogether cut off from the Church.

Canon XXIX.   (XXX.)

If any bishop, presbyter, or deacon, shall obtain possession of that dignity by money, let both him and the person who ordained him be deposed, and also altogether cut off from all communion, as Simon Magus was by me Peter.

Canon XXX.   (XXXI.)

If any bishop obtain possession of a church by the aid of the temporal powers, let him be deposed and excommunicated, and all who communicate with him.

Canon XXXI.   (XXXII.)

If any presbyter, despising his own bishop, shall collect a separate congregation, and erect another altar, not having any grounds for condemning the bishop with regard to religion or justice, let him be deposed for his ambition; for he is a tyrant; in like manner also the rest of the clergy, and as many as join him; and let laymen be excommunicated. Let this, however, be done after a first, second, and third admonition from the bishop.

Canon XXXII.   (XXXIII.)

If any presbyter or deacon has been excommunicated by a bishop, he may not be received

---

[1] Hammond has omitted these words.

[2] I have changed Hammond's rendering of this last phrase, "in like manner with respect to the other clergy."

into communion again by any other than by him who excommunicated him, unless it happen that the bishop who excommunicated him be dead.

Canon XXXIII. (XXXIV.)

No foreign bishop, presbyter, or deacon, may be received without commendatory letters; and when they are produced let the persons be examined; and if they be preachers of godliness, let them be received. Otherwise, although you supply them with what they need, you must not receive them into communion, for many things are done surreptitiously.

Canon XXXIV. (XXXV.)

The bishops of every nation must acknowledge him who is first among them and account him as their head, and do nothing of consequence without his consent; but each may do those things only which concern his own parish, and the country places which belong to it. But neither let him (who is the first) do anything without the consent of all; for so there will be unanimity, and God will be glorified through the Lord in the Holy Spirit.[1]

Canon XXXV. (XXXVI.)

Let not a bishop dare to ordain beyond his own limits, in cities and places not subject to him. But if he be convicted of doing so, without the consent of those persons who have authority over such cities and places, let him be deposed, and those also whom he has ordained.

Canon XXXVI. (XXXVII.)

If any person, having been ordained bishop, does not undertake the ministry, and the care of the people committed to him, let him be excommunicated until he does undertake it. In like manner a presbyter or deacon. But if he has gone and has not been received, not of his own will but from the perverseness of the people, let him continue bishop; and let the clergy of the city be excommunicated, because they have not corrected the disobedient people.

Canon XXXVII. (XXXVIII.)

Let there be a meeting of the bishops twice a year, and let them examine amongst themselves the decrees concerning religion and settle the ecclesiastical controversies which may have occurred. One meeting to be held in the fourth week of Pentecost [*i.e.*, the fourth week after Easter], and the other on the 12th day of the month Hyperberetæus [*i.e.*, October].

Canon XXXVIII. (XXXIX.)

Let the bishop have the care of all the goods of the Church, and let him administer them as under the inspection of God. But he must not alienate any of them or give the things which belong to God to his own relations. If they be poor let him relieve them as poor; but let him not, under that pretence, sell the goods of the Church.

Canon XXXIX. (XL.)

Let not the presbyters or deacons do anything without the sanction of the bishop; for he it is who is intrusted with the people of the Lord, and of whom will be required the account of their souls.

Canon XL. (XL. continued.)

Let the private goods of the bishop, if he have any such, and those of the Lord, be clearly distinguished, that the bishop may have the power of leaving his own goods, when he dies, to whom he will, and how he will, and that the bishop's own property may not be lost under pretence of its being the property of the Church: for it may be that he has a wife, or children, or relations, or servants; and it is just before God and man, that neither should the Church suffer any loss through ignorance of the bishop's own property, nor the bishop or his relations be injured under pretext of the Church: nor that those who belong to him should be involved in contests, and cast reproaches upon his death.

Canon XLI.

We ordain that the bishop have authority over the goods of the Church: for if he is to be intrusted with the precious souls of men, much more are temporal possessions to be intrusted to him. He is therefore to administer them all of his own authority, and supply those who need, through the presbyters and deacons, in the fear of God, and with all reverence. He may also, if need be, take what is required for his own necessary wants, and for the brethren to whom he has to show hospitality, so that he may not be in any want. For the law of God has ordained, that they who wait at the altar should be nour-

---

[1] The text here differs; I follow Beveridge. Hammond reads, "Through the Lord Jesus Christ, and the Father through the Lord by the Holy Spirit, even the Father, the Son, and the Holy Spirit."

ished of the altar. Neither does any soldier bear arms against an enemy at his own cost.

Canon XLII.

If a bishop or presbyter, or deacon, is addicted to dice or drinking, let him either give it over, or be deposed.

Canon XLIII.

If a subdeacon, reader, or singer, commits the same things, let him either give over, or be excommunicated. So also laymen.

Canon XLIV.

Let a bishop, presbyter, or deacon, who takes usury from those who borrow of him, give up doing so, or be deposed.

Canon XLV.

Let a bishop, presbyter, or deacon, who has only prayed with heretics, be excommunicated: but if he has permitted them to perform any clerical office, let him be deposed.

Canon XLVI.

We ordain that a bishop, or presbyter, who has admitted the baptism or sacrifice of heretics, be deposed. For what concord hath Christ with Belial, or what part hath a believer with an infidel?

Canon XLVII.

Let a bishop or presbyter who shall baptize again one who has rightly received baptism, or who shall not baptize one who has been polluted by the ungodly, be deposed, as despising the cross and death of the Lord, and not making a distinction between the true priests and the false.

Canon XLVIII.

If any layman put away his wife and marry another, or one who has been divorced by another man, let him be excommunicated.

Canon XLIX.

If any bishop or presbyter, contrary to the ordinance of the Lord, does not baptize into the Father, the Son, and the Holy Ghost, but into three Unoriginated Beings, or three Sons, or three Comforters, let him be deposed.

Canon L.

If any bishop or presbyter does not perform the one initiation with three immersions, but with giving one immersion only, into the death of the Lord, let him be deposed. For the Lord said not, Baptize into my death, but, "Go, make disciples of all nations, baptizing them in the name of the Father, and of the Son, and of the Holy Ghost."

Canon LI.

If any bishop, presbyter, or deacon, or any one of the sacerdotal list, abstains from marriage, or flesh, or wine, not by way of religious restraint, but as abhorring them, forgetting that God made all things very good, and that he made man male and female, and blaspheming the work of creation, let him be corrected, or else be deposed, and cast out of the Church. In like manner a layman.

Canon LII.

If any bishop or presbyter,[1] does not receive him who turns away from his sin, but rejects him, let him be deposed; for he grieveth Christ who said, "There is joy in heaven over one sinner that repenteth."

Canon LIII.

If any bishop, presbyter, or deacon, does not on festival days partake of flesh and wine, from an abhorrence of them, and not out of religious restraint, let him be deposed, as being seared in his own conscience, and being the cause of offence to many.

Canon LIV.

If any of the clergy be found eating in a tavern, let him be excommunicated, unless he has been constrained by necessity, on a journey, to lodge in an inn.

Canon LV.

If any of the clergy insult the bishop, let him be deposed: for "thou shalt not speak evil of the ruler of thy people."

Canon LVI.

If any of the clergy insult a presbyter, or deacon, let him be excommunicated.

Canon LVII.

If any of the clergy mock the lame, or the deaf, or the blind, or him who is infirm in his legs, let him be excommunicated. In like manner any of the laity.

Canon LVIII.

If any bishop or presbyter neglects the clergy or the people, and does not instruct them in the way of godliness, let him be ex-

---

[1] Hammond adds " or deacon."

communicated, and if he persists in his negligence and idleness, let him be deposed.

Canon LIX.

If any bishop, presbyter, or deacon, when any of the clergy is in want, does not supply him with what he needs, let him be excommunicated ; but if he persists, let him be deposed, as one who has killed his brother.

Canon LX.

If any one reads publicly in the church the falsely inscribed [1] books of impious men, as if they were holy Scripture, to the destruction of the people and clergy, let him be deposed.

Canon LXI.

If any accusation be brought against a believer of fornication or adultery, or any forbidden action, and he be convicted, let him not be promoted to the clergy.

Canon LXII.

If any of the clergy, through fear of men, whether Jew, heathen, or heretic, shall deny the name of Christ, let him be cast out. If he deny the name of a clergyman, let him be deposed. If he repent, let him be received as a layman.

Canon LXIII.

If any bishop, presbyter, or deacon, or any one of the sacerdotal order, shall eat flesh with the blood of the life thereof, or anything killed by beasts, or that dies of itself, let him be deposed. For the law has forbidden this. If he be a layman, let him be excommunicated.

Canon LXIV.

If any clergyman or layman shall enter into a synagogue of Jews or heretics to pray, let the former be deposed and let the latter be excommunicated.[2]

Canon LXV.

If any clergyman shall strike anyone in a contest, and kill him with one blow, let him be deposed for his violence. If a layman do so, let him be excommunicated.

Canon LXVI.

If any of the clergy be found fasting on the Lord's day, or on the Sabbath,[3] excepting

the one only, let him be deposed. If a layman, let him be excommunicated.

Canon LXVII.

If anyone shall force and keep a virgin not espoused, let him be excommunicated. And he may not take any other, but must retain her whom he has chosen, though she be a poor person.

Canon LXVIII.

If any bishop, presbyter, or deacon, shall receive from anyone a second ordination, let both the ordained and the ordainer be deposed ; unless indeed it be proved that he had his ordination from heretics ; for those who have been baptized or ordained by such persons cannot be either of the faithful or of the clergy.

Canon LXIX.

If any bishop, presbyter, or deacon, or reader, or singer, does not fast the holy Quadragesimal fast of Easter, or the fourth day, or the day of Preparation, let him be deposed, unless he be hindered by some bodily infirmity. If he be a layman, let him be excommunicated.

Canon LXX.

If any bishop, presbyter, or deacon, or any one of the list of clergy, keeps fast or festival with the Jews, or receives from them any of the gifts of their feasts, as unleavened bread, or any such things, let him be deposed. If he be a layman, let him be excommunicated.

Canon LXXI.

If any Christian brings oil into a temple of the heathen or into a synagogue of the Jews at their feast, or lights lamps, let him be excommunicated.

Canon LXXII.

If any clergyman or layman takes away wax or oil from the holy Church, let him be excommunicated, [and let him restore a fifth part more than he took.] [4]

Canon LXXIII.

Let no one convert to his own use any vessel of gold or silver, or any veil which has been sanctified, for it is contrary to law ; and if anyone be detected doing so, let him be excommunicated.

---

[1] Hammond translates " bearing false inscriptions," the Greek is ψευδεπίγραφα.

[2] Hammond translates differently with the same meaning.

[3] Hammond substitutes " any Saturday," and omits the word " only."

[4] This last phrase is omitted by Hammond, but is found in the Latin and in some of the Greek texts.

Canon LXXIV.

If any bishop has been accused of anything by men worthy of credit, he must be summoned by the bishops; and if he appears, and confesses, or is convicted, a suitable punishment must be inflicted upon him. But if when he is summoned he does not attend, let him be summoned a second time, two bishops being sent to him, for that purpose. [If even then he will not attend, let him be summoned a third time, two bishops being again sent to him.[1]] But if even then he shall disregard the summons and not come, let the synod pronounce such sentence against him as appears right, that he may not seem to profit by avoiding judgment.

Canon LXXV.

An heretic is not to be received as witness against a bishop, neither only one believer; for, "in the mouth of two or three witnesses, every word shall be established."

Canon LXXVI.

A bishop must not out of favour to a brother or a son, or any other relation, ordain whom he will to the episcopal dignity; for it is not right to make heirs of the bishopric, giving the things of God to human affections. Neither is it fitting to subject the Church of God to heirs. But if anyone shall do so let the ordination be void, and the ordainer himself be punished with excommunication.

Canon LXXVII.

If any one be deprived of an eye, or lame of a leg, but in other respects be worthy of a bishopric, he may be ordained, for the defect of the body does not defile a man, but the pollution of the soul.

Canon LXXVIII.

But if a man be deaf or blind, he may not be made a bishop, not indeed as if he were thus defiled, but that the affairs of the Church may not be hindered.

Canon LXXIX.

If anyone has a devil, let him not be made a clergyman, neither let him pray with the faithful; but if he be freed, let him be received into communion, and if he is worthy he may be ordained.

Canon LXXX.

It is not allowed that a man who has come over from an heathen life, and been baptized or who has been converted from an evil course of living, should be immediately made a bishop, for it is not right that he who has not been tried himself should be a teacher of others. Unless indeed this be done upon a special manifestation of Divine grace in his favour.

Canon LXXXI.

We have said that a bishop or presbyter must not give himself to the management of public affairs, but devote himself to ecclesiastical business. Let him then be persuaded to do so, or let him be deposed, for no man can serve two masters, according to the Lord's declaration.

Canon LXXXII.

We do not allow any servants to be promoted to the clergy without the consent of their masters, [to the troubling of their houses.[2]] But if any servant should appear worthy of receiving an order,[3] as our Onesimus appeared, and his masters agree and liberate him, and send him out of their house, he may be ordained.

Canon LXXXIII.

If a bishop, presbyter, or deacon, shall serve in the army, and wish to retain both the Roman magistracy and the priestly office, let him be deposed; for the things of Cæsar belong to Cæsar, and those of God to God.

Canon LXXXIV.

Whosoever shall insult the King, or a ruler, contrary to what is right, let him suffer punishment. If he be a clergyman, let him be deposed; if a layman, excommunicated.

Canon LXXXV.

Let the following books be counted venerable and sacred by all of you, both clergy and Laity. Of the Old Testament, five books of Moses, Genesis, Exodus, Leviticus, Numbers, Deuteronomy; of Joshua the Son of Nun, one; of the Judges, one; of Ruth, one; of the Kings, four; of the Chronicles of the book of the days, two; of Ezra, two; of Esther, one; [some texts read "of Judith, one";] of the Maccabees, three; of Job, one; of the Psalter, one; of Solomon, three, viz.: Prov-

---

[1] According to Hefele. these words are only in the Latin, but they are in the Greek text of Beveridge.

[2] According to Hefele this is only in the Latin, but it is found in the Greek of Beveridge.
[3] I have changed Hammond's translation here.

erbs, Ecclesiastes, and the Song of Songs; of the Prophets, twelve; of Isaiah, one; of Jeremiah, one; of Ezekiel, one; of Daniel, one. But besides these you are recommended to teach your young persons the Wisdom of the very learned Sirach. Our own books, that is, those of the New Testament, are: the four Gospels of Matthew, Mark, Luke, and John; fourteen Epistles of Paul; two Epistles of Peter; three of John; one of James, and one of Jude. Two Epistles of Clemens, and the Constitutions of me Clemens, addressed to you Bishops, in eight books, which are not to be published to all on account of the mystical things in them. And the Acts of us the Apostles.[1]

I

THE LETTER OF THE BLESSED DIONYSIUS, THE ARCHBISHOP OF ALEXANDRIA TO BASILIDES THE BISHOP, WHO MADE ENQUIRIES ON VARIOUS SUBJECTS, TO WHICH DIONYSIUS MADE ANSWER IN THIS EPISTLE, WHICH ANSWERS HAVE BEEN RECEIVED AS CANONS.[2]

Dionysius to my beloved son, and brother, and fellow minister in holy things, Basilides faithful to God, salutation in the Lord.

NOTE.

Dionysius, Johnson says, wrote in about A.D. 247.

CANON I.[3]

When the Paschal fast is to be broken depends on the precise hour of our Saviour's resurrection, and this was not certainly to be known from the Four Evangelists; therefore they who have not fasted the Monday, Tuesday, Wednesday, and Thursday before Easter, do no great thing if they fast the Friday and Saturday, and so till past three on Easter morning. But they who have fasted the whole six days, are not to be blamed if they break their fast after midnight. Some do not fast any of these days.

CANON II.

Menstruous women ought not to come to the Holy Table, or touch the Holy of Holies,[4] nor to churches, but pray elsewhere.

NOTE.

Balsamon notes how the canon educes the example of the woman who had had an issue of blood for twelve years and who therefore did not dare to touch the Lord, but only the "hem of his garment." He also notes that the question proposed, was whether Christian women should be excluded from the church and need follow the example of the Hebrews, who "when the menstrual flux was upon them, sat in a solitary place by themselves and waited for seven days to pass, and their flux should be over." The answer given is as above.

CANON III.

They that can contain and are aged ought to judge for themselves. They have heard St. Paul say; that they should "for a time give themselves to prayer, and then come together again."

NOTE.

In this epitome Johnson has set forth the meaning of the canon, as understood by the Greek scholiasts, rather than translated and epitomized the canon itself.

CANON IV.

They who have had involuntary nocturnal pollutions be at their own discretion [whether to communicate or not].

NOTE.

The Saint ends this canon with these words: "I have given opinion on the points about which you have consulted me, not as a doctor, but in all simplicity as it is suitable the relation between us should be. And when you have examined, my most learned son, what I have written you will let me know what seems to you better or whether you agree with my opinions. Farewell, dear son, may your ministry be in the peace of the Lord."

---

[1] The text of this canon is quite different in the different codices and versions. I have departed from Hammond's version.
[2] I have followed in the captions to all these non-conciliar canons the Greek text of Beveridge in his *Synodicon* (Tom. II.).
[3] I have here placed Johnson's epitome of these canons; the Ancient Epitome is lacking.
[4] In the Greek "the body and blood of Christ."

II.

THE CANONS OF THE BLESSED PETER, ARCHBISHOP OF ALEXANDRIA, AND MARTYR,[1] WHICH ARE FOUND IN HIS SERMON ON PENITENCE.

CANON I.

The fourth Easter from the beginning of the persecution was now come; and orders, that they who did not fall till after they had endured severe torments, and have already been "Mourners" three years, after forty days' fast, are to be admitted to communion, although they have not been before received [to penance].[2]

CANON II.

But if they endured imprisonment only, without torments, let a year be added to their former penance.

CANON III.

If they fell voluntarily, without torments or imprisonments, but are come to repentance, four years are added to their former penance.

CANON IV.

The case of them who do not repent pronounced desperate.

CANON V.

They that used evasion, and did not right down subscribe the abnegation, or with their own hands incense the idols, but sent a heathen to do it for them, are enjoined six months' penance, though they have been pardoned by some of the Confessors.

CANON VI.

Slaves forced by their masters to incense idols, and doing it in their master's stead, are enjoined a year's penance.

CANON VII.

The masters who forced them to it, are enjoined three years' penance, as being hypocrites, and as forcing their slaves to sacrifice.

CANON VIII.

They who first fell, and afterwards recovered themselves, by professing themselves Christians, and endured torments, are forthwith admitted to communion.

CANON IX.

That they who provoked the magistrates to persecute themselves and others are to be blamed, yet not to be denied communion.

CANON X.

That clergymen, who run themselves into persecution, and fell, though they did afterward recover themselves, and suffer torments, yet are not to be admitted to perform the sacred offices.

CANON XI.

That they who prayed for them who fell after long torments, be connived at, and we pray together with them, since they lament for what they have done, with anguish and mortification.[3]

CANON XII.

That they who with money purchased their ease and freedom, are to be commended.

CANON XIII.

Nor should we accuse those who ran away, and left all, though others left behind might fare the worse for it.[4]

CANON XIV.

That they who endured tortures, and afterwards, when they were deprived of speech and motion, had their hands forced into the fire, to offer unholy sacrifice, be placed in the Liturgy [i.e., in the diptychs] among the Confessors.

CANON XV.

Wednesday is to be fasted, because then the Jews conspired to betray Jesus; Friday, because he then suffered for us. We keep the Lord's Day as a day of joy, because then our Lord rose. Our tradition is, not to kneel on that day.

---

[1] According to Johnson, St. Peter of Alexandria was martyred A.D. 311 in the persecution in the time of Diocletian. carried on by Maximian.

[2] In Beveridge will be found Balsamon's and Zonaras's notes.

[3] Johnson remarks, "The truth is, there is occasion for a critic, for the Greek is certainly corrupted."

[4] This canon contains the legend, refuted by St. Jerome, that St. John the Baptist was taken by St. Elizabeth away from the danger of Herod's edicts against the Innocents and escaped by flight, his father, Zacharias, the meanwhile being slain between the temple and the altar.

III.

THE CANONICAL EPISTLE OF ST. GREGORY, ARCHBISHOP OF NEOCÆS-AREA, WHO IS CALLED THAUMATURGUS, CONCERNING THEM THAT, DURING THE INCURSION OF THE BARBARIANS, ATE OF THINGS OF-FERED TO IDOLS AND COMMITTED CERTAIN OTHER SINS.[1]

Canon I.

That they who have been taken captives by the barbarians, and have eaten with them, be not treated as persons that have eaten things offered to idols; especially because it is universally reported, that they do not sacrifice to idols; nor shall those women who have been ravished by them, be treated as guilty of fornication, unless they were before of lewd lives.

Canon II.

That those Christians who plundered their brethren during the invasion, be excommunicated, lest wrath come on the people, and especially on the presidents,[2] who enquire not into these matters.

Canons III., IV., V.

The pretence of having found those goods, or that they themselves lost things of equal value, shall stand them in no stead, but that they be excluded from prayer.[3]

Canon VI.

Against those who detain them prisoners who had escaped from the barbarians, the holy man[4] expects that such should be thunder-struck, and therefore desires that some enquiry be made upon the spot by persons sent for this purpose.

Canon VII.

That they who joined the barbarians in their murder and ravages, or were guides or informers to them, be not permitted to be hearers, till holy men assembled together do agree in common upon what shall seem good, first to the Holy Ghost, then to themselves.

Canon VIII.

But if they discover themselves, and make restitution, they shall be admitted to be Prostrators.

Canon IX.

They that are convicted to have found (though in their own houses) anything [of their neighbours'] left by the barbarians shall also be Prostrators; but if they shall confess themselves they shall communicate in prayer.

Canon X.

This last privilege is restrained to such as demand nothing as a reward for their discovery, and salvage, or under any pretence whatsoever.

Canon XI.

The station of Mourners is without the gate of the oratory; the station of the Hearers is within the oratory, in the porch with the catechumens; the station of Prostrators is within the door of the temple; the station of Costanders is among the communicants; the last is the participation of Holy Mysteries.[5]

IV.

THE EPISTLE OF ST. ATHANASIUS TO THE MONK AMMUS.[6]

(Παντα μὲν καλὰ, κ. τ. λ.)

(*This*, as Epistle XLVIII, *will be found translated in Vol. IV. of the* Nicene and Post-Nicene Fathers (*2d Series*) p. 556 *et seq.*)

Involuntary nocturnal pollutions are not sinful, [I add to Johnson the exact words of the Saint. "For what sin or uncleanness can any natural excrement have in itself? Think of the absurdity of making a sin of the wax which comes from the ears or of the spittle from the mouth. Moreover we might add many things and explain how the excretions from the

[1] Johnson says this was about the year of grace 240, after the Goths had ravaged Asia, during the reign of Gallienus. The letter, he thinks, was an Encyclical sent to every bishop of his province, by Euphrosynus, who was one of these bishops and whom he calls his "old friend." In the beginning of the letter he addresses each one of the bishops as "most holy pope."
[2] I.e., The bishops, cf. St. Justin Martyr, Tertullian, etc.
[3] Literally "abdicate from Prayers." Johnson explains this to mean that they became Prostrators.
[4] I.e., St. Gregory.
[5] Johnson has a note that this canon is not "St. Gregory's but an addition by some other hand."
[6] In English translation named Amun.

belly are necessary to animal life. But if we believe that man is the work of God's hand, as we are taught in holy Scripture, how can it be supposed necessary that we perform anything impure? And if we are the children of God, as the holy Acts of the Apostles teaches, we have in us nothing unclean, etc., etc."]; nor is matrimony unclean, though virginity ["which is angelic and than which nothing can be more excellent"] is to be preferred before it.

THE EPISTLE OF THE SAME ATHANASIUS TAKEN FROM THE XXXIX. FESTAL EPISTLE.

(*Found translated in Vol. IV. of* Nicene and Post-Nicene Fathers (*2d series*), *pp. 551 and 552.*)

[*Johnson's epitome is so unsatisfactory that I have been compelled to relegate it to a footnote and to make one in its room of my own.**]

As the heretics are quoting apocryphal writings, an evil which was rife even as early as when St. Luke wrote his gospel, therefore I have thought good to set forth clearly what books have been received by us through tradition as belonging to the Canon, and which we believe to be divine. For there are in all twenty-two books of the Old Testament. Genesis, Exodus, Leviticus, Numbers, Deuteronomy. After this comes Joshua, and Judges, and Ruth. The four books of the Kings, counted as two. Then Chronicles, counted the two as one. Then First and Sec-

---

* Johnson says: " This contains the Canon of Scripture as we now receive it in all respects, save that the Epistle of Baruch is reckoned in the Canon, but Esther is not. He tells us, there are other books never reckoned in the Canon but authorized by the fathers to be read by the Catechumens, viz. : Wisdom of Solomon, of Sirach, Esther, Judith, and Tobias, and that which is called *The Doctrine of the Apostles*, and *Pastor*. These (says he) are read, the other reckoned of the Canons : Apocryphal books are the invention of heretics." To this Johnson appends a note, to wit : " It is the common opinion of learned men that the reason why some of the ancients reckoned the book of Esther not to belong to the Canon, was the Apocryphal chapters added to it by another hand. That *The Doctrine of the Apostles* is a book now lost, see Dr. Grabe's *Essay* on this subject."
Who these " learned men " may be, I do not know, but at the time of the writing of St. Athanasius the position of the Hebrew Esther was not well assured in the restricted Palestinian Jewish Canon. On this point the reader should make himself familiar with *The Canon of the Old Testament* by the Rt. Rev. Tobias Mullen, Roman Catholic Bishop of Erie, U. S. A.

ond Esdras [i.e. Ezra and Nehemiah]. After these Psalms, Proverbs, Ecclesiastes, and Cantica. To these follow Job, and the Twelve Prophets, counted as one book. Then Isaiah, Jeremiah together with the Epistle of Baruch, the Lamentations, Ezekiel, and Daniel.

Of the New Testament these are the books [then follows the complete list ending with " the Apocalypse of John "]. These are the fountains of salvation, that whoso thirsteth, may be satisfied by the eloquence which is in them. In them alone (ἐν τούτοις μόνοις) is set forth the doctrine of piety. Let no one add to them, nor take aught therefrom.

I also add for further accuracy that there are certain other books, not edited in the Canon, but established by the Fathers, to be read by those who have just come to us and wish to be instructed in the doctrine of piety. The Wisdom of Solomon, the Wisdom of Sirach, Esther, Judith, Tobit, the Doctrine (Διδαχή) of the Apostles and the Pastor. And let none of the Apocrypha of the heretics be read among you.

THE EPISTLE OF ST ATHANASIUS TO RUFFINIAN.

Σὺ μὲν τὰ υἱῷ, κ. τ. λ.

(*Found translated as* Epistle LV. *in Vol. IV. of the* Nicene and Post-Nicene Fathers (*2d Series*) *pp. 566 and 567.*)

It has been determined by synods in Greece, Spain, France, that they who have fallen, or been leaders of impiety [Arianism], be pardoned upon repentance, but that they have not the place of the clergy ; but that they who were only drawn away by force, or that complied for fear the people should be corrupted, have the place of the clergy too. Let the people who have been deceived, or forced, be pardoned, upon repentance and pronouncing anathema against the miscreancy of Eudoxius and Euzoius, ringleaders of the Arians (who assert that Christ is a creature); and upon professing the faith of the Fathers at Nice, and that no synod can prejudice that.

V.

THE FIRST CANONICAL EPISTLE OF OUR HOLY FATHER BASIL, ARCHBISHOP OF CÆSAREA IN CAPPADOCIA TO AMPHILOCHIUS, BISHOP OF ICONIUM.[1]

(This Epistle, number ct xxxviij., is found translated in Volume VIII. of the Second Series of the Nicene and Post-Nicene Fathers, *p. 223 et seqq.)*

CANON I.

As to the question concerning the Puritans the custom of every country is to be observed, since they who have discussed this point are of various sentiments. The [baptism] of the Pepuzenes I make no account of, and I wonder that Dionysius the canonist was of another mind. The ancients speak of heresies, which entirely break men off, and make them aliens from the faith. Such are the Manichæans, Valentinians, Marcionites and Pepuzenes, who sin against the Holy Ghost, who baptize into the Father, Son and Montanus, or Priscilla. Schisms are caused by ecclesiastical disputes, and for causes that are not incurable, and for differences concerning penance. The Puritans are such schismatics. The ancients, viz. Cyprian and Fermilian, put these, and the Encratites, and Hydroparastatæ, and Apotactites, under the same condemnation; because they have no longer the communication of the Holy Ghost, who have broken the succession. They who first made the departure had the spiritual gift; but by being schismatics, they became laymen; and therefore they ordered those that were baptized by them, and came over to the Church, to be purged by the true baptism, as those that are baptized by laymen. Because some in Asia have otherwise determined, let [their baptism] be allowed: but not that of the Encratites; for they have altered their baptism, to make themselves incapable of being received by the Church. Yet custom and the Fathers, that is bishops, who have the administration, must be followed; for I am afraid of putting an impediment to the saved; while I would raise fears in them concerning their baptism. We are not to allow their baptism, because they allow ours, but strictly to observe the canons. But let none be received without unction. When we received Zois and Saturninus to the Episcopal chair, we made, as it were, a canon to receive those in communion with them.

CANON II.

Let her that procures abortion undergo ten years' penance, whether the embryo were perfectly formed, or not.

CANON III

A deacon guilty of fornication, is deposed, not excommunicated; for the ancient canon forbids a single crime to be twice punished. And further, a layman excommunicated may be restored to the degree from which he falls, but a clergyman deposed cannot. Yet it is better to cure men of their sins by mortification, and to execute the canon only in cases where we cannot reach what is more perfect.

CANON IV.

They that marry a second time, used to be under penance a year or two. They that marry a third time, three or four years. But we have a custom, that he who marries a third time be under penance five years, not by canon, but tradition. Half of this time they are to be hearers, afterwards Co-standers; but to abstain from the communion of the Good Thing, when they have shewed some fruit of repentance.

CANON V.

Heretics, upon their death-bed, giving good signs of their conversion, to be received.

CANON VI.

Let it not be counted a marriage, when one belonging to the canon commits fornication, but let them be forced to part.[2]

CANON VII.

They who have committed sodomy with men or brutes, murderers, wizards, adulterers, and idolaters, have been thought worthy of the same punishment; therefore observe the same method with these which you do with others. We ought not to make any doubt of receiving those who have repented thirty years for the uncleanness which they committed through ignorance; for their ignorance pleads their pardon, and their willingness in confessing it; therefore com-

---

[1] These canons of St. Basil's are annotated by Zonaras, Balsamon and Aristenus, and of them there is also the Ancient Epitome which will be found in Beveridge (*Synod.*, Tom. II., p. 47). Johnson gives the date of these canons as later than the year 370.

[2] Johnson adds this note, "i.e. a clergyman, Monk, Deaconess, etc." See *Can. Nic.*, xvj.

mand them to be forthwith received, especially if they have tears to prevail on your tenderness, and have [since their lapse] led such a life as to deserve your compassion.

Canon VIII.

He that kills another with a sword, or hurls an axe at his own wife and kills her, is guilty of wilful murder; not he who throws a stone at a dog, and undesignedly kills a man, or who corrects one with a rod, or scourge, in order to reform him, or who kills a man in his own defence, when he only designed to hurt him. But the man, or woman, is a murderer that gives a *philtrum*, if the man that takes it die upon it; so are they who take medicines to procure abortion; and so are they who kill on the highway, and rapparees.

Canon IX.

Our Lord is equal, to the man and woman forbidding divorce, save in case of fornication; but custom requires women to retain their husbands, though they be guilty of fornication. The man deserted by his wife may take another, and though he were deserted for adultery, yet St. Basil will be positive, that the other woman who afterward takes him is guilty of adultery; but the wife is not allowed this liberty. And the man who deserts an innocent wife is not allowed to marry.

Canon X.

That they who swear that they will not be ordained, be not forced to break their oath. Severus, Bishop of Masada, who had ordained Cyriacus priest to a country church, subject to the Bishop of Mesthia, is referred to the divine tribunal, upon his pretending that he did it by surprise. Cyriacus had upon his ordination, been forced, contrary to canon, to swear that he would continue in that country church; but the Bishop of Mesthia, to whom that church properly belonged, forced him out. St. Basil advises Amphilochius to lay the country church to Masada, and make it subject to Severus, and to permit Cyriacus to return to it and save his oath; and by this means he supposes that Longinus, the lord of that country, would be prevailed upon to alter his resolution of laying that church desolate, as he declared he would upon Cyriacus's expulsion.

Canon XI.

He that is guilty of involuntary murder, shall do eleven years' penance—that is, if the murdered person, after he had here received the wound, do again go abroad, and yet afterward die of the wound.

Canon XII.

The canon excludes from the ministry those who are guilty of digamy.

Canon XIII.

Our fathers did not think that killing in war was murder; yet I think it advisable for such as have been guilty of it to forbear communion three years.

Canon XIV.

An usurer, giving his unjust gain to the poor, and renouncing his love of money, may be admitted into the clergy.

Canons XV. and XVI.

Not properly canons, but explications of Scripture, and therefore neither Balsamon, nor Aristenus, regard them as canons.

THE SECOND CANONICAL EPISTLE OF THE SAME.

(*This is found translated in the same volume last referred to,* Epistle cxcix., *p.* 236 *et seqq.*)

Canon XVII.

I made a canon, that they at Antioch, who had sworn not to perform the sacred offices should not do it publicly, but in private only: As to Bianor, he is removed from thence to Iconium, and therefore is more at liberty; but let him repent of his rash oath which he made to an infidel for avoiding a small danger.

Canon XVIII.

That the ancients received a professed virgin that had married, as one guilty of digamy, viz., upon one year's penance; but they ought to be dealt with more severely than widows professing continency, and even as adulterers: But they ought not to be admitted to profess virginity till they are above sixteen or seventeen years of age, after trial, and at their own earnest request; whereas relations often offer them that are under age, for their own secular ends, but such ought not easily to be admitted.

Canon XIX.

That men, though they seem tacitly to promise celibacy, by becoming monks, yet do it not expressly; yet I think fit that they be interrogated too, and that a profession should be demanded of them, that if they betake themselves to a carnal life, they may be punished as fornicators.

Canon XX.

Women professing virginity, though they did marry while they were heretics, or catechumens, yet are pardoned by baptism. What is done by persons in the state of catechumens, is never laid to their charge.

Canon XXI.

A married man committing lewdness with a single woman, is severely punished as guilty of fornication, but we have no canon to treat such a man as an adulterer; but the wife must co-habit with such a one: But if the wife be lewd, she is divorced, and he that retains her is [thought] impious; such is the custom, but the reason of it does not appear.

Canon XXII.

That they who have stolen virgins, and will not restore them, be treated as fornicators; that they be one year mourners, the second hearers, the third received to repentance and the fourth be co-standers, and then admitted to communion of the Good Thing. If the virgins be restored to those who had espoused them, it is at their discretion to marry them, or not; if to their guardians, it is at their discretion to give them in marriage to the raptors, or not.

Canon XXIII.

That a man ought not to marry two sisters, nor a woman two brothers: That he who marries his brother's wife, be not admitted till he dismiss her.

Canon XXIV.

A widow put into the catalogue of widows, that is, a deaconess being sixty years old, and marrying, is not to be admitted to communion of the Good Thing, till she cease from her uncleanness; but to a widower that marries no penance is appointed, but that of digamy. If the widow be less than sixty, it is the bishop's fault who admitted her deaconess, not the woman's.

Canon XXV.

He that marries a woman that he has corrupted, shall be under penance for corrupting her, but may retain her for his wife.

Canon XXVI.

Fornication is neither marriage, nor the beginning of marriage. If it may be, it is better that they who have committed fornication together be parted; but if they be passionate lovers, let them not separate, for fear of what is worse.

Canon XXVII.

As for the priest that is engaged, through ignorance, in an unlawful marriage, I have decreed, that he retain the honour of the chair; but forbear all sacred operations, and not give the blessing either in private, or public, nor distribute the Body of Christ to another, nor perform any liturgy; but let him bewail himself to the Lord, and to men, that his sin of ignorance may be pardoned.

Canon XXVIII.

That it is ridiculous to vow not to eat swine's flesh, and to abstain from it is not necessary.

Canon XXIX.

That princes ought not to swear to wrong their subjects: that such rash oaths ought to be repented of, and evil not to be justified under pretence of religion.

Canon XXX.

That they who steal women, and their accomplices, be not admitted to prayers, or be co-standers for three years. Where no violence is used, there no crime is committed, except there be lewdness in the case. A widow is at her own discretion. We must not mind vain pretences.

Canon XXXI.

She, whose husband is absent from home, if she co-habits with another man, before she is persuaded of his death, commits adultery.

Canon XXXII.

The clergyman who is deposed for mortal sin, shall not be excommunicated.

Canon XXXIII.

That a woman being delivered of a child in a journey, and taking no care of it, shall be reputed guilty of murder.

Canon XXXIV.

That the crime of women under penance for adultery, upon their own confession, or otherwise convicted, be not published, lest it occasion their death ; but that they remain out of communion the appointed time.

Canon XXXV.

If a woman leave her husband, and if it do upon inquiry appear, that she did it without reason, she deserves to be punished ; but let him continue in communion.

Canon XXXVI.

A soldier's wife marrying after the long absence of her husband, but before she is certified of his death, is more pardonable than another woman, because it is more credible that he may be dead.

Canon XXXVII.

That he, who having another man's wife or spouse taken away from him, marries another, is guilty of adultery with the first, not with the second.

Canon XXXVIII.

If a woman run after him that has corrupted her, she shall be under penance three years, though the parents be reconciled to her.

Canon XXXIX.

She, who continues to live with an adulterer, is all that time an adulteress.

Canon XL.

She that [being a slave] gives herself up to the will of a man, without the consent of her master, commits fornication ; for pacts of those who are under the power of others are null.

Canon XLI.

A widow being at her own discretion, may marry to whom she will.

Canon XLII.

Slaves marrying without the consent of their masters, or children without consent of their fathers, it is not matrimony but fornication, till they ratify it by consenting.

Canon XLIII.

That he who gives a mortal wound to another is a murderer, whether he were the first aggressor, or did it in his own defence.

Canon XLIV.

The deaconess that has committed lewdness with a pagan is not to be received to communion, but shall be admitted to the oblation, in the seventh year—that is, if she live in chastity. The pagan, who after [he has professed] the faith, betakes himself again to sacrilege, returns [like the dog] to his vomit : we therefore do not permit the sacred body of a deaconess to be carnally used.

Canon XLV.

He that assumes the name of a Christian, but reproaches Christ, shall have no advantage from his name.

Canon XLVI.

She that marries a man who was deserted for a while by his wife, but is afterward dismissed upon the return of the man's former wife, commits fornication, but ignorantly : she shall not be prohibited marriage, but it is better that she do not marry.

Canon XLVII.

Encratites, Saccophorians, and Apotactites, are in the same case with the Novatians. We re-baptize them all. There is a diversity in the canons relating to the Novatians, no canon concerning the other. If it be forbid with you, as it is at Rome for prudential causes, yet let reason prevail. They are a branch of the Marcionists ; and though they baptize in the name of the three divine Persons, yet they make God the author of evil, and assert, that wine and the creatures of God, are defiled. The bishops ought to meet, and so to explain the canon, that he who does [baptize such heretics] may be out of danger, and that one may have a positive answer to give to those that ask it.

Canon XLVIII.

A woman dismissed from her husband, ought to remain unmarried, in my judgment.

Canon XLIX.

If a slave be forced by her master, she is innocent.

Canon L.

We look on third marriages as disgraceful to the Church, but do not absolutely condemn them, as being better than a vague fornication.

THE THIRD EPISTLE OF THE SAME TO THE SAME.

(*Found in* lib. cit., p. 255, *et seqq.* Epistle ccxvij.)

Canon LI.

That one punishment be inflicted on lapsing clergymen, viz. : deposition, whether they be in dignity, or in the ministry which is given without imposition of hands.

Canon LII.

A woman delivered in the road, and neglecting her child, is guilty of murder, unless she was under necessity by reason of the solitude of the place, and the want of necessaries.

Canon LIII.

A widow slave desiring to be married a second time, has, perhaps, been guilty of no great crime in pretending that she was ravished; not her pretence, but voluntary choice is to be condemned; but it is clear, that the punishment of digamy is due to her.

Canon LIV.

That it is in the bishop's power to increase or lessen penance for involuntary murder.

Canon LV.

They that are not ecclesiastics setting upon highwaymen, are repelled from the communion of the Good Thing; clergymen are deposed.

Canon LVI.

He that wilfully commits murder, and afterwards repents, shall for twenty years remain without communicating of the Holy Sacrament. Four years he must mourn without the door of the oratory, and beg of the communicants that go in, that prayer be offered for him; then for five years he shall be admitted among the hearers, for seven years among the prostrators; for four years he shall be a co-stander with the communicants, but shall not partake of the oblation; when these years are completed, he shall partake of the Holy Sacrament.

Canon LVII.

The involuntary murderer for two years shall be a mourner, for three years a hearer, four years a prostrator, one year a co-stander, and then communicate.

Canon LVIII.

The adulterer shall be four years a mourner, five a hearer, four a prostrator, two a co-stander.

Canon LIX.

The fornicator shall be a mourner two years, two a hearer, two a prostrator, one a co-stander.

Canon LX.

Professed virgins and monks, if they fall from their profession, shall undergo the penance of adulterers.

Canon LXI.

The thief, if he discover himself, shall do one year's penance; if he be discovered [by others] two; half the time he shall be a prostrator, the other half a co-stander.

Canon LXII.

He that abuses himself with mankind, shall do the penance of an adulterer.

Canon LXIII.

And so shall he who abuses himself with beasts, if they voluntarily confess it.

Canon LXIV.

The perjured person shall be a mourner two years, a hearer three, a prostrator four, a co-stander one.

Canon LXV.

He that confesses conjuration, or pharmacy, shall do penance as long as a murderer.

Canon LXVI.

He that digs the dead out of their graves, shall be a mourner two years, a hearer three years, a prostrator four years, a co-stander one year.

Canon LXVII.

Incest with a sister is punished as murder.

Canon LXVIII.

All incestuous conjunction, as adultery.

Canon LXIX.

A reader or minister lying with a woman he has only espoused, shall cease from his function one year; but if he have not espoused her, he shall [wholly] cease from his ministry.

Canon LXX.

The priest or deacon that is polluted in lips, shall be made to cease from his function, but shall communicate with the priests or deacons. He that does more shall be deposed.

Canon LXXI.

He that is convicted to have been conscious to any of these crimes, but not discovered it, shall be treated as the principal.

Canon LXXII.

He that gives himself to divination, shall be treated as a murderer.

Canon LXXIII.

He that denied Christ, is to be communicated at the hour of death, if he confess it, and be a mourner till that time.

Canon LXXIV.

[The bishop] that has the power of binding and loosing, may lessen the time of penance, to an earnest penitent.

Canon LXXV.

He that commits incest with a half-sister, shall be a mourner three years, a hearer three years, a co-stander two years.

Canon LXXVI.

And so shall he be who takes in marriage his son's wife.

Canon LXXVII.

He that divorces his wife, and marries another, is an adulterer ; and according to the canons of the Fathers, he shall be a mourner one year, a hearer two years, a prostrator three years, a co-stander one year, if they repent with tears.

Canon LXXVIII.

So shall he who successively marries two sisters.

Canon LXXIX.

So shall he who madly loves his mother-in-law, or sister.

Canon LXXX.

The Fathers say nothing of polygamy as being beastly, and a thing unagreeable to human nature. To us it appears a greater sin than fornication : Let therefore such [as are guilty of it] be liable to the canons, viz. : after they have been mourners one year—let them be prostrators three years—and then be received.

Canon LXXXI.

They who in the invasion of the barbarians have after long torments, eaten of magical things offered to idols, and have sworn heathen oaths, let them not be received for three years ; for two years let them be hearers, for three years prostrators, so let them be received ; but they who did it without force, let them be ejected three years, be hearers two years, prostrators three years, co-standers three years, so let them be admitted to communion.

Canon LXXXII.

They who by force have been driven to perjury, let them be admitted after six years ; but if without force, let them be mourners two years, hearers two years, the fifth year prostrators, two years co-standers.

Canon LXXXIII.

They that follow heathenish customs, or bring men into their houses for the contriving pharmacies, or repelling them, shall be one year mourners, one year hearers, three years prostrators, one year co-standers.

Canon LXXXIV.

We do not judge altogether by the length of time, but by the circumstances of the penance. If any will not be drawn from their carnal pleasures, and choose to serve them rather than the Lord, we have no communication with them.

Canon LXXXV.

Let us take care that we do not perish with them ; let us warn them by night and day, that we may deliver them out of the snare or however save ourselves from their condemnation.

FROM AN EPISTLE OF THE SAME TO THE BLESSED AMPHILOCHIUS ON THE DIFFERENCE OF MEATS.

(*Found translated in* lib. cit., *p.* 287, *part of* Epistle ccxxxvj.)

Canon LXXXVI.

Against the Encratites, who would not eat flesh.

OF THE SAME TO DIODORUS BISHOP OF TARSUS, CONCERNING A MAN WHO HAD TAKEN TWO SISTERS TO WIFE.

(*Found translated in* lib. cit., *p.* 212 *et seqq.* Epistle clx.)

Canon LXXXVII.

Contains the preface of his letter to Diodorus Bishop of Tarsus, in which he tells him of a letter shewed him in justification of a man's marrying two sisters bearing his name ; but he hopes it was forged.

Canon LXXXVIII.

Contains the rest of the letter, in which he argues and inveighs against this practice.

OF THE SAME TO GREGORY A PRESBYTER, THAT HE SHOULD SEPARATE FROM A WOMAN WHO DWELT WITH HIM.

Canon LXXXIX.

A letter to Gregory, an unmarried priest, charging him to dismiss a woman whom he kept, though he was 70 years of age, and declared himself free from all amorous affections; and St. Basil would seem to believe him in this particular; but cites the III. canon of Nice against this practice, bids him avoid scandal, place the woman in a monastery, and be attended by men: he threatens him that if he does not comply, he shall die suspended from his office, and give account to God: that he shall be an anathema to all the people, and they who receive him [to communion] be excommunicated.

OF THE SAME TO THE CHOREPISCOPI, THAT NO ORDINATIONS SHOULD BE MADE CONTRARY TO THE CANONS.

(*Found translated in Vol. VIII.* Nicene and Post-Nicene Fathers, *p.* 157. Epistle liv.)

Canon XC.

A letter to his Village-bishop:[1] he complains of the want of discipline of the multiplying of the clergy, and that without due examination and enquiry into their morals; that they had dropped the old custom, which was for the priests and deacons to recommend to the Village Bishop, who taking the testimonial, and giving notice of it to the [City] Bishop, did afterwards admit the minister into the sacerdotal list; that the number of the inferior clergy was unreasonably increased, especially in time of war, when men got into orders to avoid the press: he orders a list of the clergy in every village to be sent to him, and who admitted him, if any have been admitted into the inferior orders by priests, that they be looked on as laymen. Let not who will, put his name into the list. Re-examine those who are there, expel the unworthy, admit none without my consent for the future; if you do he shall be counted a layman.

---

[1] Johnson by mistake has the singular instead of the plural.

OF THE SAME TO HIS SUFFRAGANS THAT THEY SHOULD NOT ORDAIN FOR MONEY.

(*Found translated in* lib. cit., *pp.* 156 *and* 157. Epistle liii.)

Canon XCI.

One letter to the bishop subject to him, wherein he prohibits to take money for orders, and to bring merchandize into the church, which is entrusted with the Body, and Blood of Christ; they had their pay after the ordination was performed; this he calls an artifice, and declares, that he who is guilty of it shall depart from the altar in his country, and go buy and sell the gift of God where he can.

FROM CHAPTER XVII. OF THE BOOK ST. BASIL WROTE TO BLESSED AMPHILOCHIUS ON THE HOLY GHOST.

(*Found translated in* lib. cit., *p.* 40 *et seqq.*)

Canon XCII.

He speaks of the written doctrine, and the unwritten tradition of the Apostles, and says, that both have the same efficacy as to religion. The unwritten traditions which he mentions, are the signing those who hope in Christ with the Cross; praying toward the East, to denote, that we are in quest of Eden, that garden in the East from whence our first parents were ejected (as he afterwards explains it), the words of invocation at the consecration of the Bread of Eucharist, and the cup of eulogy; the benediction of the baptismal water, the chrism and of the baptized person; the trine immersion, and the renunciations made at baptism; all which the Fathers concealed from those who were not initiated. He says the dogmata were always kept secret, the *Kerugmata* published; he adds the tradition of standing at prayer on the first day of the week, and the whole Pentecost (that is, from Easter to Whitsunday), not only to denote our rising with Christ, but as a prefiguration of our expecting an eternal perfect day, for the enjoyment of which we erect ourselves; and lastly, the profession of our faith in Father, Son and Holy Ghost at baptism.

Canon XCIII.

He asserts the Doxology [in these words] "with the Holy Spirit," to be an unwritten, Apostolic tradition. For this is a dogma full of authority, venerable for its antiquity.

FROM THE LETTER OF BASIL THE GREAT TO THE NICOPOLITANS.

There is also in Tilius and Bishop Beveridge here[1] inserted an epistle of St. Basil the Great to the Nicopolitans, comforting them under the loss of their church or oratory, and telling them, that they ought not to be concerned that they worship God in the open air, for that the eleven Apostles worshipped God in an upper room, where they were cooped up, while they that crucified Jesus performed their worship in a most famous Temple.

VI.

THE CANONICAL EPISTLE OF ST. GREGORY, BISHOP OF NYSSA, TO ST. LETOÏUS, BISHOP OF MELITENE.[2]

Canon I.

At Easter not only they who are transformed by the grace of the laver, i.e. baptism, but they who are penitents and converts, are to be brought to God, i.e. to the Communion : for Easter is that Catholic feast in which there is a resurrection from the fall of sin.

Canon II.

They who lapse without any force, so as to deny Christ, or do by choice turn Jews, idolaters, or Manichees, or infidels of any sort, not to be admitted to communion till the hour of death ; and if they chance to recover beyond expectation, to return to their penance. But they who were forced by torments, to do the penance of fornication.

Canon III.

If they who run to conjurers or diviners, do it through unbelief, they shall be treated as they who wilfully lapse, but if through want of sense, and through a vain hope of being relieved under their necessities, they shall be treated as those who lapse through the violence of torment.

Canon IV.

That fornicators be three years wholly ejected from prayer, three years hearers, three years prostrators, and then admitted to communion ; but the time of hearing and prostrating may be lessened to them who of their own accord confess, and are earnest penitents. That this time be doubled in case of adultery, and unlawful lusts, but discretion to be used.

Canon V.

Voluntary murderers shall be nine years ejected out of the church, nine years hearers, nine years prostrators ; but every one of these nine years may be reduced to seven or six, or even five, if the penitents be very diligent. Involuntary murderers to be treated as fornicators, but still with discretion, and allowing the communion on a death-bed, but on condition, that they return to penance if they survive.

Canon VI.

That the Fathers have been too gentle toward the idolatry of covetous persons, in condemning to penance only robbery, digging of graves, and sacrilege, whereas usury and oppression, though under colour of contract, are forbidden by Scripture. That highwaymen returning to the Church, be treated as murderers. They that pilfer, and then confess their sin to the priest, are only obliged to amendment, and to be liberal to the poor ; and if they have nothing, to labour and give their earnings.

Canon VII.

They who dig into graves, and rake into the ashes and bones of the dead, in order to find some valuable thing buried together with the corpse, (not they who only take some stones belonging to a sepulchre, in order to use them in building) to do the penance of fornicators.

Canon VIII.

He observes that by the law of Moses, sacrilege was punished as murder, and that the guilty person was stoned to death, and thinks the Fathers too gentle, in imposing a shorter penance on sacrilege than adultery.

---

[1] I.e., at the end, after the Epistle of Gennadius.
[2] These Canons, in Beveridge's *Synodicon*, are annotated only by Balsamon.

VII.

FROM THE METRE POEMS OF ST. GREGORY THEOLOGUS, SPECIFYING WHICH BOOKS OF THE OLD AND NEW TESTAMENT SHOULD BE READ.[1]

Let not other books seduce your mind : for many malignant writings have been disseminated. The historical books are twelve in number by the Hebrew count, [then follow the names of the books of the Old Testament but Esther is omitted, one Esdras, and all the Deutero-Canonical books]. Thus there are twenty - two books of the Old Testament which correspond to the Hebrew letters. The number of the books of the New Mystery are Matthew, who wrote the Miracles of Christ for the Hebrews; Mark for Italy ; Luke, for Greece ; John, the enterer of heaven,[2] was a preacher to all, then the Acts, the xiv. Epistles of Paul, the vij. Catholic Epistles, and so you have all the books. If there is any beside these, do not repute it genuine.

VIII

FROM THE IAMBICS OF ST. AMPHILOCHIUS THE BISHOP TO SELEUCUS, ON THE SAME SUBJECT.[3]

We should know that not every book which is called Scripture is to be received as a safe guide. For some are tolerably sound and others are more than doubtful. Therefore the books which the inspiration of God hath given I will enumerate. [Then follows a list of the proto-canonical books of the Old Testament, Esther alone being omitted. All the deutero-canonical books are omitted. He then continues] to these some add Esther. I must now show what are the books of the New Testament. [Then follow all the books of the New Testament except the Revelation. He continues,] But some add to these the Revelation of John, but by far the majority say that it is spurious. This is the most true canon of the divinely given Scriptures.

NOTE.

We have thus four [five if we accept the Laodicean list as genuine,] different canons of Holy Scripture, all having the approval of the Council in Trullo and of the Seventh Ecumenical. From this there seems but one conclusion possible, viz. : that the approval given was not specific but general.

IX.

THE CANONICAL ANSWERS OF TIMOTHY, THE MOST HOLY BISHOP OF ALEXANDRIA, WHO WAS ONE OF THE CL FATHERS GATHERED TOGETHER AT CONSTANTINOPLE, TO THE QUESTIONS PROPOSED TO HIM CONCERNING BISHOPS AND CLERICS.[4]

QUESTION I.

If a lad of seven years old, or a man, being a catechumen, being present at the oblation, does eat of it through ignorance, what shall be done in this case ?

Answer. Let him be illuminated, i.e. baptized, for he is called by God.

QUESTION II.

If baptism be desired for a catechumen that is possessed, what shall be done ?

Answer. Let him be baptized at the hour of death, not otherwise.

QUESTION III.

Ought a communicant to communicate, if he be possessed ?

Answer. If he do not expose or blaspheme the Mysteries, let him communicate not always, but at certain times.

QUESTION IV.

If a catechumen be sick, and in a frenzy, so that he cannot make profession of his faith, can he be baptized, at the entreaty of his friends ?

Answer. He may, if he be not possessed.

---

[1] Not being satisfied with Johnson, I have supplied a translation from Beveridge. It also is found in Aristenus's *Epitome.* Balsamon has written a brief scholion adding nothing of importance to the text.
[2] This seems to imply a knowledge of the Revelation, although it is not mentioned.

[3] That is the Canon of Holy Scripture. I have substituted my own Epitome, in the room of Johnson's, translating the original as it is found in Beveridge's *Synodicon*, Tom. II., p. 179. It is also in Aristenus's *Epitome*. Balsamon has no scholion on this passage.
[4] Beveridge's *Synodicon* gives notes by Balsamon only.

QUESTION V.

Can a man or woman communicate after performing the conjugal act over night?
Answer. No. 1 Cor. vii. 5.

QUESTION VI.

The day appointed for the baptism of a woman; on that day it happened that the custom of women was upon her; ought she then to be baptized?
Answer. No, not till she be clean.

QUESTION VII.

Can a menstruous woman communicate?
Answer. Not until she be clean.

QUESTION VIII.

Ought a woman in child-bed to keep the Paschal fast?
Answer. No.

QUESTION IX.

Ought a clergyman to perform the oblation, or pray, while an Arian or heretic is present?
Answer. As to the divine oblation, the deacon, after the kiss, makes a proclamation, "Let all that are not Communicants walk off;" therefore such persons ought not to be present, except they promise to repent, and renounce their heresy.

QUESTION X.

Is a sick man obliged to keep the Paschal fast?
Answer. No.

QUESTION XI.

If a clergyman be called to celebrate a marriage, and have heard that it is incestuous; ought he to comply, and perform the oblation?
Answer. No; he must not be partaker of other men's sins.

QUESTION XII.

If a layman ask a clergyman whether he may communicate after a nocturnal pollution?
Answer. If it proceed from the desire of a woman, he ought not: but if it be a temptation from Satan, he ought; for the tempter will ply him when he is to communicate.

QUESTION XIII.

When are man and wife to forbear the conjugal act?
Answer. On Saturday, and the Lord's day; for on those days the spiritual sacrifice is offered.

QUESTION XIV.

Shall there be an oblation for him, who being distracted, murders himself?
Answer. Not except the case be very clear that he was distracted.

QUESTION XV.

If one's wife be possessed to such a degree, as that she be bound with irons, and the man cannot contain, may he marry another?
Answer. I can only say it would be adultery so to do.

QUESTION XVI.

If a man in washing or bathing, swallow a drop of water, may he communicate after it?
Answer. If Satan find an occasion of hindering us from the communion, he will the oftener do it.

QUESTION XVII.

Are they, who hear the Word, and do it not, damned?
Answer. If we neither do it, or repent that we have not done it.

QUESTION XVIII.

At what age are sins imputed to us by God?
Answer. According to every one's capacity and understanding; to one at ten, to another when older.

X.

THE PROSPHONESUS OF THEOPHILUS, ARCHBISHOP OF ALEXANDRIA, WHEN THE HOLY EPIPHANIES HAPPENED TO FALL ON A SUNDAY.[1]

CANON I.

Because the fast of Epiphany chances to fall on a Lord's day, let us take a few dates, and so break our fast, and honour the Lord's day, and shew our dislike of heresy, and yet not wholly neglect the fast which should be observed on this day; eating no more till our evening assembly at three afternoon.

---

[1] Johnson gives the date as about A.D. 385. These are annotated only by Balsamon.

THE COMMONITORY OF THE SAME WHICH AMMON RECEIVED ON ACCOUNT OF LYCUS.

Canon II.

Let [the priests] who have communicated with the Arians, be retained or rejected, as the custom of every church is; but so, that other orthodox [priests] be ordained, though the others continue. As the orthodox bishops did in Thebais, so let it be in other cities. They who were ordained by Bishop Apollo, and afterwards communicated with the Arians, if they did it of their own accord, let them be censured; but if they only did it in obedience to the bishop, let them be continued; but if all the people abdicate them, others must be ordained. And if Bistus the priest be found to have committed uncleanness with a woman dismissed from her husband, let him not be permitted to be a priest. But this is no prejudice to the bishop who ordained him, if he did it ignorantly; since the Holy Synod commands unworthy men to be ejected, though they be not convicted until after ordination.

Canon III.

Let Bishop Apollo's sentence against his priest Sur prevail, though he has the liberty of being further heard.

Canon IV.

If Panuph the deacon married his brother's daughter before baptism, let him continue among the clergy, if she be dead, and he had not to do with her after his baptism; but if he married her, and cohabited with her while he was a communicant, let him be ejected from the clergy, without prejudice to the bishop who ordained him, if he did it ignorantly.

Canon V.

If it do evidently appear, that Jacob, while he was reader, did commit fornication, and was ejected by the priests ($\pi\rho\epsilon\sigma\beta\upsilon\tau\acute{\epsilon}\rho\omega\nu$), and yet afterwards ordained, let him be ejected, and not otherwise.

Canon VI.

That all in holy orders unanimously choose those who are to be ordained, and then the bishop examine [them]; or that the bishop ordain them in the midst of the church, all that are in holy orders consenting, and the bishop with a loud voice asking the people, who are then to be present, whether they can give their testimony [to the parties to be ordained]; and that ordination be not performed in private; if there be in the remote country, who while they were communicants [with the Arians] communicated in their opinions, let them not be ordained until they be examined by orthodox clergymen, in the presence of the bishop, who is to charge the people, that there be no running up and down in the middle of the church, or service.

Canon VII.

Let the clergymen distribute all that is offered by way of sacrifice, after so much as was necessary has been consumed in the Mysteries. Let not the catechumens taste of them, but clergymen and communicants only.[1]

Canon VIII.

One, Hierax, had delated a clergyman as guilty of fornication. Bishop Apollo defended him. Theophilus orders the matter to be examined.

Canon IX.

That an Œconomus be created, by the consent of all that are in Holy Orders, with the concurrence of Bishop Apollo, that so the goods of the Church be expended as they ought.

Canon X.

That the widows, poor, and travellers be not disturbed; and that no one make a property of the goods of the Church.

OF THE SAME TO AGATHO THE BISHOP.

Whereas Maximus has for ten years lived in unlawful marriage, but pretends that it was through ignorance, and that they are now parted by mutual consent, let them stand among the catechumens, if it appear that they be in earnest.

OF THE SAME TO MENAS THE BISHOP.

Theophilus was informed, that the priest in Geminus, a village, had repelled Kyradium (a woman) from the communion: Theophilus approves of it, because she had done wrong, and was unwilling to make satisfaction; but orders her to be admitted to communion upon repentance.

---

[1] Johnson gives this note. "To eat the main of what was left, was not at all inconsistent with reserving so much as was necessary for foreseen and unforeseen emergencies."

THE NARRATIVE OF THE SAME CONCERNING THOSE CALLED CATHARI.

Because the great synod held at Nice has decreed, That [the clergymen] who come over to the Church from the Novatians be ordained ; do you ordain those that come over, if their life be upright, and there be no objection.

XI.

THE CANONICAL EPISTLE OF OUR HOLY FATHER AMONG THE SAINTS, CYRIL, ARCHBISHOP OF ALEXANDRIA, ON THE HYMNS.[1]

CYRIL TO DOMNUS.

This letter contains a complaint of one, Peter, deposed from his See, yet retaining the character of a bishop, who thought his cause good, but complains that he had not time and opportunity given him for his defence ; and that whatever he had, was taken away from him. He desires Domnus, who was a Metropolitan, that he would call a synod, and let him have a hearing ; and that such bishops as Peter suspected of prejudice against him should not be permitted to be his judges. He thinks it very hard, that not only what belonged to the Church, but every thing else was taken from him ; and complains that all bishops were called to account for every thing they received, whether from the Church, or by any other means. Peter had indeed signed an instrument of resignation ; but Cyril says, that he was terrified into it ; and that he would have no such resignation be of force except he that made it deserved deposition.

OF THE SAME TO THE BISHOPS OF LIBYA AND PENTAPOLIS.

There is another Epistle of the same father, complaining to the bishops of Libya and Pentapolis. That some who had been refused ordination by their own bishop, or cast out of the monasteries for their irregularity, were ordained by a surprise upon some other bishop, and that just as they came from their bride-bed, and then went and performed the oblation, or any other office, in the monasteries from which they had been ejected, which gave great offence. He charges the bishops to take care of this for the future and, if any were to be ordained, to enquire into their lives, and whether they are married, and when, and how ; and orders, that catechumens, who had been separated for lapsing, be baptized at the hour of death.

XII. [2]

THE ENCYCLICAL LETTER OF GENNADIUS, PATRIARCH OF CONSTANTINOPLE AND OF THE HOLY SYNOD MET WITH HIM TO ALL THE HOLY METROPOLITANS AND TO THE POPE OF THE CITY OF ROME.[3]

To the most beloved of God, fellow-minister, Gennadius and the most holy synod assembled in the royal city which is New Rome, sendeth greeting.

As our Lord without money and without price ordained his Apostles, so should we ordain the clergy, for the Lord has placed us in their grade and in their stead (εἰς τὸν ἐκείνων βαθμόν τε καὶ τόπον). Nor should we use any ingenious sophisms to avoid this plain duty, explicitly laid upon us, not only by the words of the Gospel but also by a canon of the great Ecumenical Synod of Chalcedon.

---

[1] Johnson gives the date of this as about the year 412 A.D..
[2] The Greeks speak of the canons of The Thirteen Holy Fathers, counting in the number St. Cyprian's canon, but as this was really Synodal I have placed it in that category.

[3] In this I have not followed Johnson, but translated from Beveridge, *Synod.*, Tom. II., p. 181.

INDEXES

As this volume is composed (1) of the "Decrees and Canons" of the Councils, along with extracts from the proceedings of some of the principal ones, and (2) of *Scholia* that are given to explain and illustrate those other main parts in the collection, an attempt is made to combine in the same set of indexes the references to these two parts, and at the same time to easily distinguish them to the eye by the character of the types that are used. This is thought to be simpler and more generally useful than either to have separate indexes for the text and *Scholia*, or to index all the references without distinction. The references that belong to the Decrees, Canons, and Extracts, are placed in heavy face type, while those that belong to the *Scholia* are in the usual lighter face type of the volume. Where the same figures in different type are found together, it means that a reference is made to some fact in the text on that page, and also to some comment in the *Scholia* upon the same page.

INDEX OF AUTHORS

INDEX OF NAMES

INDEX OF WORDS AND PHRASES

INDEX OF PLACES.

INDEX OF SUBJECTS

Clergy—*Continued.*

given him by God, **118, 594**; is not to be translated by compulsion of the bishops, **118, 594**; can ordain in another jurisdiction with the other bishop's consent, **119**; for irregularity a bishop is amenable to the synod, **119**; his interference in another parish must have been frequent, 119 ; if chosen by his predecessor he is disqualified, **119**; must be appointed by a synod, and with the judgment of the bishops, **119, 120**; a coadjutor *cum jure successionis*, 120 ; with the presbyters and deacons, bishop has charge of all church property, **120, 120, 121, 596**; his property at his decease must be honestly cared for, **120, 596**; his heirs must not be vexed and harried with lawsuits, **120, 596**; he may bequeath all his private property to any one, **120, 596**; he controls the funds of the church, **121, 596**; must dispense them in piety and godly fear, **121, 596**; may apply church-funds to necessary uses, **121, 596**; shall not appropriate or waste church revenue, **121, 283, 381, 458, 596**; shall not allow friends or relatives to do so, **121, 596**; if accused of dishonest dealing, he shall appeal to the synod, **121, 183**; qualifications necessary for his election, **131**; not to be elected by popular tumult, 131, **415**; his sermon in the liturgy, **136, 138**; his place and duty in the liturgy, **136, 138, 139**; his place among the clergy, **140**; his distinctive dress, 141, 142 ; wore golden mitre or fillet, **141**; when called to a synod, he must attend, **152, 282, 420**; and either teach or be taught, **152**; he can only be excused by ill-health from attending synod, **152, 282**; or by other unavoidable hindrance, 152, **282**; should not be guilty of contempt, **152, 282**; enters the *bema* accompanied by the clergy, **157**; presbyters form the bishop's guard of honour, 157, 158 ; must not be appointed in village or country district, **158**; must not make the oblation in a private house, **152**; the bishops of the east are to manage the east alone, **176**; the bishops of the Asian diocese administer Asian affairs alone, **176**; the Pontic bishops administer only Pontic matters, **176**; and the Thra-

Clergy—*Continued.*

cian bishops only Thracian affairs, **176**; his enthronization, **177**; one setting aside the decrees of the Council of Ephesus shall be deposed, **230**; one teaching contrary to the faith established at Nicæa shall be deposed, **231**; is not to ordain for money payment, **268, 559, 595**; is not to sell a grace which cannot be sold, **268, 559**; shall not be ordained simoniacally, **268, 559, 595**; simoniacal ordination is invalid, **268**; must not engage in secular management, **269, 599**; he may be called by law to manage for orphans, etc., **269**; must be watchful over the monks, 270 ; is judge, in the first instance, between clergy, **274**; against another bishop appeals to the synod of the province, **274, 417**; against his metropolitan appeals to the Exarch of the diocese, **274**; against his Exarch appeals to the Patriarch in Constantinople, **274**; appealing to secular powers to divide a province he shall be degraded, **276-7**; may grant indulgence to his virgins and monks, **280**; charges against one shall not be loosely received, **283**; the accuser of a bishop must have his own character investigated, **283, 446, 451**; often accused slanderously in order to cause confusion, 183, **446**; the accusers must be strictly examined, **183, 283**; all accusers are not to be received or all excluded, **183, 446**; accusers of a bishop for fraud and such things have open court, **183**; heretic may not accuse a bishop on ecclesiastical grounds, 183 ; neither may one be excommunicated, **183**; those under charge of faults cannot accuse until themselves cleared, 183 ; an eligible accuser brings the case first before the provincial bishops, 183 ; then the case may be appealed to the bishops of the diocese, 183 ; but the case should not be carried before the Emperor or ecumenical synod, 183 ; the goods of a bishop deceased shall not be seized by the clergy, **283, 381, 596**; shall have a steward to manage the church's business, **235, 476**; may not be married before or after ordination, 363 ; deposed if he has had intercourse with a nun, **364**; shall not put away his wife on pretence of piety, 370, **594**; was allowed by Eastern custom to have his

Clergy—*Continued.*

wife, 371 ; the higher aim of bishop's position, 371 ; depriving for lawful cohabitation he shall be deposed, **371**; age for consecration, **372, 372**; the name a later introduction behind apostle, 373 ; liable to deposition for receiving a cleric who should have gone home, **374, 595**; shall not teach publicly in any foreign city, **375, 594**; under pain of acting only as a presbyter, **375**; on his consecration he must remove his wife to a distance, **388**; supports his wife who is so removed, **388**; they must separate by mutual consent, **388**; absent three Sundays from church without necessity, he is under penalty, **400, 425**; opinion upon bishop's translations, **415**; shall not be elected by bribery or intrigue, **416**; or on fraudulent commendations, **416**; one so appointed is deprived of communion even *in extremis*, **416**, 416 ; was in earlier days elected by the people, 416, 426 ; shall not pass uncalled into another province, **416, 594**; his form of procedure in dispute with another bishop, **417**; his appeal to Julius, bishop of Rome, **417**, 417 seq., **418**, 418 seq.; shall not be ordained for a village or petty town, **420**, 421 ; let him be ordained for a former see or large town, **420**, 421 ; should specially care for the widows and orphans, **422**; should not go up to court unless summoned by letter, **422**; and then use his influence for truth and right, **422**; was often summoned by the princes for consultation and advice, **422**; should not be long absent from his diocese, 422 ; should intercede at court for criminals, 422 ; on appeal to court he should send a deacon as delegate, **423**; the bishop's going to court excites jealousy and suspicion, **423, 423**; the form of procedure in sending a petition to court, 423 seq., **432, 502**; may use the influence of friends at court, **423, 424**; must have passed slowly through all the orders of the priesthood, **424, 425**; must have shown himself worthy of the episcopate, **425**; should not have been merely a rich man, or lawyer, or courtier, **425**; should not be a novice, **425, 599**; stranger shall not boast and bring the proper bishop into contempt, **425, 426**; stranger shall not in-

Council (Ecumenical) disliked by Gregory Nazianzen, 13 ; tests writings on the faith, and approves or condemns, 299 seq. ; ecumenicity of a council considered, 524 seq. ; question over the second Nicene, 524 seq. ; the four were revered by Gregory Great, 525 ; the six Ecumenical were confirmed and adopted, **555, 555, 556.**

Council (Provincial) held twice a year, **46.**

Courts of Appeal. [See CLERGY.]

Creed, the Nicene, 1, 3, 249, 263 ; of Eusebius, 1, 3 ; to be learned by the catechumens and repeated to the bishop, **154, 399;** or to be repeated to the presbyters, **154;** to be repeated by the catechumens on the Thursday before baptism, **154,** 154 ; of Constantinople, difficulties about the, 162, 162 n., 163, 167, 168 ; text of that of Constantinople, 163, 263 ; text of those in Epiphanius's *Ancoratus,* 164, 165 ; additions to, were forbidden, 162, 163, 167-9 ; that of Ephesus, 197 ; in Cyril's letter to Nestorius, **202;** those of Constantinople and Nicæa are one creed, 234 ; that given out by the seventh ecumenical, Nicæa II., **540. 549.**

Cresconius bishop of Villa Regis, **464, 480;** left his see and invaded Tubinia, **464;** refused to leave and return to his own church, **464;** was deposed for contempt and handed over to the magistrate, **454, 480.**

Crime should not be punished twice, **604.**

LIST OF WORDS AND PHRASES.